European Union Law

SECOND EDITION

Elspeth Berry LLB, Solicitor
Senior Lecturer in Law, Nottingham Law School

and

Sylvia Hargreaves BA, LLM, PhD, Solicitor
Principal Lecturer in Law, Nottingham Law School

OXFORD
UNIVERSITY PRESS

OXFORD
UNIVERSITY PRESS

Great Clarendon Street, Oxford OX2 6DP

Oxford University Press is a department of the University of Oxford. It furthers the University's objective of excellence in research, scholarship, and education by publishing worldwide in

Oxford New York

Auckland Cape Town Dar es Salaam Hong Kong Karachi Kuala Lumpur Madrid Melbourne Mexico City Nairobi New Delhi Shanghai Taipei Toronto

With offices in

Argentina Austria Brazil Chile Czech Republic France Greece Guatemala Hungary Italy Japan Poland Portugal Singapore South Korea Switzerland Thailand Turkey Ukraine Vietnam

Oxford is a registered trade mark of Oxford University Press in the UK and in certain other countries

Published in the United States by Oxford University Press Inc., New York

First published 2004

This edition published 2007

British Library Cataloguing in Publication Data
Data available

Library of Congress Cataloging in Publication Data
Data available

Typeset by Newgen Imaging Systems (P) Ltd., Chennai, India
Printed in Great Britain
on acid-free paper by
CPI Bath Press

ISBN 978-0-19-928244-9

10 9 8 7 6 5 4 3 2 1

PREFACE

EU law is a subject which students have traditionally found difficult. Although many students will have come across EU law at work, or will have an interest in the politics, economics, or history of the EU, many others find it a particularly inaccessible subject. This book aims to, and in previous editions has succeeded in, demystifying the key areas of EU law for undergraduate and graduate students approaching the subject for the first time.

We start with the background to EU law—the history of the EU, which is fundamental to an understanding of the content and function of EU law, and the institutional structure and the sources of law which it produces. We then examine the EU's legal system, explaining and analysing the way in which EU law can be utilized in actions before the domestic courts, and the actions which may be brought against the EU for illegal conduct. The remainder of the book is devoted to the major areas of substantive law—freedom of movement and competition law. In all these areas we explain the basic concepts, with full cross-references to the *Cases and Materials* in the Online Resource Centre. Students are able to test and consolidate their understanding in considering the questions and undertaking the exercises that appear throughout the book. There is also the opportunity to tackle more extended sample questions in each chapter, both problems and essays, to which guide answers are provided.

We have found in the past that students consider this to be more user-friendly text for EU law than many of its competitors, but we also ensure that its coverage is sufficient for standard EU courses.

Elspeth Berry and Sylvia Hargreaves
Nottingham Law School

OUTLINE TABLE OF CONTENTS

CONTENTS

SOURCE ACKNOWLEDGEMENTS

Grateful acknowledgement is made to the publishers of copyright material which appears on the Online Resource Centre.

Extracts from the reports of the European Court of Justice and Court of First Instance (ECR) are taken from www.curia.europa.eu. These are unauthenticated reports and are reproduced free of charge. The definitive versions are published in Reports of Cases before the Court of Justice or the Official Journal of the European Union.

If notified, the publisher will undertake to rectify any errors or omissions at the earliest opportunity.

TABLE OF CASES

European Commission Decisions

European Court of Justice and Court of First Instance

United Kingdom

TABLE OF LEGISLATION

Decisions

Directives

Regulations

France

Ireland

Netherlands

United Kingdom

HOW TO USE THIS BOOK

This book will give students of European Union law a clear and accurate introduction to the subject. Our aim has been to make the material as accessible as possible for those students coming to the subject for the first time. To this end we have included a number of features throughout the text to allow for interactive use of the book by students, in testing their knowledge and checking their understanding.

Cases and Materials

The Online Resource Centre that accompanies this book features additional cases and materials that complement the textbook. These resources can be downloaded free of charge, and can be used either as material for independent study, or integrated into your institution's existing virtual learning environment.

To access the online cases and materials:

1. Go to **www.oxfordtextbooks.co.uk/orc/berry-hargreaves2e/**
2. Click on the *Cases and Materials* link
3. Login using the following details:

   username: **berry2e**

   password: **Materials**

Wherever there are cases or materials relating to the text, the Online Resource Centre symbol appears in the margin of the textbook.

Chapter Objectives

Each chapter opens with a set of objectives to help students identify the areas they should understand by the end of the chapter.

Summaries of Key cases

Summaries of Key cases are highlighted in boxes throughout the text to illustrate and reinforce Key principles.

Question boxes 

Questions are included throughout the text to encourage students to engage critically with the issues discussed. They also provide a useful means for students to test their knowledge while reading the chapter or during the revision process. Where the Online Resource Centre (www.oxford textbooks.co,uk/orc/berry-hargreaves2e/) contains cases or materials relating to a question the symbol will appear in the question box.

Exercises 

Exercises are included throughout the text for students to test their understanding of the issues raised by key cases, and to encourage deeper reading and analysis of cases. Where the Online Resource Centre (www.oxfordtextbooks.co.uk/orc/berry-hargreaves2e/) contains cases or materials relating to an exercise, the @ symbol will appear in the exercise box.

Chapter Summaries

Chapters end with a summary of the main issues discussed in the chapter. This is not intended as a substitute for reading the chapter, but rather as a section to refresh the student's memory on the key issues discussed. The summaries provide a useful reminder of areas that should be considered in relation to revision, assessments, and exams.

Further Reading

Sources recommended in the text for additional reading assist the student to understand the important issues, and encourage a broader knowledge of the subject.

Assessment Exercises 

All chapters end with an 'Assessment Exercise' that asks a question or sets up a scenario for the students to assess and answer using the knowledge gained through reading the chapter. Full specimen answers to the Assessment Exercises appear in the Online Resource Centre.

Glossary

The glossary contains many key terms and ensures students are able to understand the terminology specific to European Union law.

Updates

Updates to the text can be found on the Online Resource Centre. This indispensable resource allows students to access changes in the law that have occurred since publication of the book: students can keep up to date with new developments without buying a new book. Updates are available in pdf format, so can be printed for easy reference.

GLOSSARY

Definitions

The Treaty of Paris establishing the European Coal and Steel Community 1951	The ECSC Treaty
The Treaty establishing the EEC 1957 (note that 'EEC' has been amended to 'EC')	The EC Treaty
The EC Treaty establishing the European Atomic Energy Community 1957	The EURATOM Treaty
The Single European Act 1986	The SEA
The Treaty on European Union 1992	The EU Treaty
The Council of the European Communities (also known as the Council of Ministers)	The Council
The Commission of the European Communities	The Commission
The Parliament of the European Communities	The Parliament
The Court of Justice of the European Communities	The Court of Justice
The Common Agricultural Policy	The CAP
Economic and Monetary Union	EMU

Cartel A group of independent companies or businesses, operating in the same market, that collude to fix prices, share markets or engage in other forms of anti-competitive behaviour—see further **Chapter 12**

Charge having equivalent effect to a customs duty ('CEE') A levy charged on goods by virtue of the fact that they cross a frontier, which is not a customs duty in the strict sense—see further **Chapter 8**

Citizen of the European Union A national of a Member State—see further **Chapters 9, 10, 11**

Commission A body made up of representatives from Member States but who take an oath of independence. It drafts the legislation of the European Community and, in some cases, of the European Union—see further **Chapter 2**

Concerted practice A form of coordination between undertakings falling short of an agreement by which, through their cooperation, the parties eliminate or reduce competition between them—see further **Chapter 13**

Council A body made up of national politicians which takes the major decisions in the European Community and the European Union—see further **Chapter 2**

Customs duty A levy charged on goods by virtue of the fact that they cross a frontier—see further **Chapter 8**

Customs Union An agreement between countries to operate a free trade area, in which goods circulate without restrictions, and a system whereby a common level of duty is charged on goods entering the free trade area from non-member countries—see further **Chapter 8**

Decision A form of secondary legislation which is directly applicable to those entities to which it is addressed—see further **Chapter 3**

Derogation A permissible exception to a legal rule or principle—see further **Chapters 8, 11**

Direct applicability The capacity of Community law to become law in Member States—see further **Chapter 4**

Direct concern The impact that Community law may have on an individual or business when Member States have no intervening discretion or have exercised this discretion prior to the adoption of the law. Together with individual concern, this is often a precondition for an applicant to bring an action for annulment under Article 230 EC—see further **Chapter 7**

Direct effect The ability of Community law to be enforced directly in national courts—see further **Chapter 4**

Directive A form of secondary legislation which is addressed to the Member States and requires them to change their national law to achieve Community objectives—see further **Chapter 3**

Distinctly applicable measure An MEQR that does not apply equally to domestic and imported products (i.e. makes a distinction between them)—see further **Chapter 8**

European Community A supranational body with 27 Member States and run by the Commission, the Council and the Parliament. It is part of the European Union—see further **Chapter 1**

European Union A supranational body with 27 Member States and run by the Commission, the Council, and the Parliament. It includes the European Community and the policy areas of judicial and police cooperation in criminal matters and the common foreign and security policy—see further **Chapter 1**

Horizontal agreement An agreement between undertakings operating at different levels of the market—see further **Chapter 13**

Indirect effect The ability of Community law to influence the interpretation of national law and thus, itself to be enforced indirectly in the national courts—see further **Chapter 4**

Indistinctly applicable measure An MEQR that applies equally to domestic and imported products (i.e. makes no distinction between them)—see further **Chapter 8**

Individual concern The impact that a particular piece of Community law may have on an individual or business (or a group thereof) when it is affected by it in a way in which no other individual, business, or group is. Together with individual concern, this is often a precondition for an applicant to bring an action for annulment under Article 230 EC—see further **Chapter 7**

Internal market An area within which goods, persons, services, and capital move freely without restrictions—see further **Chapter 8**

Legal or legislative base A Treaty Article which gives the Community the power to pass secondary legislation on a particular issue—see further **Chapters 3** and **6**

Measure having equivalent effect to a quantitative restriction ('MEQR') A non-tariff barrier to trade which is not quantitative but has a similar effect to a quantitative restriction, for instance a technical requirement relating to a product—see further **Chapter 8**

Non-tariff barrier to trade A restriction on the free movement of goods which is not of a pecuniary nature (i.e. does not involve any direct payment of money)—see further **Chapter 8**

Parliament A directly elected body which in some areas takes the decisions in the European Community jointly with the Council, but in others merely has the right to be consulted—see further **Chapter 2**

Preliminary reference A request by a national court for a ruling by the Court of Justice on the meaning or validity of Community law—see further **Chapter 5**

Preliminary ruling A ruling by the Court of Justice on the meaning or validity of Community law in response to a request by a national court—see further **Chapter 5**

Proportionality A general principle of Community law: measures, decisions, or actions must go no further than is necessary to achieve their objective—see further **Chapters 8, 11, 13**

Protectionist measure A measure, such as a customs duty or charge having equivalent effect, which is intended to protect domestic products from competition from imported products—see further **Chapter 8**

Quantitative restriction A non-tariff barrier to trade imposing a limit on the quantity of goods that may be imported or exported, and comprising a quota or a ban—see further **Chapter 8**

Regulation A form of secondary legislation which is directly applicable in the Member States—see further **Chapter 3**

Tariff barrier to trade A restriction on the free movement of goods consisting in a duty or levy—see further **Chapter 8**

Treaties The founding documents of the European Union and the European Community—see further **Chapter 3**

Undertaking (competition law) A legal or natural person engaged in economic activity (i.e. a business)—see further **Chapters 12, 13, 14**

Vertical agreement An agreement between undertakings operating at different levels of the market—see further **Chapter 13**

1 Origins of European Community and European Union law

1.1 OBJECTIVES

By the end of this chapter you should be able to:

1 Explain the basic economic principles underlying the formation and policies of the Community

2 Assess whether the economic and political aims of the founders of the Community have been achieved

3 Describe the changes which have taken place in the ambitions of the Community in social, economic and political spheres

4 Understand the development of the Community since its inception, including the effect of the treaties amending and supplementing the EC Treaty (the SEA, the EU Treaty and the Treaties of Amsterdam and Nice)

5 Explain the structure and underlying objectives of the EU

1.2 Introduction

The legal framework of the Community has developed specifically in order to support and further the aims of the Community organization, and therefore an awareness of the origins of the Community is essential in order to understand the nature of its laws and their impact on UK law.

The 'European Community' or 'EC' is now the correct term for what was formerly the 'European Economic Community' or 'EEC'. It is only one of the three 'European Communities' (see 1.5), which in turn form part of the European Union or EU (see 1.9.2.1). Throughout this book the term 'the Community' will be used for the organization at all stages of its development and may, where appropriate, include the other two Communities.

The EC and EU Treaties were renumbered by the Treaty of Amsterdam (see 1.9.3) which came into force on 1 May 1999. In this textbook the new Article numbers are used and where this number is different to the previous number, the previous number is given in brackets. In the corresponding *Cases and Materials* a table of equivalence of old and new Article numbers is included.

The official convention is that references to Treaty articles as they were prior to 1 May 1999 are made in the form 'Article 1 of the [EC/EU/ECSC/Euratom] Treaty'. References to Treaty Articles as they exist from that date are made in the form 'Article 1 [EC/EU/ECSC/Euratom]'.

1.3 The economic origins of the Community

The original aims of the Community were set out in Article 2 of the Treaty and included balanced economic expansion, increased stability, improved living standards, and closer relations between Member States. These were to be achieved by establishing a common market and harmonizing economic policies. Article 3 of the Treaty set out a number of specific activities to be carried out for the purpose of achieving the aims of Article 2. Articles 2 and 3 have since been amended. In addition to its original provisions, Article 2 EC (*Cases and Materials* (1.1)) now sets out the specific aim of economic and monetary union (known as EMU for short) as well as more general aims, such as equality between men and women, a high level of employment, and of social protection. Article 3 EC (*Cases and Materials* (1.1)) now omits provisions which have been fulfilled, for instance the Common Customs Tariff, and adds a number of new activities for the Community, including some which go beyond purely economic matters, such as consumer protection and the establishment of a Social Fund. It also lists what the Community may do in order to achieve a common market.

The philosophy behind the economic policies of the Community was (and still is) that every individual, company and so forth, based in the Community should be free to invest, produce, work, buy, sell, or supply services wherever in the Community this can be done most efficiently and without competition being artificially distorted. This policy was to be achieved through the establishment of a common market.

? QUESTION 1.1

What do you think the term 'common market' means?

The definition of a common market will be considered shortly but it is a relatively advanced stage on the road to economic integration. At the most basic level, there is simply trade between countries.

Prior to any economic cooperation between countries, each country trades as an independent entity. It makes most sense for each country to concentrate on the goods or services which it can produce most efficiently. To take a hypothetical example, suppose that France produces wine much more efficiently than the UK, but only produces cheese slightly more efficiently.

? QUESTION 1.2

In this example, what might France and the UK gain from trading with each other?

Since France is most efficient in wine production, it should concentrate on that. Since the UK is most efficient (or least inefficient) at producing cheese, it should concentrate on that. However, the two countries can only optimize their efficiency in this way if they trade with each other in order to meet the demand for the product of which they now produce less.

QUESTION 1.3

Can you see any potential problems for these countries in this scenario?

If there are no restrictions at all on trade, i.e. it is 'free trade', then there may be disadvantages. For instance, if France produces less cheese and the UK produces less wine, there will be unemployed workers in the French cheese and UK wine industries. Another problem is that few countries would wish to be totally dependent on one country of supply if the commodity involved was an essential one, such as oil or grain. A third problem is that we have been looking at two countries in isolation. In the real world, free trade does not exist between all countries because of protectionist measures by some, and economic integration between others. The Community has adopted the approach of economic integration.

The first stage of integration is a free trade area. This is where a number of countries agree to remove all customs duties and quotas between themselves, so that when goods, capital, and so forth are moved from one country to another, there is no restriction on the amount and no border taxes on them, **but** each country keeps its own (i.e. different) duties and quotas as regards countries outside the area.

Example

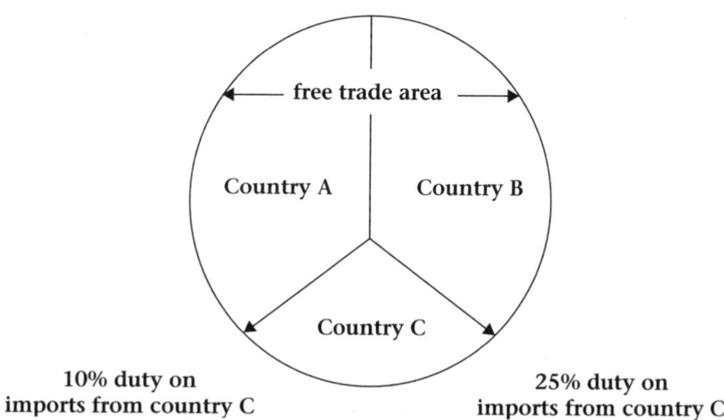

Country A and Country B have joined together to create a free trade area. Country C borders on both of them, but is not part of the free trade area. Country A levies a duty of 10% on goods from countries outside the free trade area, whereas Country B levies a duty of 25% on such imports.

It will be cheaper for Country C to market goods to the whole of the free trade area (Countries A and B) through Country A. The goods will be taxed at 10% when they enter A but can then pass into B without further payment because of the free trade area.

This is good for consumers in the free trade area because the goods will be cheaper than if a 25% duty had been added, but it may affect the relative competitiveness of industry in B (which has to compete with goods from C which are cheaper than before), the trade balance (because C's exports to A will rise and to B will fall, while exports from A to B will also rise) and the customs duties received by each country.

The next stage of integration is a customs union. This consists of a free trade area **plus** an agreement by all members of the area to impose a common level of duty on goods coming into the area from non-member countries.

This common level of duty for the Community is known as the Common Customs Tariff or CCT for short.

A customs union would avoid the imbalance outlined above because the same level of duty would be charged by all the countries within the free trade area to countries outside it. In the example given above, goods from Country C would incur the same level of duty whether they enter the free trade area through A or B.

? QUESTION 1.4

Jack, a chocolate manufacturer within a free trade area, can either buy cheap sugar from outside the area (on which he has to pay a 40% duty), or slightly more expensive sugar from another country within the area (on which he does not have to pay duty). Which do you think he will choose? Will this cause any problems?

The problem with a customs union from an economist's point of view is that it may encourage inefficiency. It is cheaper for Jack to buy from an inefficient producer in another country within the free trade area than from an efficient producer in a country outside the area on whose products he then has to pay import duties. Of course from the point of view of the inefficient producers, being in a customs union is not a problem at all.

Another problem is that such policies lead to international trade diversion, which may cause economic difficulties for countries outside the free trade area. This was a factor in the creation of the European Free Trade Area (EFTA), which was set up in 1960 by a number of European countries outside the Community in an attempt to counter the negative effects on trade.

The next step is a common market. This consists of a customs union **plus** an agreement by all members to remove restrictions on what are known as factors of production, e.g. labour, capital, materials, etc, between themselves. So, for example, there should be no restrictions on working in another country within a common market.

In the Community this requirement has been translated into 'freedom of movement of goods, persons, services and capital'.

The term 'common market' is an economic term used to describe an abstract model. In the context of the Community, the Single European Act 1986 has introduced a further term, the 'internal market', also known as the 'Single Market'. This has a broadly similar meaning but is a term particular to the Community, implying a common market in the precise form laid down by the Act. In the Single Market, certain restrictions on the factors of production continue to exist.

The final stage of the economic integration process is an economic and monetary union. This consists of a common market (including the Community's 'Single Market') **plus** unified monetary and fiscal policies. These include, inter alia, a single currency for all members, common policies on interest rates and central control by the union of each country's budget.

The process of economic and monetary union of the Community is now outlined in the EU Treaty (see 1.9.2). This was not one of the original aims of the Community.

1.4 The political origins of the Community

Ideas of European political integration existed prior to the Second World War, but these ideas only really began to look realistic in the post-war years. Across Europe, memories were scarred by two devastating wars, successive severe winters led to a fuel crisis, there was a series of bad harvests, and foreign reserves were drained by the lack of exports. It seemed that political cooperation might be the way to a better future.

The military threat from the USSR at this time, which marked the beginning of the Cold War, was perceived as particularly acute, and in order to promote post-war stability in Europe the USA offered support in the form of the Marshall Plan (which gave aid to European countries for post-war reconstruction) and the Truman Doctrine (which pledged military support to countries resisting aggression). The founding members of the EC felt that the likelihood of a third world war centred on Europe would be decreased by constructing close economic and political ties between European countries. A cooperative effort, including the pooling of resources, was needed for Europe to recover from the war and cope with the economic problems of the post-war years. In addition, while as individual countries they were too small to compete economically or militarily with either the USA or the then USSR, working together they might have more global influence.

? **QUESTION** 1.5

Despite these cogent reasons, the 1940s did not see the formation of a European union. In the light of what you have read so far, can you think of a reason why the EC Treaty was not signed until 1957 rather than a decade earlier?

The problems of the immediate post-war era—depleted national reserves, decimated industries and large numbers of unemployed ex-servicemen, together with a series of bad winters—meant that national reconstruction took priority over more grandiose European plans. In addition, some of the most ardent supporters of the ideal of a European union were not in a position to influence events. West Germany, which saw a European union as a way to gain re-acceptance by its neighbours had, in the immediate post-war era, little political influence and Winston Churchill, the British Prime Minister who had argued for a United States of Europe, had fallen from power. However, during the late 1940s a number of organizations were set up which involved the close cooperation of European and other states. These included the Organization for European Cooperation (now the Organization for Economic Cooperation and Development), the North Atlantic Treaty Organization and the Council of Europe. A European Defence Community was also proposed, but failed to materialize.

1.5 The original Treaties

1.5.1 The Treaty of Paris establishing the European Coal and Steel Community (ECSC)

A number of countries, particularly France, recognized that if West Germany's coal and steel industries were tied to that of other countries, that country would be seriously hampered in any war effort. In addition it was recognized that cooperation in this area could be economically advantageous.

As a result, in 1951 the Benelux countries together with France, Italy and Germany signed the ECSC Treaty, removing trade restrictions between them on coal and steel and creating a supranational authority (i.e. with powers over the Member States) to oversee the expansion of production.

In the preamble to the ECSC Treaty the signatories declared it to be only the first step towards a federal Europe, but all the members recognized the importance of establishing solidarity in fact before progressing to grander ideals. The ECSC had the same Member States as the European Community and EURATOM and shared their institutions from 1967.

The ECSC Treaty expired in July 2002.

1.5.2 The Treaty of Tome establishing the European Economic Community (now the European Community)

The six members of the ECSC, particularly the Benelux countries which were already closely linked economically by the Benelux Union, became increasingly anxious to extend their fledgling alliance to other economic and political areas. In 1957, on the basis of the Spaak Report on the feasibility of European integration, the Treaty establishing the EEC was signed.

? QUESTION 1.6

Summarize in not more than one hundred words the economic and political events which led to the creation of the Community in 1957. Check your answer against the foregoing text to make sure that you have included the most important points.

1.5.3 The EC Treaty establishing the European Atomic Energy Community (EURATOM)

In 1957 the six Community countries signed this treaty, formally agreeing to cooperate in the development of the peaceful use of atomic energy. EURATOM has the same Member States as the European Community and the ECSC and has shared their institutions since 1967.

1.6 The early years of the Community

The economic boom of the late 1950s and early 1960s made the Community's task easier. Many quotas and duties were removed and a common external tariff put in place. Steps were taken towards establishing the free movement of workers and protecting their social security interests, regulating competition and establishing a common agricultural policy.

Initially, all Community decisions were taken by consensus. However, during the 1960s provisions gradually came into effect requiring certain decisions to be taken by a qualified majority vote. Qualified majority voting (QMV) requires a specific number of votes (rather than a simple majority) to be cast in favour of a measure in order for it to be passed. The number of votes given to a country is determined by the relative size of its population, thus giving greater power but, crucially, no veto to the larger countries such as Italy and France. Qualified majority decisions were to include, from 1966, those concerning agricultural prices, the area which absorbed most of the Community's expenditure and an area of key importance to France. The French president, Charles de Gaulle, believed that it was not in French interests for decisions in this area to be taken without French approval. He therefore refused to exercise France's vote in the final period of consensus voting so that no decisions could be taken. This tactic succeeded in forcing the other countries to compromise on the issue of QMV. The compromise was known as the Luxembourg Accords.

The Luxembourg Accords stated that where the Treaty provided for qualified majority voting **and** the vitally important interests of one or more Member States were involved, the Community must try to find a unanimous solution. In practice the Accords meant that all decisions had to be unanimous. Either all Member States agreed with a decision in the first place or those which did not claimed that their vital interests were affected and refused to vote in favour until a solution was reached which they could accept. The decision would then be unanimous. QMV was effectively sidelined, and only once were the Accords ignored prior to the introduction of the Single European Act (see 1.9.1). This was in 1982 when the UK opposed the adoption of certain agricultural prices as part of its campaign to limit Community expenditure. Despite this opposition, the measure was passed using QMV.

The Single European Act 1986, the Treaty on European Union 1992 (EU Treaty) and the Treaty of Amsterdam have extended the areas to which QMV applies and made it less practical for the Luxembourg Accords to operate. In addition, with the continued expansion of Community membership, it would become increasingly difficult to make decisions unless QMV is strictly applied.

However, it is interesting to note that the Treaty of Amsterdam has inserted into the EC Treaty and the EU Treaty a formula similar to the Luxembourg Accords applicable in the procedures for establishing closer cooperation. The details of closer cooperation will be discussed further at 3.6.3 but, effectively, where some but not all Member States wish to establish closer cooperation they may do so, subject to certain conditions. However, if a Member State opposes this cooperation for 'important and stated reasons of national policy' the Council may not authorize it, but must instead refer the matter to the Council meeting as Heads of Government or State, which may only authorize the cooperation by unanimous agreement. This effectively applies the Luxembourg Accords to closer cooperation, since a Member State which declares that it has important reasons for opposing closer cooperation may force a decision to be taken unanimously, enabling it to block the decision.

1.7 A period of stagnation for the Community

From the mid-1960s there was a falling away of interest in the Community which lasted until well into the 1980s. The boom of the early 1960s had not been sustained and Community membership no longer appeared to guarantee economic success. In the 1970s the Member States became even less interested in the Community, as they concentrated on their own economic ills in the wake of the Organization of Petroleum Exporting Countries (OPEC) crisis of 1973, when oil prices rocketed and a world-wide slump set in.

The Merger Treaty (1965) merged the institutions of the three Communities (the ECSC, the Community, and EURATOM), but the 1969 deadline for the completion of the common market came and went, scarcely noticed and certainly unfulfilled.

The Budgetary Treaties of 1970 and 1975 introduced a special procedure for drafting and approving the Community budget which gave the Parliament greater powers (although these were still woefully inadequate by the standards of many members of the Parliament and of the public who saw the Community as alarmingly undemocratic). The 'own resources' concept was also introduced, that is to say, in addition to money contributed by the Member States, the Community had its own resources coming from the levies under the Common Agricultural Policy, the CCT and other Community inspired taxes. A Court of Auditors was appointed as a financial watchdog over Community spending.

The most important activities in this period were the development of the Community's legal system and the expansion of its membership (see 1.10).

EXERCISE 1.1

Make a note of the names of the cases listed below, which will be discussed in more detail later as indicated. When you reach each of these cases in later chapters, think about the impact that they had on the development of Community law and contrast this with the lack of development of other aspects of the Community at that time.

Important legal developments included the following Court of Justice decisions.

(a) Once Community measures had been taken in a particular area, Member States could no longer act independently in that area, since this would prevent the uniform application of

Community law; *Commission* v *Council (ERTA)* (Case 22/70) [1971] ECR 263. (See 3.4.2.)

(b) In certain circumstances an individual could rely on Community Directives in national courts; *Van Duyn* v *Home Office* (Case 41/74) [1974] ECR 1337. (See 4.3.2.)

(c) Since Community law was supreme, national legislation which conflicted with it should be disapplied; *Amministrazione delle Finanze dello Stato* v *Simmenthal SpA (Simmenthal II)* (Case 106/77) [1978] ECR 629. (See 3.3.2.2.)

(d) Legislation enacted by the Council without consulting the Parliament where required was invalid; *Roquette Frères* v *Council* (Case 138/79) [1978] ECR 3333. (See 6.8.2.)

1.8 The re-launch of the Community

In 1984 the Draft EU Treaty, which was designed to create a federal Europe with a more powerful Parliament, was adopted by the Parliament. Although the Draft was not accepted by the Council, the Dooge Committee was set up to look into possible reforms of the EC Treaty.

The French Presidency under François Mitterrand managed to resolve the long-running dispute over the UK's contribution to the budget, and pressurized the UK into accepting the work of the committee by making references to a future scenario involving a two-tier Europe, with the UK firmly in the second tier. The UK had fallen behind its more integrationist neighbours once before, when it had refused to join the Community in the 1950s. It was not an experience which the UK, even under Margaret Thatcher, wished to repeat.

At the same time, a new President of the Commission was appointed, Jacques Delors. It was he who oversaw the White Paper on European Union which became the Single European Act (see 1.9.1). Ironically, given the view of the then UK government under Margaret Thatcher on European union, it was a British Commissioner, Lord Cockfield, who actually masterminded the White Paper.

In 1988 the European Regional Development Fund and the European Social Fund were restructured to channel more Community funds away from the Common Agricultural Policy (CAP) and towards regional development, as part of the Community's commitment to the harmonization of development throughout the Community, and to counter fears that the Single Market would exacerbate regional inequalities.

In 1989 all of the Member States, except the UK, adopted the Community Charter of Fundamental Social Rights of Workers. This was in addition to provisions in the EC Treaty on health and safety at work, and the prohibition of discrimination at work on grounds of sex. The Charter stated the basic rights of, amongst others, freedom of movement, fair remuneration and adequate social protection, but was not binding and conferred no new powers. It was simply a statement of recommended standards of worker welfare which were to be a goal for its signatories. It was the basis for the Social Protocol of the EU Treaty, the so-called 'Social Chapter', which extended the ambit and powers of Community social policy and into which the UK eventually opted. These provisions have now been incorporated into the EC Treaty (Articles 136–45 (ex 117–22) EC).

1.9 The amending Treaties

There have been four major amending Treaties: the Single European Act 1986 (SEA), the Treaty on European Union 1992 (the EU Treaty), the Treaty of Amsterdam 1997 and the Treaty of Nice 2001. The SEA and the Treaties of Nice and Amsterdam consisted of provisions amending the EC, EU, ECSC, and EURATOM Treaties. The EU Treaty (sometimes known as the TEU) also consists largely of provisions amending the EC Treaty, but certain provisions remain outside.

This Chapter will summarize each of these four Treaties and consider the current status of the provisions introduced by them in more detail.

1.9.1 The Single European Act 1986 (SEA)

The key provisions of the SEA were:

* **Amendments to the EC Treaty to ensure completion of the single internal market by the end of 1992**

The EC Treaty laid down a twelve-year period for the establishment of a common market, but by the end of 1969 it was far from complete. The Court of Justice had tried to assist by prohibiting many interferences with free movement, but it could not achieve the necessary advances alone. The Commission, under the presidency of Jacques Delors, was particularly keen to set the wheels in motion.

The SEA provided the following:

- a detailed definition of the Single Market (in Article 14 (ex 7a) EC);

Article 14 (ex 7a)

1. The Community shall adopt measures with the aim of progressively establishing the internal market over a period expiring on 31 December 1992, in accordance with the provisions of this Article and of Articles 15, 26, 47(2), 49, 80, 93, and 95 and without prejudice to the other provisions of this Treaty.
2. The internal market shall comprise an area without internal frontiers in which the free movement of goods, persons, services and capital is ensured in accordance with the provisions of this Treaty.
3. The Council, acting by a qualified majority on a proposal from the Commission, shall determine the guidelines and conditions necessary to ensure balanced economic progress in all the sectors concerned.

- a deadline of the end of 1992 for the completion of the Single Market;
- a specific obligation on the Community to adopt the necessary measures to achieve the Single Market;
- a new law-making power to be applied to such measures, requiring the approval of either a qualified majority of the Council and a majority of the Parliament or of the Council acting unanimously. This was known as the cooperation procedure (but has now been replaced by other procedures—see 3.6.)

* **Amendments to the EC Treaty to include new areas of competence**

These new areas of competence were those that the Community had in practice already taken upon itself, for example, environmental matters, research and development, and regional development. They constituted new legislative bases, that is to say, legal foundations on which the Community is empowered to base legislation. For further details of the importance of legislative bases, see 3.4, 3.6, 6.3.3.2 and 6.8.

* **Amendments to the EC Treaty to introduce the Court of First Instance**

This court was introduced in order to reduce the workload of the Court of Justice and thereby ease the problem of delays in the judicial process. However, it largely failed to do this.

* **Provisions (operating outside the EC Treaty) formalizing the role of the European Council**

The European Council (the Council operating at the level of heads of government or state) was originally an informal forum for discussion, but was brought into the Community framework by Article 2 SEA and given a more formal role by Article 4 (ex D) EU.

* **Provisions (operating outside the EC Treaty) for European Political Cooperation**

The SEA set out a number of principles to bring about closer and more systematic cooperation in the formulation and implementation of foreign policy. This was built upon both by the EU Treaty (see 1.9.2) and the Treaty of Amsterdam (see 1.9.3).

1.9.2 The Treaty on European Union 1992

The EU Treaty represents potentially the most significant advance in the Community's development since its foundation in 1957. It created an entirely new structure, the European Union, based on the Community and with the same membership, but with a much greater sphere of competence. The Community continues to exist in the form already outlined but is now part of the European Union, rather as Scotland continues to exist as a separate entity although it is also part of the UK. The EU shares the institutions of the Community (see **Chapter 2**).

As mentioned above, the EU Treaty created the EU. This is closely related to the Community, but is a separate entity and must be considered in a little more detail.

1.9.2.1 Structure of the EU

The EU consists of the Communities (the Community, EURATOM and, originally, the ECSC), a common foreign and security policy and cooperation on justice and home affairs. It has no legal personality of its own and uses the Community's institutions and resources.

? QUESTION 1.7

What do you think is meant by the expression 'the three pillars of the EU'? Draw a diagram illustrating the structure of the EU.

The 'three pillars' of the EU are the central pillar of the Communities and the two side pillars of foreign and security policy, and justice and home affairs. To make this clear, a diagram may be drawn as follows.

Structure of the EU

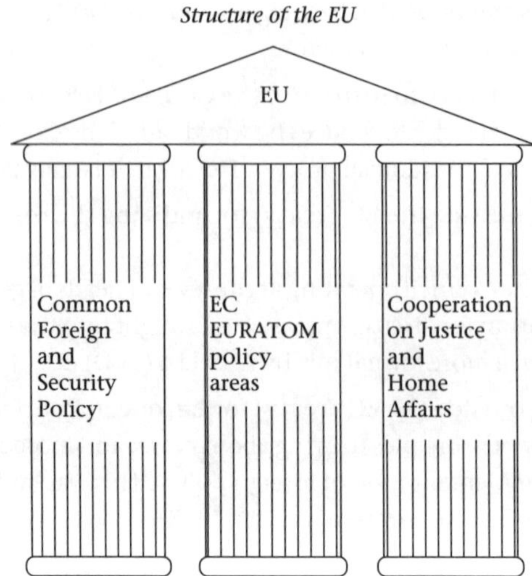

1.9.2.2 Objectives of the EU

These are set out in Article 2 (ex B) EU and were amended by the Treaty of Amsterdam. Article 2 provides that the objectives of the EU are as follows:

(a) to promote economic and social progress, a high level of employment and balanced and sustainable development through economic and social cohesion and EMU (see 1.9.2.3);

(b) to assert its international identity, in particular through a common foreign and security policy (see 1.9.2.3);

(c) to strengthen individual rights by the introduction of EU citizenship (see 1.9.2.3);

(d) to maintain and develop the EU as an area of freedom, security and justice (see 1.9.2.3);

(e) to maintain the '*acquis communautaire*' (the existing laws and conventions of the Community).

Article 6 EU states that the national identity of the Member States should be respected, indicates that democracy is a prerequisite for membership, and states that fundamental human rights must be observed by the EU. Article 6 was amended by the Treaty of Amsterdam to refer additionally to the principles of liberty and the rule of law.

1.9.2.3 Key provisions of the EU Treaty

- **Change of name**

The EU Treaty changed the name of the Community from the European Economic Community to the European Community. This change of name reflects the change of emphasis within the organization, from an economic and market oriented body to one with competences in areas such as education, culture, and consumer protection.

- **Subsidiarity** (see **3.4.3**)

- **Citizenship**

The rights granted by Article 19 (ex 8b) EC to stand and vote in local and European elections in another Member State in which the citizen is resident, were new, but it should be noted that national elections are excluded. The right to participate in such elections is governed by national law and does not arise merely by virtue of EU citizenship.

The right given by Article 20 (ex 8c) EC to diplomatic protection provided by another Member State in a non-EU country where the citizen's own Member State is not represented was officially new, but reflected what formerly happened in practice. The rights given by Article 21 (ex 8d) EC to petition the Parliament or the EU Ombudsman were also technically new, although in practice it was always possible to petition the local MEP.

For both the Parliament and the citizen, the key importance of these rights is the element of democracy. The ability to receive petitions gives the Parliament (the only directly elected Community institution) direct contact with the people of the Community. Equally, the right to present petitions to the Parliament or the Ombudsman gives citizens their most direct influence on the activities of the Parliament and through it, on those of the Community generally.

As mentioned above, Articles 17–22 (ex 8–8e) EC are as much a restatement of existing rights (free movement of workers) and practices (diplomatic protection) as a grant of new ones (participation in elections, petitioning the Parliament). However, Article 17 EC is of some importance because, for the first time, individual political rights were gathered together and bestowed directly on the citizens of the EU, rather than simply on the nationals of individual Member States.

- **Economic and social cohesion**

As a result of the EU Treaty, the strengthening of economic and social cohesion is now included in the activities of the Community listed under Article 3 EC and in the Protocol on Economic and Social Cohesion annexed to the EC Treaty. The Community decided that, in order to spread the benefits of the Single Market, it must take positive action to reduce the economic and social disparities between different regions. This was considered to be particularly important if economic and monetary union is to be achieved. A Cohesion Fund was set up to contribute to projects involving the international transport infrastructure or the environment.

- **Economic and monetary union**

Article 4 (ex 3a) EC now provides that the activities of the Member States and the Community are to include:

(a) an economic policy involving:

  (i) the coordination of the Member States' economic policies;
  (ii) the internal market;
  (iii) the definition of common objectives; and
  (iv) an open market economy with free competition

(b) a monetary policy involving:

  (i) the permanent fixing of exchange rates leading to the introduction of a single currency, the ECU; and
  (ii) a single monetary and exchange rate policy.

In December 1995, the European Council decided that when the ECU became the single currency it would be known as the Euro.

- **Cooperation on justice and home affairs** (now police and judicial cooperation in criminal matters).

As introduced by the EU Treaty, Cooperation on Justice and Home Affairs covered the treatment of non-Member State, nationals and aspects of law enforcement which fell outside Community competence but which had the potential to affect the operation of the Single Market.

More specifically, Article 29 (ex K.1) of the EU Treaty listed nine areas which are of 'common interest' to the Member States, and over which therefore they could be required to cooperate. These included areas such as asylum policy and immigration policy, which were moved from the Treaty of Amsterdam into the EC Treaty itself (see 1.9.3). The remaining areas of competence in this pillar were renamed Police and Judicial Cooperation in Criminal Matters.

The aim of these provisions (contained in Title VI EU (Articles 29–42 EU) (ex K.1–K.14) EU) is to provide citizens with a high level of safety within 'an area of freedom, justice and security'. This is to be achieved by three methods:

(a) closer cooperation between police forces and customs authorities, involving:
   (i) operational cooperation including Europol;
   (ii) exchange of information;
   (iii) joint initiatives in training and exchanges;
   (iv) common development of detective techniques;

(b) closer judicial cooperation in criminal matters, such as:
   (i) enforcement of judgments;
   (ii) extradition;

(c) harmonization of criminal law.

The legislative procedure is different to that applicable under the EC Treaty. A measure may be proposed by a Member State or the Commission, Parliament need only be consulted and the Council takes the final decision (unanimously or by qualified majority according to the type of measure).

The jurisdiction of the Court of Justice in this area is limited (see 2.3.4). It may only give preliminary rulings under Article 234 EC (ex 177) EC (see **Chapter 5**) on questions of interpretation and validity relating to Articles 29–42 EU where those questions are referred by courts of a Member State which has declared that it will accept such jurisdiction. A Member State may limit this jurisdiction to questions referred by the highest court, rather than by all courts. The Court of Justice has no jurisdiction in respect of law and order or internal security measures taken under Articles 29–42 EU. No jurisdiction is provided in relation to Article 230 (ex 173) EC (see **Chapter 6**).

The Treaty of Nice (see 1.9.4) provided limited amendments to this pillar. The European Judicial Cooperation Unit (Euro Just) was set up, composed of national prosecutors, magistrates or police officers of equivalent competence. Euro Just facilitates coordination between national prosecuting authorities, supports international criminal investigations, and cooperates with the European Judicial Network.

- **The common foreign and security policy.**

The Common Foreign and Security Policy introduced by the EU Treaty represents an advance on the SEA's Political Cooperation and covers all areas of foreign and security policy, eventually including a common defence policy and possibly a common defence. The defence role is fulfilled by the existing Western European Union, of which ten Member States are members and five Member States are observers. This pillar was further developed by the Treaties of Amsterdam and Nice.

These provisions (contained in Title V EU (Articles 11–28) (ex J.1–J.18)) potentially cover all areas of foreign and security policy.

This policy is to be achieved by:

(a) the definition of general principles (by the European Council (see 2.4.1));

(b) common strategies (to be implemented by the EU where Member States have important interests in common);

(c) joint actions (that is to say, operational action in specific circumstances);

(d) common positions (to which Member States must conform in their national policies);

(e) the strengthening of systematic cooperation between Member States.

The legislative procedure is different to that applicable under the EC Treaty. A measure may be proposed by a Member State or the Commission, Parliament need only be consulted and the Council takes the final decision (unanimously or by qualified majority according to the type of measure).

Article 23 EU provides that where Member States are required to act unanimously in the common foreign and security policy, a Member State may abstain without prejudice to action being taken ('constructive absention'). In effect, this means that other Member States may proceed to act. However, Article 23 further provides that abstentions may be qualified and that if more than a third of weighted votes are thus qualified, the decision may not be adopted.

Article 23 EU also provides that where Member States are required to act by qualified majority in the common foreign and security policy, and no decision having military or defence implications is involved, a vote may not be taken if a Member State declares that it opposes this 'for important and stated reasons of national policy'. The matter may then be referred to the Council acting in the composition of Heads of Government or State, which must act unanimously to authorize the action.

The Court of Justice has no jurisdiction in this area (see 2.3.4.1).

The Treaty of Nice provided limited amendments to this pillar. The role of the WEU is reduced and that of NATO emphasized.

QUESTION 1.8

What significance, if any, do you consider that this change of name might have?

1.9.3 The Treaty of Amsterdam

This Treaty was negotiated against the background of anticipated enlargement, requiring both institutional reform to ensure that a larger Community would be administratively workable, and greater flexibility to ensure that those Member States which wish to do so can proceed to greater integration. The Treaty of Amsterdam was also intended to build on the achievements of the EU Treaty. The Treaty of Amsterdam was heralded as another major amending Treaty like the EU Treaty, but has in fact achieved much less. One of its main functions should have been to make institutional reforms to prepare the Community for enlargement, but it has not succeeded in this aim. As a result, a further Treaty was required, the Treaty of Nice 2001 (see 1.9.4).

The key provisions of the Treaty of Amsterdam were

- **Renumbering of the Treaties**

As mentioned at 1.2 the Treaty of Amsterdam provided for the renumbering of the EC and EU Treaties.

- **Institutional reform**
  - the reform of the co-decision procedure (see 3.6.2);
  - the extension of the co-decision procedure, giving equal rights of decision making to the Parliament and the Council in most areas (see 3.6.2);
  - the extension of QMV (see 1.6);
  - amendments to subsidiarity (see 3.4.3).

  However, the Treaty of Amsterdam failed to deal with the following institutional problems which would arise on enlargement to over twenty Member States:
  - the system of the Presidency, since the system of each Member State holding the Presidency for six months in turn would mean that Member States would hold the Presidency less than once every ten years, with possible adverse consequences politically and in terms of consistency.
  - the number of Commissioners, since the system of one Commissioner per Member State and two for larger States would mean that there would be almost thirty Commissioners, with possible adverse consequences for effective decision-making in the Commission;
- **Introduction of new Title IV EC on visas, asylum, immigration, and other policies relating to the free movement of persons**
- **Introduction of new EC Titles on Employment and Social Policy**
- **The renaming and amending of Cooperation on Justice and Home Affairs—now Police and Judicial Cooperation in Criminal Matters**
- **Amendments to the Common Foreign and Security Policy** (see 1.9.2.3)
- **Introduction of Article 7 EU**

Article 7 EU, as introduced by the Treaty of Amsterdam, provides that if a Member State seriously breaches the fundamental principles set out in Article 6 EU (liberty, democracy, respect for human rights and fundamental freedoms, and the rule of law) its Treaty rights, including voting rights, may be suspended. A breach is determined unanimously by the Council on a proposal by one-third of the Member States or by the Commission, and the Parliament's assent is required. A decision on whether to suspend the rights of the Member State is broken by the Council by QMV.

Under the Treaty of Amsterdam, the first and only step which the EU could take if a Member State seriously breached the fundamental principles enshrined in Article 6 EU was the suspension of its Treaty rights, including voting rights. The Treaty of Nice permits the Council to take lesser measures designed to give the Member State an opportunity to stave off this more serious sanction. The Parliament, Commission, or one-third of the Member States may make a proposal and if the Parliament assents, the Council may by a four-fifths majority determine the existence of a 'clear risk' of a serious breach of the principles in Article 6 and address recommendations to the Member State. Before doing so it must hear the Member State and may commission an independent report on the Member State concerned.

- **Introduction of 'closer cooperation'—now 'enhanced cooperation'** (see 3.6.3)

- **Incorporation of Schengen**

The Protocol (No 2) integrating the Schengen acquis into the framework of the European Union (1997) provides that those Member States which had signed the Schengen Agreements (all Member States except the UK and Ireland) now conduct their cooperation on the abolition of internal borders under the institutional and legislative framework of the EU. Ireland and the UK may take part in such arrangements subject to the unanimous approval of the other Member States. Denmark is not involved in the incorporation into the EC Treaty, and further development, of the Schengen acquis, but retains its existing obligations under Schengen. The term 'acquis' refers to existing laws, conventions, and decisions. In this context it refers to those existing measures passed pursuant to the Schengen agreements.

1.9.4 The Treaty of Nice 2001

As discussed above, the Treaty of Nice was intended to achieve those institutional reforms which the Treaty of Amsterdam failed to achieve. However, its lack of success has been highlighted by the subsequent need to attempt to produce a European Constitution.

The key provisions of the Treaty of Nice were:

- **Institutional reform**

Certain of these amendments—in relation to the number and allocation of MEPs, the requirements of QMV and the number of Commissioners—are contained in the Protocol on the Enlargement of the European Union which is annexed to the Treaty of Nice, rather than in the body of the Treaty itself:

  - reforms to the Commission (see 2.3.1);
  - extension and reweighting of QMV (see 1.6);
  - reforms to the Parliament (see 2.3.3);
  - reforms to the procedures of the Court of Justice (see 2.3.4);
  - extension of the jurisdiction of the Court of First Instance (see 2.3.5);
  - reforms to the Court of Auditors (see 2.3.6);
  - extension of co-decision (see 3.6.2);
  - alterations to the *locus standi* of the Parliament under Article 230 EC (see 6.3.3.1 and 6.3.3.2).

- **Amendments to Police and Judicial Cooperation**
- **Amendments to the Common Foreign and Security Policy** (see 1.9.3)
- **Amendments to Social Policy**
- **Amendments to Article 7 EU** (see 1.9.2.3)
- **Enhanced Cooperation** (see 3.6.3)

The Treaty of Nice provides a number of amendments to the scope, conditions, and procedure for closer cooperation which it renames 'enhanced cooperation'.

EXERCISE 1.2

Briefly describe and explain the events leading to the introduction of the Single European Act. Check your answer against the foregoing text to make sure that you have included the most important points.

1.10 Enlargement

> **? QUESTION 1.9**
>
> From your own knowledge, can you identify the current Member States of the Community?

The original six members of the Community were Belgium, The Netherlands, Luxembourg, Italy, France, and Germany. In 1973 the UK, Denmark, and Ireland joined them, followed by Greece in 1981, Spain and Portugal in 1986, and Austria, Finland, and Sweden in 1995. In 2004, Cyprus, Malta, Estonia, Latvia, Lithuania, the Czech Republic, Hungary, Poland, Slovakia and Slovenia joined the Community, and in 2007 Bulgaria and Romania, bringing the total to 27.

The Community is conducting negotiations for accession with a number of other countries.

1.11 The current economic status of the Community

> **? QUESTION 1.10**
>
> Can you identify from your own knowledge which stage the Community has now reached? Give reasons for your answer.

If you have any difficulty in answering this question, look back at the definition of each stage and think about your own experience. Have you ever wanted to work in another Community country or bring back expensive goods from a European holiday? What sort of restrictions, if any, have you encountered or think that you might encounter?

Despite the widespread use in the UK in the 1970s of the term 'Common Market', meaning the Community, the deadline originally envisaged by the EC Treaty for the completion of the common market (the end of 1969) passed without fulfilment. It was only the completion in the early 1990s of the Single Market which brought the Community close to achieving a full common market. In fact, as stated above, the Single Market is not a perfect market. For instance, there are still more restrictions on the right of a Briton to work in Germany than for a German to work there, and restrictions on the value of goods which that Briton might bring back into the UK with him. These are not features that one would expect to see in a genuine common market. However, the Single Market as defined by the Community has now been fulfilled.

Note also that the Schengen Agreements on the abolition of frontier controls were agreed by all Member States except the UK and Ireland, and have now been incorporated into the EU (see 1.9.3). The Agreements are intended to achieve the free movement of persons between these countries.

1.12 The current political status of the Community

The draft Treaty Establishing a Constitution for Europe (http://europa.eu.int/constitution) is designed to replace the EC and EU Treaties with a single Treaty, and the EC and EU with a single body. A number of amendments to the institutions are included, in order to streamline procedures after the recent enlargement, and in the expectation of further enlargement in the future. It also incorporates the EU Charter of Fundamental Rights, thus making human rights enforceable against the institutions of the EU. However, the Treaty establishing the Constitution will enter into force only when—and if—ratified by all Member States. At the date of writing, although many States have ratified the Treaty, at least two are unlikely to do so in the near future after their populations rejected the Treaty in referenda.

CONCLUSION

The Community has come a long way since 1957. A rather imperfect common market is in place and full economic and monetary integration is envisaged. The Member States have achieved much in terms of political cooperation. The EU Treaty (and to a lesser extent the SEA and the Treaties of Amsterdam and Nice) fundamentally changed the political, economic, and legal assumptions underlying the Community. However, how the tension between 'deepening' the level of integration and 'widening' the number of countries to be integrated will be resolved remains to be seen.

In political terms, the agenda for EMU and the new policy areas relating to foreign and defence policy, and justice and home affairs, gave a radical new direction to the Community.

In economic terms, the move to economic and monetary union has been far from smooth and a degree of scepticism still surrounds the project.

In legal terms, the EU Treaty has firmly established the principle of subsidiarity and inserted into the EC Treaty some of its most detailed provisions (those on EMU). It has also introduced new policy areas which are outside the legal framework of the Community.

The Treaty of Amsterdam built on these policy areas and began to incorporate some of them into the Community's legal framework. It also introduced for the first time a general principle of closer cooperation among some Member States. The potential significance of this principle remains to be seen.

The Treaty of Nice attempts to prepare for enlargement by reforming the institutions and procedures of the EU. Although it achieves a number of reforms, not all of these are in force as yet, and the true test of their success will come when enforcement actually takes place.

SUMMARY

- The EEC (now the EC) was founded in 1957 as a result of the EEC (now the EC) Treaty. Its **origins** lie in the desire of the original Member States to avoid another major war developing in Europe and to develop a trading bloc with global influence. It was preceded by the ECSC, which attempted to integrate the traditional war industries, coal and steel, so that Member States could engage in a war effort.

- Since then, the EC has proceeded along the path of **economic integration** (see further **Chapter 8** on the free movement of goods), and in 1992 the EU Treaty established economic and monetary union as an objective of the Member States.
- However, there have been, and remain, **difficulties**. As the number of Member States increases, decision-making becomes more complex, not least because of the corresponding increase in the diversity of views as to what the EC should be about. The rejection of the Constitution by the populations of a number of Member States is evidence of this.
- The first major amending Treaty, **the SEA**, provided momentum to achieve the single market within the EC. It also extended the competences of the EC and set up the CFI.
- The most important amending Treaty, **the EU Treaty** or TEU, established a new body, the EU. This is almost identical to the EC but has additional competences (police and judicial cooperation in criminal matters and a common foreign and security policy) which are outside the institutional structure of the EC (particularly the input of the Parliament and the Court of Justice).
- The **Treaties of Amsterdam and Nice** were primarily intended to streamline the institutional structures of the EC in anticipation of enlargement. However, they have not been entirely successful in enabling the EC to function more efficiently.

CHAPTER 1: ASSESSMENT EXERCISE

(a) Explain the underlying philosophies behind the formation of the Community.
(b) How have these philosophies changed since formation?
(c) Why was the Single European Act necessary and how did it provide for the achievement of its objectives?
(d) Briefly summarize the provisions on EMU as introduced by the EU Treaty.

See *Cases and Materials* (1.3) for a specimen answer.

FURTHER READING

Duff, A. (1997). 'The Treaty of Amsterdam: Text and Commentary', *Federal Trust*. London: Sweet Maxwell.

Editorial Comments (1995). 'Schengen: The Pros and Cons' *Cases and Materials* 32 (3) *CMLRev* 675.

George, S. and Burke, I. (2001). 'Politics in the European Union' Oxford: Oxford University Press.

Marias, E. (1994). 'The Right to Petition the European Parliament after Maastricht' in *ELRev* 169.

Piris, J. C. (1994). 'After Maastricht, are the Community Institutions More Efficacious, More Democratic and More Transparent?' 19 *EL Rev* 449.

Raworth, P. (1994). 'A Timid Step Forwards: Maastricht and the Democratisation of the EC', 19(1) *ELRev* 16.

2 The institutions of the Community and the EU

2.1 OBJECTIVES

By the end of this chapter you should be able to:

1 Describe the composition and functions of the institutions of the Community and the EU

2 Analyse the relative importance and power of these institutions, including the extent of the so-called 'democratic deficit'

3 Explain the role of the Court of Justice within the framework of the Community

2.2 Introduction

When politicians and others talk of 'Brussels' what do they actually mean? Are they referring to the democratically elected Parliament, representatives of the Member State governments meeting in Council, or the full-time and independent Commissioners? The aim of this chapter is to give you an overview of the composition and functions of these and the other main institutions of the Community. While this is not a difficult topic, it is important that you are familiar with the roles of the institutions in order to understand the balance of power within the Community and the legislative framework outlined in **Chapter 3**. The most important institutions are the five referred to in Article 7 (ex 4) EC (the Parliament, the Council, the Commission, the Court of Justice (to which the Court of First Instance is attached) and the Court of Auditors), but in order to gain a true picture of the Community's organization we will be considering a number of the other institutions.

2.3 The 'Big Five' Institutions

EXERCISE 2.1

From your own knowledge, try to fill in as much information as you can about the five main institutions in the following table.

Which people make up this institution?	What kind of work do they do?
The Commission	
The Council	
The Parliament	
The Court of Justice	
The Court of Auditors	

Exercise 2.2 is also related to this chart.

2.3.1 The Commission

This body is based in Brussels but has an outpost in Luxembourg. It consists of one Commissioner from each Member State. They are appointed for five-yearly periods by the common accord of the Member States and must be approved by the Parliament. Once the number of Commissioners exceeds 27, a system of rotation, to be decided unanimously by the Council, will be used.

Commissioners are expected to possess general competence, and to be independent. They are not national representatives, and should not take instructions from their Member State (or indeed anyone else). You might, however, have noted that since they ultimately owe their appointment and re-appointment to the exercise of national discretion and to Parliamentary approval, these factors may influence the exercise of their powers.

Commissioners meet weekly and take decisions by a simple majority vote (Article 219 (ex 163) EC). They have specific duties according to the policy portfolio which is allocated to them by the President of the Commission (a Commissioner nominated by the Council and approved by the Parliament). Each Commissioner has a personal staff of civil servants, and they are also assisted by departments of civil servants that each cover a policy area.

The power of the Commission to delegate is severely limited, for example, decisions under Article 226 (ex 169) EC must be the subject of collective deliberation (see 2.3.1.1) and it cannot keep pace with its increasing volume of work. This causes delays in the enactment of legislation.

The Commission has three principal roles as outlined below: guardianship of the EC Treaty, formulation of policy, and execution of policy. In addition to these functions, the Commission also has a representative function. The Commission President may speak on behalf of the Community, often with the head of government or state of the Member State which holds the Presidency of the Community, and it is the Commission which negotiates international agreements on behalf of the Community. It is also responsible for the establishment of Community diplomatic missions abroad and the accreditation of those sent to the Community.

2.3.1.1 Guardianship of the EC Treaty

The Commission's chief weapon in enforcing the EC Treaty is Article 226 (ex 169) EC. Article 226 (ex 169) EC empowers the Commission to bring enforcement proceedings before the Court of Justice against a Member State which it considers to have failed to fulfil its Treaty obligations. The Commission must first allow the Member State to state its case, and will then give its opinion. If the Member State does not comply with the opinion, the Commission may bring proceedings in the Court of Justice. Decisions by the Commission under Article 226 EC must be made collectively by the Commission (C-191/95 *Commission* v *Germany* [1998] ECR I-5449).

Under Article 227 (ex 170) EC, if a Member State considers that another Member State has failed to fulfil its Treaty obligations, it must notify the Commission, which will allow the other Member State to state its case and then give its opinion. The Commission or the complainant Member State may then bring proceedings in the Court of Justice.

An example of the effect of rulings under Articles 226 and 227 (ex 169 and 170) may be seen in *Commission* v *France* (Cases 24 and 97/80) [1980] ECR 1319. The Court of Justice had ruled that French restrictions on imports of lamb and mutton from the UK were contrary to Community law. Despite this, the restrictions were continued by France on the ground that their sudden withdrawal could lead to economic damage and possibly problems of public order. The Court of Justice ruled that a judgment that a Member State had failed in its obligations amounted to a prohibition on applying the inconsistent national measures and the imposition of a duty to take all necessary action. The restrictions should therefore have been lifted with effect from the date specified in the earlier judgment.

Under Article 228 (ex 171) EC the Court of Justice, on the application of the Commission, may fine a Member State which is guilty of a continued failure to comply with a judgment against it given by the Court of Justice.

Additionally, under Articles 230 and 232 (ex 173 and 175) EC (see **Chapter 6**) any Member State or institution (including the Commission) may refer an act or omission which is contrary to Community law to the Court of Justice for annulment; and the Commission has enforcement powers in relation to the EC Treaty and secondary legislation relating to competition policy.

2.3.1.2 Formulation of policy

There are three ways in which the Commission can formulate policy:

(a) **A proposal for action**
This can relate to any area of Community competence and may take the form of draft legislation for the Council to adopt or more general proposals for consideration by the Council, for example the White Paper 'Completing the Internal Market'. Note that under Title VI EU, judicial cooperation in criminal matters, legislation may be proposed by either the Commission or a Member State.

(b) **The draft budget**
The Commission is responsible for drafting the annual Community budget.

(c) **Policy decisions**
The Commission may take policy decisions where the EC Treaty so provides. Article 137 (ex 118) EC gives the Commission the task of promoting close cooperation between Member States in social matters. In *Germany and Others* v *Commission* (Cases 281/85 etc.) [1987] ECR 3202, a number of Member States challenged certain Decisions taken by the Commission pursuant to this Article. The Court of Justice ruled that where the Treaty gave the Commission a specific task, it must be interpreted as giving the Commission all powers necessary to carry out the task, including the power to adopt binding legislation, such as Decisions.

2.3.1.3 Execution and administration of policy

The Commission's role here is generally an indirect one. For example, under powers delegated by the Council, it enacts rules and checks that the Member States are observing them. The use of these delegated powers is supervised by a committee of officials from the Member States, chaired by a representative of the Commission. This practice is known as 'comitology'.

? QUESTION 2.1

Can you see how the practice of comitology might undermine the powers of the Commission?

The use of supervising committees made up of representatives of the Member States gives the Member States an indirect, but pervasive influence over the work of the Commission in addition to the direct influence which they already have over the work of the Council.

The Commission also manages Community finances and enforces Community competition policy. It is responsible for the collection and expenditure of finance.

2.3.2 The Council of the European Union (formerly known as the Council of Ministers)

This is based in Brussels, but has an outpost in Luxembourg. Unlike the Commission, it does not have a fixed membership. The 'basic' Council consists of the Foreign Ministers of the Member States, who discuss not only foreign affairs but issues of general concern. However, when a more specialized area is under discussion, the Council will consist of ministers from that policy area, for example the ministers for agriculture or for trade.

? QUESTION 2.2

Compare the composition of the Council with that of the Commission. Which do you think will represent the interests of the individual Member States more strongly?

Not only must Commissioners be independent of their Member States but their weekly meetings allow for the development of a certain solidarity along Community lines. In contrast, the fluidity of the Council means that its individual members meet rarely and develop little Community solidarity. Since they are not constrained by any formal requirement of independence, the Council is where national interests are represented more strongly. As a result, the Council is not as cohesive and forceful as the other institutions. It might be said that it is not, in effect, as 'European' as the others.

Some Council decisions must be unanimous, but most are taken by a simple majority or a qualified majority ('QMV') (see 1.6).

The tasks of the Council include taking decisions, coordinating the economic policies of the Member States and delegating the necessary implementing powers to the Commission. The Council may also request the Commission to undertake studies and submit proposals for legislation.

2.3.2.1 The Presidency

The Presidency of the Council, which is in effect the Presidency of the Community, is held by the Member States in turn for six-monthly periods. The minister from the country holding the Presidency convenes and chairs Council meetings and signs Council Acts. The government of the Member State holding the Presidency controls the Council agenda and therefore, at the start of its term, it prepares and presents a programme of action. The relevant country usually sees its Presidency as a time to make its mark upon the Community, but it may be hamstrung by the need to complete work already underway. This was the position of the British Presidency in the latter half of 1992 which inherited the final stages of the EU Treaty, and was obliged to oversee its ratification.

2.3.3 The Parliament

The chief provisions governing the Parliament are to be found in Articles 189 to 201 (ex 137–44) EC.

> **? QUESTION 2.3**
>
> The Commission and the Council are based in Brussels, and the Court of Justice and Court of Auditors are based in Luxembourg. If you were an architect in charge of a project to design a new Parliament building, in which European city would you locate it?

You might have suggested that the Parliament should, like the other two legislative institutions, be based in Brussels. Alternatively you might have said that it should be located in Luxembourg alongside the courts, or even that it should be based in a third city, in order to spread the institutions evenly across the Community. What you are unlikely to have proposed is that the Parliament should be based in Strasbourg, Luxembourg, and Brussels; the current, and inefficient, state of affairs which increases the workload of the MEPs and the overall cost to the Community of the institution. It is, rather like the old air travel joke of 'breakfast in London, dinner in New York, luggage in Tokyo', with plenary (i.e. full) meetings in Strasbourg, committee meetings in Brussels, and bureaucracy in Luxembourg.

Members of the European Parliament (MEPs) are elected five-yearly. The electoral procedure is not uniform but is determined individually by the Member States.

In the early years of the Community, members of the Parliament (then known as the Assembly) were delegates from national Parliaments, and were therefore unlikely to develop strong political links with members from other Member States. However, the introduction of direct and universal elections to the Parliament in 1979 loosened the ties between members of the European Parliament and their national Parliaments, and this has been reinforced by the

Parliament's continuing struggle for increased powers, largely against the interests of the individual Member States. Article 191 (ex 138a) EC asserts the importance of political parties at the European level as a factor promoting integration between the Member States.

Plenary sessions are held eleven times a year and decisions are generally taken by a majority of the MEPs present at plenary session.

2.3.3.1 Powers

Legislative

The Parliament can make informal representations prior to the drafting of legislation, either in Parliamentary sessions, or in committee meetings (which are attended by a representative of the Commission). It may also request the Commission to submit proposals for legislation which it feels is required (Article 192 (ex 138b) EC).

Once legislation has been drafted, the Parliament must normally give a formal opinion on it to the Council. The procedure is that a committee scrutinizes the draft and reports to Parliament, and the Parliament passes a resolution which is presented to the Council along with the Commission's proposal.

The exact input of the Parliament into the legislative procedure is dependent upon the particular procedure which is used (see 3.6). For present purposes, the position under the most important procedures can be summarized as follows:

Legislative procedure	Parliamentary input
Consultation	The Parliament is consulted and its views may or may not be taken into account.
Co-decision	The Parliament has the right of co-decision with the Council and therefore if the Parliament rejects the measure, the Council cannot adopt it.

The Parliament has co-budgetary authority with the Council and therefore may amend or reject the Budget. The Budget must ultimately be approved by the Parliament.

Supervisory

Articles 193–201 (ex 138c–144) EC give the Parliament the following supervisory powers:

(a) It can set up Committees of Inquiry to investigate alleged maladministration (Article 193 (ex 138c) EC). It did this in early 1999 in respect of allegations of fraud, maladministration, and nepotism against the Commission, and the Commission subsequently resigned.

(b) It may receive petitions from EU citizens (Article 194 (ex 138d) EC).

(c) It may appoint an Ombudsman to investigate complaints by EU citizens (Article 195 (ex 138e)).

(d) It has the right to put questions to the Commission (Article 197 (ex 140) EC) at Parliamentary debates and in committee meetings.

(e) It may question the Council at Parliamentary debates (although the Council determines its own attendance at such debates (Article 197 (ex 140) EC) or in writing (Article 25 of the Council's Rules of Procedure as adopted by Council Decision 93/662/OJ 1993 L304/1)).

(f) It has the right to debate the Commission's annual report (Article 200 (ex 143) EC).

(g) It can, by a two-thirds majority, require the whole Commission to resign (Article 201 (ex 144) EC).

? QUESTION 2.4

Can you think of any reason why the Parliament might be reluctant to require the Commission to resign? In the light of what you have learned about the appointment of the Commission, what might Member States do about any such dismissal?

This power has never been used and it is arguable that it is so Draconian—because it applies to the whole Commission only—that it never will be. It would be theoretically possible for the Member States to re-appoint the same Commissioners, which could lead to a constitutional crisis. However, similar reasons were advanced for the non-use of the power to veto the Budget, and the Parliament has in fact exercised this power twice. The Parliament has never voted to sack the Commission, but the fact that it came close to doing so in early 1999 may have been influential in the Commission's subsequent decision to resign.

Other supervisory powers of the Parliament are as follows:

(h) It must approve the incoming Commission (Article 214 (ex 158) EC).

(i) It may initiate proceedings before the Court of Justice in respect of certain acts or omissions by the other institutions (see **Chapter 6** concerning Articles 230 and 232 (ex 173 and 175) EC).

Other powers

The Parliament has a veto over a number of issues including the admission of new members to the Community, and certain aspects of the work of the European Central Bank (ECB), (Article 105(6) EC). It also has a veto in all areas where the co-decision procedure (see 3.6.2) is used.

? QUESTION 2.5

It has been said that there is a 'democratic deficit' within the Community. In the light of what you have now read about the composition and powers of the Council, the Commission, and the Parliament, to what extent do you agree with this statement?

In **Chapter 3** it will be seen that the Community exercises sovereign powers. Within the Community it is the Council and the Commission which exercise most of these powers. The Council is not directly elected, although its ministers are usually members of their national Parliaments, and they are not collectively responsible to any representative body. The Commission is not elected at all, although its composition must be approved by the Parliament, and it similarly lacks accountability. The Parliament, which by contrast is directly and universally elected and therefore accountable to individual constituents, has relatively little legislative input. While the democratic deficit is not total, it provides a ready-made line of argument for those who oppose the grant of further powers to the Community (although it is usually these people who also oppose the extension of Parliamentary powers).

In the light of this deficit, it is not surprising that the Parliament has been keen to protect what powers it does have, and in these endeavours it has often been assisted by the Court of Justice (see 2.3.4 and **Chapter 6**).

2.3.4 The Court of Justice

The Court of Justice is based in Luxembourg and consists of one judge from each Member State, who are required to be independent and to have the ability required for appointment to the highest judicial office in their country or to be a jurisconsult of recognized competence.

The judges are assisted by Advocates General, one of whom will be assigned to each case. They deliver a reasoned and impartial Opinion to assist the judges. The Treaty of Nice provides that an Opinion will be given only in certain cases. The Opinion of the Advocate General is always delivered at the conclusion of the parties' arguments and before judgment is given. (It should be noted that this order is occasionally reversed in the report of the case, with the Opinion being placed at the end, after the judgment.) The Opinion will contain a review of the facts, the parties' submissions and the applicable law, including previous decisions of the Court of Justice itself.

Unlike the system in England and Wales, only one judgment is given by the Court of Justice and so no dissenting judgments are ever given.

2.3.4.1 Jurisdiction

The Court of Justice has often been involved in pushing forward the frontiers of Community law (see **Chapter 6**) within the confines of its jurisdiction as outlined below. It should be noted that the Court of Justice is not bound by its own previous decisions, although they are persuasive, and is therefore well able to respond to changing needs and attitudes within the Community and the Member States.

The jurisdiction of the Court of Justice stems from Article 220 (ex 164) EC and can be categorized as follows.

Disputes about power

The Court of Justice deals with disputes between the Member States and/or the Community institutions about the balance of power between them. An action may be brought under either Article 230 (ex 173) EC or Article 232 (ex 175) EC (see **Chapter 6**) involving either a Member State or an individual alleging the wrongful exercise of power by the Community, or an institution alleging the wrongful exercise of power by another institution. An example of the latter would be the allegation by the Parliament that the Council had relied on the wrong 'legislative base' to pass a measure (see 3.4, 3.6, 6.3.3.2 and 6.8).

Disputes about the obligations of Member States

The Court of Justice deals with cases where the Commission (under Article 226 (ex 169) EC) or a Member State (under Article 227 (ex 170) EC) alleges that another Member State has failed to fulfil its Treaty obligations (these include obligations under secondary legislation). If an action under Article 226 (ex 169) EC or 227 (ex 170) EC is successful, Article 228 (ex 171) EC will apply.

Article 228 (ex 171) EC requires that the Member State comply with the judgment of the Court of Justice. If it fails to do so, a penalty payment may be imposed.

Damages

The Court of Justice has jurisdiction in cases concerning the award of non-contractual damages against the Community (Articles 235 (ex 178) and 288 (ex 215) EC; see **Chapter 7**).

Disputes about interpretation

National courts may, in certain circumstances, ask the Court for clarification of the meaning of a piece of Community legislation (under Article 234 (ex 177) EC; see **Chapter 5**).

Appellate jurisdiction

The Court of Justice has jurisdiction in appeals from the Court of First Instance (see below). These mostly involve disputes in the sphere of competition policy as to the exercise of the Commission's powers under Articles 81–9 (ex 85–94) EC.

Limitations on jurisdiction

In the EU Treaty and the Treaty of Amsterdam (see 1.9.2 and 1.9.3) the jurisdiction of the Court of Justice in certain areas has been limited as follows.

Articles 61–9 EC (provisions establishing an area of freedom, security, and justice)

(a) It may only give preliminary rulings under Article 234 (ex 177) EC (see **Chapter 5**) on questions relating to Articles 61–9 EC (visas, asylum, immigration, and certain other matters relating to the free movement of persons) where those questions are referred by the highest courts in the Member States, rather than by any court.

(b) It has no jurisdiction at all in relation to measures under Article 62(1) EC (removing controls on persons crossing internal borders) relating to law and order or internal security.

(c) In addition, however, the Court may be required to give an interpretative ruling at the request of the Commission, the Council, or a Member State.

Articles 29–42 EU (provisions on police and judicial cooperation in criminal matters)

(a) It may only give preliminary rulings under Article 234 (ex 177) EC (see **Chapter 5**) on questions relating to Articles 29–42 EU (see 4.11) where those questions are referred by courts of a Member State which has declared that it will accept such jurisdiction.
A Member State may choose to limit this jurisdiction to questions referred by the highest court, rather than by all courts.

(b) It has no jurisdiction at all in respect of law and order or internal security measures taken under Articles 29–42 EU.

(c) It has no jurisdiction under Articles 230 and 232 EC (see **Chapter 6**) to review the validity of action/inaction under Articles 29–42 EU.

Articles 11–28 EU (provisions on foreign policy)

- It has no jurisdiction at all in respect of foreign policy measures taken under Article 11–28 EU (see 1.9.2.3).

2.3.4.2 Procedure

The increasing workload of the Court of Justice has resulted in longer delays, both in the hearing of direct actions, and in the giving of preliminary rulings.

> **? QUESTION 2.6**
>
> Given what you have learned so far about the Court of Justice and the Community legal system, what factors particular to the Court of Justice can you think of to account for these delays? Can you think of any solution(s) to the problem of delay?

The Court of Justice will generally follow one of two procedures, according to whether the case has started in the Court of Justice or has been referred from a national court. (Special rules apply to appeals from the Court of First Instance to the Court of Justice and certain other categories of case.)

Procedure in direct actions (i.e. those which began in the Court of First Instance or the Court of Justice itself)

(a) written proceedings consisting of:
 (i) application;
 (ii) service of the application on the defendant;
 (iii) defence;
 (iv) reply and rejoinder (not always);

(b) preliminary enquiries by a judge (not always);

(c) oral proceedings in court or in Chambers consisting of:
 (i) report of the preliminary enquiries (where applicable);
 (ii) legal arguments by the parties;
 (iii) Opinion of the Advocate General (note that the Treaty of Nice (see 1.9.4) provides that an Opinion will only be essential where a new point of law is raised);

(d) judgment.

Procedure in preliminary rulings (i.e. where, in an action before a national court, that court has referred a question (or questions) to the Court of Justice)

(a) decision to refer by national court;

(b) service of the decision to refer on the parties, the Member States (accompanied by a translation into the official language of that State), the Commission and the Council;

(c) written observations by the parties, Member States, and institutions (not mandatory);

(d) preliminary enquiries by a judge (not always);

(e) oral proceedings in court or in Chambers (as for direct actions (see above) but the Court may dispense with legal arguments by the parties);

(f) judgment.

QUESTION 2.7

Imagine that you are a lawyer based in the UK and that you have a client who is a party to proceedings before the Court of Justice in Luxembourg. What advantage does the mainly written procedure adopted by that court have for you?

The advantages of such a procedure are first, that the bulk of the work for the case may be done in your own office, with all your usual resources to hand, and secondly, that by minimizing the time spent at court in Luxembourg, the cost to your client is reduced.

2.3.5 The Court of First Instance

The Court of First Instance consists of one judge from each Member State, who must be independent and have the ability required for appointment to judicial office in their own country. It was introduced by the SEA (see 1.9.1) to reduce delays in the judicial process.

QUESTION 2.8

Given this aim, and the name of the new court, what sort of jurisdiction would you expect it to be given? Write down your answer and look at it again when you have studied this section.

The Court of First Instance has jurisdiction in the following cases:

(a) Cases brought by non-privileged applicants under Articles 230, 232, 235, and 238 (ex 173, 175, 178, and 181) EC. Articles 230 and 232 (ex 173 and 175) EC will be discussed further in **Chapter 6**. Article 235 (ex 178) EC concerns actions for compensation against the Community under Article 288 EC and will be discussed in **Chapter 7**. Article 238 (ex 181) EC concerns contracts concluded with the Community which contain an arbitration clause.

(b) Cases between the Community and its staff.

QUESTION 2.9

Look back at your answer to Question 2.8. Is the jurisdiction of the Court of First Instance what you expected it to be?

In the UK, the court in which any particular case is first heard is described as being the court of first instance, and is often the only court to deal with that case. It might therefore be supposed that a Court of First Instance for the Community, created to lessen the workload of the Court of Justice, would deal with all cases on a preliminary basis.

However, the jurisdiction of the Court of First Instance is considerably less than that of the Court of Justice. For instance, it does not yet hear cases brought under Article 234 (ex 177) EC (see **Chapter 5**) which constitute the bulk of cases before the Court of Justice. However, the Treaty of Nice (see 1.9.4) provides that Article 234 jurisdiction be given to the Court of First Instance in areas to be laid down in the Statute of the Court of Justice. Rulings could exceptionally be reviewed by the Court of Justice where there is a serious threat to the consistency of Community law.

Article 234 will be considered in more depth in **Chapter 5**. For the time being, note that Article 234 provides a procedure whereby national courts may, where a point of Community law is raised in a case before them, ask the Court of Justice certain questions about that Community law.

Together with the increased number of cases being received by the Court of Justice, and the fact that that Court must now hear appeals from the Court of First Instance, this unlimited jurisdiction has meant that the workload of the Court of Justice has not decreased. Delays in cases being heard are now substantial in both courts.

In an attempt to reduce delays, the possibility was introduced of decisions by single judges (rather than groups of judges in chambers) in the Court of First Instance (Decision 99/291 (OJ 1999 L 114/52) amending Decision 88/591). However, this is the exception rather than the rule. The procedure before the Court of First Instance is similar to that before the Court of Justice, except that judges perform the task of Advocate Generals where a case requires an Opinion to be given.

Article 225a EC provides that judicial panels be created to give first instance decisions in direct actions in areas such as staff disputes with the Community. Appeal will lie to the Court of First Instance and only then to the Court of Justice where there is a serious threat to the consistency of Community law.

2.3.6 The Court of Auditors

This body was established in 1977, and was introduced by the EU Treaty as the 'fifth' major institution (after the Council, the Commission, the Parliament, and the Court of Justice). It consists of 15 members, one from each of the Member States, who are qualified to carry out a Community audit, and whose independence is beyond doubt. Members are appointed for six-yearly terms by the Council, which is required to consult the Parliament on the appointments. Article 247 EC as amended by the Treaty of Nice (see 1.9.4) provides that there should be one member from each Member State.

The name 'Court' is something of a misnomer, as the function of the Court of Auditors is to examine the accounts of the Community and confirm their reliability and legality. It draws up an annual report, approved by a majority of its members, and may submit opinions or observations at any time at the request of any institution. The annual report is by no means a rubber stamp on Community finances; the Court frequently highlights inadequate documentation and control over expenditure, particularly in the Common Agricultural Policy (CAP) and recommends tighter controls.

EXERCISE 2.2

Now that you have learned about the main institutions, go back to the chart at Exercise 2.1 and try to amend it, or add further information as necessary, without looking at the text.

2.4 The other institutions

2.4.1 The European Council

The position of the European Council is set out in Article 4 (ex D) EU. It is composed of all the heads of government or state of the Member States who meet twice a year (at the end of each Presidency) to provide the EU, which includes the Community, with its political impetus. The President of the Commission and the national foreign ministers also attend these meetings. There are also occasional interim meetings of the European Council.

2.4.2 The Economic and Social Committee (ECOSOC)

This issues and policy body consists of approximately 200 independent members (i.e. not influenced by their own Member State) appointed, in proportion to the population of each Member State, by the Council on the recommendation of the Member States. Various categories of economic and social activity are to be represented on the Committee such as employers, workers, farmers, and professional associations.

ECOSOC is to be consulted by the Council and the Commission where the EC Treaty so provides or where those institutions so wish. It can also issue its own opinions on social and economic matters.

Article 258 EC provides that maximum membership be set at 350, and that representatives must be elected or accountable to an elected assembly.

2.4.3 The Committee of the Regions

The composition and appointment of this body is similar to that of ECOSOC, except that the interests to be represented are specified as those of regional and local bodies. The UK representatives are from local authorities.

The Committee of the Regions is to be consulted by the Council and the Commission where the EC Treaty so provides or where those institutions so wish. It can also issue its own opinions where it believes that significant regional issues are affected.

Article 263 EC provides that maximum membership be set at 350 and that representatives must be elected or accountable to an elected assembly.

2.4.4 The European Investment Bank

This was established by the EC Treaty to provide investment loans to assist the funding of projects to promote regional development in the Community. It receives money from the Member States, but also raises its own funds on the international capital markets.

2.4.5 The Committee of Permanent Representatives (COREPER)

This body consists of the ambassadors of the Member States to the Community. It carries out preparatory research and drafting for Council proposals, and divides them into those on which it has already reached a unanimous decision and which can therefore be agreed by the Council without further discussion, and those which require further discussion by the Council in order to reach an agreement.

2.4.6 The institutions of economic and monetary union (EMU)

The following institutions were introduced by the EU Treaty solely to further the objective of economic and monetary union.

(a) The European Central Bank.

(b) The European System of Central Banks.

CONCLUSIONS

The key institutions from a legal perspective are the Commission, the Council, and the Parliament, which have power (to a greater or lesser extent, depending on the legislative procedure (see 3.6)) and, of course, the Court of Justice, which has been in the forefront of promoting Community law and its enforcement in the Member States. However, despite the criticisms often levelled at the Community institutions and their powers, it should be remembered that ultimate power still lies with the Council and therefore with the Member States.

SUMMARY

- The **Commission** is made up of full-time Commissioners, one from each Member State. It has the almost exclusive right to initiate legislation and it enforces the Treaty against Member States that are in breach.
- The **Council of the EU** is formed of one representative government minister for the policy area under discussion from each Member State. It takes the final decision on legislation, sometimes jointly with the Parliament, and gives political direction to the EU. Each Member State holds the Presidency of the Council for six months in turn.
- The **Parliament** is made up of MEPs directly elected from each Member State. Its powers have gradually increased over the years, but it remains much less powerful in the EU structure than are national parliaments in the Member States. However, in some areas it has the joint right of final decision on legislation with the Council, and the areas to which this right of co-decision applies are gradually being extended.
- The **Court of Justice** consists of one judge from each Member State. A single judgment is given in each case; there are no dissenting judgments. Judgments are generally preceded by an advisory

Opinion from an Advocate General. It is the supreme judicial authority on issues of Community law, but is not a court of appeal from Member State courts. Instead, it is possible under Article 234 EC (see **Chapter 5**) to refer questions of Community law to the Court of Justice during the course of legal proceedings before a national court. Actions against the Community institutions (for example under Articles 230 (see **Chapter 6**) or 288 EC (see **Chapter 7**)) may be brought directly before the Court of Justice. The jurisdiction of the Court is limited in certain sensitive policy areas, namely establishing an area of freedom, security and justice (see **Chapter 9**), police and judicial cooperation in criminal matters (see **Chapter 9**) and the common foreign and security policy (see 1.9.2.3).

- The **Court of First Instance** also consists of one judge from each Member State. Certain actions against the Community institutions must start in the CFI, but can be appealed to the Court of Justice (see **Chapter 6**). Although the CFI does not yet hear preliminary references (see **Chapter 5**), the possibility of it doing so has been established.

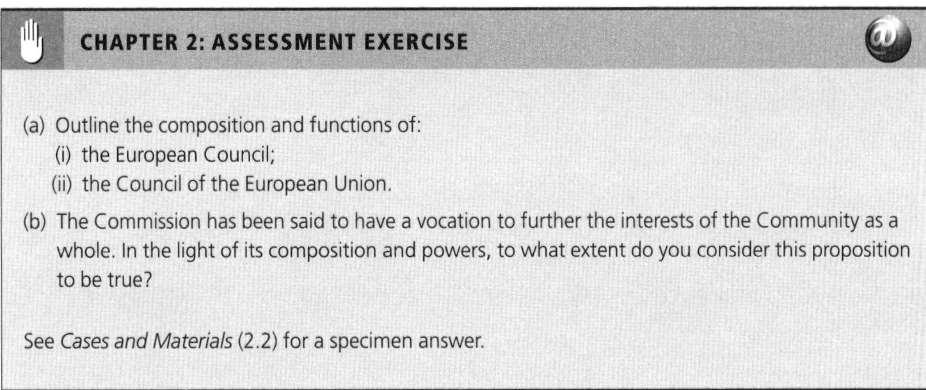

CHAPTER 2: ASSESSMENT EXERCISE

(a) Outline the composition and functions of:
  (i) the European Council;
  (ii) the Council of the European Union.

(b) The Commission has been said to have a vocation to further the interests of the Community as a whole. In the light of its composition and powers, to what extent do you consider this proposition to be true?

See *Cases and Materials* (2.2) for a specimen answer.

FURTHER READING

Arnull, A. (1994). 'Judging the New Europe', 19 *ELRev* 3.

Edward, D. (1995). 'How the Court of Justice Works' 20 *ELRev* 539.

Lenaerts, K. and Arts D. (1999). *'Procedural Law of the European Union'*. London: Sweet & Maxwell.

(1996). *The Role and Future of the European Court of Justice*. The British Institute of International and Comparative Law (BIICL).

3 Sovereignty and sources of law

3.1 OBJECTIVES

By the end of this chapter you should be able to:

1 Explain the impact of Community membership on the UK's sovereignty

2 Understand the concept of federalism and how it relates to the Community

3 Describe the various sources of Community law and discuss their effect and relative importance

4 Outline the main legislative processes of the Community and analyse the relative degree of power which they give to each of the institutions

5 Explain the concept of subsidiarity and its importance to the Community

3.2 Introduction

What has been the impact of the UK's accession to the Community on national sovereignty? This is a much debated topic. It is often argued by opponents of UK membership that we have entirely ceded our national sovereignty to 'Brussels'. The truth of the matter is not so simple, and in the first part of this chapter the extent to which there is now a source of law which ranks above our national laws will be examined.

In the second part of this chapter, the exact nature of these sources of law will be considered. The EC Treaty is the starting point but since 1957 a vast body of Community law has grown up which pervades virtually every aspect of UK law. It is vital for today's lawyer to be aware of these sources and to understand their potential importance as legal authorities.

3.3 Sovereignty

3.3.1 The political problem

The problem of sovereignty has both a political and a legal dimension. By way of introduction, we will consider briefly the political dimension.

? **QUESTION 3.1**

What do you understand by the term 'national sovereignty'? Is it your opinion that this has been affected by the membership of the Community?

In the political arena, the term 'national sovereignty' is often used to mean the power of the British people, through their national government, to govern their own affairs as they see fit. There is little doubt that membership of the Community limits the power of the UK government, since decisions in certain policy areas are now taken by the Community. In theory, the position could be restored at any time by repealing the European Communities Act 1972 and leaving the Community, but it is unlikely that such extreme action will be taken in the foreseeable future.

The reality for the time being, therefore, is that absolute national sovereignty has been lost. The question, and this is more a matter of politics than of law, is whether this is a price worth paying for the benefits of Community membership. Lord Slynn of Hadley, in one of the Hamlyn Lecture series, *Introducing a European Legal Order*, contrasts the negative view of membership, that the Community endangers 'national sovereignty, national independence and national identity', with the positive view that the situation is not one 'of surrendering sovereignty but of pooling sovereignty in certain areas for the good of all'.

3.3.2 The legal problem

The legal dimension to the question of sovereignty is more complex.

3.3.2.1 Parliamentary sovereignty

In the UK, the long-established doctrine of Parliamentary sovereignty means, first, that the courts may not question the validity of Parliamentary legislation (*Pickin* v *BR Board* [1994] 4 All ER 609) and, secondly, that Parliament cannot bind its successors, so a later Act of Parliament will impliedly repeal an earlier Act insofar as they are inconsistent (*Vauxhall Estates* v *Liverpool Corporation* [1932] 1 KB 733; *Ellen Street Estates* v *Minister of Health* [1934] 1 KB 590). In summary, this doctrine establishes the supremacy of Parliamentary legislation.

QUESTION 3.2

In what way might this doctrine conflict with giving full effect to Community law?

This doctrine is clearly in conflict with the full recognition of Community law in the UK. First, if Community law is to be fully effective, the UK courts must be able to question the validity of Acts of Parliament which conflict with, or inadequately transpose it. Secondly, if UK legislation which is inconsistent with Community law has the effect of repealing it, this would destroy any possibility of Community law applying uniformly across the Community, and in fact s. 2(4) of the European Communities Act 1972 (*Cases and Materials* (3.1)) provides that any future enactment is to take effect subject to Community law. The latter point was clearly accepted by the House of Lords in *R* v *Secretary of State for Transport ex parte Factortame Ltd (Factortame I)* (Case C-213/89) [1990] ECR I-2433 (*Cases and Materials* (3.1)), which we shall be considering shortly.

It would appear that the doctrine of Parliamentary sovereignty has been considerably qualified by UK membership of the Community. If absolute Parliamentary sovereignty no longer exists, then although it could be restored by repealing the European Communities Act 1972 (see 3.3.1), the practical reality is that a 'new legal order' has been created, in which Community law has supremacy over national law.

3.3.2.2 The role of the Court of Justice

The Court of Justice has, on a number of occasions, taken the view that the supremacy of Community law is implicit in the obligation imposed upon Member States by Article 10 (ex 5) EC.

Article 10 (ex 5) EC provides that:

> Member States shall take all appropriate measures, whether general or particular, to ensure fulfilment of the obligations arising out of this Treaty or resulting from action taken by the institutions of the Community. They shall facilitate the achievement of the Community's tasks.
>
> They shall abstain from any measure which could jeopardise the attainment of the objectives of this Treaty.

The national courts are therefore obliged to give effect to those Treaty obligations, even if this means disapplying national law.

All appropriate measures might include, as we shall see, repealing or refusing to apply inconsistent national law, referring all questions of interpretation of Community law to the Court of Justice, or refusing to take account of the Member State's excuses for its own non-compliance with national law. The obligation to refer certain questions as to the interpretation of a piece of Community law to the Court of Justice, and to follow decisions which it has made, limits, in effect, the right of UK courts to interpret the law which applies in this country.

Costa v _ENEL_ (Case 6/64) [1964] ECR 585

The classic statement of the supremacy of Community law is contained in the judgment of the Court of Justice in *Costa* v *ENEL* (*Cases and Materials* 3.1). Costa argued that the nationalization of the Italian electricity industry was contrary to Community law. ENEL and the Italian government argued that this was irrelevant, since the Italian courts were obliged to apply the later Italian law under which nationalization was legal. The case was referred to the Court of Justice under Article 234 EC (see **Chapter 5**) for an interpretation of Community law.

The Court of Justice ruled that Community law was part of the legal systems of the Member States and had to be applied by national courts. There had been a transfer of sovereignty to the Community and it was integral to this new legal system that Community law took precedence over later, inconsistent national law.

Amministrazione delle Finanze dello Stato v Simmenthal SpA (Case 106/77) [1978] ECR 629

In *Simmenthal II* (*Cases and Materials* (3.1)) (see also 1.7) the Court of Justice clarified its position still further. The Court of Justice had ruled, in *Simmenthal SpA* v *Italian Minister of Finance (Simmenthal I)* (Case 35/76) [1976] ECR 1871 that a fee charged on Simmenthal's imports of beef into Italy was contrary to Community law on the free movement of goods. The Italian court ordered the fee to be repaid but the Amministrazione delle Finanze appealed. Under Italian law, the constitutionality of the law imposing the fee had to be referred to the Constitutional Court. The Italian court seized of the case referred the issue to the Court of Justice.

The Court of Justice referred to the 'principle of the precedence of Community law' and stated expressly that a national court should disapply national legislation which conflicted with Community law, without waiting for it to be repealed by legislative or other means (such as a ruling by the Constitutional Court). In addition to the grounds set out in *Costa*, the Court of Justice based its ruling on the nature of Article 234 (ex 177) EC (see **Chapter 5**), under which this action was brought. Article 234 (ex 177) permits a national court to seek clarification from the Court of Justice as to the meaning or validity of Community law. The Court of Justice argued that its effect would be limited if the national court did not then apply Community law in accordance with the ruling of the Court of Justice.

In *Commission* v *Belgium* (Case 77/69) [1970] ECR 237, the Belgian government had attempted to reform a timber tax which the Commission had indicated to be in contravention of Community law. However, the necessary legislation lapsed when the Belgian Parliament was dissolved, and under the Belgian constitution the government was separate from, and unable to dictate to, the Parliament. The Court of Justice held that this was not a valid defence to the charge that Belgium had failed to fulfil its Treaty obligations. A Member State which had contravened Community law could not plead in its defence that its national law forced it to do so or that it had particular problems in complying.

A different problem in according supremacy to Community law arose in the *Factortame* litigation (*R* v *Secretary of State for Transport ex parte Factortame Ltd*) which involved a number of references to the Court of Justice. *Factortame II* (Case C-221/89) [1991] ECR I-3905 concerned the validity of certain provisions of the Merchant Shipping Act 1988, which the applicants, a group of Spanish fishermen, claimed were in contravention of directly enforceable Community rights.

Factortame I (Case C-213/89) [1990] ECR I-2433

Factortame I (*Cases and Materials* (3.1)) concerned the possibility of interim relief being granted, in the form of a suspension of the disputed parts of the Act pending a final ruling on their validity from the Court of Justice. It was held by the House of Lords that the remedy was not available under English law, but in the light of conflicting Court of Justice case law on an interim measure a reference would be made to the Court of Justice under Article 234 (ex 177) of the EC Treaty concerning the award of interim protection. The Court of Justice ruled that despite the provisions of national law, the national legislation could and should be suspended pending a conclusive ruling on its validity. Rights under Community law could not be truly effective if those who sought to enforce them were prejudiced by the operation of the allegedly conflicting national legislation while the issue was being resolved. (The contested provisions of the Merchant Shipping Act were ultimately found to be contrary to Community law, and therefore invalid under s. 2(4) of the European Communities Act 1972—see *Factortame II*.)

3.3.3 Conclusion

QUESTION 3.3

Consider your initial reaction to the question of national sovereignty (Question 3.1: see 3.3.1). What do you now consider to be the position of UK sovereignty, legal or otherwise?

The UK, and for that matter all the Member States, have surrendered, or pooled, their absolute national sovereignty. In terms of legal sovereignty, not only has the UK Parliament lost its exclusive right to legislate, but Community law will prevail over national laws. This position is subject to two provisos. First, sovereignty may be regained by withdrawing from the Community; and secondly, in those areas where the Community has no competence, such as defence, sovereignty is, for the time being, intact (although, of course, many of these areas are affected indirectly by Community law).

3.3.4 Federalism

Having noted that the sovereignty of the Member States in certain areas has been surrendered to the Community, the question of the legal status of the Community itself must be considered.

QUESTION 3.4

In the light of what you have learned about the Community so far, would you describe it as a federation along the lines of, say, the United States of America?

In the classic federal pattern, the powers of the central or federal government and those of its Member States are exercised independently. By contrast, in the Community the lines are not always so clearly drawn and competences in some areas are shared. Other elements of a federal state are also absent. The Community has only limited powers in the policy areas of defence or foreign affairs (see 1.9.2.3) and its few powers of taxation are insufficient to fund its activities. The Parliament is excluded from decision-making in a number of key areas, such as foreign policy, a situation inconceivable in a federation such as the USA, where the federal legislature composed of representatives from the member states, is able to influence and control the activities of the federal government.

Despite these comments, it may be argued that the Community has increasingly federal tendencies. For instance, the insertion of the principle of subsidiarity into the EC Treaty (see 3.4.3) may lead to a clearer separation of powers between the Community and Member States, a majority of Member States are implementing a single currency, and a Briton or an Italian is now also a Community national, just as a Texan or a Californian is an American national. In addition, the Community has gradually increased its competence in all areas, including foreign policy (see 1.9.2.3).

? QUESTION 3.5

In what ways do you think that federal ideas have influenced the Community?

As discussed in 1.4, the events of the Second World War greatly influenced the move towards European integration. Amongst the myriad of ideas put forward at that time were those which envisaged a federal Europe with independent members as a counter-balance to the nation State, with its destructive capabilities. Although these were not taken up by the founders of the Community, the Preamble to the EC Treaty refers to an 'ever closer union of peoples' and it can be seen that the potential for a federal state does exist. The Community has put in place a supranational authority with sovereign power in certain policy areas, and the EU Treaty introduced a timetable of events leading to a single currency and a single economic and monetary policy. The EU Treaty also formalized, for the first time, a framework for intergovernmental cooperation between the Member States in foreign policy and defence, and in certain areas relating to justice and home affairs, which was built on by the Treaty of Amsterdam (see 1.9.3).

3.4 Attribution of powers to the Community

The issues of sovereignty and federalism discussed above are concerned with the sharing of power. The fundamental rule is that the Community may act only if the EC Treaty has given it power to do so. (The exercise of such power is subject to the principle of subsidiarity discussed in 3.4.3.) Articles 2 and 3 EC (see 1.3) set out the broad aims and activities of the Community, and other Treaty Articles give more specific powers. The Treaty Article on which a particular Community measure is based is known as its legislative or legal base (see 3.4, 3.6, 6.3.3.2, and 6.8). For example, Article 175 (ex 130s) EC gives the Community the power to adopt measures to achieve its environmental objectives as set out in Article 174 (ex 130r) EC. If the Treaty does not specifically give the Community the power to act, Article 308 (ex 235) EC provides a fall-back position.

3.4.1 **Article 308 EC**

Article 308 (ex 235) empowers the Community to take action where two conditions are fulfilled. First, the action must be necessary in order to achieve one of the objectives of the Community; and secondly, the EC Treaty must have failed to provide the necessary power in another Article.

3.4.2 **Power to act externally**

Where the power in question relates to external matters, that is to say the international relations of the Community, a further rule governing the grant of power to the Community has been established.

In *Commission* v *Council (ERTA)* (Case 22/70) [1971] ECR 263) the EC Treaty gave competence to the Community in Community-wide transport matters, but did not expressly extend this to transport matters involving other countries. The Court of Justice held that, in the absence of any express provision to the contrary in the EC Treaty, the express power to act internally gave the Community the implied power to act externally, and therefore to negotiate and conclude international agreements. If Member States could act independently outside the Community, this might affect the uniform policy within the Community.

This rule applies only where the Community has internal competence in all areas covered by the proposed measure. Where an international agreement relates both to areas where the Community has internal competence and areas where it does not, both the Community and the Member States may negotiate.

3.4.3 **Subsidiarity**

The EU Treaty broadened the definition of subsidiarity, a principle first introduced by the SEA in 1986, and concerning the effective allocation of power between the different authorities of the Community, namely the Community institutions and the Member States. The key provision is now Article 5 EC.

Article 5 (ex 3b) states:

> The Community shall act within the limits of the powers conferred upon it by this Treaty and of the objectives assigned to it therein.
>
> In areas which do not fall within its exclusive competence, the Community shall take action, in accordance with the principle of subsidiarity, only if and insofar as the objectives of the proposed action cannot be sufficiently achieved by the Member States and can therefore, by reason of the scale or effects of the proposed action, be better achieved by the Community.
>
> Any action by the Community shall not go beyond what is necessary to achieve the objectives of this Treaty.

Article 5 (ex 3b) EC thus sets out three principles to be observed by the Community when it takes action. It must act:

- within the powers laid down in the EC Treaty;
- in accordance with subsidiarity, except in areas which fall within its exclusive competence;
- in proportion to the objective to be achieved.

The second of these conditions means that the Community may take action only where it has exclusive competence, **or** where its action would be in accordance with the principle of subsidiarity. If a proposed measure relates to an area of exclusive competence, the Community may take action without regard to subsidiarity because by definition the Member States have no power to take action in that area. It is therefore useful to understand a little more about the areas in which the Community has 'exclusive competence'.

Article 70 (ex 74) EC provides that transport matters should be dealt with by Member States within the framework of a common transport policy drawn up by the Community. In *Commission* v *Council (ERTA)* (Case 22/70 [1971] ECR 263), the Court of Justice ruled that once the Community had drawn up such a policy, the Member States could no longer make rules (in this case by entering into an international transport agreement) which affected that policy. The Community, not the Member States, therefore had competence to negotiate and conclude the agreement in question. It can therefore be said that once the Community has taken action, it has exclusive competence in that area and can act regardless of subsidiarity.

? **QUESTION** 3.6

Can you identify a problem with the application of subsidiarity if 'exclusive competence' is taken to refer to all areas in which the Community has already acted?

If subsidiarity is only applicable to measures concerning policy areas where the Community has not yet acted, its scope and importance will be gradually diminished as the Community continues to legislate. However, it is difficult to identify an alternative rule for identifying areas of exclusive competence. There are some areas, such as EU citizenship (see 1.9.2.3) where the Community must, logically, have exclusive competence, and it also seems clear that the Community has sole power to pass measures relating to the Single Market (under Article 14 (ex 7a—see 1.9.1). If Member States could pass their own measures in this area, markets would continue to be partitioned along national lines and it would be impossible to achieve the Single Market. The Treaty of Amsterdam introduced a Protocol (*Cases and Materials* (3.2)) dealing, inter alia, with subsidiarity. Subsidiarity certainly acts as a political guideline to be borne in mind by the Community institutions when deciding whether they have power to take a particular measure. Subsidiarity is already affecting political decision-making, particularly by the Commission (see, for example, the Conclusions of the Presidency at the Edinburgh European Council meeting 11–12 December 1992.

Subsidiarity can also be used by the Court of Justice as a guide in interpreting Community legislation, in particular its scope.

However, whether the Court of Justice would have to be prepared to use it as a test of the validity of legislation, so that a Community measure which deals with a matter which might be dealt with equally well (or better) by Member States would be annulled by the Court of Justice, is unclear.

? **QUESTION** 3.7

Why do you think that the Member States themselves might favour this possibility?

This would give Member States a second chance after their initial input in the legislative process (in Council) to restrict Community competence to those areas where the Community is better placed than individual Member States to take action. However, in order for Member States to enforce this restriction, they must be able to challenge the validity of Community measures before the Court of Justice, on the ground of failure to comply with subsidiarity. It remains to be seen whether the Court would be prepared to annul legislation on this ground.

In conclusion, although cases such as *ERTA* indicate that the Community has exclusive competence in areas where it has already acted, it remains to be seen whether this definition will be applied when considering the scope of subsidiarity, given the disadvantage of this mentioned above. The Community also has exclusive competence in specific areas such as the Single Market. Certainly, in all situations where Community competence is not exclusive, its actions will be liable to be tested, at some stage, against the requirement of subsidiarity.

3.5 Sources of Community law

Having considered the supremacy of Community law in the national legal systems of the Member States, it is now necessary to examine the sources of law.

QUESTION 3.8

In the light of what you have learned so far about the Community and its legal system, can you identify the fundamental source(s) of Community law?

3.5.1 The Treaties

These are the fundamental sources of Community law.

The founding Treaties are:

(a) The ECSC Treaty 1951 (expired July 2002).

(b) The EEC Treaty 1957 (now the EC Treaty).

(c) The Euratom Treaty 1957.

These have been revised by:

(a) The Merger Treaty 1965.

(b) The Budgetary Treaties of 1970 and 1975.

(c) The Treaties of Accession of new Member States (i.e. one Treaty for each Member State other than the original six).
(d) The Single European Act 1986.
(e) The Treaty on European Union 1992.
(f) The Treaty of Amsterdam 1997.
(g) The Treaty of Nice 2001.

For the purposes of this chapter it is only necessary to consider the EC Treaty, as amended.

The major amending Treaties (the Single European Act, the Treaty on European Union, the Treaty of Amsterdam, and the Treaty of Nice) are discussed in 1.9.

The EC Treaty is 'self-executing', that is to say, it becomes law in a Member State immediately upon ratification by that State, which therefore need not pass national legislation in order to implement it. The UK, in fact, chose to do so because of its approach to the status of non-national law. Unlike our European neighbours we see international law as separate from, rather than simply a superior part of, national law. In order for it to become part of our legal system it must actually be written into national law. This was achieved by s. 2(1) of the European Communities Act 1972 (*Cases and Materials* (3.3)).

As a result, the EC Treaty is directly applicable in the Member States. It is not, however, always directly effective. The importance of this distinction will be examined in 4.3, but for the time being it is sufficient to say that the EC Treaty is part of the law of this country in the same way as the Police and Criminal Evidence Act 1984 or the Unfair Contract Terms Act 1977, for example.

The EC Treaty consists of the following:

(a) the Preamble setting out the objectives of the Community;
(b) the body of the Treaty dealing with six broad areas (further divided into Titles):
    (i) Principles
    (ii) Citizenship of the EU (see 1.9.2.3)
    (iii) Community policies, including policies on
        - free movement of goods (see **Chapter 8**)
        - free movement of persons (see **Chapter 9**)
        - visas, asylum, and immigration
        - competition (see **Chapters 10–11**)
        - economic and monetary policy (see 1.9.2.3)
        - employment
        - social policy
        - consumer protection
        - the environment
    (iv) Association of overseas territories and territories
    (v) Institutions of the Community
    (vi) General and final provisions
(c) Protocols on various issues, for example, the incorporation of Schengen (see 1.9.3).

3.5.2 Secondary legislation

QUESTION 3.9

In the light of what you learned about the institutions in Chapter 2, can you identify the body/bodies responsible for making secondary legislation? Is it always the responsibility of the same body/bodies?

The Council, Commission, and Parliament are responsible for law-making insofar as they are granted the power to pass legislation by the Treaty. Legislative acts may be adopted by the Council (e.g. under the consultation procedure (see below)), or the Commission (e.g. in competition policy) alone, or the Council and the Parliament jointly (e.g. under the co-decision procedure (see below)). Secondary legislation of the Community can be compared with statutory instruments under UK law. The Treaty or Act of Parliament confers powers and provides an outline of the law, and cannot (with some rare exceptions in the case of Acts) be challenged, whereas the secondary legislation or statutory instrument provides the detail and can be challenged in the courts. The Treaty, however, lays down a more basic framework than most Acts of Parliament, and secondary legislation is correspondingly more important in the context of Community law.

Article 249 (ex 189) EC defines five types of legal act which the Community may use: These are Regulations, Directives, Decisions, Recommendations, and Opinions. Neither Recommendations nor Opinions have binding force, but it is wise to take note of them because they are often followed by binding measures along the same lines.

Article 249 (ex 189) EC provides that:

> In order to carry out their task and in accordance with the provisions of this Treaty, the European Parliament acting jointly with the Council, the Council, and the Commission shall make regulations and issue directives, take decisions, make recommendations, or deliver opinions.
>
> A regulation shall have general application. It shall be binding in its entirety and directly applicable in all Member States.
>
> A directive shall be binding, as to the result to be achieved, upon each Member State to which it is addressed, but shall leave to the national authorities the choice of form and method.
>
> A decision shall be binding in its entirety upon those to whom it is addressed.
>
> Recommendations and opinions shall have no binding force.

EXERCISE 3.1

Read Article 249 EC (above). Try to summarize the differences between Regulations, Directives, and Decisions.

Regulations have the following characteristics:

(a) they are binding in their entirety, i.e. everything in the Regulation has binding force upon those to whom it applies;

(b) they are of general application, i.e. they apply to everyone in the Community (Member States, companies, individuals);

(c) they are directly applicable, i.e. implementing legislation is unnecessary for Regulations to become law in Member States.

Directives have the following characteristics:

(a) they are binding as to the result, i.e. it is only the result of the Directive which is binding, not the detail;

(b) they are only binding upon the Member State(s) to whom they are addressed;

(c) they require the Member State(s) to implement the Directive, i.e. the Member State must pass implementing legislation but the form and methods of implementation are for it to decide.

Decisions have the following characteristics:

(a) they are binding in their entirety;

(b) they bind only those to whom they are addressed (Member States, companies, or individuals);

(c) there is no need for implementing legislation.

The key differences are therefore as to

(a) *What* elements of measure apply

(b) To *whom* they apply

(c) *How* they apply.

? QUESTION 3.10

Which of the following measures could affect you directly?

(a) A Regulation concerning public holidays.

(b) A Directive addressed to the UK concerning public holidays.

(c) A Decision addressed to your employer, concerning holiday entitlement.

(d) An Opinion concerning public holidays.

A Regulation applies directly across the whole Community and will affect you directly if the subject matter, as here, is relevant to you. A Directive will generally not have direct effect (although see 4.3.2), and it is the UK legislation passed to implement it that will directly affect you. The Decision will affect your employer directly, but it is the resulting action taken by the employer that affects you directly. An Opinion does not affect anyone directly.

3.5.3 Decisions of the Court of Justice

The rulings of the Court of Justice are authoritative on all aspects of the Treaties and other (secondary) legislation. The Court has also developed certain legal principles, some of which it has implied into the Treaties, and others of which are part of the legal traditions of the Member States.

3.5.4 General principles of Community law

3.5.4.1 What are they?

Principles derived from the legal traditions of the Member States include equality, proportionality (legislation should not go beyond what is necessary to deal with the relevant problem or to achieve the desired objective), and legal certainty (it should always be possible to ascertain the law applicable to the circumstances at the time and therefore laws should not be ambiguous, nor apply retrospectively to the detriment of those who have fairly relied on them). Principles derived from both Member States and international law include respect for fundamental rights, and the Court of Justice has derived from the Treaty the principles of non-discrimination (on grounds of sex or nationality) and solidarity between Member States, which includes the duty to fulfil Treaty obligations.

3.5.4.2 Are they useful?

The principles can be used by all courts to interpret Community law, and can be used by the Court of Justice to test the legality of Community acts, and of implementing measures enacted by the Member States.

3.5.4.3 What is the basis for relying on them?

The most important of these as authority for relying on general principles of Community law is Article 220 (ex 164) EC, which states that they should be observed in the application of the EC Treaty (the words 'the law' refer to a body of principles). Article 230 (ex 173) EC gives authority for the Court of Justice to rely on 'any rule of law' when determining the validity of a Community measure (see 6.8.3).

3.6 Legislative procedures

In the UK, most legislation must be proposed by the government, approved by both Houses of Parliament and given Royal Assent, in order for it to become law. There are minor variations in the detail of this procedure according to the importance of the legislation and to what extent it is opposed. In some cases a different procedure is used. For example, a Private Members' Bill is proposed by a Member of Parliament, rather than the government, and certain types of delegated legislation may become law without Parliamentary approval. To a certain extent, an analogy may be drawn with Community law. The usual procedure is for a measure to be proposed by the Commission, discussed by the Parliament and adopted by the Council but there are considerable variations on this procedure, and the two most important of these are set out below. The correct legislative procedure in respect of a proposed piece of legislation is determined by the legal base of the proposed legislation (see 3.4, 6.3.3.2, and 6.8), that is to say the Treaty Article which gives the Community power to act in that area.

It is also necessary to note that, in some cases, a completely different procedure may be used. For example, the Parliament rather than the Commission may propose legislation concerning elections to the Parliament (Article 190 (ex 138) EC); and the Commission may enact legislation on its own in certain areas of competition policy (Article 86 (ex 90) EC) or where the Council has delegated power to it.

The Commission acts by majority (Article 219 (ex 163) EC) as does, in general, the Parliament (Article 198 (ex 141) EC). The Council also acts by majority unless a qualified majority or unanimity is expressly required (Article 205 (ex 148) EC).

3.6.1 Consultation procedure

This procedure is set out in each Article to which it applies.

This procedure will be applied where the EC Treaty so specifies, e.g. measures involving the CAP (Article 37(2) (ex 43(2) EC), certain environmental measures (Article 175(2) (ex 130s(2) EC).

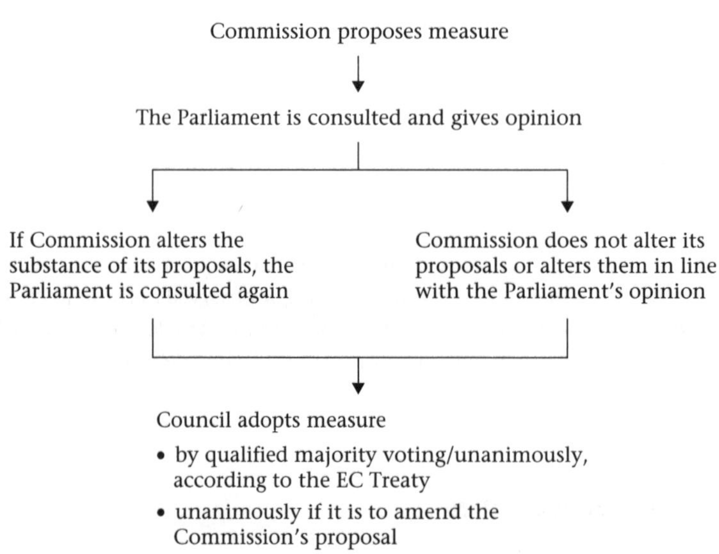

3.6.2 Co-decision procedure

This is set out in Article 251 (ex 189b) EC (see *Cases and Materials* (3.4)).

This procedure will be applied where the EC Treaty specifies that the Article 251 (ex 189b) EC procedure be used, e.g. measures concerning the internal market (Article 95 (ex 100a) EC), public health (Article 152 (ex 129) EC), vocational training (Article 150 (ex 127) EC). Note that the Treaty of Nice (see 1.9.4) provides that this procedure be applied to still more areas.

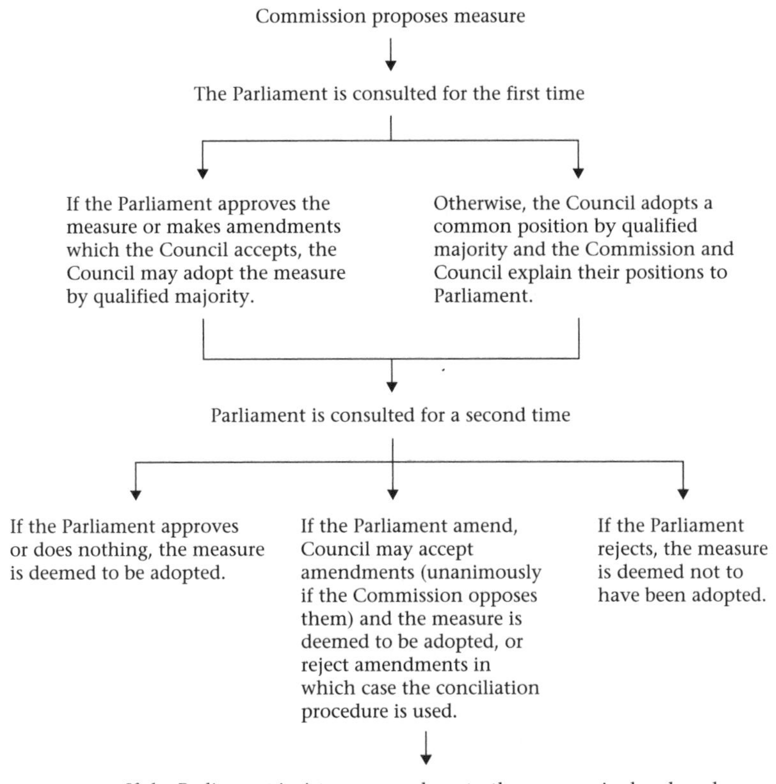

3.6.2.1 Conciliation procedure

Where the conciliation procedure is used, a Conciliation Committee, composed of equal numbers of representatives from the Council and the Parliament, has six weeks to reach agreement by a qualified majority of the Council representatives **and** a majority of the Parliamentary representatives. The agreed proposal is then adopted by both institutions. If there is no agreement the measure is deemed not to have been adopted.

EXERCISE 3.2

Summarize as briefly as possible the procedures that will apply to the following proposed legislation:

(a) The Commission has proposed a measure reducing subsidies to llama farmers. The Parliament's opinion is that the reduction should apply only to farmers with more than ten llamas but the Commission disagrees. The Council agrees with the Parliament.

(b) The Commission has proposed a measure that would restrict admission to the professional stage of legal education (including the Legal Practice Course and the Bar Finals course) to those with fluency in at least two European languages.

Assuming that the measure proposed at (a) is part of the CAP, the consultation procedure will apply (Article 37(2) (ex 43(2) EC). The Parliament has already been consulted once and its opinion referred back to the Commission. The Council is now free to adopt the measure, but since it wishes to adopt amendments which the Commission opposes, it must adopt the measure unanimously.

Since the measure proposed at (b) relates to vocational training, the co-decision procedure applies (Article 150 (ex 127) EC). The Parliament will be consulted on the Commission's proposal, and if it approves the proposal or amends it, it will be adopted if the Council accepts any amendments. Otherwise the Council and the Commission will explain their positions to Parliament which will consider the issue again. If the Parliament then approves the measure or makes amendments which the Council can accept, the measure is adopted. If not, it goes to the Conciliation Committee. If agreement is reached the measure is adopted; if it is not, the measure is dropped.

3.6.3 Enhanced cooperation

The Treaty of Amsterdam authorized 'closer cooperation' in the context of the EC Treaty generally and Title VI EU (police and judicial cooperation). This was a revolutionary concept, as it recognized the general principle that EU action could be taken by just some Members. Previously this had been limited to opt outs by particular Member States in specific areas. The Treaty of Nice renamed 'closer cooperation' 'enhanced cooperation' and made substantial amendments to it. It also extended it to the implementation of joint actions and common positions under the common foreign and security policy. Such cooperation may not apply to matters with military or defence implications.

3.6.3.1 Conditions

Articles 43, 43a, and 43b EU provide that the general conditions for cooperation are that it must:

(a) be aimed at furthering the objectives of the Community the EU and reinforcing integration;

(b) respect the Treaties;

(c) respect the acquis communautaire;

(d) not undermine the internal market;

(e) involve an area of joint competence;

(f) not constitute a barrier to, or discrimination in, trade between Member States, or the distortion of competition;

(g) involve at least eight Member States;

(h) respect the rights of non-participating Member States;

(i) not affect the Schengen Protocol;

(j) be open to all Member States.

Article 27a EC provides that enhanced cooperation in the area of police and judicial cooperation in criminal matters must also have as its objective enabling the EU to develop more rapidly into an area of freedom, security, and justice.

Enhanced cooperation in the common foreign and security policy must also:

(a) be aimed at safeguarding the interests and values of the EU by asserting its internal identity;

(b) respect the principles and decisions of the common foreign and security policy;

(c) respect the powers of the Community;

(d) respect consistency between the EU's internal and external policies.

3.6.3.2 Procedure

Under both Treaties, with the exception of the Common Foreign and Security Policy, the Member States request the Commission to make a proposal for enhanced cooperation, and the Commission must give reasons if it refuses to make a proposal. Under the EU Treaty (Article 40a EU) the Member States may then submit a proposal directly to the Council, but under the EC Treaty there is nothing more they can do. The Parliament is consulted unless it is an area of the EC Treaty to which the co-decision procedure (see 3.6.2) applies, in which case, Parliament's assent is required (Articles 40a EU and 11 EC). Under the EU Treaty, the Parliament is only informed.

Under the Common Foreign and Security Policy, Member States make a request to the Council (Article 27c EU). The Commission and Parliament are informed and the former may offer its opinion. Under both Treaties the final decision is taken by the Council by qualified majority voting (Articles 40b EU and 11 EC) and (Article 23(2) EU).

If States wish to opt in to cooperation under the EC Treaty by qualified majority voting, it is for the Commission to approve this (Article 11a EC). Under the EU Treaty (Articles 27e and 40b EU) it is the Council which decides, but this need not simply be a positive or negative decision; a decision may be held in abeyance and reconsidered at a later date.

CONCLUSIONS

Although it remains open to the UK to repeal the European Communities Act 1972 and leave the Community, this seems unlikely to happen in the near future, and in the meantime the supremacy of Community law has fundamentally qualified the doctrine of Parliamentary sovereignty. However, it is not yet true to say that our sovereignty has given way to an emerging federation. While the Community certainly has the potential to become a federation, this potential is some way from being converted into reality.

The measures which have had the greatest practical impact on our Parliamentary sovereignty have been Treaty Articles, Regulations, Directives and last, but by no means least, the decisions of the Court of Justice. In **Chapter 4** the impact of Treaty Articles and secondary legislation will be considered in detail and, throughout this textbook, the impact of judgments from the Court of Justice will be apparent.

SUMMARY

- The ECA 1972 provides that future UK legislation takes effect subject to EC law. This represents a significant erosion of **Parliamentary sovereignty**. However, the UK may at any time leave the EC (although this is becoming increasingly difficult, politically and economically) and regain Parliamentary sovereignty.
- The **powers of the EC** are granted to it by the Member States in the EC Treaty. These powers are subject to many limitations, including those laid down expressly in the Treaty and principles such as subsidiarity.
- The **sources of EC law** are the Treaties, secondary legislation, judgments of the Court of Justice, and general principles laid down by the Court.
- **Secondary legislation** is of three main types; Regulations, Decisions, and Directives. **Regulations** apply across the EC and have the force of law as soon as they are adopted. **Decisions** are addressed to particular entities and are legally binding on them as soon as they are adopted. **Directives** set out provisions which Member States must ensure are reflected in national law. The legal effect of these measures will be discussed further in **Chapter 4**).
- The EC has a variety of *legislative procedures*, the two most important of which are consultation and co-decision. In both, the Commission proposes legislation and the Council takes the final decision, but in consultation the Parliament is merely consulted, whereas in co-decision it has the joint right of decision with the Council.
- Enhanced cooperation allows a smaller group of Member States than the entire EC/EU membership to take action within the framework of the EC or EU.

CHAPTER 3: ASSESSMENT EXERCISE

(a) Explain the impact of Community membership on British Parliamentary sovereignty.

(b) (i) Briefly outline the main sources of Community law.

(ii) Explain the importance of the decisions of the Court of Justice, and give three principles which it has developed.

(c) Briefly explain the concept of subsidiarity.

See *Cases and Materials* (3.6) for a specimen answer.

FURTHER READING

Amministrazione delle Finanze dello Stato v *Simmenthal SpA (Simmenthal II)* (Case 106/77) [1978] ECR 629.

Articles 5, 251, and 308.

Costa v *ENEL* (Case 6/64) [1964] ECR 585.

MacCormick, N. (1993). 'Beyond the Sovereign State', 56 *MLR* 1.

R v *Secretary of State for Transport ex parte Factortame Ltd (Factortame I)* (Case C-213/89) [1990] ECR I-2433.

4 Enforcement of Community law in national courts

4.1 OBJECTIVES

By the end of this chapter you should be able to:

1. Understand and analyse the concept of direct effect
2. Explain the concept of indirect effect and the way in which it has been interpreted by the courts
3. Discuss the rules which apply to the grant of remedies for breach of Community law
4. Explain generally the rights of an individual or company to rely on a provision of Community law in their national courts

4.2 Introduction

The ability of litigants to enforce Community law in national courts is an essential feature of the integrated legal system set up by the Community. Although the Court of Justice is the supreme court in that system, the lower, that is to say national, courts must also be able to apply Community law. In later chapters it will be seen that certain remedies in respect of Community law may be administered only by the Court of Justice, and of course if national law grants the same rights as Community law, it will be sufficient for the applicant to rely directly on national law. However, where national law provides lesser rights than Community law, it is vital that an applicant can enforce his Community rights in the national courts. In the case of Community law which should have been transposed into national law, such as Directives, the applicant may request the Commission to take proceedings under Article 226 (ex 169) EC against the Member State for failing to do so, but this is a relatively circuitous route and increases both delay and expense for the applicant. Where the measure is not designed to be transposed, the applicant has no alternative but to rely directly on the Community measure. It is therefore necessary to identify those rights which may be enforced in the national courts.

4.3 Direct effect

Although, as discussed in **Chapter 3**, Community law is part of our legal system, and is therefore directly applicable in the UK, not all Community law is directly effective, that is to say, capable of judicial enforcement. In practice, the same situation arises under national law. For example, if a statute is passed enabling the government to privatize the roads, the provisions of the statute could not be enforced against the government if it in fact decided not to go ahead with the privatization.

The Court of Justice has ruled in a number of cases that in order for a Treaty Article, Regulation, or Decision to be directly effective it must be sufficiently clear and unconditional for reliance to be placed on it, and there must be no scope for the exercise of Member State discretion in implementing it. The position with regard to Directives is slightly different and will be considered separately.

4.3.1 Treaty Articles, Regulations, and Decisions

The case which first established the concept of direct effect of Community law related to Treaty Articles.

***Van Gend en Loos v Nederlandse Administratie der Belastingen* (Case 26/62) [1963] ECR 1**

In *Van Gend en Loos* (*Cases and Materials* (4.1)), Van Gend en Loos was required by Dutch law to pay an increased customs duty on imports. It argued in the Dutch courts that this was a violation of Article 25 (ex 12) of the EC Treaty which provided inter alia that Member States should not increase such charges. The Dutch court referred to the Court of Justice the question of whether a litigant before a national court could rely directly on the EC Treaty, and in particular, on Article 25 (ex 12). It was held that those Treaty obligations which were clear, unconditional, and not subject to intervening action by Member States, such as Article 25 (ex 12), could be relied upon in national courts.

After its ruling in *Van Gend en Loos* the Court of Justice went on in other cases to rule that Regulations and Decisions could also have direct effect.

In *Politi SAS* v *Ministero delle Finanze* (Case 43/71) [1973] ECR 1039 Italy levied import taxes on pork, contrary to the provisions of a Regulation. An importer, Politi, sought to rely on the Regulation. The Italian court made a reference to the Court of Justice under Article 234 (ex 177) of the EC Treaty. The Court of Justice ruled that Regulations could be directly effective because, by reason of their nature and function within the Community legal system, they created individual rights which national courts must protect.

The direct effect of Decisions was recognized in *Grad* v *Finanzamt Traunstein* (Case 9/70) [1970] ECR 825. A Decision provided for the replacement of national freight taxes by a common Community freight tax. A freight transporter sought to rely on the Decision to challenge a German freight tax. The German court made a reference to the Court of Justice under Article 234 (ex 177) of the EC Treaty. The Court of Justice ruled that since Decisions had binding effect, they must be capable of enforcement by those who were affected by them. The Court also adduced the argument that since Article 234 (ex 177) EC (see **Chapter 5**) permitted national courts to refer to the Court of Justice questions concerning 'all acts' of the Community, this presupposed that those courts could in the first place apply 'all acts'. On the facts, however, Grad lost because the date for the Decision to come into effect had not yet passed and therefore it had not yet become directly effective.

The two preconditions for the direct effect of Treaty Articles, Regulations, and Decisions will now be considered in more detail.

4.3.1.1 The measure must be clear and unconditional

In practice there is some overlap between clarity and unconditionability. For example, a provision may be unclear because it is conditional on other factors, or it may be conditional because it is for the Member State to implement it in detail. However, a measure may be sufficiently clear even if its precise scope requires interpretation by the Court of Justice under the Article 234 (ex 177) EC procedure (see **Chapter 5**).

In *Van Gend en Loos*, the Court of Justice ruled that the statement in Article 25 (ex 12) EC that 'Member States shall refrain from introducing any new customs duties . . . and from increasing those which they already apply . . .' imposed a clear prohibition on such measures.

A further example is provided by *Defrenne* v *SABENA* (Case 43/75) [1976] ECR 455 which involved a dispute over the policy of the Belgian airline, SABENA, compulsorily to retire its female air hostesses, but not its male crew, at age 40. Belgian legislation concerning the provision of retirement pensions for civil aviation air crews excluded air hostesses from the pension scheme in question. Ms Defrenne, an air hostess employed by SABENA airlines, claimed that this exclusion infringed the principle of equality contained in Article 141 (ex 119) EC. The Belgian court made a reference, inter alia, as to the effect of Article 141 to the Court of Justice under Article 234 (ex 177) of the EC Treaty.

The Court of Justice held that this imposed a clear and unconditional prohibition on direct discrimination (discrimination based directly on grounds of sex) and was directly effective to this extent but was not sufficiently clear in respect of more indirect discrimination (discrimination purportedly based on factors other than sex, but resulting in discrimination between men and women), since it did not identify what might constitute such discrimination.

Similarly, Regulations and Decisions must be sufficiently clear and unconditional. As Advocate General Warner stated, in *R* v *Secretary of State for Home Affairs, ex parte Santillo* (Case 131/79) [1980] ECR 1585, 'not every provision of every Regulation has direct effect, in the sense of conferring on private persons rights enforceable by them in national courts'.

In *Grad* the Court of Justice ruled that decisions must be 'unconditional and sufficiently clear and precise to be capable of creating direct effects'.

4.3.1.2 There must be no scope for the exercise of Member State discretion in implementation

In the context of Treaty Articles, Regulations, and Decisions it is relatively rare for Member States to be required to pass implementing legislation (see 3.5). However, where such implementation is required, as with Article 141 (ex 119) EC as originally drafted, it seems that as long as the deadline date for implementation has passed, the measure can take effect directly as it did in *Defrenne*, so long as it is sufficiently clear and unconditional.

4.3.2 Directives

Directives, as we saw in **Chapter 3**, are binding as to their result, but unlike Treaty Articles, Regulations, and Decisions, leave the detail of implementation to the Member States. Direct effect should therefore not be an issue since it should be possible to rely on the national, implementing measure before a national court. Unfortunately, the position is not so simple, as the implementing measure may be defective or non-existent. The Court of Justice has therefore recognized that in certain circumstances a Directive may have direct effect.

***Van Duyn* v *Home Office* (Case 41/74) [1974] ECR 1337**

The case in which the concept of direct effect was established in relation to Directives is *Van Duyn* (*Cases and Materials* (4.1)). Van Duyn, a Dutch national, applied for permission to enter the UK to work for the Church of Scientology. As the UK authorities officially disapproved of this organization, permission was refused under Article 39 (ex 48) EC, which allowed Member States to derogate on public policy grounds from the right to freedom of movement for workers. Van Duyn sought to enforce Directive 64/221 which stated that such derogations could be based only on the personal conduct of the applicant. It was held that it was possible to rely directly on an unimplemented Directive (such as Directive 63/22) if it was sufficiently clear. She lost on the facts because the Court of Justice held that personal conduct could include membership of a particular organization.

The Court of Justice ruled that in order for Directives to have a useful effect, they must be capable of producing direct effects, subject to the nature and wording of the Directive in question.

The preconditions which Directives must satisfy in order to have direct effect will now be considered.

4.3.2.1 The directive must be sufficiently clear and unconditional

This is the same requirement as for Treaty Articles, Regulations, and Decisions (see 4.3.1.1). In *Van Duyn* (see 4.3.2) the Court of Justice ruled that the Directive at issue was sufficiently clear and unconditional to be given effect to.

4.3.2.2 The deadline for implementation must have passed

As noted at 4.3.1.2, Treaty Articles, Regulations, and Decisions may only have direct effect if there is no scope for the exercise of Member State discretion in implementation. This requirement is not appropriate for Directives.

QUESTION 4.1

Given what you have learned about the nature of Directives, why do you think that this requirement would be problematic for Directives? (If you have difficulty in answering this question, look back at 3.5.2).

The problem with Directives is that they are simply instructions to Member States to transpose particular provisions into national law, and so it is almost inevitable that some discretion is left to Member States. The Court of Justice has therefore adapted this requirement for Directives, which can have direct effect so long as the deadline for implementation has passed.

Pubblico Ministero v _Ratti_ (Case 148/78) [1979] ECR 1629

In *Pubblico Ministero* v *Ratti*, Ratti's company had complied with a Directive as to the information to be supplied on labels on chemicals. However, Italy had failed to implement the Directive and prosecuted Ratti under its own, stricter laws. The Italian court made a reference to the Court of Justice.

The Court of Justice ruled that the Directive had not become directly effective because the deadline for its implementation had not passed. Until that time, it was not intended to have legal effect and Ratti could not rely on it.

This means that if a Member State wishes to take advantage of the discretion provided by a Directive, it must pass implementing legislation. If it does not, it cannot rely on an option in the Directive which it has failed to exercise. For example, in *East Riding of Yorkshire Council* v *Gibson* [2000] 3 CMLR 329, a swimming instructor employed by a local authority sought to rely directly on Directive 93/104 (the Working Time Directive), which provided for four weeks paid leave annually, and which the UK had not implemented by the deadline. The House of Lords held that the provision on paid leave was not directly effective. However, the House of Lords stated that had the provision been directly effective, the local authority could not have relied on the provision in the Directive permitting Member States to opt for a three-week leave period, rather than four, during a transitional period. It was not open to the State, or an emanation of it, to rely upon an option which it had not exercised.

Before leaving this issue, brief mention should be made of a rather exceptional point. If it is a principle of law of the Member State in question that more favourable laws should apply retroactively, a Directive may be applied retroactively by the courts of that Member State, even where the cause of action arose before the date set for compliance with the Directive. For example, in *Criminal proceedings against Ibiyinka Awoyemi* (Case C-230/97) [1998] ECR I-6781 the Court of Justice ruled that Awoyemi could rely on the directly effective provisions of Directive 91/439 on the mutual recognition of driving licences even before the deadline for transposition of that Directive into national law had passed, if the relevant Member State recognized the principle that more favourable provisions of criminal law had retroactive effect. However, the Court stressed the fact that the Directive was directly effective, because it was clear and precise and the deadline date had passed (albeit after the cause of action arose) without the Member State having taken the measures necessary to implement it. It therefore appears that this exception will apply only where the Member State in question has a rule of law that more favourable criminal laws should apply retroactively and where the Directive in question is capable of direct effect.

4.3.2.3 Directives only have vertical direct effect

The term 'vertical direct effect' is used where an individual, at one level of the legal system, seeks to enforce a Community measure against the State, which occupies a different level in the system. It can be contrasted with the concept of horizontal direct effect (see below) where an individual wishes to rely on a Community measure against someone at the same level in the system, i.e. an individual. (You should note that 'individual' here refers to any private party and can include businesses.)

The law as to the direct effect of Directives draws a clear distinction between cases where the applicant seeks to enforce a Directive against a Member State, and those where enforcement is sought against a private party. In the latter situation a Directive cannot have direct effect (although a Treaty, Article, Regulation, or Decision could).

***Marshall* v *Southampton and South West Area Health Authority (Teaching) (No 1)* (Case 152/84) [1986] ECR 723**

In *Marshall* (*Cases and Materials* (4.1)), Miss Marshall, a dietician, sought to rely on the provisions of Directive 76/207 (*Cases and Materials* (4.1)) which prohibited discrimination at work on grounds of sex, in opposing her enforced retirement at the age of 62 which was three years earlier than her male colleagues. She sought to rely on Directive 76/207 which had not been properly implemented by the UK, and which prohibited discrimination at work on grounds of sex. The UK court made a reference to the Court of Justice under Article 234 (ex 177) of the EC Treaty.

The Court of Justice ruled that the Directive was directly effective against the Area Health Authority. Directives were binding only against the State (and emanations of the State), but the capacity in which the State or emanation thereof acted (here as public authority or employer) was irrelevant. Miss Marshall thus succeeded in her claim.

Subsequent cases have given further guidance on which bodies may be included in the definition of the State.

***Foster* v *British Gas* (Case C-188/89) [1990] ECR 1–3313**

The most important of these cases is *Foster* (*Cases and Materials* (4.1)). British Gas employees were compulsorily retired at age 60 if female but at age 65 if male. Mrs Foster was compulsorily retired by British Gas, at the age of 60, in accordance with this retirement policy. Mrs Foster alleged that this was contrary to Directive 76/207 (above).

A reference was made by the national court under Article 234 (ex 177) of the EC Treaty.

The Court of Justice ruled that, as the deadline for implementation of the Directive had passed without transposing measures having been taken by the UK, the directive itself could be directly effective. It relied on *Marshall* as authority for the proposition that the State could not take advantage of its own failure to implement a Directive. The Court of Justice held that the Directive could be relied upon against British Gas, since it was an emanation of the State. Organizations which were to be treated as an emanation of the State, and against which direct effect could be pleaded were those which, like British Gas:

(a) had been made responsible by the State for providing a public service; and

(b) provided that service under the control of the State; and

(c) had special powers to provide that service, beyond those normally applicable in relations between individuals.

In *Doughty* v *Rolls Royce plc* [1992] 1 CMLR 1045 Rolls Royce had a policy similar to that of British Gas (above), and a female employee sought to rely on Directive 76/207. Mrs Doughty was compulsorily retired by her employer, Rolls Royce, at the age of 60, in accordance with their retirement policy which applied a retirement age of 65 to her male colleagues. She sought to rely on Directive 76/207 which had not been properly implemented by the UK, and which prohibited discrimination at work on grounds of sex. It was held that the Directive could not be directly effective against Rolls Royce because it did not fulfil the test set out in *Foster* and so was not an emanation of the Member State. It was 100% owned by the State and therefore any service it provided was under the control of the State. However, it was involved in a commercial undertaking, and was therefore not responsible for any public service, and it did not exercise any special powers of the type enjoyed by British Gas.

It is clear that all elements of the test in *Foster* must be proved. They are not alternatives, and therefore State control of an organization is not sufficient by itself to make that organization an emanation of the State and liable to direct effect. The fact that British Gas has now been privatized would not, of itself, prevent it from being treated as an emanation of a Member State, provided that all the elements of the *Foster* test were present (i.e. so long as it provides a public service under the control of the State and has special powers to do so).

In other cases, local authorities and the police force have been held to be emanations of the State. In *Fratelli Costanzo SpA* v *Comune di Milano* (Case C 103/88) [1989] ECR 1–1839 Fratelli Costanzo submitted a tender to a municipal authority for a public works contract. The municipal authority eliminated this tender from the tendering procedure, and Fratelli Costanzo sought the annulment of the decision to eliminate its tender. The national court referred to the Court of Justice a number of questions on the interpretation of the Directive 71/305 on procedures for the award of public works contracts. The Court of Justice ruled, inter alia, that directives could be relied upon directly against the authority.

In *Johnston* v *Chief Constable of the RUC* (Case 222/84) [1986] ECR 1651 the Chief Constable of the RUC decided that in view of the high numbers of police officers assassinated in Northern Ireland, it was not appropriate to continue with the policy that they should not carry firearms. He decided that men should carry firearms in the regular course of their duties, but that women police officers would not be equipped with firearms and would not receive training in firearms. As a result, fewer women were required. The Chief Constable therefore refused to renew Mrs Johnston's contract as a police constable. Mrs Johnston challenged that refusal before an Industrial Tribunal. The Tribunal referred to the Court of Justice a number of questions on the interpretation of Directive 76/207 on equal treatment. The Court of Justice ruled, inter alia, that directives could be relied upon directly against an authority such as Chief Constable of the RUC.

In *Mighell and others* v *Motor Insurers Bureau* ([1999] 1 CMLR 1251) claimants in three actions, who were victims of motor accidents, sought to rely on Directive 84/5 (the Second Directive on Motor Insurance), which provided for Member States to compensate the victims of accidents caused by uninsured drivers. In the UK this role was performed by the Motor Insurers' Bureau (MIB). The Court of Appeal agreed (two of them expressing the opinion *obiter*) that the MIB was not an emanation of the State and therefore the Directive could not be relied upon against it.

One further complication is that in *National Union of Teachers* v *Governing Body of St. Mary's Church of England (Aided) Junior School* [1997] 3 CMLR 630 the Court of Appeal suggested that there might be bodies which did not satisfy the *Foster* test but which might nonetheless constitute emanations of the State. However, no further tests have been provided by the Court of Justice, and so *Foster* remains the prime test.

EXERCISE 4.1

Try to summarize the *Foster* test in your own words without looking at the text. If you have difficulty in doing this, re-read this section.

Before leaving the topic of the direct effect of Directives, brief mention should be made of the concept of horizontal direct effect. This refers to the situation where an individual seeks to rely on a direct effect of a measure against another individual. Treaty Articles, Regulations and Decisions may have horizontal as well as vertical direct effect. However, in *Marshall*, the Court of Justice ruled out the possibility of horizontal direct effect on the grounds that the binding nature of a Directive applied only to its Member State addressee(s). It could not impose obligations on an individual and should not be relied upon against them. The Court of Justice restated this position in *Faccini Dori v Recreb Srl* (Case C-91/92) [1994] ECR I-3325, despite the Opinion of Attorney General Lenz in which he persuasively argued that Directives should have horizontal direct effect.

QUESTION 4.2

Would a woman in the same position as Miss Marshall, but employed by a private hospital, be able to rely on the equal pay Directive in the same way?

In *Marshall* the Court of Justice clearly stated that a Directive could not be relied upon against another individual. It would therefore be possible to rely on the Directive in this situation only if the private hospital could be shown to be an emanation of the Member State. In the light of *Foster* and *Doughty* it would be necessary for the hospital to be operating a public service under the control of the State and to have special powers to do so. It is unlikely that these criteria would be fulfilled (since private healthcare is not a public service) and if they were not, the woman would be unable to rely on the terms of the Directive.

4.3.4 Recommendations and Opinions

The key case concerning the direct effect of Recommendations is *Grimaldi* v *Fonds des Maladies Professionnelles* (Case C-322/88) [1989] ECR 4407. Grimaldi suffered from a disease which was classified under a Recommendation as an occupational disease, and thereby entitled him to compensation. Under French law, however, it was not so classified, and therefore under French law, Grimaldi was not entitled to any compensation. Grimaldi sought to rely on the Recommendation. The French court made a reference to the Court of Justice under Article 234 (ex 177) of the EC Treaty. The Court of Justice ruled that since Recommendations were not intended to have binding effect, it would clearly be inappropriate for them to have direct effect, and therefore Grimaldi could not rely directly on the Recommendation. However, although Recommendations could not be directly effective, they could be taken into consideration when interpreting other measures.

Opinions are similar to Recommendations in effect, and therefore this ruling is equally applicable to them.

We have now covered the concept of direct effect. This is one of the most important concepts in EU law, and if you have difficulty in understanding this topic, you should review the foregoing text before passing on to the next topic.

4.4 Indirect effect

This term refers to the use of Community law to interpret national law. Community law is then said to have an 'indirect effect' since it influences the interpretation of national law (as opposed to a direct effect where it is relied upon directly).

4.4.1 Treaty Articles, Regulations, and Decisions

Although Treaty Articles, Regulations, and Decisions can have indirect effect, it is a relatively unimportant concept in relation to them. This is because they will generally only fail to have direct effect if they are unclear or conditional, in which case they are unlikely to be of much assistance in interpreting national law.

4.4.2 Recommendations and Opinions

Indirect effect has more importance in relation to Recommendations and Opinions because they cannot have direct effect (see 4.3.4).

Although in *Grimaldi* the Court of Justice ruled out direct effect, it stated that Recommendations could have indirect effect. It argued that since Recommendations must have some legal effect, they should be taken into consideration when interpreting national implementing measures, or Community measures which the Recommendations were designed to supplement. As with direct effect, this ruling can be taken to apply equally to Opinions.

Indirect effect is of most importance in relation to Directive and so this topic will be examine in some detail.

4.4.3 Directives

Since direct effect is restricted to those Directives which are sufficiently clear and unconditional, and may be relied upon only against the State, the doctrine of direct effect is of somewhat limited use. However, the possibility exists that a Directive may have indirect effect, that is to say, it may be used in a national court in interpreting the relevant national legislation, even if the Directive is too vague to be applied itself, or if the action is against another individual.

Von Colson and Kamann v _Land Nordrhein-Westfalen_ (Case 14/83) [1984] ECR 1891

Von Colson (*Cases and Materials* (4.2)) involved the appointment of two men as social workers. Two disappointed female applicants alleged that they had been discriminated against contrary to Directive 76/207 which prohibited discrimination at work on grounds of sex. Under German law, the applicants were only entitled to recover their travel expenses.

The German court made a reference to the Court of Justice under Article 234 (ex 177) of the EC Treaty.

The Court of Justice held that the provisions of the Directive as to remedies were not sufficiently precise and unconditional to be directly effective. However, national law should be interpreted in the light of its provisions, which required that an effective remedy be available. The nominal remedy available under German law (the award of expenses) was not adequate.

The case left open the question of precisely **which** national legislation should be construed in this way. The domestic legislation in *Von Colson* had been passed specifically in order to implement the Directive, but in its judgment the Court of Justice referred to 'national law **and** in particular the provisions of a national law specifically introduced in order to implement Directive 76/207' (emphasis added). This implies that legislation not specifically passed to implement a Directive could also fall to be construed in accordance with it. In particular, where the national legislation predates the Directive, such an interpretation might prove difficult, but it could be argued that if indirect effect were to be limited to implementing legislation, an unscrupulous Member State could simply fail to pass any implementing legislation, and thus avoid both actions based on national implementing law and actions based on the Directive itself.

It should be noted that the duty of consistent interpretation applies only to legislation. In *White (A.P.)* v *White and the Motor Insurers Bureau* [2001] 2 CMLR 1, the victim of a motor accident caused by an uninsured driver sought to rely on the agreement made between the Secretary of State for the Environment, Transport, and the Regions and the Motor Insurers Bureau ('MIB') in implementation of Directive 84/5 (the Second Directive on Motor Insurance). The agreement provided, inter alia, for the compensation of victims who had obtained judgment against an uninsured driver, unless he 'knew or ought to have known' that the driver was uninsured. The Directive only referred to victims who 'knew'.

In determining the meaning of this phrase, the House of Lords ruled that there was no obligation to interpret the agreement in line with the Directive since it was not legislation. This is surprising given that the agreement was made with the Secretary of State, and that it was made in fulfilment of the UK's obligations under the Directive. However, the House of Lords ruled that a purposive approach to the interpretation of the agreement should be taken. Account must therefore be taken of the Directive, since the purpose of the agreement was to give effect to the provisions of the Directive. The result of this was that the House of Lords took account of the Directive in interpreting the agreement, but did so not in order to give indirect effect to the Directive, but in accordance with the usual domestic rules of statutory interpretation.

Although courts in the UK have recognized the concept of indirect effect, they have tended to rely on it somewhat sparingly. One example of its use is in *Litster* v *Forth Dry Dock and*

Engineering Co. Ltd [1989] 2 CMLR 194. Litster and others were dismissed by their employer, a shipyard, one hour before it was sold to another company and new employees taken on. UK law designed to implement a Directive provided the employees with a remedy only if they had been employed immediately before such a transfer. Litster argued that 'immediately before' must be interpreted in the light of the Directive, which was clearly intended to protect all employees dismissed in the event of a transfer of employer. The House of Lords accepted the principle of indirect effect but restricted its scope. It took the view that the duty of construction imposed on national courts by *Von Colson* applied to legislation 'issued for the purpose of complying with directives'. On the facts, the relevant UK law had been so intended, and therefore the employees were entitled to compensation.

Marleasing SA v *La Comercial Internacional de Alimentación SA* (Case C-106/89) [1990] ECR I-4135

The Court of Justice subsequently clarified its position in *Marleasing* (*Cases and Materials* (4.2)). Spanish law laid down a number of grounds on which a company could be struck off the register, including lack of cause, meaning that the company had no real function. Spain had failed to implement a company law Directive which omitted this particular ground. La Comercial sought to rely on the Directive when Marleasing attempted to have it struck off for lack of cause. It was held that Spanish law must be interpreted in accordance with the Directive and therefore a company could not be struck off for lack of cause.The Court of Justice confirmed that the Directive could not have horizontal direct effect against Marleasing but ruled that Spanish law, even though it predated the Directive, must be interpreted 'as far as possible' in accordance with it. This meant that lack of cause was not a ground on which a company could be struck off and therefore La Comercial could not be struck off.

It should be borne in mind that the Court of Justice has consistently attempted to promote and expand the application of Community law, and to have given indirect effect a more narrow application would have gone against this policy.

The first case involving indirect effect to come before the UK courts after *Marleasing* was *Webb* v *EMO Air Cargo (UK) Ltd*. Ms Webb was employed to cover the maternity leave of another colleague. Prior to taking employment, Webb discovered that she was pregnant, and was dismissed as a result.

Webb's argument that her dismissal was contrary to the Sex Discrimination Act 1975 was rejected by the House of Lords. As to Webb's argument that her dismissal was contrary to Directive 76/207, which prohibited discrimination at work on grounds of sex, the House of Lords accepted that *Marleasing* required it to interpret the Sex Discrimination Act consistently with the later Directive, but 'only if it is possible to do so'. A reference was therefore made to the Court of Justice as to whether the dismissal was contrary to Directive 76/207.

The Court of Justice ruled that Webb's dismissal did indeed contravene Directive 76/207. The House of Lords was therefore left with the task of attempting to interpret the Sex Discrimination Act consistently with the requirements of the Directive. The House of Lords concluded that the Sex Discrimination Act could be interpreted consistently with the Directive.

Section 1(1)(a) of the Act prohibits the discriminatory treatment of women on the ground of their sex. Section 5(3) of the Act states that in order to show discrimination, any comparison between the treatment of women and that of men must be made on the basis of similar 'relevant circumstances'. Prior to the ruling of the Court of Justice, the House of Lords had interpreted 'relevant circumstances' in Webb's case to mean her unavailability for work. Since a male employee who was unavailable to work would have been treated in the same way, there was no discrimination.

In the light of the Court of Justice ruling that Webb's dismissal contravened Directive 76/207, the House of Lords interpreted 'relevant circumstances' to mean Webb's unavailability for work due to pregnancy. Since a male employee could not have been dismissed for this reason, the dismissal was discriminatory.

The *Webb* case clearly indicates that the House of Lords has accepted the ruling of the Court of Justice in *Marleasing* that even national legislation which pre-dates Community law must be interpreted consistently with it.

However, the 'as far as possible' caveat in *Marleasing* provides a potential loophole.

Wagner Miret* v *Fondo de Garantía Salarial **(Case C-334/92) [1993] ECR I-6911**

In the case of *Wagner Miret* (*Cases and Materials* (4.2)), the Court of Justice confirmed the existence of this loophole and took a more restrictive approach to indirect effect. Wagner Miret was a senior manager in a company which became insolvent. Directive 80/897 obliged Member States to set up a fund to recompense employees whose employers became insolvent. Although Spain had set up such a fund, it did not cover payments to higher management staff. The Spanish court made a reference to the Court of Justice under Article 234 (ex 177) of the EC Treaty. The Court of Justice ruled that Directive 80/897 was not sufficiently precise to be directly effective. The relevant Spanish law clearly restricted the coverage of the existing fund and the Court of Justice accepted that the law governing the fund could not be interpreted as permitting higher management employees to claim from it. The only possible remedy for Wagner Miret was that the State should recompense him for his losses since its failure to transpose the Directive had caused his loss. (This is sometimes referred to as the *Francovich* remedy, and will be discussed at 7.4.1.)

4.4.4 Relationship between indirect effect and the sovereignty of Community law

? **QUESTION** 4.3

How does the concept of indirect effect relate to what you learned about the sovereignty of Community law in 3.3?

First, indirect effect is a practical manifestation of the sovereignty of Community law, because an interpretation of national law which is consistent with Community law takes precedence over an interpretation which does not. Secondly, where national law clearly conflicts with

Community law and cannot be interpreted consistently with it, the national court is under a duty to refuse to apply the conflicting elements of national law.

Where national law imposes a duty or prohibition on an applicant which is contrary to Community law, the applicant could benefit from it being disapplied. For example, in *R* v *Secretary of State for Transport ex parte Factortame ('Factortame II')* (see 3.3.2.2) the applicants were Spanish fishermen who were prevented from fishing in British waters by the provisions of the Merchant Shipping Act 1988. They therefore sought to have the Act disapplied so that they could legally resume fishing.

By contrast, where national law gives the applicant certain rights which are not as favourable as those granted by Community law, the applicant could be worse off if the national law is disapplied. This is because, if the Community measure in question has no direct or indirect effect, the applicant's only rights are under national law. In these circumstances, national law would not be disapplied.

We have now covered the concept of indirect effect. If you have difficulty in understanding this topic, or its application by the UK courts (and most students do!) you should review this section of the text before going on to the next topic.

4.5 Remedies available

The full range of remedies available in respect of national law is applicable to Community law. However, the two most important remedies for breach of Community law are the disapplication of national law (see 3.3), and damages.

4.5.1 Disapplying national legislation

The Court of Justice clearly stated in *Amministrazione delle Finanze dello Stato* v *Simmenthal (Simmenthal II)* (see 3.3.2.2) that national courts had a responsibility to disapply national law which conflicted with Community law.

In *Factortame I* (see 3.3.2.2), the applicants sought to suspend an Act which allegedly conflicted with Community law, pending a decision by the Court of Justice. Under national law, such a remedy was not available. However, the Court of Justice ruled that in order for the Community right to be fully effective, this remedy must be granted and the Act temporarily suspended.

4.5.2 Damages

As we have seen in this chapter, damages may be awarded in any of the following circumstances for breach of Community law:

(a) Against an individual or private or public body for breach of a directly effective Treaty Article, Regulation, or Decision (see 4.3.1);

(b) Against a public body which is an 'emanation of the Member State' for breach of a directly effective Directive (see 4.3.2).

We will see, in **Chapter 7**, that damages may also be awarded for breach of Community law:

(c) against the Community for breaches committed by its institutions, employees, or agents (see 7.3);

(d) against a Member State for its breaches (see 7.4).

In all these cases the damages will actually be awarded by the national courts, and so national laws governing the award of damages will apply subject to the conditions which the Court of Justice has laid down (see below). In addition, damages may be awarded for breach of national law interpreted in the light of Community law, but this is an action under national, rather than Community, law and the principles set out do not apply.

4.6 Principles governing the award of a remedy

Although, in an action in the national courts, the award of any remedy for breach of Community law is governed by national law, the Court of Justice has laid down a number of principles with which the award of this remedy must comply. These principles have been developed over time and in some cases appear to conflict.

4.6.1 Non-discrimination

The remedy must be available on conditions as favourable as those applicable to an equivalent breach of national law.

For example, if certain time limits or rights of appeal are laid down for actions based on national law, no lesser time limits or more restricted rights of appeal may be imposed for an action based on Community law.

4.6.2 The remedy must be effective

The Court of Justice has repeatedly stated that national laws must not make the obtaining of a remedy in practice 'impossible or excessively difficult'. In two areas in particular, national laws have often fallen foul of this principle: the time limits imposed, and the amount of damages awarded. Each of these will be considered in turn.

4.6.2.1 Time limits

Although the question of time limits on bringing an action is governed by national procedural rules (three years for most actions in the UK), these will not apply if they make it virtually impossible to exercise Community law rights. In *Emmott* v *Minister for Social Welfare and another* (Case C-208/90) [1991] ECR I-4269 Ireland had not implemented the necessary measures to comply with a Directive equalizing disability benefits until two years after the implementation deadline. Emmott claimed compensation in respect of underpaid benefit during this two-year period, but the Irish authorities alleged that her claim was outside the three-month time limit set by Irish law.

The national court made a reference to the Court of Justice under Article 234 EC. The Court of Justice ruled that the time limit should not start to run until the Directive had been properly transposed, and therefore that the claim was admissible.

The key to this ruling was that the time limit made it **virtually impossible** for Emmott to exercise her Community law rights since the three-month time limit expired long before the relevant Directive was implemented, and therefore before Emmott could have become aware of her rights.

However, where a time limit on the bringing of another action does **not** make the exercise of Community law rights virtually impossible, that time limit will not be in conflict with Community law and will therefore be valid. In *Edilizia Industriale Siderurgica Srl (Edis)* v *Ministero delle Finanze* (Case C-231/96) [1998] ECR I-4951 the Court of Justice ruled that a time limit of three years on the commencement of actions to recover charges levied in contravention of Community law was compatible with Community law, even though at the time those charges were levied, the relevant Directive had not been properly implemented under national law. The charges had been levied between 1986 and 1992 and the Directive was correctly implemented in 1993, so it was still possible to bring an action for recovery of the charges once the Directive had been implemented (albeit not for all the charges paid).

In later cases such as *Johnson* v *Chief Adjudication Officer* (Case C-410/92) [1994] ECR I-5493 and *Steenhorst-Neerings* v *Bestuur van de Bedrifsvereniging voor Detailhandel* (Case C 338/91) [1993] ECR I-5475 the Court of Justice has made it clear that time limits which do not prevent the bringing of an action, but simply limit the arrears of benefit payable, are applicable.

4.6.2.2 The amount of damages

Where national law imposes an unduly severe limit on the maximum amount of damages that can be awarded, this may make the remedy ineffective to protect the applicant's Community law rights.

In *Marshall* v *Southampton and South West Area Health Authority (No. 2)* (Case C-271/91) [1993] ECR I-4367 (for the facts, see *Marshall (No. 1)* at 4.3.2.3), Marshall disputed the severe restrictions which the Sex Discrimination Act imposed on the amount of damages which could be awarded. The national court made a reference to the Court of Justice under Article 234 EC. The Court of Justice ruled that the Act conflicted with Article 249 (ex 189) EC which provided that Member States must ensure that the objectives of Directives were fulfilled. The objective of Directive 76/207 was to achieve real equality of opportunity. This required that where such equality had not been achieved, the victim of discrimination could be reinstated or compensated in full for the loss and damage sustained. The limit on damages was contrary to Community law because it was unrelated to the loss suffered.

It should be noted that this Directive expressly imposed a duty on Member States to take the necessary measures to enable applicants to pursue their claims. It has been argued that had such a specific duty been absent, the Court of Justice might have been less willing to override the provisions of national law.

However, there have been other cases in which the Court of Justice has made it clear that a national limit on the amount of damages is incompatible with Community law if it renders the remedy ineffective.

In a case considered earlier (at 4.4.3), *Von Colson*, two women who had attended an interview, but failed to secure the post, brought a claim for damages on the grounds of sex discrimination. The Court of Justice ruled that the compensation must be adequate in relation to the damage sustained and that a German law which limited the amount of damages to a 'purely nominal amount such as . . . the expenses incurred by them in submitting their application', did not effectively protect the applicants' rights under Community law.

In *Draehmpaehl* v *Urania Immobilienservice OHG* (Case C-180/95) [1997] ECR I-2195 the Court of Justice ruled that a national law which prescribed an upper limit of three months' salary for compensation for sex discrimination in the appointment of candidates to a job was contrary to Community law. However, the Court qualified this ruling by stating that such a rule was only invalid insofar as it applied to applicants who would have obtained a post had it not been for the selection process. Where an applicant would not have obtained the position anyway, and therefore suffered little or no loss, the ceiling of three months' salary was compatible with Community law.

Similar problems occur in the context of business as well as personal losses. In *Factortame III* (see 7.4.2), the Court of Justice ruled that the total exclusion of loss of profit as a head of damages which could be awarded for breach of Community law was incompatible with Community law. It stated that in the context of commercial litigation, such a total exclusion would make genuine reparation of losses suffered practically impossible.

4.6.3 New remedies need not be created

In the case of *Rewe Handelsgesellschaft Nord mbH and Rewe-Markt Steffen* v *Hauptzollamt* (Case 158/80) [1981] ECR 1005 cruises which went beyond German territorial waters were organized by certain retailers so that goods could be technically 'exported', traded, and 'imported' again, thus incurring certain customs and tax advantages. Land-based retailers claimed that this practice was in breach of Community law. The German court made a reference to the Court of Justice under Article 234 (ex 177) of the EC Treaty on the interpretation and validity of the Community law in question, and on the remedies which should be available for any breach.

It was held that all actions available to enforce national law, must be available to enforce Community law, but new actions need not be created. The remedies available for breach of Community law in this instance depended on provisions of German law. The Court of Justice acknowledged that national courts need not create new remedies to ensure that Community law is fully effective if those remedies do not exist in national law. The remedy available therefore depended on the provisions of national law.

This principle may, on occasion, conflict with the principle of effectiveness. More recent case law (*Marshall No. 2* , *Factortame III*) appears to indicate that new remedies may be necessary in the interests of effectiveness.

4.6.4 No further substantive conditions

Where liability has arisen under Community law, no further substantive conditions may be imposed by national law. In the case which established this principle, *Dekker* v *Stichting VJV* (Case C-177/88) [1990] ECR I-3941, Dekker's name had been put forward as the most suitable candidate for a job, but after she informed the employer that she was pregnant, she was rejected because his insurance would not cover the cost of a replacement worker during her maternity leave. She sought to rely on Directive 76/207 which prohibited discrimination at work on grounds of sex. Under Dutch law, Dekker was required to prove not merely discrimination, but unjustified discrimination. The employer claimed that his action was justified because his insurance would not cover the cost of her maternity leave in these circumstances. The Dutch court made a reference to the Court of Justice under Article 234 (ex 177) of the EC Treaty. It was held that the Directive imposed liability purely on the basis of discrimination, and therefore the extra requirement under Dutch law could not be applied. The Court of Justice held that since the Directive imposed liability purely on the basis of discrimination, regardless of any fault, national provisions requiring such fault to be proved could not be applied.

A further example of this principle is the statement in *Factortame III* that if the conditions for Member State liability are satisfied, no further requirement of proof of fault may be imposed by national law.

You should now have achieved all the learning objectives set out in 4.1. If you are still unsure about any area, don't panic. This chapter contains some complex material. However, it is a vital area of Community law for you to grasp and you should be prepared to review those elements of it which you do not understand as many times as is necessary.

CONCLUSIONS

It is essential to the supremacy and effectiveness of Community law that that law should be capable of being enforced in national courts, as a matter both of principle and of practice. In the national courts the most satisfactory course of action for a litigant is, of course, to rely directly on Community law or on any implementing legislation. Where this is not possible, he or she may seek to rely on the indirect effect of the measure; this is to say, its effect on the interpretation of national law. Where a Directive is concerned, there is a fall-back position, namely to seek damages from the Member State which has failed properly, or indeed at all, to implement it. As a result of the decision in Factortame III , individuals may also have a remedy in respect of national law which conflicts with Community law.

If the applicant is successful under any of these headings, the availability and nature of any remedy will be governed by national law, subject to a number of guidelines laid down by the Court of Justice. While this system has its loopholes, the effects of the Court of Justice in this area have been quite remarkable in changing the approach of the national courts.

SUMMARY

- **Direct effect** refers to a characteristic possessed by some Community legislation—that it may be enforced directly and produce legal effects. Treaty Articles, Regulations, Decisions, and Directives are all—in principle—capable of direct effect. However, a particular measure will only have direct effect if it is clear and precise (*Van Duyn* ; *Politi* ; *Grad* ; *Van Duyn*). In addition, if it is a Directive, the deadline for its transposition into national law must have passed (*Ratti*) it may only be enforced against an emanation of the State (*Marshall*). An emanation of the State is an entity of the State, and it has specific powers to do so (*Foster*).

- **Indirect effect** refers to another characteristic of some Community legislation—that it may be enforced indirectly through informing the interpretation of national law. All national law, whatever its date or purpose, must be interpreted in line with Community law (*Marleasing*). However, sometimes the national law in question is so different from the relevant Community law that it simply cannot be interpreted in that way (*Wagner Miret*).
- **Remedies** may be awarded for breach of directly effective Community law, or for breach of national law as interpreted in accordance with Community law. In either event, remedies are governed by national law, both in substance and procedure, and new remedies for breach of Community law need not be created. However, the Court of Justice has ruled that the remedy awarded must be non-discriminatory and effective, and must not be subjected to fulfilment of further substantive conditions.

CHAPTER 4: ASSESSMENT EXERCISE

Alf works for Humber plc, a company created to build and operate a railway bridge across the Humber estuary. It is authorized to do so under s. 1 of the (fictitious) Estuary Bridges Act 1990, which also gives it powers to regulate the connecting train service.

(Fictitious) Directive 999/93 requires Member States to take all measures necessary to ensure that bridge workers are provided with appropriate safety equipment, including hard hats. The deadline for implementation of the Directive has passed without UK compliance. The Estuary Bridges Act merely provides that licence holders must ensure that their employees are aware of safety hazards and advised to wear appropriate clothing.

Alf sustained a serious head injury when a cable fell on him during construction of the bridge, and as a result is unfit to work. He claims that his injury was caused by the company's failure to provide workers with hard hats. Humber plc claims that it had made Alf aware of the risks and had advised him to wear a hard hat, although the company itself was unable to provide them. It argues that the Act requires only the provision of information and advice.

(a) Advise Alf as to whether he has any cause of action against Humber plc.

(b) Would it make any difference to your answer if the company did not have the power to regulate the train service referred to above but was wholly owned by the State?

See *Cases and Materials* (4.4) for a specimen answer.

FURTHER READING

Drake, S. (2005). 'Twenty years after *Von* Colson: the impact of "Indirect effect" on the protection of the individual's Community rights', 30(3) *ELRev* 329.

Foster v *British Gas* (C-188/89) [1990] ECR 1–3313.

Lenz, M. (2000). 'Horizontal What? Back to Basics', 25(5) *ELRev* 509.

Marleasing SA v *La Comercial Internacional de Alimentación SA* (C-106/89) [1990] ECR I-4135.

Steiner, J. (1993). 'From direct effects to *Francovich*; shifting means of enforcement of Community law', 18 *ELRev* 3.

Van Duyn v *Home Office* (Case 41/74) [1974] ECR 1337.

Wagner Miret v *Fondo de Garantía Salarial* (C-334/92) [1993] ECR I-6911.

5 Preliminary references

5.1 OBJECTIVES

By the end of this chapter you should be able to:

1 Identify the types of issue which may be the subject of a preliminary reference under Article 234 (ex 177) EC

2 Explain the circumstances in which national courts are obliged to make a reference and those in which they merely have a discretion as to whether to do so

3 Analyse the approaches taken to Article 234 (ex 177) EC by the Court of Justice and the UK courts in respect of discretionary and mandatory references

4 Explain the ***CILFIT*** guidelines

5 Discuss the importance of Article 234 (ex 177) EC references to the difference between questions of validity and those of interpretation

5.2 Introduction

What fundamental problem underlies the Community's legal system? It is that, although it purports to be part of the legal system of each Member State, the initiation, enactment, and interpretation of Community law are performed by entities entirely distinct and indeed distanced from those national courts which are, as we saw in **Chapter 4**, expected to apply Community law. Not only that, those national courts apply Community law independently of one another, leading potentially to different interpretations of the same piece of legislation or decision of the Court of Justice. If Community law is to be supreme it must have the same meaning and effect in all Member States, and therefore that meaning and effect must be determined by the Court of Justice.

To overcome this problem, the EC Treaty provides a procedure whereby national courts may consult the Court of Justice on particular issues of Community law. The national court will deliver judgment in the case, but is able to clarify certain issues of Community law with the Court of Justice before doing so. This is known as the preliminary reference or preliminary rulings procedure and is to be found in Article 234 (ex 177) EC (see below). The Treaty of

Nice (see 1.9.4) provides for the transfer of some Article 234 jurisdiction to the Court of First Instance (see 2.3.5).

This chapter will concentrate on the distinction between situations where a national court is generally **obliged** to make a reference ('mandatory references') and those in which it may make a reference but is **not obliged** to do so ('discretionary references'). As a general rule, it is the status of the court in the national legal system which determines this.

THE EC TREATY

Article 234 (ex 177)

The Court of Justice shall have jurisdiction to give preliminary rulings concerning:

(a) the interpretation of this Treaty;

(b) the validity and interpretation of acts of the institutions of the Community and of the ECB;

(c) the interpretation of the statutes of bodies established by an act of the Council, where those statutes so provide.

Where such a question is raised before any court or tribunal of a Member State, that court or tribunal may, if it considers that a decision on the question is necessary to enable it to give judgment, request the Court of Justice to give a ruling thereon.

Where any such question is raised in a case pending before a court or tribunal of a Member State against whose decisions there is no judicial remedy under national law, that court or tribunal shall bring the matter before the Court of Justice.

Article 234 (ex 177) EC provides that a national court may, or in certain circumstances must, refer certain questions to the Court of Justice if it considers that a decision on the question is necessary to enable it to give judgment. The questions that may be referred are those as to the **interpretation** of the EC Treaty or of secondary legislation and those as to the **validity** of secondary legislation.

? QUESTION 5.1

In what areas has the Court of Justice's jurisdiction under Article 234 EC (ex 177) EC been limited? (If you cannot remember the answer to this question, refer back to 2.3.4)

Note that jurisdiction is limited to Community law and does not extend to national law. Once the Court of Justice has interpreted Community law, it is for the national courts to apply it to the facts and, if appropriate, decide on the compatibility of national law. In *Brasserie du Pêcheur SA* v *Germany* and *R* v *Secretary of State for Transport ex parte Factortame (Factortame III)* (see 7.4.2), the Court of Justice strayed beyond this and asserted that since it had sufficient information, it would apply its ruling on Community law to the facts. The national court accepted this application. However, it was not strictly obliged to do so. In *Arsenal Football Club plc* v *Matthew Reed* [2002] EWHC 2695 (Ch) [2003] 2 CMLR 25 (*Cases and Materials* (5.1)), the High Court referred a question to the Court of Justice concerning the interpretation of Directive 89/104 on trade marks. On receipt of the ruling by the Court of Justice, the High

Court rejected the Court's application of the law to the facts on the ground that it had exceeded its jurisdiction and had erred as to the facts.

Criminal and civil legal aid are available for Article 234 (ex 177) EC references. Any existing criminal legal aid certificate will automatically cover Article 234 (ex 177) EC proceedings, but an existing civil legal aid certificate will need to be amended. Where there is no certificate, a legal aid application may be made for the proceedings in the UK, which will then include the reference to the Court of Justice.

5.3 The meaning of 'court or tribunal'

These terms have an autonomous meaning in Community law, and the fact that a body is classified as a court or tribunal under national law is not conclusive (*Politi* v *Italy* (Case 43/71) [1971] ECR 1039).

The factors to be taken into account include whether the body is established by law, whether it is permanent, whether its jurisdiction is mandatory, whether its procedure is *inter partes*, whether it applies rules of law, and whether it is independent (*Dorsch Consult Ingenieurgesellschaft mbH* v *Bundesbaugesellschaft Berlin mbH* (Case C-54/96)[1997] ECR I-4961).

5.4 The status of the national court

QUESTION 5.2

Article 234 (ex 177) EC provides that while some national courts have a discretion as to whether to refer an issue to the Court of Justice, others have no choice. From which courts is a reference obligatory?

Article 234 (ex 177) EC provides that a reference is obligatory from a court 'against whose decisions there is no judicial remedy under national law'. The House of Lords is such a court. A court against whose decision there *is* such a remedy is not obliged to refer, although it has a discretion to do so.

In *Costa* v *ENEL* (Case 6/64) (see 3.3.2.2) an Italian magistrates' court made a reference to the Court of Justice under Article 234 (ex 177). The Court of Justice ruled that 'national courts against whose decisions, as in the present case, there is no judicial remedy, must refer the matter to the Court of Justice'.

Under the Italian legal system, certain categories of case could be appealed from the magistrates' court while other categories could not. The present case fell into the latter category, that is to say, there was no possibility of an appeal.

As a result of this decision, a reference is obligatory from lower courts whose decision in a particular case is automatically final. In the English legal system this would include, for example, the Court of Appeal in certain probate and insolvency proceedings, since statute provides that its decisions in such actions are final (County Courts Act 1984, s. 82 and Insolvency Act 1986, s. 375(2), respectively).

The question we now need to consider is whether a court from which an appeal is theoretically possible in a particular case should be considered to be a final court if leave to appeal is, in fact, refused.

***Magnavision* v *General Optical Council* (No. 2) [1987] 2 CMLR 262**

In *Magnavision* (*Cases and Materials* (5.2)), in the main proccedings, a Belgian company had been fined for marketing spectacles contrary to the Opticians Act. It had argued that the Act was in breach of Community law, but the High Court had declined to make a reference to the Court of Justice. Leave to appeal was refused whereupon counsel for the Belgian company argued that a reference must now be made. It was held that a reference would not be made because the meaning of the Community legislation was clear. Counsel argued that, since the High Court had refused leave to appeal, it had turned itself into a final court and was obliged to make the reference to the Court of Justice which it had refused to make during the case. The High Court dismissed this argument. It stated that the prospect of leave being refused could not affect its decision as to whether to make the reference. The High Court also pointed out that it had declined to exercise its discretion to refer because it considered the relevant Community law to be clear. As we shall see, this is a ground on which even a final court may refuse to make a reference.

***R* v *Pharmaceutical Society of Great Britain, ex parte the Association of Pharmaceutical Importers* [1987] 3 CMLR 951**

In *R* v *Pharmaceutical Society* (*Cases and Materials* (5.2)), UK law prohibited the dispensing of products which were identical to those prescribed, but were of a different brand. A pharmaceutical association alleged that this was contrary to Article 28 (ex 30) EC. The Court of Appeal exercised its discretion to refer this issue to the Court of Justice but remarked, obiter dicta, that a judicial remedy from its decisions lay in the possibility of applying for leave to appeal and that a court or tribunal below the House of Lords could be a final court only if there was no possibility of appeal (for instance the Court of Appeal in certain proceedings—see above).

It is evident from these cases that the UK courts have accepted that a court below the House of Lords will constitute a final court for the purposes of Article 234 (ex 177) EC only where, as a matter of procedure, there is no possibility of appeal. This may be perceived as unfair by parties who are in fact denied leave to appeal, but preferable to the alternative, which would be to re-open decided cases in which leave to appeal is subsequently refused.

5.5 Discretionary references

5.5.1 Courts from which a reference is discretionary

You might have listed, among others, the Court of Appeal, the High Court, the county court, magistrates' courts, and employment tribunals. The key question to be asked is whether the

EXERCISE 5.1

Try to think of as many examples as you can of English courts or tribunals from which there is generally a judicial remedy under national law.

alleged court or tribunal exercises a judicial function. Thus, the Employment Appeal Tribunal has been held to be able to make a reference under Article 234 (ex 177) EC (*Jenkins* v *Kingsgate (Clothing Productions) Ltd* (Case 96/80) [1981] ECR 911) as has the Social Security Commissioner (*Drake* v *Chief Adjudication Officer* (Case 150/85) [1986] ECR 1995) and the Special Commissioners for Income Tax (*Lord Bruce of Donington* v *Aspden* (Case 208/80) [1981] ECR 2205).

5.5.2 Guidelines governing the exercise of the discretion

Although the exercise of the discretion to refer is a matter for the court seized of a particular case, both the Court of Justice and national courts have purported to lay down guidelines as to when and how the discretion should be exercised. You should remember that the view of the Court of Justice is that the extent of the national courts' discretion is dependent on the correct interpretation of Article 234 (ex 177) EC and that it (the Court of Justice) is the only body which is competent to make authoritative pronouncements on such an interpretation.

There are a number of significant Court of Justice cases on the issues surrounding the making of a reference, but the leading English cases will also be considered.

5.5.2.1 Acte clair

Note that this concept is equally relevant to mandatory references (see 5.6) and therefore some of the caselaw discussed relates to mandatory references. However, the concept has only one meaning, which applies to both types of reference.

The court must believe that there is no reasonable doubt as to the answer to the question, and that this answer would be equally clear to the Court of Justice and to the national courts of other Member States. This raises the question of whether a measure can ever be so clear that no query can be raised.

QUESTION 5.3

Can you think of any problems which might arise in applying this condition?

First, there is a difference between absolute clarity and the clarity necessary to apply the measure to the facts in question. How clear, exactly, need a measure be to obviate a compulsory reference? Secondly, a measure might clearly mean one thing to one court and another to a different court.

***CILFIT and Lanificio di Gavardo SpA* v *Ministry of Health* (Case 283/81) [1982] ECR 3415**

The Court of Justice in *CILFIT* (*Cases and Materials* (5.3.1)) indicated that a number of factors should be taken into account. A number of textile firms complained that an Italian levy on wool was in contravention of Community law. The Italian government claimed that a reference was unnecessary because the meaning of the Community law in question was clear. The Italian court made a reference to the Court of Justice on the obligations of a court from whose decisions there was no judicial remedy. The Court of Justice ruled that there was no obligation to refer if the measure was acte clair. In order to determine whether this was so, three issues must be considered.

First, since Community legislation is drafted in different languages, each version being equally authentic, it is possible to say that the meaning of the measure is clear only if it has the same meaning in all the languages and is equally clear in all. If there is any discrepancy or lack of clarity in even one language then it is not possible to say that the application of Community law is obvious, and therefore a reference would be mandatory.

Secondly, the doctrine of *acte clair* is applicable only where legal concepts in Community law have the same meaning in all Member States. For instance, if a measure concerns 'contracts', and the concept of a 'contract' differs under French and English law, then *acte clair* cannot apply and a reference is mandatory.

Thirdly, measures must be interpreted in the context of Community law as a whole, with particular regard to the objectives and progress of Community law at the time the measure was to be applied. For instance, the interpretation of a measure concerning the Single Market might become clear when looked at in the context of the state of the Single Market at the time in question.

To summarize, the third consideration referred to above may assist a national court, but the first two considerations appear effectively to remove the possibility of relying on *acte clair*. Realistically, it is beyond the scope of a national court accurately to compare texts and legal concepts in several different languages, and it will only be those courts which are prepared to adopt a somewhat cavalier attitude to these considerations that can avoid mandatory references.

***R* v *International Stock Exchange of the UK and the Republic of Ireland Limited ex parte Else (1982) Limited and others* [1993] 2 CMLR 677**

In *ELSE* (*Cases and Materials* (5.3.1)) shareholders in a company whose Stock Exchange listing was suspended sought to challenge the suspension. The Court of First Instance referred to the Court of Justice a number of questions on the interpretation of Directive 79/279 on the admission of securities to official Stock Exchange listing. The Stock Exchange appealed against the decision to refer. The Court of Appeal allowed the appeal. It held that a national court should consider whether it could 'with complete confidence resolve the issue itself'. In deciding whether this was so, a court should take into account a number of factors:

(a) the differences between national and Community legislation;

(b) the difficulties in dealing with what might be an unfamiliar field;

(c) the need for a uniform interpretation throughout the Community;

(d) the advantages enjoyed by the Court of Justice in interpreting Community law.

In *R* v *Henn and Darby* [1980] 1 CMLR 246, which was decided prior to the ruling in *CILFIT*, importers of pornographic material argued that UK restrictions on such imports were in contravention of Article 28 (ex 30) EC, which prohibited restrictions on imports, and were not saved by Article 30 (ex 36) EC, which permitted restrictions on grounds of public policy. The Court of Appeal refused to make a reference on the ground that the application of Community law was clear. The House of Lords reversed this decision and requested a preliminary ruling.

Lord Diplock warned that a court should not be too ready to apply *acte clair* and treat a reference as purely discretionary, simply because the meaning of the English text was clear to that court. First, the English text was only one of six of equal authority (at that time there were only nine Member States and six official languages), any one of which might be unclear or capable of a different interpretation. Secondly, the possibility of judicial disagreement over the 'clear' meaning of Community law was highlighted in this case by the contrasting views of the House of Lords, which considered that Article 28 (ex 30) EC had been breached, and the Court of Appeal, which considered that it had not.

In *R* v *Secretary of State for Transport ex parte Factortame (Factortame I)* [1989] 3 CMLR 1 (see 3.3.2.2), the House of Lords considered a reference to be mandatory in the light of the ambiguous rulings made by the Court of Justice on the particular point in question and in application of the *CILFIT* guidelines. Lord Bridge noted that in *Granaria BV* v *Hoofdproduktschap voor Akkerbouwprodukten* (Case 101/78) [1979] ECR 623 the Court of Justice held that every regulation which is brought into force in accordance with the Treaty must be presumed to be valid and must be treated as fully effective so long as a competent court has not made a finding that it is invalid, whereas in *Firma Foto-Frost* v *Hauptzollamt Lübeck-Ost* (Case 314/85) [1987] ECR 4199 (5.9) it had held that the rule that national courts may not themselves declare Community acts invalid may have to be qualified in certain circumstances in the case of proceedings relating to an application for interim measures. He concluded that in the light of these two authorities, and in application of the principles laid down by the Court of Justice in *CILFIT*, it was not possible to decide whether, in relation to the grant of interim protection in the instant case, Community law overrides English law and either empowers or obliges an English court to make an interim order protecting the putative rights claimed by the applicants. It was therefore necessary for a reference to be made on this issue to the Court of Justice.

R v *Secretary of State for the Environment ex parte RSPB* [1997] Env LR 431

In *RSPB* the RSPB challenged the decision of the Secretary of State for the Environment to exclude an area known as Lappel Bank from a designated Special Protection Area for Birds ('SPA'), on the ground that the Birds Directive did not permit economic considerations to be taken into account in the particular circumstances of the case. It was held by the House of Lords that a reference to the Court of Justice should be made.

The Divisional Court and the majority of the Court of Appeal had held that the Directive was *acte clair* and that the Secretary of State was indeed entitled to take into account such considerations. The dissenting judge in the Court of Appeal also considered that the Directive was *acte clair*, but argued that it was clear that the Secretary of State could **not** take economic factors into account. The House of Lords considered that these conflicting judgments made a reference obligatory.

It may be that this cautionary approach will only be used if a court is genuinely uncertain as to the meaning of the measure and that if it is certain in its own mind as to that meaning, the *CILFIT* criteria will continue to be ignored.

5.5.2.2 The reference must be relevant

As with acte clair, this is an issue of equal importance to discretionary and mandatory references. *Dzodzi* v *Belgian State* (Cases C-297/88 & C-197/89) [1990] ECR I-3763 involved a rather unusual reference. The Togolese widow of a Belgian national claimed Belgian residency under a Belgian law which gave the spouses of Belgian nationals the same residency rights as Community nationals. The Belgian government argued that since the case turned on the meaning of Belgian law, a reference to the Court of Justice was unnecessary. The Court of Justice ruled that it was for the Belgian court to determine the relevance of Community law in these circumstances, but that if a ruling was requested, the Court of Justice had jurisdiction. Article 234 (ex 177) EC did not preclude jurisdiction in such circumstances, and it would destroy the system of uniform interpretation of Community law envisaged by that Article if national courts could interpret Community law themselves in purely internal cases.

_R_ v _ex parte Else_ cont.

In *R* v *International Stock Exchange of the UK and the Republic of Ireland Limited ex parte Else (1982) Limited and others* [1993] 2 CMLR 677 the Court of Appeal held that the issue must be 'critical' to the final decision. Since it is impossible to access this until the reference is made and a ruling given, this must require that the issue could be critical to the final decision.

Commissioners of Customs and Excise v _Samex ApS_ [1983] 3 CMLR 194

In *Samex* the UK issued Samex with an import licence for textiles shipped on or before 31 December 1979. The goods were imported in January 1980 and were seized by Customs. Samex argued that the time limit on the licence was contrary to Regulation 3059/78 on import licences. It was held that a reference to the Court of Justice under Article 234 (ex 177) EC should be made. Bingham J stated that the reference should be 'substantially, if not quite totally, determinative of [the] litigation'.

5.5.2.3 The existence of Court of Justice authority on the issue may make a reference unnecessary

The Court of Justice has ruled in *Da Costa en Schaake NV, Jacob Meijer NV and Hoechst-Holland NV* v *Nederlandse Belastingadministratie* (Cases 28–30/62) [1963] ECR 31 (in the context of mandatory references), that the existence of a previous Court of Justice ruling on a similar question does not preclude a reference. However, the Court of Justice was not bound by its decisions and a decision could be necessary where new factors exist or where the national court considers that the Court of Justice was wrong in its earlier ruling and might be ready to correct its approach.

5.5.2.4 The advantages of the Court of Justice

These were referred to in *Else* and had previously been elaborated upon in *Samex* (*Cases and Materials* 5.3.2).

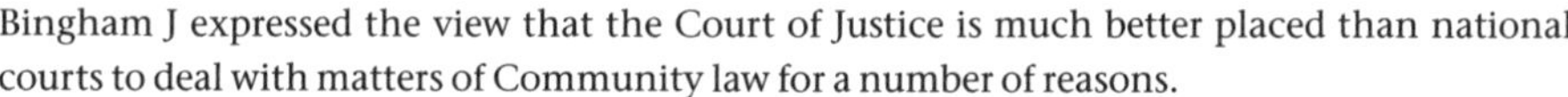

***Samex* cont.**

Bingham J expressed the view that the Court of Justice is much better placed than national courts to deal with matters of Community law for a number of reasons.
The following advantages are, according to Bingham J, possessed by the Court of Justice:

(a) the ability to take an overall view of the Community and its legal framework;

(b) the opportunity to receive submissions from the other institutions and Member States on the issue in question;

(c) the linguistic advantage of being able to consider all the authentic texts, which might make the meaning clearer;

(d) familiarity with the purposive and creative approach to interpretation required by Community law, which tended to be less detailed than English law.

5.5.2.5 The existence of domestic precedent on the issue cannot prevent a reference being made

In *Rheinmühlen-Dusseldorf* v *Einführ-und Vorratsstelle für Getreide und Futtermittel* (Cases 146 & 166/73) [1974] ECR 33, A German appeal court ruled that the withdrawal of exports refunds from a barley exporter was contrary to Community law, and the case was referred back to the lower court, which had reached a different decision, to reconsider. The lower court attempted to make a reference under Article 234 (ex 177) EC. Under German law, the lower court was bound by the decision of the higher court. The higher court referred to the Court of Justice the question of whether the lower court could make a reference despite the national rules of precedent. The Court of Justice ruled that the lower court could exercise its discretion to refer. A national court was not precluded from making a reference on a particular issue by the existence of a domestic rule of law which required that court to follow the judgment of a higher court on that issue.

In *Trent Taverns Ltd* v *Sykes* [1999] Eu LR 492 the Court of Appeal ruled that this principle applied equally to the domestic rule of law requiring the Court of Appeal to follow its own judgments. However, on the facts, the Court of Appeal concluded that a reference need not be made.

? QUESTION 5.4

Suppose that the House of Lords had ruled, as a matter of law in the case of ***Smith***, that the word 'workers' in Article 39 (ex 48) EC should be interpreted as meaning 'male workers'. The case of ***Brown***, which also involves a dispute as to the meaning of 'workers' in Article 39 (ex 48) EC is now before the High Court. Could the English law doctrine of precedent prevent the High Court from making a reference?

Even if the doctrine of precedent obliged the High Court to apply the previous ruling of the House of Lords on the matter, the ruling of the Court of Justice in the *Rheinmühlen* case makes it clear that the High Court could still make a reference if it so wished.

5.5.2.6 **Other factors**

In *Bulmer Ltd and Another* v *Bollinger SA and Others* [1974] 2 CMLR 91, Lord Denning indicated that the national court should bear in mind the delay and expense, the danger of overloading the Court of Justice, the difficulty and importance of the point, and the wishes of the parties.

Although a delay of more than 18 months in receiving a preliminary ruling from the Court of Justice is not unusual, it is open to the referring court to request that the matter be treated as one of urgency. For example, in referring to the Court the question of whether interim relief should be granted, Lord Bridge of Harwich in the House of Lords in *R* v *Secretary of State for Transport ex parte Factortame (Factortame I)* stated:

> 'The adjournment of further consideration of appeal which must necessarily follow is . . . a most unsatisfactory result from the appellant's point of view, and I venture to express the hope that the Court of Justice will . . . treat the reference made by your Lordships' House as one of urgency to which priority can be given.'

The President of the Court decided, in accordance with the Rules of Procedure of the Court, that the case should be given priority. Judgment was given on 19 June 1990, less than a year after the reference was received by the Court of Justice.

5.5.2.7 **Conclusion on guidelines**

In *Wiener S.I. GmbH* v *Hauptzollamt Emmerich* (C-338/95 [1997] ECR I-6495), Advocate General Jacobs considered the division of competence between the national courts and the Court of Justice under Article 234 EC. He argued that the Court of Justice could not cope with the workload which would result from the reference of all cases in which a point of Community law was at issue, particularly in view of the expanding volume of Community legislation. Since the Court could not rule inadmissible questions on interpretation which were properly referred, the national courts must exercise self-restraint in deciding whether to refer them. Where the Court had already established a body of principles as a result of previous references, national courts should be in a position to apply these principles to the specific facts of a case before them without making a reference. The Article 234 EC procedure should instead focus on the reference of general questions in areas of law in which there was no comprehensive body of principles. Rulings on these questions would then enable national courts to deal with more detailed questions themselves.

It should be noted that the question of when references should be made was not in fact among the questions referred by the national court in *Wiener*, and the Court of Justice subsequently answered the questions actually referred (on the interpretation of certain Regulations) without commenting on it. However, despite the fact that Court of Justice did not approve Advocate General Jacobs's comments, they have been cited by the Court of Appeal in a number of cases. In *Trinity Mirror plc* v *Commissioners of Customs and Excise* ([2001] EWCA Civ 65, [2001] 2 CMLR 33) the Court of Appeal refused to make a reference. It cited *ex parte Else* as authority for the need to refer where the national court had any real doubt, but then cited Advocate General Jacobs's comments on the need for self-restraint. It concluded that there was ample guidance from the Court of Justice on the question of principle in the area of law at issue, and that it was confident in applying that principle to the facts of the case. A similar view was taken in *The Littlewoods Organisation plc and others* v *Commissioners of Custom and Excise and others* ([2001] EWCA Civ 1542, [2001] STC 1568) and *Professional Contractor's Group and others* v *Commissioners of Inland Revenue* ([2001] EWCA Civ 1945, [2002] STC 165).

Of course, an Opinion of an Advocate General is not binding on national courts, unlike the decision of the Court of Appeal in *ex parte Else*. However, the fact that the Court of Appeal is consistently citing Advocate General Jacobs's comments indicates that the national courts may now be prepared to refuse to refer where they feel that the Court of Justice has established general principles which they themselves can apply to new situations.

In summary, the Court of Justice and the national courts have provided lower courts in the UK with a wealth of guidelines.

EXERCISE 5.2

Try to summarize the guidelines, which UK courts should take into account when exercising the discretion to refer.

The key guidelines applicable to a court from which a reference is only discretionary may be summarized as follows:

(a) In all the circumstances of the case, is the question sufficiently relevant for an answer to it to be necessary in order for the court to give judgment in the case?

(b) Is the existence of a preliminary ruling on a similar point such as to assist the court with the issue before it?

(c) Is the measure so clear that future rulings on it by the Court of Justice or a court in another Member State would be consistent with that of the court?

In addition, the court may also consider:

(d) whether the facts have been established;

(e) the advantages possessed by the Court of Justice in interpreting Community law;

(f) the differences between domestic and Community law;

(g) the need for uniform interpretation.

R v *Ministry of Agriculture, Fisheries and Food, ex parte Portman Agrochemicals Ltd* ([1994] 3 CMLR 18) provides an instructive example. The judge referred to *ex parte Else* and concluded that he did not have 'complete confidence' that he could resolve the issue himself. However, he declined to make a reference because neither party wished the case to be referred and by the time a reference was given, the matter would have become academic as far as the parties were concerned. The issue was whether MAFF could use Portman's confidential data, but by the time a ruling was given, any right of confidentiality would have expired anyway. The interests of justice would therefore not have been served by making a reference.

5.6 Mandatory references

As stated in 5.4, where there is no judicial remedy from a particular court, that court has no choice but to make a reference to the Court of Justice if the necessary pre-conditions are fulfilled. This may sound simple enough, but as we are about to see, mandatory references have provoked as much argument as discretionary references.

 **EXERCISE** 5.3 

To refresh your memory, refer back to Article 234 (ex 177) EC and write down the questions that must be referred by a court from whose decisions there is no judicial remedy.

A reference is mandatory from such a court if a question arises as to the interpretation of the EC Treaty or the validity or interpretation of the acts of the institutions. A decision on the question need not be necessary to the resolution of the case.

Under Article 234 (ex 177) EC, references from a final court would appear to be mandatory. However, the Court of Justice has ruled that this is not as straightforward as it might appear.

***CILFIT and Lanificio di Gavardo SpA* v *Ministry of Health* (Case 283/81) [1982] ECR 3415**

The leading case is *CILFIT* (see *Cases and Materials* 5.4), in which a number of textile firms complained that an Italian levy on wool was in contravention of Community law. The Italian government claimed that a reference was unnecessary because the meaning of the Community law in question was clear. The Italian court made a reference to the Court of Justice on the obligations of a court from whose decisions there was no judicial remedy. The Court of Justice ruled that there was no obligation to refer, even from a court whose decision was final, if one of three conditions was fulfilled. (Remember that a court which thereby avoids the obligation to refer nonetheless retains the discretion to do so.)

The three conditions are as follows:

5.6.1 The measure is *acte clair*

See 5.5.2.1.

5.6.2 The question of law is not relevant

There is no obligation to refer a question if the answer to it cannot in any way affect the outcome of the case (see 5.5.2.2).

5.6.3 The question has been decided before by the Court of Justice

In *Da Costa En Schaake N.V., Jacob Meijer N.V., and Hoechst-Holland N.V.* v *Nederlandse Belastingadministratie*, (Cases 28–30/62) [1963] ECR 31, a Dutch chemical exporter alleged that certain Dutch import taxes were contrary to Community law. On a reference for a preliminary ruling under Article 234 (ex 177) EC the Court of Justice ruled that the existence of a prior ruling by it on the point did not preclude a reference, although it could render it unnecessary (see 5.5.2.3).

In *CILFIT* the Court of Justice cited *Da Costa* and reiterated that if exactly the same question has already been decided by the Court of Justice, the court is not obliged to make a reference. The discretion to refer would, of course, remain.

? **QUESTION** 5.5

Do you remember any particular circumstances in which a national court might wish to refer a question which has already been decided by the Court of Justice? If you have difficulty in doing this, refer back to guideline 5.5.2.3.

EXERCISE 5.4

Try to list the problems which you think could be caused if courts from which there is no judicial remedy under national law make use of the grounds given in ***CILFIT*** in order to avoid making a reference.

Among the problems which may result are inconsistent interpretation and application of Community law across the Member States, injustice to particular applicants, and a reduction in the importance of the Court of Justice.

5.7 The timing of the reference

Note that this guideline relates not to **whether** a reference should be made but **when**. In *Irish Creamery Milk Suppliers Association* v *Ireland* (Cases 36 & 71/80) [1981] ECR 735, agricultural producers argued that an Irish levy on certain agricultural products was contrary to Community law. The Irish government wished to delay the Article 234 (ex 177) EC reference until the facts had been established. In its reference to the Court of Justice, the Irish court asked not only for an interpretation of the Community law involved, but also for clarification as to the timing of the reference. The Court of Justice ruled that it was for the national court to decide on the most appropriate time to make a reference. However, the Court also stated that it might therefore be more convenient to make a reference after the facts of the case and questions of national law had been determined. The Court of Justice would then have a clear legal context in which to give its ruling and so the ruling would be more likely to assist the national court.

5.8 Misuse of Article 234 (ex 177) EC

The Court of Justice has, on occasion, been prepared to reject a reference where it has felt that Article 234 (ex 177) EC is being misused. The three main grounds which the Court has given for such a rejection are that the referring court has failed to explain the context, that there is no genuine dispute, or that the questions referred are purely hypothetical. We shall consider each of these in turn.

5.8.1 Failure to explain the factual or legal context

The commonest reason for the Court of Justice to refuse to provide a preliminary ruling is that the order from the referring court contains an inadequate explanation of the factual or legal context.

> **? QUESTION 5.6**
>
> Why do you think it is so important that the Court has sufficient information about the facts and the national law? Could the absence of information prejudice the role of anyone other than the Court of Justice?

As the Court pointed out in *Criminal Proceedings against Saddik* (Case C-458/93) [1995] ECR I-511 a lack of information may mean that the Court cannot give a meaningful answer to the questions referred, or that Member States and other interested parties are not in a position to submit their observations.

In assessing whether it has sufficient information to provide answers to the questions referred, the Court of Justice may take into account the written and oral observations submitted by the parties, as well as the order from the national court (C-18/93 *Corsica Ferries* v *Corpo dei Piloti del Porto di Genova* [1994] ECR I-1783)). However, it is not obliged to do this and may simply reject the reference.

> ***Criminal Proceedings against Grau Gomis and others* (Case C-167/94) [1995] ECR I-1023**
>
> In *Grau Gomis* (*Cases and Materials* (5.5.1)) Grau Gomis and others were charged with smuggling tobacco contrary to Spanish law. The national court was uncertain as to the compatibility of the relevant national provisions with Community law, and referred to the Court of Justice a number of questions on the interpretation of Community law. The Court of Justice ruled that the reference was inadmissible. In order to provide an interpretation of Community law which would be helpful to the national court, it was necessary for that court to define the factual and legislative context of the questions it is asking or, at least, explain the factual basis for those questions. It was essential for the national court to give at the very least some explanation of the reasons for the choice of the Community provisions of which it requests an interpretation, and on the link it establishes between those provisions and the national legislation applicable to the dispute. This information not only enabled the Court to give helpful answers but also enabled the Member States and other interested parties to submit observations pursuant to the Court. It was the Court's duty to ensure that the opportunity to submit observations is safeguarded.

Lack of factual or legal information may also mean that the questions referred are purely hypothetical (see 5.8.3).

5.8.2 No genuine dispute

***Foglia* v *Novello (No. 1)* (Case 104/79) [1980] ECR 745**

The leading case here is *Fogila* (*Cases and Materials* (5.5.2)), where a contract between the buyer (Novello) and the seller (Foglia) provided that Novello would not be liable for any unlawfully levied taxes. The contract between Foglia and the shipper provided that Foglia was similarly not liable.

A tax was levied by France on the goods, which Foglia paid and which Novello refused to reimburse on the ground that it was contrary to Community law. Foglia and Novello brought the dispute before an Italian court, alleging that the duty was illegal, and the Italian court made a reference to the Court of Justice.

The Court of Justice refused to accept the reference on the ground that it had no jurisdiction because there was no real dispute between the parties. Article 234 (ex 177) EC references were designed to provide interpretations of Community law which were required for the resolution of genuine disputes. The terms of the two contracts in question had the result that the parties had the same interest in the outcome of the case (since, contractually, neither of the parties was liable to pay the tax if it was unlawful), and therefore there was no genuine dispute. The shipper had not appealed, as he was entitled to do, against the imposition of the tax, and Foglia had reimbursed the shipper contrary to the terms of their contract, which suggested that they expected the tax to be struck down. Article 234 (ex 177) EC did not confer jurisdiction on the Court of Justice in the context of a collusive action such as this, which disguised an attempt to have a foreign law struck down.

In *Foglia* v *Novello (No. 2)* (Case 244/80) [1981] ECR 3045 the Italian court made another attempt to refer the matter to the Court of Justice. It repeated its request for a preliminary ruling on the grounds that it was for the national court to exercise its discretion as to whether to refer. The Court of Justice accepted this argument but again refused to accept the reference on the basis that it retained the right to check its jurisdiction to hear a case, and that under Article 234 (ex 177) EC the issue referred must be one on which a decision was necessary to the resolution of the case. Where there was no genuine dispute between the parties on a particular issue, it was clearly not susceptible to a reference under Article 234 (ex 177) EC.

The fact that the parties are in effect trying to challenge the laws of one Member State in the courts of another, as in *Foglia*, makes a finding that there is no genuine dispute, and hence a refusal to accept the reference, more likely. However, such a finding is not automatic, as can be seen in *Eau de Cologne* v *Provide* (Case C-150/88) [1989] ECR I-3891.

Provide, an Italian company, ordered cosmetics from Eau de Cologne, a German company. The packaging complied with Community law, but not with Italian law, and therefore the goods could not be marketed in Italy. Provide refused to accept or pay for the goods and was sued by Eau de Cologne in the German courts. The German court made a reference to the Court of Justice on whether the Italian law was compatible with Community law. The Italian government alleged that the reference was inadmissible. The Court of Justice accepted the reference, despite the fact that the parties were questioning, in German courts, the compatibility of Italian law with Community law. It stated that the case involved a genuine dispute. When giving a ruling on the interpretation of Community law in order to assist a national court in determining the compatibility of national law with Community law, it made no difference that the disputed law was that of a different Member State.

The issue of whether there is a genuine dispute will also turn very much on the facts of the individual case. In *Celestini* v *Saar-Sektkellerie Faber* (C-105/94) [1997] ECR I-2971 certain of the facts were similar to *Foglia* v *Novello*. A German buyer bought wine from an Italian seller, but the German authorities impounded the wine and subsequently declared it unfit for human consumption. The seller sued the buyer in the Italian courts and a reference was made to the Court of Justice. Although the buyer had not contested the actions of the German authorities, and no case had been brought in the German courts, which had sole jurisdiction to rule on the validity of those actions, the Court accepted the reference. It expressly stated that there was nothing to indicate that the parties had jointly fabricated the dispute as a device to obtain a preliminary ruling.

Where it is alleged that there is no genuine dispute, the Court of Justice may request further information before it decides whether or not to accept the reference, as happened in *Vinal* v *Orbat* (Case 46/80) [1981] ECR 77. An Italian importer of pure alcohol, Vinal, contracted to supply French alcohol to Orbat. The Italian authorities imposed a duty on the goods, which Orbat refused to pay. A preliminary reference was opposed by the Italian government on the grounds that there was no real dispute and that the parties simply wished to impeach the duty so as to avoid paying it. The Court of Justice requested further information, which in the event satisfied it that there was a genuine dispute and therefore valid grounds for an Article 234 (ex 177) EC reference. However, it should be noted that the Court is not obliged to request further information and it may simply reject the reference.

5.8.3 Hypothetical questions

This category concerns questions which the Court rejects because they are not relevant on the facts, or because the facts are so unclear that there is no evidence that they are relevant. Examples of the former include *Lourenço Dias* and *Borsana*.

Lourenço Dias v _Director da Alfandega do Porto_ (Case C-343/90) [1992] ECR I-4573

In *Lourenço Dias* (*Cases and Materials* (5.5.3)) Lourenço Dias purchased a new van which he subsequently modified. Prior to the purchase the van had been imported into Portugal without paying the tax to which that modification would have given rise. The authorities fined Lourenço Dias for failing to declare the changes to the van which determined its tax classification. Lourenço Dias challenged on the ground that they were contrary to Article 90 (ex 95) EC (see **Chapter 8**). The national court referred a number of questions on the interpretation of Community law, some of which the Court of Justice rejected as hypothetical. For example, the Court refused to answer a question about taxation of imports of second-hand vehicles since the van in question was new when imported.

In *Borsana* (*Cases and Materials* (5.5.3)) the Court of Justice refused to answer a question on the compatibility of certain criminal penalties laid down by national law with Community law because the dispute before the national court was a civil case.

? QUESTION 5.7

Suppose, in proceedings concerning the compatibility with Community law of a (fictitious) UK law on the transportation by air of live animals, the following questions were referred to the Court of Justice under Article 234 (ex 177) EC:

(a) the meaning of 'air transport';
(b) the meaning of 'sea transport';
(c) the meaning of 'animals';
(d) whether 'animals' could be interpreted as including elephants.

Which of the above questions do you suspect that the Court of Justice might reject, and why?

In this example, question (b) is clearly hypothetical since the UK law does not apply to sea transport. Question (d) would also be hypothetical if the case in which the questions were referred did not on the facts, concern elephants. Questions (a) and (c) would be accepted (unless of course, the facts revealed that there was no genuine dispute, in which case all the questions would be rejected—see 5.8.2).

An example of a case where the facts and legal context are so unclear that the questions referred are regarded as hypothetical is *Meilicke*.

Meilicke v _ADV/ORGA AG_ (Case C-83/91) [1992] ECR I-4871

In *Meilicke* (*Cases and Materials* (5.5.3)) a German shareholder in ADV/ORGA, sought information from that company concerning the payment received by it in return for a new issue of shares. When this was not forthcoming he sought to rely on the Second Company Law Directive which he alleged gave him greater rights to information than German law where the company had received payment otherwise than in cash for its shares. The parties disputed whether German law required this information to be given, and agreed that the question of the compatibility of German law with the Second Directive on company law should be referred to the Court of Justice.

The Court of Justice refused to answer the questions referred on the interpretation of the Directive on the ground that they were hypothetical. It had not been established on the facts whether the payment received by Meilicke's company should be categorized as cash or not and it was therefore unclear how German law, which gave greater rights to information where payments other than cash were concerned than where payments were in cash, applied, and whether the Directive, which only applied to non-cash payments, applied at all.

5.9 Issues of validity

We have been looking so far at preliminary rulings on the interpretation of Community law, either Treaties or secondary legislation. However, Article 234 (ex 177) EC also permits preliminary references to be made concerning the validity of secondary legislation. (The validity of the Treaty may not be questioned.) Whereas a national court may often be able to interpret Community law itself, either because it is clear, or because there has been a previous Court of Justice ruling, it is less likely that it will be competent to deal with questions of validity.

Firma Foto-Frost v _Hauptzollamt Lübeck-Ost_ (Case 314/85) [1987] ECR 4199

In *Firma Foto-Frost* (*Cases and Materials* (5.6)) a Community levy was payable on imports of binoculars into Germany by Frost. The levy was subject to a waiver in certain circumstances, but the Commission ruled that in this instance, the waiver could not apply. Frost applied to the German courts to have a Commission Decision set aside. The German court requested a preliminary ruling as to whether it could review the validity of the Decision. The Court of Justice ruled that no national court could declare a Community act invalid, although it could make a declaration of validity. Any other conclusion would destroy the uniform application of Community law.

A national court should therefore make a reference to the Court of Justice whenever there is some doubt as to the validity of a measure.

5.10 Interim measures

As has already been mentioned, it is not uncommon for up to eighteen months to elapse between the making of a reference by a national court and the giving of a ruling by the Court of Justice. Given this potential delay, in certain circumstances one party may wish to request interim relief in the form of the suspension of national law. Guidelines have laid down two possibilities: the suspension of national measures implementing allegedly invalid Community law, and the suspension of national law which may, depending on the correct interpretation of Community law, be inconsistent with it.

5.10.1 National measures based on allegedly invalid Community law

In *Atlanta Fruchthandelsgesellchaft mbH and others* v *Bundesamt für Ernahrung und Forstwirtschaft* (Case C-465/93) [1995] ECR I-3761 the Court of Justice laid down conditions to be applied by national courts when granting interim relief, in the form of the suspension of national law implementing the disputed Community law, pending the outcome of a reference to the Court of Justice on the **validity** of that Community law. These conditions are as follows:

(a) the national court seriously doubts the validity of Community law and the issue has already been referred to the Court of Justice; and

(b) interim relief is necessary as a matter of urgency to avoid serious and irreparable damage to the applicant; and

(c) due account of the effect of any suspension on the whole regime of Community law has been taken; and

(d) due account of any decisions of the Court of Justice or the Court of First Instance on the validity of the Community law or on any similar application for interim relief has been taken.

5.10.2 Suspension of national measures which may, on the correct interpretation of Community law, be in conflict with it

An example of this is *Factortame I* (see 3.3.2.2), but although the Court of Justice ruled that such suspension must be possible, it was left for the House of Lords on receipt of this ruling to lay down guidelines. The House of Lords ruled that the applicants must demonstrate:

(a) a strong *prima facie* case that the national law was incompatible with Community law; and

(b) that the balance of convenience favoured the granting of an injunction suspending the Act.

The House of Lords concluded that a strong prima facie case had been shown by the Spanish fishermen that the Merchant Shipping Act was incompatible with Community law. It also concluded that the balance of convenience favoured an injunction since the damage likely to be caused (to the British fishing industry) by the injunction was outweighed by that likely to be caused (to the Spanish fishermen) by the continuance of the national law.

5.11 The effect of a ruling

A Court of Justice ruling as to the interpretation or validity of a measure provides a binding precedent for national courts. It is thus a further example of the way in which Community law (in this instance, a decision of the Court of Justice) takes precedence over national law (in this instance, the decision which the national court would otherwise have taken).

In the case of an interpretative ruling or a ruling that a measure is valid, national courts are not precluded from making further references on the point, but generally they will do so only where new evidence has come to light or where there is reason to believe that the Court of Justice may have changed its mind. In the case of a ruling of invalidity, the measure is void, that is to say, of no effect.

In general, the effect of a ruling is retrospective, but the Court of Justice may place a limitation on this.

EXERCISE 5.5

Look back at the comments already made about *Defrenne* (4.3.1.1) (and then read the extract in *Cases and Materials* (5.7)).

In *Defrenne (Defrenne* v *SABENA* (Case 43/75) [1976] 2 ECR 455), the Court of Justice took account of the fact that several Member States had failed to comply with Article 141 (ex 119) EC by the original deadline, and yet the Commission had failed to take enforcement proceedings against them. It therefore held, in the interests of legal certainty, that its ruling that Article 141 (ex 119) EC was directly effective should not be applied retrospectively except in the case of proceedings already issued.

CONCLUSIONS

It is essential to the uniformity and effectiveness of Community law that a system exists whereby national courts, faced with a dispute as to the interpretation or validity of Community law, may ask the Court of Justice for a ruling. This system is outlined in Article 234 (ex 177) EC.

However, the system is only as good as its constituent parts, and the national courts, at least in the UK, have regularly declined to refer matters which are properly the province of the Court of Justice. While this approach has its advantages in terms of speed and cost, it does make it more likely that Community law will not be applied effectively and uniformly across the Community.

SUMMARY

- Article 234 EC provides that preliminary references may be made to the Court of Justice **by any national court** or tribunal **on a question of the interpretation or validity of Community law**. The case will be stayed in the national court until the Court of Justice provides a ruling, which will then be used by the national court in giving judgment.
- A court from which an appeal at national level is automatic or may be requested in the case in question has a **discretion** to refer (Article 234 EC). In exercising this discretion, it must take account of a number of guidelines, including *acte clair* (*CILFIT*), the relevance of the issue to be referred (*Else*), the existence of any Court of Justice authority on the issue (*Da Costa*), and the advantages of the Court of Justice in interpreting EC law (*Samex*).
- A court from which no appeal is possible in the case in question has no discretion and a reference is **mandatory** (Article 234 EC). However, the Court of Justice has established three exceptions to this: a reference need not be made if the issue would be irrelevant, if there is already Court of Justice authority on the issue, or if the issue is *acte clair* (*CILFIT*).
- The Court of Justice has also developed a number of grounds on which it will **reject a reference** and refuse to give a ruling; if the national court has provided an inadequate explanation of why a ruling on the question referred is required (*Saddik*), if there is no genuine dispute (*Foglia*), or if the question is hypothetical (*Lourenço Dias*).
- Issues relating to the **validity of EC law** must be referred unless the national court is satisfied that the measure is valid, as national courts have no power to declare EC law invalid (*Foto Frost*).

CHAPTER 5: ASSESSMENT EXERCISE

Critically discuss, with examples from case law, the obligations of national courts under Article 234 (ex 177) EC.

See *Cases and Materials* (5.9) for a specimen answer.

FURTHER READING

Barav, A. (1977). 'Some Aspects of the Preliminary Rulings Procedure in EEC Law', 2 *EL Rev* 3.

CILFIT and Lanificio di Gavardo SpA v *Ministry of Health* (Case 283/81) [1982] ECR 3415.

Commissioners of Customs and Excise v *Samex ApS* [1983] 3 CMLR 194.

Editorial Comments (1991). 'Use of the preliminary procedure'. 28 *CML Rev* 241.

R v International Stock Exchange of the UK and the Republic of Ireland Limited ex parte Else (1982) Limited and others [1993] 2 CMLR 677.

The British Institute of International and Comparative Law (1996). *The Role and Future of the European Court of Justice.* BIICL.

The Court of Justice of the European Communities 'Information Note on References by National Courts for Preliminary Rulings'.

6 Challenging Community action or inaction

6.1 OBJECTIVES

By the end of this chapter you should be able to:

1. Explain the ability of the Parliament to bring actions under Article 230 (ex 173) EC and relate changes in this area of law to the development of the Parliament's role generally
2. Illustrate the importance of relying on the correct legislative base
3. Analyse the concepts of direct and individual concern
4. Identify the circumstances in which a plea of illegality under Article 241 (ex 184) EC may be made
5. Identify the circumstances in which an action under Article 232 (ex 175) EC is likely to be successful
6. Explain the effect of a successful action under Article 230 (ex 173) or Article 232 (ex 175) EC

6.2 Introduction

The most usual way of challenging Community measures is to rely on Article 230 (ex 173) EC, alleging that the Community has done something which it should not have done. The Parliament has, on occasion, alleged that the Community has adopted a measure on an incorrect legal base, a flaw which could be detrimental to the Parliament since it is that base (see 3.4, 3.6, 6.3.3.2 and 6.8) which determines the appropriate legislative procedure, and hence the degree of input of the Parliament.

Although individuals and companies are also entitled to challenge measures under this Article, their capacity to do so has been hampered by the wording of Article 230 (ex 173) EC and its interpretation by the Court of Justice, which has meant that only persons immediately concerned by the measure may challenge it. This test of 'direct and individual concern' involves a number of elements which combine to create a considerable hurdle for private applicants under Article 230 (ex 173) EC.

The partner to Article 230 (ex 173) EC is Article 232 (ex 175) EC, which may be relied on where the Community has failed to do something which it ought to have done. This is far less commonly relied on than Article 230 (ex 173) EC and there has been a particular difficulty in establishing whether it, or Article 230 (ex 173) EC, should be used to challenge a positive refusal to act. The third possible challenge to Community EC law is the so-called plea of illegality under Article 241 (ex 184) EC.

6.3 Article 230 (ex 173) EC

Article 230 (ex 173) EC permits certain Community acts to be challenged, by certain applicants, in certain circumstances. Let us consider each element of Article 230 (ex 173) EC in turn.

THE EC TREATY

Article 230 (ex 173) EC

The Court of Justice shall review the legality of acts adopted jointly by the European Parliament and the Council, of acts of the Council, of the Commission and of the ECB, other than recommendations and opinions, and of acts of the European Parliament intended to produce legal effects *vis-à-vis* third parties.

It shall for this purpose have jurisdiction in actions brought by a Member State, the European Parliament, the Council or the Commission on grounds of lack of competence, infringement of an essential procedural requirement, infringement of this Treaty or of any rule of law relating to its application, or misuse of powers.

The Court shall have jurisdiction under the same conditions in actions brought by the Court of Auditors and by the ECB for the purpose of protecting their prerogatives.

Any natural or legal person may, under the same conditions, institute proceedings against a decision addressed to that person or against a decision which, although in the form of a regulation or a decision addressed to another person, is of direct and individual concern to the former.

The proceedings provided for in this Article shall be instituted within two months of the publication of the measure, or of its notification to the plaintiff, or, in the absence thereof, of the day on which it came to the knowledge of the latter, as the case may be.

6.3.1 Acts which may be challenged EC

6.3.1.1 Acts of the legislative institutions

Article 230 (ex 173) EC permits challenges to be made to acts of the:

(a) Parliament and Council;

(b) Council;

(c) Commission;

(d) European Central Bank;

(e) Parliament, insofar as those acts are intended to produce legal effects.

6.3.1.2 Acts with binding legal effect

In the case of *IBM Corporation* v *Commission* (Case 60/81) [1981] ECR 2639, IBM challenged both:

(a) a Commission Decision to initiate proceedings under Community competition law, and

(b) a statement of objections to its marketing practices (which the Commission alleged were contrary to Article 243 (ex 186) EC) which was provided with the notification of this decision.

The Court of Justice ruled that neither the initiation of proceedings nor the statement of objections were, on the basis of their nature and legal effect, acts capable of challenge under Article 230 (ex 173) because they did not have binding legal effect. The act to be challenged must be a final statement of an institution's position and not merely an interim position.

QUESTION 6.1

In the light of this case, can you explain why Article 230 (ex 173) EC expressly excludes Recommendations and Opinions from the acts which may be challenged?

Recommendations and Opinions are expressly excluded from challenge under Article 230 (ex 173) for the very reason that they do not produce legal effects (see 3.5.2).

6.3.2 Applicants under Article 230 (ex 173) EC

Community institutions, Member States and private parties are all referred to in Article 230 (ex 173) EC, but some of them are restricted as to the acts which they may challenge.

EXERCISE 6.1

Read Article 230 (ex 173) EC and attempt to summarize the acts which may be challenged by the different types of applicant.

Not all acts may be challenged by all applicants. The position may be summarized as follows:

Applicant	Acts which may be challenged
Privileged applicants (the Council, the Commission, the Parliament and Member States).	Any act (provided that it is a final statement of an institution's position and produces legal effects; see 6.3.1.2).
'Intermediate' category of applicants (the Court of Auditors and the ECB).	Any act (as above), subject to certain restrictions.
Non-privileged applicants (companies and individuals).	Regulations and Decisions only, subject to certain restrictions.

? QUESTION 6.2

Since Article 230 (ex 173) EC does not permit non-privileged applicants to challenge Regulations or Directives, in what other ways might the terms of these measures be subject to review by such applicants? Try to think of as many ways as possible. (If you have difficulty in doing this, look back at **Chapters 4** and **5**.)

Individuals or companies (or indeed the Member State) may rely on Regulations, national legislation transposing a Directive, and in certain circumstances the Directive itself (see 4.3.2) before the national courts. National courts are then able to review the Community measure or the transposing legislation although only the Court of Justice may declare a Community measure invalid (see 5.9). Such national judicial protection is important to the Community legal system and has been expressly recognized as such by the Court of Justice, for example, in *ASOCARNE* v *Council* (Case C-10/95) P [1995] ECR I- 4149.

The restrictions on certain applicants will now be considered.

6.3.3 *Locus standi*

What is meant by the term *'locus standi'*? It means the standing, or legal ability, to bring an action. The *locus standi* of each type of applicant considered above is different, and we shall consider the position of each in turn.

6.3.3.1 Privileged applicants

As mentioned at 6.3.2, these include the Commission, the Council, the Parliament, and the Member States. They have locus standi to challenge any act.

6.3.3.2 The intermediate category of applicants

This consists of the Court of Auditors and the ECB. These bodies may challenge any act, but only in order to protect their prerogatives. Although the cases discussed in this section relate to the Parliament which, prior to the Treaty of Nice, was an intermediate applicant, they are still relevant to what is meant by the protection of an applicant's prerogatives.

***Parliament* v *Council (Chernobyl)* (Case C-70/88) [1970] ECR I-2041**

In *Chernobyl* (*Cases and Materials* (6.1)) a Regulation concerning radioactivity in foodstuffs was adopted on the basis of a public health provision in the Euratom Treaty which specified that the consultation procedure should be used in adopting legislation. The Parliament argued that the measure should properly have been based on the internal market provisions of the EC Treaty, which at that time specified the use of the cooperation procedure. It brought an action under Article 146 of the Euratom Treaty and Article 230 (ex 173) of the EC Treaty, arguing that its prerogatives had been infringed, since under the consultation procedure it had less input than under the cooperation procedure. It was held that the Parliament had *locus standi* to bring an action under Article 230 (ex 173) EC in order to protect its prerogatives. The proceedings would be continued with regard to the substance of the case.

According to *Chernobyl*, the Parliament's prerogatives include the right to influence the legislative process to the extent provided for in the EC Treaty. This prerogative would be infringed if the Parliament had been accorded less influence than it was entitled to, because of the use of the wrong legislative base (see 3.4, 3.6, 6.3.3.2 and 6.8), and therefore the wrong legislative procedure, in passing a measure.

In order for the Parliament to bring an action on this ground, it must identify the legal base which was used, and then show that this was an incorrect base for the particular legislation. The legal base will normally be a Treaty provision, but may be secondary legislation.

Commission v _Council (Generalised Tariff Preferences)_ (Case 45/86) [1987] ECR 1493

In the case of *Generalised Tariff Preferences* (*Cases and Materials* (6.1), a Regulation suspended duties on certain imports from developing countries, but did not include identification of its legislative base.

The Court of Justice held that the obligation under Article 253 (ex 190), to include in measures a statement of the reasons behind them, required as part of those reasons a sufficient identification of the legal base. Where the choice of legislative base was unclear or incorrect, the measure would, as here, be annulled.

One of the factors which may determine the correct choice of base is the relative degree of Parliamentary input.

The Court of Justice gave guidelines on the choice of legislative base in the case of Titanium Dioxide:

Commission v _Council (Titanium Dioxide)_ (Case C-300/89) [1991] ECR I-2867

In *Titanium Dioxide* (*Cases and Materials* (6.1)) a Directive harmonizing programmes for the reduction of titanium dioxide pollution had been based on Article 175 (ex 130s) EC, which concerned environmental measures. The Commission challenged the Directive on the ground that the correct legal base was in fact Article 95 (ex 100a) EC, which dealt with the internal market. Article 95 (ex 100a) EC specified the use of the cooperation procedure, whereas Article 175 (ex 130s) utilized the consultation procedure. As the cooperation procedure gave the Parliament a greater input into decision making, you will not be surprised to learn that the Parliament also favoured Article 95 (ex 100a) EC, rather than Article 175 (ex 130s) EC.

The Court of Justice stated that where two bases were appropriate, both should usually be cited. However, this was not possible here because the two bases specified the use of different legislative procedures. A joint base which effectively gave a choice of procedures would allow the consultation procedure to be used at the expense of the cooperation procedure, and thus at the expense of the Parliament's involvement in the legislative process. The Court stressed the importance of the fundamental democratic principle of Parliament's involvement in the cooperation procedure and concluded that Article 95 (ex 100a) EC was the more appropriate legislative base for the following reasons:

(a) If the burdens on businesses of measures relating to the environment were not harmonized the internal market would be distorted.

(b) Article 175 (ex 130s) EC was not the only suitable legislative base for environmental measures since Article 174 (ex 130r) EC provided that environmental protection should be a component of all Community policies. Indeed, Article 95 (ex 100a) EC specifically provided for environmental protection to be taken into account.

The Court of Justice therefore annulled the Directive on the ground that the wrong legislative base had been used.

6.3.3.3 Non-privileged applicants

This category covers individuals and other private parties such as companies—in other words, anyone other than an institution or a Member State.

? QUESTION 6.3 

Can you remember which of the cases you have learned about so far involved a non-privileged applicant? If not, look back at the cases referred to so far in this chapter, and try to identify a case which involved such an applicant.

In *IBM Corporation* v *Commission*, IBM was a non-privileged applicant.

Article 230 (ex 173) EC restricts the *locus standi* of such applicants to actions against:

(a) a Decision addressed to the applicant; or

(b) a Decision addressed to a third party which is of direct and individual concern to the applicant; or

(c) a Decision in the form of a Regulation (i.e. a disguised Decision), which is of direct and individual concern to the applicant.

The first category is fairly straightforward, but problems have arisen in the context of the second and third categories over the meaning of 'direct and individual concern' and over which Regulations can truly be said to be disguised Decisions. We shall examine each of these problems in turn but before doing so, it should be noted that true Regulations may not be challenged by non-privileged applicants.

? QUESTION 6.4

Since Article 230 (ex 173) EC does not permit non-privileged applicants to challenge Directives or genuine Regulations, in what other ways might the terms of these measures be subject to review? Try to think of as many ways as possible. (If you have difficulty in doing this, look back at 2.3.2 in conjunction with 3.6, and at 3.5.2, 4.3, 5.9 and 6.3.3.1.)

As we have seen at 6.3.3.1, privileged applicants (the Member States, the Council, the Commission, and the Parliament) may challenge any acts under Article 230 (ex 173) EC. They may therefore challenge Regulations and Directives. Member States also have the opportunity, through their representatives in the Council (see 2.3.2), to review the framing of Regulations and Directives before they are adopted (see 3.6). They also have a discretion when transposing Directives into national law (see 3.5.2). Individuals or companies (or indeed the Member State) may rely on national legislation transposing a Directive or, in certain circumstances, Treaty Articles, Regulations, Decisions, or Directives (see 4.3), before the national courts. National courts are then able to review the Community measure or the transposing legislation, although only the Court of Justice may declare a Community measure invalid (see 5.9). Such national judicial protection is important to the Community legal system, and has been expressly recognized as such by the Court of Justice in, for example, *ASOCARNE* v *Council* (Case C-10/95) P [1995] ECR I- 4149.

6.4 Direct concern

The act complained of must have a direct effect on the applicant. What does this mean? For the effect to be direct the act of the Community must cause an effect on the applicant without any intervening act. Intervening acts may occur where a Member State has some discretion in the application of a measure.

***UNICME and Others* v *Council* (Case 123/77) [1978] ECR 845**

UNICME (*Cases and Materials* (6.2)) involved a Council Regulation which, inter alia, made the importing of Japanese motor cycles subject to the issue of a licence from the Italian government. Italian importers of such motor cycles, together with their trade association, UNICME, attempted to challenge the Regulation under Article 230 (ex 173) EC. As it was not a decision addressed to them, the importers had to show that they were directly and individually concerned by the Regulation.

The Court of Justice held that the importers were not directly concerned because the Italian government retained a discretion over the grant of import licences. It was not the Regulation which directly concerned the importers, but any subsequent refusal by the Italian government to issue import licences to them.

? QUESTION 6.5

Can you think of an alternative action that the importers might have been able to bring?

The Court of Justice stated that if the Italian government did indeed refuse licences to the importers, they could bring an action in the national courts. A national court could then, if necessary, refer the question of the validity of the Regulation to the Court of Justice under Article 234 (ex 177) EC.

***Bock* v *Commission* (Case 62/70) [1971] ECR 897**

In *Bock* (*Cases and Materials* (6.2)), Bock applied for a licence to import Chinese mushrooms, but the German authorities replied that they would refuse to grant the licence as soon as they were authorized by the Commission to do so. The Commission issued a Decision allowing Germany to refuse to issue import licences for Chinese mushrooms. The Court of Justice ruled that Bock was directly concerned by the Decision. A Decision was issued giving this authorization. Bock challenged the Decision under Article 230 (ex 173) EC.

The Court of Justice held that there was no intervening discretion, because the German authorities had already exercised their discretion when they notified Bock of their intention to refuse his application as soon as they were able. It was therefore the Decision itself which actually affected Bock who therefore had *locus standi* to challenge the Decision. The Decision was annulled insofar as it applied to importers with licence applications pending at the time the Decision came into force. In contrast, in UNICME the Regulation did not directly concern UNICME because the Member State involved had yet to exercise its discretion at the time the Regulation was issued.

***Piraiki-Patraiki and others* v *Commission* (Case 11/82) [1985] ECR 207**

In *Piraiki-Patraiki* (*Cases and Materials* (6.2)) a Commission Decision authorized France to impose quotas on imports of yarn from Greece. The Greek importers sought to challenge this Decision under Article 230 (ex 173) EC.

The Court of Justice held that Greek importers with prior contracts had *locus standi* to challenge the Decision. The Decision would be annulled insofar as it applied to contracts entered into before the date of its notification and to be performed during the period of its application.

The crucial distinction between this case and *UNICME* is that, on the facts, the possibility of an exercise of intervening discretion by the French government could be disregarded. France already severely restricted such imports, and in fact had requested a quota more strict than that given, so the chance that it would not utilize the permission to impose quotas was 'purely theoretical'.

Whereas in *Bock* the German authorities had actually stated that the Decision would be applied directly to the applicant, in *Piraiki-Patraiki* it was simply the opinion of the Court of Justice that the French authorities would apply the Decision directly to the applicants. The test would therefore seem to be whether the Member State has given a sufficiently clear indication of how it will use its discretion. In *Bock* and *Piraiki-Patraiki* the Court of Justice considered that the respective governments had given such an indication, whereas in *UNICME* it was clear that the Italian government had not.

6.5 Individual concern

The classic statement of the law in this area comes from the case of *Plaumann*:

***Plaumann & Co.* v *Commission* (Case 25/62) [1963] ECR 95**

In *Plaumann* (*Cases and Materials* (6.3)) the German government applied for permission to reduce the duty on imports of clementines. The Commission issued a Decision refusing permission and Plaumann, a clementine importer, challenged it.

The Court of Justice held that Plaumann was not individually concerned by the Decision and therefore had no *locus standi* to challenge it.

In order to show individual concern, an applicant must show that it was affected by the Decision by reason of certain attributes or circumstances:

(a) which differentiated it from all others; and

(b) which distinguished it as individually as if the Decision had been addressed to it.

In this instance, the Decision applied to all the clementine producers, and Plaumann could not be said to be in any way differentiated from the others.

Clearly, then, individual concern requires that the applicant be singled out in some way by the measure. This means that it will be more difficult to prove individual concern where the measure challenged is a Regulation, than where it is a Decision.

QUESTION 6.6

Why do you think this is so? If you have difficulty answering this question, look back at the difference between these types of measure at 3.5.2.

This is because Regulations apply generally and are unlikely to concern potential applicants particularly, whereas Decisions apply to a specific entity or group of entities, and are therefore more likely to have a particular impact on them.

Unfortunately for all concerned, the Court of Justice has not developed a consistent approach to the question of whether an applicant is sufficiently singled out by a measure. A number of approaches have been discernable for some years. First, the 'closed class' test (see 6.5.1) often provides a starting point for establishing locus standi. Secondly, where an applicant fails to satisfy this test when strictly applied, the Court of Justice may consider whether it fulfils a more generous test based on the facts (see 6.5.2). Thirdly and fourthly, where the measure in question has been issued as a result of proceedings issued by the applicant or is an anti-dumping measure, the Court has developed a special test (see 6.5.3 and 6.5.4).

Each of these possibilities will be considered in turn. It should also be noted that a number of new approaches have been proposed, although not yet accepted by the Court of Justice, in relation to Regulations. These will be discussed at 6.6.2.

6.5.1 The 'closed class' test

One approach, often called the 'closed class' test, involves a consideration of whether it was possible to identify all the potential applicants at the time the measure allegedly affecting them was passed. In order to do this, the membership of the class must have been fixed at that time, and it must have been possible to ascertain the identity of those members. Where is the burden of proof? It is on an applicant to show that it is a member of such a class (possibly the only member).

The test is a strict one, as can be seen from *Spijker:*

***Spijker Kwasten BV* v *Commission* (Case 231/82) [1983] ECR 259**

In *Spijker* (*Cases and Materials* (6.3.1)) a Dutch importer of Chinese brushes, applied for an import licence which the Dutch authorities stated that they would refuse if the Commission authorized them to do so. The Commission Decision authorized the Dutch government, for a period of six months, to ban imports of Chinese brushes. Not only had the Dutch request for such a Decision been made in response to Spijker's imports, but Spijker was the only importer of such goods into the Netherlands at the time. Despite these facts, the Court of Justice concluded that Spijker was not individually concerned by the measure.

The Court of Justice ruled that the class of those potentially affected was not closed (and therefore not ascertainable) at the time of the Decision because other importers might materialize during the six-month period, who would then be adversely affected by the Decision and form part of the class of potential applicants.

***International Fruit Company and others* v *Commission* (Cases 41–4/70) [1971] ECR 411**

International Fruit Company (*Cases and Materials* (6.3.1)) involved two Regulations. The first provided that Member States were required to notify the Commission, on a weekly basis, of the quantity of apples for which import licences had been requested. This enabled the Commission to determine the percentage of licences which should be granted. The second Regulation provided that only 80% of licence applications in the week in which the applicants had applied should be granted. Their applications were amongst those refused and they challenged the second Regulation.

The Court of Justice held that the Regulation must be regarded as a conglomeration of individual Decisions which individually concerned the applicant. It applied to a fixed and ascertainable class, that is to say, applicants in a particular week, and although it took account only of the total quantity of applications, the decision then had to be applied to each individual application. This necessarily involved a decision on each application.

A similar approach was taken in one of the many 'isoglucose cases', a series of cases in the late 1970s and early 1980s involving the introduction of quotas and levies, and the abolition of subsidies, on the production of isoglucose, a liquid sugar substitute.

***Roquette Frères* v *Council* (Case 138/79) [1980] ECR 3333**

In *Roquette Frères* v *Council* (*Cases and Materials* (6.3.1)), a Regulation established quotas for the production of isoglucose and listed in an annex the companies to which these quotas applied. Roquette Frères, one of the companies listed, challenged the validity of the Regulation.

? QUESTION 6.7

How might Roquette be considered to be individually concerned?

The Court of Justice ruled that the Regulation was of individual concern to the applicants and other producers listed in the annex because specific quotas were allotted to them by name and therefore the Regulation was susceptible to challenge under Article 230 (ex 173) EC. Under the terms of Article 230 (ex 173) EC, this could only have been possible if the Court of Justice had regarded the Regulation as, in substance, a Decision.

6.5.2 A test based on the facts

In many cases, the Court of Justice has found that the contested measure potentially applies to a group of applicants which is neither fixed nor ascertainable, but has then gone on to accept that the applicant in the case before it is nonetheless individually concerned. This involves a careful examination of the particular facts of the case, and an assessment as to whether the applicant is affected by the measure in a way that no other potential applicant is affected. There are a number of examples of this approach in the case law of the Court of Justice.

***Toepfer Getreide-Import Gesellschaft* v *Commission* (Cases 106 & 107/63) [1965] ECR 405**

In *Toepfer* (*Cases and Materials* (6.3.2)) a zero levy was imposed on maize imports into Germany from 1 October 1963. A Commission Decision of 1 October then raised the levy with effect from 2 October and a second Commission Decision, of 4 October, authorized Germany to refuse applications for import licences made between 1 and 4 October. Toepfer, a German maize importer who had made an application on 1 October, challenged the second Decision under Article 230 (ex 173) EC.

The Court of Justice held that Toepfer and other importers who had made applications on 1 October were individually concerned by the second Decision. The effect of the first Decision was that the 0% levy was available only on 1 October, and so only those importers which had applied for a licence on that day were adversely affected by the second Decision authorizing the refusal of their licences. Applications made on 2–4 October which were refused, could be resubmitted thereafter without loss to the applicants, since the applicable levy would be the same. The class of potential applicants was therefore fixed and ascertainable at the time the Decision was taken, and the factual situation differentiated them from all others in the same way that a Decision addressed to them would have done.

? EXERCISE 6.2

Try to apply the 'factual' test set out above to these facts. Do you think that Toepfer was individually concerned by this Decision?

In effect, Toepfer and the other 1 October applicants created a closed class within a larger class of 1–4 October applicants. This larger class was not closed at the date of the Decision because the Decision was issued on 4 October.

In *Bock* and *Piraiki-Patraiki* (both at *Cases and Materials* (6.3.2)) the classes of potential applicant (all importers of Chinese mushrooms and all importers of Greek yarn into France, respectively) were not closed. However, the Court of Justice held that the applicant importers were individually concerned. In these cases, the Court of Justice adopted a similar test to that in *Toepfer* to find that the applicants were differentiated on the facts from all other potential applicants.

In the case of *Bock* (see 6.4), Bock did not challenge the Decision in its entirety, but only insofar as it applied to importers who had already applied for import licences. The Court of Justice considered that Bock was individually concerned by this part of the Decision because such importers constituted a fixed and ascertainable class. It therefore annulled the Decision insofar as it applied to existing licence applications.

The reasoning in *Piraiki-Patraiki* (see 6.4) was similar. The Decision applied to all potential importers of Greek yarn into France, but the Court of Justice accepted that importers already bound by contractual arrangements (and who would therefore be particularly prejudiced by the Decision when it was passed) could be distinguished from importers who were not so bound. The class of such importers was therefore fixed at the date of the Decision. The Commission could scarcely argue that it was not possible to identify the members of this class, since it was required to carry out precisely that task as part of the inquiry which the Greek Act of Accession obliged it to conduct into the effects of any proposed protective measure.

Codorniu SA v _Council_ (Case C-309/89) [1994] ECR I-1853

The Court of Justice adopted a similar line of reasoning in *Codorniu* (*Cases and Materials* (6.3.2)) which concerned a Regulation which restricted the use of the description 'crémant' to quality sparkling wines originating in France and Luxembourg.

Codornui, a Spanish producer of quality sparkling wine, applied under Article 230 (ex 173) EC for the annulment of the Regulation. It was held by the Court of Justice that Codornui had *locus standi* and the Regulation would be annulled.

The Court ruled that *Codorniu* was differentiated from other producers who might be affected by the Regulation because it had registered and used the word 'crémant' as part of its trademark since 1924.

Sofrimport SARL v _Commission_ (Case C-152/88) [1990] ECR I-2477

In the case of *Sofrimport SARL* v *Commission* (*Cases and Materials* (6.3.2)), Sofrimport had shipped apples from Chile prior to the issue of a Regulation which suspended import licences for Chilean apples. Sofrimport's subsequent application to the French authorities for an import licence was refused and it then applied for annulment of the Regulation and damages under Article 288 EC (see **Chapter 7**).

The Court of Justice held that Sofrimport had locus standi to challenge the Regulation and that it should be annulled insofar as it applied to goods in transit. When taking protectionist measures, the Commission was required, under a previous Regulation, to take into account the position of importers with goods in transit, and since such importers constituted a fixed and ascertainable class, they could be said to be individually concerned. These importers therefore had *locus standi* to challenge the Regulation insofar as it applied to them.

***Unifruit Hellas* v *Commission* (Case T-489/93) [1994] ECR II-1201**

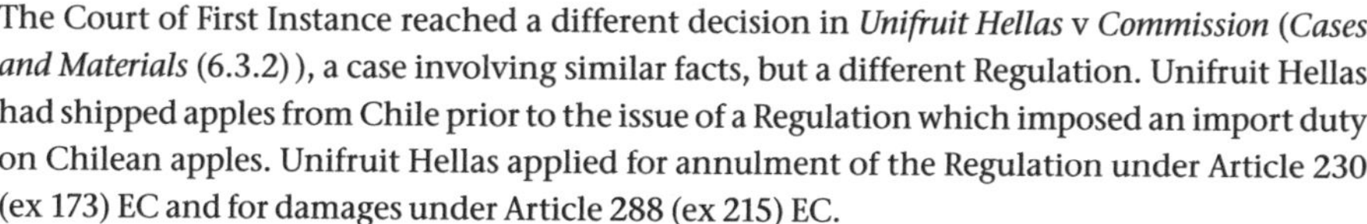

The Court of First Instance reached a different decision in *Unifruit Hellas* v *Commission* (*Cases and Materials* (6.3.2)), a case involving similar facts, but a different Regulation. Unifruit Hellas had shipped apples from Chile prior to the issue of a Regulation which imposed an import duty on Chilean apples. Unifruit Hellas applied for annulment of the Regulation under Article 230 (ex 173) EC and for damages under Article 288 (ex 215) EC.

It was held that the action under Article 230 EC was inadmissible (but that the action under Article 288 EC was admissible). The Court of First Instance ruled that although importers whose goods were in transit to the Community when the Regulation introduced a charge on those goods constituted a fixed and identifiable class of persons, that was not sufficient. The Regulation in question did not require the Commission to take into account the special position of products in transit (unlike the Regulation in *Sofrimport*) and so there was no individual concern.

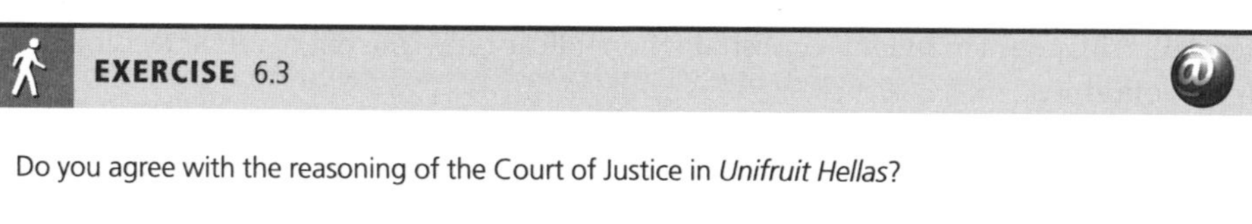

EXERCISE 6.3

Do you agree with the reasoning of the Court of Justice in *Unifruit Hellas*?

6.5.3 Measures issued as a result of proceedings initiated by applicant

Where the measure complained of was adopted as a result of proceedings in which the applicant was involved, the Court of Justice has been prepared to rule that the applicant is individually concerned. This is most likely to be the case where the measure concerns competition policy or is an anti-dumping measure (designed to stop the import into the Community of goods priced below the normal price where this could cause economic harm within the Community).

For example, in *Metro-SB-Grossmärkte GmbH & Co KG* v *Commission* (Case 26/76) [1977] ECR 1875 the applicant sought to challenge a Decision addressed to another company. However, the Decision had been issued in response to a complaint made by the applicant to the Commission that the other company was in breach of Community competition policy. Similarly, in *Timex Corporation* v *Council* (Case 264/82) [1985] ECR 849 an applicant which had initiated the complaint and given evidence in the proceedings giving rise to the anti-dumping measure was held to be individually concerned by it.

6.5.4 Anti-dumping measures

As well as those who initiate the procedure leading to the adoption of an anti-dumping measure, the Court of Justice has also recognized that producers, exporters or importers of the product at which the measure is directed may be individually concerned by it.

In *Allied Corporation* v *Commission* (Joined Cases 239 & 275/82) [1984] ECR 1005 the Court of Justice identified as relevant the fact that the producers and exporters had given undertakings pursuant to one of the contested Regulations, were referred to in the other contested Regulation, and their individual circumstances formed the subject matter of the two Regulations.

Where the applicant is not an exporter or a producer, but only an importer, it must prove that it is particularly singled out by the measure. For example, in *Extramet Industrie SA* v *Council* (Case C-358/89) [1991] ECR I-2501 the Court of Justice ruled that an importer was individually concerned where it was the largest importer and end user of the product, its business was dependent to a large extent upon the product and it was difficult to obtain supplies elsewhere.

6.6 Decisions in the form of Regulations

6.6.1 The current position

An applicant may prove that a purported Regulation is, in fact, a Decision, in one of two ways. First, the nature and scope of the Regulation may be such that it is not legislative in character and thus not a true Regulation but a Decision. Secondly, and in the alternative, a true Regulation may be of individual concern to the applicant and thus effectively a Decision so far as it is concerned.

***KSH NV* v *Council and Commission* (Case 101/76) [1977] ECR 797**

For example, in *KSH* (*Cases and Materials* (6.4.1)), an isoglucose producer challenged a Regulation which provided for the reduction, and eventual abolition, of subsidies on isoglucose production. The producer was one of only three or four such producers in the Community, and because of the technology and expense involved, any potential producers would not be in a position to enter the market for at least two years.

The Court of Justice ruled that the wording of this Regulation indicated that it was a measure of general application, applying objectively to a general and abstract category of persons. The fact that those persons were fixed and ascertainable at any given time was insufficient. The producer therefore had no *locus standi* to challenge it. It is possible that the Court of Justice was influenced in this case by the problem of massive isoglucose overproduction. If it had not invented this extra hurdle for applicants, it would have had to annul the Regulation, and the overproduction would have continued.

***Calpak* v *Commission* (Cases 789–790/79) [1980] ECR 1949**

In *Calpak* (*Cases and Materials* (6.4.1)), the Court of Justice again considered the wording of the measure. A Regulation altered the calculation of subsidies to producers of processed pears, so that reference was made only to the previous year's production rather than to the average production over the previous three years. Since the reference year in question had been a bad one for Italian producers, but not for French producers (who were their sole rivals in the Community), the Italian producers challenged the Regulation under Article 230 EC.

The Court of Justice ruled that the Regulation applied to all producers, that is to say, it applied objectively to a category of persons described in a general manner. The fact that the number, and even the identity, of those producers could be determined was insufficient for it to be categorized as a Decision.

In earlier years, the Court on occasion applied only the first, stricter test and not the second, more generous test.
However, in other cases such as *Codorniu* and *Sofrimport* (see 6.5.2), the Court applied the more generous test. More recently in *Union de Pequeños Agricultores (UPA)* v *Council* (C-50/00 P) [2002] ECR I-6677 *Cases and Materials* (6.4.1)) the Court has referred to both tests as alternatives, either of which will be sufficient to establish that the Regulation is open to challenge if the applicant is directly and individually concerned by it.

6.6.2 **Possibilities for reform**

The difficulties for non-privileged applicants of challenging measures of general application have been considered in two recent cases.

UPA v Council, Court of justice Case C-50/00 P [2002] ECR I-6677

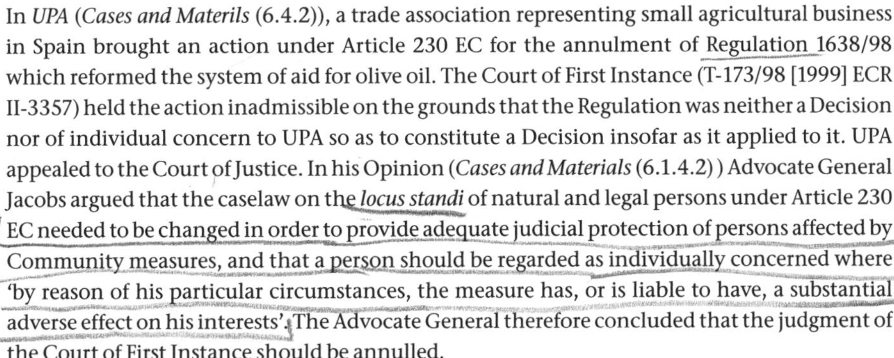

In *UPA* (*Cases and Materils* (6.4.2)), a trade association representing small agricultural business in Spain brought an action under Article 230 EC for the annulment of Regulation 1638/98 which reformed the system of aid for olive oil. The Court of First Instance (T-173/98 [1999] ECR II-3357) held the action inadmissible on the grounds that the Regulation was neither a Decision nor of individual concern to UPA so as to constitute a Decision insofar as it applied to it. UPA appealed to the Court of Justice. In his Opinion (*Cases and Materials* (6.1.4.2)) Advocate General Jacobs argued that the caselaw on the *locus standi* of natural and legal persons under Article 230 EC needed to be changed in order to provide adequate judicial protection of persons affected by Community measures, and that a person should be regarded as individually concerned where 'by reason of his particular circumstances, the measure has, or is liable to have, a substantial adverse effect on his interests'. The Advocate General therefore concluded that the judgment of the Court of First Instance should be annulled.

Subsequently the Court of First Instance gave judgment in Jégo-Quéré:

Jégo-Quéré SA v *Commission* (Case T-177/01 [2002] ECR II-2365)

In *Jégo-Quéré* (*Cases and Materials* (6.4.2)). Jégo-Quéré, a fishing company, applied for partial annulment of Regulation 1162/2001 establishing measures for the recovery of the stock of hake. The Regulation imposed minimizing mesh sizes on fishing vessels operating in certain areas and Jégo-Quéré alleged that its ability to carry on its business was adversely affected by the Regulation.

The Court of First Instance held that Jégo-Quéré had *locus standi*. It was concerned that if Jégo-Quéré's action was inadmissible, it would be denied any legal remedy enabling it to challenge the legality of the contested provisions. Access to the courts was an essential element of a community based on the rule of law, and was guaranteed by the establishment in the EC Treaty of a complete system of remedies and procedures enabling the Court to review the legality of acts of the institutions, and by the establishment by the Court of a right to an effective remedy. The latter had also been reaffirmed by Article 47 of the Charter of Fundamental Rights of the EU.

? QUESTION 6.8

What other actions might have provided a remedy?

There were two other routes by which an individual might obtain a declaration that a Community measure was unlawful: Article 234 EC and Article 288 EC. However, an Article 234 EC ruling was not possible in the present case because there were no acts of implementation capable of giving rise to an action in the national courts. Although Jégo-Quéré could breach the Regulation and then assert its illegality in proceedings against it, individuals could not be required to breach the law in order to gain access to justice. An Article 288 EC action could also not provide a solution because it could not result in the annulment of a Community measure which was held to be unlawful. (Actions under Article 288 EC will be discussed in depth in **Chapter 7**.)

The Court held that a person must be regarded as individually concerned by a Community measure of general application (i.e. a Regulation) if 'the measure in question affects his legal position, in a manner which is both definitive and immediate, by restricting this right or by imposing obligations on him'. It stressed that 'the number and position of other persons who are likewise affected by the measure, or who may be so, are of no relevance in that regard'. Although it was necessary for a non-privileged applicant to satisfy the conditions laid down by Article 230 EC in order to bring an action for annulment, an applicant seeking to challenge a general measure need not be differentiated from all others affected by it in the same way as an addressee.

In *UPA* (Case C-50/00 P [2002] ECR I-6677 (see 6.6.1), the Court of Justice rejected the reasoning of the Court of First Instance in *Jégo-Quéré*, and confirmed its judgment in Case C-321/95 P *Greenpeace* [1998] ECR I-1651 that a non-privileged applicant could only challenge a Regulation if it was in fact a Decision, or if the applicant was individually concerned by it so that it was a Decision in respect of that applicant. The judgment of the Court of Justice in *Jégo-Quéré* (Case C-263/02 P [2004] ECR I-3425) followed that in *UPA* .

? QUESTION 6.9

Which of these arguments do you find most convincing?

Even if you find the arguments of the Court of First Instance convincing, remember that it is the judgment of the Court of Justice which is authoritative. Note that the Court of Justice accepted that applicants had rights of access to the courts and to an effective remedy, but concluded that Articles 230, 234, and 241 EC provided 'a complete system of legal remedies'. (Article 241 EC is discussed in more detail at 6.11.)

6.7 Directives

Although not mentioned in Article 230 EC as subject to challenge by non-privileged applicants, it has been held that Directives are open to challenge if an applicant is directly and individually concerned by them (see, e.g., *Salamander AG* v *Parliament* (Case T-172/98) [2000] ECR II-2487 and *Japan Tobacco Inc and JT International SA* v *Parliament and Council* (Case T-223/01) [2002] ECR II-3259).

> **? QUESTION** 6.10
>
> What problems do you think might be encountered in relation to direct concern and Directives?

> **? QUESTION** 6.11
>
> Article 230 (ex 173) EC gives four grounds on which an application for annulment may be made. What are they?

Since Directives leave some discretion to Member States and cannot produce direct legal effect until their implementation deadline has passed, it will be rare for a Directive to directly concern an applicant.

6.8 Grounds for annulment

The four grounds outlined below may be relied upon by all applicants (subject to the fulfilment of the further requirements outlined above by non-privileged applicants and those in the intermediate category). The grounds overlap and an applicant may rely on one or more in its challenge. The decision of the Court of Justice need not identify the ground on which the challenge is successful.

The four grounds are as follows.

6.8.1 Lack of competence

If an institution acts beyond its powers, that act can be annulled. An example would be an act which had no legal base in the EC Treaty or in secondary legislation, and which the Community therefore had no power to take. This ground is rarely used because of the fall-back power given by Article 308 (ex 235) EC (see 3.4.1).

In *UK* v *Council (Working Time Directive)* (Case C-84/94) [1996] ECR I-5755 the UK requested the annulment of a Directive imposing a maximum working week of 48 hours on the ground, inter alia, that the Council had no competence to adopt the Directive. The UK argued that the measure did not relate to health and safety at work and therefore should not have been adopted under Article 138 (ex 118a) EC. Instead, its legal base (see 3.4, 3.6, and 6.3.3.2) should either have been Article 94 (ex 100) EC (as an internal market measure) or Article 308 (ex 235) (as a measure not covered by any specific Treaty Article). In either case the Council Decision adopting the measure would have had to be unanimous and since the UK would have opposed the Directive, the Council would not have had the competence to adopt the Regulation.

The Court of Justice ruled that Article 138 (ex 118a) EC was the appropriate legislative base for the Directive and therefore the Council was competent to adopt it.

In *Parliament* v *Council and Commission* (Cases C-317 & 318/04) [2006] ECR I-471, the Parliament challenged two measures concerning the transfer of air passenger data from the Community to the US authorities. On the basis of Article 95 EC, which empowers the Council to take measures to approximate national law to further the single market, the Community had adopted Directive 95/46 on the protection of personal data. The protection of this Directive was stated expressly not to apply to, inter alia, the processing of data in the course of an activity which fell outside Community law, including processing operations concerning public security or State activities in the area of criminal law. Where the protection of the Directive did apply, an exception was provided whereby data could be transferred to a third country if that country ensured an adequate level of data protection.

On the basis of Directive 95/46, the Commission adopted a decision stating that the US authorities ensured an adequate level of protection for personal data contained in the passenger name records of air passengers arriving in the US ('the decision on adequacy'). On the basis of Article 95, the Council adopted Decision 2004/96 approving an Agreement between the Community and the USA allowing the USA authorities to access the airlines' passenger name records for passengers travelling to the USA from the Community.

The Parliament challenged both measures.

The Court of Justice held that the decision on adequacy should be annulled because it concerned the processing of data for the purposes of national security and State activities in the area of criminal law, areas which were outside the scope of the Directive. It also ruled that Decision 2004/96 should be annulled because it concerned the processing of data for these purposes, rather than for the fulfilment of the single market, and was thus outside the scope of Article 95 EC.

6.8.2 Infringement of an essential procedural requirement

Although there are a number of possibilities here, the commonest infringements are a failure to give proper reasons for an act as required by Article 253 (ex 190) EC, and use of the wrong legislative procedure (often because of use of the wrong legal base—see 3.4, 3.6 and 6.3.3.2), in particular involving a failure to consult the Parliament.

***Roquette Frères* v *Council* Case 138/79 [1980] ECR 3333**

In *Roquette Frères* (*Cases and Materials* (6.5) and see also 6.5.1) the measure challenged should have been adopted under the consultation procedure. The Council asked the Parliament for its opinion but adopted the measure without waiting for it to be given. The Court of Justice ruled that this amounted to an infringement of an essential procedural requirement.

6.8.3 Infringement of the EC Treaty or of any rule of law relating to its application

This ground is commonly relied upon in Article 230 (ex 173) EC actions.

EXERCISE 6.4

Try to list as many 'rules of law' as possible. If you have difficulty in doing this, you should refer back to 3.5.4.

You might have mentioned legal certainty, non-discrimination, proportionality, fundamental human rights, or any other general principle of law.

6.8.4 Misuse of powers

Where an institution has been given power to act, but only for a particular purpose or purposes, then if that power is used for an illegal end or in an illegal way, this may give grounds for a challenge.

6.9 Procedure

The applicant has two months in which to challenge the measure in the Court of Justice. This time limit runs from the fifteenth day after publication of the measure in the Official Journal or, if the measure has not been published, from the day after receipt of notification by the applicant. If neither of these events has occurred, the time limit runs from the day on which the measure came to the applicant's knowledge.

6.10 Effect of annulment

If an Article 230 (ex 173) EC action is successful, the measure will be annulled, either in whole or in part. According to Article 231 (ex 174) EC, such a measure (to the extent to which it is annulled) is void, that is to say, has no legal effect. It may not be reviewed or enforced and, according to Article 233 (ex 176) EC, the defendant institution must take such steps as are necessary to comply with the judgment of the Court of Justice. The Court of Justice will determine the time from which the annulment takes effect, which may be from the date of judgment, from the future date on which the measure is replaced, or retrospectively to an earlier date. For example, in *Parliament v Council and Commission* Cases C-317 & 318/04 (see 6.8.1), the Court held that annulment of the decision on adequacy would not take effect until 30 September 2006, four months after the date of judgment. This was because the decision approved an Agreement between the Community and the USA which could only be terminated on 90 days' notice, and also because a period of time was required to adopt measures to comply with the annulment judgment.

6.11 The plea of illegality

Article 241 (ex 184) EC provides that in proceedings where a Regulation is at issue, an applicant may rely on the grounds for an Article 230 (ex 173) EC action (lack of competence and so forth) in order to allege that the Regulation is inapplicable in that case. This form of indirect challenge is known as the 'plea of illegality'.

EXERCISE 6.5

Read Article 241 (ex 184) EC. Can it give rise to an independent cause of action?

THE EC TREATY

Article 241 (ex 184)

Notwithstanding the expiry of the period laid down in the fifth paragraph of Article 230 (ex 173) EC, any party may, in proceedings in which a regulation adopted jointly by the European Parliament and the Council, or a regulation of the Council, of the Commission, or of the ECB is at issue, plead the grounds specified in the second paragraph of Article 230 (ex 173) EC in order to invoke before the Court of Justice the inapplicability of that regulation.

Article 241 (ex 184) EC cannot give rise to a separate cause of action, but can be raised in the course of other proceedings. A declaration of inapplicability means that any measures adopted under the Regulation are invalid. In theory, the declaration is relevant only to the case in question but in practice, since the Court of Justice would be likely to annul the Regulation or any measures based on it if challenged correctly under Article 230 (ex 173) EC, the other institutions would be likely to replace the Regulation in question as soon as possible. The relevant time limits and rules of *locus standi* are those applicable to the underlying action, whatever that may be.

6.12 Article 232 (ex 175) EC

Article 232 (ex 175) EC provides that the Court of Justice may declare an institution's failure to act to be an infringement of the EC Treaty.

THE EC TREATY

Article 232 (ex 175)

Should the European Parliament, the Council or the Commission, in infringement of this Treaty, fail to act, the Member States and the other institutions of the Community may bring an action before the Court of Justice to have the infringement established.

The action shall be admissible only if the institution concerned has first been called upon to act. If, within two months of being so called upon, the institution concerned has not defined its position, the action may be brought within a further period of two months.

Any natural or legal person may, under the conditions laid down in the preceding paragraphs, complain to the Court of Justice that an institution of the Community has failed to address to that person any act other than a recommendation or an opinion.

The Court of Justice shall have jurisdiction, under the same conditions, in actions or proceedings brought by the ECB in the areas falling within the latter's field of competence and in actions or proceedings brought against the latter.

6.12.1 *Locus standi*

6.12.1.1 Privileged applicants

Privileged applicants for the purpose of Article 232 (ex 175) EC are the Commission, the Council, the Parliament, and the Member States.

6.12.1.2 The intermediate category

The intermediate category under Article 232 (ex 175) EC consists solely of the ECB. The ECB may bring an action, or have an action brought against it, only in respect of areas within its field of competence.

6.12.1.3 Non-privileged applicants

Such applicants are not entitled to complain about **all** failures to act but only about a failure to address **to them** an act (other than a Recommendation or an Opinion) which they were legally entitled to claim. Since a non-privileged applicant cannot be the addressee of a Regulation or a Directive, they may only challenge a failure to adopt a Decision.

Lord Bethell v _Commission_ (Case 246/81) [1982] ECR 2277

In the case of *Bethell* (*Cases and Materials* (6.6.1)), the applicant had notified the Commission of alleged anti-competitive practices by European airlines, contrary to Community law, and had requested an inquiry and a Decision on the matter. When the Commission failed to take such action, Lord Bethell challenged this failure under Article 232 (ex 175) EC.

The Court of Justice ruled that where a non-privileged applicant such as Lord Bethell was concerned, an action for a failure to act lay only where there had been a failure to adopt a measure which the applicant was 'legally entitled to claim' under Community law. The applicant must therefore be the potential addressee of the act.

? QUESTION 6.12

To whom do you think a Commission Decision in this case would have been addressed?

In this case, the potential addressees of any Decision on the anti-competitive behaviour of the airlines would have been the airlines themselves, and not Lord Bethell (who would also have been unlikely to have been able to prove that any such Decision would have directly and individually concerned him). It was held that Lord Bethell had no *locus standi* to challenge the Commission's alleged failure to act.

In *Gestevisión Telecinco SA* v *Commission* (Case T-95/96 [1998] ECR II-3407) the Court of Justice ruled that an undertaking would be directly concerned by a decision on State aid where the national authorities clearly intended to grant the aid, and would be individually concerned where the decision would have affected them by reason of attributes or circumstances which differentiated them from all others. Where the Commission took a decision that a measure did not constitute aid, or constituted aid but was nonetheless compatible with the common market, without initiating the procedure under Article 88(2) (ex 93(2)) EC on the investigation of State aids, the beneficiaries of that procedure (in particular, competing companies) could secure compliance with the procedure only by challenging the decision to grant aid before the Court of Justice. A competing company, whose interests would be affected by the grant of that aid, was therefore directly and individually concerned by the Commission's failure to act.

6.12.2 Grounds

A failure to act on the part of the Parliament, the Council, or the Commission is open to challenge only on the ground that:

(a) the defaulting institution has been called upon to act (as it would be inequitable to sue an institution before notifying it of the complaint and calling upon it to take the action required by the complainant); and

(b) the institution has failed to act.

EXERCISE 6.6

Write down what you think 'fail to act' should mean in this context. Check, and if necessary correct, it when you have read the following section of text.

***Alfons Lütticke* v *Commission* (Case 48/65) [1966] ECR 19**

In *Lütticke* (*Cases and Materials* (6.6.2)), the applicants alleged that a German tax on imports of dried milk was contrary to Community law. They made a formal application requiring the Commission to take infringement proceedings against Germany under Article 226 (ex 169). The Commission responded that the tax was not contrary to Community law and that therefore it would not take such proceedings. The Court of Justice ruled that proceedings for a failure to act could be brought only if the institution had failed to define its position. The Commission had defined its position by taking the decision not to initiate proceedings against Germany, and therefore it had not 'failed to act' within the meaning of Article 232 (ex 175) EC.

The institution is thus not obliged to take the action required by the complainant in order to avoid an Article 232 (ex 175) EC action. It is simply obliged to define its position.

As a result of this interpretation of 'fail to act', actions under Article 232 (ex 175) EC are rarely successful.

6.12.3 Procedure

 **EXERCISE** 6.7 

Look back at Article 232 (ex 175) EC and try to summarize the procedure that an applicant should follow in order to bring a claim under this Article.

The applicant must first make a formal request to the relevant institution to act. If the institution fails to define its position within two months, the applicant may apply directly to the Court of Justice within a further period of two months.

6.12.4 Effect

If the Court of Justice finds that a failure to act infringes the Treaty, it will order the institution concerned to take any necessary steps to remedy the omission. These steps are not necessarily those requested by the applicant.

6.13 The relationship between Article 230 (ex 173) EC and Article 232 (ex 175) EC

If the institution has not defined its position, Article 232 (ex 175) EC is the appropriate provision; but if the position has been defined, Article 230 (ex 173) EC should be used since the definition in itself amounts to an act which can be challenged. The two actions are often pleaded in the alternative, but a particular measure must amount either to an act, or to a failure to act, and so only one action can be correct. If the requirements of the appropriate action are not fulfilled, for example because a challenge to an act under Article 230 (ex 173) EC is made by an individual lacking direct and individual concern, it is not open to that individual to bring an action under Article 232 (ex 175) EC instead.

In *Eridania and others* v *Commission* (Cases 10 & 18/68) [1969] ECR 459, a Commission Decision granted aid to three Italian sugar refineries. A number of other sugar producers asked the Commission to annul this Decision, which it refused to do. The other producers then made both an Article 230 (ex 173) EC, and an Article 232 (ex 175) EC application to the Court of Justice. The Court of Justice held that the Article 232 (ex 175) EC action could not succeed because the Commission's positive refusal to annul the Decision amounted to an act, rather than a failure to act. The Article 230 (ex 173) EC action could not succeed because there was no direct and individual concern. The Court of Justice stressed that Article 232 (ex 175) EC should not be used to circumvent the restrictions of Article 230 (ex 173) EC. If an institution refused to annul an act, recourse against that refusal was provided by the Treaty under Article 230 (ex 173) EC, and the refusal should not therefore be treated as a failure to act giving rise to an Article 232 (ex 175) EC action.

CONCLUSIONS

Although Articles 230, 232, and 241 (ex 173, 175, and 184) EC permit actions taken by the Community to be challenged, these Articles will not provide a remedy in every case. Under Article 230 (ex 173) EC, both the intermediate category of applicants and non-privileged applicants are extremely restricted, albeit in different ways, in their opportunities to challenge Community acts.

Under Article 232 (ex 175) EC, only total inaction may be challenged, rather than positive refusals to act and non-privileged applicants must prove that the measure they are seeking would have been addressed to them. Given that Article 241 (ex 184) EC does not provide for an independent cause of action at all, it is evident that the Community is not over-anxious to encourage challenges to its measures. However, it should be remembered that the Member States are equally cautious about challenges to national law and that under Community law, as we shall see in **Chapter 7**, it is possible to claim damages in respect of a Community measure which has not been successfully challenged under Articles 230, 232, or 241 (ex 173, 175, or 184) EC.

SUMMARY

Article 230 EC

- Article 230 EC provides for the judicial review of EC measures. **Privileged applicants** (the Member States and the major EC institutions) have standing to bring a challenge to any measure. The **intermediate category of applicants** (certain other EC institutions) may only challenge a measure for the purpose of protecting their prerogatives. **Non-privileged applicants** (individuals and companies) may only challenge measures which are addressed to them, or are of direct and individual concern to them and, if the measure is a Regulation, is truly a Decision.
- A measure will be of **direct concern** to an applicant if its impact on the applicant is direct at the time of its adoption, and does not depend on the exercise of discretion by a Member State (*Bock*).
- A measure will be of **individual concern** to an applicant if, at the date the measure is adopted, it is part of a closed class of those affected by the measure, or is part of a group which is more seriously affected by the measure than others affected (*International Fruit*, *Toepfer*).
- A **Regulation can regarded as a Decision** either if its terms are precise and specific, rather than general and abstract, so that in reality it is a Decision (*KSH*), or if it applies to the applicant in a precise and individualized way, so that it is in effect a Decision insofar as that applicant is concerned (*Codornui*).
- A number of possibilities for the **reform** of the system for challenging Regulations have been mooted, in particular by the Court of First Instance in *Jégo-Quéré* and by Advocate General Jacobs in *UPA* and *Jégo-Quéré*. However, these have so far been rejected by the Court of Justice (in *UPA* and *Jégo-Quéré*).

- Once the applicant has established its standing to bring the challenge, it must prove that at least one of the **grounds** listed in Article 230 EC is satisfied; lack of competence, infringement of an essential procedural requirement, infringement of the EC Treaty or any rule of law relating to its application, or misuse of powers.

Article 241 EC

- This allows an applicant to rely on one of the Article 230 grounds to **avoid the application of a Regulation** in legal proceedings. If successful, the Regulation is declared inapplicable in the proceedings, rather than invalid.

Article 232 EC

- Article 230 EC provides for the judicial review of the Community's **failure to take measures**. It is rarely used because any action by the EC, including a refusal to take measures, constitutes a positive act, and is thus open to challenge under Article 230 and not Article 232.

CHAPTER 6: ASSESSMENT EXERCISE

The Community operates a system of production licences, administered by the Member States, in respect of soft toys, in order to avoid the development of a soft toy mountain. The Council has recently issued a Regulation, which has immediate effect, permitting Member States to prohibit the grant of production licences in respect of cuddly toy penguins.

The two Community producers of cuddly toy penguins wish to challenge the Regulation. Do they have *locus standi* to do so?

See *Cases and Materials* (6.8) for a specimen answer.

FURTHER READING

Berry E., and Boyes S. (2005). 'Access to Justice in the Community Courts: a Limited Right?' 24 *CJQ* 224.

European Convention Discussion Circle (2003). 'Final report of the discussion circle on the Court of Justice', 25 March 2003.

European Convention Secretariat (2003). 'Access to the Court of Justice for individuals—possible amendments to Article 230, paragraph 4, of the EC Treaty', 26 February 2003.

Jégo-Quéré SA v *Commission* (T-177/01 [2002] ECR II-2365).

Neuwahl, N. A. E. M. 'Article 173 Paragraph 4 EC: Past, Present and Possible Future' (1996) 21 *ELRev* 17.

Union de Pequeños Agricultores (UPA) v *Council* (C-50/00 P ECR I-6677).

Varju, M. (2004). 'The Debate on the Future of Standing under Article 230(4) TEC in the European Convention' 10(1) *EJPL* 43.

7 Community and Member State liability in damages

7.1 OBJECTIVES

By the end of this chapter you should be able to:

1 Explain all elements of the test which must be satisfied before damages will be awarded in respect of the Community's non-contractual liability under Article 288 EC

2 Assess the factors which may lead to the reduction of damages under Article 288 EC

3 Explain and analyse the test for a wrongful act as outlined in the *Schöppenstedt* and *Second Skimmed Milk Powder* cases

4 Explain the relationship between an action under Article 288 (ex 215) EC and other actions under the EC Treaty

5 Explain the key elements of the decisions in *Francovich* and *Factortame III* and the differences between them

6 Apply the conditions laid down in *Factortame III* to a range of factual situations

7 Analyse the relationship between the Court's jurisprudence on Article 288 EC and its jurisprudence on Member State liability.

8 Explain (in conjunction with **Chapter 4**) the relationship between *Francovich* liability, and the direct and indirect effect of Directives.

7.2 Introduction

If loss is suffered as a result of Community action or inaction, it may be possible to claim damages against it under Article 288 (ex 215) EC if the Community is found to have acted wrongfully. The rules regarding the liability of the Community differ according to whether the claim is contractual or non-contractual. This chapter, for reasons which will become apparent, will concentrate on the latter.

Acts which may give rise to non-contractual claims against the Community include negligence and the adoption of defective legislation. Although Community law provides other remedies, such as annulment under Article 230 (ex 173) EC (see **Chapter 6**), damages are often claimed in addition, for instance to compensate for loss incurred prior to annulment. The facts of many of the cases already considered in this textbook in relation to other issues have led also to an action for damages, for example *Alfons Lütticke* v *Commission* (see 6.12.2 and 7.3) and *KSH* v *Council and Commission* (see 6.6.1 and 7.3.2.2).

A Member State may, in certain circumstances, be liable in damages for its own breach of Community law. For this purpose, the 'Member State' includes not only the national government, but other public-law bodies such as territorial bodies to which certain legislative or administrative tasks have been devolved (*Haim* v *Kassenzahnärztliche Vereinigung Nordrhein* (Case C-424/97 [2000] ECR I-5123)). The Court of Justice has developed two different sets of conditions governing such liability, commonly known as the *Francovich* conditions and the *Factortame III* conditions. These will now be examined.

7.3 Non-contractual liability of the Community

THE EC TREATY

Article 288 (ex 215)

...

In the case of non-contractual liability, the Community shall, in accordance with the general principles common to the laws of the Member States, make good any damage caused by its institutions or by its servants in the performance of their duties.

The preceding paragraph shall apply under the same conditions to damage caused by the ECB or by its servants in the performance of their duties.

The personal liability of its servants towards the Community shall be governed by the provisions laid down in their Staff Regulations or in the Conditions of Employment applicable to them.

In *Dubois et Fils SA* v *Council and Commission* (Case T-113/96) [1998] ECR II-125 the Court of First Instance ruled that the Treaties of the EC and the EU were not 'acts of the institutions' but agreements by the Member States. They could not, therefore, give rise to liability on the part of the Community under Article 288 (ex 215) EC.

Article 235 (ex 178) EC confers jurisdiction upon the Court of Justice to award damages under Article 288 (ex 215) EC.

EXERCISE 7.1

Look back at 2.3.5 above. Does the Court of First Instance have any jurisdiction in this area?

The Court of First Instance has jurisdiction to hear actions brought under Article 288 (ex 215) EC by legal and natural persons.

Article 288 (ex 215) EC states that Community liability is to be determined in accordance with the general principles common to the law of the Member States.

***Alfons Lütticke* v *Commission* (Case 4/69) [1971] ECR 325**

In the course of its judgment in *Lütticke* (*Cases and Materials* (7.1)). Lütticke alleged that a German levy on its imports was contrary to Community law, and requested the Commission to bring proceedings against the German government. The Commission refused to do this and Lütticke brought an Article 288 (ex 215) EC action to recover damages caused by the Commission's inaction.

It was held that damages could not be awarded because the Commission's conduct ad not been illegal.

The Court of Justice explained the meaning of the requirement in Article 288 (ex 215) EC that damages be awarded in accordance with 'the general principles common to the law of the Member States'. Lütticke had first brought an unsuccessful action under Article 232 (ex 175) EC (Case 48/65; see **Chapter 6**). Case 4/69 involved an action under Article 288 (ex 215) EC to recover damages caused by the Commission's inaction.

? QUESTION 7.1

Remember that these general principles are those which are common to the laws of Member States on liability. From your knowledge of English law can you guess what might have to be proved before damages will be awarded under Article 288 (ex 215) EC?

In this case, the Court of Justice stated that the reference to 'the general principles common to the law of the Member States' meant that the Community would be liable in damages if three elements were proved:

(a) actual damage to the applicant (personal or property damage);

(b) illegal conduct by a Community institution;

(c) a causal link between the illegal conduct and the damage.

On the facts, the Court of Justice held that the Commission's conduct had not been illegal and that therefore damages could not be awarded.

Each of these three principles will now be examined in turn.

7.3.1 Actual damage

It can be surprisingly difficult to prove this element of liability, as can be seen from the case of *GAEC*.

***GAEC* v *Council and Commission* (Case 253/84) [1987] ECR 123**

In *GAEC*, subsidies had been provided to German farmers pursuant to a Council Decision, and aggrieved French farmers brought an Article 288 (ex 215) action claiming damages for losses caused to them by competition from subsidized German milk, poultry, and cattle products. The Court of Justice held that in respect of sales of milk and poultry, actual damage was not proved because the farmers had produced no evidence of their losses. (The result of their claim for losses in respect of cattle products will be discussed at 7.3.6.)

Even where the applicant is able to prove its loss, the level of damages awarded may be less than the loss sustained if the applicant has been guilty of contributory negligence or has failed to mitigate its loss.

> **? QUESTION 7.2**
>
> From your own knowledge, can you attempt to explain, or give an example of, either of these principles?

These principles are both enshrined in English law. In the law of tort it has been established that a plaintiff who has contributed through his own negligence to the tort or to the resulting damage, may be expected to bear some or all of his own loss. For example, damages awarded to a plaintiff injured in a car accident may be reduced if it is shown that he contributed to the accident by driving too fast, or contributed to the resulting damage by failing to wear a seatbelt.

In both contract and tort, English law recognizes that a plaintiff should do his best to minimize the loss that he has suffered as a result of the tort or breach of contract. If he does not do so, then in effect he has brought some of his loss upon himself and should therefore bear a proportion of it. In the example given above, damages awarded in respect of lost earnings while the plaintiff is unable to undertake his normal work may be reduced if he fails to take reasonable alternative work.

The use of both principles in Community law is similar.

7.3.1.1 Duty to mitigate any loss

> ***Mulder* v *Council and Commission (Mulder II)* (Cases C-104/89 & C-37/90) [1992] ECR I-3061**
>
> *Mulder* concerned two Council Regulations. The first allocated milk quotas (the amount of milk which a particular undertaking could produce without incurring a levy) to producers on the basis of the previous year's production. A number of producers, such as Mulder, had not produced any milk in the previous year as a result of a Community agreement aimed at reducing overproduction. They were therefore disadvantaged by the terms of the Regulation. These producers had successfully applied for partial annulment of the measure under Article 230 (ex 173), for breach of their legitimate expectation that they would be able to resume milk production when the agreement came to an end (*Mulder* v *Minister van Landbouw en Visserij (Mulder I)* (Case 120/86) [1988] ECR 2321 and *Von Deetzen* v *Hauptzollampt Hamburg-Jonas* (Case 170/86) [1988] ECR 2355). A second Regulation was introduced which provided quotas for these producers, but at a lower rate than for other producers. The producers then claimed damages under Article 288 (ex 215) EC. It was held that reduced damages would be awarded in respect of the first Regulation, but no damages at all would be awarded in the respect of the second Regulation.
>
> The Court of Justice reduced the damages awarded by the amount of profit which the producers could reasonably have earned had they undertaken alternative activities. However, it failed to give examples of such activities. Although the word 'reasonably' would presumably exclude activities which were fundamentally different from the original business, such as manufacturing, no guidance was given.

A potential applicant would therefore be wise to undertake some kind of alternative activity in order to reduce the actual loss, unless it is confident of proving that there is no possible alternative.

7.3.1.2 Contributory negligence

In the case of *Adams* v *Commission* (Case 145/83) [1985] ECR 3539, Adams had supplied the Commission with confidential information concerning breaches of Community competition law by his employer, Hoffman-La Roche. In the course of proceedings, the Commission gave papers to Hoffman-La Roche which enabled it to identify Adams as the source of the leaked information. It then failed to warn Adams that Hoffman-La Roche was planning to prosecute him, and when Adams returned to Switzerland, he was arrested and convicted of industrial espionage under Swiss law.

The Court of Justice awarded damages for Adams's loss of earnings and loss of reputation as a result of his conviction and imprisonment, which the Court of Justice attributed to the Commission's wrongful actions in allowing Adams to be identified and in failing to warn him that his identity was known. However, the damages awarded were reduced by half as a result of Adams's contributory negligence. The Court of Justice ruled that Adams had been contributorily negligent in failing to warn the Commission that he could be identified from the documents, in failing to ask that he be kept informed of progress in the case, particularly with regard to the use of the documents, and in returning to Switzerland without inquiring as to the current status of the proceedings and the use of the documentation. This decision appears to be rather harsh, both as to the existence and the level of the contributory negligence, but it is true to say that the Court of Justice has tended to be cautious in imposing liability on the Community.

7.3.2 Wrongful act: General legislative measures

The greatest number of applications for damages under Article 288 (ex 215) EC has been in respect of general legislative acts. As a result the Court of Justice appears to have attempted to stem the flow by applying a restrictive test as to what constitutes a 'wrongful act' where legislative acts are concerned. This test is commonly referred to as the *Schöppenstedt* or *Second Skimmed Milk Powder* test, after the cases in which it was respectively introduced and clarified.

Zuckerfabrik Schöppenstedt v _Council_ (Case 5/71) [1971] ECR 975

In *Schöppenstedt* (*Cases and Materials* (7.1)), a number of German sugar producers alleged that a Regulation imposing minimum and maximum prices for raw sugar was, in its detail, discriminatory. The Court of Justice refused to award damages on the ground that the Community could not incur liability for legislative action involving economic policy unless there had been:

(a) a sufficiently flagrant violation;

(b) of a superior rule of law;

(c) for the protection of the individual.

For this instance, the Court of Justice held that the alleged differences in the system were not discriminatory, and therefore that there had not been a 'sufficiently flagrant violation' of the principle of non-discrimination.

***Bayerische HNL Vermehrungsbetriebe GmbH & Co KG and others* v *Council and Commission* (Cases 83 etc./76) [1978] ECR 1209**

The Court of Justice confirmed the test laid down in *Schöppenstedt* in *Bayerische* (*Cases and Materials* (7.1)), commonly referred to as the *Second Skimmed Milk Powder* case, a Regulation provided for the compulsory purchase of skimmed milk powder for use in animal feedstuffs in order to reduce Community milk stocks. Poultry producers claimed damages against the Community for the increased price of animal feed. The Court of Justice had already accepted, in other cases referred under Article 234 EC, that the Regulation was void, because it discriminated between different agricultural sectors (against poultry producers for the benefit of the dairy industry) and was out of proportion to the achievement of a reduction in milk stocks.

? QUESTION 7.3

In the light of the *Schöppenstedt* test, do you think that the producers in the *Second Skimmed Milk Powder* case succeeded?

The Court of Justice effectively repeated the *Schöppenstedt* test, substituting the words 'sufficiently serious breach' for 'sufficiently flagrant violation'. However, it refused to award damages to the producers on the grounds that it was essential for the Community to have a wide discretion in adopting economic legislation. The Community should not be hindered, in making economic policy, by the prospect of continual applications for damages.

The key elements of the *Schöppenstedt* test will now be examined in greater detail.

7.3.2.1 A superior rule of law for the protection of individuals

Superior rules of law have been taken to include those general principles of law discussed in 3.5.4 and 6.8.3.

In *Sofrimport* v *Commission* (see 6.5.2), which concerned the prohibition of import licences in respect of Chilean apples, the Court of Justice gave damages for breach of the legitimate expectation of importers that goods in transit would be protected against the sudden introduction of such a prohibition.

In *Dumortier Frères* the Court of Justice ruled that the principle of equality 'occupies a particularly important place among the rules of Community law intended to protect the interests of the individual'.

In the *Second Skimmed Milk Powder* case, the Court of Justice ruled that the Regulation requiring the compulsory purchase of Community stocks of skimmed milk powder was in breach (albeit not a flagrant breach) of the principle of non-discrimination and that it was 'impossible to disregard the importance of this prohibition on discrimination in the system of the Treaty'.

In an Article 234 (ex 177) EC ruling concerning the same Regulation (*Bela-Mühle* v *Grows-Farm* (Case 114/76) [1977] ECR 1211), the Court of Justice had ruled that the measure was void not only because it was discriminatory, but also because it was out of all proportion to the end to be achieved.

In *CNTA* v *Commission* (Case 74/74) [1975] ECR 533, a Regulation abolished, without warning, compensation for the effect of exchange rate fluctuations on trade in colza and rape seeds. The Court of Justice awarded damages in respect of transactions which had already been entered into at the date of abolition of the compensation scheme, and for which export licences fixing the amount of compensation in advance had already been obtained. It stated that, in respect of such transactions, there was a legitimate expectation that the compensation would not be withdrawn.

In addition to these general principles, Treaty Articles will generally constitute superior rules of law, but this is not always the case. For example, in *Kind* v *EEC* (Case 106/81) [1982] ECR 2885, Kind alleged that a Community export levy on meat was in breach of Article 253 (ex 190) EC, which required the reasons for a measure to be given. His claim for damages was rejected because a failure to state the reasons for a measure did not amount to a manifest and grave disregard of the limits on the Community's powers.

Not only must the rule of law infringed be a superior one, it must also be for the protection of individuals. The case of *Kampffmeyer and others* v *Commission* (Cases 5, 7, & 13–24/66) [1967] ECR 245 involved similar facts to those of *Toepfer* (see 6.5.2). The Commission had upheld a wrongful refusal by Germany to allow the applicants to import maize at a time when large profits could be made because of the zero levy imposed by a Regulation.

In *Kampffmeyer*, the Regulation establishing levies on maize also provided that the Commission must investigate protective measures imposed by the Member States. The Court of Justice ruled that in failing to investigate fully, the Commission had infringed a rule of law which was for the protection of individuals. The fact that the interests protected were of a general nature (free trade, support for the relevant markets and the establishment of a single market), did not preclude their protection from being for the ultimate protection of individuals.

7.3.2.2 A sufficiently serious breach

The Court of Justice stated that the institution concerned must have 'manifestly and gravely disregarded the limits on the exercise of its powers'. In its application of this test to the facts, the Court of Justice indicated that both the unlawfulness of the act, and the nature of its effect, must be considered. In this case, the measure in question affected a wide range of traders, so that its impact on any particular undertaking was less evident; and the effect of the measure on the price of feed was relatively small in comparison to the price increases resulting from other factors. The effect of the action was therefore within the inherent economic risks of that business sector and the Community could not be said to have manifestly and gravely exceeded the limits on its powers.

Dumortier Frères SA and others v Council and Commission (Cases 64 & 113/76) [1979] ECR 3091

Dumortier Frères (*Cases and Materials* (7.1)) involved a Regulation under which production refunds in respect of maize grits were abolished while those for maize starch were not. Both products were used in brewing and in baking, and were in direct competition with each other. The Court of Justice concluded that the Community had manifestly and gravely disregarded the limits on its powers by withdrawing refunds from the production of maize grits, but not from the production of maize starch, which was a competing product.

The Court of Justice ruled that the disregard of the principle of non-discrimination was manifest, and grave, because the damage went beyond the bounds of the inherent economic risks and the Council had ignored the advice of the Commission to reintroduce the refunds.

In *Mulder I* and *Von Deetzen* (see 7.3.1.1), the exclusion of certain producers from the milk quota system was held to be invalid. When a subsequent Regulation allocated to such producers quotas which were less generous than those given to other producers, this too was held to be invalid on the ground that it was discriminatory (*Spagl* v *Hauptzollamt Rosenheim* (Case C-189/89) [1990] ECR I-4539) and *Pastätter* v *Haupzollamt Bad Reichenhall* (Case C-217/89) [1990] ECR I-4585).

As outlined above, in *Mulder II*, the Court of Justice granted damages in respect of the original exclusion. However, it declined to do so in respect of the discriminatory quotas.

? QUESTION 7.4

Bearing in mind the requirement that the Community's wrongful action must have been manifest and grave, why do you think that the Court of Justice in *Mulder* came to this decision about damages?

In excluding the producers completely, the Commission had seriously breached the principles of non-discrimination and legitimate expectation but in simply granting them lower quotas than other producers, the infringement of those principles was not manifest or grave.

In *G. R. Amylum NV and Tunnel Refineries Limited* v *Council and Commission* (Cases 116 & 124/77) [1979] ECR 3497 and *Koninklijke Scholten Honig NV* v *Council and Commission* (Case 43/77) [1979] ECR 3583

In this case (*Cases and Materials* (7.1)), a number of isoglucose producers brought actions for damages in respect of certain production levies on isoglucose which the Court of Justice, in *RSH and Tunnel Refineries* v *Commission and Council* (Joined Cases 103 & 145/77) [1978] ECR 2037 had ruled to be invalid. As outlined in 6.6.1, there were only three or four isoglucose producers in the Community, and other potential producers would not be in a position to enter the market for at least two years. The effect of the levies was clearly serious, given that one producer had been forced to close down its isoglucose business altogether.

The Court of Justice refused to award damages, despite the factors referred to above. It stated that the Community would be liable only if its errors were so grave that its conduct could be said to be 'verging on the arbitrary' and this was not so in the present case. This appears to be an additional test, since the Community's wrongful act in this instance was both manifest and grave.

QUESTION 7.5

In the light of what you have read so far, what would you expect the decision of the Court of Justice to have been in this case?

In *Roquette Frères SA* v *French Customs Administration* (Case 145/79) [1980] ECR 2917 the Court of Justice had declared invalid a Regulation which provided for compensation to be given, or levies imposed, on agricultural imports and exports, in order to compensate fully for the effect of exchange rate fluctuations. In *Roquette Frères* v *Commission* (Case 20/88) [1989] ECR 1553, Roquette Frères claimed damages for the effects of the Regulation.

QUESTION 7.6

Do you consider this to have been an appropriate case for the award of damages against the Community?

You might have concluded that if the case of the producers in *Amylum* was not considered to be sufficiently meritorious for an award of damaes, then the case of these applicants would certainly not be. Indeed, despite its ruling that the Regulation was invalid, the Court of Justice refused to award damages to Roquette. It stated that the applicant's loss had been caused by the use of an incorrect basis for calculation but that this was merely a 'technical error' by the Commission, and did not amount to a manifest and grave disregard of its powers.

It can therefore be concluded that liability will exist only if the Community has obviously, and to a serious extent, disregarded the limits on its discretion, as evidenced by effects on the producers which go substantially beyond the normal risks of the economic sector in question. However, if the Community has little or no discretion in the relevant area, any infringement of Community law will be regarded as sufficiently serious: *Commission* v *Fresh Marine Company A/S* (Case C-472/00) [2003] ECR I-7541.

7.3.4 Wrongful acts: Administrative acts

Although the *Second Skimmed Milk Powder* test was expressed as applying only to general legislative acts of an economic nature, it may be that this reflected the fact that all Community legislation at that time was of an economic nature. Indeed, the only acts excluded from the test were administrative acts. As Community powers are extended beyond economic matters, it remains to be seen whether the test will be applied to general legislative measures other than those which involve choices of economic policy. In any event, it is clear that the test will not be applied to purely administrative measures.

Where the act complained of is an administrative measure (and, possibly, where it is a general, but non-economic legislative measure), the applicant need prove only the general principles outlined in *Alfons Lütticke* v *Commission* (Case 4/69) [1971] ECR 325, namely damage, a wrongful act and causation. No further conditions attach to the nature of the wrongful act. In other words, it need not also amount to a sufficiently serious breach of a superior rule of law. The test is therefore more straightforward, and generally easier for an applicant to fulfil, than that applicable to general economic legislative measures.

This simpler test was applied in *Adams* (see 7.3.1.2), where the wrongful acts in question were not general legislative acts, but the negligent acts of the Commission in revealing sensitive documents and failing to warn Adams. Adams therefore needed to prove only that the acts were wrongful, and not that they constituted a serious breach of a rule of law for the protection of individuals.

However, the Court of Justice has been as unwilling to impose liability on the Community for non-legislative acts, as it has been to impose liability for economic measures. In *Adams*, as we have seen, a wide definition of contributory negligence was applied so as to limit the liability of the Community.

An administrative issue was also considered in *Cato* v *Commission* (Case C-55/90) [1992] ECR I-2533. Cato had failed to qualify for compensation (in respect of a decommissioned fishing vessel) under a scheme which the UK had introduced pursuant to a Directive. He applied for damages under Article 288 (ex 215) EC on the basis that the UK scheme was in fact contrary to the Directive, and that the Commission had therefore not acted wrongfully in approving the scheme. The Court of Justice ruled that on the facts, the scheme did not contravene the Directive. The Court was therefore not obliged to address the possibility that Community approval of a **wrongful** implementing measure could in itself be wrongful, and render the Community liable in damages. However, it seems unlikely that the Court would find the Community liable in such circumstances. First, the Community has limited resources available for such supervision. Second, subsequent to the judgment in *Cato*, the Court of Justice has ruled that individuals may seek redress from a Member State where its defective implementation (or non-implementation) is the cause of the applicant's losses (see 7.4).

7.3.5 Wrongful acts: acts by Community servants

Article 288 (ex 215) EC provides that the Community must make good any damage caused, not only by its institutions, but also by its servants in the performance of their duties. Although the *Second Skimmed Milk Powder* test is inapplicable here, since individuals are not directly responsible for general legislative measures, the Court of Justice has adopted a strict approach to the causation element of the 'general principles' in order to limit the likelihood of the Community being liable.

In *Sayag* v *Leduc* (Case 9/69) [1969] ECR 329, Leduc was injured in a road accident caused by a Euratom official, Sayag, who was driving his private car in performance of his official duties. Sayag alleged that any liability in damages lay with his employer, Euratom, rather than himself, under a provision of the Euratom Treaty which was equivalent to Article 288 (ex 215) EC. The Court of Justice held that Euratom was not liable because the wrongful act by its servant had not been committed 'in the performance of his duties'. The Community could be liable only for acts of its servants which were a necessary extension of the tasks of its institutions. Therefore 'in the performance of his duties' in this context must be limited to occasions when the Community would be unable to fulfil its tasks unless Sayag used his private car. This test seems unduly restrictive, and would fix liability on Euratom only in the event that no official car or public transport was available to Sayag to reach his destination, and that his doing so was essential to the work of the Community.

7.3.6 Causation

The applicant must prove that the wrongful act actually led to his loss. The Court of Justice will not simply assume causation after a wrongful act by the Community, and loss to the applicant, have been proved.

Although the French farmers in *GAEC* v *Council and Commission* (see 7.3.1) produced statistics to prove their losses in respect of beef and veal, they failed to show causation because there was evidence that French prices for these products had fallen prior to the German subsidy becoming effective.

The test is a strict one, as can be seen from *Dumortier Frères* (see 7.3.2.2). The maize grits producers claimed compensation under Article 288 (ex 215) EC for:

(a) the loss of refunds prior to this date;

(b) lost sales;

(c) the resulting factory closures by two producers and bankruptcy of one.

The Court of Justice ruled that damages should be awarded only in respect of the lost refunds. First, the reduction in sales could not be attributed to the withdrawal of the refunds, since the producers had not chosen to pass on the loss of refunds in increased prices. Secondly, even if the abolition of refunds had exacerbated the problems of certain producers, the factory closures and bankruptcy were not a sufficiently direct result of the abolition to render the Community liable. There was no obligation to make good every unfortunate consequence, however remote, of unlawful legislation.

It can be observed from this case that not only must causation be proved, but that causation must be sufficiently direct. A further illustration of this point is provided by *Kampffmeyer* v *Commission* (Cases 5, 7, & 13–24/66 [1967] ECR 245), where the alleged damage had been caused by the Commission's approval of a German ban on maize importers. Only those importers which had concluded contracts prior to the refusal of licences were awarded damages. Of these, those which had chosen to fulfil their contracts were awarded damages in respect of the higher levies which they had had to pay in order to do so. Those which had chosen to repudiate their contracts were awarded damages in respect of penalties payable for breach of contract.

The Court of Justice ruled that the expected profit was of a purely speculative nature and therefore damages should be limited to an amount equivalent to 10% of the sums which the importers would have paid by way of levy if they had carried out the contracts.

7.3.7 The relationship between Article 288 EC and other actions

The success of an action under Article 288 (ex 215) EC is independent of any other action (for instance, under Articles 230, 234, or 241 (ex 173, 177, or 184) EC), so that the fact that there has been no other action or that such an action has been unsuccessful is irrelevant. Indeed, Article 233 (ex 176) specifically provides that where an act of an institution is annulled, the obligations imposed on that institution as a result do not affect any liability it might also incur in damages.

In the case of *Krohn and Co. Import–Export (GmbH and Co. KG)* v *Commission* (Case 175/84) [1986] ECR 753, the Commission had authorized the German authorities to refuse to grant an import licence to Krohn for Thai manioc. Krohn brought an action for damages after it had become time barred from bringing an Article 230 (ex 173) EC action. The Court of Justice held that an action under Article 288 (ex 215) EC was admissible on the grounds that it was an independent action with a particular purpose. The fact that the time limit for an Article 230 (ex 173) EC action had passed, and that the measure had thereby become definitive, was irrelevant.

In Case 4/69 *Alfons Lütticke* (7.3) the Court of Justice stated that 'The action for damages provided for by . . . Article 288 (ex 215) was established by the Treaty as an independent form of action with a particular purpose to fulfil'.

Despite the fact that an Article 288 (ex 215) EC action is self-contained, it is common for a measure which is the subject of Article 288 (ex 215) EC proceedings to have been annulled under Article 230 (ex 173) EC or declared invalid under Article 234 (ex 177) EC. For example, the 'isoglucose cases' referred to above (see 7.3.2.2) had been preceded by an unsuccessful action under Article 230 (ex 173) EC and a successful action under Article 234 (ex 177) EC. In *Sofrimport* (see 6.5.2), the applicants successfully requested in the same action both the annulment of a Regulation and damages in respect of the losses caused to them.

7.3.8 Time limits

Under Article 43 of the Statute of the Court of Justice, an applicant has five years from the event giving rise to the claim in which to bring an action. However, this period does not start to run until the damage has materalized and will be suspended by any other Court of Justice proceedings.

In *Saint and Archer* v *Council and Commission* (Case T-554/93) [1997] ECR II-563, a case involving similar facts to those of *Mulder I* and *II* , the Court ruled that where damage was not caused instantaneously but continued for a period, entitlement to compensation related to successive periods starting each day when damage occurred. There was therefore a separate time limit for damage claims for each day when it was impossible to deliver milk and so the time limit only excluded damage incurred on days preceding the date of action by more than five years.

7.4 Member State liability

There is no provision in the EC Treaty for Member States to be liable in damages for their breaches of Community law. However, the Court of Justice has established that such liability does exist—the conditions governing such liability are not uniform, but depend on the nature of the breach of law. There are two sets of conditions; each governing different types of breach. These will be examined in turn.

7.4.1 *Francovich* liability

***Francovich and Others* v *Italy* (Cases C-6/90 & C-9/90) [1991] ECR I-5357**

In *Francovich* (*Cases and Materials* (7.2.1)), Francovich was owed wages by his employer, a company which had become insolvent. Under Italian law, Francovich had no remedy. However, under a Directive which Italy had failed to transpose, the State was required to set up a scheme under which employees of insolvent companies would receive at least some of their outstanding wages.

The Court of Justice ruled that the Directive was not sufficiently precise to have direct effect. It could not be indirectly effective because there was no relevant Italian legislation in accordance with which it could fall to be construed. The Court of Justice ruled instead that the Italian State could be liable in damages. It gave two reasons for the imposition of liability on Member States. First, the full effectiveness of Community law would be impaired if individuals could not obtain redress directly from a State which was responsible for a breach of Community law that had caused them loss. Secondly, Article 10 (ex 5) EC obliged Member States to take all measures to ensure that they fulfilled their Treaty obligations, and this included making good the consequences of a breach of these obligations.

The Court of Justice restricted Member State liability for failure to implement a Directive to situations where three conditions were fulfilled:

(a) The result prescribed by the Directive must involve the grant of rights to individuals.

(b) The content of those rights must be clear from the Directive.

(c) There must be a causal link between the breach of the State's obligation and the damage suffered by the individual.

In this case, the Directive gave employees the right to be paid their wages and it was clear from the Directive that these were to be paid in full up to a certain time. However, the Directive only applied to employees whose employer had been made subject to specified types of insolvency proceedings. Under Italian law, Francovich's employer could not be subjected to such proceedings, and so in the later case of *Francovich* v *Italian Republic* (Case C-479/93) [1993] ECR I-3843 (*Francovich II*), the Court of Justice ruled that Francovich was not covered by the protection of the Directive. Italy's failure to implement the Directive by setting up an appropriate scheme had therefore not caused Francovich loss.

From the judgment in *Francovich* (and in later cases on Member State liability—see below), it appears that the Court of Justice will only consider Member State liability where direct and indirect effect cannot provide a remedy.

? QUESTION 7.7

Look back at 4.3.2 and 4.4.3. Do you agree with this approach? Should this remedy be used in preference to direct and indirect effect, or only where those doctrines are inapplicable?

The basic requirement for liability is that there has been a breach of Community law which has caused loss to the applicant. Beyond this, as the Court stated in *Francovich*, 'the conditions under which that liability gives rise to a right to reparation depend on the nature of the breach of Community law giving rise to the loss and damage'. In other words, further conditions may attach to liability, depending on the type of wrongful act. Where the wrongful act consists of a failure to transpose a Directive, as in *Francovich*, the applicant must show that the Directive would have conferred clear rights on him. This is part of causation.

If a Member State's wrongful act consists of something other than the failure to transpose a Directive, the *Francovich* conditions will not apply. However, the conditions in *Brasserie du Pêcheur SA* v *Germany and R* v *Secretary of State for Transport ex parte Factortame* (Factortame III) (Joined Cases C-46 & C-48/90) [1996] ECR I-1209 (see 7.4.2) which are slightly different, may apply. In *Dillenkofer and others* v *Germany* (Joined Cases C-178 and 179/94 & C-188 to 190/94) [1996] ECR I-4845, a case involving the total non-transposition of a Directive, the Court of Justice applied the *Francovich* conditions but also attempted to reconcile them with the *Factortame III* conditions.

7.4.2 *Factortame III* liability

After the judgment in *Francovich*, it was unclear whether Member States would incur liability in damages for any other sort of breach of Community law and, if so, what sort of breaches and under what conditions. In *Brasserie du Pêcheur SA* v *Germany* and *R* v *Secretary of State for Transport ex parte Factortame ('Factortame III')* (Joined Cases C-46 and C-48/93) [1996] ECR I-1029 (*Cases and Materials* (7.2.2) the Court held that the principle of Member State liability applied where a State had enacted legislation which was contrary to Community law, but under conditions different to those laid down in *Francovich*.

? EXERCISE 7.2

We have already looked at other aspects of the *Factortame* litigation (see 3.3.2.2 and 5.5.2.1). Try to summarize in writing the facts giving rise to the litigation and the judgments prior to this particular ruling. This will help you to understand the nature of the claim for damages. (If in doubt, see 3.3.2.2 above.)

Brasserie du Pêcheur SA v Germany and R v Secretary of State for Transport ex parte Factortame ('Factortame III') (Joined Cases C-46 & 48/93) [1996] ECR I-1029

In *Brasserie du Pêcheur* (*Cases and Materials* (7.2.2), the Court of Justice considered together claims for damages by a French brewery against the German government, and by Spanish fishermen against the UK government, in respect of national legislation which conflicted with Community law. Factortame and other Spanish fishermen claimed damages from the UK government after the Merchant Shipping Act 1988, which had made it unlawful for them to fish in UK waters, was declared by the Court of Justice to be contrary to Community law. They alleged, in particular, that this was contrary to Article 52 (now Article 43) EC which gave Member State nationals the right to establish themselves in another Member State as self-employed persons, and to set up and manage undertakings. Their action for damages was joined by the Court with that of Brasserie du Pêcheur, a French brewery. It claimed damages from the German government after the prohibition on its export from France imposed by Germany was declared by the Court of Justice to be contrary to Community law.

The Court of Justice held that the UK government could be sued for damages for its breach of Community law in enacting the invalid Act.

In *Factortame III* the Court restated the principles of State liability which it had outlined in *Francovich*. It stated that although the Treaty did not expressly provide for Member State liability in damages, such liability must be possible in order to ensure the full effectiveness of Community law and as part of the duty of Member States under Article 5 to fulfil their Treaty obligations. Indeed, the Court considered that this reasoning applied even more strongly in the present case, which involved rights upon which individuals were entitled to rely in national courts, than in *Francovich*, in which the rights infringed were not enforceable in the national courts.

As to the conditions under which Member State liability would arise, the Court reasoned that these must be similar to those laid down in Article 288 (ex 215) EC of the Treaty under which the Community institutions could incur liability for breach of Community law. Put simply, Article 288 (ex 215) EC imposes liability where there is a wrongful act, damage to the applicant and causation. In addition, if the allegedly wrongful act is a piece of legislation over which the institution has been given a wide degree of discretion (which the Court assumed to be the case in both *BT* (see below) and *Factortame III*), a further test, known as the *Schöppenstedt* test, applies.

In *Factortame III* the Court of Justice reformulated this test and ruled that where the Member State acts pursuant to a wide discretion, the State will be liable for its breach of Community law if:

(a) the breach infringes a rule of law intended to confer rights on individuals;

(b) the breach is sufficiently serious;

(c) there is a direct causal link between the breach of the State's obligation and the damage to the applicant.

7.4.2.1 Infringement of a rule of law intended to confer rights on individuals

The Court of Justice appears to have accepted that almost any rule of law breached is a law intended to confer rights on individuals, since in none of the cases on Member State liability so far decided has the Court found that this condition is not satisfied.

In *Factortame III* the Court of Justice accepted that Article 43 (ex 52) EC, which provides that Member State nationals may move to another Member State as self-employed persons or in order to manage a business, confers rights on individuals which national courts must protect.

7.4.2.2 Sufficiently serious breach

The Court of Justice stated in *Factortame III* that a breach of Community law would be sufficiently serious if the Member State had 'manifestly and gravely disregarded the limits on its discretion'. it might be expected that, in line with the Article 288 EC jurisprudence, the number of applicants in *Factortame III* would have been taken as an indication that the breach was not manifest, since it affected a wide range of persons. However, in dealing with the liability of the Member State in *Factortame III*, the Court made no mention of the numbers of those potentially affected by the measure, even though there were ninety-seven applicants in that case.

Instead, in determining whether this was so, the Court set out a number of factors which could be taken into account.

The factors which the Court suggested could be taken into account were:

(a) the clarity and precision of the rule breached;

(b) the extent of any discretion left to the Member State;

(c) whether the breach was intentional or involuntary;

(d) whether the error of law was excusable or inexcusable;

(e) whether the position taken by a Community institution had contributed towards the Member State's action;

(f) the adoption or retention of practices contrary to Community law.

There is potential overlap between these factors. For example, an error of law might be considered excusable if the rule of law breached is extremely unclear.

? QUESTION 7.8

What other information do you think you might need in order to assess whether the error of law was excusable? (If you have difficulty in answering this question, think about the sources you might consult in order to try to understand a piece of legislation.)

Whether an error of law is excusable or inexcusable will turn largely on the clarity of that law, as mentioned above, and also on the existence of any judgments of the Court of Justice on the meaning of the particular law. For example, in *BT* (see below), the Court of Justice ruled that the UK's error of law was excusable because the law in question was unclear, and there had been no previous rulings as to its meaning.

In applying these factors in *Factortame III*, the Court of Justice ruled that regard should be had, *inter alia*, to the common fisheries policy, the fact that proceedings before the Court of Justice had indicated that the Act was likely to be found invalid, the fact that the Commission had warned the UK that its actions could be contrary to Community law, and the allegation by one of the claimants that the UK had delayed complying with the ruling from the Court of Justice in *Commission* v *UK* (Case C-246/89) [1989] ECR I-3125, that parts of the Merchant Shipping Act 1988 were unlawful. These factors made the Member State's breach of the Community law all the more blatant, and therefore all the more 'manifest'. In fact, the Court indicated that one of these factors—the alleged failure of the UK to comply immediately with a judgment of the Court of Justice—was so serious that, if proved, it would automatically constitute a 'sufficiently serious breach' without any need to consider the factors set out above for determining the existence of such a breach.

***R* v *Ministry of Agriculture, Fisheries and Food ex parte Hedley Lomas* (Case C-5/94) [1996] ECR I-2553**

This approach has been taken by the Court of Justice in another case: that of *Hedley Lomas* (*Cases and Materials* (7.2.2)) which involved a breach by the UK of Article 28 (ex 30) EC on the free movement of goods. The UK refused to grant export licences for live animals to Spain on the ground that Spanish slaughterhouses were not complying with Directive 74/577 on the stunning of animals before slaughter. Hedley Lomas, a sheep exporter, sought damages from the British government.

The Court of Justice held that the UK government could be liable in damages. The Court applied the *Factortame III* test but ruled that the Member State had no discretion as to whether to comply with Article 28 (ex 30) EC, and so any infringement of it must be a sufficiently serious breach. The UK was therefore liable in damages to Hedley Lomas.

This judgment has been criticized as going beyond *Factortame III*. In *Factortame III* the Court of Justice referred to a breach of law—the failure to comply with a judgment by it—over which the Member State clearly had no discretion. After all, Member States cannot choose whether to comply with judgments of the Court of Justice; they are under a strict duty to do so. However, Member States do effectively have a discretion over the implementation of Article 28 (ex 30) EC, because they can restrict the free movement of goods if one of the exceptions contained in Article 30 (ex 36) EC applies. In *Hedley Lomas*, the UK had argued that one of these exceptions did indeed apply. Admittedly the Court did not accept this argument, but it seems a little unjust for the Court then to rule that since the UK had been wrong about the application of Article 30 (ex 36) EC, it had had no discretion and therefore must be guilty of a sufficiently serious breach. After all, the UK could not have known that its interpretation of Article 30 (ex 36) EC would be adjudged to be incorrect until the Court of Justice gave judgment.

A further criticism which may be levied at the whole idea of according to certain breaches the automatic status of a 'sufficiently serious breach', is that the main element of the *Factortame III* test—and the feature which distinguishes it from *Francovich*—is the very examination of **whether** there has been a sufficiently serious breach, and yet the Court appear to be prepared to omit that examination on a rather arbitrary basis.

Perhaps the best approach is to treat this possibility as a rather anomalous exception to the general application of the *Factortame III* test, and to concentrate on understanding and applying *Factortame III* and the following case , namely *BT* .

***R* v *HM Treasury ex parte British Telecommunications plc* (Case C-392/93) [1996] ECR I-1631**

In *BT* (*Cases and Materials* (7.2.2)), the Court of Justice held that there was no sufficiently serious breach because the interpretation of the Directive on which the flawed implementing measures were based was reasonable in the circumstances. There was no appropriate case law for the UK to consult, and the Commission had not raised the matter when the UK adopted the implementation measures. The UK did not, therefore, incur liability in damages. BT brought proceedings claiming that the UK had incorrectly implemented Directive 90/531 on procurement procedures for organizations operating in the telecommunications sector. The national court referred to the Court of Justice a number of questions on the interpretation of the Directive and on the rules for Member State liability. It was held, inter alia, that the UK government was not liable in damages.

The Court of Justice came to a similar conclusion in *Denkavit International BV and VITIC Amsterdam BV and Voormeer BV* v *Bundesamt für Finanzamt* (Cases C-283, C-291, and C-292/94) [1996] ECR I-5063. In that case the German government had failed to implement correctly a Directive on the taxation of parent and subsidiary companies. The Court ruled that the Member State was not liable in damages for this breach of Community law because the rule breached was not clear and precise. Almost all Member States had adopted the same, incorrect interpretation as Germany, and there had been no case law from the Court of Justice as to how this Directive was to be interpreted.

In *R* v *Secretary of State for the Home Department ex parte Gallagher* [1996] 2 CMLR 951, the Court of Appeal applied the *Factortame III* test to the UK's failure, in the form of the Prevention of Terrorism (Temporary Provisions) Act 1989, to transpose correctly a Directive on the free movement of persons. It ruled that the UK's breach of Community law was not sufficiently serious because persons subject to the Act were not 'obviously worse off' as a result of that breach, and the Commission had not objected to the Act when notified of it.

***Köbler* v *Austria* (Case C-224/01) [2003] ECR 1–10239**

In *Köbler* v *Austria* (*Cases and Materials* (7.2.2)) Köbler alleged that an increment payable to university professors with 15 years' service in Austrian universities was discriminatory because no account was taken of periods of service in universities in other Member States. The *Verwaltungsgerichtshof* (Supreme Administrative Court) dismissed his claim. Köbler then brought an action for damages against the State on the grounds that the judgment infringed Community law. The Court of Justice ruled that the breach of law was insufficiently serious. Community law did not expressly state whether discrimination such as that at issue could be justified, this point had not been dealt with previously by the Court, and the answer was not obvious. In reaching an incorrect conclusion and refusing to make a reference, the national court had not committed a sufficiently serious breach of Article 39 EC and Regulation 1612/68 on the free movement of workers.

7.4.2.3 Causation of damage

The issue of causation is for the national court to determine on the facts (see *Francovich II* above).

In *Gallagher* (see 7.4.2.2), the Court of Appeal ruled that in addition to the fact that the breach of Community law was not sufficiently serious, there was no causal link between the breach and Gallagher's losses. Even if the UK had properly implemented the Directive, Gallagher could properly—and indeed would—have been excluded from the UK. Gallagher was arrested, and excluded from the UK under the Prevention of Terrorism (Temporary

Provisions) Act 1989 on the ground that he had been involved in acts of terrorism. On a preliminary ruling the Court of Justice ruled that the procedure under the Act was contrary to Directive 64/221 on the free movement of persons. Gallagher sought damages from the UK government. It was held that the UK government was not liable in damages because there was nothing whatever to suggest that the Home Secretary's decision would have been any different had he awaited receipt of Gallagher's representations, and the report of the nominated person before making an exclusion order.

An important point to note is that in *Factortame III* the Court of Justice stated that in determining the extent of the loss or damage for which compensation would be awarded, the national court should have regard to 'whether the injured person showed reasonable diligence in order to avoid the loss or damage or limit its extent and whether, in particular, he availed himself in time of all the legal remedies available to him'. So not only must the applicant mitigate his loss, but this mitigation could include the duty to take legal action against other parties. Therefore, an applicant who has a potential claim against another defendant, by relying on the direct or indirect effect of Community law against that defendant, will be expected to pursue that claim before making a claim against the State for damages. If he does not do so, then the amount of damages payable by the State may be reduced.

7.4.2.4 Application of the *Factortame III* test

In *Factortame III* itself, the test was applied where the Member State had enacted legislation which was contrary to Community law. Subsequently, the Court of Justice has applied the *Factortame III* test to a number of other types of breach. In *R* v *HM Treasury ex parte British Telecommunications plc* (Case C-392/93) [1996] ECR I-1631 (*Cases and Materials* (7.2.2)) it applied it to a Member State's failure to implement a Directive correctly. In *R* v *Ministry of Agriculture, Fisheries and Food ex parte Hedley Lomas* (Case C-5/94) [1996] ECR I-2553 (*Cases and Materials* (7.2.2)) it applied it to a Member State's administrative policy which contravened Community law. In *Köbler* v *Austria* (Case C-224/101 [2003] ECR 1-10239 (*Cases and Materials* (7.2.2)) it applied the test to a court of last instance's incorrect ruling on Community law after a failure to make a preliminary reference (see 5.6).

7.5 Concurrent liability

Cases of potentially concurrent liability arise where a Community measure implemented by a Member State has adversely affected the applicant. In *Kampffmeyer* v *Commission* (see 7.3.2.1 and 7.3.6) in the Court of Justice ruled that the applicants must exhaust their rights of action against the national authorities before the Court of Justice would issue final judgment as to any Community liability in damages. In its reasoning, it stated that, 'It is necessary to avoid the applicants being insufficiently or excessively compensated for the same damage by the different assessment of two different courts applying different rules of law.' However, as the Court made clear in *Krohn* v *Commission* (see 7.3.7) this applies only where the rights of action against the national authorities will effectively compensate the applicant. Since the annulment by the German authorities of their decision to refuse Krohn an import licence would not adequately compensate it, the Court accepted that an action under Article 288 (ex 215)EC should not be made dependent on exhausting national remedies.

CONCLUSIONS

In order for the Community to be liable in damages, an applicant must at the very least prove that it has suffered loss, and that this is due to a wrongful act by the Community. In addition, where the alleged wrongful act consists of a general legislative measure, the applicant must also prove that there has been a sufficiently serious breach of a superior rule of law for the protection of the individual. The Court of Justice has applied these tests strictly and as a result there has been no opening of the floodgates to Community liability. There are, of course, policy reasons behind Article 288 (ex 215) EC and the related jurisprudence. The Community institutions should not be hampered in their legislative activities by the threat of mass litigation, and indeed the cost to the Community—and therefore ultimately to the citizens of the Member States—would be too great. Whether a correct balance has been achieved between policy decisions and providing justice for those affected by Community measures is a matter of opinion, but this question has assumed greater importance with the extension of Member State liability on principles similar to Article 288 (ex 215) EC.

There are now two tests for Member State liability: the *Francovich* test, applicable where a Member State has completely failed to transpose a Directive; and the *Factortame III* test, applicable in a number of other situations. While this is perhaps the simplest way to approach the issue, the Court of Justice has attempted to reconcile the two tests.

In *Dillenkofer and others* v *Germany*, Dillenkofer and others purchased package holidays. Following the insolvency of their tour operators, some never received their holiday and others had to return home at their own expense. They did not receive reimbursement of their expenses, and they therefore brought actions for compensation against the German government. The German government had failed to implement by the deadline date the Package Travel Directive which provided for a fund to be set up to compensate or repatriate travellers in the event of the insolvency of their tour operator. It was held that the German government could be liable in damages.

In *Dillenkofer* the Court observed that the two sets of conditions were in fact very similar. Both required: (a) a sufficiently serious breach of (b) a rule of law which gave rights to individuals which (c) caused loss to the applicant. The key difference, according to the Court, was that instead of expressly requiring a sufficiently serious breach, the *Francovich* test required the total non-transposition of a Directive, which is, of course, simply a clear example of a sufficiently serious breach.

Despite the Court's comments in *Dillenkofer and others* v *Germany* it did not attempt to produce or apply a combined test on the facts, and so it seems that it will be acceptable to go on applying the *Francovich* or *Factortame III* tests separately, as applicable.

As a final point it is also worth noting that although the rules on Member State liability have been based on those applicable to Community liability, the two areas of law are quite separate. For example, in imposing liability on Community institutions the Court of Justice has interpreted 'manifest' as meaning that the measure affected a limited and ascertainable group (see, e.g., *Dumortier Frères*).

SUMMARY

EC liability

- Article 288 EC provides that the Community is liable for the acts of its institutions and servants according to the general principles common to the laws of the Member States. In *Alfons Lütticke* the Court of Justice interpreted this as requiring proof of a **wrongful act** which has **caused damage** to the applicant. Where the wrongful act consists of a general legislative measure, the EC will only incur liability if it has committed a sufficiently serious breach of a rule of law for the protection of individuals (*Schöppenstedt, Second Skimmed Milk*).

Member State liability

- From **Article 288 EC** the Court of Justice has developed the principle that Member States are liable in damages for their breaches of EC law.
- Where the Member State's breach consists of a **failure to transpose a Directive**, it will incur liability if the Directive gave rights to individuals, the content of those rights is clear from the Directive and the State's breach cased loss to the applicant (*Francovich*).
- Where the Member State's breach consists of **enacting legislation which is contrary to EC law** (*Factortame III*), **incorrect transposition of a Directive** (*BT*), **administrative practices** which are contrary to EC law (*Hedley Lomas*), or a **wrongful judgment on Community law** after a refusal to make a reference under Article 234 EC by a court from which there is no appeal under national law (*Köbler*), the State will incur liability if the breach is of a rule of law for the protection of individuals and is sufficiently serious (*Factortame III*).

CHAPTER 7: ASSESSMENT EXERCISE

(a) Critically discuss the development by the Court of Justice of the 'general principles' referred to in Article 288 (ex 215) EC.

(b) Briefly compare the jurisprudence of the Community Courts regarding the action for damages under Article 288 EC with that regarding Member State liability.

See *Cases and Materials* (7.4) for a specimen answer.

FURTHER READING

Deards E. (1997). 'Curiouser and Curiouser? The Development of Member State liability in the Court of Justice' 3 *EPL* 117.

Durdan, A. (1976). 'Restitution or Damages: National Court or European Court?' 1 *EL Rev* 431.

Van Gerven, W. (1995). 'Taking Article 215 EC Seriously' in New Directions in European Public Law, Oxford: Hart Publishing.

Van Gerven, W. (1994). 'Non contractual Liability of Member States, Institutions and Individuals for Breaches of Community Law with a View to a Common Law for Europe', *Maastricht Journal of European and Comparative Law* 11(1) 6.

8 Free movement of goods

8.1 OBJECTIVES

By the end of this chapter you should be able to:

1 Explain the principle of free movement of goods and its significance within the Community internal market

2 Discuss and analyse the key Treaty provisions relating to the elimination of customs duties, charges having equivalent effect, discriminatory internal taxation, quantitative restrictions, and measures having equivalent effect

3 Discuss the nature and scope of the exceptions to the principle of free movement of goods

8.2 Introduction

Article 14 (ex 7a) EC underlines the importance of the principle of freedom of movement of goods as one of the four freedoms of the Community, defining the internal market as 'an area without internal frontiers in which the free movement of goods, persons, services, and capital is ensured in accordance with the provisions of this Treaty'. This element of the internal market has as its objective the removal of all obstacles to the free circulation of goods between Member States.

Such obstacles can take a number of different forms, ranging from customs duties charged on goods as they cross internal frontiers to 'hidden barriers' to trade, which are more difficult to identify. This chapter will consider the nature of these obstacles to interstate trade, at the Treaty provisions which prohibit them, and at the exceptions to the principle of free movement of goods.

8.3 Overview of the Community free movement provisions

8.3.1 The customs union

The European Community is a customs union, incorporating both internal and external elements. The internal element is a free trade area, in which goods move freely between Member

States, and which is a key component of the Community internal market. This chapter deals with the internal aspects of the free movement of goods provisions. Although the external elements of the customs union fall outside the scope of this book, it is nevertheless useful to begin with an understanding of the basic principles underlying the overarching concept of the customs union.

EXERCISE 8.1

Turn back to Chapter 1. Write down the two essential features of a customs union.

In simple terms, a customs union consists of an agreement between countries to operate:

(a) a free trade area in which goods pass between them without restrictions, together with

(b) a system whereby a common level of duty is charged on goods coming into the free trade area from non-member countries.

In the European Community these are sometimes referred to, respectively, as the internal and external aspects of the customs union. Non-Member States are termed 'third countries'.

8.3.2 Articles 23 (ex 9) and 24 (ex 10) EC

Article 23 (ex 9) sets out the Treaty definition of the Community customs union:

THE EC TREATY

Article 23 (ex 9)

1. The Community shall be based upon a customs union which shall cover all trade in goods and which shall involve the prohibition between Member States of customs duties on imports and exports and of all charges having equivalent effect, and the adoption of a common customs tariff in their relations with third countries.
2. The provisions of Article 25 and of Chapter 2 of this Title shall apply to products originating in Member States and to products coming from third countries which are in free circulation in Member States.

Article 24 (ex 10)

1. Products coming from a third country shall be considered to be in free circulation in a Member State if the import formalities have been complied with and any customs duties or charges having equivalent effect which are payable have been levied in that Member State, and if they have not benefited from a total or partial drawback of such duties or charges.

? **QUESTION** 8.1

(a) What does Article 23 (ex 9) prohibit between Member States?

(b) What term is used for the common level of duty charged upon goods from third countries?

The internal aspect of the customs union is the prohibition between Member States of 'customs duties on imports and exports and of all charges having equivalent effect'. This prohibition, which will be examined in detail in this chapter, applies to goods passing across any of the Community's internal borders.

When goods enter the Community from third countries, the Common Customs Tariff (known as the CCT) applies. The CCT, sometimes referred to as the Common External Tariff (CET), is governed by Articles 26 and 27 (ex 28 and 29) EC. These articles provide for the fixing of Common Customs Tariff duties by the Council, acting on a proposal from the Commission.

? QUESTION 8.2

What do you think is meant by products in 'free circulation' referred to in Articles 23 and 24 (ex 9 and 10)?

The Treaty makes no distinction between 'products' and 'goods'. When goods have passed into the Community from third countries, the necessary formalities have been complied with and the appropriate duties paid, those goods are allowed to move freely between Member States without any further restriction. Such goods, like goods which originate in the Community itself, are said to be in free circulation.

This chapter is concerned with the free movement of goods in the Community internal market, between Member States.

8.3.3 Application of the principle of free movement of goods in the internal market

The principle of free movement of goods in the internal market is one of the fundamental freedoms upon which the Community is founded. Any measure adopted by a Member State government, be it protectionist or not, which sets up a barrier to the free movement of goods will be condemned by the Court of Justice unless it falls within the scope of the exceptions provided for in the Treaty and in the case law of the Court. As will be seen later in this chapter, those exceptions are interpreted restrictively.

? QUESTION 8.3

What do you think the term 'protectionist' means?

Although the Community comprises an internal market in which goods can circulate freely without restrictions, it is important to understand that Member States may seek to protect their own domestic products from competition from similar products crossing the Community's internal borders. A measure such as the imposition of a customs duty, which has the effect of raising the price of imported goods and making them less competitive, is protectionist if it is designed for that purpose. If a charge is imposed on imported goods for other reasons, that charge is not protectionist.

***Sociaal Fonds voor de Diamantarbeiders* v *Chougol Diamond Co* (Cases 2 & 3/69) [1969] ECR 211**

A good example of a non-protectionist measure can be found in *Diamonds* (*Cases and Materials* (8.1.1)). A Belgian law imposed a levy on imported diamonds, the proceeds of which were paid into a social security fund for workers in the Belgian diamond industry. The charge was not protectionist, for Belgium did not produce diamonds.

The Court of Justice found that the distinction between protectionist and non-protectionist measures was irrelevant. The Court would examine the effect of the measure, not its purpose, and would find any charge which hindered interstate trade to be in violation of the principle of the free movement of goods.

8.3.4. Outline of the Treaty Articles providing for the free movement of goods

THE EC TREATY

Article 3 (ex 3)

For the purposes set out in Article 2, the activities of the Community shall include, as provided in this Treaty and in accordance with the timetable set out therein:

(a) the prohibition, as between Member States, of customs duties and quantitative restrictions on the import and export of goods, and of all other measures having equivalent effect.

Article 14 (ex 7a)

1. The Community shall adopt measures with the aim of progressively establishing the internal market over a period expiring on 31 December 1992. . . .
2. The internal market shall comprise an area without internal frontiers in which the free movement of goods, persons, services, and capital is ensured in accordance with the provisions of this Treaty.

Articles 23–31 (ex 9–37), headed 'Free Movement of Goods', deal with the internal and external aspects of the customs union. In addition, there are other provisions contained in the competition and taxation section of the Treaty (Articles 81–97 (ex 85–102) which are aimed at the elimination of measures restricting trade between Member States or threatening or distorting competition within the common market. Although the main competition rules (Articles 81 and 82 (ex 85 and 86)) are considered separately in **Chapters 13** and **14**, it should be noted that, together with the rules relating to free movement of goods, they constitute the means to achieve a unified Community internal market which functions efficiently and which allows the Community to compete effectively on a global scale.

The following Treaty Articles contain detailed rules concerning the free movement of goods:

- Article 25 (ex 12): the prohibition of customs duties and charges having equivalent effect to customs duties.
- Article 90 (ex 95): the prohibition of discriminatory taxation.

- Articles 28 and 29 (ex 30 and 31): the prohibition of quantitative restrictions and all measures having equivalent effect.

This chapter will consider in detail Articles 25, 90, 28, and 30 (ex 12, 95, 30, and 36).

8.4 Article 25 (ex 12): the prohibition of customs duties and charges having equivalent effect ('tariff' barriers to trade)

THE EC TREATY

Article 25 (ex 12)

Customs duties on imports and exports and charges having equivalent effect shall be prohibited between Member States. This prohibition shall also apply to customs duties of a fiscal nature.

? **QUESTION** 8.4

What does Article 25 EC prohibit?

Article 25 (ex 12) prohibits customs duties on imports and exports and charges having equivalent effect.

8.4.1 Direct effect of Article 25 (ex 12)

EXERCISE 8.2

Turn back to **Chapter 4** and remind yourself of the meaning of 'direct effect'. Write down the name of the case in which the Court of Justice established that Treaty Articles are capable of direct effect. Which Treaty Article did this case concern?

Van Gend en Loos **v** ***Nederlandse Administratie der Belastingen*** **(Case 26/62) [1963] ECR 1**

The Court first considered the direct effect of Treaty Articles in a case concerning Article 25 (ex 12) and the increase in a customs duty imposed by the Dutch authorities on imports of ureaformaldehyde. In this case, not only did the Court establish that Treaty Articles are capable of direct effect, it also held that Article 25 (ex 12) itself is directly effective.

8.4.2 Meaning of 'customs duties' and 'charges having equivalent effect'

QUESTION 8.5

How would you define a 'customs duty'? Glance back at **Chapter 1** for guidance.

The term 'customs duty' combines two elements, referred to by the Court of Justice in *Sociaal Fonds voor de Diamantarbeiders* v *Chougol Diamond Co* (Cases 2 & 3/69) [1969] ECR 211 (*Cases and Materials* (**8.1.1**)). First, it comprises a pecuniary charge on goods, which might be referred to as a 'tax' or a 'levy'. Secondly, that charge is imposed by reason of the fact that the goods cross a frontier.

A prohibition on customs duties alone would leave the way open for Member States to justify charges on imported goods which are not customs duties in the strict sense. Consequently, the Article 25 (ex 12) prohibition also encompasses charges of equivalent effect to customs duties. The Court of Justice has used the concept of 'charges having equivalent effect' (or, as they are commonly referred to, CEEs) to give broad scope to Article 25 (ex 12). This is illustrated by *Commission* v *Luxembourg and Belgium (Gingerbread)* (Cases 2 & 3/62) [1962] ECR 425 (*Cases and Materials* (8.2.1)) and *Sociaal Fonds voor de Diamantarbeiders* v *Chougol Diamond Co* (Cases 2 & 3/69) [1969] ECR 211 (*Cases and Materials* (8.1.1)).

EXERCISE 8.3

Consider the extracts from *Gingerbread* and *Diamonds* (*Cases and Materials* (8.2.1 and 8.1.1)). In each case, what was the purpose of the charge imposed and how did the Court of Justice view the charge? Make a written note of your answers.

Commision v *Luxembourg and Belgium* (*Gingerbread*) (Cases 2 & 3/62) [1962] ECR 425, Court of Justice

Gingerbread concerned the increase of a charge imposed by Luxembourg and Belgium on imports of gingerbread. The two governments claimed that the reason for the charge was to offset the effects on the price of domestically produced gingerbread of an internal tax on rye, one of the ingredients of gingerbread. The Court of Justice held that the purpose of Article 25 (ex 12) was to prohibit not only those measures which are clearly customs duties in the strict sense but also other measures, perhaps called by different names or with non-protectionist purposes, which nonetheless have a similar effect to customs duties. Such measures constitute CEEs. The charge on imported gingerbread resulted in the alteration of the price of the product, thereby reducing its competitiveness in the Luxembourg and Belgian markets and affecting trade between Member States.

***Diamonds* cont.**

The Court of Justice reached similar conclusions in *Diamonds*. Here, a charge on diamonds imported into Belgium was held to be a CEE, despite the fact that the charge was not protectionist (Belgium did not produce diamonds), and was levied to provide social security benefits for Belgian diamond workers.

CEEs have been defined by the Court of Justice in similar terms in a number of cases. The definition in *Diamonds* is typical:

***Diamonds* cont.**

'. . . any pecuniary charge, however small and whatever its designation and mode of application, which is imposed unilaterally on domestic or foreign goods by reason of the fact that they cross a frontier, and which is not a customs duty in the strict sense, constitutes a charge having equivalent effect . . . even if it is not imposed for the benefit of the State, is not discriminatory or protective in effect or if the product on which the charge is imposed is not in competition with any domestic product.'

8.4.3 Charges for services rendered

Member States have frequently argued that charges imposed upon imported goods escape the Article 25 (ex 12) prohibition because they are levied for services rendered to the importer.

? QUESTION 8.6

What kinds of service might be relevant here?

The argument has been put forward in relation to a wide range of 'services', including, for instance, health and safety or quality control inspection services, a statistical service provided for importers and exporters and storage services.

The Court of Justice has made clear that a charge for services will fall outside the Article 25 (ex 12) prohibition only if those services are of direct benefit to the goods or traders and if the charge is proportionate to the services provided.

***Commission* v *Italy* (*Statistical levy*) (Case 24/68) [1969] ECR 193, Court of Justice**

Statistical Levy (*Cases and Materials* (8.2.2)) concerned a levy imposed by the Italian government on all imports and exports. The proceeds were used to compile statistics which, it was claimed, were of benefit to traders.

The Court of Justice held that any advantage gained by importers and exporters from the statistical information was so general and difficult to assess that the charge did not constitute consideration for 'a specific benefit actually conferred' and consequently comprised a CEE.

Commission v _Belgium (Customs Warehouses)_ (Case 132/82) [1983] ECR 1649

In *Customs warehouses* (*Cases and Materials* (8.2.2)), the Court of Justice considered charges levied for the storage of imported goods. Community rules enabled imported goods to be given customs clearance at public warehouses located in the interior of a Member State, rather than at the point of entry on to the territory. Belgium imposed storage charges upon goods deposited at such warehouses to await customs formalities. Charges were also imposed on imported goods which were simply presented at the warehouses for customs clearance. It was held that when a charge is payable exclusively on imported products, it is a CEE unless it is 'the consideration for a service actually rendered to the importer'. Moreover, that charge must be 'of an amount commensurate with that service'—it must not exceed the cost of the service or the value to the trader of the service provided.

A number of cases have dealt with charges imposed in relation to health controls:

Rewe-Zentralfinanz v _Direktor der Landwirtschaftskammer Westfalen-Lippe_ (Case 39/73) [1973] ECR 1039 (charges for plant health inspections)

(**_Commission_ v _Belgium (Health Inspection Service)_ (Case 314/82) [1984] ECR 1543**
(fees for the inspection of poultry-meat)

Commission v _Germany_ (Case 18/87) [1988] ECR 5427 (fee for veterinary inspections carried out on live animals on their importation into Germany).

In the first two of these judgments, the Court of Justice held that charges for inspections imposed in the 'general interest' (the plant health inspections case), and those which are expressly permitted under Community law (*Commission* v *Belgium*, inspections of poultry meat) do not, for those reasons alone, escape classification as CEEs. However, charges for inspections which are mandatory under Community law are lawful, provided the charges do not exceed the cost of the inspection, and the inspections themselves are obligatory and uniform for all the products concerned in the Community, are provided in the general interest of the Community and promote the free movement of goods (*Commission* v *Germany*, veterinary inspections).

The principle that charges for inspections mandated by Community law are not CEEs was first established in *Bauhuis* v *Netherlands State* (Case 46/76) [1977] ECR 5. The same principle applies to charges for inspections that are mandatory under international agreements entered into by the Community (*Commission* v *Netherlands* (Case 89/76) [1977] ECR 1355).

8.5 Article 90 (ex 95): the prohibition of discriminatory taxation

8.5.1 The scope of Article 90 (ex 95)

It has already been noted that customs duties and CEEs are charges imposed on goods by reason of the fact that they cross a frontier. Such charges are an obstacle to free movement because they increase the trader's costs. They also affect the competitive structure of the internal market by raising the price of products to the consumer. Similar effects may flow from the imposition of taxes on imported goods. The kinds of tax referred to here are those which are levied by Member States not by reason of importation but as part of a system of internal taxation. They have been defined by the Court of Justice as charges relating to 'a general system of internal dues applied systematically and in accordance with the same criteria to domestic products and imported products alike' (*Denkavit* v *France* (Case 132/78) [1979] ECR 1923).

Where a charge is classified as a genuine internal tax, rather than a customs duty or a CEE, Article 25 (ex 12) does not apply. Internal taxes fall within the scope of Article 90 (ex 95). This provision does not prevent Member States from setting up taxation systems which they consider suitable in relation to particular products but prohibits the discriminatory taxation of imported and domestically produced goods. The distinction between a charge having equivalent effect and a genuine tax is important. If a charge is classified in the former category, it will be unlawful under Article 25 (ex 12). If on the other hand it is a genuine tax, it will be permissible provided that it complies with Article 90 (ex 95).

8.5.2 The Article 90 (ex 95) prohibition

THE EC TREATY

Article 90 (ex 95)

No Member State shall impose, directly or indirectly, on the products of other Member States any internal taxation of any kind in excess of that imposed directly or indirectly on similar domestic products.

Furthermore, no Member State shall impose on the products of other Member States any internal taxation of such a nature as to afford indirect protection to other products.

EXERCISE 8.4

Compare the two paragraphs of Article 90 (ex 95). You will see that both relate to the imposition by a Member State of internal taxes on the products of other Member States. How do the provisions of the two paragraphs differ? Make a brief note of your answer.

Clearly, there would be little point in eliminating cross-frontier charges if Member States were still able to obstruct interstate trade and reduce competition from imported products by means of discriminatory internal taxation. Under Article 90 (ex 95), internal taxation is discriminatory and therefore prohibited where:

- taxes imposed on imported goods exceed those levied on similar domestic products (Article 90(1)) or where
- taxes imposed on imported goods give indirect protection to other products (Article 90(2)).

The Court of Justice declared Article 90 (ex 95) to be directly effective in a case concerning a German tax on imported powdered milk (*Lütticke (Alfons) GmbH* v *Hauptzollamt Saarlouis* (Case 57/65) [1966] ECR 205).

8.5.3 Article 90(1) (ex 95(1)): the prohibition of discriminatory taxation of similar products

The first paragraph of Article 90 (ex 95) prohibits internal taxation of any kind on imports in excess of that imposed directly or indirectly on similar domestic products. In *Molkerei-Zentrale* v *Hauptzollamt Paderborn* (Case 28/67) [1968] ECR 143 the Court of Justice indicated that the words 'directly or indirectly' must be widely construed to include taxes imposed on the domestic products at various stages of the manufacturing and marketing process.

Discrimination may result not from different rates of taxation but from other connected factors, such as the rules relating to tax collection, or the basis of assessment.

Commission v _Ireland (Excise Payments)_ (Case 55/79) [1980] ECR 481

Excise Payments (*Cases and Materials* (8.3.1)) concerned Irish rules relating to tax collection. These allowed domestic producers of spirits, beer and wine deferment of tax payments beyond the date on which the products were put on the market, whilst importers had to pay tax on importation of the products. Although the level of tax was equal, the discrimination arising from the system of collection amounted to a breach of Article 90 (ex 95).

Outokumpu Oy (Case C-213/96) [1998] ECR I-1777

In a later case, the Court of Justice considered rules relating to the basis of tax assessment. Finnish legislation subjected domestically produced electricity to tax rates that varied according to the method of production but subjected imported electricity to a flat-rate tax. That rate was higher than the lowest tax charged on domestically produced electricity.

The Court of Justice held that Article 90 (ex 95) does not preclude the rate of an internal tax on electricity from varying according to the way in which the electricity is produced, on the basis of environmental considerations. However, Article 90 (ex 95) is infringed where the tax on the imported product and that on the similar domestic product are calculated in a different manner and on the basis of different criteria which lead, if only in certain cases, to higher taxation being imposed on the imported product.

Tax measures which openly treat domestic goods and imports differently are directly discriminatory. Because this form of discrimination is easily identifiable, Member States are generally careful to avoid it, though some cases of direct discrimination have reached the Court of Justice. A good example is to be found in *Lütticke (Alfons) GmbH* v *Hauptzollamt Saarlouis*. A taxation system which appears neutral but has the effect of discriminating against imported products is indirectly discriminatory and will infringe Article 90 (ex 95).

Humblot v _Directeur des Services Fiscaux_ (Case 112/84) [1985] ECR 1367

This situation occurred in *Humblot* (*Cases and Materials* (8.3.1)), in which the applicant claimed a refund of the tax he had paid on his 36 horsepower car. The French system of annual motor vehicle taxation imposed a lower rate of tax on cars of 16 horsepower or less than on cars over 16 horsepower. France did not produce high-powered cars falling into the higher tax category.

Consequently, whilst the two-tier taxation system did not directly discriminate between imported and domestically produced vehicles, the effect of the tax system was to place imported cars at a competitive disadvantage.

The Court of Justice held that the system breached Article 90(ex 95).

8.5.4 Objective justification

A Member State may seek to counter an allegation of indirectly discriminatory taxation by providing an objective justification for the rule in question. Two notable cases concerned apparently indirectly discriminatory internal taxation imposed, respectively, by France and Italy.

***Commission* v *France* (Case 196/85) [1987] ECR 1597**

Under the French General Tax Code, the duty payable on natural sweet wines was less than that imposed upon other kinds of liqueur and similar wines. The Commission claimed that this scheme of taxation was discriminatory because its effect was to favour the domestic products (*Cases and Materials* (8.3.2)).

***Chemial Farmaceutici SpA* v *DAF SpA* (Case 140/79) [1981] ECR 1**

In Italy, synthetic alcohol attracted a higher rate of taxation than alcohol produced by fermentation, despite the fact that the two products had identical uses. Italy produced very little synthetic alcohol (*Cases and Materials* (8.3.2)).

 **EXERCISE** 8.5 

Look at the extracts from these two cases.

How did the respective governments seek to justify the allegedly indirectly discriminatory taxation?

***Commission* v *France* and *Chemical Farmaceutici* cont.**

The French government sought to justify the scheme of taxation of wines on the basis of its regional policy, designed to encourage production in poor growing areas. The Italian government maintained that the higher taxation of synthetic alcohol constituted a 'legitimate choice of economic policy' aimed to encourage production of alcohol by fermentation rather than from ethylene, a raw material which, it was said, should be reserved for more important economic uses.

Although in both cases the Court of Justice rejected allegations that the effect of the taxation systems was to favour the domestic products over imports, the judgments suggest a willingness to allow legitimate policy objectives, which are compatible with Community aims, to preclude too strict an application of Article 90 (ex 95).

This point was further illustrated in *Commission* v *Greece* (Case C-132/88) [1990] ECR I-1567, in which the Court of Justice considered an environmental justification for a car taxation system providing for differential rates of taxation according to power rating. Here, the Court held that such a taxation system would escape the Article 90 prohibition, notwithstanding that all cars in the highest tax band were imported, provided that no discriminatory effect disadvantaging imports could be established.

8.5.5 'Similar' products

Since the first paragraph of Article 90 (ex 95) applies to 'similar' products, the issue of similarity between non-identical products which are subject to different rates of taxation has been the focus of much of the caselaw. This issue was prominent in a number of cases concerning alcoholic beverages. Here, the Commission challenged taxation regulations which, it alleged, favoured domestic alcoholic products. In these, as in other cases, Member States have sought to defend their taxation systems by arguing that the products concerned were not sufficiently similar to bring the first paragraph of Article 90 (ex 95) into play. Such claims were presented, for instance, in *John Walker*.

? QUESTION 8.7

What factors did the Court of Justice examine in *John Walker* (*Cases and Materials* (8.3.3)), when it was considering the question of product similarity? What conclusion did the Court reach?

***John Walker* v *Ministeriet for Skatter* (Case 243/84) [1986] ECR 875**

Under Danish legislation, Scotch whisky was taxed at a higher rate than fruit wine of the liqueur type. John Walker, a Scotch whisky producer, claimed that this taxation system infringed Article 90 (ex 95). The Court first examined the characteristics of the products—origin, method of manufacture, and organoleptic properties. It then went on to consider whether the products 'are capable of meeting the same needs from the point of view of the consumer'. The Court concluded that the products may not be regarded as similar products for the purposes of Article 90(1). (*Cases and Materials* (8.3.3)).

Here, and in other cases, the Court of Justice emphasized that the term 'similar products' should be interpreted widely to encompass similar characteristics and comparable use. These tests were also applied, for instance, in *Commission* v *France (French Taxation of Spirits)* (Case 168/78) [1980] ECR 347 in which the 'similarity' of non-fruit spirits (whisky, gin, and vodka) and fruit spirits (brandy, armagnac, and calvados) were examined.

8.5.6 'Indirect protection to other products'

As has been seen, the first paragraph of Article 90 (ex 95) prohibits the unequal taxation of similar products. The second paragraph of Article 90 (ex 95) prohibits internal taxation giving indirect protection to domestic products which, though they are not similar to the imported products, are nevertheless in competition with them. The Court of Justice's approach to the distinction between the two paragraphs of Article 90 (ex 95) can be traced through the series of alcohol cases referred to above. In the earlier judgments, the Court of Justice did not distinguish between the two paragraphs at all and treated the concepts of 'similar' and 'competing' products as interchangeable.

? QUESTION 8.8

What do you think was the problem with this approach?

The problem with the Court of Justice's approach was that it concealed the distinction between the different effects of breaches of the two paragraphs of Article 90 (ex 95). If goods are similar, Member States are required to equalize taxation. If they are merely in competition, Member States are only required to remove the competitive effect of the tax regulation. In one particularly difficult case, *Excise Duties on Wine* the nature of the products led the Court of Justice to treat the two paragraphs separately.

Commission* v *United Kingdom (Excise Duties on Wine)
(Case 170/78) [1980] ECR 417, [1983] ECR 2265

In the UK, wine was taxed at a higher rate than beer. Since the two products were clearly not similar within the terms of Article 90(1) (ex 95(1)), the Commission relied on Article 90(2) (ex 95(2)), claiming that wine and beer were in competition and that the higher tax on wine gave indirect protection to beer producers in the UK. Initially, the Court of Justice declined to deliver a final judgment, asking the parties to come back with further information regarding consumer prices and annual consumption of the two products. When judgment was finally delivered three years later, the Court based its examination on a comparison between beer and the cheaper varieties of wine. It concluded that the two beverages were 'capable of meeting identical needs' and so there was a degree of substitution between them. The Court considered not only current consumer preferences and purchasing habits but also possible future market developments which might place wine and beer in direct competition with each other. Taxation policy must not be allowed to 'crystallize' consumer habits by taxing one product more heavily than another. Also satisfied that the taxation system favoured the domestic product, the Court ruled that there was a breach of the second paragraph of Article 90 (ex 95). (*Cases and Materials* (8.3.4)).

8.6 Harmonization of taxation

The problems arising from discriminatory taxation could be solved by the harmonization of taxation between Member States. Although progress has been made in relation to the approximation of VAT, excise duty, and corporation tax regulation, Member States remain unwilling to transfer control to the Community in an area which symbolizes national sovereignty.

8.7 Articles 28 and 29: the prohibition of quantitative restrictions and all measures having equivalent effect ('non-tariff' barriers to trade)

So far, barriers to trade of a pecuniary nature have been considered—customs duties, charges having equivalent effect, and discriminatory taxes. These are comparatively easy to identify because they involve payments of money. There are other kinds of obstacle to the free movement of goods, 'non-tariff' barriers to trade, which are often more difficult to identify. These comprise physical and technical barriers to the free flow of goods between Member States. Articles 28 and 29 prohibit such barriers in relation to imports (Article 28) and exports (Article 29).

THE EC TREATY

Article 28 (ex 30)

Quantitative restrictions on imports and all measures having equivalent effect shall be prohibited between Member States.

Article 29 (ex 34)

Quantitative restrictions on exports and all measures having equivalent effect shall be prohibited between Member States.

This section will consider the most important of these provisions, Article 28 (ex 30).

QUESTION 8.9

Which two kinds of barrier to trade does Article 28 prohibit? Write down your answer.

Article 28 (ex 30) concerns restrictions on imports. It prohibits two kinds of barrier to trade:

- quantitative restrictions and
- all measures having equivalent effect.

The similar prohibition in Article 29 (ex 34) relates to exports.

Although Article 28 (ex 30) is addressed to Member States the Court of Justice has applied the Article widely to include measures adopted by public and semi-public bodies, such as the Royal Pharmaceutical Society (*R.* v *Royal Pharmaceutical Society of Great Britain* (Cases 266 and 267/87) [1989] ECR 1295 (*Cases and Materials* (8.7.3)) which have powers conferred on them by national legislation. Article 28 covers not only measures applied by a Member State to the whole of its territory, but also those applying to only part of its territory.

Ditlev Bluhme **(Case C-67/97 [1998] ECR 1-8033)**

This was confirmed by the Court of Justice in *Ditlev Bluhme*. Here it was held that a Danish prohibition on the keeping on the Danish island of Læsø of any species of bee other than the Læsø brown bee, effectively prohibiting the importation of other kinds of bee, constituted a measure having equivalent effect to a quantitative restriction.

One further key provision which should be mentioned at this point is Article 30 (ex 36). This Article allows national laws to restrict the free movement of goods on certain specified grounds. The Article 30 (ex 36) grounds of derogation from Articles 28 and 29 (ex 30 and 34) will be considered later in this chapter.

8.8 Quantitative restrictions on imports

Quantitative restrictions are measures which limit the import (or indeed the export) of goods by reference to amount or value. Quantitative restrictions on imports are prohibited by Article 28 (ex 30).

> **? QUESTION 8.10**
>
> What form do you think a quantitative restriction might take?

Quantitative restrictions can take different forms but are generally easily recognized. They have been defined by the Court of Justice as 'measures which amount to a total or partial restraint of . . . imports, exports, or goods in transit' (*Geddo* v *Ente Nazionale Risi* (Case 2/73) [1973] ECR 865), in other words import (or export) quotas and bans. For instance, in *R.* v *Henn and Darby* (Case 34/79) [1979] ECR 3795 (*Cases and Materials* (8.7.1)), a ban on the import of pornographic materials was held to amount to a quantitative restriction under Article 28 (ex 30). Quotas are limitations on imports or exports by quantity. They are sometimes concealed behind a licensing system under which certain importers are permitted to import a specified quantity of a product, determined according to value, weight, or another quantitative criterion.

8.9 Measures having equivalent effect to quantitative restrictions (MEQRs)

8.9.1 Scope of 'MEQR': Directive 70/50

The concept of measures having equivalent effect to quantitative restrictions has proved both more complex and more difficult to define than that of quantitative restrictions. Some guidance on the meaning of 'measures having equivalent effect to quantitative restrictions' (referred to in the rest of this chapter as MEQRs) is provided by secondary legislation, in the form of Directive 70/50.

Although Directive 70/50 was a transitional measure and is therefore no longer formally applicable, it indicates the Commission's view of the scope of MEQRs.

DIRECTIVE 70/50

Article 2

1. This Directive covers measures, other than those applicable equally to domestic or imported products, which hinder imports which could otherwise take place, including measures which make importation more difficult or costly than the disposal of domestic production.
2. In particular, it covers measures which make imports or the disposal, at any marketing stage, of imported products subject to a condition—other than a formality—which is required in respect of imported products only, or a condition differing from that required for domestic products and more difficult to satisfy. Equally, it covers, in particular, measures which favour domestic products or grant them a preference, other than an aid, to which conditions may or may not be attached.

Article 3

This Directive also covers measures governing the marketing of products which deal, in particular, with shape, size, weight, composition, presentation, identification, or putting up and which are equally applicable to domestic and imported products, where the restrictive effect of such measures on the free movement of goods exceeds the effects intrinsic to trade rules.

This is the case, in particular, where:

— the restrictive effects on the free movement of goods are out of proportion to their purpose;

— the same objective can be attained by other means which are less of a hindrance to trade.

? QUESTION 8.11

Can you identify the two categorie of measures to which Directive 70/50 refers? Make a written note.

Directive 70/50 divides MEQRs into two categories: measures which apply equally to domestic and imported products and measures other than those which apply equally to domestic and imported products. These are frequently referred to, respectively, as 'distinctly applicable measures' (they do not apply equally to, or make a distinction between, domestic and imported products) and 'indistinctly applicable measures' (they apply equally to, or make no distinction between, domestic and imported products). The importance of distinguishing between these two categories of MEQRs will emerge later in this chapter.

Directive 70/50 also provides examples of the kinds of measures which constitute MEQRs. Article 2 covers distinctly applicable measures which 'hinder imports which could otherwise take place, including measures which make importation more difficult or costly than the disposal of the domestic product' and provides an extensive non-exhaustive list of examples of such measures. These include, for instance, restrictions on the advertising of imported products, laying down less favourable prices for imported products, and subjecting imported products to controls that are stricter or not applied to the domestic product. Article 3 covers indistinctly applicable measures concerning the marketing of products, in particular those which deal with 'shape, size, weight, composition, presentation, identification, or putting up'.

? QUESTION 8.12

If a measure applies equally to the imported and the domestic product, how can it discriminate against imports and hinder trade between Member States, in breach of Article 28 (ex 30)?

Although indistinctly applicable measures appear not to discriminate against imports because they apply equally to imported and domestic products, they frequently have discriminatory effects, thereby restricting trade between Member States. *Walter Rau* illustrates this point:

***Walter Rau Lebensmittelwerke* v *de Smedt PvbA* (Case 261/81) [1982] ECR 3961**

A Belgian requirement that all margarine for retail sale, both imported and domestically produced, be in cube-shaped form or cube-shaped packaging did not overtly discriminate against imported margarine. However, the requirement was discriminatory in effect. In practice, imports of the product would become more costly, since importing producers would be obliged to adapt their packaging processes in order to comply with requirements which were not imposed upon them by their own national legislation. The issue of justification of the requirement on grounds of consumer protection is considered below (see 8.11.4) (*Cases and Materials* (8.4.1)).

Article 3 does however provide that the measures within its scope contravene Article 28 (ex 30) only 'where the restrictive effect of such measures on the free movement of goods exceeds the effects intrinsic to trade rules', that is 'where the restrictive effects on the free movement of goods are out of proportion to their purpose' or where 'the same objective can be attained by other means which are less of a hindrance to trade'. In other words, the measures are lawful provided they satisfy the principle of proportionality.

? QUESTION 8.13

Do you remember the meaning of 'proportionality'? Look back at **Chapter 3** to refresh your memory. Write down the meaning of the term in one sentence.

The principle of proportionality is one of the general principles of Community law. To be proportionate, a measure must be suitable for the purpose of achieving the desired objective and go no further than is necessary to achieve that objective. The importance of this principle to the rules governing the free movement of goods will become apparent presently.

8.9.2. Definition of 'MEQR': *Dassonville*

The Court of Justice, whilst it has occasionally referred to Directive 70/50 in considering whether a particular measure constitutes an MEQR, introduced its own definition in *Dassonville*.

***Procureur du Roi* v *Dassonville* (Case 8/74) [1974] ECR 837**

Criminal proceedings were instituted in Belgium against traders who had imported Scotch whisky from France without being in possession of the certificate of origin required by a Belgian provision for all imported goods bearing a designation of origin.

In considering whether this requirement constituted an MEQR, the Court of Justice formulated and applied its own definition of 'MEQR' and, in doing so, held that the national provision fell within that definition and constituted a breach of Article 28 (ex 30) (*Cases and Materials* (8.4.2)).

This definition, known as the '*Dassonville* formula', provides that:

> All trading rules enacted by Member States which are capable of hindering, directly or indirectly, actually or potentially, intra-Community trade are to be considered as measures having an effect equivalent to quantitative restrictions.

The scope of the formula is wide, since it covers those measures which, although they do not actually hinder trade between Member States, are capable of doing so. Unlike Directive 70/50, the formula does not distinguish between distinctly and indistinctly applicable measures but is concerned with the restrictive effects of a measure on inter-state trade rather than its form. However, in *Dassonville*, the Court did accept that 'reasonable' restraints may not be caught by Article 28 (ex 30). The further development of what has become known as the 'rule of reason' will be considered presently.

8.9.3 Examples of distinctly applicable measures caught by Article 28 (ex 30)

The following cases provide examples of distinctly applicable measures which have been found by the Court of Justice to fall within Article 28 (ex 30).

EXERCISE 8.6

Read the extracts from the following cases in *Cases and Materials*. For each case, write down a short phrase which describes the relevant measure.

- *Rewe-Zentralfinanz* v *Landwirtschaftskammer Bonn* (Case 4/75) [1975] ECR 843 (*Cases and Materials* (8.4.3)) *(San Jose Scale)*.

- *Procureur du Roi* v *Dassonville* (Case 8/74) [1974] ECR 837 (*Cases and Materials* (8.4.2)).

- *Commission* v *Ireland ('Buy Irish' Campaign)* (Case 249/81) [1982] ECR 4005 (*Cases and Materials* (8.4.3))

A brief summary of each case can be found at the end of this section.

You may have written down something like this:

- *San Jose Scale*: plant health inspections applied by the West German authorities to imported but not domestically produced apples (note that the Court of Justice held the inspections to be justified in principle on health grounds under Article 30 (ex 36), considered below).

- *Dassonville*: a Belgian rule requiring the production of certificates of origin for imported goods bearing a designation of origin.
- *Buy Irish*: the introduction by the Irish government of a 'Buy Irish' campaign in order to promote Irish products to the disadvantage of imports.

***Rewe-Zentrolfinanz* v *Landwirtschaftskammer Bonn* (Case 4/75) [1975] ECR 843**

Germany carried out phytosanitary inspections on imported plant products, such as apples, to prevent the spread of a pest known as San Jose Scale. Similar domestic products were not subject to compulsory inspections before being distributed in Germany.

Applying Article 2 of Directive 70/50, the Court of Justice held that the inspections constituted MEQRs.

***Procurer du Roi* v *Dassonville* (Case 8/74) [1974] ECR 837**

Belgian rules required imported goods bearing a designation of origin to be accompanied by an official document issued by the state of origin certifying the origin of the goods. Criminal proceedings were instituted in Belgium against traders who had imported Scotch whisky from France without being in possession of the required certificate.

The Court of Justice formulated and applied its own definition of 'MEQR' and, in doing so, held that the national provision fell within that definition and constituted a breach of Article 28 (ex 30).

***Commission* v *Ireland* (Case 249/81) [1982] ECR 4005**

The Irish Government introduced a three-year, programme to help promote Irish products with the aim of achieving 'a switch from imports to Irish products equivalent to 3% of total consumer spending'. The two main elements of the campaign were widespread advertising of Irish products and the use of the 'Guaranteed Irish' symbol.

The Court of Justice upheld the Commission's claim that the campaign constituted an MEQR *('Buy Irish' Campaign).*

***Commission* v *Germany* (Case C-325/00) [2002] ECR 1–9977**

Similarly, the awarding of a 'quality label' by a German public body to finished products of a certain quality produced in Germany constituted an infringement of Article 28.

The Court of Justice held that a label of this kind, which was designed to promote the distribution of agricultural and food products made in Germany and which indicated the German origin of the products to which it was attached, was likely to encourage consumers to buy products carrying the label in preference to imported products. Thus, even though its use was optional, the label was, at least potentially, a hindrance to the free movement of goods.

It will be seen from all these cases that the national provisions constituted a hindrance or disincentive to the importer, either because they imposed conditions which were difficult or costly to satisfy and/or because they gave an advantage to the domestic product in the domestic market.

8.9.4 Examples of indistinctly applicable measures caught by Article 28 (ex 30)

The following cases provide examples of indistinctly applicable measures which have been found by the Court of Justice to fall within Article 28 (ex 30).

EXERCISE 8.7

Read the extracts from the following cases in *Cases and Materials*. For each case, write down a short phrase which describes the relevant measure.

- *Commission* v *United Kingdom (Origin Marking of Goods)* (Case 207/83) [1985] ECR 1202 (*Cases and Materials* (8.4.4)).
- *Walter Rau Lebensmittelwerke* v *de Smedt PvbA* (Case 261/81) [1982] ECR 3961 (*Cases and Materials* (8.4.1)).

A brief summary of each case can be found at the end of this section.

You may have written down something like this:

- *Origin Marking of Goods*: a UK requirement that certain goods offered for retail sale in the UK be marked with their country of origin.
- *Walter Rau*: a Belgian law requiring margarine for retail sale to be in cube-shaped form or packaging.

***Commission* v *United Kingdom* (Case 207/83) [1985] ECR 1202**

Under English legislation, certain categories of goods—clothing and textiles, domestic electrical appliances, footwear, and cutlery—could not be sold in the UK unless they were marked with or accompanied by an indication of origin. Although the requirement applied equally to imports and domestic products, the Court of Justice held that, in enabling consumers to distinguish between domestic and imported products, this allowed them to assert any prejudices they might have against foreign products. Consequently, the measure amounted to an MEQR *(Origin Marking of Goods)*.

> ***Walter Rau Lebensmittelwerke* v *de Smedt PvbA* (Case 261/81) [1982] ECR 3961**
>
> Belgium required all margarine for retail sale, both imported and domestically produced, to be in cube-shaped form or cube-shaped packaging. Although there was no distinction between imports and the domestic product, the practical effect of this requirement was to increase importers' costs. In order for the product to be sold lawfully in Belgium, importers would be obliged to adapt their packaging, in compliance with a requirement which was not imposed upon them by their own national legislation. The Court of Justice found that the measure constituted an MEQR.

8.10 Member States' obligation to ensure the free movement of goods

The Court of Justice has affirmed that, in addition to their duty to refrain from introducing measures restricting the free movement of goods, Member States are also under a positive obligation to take all necessary and proportionate steps to ensure the free movement of goods within their territory.

> ***Commission* v *France* (Case C-265/95) [1997] ECR 1-6959**
>
> *Commission* v *France* concerned a complaint by the Commission that for more than a decade, the French authorities had failed to prevent violent protests by French farmers directed against agricultural products being imported from other Member States. There had been interception of lorries, destruction of loads, violence against lorry drivers, threats against supermarkets selling produce from other Member States, and damage to goods on display in French shops. The Court of Justice held that, in failing to adopt adequate measures to prevent such acts, France was in breach of its obligations under Article 10 EC, which requires Member States to take all appropriate measures to ensure the fulfilment of the obligations arising out of the Treaty.

Susbequently, in *Schmidberger* v *Austria* (Case C-112/00) [2003] ECR I-5659, the Court of Justice held that the Austrian authorities' decision to permit a demonstration by environmental protesters, causing a 30-hour motorway closure, was an obstacle to free movement but was justified on the grounds of the ECHR fundamental rights to freedom of expression and assembly. The judgment is unclear as to whether these grounds are to be regarded as falling within the Article 30 derogation or the *Cassis* mandatory requirements, discussed below.

8.11 *Cassis de Dijon*: measures falling outside the scope of Article 28 (ex 30)

Rewe-Zentral AG v *Bundesmonopolverwaltung für Branntwein* (Case 120/78) [1979] ECR 649 (*Cases and Materials* (8.5)), otherwise known as *Cassis de Dijon* (because it concerned the blackcurrant liqueur 'cassis'), marks a very important stage in the development of the Court of Justice's jurisprudence on the free movement of goods. The decision builds upon the *Dassonville* judgment by developing the idea of 'reasonableness' introduced in that case and to which reference was made earlier.

***Rewe-Zentral AG* v *Bundesmonopolverwaltung für Branntwein* (Case 120/78) [1979] ECR 649**

In *Cassis de Dijon*, the applicant had been refused authorization to import a consignment of 'Cassis de Dijon' (blackcurrant liqueur) into Germany from France because the product did not meet German requirements. To be marketed lawfully in Germany, fruit liqueurs were required to have a minimum alcohol content of 25%. The alcohol content of 'Cassis de Dijon', which was freely marketed in France, was between 15% and 20%. The applicant claimed that the legislation constituted a measure having equivalent effect to a quantitative restriction on imports contrary to Article 28 (ex 30). In considering this claim, the Court of Justice applied the rule which has become known as the 'rule of reason' (*Cases and Materials* (8.5)).

8.11.1 The *Cassis* rule of reason

In *Cassis de Dijon*, the Court of Justice stated that:

***Cassis* cont.**

Obstacles to movement within the Community resulting from disparities between the national laws relating to the marketing of the products in question must be accepted insofar as those provisions may be recognized as being necessary in order to satisfy mandatory requirements relating in particular to the effectiveness of fiscal supervision, the protection of public health, the fairness of commercial transactions and the defence of the consumer.

This is often referred to as the *Cassis* 'rule of reason'. A paraphrase might help you to remember this important 'first *Cassis* principle': when the rule of reason is applied, certain measures within the *Dassonville* formula will not contravene Article 28 (ex 30) if they are necessary to protect 'mandatory requirements'.

Although the *Cassis* judgment does not state this in so many words, later case law indicates that the rule of reason applies only to measures which are formally non-discriminatory, in other words to indistinctly applicable measures. Distinctly applicable measures cannot be justified by mandatory requirements, though they may be considered under one of the derogations contained in Article 30 (ex 36) (to be considered presently).

***Commission* v *Ireland (Restrictions on Importation of Souvenirs)* (Case 113/80) [1981] ECR 1625**

Here the Court of Justice refused to apply *Cassis* principles to a distinctly applicable measure adopted by the Irish government allegedly in the interests of fair trading and to protect consumers, which required imported souvenirs depicting Irish motifs (such as shamrocks) to be marked 'foreign' or with their country of origin.

The Court further held that the Article 30 derogation did not apply, since neither the protection of the consumer nor the fairness of commercial transactions is included amongst the Article 30 exceptions. (*Cases and Materials* (8.5.1))

It should be emphasized that the rule of reason can only be applied in the absence of Community rules governing the interest concerned. If the Community has adopted harmonizing legislation in a particular area, Member States are not at liberty to apply their own additional requirements, unless that legislation expressly permits this.

8.11.2 The mandatory requirements

You should note the guidance given by the Court as to the meaning of 'mandatory requirements' within the rule of reason:

(a) effectiveness of fiscal supervision;

(b) protection of public health;

(c) fairness of commercial transactions; and

(d) defence of the consumer.

8.11.3 Extension of the mandatory requirements

There have been many cases in which Member States have sought to rely on one or more of the four mandatory requirements listed specifically in the *Cassis* judgment. In *Italy* v *Gilli and Andres* (Case 788/79) [1980] ECR 207, for example, Italy argued that its prohibition on the sale of vinegar not produced from wine was justified on grounds of public health and the protection of the consumer. Nonetheless, the Court of Justice has made clear that the list of mandatory requirements set out in the *Cassis* judgment is non-exhaustive and has extended the list in subsequent cases, to include further mandatory requirements.

EXERCISE 8.8

Read the extracts from the following cases in *Cases and Materials*. Make a note of the further mandatory requirements which the Court of Justice has added to those set out in *Cassis*:

- *Danish Bottles* (*Cases and Materials* (8.5.2)).
- *Oebel* (*Cases and Materials* (8.5.2)).
- *Cinéthèque* (*Cases and Materials* (8.5.2)).
- *Torfaen* (*Cases and Materials* (8.5.2)).

A brief summary of each case can be found at the end of this section.

The list of mandatory requirements originally set out in *Cassis* has been extended by the Court of Justice to include environmental protection (*Danish Bottles*), legitimate interests of social and economic policy (*Oebel*), the creation of cinematographic works (*Cinéthèque*) and 'national and regional sociocultural characteristics' (*Torfaen Borough Council*).

Commission v *Denmark* (Case 302/86) [1988] ECR 4607

Denmark introduced legislation for the protection of the environment. This required all containers for beer and soft drinks to be re-usable and subject to a deposit-and-return system. The legislation also provided that all containers must be approved by the National Agency for the Protection of the Environment but allowed drinks producers to use non-approved containers for quantities not exceeding 3,000 hectolitres a year and for the sale of imported drinks introduced to test the market in Denmark, provided a deposit-and-return system was set up.

The Court of Justice held that the protection of the environment is 'one of the Community's essential objectives', which may justify limitations on the free movement of goods *(Danish Bottles)*.

Oebel (Case 155/80) [1981] ECR 1993

German legislation prohibited night working in bakeries and night deliveries of bakery products. This, it was claimed, constituted a barrier to interstate trade with regard to products which had to be delivered in time for breakfast in neighbouring Member States. On the facts, the Court of Justice ruled that the prohibitions were compatible with Articles 28 (ex 30) and 29 (ex 34) because 'trade within the Community remains possible at all times' and it was consequently not necessary for the German Government to justify the legislation. However, the Court accepted that legitimate interests of economic and social policy, designed to improve the working conditions in a particular industry, could constitute a mandatory requirement.

Cinéthèque SA v *Fédération Nationale des Cinémas Françaises* (Cases 60 & 61/84) [1985] ECR 2605

Under French legislation, films could not be re-issued on video for sale or hire within a period of one year from cinema showing. Cinéthèque, which had offered for sale video recordings of a certain film within the stipulated period and whose recordings had been seized by the National Federation of French Cinemas, claimed that the legislation infringed the free movement provisions. The Court of Justice held that a national system for the protection of cinematographic works which, irrespective of their origin, gives priority, for a limited period, to the distribution of such works through the cinema, is justified.

Torfaen Borough Council v *B&Q plc* (Case 145/88) [1989] ECR 3851

B&Q claimed that s. 47 of the Shops Act 1950, which (with certain exceptions) prohibited Sunday trading in the UK, was a measure having equivalent effect to a quantitative restriction on imports within the meaning of Article 28 (ex 30) and that it was not justified under Article 30 (ex 36) or by virtue of any 'mandatory requirement'. Referring to its decision in *Oebel*, the Court of Justice held that the Sunday trading rules were justified on the ground that they were in accord with national or regional socio-cultural characteristics.

It is clear that the Court of Justice remains willing to continue considering further justifications for restrictions on the free movement of goods, thereby extending the mandatory requirements (or 'overriding requirements', as it has referred to them more recently), and that Member States will continue to present novel and interesting justifications. *Familiapress* is yet one more example.

***Vereinigte Familiapress Zeitungsverlags- und Vertriebs GmbH* v *Heinrich Bauer Verlag* (Case C-368/95) [1997] ECR I-3689**

The Court of Justice indicated that the maintenance of press diversity may constitute an 'overriding requirement' justifying a restriction on the free movement of goods. The reference from the Austrian court concerned national legislation prohibiting publishers from including prize competitions in their magazines. The Austrian government claimed that the measure was aimed to protect small publishers whose commercial survival was threatened because they could not afford to compete with large publishers offering big prizes. The Court held that, assuming that there was indeed a competitive relationship of this kind between small and large publishers, such a prohibition would not breach Article 28 (ex 30) provided that it was proportionate to the maintenance of press diversity and that that objective could not be achieved by less restrictive means.

8.11.4 Proportionality

You may have noticed that the extracts from the cases above and the brief summary of *Familiapress* refer to the principle of proportionality. The rule of reason requires that indistinctly applicable measures adopted to satisfy a mandatory requirement be proportionate. This means that measures must go no further than is necessary to protect the relevant interest—the protection of public health, the defence of the consumer or any other mandatory requirement.

? QUESTION 8.14 

How did the German government seek to justify its law on alcohol content in *Cassis* (*Cases and Materials* (8.5))?

***Cassis* cont.**

In *Cassis*, the German government argued that the measure was adopted in order to protect public health (low-alcohol spirits create a tolerance to alcohol and cause alcoholism) and the fairness of commercial transactions (the high rate of tax on high-alcohol drinks gave low-alcohol drinks a competitive advantage). The Court was unconvinced. Moreover, although the restriction allegedly fell within the mandatory requirements relating to public health and the fairness of commercial transactions, the German measure was not necessary to satisfy those requirements.

? QUESTION 8.15

What other means could the German government have used to achieve its stated objectives in relation to alcohol levels?

The government could have used other means which were less of a hindrance to trade, such as a requirement that products be labelled to indicate alcohol content. You have no doubt recognized the use of the word 'necessary' (meaning in this context 'no more than is necessary') as a reiteration of the proportionality principle.

For more examples of the proportionality principle in this context, consider *Walter Rau* (*Cases and Materials* (8.4.1)) and *Danish Bottles* (*Cases and Materials* (8.5.2)).

***Walter Rau Lebensmittelwerke* v de *Smedt PvbA* (Case 261/81) [1982] ECR 3961**

Belgian legislation prohibited the retailing of margarine which was not in cube-shaped form or packed in cube-shaped packaging. The Belgian Government maintained that this provision could not be classified as a measure having equivalent effect to a quantitative restriction and, even if it could be so classified, the provision was necessary for the protection of the consumer in order to prevent confusion between margarine and butter. The Court of Justice, having found that this provision was indeed an MEQR, turned to consider its justification by the Belgian Government. Whilst the Court accepted that, in principle, legislation designed to prevent confusion in the mind of the consumer is justified, legislation that prescribes a particular form of packaging goes further than is necessary to achieve that desired objective. Consumers may be protected just as effectively by other measures which are less of a hindrance to inter-state trade, such as a labelling requirement.

***Commission* v *Denmark* (Case 302/86) [1988] ECR 4607**

It will be recalled that in *Danish Bottles*, the Court of Justice accepted that the protection of the environment could constitute a justification for measures restricting the free movement of goods. In order to fall outside the scope of Article 28 (ex 30), such measures must comply with the principle of proportionality. The Court found the Danish deposit-and-return system for beer and soft drinks containers to be proportionate, since this was an indispensable element of a system intended to ensure the re-use of containers. By contrast, the restriction on the quantity of beer and soft drinks that could be marketed in non-approved containers was disproportionate to the objective pursued. Although only approved containers could be returned to any retailer, ensuring maximum rate of re-use, the re-use of non-approved containers could be achieved if they were returned to the retailer who sold the drinks. Consequently, a limitation on the use of non-approved containers went further than was necessary to protect the environment.

8.11.4 The principle of mutual recognition

The *Cassis* judgment established a further principle, known as the principle of 'mutual recognition': where goods have been lawfully produced and marketed in one Member State there is no reason why they should not be introduced into another Member State. The principle operates as a presumption which, because of the importance of the principle of free movement of goods, is not easily displaced. The presumption will be displaced if it can be shown that restrictive measures are necessary to satisfy mandatory requirements. For an illustration of the application of the principle of mutual recognition, look at Prantl (*Cases and Materials* (8.5.3)).

> ***Criminal proceedings against Karl Prantl*** **(Case 16/83) [1984] ECR 1299**
>
> An Italian national, Karl Prantl, imported into Germany Italian red wine bottled in 'Bocksbeutel' bottles. Such bottles, of a characteristic bulbous shape, were traditional to certain regions of both Italy and Germany. German legislation restricted the use of the 'Bocksbeutel' in Germany to wine produced in those German regions. Prantl was charged in criminal proceedings in Germany with making improper use of the 'Bocksbeutel'. The Court of Justice applied the principle of mutual recognition. It held that national legislation may not bar imports of wines from another Member State by reserving the right to use a particular shape of bottle to its own national product, where bottles of a similar shape were also used traditionally in the state of origin.

A further reference to this principle can be found, for instance, in *Walter Rau* (*Cases and Materials* (8.4.1)) (at paragraph 17).

8.12 Article 28 (ex 30) as a defence in national court proceedings

It is sometimes said that Article 28 (ex 30) may be used either as a 'sword' or a 'shield'. It is used as a 'sword' by the Commission in Article 226 (ex 169) enforcement proceedings where Member States have introduced unlawful restrictions, and was used, for instance, in *Commission* v *Ireland ('Buy Irish' Campaign)* (Case 249/81) [1982] ECR 4005 (*Cases and Materials* (8.4.3)) and *Commission* v *United Kingdom (Origin Marking of Goods)* (Case 207/83) [1985 ECR 1202 (*Cases and Materials* (8.4.4)).

As a 'shield', Article 28 (ex 30) has frequently been raised as a defence by individuals in national courts. Good examples of this can be found in *Procureur du Roi* v *Dassonville* (Case 8/74) [1974] ECR 837 (*Cases and Materials* (8.4.2)) and *Criminal Proceedings against Karl Prantl* (Case 16/83) [1984] ECR 1299 (*Cases and Materials* (8.5.3)). The use of Article 28 (ex 30) as a defence to criminal prosecutions came under close scrutiny with a series of cases concerning alleged infringements of the UK Sunday trading legislation. Here, UK traders facing prosecution argued that limitations on Sunday trading restricted the free movement of goods in breach of Article 28 (ex 30). Ultimately, in *Stoke-on-Trent City Council* v *B&Q.* (Case C-169/91) [1992] ECR I-6635, the Court of Justice, applying *Cassis* principles, found the legislation to be

both justified and proportionate. However, these cases prepared the ground for the next development relating to indistinctly applicable MEQRs, in *Keck and Mithouard* (Cases C-267 & 268/91) [1993] ECR I-6097.

8.13 *Keck* and beyond: judicial developments on indistinctly applicable measures

Judicial developments on Article 28 (ex 30) raise the distinction between:

(a) those indistinctly applicable measures which hinder, directly or indirectly, actually or potentially, trade between Member States within the meaning of *Dassonville*; and

(b) those indistinctly applicable measures which have an effect on the overall volume of trade because they are restrictive or regulatory but which are neither intended to be protectionist nor affect imports any more than they affect domestic products.

Criminal proceedings against Keck and Mithouard **(Cases C-267 & 268/91) [1993] ECR I-6097**

This distinction was articulated by the Court of Justice in *Keck*. Mr Keck and Mr Mithouard had been prosecuted for reselling products at a loss, contrary to French unfair competition legislation. They raised Article 28 (ex 30) as a defence, claiming that the national provisions were incompatible with the Community principle of free movement of goods. Whilst the Court of Justice recognized that the legislation restricted the overall volume of sales and hence the volume of sales of products from other Member States, it declared that national measures affecting imports and restricting or prohibiting certain selling arrangements do not fall within the *Dassonville* formula:

> provided that those provisions apply to all affected traders operating within the national territory and provided that they affect in the same manner, in law and in fact, the marketing of domestic products and of those from other Member States.

Where these conditions are satisfied, declared the Court, such provisions do not impede market access for imported products any more than for domestic products. Consequently such measures fall outside the scope of Article 28 (ex 30) altogether (*Cases and Materials* (8.6)).

The Court indicated in *Keck* that its judgment was aimed at traders who invoke Article 28 (ex 30) to challenge national rules which restrict their commercial freedom. *Keck* refers to restrictions relating to 'selling arrangements' (rather than rules concerning the goods themselves—packaging, content, labelling) which apply to all traders in the national territory and which affect in the same manner, in law and in fact, both imported and domestic products. It might be anticipated that, in practice, this distinction will prove difficult to apply. The Court of Justice has provided some guidance as to the scope of 'selling arrangements' in decisions subsequent to *Keck*.

 **EXERCISE** 8.9 

Read the extract from *Tankstation 't Heukske* (*Cases and Materials* (8.6)). What was the view of the Court of Justice on the application of Article 28 (ex 30) to national rules on shop closing hours? Make a written note of your answer.

***Criminal Proceedings against Tankstation 't Heukske vof and J.B.E Boermans* (Joined Cases C-401/92 & C-402/92) [1994] ECR I-2199**

Dutch legislation restricted the times at which certain goods could be sold, though it applied less rigorous regulation to petrol stations and motorway shops. Tankstation t'Heukske and Mr Boermans appealed against their convictions for infringement of the legislation in the Dutch court, arguing that the national legislation constituted an MEQR and a breach of Community law.

The Court of Justice held that Article 28 (ex 30) does not apply to national rules on shop opening hours which apply to all traders operating within the national territory and affect in the same manner, in law and in fact, the marketing of domestic products and of products from other Member States.

The same principles have been applied to Greek rules requiring processed milk for infants to be sold only by pharmacies (*Commission* v *Greece* (Case C-391/92) [1995] ECR I-1621) and to Belgian legislation prohibiting sales yielding very low profit margins (*Groupement National des Négotiants en Pommes de Terre de Belgique (Belgapom)* v *ITM Belgium SA and Vocarex SA* (Case C-63/94) [1995] ECR I-2467).

However, it is clear that any restriction with a discriminatory effect on imports will constitute an MEQR, even where it may be characterized as a 'selling arrangement'.

***Schutzverband gegen unlauteren Wettbewerb* v *TK-Heimdienst Sass GmbH* (Case C-254/98) [2000] ECR I-151**

The Court considered Austrian legislation prohibiting butchers, bakers, and grocers from selling their goods on rounds from door to door unless they also carried on business selling the same type of goods from permanent establishments in the same district or an adjacent municipality. Although the legislation concerned selling arrangements applying to all traders in the national territory, traders from other Member States, in order to have the same access to the Austrian market as local traders, would be obliged to incur the additional cost of setting up a permanent establishment in the relevant locality. The legislation had the effect of impeding access to the Austrian market for imported products and was therefore incompatible with Article 28 (ex 30).

In other cases, the Court of Justice has left it to the national court to assess the impact of restrictions. For instance, in *Burmanjer, van Der Linden and De Jong* (Case C-20/03) [2005] ECR I-4133 the Court held that Belgian rules applying to itinerant sales on the public highway constituted 'selling arrangements'. However, the assessment of the impact of the Belgian restrictions on domestic products and products for other Member States, respectively, was left to the national court.

In the particular context of advertising, the Court of Justice has recognized that national rules restricting or prohibiting product advertising can be a greater impediment to market access for imported products than for domestic products.

 **EXERCISE** 8.10 

Read the extract from *De Agostini* (*Cases and Materials* (8.6)). What was the Court's view of the potential impact of advertising restrictions on imports?

***Konsumentombudsmannen (KO)* v *De Agostini (Svenska) Förlag AB* and *Konsumentombudsmannen (KO)* v *TV Shop i Sverige AB* (Cases C-34–6/95) [1997] ECR I-3843**

Swedish legislation prohibited television advertising that was misleading or was designed to attract the attention of children under twelve years of age. The Court of Justice took the view that a producer which is unable to promote its products in another Member State may well be prevented from penetrating a new market, whereas advertising restrictions may have less impact upon the marketing of the domestic product. In these circumstances, whilst the restrictions may be classified as 'selling arrangements', the *Keck* exception does not apply because of their discriminatory effect. In this case, the Court of Justice left consideration of the effects of the prohibition on advertising to the national court.

Subsequently, in *Konsumentombudsmannen* v *Gourmet International Products Aktiebolag* (Case C-405/98) [2001] ECR 1-1795, the Court of Justice considered Swedish legislation restricting the advertising of alcoholic drinks. The Court concluded that, even without a close analysis of the underlying facts, the prohibition of certain kinds of advertising of these products is liable to impede access to the market by products from other Member States more than it impedes access by domestic products.

8.14 Article 29 (ex 34)

This section has concentrated on Article 28 (ex 30) and the prohibition relating to imports. It should be noted that similar principles apply to exports under Article 29 (ex 34). However, whereas distinctly applicable measures which discriminate against exports will generally breach Article 29 (ex 34), indistinctly applicable measures will not unless they are protectionist.

8.15 Article 30 (ex 36): derogation from Articles 28 and 29 (ex 30 and 34)

8.15.1 The Article 30 (36) grounds

Article 30 (ex 36) sets out a list of grounds on which Member States may justify measures which obstruct interstate trade. Measures which are justified under Article 30 (ex 36) will be lawful even though they breach Article 28 (ex 30). The provisions of Article 30 (ex 36) allow what is called 'derogation' from the principle of free movement of goods. Because this principle is fundamental to the Community system, the Article 30 (ex 36) exceptions are interpreted very strictly by the Court of Justice.

THE EC TREATY

Article 30 (ex 36)

The provisions of Articles 28 and 29 shall not preclude prohibitions or restrictions on imports, exports, or goods in transit justified on grounds of public morality, public policy or public security; the protection of health and life of humans, animals or plants; the protection of national treasures possessing artistic, historic or archaeological value; or the protection of industrial and commercial property. Such prohibitions or restrictions shall not, however, constitute a means of arbitrary discrimination or a disguised restriction on trade between Member States.

EXERCISE 8.11

List the Article 30 (ex 36) grounds.

Under Article 30 (ex 36), derogation from the free movement of goods principle is allowed on grounds of:

(a) public morality, public policy, public security;

(b) the protection of health and life of humans, animals or plants;

(c) the protection of national treasures possessing artistic, historic or archaeological value;

(d) the protection of industrial and commercial property.

8.15.2 An exhaustive list

Unlike the mandatory requirements within the *Cassis* rule of reason, the list of exceptions in Article 30 (ex 36) is exhaustive. Thus, in *Commission* v *Ireland (Restrictions on Importation of Souvenirs)* (Case 113/80) [1981] ECR 1625 in *Cases and Materials* (8.5.1), the Court of Justice refused to accept a justification based on consumer protection, since this justification is not specified in Article 30 (ex 36). (It will be recalled that the *Cassis* rule of reason could not be applied in this case because the Irish legislation was distinctly applicable). However, unlike the rule of reason, the Article 30 (ex 36) exceptions can apply both to distinctly and indistinctly applicable measures, though the latter would normally be considered under *Cassis*.

8.15.3 Proportionality

Article 30 (ex 36) does not give Member States complete discretion to adopt any measures which fall within the exceptions but requires such measures to be 'justified' on one of the specified grounds. To be 'justified', measures must be no more than is necessary to achieve the desired aim.

QUESTION 8.15

What general principle of Community law do you recognize here?

You will no doubt recall that reference has been made already in this chapter to this important general principle, the principle of proportionality, which is also an essential element of the *Cassis* rule of reason.

8.15.4 No arbitrary discrimination or disguised restriction on trade

EXERCISE 8.12

Read Article 30 (ex 36) and note the two 'negative' conditions relating to national prohibitions or restrictions.

In addition to the proportionality requirement, Article 30 (ex 36) also lays down two other conditions which must be satisfied before restrictions can be considered lawful. Measures must not constitute 'a means of arbitrary discrimination or a disguised restriction on trade between Member States'. In *Imports of Poultry Meat*, the Court of Justice decided that a UK measure effectively imposing a ban on the import of turkey meat, introduced purportedly to prevent the spread of Newcastle disease, was arbitrary and a disguised restriction on trade because it was designed to protect domestic producers. Several factors pointed to this conclusion, including the haste with which the measures had been introduced, their timing (the beginning of the Christmas season) and the measures which the French had themselves introduced to prevent Newcastle disease (*Commission* v *United Kingdom (Imports of Poultry Meat)* (Case 40/82) [1982] ECR 2793). Similarly, in *Italian Table Wines*, French quality checks on Italian imported wines were held to be arbitrary. Quality checks on French wines were much less frequent and there was no evidence supporting the need for systematic checks on the imported product (*Commission* v *France (Italian Table Wines)* (Case 42/82) [1983] ECR 1013).

Here, as under *Cassis*, the principle of mutual recognition applies. Unless restrictions are objectively justified, where goods have been lawfully produced and marketed in one Member State there is no reason why they should not be introduced into another Member State.

Discussion now turns to the scope of the Article 30 (ex 36) grounds of justification.

8.15.5 **Public morality**

This exception to the free movement provisions has been considered by the Court of Justice in relation to restrictions on the trade in pornographic or obscene material.

R v Henn and Darby (Case 34/79) [1979] ECR 3795

Here the defendants appealed against convictions under English customs legislation which prohibited the importation of indecent or obscene articles. The articles in question formed part of a consignment of obscene films and magazines which had arrived at Felixstowe from Rotterdam.

The Court of Justice ruled that a ban on the import of pornographic articles into the UK breached Article 28 (ex 30) but was justified on grounds of public morality under Article 30 (ex 36).

The Court stated that 'it is for each Member State to determine in accordance with its own scale of values and in the form selected by it the requirements of public morality in its own territory' and this was not affected by the fact that different rules applied in different parts of the UK. Moreover, there was no arbitrary discrimination or disguised restriction on trade despite the fact that national law did not place an absolute ban on the possession of or trade in pornographic material. Such restrictions as did exist had the clear purpose of restraining the manufacture and marketing of obscene material and from this the Court concluded that there was no 'lawful trade' in such material in the UK (*Cases and Materials* (8.7.1)).

Similar issues arose in *Conegate* (*Cases and Materials* (8.7.1)) but the outcome was different in this case.

***Conegate Ltd* v *Customs and Excise Commissioners* (Case 121/85) [1986] ECR 1007**

Here, a consignment of inflatable dolls of a sexual nature and other erotic articles imported from Germany by Conegate Ltd had been seized by the UK customs authorities on the grounds that they were 'indecent or obscene' under English customs legislation. Subsequently, the national court had ordered the forfeiture of the goods. Conegate Ltd argued that the forfeiture infringed Article 28 (ex 30) and could not be justified on grounds of public morality under Article 30 (ex 36).

The Court of Justice confirmed that it is for Member States to decide upon the obscene or indecent nature of goods. However, the Court undertook a closer examination of the national rules and concluded that the restrictions placed on domestic goods—prohibition on transmission by post, restrictions on public display, licensing systems in some areas for premises from which the goods were sold—did not amount to a prohibition on manufacture and sale. Consequently, the UK could not rely on Article 30 (ex 36) to prohibit the importation of similar goods, though it was not precluded from applying the same restrictions upon imported goods once they had entered the country.

8.15.6 **Public policy**

Very few cases have raised issues of public policy and where this ground of justification has been considered by the Court of Justice, it has been very strictly interpreted. It is clear that 'public policy' cannot be used as a general justification which embraces more specific defences (such as consumer protection or economic justifications) but must be given its own independent meaning (*Commission* v *Italy (Re Ban in Pork Imports)* (Case 7/61) [1962] CMLR 39. One case in which the public policy justification was accepted by the Court of Justice is *R.* v *Thompson* (Case 7/78) [1978] ECR 2247. Here, the Court recognized a state's need to protect its right to mint coinage as one of its fundamental interests and held that the right to protect coinage from destruction stems from that right. Thus a prohibition on the import and export of coins was justified on public policy grounds.

8.15.7 Public security

EXERCISE 8.13

Read the extracts from *Campus Oil* (*Cases and Materials* (8.7.2)). How were the Irish national rules on the purchase of petroleum products justified?

***Campus Oil Ltd* v *Minister for Industry and Energy* (Case 72/83) [1983] ECR 2727**

The Court of Justice held that Irish legislation requiring importers to purchase a certain percentage of their requirements from a state-owned oil refinery was justified on public security grounds. The measure ensured that Ireland was able to maintain its own refining capacity in relation to products which were fundamental to the provision of essential services. An interruption of supplies could seriously threaten public security.

EXERCISE 8.14

Turn back to *Campus Oil* (*Cases and Materials* (8.7.2)) and note the issues relating to proportionality.

However, the prices charged must be set at a competitive level and the quantity of oil that must be purchased by importers must not exceed the minimum supply requirements of the state without which its public security could be ensured.

8.15.8 Protection of health and life of humans, animals or plants

? **QUESTION** 8.16

What kinds of measure do you think Member States might seek to justify on health grounds?

You may recall three specific health measures which have already been referred to earlier in this chapter. In *San Jose Scale*, the Court of Justice held that German inspections of imported (but not domestically produced) apples were justified on health grounds (*Rewe-Zentralfinanz* v *Landwirtschaftskammer Bonn* (Case 4/75) [1975] ECR 843 (*Cases and Materials* (8.4.3))). By contrast, the Court refused to accept health justifications for UK measures which effectively imposed a ban on poultry meat imports from most other Member States (*Commission* v *United Kingdom (Imports of Poultry Meat)* (Case 40/82) [1982] ECR 2793) and delays in the customs clearance of imported Italian wines at the French border caused by systematic checks on quality (*Commission* v *France (Italian Table Wines)* (Case 42/82) [1983] ECR 1013).

In order to succeed under this head, Member States must show that there is a real health risk. In *San Jose Scale*, there was a real risk that the pest would spread to domestic apples. The Court of Justice held that the inspections were justified in principle under Article 30 (ex 36). They would not constitute arbitrary discrimination where effective measures were taken to prevent the distribution of contaminated domestic apples. Measures must also satisfy the proportionality requirement and must not constitute 'arbitrary discrimination or a disguised restriction on trade between Member States'. As noted earlier, the Court found that there was arbitrary discrimination and a disguised restriction on trade in both *Poultry Meat* and *Italian table Wines*.

On occasions, indistinctly applicable measures have been considered under Article 30 (ex 36), for instance prohibitions on the use of certain additives in beer (*Commission* v *Germany (Beer Purity Laws)* (Case 178/84) [1987] ECR 1227 (*Cases and Materials* (8.7.3)) and rules prohibiting pharmacists from substituting any other product for the product specified in a doctor's prescription (*Royal Pharmaceutical Society*) (*Cases and Materials* (8.7.3)).

EXERCISE 8.15

Read the extracts from *Beer Purity Laws* (*Cases and Materials* (8.7.3)). The German government argued that the use of additives in beer was particularly harmful to the German population. Why?

***Commission* v *Germany (Beer Purity Laws)* (Case 178/84) [1987] ECR 1227**

German legislation required all drinks marketed in Germany under the designation 'Bier' to be produced only from certain ingredients and imposed an absolute ban on the marketing of beers containing additives. The German government pointed to the high consumption of beer in Germany and claimed that because of this, the use of additives presented a greater risk to public health in Germany than in other Member States. Noting that Germany permitted the use of additives in the manufacture of all, or virtually all, other drinks, the Court of Justice held that the fact that the German population consumes large quantities of beer did not justify stricter rules for beer.

Nonetheless, the Court of Justice has recognized more recently that 'national nutritional habits', together with the results of international scientific research, may justify restrictive measures. Moreover, scientific data may not be able to provide an accurate assessment of the risks to human health. In *Greenham and Abel* (Case C- 95/01 [2004] ECR I-1333, the Court considered French rules that prohibited the marketing of products containing unauthorized additives which, it was claimed, were already lawfully marketed in other Member States. The Court reiterated that, in the absence of Community harmonizing legislation, such rules would be justified under Article 30 EC only where there is a genuine risk to public health. The necessary risk assessment must be based upon the latest scientific data, to establish the degree of probability of harmful effects. However, the Court accepted that there may be scientific uncertainty about the existence or extent of any risk to human health. In these circumstances, Member States may, in accordance with the precautionary principle, take protective measures without having to wait until the existence and gravity of those risks are fully demonstrated.

In view of the Court of Justice's generally restrictive interpretation of the Article 30 (ex 36), it is perhaps surprising that in *R* v *Royal Pharmaceutical Society of Great Britain* (*Cases and Materials* (8.7.3)) rules concerning the dispensing of medicines by pharmacists in the UK were held to be both justified and proportionate.

***R* v *Royal Pharmaceutical Society of Great Britain* (Cases 266 & 267/87) [1989] ECR 1295**

Rules of the Royal Pharmaceutical Society of Great Britain prohibited pharmacists from substituting, except in an emergency, any other product for the product specifically named in prescriptions written by doctors, dentists, and vets. The Association of Pharmaceutical Importers claimed that the rules infringed Article 28 (ex 30). The Court of Justice disagreed. The rules did not go beyond what was necessary to achieve the objective in view, namely to leave the entire responsibility for the treatment of a patient in the hands of the doctor. Moreover, the Court could not discount the psychosomatic factor. Patients had greater confidence in the specific medicine prescribed than in a substitute, even though the latter has exactly the same therapeutic effect.

8.15.9 Protection of national treasures possessing artistic, historic, or archaeological value

The scope of this derogation remains uncertain, though in *Commission* v Italy *(Export Tax on Art Treasures, No. 1)* (Case 7/68) [1968] ECR 423, the Court indicated that quantitative restrictions (but not charges) would be justified where the object of those restrictions was to prevent art treasures from being exported from a Member State.

8.15.10 Protection of industrial and commercial property

The various kinds of industrial and commercial property rights (or 'intellectual property rights') include patents, copyright, trade marks, and design rights. The use of such rights can impede the free movement of goods throughout the Community because national intellectual property law tends to partition markets along national lines. Although in principle Article 30 (ex 36) (together with Article 295 (ex 222), which precludes Community interference with national rules relating to property ownership) protects industrial property rights, these rights have been curtailed by the Court of Justice. This has been done by means of the distinction drawn between the ownership or existence of the rights and their exercise. Whilst the ownership of the right is protected, any improper exercise of it—which is anti-competitive or constitutes an obstacle to trade—will be condemned by the Court.

8.15.11 No economic justifications under Article 30 (ex 36)

Economic interests do not justify restrictions on the free movement of goods. This was made clear in *Duphar BV* v *Netherlands* (Case 238/82) [1984] ECR 523 and in *Campus Oil Ltd* v *Minister for Industry and Energy* (Case 72/83) [1983] ECR 2727 (*Cases and Materials* (8.7.2)) and was later reaffirmed by the Court of Justice in *Evans Medical*.

EXERCISE 8.16

Read the extracts from *Evans Medical* (*Cases and Materials* (8.7.4)). Summarize the conclusions of the Court of Justice on the application of the Article 30 (ex 36) to the UK's refusal of import licences for the drug diamorphine.

***R* v *Secretary of State for Home Department ex parte Evans Medical Ltd* (Case C-324/93) [1995] ECR I-563**

Under government policy aimed to prevent diamorphine being diverted to illicit trade, until 1992 Evans Medical and Macfarlan Smith had exclusive rights in the UK regarding the importation, manufacture and processing of the drug. When Generics (UK) Ltd sought judicial review of the Secretary of State's refusal, in 1990, to grant the company an import licence for diamorphine, the Secretary of State acknowledged that the refusal of the licence was not justified. He announced a review of his decision, stating that the policy on importation was a hindrance to intra-Community trade and that reliability of supplies could be guaranteed by the introduction of a tendering scheme. Evans and Macfarlan brought proceedings against the Secretary of State in the High Court. On an Article 234 (ex 177) reference, the Court of Justice held that the refusal of the licence could not be justified on economic grounds—here, the Member State's desire to ensure the survival of Macfarlan. However, the derogation might apply if the maintenance of a reliable supply of drugs for essential medical purposes was necessary for the protection of the life and health of humans.

Similarly, purely economic reasons did not justify Greek legislation which, in effect, obliged petroleum marketing companies to obtain a significant part of their supplies from refineries established in Greece (*Commission* v *Greece* (Case C-398/98) [2001] ECR I-7915).

8.15.12 Environmental justifications for distinctly applicable measures?

It has been suggested that two decisions of the Court of Justice concerning national measures for the protection of the environment, *Commission* v *Belgium* (Case C-2/90 [1992] ECR I-4431 and *PreussenElektra AG* v *Schleswag AG* (Case C-379/98) [2001] ECR I-2099, call into question the established view that the Article 30 list of justifications is exhaustive. As previously noted, according to that established view, the Article 30 list cannot be extended in the way that the *Cassis* list of mandatory requirements, relating to indistinctly applicable measures only, has been extended.

Some commentators have argued that, in these two cases, the Court of Justice allowed environmental objectives to justify distinctly applicable measures caught by Article 28. However in *Commission* v *Belgium*, whilst the Court Justice took account of environmental protection in considering apparently unlawful national legislation concerning the disposal of waste, it held that, because of the special nature of that product, the provisions in question did not discriminate against imports.

In *PreussenElektra*, in which the Court of Justice considered German legislation requiring German electricity suppliers to purchase the electricity produced from renewable sources in their area of supply, the Court avoided discussion of the distinctions between the Article 30 justifications and the *Cassis* mandatory requirements. It held that the legislation was not incompatible with Article 28.

Notwithstanding these outcomes, neither of the two judgments is a model of clarity. It will be interesting to follow any evolution of the relevant legal principles in future decisions.

8.16 Harmonization

As is evident from many of the cases discussed in this chapter, the application of different product standards by different Member States, in relation for instance to health and safety requirements and consumer protection, creates a hindrance to the free movement of goods. The process of harmonization aims to eliminate these disparities by laying down Community-wide standards which are binding on all Member States.

Article 94 EC provides for the adoption of Directives for this purpose, but early progress on harmonization was slow. The adoption of Directives under Article 94 requires unanimous approval in the Council of Ministers. Because of this and because the initial approach to harmonization was to adopt comprehensive and detailed rules covering particular areas, consensus was difficult to achieve. However, where a measure harmonizing an area comprehensively has been put in place, a Member State has no recourse to Article 30 derogation from the free movement principles in that particular area.

A new approach to harmonization moved away from comprehensive rules and focused on a minimum level of Community regulation. A Council Resolution of 7 May 1985 stated that, in relation to technical harmonization and standards, Directives were to be based upon the 'essential safety requirements (or other requirements in the general interest) with which products put on the market must conform and which should therefore enjoy free movement throughout the Community'. The detailed technical specifications needed to ensure that products meet the essential requirements are not a matter for Community legislation but for 'organizations competent in the standardization area'.

The process of harmonization was further facilitated after the insertion into the EC Treaty by the Single European Act 1986 of Article 95(1), which provides for qualified majority voting for the adoption of measures concerning the establishment and functioning of the internal market. Under Article 95(4), Member States wishing to apply stricter or higher standards than those comprising the essential requirements may seek approval for these from the Commission on the basis of 'major needs' referred to in Article 30 or in relation to the environment or the working environment. Similarly, after the adoption of a harmonizing measure, approval may be sought under Article 94(5) for the introduction of new national provisions based on new scientific evidence relating to the protection of the environment or the working environment.

CONCLUSIONS

This chapter has underlined the importance of the free movement of goods to the Community internal market. It has been seen that obstacles to trade can take the form of customs duties, charges, taxes, quantitative restrictions and measures having equivalent effect. Member States seeking to rely on the *Cassis* rule of reason or the Article 30 (ex 36) derogation in order to justify measures breaching Article 28 (ex 30) must be able to establish not only that the measures in question are not protectionist but also that they are no more than is necessary to achieve the objective in view, in other words that they satisfy the principle of proportionality.

SUMMARY

- **The free movement of goods** is one of the four fundamental freedoms of the Community internal market, defined by Article 14 (ex 7a) EC as 'an area without internal frontiers in which the free movement of goods, persons, services and capital is ensured . . . .'
- **Obstacles to the free movement of goods** may take the form of customs duties, charges having equivalent effect (CEEs), discriminatory national taxation, quantitative restrictions, and measures having equivalent effect (MEQRs)
- **Customs duties and CEEs** are tariff barriers to trade. They are charges imposed on goods by virtue of the fact that the goods cross a frontier between Member States (*Diamonds, Statistical Levy, Gingerbread*). Customs duties and CEEs are prohibited by Article 25 (ex 12) EC, even when they have no protectionist purpose (*Diamonds*). Charges for services rendered to the importer or the trader are outside the scope of Article 25 (ex 12) EC, provided the service confers a genuine benefit and that the charge imposed is proportionate to the value of the service.
- **Discriminatory national taxation** is prohibited by Article 90 (ex 95) EC. Discrimination may be direct (open discrimination between imported and domestic products) (*Lüttick*) or indirect (the taxation, whilst not openly discriminatory, has a discriminatory effect) (*Humblot*). Indirect discrimination may be objectively justified (*Natural Sweet Wines, Chemial Farmaceutici, Commission* v *Greece*). The EC Treaty provides that 'similar' products must be taxed equally (Article 90(1) (ex 95(1)), whilst products that are not similar but in competition with each other must not be subject to taxation that gives advantage to the domestic product (Article 90(2) (ex 95(2)).

- **Quantitative restrictions** are non-tariff barriers to trade. They are total or partial restraints on the import or export of goods (*Geddo*), in other words import or export quotas or bans. They are prohibited by Article 28 (ex 30) EC.
- **MEQRs** are non-tariff barriers to trade. They take various forms, such as technical or health and safety requirements imposed by Member States. MEQRs were defined by the Court of Justice in *Dassonville* and guidance as to their scope is given in Directive 70/50. MEQRs are either distinctly applicable (they do not apply equally to domestic and imported goods) or indistinctly applicable (they apply equally to domestic and imported goods). MEQRs are prohibited by Article 28 (ex 30) EC.
- **In *Cassis de Dijon*** the Court of Justice declared that measures satisfying certain 'mandatory requirements', provided they are proportionate, do not constitute MEQRs and consequently do not infringe Article 28 (ex 30) EC. This is the *Cassis* 'rule of reason'. It applies only to indistinctly applicable measures. The list of mandatory requirements has been extended in subsequent cases. In *Cassis*, the Court also established the principle of mutual recognition: where goods have been lawfully produced and marketed in one Member State, there is no reason why they should not be introduced into another Member State.
- **In *Keck*** the Court of Justice declared that 'selling arrangements' which apply to all traders in the national territory and which affect in the same manner, in law and in fact, both imported and domestic products are outside the scope of Article 28 (ex 30) EC.
- **Article 30 (ex 36) EC** provides of derogation from the principle of free movement of goods, setting out grounds on which Member States may justify restrictions. These grounds are exhaustive but apply to both distinctly and indistinctly applicable measures. To fall within the Article 30 derogation, measures must be proportionate and must not constitute arbitrary discrimination or a disguised restriction on trade.

CHAPTER 8: ASSESSMENT EXERCISE

1 (a) Explain the distinction between distinctly applicable measures and indistinctly applicable measures. Give one example of each drawn from cases decided by the Court of Justice.

(b) Why is this distinction important?

2 Consider the following (fictitious) measures and comment on their compatibility with Community provisions on the free movement of goods.

(a) A recently introduced Italian tax on wine with an alcohol content exceeding 9%. Importers from other Member States are required to pay the tax at the date of importation. Domestic producers may defer payment until up to six weeks after the product has been put on the market.

(b) A Belgian regulation requiring all imported (but not domestically produced) onions to undergo inspections. The Belgian government claims that the measure is designed to control the spread of the onion beetle, which is a very destructive pest.

(c) German legislation requiring vegetarian cheese to be packed in triangular boxes. The government claims that the measure is aimed to protect the consumer.

(d) English legislation which prohibits video shops and all other video retail outlets from opening between 9 p.m. and 8 a.m.

See *Cases and Materials* (9.8) for specimen answers.

FURTHER READING

Barnard, C. (2001). 'Fitting the Remaining Pieces into the Goods and Persons Jigsaw?' 26 EL Rev 35.

Connor, T. (2005). 'Accentuating the Positive: the 'Selling Arrangement', the First Decade, and Beyond' 30 ICLQ 127.

Greaves, R. (1998). 'Advertising Restrictions and the Free Movement of Goods and Services' 23 EL Rev 305.

Koutrakos, P.(2001). 'On Groceries, Alcohol and Olive Oil: More on Free Movement of Goods after *Keck*' 26 EL Rev 391.

Shuibhne, N. (2002). 'The Free Movement of Goods and Article 28: an Evolving Framework' 27 EL Rev 408.

Weatherill, S. (1996). 'After *Keck*: Some Thoughts on how to Clarify the Clarification' 33 CML Rev 51.

Weatherill, S. (1999). 'Recent Case Law concerning the Free Movement of Goods: Mapping the Frontiers of Market Deregulation'. 36 CML Rev 51.

Wils, W. (1993). 'The Search for the Rule in Article 30: Much Ado about Nothing?' 18 EL Rev 475.

9 Free movement of persons: citizens of the European Union

9.1 OBJECTIVES

By the end of this chapter you should be able to:

1 Detail the Treaty Articles and secondary legislation which give effect to the principle of freedom of movement of persons

2 Describe the rights granted to citizens of the European Union by the free movement provisions

9.2 Introduction

The free movement of persons is identified by Article 3(1)(c) (ex 3(c)) EC as one of the four essential freedoms of the Community internal market and, as noted in Chapter 8, Article 14 (ex 7a) EC defines the internal market as an area without internal frontiers in which the free movement of goods, persons, services, and capital is ensured. Other Treaty provisions relate to the movement of persons across the European Union's external borders, concerning visas, asylum, and immigration. They are contained in Articles 61–69 of the EC Treaty, which seek to establish progressively an area of freedom, security, and justice. In particular, they include measures establishing standards and procedures to be followed by Member States in carrying out checks on persons at external borders. The rules relating to the European Union's external borders lie outside the scope of this book. **Chapters 9**, **10**, and **11** deal with the free movement of persons within the internal market.

The purpose of the original Treaty provisions was to ensure that the economically active—workers, the self-employed, and those providing services—are able to move freely and reside throughout the Community in locations where their skills and labour are in demand. On a broader view, these provisions are concerned also with the right of a national of a Member State to be free from discrimination on account of nationality and to raise his or her standard of living and quality of life through working and residing in another Member State. In addition to the free movement rights, Article 12 (ex 6) EC establishes the principle of non-discrimination on grounds of nationality.

Rights of free movement and residence were subsequently extended by secondary legislation to the families of the economically active and also to economically inactive persons who could demonstrate the required degree of financial independence. Although these provisions represented a weakening of the link between free movement rights and economic activity, such rights were still to an appreciable extent tied to economic status. As will become apparent in this chapter, the introduction of the concept of citizenship of the European Union by the Treaty on European Union proved to be a further significant step towards the breaking of that link. In this respect, there have been notable developments in the European Court of Justice and in the form of new secondary legislation, Directive 2004/38.

9.3 Treaty provisions

The key provisions are:

(a) Article 12 (ex 6) EC: prohibits discrimination on grounds of nationality 'within the scope of application of the Treaty'.

(b) Article 17 (ex 8) EC: established citizenship of the European Union.

(c) Article 18(1) (ex 8a(1)) EC: right of free movement and residence of Union citizens.

(d) Article 39 (ex 48) EC: free movement of workers.

(e) Article 43 (ex 52) EC: freedom of establishment—free movement of the self-employed.

(f) Article 49 (ex 59) EC: freedom to provide services.

The Union citizenship provisions, Articles 17 and 18, were incorporated into the EC Treaty by the Treaty on European Union. These form the basis of the rights discussed in this chapter. The rights relating specifically to economically active Union citizens, Articles 39, 43, and 49, are discussed in **Chapter 10**.

THE EC TREATY

Article 12 (ex 6)

Within the scope of application of this Treaty and without prejudice to any special provisions contained therein, any discrimination on grounds of nationality shall be prohibited.

Article 17 (ex 8)

1. Citizenship of the Union is hereby established. Every person holding the nationality of a Member State shall be a citizen of the Union. Citizenship of the Union shall complement and not replace national citizenship.

Article 18 (ex 8a)

1. Every citizen of the Union shall have the right to move and reside freely within the territory of the Member States, subject to the limitations and conditions laid down in this Treaty and the measures adopted to give it effect.

9.4 Limitations on free movement

9.4.1 The qualification to Union citizens' rights

QUESTION 9.1

What qualification is applied to Union citizens' right to move and reside freely within th
Member States?

The Article 18(1) EC right is made subject to 'the limitations and conditions laid down in this Treaty and by the measures adopted to give it effect'. The Court of Justice's interpretation of this qualification is discussed presently.

9.4.2 The right of Member States to restrict entry and residence

There are circumstances in which Member States may legitimately restrict entry and residence, set out in the Treaty and in secondary legislation. The scope of the three grounds of limitation—public policy, public security, or public health—is discussed in **Chapter 11**.

9.5 Extension of rights to the economically inactive

Before Treaty amendments created Union citizenship, Treaty rights were confined to the economically active—workers, the self-employed, and persons providing services. Secondary legislation had granted rights to family members and to persons of independent means (Directive 90/364), retired persons (Directive 90/365), and students (Directive 90/366, replaced by Directive 93/96). Rights under these three directives were conditional on the possession of sufficient resources to avoid becoming a burden on social security, and sickness insurance.

9.6 Union citizens' rights: the European Court of Justice

This secondary legislation apart, free movement rights were still to an appreciable extent tied to worker status. However, the introduction of Union citizenship allowed the Court of Justice to extend the rights yet further. The Court declared that 'Union citizenship is destined to be the fundamental status of the nationals of the Member States (see *Grzelczyk*, below). The Court used this as the starting point for granting Union citizens a right associated with free movement, the right to non-discrimination on grounds of nationality enshrined in Article 12 (ex 6) EC. It did so in *Sala*.

EXERCISE 9.1 

Look at the extract from *Sala* (*Cases and Materials* (9.1)). How did the Court of Justice define the scope of the rights attached to Union citizenship?

Sala v *Freistaat Bayern* (Case C-85/96) [1998] ECR I-2691

Mrs Sala, a Spanish national who was lawfully resident in Germany but whose status as a worker had not been established, had been refused the grant of a child-raising allowance because she could not produce a residence permit issued by the national authorities, as required by the national legislation. The legislation did not impose a similar requirement on claimants of German nationality who, to be eligible for the benefit, were simply required to be permanently or ordinarily resident in Germany.

The Court held that Article 8(2) (now 17(2)) EC attaches to the status of Union citizenship the rights and duties laid down by the Treaty. Thus, a Union citizen lawfully resident in a Member State of which he or she is not a national, can rely on the non-discrimination provisions of Article 12 (ex 6) EC in all matters falling within the scope of application of the Treaty.

The Court of Justice adopted similar reasoning in *Grzelczyk* v *Centre Public d'Aide Sociale d'Ottignies-Louvain-la-Neuve* (Case C-184/99) [2001] ECR I-6193.

Grzelczyk v *Centre Public d'aide social d'Ottignies-Louvain-la-Neuve* (Case C-184/99 [2001] ECR I-6193)

Rudy Grzelczyk was a French student studying in Belgium. He had applied for a welfare benefit, the 'minimex', during the final year of his studies. This had been granted by the Belgian authorities but then had been withdrawn, on grounds of his nationality. Having established Gzelczyk's right of residence in Belgium on the basis of Directive 93/96, the Court of Justice upheld Gzelczyk's right, as a Union citizen lawfully resident in another Member State, not to be discriminated against on account of his nationality.

 **EXERCISE** 9.2 

Read the extract from *Grzelczyk* (*Cases and Materials* (9.1)). Note, in paragraph 31, the Court's future vision of Union citizenship as the fundamental status of nationals of the Member States.

***D'Hoop* v *Office national de l'emploi* (Case C-224/98) [2002] ECR I-6191**

Subsequently, the non-discrimination principle was extended to a Union citizen whose claim was against her state of origin. Ms D'Hoop, a Belgian national, had obtained her baccalauréat in France and then returned to Belgium where she completed a university course. She was refused the 'tide-over' allowance for persons seeking their first employment because she had undertaken her secondary education outside Belgium. The Court of Justice held that Union citizens should not be disadvantaged because they have exercised their freedom to move in order to pursue education in another Member State; Union citizenship formed the basis of rights to equal treatment in law, irrespective of nationality.

Nonetheless, under Article 18(1) EC, Union citizens' rights are 'subject to the limitations and conditions laid down in the Treaty and by the measures adopted to give it effect'. This qualification was significant in *Grzelczyk*, where the Court of Justice applied the 'sufficient resources' and 'sickness insurance' conditions attached to student rights in Directive 93/96 in upholding *Grzelczyk*'s right, as a Union citizen, to residence in Belgium.

***Baumbast* v *Secretary of State for the Home Department* (Case C-413/99) [2002] ECR I-7091**

In *Baumbast* the Court of Justice again used Union citizenship as the basis for residency rights, subject to the same conditions in the relevant secondary legislation—in this case Directive 90/364, which granted rights to financially independent persons. The UK had refused to renew Mr Baumbast's residence permit on the grounds that he no longer held the status of worker.

The Court held that Mr Baumbast had a right of residence in the UK, despite the fact that his sickness insurance fell short of what was required. Since Mr Baumbast had sufficient means not to become a financial burden on the UK system, it would be disproportionate to refuse him rights. (*Cases and Materials* (9.1)).

However, in *Trojani* (Case C-456/02) [2004] 3 CMLR 38, the Court of Justice declared that Union citizenship does not give rise to an unconditional residency right.

EXERCISE 9.3

Look at *Trojani* (*Cases and Materials* (9.1)). What were the Court's conclusions on Mr Trojani's rights as a citizen of the Union? What were its conclusions on his rights under Article 12 (ex 6) EC ?

***Trojani* v *Centre public d'aide sociale de Bruxelles* (Case C-456/02)**

Mr Trojani was a French national who had temporary leave to reside in Belgium. His application for the minimex benefit had been refused on grounds of his nationality and on the basis that he had no entitlement to the benefit as a 'worker' under Community law. Mr Trojani had challenged this decision in the Belgian court.

The Court of Justice reaffirmed the right of residence arising from citizenship status subject, in Mr Trojani's case, to the limitations contained in Directive 90/364. Mr Trojani did not have sufficient resources within the meaning of the Directive and therefore did not derive a residency right from Article 18 (ex 8a) EC. However, since he was lawfully resident in Belgium, he could benefit from the principle of equal treatment laid down in Article 12 (ex 6) EC.

The Court of Justice's decision in *Wijsenbeek* (Case C-378/97) [1999] ECR I-6207 is a further reminder of the conditions and limitations placed upon free movement rights. Here, the Court held that neither Article 14 (ex 7a) EC (the principle of free movement 'in accordance with the provisions of the Treaty') nor Article 18 (ex 8a) EC preclude a Member State from requiring a person, whether or not a citizen of the European Union, to establish his nationality on entry.

As will become apparent in the sections that follow, many of the principles applied by the Court of Justice in the cases discussed above concerning rights attached to citizenship of the Union, including the right to equal treatment and rights of residence, are now incorporated into Directive 2004/38 on the right of citizens of the Union and their family members to move and reside freely within the territory of the Member States.

9.7 Free movement rights: secondary legislation

9.7.1 The original provisions

Before the introduction of the new Citizenship Directive 2004/38, in addition to the residency Directives covering students, retired persons, and persons of independent means, a range of secondary provisions granted free movement and non-discrimination rights:

(a) Directive 68/360: rights of workers and their families.

(b) Directive 73/148: rights of the self-employed and their families.

(c) Regulation 1612/68: freedom from discrimination in employment.

(d) Directive 75/34: right to remain after employment has ceased.

(e) Directive 64/221: derogation on grounds of public policy, public security or public health.

Much of this legislation has now been repealed, the provisions being consolidated and extended in the new Citizenship Directive 2004/38.

9.7.2 Directive 2004/38: the Citizenship Directive

With the establishment of Union citizenship, and the Treaty right to free movement attached to it, came the opportunity for a new approach to the review of the existing complex and fragmented body of secondary legislation on free movement of persons. Articles 17 and 18 (ex 8 and 8a) EC, together with the non-discrimination provision in Article 12 (ex 6) EC, provided the basis for the new Citizenship Directive 2004/38. The pre-existing secondary legislation was repealed or amended with effect from 30 April 2006, the Directive's implementation deadline.

? QUESTION 9.2

When did Directive 2004/38 become capable of direct effect?

To refresh your memory on the meaning of 'direct effect', look back at **Chapter 4**. Directive 2004/38 became capable of direct effect as soon as the implementation deadline had passed. This means that individuals are able to rely on its provisions in the national court, provided the conditions for direct effect are satisfied.

Significantly, Directive 2004/38 shifts the focus of free movement and residence rights away from economic status to the status of citizenship of the Union. The preamble declares that '... citizenship should be the fundamental status of the nationals of the Member States when they exercise their right of free movement and residence ... ' (Recital 3).

? QUESTION 9.3

Do you recall the case in which the Court of Justice first made this declaration about the significance of Union citizenship?

This declaration was made in *Grzelczyk* v *Centre Public d'aide social d'Ottignies-Louvain-la-Neuve* (Case C-184/99 [2001] ECR I-6193) and subsequently reiterated by the Court in later cases.

9.8 Directive 2004/38: beneficiaries and their rights

Directive 2004/38 applies to all Union citizens who move to or reside in another Member State and their family members, as defined. The host State must also facilitate the entry and residence of certain other family members and of the partner with whom the citizen has a durable relationship, 'duly attested'. The rights apply irrespective of nationality, though the person claiming the primary entry and residence right must be a Union citizen. The precise scope of 'family member' and the associated provisions will be considered presently.

Any person having the nationality of a Member State is also a citizen of the Union.

QUESTION 9.4

How is 'Union citizen' defined? Look back at Article 17 (ex 8) EC.

The rights granted under the Directive may be grouped into the following five broad categories. It should be noted that the rights are subject to limitations on grounds of public policy, public security, or public health. These limitations are discussed in detail in **Chapter 11**.

9.8.1 All Union citizens and their families

It will be recalled that, under Article 18 (ex 8a) EC Union citizens have the right to move freely within the Community, subject to the limitations and conditions in the Treaty and secondary legislation. This includes the conditions and limitations contained in Directive 2004/38.

Directive 2004/38, Articles 4–6, grants Union citizens the right to leave their home state, enter another Member State, and reside there for up to three months without conditions or formalities, other than the requirement to hold a valid identity card or passport. Family members who are not Union citizens have similar rights, subject to the possession of a passport and, if required by the Member State, an entry visa.

For those who are not economically active or job-seekers, the right of residence applies provided the individual does not become an unreasonable burden on the social assistance system of the host State, but expulsion must not be an automatic consequence of recourse to social welfare (Article 14). Member States are not obliged to grant entitlement to social assistance during the first three months of residence to Union citizens other than workers, self-employed persons, or their families (Article 24).

9.8.2 Workers, the self-employed, and their families

They have the right to reside in another Member State for more than three months.

Directive 2004/38 also reaffirms the right of jobseekers to entry and residence, which is enshrined in previous case law. The extent of all these rights is considered in detail in **Chapter 10**.

9.8.3 Persons of independent means and their families

Union citizens who have sufficient resources for themselves and their family members not to become a burden on the social assistance system of the host State and who have sickness insurance have the right to reside in another Member State for more than three months (Article 7(1)(b)). This right and the two conditions attached to it were originally contained in Directive 90/364. You may recall that the Court of Justice applied the two conditions in *Baumbast* v *Secretary of State for the Home Department* (Case C-413/99) [2002] ECR I-7091.

? **EXERCISE** 9.4 

Look again at *Baumbast* (*Cases and Materials* (9.1)). What was the Court of Justice's approach to the application of the condition relating to sickness insurance?

Baumbast **cont.**

Mr Baumbast's application to the UK authorities for renewal of his residence permit had been refused on the grounds that he was no longer a worker or self-employed in the UK. As a citizen of the Union, he sought to rely on the residence rights in Article 18(1) (ex 8a) EC. Applying the conditions attached to the rights of persons of independent means contained in Directive 90/364, the Court of Justice insisted that these must be applied proportionately. Mr Baumbast's financial circumstances were sound and the family had lived in the UK for several years without becoming a burden on public funds. It would be disproportionate to deny his rights on the basis that his sickness insurance did not cover emergency medical treatment in the UK.

In determining whether Union citizens have sufficient resources, Member States may not lay down a fixed amount but must take account of an individual's personal situation. The applicable amount must be no higher than the threshold level at which claimants become eligible for social assistance in the host State (Article 8, Directive 2004/38).

9.8.4 Students and their families

Students who are Union citizens and their family members have a right of residence in another Member State, provided they have sickness insurance and make a declaration that they have sufficient resources not to become a burden on the social assistance system of the host State. This right was originally contained in Directive 93/96. It was considered by the Court of Justice in *Grzelczyk* v *Centre Public d'aide social d'Ottignies-Louvain-la-Neuve* (Case C-184/99 [2001] ECR I-6193).

 **EXERCISE** 9.5 

Look again at *Grzelczyk* (*Cases and Materials* (9.1)). You may remember that Rudy Grzelczyk had applied for a welfare benefit during the final year of his studies in Belgium. Explain the reasoning applied by the Court of Justice in reaching its conclusion that Grzelczyk satisfied the 'sufficient resources' condition.

Grzelczyk **cont.**

The Court of Justice held that Mr Grzelczyk's right to equal treatment with nationals of the host State was, in accordance with Article 18(1)(ex 8a(1)) EC, subject to the conditions and limitations in Directive 93/96. With regard to 'sufficient resources' the Court declared that recourse to social assistance must not lead automatically to the conclusion that this condition is no longer fulfilled, particularly if the individual's difficulties are temporary. Moreover, a student's financial circumstances may change. The truthfulness of the declaration on this matter must be assessed only as at the time when it is made.

Grzelczyk predates Directive 2004/38 which provides that, although students and their families have, generally, a right to equality of treatment with the host State's nationals, they have no entitlement to welfare during the first three months of residence. Nor is a Member State obliged to provide maintenance grants and student loans for persons other than workers, the self-employed and their families (Article 24).

9.8.5 Right of permanent residence

Article 16 of Directive 2004/38 grants a right of permanent residence to Union citizens who have resided legally in a host State for at least five years. Once the right has arisen, individuals need no longer be workers, self-employed, students, or persons of independent means. The right extends to family members, irrespective of nationality, though family members who are not Union citizens must normally have resided legally with the Union citizen in the host State for five years. The right is lost only through absence from the host State for more than two years. In some circumstances, such as retirement, a Union citizen acquires the right to remain permanently before completing five years' residence (Article 17).

The right to remain permanently provides additional safeguards in relation to Member States' right to expel individuals on grounds of public policy or public security. No such decision may be taken against persons with permanent residency rights except on 'serious' grounds of public policy or public security. Further, an expulsion decision taken against a Union citizen who has resided in the host State for ten years or is a minor (unless in the best interests of the child) must be based on 'imperative' grounds of public security (Article 28). The public policy and public security grounds are discussed in detail in **Chapter 11**.

9.9 Freedom from discrimination

You may recall the cases in which the Court of Justice affirmed that Union citizens lawfully resident in another Member State are entitled to be free from discrimination on grounds of nationality, on the basis of Article 12 (ex 6) EC.

EXERCISE 9.6

Look back at the relevant cases, *Sala*, *Grzelczyk*, *D'Hoop*, and *Trojani* (9.6) (*Cases and Materials* (9.1)).

A similar, though slightly less extensive, right is now enshrined in Directive 2004/38, which provides that all Union citizens exercising residency rights under the Directive, and their family members, are entitled to equal treatment with the nationals of the host State 'within the scope of the Treaty' (Article 24).

QUESTION 9.5

Are there any exceptions? Refer back to (9.8.4).

One exception applies to students and their families. Member States are not obliged to provide maintenance grants and student loans for persons other than workers, the self-employed, and their families. In relation to welfare benefits, the derogation from the equality principle applies to students but also more widely. Article 24 provides that persons exercising rights under the Directive have no right to welfare during the first three months of residence, other than workers, the self-employed, and their families.

Directive 2004/38 also provides that those who enter in search of work have no right to welfare at any time. However, in the light of its decisions in *Collins* and *Ioannidis*, it could well be that the Court of Justice will in future admit exceptions to this rule insofar as benefits intended to facilitate access to the labour market are concerned. (*Collins* v *Secretary of State for work and pensions* (Case C-138/02), judgment of 23 March 2004; *Ioannidis* (Case C-258/04) [2005] 3 CLMR 47 (see **Chapter 10**).

9.10 Administrative formalities

9.10.1 Reporting requirements

Member States may require persons to report to the authorities within a reasonable period of time after entry (Directive 2004/39, Article 5) but it is clear that reporting requirements must not be unduly restrictive. An Italian requirement that immigrant workers report to the police within three days of arrival was considered in *Criminal Proceedings against Lynne Watson and Alessandro Belmann* (Case 118/75) [1976] ECR 1185 and *Messner* (Case C-265/88) [1989] ECR 4209. *Watson and Belmann* confirmed the right of Member States to keep track of population movements and, in particular, to specify a period of time within which foreign nationals must report. However, that period must not be unreasonable. In *Messner*, the Court of Justice held that three days was unreasonably short. Where requirements are lawful, Member States may apply proportionate sanctions (*Watson and Belmann*).

EXERCISE 9.7

Look at the extract from *R* v *Pieck* (Case 157/79) [1980] ECR 2171 (*Cases and Materials* (9.2)). What views did the Court of Justice express on deportation, fines, and imprisonment as penalties for non-compliance with formalities by Community migrant workers?

The Court viewed deportation in these circumstances as incompatible with Community law, since it negates the very right conferred and guaranteed by the Treaty. National authorities are not entitled to impose penalties which are so disproportionate to the gravity of the infringement that they become obstacles to the free movement of persons. Whilst fines may be proportionate, imprisonment is not.

9.10.2 Registration: Union citizens

In addition to any reporting requirements and for periods of residence over three months, Member States may require Union citizens, including family members who are also Union citizens, to register with the relevant authorities. A registration certificate must be issued immediately. Proportionate and non-discriminatory penalties may be applied for failure to comply.

9.10.3 Residence cards: third country nationals

If they plan to reside in the host State for more than three months, family members who are not Union citizens must apply for a residence card. The 'Residence card of a family member of a Union citizen' must be valid for five years or for the intended period of residence, if shorter. Again, proportionate and non-discriminatory penalties may be applied for failure to comply.

9.10.4 Other administrative requirements

It is clear that the Court of Justice will insist on the proportionality of penalties applied for infringements of other kinds of administrative requirement too. This point is illustrated by *Skanavi*.

***Criminal Proceedings against Sofia Skanavi and Constantin Chryssanthakopoulos* (Case C-193/94) [1996] ECR I-929**

Mrs Skanavi, a Greek national residing in Germany, had failed to exchange her Greek driving licence for a German licence, as required by Community law. She was charged with driving without a licence and faced a criminal penalty of up to one year's imprisonment or a fine. The Court of Justice held that the requirement was administrative and that to treat a person who has failed to exchange a licence as driving without a licence, triggering criminal penalties, would be disproportionate to the gravity of the infringement. It would constitute a lasting restriction on free movement, since a criminal conviction may have serious consequences for the individual's employment or self-employment activity.

9.11 Community rights in the State of origin

Community free movement rights cannot be claimed against a person's State of origin unless that individual has already exercised the right of free movement.

***Morson and Jhanjan* v *Netherlands* (Cases 35 & 36/82) [1982] ECR 3723**

This issue arose in *Morson*, in which the Court of Justice held that two Surinamese women who wanted to join their adult children (on whom they were dependent) in Holland had no right to do so under Community law. Since the children had Dutch nationality and 'had never exercised their right to free movement within the Community', this was a purely internal matter which had no Community element.

Whilst the Court of Justice has continued to reiterate this principle, numerous claimants have succeeded in establishing the necessary Community element in a variety of ways. Some of the cases have concerned individuals who have returned to their State of origin following a period of economic activity in another Member State.

***R* v *Immigration Appeal Tribunal and Singh, ex parte Secretary of State for the Home Department* (Case C-370/90) [1992] ECR I-4265**

Here, the Court of Justice upheld the Community right of the Indian husband of a British woman to re-enter the UK following a period when the couple had been working in Germany. By leaving the UK to work in Germany, Mr Singh's wife had become a Community migrant worker, acquiring all the rights attached to that status. That included the right of family members to re-enter and reside in the Member State of origin.

In order to benefit from Community rights of re-entry and residence in such circumstances, the spouse must be lawfully resident in a Member State when moving to the Member State to which the Union citizen is migrating. Nonetheless where this is not so, in assessing the spouse's application to enter and remain with the returning Union citizen, the authorities must have regard to the right to respect for family life under Article 8 of the European Convention on Human Rights, provided the marriage is genuine (*Akrich* (*Secretary of State for the Home Department* v *Akrich* (Case C-109/01) [2003] ECR I-9607)). It is worth noting that under Article 35 of Directive 2004/38, Member States may refuse, terminate, or withdraw rights in cases of abuse or fraud, including marriages of convenience.

Like *Singh, Terhoeve* concerned an individual who had exercised free movement rights by pursuing economic activity in another Member State.

***Terhoeve* v *Inspecteur van de Belastingdienst Particulieren/Ondernemingen Buitenland* (Case C-18/95) [1999] ECR I-345**

The Court of Justice held that a Dutch national who had been posted to the UK by his Dutch employer could rely on Article 39 (ex 48) EC and Regulation 1612/68 to challenge Dutch social security legislation which operated to his disadvantage as a result of his residence in another Member State.

EXERCISE 9.8

Look back at *D'Hoop* (9.6) and read the extracts from *Carpenter* (*Cases and Materials* (9.3)). What factors brought the respective applicants within the scope of Community law?

In *D'Hoop* the Court of Justice extended the right to rely on Community law against one's own Member State, which in *Singh* and *Terhoeve* was applied to workers, to an individual who had resided in another Member State for completion of her secondary education (*D'Hoop* v *Office national de l'emploi* (Case C-224/98) [2002] ECR I-6191). Mrs Carpenter's claim concerned rights derived from her husband's status.

***Carpenter* v *Secretary of State for the Home Department* (Case C-60/00) [2002] ECR 1-6279, Court of Justice**

Mrs Carpenter, a national of the Philippines, had stayed on in the UK after the expiry of her leave to remain as a visitor. She claimed that she was entitled to stay under Community law, her right being derived from her husband's rights under Article 49 (ex 59) EC and secondary legislation relating to the provision of services. Although, unlike the British spouse in *Singh*, Mr Carpenter had not established himself in another Member State, he had travelled to other Member States to provide and receive services.

The Court of Justice accepted Mrs Carpenter's claim, referring to the importance of the protection of family life of nationals of the Member States in eliminating obstacles to the exercise of fundamental Treaty rights.

Other cases affirmed the Community rights of persons who had always been resident in one Member State but held the nationality of another.

***Avello* v *Belgian State* (Case C-148/02) [2003] ECR I-11613**

In *Avello* the Court of Justice held that children with dual Belgian and Spanish nationality who had been resident in Belgium since their birth there, had the right to be free from discrimination under Community law, in relation to Belgian rules governing their surname.

***Zhu and Chen* v *Secretary of State for the Home Department* (Case C-200/02) [2004] ECR I-9925**

Similarly, a child with Irish nationality who had been born in the UK and had always lived there was entitled to remain in the UK for an indefinite period, by virtue of her rights under Article 18 EC and Directive 90/364.

CONCLUSIONS

The principle of freedom of movement for persons has undergone remarkable development over the course of the Community's history. Interpreted and applied in the early years within the context of the economic origins of the internal market, this principle initially related only to those persons with economic status—workers, the self-employed, and their families. Then, secondary legislation conferred free movement rights on certain groups of economically inactive persons—students and persons of independent means. Subsequently, following the creation of citizenship of the European Union by the Treaty on European Union, the Court of Justice extended non-discrimination and residency rights to Union citizens, within the scope of application of the Treaty. Finally, with the adoption of Directive 2004/38, rights to enter and a limited right to reside in another Member State are extended to all Union citizens. This chapter has considered the scope of free movement rights for Union citizens. **Chapters 10** and **11** concern the more specific rights granted to the economically active and their families and the limitations on those rights.

SUMMARY

- **Free movement of persons** is one of the four fundamental freedoms of the Community internal market.
- **Originally, rights were granted to the economically active**: workers, the self-employed (Articles 39 (ex 48), 43 (ex 52), 49 (ex 59) EC), and their families (Directive 68/360, Regulation 1612/68).
- **Subsequently, rights were extended to:** three groups of economically inactive persons—persons with independent means, retired persons, and students, provided they had sufficient financial resources (Directive 90/ 364, 90/365, 90/366 (later Directive 93/96)).
- **Free movement rights** relate to not only freedom of movement and residence but also incorporate the right to be free from discrimination on grounds of nationality 'within the scope of application' of the Treaty (Article 12 (ex 6) EC).
- **Citizenship of the European Union**, together with free movement rights for Union citizens, was introduced into the EC Treaty by the Treaty on European Union (Articles 17 (ex 8), 18 (ex 8a) EC).
- **The Court of Justice applied Article 18 (ex 8a)** in a number of cases (*Sala*, *Grzelczyk*, *D'Hoop*, *Baumbast*), though Union citizens 'free movement rights remain' subject to the limitations and conditions laid down in [the] Treaty and the measures adopted to give it effect (Article 18 (ex 8a) EC).
- **The Citizenship Directive 2004/38** repealed much of the pre-existing secondary legislation on free movement of persons, consolidating and extending the former provisions. Echoing the declaration of the Court of Justice, the Directive states that '... citizenship should be the fundamental status of the nationals of the Member States when they exercise their right of free movement and residence ...' The Directive grants limited rights to all Union citizens. It affirms and extends the rights of those groups who were already beneficiaries of rights under the former provisions (subject to derogation, considered in **Chapter 11**) and creates a new right of permanent residence.

CHAPTER 9 ASSESSMENT EXERCISE

Outline the development of Community law on the free movement of persons in the internal market.

See *Cases and Materials* (9.5) for specimen answer

FURTHER READING

Barber, N. (2002). 'Citizenship, Nationalism and the European Union' 27 *EL Rev* 241.

Jacqueson, C. (2002). 'Union Citizenship and the Court of Justice: Something New under the Sun? Towards Social Citizenship' 27 *EL Rev* 260.

White, R. (2005). 'Free Movement, Equal Treatment and Citizenship of the Union' 54 *ICLQ* 885.

10 Free movement of persons: workers, the self-employed, and their families

10.1 OBJECTIVES

By the end of this chapter you should be able to:

1 Detail the Treaty Articles and secondary legislation granting free movement rights to workers, the self-employed and their families.

2 Describe the scope of the right of workers, the self-employed and their families to move freely to and reside in another Member State and to be free from discrimination on grounds of nationality.

10.2 Introduction

As noted in **Chapter 9**, the original Treaty provisions on free movement of persons were designed to ensure that economically active nationals of the Member States are able to move around the Community and to reside in locations where their skills and labour are in demand. These provisions give free movement rights to workers and set out the right of establishment and to provide services in another Member State, all subject to limitations on grounds of public policy, public security, or public health. Secondary legislation conferred rights on family members and, additionally, the Court of Justice recognized limited rights, now contained in secondary legislation, for persons moving to another Member State in search of work. The Citizenship Directive 2004/38 repealed, consolidated, and extended much of the original secondary legislation. The rights of workers, the self-employed, and their families are the focus of this chapter. **Chapter 11** considers derogation from the rights.

10.3 Key provisions

The key provisions are:

(a) Article 39 (ex 48) EC: rights of workers.

(b) Article 43 (ex 52) EC: freedom of establishment.

(c) Article 49 (ex 59) EC: freedom to provide services.

(d) Directive 2004/38: Citizenship Directive.

It should be remembered that all Union citizens derive their primary rights of free movement and residence and of freedom from discrimination from Articles 18 (ex 8(a)) and 12 (ex 6) EC, respectively.

EXERCISE 10.1

Do you recall Articles 12 and 18 EC? Look back at **Chapter 9** to refresh your memory.

10.4 Free movement of workers

10.4.1 Treaty rights

THE EC TREATY

Article 39 (ex 48)

1. Freedom of movement for workers shall be secured within the Community.
2. Such freedom of movement shall entail the abolition of any discrimination based on nationality between workers of the Member States as regards employment, remuneration, and other conditions of work and employment.
3. It shall entail the right, subject to limitations justified on grounds of public policy, public security, or public health:
   (a) to accept offers of employment actually made;
   (b) to move freely within the territory of Member States for this purpose;
   (c) to stay in a Member State for the purpose of employment in accordance with the provisions governing the employment of nationals of that State laid down by law, regulation, or administrative action;
   (d) to remain in the territory of a Member State after having been employed in that State, subject to conditions which shall be embodied in implementing regulations to be drawn up by the Commission.
4. The provisions of this Article shall not apply to employment in the public service.

EXERCISE 10.2

Article 39 grants much wider rights to workers than simply the right to move freely within the Community. Write down a brief summary of these rights.

In addition to the right of free movement, Article 39 (ex 48) EC grants workers the right to accept offers of employment in other Member States, to stay there during that employment, and, (subject to conditions) to remain after employment has ceased. Note also the specific application of the general principle of non-discrimination on grounds of nationality, providing for the abolition of discrimination based on nationality between the workers of the Member States with respect to pay and conditions of employment. These scope of these rights is defined by secondary legislation, Directive 2004/38 and Regulation 1612/68.

10.4.2 **Who is a 'worker'?**

The rights apply to Union citizens who are workers. How then is 'worker' defined?

There is no Treaty definition, however the Court of Justice has emphasized that the term may not be defined by national laws but has a Community meaning (*Hoekstra (née Unger)* v *Bestuur der Bedrijfsvereniging voor Detailhandel en Ambachten* (Case 75/63) [1964] ECR 177 and *Levin* v *Staatssecretaris van Justitie* (Case 53/81) [1982] ECR 1035 (*Cases and Materials* (10.1.1)).

QUESTION 10.1

Why has the Court of Justice insisted that 'worker' be given a Community meaning?

If Member States were able to decide and modify the meaning of 'worker', the free movement rules would be frustrated because national laws would be able to 'eliminate at will the protection afforded by the Treaty to certain categories of person' (*Hoekstra*).

The Court of Justice defined 'worker' in *Lawrie-Blum* v *Land Baden-Württemberg* (Case 66/85) [1986] ECR 2121 (*Cases and Materials* (10.1.1)) and has frequently referred to this definition in later judgments. The 'essential feature of an employment relationship . . . is that for a certain period of time a person performs services for and under the direction of another person in return for which he receives remuneration'.

QUESTION 10.2

Can you think of any particular circumstances in which an individual's status as a worker might be open to doubt?

Look at the cases in the next exercise.

EXERCISE 10.3

Read the extracts from the following cases. Summarize each applicant's circumstances. Was the individual concerned held to be a 'worker' under Community law? Write down your answers.

(a) *Hoekstra (née Unger)* v *Bestuur der Bedrijfsvereniging voor Detailhandel en Ambachten* (Case 75/63) [1964] ECR 177 (*Cases and Materials* (10.1.1)).

(b) *Levin* v *Staatssecretaris van Justitie* (Case 53/81) [1982] ECR 1035 (*Cases and Materials* (10.1.1)).

(c) *Kempf* v *Staatssecretaris van Justitie* (Case 139/85) [1986] ECR 1741 (*Cases and Materials* (10.1.1)).

(d) *Steymann* v *Staatssecretaris van Justitie* (Case 196/87) [1988] ECR 6159 (*Cases and Materials* (10.1.1)).

(e) *Bettray* v *Staatssecretaris van Justitie* (Case 344/87) [1989] ECR 1621 (*Cases and Materials* (10.1.1)).

(f) *Trojani* v *Centre public d'aide social de Bruxelles* (Case C-456/02 [2004] 3 CMLR 38 (*Cases and Materials* (10.1.1)).

The concept of 'worker' included:

(a) *Hoekstra*: a person who, having left her job, was not currently in employment but was capable of taking another job.

(b) *Levin*: a part-time worker whose income from employment did not provide sufficient means of support and fell below the nationally recognized minimum subsistence level, where the work was 'effective and genuine' and not on such a small scale as to be 'purely marginal and ancillary' (*Levin*).

In *Levin*, the Court of Justice did not consider the position of a worker whose below-subsistence income is supplemented by state benefit rather than from private funds. This issue arose in *Kempf*. Note also that in *Levin* the Court of Justice indicated that, provided the work is 'effective and genuine', a person's motives in seeking employment in another Member State are irrelevant.

Levin v *Staatssecretaris van Justitie* (Case 53/81) [1982] ECR 1035

The Dutch authorities refused Mrs Levin (a British national and the wife of a national of a non-member country) a permit to reside in the Netherlands on the grounds that she was not engaged in a gainful occupation. She had subsequently taken up part-time work, earning less than the income considered in the Netherlands to be the minimum necessary for subsistence. She claimed that she and her husband had more than sufficient income to support themselves. The Netherlands Government maintained that the Article 39 (ex 48) rights applied only to persons whose income from employment reaches at least the subsistence level laid down by the host State or who work the number of hours considered normal for full-time employment in any particular sector.

(c) *Kempf*: a part-time worker whose income was below the minimum means of subsistence in the host State and who needed to supplement that income by drawing supplementary state benefit.

Kempf v _Staatssecretaris van Justitie_ (Case 139/85) [1986] ECR 1741

Mr Kempf, a German national, was resident in the Netherlands where he worked as a part-time music teacher, giving twelve lessons per week. His income was supplemented by social security benefit. Kempf was refused a residence permit on the grounds that he was not a worker (and therefore not a 'favoured EEC citizen') because his income from employment did not meet his needs. The national court had found that Kempf's work was not on such a small scale as to be purely a marginal and ancillary activity.

(d) *Steymann*: a member of a religious community who performed general household duties and was engaged in commercial activity on behalf of the community. Although he did not receive formal wages but only his 'keep' and pocket money, the work constituted an 'economic activity'.

Steymann v _Staatssecretaris van Justitie_ (Case 196/87) [1988] ECR 6159

Following a short period of employment as a plumber in the Netherlands, Mr Steymann, a German national, joined a Dutch religious community known as the Bhagwan Community. Here, he undertook plumbing work and general household duties and participated in the Community's commercial activities which included running a discotheque, a bar, and a launderette. His application for a residence permit was turned down on the grounds that he was not a 'favoured EEC national'.

(e) *Bettray*: the concept of 'worker' did not include a person who was taking part in a drug-rehabilitation programme aimed to reintegrate people into the workforce and which involved work carried out under supervision and for remuneration. Here, since the objective was the rehabilitation of the individual, the work could not be regarded as an 'effective and genuine economic activity'.

Bettray v _Staatssecretaris van Justitie_ (Case 344/87) [1989] ECR 1621

The Netherlands authorities had refused to grant Mr Bettray a residence permit on three occasions. Bettray had given as one of the reasons for his residence in the Netherlands 'a stay in a rehabilitation centre for drug addicts'. At the centre, under a scheme set up under the Dutch Social Employment Act, individuals were engaged in work for which they received payment but which was aimed to enable them eventually to take up ordinary employment or lead as normal a life as possible.

(f) In *Trojani*, the Court of Justice left the decision as to Mr Trojani's worker status to the national court:

***Trojani* v *Centre public d'aide sociale de Bruxelles* (Case C-456/02) [2004] 3 CMLR 38**

Mr Trojani was a French national who had worked as a self-employed person for a short time in Belgium, had left and then returned some years later, obtaining temporary leave to reside. After living at a campsite and a youth hostel, he was given accommodation at a Salvation Army hostel in Brussels. Here, in return for board and lodging and some pocket money, he did various jobs around the hostel for around thirty hours per week as part of a 'personal socio-occupational reintegration programme'. Mr Trojani's application for the minimex welfare benefit was refused on grounds of his nationality and on the basis that he had no entitlement to it as a 'worker'. The Court of Justice, having established that the benefits in kind and money received by Mr Trojani constituted consideration for work for and under the direction of the hostel, held that the national court must decide whether that work was real and genuine and part of the 'normal labour market'. This could entail consideration of the status and practices of the hostel, the content of the reintegration programme, and the nature and detail of the work.

With the exception of *Bettray*, these cases illustrate the Court of Justice's concern to extend individual rights through a broad definition of 'worker'.

***Franca Ninni-Orasche* v *Bundesminister für Wissenschaft, Verkehr und Kunst* (Case C-413/01) [2004] 1 CMLR 19**

The same approach is apparent here, where the Court considered the situation of an Italian woman who had been resident in Germany since 1993. She had taken up employment some years after her arrival in Germany and had worked for only two and a half months under a fixed-term contract. In the meantime she had gained qualifications for university entry, looking for other work between the expiry of her fixed-term contract and taking up studies. The Court held that none of these factors would be relevant in the determination of worker status, provided the activity performed as an employed person was not purely marginal and ancillary.

Directive 2004/38 extends the scope of 'worker' to include, for instance, persons who are temporarily unable to work because of illness or accident and involuntarily unemployed after at least a year in employment (Article 7(3)).

10.4.3 Right to enter and remain

QUESTION 10.3

Under secondary legislation, what is the precise scope of workers' rights to enter and remain in another Member State? If you have forgotten, glance back at **Chapter 9**.

Under Directive 2004/38 workers who are Union citizens have a right to enter and reside in another Member State for more than three months (Articles 5, 7). The right of permanent residence arises after five years (see **Chapter 9**).

10.4.4 Freedom from discrimination

The general principle of non-discrimination contained in Article 12 (ex 6) EC is given specific application to workers in Article 39(2) (ex 48(2)), which provides for the abolition of any discrimination based on nationality between the workers of the Member States as regards pay and other conditions of employment. The Court of Justice has confirmed that the right may be invoked not only against the Member States and public authorities but also against private individuals (*Angonese* v *Cassa di Risparmio di Bolzano SpA* (Case C-281/98) [2000] ECR I-4139).

Article 24 of Directive 2004/38 confers a right to equality of treatment with nationals of the host State on all Union citizens exercising their rights under the Directive and their families. More specifically, Regulation 1612/68 elaborates on a workers' primary Treaty right to freedom from discrimination.

10.4.5 Regulation 1612/68

Unlike the other pre-existing secondary legislation concerning free movement of persons, Regulation 1612/68 escaped repeal by Directive 2004/38, save for two of its provisions relating to workers' families, Articles 10 and 11, which have been amended and absorbed into the new Directive.

Regulation 1612/68 gives substance to the provisions of Article 39 (ex 48) EC in three important areas: eligibility for employment, equal treatment in employment, and children's rights.

10.4.5.1 Eligibility for employment (Articles 1–6)

The Regulation provides that any national of a Member State has the right to take up and pursue employment in another Member State with the same priority and under the same conditions as host State nationals. It prohibits discrimination such as limits on applications or offers of employment, special recruitment procedures, advertising restrictions, and any other impediments to the recruitment of non-resident workers.

***Commission* v *France (French Merchant Seamen)* (Case 167/73) [1974] ECR 359**

This case concerned Article 4 of Regulation 1612/68, which prohibits national measures restricting the employment of nationals of other Member States by number or percentage. The offending French provision was Article 3(2) of the *Code du Travail Maritime* of 1926. Ministerial orders issued pursuant to this Article imposed an overall ratio of three French to one non-French crew members on ships of the merchant fleet. By refusing to amend Article 3(2), France was found to be in breach of its Community obligations.

In a later decision, the Court of Justice held that rules laid down by sporting associations limiting the number of professional footballers who are nationals of other Member States which football clubs can field in official matches infringe the free movement provisions of the Treaty (*Union Royale Belge des Sociétés de Football Association ASBL* v *Bosman* (Case 415/93) [1995] ECR I-4921).

Article 3(1) does, however, permit the application of language requirements, provided these are necessary 'by reason of the nature of the post to be filled'.

Groener v _Minister for Education_ (Case 379/87) [1989] ECR 3967

This issue arose in *Groener* (*Cases and Materials* (10.1.2)) which concerned an Irish requirement that lecturers in Irish vocational schools be competent in the Irish language. Although this had the effect of discriminating against non-nationals, it was held to be compatible with Regulation 1612/68.

This is a somewhat surprising decision, since the teaching of art in these schools was conducted in English.

QUESTION 10.4

Why, then, did the Court of Justice consider that it was not unreasonable to require teachers to have some knowledge of the national language?

Groener cont.

The Irish government had for some years been promoting the use of the Irish language, which was recognized by the Irish Constitution as the first official language. The Court considered that education was important in the implementation of this policy. In view of the privileged relationship of teachers with their pupils, in a role which was not confined to the classroom but extended to participation in the general life of the school, the language requirement was not disproportionate to the government's policy objective.

However, a requirement to hold a particular language qualification would be unlawful, unless it could be justified by factors unrelated to nationality and was proportionate to its objective. The Court of Justice so held in *Angonese* v *Cassa di Risparmio di Bolzano SpA* (Case C-281/98) [2000] ECR I-4139, which concerned a requirement of this kind imposed by an Italian bank. Although the applicant, Mr Angonese, did not possess the language certificate required by the bank, he could provide other evidence of his linguistic ability.

QUESTION 10.5

The language requirement considered in *Groener* was indirectly discriminatory. What does this mean?

Measures which openly differentiate between nationals and non-nationals are directly discriminatory. Measures which appear on their face to treat nationals and non-nationals alike but in practice have a discriminatory effect are indirectly discriminatory. The language requirement in *Groener* applied to all applicants, irrespective of nationality, and was therefore not directly discriminatory. However, the requirement was indirectly discriminatory because it had a greater impact on non-Irish applicants who would be less likely than Irish applicants to have knowledge of the Irish language. Despite this, as has been noted, the Court of Justice held the requirement to be objectively justified under Article 3(1) of Regulation 1612/68.

10.4.5.2 Equal treatment in employment

Migrant workers may not be treated differently from national workers by reason of their nationality with respect to conditions of employment such as pay, dismissal, reinstatement, and re-engagement (Article 7, Regulation 1612/68). Discrimination is unlawful, whether it be direct or indirect.

Marsman v _Rosskamp_ (Case 44/72) [1972] ECR 1243

This case concerned directly discriminatory German legislation. The legislation accorded a degree of employment protection in the event of injury at work to all national workers irrespective of their State of residence but only to those non-national workers who were living in Germany. This directly discriminatory measure was found to be an infringement of the principle of equality in employment.

Sotgiu (*Cases and Materials* (10.1.3)) provides a good illustration of indirect discrimination.

Sotgiu v _Deutsche Bundespost_ (Case 152/73) [1974] ECR 153

The German Federal Post Office had increased the separation allowance paid to post office employees in Germany who lived away from home. Those who were living in Germany at the time of their recruitment were paid at a higher rate than those who had been living abroad at that time. Whilst this arrangement did not discriminate directly against non-nationals, in practice it was likely to operate to the disadvantage of non-nationals. The Court of Justice found that the arrangement was capable of amounting to inequality of treatment, though left open the possibility that it might be objectively justified because the higher allowance was temporary and had conditions attached to it.

10.4.5.3 Social and tax advantages

Article 7(2) guarantees non-national workers the same social and tax advantages as national workers. This provision has been interpreted widely by the Court of Justice.

QUESTION 10.6

Must a 'social advantage' be attached to a contract of employment? Look at *Cristini* (*Cases and Materials* (10.1.4)).

***Cristini* v *SNCF* (Case 32/75) [1975] ECR 1085**

The widow of an Italian worker, herself an Italian national, who had four infant children, was refused the French Railways (SNCF) fare reduction card for large families, on grounds of her nationality. SNCF argued that the card did not amount to a 'social advantage' under Article 7(2) because that Article applied only to advantages attaching to worker status. The Court disagreed, holding that the provision applied to all social and tax advantages, whether or not they are attached to the contract of employment. Moreover, since the card was available to the families of deceased French workers, it would be contrary to the purpose and spirit of the Treaty to deny the same benefit to the families of deceased workers of other Member States.

'Social and tax advantages' have included a disability allowance claimed by an Italian worker in France for his adult son (*Inzirillo* v *Caisse d'Allocations Familiales de l'Arondissement de Lyon* (Case 63/76) [1976] ECR 2057); a discretionary childbirth loan (*Reina* v *Landeskreditbank Baden-Württemberg* (Case 65/81) [1982] ECR 33); a guaranteed income for old people in Belgium claimed by an Italian widow living there with her retired son (*Castelli* v *ONPTS* (Case 261/83) [1984] ECR 3199); and the Belgian 'minimex' (minimum income allowance) claimed by an unemployed worker (*Hoeckx* v *Centre Public d'Aide Sociale de Kalmthout* (Case 249/83) [1985] ECR 973) and by members of the family of an unemployed worker (*Scrivner* v *Centre Public d'Aide Sociale de Chastre* (Case 122/84) [1985] ECR 1027).

Whilst in *Lebon*, the Court of Justice held that the right to equal social and tax advantages does not extend to jobseekers (*Centre Public d'Aide Sociale de Courcelles* v *Lebon* (Case 316/85) [1987] ECR 2811 (*Cases and Materials* (10.1.4))), the later *Sala* judgment suggests that the Court of Justice has moved towards the recognition of broader rights for jobseekers. Here, in the context of Article 39 (ex 48) EC and Article 7(2) of Regulation 1612/68, the Court declared that a person who is genuinely seeking work must be classified as a worker. However, it is unclear whether this classification might be applied to a national of a Member State who enters another Member State as a jobseeker as well as to a non-national Community worker whose employment in another Member State has ended and who is consequently seeking further employment in that Member State. (*Sala* v *Freistaat Bayern* (Case C-85/96) [1998] ECR I-2691).

Equality of treatment accorded to workers under Regulation 1612/68 also includes equal trade union rights and equal treatment in matters of housing and house ownership (Articles 8, 9).

10.4.6 Access to education and training

Workers' children residing in the host State have the same right as nationals to general education, apprenticeship, and vocational training courses (Article 12, Regulation 1612/68). This provision has been interpreted liberally to include not only equal access to educational courses but also equal eligibility for 'any general measures intended to facilitate educational attendance', including grants (*Casagrande* v *Landeshauptstadt München* (Case 9/74) [1974] ECR 773 (*Cases and Materials* (10.1.5))).

Before its decision in *Bidar* (*R* v *London Borough of Ealing & Secretary of State for Education ex parte Bidar*) (Case C-209/03) [2005] ECR I-2119), the Court of Justice had interpreted student rights and worker rights in this area much more restrictively. Whilst the right to non-discrimination covers tuition fees (*Gravier* v *City of Liège* (Case 293/83) [1985] ECR 593 (*Cases and Materials* (10.1.5))), the Court of Justice held in *Lair* that students were not entitled to maintenance grants and loans from a host State, since these were matters of social and educational policy, falling outside the scope of the Treaty. Moreover, a worker's right of equal access to education did not include eligibility for maintenance grants and loans, save in specific circumstances. A worker who gave up work voluntarily in order to undertake a course of study in the host State could claim maintenance aid for study as a 'social advantage', but only if s/he could establish continuity between the previous work and the course of study. A person who had pursued employment in the host State purely as a means to becoming a student would not be eligible for such benefits. (*Lair* v *Universität Hannover* (Case 39/86) [1988] ECR 3161 (*Cases and Materials* (10.1.5)); *Brown* v *Secretary for State for Scotland* (Case 197/86) [1988] ECR 3205). Subsequently, the Court of Justice considered the position of workers with fixed term contracts.

Ninni-Orasche cont.

Ninni-Orasche concerned an Italian woman who had worked in Germany until the expiry of her two-and-a-half-month fixed-term contract. She had subsequently gained qualifications for university entry, whilst at the same time continuing, unsuccessfully, to seek other employment. Her request for a maintenance grant for her studies had been refused. The Court of Justice held that the expiry of a fixed-term contract does not necessarily amount to voluntary unemployment. The national court may take account of factors such as the employment practices in that sector and the individual's chances of finding that particular kind of employment on a permanent basis. Nonetheless, the Court reiterated its previous rulings in *Lair* and *Brown* concerning individuals who pursue employment in the host State solely for the purpose of benefiting from the host State's system of student assistance. Here, unemployment would be voluntary.

The right to equal treatment conferred by Article 24 of Directive 2004/38 on all Union citizens and their family members will undoubtedly be interpreted to include equality of access to education with nationals of the host State. However, the Directive incorporates the *Lair* and *Brown* rulings on entitlement to grants and loans for studies, including vocational training, by restricting that entitlement to workers, the self-employed, persons who retain such status, and their families. In this regard, Article 7(3) provides that a Union citizen who is no longer a worker or a self-employed person may nevertheless retain that status. This will be the case if s/he is involuntarily unemployed and embarks upon vocational training or if s/he is voluntarily unemployed and the training is related to the previous employment.

Notwithstanding these unequivocal statements about student maintenance grants and loans, in a remarkable judgment delivered before Directive 2004/38 came into effect, the Court of Justice effectively ignored the Article 24 exception to the equality principle and brought student loans within the scope of Community law.

***R* v *London Borough of Ealing & Secretary of State for Education ex parte Bidar* (Case C-209/03) [2005] ECR I-2119**

Dany Bidar, a French national, had come to the UK with his mother, who died soon after their arrival. Mr Bidar had remained in the UK, living with his grandmother, completing his secondary education and then, in 2001, starting a course at University College, London. He had not previously received any social assistance but now applied for a student loan. This was refused on the ground that he was not settled in the UK. On a reference from the High Court, the Court of Justice revisited the issue of student entitlement to maintenance aid for studies from a host State. The Court referred to two significant developments introduced by the Treaty on European Union since the *Lair* and *Brown* judgments: the creation of Union citizenship and the new Article 149(1) EC, which provides for Community encouragement and support for cooperation between Member States in education matters.

The Court held that, in view of these developments, Article 12 EC conferred a right to equality with British nationals in relation to student grants and loans. However, a Member State would be justified in requiring a certain degree of integration into the society of that State, though would not be justified in insisting upon any link with the employment market. *Bidar* (*Cases and Materials* (10.1.5)).

10.4.7 Employment in the public service

EXERCISE 10.4

Look back to the beginning of this chapter, to Article 39(4) (ex 48(4)) EC. What does this Article provide?

Article 39(4) (ex 48(4)) EC allows Member States to deny or restrict access to employment in the public service on grounds of a worker's nationality. Potentially, this provision gives wide scope for discrimination, particularly in those Member States where the term 'public service' covers a broad spectrum of activities. However, the meaning of 'public service' is to be determined not by the Member States but by the Court, which has defined the term restrictively.

It is clear that Article 39(4) (ex 48(4)) EC applies only to admission to the public service. Once a national of another Member State has been appointed to a public service post, any discrimination on grounds of nationality with regard to remuneration or other conditions of employment will infringe the free movement provisions (*Sotgiu* v *Deutsche Bundespost* (Case 152/73) [1974] ECR 153 (*Cases and Materials* (10.1.3)).

QUESTION 10.7

In *Commission* v *Belgium* (*Public Employees*) (Case 149/79) [1980] ECR 3881 (*Cases and Materials* (10.1.6)) what posts did the Belgian government claim were in the public service?

***Commission* v *Belgium (Public Employees)* (Case 149/79) [1980] ECR 3881**

Under Belgian law, only Belgian nationals could work for local authorities and public undertakings in positions such as trainee drivers, loaders, platelayers, shunters and signallers on Belgian railways, unskilled workers on local railways and nurses, night-watchmen, plumbers, carpenters, electricians, garden hands, architects, and supervisors. The Belgian government argued that entry to public office was a matter for Member States and that 'public service' did not have a Community meaning. The Court of Justice disagreed, insisting upon the uniform interpretation and application of Article 39(4) (ex 48(4)) EC throughout the Community and defining 'public service' posts as those involving 'the exercise of power conferred by public law' where there was a 'responsibility for safeguarding the general interests of the State'.

Later judgments have excluded from 'public service' trainee school teachers (*Lawrie-Blum* v *Land Baden-Württemberg* (Case 66/85) [1986] ECR 2121 (*Cases and Materials* (10.1.1), university foreign language assistants (*Allué and Coonan* v *Universita degli studi di Venezia* (Case 33/88) [1989] ECR 1591), secondary school teachers (*Bleis* v *Ministère de l'Education Nationale* (Case C-4/91) [1991] ECR I-5627) and primary school teachers (*Commission* v *Luxembourg* (Case C-473/93) [1996] ECR I-3207). The Court of Justice has also confirmed that Article 39(4) applies only where the activities 'safeguarding the interest of the state' or requiring 'special allegiance to the state' are exercised on a regular basis and do not represent only a minor part of the activities of the post (*Anker, Ras, and Snoek* v *Germany* (Case C-47/02) [2004] 3 CMLR 14).

10.5 Jobseekers

Whilst originally neither the Treaty nor secondary legislation granted rights to Member State nationals who move in search of work, in *Royer* the Court of Justice established the right to enter another Member State as a jobseeker.

***Procureur du Roi* v *Royer* (Case 48/75) [1975] ECR 497**

It was perhaps not surprising that the Belgian authorities were unhappy about Mr Royer's presence in Belgium. In France, his country of origin, he had been convicted of procuring and prosecuted for armed robberies. He faced criminal proceedings for illegal entry and illegal residence in Belgium, where his wife, also a French national, ran a café and dance hall. In responding to questions referred by the Belgian court, the Court of Justice confirmed the right of entry to 'look for or pursue an occupation or activities as employed or self-employed persons'.

Subsequently, *Antonissen* made clear that there was no an absolute right to remain indefinitely. Here, the Court of Justice held that the UK could lawfully deport a Community migrant who had not found employment after six months. However, an individual would be entitled to stay on if they were making genuine efforts to find work and there was a real chance of being

employed (*R* v *Immigration Appeal Tribunal, ex parte Antonissen* (Case C-292/89) [1991] ECR I-745 (*Cases and Materials* (10.2))). A provision automatically requiring a national of another Member State to leave the country at the end of a specified period infringes Community law (*Commission* v *Belgium* (Case C-344/95) [1997] ECR I-1035).

These principles are now incorporated into Directive 2004/38, which, in Recital 9 states that the three-month maximum residency period in Article 6 does not preclude jobseekers' entitlement to the more favourable rights under the case law. Jobseekers may not be expelled for so long as they '. . . can provide evidence that they are continuing to seek employment and that they have a genuine chance of being engaged'. This applies even if they become an 'unreasonable burden on the social assistance system of the host State' (Article 14 (4)). However, jobseekers have no entitlement to social assistance in the host State (Article 24). Interestingly, *Collins*, judgment of 23 March 2004), decided only weeks before the adoption of Directive 2004/38, is in apparent conflict with this provision.

EXERCISE 10.5

Look at the extracts from *Collins* (*Cases and Materials* (10.2)). What were the Court of Justice's conclusions on jobseekers' eligibility to jobseeker's allowance?

***Collins* v *Secretary of State for Work and Pensions* (Case C-138/02)**

Mr Collins, who had dual Irish and American nationality, had come to the United Kingdom to look for work. His claim to jobseeker's allowance had been refused on the ground that he was not habitually resident in the UK since he had not been resident for an appreciable time and he was not a 'worker' under Community law.

The Court referred to its earlier judgment in *Antonissen*, in which it confirmed that jobseekers' rights are derived from Article 39 (ex 48) EC. Those rights included the right to equality with national workers. The Court acknowledged that its earlier decisions had denied jobseekers entitlement to financial benefits. However, the Court now reasoned that in view of its more recent judgments on Union citizens' right to non-discrimination, under Article 12 (ex 6) EC, the principle of equality in Article 39(2) (ex 48(2)) must be interpreted to include a right to a financial benefit 'intended to facilitate access to employment in the labour market of a Member State'.

Whilst this represents an extension of jobseeker rights, the Court was careful to underline the link between the entitlement to this benefit and its purpose, namely to facilitate access to work. Moreover, the Court went on to confirm that a residence requirement attached to a jobseeker's allowance may be justified by objective considerations provided these are proportionate and non-discriminatory. If that requirement demands a period of residence, that period must be no longer than is necessary for the authorities to satisfy themselves that the individual is genuinely seeking work.

Later, the Court of Justice took the same approach in *Ioannidis*, in considering the Belgian authorities' refusal to grant the 'tide-over' allowance, for persons seeking their first employment, to a Greek national because he had not completed his secondary education in Belgium, as was required under national law. Whilst it would be legitimate for national law to require a link between the applicant for the allowance and the relevant geographic employment market, it would be disproportionate to insist that the completion of education in that Member State constituted a necessary element of that link. (*Ioannidis* (Case C-258/04) [2005] 3 CLMR 47)

10.6 Free movement rights for the self-employed

The two key Treaty provisions relating to free movement of the self-employed are Articles 43 (ex 52) EC (the right of establishment) and 49 (ex 59) EC (freedom to provide services). These two Articles apply not only to individuals but also to companies and there is a substantial body of case law concerning companies that operate in more than one Member State. Issues relating to companies lie outside the scope of this book. This chapter focuses on the rights of self-employed persons under the Treaty and the Citizenship Directive 2004/38. As is the case for workers, entitlement to independent rights of entry, residence, and non-discrimination apply only to Union citizens, although, as will be seen later, family members have derived rights under Community law, irrespective of their nationality.

10.6.1 Right of establishment and freedom to provide services

THE EC TREATY

Article 43 (ex 52)

Within the framework of the provisions set out below, restrictions on the freedom of establishment of nationals of a Member State in the territory of another Member State shall be prohibited. Such prohibition shall also apply to restrictions on the setting up of agencies, branches, or subsidiaries by nationals of any Member State established in the territory of any Member State.

Freedom of establishment shall include the right to take up and pursue activities as self-employed persons and to set up and manage undertakings, in particular companies or firms within the meaning of the second paragraph of Article 48, under the conditions laid down for its own nationals by the law of the country where such establishment is effected, subject to the provisions of the chapter relating to capital.

Article 49 (ex 59)

Within the framework of the provisions set out below, restrictions on freedom to provide services within the Community shall be prohibited in respect of nationals of Member States who are established in a State of the Community other than that of the person for whom the services are intended.

? QUESTION 10.8

What is the distinction between 'establishment' and the 'provision of services'?

Establishment in another Member State involves setting up a business or practising a professional activity there (for instance as a doctor or a lawyer) on a permanent or semi-permanent basis. When an individual is established in one Member State and simply provides services in another without being installed there, this constitutes the 'provision of services'. This includes a situation where a service provider does not move to another Member State but provides services there, for instance through telephone marketing (*Alpine Investments BV* v *Minister of Finance* (Case C-384/93) [1995] ECR I-1141).

10.6.2 Entry, residence, and limitation on the rights

The Treaty rights of establishment and to provide services are reaffirmed in Directive 2004/38 in the form of entry and residence rights for the self-employed. As in the case of workers, the rights are subject to limitations on grounds of public policy, public security, or public health (Articles 46 (ex 56) EC (establishment) and 55 (ex 66) EC (services) and Directive 2004/38). These limitations are considered in detail in **Chapter 11**.

10.6.3 Exercise of official authority

Article 45 (ex 55) EC contains an exception similar to that contained in Article 39(4) (ex 48(4)) EC concerning employment in the public service. It provides that the right of establishment shall not apply to activities which are connected with the exercise of official authority. This derogation, which also applies to services (Article 55 (ex 66) EC) has, like the Article 39(4) (ex 48(4)) EC derogation, been construed narrowly by the Court of Justice.

10.6.4 Freedom from discrimination

In two early cases, the Court of Justice held Articles 43 (ex 52) and 49 (ex 59) EC to be directly effective. Both cases concerned the right of self-employed persons to be free from discrimination on grounds of nationality. In one case, concerning a nationality requirement, the discrimination was direct. In the other, concerning a residence requirement, it was indirect.

EXERCISE 10.6

Look back at 10.4.5.1 if you have forgotten the meaning of 'direct discrimination' and 'indirect discrimination'.

***Reyners* v *Belgium* (Case 2/74) [1974] ECR 631**

A Dutch national resident in Belgium who held the qualification of *Docteur en Droit Belge* could not be admitted to the profession of advocate in Belgium because he did not satisfy the nationality requirement of the Belgian *Code Judiciaire*. The Court of Justice, declaring that Article 43 (ex 52) EC provides for the implementation of the general principle of non-discrimination contained in Article 12 (ex 6) EC, ruled that Article 43 had direct effect and thus could be invoked by Reyners.

Van Binsbergen* v *Bestuur van de Bedrijfsvereniging voor de Metaalnijverheid
(Case 33/74) [1974] ECR 1299

A Dutch national who had qualified as an advocate in Holland and was providing legal services to a client there was informed, when he moved from Holland to Belgium, that he could no longer represent his client because under Dutch law only lawyers established in Holland had rights of audience before certain tribunals. The Court of Justice held that Articles 49 and 50 (ex 59 and 60) EC were directly effective and could therefore be invoked by an individual who was the victim of discrimination either on grounds of nationality or State of residence.

QUESTION 10.9

Which Treaty provision prohibits discrimination on grounds of nationality 'within the scope of application of this Treaty'?

This principle is set out in Article 12 (ex 6) EC. In addition, as noted in **Chapter 9**, all Union citizens residing in a host State on the basis of Directive 2004/38 have the right to equal treatment with nationals (Article 24, Directive 2004/38).

It is uncertain whether full equality of treatment extends to Union citizens who are simply providing services, rather than being established, in another Member State. For instance, a service provider's entitlement to welfare benefits, irrespective of his or her length of residence in the host State, would, arguably, be more properly claimed from the State of establishment than from the host State.

Equality of treatment is problematic for the self-employed in other respects too. The difficulties stem from Articles 43 and 50 (ex 52 and 60) EC, which provide that the rights of establishment and to provide services are to be exercised under the same conditions as for nationals of the host State. Two areas in particular have been contentious: the recognition of qualifications and rules of professional conduct.

10.6.5 Recognition of qualifications

Applying the non-discrimination principle, it would be logical to expect that a Union citizen in self-employment in another Member State would be required to satisfy any qualification requirements applying to nationals in the same trade or profession. Because host State education and qualification requirements may not be easily satisfied by a non-national, they can constitute a very serious obstacle to the free movement of self-employed persons within the Community. The Court of Justice has set out guiding principles to deal with this issue.

It is an unjustified restriction on freedom of establishment to refuse admission to a profession to a person who has a qualification recognized as equivalent to a national qualification in the state of establishment and who has satisfied professional training requirements.

***Thieffry* v *Conseil de l'Ordre des Avocats à la Cour de Paris* (Case 71/76) [1977] ECR 765**

Mr Thieffry, a Belgian advocate, applied for admission to the Paris Bar. His application was rejected on the ground that he did not hold the necessary French qualifications and despite the fact that his Belgian qualifications were officially recognized in France as equivalent. The Court of Justice held that in circumstances such as these it is incompatible with Article 43 (ex 52) EC to restrict admission to a profession to individuals holding a national diploma. (*Cases and Materials* (10.3.1)).

Where qualifications are not already recognized as equivalent in the host State, the national authorities must compare an individual's education and training with national requirements and must recognize a non-national's qualifications if they are equivalent. If they are not, the authorities may require evidence of the necessary knowledge and experience (*Vlassopoulou* v *Ministerium für Justiz* (Case C-340/89) [1991] ECR I-2357 (*Cases and Materials* (10.3.1)).

10.6.6 Mutual recognition of qualifications

In order to overcome the problems surrounding the recognition of qualifications, a programme of harmonization was instigated, consisting in the adoption of twelve sectoral Directives setting out the requirements for particular trades and professions, including those of doctor, dentist, veterinary surgeon, pharmacist, nurse, and architect. As progress was very slow, a new approach was adopted with Directive 89/48. This provides for the mutual recognition of qualifications in professions requiring a higher education diploma, other than those already covered by the sectoral Directives, including law, accountancy, and surveying. An individual who holds a higher education diploma awarded on completion of at least three years' professional education and has completed the professional training required for that profession is, in principle, entitled to pursue that profession in another Member State.

Where training and education fall short of that required by the host State by at least one year or the individual has not undertaken the necessary period of supervised practice, evidence of professional experience may be required. In certain circumstances, Member States may require non-nationals to pass an aptitude test or complete a period of supervised training. This applies, for instance, where there is a substantial difference between the matters covered by training in the host State and the State where training was undertaken. In relation to the practice of the law, Directive 98/5 allows lawyers qualified in one Member State to be integrated into the profession in another Member State following a period of professional practice in the host State under their home State professional title. Directive 89/48 is supplemented by Directive 92/51 on the mutual recognition of qualifications obtained on completion of non-degree post-secondary education.

More recently, the Commission has undertaken a review of the system for the recognition of professional qualifications and new legislation, Directive 2005/36, has been adopted. This consolidates the existing secondary legislation in this area, which will be repealed on the expiry of the implementation deadline for Directive 2005/36 on 20 October 2007. The Directive aims to liberalize the provision of services and simplify administrative procedures.

It allows service providers in 'regulated' professions to operate in another Member State under their original professional title without applying for recognition of their qualifications, subject to safeguards, including Members States' right to require information such as proof of qualifications and details of insurance cover. In relation to the right of establishment, the existing systems of mutual recognition and recognition of qualifications covered by the sectoral Directives are retained.

10.6.7 Rules of professional conduct

Rules of professional conduct regulating, for instance, professional ethics and organization can constitute real obstacles to the movement of self-employed persons because non-nationals may find it difficult or costly to comply with them.

The Court of Justice has recognized that the problem of compliance with professional rules of conduct can be particularly acute for persons providing services, who are likely to be bound by the regulations of their State of establishment. A requirement that they also comply with the professional rules of the State where the services are provided might well be an unnecessary hindrance to free movement. The Court has held that such rules must be scrutinized to see whether they are objectively justified and proportionate and whether national rules in the State of establishment already achieve the aims in view.

EXERCISE 10.7

Read the extract from *Säger* (*Cases and Materials* (10.3.2)). Summarize the reasoning of the Court of Justice on the proportionality of the national legislation.

***Säger* v *Dennemeyer & Co. Ltd* (Case C-76/90) [1991] ECR I-4221**

Under German legislation, only persons holding the necessary licence were permitted to provide legal services. Licences were available to patent agents, but were not issued to persons who, like Dennemeyer (who was based in the UK) , only offered patent renewal services. Säger, a German patent agent, challenged Dennemeyer's right to provide patent renewal services in Germany.

The Court held that the freedom to provide services may be limited only by non-discriminatory rules which are justified in the public interest and only insofar as that interest is not already protected by rules applying to the service provider in the State of establishment. Requirements limiting freedom to provide services must be proportionate to their objective. The aim of the German legislation was to protect the recipients of legal services by ensuring that they were advised by suitably qualified persons. This objective justified a restriction of the freedom to provide services. However, national measures would be disproportionate if they required the service provider to have professional qualifications which were unnecessary for the tasks to be carried out. Here, the tasks—warning clients when renewal fees were due and paying fees on their behalf—did not require specific professional skills.

Similar principles have been developed by the Court of Justice in relation to the right of establishment and are set out clearly in *Gebhard.*

***Gebhard* v *Consiglio dell'Ordine degli Avvocati e Procuratori di Milano* (Case C-55/94) [1995] ECR I-4165.**

Disciplinary proceedings had been opened in Milan against Gebhard, a lawyer qualified in Germany, who was accused of contravening Italian legislation by practising in Italy under the title *avvocato*. The Court of Justice confirmed that a Community national exercising the right of establishment in another Member State must comply with the conditions laid down for the pursuit of that activity, such as conditions relating to the use of a professional title. However, measures constituting a limitation on a fundamental freedom guaranteed by the Treaty must be applied in a non-discriminatory manner, must be justified in the general interest, and must be suitable for and proportionate to attaining their objective.

10.6.8 Other kinds of restriction on the freedom to provide services

The range of possible restrictions on freedom to provide service is not limited to educational and professional requirements.

EXERCISE 10.8

Look at *Schindler* (*Cases and Materials* (10.3.3)). What was the nature of the obstacle to the free provision of services in this case? What was the Court's conclusion?

***HM Customs and Excise* v *Schindler* (Case C-275/92) [1994] ECR I-1039**

Customs and Excise confiscated invitations to participate in a lottery organized in Germany, dispatched from Germany to the UK by Gerhart and Jörg Schindler, on the grounds that they contravened lotteries legislation. Holding that lottery activities constitute services, the Court of Justice considered whether national legislation prohibiting lotteries restricts the freedom to provide services and, if so, whether such restriction may be justified. The legislation aimed to protect public morality, to protect the consumer, to prevent crime and fraud, and to restrict demand for gambling. The Court held that that such legislation would be justified provided it was not discriminatory and was a 'necessary part of the protection which that Member State seeks to secure in its territory', in other words was proportionate.

10.6.9 The proposed Services Directive

Proposed new legislation aims to extend free movement principles in the services sector by removing legal and administrative barriers to the provision of services within the internal market. At the time of writing, the proposed Services Directive was still under consideration.

The European Parliament had voted to remove the controversial 'country of origin principle' under which a service provider operating in another Member State would be governed by home State regulations. The revised draft provides for regulation under the rules of the Member State where the service is provided.

10.7 Recipients of services

The Treaty makes no express reference to recipients of services, but the right of Member State nationals to enter and remain in another Member State for the purpose of receiving services is enshrined in the case law of the Court of Justice, as well as in secondary legislation. The Court has recognized that Article 49 includes within its scope the right to receive, as well as to provide, services. In early decisions, the Court of Justice included within the scope of 'recipients of services' tourists and persons travelling to another Member State for medical treatment and for education and business purposes. *Cowan* concerned a recipient of tourist services.

EXERCISE 10.9

Read the extracts from *Cowan* (*Cases and Materials* (10.4)). What was Mr Cowan's claim? What did the Court of Justice decide?

Cowan v _Le Trésor Public_ (Case 186/87) [1989] ECR 195

Mr Cowan, a British national, was violently attacked at the exit of a metro station whilst on a short visit to Paris. The French Treasury refused him, on the basis of his nationality, the compensation to which a French national would have been entitled in such circumstances under the French code of penal procedure. He challenged this decision, relying on the non-discrimination provision, Article 12 (ex 6) EC. The French government argued that the national law did not create a barrier to free movement and that the right to compensation concerned national solidarity, presupposing a 'closer bond with the State than that of a recipient of services'. The Court of Justice disagreed, holding that the prohibition of discrimination applied to recipients of services in such circumstances. The fact that the compensation was financed by the Public Treasury could not alter the rules regarding the protection of the rights guaranteed by the Treaty.

Nonetheless, Member States may restrict the rights of recipients of services, including tourists, in accordance with the principles applying to workers, the self-employed, students, and family members, on grounds of public policy, public security, or public health. (*Criminal proceedings against Donatella Calfa* (Case C-348/96) [1999] ECR I-11). These limitations are considered in **Chapter 11**.

Difficult issues remain concerning the extent to which persons claiming the right to receive services have rights of access to publicly funded services on the basis of equality with nationals. In the educational context, the *Lair* and *Brown* judgments confirmed rights of access to university courses, including payment of fees, on the same basis as nationals. (*Lair* v *Universität Hannover* (Case 39/86) [1988] ECR 3161 (*Cases and Materials* (10.1.5); *Brown* v *Secretary for State for Scotland* (Case 197/86) [1988] ECR 3205). Although in these two cases the Court ruled out entitlement to maintenance grants, this position was reversed in *Bidar* (*R* v *London Borough of Ealing & Secretary of State for Education ex parte Bidar*) (Case C-209/03) [2005] ECR I-2119). In relation to publicly funded medical services, the Court has held that these fall within Article 49, though Member States are entitled to take account of the needs of their own population and restrictions may be justified on public policy or public health grounds (*Kohll* v *Union des Caisses de Maladie* (Case C-158/96) [1998] ECR I-1931)

10.8 Rights of family members

As noted earlier, Directive 2004/38 grants rights of entry and residence to family members of Union citizens who exercise free movement rights as workers, self-employed persons, persons of independent means, students, and jobseekers. The rights are extended to family members of Union citizens who exercise their right to enter and remain in a host Member State for up to three months. Recital 5 sets out the underlying rationale for family rights: to allow Union citizens to exercise free movement rights 'under objective conditions of freedom and dignity'.

Notwithstanding that family rights are granted 'irrespective of nationality', the Directive makes distinctions between Union citizens and third-country nationals. Whilst the substance of their respective rights is generally the same, there are notable differences relating, in particular, to the right to remain in the host State following the death or departure of the Union citizen and on divorce. It is important to note that family member rights do not exist independently but are derived from the Union citizen with the primary free movement rights. Family members who are Union citizens may of course themselves acquire independent rights under Community law.

10.8.1 Who are 'family members'?

QUESTION 10.10

Who do you think is included within the definition of 'family member'?

'Family member' is defined in Article 2 of Directive 2004/38. It includes the Union citizen's spouse and registered partner; direct descendants under 21 or who are dependant and those of the spouse or registered partner; and dependent direct relatives in the ascending line and those of the spouse or registered partner. The status of dependant results from a factual situation in which the Union citizen is actually providing support. The reasons for dependence on the Union citizen are irrelevant (*Centre Public d'Aide Sociale de Courcelles* v *Lebon* (Case 316/85 [1987] ECR 2811 (*Cases and Materials* (10.1.4))).

Additionally, Member States must facilitate the entry and residence of any other family members, irrespective of their nationality, who are dependent or members of the Union citizen's household in the home State or need his/her personal care on serious health grounds; and the partner with whom the Union citizen has a durable relationship.

10.8.2 Spouses and partners

'Family member' has always included the spouse. The Court of Justice made clear that 'spouse' was restricted to persons married to each other, thus excluding cohabitees (*Netherlands State* v *Reed* (Case 59/85) [1985] ECR 1283) Now, under Directive 2004/38 'family member' also includes

> the partner with whom the Union citizen has contracted a registered partnership, on the basis of the legislation of a Member State, if the legislation of the host Member State treats registered partnerships as equivalent to marriage and in accordance with the conditions laid down in the relevant legislation of the host Member State (Article 2(2)(b)).

Unfortunately, this provision is likely to give rise to differences in treatment across the Community, since Member States retain competence in the legal regulation of non-marital relationships.

10.8.3 Marriages of convenience

Doubtless acutely aware of Member State sensitivities about immigration from outside the Community and the possibilities of abuse, the Court of Justice made clear that rights were not applicable in relation to marriages of convenience between Member State nationals and third-country nationals (*Secretary of State for the Home Department* v *Akrich* (Case C-109/01) [2003] ECR I-9607). This is confirmed in Directive 2004/38, which allows Member States to refuse, terminate, or withdraw rights in cases of abuse or fraud, such as marriages of convenience, provided such action is proportionate (Article 35).

10.8.4 Entry, residence, and permanent residence

QUESTION 10.11

Family members may themselves be Union citizens. If so, what entry and residence rights do they have? If you have forgotten, look back at **Chapter 9**.

Directive 2004/38 (Articles 5–7) grants rights of entry and residence to family members. All Union citizens may enter another Member State and reside there for up to three months. They must hold a valid identity card or passport. Thereafter, they are entitled to remain for more than three months, by virtue of their relationship with the Union citizen from whom their rights are derived. Third-country nationals 'accompanying or joining the Union citizen' also have derived rights of entry and residence. They must have an entry visa, unless they hold a valid residence card.

Family members can acquire permanent residency rights, though there is a subtle difference between the rights of Union citizens and third-country nationals. The former must have resided legally 'in the host Member State' for five years, whilst the latter must have 'resided with the Union citizen in the host Member State' for five years.

QUESTION 10.12

When does the right of permanent residence arise and what additional safeguards against expulsion does it provide? Look back at **Chapter 9** to find the answers.

10.8.5 Retention of residence rights following the death or departure of the Union citizen

Here again, Directive 2004/38 distinguishes between family members who are Union citizens and third-country nationals. The rights of the former are unaffected by the departure from the host State or the death of the Union citizen, though before acquiring the right of permanent residence, they must meet the conditions in Article 7(1) (hold worker, self-employed, financially independent, or student status) (Article 12). In the event of the Union citizen's death, the residence rights of family members who are third-country nationals are contingent on their having lived with the Union citizen in the host State for at least a year; in addition, before acquiring the right of permanent residence, their residence right is subject to them showing that they are workers or self-employed persons or that they have sufficient resources not to become a burden on the host State's social assistance system. Third-country nationals have no right to remain following the Union citizen's departure from the host State, save in the particular circumstances next considered, where more extensive rights apply, irrespective of nationality.

In the event of the Union citizen's death or departure, if there is a child still in education in the host State, the child and the parent who has actual custody are entitled, irrespective of nationality, to remain until completion of the studies (Article 12(3)). These rights reflect the previous decisions in *Eternach* and *Baumbast, R* v *Secretary of State for the Home Department* (Case C-143/99) [2002] ECR I-7091.

***Eternach and Moritz* v *Minister van Onderwijs en Wetenschappen* (Cases 389/87 and 390/87) [1989] ECR 723**

Here, the Court of Justice considered the position of a child of a German migrant worker who had received his primary and secondary education in the Netherlands where his father was working and who had returned to Germany with his family. Subsequently, because his Netherlands diplomas were not recognized in Germany, he had returned alone to continue his studies. The Court of Justice held that, in circumstances such as these, a child retains rights of residence in order to complete his education.

The Court went further in *Baumbast*, holding that the children's right to remain to complete their education included the right of their 'primary carer' parent, irrespective of nationality, to remain with them.

10.8.6 The effect of separation and divorce

The Court of Justice has made clear that a spouse's status as spouse is unaffected by separation.

Diatta v Land Berlin (Case 267/83) [1985] ECR 567

Mrs Diatta, a Senegalese national, was married to a French national who resided and worked in Berlin. After living with her husband for some time, she moved into separate accommodation, intending to seek a divorce. The questions referred by the national court concerned the former Articles 10 and 11 of Regulation 1612/68 (family members' right to install themselves with the worker and to take up employment). The Court of Justice held that a marital relationship is 'not dissolved merely because the spouses live separately, even where they intend to divorce at a later date'. (*Cases and Materials* (10.5.1)).

The Court of Justice has been more reluctant to express an opinion on the impact of divorce.

***Singh* (*R* v *Immigration Appeal Tribunal ex parte Secretary of State for the Home Department* (Case C-370/90) [1992] ECR I- 4265**

The Court of Justice avoided the opportunity to do so here. You may recall that this case concerned the free movement rights of an English woman's Indian husband on the couple's return from Germany, where they had both been working. Some time after their return, the couple had divorced. The Court chose not to comment on the effects of the divorce on Mr Singh's rights, on the basis that the question referred by the English High Court related to the period prior to the decree absolute.

? QUESTION 10.13

What may be the impact of separation on permanent residency rights? Look back at 10.8.4 to find the answer.

? QUESTION 10.14

Look again at the rights of spouses on the death or departure of the Union citizen, under Directive 2004/38. What do you think is the position of the spouse, under the Directive, following divorce?

The residence rights of family members who are Union citizens are unaffected by the termination of marriage or registered partnership, though before acquiring the right of permanent residence, they must meet the conditions in Article 7(1).

By contrast, family members who are third-country, nationals retain the right of residence only in limited circumstances:

(a) where a marriage or partnership lasts at least three years, with one year in the host State;

(b) where the spouse or partner has custody of the Union citizen's children;

(c) where there are 'particularly difficult circumstances, such as domestic violence during the marriage or registered partnership';

(d) where the spouse has right of access to a minor child and a court has ruled that access must be in the host State.

In addition, before acquiring the right of permanent residence, their rights are subject to them showing that they are workers or self-employed, or have sufficient resources for themselves and their family members not to become a burden on the social assistance system of the host State (Article 13 (2), Directive 2004/38).

There is no express reference to children's rights in such circumstances, though in *Baumbast, R v Secretary of State for the Home Department* (Case C-413/99) [2002] ECR I-7091), the Court of Justice confirmed children's rights to continue to reside in the host State in order to continue their education, in circumstances of divorce.

10.8.7 Right to take up employment

Irrespective of nationality, family members may take up employment or self-employment in the host State (Article 23, Directive 2004/38). This incorporates the previous provision in Article 11 of Regulation 1612/68 (now repealed), which was applied in *Gül*.

Gül v _Regierungspräsident Düsseldorf_ (Case 131/85) [1986] ECR 1573

The German authorities had refused to grant authorization to Gül to practise medicine, a Cypriot doctor married to a British woman. The Court of Justice held that Article 11 granted the right to take up any kind of employment activity under the same conditions as nationals of the host State (*Cases and Materials* (10.5.2)).

10.8.8 Equal treatment

Under Directive 2004/38, the right to equal treatment applies without limitation to the family members of workers and the self-employed. For family members of other Union citizens, namely persons of independent means and students, there is no entitlement to social assistance during the first three months of residence, or to student grants and loans. In any event, their residency rights remain subject to the general conditions relating to sufficient resources and sickness insurance (see **Chapter 9**).

CONCLUSIONS

In accordance with the Community's original economic goals and the common market ideal, the founding Treaty of Rome, 1957 and early secondary legislation granted free movement rights to the economically active and their families.

These rights incorporated another fundamental right—freedom from discrimination on grounds of nationality, within the Treaty's scope of application. The European Court of Justice, through its liberal interpretation and application of the free movement provisions, has not only extended the scope of the rights but has also affirmed their social, as well as their economic, significance. Establishment of citizenship of the European Union and the adoption of the Citizenship Directive adds yet a further dimension by superimposing the over-arching status of Union citizenship. Nationals of the Member States possessing worker or self-employed status continue to enjoy rights which have been long-established and extended, but now do so as European Union citizens. Whilst this undoubtedly represents a significant conceptual shift, its practical impact is debatable. This chapter has covered free movement rights. It should not be forgotten that these rights may be subject to limitations on grounds of public policy, public security, or public health. The limitations are discussed in **Chapter 11**.

SUMMARY

- **Free movement rights for workers and the self-employed** are enshrined in original EC Treaty provisions: Articles 39 (ex 48) EC (free movement of workers), 43 (ex 52) EC (right of establishment), and 49 (ex 59) EC (freedom to provide services).
- **Free movement rights** include the right to freedom from discrimination on grounds of nationality within the scope of application of the Treaty (Article 12 (ex 6) EC) and this right finds expression specifically for workers in Article 39 (2) (ex 48 (2)) and Regulation 1612/68 (equal treatment in employment).
- **The scope of the Treaty rights** of entry and residence for workers and the self-employed is defined and elaborated in the Citizenship Directive 2004/38, which also creates a new right of permanent residence.
- **The European Court of Justice** has interpreted and applied the rights widely, for instance in its broad definition of 'worker' (e.g. *Hoekstra*, *Levin*, *Kempf*, *Steymann*). The Court has also granted entry and residence rights to nationals of the Member States who move in search of work (*Royer*). These rights are now confirmed in Directive 2004/38.
- **Family members were granted rights** by early secondary legislation, now consolidated and extended in the Citizenship Directive 2004/38. Unless they are themselves Union citizens with independent rights under the Directive, family members' rights are derived from the rights of the worker or self-employed Union citizen.
- **Directive 2004/38 distinguishes** between family members who are nationals of a Member State and those who are third-country nationals and the latter have less extensive rights in a number of circumstances.

CHAPTER 10: ASSESSMENT EXERCISE

1. George, a British national, has taken up employment in Paris as a journalist with a French magazine, working 12 hours per week. He is joined by his wife Sue and daughter Anne (aged 23), also British nationals. George has been told by the French authorities that because he is a part-time worker whose earnings are insufficient to support himself and his family financially, neither he nor his family are entitled to remain in France. Advise George, Sue, and Anne.

See *Cases and Materials* (10.7) for a specimen answer.

FURTHER READING

Acierno, S. (2003). 'The *Carpenter* Judgment: Fundamental Rights and the Limits of the Community Legal Order' 28 *EL Rev* 398.

Barnard, N. (1996). 'Discrimination and Free Movement in EC Law' *ICLQ* 82.

Daniel, L. (1997). 'Non-discriminatory Restrictions to the Free Movement of Persons' 22 *EL Rev* 191.

Golynker, O. (2006). 'Student Loans: the European Concept of Social Justice according to *Bidar*' 31 *EL Rev* 390.

White, R. (2005). 'Free movement, Equal Treatment and Citizenship of the Union' 54 *ICLQ* 885.

11 Free movement of persons: limitations on grounds of public policy, public security, or public health

11.1 OBJECTIVES

By the end of this chapter you should be able to:

1 Describe and discuss the permissible limitations on the free movement of persons, comprising the public policy, public security, and public health grounds

2 Outline the relevant provisions of the EC Treaty and Directive 2004/38

3 Understand and describe the approach of the Court of Justice to the interpretaton and application of the limitations

4 Outline the procedural rights granted to individuals facing limitations on their free movement rights

11.2 Introduction

As indicated in **Chapters 9** and **10**, rights of free movement and residence for Union citizens and their families are subject to various qualifications and limitations. Article 18(1) makes the rights of free movement and residence of Union citizens 'subject to the limitations and conditions laid down in this Treaty and the measures adopted to give it effect'. **Chapter 9** considered a number of cases in which the European Court of Justice has applied relevant 'conditions and limitations' in confirming rights of residence and non-discrimination for Union citizens. Articles 39(4) (ex 48(4)), 45 (ex 55), and 55 (ex 66) EC allow Member States to restrict access to employment in public service posts for workers, the self-employed, and those providing services, respectively. The 'public service proviso' was discussed in **Chapter 10.** Additionally, Member States may restrict entry and residence on grounds of public policy, public security, or public health. These three grounds of limitation form the subject of this chapter.

11.3 The right of Member States to restrict entry and residence

Articles 39(3) (ex 48(3)), 46 (ex 56), and 55 (ex 66) EC allow Member States to restrict the rights, respectively, of workers, persons exercising the right of establishment and those providing services in another Member State on grounds of public policy, public security, or public health. These limitations, previously fleshed out in Directive 64/221, are now elaborated in Directive 2004/38 and, under this secondary legislation, apply to all categories of persons exercising rights under the Directive—family members, students, and persons of independent means, as well as to the economically active. The limitations apply only to entry and residence rights and not to rights of access to employment and, because of the fundamental importance of the principle of freedom of movement within the Community internal market, the Court of Justice interprets them very restrictively. Directive 2004/38 also sets out important procedural safeguards for individuals who face restrictions on their rights.

11.4 Partial restrictions on residence

Whilst the Treaty and Directive 64/221 clearly allowed a Member State to exclude or deport a non-national exercising Community rights of free movement on grounds of public policy, public security, or public health, it was less clear whether the limitations included the right to impose partial restrictions on free movement within a Member State. This issue was first considered by the Court of Justice in *Rutili* v *Ministre de l'Intérieur* (Case 36/75) [1975] ECR 1219.

 **QUESTION** 11.1 

What internal restrictions were placed by the French authorities upon the applicant in *Rutili* (*Cases and Materials* (11.1)

Rutili **v** ***Ministre de l'Intérieur*** **(Case 36/75) [1975] ECR 1219**

Mr Rutili, an Italian national resident in France, was well-known for his trade union activities and political activism. It was alleged that he was 'likely to disturb public policy' and consequently his residence permit prohibited him from living in four particular *départements*., including the one in which he and his family were habitually resident.

The Court of Justice held that prohibitions on residence under Article 39(3) (ex 48(3)) EC may be imposed only in respect of the whole of the national territory, unless nationals are subject to the same limitations. Otherwise, they amount to inequality of treatment between nationals and non-nationals which, if within the field of application of the Treaty, breach the non-discrimination provision contained in Article 12 (ex 6) EC.

 **EXERCISE** 11.1 

Look again at paragraph 50 the *Rutili* judgment (*Cases and Materials* (11.1)) How did the Court of Justice put the dictum it contains 'in context' in the later case of *Olazabal*? (*Cases and Materials* (11.1)).

***Ministre de l'Intérieur* v *Olazabal* (Case C-100/01), [2002] ECR I-10981**

Mr Olazabal, a Spanish national of Basque origin, had been sentenced in France to 18 months' imprisonment and a four-year ban on residence for conspiracy to disturb public order by intimidation or terror. Subsequently, having been granted provisional authorization to remain, he planned to move to Aquitaine, which borders Spain. In the light of police reports that Mr Olazabal maintained contact with the Basque separatist group ETA, the Minister for the Interior prohibited him from residing in 31 départements in order to keep him away from the Spanish border.

The Court of Justice distinguished the circumstances of Mr Rutili and Mr Olazabal. In *Rutili*, the national court had doubts as to whether the prohibition was justified on public policy grounds. By contrast, in *Olazabal* it was accepted not only that public policy reasons justified partial restrictions but that, if partial restrictions could not be imposed, public policy reasons would justify his exclusion from the whole of the national territory. The Court reasoned that, where nationals of other Member States are liable to deportation or prohibition of residence, they may also be subject to less severe measures imposing partial limitations, even though the Member State concerned cannot apply such measures to its own nationals. Such measures, the Court held, were compatible with the free movement provisions provided they are based on the non-national's individual conduct and are proportionate.

The issue of partial restrictions on residence is addressed by Directive 2004/38, which provides that the right of residence covers the whole territory of a Member State. Partial restrictions may be imposed only where the same restrictions apply to the host State's own nationals. (Article 22) In the light of its judgment in *Olazabal*, it will be interesting to see how the Court of Justice interprets this provision.

11.5 'Measures' taken by Member States

Directive 2004/38 refers to 'measures' taken by Member States (Article 27). In the context of free movement of workers, 'measures' were defined by the Court of Justice in *Bouchereau* as any action which affects the right of persons . . . to enter and reside freely in the Member States under the same conditions as nationals of the host State' (*R* v *Bouchereau* (Case 30/77) [1977] ECR 1999).

Member States may restrict the freedom of movement and residence of Union citizens and their family members, irrespective of nationality, on grounds of public policy, public security, or public health, but these grounds may not be invoked for economic ends. (Article 27, Directive 2004/38).

11.6 Public policy and public security

11.6.1 General principles

Directive 2004/38 sets out a number of general principles in Article 27:

(a) Measures taken on grounds of public policy and public security must be proportionate and based exclusively on the personal conduct of the individual concerned.

(b) That conduct must represent a 'genuine, present and sufficiently serious threat affecting one of the fundamental interests of society'.

(c) Justifications unconnected with the particular case or based on 'considerations of general prevention' will not be accepted.

(d) Previous criminal convictions shall not in themselves constitute grounds for taking restrictive measures. Nevertheless, the host State may request an individual's previous police record from the Member State of origin or another Member State, if this is essential to ascertain whether he or she is a danger to public policy or public security. Such enquiries, which must not be a matter of routine, will generally be made when the individual reports to or registers with the host State's authorities and, in any event, within the first three months of arrival.

These provisions incorporate many of the pre-existing provisions of Directive 64/221, as interpreted by the Court of Justice. A consideration of the Court's previous judgments is important to an understanding of the scope and application of the current provisions.

11.6.2 Scope of 'public policy' and 'public security'

In order to justify restrictive measures on public policy or public security grounds, the personal conduct of the individual concerned must represent a 'genuine, present and sufficiently serious threat affecting one of the fundamental interests of society' (Directive 2004/38, Article 27(2)). This provision incorporates the Court's definition of 'public policy' in *Bouchereau*.

In earlier cases, the Court of Justice had defined 'public policy' more broadly.

 **EXERCISE** 11.2 

Read the extract from *Van Duyn* (*Cases and Materials* (11.2.1)) concerning the meaning of 'public policy'. Did the Court of Justice consider that activities must be unlawful to fall within the scope of the public policy ground?

***Van Duyn* v *Home Office* (Case 41/74) [1974] ECR 1337**

Yvonne Van Duyn, a Dutch national, came to the UK to work as a secretary for the Church of Scientology. She was refused entry on grounds of public policy because the UK government regarded the Church as socially harmful. However, the Church was not illegal in the UK and there were no restrictions on UK nationals who wished to join or take up employment with it. Van Duyn sought a declaration that she had the right, under Article 39 (ex 48) EC, to enter and remain in the UK.

The Court of Justice, whilst insisting that the concept of public policy be interpreted strictly, allowed an area of discretion to the Member States. The Court held that where a Member State has taken administrative measures to counteract the activities of an organization, that State may rely on the public policy ground even though it has not made those activities unlawful. It may place restrictions on a national of another Member State who wishes to take up a particular employment even though no similar restrictions are placed on its own nationals.

The Court moved to a narrower definition in *Rutili*. It will be remembered that this case concerned the imposition of partial restrictions on Mr Rutili's residence in France on the grounds that he was 'likely to disturb public policy'. The Court of Justice declared that whilst Member States are entitled to determine the requirements of public policy in the light of their national needs, the determination of the scope of public policy must be subject to control by the Community institutions. Restrictions cannot be imposed unless there is a 'genuine and sufficiently serious threat to public policy' (*Rutili* v *Ministre de l'Intérieur* (Case 36/75) [1975] ECR 1219 (*Cases and Materials* (11.1)).

Then followed the yet narrower definition in *Bouchereau*.

R v Bouchereau (Case 30/77) [1977] ECR 1999

Following Mr Bouchereau's second conviction for drugs offences, the Marlborough Street Magistrates were considering recommending his deportation from the UK. Whilst recognizing the need to allow Member States an area of discretion, as it had stated in *Van Duyn*, the Court of Justice declared that the concept of public policy presupposes the existence of 'genuine and sufficiently serious threat to the requirements of public policy affecting one of the fundamental interests of society' (*Cases and Materials* (11.2.1)).

11.6.3 Measures of a general preventative nature

Whilst *Bouchereau* may leave scope for an element of discretion in the interpretation of 'public policy' and 'public security' in Article 27, it is clear that such discretion does not extend to the adoption of measures of a general preventative nature. The Court of Justice considered a measure of this kind in *Bonsignore*.

EXERCISE 11.3

Look at *Bonsignore* (*Cases and Materials* (11.2.2)). What was the 'measure of a general preventative nature' in this case?

***Bonsignore* v *Oberstadtdirektor of the City of Cologne* (Case 67/74) [1975] ECR 297**

The German authorities had ordered the deportation of Mr Bonsignore, an Italian national, following his conviction for unlawful possession of a firearm and causing death by negligence. He had been fined for the first offence but no punishment was imposed for the second offence, which involved the accidental killing of his brother through careless handling of the firearm. The national court considered that the only possible justification for the deportation would be 'reasons of a general preventive nature', based on 'the deterrent effect which the deportation of an alien found in illegal possession of a firearm would have in immigrant circles having regard to the resurgence of violence in the large urban centres'. The national court asked the Court of Justice whether 'reasons of a general preventive nature' justified expulsion, in particular where it was clear that the individual concerned would not commit further offences. The Court held that such reasons do not justify restrictive measures.

This ruling is incorporated into Article 27 of Directive 2004/38 which, as noted earlier, provides that justifications unconnected with the particular case or based on 'considerations of general prevention' will not be accepted.

11.6.4 Personal conduct

Like the current provision in Directive 2004/38, Directive 64/221 required that measures justified on grounds of public policy or public security be based exclusively on the personal conduct of the individual concerned. This requirement was invoked in *Van Duyn*. Here, the Court of Justice was asked to consider whether an individual's association with an organization constituted personal conduct.

 **EXERCISE** 11.4 

Read the extracts from *Van Duyn* (*Cases and Materials* (11.2.1)). What did the Court of Justice conclude?

***Van Duyn* cont.**

As noted earlier, Yvonne van Duyn, a Dutch national, challenged the UK's refusal to allow her entry to take up a post as secretary with the Church of Scientology, an organization considered by the UK Government to be 'socially harmful'. Relying on Article 39 (ex 48) EC and Directive 64/221, Ms van Duyn maintained that the public policy ground did not apply, since the justification for the refusal of entry was not based upon her personal conduct but on the UK Government's general policy of refusing work permits to all foreign nationals wishing to take up employment with the Church. She argued that her association with the Church of Scientology did not constitute 'personal conduct'. The Court of Justice disagreed, holding that present association with an organization, reflecting a participation in its activities and identification with its aims, constitutes personal conduct. In general, past association would not justify restrictions.

11.6.5 Automatic expulsion

Other cases have concerned national measures applying the penalty of automatic expulsion for particular criminal offences.

EXERCISE 11.5

Look at the extracts from *Calfa* (*Cases and Materials* (11.2.3)). What was the precise nature of the penalty imposed under Greek law?

In *Calfa* the Court of Justice considered Greek provisions imposing the penalty of automatic expulsion for life on non-nationals convicted of drugs offences. It should be noted that, before turning to consider this penalty, the Court of Justice first addressed Ms Calfa's rights under Community law as a tourist and recipient of services.

Criminal Proceedings against Donatella Calfa **(Case C-348/96) ECR I-11**

Ms Calfa, an Italian national, had been convicted by a Greek court of possession and use of prohibited drugs whilst on holiday in Crete. She was sentenced to three months' imprisonment and the court, as required by national legislation in such cases concerning non-nationals, ordered her to be expelled for life from Greek territory. Ms Calfa claimed that the free movement provisions of the Treaty did not allow a Member State to adopt measures requiring the automatic expulsion of nationals of other Member States when there were no provisions requiring a comparable measure to be taken against the Member State's own nationals. The Court of Justice emphasized that Member States may adopt against nationals of other Member States measures which they cannot apply to their own nationals, in particular on public policy grounds. However, the public policy exception could not be relied on to justify an automatic expulsion for life. Such a measure, because it was imposed automatically, took no account of the personal conduct of the offender.

The Court of Justice reached a similar conclusion in the *Oliveri* case. The joined cases *Orfanopoulos* and *Oliveri* concerned automatic expulsion orders issued by the German authorities against Orfanopoulos, a Greek national, and Oliveri, an Italian national, both of whom were drug addicts and had been convicted of narcotics offences.

QUESTION 11.2

What was the Court's view of the automatic expulsion in Mr Oliveri's case? Look at the case extracts (*Cases and Materials* (11.2.3)).

***Orfanopoulos and Oliveri* v *Land Baden-Württemberg* (Joined cases C-482/01 and C-493/01) [2004] ECR I-5257**

In *Oliveri,* the Court of Justice considered German legislation that required the competent authorities to expel nationals of other Member States who had been sentenced to at least two years' youth custody or a custodial sentence for narcotics offences. Referring to its judgments in *Bonsignore* and in *Calfa*, the Court held that Community law precludes expulsion based on reasons of a general preventative nature, that is with the purpose of deterring other aliens, in particular where expulsion automatically follows a criminal conviction and no account is taken of the personal conduct of the offender or of the danger that person represents to public policy.

The general principles set out by the Court of Justice in these decisions are now incorporated into Article 33 of Directive 2004/38. This provides that expulsion orders may not be issued by the host Member State as a penalty or legal consequence of a custodial penalty, unless they conform to the requirements of Articles 27 (general principles (11.6.1)), 28 (protection against expulsion (11.6.8)) and 29 (public health (11.6.9)).

11.6.6 **Proportionality**

As in other areas of Community law, restrictive measures taken by Member States must be proportionate to their legitimate aim.

? **QUESTION** 11.3

Can you remember any circumstances in which the expulsion of a national of another Member State would be disproportionate? Look back at 9.10.1 and *R* v *Pieck* (Case 157/79) [1980] ECR 2171 (*Cases and Materials* (9.2)).

In *Pieck,* the Court of Justice held that expulsion would be a disproportionate penalty for non-compliance with administrative formalities. It is clear that, even for much more serious offences, proportionality must still be applied. In *Orfanopoulos*, which, it will be recalled, concerned an expulsion order impose automatically following a conviction for narcotics offences, the Court of Justice emphasized the need for an assessment of the proportionality of the restriction to the legitimate aim pursued, here the protection of public policy.

? **QUESTION** 11.4

Which paragraph of the *Orfanopoulos* judgment sets out the factors relating to the proportionality of the penalty to be imposed? Look at the case extracts (*Cases and Materials* (11.2.3)).

***Orfanopoulos and Oliveri* cont.**

Georgios Orfanopoulos, a Greek national living in Germany and an intermittent worker, was a drug addict who had been convicted on nine occasions for drugs offences and acts of violence, eventually being sentenced to a term of imprisonment. At the end of his sentence, he was to be deported under national legislation providing 'as a general rule' for the expulsion of aliens on 'serious' grounds of public security and public policy. Mr Orfanopoulos had lived in Germany for many years. He had married a German national and there were three children of the marriage. On a reference from the national court, the Court of Justice considered the compatibility of the expulsion with Community law, particularly with the principle of proportionality.

At paragraph 99 of its judgment, the Court of Justice declared that, in assessing the proportionality of the penalty imposed, the national court must take account of a range of relevant factors. These comprised the nature and seriousness of the offences, the length of the offender's residence in the host State, the period which has elapsed since the offences were committed, the family circumstances, and the difficulties which the spouse and children face in the offender's country of origin.

11.6.7 Previous criminal convictions

? QUESTION 11.5

What does Directive 2004/38 provide on previous criminal convictions? Look back at 11.6.1.

Like its predecessor, Directive 64/221, Directive 2004/38 provides that previous criminal convictions shall not in themselves constitute grounds for measures taken on public policy or public security grounds. If previous criminal convictions are not *in themselves* grounds, can they be taken into account at all? This question was addressed in *Bouchereau.*

EXERCISE 11.6

Look at the *Bouchereau* case *(Cases and Materials* (11.2.1)). The Court of Justice held that previous criminal convictions may be taken into account in certain circumstances. Copy out the words used by the Court to describe those circumstances.

***Bouchereau* cont.**

Bouchereau was a French national working in England who had been convicted on two occasions of unlawful possession of drugs. The magistrates' court which heard the second of these cases proposed to recommend his deportation and asked the Court of Justice for clarification of the provision relating to previous convictions in Directive 64/221.

The Court of Justice held that previous criminal convictions can only be taken into account when 'the circumstances which gave rise to that conviction are evidence of personal conduct constituting a *present threat to the requirements of public policy*'. This will be the case where the individual concerned shows *'a propensity to act in the same way in the future'* (emphases added). Note, however, that the Court did not rule out the possibility that past conduct alone may be a sufficiently serious threat to the requirements of public policy.

The issue of previous criminal convictions arose again in *Criminal proceedings against Donatella Calfa* (Case C-348/96) [1999] ECR I-11. In this judgment, the Court of Justice made clear the close relationship between the scope of the 'public policy' ground, the provision on previous criminal convictions and assessment of personal conduct.

 **EXERCISE** 11.7 

Read the extracts from *Calfa* (*Cases & Materials* (11.2.3)). Summarize, in a few sentences, the reasoning of the Court of Justice in relation to the public policy ground, previous criminal convictions and personal conduct.

***Calfa* cont.**

The Court of Justice reiterated that the public policy exception, like all derogations from a fundamental Treaty principle, must be interpreted strictly. The Court pointed out that Article 3 of Directive 64/221 (now incorporated into Article 7 of Directive 2004/38) states that measures taken on grounds of public policy must be based exclusively on the personal conduct of the individual concerned. Further, previous criminal convictions cannot, in themselves, constitute grounds for taking such measures. Such a conviction can only be taken into account insofar as the circumstances giving rise to that conviction are evidence of personal conduct constituting a present threat to the requirements of public policy. The national legislation at issue imposed automatic expulsion for life without taking into account the personal conduct of the offender or of the danger posed by him for the requirements of public policy. Consequently, the public policy exception cannot be relied on to justify a restriction such as that imposed by the Greek legislation.

Similarly in *Orfanopoukops* and *Oliveri*, the interrelationship between the scope of the public policy ground, the provision on previous criminal convictions, and assessment of personal conduct was made very clear. Moreover, in *Oliveri*, the Court of Justice stressed the need for any threat to public policy to be present and continuing at the time when the penalty is imposed.

 **EXERCISE** 11.8 

Look at paragraphs 72, and 77–81 of the *Oliveri* judgment, which concern the requirement for a 'present threat' to be satisfied at the time of the expulsion (*Orfanopoulos* and *Oliveri* v *Land Baden-Württemburg* (Joined cases C-482/01 and C-493/01) [2004] ECR I-5257) (*Cases and Materials* (11.2.3)).

***Orfanopolos and Oliveri* cont.**

In relation to Mr Oliveri's case, the Court of Justice ruled that the German legislation requiring the expulsion of an offender convicted and sentenced for a drugs offence was incompatible with Community law: An automatic penalty takes no account of the individual's personal conduct or of the danger to public policy that he or she represents. Further, the national competent authorities must assess, on a case-by-case basis, whether the circumstances giving rise to that expulsion establish personal conduct which is a present threat to the requirements of public policy. That requirement must, as a general rule, be satisfied at the time of the expulsion. Thus, in reviewing expulsion decisions of the national competent authorities, national courts must be able to take into consideration matters occurring after the original decision was made which indicate a diminution of the threat to public policy, especially where a long time has elapsed between the date of the decision and review by the national court.

As noted earlier, Article 33 of Directive 2004/38 provides that expulsion orders may not be issued as a penalty or legal consequence of a custodial penalty, unless they comply with Articles 27, 28, and 29. Article 33 also provides that if an expulsion order is enforced more than two years after its issue, the Member State must check that the individual concerned is currently and genuinely a threat to public policy or public security and assess whether there has been any material change in the circumstances since the order was issued.

11.6.8 **Protection against expulsion**

Even where an individual's conduct is sufficiently serious to justify restrictions on his or her rights, before taking an expulsion decision on grounds of public policy or public security Member States must take additional factors into account. Article 28 of Directive 2004/38 provides guidance, in a non-exhaustive list, on the matters that are to be considered:

(a) how long the individual has resided in the host State;

(b) his/her age, state of health, family and economic situation, social and cultural integration into the host State;

(c) the extent of his/her links with the country of origin.

These considerations reflect the Court of Justice's approach in *Orfanopoulos and Oliveri*. (*Cases and Materials* (11.2.3)). Here, typically, the Court emphasized that derogations from the principle of freedom of movement must be interpreted restrictively and, moreover, with proper regard for fundamental rights. The Court referred specifically to the right to family life guaranteed by Article 8 of the European Convention on Human Rights (ECHR).

***Orfanopoulos and Oliveri* cont.**

It will be recalled that Georgios Orfanopoulos, a Greek national, was facing automatic expulsion from Germany following a conviction on drugs charges. Mr Orfanopoulos had been resident in Germany for many years. He had married a German national and there were three children of the marriage. According to the national court, his wife and children could not reasonably be expected to live in Greece. The Court held that, whilst Article 39 EC and Directive 64/221 did not preclude the national measure, a fair balance must be struck between the Member State's legitimate interests and respect for fundamental rights. In assessing the proportionality of the measure, the national court must take all these factors into account.

Further protection is afforded by Directive 2004/38 to Union Citizens and their family members who have permanent rights of residence. They may be expelled only on 'serious' grounds of public policy or public security. Moreover, an expulsion decision taken against a Union citizen who has resided in the host State for the previous ten years or is a minor (unless in the best interests of the child) must be based on 'imperative' grounds of public security. It remains to be seen how the Court will interpret these more rigorous grounds.

11.6.9 Public health

As has been noted throughout this section, the scope of the limitations on individuals' rights to free movement within the internal market are formulated and interpreted narrowly; restrictions must be proportionate to their legitimate aim and proportionality must be assessed on a case-by-case basis. This approach adopted by the Court of Justice, and Directive 2004/38, in incorporating many of the principles set out by the Court in this area of Community law, has narrowed even further Member States' ability to restrict or deny individual rights. The interpretation of the public health ground of limitation further demonstrates the development of strengthened individual rights for Union citizens and their families.

In relation to this ground of limitation, Directive 2004/38 is drafted more narrowly than its predecessor, Directive 64/221. The previous provisions referred to 'diseases and disabilities' affecting public health or public policy and thereby justifying restrictions. These comprised not only specified diseases (tuberculosis and syphilis), diseases subject to quarantine listed by the World Health Organization and 'other infectious diseases or contagious parasitic diseases' but also to drug addiction and various kinds of mental illness, including 'profound mental disturbance'. Directive 2004/38 refers only to 'diseases' and provides that the only diseases justifying measures restricting freedom of movement are those with epidemic potential (as defined by the relevant instruments of the World Health Organization) and other infectious or contagious parasitic diseases. As previously, diseases occurring beyond a specified point do not justify expulsion. In Directive 64/221, that point was the issue of the first residence permit. In Directive 2004/38, it is the completion of three months' residence in the host State. During that three-month initial period, Member States may insist upon a medical examination, free of charge, though not as a matter of routine (Directive 2004/38, Article 29).

11.6.10 Procedural rights

Articles 30 and 31 of Directive 2004/38 provide important procedural rights for individuals who are denied the rights of entry and residence granted by the Treaty and secondary legislation. These include the right to be notified in writing, in a comprehensible way, of any decision taken against them and to be informed of the grounds on which that decision is based, unless this is contrary to the interests of State security. The notification must specify the court or authority with which an appeal may be lodged, the time limit for the appeal and, where applicable, the time limit for the person to leave the territory of the host State. Save in cases of urgency, the time allowed for the person to leave the Member State must be no less than one month from the date of notification. There must be a right of appeal or review of decisions and where an appeal is accompanied by an application for an interim order suspending the expulsion decision, actual removal from the territory must not take place, save in limited specified circumstances, until a decision on that application has been taken.

After a reasonable period, and in any event after three years from enforcement of an exclusion order, persons excluded on public policy or public security grounds may submit an application to have the order lifted, on the grounds that there has been a material change in the circumstances which justified the exclusion decision. Such applicants have no right of entry while their application is being considered.

CONCLUSIONS

Despite the centrality of the principle of free movement of persons to the internal market concept, from its beginnings Community law has recognized the right of Member States to impose limitations on entry and residence within their territory. The original Treaty provisions, permitting restrictions on grounds of public policy, public security, or public health, have survived without amendment. Nonetheless, the three grounds of limitation have been interpreted restrictively by the Court of Justice which, in gradually narrowing their scope, has continued to enhance individual rights. The Court's approach is reflected in developments in secondary legislation. Directive 64/221, which defined the scope of 'public policy', 'public security', and 'public health', has now been superseded by Directive 2004/38. This Directive incorporates many of the principles applied by the Court of Justice in its restrictive interpretation of the limitations. Secondary legislation, currently Directive 2004/38, also provides important procedural safeguards to individuals faced with the limitation of their Community rights.

SUMMARY

- **Member States may limit individuals' right to entry and residence on their territory on grounds of pubic policy, public security, or public health:** the limitations are set out in the EC Treaty in Article 39 (3) (ex 48 (3)) (workers), Article 46 (ex 56) (persons exercising the right of establishment) and Article 55 (ex 66) (persons providing services).
- **The Court of Justice has interpreted the limitations restrictively**, thereby enhancing individual rights, for instance by gradually narrowing the scope of 'public policy' (*Van Duyn*, *Rutili*, *Bouchereau*), by insisting on the proportionality of measures adopted by Member States and by drawing proportionality in the broadest of terms (*Orfanopoulos*).
- **Directive 64/221**, now repealed by Directive 2004/38, defined the scope of the three limitations and set out important procedural safeguards for individuals.
- **Directive 2004/38** repealed Directive 64/221. Directive 2004/38, which delineates the scope of 'public policy', 'public security', and 'public health', incorporates many of the principles laid down by the Court of Justice in this area of Community law.

- **Directive 2004/38 sets out general principles,** incorporating some of the provisions of Directive 64/221 and reflecting some of the previous decisions of the Court of Justice. Measures based on public policy or public security must be proportionate and based exclusively on the personal conduct of the individual concerned (*Calfa, Oliveri,* and *Orfanopoulos*). Conduct must represent 'a genuine, present, and sufficiently serious threat affecting one of the fundamental interests of society (*Bouchereau*). Justifications based on 'considerations of general prevention will not be accepted (*Bonsignore*). Previous criminal convictions do not in themselves constitute grounds for taking measures (*Bouchereau*).
- **Directive 2004/38 defines the scope of 'public health'** more narrowly than did Directive 64/221, referring only to 'diseases' and not to 'diseases and disabilities'.
- **Directive 2004/38 also sets out important procedural rights:** the right to be informed of decisions and the grounds on which they have been taken; the right to appeal and to be allowed no less that one month to leave the host State; and the right have an expulsion order lifted after a reasonable period of time.

CHAPTER 11: ASSESSMENT EXERCISE

For the past four years Gertrude, a British national, has lived in Paris, where she is employed as a waitress. Three years ago, Gertrude married Pierre, a French national who has always lived in Paris, has never travelled abroad, and speaks no English. Gertrude and Pierre have a child, aged three who speaks only French. All the members of Pierre's large extended family live within the Paris conurbation. Gertrude has no surviving relatives, save for her husband and child and an elderly aunt who lives in Italy.

Ten years ago, Gertrude took part in an animal rights demonstration in Trafalgar Square in London. She was subsequently convicted of public order offences by an English court and received a small fine. Although since then Gertrude has led a conventional and quiet life, she still worries that the French authorities will become aware of her conviction and seek to deport her from France.

Advise Gertrude of her rights (if any) under Community law.

See Cases *and Materials* (10.6) for a specimen answer.

FURTHER READING

Connor, T.C. (1998). 'Migrant Community Nationals: Remedies for Refusal of Entry by Member States'. 28 *EL Rev* 157.

Hall, S. (1991). 'The European Convention on Human Rights and Public Policy Exceptions to the Free Movement of Workers under the EEC Treaty'. 16 *EL Rev* 466.

Vincenzi, C. (1994). 'Deportation in Disarray: the Case of EC Nationals'. *Crim LR* 163.

12 Introduction to EC Competition Law

12.1 OBJECTIVES

By the end of this chapter you should be able to:

1 Outline the general aims of Community competition law

2 Understand the focus of the regulation contained in Articles 81 and 82 (ex 85 and 86) EC

3 Outline the main provisions relating to the enforcement of EC competition law

12.2 Introduction

The Community rules on the free movement of goods have been fundamental to the establishment of the internal market and they continue to be key to the maintenance of free trade between Member States. As has been seen in **Chapter 8**, Articles 25 and 28 (ex 12 and 30) EC, which prohibit customs duties, charges having equivalent effect, quantitative restrictions, and all measures having equivalent effect, are core elements of the Community free-market project. All these provisions, together with the derogation provisions of the EC Treaty and the associated case law of the Court of Justice, seek to eliminate unjustified and disproportionate barriers to trade in the form of measures adopted by Member States.

Although actions by Member States restricting the free flow of goods constitute a major challenge to free trade, these are not the only threat to the achievement of the internal market objective. The restrictive trading practices of businesses, in the provision of both goods and services, can also have a damaging effect on free trade. Moreover, not only do such practices prejudice the effective operation of the free market, they also have a detrimental effect on business efficiency and are likely to harm consumers. The two major provisions of EC competition law, Articles 81 and 82 (ex 85 and 86) EC are concerned with harmful business practices. Article 81 governs business agreements and Article 82 aims to control the behaviour of very powerful businesses which are 'dominant' in a particular market. In the interests of the free market, business efficiency, and consumer protection, these provisions seek to ensure that restrictive business practices are investigated and eliminated. Articles 81 and 82 are enforced by the European Commission, national competition authorities and national courts under powers conferred by Regulation 1/2003.

This chapter provides a brief overview of the aims of EC competition law, Articles 81 and 82 (ex 85 and 86) EC and the provisions on enforcement. **Chapters 13**, and **14** consider Articles 81 and 82 in more depth. Whilst a text on EU law would be incomplete without some discussion of the Community competition provisions, as these lie at the very heart of the internal market concept, this area of Community law has developed so extensively that it merits separate and detailed study. This book aims to achieve no more than the presentation and explanation of the key concepts and legal principles and the analysis of the major decisions of the European Commission and the Community courts.

12.3 The aims of Community competition law

As noted already, it is possible to identify a number of different aims underlying Community competition law.

12.3.1 Achieving the internal market

The creation and maintenance of the European internal market is a fundamental Community goal. This is to be achieved primarily through the elimination of obstacles to the free movement of goods, persons, services, and capital throughout the Member States. With respect to the free movement of goods, Community law prohibits restrictions such as bans, quotas, customs duties, and other kinds of measure adopted by Member States which impede or prevent free movement within the common market. However, these rules are not in themselves sufficient. The single market objective can be frustrated by other barriers to free trade, arising from agreements between businesses.

? QUESTION 12.1

Can you think of any kinds of agreement between businesses (for instance between producers or distributors of goods) which might frustrate the internal market objective?

The kinds of agreement which threaten market integration are those which partition the common market, thereby preventing goods from moving freely throughout the Member States. Suppose, for example, that three major washing machine manufacturers operating, respectively, in the Netherlands, France, and Belgium agree that each will supply its own washing machines only to distributors located in its own national territory. The effect of such an agreement is to protect each of those manufacturers from competition from two of its potential rivals within the national market. The agreement is anti-competitive. It also partitions the market along national lines and prevents the washing machines moving freely from Member State to Member State.

On a smaller scale, the distributors of the washing machines might agree that each of them will sell to customers only within a specified area, keeping out of the territory assigned to the other parties under their agreement. Again, competition between the distributors within their own territories is eliminated and the agreement constitutes an obstacle to the free movement of the products.

Both these agreements are market-sharing agreements. Community competition law prohibits anti-competitive practices of this kind. It also prohibits abusive behaviour by single businesses that are dominant in a particular market.

? QUESTION 12.2

How might a business that supplies most of the products of a particular kind in the EU, and has thereby become dominant in the market for that product, partition the common market? Consider, for instance, a very large computer manufacturer which supplies most of the computers sold in the EU and sells its products to independent distributors across the EU, for resale to retail customers.

One way in which this dominant manufacturer might partition the EU market is by supplying its computers subject to the condition that the distributors resell the products only within the Member State in which they operate. This prevents the computers from moving freely throughout the EU.

12.3.2 Efficiency

A further aim of Community competition law is the enhancement of efficiency in all aspects of production and distribution of goods and services. Efficiency is necessary not only to ensure that the European consumer has available the highest quality products and services at the lowest possible price but also to enable the Community to compete effectively on world markets. Anti-competitive agreements can be very damaging to efficiency.

? QUESTION 12.3

Consider the market-sharing agreements described above. How might these impact on the efficiency of production?

Under each of these agreements, provided none of the parties 'cheats' by breaching the terms, the parties are all protected from competition from each other within the allocated territories. Without the threat of competition, they have no incentive to operate efficiently or maintain the quality of their products and services.

? QUESTION 12.4

Would you expect a dominant company to operate efficiently?

Where a company supplies most or a very large percentage of products or services of a particular kind, there would certainly be a tendency for it to lose sight of efficiency. With little or no threat of competition, the company might well become complacent, believing its market position to be secure.

12.3.3 The protection of the consumer

Agreements restricting competition are likely to have a detrimental effect on consumers.

QUESTION 12.5

How might the market-sharing agreement relating to the Netherlands, France, and Belgium, described in 12.3.1, harm consumers?

A consumer wishing to purchase a washing machine in the Netherlands would be precluded from choosing a machine manufactured by the French and Belgian manufacturers, unless he or she could obtain a machine which had been purchased by a third party in France or Belgium and subsequently imported into the Netherlands. Consumers in France and Belgium would be in a similar position. In addition to the reduction in consumer choice, the agreement would also be likely to result in higher prices and lower quality. Because of reduced competition, each producer would be in a position to raise its prices and pay less regard to quality, without risking lost sales.

Rather than enter into a market-sharing agreement, these producers might agree that they will charge the same price for their products. This would be referred to as a 'price-fixing' agreement. Typically, when this occurs, prices tend to be fixed at a higher level than that which could be maintained in a competitive market, resulting in a detriment to consumers.

QUESTION 12.6

How might a dominant company harm consumer interests?

A company which enjoys a position of market power because of its dominance in the market for a particular product or service may raise its prices above competitive levels, secure in the knowledge that the consumer has little or no possibility of purchasing the product or service from another source. Of course, if the price is set too high, the consumer may choose not to buy at all.

12.3.4 The protection of small and medium-sized businesses

Consumer protection is not confined to the interests of individual persons. EC competition law is also concerned to protect small and medium-sized businesses from restrictive practices and the abuse of market power. For instance, a small manufacturer might suffer at the hands of suppliers of particular raw materials or components who agree to align their trading practices. This could be an agreement to fix prices at an excessively high level. If there are few or no alternative sources of supply, the small manufacturer has little choice but to pay. Similarly, a dominant supplier of raw materials or components may abuse its market power and harm the small manufacturer by charging excessive prices or reducing the quality of its products.

12.4 Outline of the Community competition rules

Article 3 (ex 3) EC makes a clear statement of the significance of the competition rules to the internal market.

THE EC TREATY

Article 3 (ex 3)

For the purposes set out in Article 2, the activities of the Community shall include, as provided in this Treaty and in accordance with the timetable set out therein:

. . .

(g) a system ensuring that competition in the internal market is not distorted . . .

This broadly stated aim is supported by other more specific provisions including those contained in:

(a) Articles 87–9 (ex 92–4), EC concerning State aids;

(b) Article 81 (ex 85) EC, prohibiting anti-competitive agreements between businesses; and

(c) Article 82 (ex 86) EC, concerning the abuse of market power.

For reasons of space, State aids must unfortunately fall outside the scope of this book. Discussion will turn presently to more detailed consideration of Articles 81 and 82 (ex 85 and 86) EC (**Chapters 13** and **14** respectively). Before looking at the detailed rules, it will be useful to take a very brief overview of these provisions, within the context of the aims of Community competition law set out above, and to consider the provisions on the enforcement of Articles 81 and 82 under Regulation 1/2003.

12.5 Article 81 (ex 85) EC: anti-competitive agreements

In broad terms, Article 81 (ex 85) EC prohibits agreements between businesses (referred to in Article 81 as 'undertakings', a term which will be used throughout the rest of this chapter) which prevent, restrict, or distort competition within the common market and affect trade between Member States

EXERCISE 12.1

Look back at 12.3 and the business agreements described throughout that section. Make a list summarizing all the agreements that may well infringe Article 81 (ex 85) EC.

You may have picked out the following as possible infringements of Article 81 (ex 85) EC.

(a) Agreement between the three washing machine manufacturers operating in the Netherlands, France, and Belgium, respectively, to supply their products only in their own national territory (market-sharing)

(b) Agreement between the same three manufacturers that they will charge the same price for their products (price-fixing)

(c) Agreement between the distributors of the washing machines that each will sell to customers only within a specified area, keeping out of the territory assigned to the other parties (market-sharing)

(d) Agreement between suppliers of raw materials or components to fix prices at an excessively high level (price-fixing)

Market sharing and price-fixing are recognized as the two most damaging restrictions of competition. There are other kinds of restriction too, as will become apparent in the detailed discussion of Article 81 in **Chapter 13**.

12.6 Article 82 (ex 86) EC: abuse of a dominant position

Article 82 (ex 86) EC provides that any abuse by a dominant undertaking (remember that 'undertaking' means a business) in the common market shall be prohibited as incompatible with the common market.

EXERCISE 12.2

Look back at 12.3 and the business behaviour described throughout that section. Make a list summarizing all the behaviour that may well infringe Article 82 (ex 86) EC.

You may have picked out the following as possible infringements of Article 82 (ex 86) EC.

(a) A very large computer manufacturer, which supplies most of the computers sold in the EU, sells its computers to distributors across the EU subject to the condition that they resell the products only within the Member State in which they operate (market-sharing).

(b) A company which enjoys a position of market power because of its dominance in the market for a particular product or service raises its prices above competitive levels (this abusive behaviour is often referred to as 'excessive pricing').

Other examples of abuse of a dominant position are considered in detail in **Chapter 14**.

12.7 Enforcement of Articles 81 and 82 (ex 85 and 86) EC

12.7.1 The enforcement regime

The original EC competition law enforcement regime was set out in Regulation 17/62. The Commission took the central role, being empowered to investigate alleged infringements, to order termination of infringements and to fine undertakings acting in breach of the competition rules. At the same time, national courts were able to apply those provisions of Articles 81 and 82 (ex 85 and 86) which were directly effective. Following wide consultation, in September 2000 the Commission published a proposal for the reform of Regulation 17/62 and, in December 2002, Regulation 1/2003 on the implementation of the rules on competition laid down in Articles 81 and 82 was adopted. Regulation 1/2003 replaced Regulation 17/62 and introduced a new enforcement regime. It entered into force on 1 May 2004.

The basis of the current regime is a system under which the Commission (through the Directorate General for Competition or D/G Competition, the department responsible for competition matters), the national courts, and the national competition authorities cooperate in the effective enforcement of the Community competition rules. This enables the Community to meet the challenges of enlargement, whilst at the same time ensuring that Articles 81 and 82 (ex 85 and 86) EC are applied uniformly across the Community.

12.7.2 Allocation of cases between the Commission and national competition authorities

Under Regulation 1/2003, both the Commission and national competition authorities can investigate alleged infringements, issue decisions and impose fines.

? QUESTION 12.7

Do you know which is the competent competition authority in the UK?

In the UK, the investigation and enforcement powers contained in Regulation 1/2003 are exercised by the Office of Fair Trading, headed by the Director General of Fair Trading. Commonly, investigations are instigated by the Commission or national competition authorities following complaints by undertakings or individuals affected by infringements. The Commission is empowered to take over cases from national authorities and does so in accordance with criteria set out in the *Commission notice on cooperation within the network of Competition authorities*, 2004. In particular, this will occur where a similar competition issue arises in several Member States or to ensure effective enforcement. This allows the Commission to concentrate its limited resources on the most serious infringements of the competition rules, especially cartel activity operating across different Member States.

? **QUESTION** 12.8

What are the features of a cartel?

In recent years, many competition regimes across the world have increased their efforts to root out and eradicate cartels. These may operate on an international level and can have a serious impact upon competition. Typically, a cartel comprises a number of separate companies operating in the same market that collude to fix prices, share markets or engage in other kinds of anti-competitive behaviour. Cartel members are well aware that their activity infringes competition rules and consequently act secretively, making great efforts to conceal their collusion from the competition authorities.

12.7.3 Cooperation with national competition authorities

In order to ensure effective and consistent enforcement, Regulation 1/2003 (Articles 11–13) requires close cooperation between national competition authorities and the European Commission and between national authorities themselves. National authorities must, for instance, inform the Commission when they begin investigations and provide a summary of the case before adopting a final decision. The Commission must pass on copies of any important relevant documents that it holds. If the Commission decides to take over a case, the national authorities may take no further action. Any relevant information may be exchanged between national authorities and between authorities and the Commission.

12.7.4 Cooperation with national courts

National courts may apply Articles 81 and 82 (ex 85 and 86) EC in proceedings brought by private parties seeking, for instance, injunctions to prevent an infringement or damages where loss has occurred. Regulation 1/2003 (Article 15) provides for cooperation between national courts and the Commission. National courts can request information or advice from the Commission and may, of course, refer questions of interpretation of Articles 81 and 82 to the Court of Justice under the Article 234 EC preliminary reference procedure.

 **EXERCISE** 12.3

Look back at **Chapter 5** to remind yourself of Article 234 (ex 177) EC and the preliminary reference procedure.

The Commission may make observations to the national court and copies of judgments must be submitted to the Commission. However, whereas the Commission is able to relieve a national competition authority of the competence to act in any particular case by taking over the case itself, the Commission does not have a similar power in relation to cases before national courts. This means that national court proceedings and Commission proceedings may run in parallel or a national court may be called upon to consider a case on which a Commission decision has already been taken. Regulation 1/2003 (Article 15) provides that national courts must avoid judgments that conflict with Commission decisions, whether these have already been issued or are contemplated. National courts must assess whether it is necessary to stay proceedings pending a Commission decision.

12.7.5 The Commission's powers under Regulation 1/2003 (Articles 7–10): Decisions

By formal Decision, the Commission may require undertakings to bring an infringement to an end. It may impose any behavioural or structural remedy which is proportionate and necessary to end the infringement.

QUESTION 12.9

Can you think of any examples of behavioural and structural remedies?

As you might expect, a behavioural remedy relates to the behaviour of the undertaking, for example an order to resume supplies to a customer, imposed by an undertaking found to have abused its position by refusing supplies. A structural remedy entails changes in the structure of the undertaking, for instance an order to dispose of part of its business. Commission investigations are frequently protracted and for this reason, Regulation 1/2003 permits the Commission to order interim measures in urgent cases, where there is a risk of serious or irreparable damage to competition.

12.7.6 The Commission's powers of investigation

Regulation 1/2003 (Articles 17–21) gives the Commission the power to investigate sectors of the economy, to request information from undertakings and associations of undertakings, to take statements and to conduct inspections of business and other premises. Sector investigations may include requests for information and inspections of business premises, but here the Commission has no power to impose remedies. The Commission may also request information from national governments and competition authorities. In the course of its investigations into specific suspected infringements, the Commission can ask undertakings to supply all necessary information, either by simple request or by formal Decision. Articles 23–24 provide that fines of up to 1% of the previous year's turnover may be imposed for the provision of incorrect or misleading information. In the case of failure to comply with a formal Decision requesting information, similar fines plus daily penalties of up to 5% of the undertaking's daily turnover may be imposed. The Commission may interview any person in connection with its inquiries, though no penalties may be imposed for the provision of incorrect or misleading information during an interview.

The power to inspect business premises is a powerful tool, particularly if undertakings have tried to conceal their behaviour, for instance in operating a cartel or in abusing a dominant position. Such inspections may be voluntary (conducted with the agreement of the undertaking concerned) or mandatory (often referred to as 'dawn raids'). Persons authorized by the Commission have the power to enter an undertaking's premises, land, and means of transport; examine books and other business records, including computer records, and take photocopies; seal any business premises or books or records; and ask for explanations of facts or documents and record the answers. If it has a reasonable suspicion that books or records proving a serious violation are being kept at other premises, the Commission has the power, with prior authorization from a national court, to carry out inspections there.

The Commission may undertake a mandatory inspection (which requires a formal Decision) without having first attempted a voluntary inspection (which requires only written authorization). The Commission will carry out a mandatory inspection where the element of surprise is an important feature of its inquiry, but it has no power of forcible entry. If an undertaking refuses to submit to such an inspection, the Member State concerned must give necessary assistance, usually entailing the issue of a search warrant and police involvement. Refusal to allow entry to Commission officials carrying out a mandatory inspection.may give rise to daily penalties and fines of up to 1% and 5% of turnover, respectively.

12.7.7 The Commission's duty of confidentiality

Inevitably, some of the documents acquired by the Commission and the national competition authorities during their investigations will be highly sensitive because they contain business secrets. They might relate, for instance, to future business plans or to valuable know-how. Regulation 1/2003 (Article 27) allows parties access to the file for the purposes of their defence. However, that right is subject to the legitimate interest of undertakings in the protection of their business secrets. Similarly Article 30, which requires the Commission to publish Decisions finding and ordering termination of infringements and imposing fines and penalties, requires the Commission, in publishing these Decisions, to have regard to the legitimate interests of undertakings in the protection of their business secrets.

12.7.8 Right to be heard

Before the Commission adopts a Decision that is unfavourable to an undertaking—finding an infringement, ordering interim measures, or imposing fines or penalties—that undertaking must be given the opportunity of a hearing. If the Commission considers it necessary, it may hear other persons. Where they show a 'sufficient interest', those persons must be heard (Article 27).

12.7.9 Fines and penalties for breaches of Articles 81 and 82 (ex 85 and 86) EC

Substantial fines and daily penalties may be levied on undertakings found to have infringed Articles 81 and 82 (ex 85 and 86) EC. Lump sum fines of up to 10% of total turnover plus, in the case of continuing infringements, daily penalties of up to 5% of daily turnover may be imposed (Negotiation 1/2003, Articles 23–24). Fines can be heavy, since turnover figures are based upon an undertaking's worldwide turnover. Obvious and blatant breaches, such as market-sharing or price-fixing, will attract large fines. Other factors may be relevant too. The Commission considers, for instance, the economic strength of the parties to an agreement or of dominant undertakings; their share of the product market; the extent of the profits derived from the offending behaviour; any previous infringements; and whether the behaviour was inadvertent or deliberate. In order to assist it in its fight against cartels, the Commission gives full immunity from fines to cartel members who come forward with information leading to a 'dawn raid' or establishing an infringement. Reductions in fines are available to cartel members who pass on information providing 'significant added value' to an investigation.

12.7.10 **Judicial Review**

Commission Decisions under the competition rules are subject to judicial review by the Community courts. Since 1989, review of competition matters has been undertaken by the Court of First Instance rather than the Court of Justice. Appeal on points of law lies to the Court of Justice.

QUESTION 12.10

Under which Treaty Articles do you think proceedings for judicial review may be brought? Look back at **Chapter 6** for guidance.

Proceedings may be brought before the Court of First Instance in one of two circumstances. The majority of actions are those in which the complainant undertaking seeks annulment of a Commission Decision finding that it has infringed the competition rules (Article 230 (ex 173) proceedings). Alternatively, an undertaking may contest the Commission's failure to act or to take adequate action in response to its complaint against other parties (Article 232 (ex 175) proceedings). Annulment of Commission Decisions on competition matters is uncommon, though not unknown. A complainant undertaking is more likely to secure the reduction of fines rather than annulment.

CONCLUSIONS

Whereas the Community free movement of good provisions concern restrictive measures adopted by Member States, the competition rules contained in Articles 81 and 82 (ex 85 and 86) EC target harmful business behaviour. One of their primary aims is to promote free trade across the EU, but other considerations are important too. The provisions seek also to encourage business efficiency and to protect consumers and small and medium-sized enterprises from restrictive business practices and from abuse by dominant business organizations. The European Commission, the national competition authorities, and the national courts all have a part to play in the enforcement of Articles 81 and 82. Under Regulation 1/2003, the Commission has available wide powers, which are especially important in the investigation of the most serious infringements, such as cross-border cartels.

SUMMARY

- **EC competition law seeks to:** promote free trade and business efficiency and to protect consumers and small enterprises from restrictive practices and abusive behaviour by dominant undertakings
- **Article 81 (ex 85) EC** prohibits anti-competitive agreements between undertakings
- **Article 82 (ex 86) EC** prohibits any abuse of a dominant position within the common market
- **Articles 81 and 82 are enforced** by the European Commission, the national competition authorities, and the national courts
- **Regulation 1/2003** gives the Commission extensive powers for the investigation of suspected breaches, including the power to request information from undertakings, to enter business premises, and to inspect books and records
- **The Commission can issue Decisions** ordering termination of infringements and imposing fines and penalties
- **Commission Decisions are subject to review** by the Court of First Instance and the Court of Justice

CHAPTER 12: ASSESSMENT EXERCISE

Outline the powers of the European Commission in the enforcement of Articles 81 and 82 (ex 85 and 86) EC. How are the rights and interests of undertakings protected?

See *Cases and Materials* (12.2) for specimen answer.

FURTHER READING

Burnside, A. (2005). 'Co-operation in Competition: a New Era'. 30 EL Rev 234.

Gilliams, H.M. (2003). 'Modernisation: from Policy to Practice', European Competition Law Review 451.

Holmes, K. (2004). 'Public Enforcement or Private Enforcement? Enforcement of Competition Law in the EC and the UK', *European Competition Law Review* 25.

13 Anti-competitive agreements, decisions, and concerted practices

13.1 OBJECTIVES

By the end of this chapter you should be able to:

1 Outline the framework of regulation contained in Article 81 (ex 85) EC

2 Explain and analyse the scope of the Article 81(1) (ex 85(1)) prohibition of agreements between undertakings, decisions of associations of undertakings, and concerted practices which prevent, restrict, or distort competition within the common market

3 Discuss the provisions of Article 81(3) (ex 85(3))

13.2 Introduction

In the introduction to EC competition law in **Chapter 12**, it was noted that the Community rules on competition are an integral part of the internal market. One of their primary aims is the maintenance of free trade in goods and services throughout the EU. In particular, Articles 81 and 82 (ex 85 and 86) EC seek to eliminate obstacles to trade arising from restrictive agreements between businesses and from the behaviour of very powerful business organizations. These provisions are also designed to promote business efficiency, to protect consumers, and to protect small and medium-sized enterprises from unfair competition. This chapter considers Article 81 in more detail. It will be seen that the rules it incorporates are wide in scope and have been broadly interpreted by the European Commission and the Community courts. Article 81 relates not only to agreements between businesses but also to decisions of trade associations and to concerted practices.

13.3 The framework of Article 81 (ex 85) EC

13.3.1 Article 81(1)(ex 85(1)) EC

The broad scope of Article 81 is immediately apparent on a reading of the first paragraph. Article 81(1) prohibits anti-competitive agreements between undertakings, decisions of associations of undertakings, and concerted practices. It lists a number of examples of the types of agreement to which Article 81(1) (ex 85(1)) applies. These are contained in Article 81(1)(a)–(e).

THE EC TREATY

Article 81

1. The following shall be prohibited as incompatible with the common market: all agreements between undertakings, decisions by associations of undertakings, and concerted practices which may affect trade between Member States and which have as their object or effect the prevention, restriction, or distortion of competition within the common market, and in particular those which:
   (a) directly or indirectly fix purchase or selling prices or any other trading conditions;
   (b) limit or control production, markets, technical development, or investment;
   (c) share markets or sources of supply;
   (d) apply dissimilar conditions to equivalent transactions with other trading parties, thereby placing them at a competitive disadvantage;
   (e) make the conclusion of contracts subject to acceptance by the other parties of supplementary obligations which, by their nature or according to commercial usage, have no connection with the subject of such contracts.

Article 81 (ex 85) refers to 'undertakings'.

? QUESTION 13.1

Do you remember the meaning of 'undertaking'?

The precise meaning of this term is examined below. Broadly speaking, it means any person or entity involved in commercial activity, in other words a business or an individual engaged in business.

13.3.2 Article 81(2)(ex 85(2)) EC

Article 81(2) sets out the consequences of a breach of Article 81(1).

THE EC TREATY

Article 81

2. Any agreements or decisions prohibited pursuant to this Article shall be automatically void.

Although Article 81(2) provides that agreements falling within the Article 81(1) prohibition shall be automatically void, the Court of Justice has held that if it is possible to remove ('sever') restrictive clauses, then those clauses alone will be held to be void. The remainder of the agreement may remain intact.

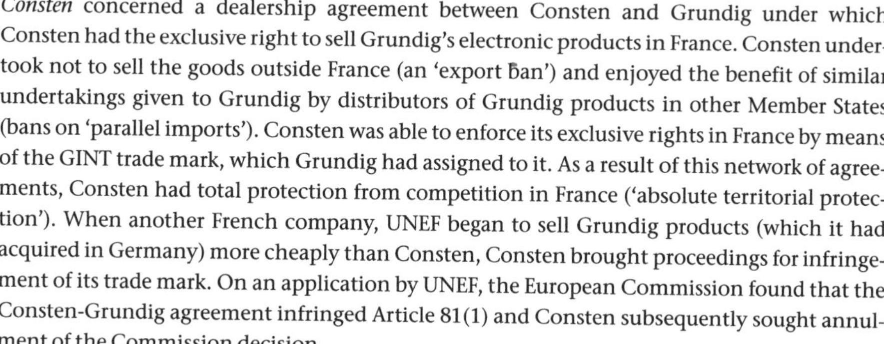

***Établissements Consten SA* v *Commission* (Cases 56 & 58/64) [1966] ECR 299**

Consten concerned a dealership agreement between Consten and Grundig under which Consten had the exclusive right to sell Grundig's electronic products in France. Consten undertook not to sell the goods outside France (an 'export ban') and enjoyed the benefit of similar undertakings given to Grundig by distributors of Grundig products in other Member States (bans on 'parallel imports'). Consten was able to enforce its exclusive rights in France by means of the GINT trade mark, which Grundig had assigned to it. As a result of this network of agreements, Consten had total protection from competition in France ('absolute territorial protection'). When another French company, UNEF began to sell Grundig products (which it had acquired in Germany) more cheaply than Consten, Consten brought proceedings for infringement of its trade mark. On an application by UNEF, the European Commission found that the Consten-Grundig agreement infringed Article 81(1) and Consten subsequently sought annulment of the Commission decision.

The Court of Justice held that the only prohibited clauses were those giving absolute territorial protection and that these could be severed, leaving the rest of the agreement intact. (*Cases and Materials* (13.1.1)).

The Court of Justice applied the same principles in (*Société Technique Minière* v *Maschinenbau Ulm GmbH* (Case 56/65) [1966] ECR 235 (*Cases and Materials* (13.1.1)).

13.3.3 Article 81(3)(ex 85(3)) EC

This paragraph sets out the exemption provisions. Under Article 81(3), Article 81(1) (ex 85(1)) may be declared inapplicable to an agreement, decision or concerted practice if certain conditions are satisfied.

THE EC TREATY

Article 81

3. The provisions of paragraph 1 may, however, be declared inapplicable in the case of:

— any agreement or category of agreements between undertakings;

— any decision or category of decisions by associations of undertakings;

— any concerted practice or category of concerted practices;

which contributes to improving the production or distribution of goods or to promoting technical or economic progress, while allowing consumers a fair share of the resulting benefit, and which does not;

(a) impose on the undertakings concerned restrictions which are not indispensable to the attainment of these objectives;

(b) afford such undertakings the possibility of eliminating competition in respect of a substantial part of the products in question.

? QUESTION 13.2

Do you remember which authorities have the power to enforce Article 81 (ex 85) EC? If you have forgotten, look back at **Chapter 12**.

Article 81 is enforced by the European Commission, the national competition authorities and the national courts.

Under Regulation 17/62, which set out the previous enforcement regime, the Commission alone had the power to apply Article 81(3) and declare Article 81(1) inapplicable to agreements satisfying its terms. It did so by means of individual exemptions, applying to individual agreements, and block exemptions, applying to categories of agreement. An undertaking seeking individual exemption for a specific agreement was required to notify the agreement to the Commission. The notification system was abolished when the current enforcement regime was introduced.

? QUESTION 13.3

Do you recall the current enforcement Regulation and when this entered into force? If you have forgotten, look back at **Chapter 12**.

The current enforcement regime, contained in Regulation 1/2003, entered into force on 1 May 2004. Now, national competition authorities and national courts are able to apply the exemption provisions and declare Article 81(1) inapplicable to agreements satisfying the conditions specified in Article 81(3). The system of block exemptions is still retained. This will be considered later in this Chapter.

13.4 Article 81(1) (ex 85(1)): the prohibition

? QUESTION 13.4

What kinds of arrangement between undertakings does Article 81(1) prohibit? Look back at 13.3.1.

The following are prohibited: agreements between undertakings, decisions by associations of undertakings, and concerted practices which may affect trade between Member States and which have as their object or effect the prevention, restriction, or distortion of competition within the common market. Thus, for a breach to occur, there must be:

- an agreement between undertakings or a decision by an association of undertakings or a concerted practice
- which may affect trade between Member States; and
- which has as its object or effect the prevention, restriction, or distortion of competition within the common market.

All three elements must be satisfied. In order to understand the scope of the Article 81(1) prohibition, each of these must be examined.

13.5 Agreements between undertakings, decisions of associations of undertakings, and concerted practices

13.5.1 Undertakings

There is no Treaty definition of 'undertaking'. The term has been interpreted widely by the Court of Justice in order to extend the application of Article 81(1) (ex 85(1)) as far as possible. 'Undertaking' has consequently been held to include both legal and natural persons engaged in commercial activity in the supply of goods or services.

? QUESTION 13.5

What do you think is meant by 'legal' persons engaged in commercial activity?

Clearly, natural persons engaged in commercial activity comprise individuals running their own businesses, as sole traders or in partnership. As for legal persons, the Court of Justice has included within the scope of Article 81(1) (ex 85(1)) various kinds of entity engaged in commercial activity, such as companies, state-owned corporations, and even sporting associations. To be classed as undertakings under Article 81(1) (ex 85(1)), such individuals or entities need not be pursuing their commercial activity with a view to profit.

13.5.2 Autonomous conduct of undertakings

Article 81 (ex 85) does not apply where the restriction of competition is not attributable to the autonomous conduct of undertakings, a point confirmed by the Court of Justice in *Ladbroke Racing*.

***Commission and France* v *Ladbroke Racing Ltd* (Joined Cases C-359 & 379/95P) [1997] ECR 1-6265, [1998] 4 CMLR 27**

Ladbroke Racing concerned French legislation requiring horse racing companies authorized to operate off-course totalizator betting to place the management of those operations in the hands of the *Pari Mutuel Urbain* (PMU). Ladbroke claimed that agreements or concerted practices between the companies and between the companies and PMU granting PMU the exclusive right to manage their betting operations infringed Article 81 (ex 85). The Court of Justice reiterated that Article 81 (ex 85) only applies where undertakings engage in anti-competitive activity on their own initiative. There is no infringement where anti-competitive conduct is required by national legislation.

The same principles apply in relation to Article 82 (ex 86) **(Chapter 14)**.

13.5.3 Agreements

Article 81(1) (ex 85(1)) is designed to catch a wide range of agreements, including those which are made informally without writing. If that were not the case, it would be possible for undertakings to avoid the competition rules without difficulty. The term 'agreement', as might be expected, covers legally enforceable contracts. It has also been held to cover less formal agreements—the so-called 'gentleman's agreement'—and simple understandings between parties. It is not necessary to define 'agreement' precisely because the Article 81(1) (ex 85(1)) concept of 'concerted practice' has such a wide scope that it includes many forms of informal understanding between undertakings whose classification as 'agreements' might be open to doubt.

13.5.4 Decisions by associations of undertakings

The coordination of trading activity between undertakings can arise from decisions taken collectively through a trade association. Such decisions are specifically covered by Article 81(1) (ex 85(1)) and, if all the other elements are satisfied, will constitute a breach of that Article. Even a non-binding recommendation—for instance to raise prices or to refuse supplies to particular categories of customer—can constitute a decision within the meaning of Article 81(1) (ex 85(1)). *IAZ* (*Cases and Materials* (13.2.1)) concerned a non-binding recommendation to its members by a trade association.

***IAZ International Belgium NV* v *Commission* (Cases 96–102, 104, 105, 108, and 110/82) [1983] ECR 3369**

A Belgian water suppliers' trade association recommended its members not to connect washing machines and dishwashers to the mains water supply system unless they carried a conformity label issued by the Belgian manufacturers' trade association indicating that they satisfied certain standards laid down by national legislation. The system was operated in such a way as to discriminate against machines produced in other Member States. The applicants sought annulment of a Commission Decision finding a breach of Article 81(1) (ex 85(1)), contending (inter alia) that a non-binding recommendation fell outside the scope of that provision.

The Court of Justice confirmed the Commission's view that a non-binding recommendation could fall within the scope of Article 81(1) if it was intended to be anti-competitive and was normally complied with, resulting in an appreciable effect on competition.

The term 'association of undertakings' is not confined to trade associations but can also include professional organizations.

***Wouters* v *Netherlands Bar* (Case C-309/99) [2002] ECR I-1577**

Here, the Court considered a regulation of the Bar of the Netherlands prohibiting multi-disciplinary partnerships of members of the Bar and accountants. The Court declared that such a regulation expresses the intention of the delegates of the members of a profession that they should act in a particular manner in carrying on their economic activity. In adopting such a regulation, the professional organization must be regarded as an association of undertakings.

13.5.5 Concerted practices

The interpretation of 'concerted practices' has given rise to many difficulties. Whilst the term is much wider in scope than 'agreements' and 'decisions of associations of undertakings', the outer limits of the concept are not easily defined. The first important case concerning concerted practices to come before the Court of Justice was *Dyestuffs*.

 **EXERCISE** 13.1 

Look at *Dyestuffs* (*Cases and Materials* (13.2.2)). How did the Court of Justice define a concerted practice at paragraph 64? Write out the definition.

***Imperial Chemical Industries Ltd* v *Commission (Dyestuffs)* (Case 48/69) [1972] ECR 619.**

Here, ICI challenged a Commission Decision concerning three price increases which had been introduced uniformly and almost simultaneously by a number of producers of aniline dyes, including ICI, during the 1960s. The Commission took the view that the prices had been fixed through concerted practices and fines were imposed.

The Court of Justice defined a concerted practice as 'a form of coordination between undertakings which, without having reached the stage where an agreement properly so-called has been concluded, knowingly substitutes practical cooperation between them for the risks of competition'. The producers argued that their behaviour did not amount to concerted practice but was part of the normal operation of an oligopolistic market (relatively few sellers dominating the market for a particular product).

It is often argued that in oligopolistic markets where pricing policies are transparent, rival undertakings will respond naturally and without collusion to each other's market strategy. If one undertaking raises prices, the others will tend to follow with similar price increases. This is a form of 'parallel' behaviour.

 **EXERCISE** 13.2 

Look again at *Dyestuffs*, in particular paragraphs 66 and 67 (*Cases and Materials* (13.2.2)). What view did the Court of Justice take on the significance of parallel behaviour in relation to concerted practices?

***Dyestuufs* cont.**

The Court ruled that whilst parallel behaviour in itself does not amount to concerted practice, it may be strong evidence of such practice. That will be the case where the conduct 'leads to conditions of competition which do not correspond to the normal conditions of the market'.

This view has been criticized on the basis that it is difficult to determine with any certainty what are 'normal conditions of the market'. The *Dyestuffs* decision itself did not, however, depend upon the Court's analysis of parallel behaviour. There was sufficient evidence of communications between the companies to establish that they had knowingly cooperated with each other to eliminate the risks of competition.

An oligopolistic market was considered once again in *Woodpulp*.

 **EXERCISE** 13.3 

Look at the extracts from *Woodpulp* and summarize the conclusions of the Court of Justice (*Cases and Materials* (13.2.2)).

***Ahlström & Ors* v *Commission (Woodpulp)* (Cases C-89, 104, 114, 116–117, 125–129/85) [1993] ECR I-1307**

Here, the Court of Justice accepted that parallel pricing, arising under a system of quarterly price announcements operated by a number of woodpulp producers, did not amount to concerted practice but was the result of the normal operation of an oligopolistic market. There was no evidence of communication between the parties and the parallel conduct could be satisfactorily explained by the nature of the woodpulp market.

A concerted practice need not entail the existence of a plan. However, whilst there would be no breach where undertakings simply responded to the current and anticipated conduct of their competitors, Article 81(1) does preclude direct contact between undertakings 'the object or effect whereof is either to influence the conduct . . . of an actual or potential competitor or to disclose to such a competitor the course of conduct which they themselves have decided to adopt or contemplate adopting on the market' (*Cooperatieve Vereniging 'Suiker Unie' UA* v *Commission* (the *Sugar Cartel* cases) (Cases 40–8, 50, 54–6, 111, 113, 114/73) [1975] ECR 1663  (*Cases and Materials* (13.2.2)). Indeed, there is a presumption that operators who have exchanged such information with their competitors and are still active on the market take account of that information in the conduct of their business. In such circumstances, a concerted practice will be established without evidence of anti-competitive effects on the market. An anti-competitive object is sufficient. (Case C-199/92P *Huls AG* v *Commission* [1999] ECR I-4287).

13.5.6 Vertical and horizontal agreements

Article 81 (ex 85) is concerned with both vertical and horizontal agreements which restrict competition and affect trade between Member States. A vertical agreement is an agreement between undertakings which operates on different levels of the production/distribution chain.

QUESTION 13.6 

Who do you think might be parties to a typical vertical agreement? Do you remember the agreement between Consten and Grundig (13.3.2)?

The most common types of vertical agreement are those which involve distribution systems, for instance an agreement between a car manufacturer and a dealer in the car retailing business. The application of Article 81 (ex 85) to vertical agreements was established in *Consten* (*Cases and Materials* (13.2.3)).

 **EXERCISE** 13.4 

Look at the extracts from *Consten*. Summarize the Court of Justice's reasoning on this point. Have a look also at *STM* (*Société Technique Minière* v *Maschinenbau Ulm GmbH* (Case 56/65) [1966] ECR 235 (*Cases and Materials* (13.2.3))), where the Court of Justice reiterated its conclusion.

Établissements Consten SA v _Commission_ (Cases 56 & 58/64) [1966] ECR 299

It will be recalled that the Consten–Grundig agreement was a dealership agreement under which Grundig supplied its electronic products to Consten for resale in France. Another French company, UNEF, acquired Grundig products in Germany. When UNEF began to sell Grundig products in France, Consten brought proceedings against UNEF for infringement of the GINT trade mark, which Grundig had assigned to it in France. Following an application by UNEF alleging that the Consten–Grundig agreement breached Article 81(1) (ex 85) EC, the Commission issued a Decision finding an infringement. Consten sought annulment of that decision, arguing (inter alia) that Article 81(ex 85) EC applied only to horizontal agreements.

The Court of Justice reasoned that Article 81 (ex 85) EC refers in a general way to all agreements that distort competition and makes no distinction based on whether they are made between competitors who operate at the same level or at different levels in the economic process. Moreover, competition may be distorted not only by agreements limiting competition between the parties themselves but also by agreements that limit competition between one of them and third parties. This would be particularly significant where, as a result, the parties to the agreement gained an unjustified advantage at the expense of consumers.

In 1997, the Commission initiated a wide consultation on the reform of the rules on vertical restraints (restrictions of competition in vertical agreements) and legislation was adopted in this area in 1999. This is considered later in this chapter.

QUESTION 13.7

How would you define a horizontal agreement? Who do you think might be parties to a typical horizontal agreement? For an example of a (fictitious) horizontal agreement, look back at the agreement between the Dutch, French and German washing machine manufacturers in **Chapter 12**.

A horizontal agreement is an agreement between undertakings which operate on the same level of the production/distribution chain, for instance between a group of manufacturers or between a number of retailers.

For Article 81 (ex 85) to apply, undertakings must be independent of each other. Consequently, agreements between a parent company and its subsidiary or within an undertaking do not fall within its scope.

13.6 'Which may affect trade between Member States'

This is the second element of Article 81(1) (ex 85(1)). A restrictive agreement, decision, or concerted practice does not breach Article 81(1) (ex 85(1)) unless it 'may affect trade between Member States'. If there is no such effect, an agreement falls to be considered under national law. The Court of Justice has extended Community jurisdiction in this area of competition law by adopting a very broad view of this element of Article 81 (ex 85). An effect on trade between Member States is not difficult to establish.

13.6.1 Actual or potential effect

The scope of 'effect on trade between Member States' was defined in *STM*.

***Société Technique Minière* v *Maschinenbau Ulm GmbH* (Case 56/65) [1966] ECR 235**

Maschinenbau Ulm (MU), a German company which produced heavy earth-moving equipment, entered into an agreement with Société Technique Minière (STM) for the supply of thirty-seven grading machines. Under the contract, STM was given the exclusive right to sell such machines in France, MU agreeing not to supply to any other distributor in the territory, nor to sell there itself. The agreement did not prevent parallel imports and exports: other French distributors were able to obtain supplies from outside France and STM could sell the machines outside the territory. A dispute arose between the parties and STM claimed that the contract was void under Article 81(1) (ex 85(1)).

EXERCISE 13.5

Look at *STM* (*Cases and Materials* (13.3.1)) What test did the Court of Justice apply to determine an effect on trade between Member States? Write down your answer.

The test laid down in *Société Technique Minière* is wide. Article 81(1) (ex 85(1)) applies wherever it is 'possible to foresee with a sufficient degree of probability on the basis of a set of objective factors of law or of fact that the agreement in question may have an influence, direct or indirect, actual or potential, on the pattern of trade between Member States'. The Court has also made clear that an agreement must be looked at in its entirety:

***Windsurfing International* v *Commission* (Case 193/83) [1986] ECR 611**

Windsurfing International sought annulment of a Commission Decision holding that a number of the restrictions in its agreements with certain Community undertakings licensing them to sell its patented windsurfing rigs infringed Article 81(1) (ex 85(1)). The company argued (inter alia) that each individual restrictive clause did not have an appreciable effect on interstate trade.

The Court of Justice held that an agreement will not escape the scope of Article 81(1) (ex 85(1)) simply because individual restrictions contained in it do not affect interstate trade (*Cases and Materials* (13.3.1).

An important feature of the *Société Technique Minière* test is that it is not necessary to show that an agreement has already affected trade between Member States. A potential effect will suffice. Thus, an agreement between undertakings currently operating within one Member State may be caught by Article 81(1) (ex 85(1)).

***Vacuum Interrupters Ltd* (Commission Decision) OJ 1977 L 48/32, [1977] 1 CMLR D67**

Here the Commission decided that a joint venture agreement between two UK companies to design and manufacture switchgear in the UK was capable of affecting trade between Member States. In the absence of an agreement between them, each company would have gone ahead with independent development of the product and would have marketed it in other Member States. Moreover, it would be more difficult for potential competitors from other Member States to enter the UK market in the product in the face of the combined economic and technical strength of the two manufacturers (*Cases and Materials* (13.3.1)).

Even where it is unlikely that an undertaking would wish to extend its trading activities beyond the boundaries of a single Member State, the potential effect of restrictions will still be sufficient to bring an agreement within the scope of Article 81(1) (ex 85(1)). This situation was considered by the Court of Justice in *Pronuptia* (*Cases and Materials* (13.3.1)).

***Pronuptia de Paris GmbH* v *Pronuptia de Paris Irmgard Schillgalis* (Case 161/84) [1986] ECR 353**

A distribution franchise agreement between Pronuptia de Paris GmbH (the franchisor) and Mrs Schillgalis (the franchisee) relating to the retail sale of wedding dresses and other clothes worn at weddings, contained many restrictive clauses. A dispute between the parties concerning the payment of royalties came before the national court, which referred to the Court of Justice a number of questions on the application of Article 81 (ex 85) to franchise agreements.

The Court ruled that, even where franchise agreements are entered into between undertakings operating in the same Member State, they are liable to affect trade between Member States if they prevent franchisees from establishing themselves in another Member State.

13.6.2 Agreements within one Member State

Although the parties to an agreement may operate exclusively in one and the same Member State, there may still be an effect—actual or potential, direct or indirect—between Member States. *Vacuum Interrupters* (13.6.1) illustrates this point. An agreement which operates within a single Member State but covers the whole territory of that State 'by its very nature has the effect of reinforcing the compartmentalization of markets on a national basis, thereby holding up the economic interpenetration which the Treaty is designed to bring about' (*Vereeniging van Cementhandelaren* v *Commission* (Case 8/72) [1972] ECR 977.

13.6.3 An increase in trade

An effect on trade between Member States means any effect, even if it results in an increase in trade.

 **EXERCISE** 13.6 

Look at the extracts from *Consten* (*Établissements Consten SA* v *Commission* (*Cases and Materials* (13.3.2)). What was the Court of Justice's view of Consten's submission that the agreement with Grundig encouraged an increase in trade between Member States? Look back at 13.3.2 if you have forgotten the details of the Consten–Grundig agreement.

In the Court's view, this would not exclude the possibility of an effect on trade between Member States. The agreement prevented Consten from exporting Grundig products to other Member States and prevented other undertakings from importing Grundig products into France. It was indisputable that the agreement affected trade between Member States, satisfying this particular element of Article 81(1).

13.6.4 Networks of agreements

The Commission and the Court will, where appropriate, look at the effect of an agreement as part of a series or a network of agreements which as a whole is capable of affecting trade between Member States. *Brasserie de Haecht* (*Cases and Materials* (13.3.3)) provides a good illustration of this principle.

***Brasserie de Haecht SA* v *Wilkin (No. 1)* (Case 23/67) [1967] ECR 407**

This case concerned loan agreements between the brewery Brasserie de Haecht and Mr and Mrs Wilkin, relating to the purchase of furniture for the café run by the couple. The borrowers agreed, for so long as the debt was not paid off and for a further period of two years, to obtain all their supplies of beer and soft drinks exclusively from the brewery. Discovering that Mr and Mrs Wilkin had not complied with the exclusive purchasing obligation, the brewery began an action for the repayment of the loan in the national court. The couple argued that the agreements breached Article 81 (ex 85) and were therefore void. On a reference to the Court of Justice, the national court asked whether it should confine itself to consideration of the agreements between the brewery and Mr and Mrs Wilkin or whether it should take into account the large number of similar contracts between a small number of Belgian breweries and a large number of liquor licensees.

The Court of Justice held that the effects of agreements must be examined in their legal and economic context. The existence of similar contracts is a factor to be taken into account in assessing whether an agreement is capable of affecting trade between Member States.

13.7 'Which have as their object or effect the prevention, restriction, or distortion of competition within the common market'

This is the third element of Article 81(1) (ex 85(1)). Any agreement which may affect trade between Member States and which prevents, restricts, or distorts competition within the common market will breach Article 81(1)(ex 85(1)). However, it will be recalled that Article 81(3) provides exemption for agreements satisfying specified conditions, to be considered presently. Additionally, an agreement will only breach Article 81(1) if it has an 'appreciable' effect on competition.

13.7.1 An 'appreciable' effect on competition: the *de minimis* principle

Despite the generally broad interpretation of Article 81(1), the Court of Justice ruled, in the early case of *Volk* v *Vervaecke* (*Cases and Materials* (13.4.1)) that an agreement falls outside Article 81(1) if it has only an insignificant effect on the market. If an agreement does not have an appreciable effect on competition, it is described as being of minor importance or *de minimis*.

***Volk* v *Établissements Vervaecke Sprl* (Case 5/69) [1969] ECR 295**

An exclusive distribution agreement between Volk, a small-scale manufacturer of washing machines and Vervaecke, a Dutch distributor, sought to establish absolute territorial protection for Vervaecke. A contractual dispute arose between the parties. The national court asked the Court of Justice whether the manufacturer's share of the market (less than 1% in this case) should be taken into account in order to decide whether the disputed contract fell within the Article 81(1) (ex 85(1)) prohibition.

The Court held that this exclusive dealing agreement, even with absolute territorial protection, escaped the Article 81(1) prohibition because of the weak position of the parties in the market covered by the agreement.

? QUESTION 13.8

Do you remember what is meant by 'absolute territorial protection'? Look back at 13.3.2 for an example of this in the Consten–Grundig agreement.

However, the Court did not specify a precise market share within which the *de minimis* principle would apply. The position has been clarified in a series of Commission notices on agreements of minor importance. The most recent Notice, issued in 2001, sets out the Commission's view that agreements affecting trade between Member States do not appreciably restrict competition within the meaning of Article 81(1) if:

(a) the parties' aggregate market share in any of the relevant markets affected by the agreement does not exceed 10% (where the parties are actual or potential competitors); or

(b) the market share of each of the parties to the agreement does not exceed 15% (where the parties are not actual or potential competitors).

Where it is difficult to classify an agreement as either an agreement between competitors or an agreement between non-competitors, the 10% threshold is applicable.

? QUESTION 13.9

What market share threshold would be applied to the following agreements in assessing whether their effect on competition was appreciable:

(a) an agreement between two computer manufacturers, which supply their products throughout the EU, to adopt the same technical specifications for their products;

(b) a distribution agreement between a French paint manufacturer and a UK paint retailer which requires the retailer to provide training to the staff it employs to sell the paint?

The agreement between the computer manufacturers is a horizontal agreement between companies that are actual competitors in the market for the supply of computers in the EU. If their aggregate market share exceeds 10%, the agreement is not *de minimis*. The distribution agreement is a vertical agreement between non-competitors, a paint manufacturer, and a paint retailer. It will have an appreciable effect on competition if each of the parties' shares in their respective markets exceeds 15%.

These *de minimis* provisions do not apply to agreements containing hardcore restrictions. Thus, agreements between competitors fixing sale prices, limiting output or sales, or allocating markets, fall within Article 81(1), as do agreements between non-competitors which, for instance, fix minimum resale prices or restrict the territory into which the buyer may sell the relevant goods or services. If the *de mimimis* provisions apply, the Commission will not institute proceedings; where undertakings assume in good faith that an agreement is covered by the notice, the Commission will not impose fines.

13.7.2 Object or effect

QUESTION 13.10 

Article 81(1) (ex 85(1)) refers to the anti-competitive 'object or effect' of an agreement. Is it necessary to prove both? Look at *Société Technique Minière* v *Maschinenbau Ulm GmbH* (Case 56/65) [1966] ECR 235 (*Cases and Materials* (13.4.2)).

The first line of enquiry is the object of an agreement. If an agreement is clearly designed to prevent, restrict or distort competition—if for instance it contains blatant price fixing or market-sharing clauses—then there will be no need to prove an anti-competitive effect. It is only necessary to consider the effects of an agreement if it has no obvious anti-competitive purpose.

13.7.3 Prevention, restriction, or distortion of competition

The words 'prevention', 'restriction', and 'distortion' used in the first paragraph of Article 81(1) (ex 85(1)) cover all forms of anti-competitive behaviour and no distinction is made between them. Article 81(1)(a)–(e) (ex 85(1)(a)–(e)) lists examples of restrictions which are likely to breach Article 81(1) (ex 85(1)). Although Article 81 refers to 'agreements', it should be noted that these examples also cover individual restrictive clauses within agreements

 **EXERCISE** 13.7

Look back at 13.3.1 and the examples of prohibited restrictions listed in Article 81(1)(a)–(e) (ex 85(1)(a)–(e)).

Although many forms of anti-competitive behaviour will fall within one of the listed categories, the list is not exhaustive. It provides examples of prohibited restrictions.

13.7.4 Price fixing: Article 81(1)(a) (ex 85(1)(a))

Price fixing is a classic form of anti-competitive behaviour. Horizontal price fixing (for instance in an agreement between manufacturers) is regarded both by the Commission and the Court as having an anti-competitive object. Price fixing in vertical agreements (for instance between a supplier and retail outlets) infringes Article 81(1) (ex 85(1)) and exemption will apply only in exceptional cases. The price-fixing agreement in *Hennessy/Henkell* (*Cases and Materials* (13.4.3)) had been notified to the Commission under the old enforcement regime contained in Regulation 17/62. 

Henessy/Henkel **(Commission Decision) OJ 1980 L 383/11, [1981] 1 CMLR 601**

An exclusive distribution agreement for the sale of Hennessy cognac in Germany contained a number of restrictions, including a clause fixing the minimum and maximum resale prices to be charged by the distributor, Henkell. The Commission decided that the fixing of maximum and minimum price levels infringed Article 81(1) (ex 85(1)) and refused to grant an exemption under Article 81(3) (ex 85(3)). Here, the Commission rejected the argument that the fixing of retail prices was justified because it protected the luxury image of the product.

? **QUESTION** 13.11 

What was the Court of Justice's view of recommended prices in *Pronuptia de Paris GmbH* v *Pronuptia de Paris Irmgard Schillgalis* (Case 161/84) [1986] ECR 353 (*Cases and Materials* (13.4.3))?

You may recall that *Pronuptia* concerned a distribution franchise agreement between Pronuptia de Paris GmbH (the franchisor) and Mrs Schillgalis (the franchisee) relating to the retail sale of wedding dresses and other clothes worn at weddings. The agreement included retail price 'guidelines'. The Court of Justice held that recommended prices would not breach Article 81(1) (ex 85(1)) provided that such recommendations were not binding on the franchisees. *(Pronuptia)*

13.7.5 Fixing other trading conditions: Article 81(1)(a) (ex 85(1)(a))

Within this category, two trading conditions in particular have been condemned by the Commission and the Court of Justice in the strongest of terms. Article 81(1) (ex 85(1)). These are the export ban and the ban on parallel imports.

 **EXERCISE** 13.8 

Explain what is meant by 'export ban' and 'ban on parallel imports' and why these particular trading conditions are incompatible with the internal market. Look back at *Établissements Consten SA* v *Commission* (Cases 56 and 58/64) [1966] ECR 299 (*Cases and Materials* 13.3.2) to find the answer.

Other kinds of trading condition, to be found in distribution agreements, may relate to the way in which goods or services are marketed. Such agreements may, for instance, set up and regulate franchise distribution systems. In *Pronuptia* the Court of Justice described the characteristics of this kind of distribution system and the restrictions that it commonly entails. Essentially, these kinds of arrangement are made between an undertaking that has established itself as a distributor of a particular product (the franchisor) and other independent traders (the franchiseees). The franchisor grants to the franchisees, for a fee, the right to establish themselves elsewhere using its business name and methods. The franchisor derives financial benefit without investing its own capital; the franchisees gain access to successful business methods and benefit from the reputation of the franchisor's business name. In order to protect its reputation, the franchisor will insist upon the franchisee accepting specific obligations: for instance, not to transfer its shop to another party or relocate without the franchisor's consent, to apply the franchisor's business methods, to use its know-how, and to lay out and decorate its premises according to the franchisor's instructions. All these obligations constitute the fixing of trading conditions and are restrictive of competition. However, although they may fall within Article 81(1), they are likely to be exempt, either under the vertical restraints block exemption or individually under Article 81(3), both discussed later in this chapter.

13.7.6 Other restrictions likely to breach Article 81(1): Article 81(1)(b)–(e)

Article 81(1)(b) (ex 85(1)(b)) refers to agreements which control production, markets, technical developments, or investments. These fall within the scope of Article 81(1) (ex 85(1)) but may be exempt under Article 81(3) An example can be found in *ACEC/Berliet*.

ACEC/Berliet (Commission Decision) JO 1968 L 201/7, [1968] CMLR D35

The agreement between ACEC and Berliet provided for technical cooperation and joint research on the development of a bus equipped with electric transmission. There were a number of restrictive clauses, including clauses controlling production and markets. Berliet was to develop the bus and ACEC the transmission system. ACEC undertook to deliver its transmission system only to Berliet in France and to only one manufacturer in each of the Member States. Berliet would buy transmission systems only from ACEC, though it was not subject to any territorial or other restrictions on the marketing of the bus. Following notification of the agreement, the Commission found that it infringed Article 81(1). However, exemption was granted under Article 81(3), subject to the condition that the parties report the progress of the agreement after three years.

Article 81(1)(c) (ex 85(1)(c)) refers to agreements to share markets or sources of supply. These fall within the Article 81(1) (ex 85(1)) prohibition but may satisfy the Article 81(3) (ex 85(3)) conditions. *Transocean Marine Paint Association* provides a good example.

Transocean Marine Paint Association (Commission Decision) [1967] CMLR D9

Several European and non-European manufacturers of marine paint created the Transocean Marine Paint Association with the aim of collaborating in the manufacture and worldwide marketing of their product. The paints were to be manufactured under a single formula determined by the Association and marketed in the same form. Each member remained free to fix its own prices. The same trade mark was to be used, though members were at liberty to add their own mark. Each member was granted a marketing territory corresponding to the country in which it was established. Sales into other members' territory could only be made with the prior agreement of the member concerned and on payment of a commission. The parties notified the agreement, requesting negative clearance or exemption.

The Commission found that the agreement infringed Article 81(1) (ex 85(1)) but granted exemption under Article 81(3) (ex 85(3)).

Article 81(1)(d) (ex 85(1)(d)) refers to agreements which apply dissimilar conditions to equivalent trading transactions with other trading parties, thereby placing them at a competitive disadvantage. Agreements to discriminate between trading parties—for instance to offer discounts to some customers but not to others in relation to identical goods or services—breach Article 81(1) (ex 85(1)) and are unlikely to be exempt.

Article 81(1)(e) (ex 85(1)(e)) refers to agreements which make the conclusion of contracts subject to acceptance by the other parties of supplementary obligations which, by their nature or according to commercial usage, have no connection with the subject of such contracts. Here, a distinction is to be made between those obligations which do have a connection and those which do not have a connection with the subject of the contract, a distinction which may not be easy to draw. The latter breach Article 81(1) (ex 85(1)) but may be exempt.

13.8 The rule of reason

The rule of reason, a concept applied in US anti-trust (i.e. competition) law, entails the balancing of the pro- and anti-competitive effects of an agreement within its market context. Where an agreement is found, on balance, not to be anti-competitive, there is no breach of competition rules. A rule of reason has never been expressly recognized in Community law; indeed the Court of First Instance in *Metropole Television* v *Commission* (case T-112/99) [2001] ECR II 2459, emphasized that its existence in Community law is doubtful. Nevertheless, the scheme of exemption contained in Article 81(3) (ex 85(3) EC) does entail an assessment of the pro- and anti-competitive effects of agreements and requires, for agreements to be exempt, that they are not unduly restrictive of competition.

13.9 Exemption: Article 81(3) (ex 85(3)) EC

Article 81(3) (ex 85(3)) allows Article 81(1) (ex 85(1)) to be declared inapplicable to agreements, decisions, or concerted practices.

THE EC TREATY

Article 81

3. The provisions of paragraph 1 may, however, be declared inapplicable in the case of:
   - any agreement or category of agreements between undertakings;
   - any decision or category of decisions by associations of undertakings;
   - any concerted practice or category of concerted practices;

which contributes to improving the production or distribution of goods or to promoting technical or economic progress, while allowing consumers a fair share of the resulting benefit, and which does not;

(a) impose on the undertakings concerned restrictions which are not indispensable to the attainment of these objectives;

(b) afford such undertakings the possibility of eliminating competition in respect of a substantial part of the products in question.

13.10 Application of Article 81(3) to individual agreements

13.10.1 Abolition of notification

Under the former enforcement regime contained in Regulation 17/62, the Commission alone had the power to exempt individual agreements under Article 81(3), following their notification to the Commission by the parties. The system was designed to ensure that the competition rules were applied uniformly throughout the Community but the Commission's heavy workload in considering agreements notified to it led to delays and consequent uncertainty for business. For these reasons, it was proposed that national competition authorities and national courts should be empowered to apply Article 81(3). This change was adopted under Regulation 1/2003, which replaced Regulation 17/62. Notification was abolished altogether under the new enforcement regime. Regulation 1/2003 provides that agreements caught by Article 81(1) but which satisfy the conditions of Article 81(3) will not be prohibited but will be valid and enforceable *ab initio*, without the adoption of an exemption decision.

Although the abolition of notification relieves undertakings of the need to spend time and resources in dealing with notifications, the system had the advantage of certainty. Now, undertakings must rely on their own assessment of whether their agreements amount to infringements of the competition rules. If that assessment is incorrect, undertakings are exposed to the risk of liability to fines or to damages claims in the national court. On the other hand, the abolition of notification has one major advantage for the Commission. It allows the concentration of resources on the investigation and elimination of the most serious infringements of the competition rules, in particular cross-border cartels.

? QUESTION 13.12

Do you remember the features of a cartel? Look back at **Chapter 12**.

13.10.2 The agreement must contribute to 'improving the production or distribution of goods or to promoting technical or economic progress'

The greater its economic benefits, the more likely it is that an agreement will be exempt. The issue is whether the restrictions in an agreement are justified by the benefits which will flow from it. Some agreements might incorporate more than one of the benefits listed in this first positive condition, others just one of them.

Improvements in production might ensue from agreements under which each party specializes in a particular area of production.

Bayer/Gist-Brocades **(Commission Decision) OJ 1976 L 30/13, [1976] 1 CMLR D98**

Under an agreement between two pharmaceutical companies, which was granted exemption by the Commission under Article 81(3) (ex 85(3)), each company agreed to give up part of its business in favour of the other, allowing one party to specialize in the production of one particular penicillin product and the other to concentrate on the production of a different penicillin product.

Technical and economic progress can result from research and development agreements. For instance, the ACEC/Berliet agreement allowed each party to concentrate on the areas within their own expertise, Berliet on research on vehicles and their manufacture and ACEC on research on electrical constructions.(*ACEC/Berliet* (Commission Decision) JO 1968 L 201/7, [1968] CMLR D35 (*Cases and Materials* (13.5.1)).

Distribution might be improved through exclusive supply or purchasing agreements. Here, the Commission has sometimes been prepared to take a surprisingly generous view of restrictions. In its Decision in *Transocean Marine Paint Association* JO 1967 163/19, [1967] CMLR D9, it granted exemption to a distribution agreement which partitioned markets on national lines (though did not give absolute territorial protection) because of its benefits in terms of improved distribution of the product.

 **EXERCISE** 13.9 

Look at paragraph 22 of *Transocean Marine Paint Association* (Commission Decision) JO 1967 163/19, [1967] CMLR D9 (in *Cases and Materials* (13.5.1)) How did the agreement improve distribution?If you have forgotten the facts of *Transocean Marine Paint*, look back at 13.7.6.

The agreement resulted in improvements to the distribution of marine paint, since it ensured that paints were available in a regular manner and in sufficient quantities in a large number of countries and ports. This sales network enabled the members of the Association to compete actively with the big marine paint manufacturers, resulting in an increased supply of the products. Without the agreement, members would have needed to set up their own distribution systems in a large number of countries, entailing excessive investment risks.

13.10.3 Allowing consumers a fair share of the resulting benefit

 **EXERCISE** 13.10 

Look at paragraph 23 of *Transocean Marine Paint Association* (Commission Decision) JO 1967 163/19, [1967] CMLR D9 (in *Cases and Materials* (13.5.2)). How did the agreement allow consumers a fair share of the resulting benefit?

Supply of the paints was increased and consumers no longer needed to carry on their ships paints required for maintenance, as they could obtain supplies in numerous ports easily and quickly. Consumers were also able to obtain technical advice and supervision locally when undertaking painting work. At the same time, it remained open to consumers to purchase supplies from members of the Association in other countries if their terms and conditions were more favourable.

The meaning of 'consumer' is not confined to the ultimate consumer of a product but includes persons (individuals or companies) at all levels of the distribution chain.

***ACEC/Berliet* cont.**

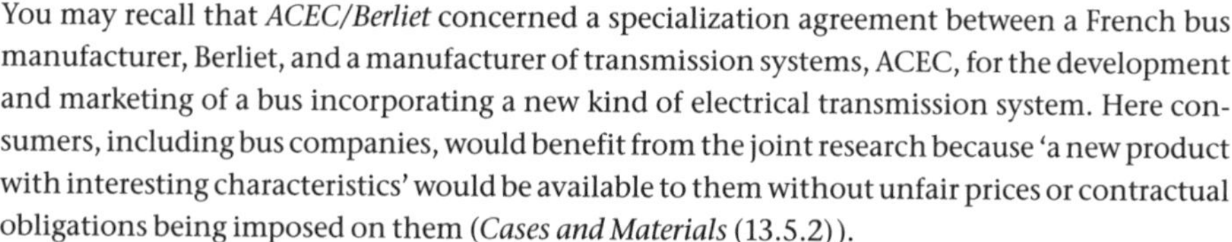

You may recall that *ACEC/Berliet* concerned a specialization agreement between a French bus manufacturer, Berliet, and a manufacturer of transmission systems, ACEC, for the development and marketing of a bus incorporating a new kind of electrical transmission system. Here consumers, including bus companies, would benefit from the joint research because 'a new product with interesting characteristics' would be available to them without unfair prices or contractual obligations being imposed on them (*Cases and Materials* (13.5.2)).

In addition to specific benefits in any particular case, the Commission has recognized that any benefits resulting from an agreement, such as a better or cheaper product or service, will be passed on to the consumer only if the parties face competition from other undertakings in the same product market. Thus, an assessment must be made of the competition faced by the parties, looking carefully at the structure of the market and the size of the parties' market share.

13.10.4 No restrictions which are not indispensable

Restrictions must not go beyond what is necessary to achieve the beneficial objectives of the agreement.

? QUESTION 13.13

Which important general principle of Community law do you recognize here?

This is another manifestation of the principle of proportionality. Certain restrictions will rarely, if ever, be regarded as indispensable. Examples are agreements, or clauses in agreements, conferring absolute territorial protection (see, for instance, *Établissements Consten SA* v *Commission*), or fixing prices. Other kinds of restriction are to be considered in their particular context.

EXERCISE 13.11

Look at paragraphs 18–23 of the *ACEC/Berliet* decision (*Cases and Materials* (13.5.2)). List the restrictions which the Commission considered to be indispensable to obtaining the objectives of improvement of production and promotion of technical progress and, in each case, the reasons for the conclusion.

Your list may look something like this:

(a) ACEC's undertaking to deliver its transmission only to Berliet and to cooperate only with Berliet in France. This allowed Berliet to concentrate its efforts on development of a single range of vehicles and gave it some protection from competition, providing an incentive to complete the project, since it would obtain a return on its investment.

(b) Prohibition on Berliet purchasing electric transmissions other than from ACEC. This made it worthwhile financially for ACEC to adapt its transmission for Berliet vehicles.

(c) ACEC's obligation to deliver its transmission only (with limited exceptions) to one single manufacturer in each Member State. This concentrated production with a limited number of manufacturers, allowing them to attain profitable production runs in the launch period, when demand for the product would be weakest.

13.10.5 No elimination of competition

There must be no elimination of competition in respect of the product in question. In *ACEC/Berliet*, for instance, the Commission concluded that the buses would be competing with buses equipped with mechanical transmission produced by several other manufacturers. Normally, before a decision can be made under this head, it will be necessary to define the relevant product and geographical markets (in the same way that this would be done in relation to Article 82 (ex 86) **(Chapter 14)**. For some agreements, competition from undertakings outside the Community will be taken into account, as the Commission did in *ACEC/Berliet*.

13.11 Block exemption

Article 81(3) (ex 85(3)) allows Article 81(1) (ex 85(1)) to be declared inapplicable not only to individual agreements but also to categories of agreement. In relation to categories of agreement, the Commission achieves this, under authority delegated by the Council, by issuing block exemptions giving automatic exemption to certain kinds of agreement. The Commission has used block exemptions as a means of reducing its own workload, which continued to increase as more and more businesses sought protection from fines by notifying any agreements which might possibly infringe Article 81(1) (ex 85(1)).

The kinds of agreement covered by block exemptions are those which, though they contain restrictions, are considered overall to have beneficial effects, such as specialization agreements and technology transfer agreements (relating to patent and know-how licensing). Each block exemption is contained in a Regulation. Most of the original Regulations followed the same basic format, setting out those restrictions which were permitted, the 'white list', and those which were not permitted, the 'black list'. More recent block exemptions, including the block exemptions for specialization agreements, research and development agreements, and vertical agreements, contain 'black-listed' restrictions but no 'white list' of restrictions. The Commission takes the view that the removal of the 'white-lists' will free business from the 'straitjacket' effect of the former Regulations, under which the parties to an agreement were limited to the use of the expressly permitted restrictions.

The system of block exemptions remains unaltered by Regulation 1/2003.

13.12 Regulation 2790/99: the block exemption for vertical agreements

Regulation 2790/99, the block exemption for certain categories of vertical agreement and concerted practice, was adopted in December 1999 and came into force in June 2000. Before turning to the detail of the block exemption, it is useful to consider, generally, the nature and potential effects of vertical restraints.

13.12.1 Vertical restraints and the background to the block exemption

There is considerable debate between economists as to the harmfulness or otherwise to competition of restrictions contained in vertical agreements, or 'vertical restraints'.

QUESTION 13.14

What is a vertical agreement? If you have forgotten, look back to 13.5.6

A vertical agreement is an agreement between undertakings operating at different levels of the production/distribution chain, for instance between a manufacturer and a distributor. Such an agreement may contain restrictions that could be regarded as both pro- and anti-competitive.

EXERCISE 13.12

Consider the following circumstances:

UK Audio, a UK manufacturer of electronic sound recording equipment is seeking to establish a market for its products in Italy. Because UK Audio has no retailing expertise, the company has decided not to set up its own retailing outlets in Italy, but instead to sell through an independent retailer, which has outlets in Rome, Milan, and Naples. The retailer is prepared to undertake extensive advertising and the provision of after-sales service, without which the marketing of the products will not be successful.

What commitment do you think the retailer may well demand from UK Audio in order to ensure that its financial investment is rewarded through maximization of its sales of the products?

The retailer may be unwilling to take on the expenditure required for advertising and for the provision of after-sales service unless it is protected from competition from other retailers. It may well require UK Audio to agree not to supply its products to other retailers in the Rome, Milan, and Naples areas. Such a commitment to exclusivity is restrictive of intra-brand competition (competition within the brand, between retailers of the UK Audio's products). It is also pro-competitive, in that it may facilitate the penetration of a new market which would otherwise not have been accessible to UK Audio, thus increasing inter-brand competition (competition between different brands of sound recording equipment on the Italian market).

Before reform of Community competition law on vertical agreements, the Commission had been criticized for its inflexible approach to vertical restraints, which led it to condemn them as anti-competitive and a breach of Article 81(1), without undertaking an adequate analysis of their potentially beneficial economic effects. In 1997, the Commission published the *Green Paper on Vertical Restraints in EC Competition policy*, which initiated a consultation on review of policy towards vertical restraints and proposed possible options for reform. The timing was significant, for three of the existing block exemption Regulations on distribution, covering exclusive buying and selling and franchising, were due to expire. When it published the results of the consultation, the Commission recognized the need for greater flexibility in the approach to vertical agreements, based upon an effects-based economic analysis. The outcome was the adoption of a new block exemption extending to all vertical agreements.

13.12.2 **The exemption: Article 2**

REGULATION 2790/99

Article 2

1. Pursuant to Article 81(3) of the Treaty and subject to the provisions of this Regulation, it is hereby declared that Article 81(1) shall not apply to agreements or concerted practices entered into between two or more undertakings each of which operates, for the purposes of the agreement, at a different level of the production or distribution chain, and relating to the conditions under which the parties may purchase, sell, or resell certain goods or services ('vertical agreements').

   This exemption shall apply to the extent that such agreements contain restrictions of competition falling within the scope of Article 81(1) ('vertical restraints').

   . . .

It will be seen from this provision that, in broad terms, Regulation 2790/99 exempts from Article 81(1) vertical agreements relating to the conditions under which the parties may purchase, sell, or resell certain goods or services, to the extent that these agreements contain otherwise prohibited restrictions. The Regulation covers, for instance, exclusive buying and selling and franchising agreements.

However, a number of points, discussed in more detail presently, should be noted. The exemption:

(a) applies only where the market share on the relevant market (for detailed discussion of the concept of the relevant market, see **Chapter 14**) of the supplier or buyer does not exceed 30%;

(b) does not apply to vertical agreements having certain specified objects, such as price fixing and absolute territorial protection;

(c) does not apply to specific obligations, such as non-competition clauses whose duration is indefinite or exceeds five years.

Whilst the block exemption contains 'blacklisted' restrictions, it does not constrain undertakings to a 'white list' of specific permitted restrictions. This means that if a restriction in an agreement is not blacklisted, it is permitted.

13.12.3 Definitions: Article 1

Article 1 defines a number of terms used in the Regulation, including 'non-compete obligation' and 'exclusive supply obligation'.

REGULATION 2790/99

Article 1

For the purposes of this Regulation:

. . .

(b) 'non-compete obligation' means any direct or indirect obligation causing the buyer not to manufacture, purchase, sell, or resell goods or services which compete with the contract goods or services, or any direct or indirect obligation on the buyer to purchase from the supplier or from another undertaking designated by the supplier more than 80% of the buyer's total purchases of the contract goods or services and their substitutes on the relevant market, calculated on the basis of the value of its purchases in the preceding calendar year;

(c) 'exclusive supply obligation' means any direct or indirect obligation causing the supplier to sell the goods or services specified in the agreement only to one buyer inside the Community for the purposes of a specific use or for resale;

EXERCISE 13.13

Consider Article 1 of Regulation 2790/99, paragraphs (b) and (c). How would the following contractual obligations relating to Alpha Co, a widget manufacturer, and Omega Co, a widget distributor, be described within the terms of the Regulation:

- an obligation imposed by Alpha Co, under a contract for the supply of widgets to Omega Co, causing Omega Co not to sell widgets which compete with those supplied under the contract;
- an obligation on Omega Co to purchase from Alpha Co more than 80% of its total widget purchases from Alpha Co;
- an obligation imposed upon Alpha Co causing Alpha Co to sell widgets for resale only to Omega Co within the Community.

The first two contractual obligations restrict Omega Co's ability to sell widgets competing with Alpha Co's widgets and comprise non-compete obligations. The third obligation is an exclusive supply obligation because it causes Alpha Co to sell to only one buyer inside the Community.

13.12.4 Market share threshold: Article 3

Article 3 of the Regulation makes the exemption contained in Article 2 subject to a market share threshold. The exemption applies only where the supplier's market share does not exceed 30%, save in the case of agreements containing exclusive supply obligations, where the market share threshold applies to the buyer's market share.

REGULATION 2790/99

Article 3

1. Subject to paragraph 2 of this Article, the exemption provided for in Article 2 shall apply on condition that the market share held by the supplier does not exceed 30% of the relevant market on which it sells the contract goods or services.
2. In the case of vertical agreements containing exclusive supply obligations, the exemption provided for in Article 2 shall apply on condition that the market share held by the buyer does not exceed 30 % of the relevant market on which it purchases the contract goods or services.

13.12.5 Hardcore, non-severable restrictions: Article 4

 **QUESTION** 13.15

From your knowledge of the Article 81(1) so far, which two kinds of restriction do you think would be seen as 'hard-core' and therefore subject to an absolute prohibition?

The benefit of the block exemption does not apply to vertical agreements which contain certain hardcore restrictions. These restrictions are set out in Article 4. They include restrictions by the supplier on the buyer's ability to determine its sale price, save for maximum or recommended sale prices (price fixing); and restrictions on the territory into which the buyer may sell the goods or services, with some specified exceptions (territorial restrictions, a form of market-sharing). The impact of Article 4 is that an agreement containing hardcore restrictions is, in its entirety, outside the scope of the block exemption. It is not possible to sever the offending clauses and leave the rest of the agreement within the exemption.

REGULATION 2790/99

Article 4

The exemption provided for in Article 2 shall not apply to vertical agreements which, directly or indirectly, in isolation or in combination with other factors under the control of the parties, have as their object:

(a) the restriction of the buyer's ability to determine its sale price, without prejudice to the possibility of the supplier's imposing a maximum sale price or recommending a sale price, provided that they do not amount to a fixed or minimum sale price as a result of pressure from, or incentives offered by, any of the parties;

(b) the restriction of the territory into which, or of the customers to whom, the buyer may sell the contract goods or services , except:

[Article 4 then lists specified restrictions relating, inter alia, agreements such as selective distribution agreements, which fall outside the scope of this book].

13.12.6 Severable restrictions: Article 5

By contrast to Article 4, Article 5 provides that the block exemption does not apply to certain obligations contained in agreements. Although the Article 5 restrictions themselves fall outside the block exemption, they may be severed, allowing the remainder of the agreement to benefit from the block exemption. Severable restrictions include certain non-compete obligations.

QUESTION 13.16

Where is 'non-compete obligation' is defined?

The block exemption does not apply to indefinite non-compete obligations, nor to non-compete obligations of more than five years' duration. However, the five-year limitation does not apply where the contract goods or services are sold by the buyer from premises and land owned or leased by the supplier, provided the non-compete obligation does not extend beyond the buyer's occupancy of the premises.

Non-compete obligations applying after the termination of the agreement are block exempted only if they are limited to one year after termination, relate to goods or services which compete with the contract goods or services, are limited to the premises from which the buyer has operated during the contract period, and are indispensable to protect know-how transferred by the supplier to the buyer.

'Non-compete obligation' is defined in the definitions section of the Regulation in Article 1 (13.12.3))

13.12.7 Withdrawal of the benefit of the Regulation: Article 6

Under Article 6, the Commission may withdraw the benefit of the Regulation from vertical agreements which are within its scope but which, nevertheless, are incompatible with Article 81(3).

CONCLUSIONS

One of the primary challenges for Community competition law is to ensure adequate regulation of restrictive practices which threaten market integration, reduce efficiency, and prejudice the consumer—but at the same time to avoid an over-interventionist approach which strikes down all restrictions, even if they are necessary to achieve overall economic benefits. The framework of Article 81 (ex 85), specifically the provisions in Article 81(3) (ex 85(3)), allows for the assessment of the pro- and anti-competitive effects of agreements and provides scope for the necessary balance to be struck. Whether this balance is always achieved is a matter of continuing debate for businesses, economists, and lawyers, alike.

SUMMARY

- **Article 81(1)** prohibits agreements between undertakings, decisions of associations of undertakings, and concerted practices which may affect trade between Member States and which have as their object or effect the prevention, restriction, or distortion of competition within the common market. Article 81(1) is wide in scope, catching not only formal and legally binding agreements but also informal arrangements between undertakings, notably concerted practices.
- **For a breach to be established**, all three elements of Article 81(1) must be satisfied.
- **Article 81(2)** provides that prohibited agreements shall be automatically void. However, the Court of Justice has held that offending restrictions may be severed from an agreement, allowing the rest of the agreement to remain in place (*STM*, *Consten*).
- **Article 81(3)** allows certain agreements to be exempt from Article 81(1). In order to be exempt, an agreement must satisfy specified conditions. It must have beneficial effects, such as improvements in distribution; those benefits must be passed on to the consumer; the restrictions must go no further than is necessary to achieve their objective (proportionality); and there must be no substantial elimination of competition.
- **Exemption applies to individual agreements** that satisfy the Article 81(3) conditions.
- **Exemption also applies to certain categories of agreement ('block exemption')**, for instance to vertical agreements below a specified market share threshold. The block exemptions are contained in Regulations.
- **Regulation 2790/99** is the block exemption relating to vertical agreements. It applies subject to a 30% market-share threshold. The block exemption excludes from its scope 'hard-core' restrictions, such as price fixing and market-sharing and agreements containing such restrictions are excluded in their entirety from the benefit of the block exemption. The block exemption also excludes certain kinds of restriction, such as certain non-compete clauses, though these may be severed, allowing the rest of the agreement to benefit from exemption.

CHAPTER 13: ASSESSMENT EXERCISE

Rainco, a UK manufacturer of raincoats which has a 20% share of the relevant market, agrees to supply raincoats for resale to Pluieco, a French wholesaler of rainwear. The contract between them provides as follows:

- Rainco agrees to supply the contract goods only to Pluieco in France but is permitted to continue to supply raincoats in other Member States ('obligation 1')
- Pluieco agrees, for a period of six years from the date of the agreement, not to sell raincoats which compete with the contract goods ('obligation 2')

Does the agreement benefit from the block exemption under Regulation 2790/99? How would your answer differ (if at all) if there were a further clause in the agreement fixing the price at which Pluieco could resell the contract goods?

See *Cases and Materials* (13.7) for a specimen answer.

FURTHER READING

Green, N. (1988). 'Article 81 in Perspective: Stretching Jurisdiction, Narrowing the Concept of a Restriction and Plugging a Few Gaps', *European Competition Law Review* 190.

Odudu, O. (2002). 'Article 81(3), Discretion and Direct Effect', *European Competition Law Review* 17.

Roitman, D. (2006). 'Legal Uncertainty for Vertical Distribution Agreements: the Block Exemption Regulation 2790/99 (BER) and Related Aspects of the New Regulation 1/2003', *European Competition Law Review* 261.

14 Abuse of a dominant position

14.1 OBJECTIVES

By the end of this chapter you should be able to:

1 Explain and analyse the prohibition of abuse of a dominant position contained in Article 82 (ex 86) EC

2 Explain and analyse the key concepts of dominance, relevant product market, relevant geographical market, and abuse

14.2 Introduction

As was noted in **Chapter 13**, Article 81 (ex 85) deals primarily with the control of restrictive agreements and concerted practices between independent undertakings. The concern of Article 82 (ex 86) is the threat posed to competition within the common market by the economic power of single undertakings which enjoy a dominant position in a particular market for goods or services. Article 82 (ex 86) does not prohibit dominance. However, it does provide that any abuse of market power which is capable of affecting trade between Member States is prohibited as incompatible with the common market. Such abuses may be anti-competitive, in that they eliminate or seriously weaken existing competition in a particular market or prevent new competitors entering that market. They may also amount to exploitative behaviour, which takes unfair advantage of the consumer. Like Article 81 (ex 85), Article 82 (ex 86) pursues the broad aim of eliminating distortion of competition in the internal market which is set out in Article 3(1)(g) (ex 3(g)) (formerly Article 3(f)) EC.

14.3 Article 82 (ex 86): the prohibition

Article 82 (ex 86) EC prohibits the abuse of market power in the common market.

THE EC TREATY

Article 82 (ex 86)

Any abuse by one or more undertakings of a dominant position within the common market or in a substantial part of it shall be prohibited as incompatible with the common market in so far as it may affect trade between Member States.

Such abuse may, in particular, consist in:

(a) directly or indirectly imposing unfair purchase or selling prices or other unfair trading conditions;

(b) limiting production, markets, or technical development to the prejudice of consumers;

(c) applying dissimilar conditions to equivalent transactions with other trading parties, thereby placing them at a competitive disadvantage;

(d) making the conclusion of contracts subject to acceptance by the other parties of supplementary obligations which, by their nature or according to commercial usage, have no connection with the subject of such contracts.

EXERCISE 14.1

Look at the first paragraph of Article 82 (ex 86). You will see that it prohibits certain behaviour by undertakings because that behaviour is incompatible with the common market. Write down the key words and phrases used to define the prohibited behaviour.

You might have written down something like this: abuse; one or more undertakings; dominant position; within the common market or a substantial part of it; affect trade between Member States.

EXERCISE 14.2

Turn back to **Chapter 13** to remind yourself of the meaning of the term 'undertaking' under Article 81 (ex 85). 'Undertaking' has the same meaning under Article 82 (ex 86).

You may have noticed that Article 82 refers to 'one or more undertakings'. The application of Article 82 to the behaviour of more than one undertaking acting together in a position of 'collective dominance' is considered briefly at the end of this chapter, which focuses on the more commonly occurring situation of single undertakings in a position of market power.

There are three essential elements to a breach of Article 82. All three must be established:

(a) dominant position within the common market or a substantial part of it; and

(b) an abuse of that dominant position; and

(c) that abuse must be capable of affecting trade between Member States.

In order to understand the scope of the prohibition in Article 82 (ex 86), all three elements must be considered.

14.4 Dominant position

14.4.1 Definition

An undertaking is dominant when it has substantial market power. In *United Brands Co* v *Commission* (Case 27/76) [1978] ECR 207 the Court of Justice, outlining the general objectives of Article 82, set out a definition a 'dominant position' which has been referred to in many subsequent cases.

 **EXERCISE** 14.3 

Look at the extract from *United Brands* (*Cases and Materials* (14.1)). Write down the Court of Justice's definition of 'dominant position'.

This definition is contained in paragraph 65 of the judgment:

> a position of economic strength enjoyed by an undertaking which enables it to prevent effective competition being maintained on the relevant market by giving it the power to behave to an appreciable extent independently of its competitors, customers, and ultimately of its consumers.

If an undertaking is dominant it may be able to prevent potential competitors entering the market, weaken existing competitors or drive existing competitors, out of the market. A dominant undertaking may also be able to exploit its customers.

? **QUESTION** 14.1

How might a dominant undertaking drive an existing competitor out of the market or prevent a new competitor entering the market?

? **QUESTION** 14.2

How might a dominant undertaking exploit its customers?

One of the most obvious ways in which a dominant undertaking might exclude or eliminate competition is by temporarily lowering its prices below cost. Another is by offering discounts to customers who agree to buy all or most of their supplies from the undertaking. Because of its economic strength, it may be able to do this for some time. Smaller and less powerful undertakings cannot afford to compete on these terms and may go out of business. The result is a distortion of competition. The dominant undertaking may be able to exploit its customers—for instance, by charging them unjustifiably high prices or by insisting that when they buy goods from that undertaking they must also buy related services—knowing that the customers are not able, or would find it difficult, to buy elsewhere.

? QUESTION 14.3

What factors do you think might indicate that an undertaking is in a dominant position? Write down your answer and look at it again at the end of this section.

As indicated in *United Brands* at paragraph 65, a dominant position is assessed in relation to a particular market, the 'relevant market', which may be a market for goods or services. In order to assess an undertaking's market power, it is necessary first to identify the market in which it is operating. There are three kinds of market which the Court of Justice and the Commission look at when considering dominant position:

(a) the relevant product market;

(b) the relevant geographic market; and

(c) the relevant temporal market.

14.4.2 Relevant product market

The definition of the relevant product market ('RPM') has been the subject of dispute in much of the case law on Article 82 (ex 86). This is partly because definition is often extremely difficult, involving detailed and sometimes controversial economic analysis. More importantly, the definition of the RPM may be the crucial factor in determining whether or not an undertaking is in a dominant position. If there is no dominance in the market, there is no breach of Article 82.

? QUESTION 14.4

A (fictitious) company, Creamy plc, makes a single product, luxury 'double cream' choc ices. What is the RPM in which the company is operating?

Your first reaction may be that Creamy plc's RPM is the choc ice market. Consider other possibilities. For instance, it could be argued that the RPM is the 'double cream' choc ice market or the ice cream market generally or even the general ice cream/ice lolly market. Perhaps you can think of other possible RPMs. That raises the question as to how the RPM is determined. The Commission and the Court of Justice define the RPM in terms of product substitution or interchangeability. To decide whether goods are interchangeable and therefore in the same product market it is necessary to look, first, at consumer perception and behaviour and, secondly, at the ability of potential competitors to enter the market. In its 1997 Notice on the Definition of the Relevant Market for the Purposes of Community Competition Law, the Commission states that its starting point for definition of the RPM is demand substitutability, supply substitutability, and potential competition.

14.4.3 Product substitution

If products are such that customers regard them as substantially interchangeable, then they are likely to be in the same product market. To go back to the Creamy plc illustration, if customers setting out to buy choc ices are prepared to buy ice creams instead (for instance if they find that there are no choc ices available) then this is an indicator that choc ices and ice creams are substitutable and are therefore in the same product market. This is called cross-elasticity of demand or demand substitutability.

? QUESTION 14.5

What factors do you think would be important to a consumer who is considering whether a certain product is acceptable as a substitute for another?

The consumer's willingness to accept one product as a substitute for another depends upon factors such as the characteristics of the products, the use to which the product is to be put, and general similarity of price. On that basis, there is probably cross-elasticity of demand between choc ices and ice creams.

Some goods, although at first sight they might appear to be in the same product market because they have similar characteristics, are not interchangeable. Consider high-quality luxury fountain pens and the kinds of fountain pen which can be bought for a few pounds. Both products are put to the same use and their basic characteristics are similar. However, a luxury fountain pen is an expensive, quality product, bought perhaps partly as a status symbol. It would be difficult to argue convincingly that these products are in the same product market.

In its 1997 Notice on the Definition of the Relevant Market, the Commission sets out a test for demand substitution based upon the consumer's response to a small but significant (between 5–10 per cent) permanent increase in the price of a product. If such an increase would cause the consumer to switch from one product to another, this indicates that the two products are in the same product market. If the consumer would not switch, this indicates that the products are in separate product markets. This test for product substitution, known as the SSNIP (Small but Significant Non-transitory Increase in Price) test indicates a more quantitative approach to the definition of the relevant market.

Product substitution also depends upon what is known as cross-elasticity of supply or supply substitutability. If other undertakings are able to supply similar products or are capable of switching their production to similar products, then the RPM is extended accordingly. This aspect of product substitution will be considered presently, when *Europemballage Corp and Continental Can Co Inc* v *Commission* (Case 6/72) [1973] ECR 215 is discussed.

14.4.4 Significance of the relevant product market

? **QUESTION** 14.6

You will remember that Creamy plc manufactures only one product, luxury 'double cream' choc ices. Suppose that the company has:

(a) a very large share of the Community 'double cream' choc ice market;
(b) a large share of the Community choc ice market;
(c) a small share of the Community general ice cream market; and
(d) a negligible share of the Community ice cream/ice lolly market.

In the course of investigations by the Commission in relation to Article 82 (ex 86), the question of the RPM is a matter of dispute between Creamy plc and the Commission. What do you think the company will claim as the RPM? Why?

Undertakings are always anxious to show that they are not dominant, so that Article 82 (ex 86) will not apply to them. Consequently, they are likely to seek to define the RPM as widely as possible. The wider the RPM, the less likely they are to be dominant in that market. Conversely, the narrower the RPM, the more likely they are to be dominant. In order to escape the scope of Article 82 (ex 86), Creamy plc will claim the widest possible market—either the general ice cream market or the ice cream/ice lolly market—as the RPM.

14.4.5 Defining the relevant product market: the Commission and the Court of Justice

An examination of demand-side substitutability was key to the definition of the RPM in *United Brands*.

 **EXERCISE** 14.4 

Look at *United Brands Co* v *Commission* (Case 27/76) [1978] ECR 207 (*Cases and Materials* (14.1.1)). Write down answers to the following questions:

(a) What did the company claim to be the RPM?
(b) What did the Commission claim to be the RPM?
(c) What did the Court of Justice decide and why?

***United Brands Co* v *Commission* (Case 27/76) [1978] ECR 207**

United Brands United Brands Company of New York and United Brands Continental BV ('United Brands'), a banana producer, sought annulment of a Commission Decision finding that it had abused a dominant position in a number of ways. In order to establish whether

United Brands was in a dominant position, the first issue addressed by the Court of Justice was the definition of the relevant product market.

The company sought to define the market broadly, as fresh fruit. The Commission claimed that the RPM was bananas. The Court of Justice agreed with the Commission. This conclusion was reached following consideration of product substitution and cross-elasticity of demand. The Court accepted the argument that bananas are unique because of their appearance, taste, softness, seedlessness, and easy handling, all characteristics which make them a particularly suitable fruit for the old, the sick, and the very young. In these important respects, the Court held, no other fruits are acceptable as substitutes and there is little cross-elasticity of demand. As will be noted later, the Court of Justice went on to confirm that the company had abused its dominant position in the banana market in various ways.

Whereas in *United Brands* the Court of Justice considered the unique characteristics of the product, bananas, and concluded that these characteristics placed bananas in a separate product market, in other cases a product's specific use has precluded interchangeability with other products.

Hugin Kassaregister AB v *Commission* (Case 22/78) [1979] ECR 1869

Here, a Swedish company, Hugin Kassaregister AB, and its British subsidiary, Hugin Cash Registers Ltd ('Hugin') sought annulment of a Commission Decision finding that they had infringed Article 82 (ex 86) by refusing to supply spare parts for Hugin cash registers to Liptons Cash Registers and Business Equipment Ltd, a British company.

The Court of Justice pointed out that the only spare parts that could be used for the repair and maintenance of Hugin cash registers were Hugin spare parts. Since these were not substitutable with spare parts for other kinds of cash register, this resulted in a specific demand for Hugin spare parts. Consequently, the RPM was the market for Hugin spare parts.

? QUESTION 14.7 

How did the Court of Justice define the RPM in *Hugin* (*Cases and Materials* (14.1.1))?

Similarly, in *Eurofix & Bauco* v *Hilti AG* [1989] 4 CMLR 677 the Commission, after examining the respective uses of nail guns and power drills, concluded that nail guns were in a separate product market. The finding of a breach was later upheld by the Court of First Instance and the Court of Justice.

Both demand substitutability and supply substitutability were carefully examined by the Court of Justic in *Continental Can*. The Court found that the Commission's assessment had been inadequate.

? QUESTION 14.8 

Look at the extract from *Continental Can Co Inc* (*Cases and Materials* (14.1.1)). Why did the Court of Justice consider the Commission's analysis of product substitution to be inadequate?

Europemballage Corp and Continental Can Co Inc* v *Commission **(Case 6/72) [1973] ECR 215**

The applicants sought annulment of a Commission Decision finding that Continental Can Company had infringed Article 82 (ex 86) EC by acquiring, through its subsidiary Europemballage Corporation, an 80% share of Thomassen & Drijver-Verbliva NV. Continental Can was a very powerful packaging company which had a large share in Schmalbach-Lubeca-Werke AG (SLW), a German packaging company. The deal increased even further Continental Can's market power in Europe.

The Court of Justice took the view that when the Commission defined the RPM, it had failed to consider demand-side substitutability, in particular whether Continental Can's products (light metal containers for meat and fish and metal closures for glass jars) formed a separate market from the general market for light metal containers used for the packaging of fruit and vegetables, fruit juices, and the like. To form a separate market, Continental Can's products must be 'individualized . . . by particular characteristics of production which make them specifically suitable for this purpose'. The Commission had also neglected to consider supply-side substitutability: how difficult would it have been for potential competitors from other sectors of the market for light metal containers to enter this market by switching their production by simple adaptation to substitutes acceptable to the consumer?

To assess supply substitutability, it is necessary to consider whether there are other operators who produce similar products and could easily and cheaply enter the product market in question by simply adapting their production. If there is high cross-elasticity of supply, an allegedly dominant firm's market position is not so powerful as it might appear at first sight.

The RPM is not necessarily the market in which the ultimate consumer purchases a product. The possibility that the RPM can be an intermediate market in which there is little cross-elasticity of demand may be crucially important, as can be seen from *Commercial Solvents*.

Istituto Chemioterapico Italiano SpA and Commercial Solvents Corporation* v *Commission **(Cases 6 & 7/73) [1974] ECR 223**

The Commission had found that Commercial Solvents Corporation (CSC) and its subsidiary Istituto Chemioterapico Italiano of Milan (Istituto) had infringed Article 82 (ex 86) by refusing supplies of the raw material aminobutanol, used in the manufacture of an anti-tuberculosis drug called ethambutol, to Laboratorio Chimico Farmaceutico Giorgio Zoja (Zoja). Istituto and CSC sought annulment of the Decision. They disputed the Commission's definition of the relevant product market.

 **EXERCISE** 14.5 

Look at *Commercial Solvents* (*Cases and Materials* (14.1.1)). Can you identify the two suggested RPMs? What was the RPM according to the Court of Justice?

As in many other Article 82 (ex 86) cases, the conclusion as to the RPM in *Commercial Solvents* was a crucial factor in determining whether or not Commercial Solvents Corporation (CSC) and its subsidiary Istituto Chemioterapico Italiano SpA (Istituto) had a dominant position. If the RPM was, as CSC and Istituto argued, the end product supplied to the ultimate consumer, namely anti-tuberculosis drugs (of which there were a number available), then the companies were not dominant. If the RPM was, as the Commission argued, the particular raw material (aminobutanol) supplied by CSC to Zoja for the manufacture of anti-tuberculosis drugs, there certainly was a dominant position. The third possibility was that the RPM was the range of raw materials which could be used to produce the drug. If this was the RPM, then the companies were probably not dominant.

***Commercial Solvents* cont.**

The Court of Justice did not accept that Zoja could easily adapt its manufacturing process to the use of raw materials other than aminobutanol and so the third suggested RPM was ruled out. The Court also rejected CSC's argument that the deciding factor should be consumer choice of the ultimate product, thus also ruling out drugs for treating tuberculosis as the RPM. The Court held that the RPM was CSC's raw material, aminobutanol.

Commercial Solvents demonstrates an aspect of Community competition law which has already been noted in the context of Article 81 (ex 85). The Court of Justice and the Commission are particularly concerned to protect the interests of small and medium-sized businesses in the face of competition from large and powerful undertakings. In this case, that policy involved the protection of competition in the common market not only at the level of the ultimate consumer of the product but also at intermediate levels of production and distribution.

Sometimes, because of the specialist nature of the products or services which they supply, undertakings can be dominant in very small and apparently insignificant markets. This was the situation with regard to the Swedish firm Hugin, which, as has been seen, was found to be dominant in the market for spare parts for its own cash registers (*Hugin Kassaregister AB* v *Commission* (Case 22/78) [1979] ECR 1869 (*Cases and Materials* (14.1.1)). Similarly, General Motors was held to be dominant in a small and specialized market, since it had the sole right, under Belgian legislation, to issue the approval certificates required for the import of second-hand Opel vehicles into Belgium (*General Motors Continental NV* v *Commission* (Case 26/75) [1975] ECR 1367.

14.4.6 The relevant geographic market

Before dominance can be assessed, it is necessary also to establish the relevant geographic market. Since all Community undertakings are operating within an internal market which is theoretically free from barriers to trade, the relevant geographic market will generally be taken to be the whole of the common market. Sometimes, however, there may be factors which cause the geographic market to be defined more narrowly. In *United Brands* the Court of Justice defined the geographic market as 'an area where the objective conditions of competition applying to the product in question' are the same for all traders.

QUESTION 14.9 

What were the 'objective conditions of competition' in *United Brands* (*Cases and Materials* (14.1.2))?

Here, the relevant geographic market consisted in all the Member States except France, Italy, and the UK, since in these three Member States there were special importing arrangements that disadvantaged United Brands' products.

One major feature of a geographic market may be low transport costs. Where goods can be easily and cheaply transported, it is economic to sell them some distance away from the point of production and here, the whole of the Community may be the geographic market. This was the case, for instance, with respect to the nail cartridges supplied by the firm Hilti, which were very cheap to transport (*Hilti AG* v *Commission* (Case T-30/89) [1991] ECR II-1439 (*Cases and Materials* (14.1.2))). Conversely, where the nature of the goods makes transportation expensive or difficult, the geographic market will be more narrowly defined.

A geographic market may also be characterized in other ways—as the market in which consumers are willing and able to travel to the source of supply, or in which they are prepared to look for substitute products. It may be the geographical area to which use of the goods or services is limited (remember that the RPM can be a market for goods or services). The latter point is illustrated by the 'TV listings' cases.

RTE v Commission (Case T-69/89) [1991] ECR II-485; BBC v Commission (Case T-70/89) [1991] ECR II-535; ITP Ltd v Commission (Case T-76/89) [1991] ECR II-575; Cases C-241 & 242/91P Radio Telefis Eireann v Commission [1995] ECR I-743

Magill TV Guide complained to the Commission that RTE, BBC, and ITP abused a dominant position by refusing to allow it to publish weekly listings for the companies' Irish television programmes, which were protected by copyright. The Commission's finding of an infringement, later upheld by the Court of First Instance and the Court of Justice, identified the relevant geographic market as Ireland and Northern Ireland, the area to which the use of the TV listings was limited.

14.4.7 'Within the common market or in a substantial part of it'

Having examined the factors that determine the extent of the geographical market, it is necessary to consider how large a geographic market needs to be to constitute a market 'within the common market or a substantial part of it'. In fact, a geographic market need not be very extensive to be caught by Article 82 (ex 86). A Community-wide market clearly falls within the scope of the Article, as in *Hilti*. So may a market which extends to a number of Member States, as in *United Brands*. The Court of Justice has held that a single Member State can be the relevant geographic market and constitute a substantial part of the common market (*Michelin*).

QUESTION 14.10 

In *Michelin*, which Member State comprised the substantial part of the common market in which Michelin was held to be dominant (*Cases and Materials* (14.1.3))?

***Nederlandsche Banden-Industrie Michelin NV* v *Commission* (Case 322/81) [1983] ECR 3461**

Michelin NV, a Dutch subsidiary of the Michelin group, challenged a Commission Decision finding that it had abused a dominant position in the market for replacement tyres for heavy vehicles. Upholding the Decision, the Court of Justice agreed with the Commission's conclusion that the relevant substantial part of the common market was the Netherlands. The Dutch market for the products was an isolated market, since Dutch dealers only obtained supplies within the Netherlands.

In some cases, particularly in the air and sea transport sector, the geographic market has been drawn very narrowly. For instance, in *Sealink/B and I–Holyhead: Interim Measures* (Commission Decision) [1992] 5 CMLR 255 the relevant market was held to be the port of Holyhead, which served the ferry route between Holyhead and Dublin.

14.4.8 The relevant temporal market

Conditions of competition between undertakings sometimes vary from season to season. Therefore, as well as examining the product and geographic markets, it may be necessary to consider the temporal (or seasonal) market.

QUESTION 14.11

You will recall that the relevant product market in *United Brands* was bananas. How might seasonal factors affect this market?

It was suggested in *United Brands* that there were two seasonal markets. Evidence of fluctuating cross-elasticity of demand from season to season indicated that during the summer months, when supplies of other fruits were plentiful, the company's market power was reduced. In the winter, when substitutes were not available to the consumer, its market power was restored. Despite this evidence both the Commission and the Court of Justice identified a single temporal market. By contrast, in its decision in *Re ABG Oil* OJ 1977 L 117/1, [1977] 2 CMLR D1, the Commission defined the temporal market for oil by reference to the oil crisis precipitated by the action of the OPEC states in the early 1970s.

14.4.9 Assessing dominance

Dominance is defined broadly as the ability of an undertaking to act independently on the market, free from competitive pressure. Once the relevant market—product, geographical and (if any) temporal—has been ascertained, it is necessary to establish whether or not an undertaking is in fact dominant in that market. This can be done by reference to a number of indicators, now considered in turn. None of these indicators, save perhaps for a very large market share, is in itself conclusive of dominance but in combination the indicators may lead to a finding of dominance. The starting point is an assessment of market share.

14.4.10 Market share

In practice, total monopoly situations (in which an undertaking is the only operator in a particular market) are comparatively rare, save where monopolies are conferred by statute (see for instance *General Motors* (*Cases and Materials* (14.1.4)). In this regard, it should be noted that statutory monopolies do not, as such, escape the scope of Article 82 (ex 86) EC.

General Motors v _Commission_ (Case 26/75) [1975] ECR 1367

General Motors had the sole right, under Belgian legislation, to provide inspection services and issue the approval certificates required for the import of second-hand Opel vehicles into Belgium. This legal monopoly, together with General Motors' ability to fix its own price for this service, resulted in a dominant position within the meaning of Article 81(ex 86) EC.

Market share is a very important factor in the assessment of dominance. A very large market share may in itself be evidence of a dominant position, as the Court of Justice made clear in *Hoffmann-La Roche* (*Cases and Materials* (14.1.4)).

Hoffmann-La Roche & Co. AG v _Commission_ (Case 85/76) [1979] ECR 461

A Commission Decision found that Roche had a dominant position in the markets for a number of vitamins and had abused that position by concluding agreements with customers obliging them or inducing them, by means of fidelity discounts, to buy all or most of their requirements of vitamins exclusively or in preference from Roche. The company sought annulment of the Decision. In assessing dominance, the Court of Justice held that a very large market share creates a position of strength which may amount to a dominant position.

In *Hilti* (Case T-30/89) [1991] ECR II-1439 (*Cases and Materials* (14.1.4)) the Court of First Instance held that a market share of between 70% and 80% in the relevant market (in this case the market for nails for use with the nails guns that Hilti manufactured) was 'in itself a clear indication of a dominant position'.

14.4.11 Other factors indicating dominance

Other factors may reinforce the market power of an undertaking with a very large market share. Where a market share is smaller, other factors may combine to indicate dominance.

 **EXERCISE** 14.6 

Look again at the extracts from *Hoffmann-La Roche* and *Hilti* (*Cases and Materials* (14.1.4)). What other factors may the Court take into account when assessing dominance in the relevant market? Write down your answer.

In *Hoffmann-La Roche* the Court of Justice referred to a large market share being held for 'some time'; the relationship between the undertaking's market share and those of its competitors, especially the next largest; the undertaking's technological lead over its competitors; the existence of a highly developed sales network; and the absence of potential competition. In *Hilti* the Court of First Instance agreed with the Commission's assessment that Hilti's patents and copyright in its products helped the company maintain and reinforce its position in the market.

14.4.12 Market structure

Frequently, as was noted by the Court of Justice in *Hoffmann-La Roche*, the structure of a market is important.

? QUESTION 14.12

Think about the following market structures:

(a) Blue Medal Drinks plc (Blue Medal) has a 40 per cent share of the Community soft drinks market. Its closest rivals, Thirst Quenchers plc and Sparkling Sunshine Ltd hold, respectively, 38 per cent and 20 per cent shares.

(b) In the Community remould tyre market, Rubber Products Ltd (Rubber Products) is the largest supplier, having a market share of 40 per cent. The company's three nearest competitors hold, respectively, 5 per cent, 2 per cent, and 1 per cent shares.

Do these figures suggest that Blue Medal and Rubber Products are dominant in their respective markets? Write down your answer, giving reasons for your conclusions.

The two companies have exactly the same share of their respective markets. The difference between them lies in the position of their competitors. Rubber Products' rivals trail a long way behind in terms of market share. With its rivals close behind, Blue Medal appears much more vulnerable to competition; only a slight fluctuation in the Community soft drinks market is required to change around the figures and put Blue Medal's nearest competitor in the lead. Consequently, Blue Medal is much less likely than Rubber Products to act without regard to its competitors and customers and is thus less likely to be in a dominant position in its particular market.

Because of a combination of factors, United Brands was held to be dominant with a market share of between 40% and 45%, even though this share and the company's profits had been falling. The structure of the market was an important factor. Although the company's share of the banana market was less than 50%, that share was several times greater than that of its nearest rival. Other competitors were even further behind. (*Cases and Materials* (14.1.5)). The Commission has indicated that, in a very fragmented market, a market share as low as 20% might be sufficient to constitute dominance.

14.4.13 **Duration of market position**

An important consideration in the assessment of dominance is the length of time that an undertaking has been in a position of market power. As has been noted, in *Hoffmann-La Roche* the Court of Justice indicated that market power held 'for some time' indicated dominance on a market. If a large market share were held only for a short time before a powerful competitor entered the market, this would indicate that there was no domination of that market.

14.4.14 **Financial and technological resources**

? QUESTION 14.13

In what ways do you think extensive financial resources might assist an undertaking to establish or maintain a dominant position? Look at *United Brands* to see how this company had used its resources (*Cases and Materials* (14.1.6)).

You may have thought of a number of ways in which an undertaking might use extensive financial resources. It could, for example, indulge in persistent price-cutting, perhaps selling below cost or, as United Brands had done, use its wealth to reduce cross-elasticity of demand by widespread advertising. The greater its financial resources, the greater an undertaking's ability to develop its technological know-how, to invest in product development, and to provide technical services to its customers. United Brands had invested in research to improve the productivity and yield of its plantations and perfected new ripening methods. These kinds of strategy can be means to weaken existing competition, to drive competitors out of the market, and to deter potential new entrants to the market.

14.4.15 **Vertical integration**

The extent of vertical integration is demonstrated by the degree of control which an undertaking exerts in the production and marketing chain, either 'upstream'—for instance in the market for raw materials—or 'downstream'—in the distribution network. The greater the vertical integration, the more likely there is to be dominance.

 **EXERCISE** 14.7 

Look at the extracts from *United Brands* (*Cases and Materials* (14.1.7)). Write down the features of the company's production and marketing network which demonstrated its 'up-stream' and 'downstream' integration.

United Brands' operations were described by the Court of Justice as 'vertically integrated to a high degree'. 'Upstream' the company owned large plantations in Central and South America and so had virtual total control over banana supplies for the purposes of its own customers' requirements. As far as 'downstream' integration was concerned, the company controlled loading operations and had its own transportation systems, including railways and a banana fleet for carriage by sea. It also had control over banana ripeners, distributors, and wholesalers through an extensive network of agents. Similarly, in *Hoffmann-La Roche & Co. AG* v *Commission* the Court of Justice recognized that the company's highly efficient sales network was a factor indicating a dominant position.

14.4.16 Conduct

In *United Brands* the Court of Justice agreed with the Commission's view that the behaviour of an allegedly dominant undertaking can provide evidence of dominance. So, for example, the fact that an undertaking has cut its prices below cost can in itself indicate that it is in a dominant position. The view that abusive behaviour (a concept which we shall examine in detail presently) can indicate dominance has been criticized, since the scheme of Article 82 (ex 86) requires a finding of dominant position followed by an analysis of conduct which could amount to an abuse of that dominant position. To hold that abusive behaviour indicates dominance is to indulge in a circular argument. Nevertheless, the Commission continues to take conduct into account when assessing dominance.

14.4.17 Intellectual property rights

 **QUESTION** 14.14

Which intellectual property rights were held by Hilti and by the three television companies BBC, RTE, and ITP in *Magill*? Look back at 14.4.11 and 14.4.6 if you have forgotten.

You may recall that Hilti held patents and copyright in its products (look at paragraph 93 of the Court of First instance decision in *Hilti* (*Cases and Materials* (14.1.4))) and that BBC, RTE, and ITP held copyright in the TV listing for their television programmes (*Cases and Materials* (14.1.8)).  

These intellectual property rights could be enforced under national law in order to exclude competition in the markets for production of the products and the publication of the information, respectively, a factor indicating dominance in the market.

14.4.18 Criticism of the approach to the assessment of dominance

All the factors indicating dominance on a market can constitute 'barriers to entry', for they may hinder or prevent the entry of potential competitors to that market. They may also weaken existing competitors or drive them out of the market. However, the indicators of dominance taken into account by the Commission and the Community courts may have beneficial effects. For instance, consumers may benefit from an undertaking's investment in technological research if that results in a higher quality product, or from the efficient distribution system of an undertaking that is highly vertically integrated. For these reasons, the approach of the Commission and the Community courts to the assessment of dominance in any particular case may be controversial. Nonetheless, it should be remembered that dominance in itself does not amount to a breach of Article 82(ex 86) EC. There must also be an abuse which is capable of affecting trade between Member States.

EXERCISE 14.8

In answering Question 14.3, you should have written down the factors which you thought might indicate that an undertaking is in a dominant position. Have a look at what you wrote and see how many of the main points you identified.

14.5 Abuse

14.5.1 Exploitative and anti-competitive abuse

Often, abuses under Article 82 (ex 86) are classified into two categories, exploitative abuses and anti-competitive abuses. Exploitative abuses are those which impose unfair conditions on consumers. Anti-competitive abuses are those which prevent or weaken competition from other undertakings in the market. Many kinds of abusive behaviour can be described as both exploitative and anti-competitive. The list of abuses in Article 82 (ex 86) **(14.3)** is not exhaustive but simply gives examples of abusive behaviour. Discussion now turns to some particular kinds of abuse which have been considered by the Commission and the Court of Justice.

14.5.2 Unfair prices

The imposition of unfair or excessively high prices is one of the most obvious ways in which a dominant undertaking might abuse its position and exploit its customers. However, the concept of an 'unfair' or 'excessive' price is not without difficulty.

? QUESTION 14.15

How would you define an 'excessive' price?

The task of defining an excessive price is not easy. In charging unfair or excessive prices the dominant undertaking relies on the fact that the consumer needs or wants the product and is prepared to pay a price which is in excess of that which would be charged in a more competitive market. One way of determining an excessive price, suggested by the Court of Justice in *United Brands* (*Cases and Materials* (14.2.1)), is to compare the selling price and the cost of production, in other words to calculate the size of the profit margin. Since the Commission had not analysed United Brands' production costs, the Court refused to uphold the Commission's charge of unfair pricing. In the same case, the Court defined an excessive price as one which 'has no reasonable relation to the economic value of the product supplied'. Of course, this begs the question as to how the economic value of a product is assessed. However careful and detailed the economic analysis employed in any particular case, it appears that conclusions as to unfair or excessive pricing are likely to be controversial.

When a dominant undertaking's prices reach a certain level there is a strong incentive to other firms to enter the market and to compete by undercutting any unfair or excessive prices. Thus, market forces provide some protection for the consumer. However, such forces will not operate where there are significant barriers to entry.

? QUESTION 14.16

What was the barrier to entry in *General Motors* v *Commission* (Case 26/75) [1975] ECR 1367? (*Cases and Materials* (14.2.1)).

It will be recalled that General Motors had an exclusive right under Belgian law to provide inspection services and to issue the certificates required for the import of second-hand Opel vehicles into Belgium. Its statutory monopoly in this market created a complete barrier to entry. The Commission claimed that General Motors had charged excessive prices for the certificates. Here, the Court of Justice characterized as an abuse the imposition of a price which is 'excessive in relation to the economic value of the service provided'. However although General Motors held a dominant position, its conduct did not, on the facts, constitute an abuse.

In a similar case, *British Leyland plc* v *Commission* (Case 226/84) [1986] ECR 3263, the Court of Justice upheld a Commission Decision finding an abuse of a dominant position by British Leyland. The Court held that the prices charged by the company for type approval certificates for imports of British Leyland cars from the continent of Europe was disproportionate to the service provided. Here, it was clear that the purpose of the excessive pricing was to reduce competition in sales of British Leyland cars on the home market by discouraging imports into the UK.

14.5.3 Price discrimination

This is one aspect of the wider abuse of discriminatory treatment. Price discrimination includes such practices as target discounting and loyalty rebating, both of which will be considered presently. In its simplest and most blatant form, discriminatory pricing consists in charging different customers different prices for the same product.

? **QUESTION** 14.17 

Why did the Court of Justice conclude that the different prices that United Brands charged different customers amounted to discriminatory pricing (*Cases and Materials* (14.2.2))?

The Court of Justice held that the company's pricing policy amounted to the application of 'dissimilar conditions to equivalent transactions with other trading parties, thereby placing them at a competitive disadvantage'. The bananas the company supplied under the brand name 'Chiquita' were of almost the same quality; unloading costs at Rotterdam and Bremerhaven were similar; and transport costs from the port to the ripening facilities were generally borne by the customer. Despite all these factors, UBC charged different prices according to the Member State where the customer was established. This pricing policy was based purely on what the market would bear.

Sometimes, a difference in pricing may be justified by objective factors concerning the varying costs involved in supplying goods or services. For instance, the different costs of transportation of goods supplied to different locations, uneven labour costs across the market, or different marketing conditions in different regions may result in significant discrepancies in the cost of supply to different customers. Where differences in prices charged by a dominant undertaking are directly related to factors such as these, there is no abuse. This behaviour amounts to lawful price differentiation and not abusive price discrimination.

14.5.4 Discounts

 **QUESTION** 14.18

What kinds of discount might a trader offer to customers?

Discounts amounting to discriminatory pricing exploit the consumer. Discounts may also be anti-competitive, for instance if they target competitors by undercutting their prices. The kinds of discount which you may have thought of are those offered to customers who buy a certain minimum quantity of goods ('quantity' discounts), who agree to purchase all or most of their requirements from the supplier ('loyalty' or 'fidelity' discounts), or who reach a specified sales target ('target' discounts). Quantity discounts are not abusive provided they apply to all purchasers (and are therefore not discriminatory) and are linked directly to the volume of goods supplied, on the basis that bulk production reduces the supplier's unit costs. Other kinds of discount are caught by Article 82 (ex 86).

QUESTION 14.19

A (fictitious) manufacturer of a range of soap powders, Exploitem plc (Exploitem), offers fidelity discounts to retail outlets which undertake to purchase all their supplies of soap powder from the company. A clause in the agreement provides that if it transpires that other manufacturers are offering similar products at lower prices, the retailers can require Exploitem to reduce its prices accordingly. If Exploitem fails to do this, the retailers may purchase elsewhere.

Write down your opinion on the following points:

(a) Is the total arrangement exploitative? Why/why not?

(b) Is the total arrangement anti-competitive? Why/why not?

EXERCISE 14.9

Now turn to *Hoffmann-La Roche & Co. AG* v *Commission* (Case 85/76) [1979] ECR 461 (*Cases and Materials* (14.2.3)). Do your conclusions in answer to Question 14.19 accord with those of the Court of Justice in *Hoffmann-La Roche*?

***Hoffmann-La Roche* cont.**

You may recall that Roche had concluded agreements with customers obliging or inducing them, by means of fidelity discounts, to buy all or most of their requirements of vitamins exclusively or in preference from Roche. In addition, most of the contracts contained the so-called 'English clause' under which a customer, if it discovered that it could buy more cheaply from another supplier, could ask Roche to reduce its prices. If Roche failed to do so, the customer was free to purchase elsewhere.

The 'English' clauses allowed customers to purchase vitamins at the lowest market price, whether from Roche or from its competitors. To that extent, the agreement was not exploitative. However, the whole arrangement did limit customers' commercial freedom to a significant degree because the fidelity discounts induced them to buy their requirements of vitamins from Roche. The agreement also permitted the company to acquire information about its rivals' pricing policies, thereby enabling it to react quickly by reducing its own prices and to undermine competition. For these reasons, the Court of Justice upheld the Commission's view that the company's practices were abusive.

The Court of Justice also found the target discounting practised by Michelin to be an abuse because it tied in dealers to purchasing tyres from Michelin (*Nederlandsche Banden-Industrie Michelin NV* v *Commission* (Case 322/81) [1983] ECR 3461). In *Hilti* ((Case T-30/89) [1991] ECR II-1439) the Court of First Instance upheld the Commission's decision that Hilti had abused its dominant position by, for example, offering favourable terms to the major customers of its competitors and withholding quantity discounts from customers who also bought from competing manufacturers.

14.5.5. Predatory pricing

Predatory pricing involves the reduction of prices, usually below cost.

? QUESTION 14.20

How do you think predatory pricing and 'normal' price competition between undertakings might be distinguished?

There is no easy answer to this question, which has caused difficulty to the Commission, the Court of Justice, and economists alike. A certain level of price competition is clearly beneficial, for it encourages efficiency and favours the consumer. However, predatory pricing is anti-competitive and ultimately harms the consumer.

? QUESTION 14.21 

How might predatory pricing by a dominant undertaking disadvantage consumers in the long term? Look at the extracts from *AKZO* (*Cases and Materials* (14.2.4)).

***AKZO Chemie* v *Commission* (Case C-62/86) [1991] ECR I-3359**

AKZO produced organic peroxides, used in the plastics industry. It also produced compounds based on benzoyl peroxide, an organic peroxide used for bleaching flour. The company had a much higher turnover in the plastics sector than the flour additives sector. Until 1979, Engineering and Chemical Supplies Ltd (ECS) produced organic peroxides only for the flour additives market but in that year decided to extend its activities to the plastics market. In response, AKZO reduced its prices in the flour additives sector. AKZO brought an action before the Court of Justice for the annulment of a Commission Decision finding that it acted in breach of Article 82 (ex 86).

The Court of Justice held that prices are predatory and therefore abusive if they are intended to eliminate competition. This will be the case where prices fall below average variable costs (those which vary depending on the quantities produced). The undertaking has no interest in applying such prices, save to eliminate competition and then subsequently increase prices, to the detriment of consumers. In other cases, where prices fall below average total coats (variable costs plus fixed costs), evidence of an anti-competitive intent will be required. However, the Court has emphasized that predatory pricing is to be penalized wherever there is a risk that competition will be eliminated, even without proof that a dominant undertaking has a realistic chance of recouping its losses (*Tetra Pak International SA* v *Commission* (Case C-333/94P) [1996] ECR I-5951).

14.5.6 Tie-ins

Tie-in arrangements oblige or induce the purchaser of goods or services to buy other goods or services from the same supplier.

? QUESTION 14.22

Sometimes the inducement is a system of price discounting or rebates, examples of which have already been considered. Do you recall the cases? If not, look back at 14.5.4.

Roche, a pharmaceutical company dominant in several vitamins markets, tied its customers to purchasing all their requirements from it by offering fidelity rebates (*Hoffmann-La Roche* v *Commission*). Hilti engaged in similar practices (*Hilti AG* v *Commission*). In both cases, this constituted an abuse. In addition, Hilti was abusing its dominant position by requiring purchasers of its patented nail cartridges also to buy nails from the company, and by refusing to honour the guarantees on its tools when non-Hilti nails were used, both classic cases of product tied to product. Tying-in can also involve the tying of products and services—for instance, where the purchaser of goods is required to enter into a servicing agreement in respect of those goods—or the tying of services and services.

14.5.7 Refusal to supply

The characterization of a refusal to supply as abusive can be controversial, since it is a general principle of the contract law of many legal systems that a party should have the freedom both to enter into agreements with other parties and to refuse to deal.

? QUESTION 14.23

Apart from general contractual freedom, what factors might justify an undertaking's refusal to supply a particular customer?

An undertaking might justifiably refuse to supply a customer because of stock shortages, because there are problems with production or because the customer has not paid for goods previously supplied. You have probably thought of other justifications. A dominant undertaking may infringe Article 82 (ex 86) if it refuses to supply a customer without justification. Such conduct will be abusive if it is intended to eliminate competition.

? QUESTION 14.24 

When it refused to supply Zoja with the raw material aminobutanol, what factors made the anti-competitive intent of Commercial Solvents so obvious? (*Istituto Chemioterapico Italiano SpA and Commercial Solvents Corporation* v *Commission* (Cases 6 & 7/73 [1974] ECR 223) (*Cases and Materials* (14.2.5)).

The anti-competitive nature of Commercial Solvent's behaviour was revealed by the fact that at the same time as it was refusing further supplies to Zoja, its own subsidiary, Istituto, was emerging as a competitor in the same market as Zoja, namely the market for the manufacture of drugs for the treatment of tuberculosis.

***Hugin Kassaregister AB* v *Commission* (Case 22/78) [1979] ECR 1869**

Here the Commission suggested that Hugin had refused to supply the UK servicing firm Liptons and other undertakings outside its own distribution network with spare parts for Hugin cash registers in order to exclude competition. Hugin maintained that its commercial policy was objectively justified. It sought to reserve maintenance and repair services to itself in order to uphold the good reputation for reliability of its cash registers. In fact, this issue was not resolved, as the Commission Decision finding an abuse was annulled by the Court of Justice because there was no effect on interstate trade (*Cases and Materials* (14.2.5)).

A further example of refusal to supply is provided by *United Brands Co* v *Commission* (Case 27/76) [1978] ECR 207. Here, however, the behaviour was retaliatory rather than anti-competitive. United Brands discontinued supplies of green bananas to Olesen, a Danish ripener and distributor, because it had taken part in an advertising campaign for one of United Brands' competitors. In condemning this as an abuse, the Court of Justice described the conduct as 'a serious interference with the independence of small and medium-sized firms in their commercial relations with the undertaking in a dominant position'. (*Cases and Materials* (14.2.5)).

So far, cases concerning refusals to supply to existing customers have been considered. The 'TV listings' cases demonstrate that refusal to supply to new customers may also constitute an abuse. Here, the television companies' refusal to supply to Magill information on weekly schedules of certain television channels prevented the introduction of a new product, a general television guide, for which there was a potential consumer demand. That refusal was likely to have the effect of excluding all competition in the market for television guides (*RTE* v *Commission* (Case T-69/89) [1991] ECR II-485; *BBC* v *Commission* (Case T-70/89) [1991] ECR II-535; *ITP* v *Commission* (Case T-76/89) [1991] ECR II-575 (*Cases and Materials* (14.2.5)) (Decisions upheld on appeal to the Court of Justice in *RTE & ITP* v *Commission* (Joined Cases C-241 & 242/91P) [1995] ECR I-743)).

On the other hand, the refusal of a media undertaking to allow a rival daily newspaper, in return for appropriate remuneration, to have access to its nationwide home-delivery scheme did not constitute an abuse under Article 82 (ex 86). In order to establish an abuse, the undertaking concerned would have to show that the refusal was incapable of objective justification and would be likely to eliminate it from the daily newspaper market and that the service was indispensable to its carrying out its business. In fact, there were no technical, legal, or economic obstacles preventing the company from setting up its own nationwide home-delivery service (Case C-7/97 *Oscar Bronner GmbH & Co KG* v *Mediaprint Zeitungs- und Zeitschriftenverlag GmbH & Co KG and others* [1998] ECR 1–7791).

14.5.8 Refusal of access to an essential facility

A refusal to supply may well involve the refusal of access to a facility, rather than refusal to supply goods or services. It is sometimes said, in relation to Article 82, that this situation falls within the 'essential facilities' doctrine. Under this doctrine, a dominant undertaking abuses its position if, as the owner or controller of a facility that is essential to the conduct of a business, it refuses access to that facility to other undertakings which cannot themselves feasibly set up a similar facility to conduct that business. Sealink, for instance, which controlled the port of Holyhead, restricted B&I's access to sailing facilities there and was found to have infringed Article 82 (ex 86) (*Sealink/B and I—Holyhead: Interim Measures* (Commission Decision) [1992] 5 CMLR 255).

14.5.9 Import and export bans

In *Hilti AG* v *Commission* (Case T-30/89) [1991] ECR II-1439 it emerged that Hilti had exerted pressure upon its distributors in the Netherlands not to supply Hilti's cartridge strips to the UK market. This conduct is a good example of the kind of import/export ban imposed by a dominant undertaking which is likely to breach Article 82 (ex 86). Such practices not only restrict competition but are also incompatible with the single market.

14.5.10 Mergers

Article 82 (ex 86) was first applied to a merger in *Europemballage Corp. and Continental Can Co Inc* v *Commission* (Case 6/72) [1973] ECR 215 which, it may be recalled, concerned a Commission Decision finding that the proposed takeover by Continental Can of Thomassen & Drijver-Verbliva NV constituted an abuse of its dominant position. Despite Continental Can's arguments to the contrary, the Court of Justice agreed with the Commission that an undertaking need not have used its market power to bring about a merger in order for there to be an abuse. It is sufficient that the merger eliminates competition in a market which the undertaking already dominates. As has been noted, the outcome of this case was the annulment of the Commission's Decision because the RPM had not been proved to the satisfaction of the Court.

Although both Article 82 (ex 86) and Article 81 (ex 85) have been used as a means of controlling mergers, their usefulness in this context has now been to a large extent overtaken by the Merger Control Regulation. However, mergers which do not fall within the scope of the Regulation may still breach Articles 81 and 82 (ex 85 and 86).

14.6 Effect on trade between Member States

This is the third element of Article 82 (ex 86). For a breach to be established there must be an abuse of a dominant position and that abuse must be capable of affecting trade between Member States. The term 'effect on trade between Member States' in Article 82 (ex 86) has the same meaning as in Article 81 (ex 85) EC. Such an effect is not difficult to establish. An effect on the competitive structure of the common market will suffice (*Istituto Chemioterapico Italiano SpA and Commercial Solvents Corporation* v *Commission* (Cases 6 and 7/73) [1974] ECR 223) (*Cases and Materials* (14.3)), as will evidence that abusive behaviour might affect trade between Member States.

Hugin Kassaregister AB v *Commission* (Case 22/78) [1979] ECR 1869 is one of the few cases in which an effect on interstate trade was not established. As has already been noted Hugin, a Swedish company, refused to supply spare parts for its cash registers to Liptons, a London-based company which serviced the machines. The Court of Justice endorsed the Commission's view that Hugin was dominant in the market for its own spare parts but found that Hugin's restrictive practices had no effect on interstate trade. Liptons operated within a very limited area in and around London and there was no indication that it intended to extend its activities further. Moreover, the 'normal' pattern of movement of the spare parts was not between Member States but between Liptons in the UK and Hugin in Sweden, at that time a non-member country.

14.7 Application of Article 82 (ex 86) EC to collective dominance

There is no doubt that the reference in Article 82 (ex 86) to the abusive behaviour and dominance of 'one or more undertakings' includes the dominant position and conduct of undertakings within the same corporate group (see *Europemballage Corp and Continental Can Co Inc* v *Commission* (Case 6/72) [1973] ECR 215 and *Istituto Chemioterapico Italiano SpA and Commercial Solvents Corporation* v *Commission* (Cases 6 & 7/73) [1974] ECR 223).

The question as to whether Article 82 (ex 86) applies to a number of independent undertakings which are collectively dominant in a particular market (an oligopoly) is more controversial. Concerted action by such undertakings would usually be caught by Article 81 (ex 85). Nevertheless, in *Società Italiano Vetro (SIV)* v *Commission* (Cases T-68, 75, 77, 78/89) [1992] ECR II-1403, the Court of First Instance left open the possibility that, where this is not so, abuse by oligopolies may fall within Article 82 (ex 86). In *SIV* the Court of First Instance emphasized the significance, to a finding of dominance, of 'economic links' between the undertakings concerned. Later, in *Municipality of Almelo and Others* v *Energiebedrijf Ijsselmij NV* Case C-393/92 [1994] ECR I-1477, the Court of Justice declared that for collective dominance to exist, the undertakings 'must be linked in such a way that they adopt the same conduct on the market'. In *Irish Sugar plc* v *Commission* (Case T-228/97) [1999] ECR II-2969 links of this kind gave rise to the Court's of First Instance's finding of joint dominance between Irish Sugar and Sugar Distributors Ltd (SDL) on the Irish Sugar Market between 1985 and 1990. These links included Irish Sugar's 51% shareholding in SDL's parent company SDH and Irish Sugar's representation on the boards of both SDH and SDL, as well as arrangements between the companies relating, for instance, to technical services, marketing, commercial strategy, and advertising and undertakings by SDL to purchase all its sugar requirements from Irish Sugar and not to compete in Irish Sugar's markets. Moreover, the Court rejected the applicant's claim that joint dominance could not exist between companies in a vertical commercial relationship (upheld on appeal in *Irish Sugar* v *Commission* (Case C-497/99P) [2001] ECR I-5333).

Recent decisions concerning joint dominance in relation to the Merger Regulation suggest that joint dominance could arise simply by virtue of the effects of a highly concentrated market, whether or not there are economic links between undertakings of the kind existing between Irish Sugar and SDL described above. It remains to be seen whether the scope of 'joint dominance' will be extended in this way in relation to Article 82. The judgment of the Court of Justice in *Compagnie Maritime Belge Transports SA, Compagnie Maritime Belge SA and Dafra Lines A/S* v *Commission* (Cases C-395–6/96P) [2000] ECR I-1365 suggests that it may be so extended. Here the Court declared that a finding of joint dominance may 'depend on an economic assessment and, in particular, on an assessment of the structure of the market in question'.

14.8 The Merger Regulation

The Merger Regulation 139/2004, which entered into force on 1 May 2004 applies to mergers, takeovers, and some joint ventures ('concentrations') which have a Community dimension. Concentrations falling within the Regulation are normally dealt with only by the Commission. Those outside the Regulation are dealt with nationally. This is known as 'one-stop shopping' because it restricts investigations and action to a single authority, either national or Community. Concentrations with a Community dimension must be notified to the Commission within the timeframe specified by the Regulation. Undertakings failing to notify or supplying incorrect information are liable to be fined. Once a notification is received, the Commission is required to examine it immediately and within 25 working days to decide whether or not to instigate detailed investigations (or, as it is called, to issue proceedings). Proceedings will not be issued if the Commission considers that the concentration falls outside the scope of the Regulation or if it finds that, although the concentration has a Community dimension, it does not raise competition concerns. Proceedings, which must be completed in 90 days, must be issued in relation to concentrations which both have a Community dimension and raise competition concerns. A merger must be blocked if it would 'significantly impede effective competition'. The merger regime gives the Commission powers of investigation similar to those conferred by Regulation 1/2003 in relation to alleged breaches of Articles 81 and 82.

CONCLUSIONS

Article 82 (ex 86) is concerned with the abuse of economic power by single undertakings which dominate a particular market for goods or services. It aims to eliminate practices which are anti-competitive, in that they seek to exclude or to weaken competition, or are exploitative, in that they take advantage of consumers. An infringement of Article 82 (ex 86) occurs when all three elements of that Article are satisfied. There must be a dominant position in the relevant market, an abuse of that position and that abuse must be capable of affecting trade between Member States.

SUMMARY

- **Article 82 (ex 86) EC prohibits**, as incompatible with the common market, any abuse by one or more undertakings of a dominant position within the common market or in a substantial part of it.
- **For a breach to be established, three elements must be satisfied:** a dominant position, abuse of that dominant position, and an effect on trade between Member States
- **'Dominance' has been defined by the Court of Justice as**

  A position of economic strength enjoyed by an undertaking which enables it to prevent effective competition being maintained on the relevant market by giving it the power to behave to an appreciable extent independently of its competitors, customers and ultimately of its consumers (*United Brands*).

- **Dominance must be assessed in relation to the relevant market**, the relevant product market, the relevant geographic market, and (sometimes) the relevant temporal or seasonal market.
- **The relevant product market** is defined in terms of product substitution, comprising demand substitutability (or cross-elasticity of demand) and supply substitutability (or cross-elasticity of supply).
- **Cross-elasticity of demand relates to consumer behaviour** and the tests applied to determine whether a consumer would regard products as substitutable or interchangeable are the price, the characteristics, and the use of the products (e.g. *United Brands*, *Hilti*, *Commercial Solvents*).
- **Cross-elasticity of supply relates to the behaviour of other producers in similar markets**. Would they be able and willing to switch production from one product to the other (*Continental Can*)?
- **The relevant geographic market** may be defined in terms of factors such as the feasibility and cost of transportation (*Hilti*) or the area to which the use of the product is limited (*'TV Listings'*). The geographic market must be the common market or a substantial part of it (*Hilti*, *United Brands*, *Michelin*, *Sealink*).
- **The temporal or seasonal market is rarely relevant** but was important, for instance, in *ABG Oil*.
- **Dominance is assessed in relation to the relevant market** on the basis of market share and any other indicators, such as market structure (*United Brands*), resources (*United Brands*), vertical integration (*United Brands*, *Hoffmann-La Roche*), intellectual property rights (*Hilti*, *Hugin*, *'TV Listings'*), and conduct (*United Brands*).
- **Dominance in itself in unobjectionable. For a breach to occur, there must be an abuse**. Abuses identified by the Commission and the Court of Justice include unfair pricing (*United Brands*, *British Leyland*), price discrimination (*United Brands*), discounts (*Hoffmann-La Roche*), predatory pricing (*AKZO*), and refusal to supply (*Commercial Solvents*, *United Brands*, *'TV Listings'*, *Hugin*).
- **The abuse must be capable of affecting trade between Member States**. Such an effect is generally easily established.

CHAPTER 12: ASSESSMENT EXERCISE

Happy Boy plc (Happy Boy) is a UK manufacturer of pet food. The company's share of the European Community pet food market is negligible. Happy Boy's most successful product is its dog food, 'Bing', which it has supplied for many years to wholesalers throughout the Community. The company's massive financial investment in extensive advertising and research and development has paid off. Bing has become so popular that it is now a leading brand in many Member States and Happy Boy has increased its share of the Community dog food market to 45%. The company's nearest rivals in this market hold, respectively, 6%, 4%, and 2% market shares.

Waggles (UK) Ltd (Waggles) has produced dog food for the domestic market since the early 1970s. Last year, the company announced its intention to start exporting to the continent of Europe. Waggles has just learned that Happy Boy is now offering Bing to new and existing customers at considerably reduced prices and is negotiating further discounts with individual wholesalers based upon agreed sales targets for the coming year. It has also emerged that the French wholesaler Ani-Domestique SA (AD) (an established customer of Happy Boy), which agreed to distribute Waggles' promotional literature to its own customers, has been informed by Happy Boy that, as from the end of the month, no further orders from AD for Happy Boy's products will be met.

Advise Waggles.

See *Cases and Materials* (14.5) for a specimen answer.

FURTHER READING

Bavasso, A. (2005). 'The Role of Intent under Article 82', *European Competition Law Review* 616.

Kallaugher, J. and B. Sher. (2004). 'Rebates Revisited: Anti-competitive Effects and Exclusionary Abuse under Article 82', *European Competition Law Review*.

Niels, G. and H. Jenkins. (2005). 'Reform of Article 82: Where the Link between Dominance and Effects Breaks Down', *European Competition Law Review* 605.

Turnbull, S. (1996). 'Barriers to Entry, Article 86 EC and the Abuse of a Dominant Position: an Economic Critique of European Community Competition Law, *European Competition Law Review* 96.

INDEX

A

B

D

E

F

Q

R

S

T

Essentials of Entrepreneurship and Small Business Management

Third Edition

Thomas W. Zimmerer
Drury University

Norman M. Scarborough
Presbyterian College

Prentice Hall Upper Saddle River, NJ 07458

Library of Congress Cataloging-in-Publication Data
Zimmerer, Thomas.
Essentials of entrepreneurship and small business management/Thomas W. Zimmerer, Norman M. Scarborough.—3rd ed.
p. cm.
ISBN 0-13-017280-4
1. Small business—Management. 2. New business enterprises—Management. I. Scarborough, Norman M. II. Title.
HD62.7 .Z55 2001
658.02′2—dc21

2001021121

Acquisitions Editor: Melissa Steffens
VP/Editor-in-Chief: Jeff Shelstad
Assistant Editor: Jessica Sabloff
Media Project Manager: Michele Faranda
Marketing Manager: Michael Campbell
Managing Editor (Production): Judy Leale
Production Editor: Theresa Festa
Production Assistant: Dianne Falcone
Permissions Coordinator: Suzanne Grappi
Associate Director, Manufacturing: Vincent Scelta
Production Manager: Arnold Vila
Manufacturing Buyer: Diane Peirano
Design Manager: Patricia Smythe
Designer: Steven Frim
Interior Design: Maureen Eide
Cover Design: Steven Frim
Cover Illustration/Photo: Allan Garns
Associate Director, Multimedia Production: Karen Goldsmith
Manager, Print Production: Christy Mahon
Composition: Rainbow Graphics
Full-Service Project Management: Rainbow Graphics
Printer/Binder: Hamilton Printing Company

Credit and acknowledgments borrowed from other sources and reproduced, with permission, in this textbook appear on appropriate page within text.

10 9 8 7 6 5 4 3
ISBN 0-13-017280-4

Brief Contents

To Cindy, whose patience is always tested during a writing project of this magnitude. Your support and understanding are a vital part of every book. You are the love of my life.

—N.M.S.

I'd like to dedicate this book to my wife, Linda W. Zimmerer, who makes my work a joy and to my mother, Anna B. Zimmerer (1912–2000), for her unconditional love and support.

—T.W.Z.

May your own dreams be your only boundaries.

—The Reverend Purlie Victorious in "Purlie"

Contents

PREFACE

There has never been a better time to launch a business. Today, increasing numbers of students are choosing to become entrepreneurs, starting businesses that spring from their dreams of freedom and independence and their hopes for meaningful careers. Entrepreneurship is now the driving force behind economic growth and rejuvenation all across the globe, but the United States remains the world leader in the field of entrepreneurship. At the same time, teaching small business and entrepreneurship has become one of the most challenging tasks in colleges and universities today. Like most practicing entrepreneurs, entrepreneurial students expect to maximize the amount of practical, "hands-on" knowledge they get from a course in the shortest possible time. This book allows students to do exactly that.

Essentials of Entrepreneurship and Small Business Management, 3/E, is designed to provide future entrepreneurs with the tools they need to master the most important issues involved in starting and managing a successful new business venture. This book uses a variety of tools to stimulate student interest and to promote learning. The following are some of the features that are included in this third edition:

"You Be the Consultant . . ." features. These short vignettes, drawn from actual small businesses, develop students' critical thinking skills by allowing them to apply the knowledge they gain to actual business problems. The best way for students to learn is to put their knowledge into practice; these exercises give them the opportunity to do just that. This edition continues the tradition of this practical feature that users and reviewers continue to rave about.

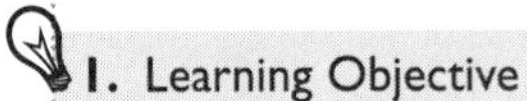

Learning Objectives. Every chapter begins with a set of learning objectives, but it doesn't end there! The learning objectives are integrated into the chapters as "markers" that appear at the beginning of the appropriate section in the chapter. The chapter summaries also are built around these learning objectives, reinforcing the key concepts covered in every chapter.

Example

Lots of "real-world" examples. Many students find that the learning process is more effective when they see examples of how entrepreneurs apply the principles they are studying. Meaningful, real-world examples are a major strength of this book. Every chapter is loaded with many examples of small companies that are living proof that the concepts and techniques covered in the text actually do work! These examples are easy to spot; they are set off in italics and include an in-margin marker containing the company's name.

- **Expanded coverage of E-Commerce and the World Wide Web.** The Web is transforming the way that companies do business, and some of the most exciting entrepreneurial stories are taking place in the world of e-commerce. This edition of *Essentials of Entrepreneurship and Small Business Management* is the first book in the field to include a complete chapter on the rapidly growing field of e-commerce (Chapter 15, "E-Commerce and the Entrepreneur"). This chapter describes the factors entrepreneurs should consider before launching into e-commerce and discusses the twelve myths of e-commerce. It also covers strategies for success in e-commerce, offers tips on building a killer Web site, and discusses security issues. In addition, many of the examples throughout the text are based on companies engaging in e-commerce.
- **A supporting Web site.** The World Wide Web brings another dimension into the modern classroom. Using the Web site that accompanies this book, professors can find online examples to enhance their in-class presentations and both students and professors can use the site as a valuable research tool. The site also includes Web activities for students, sample test questions, PowerPoint downloads, and Web links relevant to each chapter. Preparing to run a business in the twenty-first century begins at: **<www.prenhall.com/zimmerer>.**
- **Comprehensive cases drawn from highly respected case writers and the North American Case Research Association (NACRA).** Selected by the authors, these cases add another dimension to students' classroom experience. They allow students to study, analyze, and solve a small company's problems and opportunities in detail and can serve as the basis for either oral or written reports on an individual or a team basis. These cases are available as a package through the publisher.
- **High-quality tables, charts, and figures.** Thanks to computers, television, and movies, today's students are very visually-oriented, and modern textbooks should recognize this. Every chapter in this book contains helpful tables, charts, and figures designed to help students capture and retain meaningful concepts and information. The authors believe that learning should be fun and include many quality cartoons that are relevant to each chapter.
- **Thought-provoking quotations.** Every chapter begins with two or three thought-provoking quotations that set the stage for what the student will be learning.
- **A sample business plan.** A sample business plan for a children's bookstore, The Hundred Story House, that was developed by a student entrepreneur is available on the Web site. It offers a good example of how students can convert their ideas into businesses.
- **Business Plan Pro software.** Professors can have *Business Plan Pro,* the best-selling business planning software package from Palo Alto Software, packaged with their students' textbooks for a minimal fee. This software is a valuable tool that helps students build winning business plans for their entrepreneurial ideas.

Essentials of Entrepreneurship and Small Business Management, 3/E includes topics that are vital to any entrepreneur considering launching a business, all in a manageable 15 chapters. There is a right way—and a wrong way—to launch a business. This book teaches entrepreneurs and entrepreneurs-to-be the *right* way to launch their companies so they can maximize their probability of success. It progresses in a logical fashion that reflects the input of dozens of experienced, successful small business professionals. It provides a map for building a business plan to guide a business down the road to success.

This book provides valuable guidance in the critical areas entrepreneurs face as they evaluate the potential of their business ideas. Its major strengths include in-depth, practical coverage of topics such as strategic management, choosing a form of ownership or a franchise, buying an existing business, developing a marketing strategy, managing cash flow, building a financial plan, assembling a strong business plan. Once established, a business must maintain its competitive advantage. *Essentials of Entrepreneurship and Small Business Management, 3/E* addresses this need with strong chapters on advertising and pricing; building a leading a successful team; exploring global business opportunities, and, of course, e-commerce.

Students and faculty also have access to our World Wide Web page at **<www.prenhall.com/zimmerer>** that serves as a valuable resource to those interested in learning more about the exciting world of small business and entrepreneurship. It offers a handy "Before You Start Checklist" designed to help entrepreneurs make sure they have everything they need to launch a successful business and a "Business Plan Evaluation Scale" that allows entrepreneurs to measure the quality of their business plans. It also provides more than one thousand links to other Web sites relating to topics in small business management and entrepreneurship, all organized by topic. Students and faculty literally can access a world of information on small business and entrepreneurship from this one Web site. In short, it serves as a one-stop WWW location for all of your small business needs!

As you can see, the authors have used their combined 60 years of teaching experience (and their 54 years of experience writing textbooks) to produce a book that contains a multitude of both student- and professor-friendly features. We trust that this edition of *Essentials of Entrepreneurship and Small Business Management, 3/E* will help the next generation of entrepreneurs reach their full potential and achieve their dreams of success as independent business owners. It is their dedication, perseverance, and creativity that keep the world's economy moving forward.

ACKNOWLEDGMENTS

We thank the many people who played a vital role in creating this edition of *Essentials of Entrepreneurship and Small Business Management.* The contributions of the following reviewers were extremely valuable in helping us develop the features and the content of this edition:

Pamela Clark, Angelo State University
John Todd, University of Arkansas
Peter Mark Shaw, Tidewater Community College
John Phillips, University of San Francisco

In addition, we thank the members of the production team at Prentice Hall, all genuine professionals in every sense of the word. Their superb work lies at the core of the top-quality book you see before you. Creating a book is a team effort, and we could not have asked for a more cooperative, helpful group with which to work. Specifically, we thank:

Melissa Steffens, acquisition editor, who guided this project so skillfully through many obstacles. Without her, this book would not have been possible.

Theresa Festa, our outstanding production editor whose attention to detail is unsurpassed. She truly is a pleasure to work with!

Jessica Sabloff, who did an excellent job coordinating all of our ancillaries.

Samantha Steele, administrative assistant, who handled what must have been hundreds of details masterfully and always with a cheerful attitude.

Finally, we thank Natalie Anderson, our former management editor, whose vision and dedication transformed the idea for this project into reality. Her experience and support have helped make this book the success that it is. Many thanks!!!

Norman M. Scarborough
phone: (864) 833-8273
fax: (864) 833-8198
e-mail: nmscarb@presby.edu

Thomas W. Zimmerer
phone (417) 873-7241
fax (417) 873-7537
e-mail: zimmerer@drury.edu

CHAPTER 1

The Foundations of Entrepreneurship

One doesn't discover new lands without consenting to lose sight of the shore for a very long time.
—Andre Gide

Security does not lie in refusing to take risks but in taking them wisely.
—Mary Beth Grover

LEARNING OBJECTIVES

Upon completion of this chapter, you will be able to:

1. Define the role of the entrepreneur in business in the United States and across the world.
2. Describe the entrepreneurial profile and evaluate your potential as an entrepreneur.
3. Describe the benefits and drawbacks of entrepreneurship.
4. Explain the forces that are driving the growth of entrepreneurship.
5. Explain the cultural diversity of entrepreneurship.
6. Describe the important role small businesses play in our nation's economy.
7. Describe the nine deadly mistakes of entrepreneurship and explain how to avoid them.
8. Put failure into the proper perspective.
9. Explain how entrepreneurs can avoid becoming another failure statistic.

1. Define the role of the entrepreneur in business in the United States and across the world.

THE WORLD OF THE ENTREPRENEUR

Welcome to the world of the entrepreneur! Never before have more people been realizing that Great American Dream of owning and operating their own businesses. Every 11 seconds a new business is born in the United States, and there's no sign of a slowdown in our nation's interest in entrepreneurship![1] Currently, one of every 12 Americans is actively involved in trying to start a new business.[2] This resurgence of the entrepreneurial spirit is the most significant economic development in recent business history. These heroes of the new economy are rekindling an intensely competitive business environment that had all but disappeared from the landscape of U.S. business. With amazing vigor, their businesses have introduced innovative products and services, pushed back technological frontiers, created new jobs, opened foreign markets, and, in the process, enhanced the U.S. competitive edge in world markets.

Interest in entrepreneurship has never been higher than it is at the beginning of the twenty-first century. A recent study by Ernst & Young found that 78 percent of influential Americans believe that entrepreneurship will be *the* defining trend of this century. Which entrepreneurial opportunity topped their list? No surprise here: the Internet.[3] The future of entrepreneurial activity looks incredibly bright, given that the past two decades have seen record numbers of entrepreneurs launching businesses (see Figure 1.1). We appear to be on the crest of another even larger wave of entrepreneurial activity—not only in the United States but across the globe as well. The largest companies in the United States continue to engage in massive downsizing campaigns, dramatically cutting the number of managers and workers on their payrolls. This flurry of "pink slips" has spawned a new population of entrepreneurs: castoffs from large corporations (in which many of these individuals thought they would be lifetime ladder-climbers) with solid management experience and many productive years left before retirement.

This downsizing has all but destroyed the long-standing notion of job security in large corporations. As a result, members of Generation X (those born between 1965 and 1980) no longer see launching a business as being a risky career path. Having watched large companies lay off their parents after many years of service, these young people see entrepreneurship as the ideal way to create their own job security and success!

Jump Networks, Inc.

For instance, while attending Cornell University, Bill Trenchard worked as a student intern at Sony Corporation, where his father, Bob, was a vice president. Before graduating from college, however, Bill saw his father's position eliminated. Frustrated by the bureau-

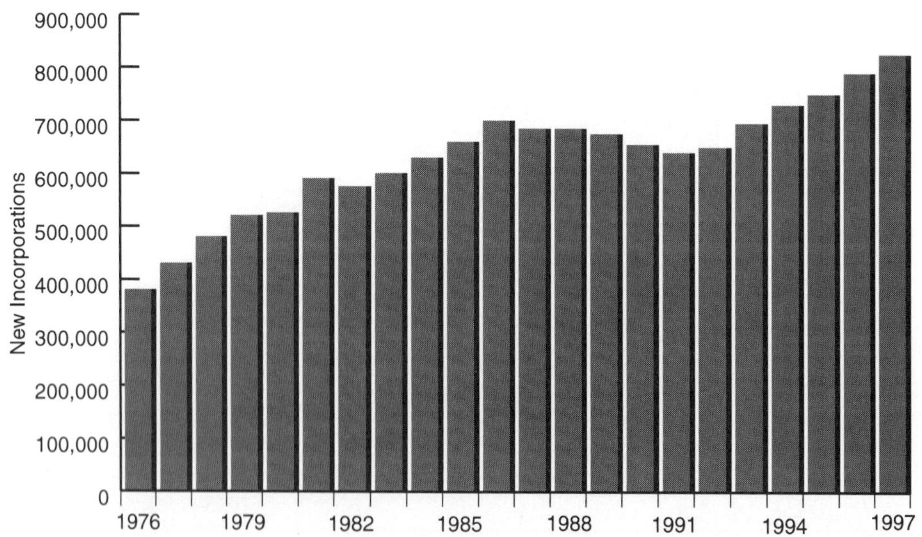

FIGURE 1.1
Number of New Incorporations
Source: Dun & Bradstreet.

cracy in the giant company and its impersonal nature, Bill decided that after college he would launch his own company rather than start on the bottom rung of some corporate ladder. He launched several Web-based technology companies, pouncing on opportunities as they arose in the fast-changing business. One of his start-ups was Jump Networks, Inc., a pioneer in Web-accessible calendars and a company for which Bill was able to attract $1.5 million in venture capital—while he was just 24! Bill recently agreed to sell Jump to Microsoft in a deal that made the twenty-something entrepreneur a multimillionaire![4]

The downsizing trend among large companies has created a more significant philosophical change. It has ushered in an age in which "small is beautiful." Twenty-five years ago, competitive conditions favored large companies with their hierarchies and layers of management; today, with the pace of change constantly accelerating, fleet-footed, agile, small companies have the competitive advantage. These nimble competitors can dart into and out of niche markets as they emerge and recede; they can move faster to exploit market opportunities; and they can use modern technology to create within a matter of weeks or months products and services that once took years and all of the resources a giant corporation could muster. The balance has tipped in favor of small, entrepreneurial companies. Howard Stevenson, Harvard's chaired professor of entrepreneurship, says, "Why is it so easy [for small companies] to compete against giant corporations? Because while they [the giants] are studying the consequences, [entrepreneurs] are changing the world."[5]

One of the most comprehensive studies of global entrepreneurship shows a significant gap in the rate of new business formation among the United States and other nations around the world. The study found that 8.5 percent of the adult population in the United States is working to start a business. Just 3.3 percent of adults in Great Britain and only 1.6 percent of adults in Japan were trying to launch companies (see Figure 1.2). The study also concluded that these different rates of entrepreneurial activity may account for as much as one-third of the variation in the rates of economic growth among these nations.[6]

Although the United States is the global leader in entrepreneurship, it is not the only nation to benefit from the surge in the small business sector. Eastern European countries, China, Vietnam, and many others whose economies were state controlled and centrally planned are now fertile ground for growing small businesses. Citizens in other countries across Europe and the Far East are also showing greater willingness to take the entrepreneurial plunge.

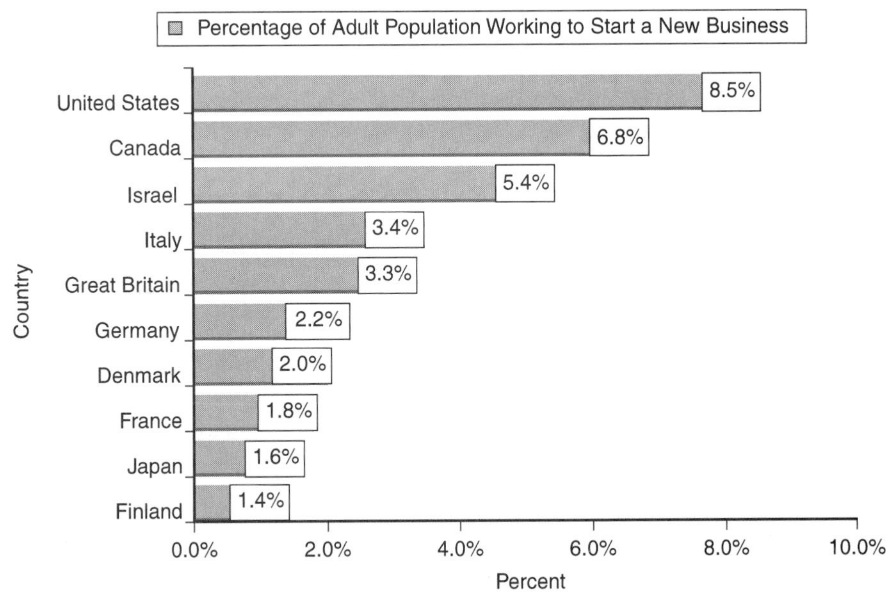

FIGURE 1.2
Entrepreneurial Activity Across the Globe
Source: 1999 Global Entrepreneurship Monitor.

Psion PLC

When David Potter decided to leave his job as a physics professor at Britain's Imperial College to launch a business, his colleagues questioned his judgment. Potter launched Psion PLC, a company that made palmtop computers. Potter recently negotiated deals with industry heavyweights Nokia Corporation, Motorola Inc., and Ericsson to license its software for use in the next generation of palmtop computers. Psion now employs more than 1,100 people and has a market value of more than $1 billion![7]

Wherever they may choose to launch their companies, these business builders continue to embark on one of the most exhilarating—and one of the most frightening—adventures ever known: launching a business. It's never easy, but it can be incredibly rewarding, both financially and emotionally. One writer calls it "life without a safety net—thrilling and dangerous."[8] Still, true entrepreneurs see owning a business as the real measure of success. Indeed, entrepreneurship often provides the only avenue for success to those who otherwise might have been denied the opportunity.

Who are these entrepreneurs, and what drives them to work so hard with no guarantee of success? What forces lead them to risk so much and to make so many sacrifices in an attempt to achieve an ideal? Why are they willing to give up the security of a steady paycheck working for someone else to become the last person to be paid in their own companies? This chapter will examine the entrepreneur, the driving force behind the U.S. economy.

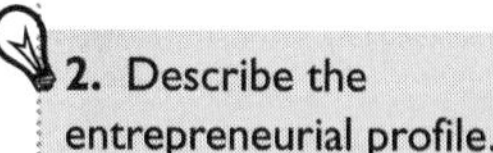

2. Describe the entrepreneurial profile.

WHAT IS AN ENTREPRENEUR?

entrepreneur—*one who creates a new business in the face of risk and uncertainty for the purpose of achieving profit and growth by identifying opportunities and assembling the necessary resources to capitalize on them.*

An **entrepreneur** is one who creates a new business in the face of risk and uncertainty for the purpose of achieving profit and growth by identifying opportunities and assembling the necessary resources to capitalize on them. Although many people come up with great business ideas, most of them never act on their ideas. Entrepreneurs do. Researchers have invested a great deal of time and effort over the last decade trying to paint a clear picture of the entrepreneurial personality. Although these studies have identified several characteristics entrepreneurs tend to exhibit, none of them has isolated a set of traits required for success. We now turn to a brief summary of the entrepreneurial profile.[9]

1. *Desire for responsibility.* Entrepreneurs feel a deep sense of personal responsibility for the outcome of ventures they start. They prefer to be in control of their resources and use those resources to achieve self-determined goals.
2. *Preference for moderate risk.* Entrepreneurs are not wild risk takers but are instead calculating risk takers. Unlike "high-rolling, riverboat" gamblers, they rarely gamble. Their goals may appear to be high—even impossible—in others' perceptions, but entrepreneurs see the situation from a different perspective and believe that their goals are realistic and attainable. They usually spot opportunities in areas that reflect their knowledge, backgrounds, and experiences, which increases their probability of success. Paul Hawken, cofounder of Smith & Hawken, a highly successful mail-order garden tool company, explains:

    > Good entrepreneurs are risk avoiders, not risk takers. They appear to be risk takers because they see the market differently than the rest of us do; they see a product or service that will converge with how the culture is changing. Once they create it, they methodically eliminate all the factors that will prevent them from getting to market. They become risk eliminators.[10]

3. *Confidence in their ability to succeed.* Entrepreneurs typically have an abundance of confidence in their ability to succeed. They tend to be optimistic about their chances for success,

YOU BE THE CONSULTANT . . .

Paradise in a Pan

Peggy Day, 72, and Jeanne Wagster, 45, spent their careers in the mortgage lending business, but each dreamed of launching a business of her own. After the two met in church and discovered a mutual talent and interest in baking, they conducted a survey of 100 people to test the idea of selling homemade pies. The survey results were convincing, so in 1994 the pair invested less than $1,000 of their own money and bought a used refrigerator, baking supplies, and groceries and went into business. They started Peggy Jean's Pies in an out-of-the-way warehouse in Columbia, Missouri, and in the early days seeded their market by giving away their homemade pies. "Peggy and I would bake up whole pies and load them in the back seats of our cars," says Wagster. "I'd double-park and she'd run into a business with a fresh, hot apple pie."

By Thanksgiving, Peggy Jean's Pies had caught on, and the partners stayed up for 36 straight hours, baking 270 pies. That spring, Day and Wagster set up four small tables in their warehouse and began selling drinks and pie by the slice. Business picked up so much that the partners decided to move into a downtown location. It was there that Wagster came up with the idea of making "baby pies," single-serving pies baked in attractive tins. Baby pies have become the company's best-selling item.

Peggy Jean's pies are just like the ones straight out of your grandmother's kitchen, and so is the service they offer. In fact, Wagster and Day trace their success not only to the quality of their pies, but also to the level of customer service they offer. They've been known to deliver pies to customers' homes and to meet rush orders with a smile. One elderly customer ordered a pie for her sister, who was to come for a visit the next day. Day and Wagster delivered the pie, but the next morning when they arrived at 4 A.M. to start the day's baking, their answering machine was full of messages from the woman. "She had eaten the whole pie and didn't have any [left] for her sister," explains Day. Could they bring her another one? Of course, they said.

Peggy Jean's Pies sells more than 2,000 whole pies and 30,000 baby pies a year, most in the Columbia area. However, the ladies recently extended their company's reach by launching a Web site **<www.peggyjeanspies.com>** and by selling pies through a local grocery chain. Peggy Jean's Pies has become so popular that their bakery/restaurant is now a regular stop for tour buses. Despite the long hours and hard work, Day and Wagster truly enjoy making "paradise in a pan" for their customers and insist that their business is a labor of love.

1. Which entrepreneurial traits do Peggy Day and Jeanne Wagster exhibit?
2. What advantages did Day and Wagster have when launching their business?
3. What obstacles did they face?

Source: Janine Latus Musick, "Upper-Crust Service," *Nation's Business,* June 1999, p. 58. Reprinted by permission, *Nation's Business,* June 1999. Copyright 1999. U.S. Chamber of Commerce.

Opportunity to Make a Difference

Increasingly, entrepreneurs are starting businesses because they see an opportunity to make a difference in a cause that is important to them. Whether it is providing low-cost, sturdy housing for families in developing countries or establishing a recycling program to preserve Earth's limited resources, entrepreneurs are finding ways to combine their concerns for social issues and their desire to earn a good living.

Sun Garden Furniture

While living in the suburbs, Steve Row watched builders put up house after house in rapid succession. What disturbed him was not the new neighbors but the large amounts of scrap wood the builders wasted. "It struck me that this wood was still in its original condition and could be usable for other things—like furniture," recalls Row. He approached the contractors, who told him to help himself to all of the scrap lumber he wanted. Today his company, Sun Garden Furniture, produces and sells a variety of unique furnishings across northern California, ranging from tables and chairs to picket fence benches and seed cabinets—all made from scrap lumber recycled from building sites.[21]

Opportunity to Reach Your Full Potential

Too many people find their work boring, unchallenging, and unexciting. But not entrepreneurs! To them, there is little difference between work and play; the two are synonymous. Entrepreneurs' businesses become their instruments for self-expression and self-actualization. They know that the only boundaries on their success are those imposed by their own creativity, enthusiasm, and vision. Tim McDonald, who had already launched several start-ups by age 31, explains, "I want to be in a situation where your growth is limited only by your own talent, your own energy—and that . . . means an entrepreneurial situation."[22]

Opportunity to Reap Unlimited Profits

Although money is not the primary force driving most entrepreneurs, the profits their businesses can earn are an important motivating factor in their decisions to launch companies. Most entrepreneurs never become superrich, but many of them do become quite wealthy. In fact, nearly 75 percent of the *Forbes* 400 Richest Americans are first-generation entrepreneurs![23] According to research by Thomas Stanley and William Danko, self-employed business owners make up two-thirds of American millionaires. "Self-employed people are four times more likely to be millionaires than people who work for others," says Danko.[24] The typical millionaire's business is not a glamorous, high-tech enterprise; more often, it is something much less glamorous—scrap metal, welding, auctioneering, garbage collection, and the like.

Dav El Chauffeured Transportation Network

Scott Solombrino has become quite wealthy through his business, Dav El Chauffeured Transportation Network. When he was a college freshman, Solombrino needed money for his tuition, so he emptied his savings account (a whopping $600) and bought a 10-year-old Cadillac limousine and started a limousine service, Fifth Avenue Limousine of Boston. Not only did the business pay Solombrino's way through school, but it also established his life's work. By the time he graduated, Fifth Avenue Limousine employed 100 people, owned 32 limousines, and generated sales of more than $2 million annually! Less than a decade after starting his company, Solombrino and two partners purchased for $12 million the franchised limousine giant Dav El Chauffeured Network whose sales now exceed $400 million.[25]

Table 1.1 offers a brief profile of some of the wealthiest Americans in history.

Opportunity to Contribute to Society and Be Recognized for Your Efforts

Often small business owners are among the most respected and most trusted members of their communities. Business deals based on trust and mutual respect are the hallmark of many established small companies. These owners enjoy the trust and recognition they receive from the customers whom they have served faithfully over the years. Playing a vital role in their local business systems and knowing that their work has a significant impact on how smoothly the nation's economy functions is yet another reward for small business managers.

Opportunity to Do What You Enjoy and Have Fun at It

A common sentiment among small business owners is that their work really isn't work. Most successful entrepreneurs choose to enter their particular business fields because they have an interest in them and enjoy those lines of work. They have made their avocations (hobbies) their vocations (work) and are glad they did! These entrepreneurs are living Harvey McKay's advice: "Find a job doing what you love, and you'll never have to work a

TABLE 1.1
Wealthiest Americans in History

Source: Adapted from "Richest Americans in History," Forbes ASAP, *August 24, 1998, p. 32; Rachel Emma Silverman, "Rich & Richer: Fifty of the Wealthiest People of the Past 1,000 Years,"* Wall Street Journal Reports: The Millennium, *January 11, 1999, pp. R6–R10.*

Who	Comment	Business	Wealth as a % of the U.S. economy[a]
1. John D. Rockefeller (1839–1937)	America's first billionaire. Created America's most powerful monopoly, the Standard Oil Company.	Oil	1.53%
2. Cornelius Vanderbilt (1794–1877)	Known as the "Commodore." Borrowed $100 from his mother at age 12 to start what became the Staten Island Ferry.	Railroad and shipping	1.15%
3. John Jacob Astor (1763–1848)	A German-born immigrant who began as a fur trader	New York real estate	0.93%
4. Stephen Girard (1750–1831)	Largest investor in the First Bank of the United States. Once loaned the U.S. Treasury $8 million to finance the War of 1812.	Shipping and banking	0.67%
5. Andrew Carnegie (1835–1919)	A "rags to riches" story. Started as a bobbin boy and went on to found U.S. Steel.	Steel	0.60%
6. Bill Gates (1955–)	Dropped out of Harvard and launched Microsoft Corporation. Wealthiest man in the world today.	Computer software	0.58%
7. Alexander Turney Stewart (1803–1876)	Founded the first department store in the United States.	Retail	0.56%
8. Frederick Weyerhauser (1834–1914)	Made his fortune as America's demand for lumber exploded.	Timber	0.55%
. . .			
66. Michael Dell (1965–)	Started Dell Computer from his dormitory room at the University of Texas.	Computers	0.12%
. . .			
90. Larry Ellison (1945–)	Started Oracle Corporation with $2,000 of his own money. (Company revenues now exceed $9 billion per year.)	Computer software	0.07%

[a] Calculated by dividing person's total wealth by the U.S. GDP at the time of death, or if person is still living, by 1997 GDP.

day in your life." The journey rather than the destination is the entrepreneur's greatest reward.

Cars on Camera

Michael Holback, owner of Cars on Camera, has transformed his hobby into a successful business venture. A longtime classic car enthusiast, Holback supplies hard-to-find cars such as classic Bentleys, Rolls Royces, Jaguars, or Stutzes for movies and television shows. "My business is truly everything I ever wanted," says Holback. "I wake up and I'm surrounded by my toys."[26] *Not only has Holback found a way to make a living, but he also is doing something he loves!*

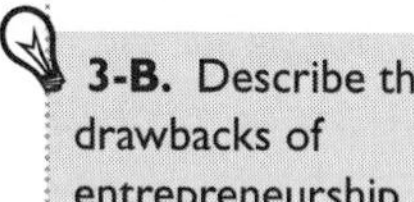

3-B. Describe the drawbacks of entrepreneurship.

THE POTENTIAL DRAWBACKS OF ENTREPRENEURSHIP

Although owning a business has many benefits and provides many opportunities, anyone planning to enter the world of entrepreneurship should be aware of its potential drawbacks. Individuals who prefer the security of a steady paycheck, a comprehensive benefit package, a two-week paid vacation, and the support of a corporate staff probably should not go into business for themselves. Some of the disadvantages of entrepreneurship follow.

Uncertainty of Income

Opening and running a business provides no guarantees that an entrepreneur will earn enough money to survive. Some small businesses barely earn enough to provide the owner-manager with an adequate income. In a business's early days the owner often has trouble meeting financial obligations and may have to live on savings. The steady income that comes with working for someone else is absent. The owner is always the last one to be paid.

Risk of Losing Your Entire Investment

The small business failure rate is relatively high. According to recent research, 24 percent of new businesses fail within two years, and 51 percent shut down within four years. Within six years, 63 percent of new businesses will have folded. Studies also show that when a company creates at least one job in its early years, the probability of failure after six years plummets to 35 percent!

Before "reaching for the golden ring," entrepreneurs should ask themselves if they can cope psychologically with the consequences of failure.

- What is the worst that could happen if I open my business and it fails?
- How likely is the worst to happen? (Am I truly prepared to launch my business?)
- What can I do to lower the risk of my business failing?
- If my business were to fail, what is my contingency plan for coping?

Long Hours and Hard Work

Business start-ups often demand that owners keep nightmarish schedules. According to a recent survey, the median workweek for small business owners increased to 56 hours from 51 hours in 1991.[27] As Figure 1.3 shows, almost three-fourths of entrepreneurs devote 50 or more hours per week to their companies. In many start-ups, six- or seven-day workweeks with no paid vacations are the norm. In fact, a recent study by American Express found that 29 percent of small business owners had no plans to take a summer vacation. The primary reason? "Too busy."[28] These owners feel the pressure because they know that when the business closes, the revenue stops coming in, and the customers go elsewhere. "Even when you own your own business," says Jil Stenn, cofounder of a business that designs edible landscapes, "you still always are working for someone else—your customers and clients."[29]

Lower Quality of Life Until the Business Gets Established

The long hours and hard work needed to launch a company can take their toll on the remainder of the entrepreneur's life. Business owners often find that their roles as husbands or wives and fathers or mothers take a back seat to their roles as company founders. Part of the problem is that most entrepreneurs launch their businesses between the ages of 25 and 39, just when they start their families (see Figure 1.4). As a result, marriages and friendships are too often casualties of small business ownership.

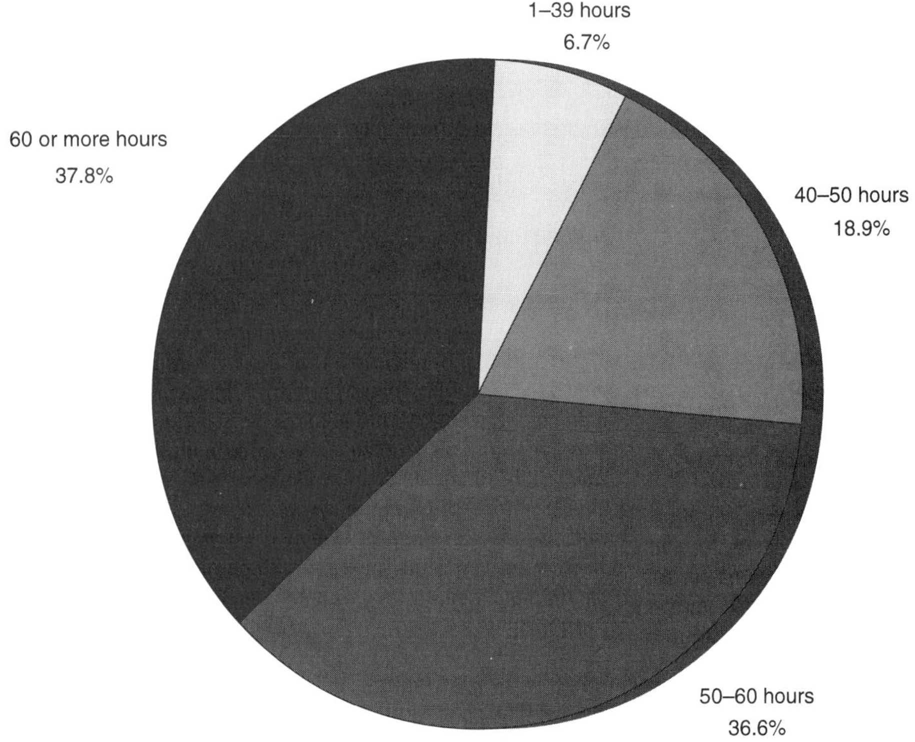

FIGURE 1.3
Number of Hours per Week Entrepreneurs Devote to Their Businesses
Source: Ernst & Young LLP.

High Levels of Stress

Starting and managing a business can be an incredibly rewarding experience, but it also can be a highly stressful one. Entrepreneurs often have made significant investments in their companies, have left behind the safety and security of a steady paycheck, and have mortgaged everything they own to get into business. Failure may mean total financial ruin, and that creates intense levels of stress and anxiety! After launching an advertising agency with a partner, one entrepreneur recalls their struggle to survive their early years: "We had

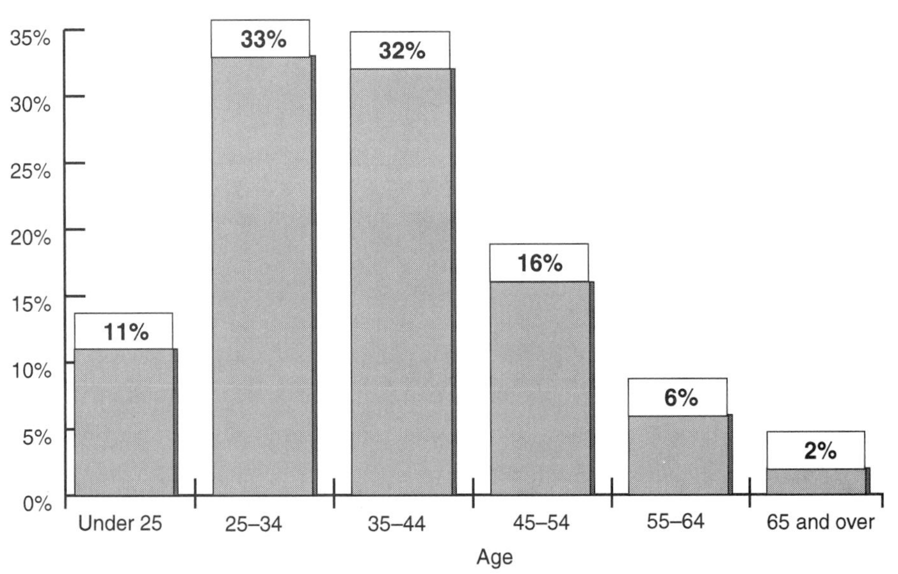

FIGURE 1.4
Owner Age When Business Formed
Source: National Federation of Independent Businesses and Wells Fargo Bank.

envisioned ourselves smiling, closing sales, and making deals, but stress headaches, pains in the neck, and unreturned phone calls marked our first year-and-a-half in business."[30]

Complete Responsibility

It's great to be the boss, but many entrepreneurs find that they must make decisions on issues about which they are not really knowledgeable. When there is no one to ask, the pressure can build quickly. The realization that the decisions they make are the cause of success or failure has a devastating effect on some people. Small business owners discover quickly that *they* are the business.

Discouragement

Launching a business is a substantial undertaking that requires a great deal of dedication, discipline, and tenacity. Along the way to building a successful business, entrepreneurs will run headlong into many different obstacles, some of which appear to be insurmountable. In the face of such difficulties, discouragement and disillusionment are common emotions. Successful entrepreneurs know that every business encounters rough spots along the way, and they wade through difficult times with lots of hard work and an abundant reserve of optimism.

4. Explain the forces that are driving the growth of entrepreneurship.

BEHIND THE BOOM: WHAT'S FEEDING THE ENTREPRENEURIAL FIRE?

What are the forces driving this entrepreneurial trend in our economy? Which factors have led to this age of entrepreneurship? Some of the most significant ones follow.

Entrepreneurs as Heroes

An intangible but very important factor is the attitude that Americans have toward entrepreneurs. As a nation we have raised them to hero status and have held out their accomplishments as models to follow. Business founders such as Bill Gates (Microsoft Corporation), Mary Kay Ash (Mary Kay Cosmetics), Jeff Bezos (Amazon.com), Michael Dell (Dell Computer Corporation), and Ben Cohen and Jerry Greenfield (Ben & Jerry's Homemade Inc.) are to entrepreneurship what Shaquille O'Neal and Emmit Smith are to sports.

Entrepreneurial Education

Colleges and universities have discovered that entrepreneurship is an extremely popular course of study. Disillusioned with corporate America's downsized job offerings and less promising career paths, a rapidly growing number of students sees owning a business as an attractive career option. Today more than 1,500 colleges and universities offer courses in entrepreneurship and small business to some 15,000 students. Many colleges and universities have difficulty meeting the demand for courses in entrepreneurship and small business.

Demographic and Economic Factors

Most entrepreneurs start their businesses between the ages of 25 and 39, and much of our nation's population falls into that age range. Plus, the economic growth that has spanned most of the 1980s and 1990s has created a significant amount of wealth among people of this age group and many business opportunities on which they can capitalize.

Shift to a Service Economy

The service sector produces 92 percent of the jobs and 85 percent of the gross domestic product (GDP) in the United States, which represents a sharp rise from just a decade ago. Because of their relatively low start-up costs, service businesses have become very popular among entrepreneurs. The booming service sector continues to provide many business opportunities, and not all of them are in high-tech fields.

Zephyr Inline Skate Tours

For example, Allen Wright's interest in the outdoors, athletics, and travel led him to launch a unique service business, Zephyr Inline Skate Tours. Wright leads his customers on vacations through diverse destinations such as New York City, the California wine country, Pennsylvania's Amish heartland, and the Netherlands—all on in-line skates! With his specialty travel business, Wright has tapped into one of the fastest-growing segments of the tourism market, and his young company already generates sales of more than $254,000, mostly through its Web site **<www.skatetour.com>.**[31]

Technological Advancements

With the help of modern business machines such as personal computers, laptop computers, fax machines, copiers, color printers, answering machines, and voice mail, even one person working at home can look like a big business. At one time, the high cost of such technological wizardry made it impossible for small businesses to compete with larger companies that could afford the hardware. Today, however, powerful computers and communication equipment are priced within the budgets of even the smallest businesses. Although entrepreneurs may not be able to manufacture heavy equipment in their spare bedrooms, they can run a service- or information-based company from their homes very effectively and look like any *Fortune* 500 company to customers and clients.

Independent Lifestyle

Entrepreneurship fits the way Americans want to live—independent and self-sustaining. People want the freedom to choose where they live, the hours they work, and what they do. Although financial security remains an important goal for most entrepreneurs, many place top priority on lifestyle issues such as more time with family and friends, more leisure time, and more control over work-related stress. In a recent study by Hilton Hotels, 77 percent of adults surveyed listed spending more time with family and friends as their top priority; 66 percent wanted more free time. Making money ranked a lowly fifth place, and spending money on material possessions came in last.[32]

E-Commerce and the World Wide Web

The proliferation of the **World Wide Web,** the vast network that links computers around the globe via the Internet and opens up oceans of information to its users, has spawned thousands of entrepreneurial ventures since its beginning in 1993. Online commerce is growing rapidly (see Figure 1.5), creating many opportunities for Web-savvy entrepreneurs. In fact, many experts compare the Internet of the 1990s to the California Gold Rush of the 1850s. Books, music, computer hardware and software, financial services, travel, and flowers are among the best-selling items on the Web, but entrepreneurs are learning that they can use this powerful tool to sell just about anything! Approximately 47 percent of small businesses have access to the Internet, and 35 percent have Web sites (although

World Wide Web—*the vast network that links computers around the globe via the Internet and opens up oceans of information to its users; a major business opportunity for entrepreneurs.*

FIGURE 1.5
Online Commerce
Source: Forrester Research Inc.

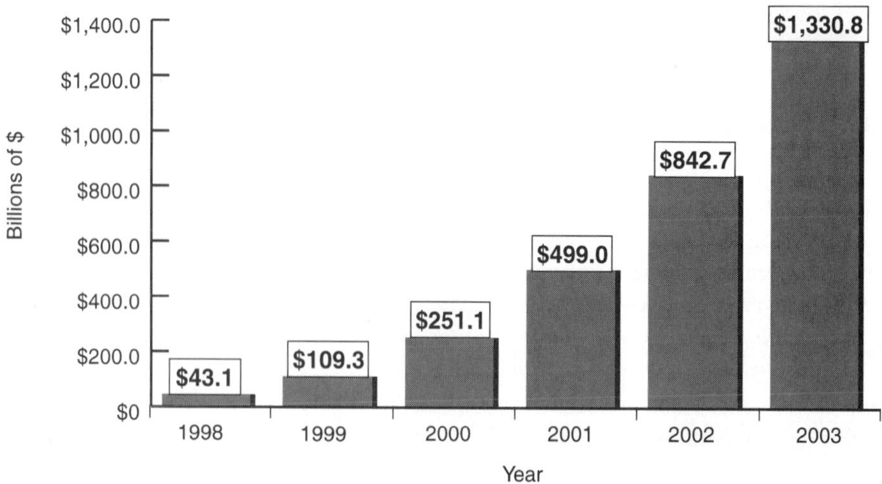

only one-third of these are actually selling on the Web).[33] Although most of them are not yet making a profit from their Web sites, the entrepreneurs behind these businesses know that they must establish a presence on the Web *now* if they are to reap its benefits in the future. These "netpreneurs" are using their Web sites to connect with their existing customers and, ultimately, to attract new ones.

The Chocolate Vault

"The 'Net has been a lifesaver for us," says Barb McCann, co-owner with her husband Jim of the Chocolate Vault, an old-fashioned candy company in Tecumseh, Michigan. Just a few years ago, the Chocolate Vault was struggling for survival, so much so that the McCanns were on the verge of closing the business. Flashier retail stores in nearby malls were outshining the McCann's downtown, small-town location. Although she had no background in technology, Barb decided to create a Web site for the Chocolate Vault in a last-ditch effort to increase sales and profits. It worked! Launched in 1997, the Web site ***<www.chocolatevault.com>*** *now accounts for one-third of the Chocolate Vault's total sales. Online sales are growing rapidly. "This has made all the difference to our business," says Barb. "The Web is bringing us customers from all over the country."*[34]

International Opportunities

No longer are small businesses limited to pursuing customers within their own borders. The shift to a global economy has opened the door to tremendous business opportunities for entrepreneurs willing to reach across the globe. Although the United States is an attractive market for entrepreneurs, approximately 95 percent of the world's population lives outside its borders. Changes such as the crumbling of the Berlin Wall, the collapse of communism, and the breaking down of trade barriers as a result of the European Community agreement have changed the world order and have opened much of that world market to entrepreneurs. Still, only 13 percent of small businesses are engaged in exporting; however, those small companies account for 20 percent of total exports.[35] International opportunities for small businesses will continue to grow rapidly in the twenty-first century.

Although going global can be fraught with dangers and problems, many entrepreneurs are discovering that selling their products and services in foreign markets is really not that difficult. Small companies that have expanded successfully into foreign markets tend to rely on the following strategies:

- Researching foreign markets thoroughly.
- Focusing on a single country initially.

- Utilizing government resources designed to help small companies establish an international presence.
- Forging alliances with local partners.

Goldenberg Candy Company

For example, Mindy and David Goldenberg, co-owners of the Goldenberg Candy Company, recently began exporting their product, Chew-ets, to global markets using connections they made with the help of the California Agricultural Department. The company's sales have climbed 10 percent since it started exporting. "Our export sales are growing, and they continue to offer great opportunities," says David.[36]

THE CULTURAL DIVERSITY OF ENTREPRENEURSHIP

5. Explain the cultural diversity of entrepreneurship.

As we have seen, virtually anyone has the potential to become an entrepreneur. Indeed, diversity is a hallmark of entrepreneurship. We now explore the diverse mix of people who make up the rich fabric of entrepreneurship.

Young Entrepreneurs

Young people are setting the pace in starting businesses. Disenchanted with their prospects in corporate America and willing to take a chance at controlling their own destinies, scores of young people are choosing entrepreneurship as their primary career path. About 30 percent of all entrepreneurs are age 30 or younger, making Generation X the most entrepreneurial generation in history! Members of this generation are responsible for 70 percent of all business start-ups.[37] There is no slowdown in sight as this generation flexes its entrepreneurial muscle. Recent surveys have found that 60 percent of 18- to 29-year-olds say they hope to launch their own businesses and that 69 percent of high school students have entrepreneurial aspirations.[38] Generation X might be more appropriately called "Generation E."

Even teenagers and preteens, those in the Millennium Generation (born after 1980), are interested in entrepreneurship. Young entrepreneur camps are popping up all around the country to teach youngsters how to launch and run a business, and a magazine, *Young Entrepreneurs,* is aimed squarely at these youthful business-building wannabes. Shawn Brennegman, 15, took a test to finish high school early so he could devote more time to running Shattered Paradigm, his computer graphics design company.[39] Because of young people such as Shawn, the future of entrepreneurship looks very bright.

Women Entrepreneurs

Despite years of legislative effort, women still face discrimination in the workforce. However, small business has been a leader in offering women opportunities for economic expression through employment and entrepreneurship. Increasing numbers of women are discovering that the best way to break the "glass ceiling" that prevents them from rising to the top of many organizations is to start their own companies. In fact, women are opening businesses at a rate about twice that of the national average.[40] Women entrepreneurs have even broken through the comic strip barrier. Blondie Bumstead, long a typical suburban housewife married to Dagwood, now owns her own catering business with her best friend and neighbor Tootsie Woodly!

Although the businesses women start tend to be smaller than those men start, their impact is anything but small. Women-owned companies employ more than 27.5 million workers, 25 percent of the nation's workforce! Women own about 38 percent of all businesses—some 9.1 million—in the United States (see Figure 1.6), a number that has more

FIGURE 1.6
Women-Owned Businesses
Source: National Foundation for Women Business Owners.

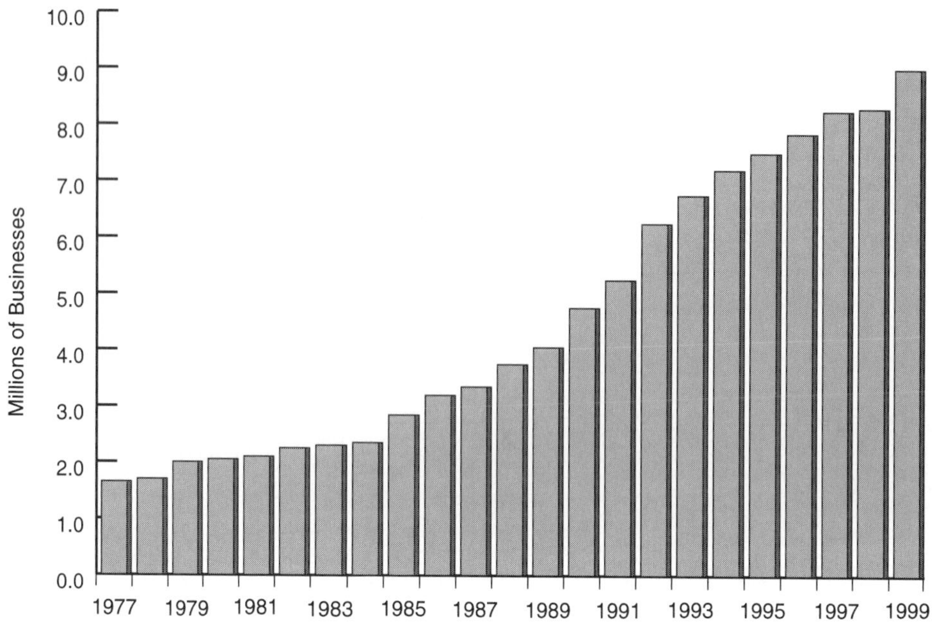

than doubled since 1987.[41] Sales revenue from women-owned companies tops $3.6 trillion.[42] Although their businesses tend to grow more slowly than those owned by men, women-owned businesses have a higher survival rate than U.S. businesses overall. One recent study found that their three-year survival rate was 72.2 percent, compared to 66.6 percent for all businesses.[43]

Although about 72 percent of women-owned businesses are concentrated in retailing and services (as are most businesses), female entrepreneurs are branching out rapidly into previously male-dominated industries. According to the National Foundation for Women Business Owners, the fastest-growing industries for women-owned companies are construction, wholesale trade, transportation, communication, agribusiness, and manufacturing.[44]

Phylway Construction Inc.

Phyllis A. Adams, founder of Phylway Construction Inc., started her highway and heavy construction company with less than $10,000 in savings and a used dump truck. She learned the basics of the construction industry from her father, who owned the general contracting company where Phyllis worked for 16 years, starting as a part-time receptionist at age 17. In 1992, she decided to strike out on her own in the construction business. Later that year, Phylway Construction was one of the companies called in to help clean up in the aftermath of Hurricane Andrew, and the company's reputation and sales soared. Phylway Construction's annual sales now exceed $14 million, and Adams was recently named Woman Entrepreneur of the Year by Entrepreneur *magazine.*[45]

Minority Enterprises

Another rapidly growing segment of the small business population are minority-owned businesses. Hispanics, Asians, and African Americans are the minority groups most likely to become entrepreneurs. Like women, minorities cite discrimination as a principal reason for their limited access to the world of entrepreneurship. Minority-owned businesses have come a long way in the past decade, however, and their success rate is climbing. Increasingly, minorities are finding ways to overcome the barriers to business ownership.

YOU BE THE CONSULTANT . . .

Just for the Fun of It!

Dell Computer Corporation has been on the *Fortune* 500 list of America's largest companies for years, and this giant of the direct computer sales industry rings up more than $18 billion in annual sales. Dell is a fierce competitor in the computer industry today, but the company's beginnings are quite humble. Michael Dell, who is the youngest person ever to head a *Fortune* 500 company, launched the business in 1984 from his dormitory room at the University of Texas with $1,000 he borrowed from his parents. His idea was and remains simple: Buy computer parts, assemble them to order, and sell them directly to customers. In his first year in business, the 19-year-old freshman sold $6 million worth of computers before deciding to take a hiatus from college. Within two years, he had 250 employees. Today Dell employs more than 23,000 workers, an indication of how rapidly his company has grown. Over its first eight years, the company grew at an annual rate of 87 percent per year; since 1992, its growth rate has averaged an astonishing 55 percent per year. Dell's stock price climbed by 26,900 percent during the decade of the 1990s alone!

Dell's business model has proved to be extremely successful because of its simplicity and because of his ability to remain focused on executing it efficiently. Dell is the proud owner of the shortest average inventory turnover in the industry—a mere seven days compared to 80 days or more at many of its competitors. That glowing statistic adds millions to the company's bottom line. Because inventory in the computer industry loses 1 percent of its value each week, reducing the amount of time inventory sits on a shelf greatly enhances a company's profitability. Part of the magic behind this impressive number lies in the fact that Dell builds computers only in response to a customer order (known as "mass customization"); the company does not build "standard" computers to place in inventory to be shipped once an order materializes. On average, it takes just four to five days for Dell to build and ship a customized computer, compared to 25 days for some competitors. Dell now builds computers on three continents and sells them all over the globe. Describing this dynamic entrepreneur's success, one analyst explains, "He's very nimble. His competitors are like Sumo wrestlers. Dell is more like a kick boxer."

Two reasons Dell kicks around so many competitors are the company's Web site and its approach to customer service. Dell introduced its Web site **<www.dell.com>** in 1996, allowing customers to specify *exactly* how they want their computers configured and to get an accurate final price. Customers loved the convenience; the Web site now brings in $10 million in sales every day! "The Internet is the ultimate form of the direct [sales] model," says Dell.

In 1987, Dell developed the industry's first on-site service program, which proved to be a major boost for sales. Until then, customers whose computers broke down had to take it back to the store where they had purchased it and hoped that someone there could fix it. With its on-site service program, Dell guaranteed that a Dell technician would come to its customers' homes or offices and repair the problem.

Despite revolutionizing the computer industry in several ways, Michael Dell is modest about his accomplishments. "At the root of it, I was probably just opportunistic," he says. "There was this business opportunity [coupled with] this product I really liked, and it all lined up together." He jokes about some of his most successful strategies that were born of necessity. "We started the company by building to the customer's order, [but] we didn't do it because we saw some massive paradigm in the future. We just didn't have any capital [to mass produce computers]!"

Michael Dell, now fourth on the *Forbes* "400 Richest Americans" list, has lost none of his entrepreneurial fervor. Recently, while speaking to an entrepreneurship class at the University of Texas, a student asked the young multibillionaire, "Why don't you just sell out, buy a boat, and sail off to the Caribbean?" Without hesitating, Dell responded, "Sailing's *boring*. Do you have any idea how much fun it is to run a billion-dollar company?"

1. What benefits has Michael Dell reaped from his entrepreneurial experience?
2. Use the World Wide Web to research the history of Dell Computer Corporation. Describe at least three strategies that have led to the company's success.
3. Which characteristics of the typical entrepreneur does Michael Dell exhibit?

Sources: Adapted from Richard Murphy, "Profile: Michael Dell," *Success,* January 1999, pp. 50–53; Michael A. Verespej, "Michael Dell's Magic," *Industry Week,* November 16, 1998, pp. 57–64; Andy Serwer, "Michael Dell Rocks," *Fortune,* May 11, 1998, pp. 59–70; Scott S. Smith, "Dell on . . ." *Entrepreneur,* April 1999, pp. 121–123.

FUBU

For instance, after several banks rejected their loan request, Daymond John, Alexander Martin, Keith Perrin, and Carl Brown refused to give up their plan to create an apparel company. To raise the capital they needed, John mortgaged his house and then converted part of it into a factory. The partners approached hometown friend, hip-hop star L.L. Cool J, who agreed to wear their fashions in his music videos, and sales took off. Today, FUBU (For Us, By Us) fashions are sold across the United States, generating sales of more than $200 million.[46]

A recent study by the Small Business Administration reported that the nation's 3.2 million minority-owned businesses generate $495 billion in annual revenues and employ almost 4 million workers.[47] The future is promising for this new generation of minority entrepreneurs, who are better educated, have more business experience, and are better prepared for business ownership than their predecessors.

Immigrant Entrepreneurs

The United States has always been a "melting pot" of diverse cultures, and many immigrants have been drawn to this nation because of its economic freedom. Unlike the unskilled "huddled masses" of the past, today's immigrants arrive with more education and experience. Although many of them come to the United States with few assets, their dedication and desire to succeed enable them to achieve their entrepreneurial dreams.

Autoweb.com Inc.

After a harrowing escape from their native Iran, brothers Frank and Payam Zamani landed in the United States with just $75 in their pockets. The Zamanis worked at various jobs while earning advanced college degrees, but their inspiration for a business came as a result of negative car-buying experiences. After buying eight clunkers, the brothers decided to use the World Wide Web to research a car purchase but found it to be of limited use. In 1995, they decided to create a Web site that would streamline the car-buying process, ***<www.autoweb.com>.*** *Within three years, their site had become the most visited automotive site on the Web. Today Autoweb.com counts more than 4,000 dealers in its network and tallies $700 million in auto sales per month!*[48]

Part-Time Entrepreneurs

Starting a part-time business is a popular gateway to entrepreneurship. Part-time entrepreneurs have the best of both worlds: They can ease into business for themselves without sacrificing the security of a steady paycheck and benefits. Approximately 15 million Americans are self-employed part-time. A major advantage of going into business part-time is the lower risk in case the venture flops. Many part-timers are "testing the entrepreneurial waters" to see whether their business ideas will work and whether they enjoy being self-employed. As they grow, many part-time enterprises absorb more of the entrepreneur's time until they become full-time businesses.

Accident Reconstruction Analysis

For more than a decade, Charles Manning Jr. ran a part-time business in an unusual niche: accident investigation, a skill he learned in the Air Force during the Korean War. Manning investigated the causes of everything from plane crashes and auto accidents to train derailments and medical accidents. In 1980, Manning's son, Charles III, convinced him to make Accident Reconstruction Analysis a full-time business. Their company has worked on high-profile cases such as the Challenger space shuttle disaster and the ValuJet explosion and generates annual revenues of $3.6 million.[49]

Home-Based Businesses

Home-based businesses are booming! Entrepreneurs operate 27.1 million businesses from their homes (a trend dubbed "HomeComing" by marketing experts), and their ranks are growing rapidly; on average, a new home-based business pops up every 11 seconds! Several factors make the home many entrepreneurs' first choice location:

- Operating a business from home keeps start-up and operating costs to a minimum.
- Home-based companies allow owners to maintain a flexible lifestyle and work style. Many home-based entrepreneurs relish being part of the "open-collar workforce."
- Technology, which is transforming many ordinary homes into "electronic cottages," allows entrepreneurs to run a variety of businesses from their homes.

Home-based companies generate $383 billion in revenues and create an estimated 8,219 new jobs each day. The average home-based entrepreneur works 61 hours a week and earns an income of just over $50,000.[50] Studies by Link Resources Corporation, a research and consulting firm, suggest that the success rate for home-based businesses is high: 85 percent of such businesses are still in operation after three years.[51]

In the past, home-based businesses tended to be rather unexciting cottage industries such as crafts or sewing. Today's home-based businesses are more diverse; modern home-based entrepreneurs are more likely to be running high-tech or service companies with millions of dollars in sales.

Digital Resource Providers

For example, Eric Schaberg and Derek Parnell found that home was the perfect location from which to start their computer programming and training company, Digital Resource Providers (DRP). At age 25, Schaberg and Parnell and their wives decided to rent a house in suburban Orlando that would serve as a low-cost headquarters for their fledgling business. "I always thought it would be neat to work from home," says Parnell. In its first full year of operation, DRP generated $100,000 in revenues and was growing rapidly. Two years later, the company was profitable enough to allow Schaberg and Parnell to earn $100,000 each. Not bad for a business operated from a suburban living room![52]

Table 1.2 offers 18 "rules" home-based entrepreneurs should follow to be successful.

Family Businesses

A **family-owned business** is one that includes two or more members of a family with financial control of the company. Family businesses are an integral part of our economy. Of the 23.3 million businesses in the United States, 90 percent are family owned and managed. These companies employ more than 50 million people, pay 65 percent of all wages, and generate 55 percent of the nation's GDP. Not all of them are small; one-third of the *Fortune* 500 companies are family businesses.[53]

family-owned business—*one that includes two or more members of a family with financial control of the company.*

"When it works right," says one writer, "nothing succeeds like a family firm. The roots run deep, embedded in family values. The flash of the fast buck is replaced with long-term plans. Tradition counts."[54] Despite their magnitude, family businesses face a major threat, a threat from within: management succession. Only 30 percent of family businesses survive to the second generation, and just 10 percent make it to the third generation. Business periodicals are full of stories describing bitter disputes among family members that have crippled or destroyed once thriving businesses.[55]

To avoid such senseless destruction of valuable assets, founders of family businesses should develop plans for management succession long before retirement looms before them.

Space Designs, Inc.

For example, Bob Baugh knew that his son Ken would take over the family business one day, but after his son earned an M.B.A., Baugh insisted that he work elsewhere first. "Experience with other companies is valuable," says Baugh. "It offers a different perspective." Five years later, Ken joined the family office furniture store and blossomed under his father's guidance. When the elder Baugh retired, Ken made a smooth transition into the top position at Space Designs, which has grown into a $50 million business under his leadership.[56]

TABLE 1.2

Follow These Rules for a Successful Home-Based Business.

Sources: Lynn Beresford, Janean Chun, Cynthia E. Griffin, Heather Page, and Debra Phillips, "Homeward Bound," Entrepreneur, *September 1995, pp. 116–118; Jenean Huber, "House Rules,"* Entrepreneur, *March 1993, pp. 89–95; Hal Morris, "Home-Based Businesses Need Extra Insurance,"* AARP Bulletin, *November 1994, p. 16; Stephanie N. Mehta, "What You Need,"* Wall Street Journal, *October 14, 1994, p. R10; Jeffery Zbar, "Home Free,"* Business Start-Ups, *June 1999, pp. 31–37.*

Rule 1. Do your homework. Much of a home-based business's potential for success depends on how much preparation an entrepreneur makes *before* ever opening for business. The library is an excellent source for research on customers, industries, competitors, and the like.

Rule 2. Find out what your zoning restrictions are. In some areas local zoning laws make running a business from home illegal. Avoid headaches by checking these laws first. You can always request a variance.

Rule 3. Choose the most efficient location for your office. About half of all home-based entrepreneurs operate out of spare bedrooms. The best way to determine the ideal office location is to examine the nature of your business and your clients. Avoid locating your business in your bedroom or your family room.

Rule 4. Focus your home-based business idea. Avoid the tendency to be "all things to all people." Most successful home-based businesses focus on a particular customer group or in some specialty.

Rule 5. Discuss your business rules with your family. Running a business from your home means you can spend more time with your family . . . and that your family can spend more time with you. Establish the rules for interruptions up front.

Rule 6. Select an appropriate business name. Your first marketing decision is your company's name, so make it a good one! Using your own name is convenient, but it's not likely to help you sell your product or service.

Rule 7. Buy the right equipment. Modern technology allows a home-based entrepreneur to give the appearance of any *Fortune* 500 company—but only if you buy the right equipment. A well-equipped home office should have a separate telephone line, a computer, a laser or inkjet printer, a fax machine (or board), a copier, a scanner, and an answering machine (or voice mail), but realize that you don't have to have everything from Day One.

Rule 8. Dress appropriately. Being an "open-collar worker" is one of the joys of working at home. But when you need to dress up (to meet a client, make a sale, meet your banker, close a deal), do it! Avoid the tendency to lounge around in your bathrobe all day.

Rule 9. Learn to deal with distractions. The best way to fend off the distractions of working at home is to create a business that truly interests you. Budget your time wisely. Your productivity determines your company's success.

Rule 10. Realize that your phone can be your best friend . . . or your worst enemy. As a home-based entrepreneur, you'll spend lots of time on the phone. Be sure you use it productively.

Rule 11. Be firm with friends and neighbors. Sometimes friends and neighbors get the mistaken impression that because you're at home, you're not working. If one drops by to chat while you're working, tactfully ask them to come back "after work."

Rule 12. Take advantage of tax breaks. Although a 1993 Supreme Court decision tightened considerably the standards for business deductions for an office at home, many home-based entrepreneurs still qualify for special tax deductions on everything from computers to cars. Check with your accountant.

Rule 13. Make sure you have adequate insurance coverage. Some homeowner's policies provide adequate coverage for business-related equipment, but many home-based entrepreneurs have inadequate coverage on their business assets. Ask your agent about a business owner's policy (BOP), which may cost as little as $300 to $500 per year.

Rule 14. Understand the special circumstances under which you can hire outside employees. Sometimes zoning laws allow in-home businesses, but they prohibit hiring employees. Check zoning laws carefully.

Rule 15. Be prepared if your business requires clients to come to your home. Dress appropriately. (No pajamas!) Make sure your office presents a professional image.

Rule 16. Get a post office box. With burglaries and robberies on the rise, you're better off using a "P.O. Box" address rather than your specific home address. Otherwise you may be inviting crime.

Rule 17. Network, network, network. Isolation can be a problem for home-based entrepreneurs, and one of the best ways to combat it is to network. It's also a great way to market your business.	
Rule 18. Be proud of your home-based business. Merely a decade ago there was a stigma attached to working from home. Today home-based entrepreneurs and their businesses command respect. Be proud of your company!	

TABLE 1.2
Follow These Rules for a Successful Home-Based Business. (Continued)

Copreneurs

copreneurs—*entrepreneurial couples who work together as co-owners of their businesses.*

Copreneurs are entrepreneurial couples who work together as co-owners of their businesses. Unlike the traditional mom and pop business (Pop as "boss" and Mom as "subordinate"), copreneurs "are creating a division of labor that is based on expertise as opposed to gender," says one expert.[57] Studies suggest that companies co-owned by spouses represent one of the fastest-growing business sectors, up by 90 percent from 1980.

Managing a small business with a spouse may appear to be a recipe for divorce, but most copreneurs say not. "There is nothing more exciting than nurturing a business and watching it grow with someone you love," says Marcia Sherrill, who, with her husband, William Kleinberg, runs Kleinberg Sherrill, a leather goods and accessories business.[58] Successful copreneurs learn to build the foundation for a successful working relationship before they ever launch their companies. Some of the characteristics they rely on include:

- an assessment of whether their personalities will mesh—or conflict—in a business setting.
- mutual respect for each other and one another's talents.
- compatible business and life goals—a common "vision."
- a view that they are full and equal partners, not a superior and a subordinate.
- complementary business skills that each acknowledges and appreciates and that lead to a unique business identity for each spouse.
- the ability to keep lines of communication open, talking and listening to each other.
- a clear division of roles and authority, ideally based on each partner's skills and abilities, to minimize conflict and power struggles.
- the ability to encourage each other and to "lift up" a disillusioned partner.
- separate work spaces that allow them to "escape" when the need arises.
- boundaries between their business life and their personal life.
- a sense of humor.
- an understanding that not every couple can work together.

Although copreneuring isn't for everyone, it works extremely well for many couples and often leads to successful businesses. "Both spouses are working for a common purpose

cathy® **by Cathy Guisewite**

but also focusing on their unique talents," says a family business counselor. "With all these skills put together, one plus one equals more than two."[59]

Christensen Designs

Before they launched Christensen Designs **<peeperpeople.com>,** *Ann and John Christensen developed a business plan to guide their entrepreneurial venture, which makes the Tree Top Peeper, a remote-controlled device that allows wildlife researchers to study the habits of endangered species. "We spent a lot of time talking about how we wanted to run the business," says John. "We also listed our talents: What can I do? What can she do? How can we put these things together?" Another integral part of the Christensens' success is their decision to separate their business responsibilities based on their abilities. Ann handles the sales and marketing functions; John is responsible for designing and manufacturing the product line.*[60]

Corporate Castoffs

Concentrating on shedding the excess bulk they took on during the 1970s and 1980s, U.S. corporations have been downsizing in an attempt to remain competitive. Throughout the 1990s, large companies reduced their employment roles by an estimated 6 million workers. One major corporation after another has announced layoffs—and not just among blue-collar workers. Companies are cutting back their executive ranks as well.

These "corporate castoffs" have become an important source of entrepreneurial activity. Some 20 percent of these discharged corporate managers have become entrepreneurs, and many of those left behind in corporate America would like to join them. A recent study by Accountemps found that nearly half of the executives surveyed believed their peers would take the entrepreneurial plunge—if they only had the money to do so. Four years before, just one-third of corporate executives were inclined to start their own companies.[61]

Many corporate castoffs are deciding that the best defense against future job insecurity is an entrepreneurial offense.

Lizzy's Homemade Ice Cream

Digital Equipment Corporation, which has shed more than 76,000 employees in recent years, has a reputation for creating entrepreneurs. Former Digital employees have launched a multitude of businesses, ranging from restaurants and wine-making to golf club design and fishing lodges. These castoffs-turned-entrepreneurs have taken the lessons they learned in corporate America and have applied them successfully in their own companies. Nick Pappas, who worked for Digital for 27 years, started Lizzy's Homemade Ice Cream in Waltham, Massachusetts, and has watched his business grow rapidly. He credits much of his success to the planning and management skills he learned at Digital.[62]

Corporate Dropouts

The dramatic downsizing of corporate America has created another effect among the employees left after restructuring: a trust gap. The result of this trust gap is a growing number of dropouts from the corporate structure who then become entrepreneurs. Although their workdays may grow longer and their incomes may shrink, those who strike out on their own often find their work more rewarding and more satisfying because they are doing what they want. When one dropout left his corporate post, he invited his former coworkers to a bonfire in the parking lot—fueled by a pile of his expensive business suits! He happily passed out marshmallows to everyone who came. Today he and his wife run an artists' gallery in California's wine country.[63]

Because they have college degrees, a working knowledge of business, and years of management experience, both corporate dropouts and castoffs may ultimately increase the small business survival rate. A recent survey by Richard O'Sullivan found that 64 percent of people starting businesses have some college education, and 16 percent have advanced

YOU BE THE CONSULTANT . . .

In Search of the Perfect Dog Biscuit

Thanks to Dan Dye and Mark Beckloff, America's canines have a place all their own to go to satisfy a yearning for a healthy snack: Three Dog Bakery, a chain of retail stores that features freshly baked, all-natural dog treats. As dog lovers, Dye and Beckloff were astounded that all of the off-the-shelf dog treats contained so many additives. Dye and Beckloff also noticed that no companies were offering healthy alternative treats for dogs, and they sensed a business opportunity. The two decided to work together to create the world's best fresh-baked dog biscuits. They spent years studying and researching their idea. They discovered that although most people are content to buy standard dog food products off the shelves of major retail stores and supermarkets, a segment of dog owners wanted only the best for their pets. They also learned that worldwide people spend more than $9 billion per year on dog food, compared to $6 billion on baby food!

Over the next three years, Dye and Beckloff spent their evenings and weekends testing and developing their dog biscuit recipes in Dye's kitchen. They interviewed veterinarians about canine nutrition and tested hundreds of recipe variations that included everything from garlic to spinach. They used their three dogs, Dottie, Gracie, and Sarah (who were the inspiration for their company's name), as taste-testers as they searched for the perfect dog biscuit. Before long, their neighbors' dogs also joined the taste-testing staff, and it became obvious to everyone that Dye and Beckloff had a hit product on their hands. The partners decided to move their operation out of Dye's kitchen, but because they were short on capital, they ended up in the low-rent district of Kansas City.

Not only did Dye and Beckloff achieve their goal of creating the world's greatest dog treat, they also created a highly successful company. The business has paid off for Dye and Beckloff, both of whom left steady jobs to launch Three Dog Bakery. The $8,000 each partner borrowed from his retirement plan to invest in the business has multiplied many times over. Both entrepreneurs now have a net worth that exceeds $5 million. Three Dog Bakery has 30 retail locations across the country and is looking to expand worldwide. The company also sells gourmet treats such as Pupcakes®, Mutt Muffins®, and Great Danish® directly to customers through its DOGalog® as well as through its Web site, **<www.threedog.com>.** Three Dog Bakery is now the largest maker of gourmet dog biscuits in the world and has been featured in various media, including *Forbes* magazine, *The Today Show, CNN,* and *The Oprah Winfrey Show* (where host Oprah Winfrey tasted a biscuit and declared it to be quite tasty).

1. What factors have contributed to the success that Dye and Beckloff have had with Three Dog Bakery?
2. Which characteristics of the entrepreneurial profile do Dye and Beckloff exhibit?

Sources: Adapted from Mary Beth Grover, "Go Ahead: Buy the Dream," *Forbes,* June 15, 1998, pp. 146–152; Lori Francisco, "Bone Appétit," *Business Start-Ups,* May 1999, p. 66; American Marketing Association, **<ama-stl.org/conf99/speaker1.shtml>.** Three Dog Bakery, **<www.threedog.com/company/sstory.html>.**

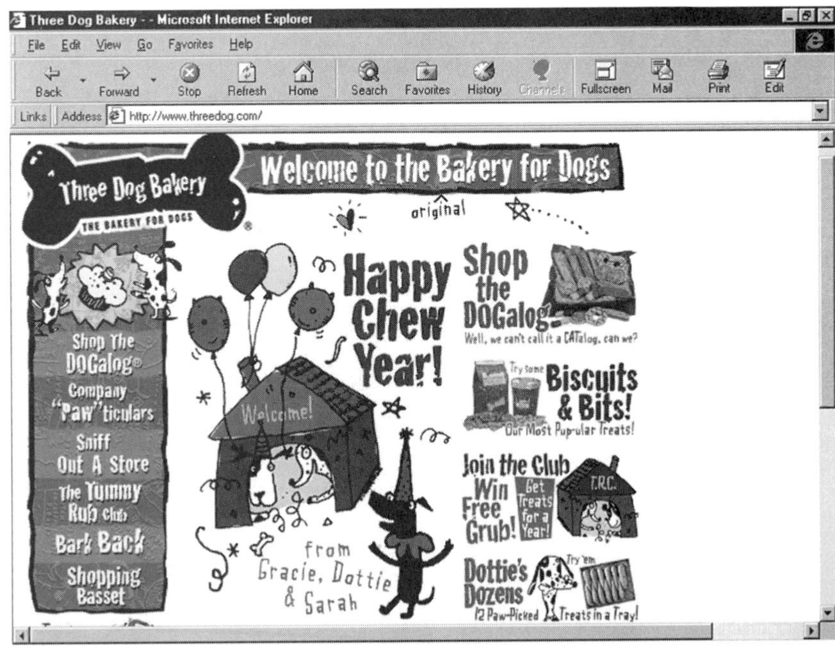

degrees.[64] Better-trained, more experienced entrepreneurs are less likely to fail. The National Federation of Independent Businesses reports that 77 percent of new companies formed since the mid-1980s were still in operation three years later.[65]

6. Describe the important role small businesses play in our nation's economy.

THE POWER OF "SMALL" BUSINESS

small business—*one that employs fewer than 100 people.*

Of the 23.3 million businesses in the United States today, approximately 23.1 million, or 99 percent, can be considered "small." Although there is no universal definition of a small business (the U.S. Small Business Administration has more than 800 definitions of a small business based on industry categories), a common delineation of a **small business** is one that employs fewer than 100 people. They thrive in virtually every industry, although the majority of small companies are concentrated in the service and retail industries (see Figure 1.7). Their contributions to the economy are as numerous as the businesses themselves. For example, small companies employ 53 percent of the nation's private sector workforce, even though they possess less than one-fourth of the total business assets. Almost 90 percent of small businesses employ fewer than 20 workers.[66] Because they are primarily labor intensive, small businesses actually create more jobs than do big businesses. In fact, small companies have created 85 percent of all the more than 12 million net new jobs in the U.S. economy since the early 1990s.[67]

gazelles—*small companies that are growing at 20 percent or more per year with at least $100,000 in annual sales.*

David Birch, president of the research firm Cognetics, says that the ability to create jobs is not distributed evenly across the small business sector, however. His research shows that just 3 percent of these small companies created 70 percent of the new jobs, and they did so across all industry sectors, not just in "hot" industries. Birch calls these job-creating small companies **"gazelles,"** those growing at 20 percent or more per year with at least $100,000 in annual sales. His research also identified "mice," small companies that never grow much

FIGURE 1.7
A Profile of Small Businesses by Industry
Source: Small Business Administration.

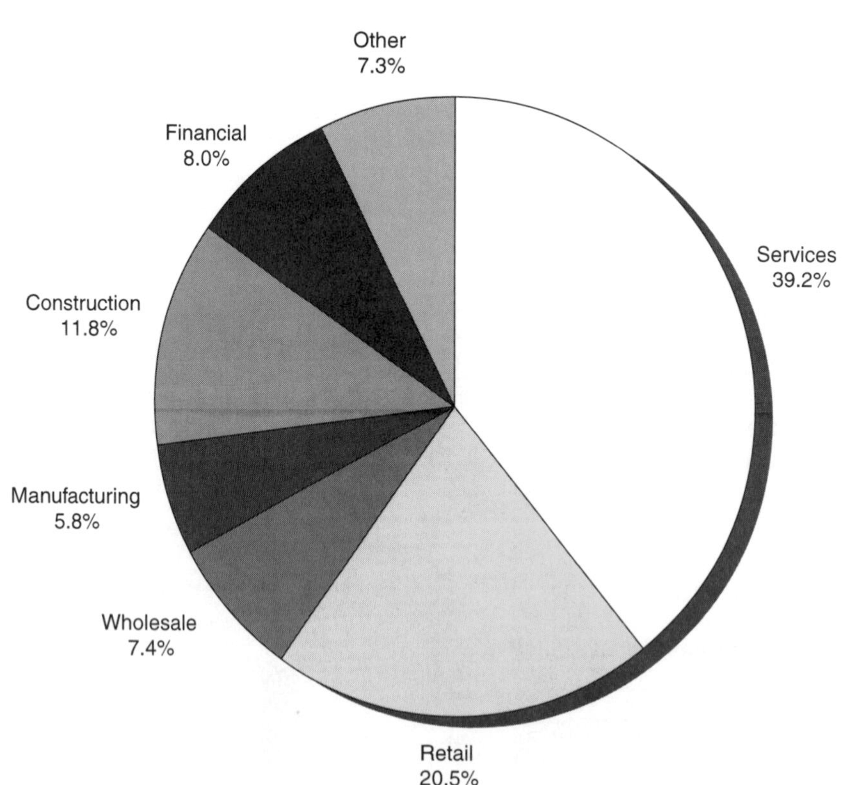

Source: By permission of Johnny Hart and Creators Syndicate, Inc.

and don't create many jobs. The majority of small companies are "mice." Birch tabbed the country's largest job-shedding businesses "elephants," who continued to lose jobs throughout the 1990s.[68]

Not only do small companies lead the way in creating jobs, but they also bear the brunt of training workers for them. A recent study by the Small Business Administration concluded that small businesses are the leaders in offering training and advancement opportunities to workers. Small companies offer more general skills instruction and training than large ones, and their employees receive more benefits from the training than do those in larger firms. Although their training programs tend to be informal, in-house, and on-the-job, small companies teach employees valuable skills, from written communication to computer literacy.[69]

Small businesses also produce 51 percent of the country's private GDP and account for 47 percent of business sales.[70] Overall, small firms provide directly or indirectly the livelihoods of more than 100 million Americans. Research conducted for the National Science Foundation concluded that small firms create four times more innovations per research and development (R&D) dollar than medium-sized firms and 24 times as many as large companies. In another study of the most important technological innovations introduced into the U.S. market, researchers found that, on average, smaller companies contributed 20 percent more of these innovations per employee than did large companies.[71] Many important inventions trace their roots to an entrepreneur, including the zipper, FM radio, the laser, air conditioning, the escalator, the light bulb, the personal computer, and the automatic transmission. The trend of small business success seems likely to continue. Currently, between 800,000 and 900,000 new companies with employees come into existence each year.

THE NINE DEADLY MISTAKES OF ENTREPRENEURSHIP

7. Describe the nine deadly mistakes of entrepreneurship and explain how to avoid them.

Because of their limited resources, inexperienced management, and lack of financial stability, small businesses suffer a mortality rate significantly higher than that of larger, established businesses. Figure 1.8 illustrates the small business survival rate over a 10-year period. Exploring the circumstances surrounding business failure may help you avoid it.

FIGURE 1.8
The Small Business Survival Rate
Source: NFIB Foundation/Visa Business Card Primer.

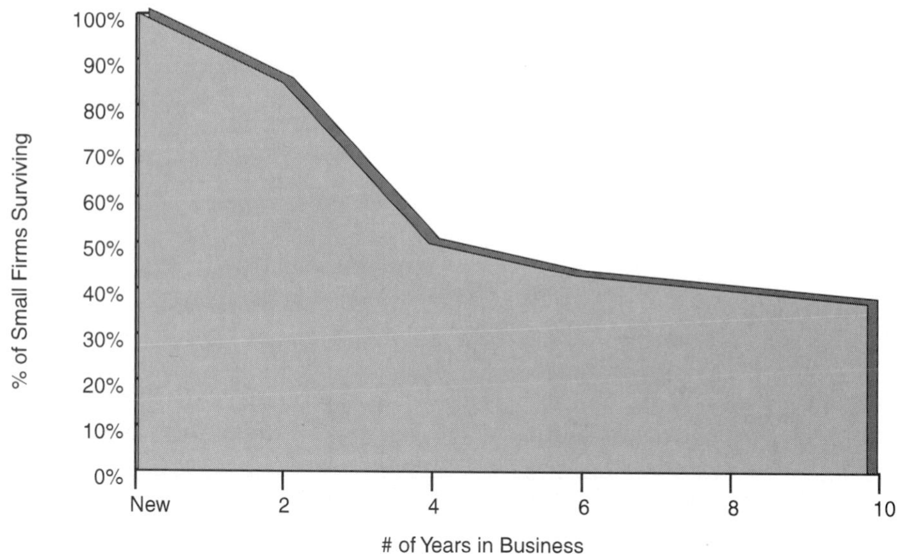

Management Incompetence

In most small businesses, poor management is the primary cause of business failure. Sometimes the manager of a small business does not have the capacity to operate it successfully. The owner lacks the leadership ability and knowledge necessary to make the business work. Many managers simply do not have what it takes to run a small enterprise. "What kills companies usually has less to do with insufficient money, talent, or information than with something more basic: a shortage of good judgment and understanding at the very top," says one business researcher.[72]

Lack of Experience

Small business managers need to have experience in the field they want to enter. For example, if a person wants to open a retail clothing business, she should first work in a retail clothing store. This will provide practical experience as well as knowledge about the nature of the business, which can spell the difference between failure and success.

Example

One West Coast entrepreneur had always wanted to own a restaurant, but he had no experience in the restaurant business. He later admitted that he thought that running a restaurant consisted primarily of dressing up in black tie, greeting his regular customers at the door, and showing them to his best tables. He invested $150,000 of his own money and found a partner to put up more capital and to help manage the restaurant. They opened and immediately ran into trouble because they knew nothing about running a restaurant. Eventually the restaurant closed, and the partners lost their original investments, their homes, and their cars; they also spent the next several years paying off back taxes.[73]

Ideally, a prospective entrepreneur should have adequate technical ability (a working knowledge of the physical operations of the business and sufficient conceptual ability); the power to visualize, coordinate, and integrate the various operations of the business into a synergistic whole; and the skill to manage the people in the organization and motivate them to higher levels of performance.

Poor Financial Control

Sound management is the key to a small company's success, and effective managers realize that any successful business venture requires proper financial control. The margin for error in managing finances is especially small for most small businesses. Two financial pitfalls are common in small business: undercapitalization and lax customer credit policies. Many small business owners make the mistake of beginning their businesses on a "shoestring," which is a fatal error. Entrepreneurs tend to be overly optimistic and often misjudge the financial requirements of going into business. As a result, they start off undercapitalized and can never seem to catch up financially as their companies consume increasing amounts of cash to fuel their growth.

The pressure for a small business to sell on credit is intense. Some managers see an opportunity to gain a competitive edge over rivals by granting credit; others feel forced to keep up with competitors who already offer their customers credit sales. Whatever the case, the small business owner must control credit sales carefully because failure to do so can devastate a small company's financial health. Poor credit and collection practices are common to many small business bankruptcies.

Failure to Develop a Strategic Plan

Too many small business managers neglect the process of strategic planning because they think that it is something that only benefits large companies. "I don't have the time" or "We're too small to develop a strategic plan," they rationalize. Failure to plan, however, usually results in failure to survive. Without a clearly defined strategy, a business has no sustainable basis for creating and maintaining a competitive edge in the marketplace. Building a strategic plan forces an entrepreneur to assess *realistically* the proposed business's potential. Is it something customers are willing and able to purchase? Who are the target customers? How will the business attract and keep those customers? What is the company's basis for serving customers' needs better than existing companies? We will explore these and other vital issues in Chapter 3, "Strategic Management and the Entrepreneur."

Uncontrolled Growth

Growth is a natural, healthy, and desirable part of any business enterprise, but it must be planned and controlled. Management expert Peter Drucker says that start-up companies can expect to outgrow their capital bases each time sales increase 40 to 50 percent.[74] Ideally, expansion should be financed by retained earnings or by capital contributions from the owner, but most businesses wind up borrowing at least a portion of the capital investment.

Expansion usually requires major changes in organizational structure, business practices such as inventory and financial control procedures, personnel assignments, and other areas. But the most important change occurs in managerial expertise. As the business increases in size and complexity, problems increase in magnitude, and the entrepreneur must learn to deal with them. Sometimes entrepreneurs encourage rapid growth, only to have the business outstrip their ability to manage it.

Buckeye Beans & Herbs

Jill and Doug Smith, co-owners of Buckeye Beans & Herbs, "got a hangover" when their specialty food company began growing rapidly. Sales were climbing by 50 percent a year, but profit margins were shrinking. To save their business, the Smiths curbed sales growth, eliminated customers that were cutting into profit margins (many of whom were large chain stores), and hired a chief financial officer. Their efforts at refocusing have their company back on track.[75]

Poor Location

For any business, choosing the right location is partly an art—and partly a science. Too often, business locations are selected without proper study, investigation, and planning. Some beginning owners choose a particular location just because they noticed a vacant building. But the location question is much too critical to leave to chance. Especially for retailers, the lifeblood of the business—sales—is influenced heavily by choice of location.

Bertucci's

Joey Crugnale created a hit pizza chain in the Boston area when he launched Bertucci's in 1981. Customers flocked to the restaurants, where they could see and smell their pizzas cooking in wood-burning ovens. Attempting to build on his success in Boston, Crugnale decided to open Bertucci's in locations in Chicago and Atlanta. Unfortunately, the company had no name recognition in either city, and sales were dismal, forcing Crugnale to close both locations. "You think you're Superman," explains Crugnale. "You do well in one market, so you assume you'll be a hit everywhere."[76]

Improper Inventory Control

Normally, the largest investment the small business manager must make is in inventory, yet inventory control is one of the most neglected managerial responsibilities. Insufficient inventory levels result in shortages and stockouts, causing customers to become disillusioned and leave. A more common situation is that the manager has not only too much inventory but also too much of the *wrong type* of inventory. Many small firms have an excessive amount of cash tied up in an accumulation of useless inventory. We will discuss both purchasing and inventory control techniques in Chapter 12.

Incorrect Pricing

Establishing prices that will generate the necessary profits means that business owners must understand how much it costs to make, market, and deliver their products and services. Too often, entrepreneurs simply charge what competitors charge or base their prices on some vague idea of "selling the best product at the lowest price," both of which are dangerous. Small business owners usually underprice their products and services.

Inability to Make the Entrepreneurial Transition

Making it over the "entrepreneurial start-up hump" is no guarantee of business success. After the start-up, growth usually requires a radically different style of management. The very abilities that make an entrepreneur successful often lead to managerial ineffectiveness. Growth requires entrepreneurs to delegate authority and to relinquish hands-on control of daily operations—something many entrepreneurs simply can't do. Growth pushes them into areas in which they are not capable, yet they continue to make decisions rather than involve others.

Table 1.3 explains some of the most common symptoms of these nine deadly mistakes.

8. Put failure into the proper perspective.

PUTTING FAILURE INTO PERSPECTIVE

Because they are building businesses in an environment filled with uncertainty and shaped by rapid change, entrepreneurs recognize that failure is likely to be part of their lives, but they are not paralyzed by that fear. "The excitement of building a new business from scratch is greater than the fear of failure," says one entrepreneur who failed in business several times before actually succeeding.[77] Entrepreneurs use their failures as a rallying point and as a means of refocusing their business ventures for success. They see failure for what it

TABLE 1.3
Symptoms of the Nine Deadly Mistakes of Entrepreneurship

Entrepreneurs whose businesses fail usually can look back on their experiences and see what they did wrong, vowing never to make the same mistake again. If you find yourself making any of the following statements as you launch your business, look out! You may become a victim of one of the nine deadly mistakes of entrepreneurship.

"We've got a great product (or service)! It will sell itself." Don't get so caught up in your product or service that you forget to evaluate whether real, live customers are willing and able to pay for it. Oh . . . and no product or service has ever "sold itself."

"With a market this big, we only need a tiny share of it to become rich." Entrepreneurs tend to be overly optimistic in their sales, profits, and cash flow estimates, especially in the beginning. Most don't realize until they get into business how tough it really is to capture even a tiny share of the market.

"Strategic plan?! We don't need a strategic plan. That's only for big corporations." One of the quickest and surest paths to failure is neglecting to build a strategic plan that defines some point of distinction for your company. A plan helps you focus on what you can do for your customers that your competitors cannot.

"What a great business idea! It's cheap, easy to start, and it's the current rage." Because a business idea is so cheap and easy to start does not necessarily make it attractive. Too many entrepreneurs get clobbered in such businesses once the market matures and the competition gets stiff or the fad passes.

"We may not know what we're doing yet, but we've got enough capital to last us until we do. We'll figure it out as we go." Everything—especially launching a business—takes longer and costs more than you think. Experienced entrepreneurs call it "the rule of two and three": Start-ups take either twice as long or need three times as much money (or both) to get off the ground as the founders forecast. Plan accordingly.

"Our forecast shows that we'll be making profits within three months, and that's very conservative . . . really." Everyone expects entrepreneurs to be optimistic about their ventures' future, but you have to temper your optimism with reality. Launching a business on the basis of one set of forecasts is asking for trouble. Make sure you develop at least three sets of forecasts—pessimistic, most likely, and optimistic—and have contingency plans for all three.

"It's a good thing that we've got enough capital to last us the few months until we hit our breakeven point." Attracting adequate start-up financing is essential to launching your business, but you also have to have access to *continuing* sources of funding. Growing businesses consume cash, and fast-growing businesses consume cash even faster. Don't become a victim of your own success; make sure you establish reliable sources of capital once your business is up and running.

"We'll make it easy for customers to buy from us. We'll extend credit to almost anyone to make a sale." One of the shortest routes to cash flow problems is failing to manage customer credit. It's easy to make a sale, but remember: Sales don't count unless you actually collect the payments from them. Watch for slow-paying customers.

"We're in the big time now. Our largest customer is [insert name of large customer here]." Landing a big customer is great, but it's dangerous to become overly dependent on a single customer for most of your sales. What happens if the customer decides to squeeze you for price concessions or to go to a competitor?

"Let's have our annual meeting in the Cayman Islands. We're the only 'stockholders,' and, besides, we deserve it. We've worked hard." Avoid the tendency to drain cash out of your business unnecessarily. A good rule of thumb: Don't start your business unless you have enough savings to support yourself (without taking cash from it) until the business breaks even.

"Let's go with this location. I know it's 'off the beaten path,' but it's so much cheaper!" For some businesses, choice of location is not a crucial issue. However, if your company relies on customers coming into your place of business to make sales, do not settle for the cheapest location. There's a reason such places are cheap! It's better to pay a higher price for a location that produces adequate sales volume.

TABLE 1.3
Symptoms of the Nine Deadly Mistakes of Entrepreneurship (Continued)

"Computer?! I don't know anything about computers. A legal pad and an adding machine are all I need to manage my business!" These days almost any business—no matter how small—can benefit from a computer. First, find the software that will help you maintain control over your business; then, buy the computer that will run it. Don't forget to budget both time and money for training and support.

"We're so small here. Everybody knows what our goals and objectives are." Just because a business is small doesn't necessarily mean that everyone who works there understands where you are trying to take the company. Do not assume that people will read your mind concerning your company's mission, goals, and objectives. You must communicate your vision for the business to everyone involved in it.

"This business is so easy it can run itself." Don't fool yourself. The only place a business will run itself is downhill! You must manage your company, and one of the most important jobs you have as leader is to prioritize your business's objectives.

"Of course our customers are satisfied! I never hear them complain." Most customers never complain about poor service or bad quality. They simply refuse to do business with you again. More often than not, the service and level of "personal treatment" that customers receive is what allows many small businesses to gain an edge over their larger rivals. Unfortunately, it's also one of the most overlooked aspects of a business. Set up a system to get regular feedback from your customers.

"What do you mean we're out of cash? We've been making a profit for months now, and sales are growing." Don't confuse cash and profits. You cannot spend profits—just cash. Many businesses fail because their founders mistakenly assume that if profits are rising, so is the company's cash balance. To be successful, you must manage both profits and cash!

Sources: Adapted from Frederick J. Beste III, "Avoiding the Traps Set for Small Firms," Nation's Business, *January 1999, p. 10; Mel Mandell, "Fifteen Start-Up Mistakes,"* Business Start-Ups, *December 1995, p. 22; Kenneth Labich, "Why Companies Fail,"* Fortune, *November 14, 1994, pp. 52–68; Sharon Nelton, "Ten Key Threats to Success,"* Nation's Business, *June 1992, pp. 22–30; Robert J. Cook, "Famous Last Words,"* Entrepreneur, *June 1994, pp. 122–128.*

really is: an opportunity to learn what does not work! Successful entrepreneurs have the attitude that failures are simply stepping-stones along the path to success. "Failure is part of the process," says Jason Olim, who at age 23 founded the online music store CDNow with his twin brother Matthew. "Mistakes are the bricks with which you build businesses."[78]

Failure is a natural part of the creative process. The only people who never fail are those who never do anything or never attempt anything new. Baseball fans know that Babe Ruth held the record for career home runs (714) for many years, but how many know that he also held the record for strikeouts (1,330)? Successful entrepreneurs know that hitting an entrepreneurial home run requires a few strikeouts along the way, and they are willing to accept them. Failure is an inevitable part of being an entrepreneur. "Everybody who is successful has had failure," says Sandy Weinberg, head of Muhlenberg College's Institute for Entrepreneurship. "And if they don't get back on the horse, they're not real entrepreneurs."[79]

One hallmark of successful entrepreneurs is the ability to fail *intelligently,* learning why they failed so that they can avoid making the same mistake again. They know that business success does not depend on their ability to avoid making mistakes but to be open to the lessons each mistake teaches. They learn from their failures and use them as fuel to push themselves closer to their ultimate target. Entrepreneurs are less worried about what they might lose if they try something and fail than about what they might lose if they fail to try.

Entrepreneurial success requires both persistence and resilience, the ability to bounce back from failure. Thomas Edison discovered about 1,800 ways *not* to build a light bulb before hitting upon a design that worked. Walt Disney was fired from a newspaper job

YOU BE THE CONSULTANT . . .

If at First You Don't Succeed, So What?

Some of the world's greatest entrepreneurs failed (some of them many times) before they finally succeeded. Henry Ford's first business, The Detroit Automobile Company, failed less than two years after Ford and his partners started it. Ford's second auto company also failed, but his third attempt in the new automobile business was, of course, a huge success. The Ford Motor Company (which is still controlled by the Ford family) is a major player in the automotive industry and is one of the largest companies in the world.

In post–World War II Japan, Masaru Ibuka and Akio Morita formed a partnership to produce an automatic rice cooker. Unfortunately, their machine burned the rice and was a flop. Their company sold just 100 cookers. Ibuka and Morita refused to give up, however, and created another company to build an inexpensive tape recorder that they sold to schools. Their tape recorder proved to be successful and the company eventually became the consumer electronics giant Sony Corporation.

Rick Rosenfield and Larry Flax wrote a screenplay that never sold, started an Italian restaurant that went bankrupt, and developed a mobile skateboard park that quickly flopped. Then, in 1984, they tried the restaurant business again, launched the California Pizza Kitchen, and struck pay dirt! The California Pizza Kitchen is now a successful national chain.

Gail Borden (1801–1874) also knew about failure because he had a great deal of experience with it. One of his first inventions, the Terraqueous Wagon, which was designed to travel on both land and water, sank on its first trial run. Several years later, returning to the United States on a steamer from London, Borden saw four babies die from tainted milk. Afterwards, he set out to make milk safer for human consumption. He knew that the key was to remove the water from milk, but the challenge was to do so without affecting its taste. For two years, he worked without success, always ending up with scorched milk. Ultimately Borden developed a vacuum condensation process that successfully removed the water from milk without adversely affecting its flavor. After three unsuccessful attempts, Borden finally won a patent for his process and set up a manufacturing plant. It failed. Undaunted, Borden convinced Jeremiah Milbank to invest in a new milk-processing venture, which was successful. The New York Condensed Milk Company supplied much needed nourishment to troops during the Civil War before becoming a staple in most American households. Today Borden Inc. is a multibillion-dollar conglomerate that still manufactures condensed milk using the same process that Borden developed more than 100 years ago. When he died in 1874, Gail Borden was buried beneath a tombstone that read, "I tried and failed; I tried again and succeeded."

1. Do these entrepreneurs exhibit the entrepreneurial spirit? If so, how?
2. How do these entrepreneurs view failure? Is their view typical of most entrepreneurs?

Sources: Adapted from Jeffrey Shuman and David Rottenberg, "Famous Failures," *Business Start-Ups,* February 1999, pp. 32–33; Francis Huffman, A Dairy Tale," *Entrepreneur,* August 1993, p. 182; Bob Gatty, "Building on Failure," *Nation's Business,* April 1987, pp. 50–51.

because, according to his boss, he "lacked ideas." Disney also went bankrupt several times before he created Disneyland.

HOW TO AVOID THE PITFALLS

9. Explain how entrepreneurs can avoid becoming another failure statistic.

We have seen the most common reasons behind many small business failures. Now we must examine the ways to avoid becoming another failure statistic and gain insight into what makes a successful business. The suggestions for success follow naturally from the causes of business failure.

Know Your Business in Depth

We have already emphasized the need for the right type of experience in the business you plan to start. Get the best education in your business area you possibly can *before* you set out on your own. Read everything you can—trade journals, business periodicals, books—

relating to your industry. Personal contact with suppliers, customers, trade associations, and others in the same industry is another excellent way to get that knowledge.

Executive Temporaries

Before she launched Executive Temporaries, Suzanne Clifton contacted other entrepreneurs in the temporary personnel services business (far enough away from her home base to avoid competitors) to find out "what it takes to operate this kind of business." She picked up many valuable tips and identified the key factors required for success. Today her company has achieved sales exceeding $4 million.[80]

Successful entrepreneurs are like sponges, soaking up as much knowledge as they can from a variety of sources.

Develop a Solid Business Plan

For any entrepreneur, a well-written business plan is a crucial ingredient in preparing for business success. Without a sound business plan, a firm merely drifts along without any real direction. Yet entrepreneurs, who tend to be people of action, too often jump right into a business venture without taking time to prepare a written plan outlining the essence of the business. "Most entrepreneurs don't have a solid business plan," says one business owner. "But a thorough business plan and timely financial information are critical. They help you make the important decisions about your business; you constantly have to monitor what you're doing against your plan."[81]

A business plan allows entrepreneurs to replace sometimes faulty assumptions with facts before making the decision to go into business.

Willowbee & Kent Travel Company

After graduating from college, Julie and Craig Poteet spent five years researching their business idea and preparing a business plan. They attended a wide array of events, from travel conventions to luggage trade shows, before they were ready to open Willowbee & Kent Travel Company. Their extensive research and thorough business plan helped them refine their concept for a travel store into a one-of-a-kind combination travel agency and travel superstore. Customers at Willowbee & Kent can sip a cup of espresso while they use interactive kiosks to take virtual trips to practically anywhere in the world or flip through travel guides before planning a trip with one of the company's travel consultants. The Poteets' planning is paying off; after just two years, Willowbee & Kent's sales topped $3 million.[82]

We will discuss the process of developing a business plan in Chapter 10, "Crafting a Winning Business Plan."

Manage Financial Resources

The best defense against financial problems is developing a practical information system and then using this information to make business decisions. No entrepreneur can maintain control over a business unless she is able to judge its financial health.

The first step in managing financial resources effectively is to have adequate start-up capital. Too many entrepreneurs begin their businesses with too little capital. One experienced business owner advises, "Estimate how much capital you need to get the business going and then double that figure." His point is well taken; it almost always costs more to launch a business than any entrepreneur expects.

The most valuable financial resource to any small business is *cash*. Although earning a profit is essential to its long-term survival, a business must have an adequate supply of cash to pay its bills and obligations. Some entrepreneurs count on growing sales to supply their company's cash needs, but it almost never happens. Growing companies usually consume more cash than they generate, and the faster they grow, the more cash they gobble up! We will discuss cash management techniques in Chapter 8, "Managing Cash Flow."

Understand Financial Statements

Every business owner must depend on records and financial statements to know the condition of her business. All too often entrepreneurs use these only for tax purposes and not as vital management control devices. To truly understand what is going on in the business, an owner must have at least a basic understanding of accounting and finance.

When analyzed and interpreted properly, these financial statements are reliable indicators of a small firm's health. They can be quite helpful in signaling potential problems. For example, declining sales, slipping profits, rising debt, and deteriorating working capital are all symptoms of potentially lethal problems that require immediate attention. We will discuss financial statement analysis in Chapter 9, "Creating a Successful Financial Plan."

Learn to Manage People Effectively

No matter what kind of business you launch, you must learn to manage people. Every business depends on a foundation of well-trained, motivated employees. No business owner can do everything alone. The people an entrepreneur hires ultimately determine the heights to which the company can climb—or the depths to which it can plunge. Attracting and retaining a corps of quality employees is no easy task, however. It remains a challenge for every small business owner. "In the end, your most dominant sustainable resource is the quality of the people you have," says one small business expert.[83] We will discuss the techniques of managing and motivating people effectively in Chapter 14, "Building and Leading a Successful Team."

Keep in Tune with Yourself

"Starting a business is like running a marathon. If you're not physically and mentally in shape, you'd better do something else," says one business consultant.[84] Your business's success will depend on your constant presence and attention, so it is critical to monitor your health closely. Stress is a primary problem, especially if it is not kept in check.

Successful entrepreneurs recognize that their most valuable asset is their time, and they learn to manage it effectively to make themselves and their companies more productive. None of this, of course, is possible without passion—passion for their businesses, their products or services, their customers, and their communities. Passion is what enables a failed entrepreneur to get back up, try again, and make it to the top.

CHAPTER SUMMARY

1. Define the role of the entrepreneur in business in the United States and around the world.

   Record numbers of people have launched companies over the past decade. The entrepreneurship boom is not limited to the United States; many nations across the globe are seeing similar growth in their small business sectors. A variety of competitive, economic, and demographic shifts have created a world in which "small is beautiful." Capitalist societies depend on entrepreneurs to provide the drive and risk taking necessary for the system to supply people with the goods and services they need.

2. Describe the entrepreneurial profile and evaluate your potential as an entrepreneur.

   Entrepreneurs have some common characteristics, including a desire for responsibility, a preference for moderate risk, confidence in their ability to succeed, a desire for immediate feedback, a high energy level, a future orientation, a skill at organizing, and a value of achievement over money. In a phrase, they are tenacious high achievers.

3-A. Describe the benefits of entrepreneurship.

   Driven by these personal characteristics, entrepreneurs establish and manage small businesses to gain control over their lives, make a difference in the world, become self-fulfilled, reap unlimited profits, contribute to society, and do what they enjoy doing.

3-B. Describe the drawbacks of entrepreneurship.

Entrepreneurs also face certain disadvantages, including uncertainty of income, the risk of losing their investments (and more), long hours and hard work, a lower quality of life until the business gets established, high stress levels, and complete decision-making responsibility.

4. Explain the forces that are driving the growth of entrepreneurship.

Several factors are driving the boom in entrepreneurship, including entrepreneurs portrayed as heroes, better entrepreneurial education, economic and demographic factors, a shift to a service economy, technological advancements, more independent lifestyles, and increased international opportunities.

5. Explain the cultural diversity of entrepreneurship.

Several groups are leading the nation's drive toward entrepreneurship: women, minorities, immigrants, part-timers, home-based business owners, family business owners, copreneurs, corporate castoffs, and corporate dropouts.

6. Describe the important role small businesses play in our nation's economy.

The small business sector's contributions are many. It makes up 99 percent of all businesses, employs 53 percent of the private sector workforce, has created 85 percent of the jobs since the early 1990s, produces 51 percent of the country's private gross domestic product (GDP), and accounts for 47 percent of all business sales.

7. Describe the nine deadly mistakes of entrepreneurship.

There are no guarantees that the business will make a profit or even survive. Small Business Administration (SBA) statistics show that 63 percent of new businesses will fail within six years. The nine deadly mistakes of entrepreneurship include incompetent management, lack of experience, poor financial control, failure to develop a strategic plan, uncontrolled growth, poor location, lack of inventory control, incorrect pricing, and inability to make the entrepreneurial transition.

8. Put failure into the proper perspective.

Entrepreneurs recognize that failure is a natural part of the creative process. Successful entrepreneurs have the attitude that failures are simply stepping-stones along the path to success, and they refuse to be paralyzed by a fear of failure.

9. Explain how entrepreneurs can avoid becoming another business failure statistic.

Entrepreneurs can employ several general tactics to avoid these pitfalls. Entrepreneurs should know their businesses in depth, prepare a solid business plan, manage financial resources effectively, understand financial statements, learn to manage people, and try to stay healthy.

DISCUSSION QUESTIONS

1. What forces have led to the boom in entrepreneurship in the United States and across the globe?
2. What is an entrepreneur? Give a brief description of the entrepreneurial profile.
3. *Inc.* magazine claims, "Entrepreneurship is more mundane than it's sometimes portrayed . . . you don't need to be a person of mythical proportions to be very, very successful in building a company." Do you agree? Explain.
4. What are the major benefits of business ownership?
5. Which of the potential drawbacks to business ownership are most critical?
6. Briefly describe the role of the following groups in entrepreneurship: women, minorities, immigrants, part-timers, home-based business owners, family business owners, copreneurs, corporate castoffs, and corporate dropouts.
7. What is a small business? What contributions do small businesses make to our economy?
8. Describe the small business failure rate.
9. Outline the causes of business failure. Which problems cause most business failures?
10. How does the typical entrepreneur view the possibility of business failure?
11. How can the small business owner avoid the common pitfalls that often lead to business failures?
12. Why is it important to study the small business failure rate and the causes of business failures?
13. Explain the typical entrepreneur's attitude toward risk.
14. Are you interested in one day launching a small business? If so, when? What kind of business? Describe it. What can you do to ensure its success?

Beyond the Classroom . . .

1. Choose an entrepreneur in your community and interview him or her. What's the "story" behind the business? How well does the entrepreneur fit the entrepreneurial profile described in this chapter? What advantages and disadvantages does the owner see in owning a business? What advice would he or she offer to someone considering launching a business?

2. Select one of the categories in the section "Entrepreneurial Profiles" in this chapter and research it in more detail. Find examples of that category. Prepare a brief report for your class.

3. Search through recent business publications (especially those focusing on small companies) and find an example of an entrepreneur, past or present, who exhibits the entrepreneurial spirit of striving for success in the face of failure. Prepare a brief report for your class.

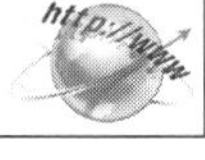

We invite you to visit this book's companion Web site at **www.prenhall.com/Zimmerer.**

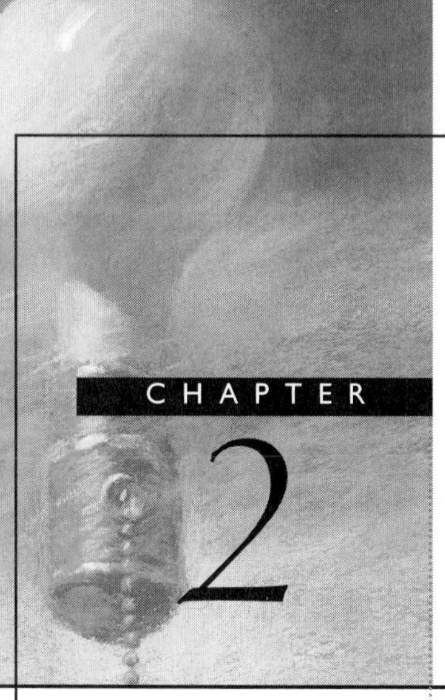

CHAPTER 2

Inside the Entrepreneurial Mind: From Ideas to Reality

Creativity is inventing, experimenting, growing, taking risks, breaking rules, making mistakes, and having fun.

—Mary Lou Cook

Discovery consists of seeing what everybody has seen—and thinking what nobody has thought.

—Albert Szent-Gyorgi

LEARNING OBJECTIVES

Upon completion of this chapter, you will be able to:

1. Explain the differences among creativity, innovation, and entrepreneurship.
2. Describe why creativity and innovation are such an integral part of entrepreneurship.
3. Understand how the two hemispheres of the human brain function and what role they play in creativity.
4. Explain the 10 "mental locks" that limit individual creativity.
5. Understand how entrepreneurs can enhance the creativity of their employees as well as their own creativity.
6. Describe the steps in the creative process.
7. Discuss techniques for improving the creative process.
8. Describe the protection of intellectual property involving patents, trademarks, and copyrights.

One of the tenets of entrepreneurship is the ability to create new and useful ideas that solve the problems and challenges people face every day. Entrepreneurs achieve success by creating value in the marketplace when they combine resources in new and different ways to gain a competitive edge over rivals. As you learned in Chapter 1, entrepreneurs can create value in a number of ways—developing new technology, discovering new knowledge, improving existing products or services, finding different ways of providing more goods and services with fewer resources, and many others. Indeed, finding new ways of satisfying customers' needs, inventing new products and services, and creating new twists on existing products and services are hallmarks of the entrepreneur!

Captivate Network

For instance, while on a business trip, Michael DiFranza stepped onto an elevator, which soon was full of strangers, all awkwardly staring at the floor display panel in an attempt to avoid making eye contact with one another. Leaning against the back wall watching this amusing scene, DiFranza came up with a simple yet innovative idea: Why not develop an elevator TV that features news, weather, sports, stock quotes, and, of course, advertisements? Researching his idea, DiFranza knew the concept had business potential when he discovered that 575 million people ride 600,000 elevators each day in the United States. DiFranza soon quit his job, developed a prototype, and launched Captivate Network **<www.captivatenetwork.com>** *after attracting $1.5 million in venture capital. Taking advantage of its first-mover position in this market, Captivate Network is on track to generate $50 million in sales in only its fifth year of operation.*[1]

Like many innovators, DiFranza created a successful business by taking two everyday items that have existed for many years and combining them in a different way.

CREATIVITY, INNOVATION, AND ENTREPRENEURSHIP

1. Explain the differences among creativity, innovation, and entrepreneurship.

What is the entrepreneurial "secret" for creating value in the marketplace? In reality, the "secret" is no secret at all: It is applying creativity and innovation to solve problems and to exploit opportunities that people face every day. **Creativity** is the ability to develop new ideas and to discover new ways of looking at problems and opportunities. **Innovation** is the ability to *apply* creative solutions to those problems and opportunities to enhance or to enrich people's lives. Harvard's Theodore Levitt says that creativity is *thinking* new things, and innovation is *doing* new things. In short, entrepreneurs succeed by *thinking and doing* new things or old things in new ways. Simply having a great new idea is not enough. One entrepreneur explains, "Creativity is only useful if it is channeled and directed. Creativity unrelated to a business plan has no value."[2]

creativity—*the ability to develop new ideas and to discover new ways of looking at problems and opportunities.*

innovation—*the ability to apply creative solutions to problems and opportunities to enhance or to enrich people's lives.*

Successful entrepreneurs come up with ideas and then find ways to make them work to solve a problem or to fill a need. In a world that is changing faster than most of us could ever have imagined, creativity and innovation are vital to a company's success—and survival. That's true for businesses in every industry—from automakers to tea growers—and for companies of all sizes. However, creativity and innovation are the signature of small, entrepreneurial businesses. Creative thinking has become a core business skill, and entrepreneurs lead the way in developing and applying that skill. In fact, creativity and innovation often lie at the heart of small companies' ability to compete successfully with their larger rivals. Even though they cannot outspend their larger rivals, small companies can create powerful, effective competitive advantages over big companies by "outcreating" and "outinnovating" them! If they fail to do so, entrepreneurs don't stay in business very long. Leadership expert Warren Bennis says, "Today's successful companies live and die according to the quality of their ideas."[3]

Sometimes creativity involves generating something from nothing. However, creativity is more likely to result in elaborating on the present, of putting old things together in new ways, or of taking something away to create something simpler or better. In some cases, a creative idea springs up from the most unexpected places. Edwin Land, one of America's most prolific inventors, credits his three-year-old daughter with the idea of the Polaroid camera. On a vacation trip in 1943, she asked why she couldn't see the photograph Land had just taken of her. During the next hour, as he walked around with his family, Land's mind was at work on his daughter's question. Before long, he had worked out the concept of building the camera that launched the era of instant photography. "The camera and the film became clear to me," Land recalls. "In my mind they were so real that I spent several hours describing them."[4]

Creative ideas often arise when entrepreneurs look at something old and think something new or different. Legendary Notre Dame football coach Knute Rockne, whose teams dominated college football in the 1920s, got the idea for his constantly shifting backfields while watching a burlesque chorus routine! Rockne's innovations in the backfield (which included the legendary "four horsemen") and his emphasis on the forward pass (a legal but largely unused tactic in this era) so befuddled opposing defenses that his teams compiled an impressive 105–12–5 record. Similarly, military tacticians, needing better camouflage designs to protect troops and equipment in World War I, borrowed ideas from the cubist art of Picasso and Braque. Their improved camouflage patterns helped the Allies win the war.[5] More recently, one entrepreneur helped solve a problem that plagued U.S. troops in the deserts of Saudi Arabia and Kuwait during Desert Storm. U.S. military experts discovered that enemy aircraft were able to detect the location of troops and equipment by looking for the repeating patterns in the camouflage used to hide them. The entrepreneur began selling the military a special camouflage whose pattern never repeated. He developed it using technology he was already employing to produce multicolored, multipatterned area rugs (each one unique) for the home market.

Entrepreneurship is the result of a disciplined, systematic process of applying creativity and innovation to needs and opportunities in the marketplace. It involves applying focused strategies to new ideas and new insights to create a product or a service that satisfies customers' needs or solves their problems. It is much more than random, disjointed tinkering with a new gadget. Millions of people come up with creative ideas for new or different products and services; most of them, however, never do anything with them. Entrepreneurs are those who connect their creative ideas with the purposeful action and structure of a business. Thus, successful entrepreneurship is a constant process that relies on creativity, innovation, and application in the marketplace.

Innovation must be a constant process because most ideas don't work and most innovations fail. Karen Anne Zien, cofounder of Polaroid Corporation's Creativity and Innovation Lab, estimates that for every 3,000 new-product ideas, four make it to the development stage, two are actually launched, and only one becomes a success in the market. These new products are crucial to companies' success, however. Robert Cooper, a researcher who has analyzed thousands of new-product launches, says that, on average, new products account for a whopping 40 percent of companies' sales.[6] Successful entrepreneurs recognize that failure often accompanies innovation, and they are willing to accept their share of failures because they know that failure is merely part of the creative process. Entrepreneurship requires business owners to be bold enough to try their new ideas, flexible enough to throw aside those that do not work, and wise enough to learn about what will work based on their observations of what did not. We now turn our attention to creativity, the creative process, and methods of enhancing creativity.

2. Describe why creativity and innovation are such an integral part of entrepreneurship.

CREATIVITY—A NECESSITY FOR SURVIVAL

In this fiercely competitive, fast-paced, global economy, creativity is not only an important source for building a competitive advantage, but it also is a necessity for survival. When developing creative solutions to modern problems, entrepreneurs must go beyond merely using whatever has worked in the past. History is not always a reliable predictor of the future in business. Making the inferential leap from what has worked in the past to what will work today (or in the future) requires entrepreneurs to cast off limiting assumptions, beliefs, and behaviors and to develop new insights into the relationship between resources, needs, and value. In other words, they must change their perspectives, looking at the world in new and different ways.

Entrepreneurs must always be on guard against traditional assumptions and perspectives about how things ought to be because they are certain killers of creativity. Such self-imposed mental constraints and other paradigms that people tend to build over time push creativity right out the door. A **paradigm** is a preconceived idea of what the world is, what it should be like, and how it should operate. These ideas become so deeply rooted in our minds that they become immovable blocks to creative thinking—even though they may be outdated, obsolete, and no longer relevant. In short, they act as logjams to creativity. Look, for example, at the following illustrations and read the text aloud:

paradigm—*a preconceived idea of what the world is, what it should be like, and how it should operate.*

Paris in the the Spring time	Once in a a Lifetime	Bird in the the Hand

If you're like most people, you didn't notice the extra word in each phrase ("Paris in the the spring time"). Why? Part of the reason is that we see what we expect to see! Past experiences shape the ways in which we perceive the world around us ("we've always done it this way"). Entrepreneurs are able to throw off these shackles on creativity and see opportunities for creating viable businesses in which most people see what they've always seen (or, worse yet, see nothing).

Many years ago, during an international chess competition, Frank Marshall made what has become known as one of the most beautiful—and one of the most creative—moves ever made on a chessboard. In a crucial game in which he was evenly matched with a Russian master player, Marshall found his queen under serious attack. Marshall had several avenues of escape for his queen available. Knowing that the queen is one of the most important offensive players on the chessboard, spectators assumed that Marshall would make a conventional move and push his queen to safety.

Using all the time available to him to consider his options, Marshall picked up his queen—and paused—and put it down on the most *illogical* square of all—a square from which the queen could easily be captured by any one of three hostile pieces. Marshall had done the unthinkable! He had sacrificed his queen, a move typically made only under the most desperate of circumstances. All the spectators—even Marshall's opponent—groaned in dismay. Then, the Russian, and finally the crowd, realized that Marshall's move was, in reality, a brilliant one. No matter how the Russian opponent took the queen, he would eventually be in a losing position. Seeing the inevitable outcome, the Russian conceded the game. Marshall had won the match in a rare and daring fashion: He had won by sacrificing his queen![7]

What lesson does this story hold for entrepreneurs? By suspending conventional thinking long enough to even consider the possibility of such a move, Marshall was able to throw off the usual paradigms constraining most chess players. He had looked beyond the traditional and orthodox strategies of the game and was willing to take the risk of trying an unusual tactic to win. The result: He won. Although not every creative business opportunity that entrepreneurs take will be successful, many who, like Frank Marshall, are willing to go beyond conventional wisdom will be rewarded for their efforts. Successful entrepreneurs, those who are constantly pushing technological and economic boundaries forward, must always ask: "Is it time to sacrifice the queen?"

Merely generating one successful creative solution to address a problem or a need usually is not good enough to keep an entrepreneurial enterprise successful in the long run, however.

Success—even survival—in this fiercely competitive, global environment requires entrepreneurs to tap their creativity (and that of their employees) constantly. An entrepreneur can be sure that if she has developed a unique, creative solution to solve a problem or to fill a need, a competitor (perhaps one six time zones away) is hard at work developing an even more creative solution to render hers obsolete. This extremely rapid and accelerating rate of change has created an environment in which staying in a leadership position requires constant creativity, innovation, and entrepreneurship. A company that has achieved a leadership position in an industry but then stands still creatively is soon toppled from its number-one perch.

Can Creativity Be Taught?

For many years, conventional wisdom held that a person was either creative—imaginative, free-spirited, entrepreneurial—or not—logical, narrow-minded, rigid. Today we know better. Research shows that anyone can learn to be creative. (Try stretching your mind's creativity with the exercise in Figure 2.1.) "Every person can be taught techniques and behaviors that help them generate more ideas," says Joyce Wycoff, author of

FIGURE 2.1
How Creative Are You? Can you recognize the well-known phrases these symbols represent?

Source: Gavin DeBecker, "Thinking Caps," USA Weekend, *July 30–August 1, 1999; April 9–11, 1999; February 5–7, 1999; June 4–6, 1999; June 11–13, 1999; July 2–4, 1999; January 22–24, 1999; January 15–17, 1999; August 6–8, 1999.*

<table>
<tr><td>Hundred
Chun Hundred
Chun Hundred
Chun Hundred
Chun Hundred</td><td>O R
H E
S W
S</td><td>Umph Umph Umph
Of the Spirit</td><td>Grace.</td></tr>
<tr><td>Standard
Standard</td><td>Stand
―
I</td><td>T42 24T</td><td>MUSTICKD</td></tr>
<tr><td>Cycle
Cycle
Cycle</td><td>SPCHIEFECTOR</td><td>Chair</td><td>Persona lity</td></tr>
<tr><td>↓
evil EVIL</td><td>D</td><td>ALL 1111 4 ALL</td><td>R|E|A|D</td></tr>
<tr><td>Knee
―
Lights</td><td>ECNALG</td><td>Blouse</td><td>Roll Roll
Roy Roy</td></tr>
<tr><td>THE DISTAGONCE</td><td>Drawing a</td><td>He's / Himself</td><td>( ) Program</td></tr>
<tr><td>T
O
U
C
H</td><td>R
ROADS
A
D
S</td><td>Man
―
Board</td><td>0
―
B.S.
M.S.
Ph.D.</td></tr>
<tr><td>Home Far</td><td>@ ee</td><td>Objection
―
Ruled</td><td>Tomb of 210, N</td></tr>
</table>

several books on creativity.[8] The problem is that in most organizations, people have never been taught—or even expected—to be creative. Many businesses also fail to foster an environment that encourages creativity among employees. Restricted by their traditional thinking patterns, most people never tap into their pools of innate creativity, and the company becomes stagnant. Not only can entrepreneurs and the people who work for them learn to think creatively, but they must for their companies' sake! "Innovation and creativity are not just for artists," says Wycoff. "These are skills with a direct, bottom-line payoff."[9]

Capitol Concierge

For instance, Mary Naylor, owner of Capitol Concierge, a company that provides concierge services in office building lobbies, looks to an unusual source for new ideas about how to promote her business: junk mail. "I collect junk mail and keep it in a box I call 'Mary's Ideas,'" says Naylor. "I get inspiration from things most people throw away. When I want to kick start my creative processes, I go to my box and see what's new."[10]

Before entrepreneurs can draw on their own creative capacity or stimulate creativity in their own organizations, they need to understand creative thinking.

CREATIVE THINKING

3. Understand how the two hemispheres of the human brain function and what role they play in creativity.

Research into the operation of the human brain shows that each hemisphere of the brain processes information differently and that one side of the brain tends to be dominant over the other. The human brain develops asymmetrically, and each hemisphere tends to specialize in certain functions. The left brain is guided by linear, vertical thinking (from one logical conclusion to the next) whereas the right brain relies on kaleidoscopic, lateral thinking (considering a problem from all sides and jumping into it at different points). The left brain handles language, logic, and symbols; the right brain takes care of the body's emotional, intuitive, and spatial functions. The left brain processes information in a step-by-step fashion, but the right brain processes it intuitively—all at once, relying heavily on images.

Left-brained vertical thinking is narrowly focused and systematic, proceeding in a highly logical fashion from one point to the next. Right-brained lateral thinking, on the other hand, is somewhat unconventional, unsystematic, and unstructured, much like the image of a kaleidoscope, whirling around to form one pattern after another. It is this right-brain-driven, lateral thinking that lies at the heart of the creative process. Those who have learned to develop their right-brained thinking skills tend to:

- always ask the question, "Is there a better way?"
- challenge custom, routine, and tradition.
- be reflective, often staring out windows, deep in thought. (How many traditional managers would stifle creativity by snapping these people out of their "daydreams," chastise them for "loafing," and admonish them to "get back to work"?)
- play mental games, trying to see an issue from a different perspective.
- realize that there may be more than one "right answer."
- see mistakes and failures as mere "pit stops" on the way to success.
- relate seemingly unrelated ideas to a problem to generate innovative solutions.
- have "helicopter skills," the ability to rise above the daily routine to see an issue from a broader perspective and then swooping back down to focus on an area in need of change.

DriveSavers Inc.

Scott Gaidano used lateral thinking to give his business an edge in serving its customers. Gaidano is the founder of DriveSavers Inc., a company that salvages data from

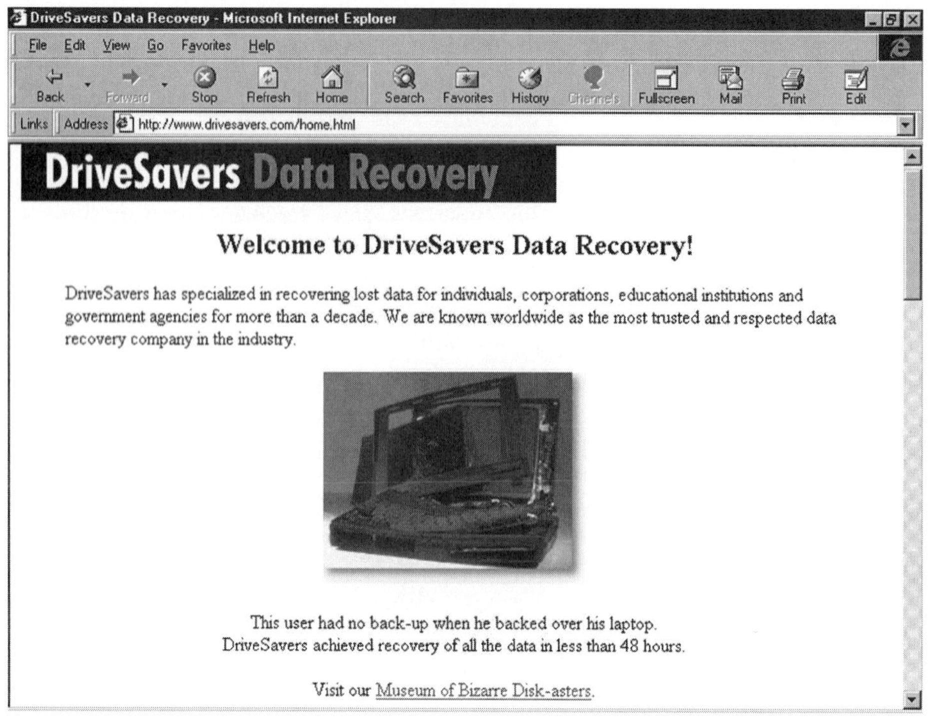

computer hard drives that have been damaged or have failed. Initially, DriveSavers would receive a customer's hard drive, extract the data from it, reload the data, and return the repaired drive (or a new one) to the customer. Gaidano saw fast turnaround times as a way to distinguish his company from its competitors, but that meant he had to count on standard carriers to deliver on time. After mulling over the problem for a few weeks, Gaidano came up with the idea of eliminating the shipping phase altogether! Instead, he would put customers' restored data on a secure Web site, where they could access it instantly. Within three weeks, DriveSavers had the Web site running ***<www.drivesavers.com>****, and now about one-third of its customers download their recovered data directly from the site.*[11]

Although each hemisphere of the brain tends to dominate in its particular functions, the two halves normally cooperate, with each part contributing its special abilities to accomplish those tasks best suited to its mode of information processing. Sometimes, however, the two hemispheres may even compete with each other, or one-half may choose not to participate. Some researchers have suggested that each half of the brain has the capacity to keep information from the other! The result, literally, is that "the left hand doesn't know what the right hand is doing." Perhaps the most important characteristic of this split-brain phenomenon is that an individual can learn to control which side of the brain is dominant in a given situation. In other words, a person can learn to "turn down" the dominant left hemisphere (focusing on logic and linear thinking) and "turn up" the right hemisphere (focusing on intuition and unstructured thinking) when a situation requiring creativity arises.[12] To get a little practice at this "shift," try the visual exercises presented in Figure 2.2. When viewed from one perspective, the picture in the middle portrays an attractive young lady with a feather in her hair and a boa around her shoulders. Once you shift your perspective, however, you will see an old woman with a large nose wearing a scarf on her head! This change in the image seen is the result of a shift from one hemisphere in the viewer's brain to the other. With practice, an individual

FIGURE 2.2

What do you see?

Source: ENTREPRENEURSHIP AND NEW VENTURE FORMATION by Zimmerer and Scarborough, © 1995. Reprinted by permission of Prentice Hall, Inc. Upper Saddle River, N.J.

A. Which do you see? The goblet or the famous twins?

B. Describe the lady you see in this drawing. How old is she, how attractive, what kind of covering on her head etc.?

C. In these patches of black and white, do you see the face of Christ?

YOU BE THE CONSULTANT . . .

The Spirit of Entrepreneurship in the Olympics

Entrepreneurs aren't the only ones who use creativity to create competitive advantages for themselves. Throughout history, Olympic athletes have pushed back the frontiers of their sports by developing new techniques, improved training methods, and innovative solutions to existing problems. Two of the best examples of applying creativity to their sports were figure skater Sonja Henie and high jumper Dick Fosbury. Although their sports are at different extremes of the Olympic spectrum, both of these athletes relied on the creative process to throw off the paradigms that bound the other athletes competing in these sports.

Before Sonja Henie came along, figure skating routines were exactly that—routine. In competitions, skaters performed a series of precise moves that emphasized accuracy and control. But when the young Norwegian glided onto the ice, skating changed forever. Bringing the beauty and movement of ballet to the skating rink, Henie transformed the sport into the graceful combination of motion, music, and muscle that it remains today. From 1927 to 1936, Henie dominated ice skating by creatively blending her graceful ballet skills with her strength on the ice. She won 10 straight world championships, eight European titles, and a record three Olympic gold medals. Trained in both dance and ballet as a child, Henie cast aside the existing paradigms of what ice skating was as she recognized the possibilities of transferring dance movements onto the ice.

After winning her last world championship in 1936, Henie used her dance and skating skills to get into show business. She became an international star in movies and in traveling ice shows that gave her the freedom to use her creative genius on the ice. Even her glamorous and daring (for the 1930s) costumes proved to be an exciting innovation in ice skating as they emphasized the grace and flow of her movements. Later generations of ice skaters would push the sport even farther. Tenely Albright (1956 Olympics) and Peggy Fleming (1968 Olympics) introduced spins, twirls, and leaps. More recently, Tara Lipinsky, Kristi Yamaguchi, Nancy Kerrigan, Katarina Witt, and others have injected an element of gymnastics to ice skating, performing triple jumps and double and triple axels. Yet every one of these champions owes a debt of gratitude to Sonja Henie, the daring young skater who had the creativity and the courage to make innovations on the ice.

Until 1968, much like ice skating, the sport of high jumping had changed little since its origins in ancient Greece. Athletes sprinted toward the bar and then leaped forward and upward, rolling over the bar face down. In the 1968 Olympics in Mexico City, Dick Fosbury revolutionized the sport with his innovative style of high jumping. He approached the bar at a different angle and then curved his body over the bar face *up,* kicking his legs over the end of the jump. Based on the principles of biomechanics, the "Fosbury Flop," as the style became known, transfers the weight of the jumper over the bar in stages. It also requires less energy and is more efficient. The result of Fosbury's innovation? An Olympic gold medal, a new world high jump record (Fosbury broke the old record by 6 cm), and the satisfaction of creating a new style of high jumping used by athletes across the world even today.

Sonja Henie and Dick Fosbury became champions by applying creativity and innovation to the sports they loved so much. Similarly, entrepreneurs can become champions in their industries by using their creative spirits to come up with new ideas, better products and services, and innovative techniques. Successful entrepreneurs rely on their ability to see the same things everyone else sees and to dream what no one else dreams.

1. What is a paradigm? How does a paradigm stifle creativity?
2. Work with a small group of your classmates to identify a local business that is bound by a paradigm. What impact is this paradigm having on the business? Identify the paradigm and then generate as many creative suggestions as you can in 20 minutes that would change this paradigm.
3. What can entrepreneurs do to throw off existing paradigms?

Source: "Innovations of the Olympic Games," *Fortune,* January 27, 1992, pp. 28–29.

can learn to control this mental shift, tapping the pool of creativity that lies hidden within the right side of the brain. This ability has tremendous power to unleash the creative capacity of entrepreneurs. The need to develop this creative ability means that exploring inner space (the space within our brains)—not outer space—becomes the challenge of the century.

Entrepreneurship requires both left- and right-brain thinking. Right-brain thinking draws on the power of divergent reasoning, which is the ability to create a multitude of original, diverse ideas. Left-brain thinking counts on convergent reasoning, the ability to evaluate multiple ideas and choose the best solution to a given problem. Entrepreneurs need to rely on right-brain thinking to generate innovative product, service, or business ideas. Then they must use left-brain thinking to judge the market potential of the ideas they generate. Successful entrepreneurs have learned to coordinate the complementary functions of each hemisphere of the brain, using their brains' full creative power. Otherwise, entrepreneurs, who rarely can be accused of being "half-hearted" about their business ideas, run the risk of becoming "half-headed."

How can entrepreneurs learn to tap their innate creativity more readily? The first step is to break down the barriers to creativity that most of us have erected over the years. We now turn our attention to these barriers and some suggested techniques for tearing them down.

BARRIERS TO CREATIVITY

4. Understand the 10 "mental locks" that limit individual creativity.

The number of potential barriers to creativity is virtually limitless—time pressures, unsupportive management, pessimistic coworkers, overly rigid company policies, and countless others. Perhaps the most difficult hurdles to overcome, however, are those that individuals impose on themselves. In his book *A Whack on the Side of the Head,* Roger von Oech identifies 10 "mental locks" that limit individual creativity.[13]

1. *Searching for the one "right" answer.* Deeply ingrained in most educational systems is the assumption that there is one "right" answer to a problem. The average student who has completed four years of college has taken more than 2,600 tests, so it is not unusual for this one-correct-answer syndrome to become an inherent part of our thinking. In reality, however, most problems are ambiguous. Depending on the questions one asks, there may be (and usually are) several "right" answers.
2. *Focusing on "being logical."* Logic is a valuable part of the creative process, especially when evaluating ideas and implementing them. However, in the early imaginative phases of the process, logical thinking may restrict creativity. Focusing too much effort on being logical also discourages the use of one of the mind's most powerful creations: intuition. Von Oech advises us to "think something different" and to freely use nonlogical thinking, especially in the imaginative phase of the creative process.

   Intuition, which is based on the accumulated knowledge and experiences a person encounters over the course of a lifetime and resides in the subconscious, can be unlocked.

Example

Royce Husted, a prolific inventor and entrepreneur, relies extensively on his intuition when creating and designing his inventions. He started with a very logical observation about bicycles ("most bicyclists ride for fun; they aren't racers, and they don't want super-skinny wheels or low handlebars"). But then he relied on his intuition to create a new bike design. He incorporated several of his existing patented ideas into the design but constantly came up with new concepts—after much deliberation. "My inner voice comes out after taking lots of mental notes," he says. "It is like a summary of observations that leads to a conclusion." Husted listened when his intuition told him to make major changes in his bike's design, and it paid off.[14]

3. *Blindly following the rules.* We learn at a very early age not to "color outside the lines," and we spend the rest of our lives blindly obeying such rules. Sometimes creativity depends on our ability to break the existing rules so that we can see new ways of doing things. Consider, for example, the top row of letters on a standard typewriter or computer keyboard:

   Q W E R T Y U I O P

   In the 1870s, Sholes & Company, a leading manufacturer of typewriters, began receiving numerous customer complaints about its typewriter keys sticking together when typists' fingers were practiced enough to go really fast. Company engineers came up with an incredibly creative solution to eliminate the problem of sticking keys. They designed a less efficient keyboard configuration, placing the letters *O* and *I* (the third and sixth most commonly used letters of the alphabet) so that the weakest fingers (the ring and little fingers) would strike them. By slowing down typists with this inefficient keyboard, the engineers solved the sticking keys problem. Today, despite the fact that computer technology has eliminated all danger of sticking keys, this same inefficient keyboard configuration remains the industry standard!

4. *Constantly being practical.* Imagining impractical answers to "what if" questions can be powerful stepping-stones to creative ideas. Suspending practicality for a while frees the mind to consider creative solutions that, otherwise, might never arise. Whenever Thomas Edison hired an assistant to work in his creative laboratory, he would tell the new employee, "Walk through town and list 20 things that interest you." When the worker returned, Edison would ask him to split the list into two columns. Then he would say, "Randomly combine objects from column A and column B and come up with as many inventions as you can." Edison's methods for stimulating creativity in his lab proved to be successful; he holds the distinction of being the only person to have earned a patent every year for 65 consecutive years![15]

5. *Viewing play as frivolous.* A playful attitude is fundamental to creative thinking. There is a close relationship between the "haha" of humor and the "aha" of discovery. Play gives us the opportunity to reinvent reality and to reformulate established ways of doing things. Children learn when they play, and so can entrepreneurs. Watch children playing and you will see them invent new games, create new ways of looking at old things, and learn what works (and what doesn't) in their games.

   Entrepreneurs can benefit from playing in the same way that children do. They, too, can learn to try new approaches and discover what works and what doesn't. Creativity results when entrepreneurs take what they have learned at play, evaluate it, corroborate it with other knowledge, and put it into practice. For instance, a group of fund-raisers discussed the arrangements for an upcoming annual fund-raising banquet (which had been the organization's primary source of income for many years). Lamenting the declining turnout over the past several years and the multitude of other organizations that used banquets as a source of revenue, one officer jokingly said, "Maybe we should have a 'non-banquet,' where people pay not to tie up several hours, eat rubber chicken, and listen to some dull speaker talk about a topic they'd rather not hear about." The other officers laughed at the idea initially and then began throwing in humorous ideas of their own. The group mustered the courage to try out their creative solution, and their "nonbanquet" was a tremendous success. It raised more money than the organization had ever raised before, and no one had to attend!

6. *Becoming overly specialized.* Defining a problem as one of "marketing" or "production," or some other area of specialty limits the ability to see how it might be related to other issues. Creative thinkers tend to be explorers, searching for ideas outside their areas of specialty. The idea for the roll-on deodorant stick came from the ballpoint pen. Velcro was invented by a man who, while hiking one day to take a break from work, had to stop to peel sticky cockleburrs from his clothing. As he picked them off, he noticed how their hooked spines caught on and held tightly to the cloth. As he resumed his hike, he began to think about the possibilities of using a similar design to fasten objects together. Thus was born Velcro!

7. *Avoiding ambiguity.* Ambiguity can be a powerful creative stimulus; it encourages us to "think something different." Being excessively detailed in an imaginative situation tends to stifle creativity. Ambiguity, however, requires us to consider at least two different, often contradictory notions at the same time, which is a direct channel to creativity. Ambiguous situations force us to stretch our minds beyond their normal boundaries and to consider creative options we might otherwise ignore. Although ambiguity is not a desired element when entrepreneurs are evaluating and implementing ideas, it is a valuable tool when they are searching for creative ideas and solutions. Entrepreneurs are famous for asking a question and then going beyond the first answer to explore other possible answers. The result is that they often find business opportunities by creating ambiguous situations.

   Tom and Sally's Handmade Chocolates

   Copreneurs Tom and Sally Fegley, owners of Tom and Sally's Handmade Chocolates, considered the possibility of other answers to the question "What uses exist for chocolate sauce?" Although most people see chocolate sauce merely as a topping for ice cream or other desserts, their friend Larry (whom they have nicknamed "Dirty Larry") came up with a different idea. The Fegleys were trying to come up with an innovative recipe that would keep their string of awards at a local fund-raising event devoted to celebrating chocolate, the Brown-Out. Their fun-loving friend suggested they shoot for the Most Decadent Award. "I'll go naked," he said. "You paint melted chocolate all over my body, and you'll win!" Although the Fegleys declined Larry's offer, his suggestion got them thinking. Before long, Tom had whipped up a batch of chocolate dessert topping, labeled it "Chocolate Body Paint," and included the following directions on the bottle: "Heat to 98.6 degrees, apply liberally, and let your imagination run wild." Today Chocolate Body Paint is the Fegleys' best-selling product, and it has won awards and has been featured in publications ranging from the Wall Street Journal *to* Playboy *magazine. "Never judge an idea by its source," advises Sally.*[16]

8. *Fearing looking foolish.* Creative thinking is no place for conformity! New ideas rarely are born in a conforming environment. People tend toward conformity because they don't want to look foolish. The fool's job is to whack at the habits and rules that keep us thinking in the same old ways. In that sense, entrepreneurs are top-notch "fools." They are constantly questioning and challenging accepted ways of doing things and the assumptions that go with them. The noted entrepreneurship theorist, Joseph Schumpeter, wrote that entrepreneurs perform a vital function—"creative destruction"—in which they rethink conventional assumptions and discard those that are no longer useful. According to Schumpeter, "The function of entrepreneurs is to reform or revolutionize the pattern of production by exploiting an invention or, more generally, an untried technological possibility for producing a new commodity or producing an old one in a new way, by opening up a new source of supply of materials or a new outlet for products, by reorganizing an industry or so on."[17] In short, entrepreneurs look at old ways of doing things and ask, "Is there a better way?" By destroying the old, they create the new.

   One way entrepreneurs often engage in creative destruction is by reversing their thinking. For example, one agricultural entrepreneur had been trying to solve a common problem that automatic picking machines have when picking the fruit from apple trees. The machines, which are quite efficient at picking apples growing on the outer limbs of the trees, often miss or damage the fruit growing on the inner limbs. For years, he worked to develop a machine with the dexterity to pick apples in both locations but to no avail. Finally, this entrepreneur reversed his thinking and began to focus his efforts, not on the picking machine but *on the apple tree!* Working with horticulturists, he was able to develop a new breed of tree whose fruit grew only on the outer limbs, where standard picking machines could easily get to it! By reversing his thinking, he solved the problem and created a new business opportunity.

9. *Fearing mistakes and failure.* Creative people realize that trying something new often leads to failure; however, they do not see failure as an end. It represents a learning experience on the way to success. As you learned in Chapter 1, failure is an important part of the creative process; it signals entrepreneurs when to change their course of action. Entrepreneurship is all about the opportunity to fail! Many entrepreneurs failed numerous times before they succeeded. Despite their initial setbacks, they were able to set aside the fear of failure and kept trying.

   The key, of course, is to see failure for what it really is: a chance to learn how to succeed. Entrepreneurs who willingly risk failure and learn from it when it occurs have the best chance of succeeding at whatever they try. Charles F. Kettering, a famous inventor (he invented the lighting and ignition systems in automobiles, among other things), explains, "You fail because your ideas aren't right, but you should learn to fail intelligently. When you fail, find out *why* you failed and each time it will bring you nearer to the goal."[18] Successful entrepreneurs equate failure with innovation rather than with defeat.

10. *Believing that "I'm not creative."* Some people limit themselves because they believe creativity belongs only to the Einsteins, Beethovens, and da Vincis of the world. Unfortunately, this belief often becomes a self-fulfilling prophecy. A person who believes he is not creative will, in all likelihood, behave that way and will make that belief come true. Successful entrepreneurs recognize that saying "I'm not creative" is merely an excuse for inaction. *Everyone* has within himself or herself the potential to be creative; not everyone will tap that potential, however.

By avoiding these 10 mental locks, entrepreneurs can unleash their own creativity and the creativity of those around them as well. Successful entrepreneurs are willing to take some risks, explore new ideas, play a little, ask "what if?", and learn to appreciate ambiguity. By doing so, they develop the skills, attitudes, and motivation that make them much more creative—one of the keys to entrepreneurial success. Table 2.1 lists some questions designed to spur imagination.

5. Understand how entrepreneurs can enhance their own creativity and that of their employees as well.

HOW TO ENHANCE CREATIVITY

Enhancing Organizational Creativity

Creativity doesn't just happen in organizations; entrepreneurs must establish an environment in which creativity can flourish—for themselves and for their workers. New ideas are fragile creations, but the right organizational environment can encourage people to develop and cultivate them. Ensuring that workers have the freedom and the incentive to be creative is one of the best ways to achieve innovation. Entrepreneurs can stimulate their own creativity and encourage it among workers in the following ways.

EXPECTING CREATIVITY. Employees tend to rise—or fall—to the level of expectations entrepreneurs have of them. One of the best ways to communicate the expectation of creativity is to give employees permission to be creative. At one small company that man-

TABLE 2.1

Questions to Spur the Imagination

Sources: Adapted from Creativity Web, "Question Summary," **<*www.ozemail.com/au/~caveman/Creative/Techniques/osb_quest.html*>**; Bits & Pieces, *February 1990, p. 20;* Bits & Pieces, *April 29, 1993, "Creativity Quiz,"* In Business, *November/December 1991, p. 18; Doug Hall,* Jump Start Your Brain *(New York: Warner Books, Inc., 1995), pp. 86–87.*

People learn at an early age to pursue answers to questions. Creative people, however, understand that good questions are extremely valuable in the quest for creativity. Some of the greatest breakthroughs in history came as a result of creative people asking thought-provoking questions. Bill Bowerman, contemplating a design for the soles of running shoes over a breakfast of waffles, asked, "What would happen if I poured rubber into my waffle iron?" He did, and that's how Nike shoes came to be. (Bowerman's rubber-coated waffle iron is on display in the Nike Town superstore and museum in Chicago.) Albert Einstein, creator of the theory of relativity, asked, "What would a light wave look like to someone keeping pace with it?" Masura Ibuka, who created the Sony Walkman, asked, "Why can't we remove the recording function and speaker and put headphones on the recorder?"

The following questions can help spur your imagination:

1. Is there a new way to do it?
2. Can you borrow or adapt it?
3. Can you give it a new twist?
4. Do you merely need more of the same?
5. Less of the same?
6. Is there a substitute?
7. Can you rearrange the parts?
8. What if you do just the opposite?
9. Can you combine ideas?
10. Can you put it to other uses?
11. What else could we make from this?
12. Are there other markets for it?
13. Can you reverse it?

ufactures industrial equipment, the owner put a "brainstorming board" in a break area. Anyone facing a sticky problem simply posts it on a brightly colored piece of paper on the board. Other workers are invited to share ideas and suggestions by writing them on white pieces of paper and posting them around the problem. The board has generated many creative solutions that otherwise would not have come up.

EXPECTING AND TOLERATING FAILURE. Creative ideas will produce failures as well as successes. People who never fail are not being creative. Creativity requires taking chances, and managers must remove employees' fear of failure. The surest way to quash creativity throughout an organization is to punish employees who try something new and fail.

ENCOURAGING CURIOSITY. Entrepreneurs and their employees constantly should ask "what if . . ." questions and to take a "maybe we could . . ." attitude. Doing so allows them to break out of the assumptions that limit creativity.

VIEWING PROBLEMS AS CHALLENGES. Every problem offers the opportunity for innovation. Entrepreneurs who allow employees to dump all of their problems on their desks to be "fixed" do nothing to develop creativity within those employees.

PROVIDING CREATIVITY TRAINING. Almost everyone has the capacity to be creative, but developing that capacity requires training. One writer claims, "What separates the average person from Edison, Picasso, or even Shakespeare isn't creative capacity—it's the ability to tap that capacity by encouraging creative impulses and then acting upon them."[19] Training—through books, seminars, workshops, and professional meetings—can help everyone learn to tap their creative capacity.

PROVIDING SUPPORT. Entrepreneurs must give employees the tools and the resources they need to be creative. One of the most valuable resources is time. 3M, a company famous for its innovations, allows its employees to spend up to 15 percent of their time working on "pet projects" that they believe have potential. Entrepreneurs should remember that creativity often requires nonwork phases, and allowing employees time to daydream is an important part of the process.

REWARDING CREATIVITY. Entrepreneurs can encourage creativity by rewarding it when it occurs. Financial rewards can be effective motivators of creative behavior, but non-monetary rewards—praise, recognition, and celebration—can be more powerful incentives. At one small company, the owner has a monthly "idea lottery." Each time an employee submits a new idea, he or she gets a numbered ticket. At the end of each month, the owner conducts a brief session to share all of the ideas generated and then holds a ticket drawing. The idea generator whose number is drawn wins a prize.

MODELING CREATIVE BEHAVIOR. Creativity is "caught" as much as it is "taught." Entrepreneurs who set examples of creative behavior, taking chances, and challenging the status quo will soon find their employees doing the same.

Building a creative environment takes time, but the payoffs can be phenomenal. 3M, a company that is famous for cultivating a creative environment, estimates that 70 percent of its annual sales comes from creative ideas that originated from its workforce. As one creativity consultant explains, "For your employees to be more creative, you have to create an environment that values their creativity."[20]

Enhancing Individual Creativity

Just as entrepreneurs can cultivate an environment of creativity in their organizations by using the techniques described previously, they can enhance their own creativity by using the following techniques.

ALLOW YOURSELF TO BE CREATIVE. As we have seen, one of the biggest obstacles to creativity occurs when a person believes that he or she is not creative. Giving yourself the permission to be creative is the first step toward establishing a pattern of creative thinking.

GIVE YOUR MIND FRESH INPUT EVERY DAY. To be creative, your mind needs stimulation. Do something different each day—listen to a new radio station, take a walk through a park or a shopping center, pick up a magazine you have never read.

Agenda Dynamics Inc.

When Janet Harris-Lange, founder of Agenda Dynamics Inc., a meeting and event management company, needs a fresh idea for an upcoming event, she makes an effort to expose her mind to new stimuli. In the past, she has walked through a secondhand thrift shop, shopped in a dime store, talked with children, and put on funny hats to generate creative ideas for her clients' events, something that is vital to her company's success. "To be better than the competition, I have to employ creative thinking," she says.[21]

KEEP A JOURNAL HANDY TO RECORD YOUR THOUGHTS AND IDEAS. Creative ideas are too valuable to waste so always keep a journal nearby to record them as soon as you get them. Patrick McNaughton invented the neon blackboards restaurants use to advertise their specials. In addition to the neon blackboard, McNaughton has invented more than 30 new products, many of which are sold through the company that he and his sister, Jamie, own. McNaughton credits much of his creative success to the fact that he writes down every idea he gets and keeps it in a special folder. "There's no such thing as a crazy idea," he insists.[22]

READ BOOKS ON STIMULATING CREATIVITY OR TAKE A CLASS ON CREATIVITY. Creative thinking is a technique that anyone can learn. Understanding and applying the principles of creativity can improve dramatically the ability to develop new and innovative ideas.

YOU BE THE CONSULTANT . . .

The Creative Side of Entrepreneurship

When St. Petersburg, one of the most splendid, harmonious cities in Europe, was being laid out early in the eighteenth century, many large boulders brought by a glacier from Finland had to be removed. One particularly large rock was in the path of one of the principal avenues that had been planned, and bids were solicited for its removal. The bids submitted were very high. This was understandable, because at that time modern equipment did not exist and there were no high-powered explosives. As officials pondered what to do, a peasant presented himself and offered to get rid of the boulder for a much lower price than those submitted by other bidders. Since they had nothing to lose, officials gave the job to the peasant.

The next morning he showed up with a crowd of other peasants carrying shovels. They began digging a huge hole next to the rock. They propped up the rock with timbers to prevent it from rolling into the hole. When the hole was deep enough, the timber props were removed and the rock dropped into the hole below the street level. Then they covered it with dirt and carted the excess dirt away.

It's an early example of what creative thinking can do to solve a problem. The unsuccessful bidders only thought about moving the rock from one place to another on the city's surface. The peasant looked at the problem from another angle. He considered another dimension—up and down. He couldn't lift it up, so he put it underground!

Managers at the Cleveland Museum used a similar kind of creative thinking to ensure the success of a dazzling exhibit of ancient Egyptian treasures. Taking a different marketing approach, museum managers held a free private showing for the city's taxi drivers. Some of the museum's snooty, blue-blooded patrons scoffed at the idea and dismissed it as an exercise in foolishness. After all, they said, taxi drivers aren't known for their polish or their culture. But the museum managers persisted. Impress the cab drivers, they reasoned, and the "cabbies" would be more likely to recommend the new exhibit to their customers, who would, in turn, flock to the museum. That's exactly what happened. During the exhibit's run in Cleveland, the museum enjoyed shoulder-to-shoulder attendance, thanks to talkative cab drivers and creative museum managers!

1. Contact a local small business owner and ask about a problem his or her company is facing. Work with a small team of your classmates and use the type of creative thinking described previously to generate potential solutions to the problem. Remember to think creatively!

Sources: Charles R. Davey, "Oddball Ideas Aren't So Odd," *Industry Week,* August 3, 1992, p. 7; *Bits & Pieces,* October 15, 1992, pp. 8–10.

TAKE SOME TIME OFF. Relaxation is vital to the creative process. Getting away from a problem gives the mind time to reflect on it. It is often this time, while the subconscious works on a problem, that the mind generates many creative solutions.

THE CREATIVE PROCESS

6. Describe the steps in the creative process.

Although new ideas may appear to strike as suddenly as a bolt of lightning, they are actually the result of the creative process, which involves seven steps:

1. Preparation
2. Investigation
3. Transformation
4. Incubation
5. Illumination
6. Verification
7. Implementation

Step 1. Preparation. This step involves getting the mind ready for creative thinking. Preparation might include a formal education, on-the-job training, work experience, and taking advantage of other learning opportunities. This training provides a foundation on which to build creativity and innovation. As one writer explains, "Creativity favors the prepared mind."[23] For example, Dr. Hamel Navia, a scientist at tiny Vertex Pharmaceuticals, recently developed a promising new drug to fight the AIDS virus. His preparation included earning an advanced degree in the field of medicine and learning to use computers to create three-dimensional images of the protein molecules he was studying.[24] How can you prepare your mind for creative thinking?

- Adopt the attitude of a lifelong student. Realize that educating yourself is a never-ending process. Look at every situation you encounter as an opportunity to learn.
- Read . . . a lot . . . and not just in your field of expertise. Many innovations come from blending ideas and concepts from different fields in science, engineering, business, and the arts. Reading books, magazines, and papers covering a variety of subject matter is a great way to stimulate your creativity.
- Clip articles of interest to you and create a file for them. Over time, you will build a customized encyclopedia of information from which to draw ideas and inspiration.
- Take time to discuss your ideas with other people, including those who know little about it as well as experts in the field. Sometimes the apparently simple questions an "unknowledgeable" person asks lead to new discoveries and to new approaches to an old problem.

American Wilderness Experience, Inc.

Dave Wiggins, president of American Wilderness Experience, Inc., an adventure travel company, gets valuable ideas from his wife, Carol, a network of business advisors, and his employees. The idea for the company's most popular trip, snowmobiling in Yellowstone National Park, came from one of the company's guides. "I find it extremely helpful to get different perspectives from people I respect and trust," says Wiggins.[25]

- Join professional or trade associations and attend their meetings. There you have the chance to brainstorm with others who have similar interests. Learning how other people have solved a particular problem may give you fresh insight into solving it.
- Invest time in studying other countries and their cultures; then travel there. Our global economy offers incredible business opportunities for entrepreneurs with the necessary knowledge and experience to recognize them. One entrepreneur began a lucrative business exporting a variety of consumer products to Latvia after he accompanied his daughter there on a missionary trip. He claims that he never would have seen the opportunity had he not traveled to Latvia with his daughter.
- Develop listening skills. It's amazing what you can learn if you take the time to listen to other people—especially those who are older and have more experience. Try to learn something from everyone you meet.

Step 2. Investigation. This step requires you to develop a solid understanding of the problem or decision. To create new ideas and concepts in a particular field, an individual first must study the problem and understand its basic components. Few people could create new chemical compounds without having a fundamental understanding of biochemistry. For example, Dr. Navia and another scientist at Vertex had spent several years conducting research on viruses and on a protein that blocks a virus enzyme called protease. His exploration on ways to block this enzyme paved the way for his discovery.

Joe Designer Inc.

For Joe Moya and Joe Raia, cofounders of Joe Designer Inc., the creative process is the key to their company's success. Joe Designer has created and developed a myriad of award-winning designs for companies ranging from Betty Crocker to Kodak. Raia explains the importance of the investigation phase as he and Moya prepare their creative team for an assignment. "We familiarize ourselves with market trends, the past history of the product," he says. "We research by flipping through magazines. We pin articles, photos, everything up on the walls and familiarize the whole team with what the history is and what we want to achieve."[26]

Step 3. Transformation. Transformation involves viewing the similarities and the differences in the information collected. This phase requires two types of thinking: convergent and divergent. **Convergent thinking** is the ability to see the *similarities* and the connections among various data and events. **Divergent thinking** is the ability to see the *differences* among various data and events. While developing his AIDS-fighting drug, Dr. Navia studied the work of other scientists whose attempts at developing an enzyme-blocking drug had failed. He was able to see the similarities and differences in his research and theirs and to build on their successes while avoiding their failures.

convergent thinking—*the ability to see the similarities and the connections among various data and events.*

divergent thinking—*the ability to see the differences among various data and events.*

How can you increase your ability to transform the information collected into a purposeful idea?

- Evaluate the parts of the situation several times, trying to grasp the "big picture." Getting bogged down in the details of a situation too early in the creative process can diminish creativity. Look for patterns that emerge.
- Rearrange the elements of the situation. By looking at the components of an issue in a different order or from a different perspective, you may be able to see the similarities and the differences among them more readily. Rearranging them also may help uncover a familiar pattern that had been masked by an unfamiliar structure.
- Before locking into one particular approach to a situation, remember that several approaches might be successful. If one approach produces a "dead end," don't hesitate to jump quickly to another. Considering several approaches to a problem or opportunity simultaneously would be like rolling a bowling ball down each of several lanes in quick succession. The more balls you roll down the lanes, the greater is the probability of hitting at least one strike. Resist the temptation to make snap judgments on how to tackle a problem or opportunity. The first approach may not be the best one.

Step 4. Incubation. The subconscious needs time to reflect on the information collected. To an observer, this phase of the creative process would be quite boring; it looks as though nothing is happening! In fact, during this phase, it may appear that the creative person is *loafing.* Incubation occurs while the individual is away from the problem, often engaging in some totally unrelated activity. Dr. Navia's creative powers were working at a subconscious level even when he was away from his work, not even thinking about his research on AIDS-fighting drugs.

How can you enhance the incubation phase of the creative process, letting ideas marinate in your mind?

- Walk away from the situation. Often doing something totally unrelated to it will give your subconscious mind the chance to work on the problem or opportunity. One expert suggests that the "three Bs"—bath, bed, and bus—are conducive to creativity. "I do some of my best thinking in my hot tub at home," says American Wilderness Experience's Dave Wiggins. "I sit there, look at the stars, and come up with some pretty good ideas."[27]
- Take the time to daydream. Although it may *look* as if you're doing nothing, daydreaming is an important part of the creative process. That's when your mind is most free from paradigms and other self-imposed restrictions on creativity. Feel free to let your mind wander, and it may just stumble onto a creative solution.

- Relax—and play—regularly. Perhaps the worst thing you can do for creativity is to work on a problem or opportunity constantly. Soon enough, fatigue walks in, and creativity walks out! Great ideas often are incubated on the golf course, on the basketball court, in the garden, or in the hammock.
- Dream about the problem or opportunity. Although you may not be able to dream on command, thinking about an issue just before you drift off to sleep can be an effective way to encourage your mind to work on it while you sleep. Surrealist painter Salvador Dali used this technique to inspire his painting. He would lie on a sofa in his studio, holding a spoon in his hand, which dangled off the edge of the sofa. As he drifted off to sleep, his hand would relax and the spoon would clatter onto the plate, waking him up. He would immediately sketch the images he had just envisioned in that netherland of semisleep.[28]
- Work on the problem or opportunity in a different environment—somewhere other than the office. Take your work outside on a beautiful day or sit on a bench in a mall. The change of scenery will likely stimulate your creativity.

Step 5. Illumination. This phase of the creative process occurs at some point during the incubation stage when a spontaneous breakthrough causes "the light bulb to go on." It may take place after five minutes—or five years. In the illumination stage, all of the previous stages come together to produce the "Eureka factor"—the creation of the innovative idea. In one study of 200 scientists, 80 percent said that at least once a solution to a problem had "just popped into their heads"—usually when they were away from the problem.[29] For Dr. Navia, the illumination stage occurred one day while he was reading a scientific journal. As he read, Dr. Navia says he was struck with an "hallucination" of a novel way to block protease.

Although the creative process itself may last for months or even years, the suddenness with which the illumination step occurs can be deceiving. For example:

The idea for the highly successful television situation comedy *Murphy Brown* came to producer Diane English during a southern California freeway drive. The idea for the show about a tough TV newswoman "came to me in a car on the Ventura Freeway. It all just happened . . . By the time I got to the San Diego Freeway, I had the first story," she says. Barry Kemp says that the idea for the TV series *Coach* popped into his head—characters, plotline, and all—at 3 o'clock in the morning. He got up and scribbled seven pages of notes that became the foundation for the successful sit-com. A professor of mathematical sciences came up with an important new theory to explain how gravity works in the rotation of spiral galaxies, a problem that has perplexed physicists and astronomers for decades while gazing at a ceiling fan in a restaurant. Like a point on the blade of a ceiling fan, he thought (he was daydreaming at the time), the speed of a star in a spinning galaxy is slower if it lies closer to the axis. He developed an equation to test his theory and then compared its results to various measurements of galactic rotation. The results were consistent with reality, and the theory worked![30]

Step 6. Verification. Validating the idea as accurate and useful, for entrepreneurs, may include conducting experiments, running simulations, test marketing a product or service, establishing small-scale pilot programs, building prototypes, and many other activities designed to verify that the new idea will work and is practical to implement. The goal is to subject the innovative idea to the test of cold, hard reality. Is it *really* a better solution to a particular problem or opportunity? Sometimes an idea that appears to have a bright future in the lab or on paper dims considerably when put to the test of reality. Will it work? Can it be produced at a reasonable price that will produce a profit for the entrepreneur? To test the value of his new drug formulation, Dr. Navia used powerful computers at Vertex

Pharmaceuticals to build three-dimensional Tinkertoy-like models of the HIV virus and then simulated his new drug's ability to block the protease enzyme. Subsequent testing of the drug verified its safety. "I was convinced that I had an insight that no one else had," he recalls.[31]

Step 7. Implementation. The focus of this step is to transform the idea into reality. Plenty of people come up with creative ideas for promising new products or services, but most never take them beyond the idea stage. What sets entrepreneurs apart is that they act on their ideas. An entrepreneur's philosophy is "ready, aim, fire . . ." not "Ready, aim, aim, aim, aim . . ." For example, the story of the common Band-Aid® illustrates the importance of the implementation phase of the creative process. Earle Dixon, an employee of Johnson & Johnson, was married to a young woman who was accident-prone. Johnson & Johnson made large surgical dressings in individual packages, but these were not practical for the small cuts and burns she always seemed to get. So Dickson would cut out a small piece of cotton gauze and put it in the center of an adhesive strip to hold it in place. He grew tired of making his bandages every time one was needed, so he got the idea to make them in quantity, using a piece of crinoline fabric to cover the adhesive strip so that it stayed fresh. When he needed a bandage, he simply peeled off the crinoline and he had a small ready-to-use bandage.

One day, James Johnson, the company's president, saw Dickson put one of his homemade bandages on his finger. Impressed by its simplicity and convenience, he agreed to start mass-producing them under the trade name Band-Aids®![32] Dickson had started out looking for a solution to a small problem and came up with an idea for a useful new product. Most importantly, he convinced his company to implement his creative idea—to turn it into a reality. As one creativity expert explains, "Becoming more creative is really just a matter of paying attention to that endless flow of ideas you generate, and learning to capture and act upon the new that's within you."[33]

For Dr. Navia and Vertex Pharmaceuticals, the implementation phase required testing the drug's ability to fight the deadly virus in humans. If it proved to be effective, Vertex would complete the process by bringing the drug to market. In this final phase of testing, Dr. Navia was so certain that he was on the verge of a major breakthrough in fighting AIDS that he couldn't sleep at night. Unfortunately, the final critical series of tests proved that Dr. Navia's flash of creativity was, as he now says, "completely, totally, and absolutely incorrect." Although his intuition proved to be wrong this time, Dr. Navia's research into fighting AIDS continues. Much of the current work at Vertex is based on Dr. Navia's original idea. Although it proved to be incorrect, his idea has served a valuable purpose: generating new ideas. "We are now applying a powerful technology in HIV research that wasn't used before, one inspired by a hunch," he says.[34]

7. Discuss techniques for improving the creative process.

TECHNIQUES FOR IMPROVING THE CREATIVE PROCESS

Teams of people working together usually can generate more and more creative ideas. Three techniques that are especially useful for improving the quality of creative ideas from teams are brainstorming, mind-mapping, and rapid prototyping.

Brainstorming

Brainstorming is a process in which a small group of people interact with very little structure with the goal of producing a large quantity of novel and imaginative ideas. The goal is

brainstorming—*a process in which a small group of people interact with very little structure with the goal of producing a large quantity of novel and imaginative ideas.*

to create an open, uninhibited atmosphere that allows members of the group to "freewheel" ideas. Participants should suggest any ideas that come to mind *without evaluating or criticizing them.* As group members interact, each idea sparks the thinking of others, and the spawning of ideas becomes contagious. For a brainstorming session to be successful, an entrepreneur should follow these guidelines:

- Keep the group small—five to eight members. If possible, include people with different backgrounds and perspectives. At Joe Design Inc., every employee in the small firm takes part in brainstorming sessions. "We bring in everybody from the bookkeeper to the office manager because they see things completely differently than we do," says Raia.[35]
- Have a well-defined problem for the group to address but don't reveal it ahead of time. Otherwise, participants will discuss their ideas, criticize them, and engage in other creativity-limiting activities. Stating the problem in the form of a "why," "how," or "what" question often helps.
- Limit the session to 40 to 60 minutes. Beyond that, participants grow weary, and creativity flags.
- Appoint someone (preferably not a brainstorming participant) to be the recorder. The recorder should write every idea on a flip chart or board so that everyone can see them.
- Use a seating pattern that encourages communication and interaction (e.g., circular or U-shaped arrangements).
- Encourage *all* ideas from the team, even wild and extreme ones. They get the group's creative juices flowing, and creativity begins to spread like wildfire!
- Establish a goal of quantity of ideas over quality of ideas. There will be plenty of time later to evaluate the ideas generated. At Ideo Inc., a Silicon Valley design firm, brainstorming teams shoot for at least 150 ideas in a 30- to 45-minute session.[36]
- *Forbid* evaluation or criticism of any idea during the brainstorming session. Criticism slams the brakes on the creative process instantly!
- Encourage participants to use "idea hitchhiking," building new ideas on those already suggested. Often some of the best solutions are those that are piggybacked on others.

Brainstorming is a powerful tool; teams of workers using brainstorming will produce a greater quantity of ideas and higher-quality ideas than individuals working alone on the same problem. Several software packages, including IdeaFisher Pro, ThoughtPath, and Inspiration, are designed to guide both individuals and teams of people through the brainstorming process.

Mind-Mapping

Another useful tool for jump-starting creativity is mind-mapping, an extension of brainstorming. One strength of mind-mapping is that it reflects the way the brain actually works. Rather than throwing out ideas in a linear fashion, the brain jumps from one idea to another. In many creative sessions ideas are rushing out so fast that many are lost if a person attempts to shove them into a linear outline. Creativity suffers. **Mind-mapping** is a graphical technique that encourages thinking on both sides of the brain, visually displays the various relationships among ideas, and improves the ability to view a problem from many sides.

mind-mapping—*a graphical technique that encourages thinking on both sides of the brain, visually displays the various relationships among ideas, and improves the ability to view a problem from many sides.*

The mind-mapping process works this way:

- Start by writing down or sketching a picture symbolizing the problem or area of focus in the center of a large blank page. Tony Buzan, originator of the mind-mapping technique, suggests using ledger paper or covering an entire wall with butcher paper to establish a wide open attitude toward creativity.
- Write down *every* idea that comes into your mind, connecting each idea to the central picture or words with a line. Use key words and symbols to record ideas in shorthand. Work as

YOU BE THE CONSULTANT . . .

Evaluating Ideas for Their Market Potential

In 1899, Charles H. Duell, U.S. Commissioner of Patents, advised President McKinley to close the U.S. Patent Office because "Everything that can be invented has been invented." Duell was way off the mark, of course; the U.S. Patent and Trademark Office has issued more than 5 million patents since 1899. However, does a great idea that earns a patent mean that the inventor has the foundation for a successful business?

Not necessarily. Alden McMurtrys, a Connecticut tinkerer, in 1911 rushed to the U.S. Patent Office with his immortal design for the bubble-hat. It used a hidden gas canister to send soap bubbles out of a hat—perfect, Mr. McMurtry thought, for show-stopping chorus numbers. It never became a commercial success.

How can an entrepreneur evaluate the market potential of a new product or service idea? The following questions can help any entrepreneur or inventor assess the profit potential of a creative idea:

- What benefits does the product or service offer customers? Is there a real need for it?
- Have you pinpointed the exact problems or difficulties your idea aims to solve? Have you considered the problems or difficulties it might create?
- On a scale of 1 to 10, how difficult will it be to execute the idea and sell it commercially?
- Does the product or service have natural sales appeal? Can customers afford it? Will they buy it? Why?
- What existing products or services would compete with your idea? Is your product or service superior to these competing products or services? If so, in what way?
- On a scale of 1 to 10, how easily can potential customers understand the benefits of your new product or service idea? Are they obvious?
- On a scale of 1 to 10, how complex is the product or service? If it is a product, can you make a prototype of it yourself?
- On a scale of 1 to 10, how complex is the distribution or delivery system necessary to get the product or service into customers' hands?
- How unique is your product or service? How easily can other companies imitate your idea?
- How much will it cost to produce or provide the product or service? To distribute it?

To evaluate creative ideas for their commercial potential, Mail Boxes Etc. relies on a set of 20 criteria, each weighted to reflect its importance, and a scoring scale of minus 2 to plus 2. By multiplying an idea's score on each criteria by the criteria's weight, managers calculate a total score that gives them a sense of an idea's market potential. Michael Michalko, author of *Cracking Creativity: The Secrets of Creative Geniuses,* suggests using the PMI (plus, minus, interesting) technique. "First, list all of the positive (plus) aspects of the idea," he says. "Then list all of the negative (minus) aspects of the idea. Last, list everything that's interesting [about it], but you're not sure if it's a plus or a minus." Evaluating an idea in this way will lead to one of three results. "You'll decide it's a bad idea, you'll decide it's a good idea, or you'll recycle it into something else," says Michalko.

Try your hand at this process. Assume the role of consultant and help Barbara Allen evaluate the market potential of her business idea: When Barbara was a little girl, her grandfather passed along to her a "secret formula" he learned growing up in the Carpathian Mountains of Transylvania. It was a concoction created by an ancestor to give the family's sheepherding dogs beautiful coats. The blend of natural oils and vitamins not only gave the dogs shiny coats, but it also stopped them from shedding. Only decades later did Barbara begin to think that this centuries-old secret formula, which she has named Mrs. Allen's Shed Stop, might have market potential. She suspects that there might be a market for a safe, all-natural product that would eliminate a shedding problem for the nation's 124 million pet owners.

1. Use the resources on the World Wide Web and your library to explore the prospects for Barbara Allen's product.
2. Use the information you collect to answer as many of the questions listed previously as possible. Conduct a PMI (plus, minus, interesting) analysis for Barbara Allen's idea.

Sources: Jane Bahls, "Got a Winner?" *Business Start-Ups,* March 1999, pp. 6–7; Patricia L. Fry, "Inventor's Workshop," *Business Start-Ups,* August 1997, pp. 34–37; Peter Carbonara, "What Do You Do with a Great Idea?" *Business Start-Ups,* August/September, pp. 28–58; Michael W. Miller, "It Seemed Like a Good Idea," *Wall Street Journal,* May 24, 1993, p. R24; Don Debelak, "Ready or Not?" *Business Start-Ups,* January 1998, pp. 62–65; Karen Axelton, "Imagine That!" *Business Start-Ups,* April 1998, p. 96; Susan Greco, "Where Great Ideas Come From," *Inc.*, April 1998, pp. 76–86.

quickly as possible for no more than 20 minutes, doing your best to capture the tide of ideas that flows from your brain. Just as in brainstorming, do not judge the quality of your ideas; just get them onto the paper. Build new ideas on the backs of existing ones. If you see a connection between a new idea and one already on the paper, connect them with a line. If not, simply connect the idea to the center symbol. You will organize your ideas later in the process.

- When the flow of ideas slows to a trickle, stop! Don't try to force creativity.
- Allow your mind to rest for a few minutes and then begin to integrate the ideas on the page into a mind map. Use colored pens and markers to connect ideas with similar themes or to group ideas into related clusters. As you organize your thoughts, look for new connections among your ideas. Sometimes the brain needs time to process the ideas in a mind map. (Recall the incubation stage of the creative process.) Walking away from the mind map and the problem for a few minutes or a few hours may lead to several new ideas or to new relationships among ideas. One entrepreneur created the format for his company's business plan with a mind map rather than with a traditional linear outline. When he finished, he not only knew what he should include in his plan but he also had a clear picture of the order in which to sequence the elements.

Rapid Prototyping

rapid prototyping—*the process of creating a model of an idea, enabling an entrepreneur to discover flaws in the idea and to make improvements in the design.*

Generating creative ideas is a critical step in the process of taking an idea for a product or a service successfully to the market. However, entrepreneurs find that most of their ideas won't work, and that's where rapid prototyping plays an important part in the creative process. The premise behind **rapid prototyping** is that transforming an idea into an actual model will point out flaws in the original idea and will lead to improvements in its design. "If a picture is worth a thousand words, a prototype is worth ten thousand," says Steve Vassallo of Ideo Inc.[37]

The three principles of rapid prototyping are the three Rs: rough, rapid, and right. Models do not have to be perfect; in fact, in the early phases of developing an idea, perfecting a model usually is a waste of time. The key is to make the model good enough to determine what works and what does not. Doing so allows an entrepreneur to develop prototypes rapidly, moving closer to a successful design with each iteration. The final R, *right,* means building lots of small models that focus on solving particular problems with an idea. "You're not trying to build a complete model," says Vassallo. "You're just focusing on a small section of it."[38]

8. Describe the protection of intellectual property involving patents, trademarks, and copyrights.

PROTECTING YOUR IDEAS

Once entrepreneurs come up with an innovative idea for a product or service that has market potential, their immediate concern should be to protect it from unauthorized use. Entrepreneurs must understand how to put patents, trademarks, and copyrights to work for them.

Patents

patent—*a grant from the federal government's Patent and Trademark Office to the inventor of a product, giving the exclusive right to make, use, or sell the invention in this country for 20 years from the date of filing the patent application.*

A **patent** is a grant from the federal government's Patent and Trademark Office (PTO) to the inventor of a product, giving the exclusive right to make, use, or sell the invention in this country for 20 years from the date of filing the patent application. The purpose of giving an inventor a 20-year monopoly over a product is to stimulate creativity and innovation. After 20 years, the patent expires and cannot be renewed. Most patents are granted for new-product inventions, but *design patents,* extending for 14 years beyond the date the patent is issued, are given to inventors who make new, original, and ornamental changes in the design of existing products that enhance their sales. Inventors who develop a new plant can obtain a *plant patent,* provided they can reproduce the plant asexually (e.g., by grafting or cross-breeding rather than planting seeds). To be patented, a device must be new (but not necessarily better!), not obvious to a person of ordinary skill or knowledge in the related field, and useful. A device *cannot* be patented if it has been publicized in print anywhere in the world or if it has been used or offered for sale in this country prior to the date of the patent application. A U.S. patent is granted only to the true inventor, not a person who discovers another's invention. No one can copy or sell a patented invention without getting a license from its creator. A patent does not give one the right to make, use, or sell an invention but the right to exclude others from making, using, or selling it.

Although inventors are never assured of getting a patent, they can enhance their chances considerably by following the basic steps suggested by the PTO. Before beginning the often lengthy and involved procedure, inventors should obtain professional assistance from a patent practitioner—a patent attorney or a patent agent—who is registered with the PTO. Only those attorneys and agents who are officially registered may represent an inventor seeking a patent. (A list of registered attorneys and agents is available at **<www.uspto.gov/web/offices/dcom/olia/oed/roster>**). Approximately 98 percent of all inventors rely on these patent experts to steer them through the convoluted process. Legal fees for filing a patent application range from $3,000 to $10,000, depending on the complexity of the product.[39]

THE PATENT PROCESS. Since George Washington signed the first patent law in 1790, the U.S. Patent and Trademark Office, **<www.uspto.gov>,** has issued patents on everything imaginable (and some unimaginable items, too), including mousetraps (of course!), animals (genetically engineered mice), games, and various fishing devices. To date the PTO has issued more than 60 million patents, and it receives more than 230,000 new applications each year![40] To receive a patent, an inventor must follow these steps:

Establish the invention's novelty. An invention is not patentable if it is known or has been used in the United States or has been described in a printed publication in this or a foreign country.

Document the device. To protect their patent claims, inventors should be able to verify the date on which they first conceived the idea for their inventions. Inventors can document a device by keeping dated records (including drawings) of their progress on the invention and by having knowledgeable friends witness these records. Inventors also can file a disclosure document with the PTO—a process that includes writing a letter describing the invention and sending a check for $10 to the PTO.

Search existing patents. To verify that the invention truly is new, nonobvious, and useful, an inventor must conduct a search of existing patents on similar products. The purpose of the search is to determine whether or not the inventor has a chance of getting a patent. Most inventors hire professionals trained in conducting patent searches to perform the research. Inventors themselves can conduct an online search of all patents granted by the PTO since 1976 from the office's Web site at **<www.uspto.gov>.** An online search of these patents does not include sketches; however, inventors can access patents, including sketches, as far back as 1971 at the IBM Patent Server Web site at **<www.patents.ibm.com>.**

Study search results. Once the patent search is finished, inventors must study the results to determine their chances of getting a patent. To be patentable, a device must be sufficiently different from what has been used or described before and must not be obvious to a person having ordinary skill in the area of technology related to the invention.

Submit the patent application. If an inventor decides to seek a patent, he must file an application describing the invention with the PTO. Most inventors hire patent attorneys or agents to help them complete their patent applications.

Prosecute the patent application. Before the PTO will issue a patent, one of its examiners studies the application to determine whether or not the invention warrants a patent. Approval of a patent normally takes about two years from the date of filing.[41] If the PTO rejects the application, the inventor can amend his application so that the PTO can accept it.

Defending a patent against "copycat producers" can be expensive and time-consuming but often is necessary to protect an entrepreneur's interest. The average cost of a patent infringement lawsuit is about $600,000 if the case goes to trial (about half that if the parties settle before going to trial), but the odds of winning are in the patent holder's favor. More than 60 percent of those holding patents win their infringement suits.[42]

Callaway Golf Company

Knockoffs of its famous "Big Bertha" golf club have kept Callaway Golf Company busy defending its patents against counterfeiters. Callaway recently discovered another company making a look-alike driver named the "Big Bursa." Experts estimate that in some cases, the knockoffs with their steeply discounted prices actually outsell the original clubs![43]

The World Wide Web has only compounded the problem of counterfeit sales, especially among luxury items such as Luis Vuitton and Coach bags, Cartier jewelry, and Chanel perfumes. The World Wide Web now accounts for 10 percent of the total counterfeit market, an amount that is double the amount of legitimate retail sales through e-commerce.[44]

Trademarks

trademark—*any distinctive word, phrase, symbol, design, name, logo, slogan, or trade dress that a company uses to identify the origin of a product or to distinguish it from other goods on the market.*

trade dress—*the unique combination of elements that a company uses to create a product's image and to promote it.*

A **trademark** is any distinctive word, phrase, symbol, design, name, logo, slogan, or trade dress that a company uses to identify the origin of a product or to distinguish it from other goods on the market. (A *service mark* is the same as a trademark except that it identifies and distinguishes the source of a service rather than a product.) A trademark serves as a company's "signature" in the marketplace. A trademark can be more than just a company's logo, slogan, or brand name; it can also include symbols, shapes, colors, smells, or sounds. For instance, Coca-Cola holds a trademark on the shape of its bottle, and NBC owns a trademark on its three-toned chime. Motorcycle maker Harley-Davidson has applied for trademark protection for the shape of its oil tanks and the throaty rumbling sound its engines make![45] Components of a product's identity such as these are part of its **trade dress,** the unique combination of elements that a company uses to create a product's image and to promote it. For instance, a Mexican restaurant chain's particular decor, color schemes, design, and overall "look and feel" would be its trade dress. To be eligible for trademark protection, trade dress must be inherently unique and distinctive to a company, and another company's use of that trade dress must be likely to confuse customers.

Urban Decay

Entrepreneur Sandy Lerner, cofounder of Urban Decay, a small cosmetics company, is locked in a battle with cosmetic industry giant Revlon over trade dress issues. Fledgling Urban Decay, launched in late 1995, introduced a hot-selling line of cosmetics with names such as "Rust," "Shattered," "Frostbite," "Pallor," and "Roach." Less than a year later, Revlon came out with its own line of similar products using the name "Street Wear." Lerner contends that Revlon's Street Wear name, its packaging, silver-and-black lettering, and design infringe upon Urban Decay's trade dress. Lerner and Urban Decay filed a lawsuit asking for damages because she says the similarities will confuse her customers and harm her company's sales.[46]

There are 1.5 million trademarks registered in the United States, 900,000 of which are in actual use. Federal law permits a manufacturer to register a trademark, which prevents other companies from employing a similar mark to identify their goods. Before 1989, a business could not reserve a trademark in advance of use. Today the first party who either uses a trademark in commerce or files an application with the PTO has the ultimate right to register that trademark. Unlike patents and copyrights, which are issued for limited amounts of time, trademarks last indefinitely as long as the holder continues to use it. However, a trademark cannot keep competitors from producing the same product and selling it under a different name. It merely prevents others from using the same or confusingly similar trademark for the same or similar products.

Many business owners are confused by the use of the symbols ™ and ®. Anyone who claims the right to a particular trademark (or service mark) can use the ™ (or ℠) symbols without having to register the mark with the PTO. The claim to that trademark or service mark may or may not be valid, however. Only those businesses that have registered their marks with the PTO can use the ® symbol. Entrepreneurs do not have to register trademarks or service marks to establish their rights to those marks; however, registering a mark with the PTO does give entrepreneurs greater power in protecting their marks. Filing an application to register a trademark or service mark is relatively easy, but it does require a search of existing names.

Bodyslimmers by Nancy Ganz

Nancy Ganz, founder of Bodyslimmers® by Nancy Ganz, registered the name she gave her hip-shaping undergarment, Hipslip®, with the PTO as soon as she coined the name. With her company's sales now exceeding $10 million, Ganz has successfully defended her trademark against several competitors who unlawfully sold similar products using the Hipslip® name. "Shielding your trademarks isn't hard," she says. "If you let things slide long enough, you could learn the hard way how much it costs to have your name taken in vain."[47]

An entrepreneur may lose the exclusive right to a trademark if it loses its unique character and becomes a generic name. *Aspirin, escalator, thermos, brassiere, super glue, yo-yo,* and *cellophane* all were once enforceable trademarks that have become common words in the English language. Such generic terms can no longer be licensed as trademarks.

Copyrights

copyright—*an exclusive right that protects the creators of original works of authorship such as literary, dramatic, musical, and artistic works.*

A **copyright** is an exclusive right that protects the creators of original works of authorship such as literary, dramatic, musical, and artistic works (e.g., art, sculptures, literature, software, music, videos, video games, choreography, motion pictures, recordings, and others). The internationally recognized symbol © denotes a copyrighted work. A copyright protects only the form in which an idea is expressed, not the idea itself. A copyright on a creative work comes into existence the moment its creator puts that work into a tangible form. Just as with a trademark, obtaining basic copyright protection does *not* require registering the creative work with the U.S. Copyright Office, **<lcweb.loc.gov/copyright>.**

Registering a copyright does give creators greater protection over their work, however. Copyright applications must be filed with the Copyright Office in the Library of Congress for a fee of $10 per application. A valid copyright on a work lasts for the life of the creator plus 50 years after his or her death. (A copyright lasts 75 to 100 years if the copyright holder is a business.) When a copyright expires, the work becomes public property and can be used by anyone free of charge.

Because they are so easy to duplicate, computer software programs and videotapes are among the most frequently pirated items by copyright infringers. Experts estimate that the U.S. software industry loses $15 billion each year to pirates who illegally copy programs and that Hollywood loses $2 billion to those who forge counterfeit videotapes and sell them. In one New York City raid of a video warehouse, police confiscated $500,000 worth of tapes, including many titles that had not yet been released in movie theaters, on their way to dishonest rental stores.[48]

Protecting Intellectual Property

Acquiring the protection of patents, trademarks, and copyrights is useless unless an entrepreneur takes action to protect those rights in the marketplace. Unfortunately, not every businessperson respects others' rights of ownership to products, processes, names, and works and infringes on those rights with impunity. In other cases, the infringing behavior simply is the result of a lack of knowledge about others' rights of ownership. The primary weapon an entrepreneur has to protect patents, trademarks, and copyrights is the legal system. The major problem with relying on the legal system to enforce ownership rights is the cost of infringement lawsuits, which can quickly exceed the budget of most small businesses.

If an entrepreneur has a valid patent, trademark, or copyright, stopping an infringer often requires nothing more than a stern letter from an attorney threatening a lawsuit. Often offenders don't want to get into expensive legal battles and agree to stop their illegal behavior. If that tactic fails, the entrepreneur may have no choice but to bring an infringement lawsuit.

Legal battles always involve costs. Before bringing a lawsuit, an entrepreneur must consider the following issues:

Can the opponent afford to pay if you win?

Do you expect to get enough from the suit to cover the costs of hiring an attorney and preparing a case?

Can you afford the loss of time, money, and privacy from the ensuing lawsuit?

CHAPTER SUMMARY

1. Explain the differences among creativity, innovation, and entrepreneurship.
   - The entrepreneur's "secret" for creating value in the marketplace is applying creativity and innovation to solve problems and to exploit opportunities that people face every day. Creativity is the ability to develop new ideas and to discover new ways of looking at problems and opportunities. Innovation is the ability to apply creative solutions to those problems and opportunities to enhance or to enrich people's lives. Entrepreneurship is the result of a disciplined, systematic process of applying creativity and innovation to needs and opportunities in the marketplace.
2. Describe why creativity and innovation are such an integral part of entrepreneurship.
   - Entrepreneurs must always be on guard against paradigms—preconceived ideas of what the world is, what it should be like, and how it should operate—because they are logjams to creativity. Successful entrepreneurs often go beyond conventional wisdom as they ask, "Why not . . . ?"
   - Success—even survival—in this fiercely competitive, global environment requires entrepreneurs to tap their creativity (and that of their employees) constantly.
3. Understand how the two hemispheres of the human brain function and what role they play in creativity.
   - For years, people assumed that creativity was an inherent trait. Today, however, we know better. Research shows that almost anyone can learn to be creative. The left hemisphere of the brain controls language, logic, and symbols, processing information in a step-by-step fashion. The right hemisphere handles emotional, intuitive, and spatial functions, processing information intuitively. The right side of the

brain is the source of creativity and innovation. People can learn to control which side of the brain is dominant in a given situation.

4. Explain the 10 "mental locks" that limit individual creativity.
   - The number of potential barriers to creativity is limitless, but entrepreneurs commonly face 10 "mental locks" on creativity: Searching for the one right answer; focusing on being logical; blindly following the rules; constantly being practical; viewing play as frivolous; becoming overly specialized; avoiding ambiguity; fearing looking foolish; fearing mistakes and failure; and believing that "I'm not creative."
5. Understand how entrepreneurs can enhance the creativity of their employees as well as their own creativity.
   - Entrepreneurs can stimulate creativity in their companies by expecting creativity, expecting and tolerating failure, encouraging curiosity, viewing problems as challenges, providing creativity training, providing support, rewarding creativity, and modeling creativity.
   - Entrepreneurs can enhance their own creativity by using the following techniques: allowing themselves to be creative, giving their minds fresh input every day, keeping a journal handy to record their thoughts and ideas, reading books on stimulating creativity or taking a class on creativity, and taking some time off to relax.
6. Describe the steps in the creative process.
   - The creative process consists of seven steps: Step 1. Preparation—involves getting the mind ready for creative thinking; Step 2. Investigation—requires the individual to develop a solid understanding of the problem or decision; Step 3. Transformation—involves viewing the similarities and the differences among the information collected; Step 4. Incubation—allows the subconscious mind to reflect on the information collected; Step 5. Illumination—occurs at some point during the incubation stage when a spontaneous breakthrough causes "the light bulb to go on"; Step 6. Verification—involves validating the idea as accurate and useful; and Step 7. Implementation—involves transforming the idea into a business reality.
7. Discuss techniques for improving the creative process. Three techniques that are especially useful for improving the creative process:
   - Brainstorming is a process in which a small group of people interact with very little structure with the goal of producing a large quantity of novel and imaginative ideas.
   - Mind-mapping is a graphical technique that encourages thinking on both sides of the brain, visually displays the various relationships among ideas, and improves the ability to view a problem from many sides.
   - Rapid prototyping is based on the premise that transforming an idea into an actual model will point out flaws in the original idea and will lead to improvements in its design.
8. Describe the protection of intellectual property involving patents, trademarks, and copyrights.
   - A patent is a grant from the federal government that gives an inventor exclusive rights to an invention for 20 years.
   - A trademark is any distinctive word, symbol, or trade dress that a company uses to identify its product and to distinguish it from other goods. It serves as a company's "signature" in the marketplace.
   - A copyright protects original works of authorship. It covers only the form in which an idea is expressed and not the idea itself and lasts for 50 years beyond the creator's death.

DISCUSSION QUESTIONS

1. Explain the differences among creativity, innovation, and entrepreneurship.
2. How are creativity, innovation, and entrepreneurship related?
3. Why are creativity and innovation so important to the survival and success of a business?
4. One entrepreneur claims, "Creativity unrelated to a business plan has no value." What does he mean? Do you agree?
5. What is a paradigm? What impact do paradigms have on creativity?
6. Can creativity be taught or is it an inherent trait? Explain.
7. How does the human brain function? In which operations does each hemisphere specialize? Which hemisphere is the "seat" of creativity?
8. Briefly outline the 10 "mental locks" that can limit individual creativity. Give an example of a situation in which you subjected yourself to one of these mental locks.
9. What can entrepreneurs do to stimulate their own creativity and to encourage it among workers?
10. Explain the steps of the creative process. What can an entrepreneur do to enhance each step?
11. Explain the differences among a patent, a trademark, and a copyright. What form of intellectual property does each protect?

Beyond the Classroom . . .

1. Your dinner guests are to arrive in five minutes, and you've just discovered that you forgot to chill the wine! Wanting to maintain your reputation as the perfect host or hostess, you must tackle this problem with maximum creativity. What could you do? Generate as many solutions as you can in five minutes working alone. Then work with two or three students in a small group to brainstorm the problem.

2. Think of as many alternative uses for the commercial lubricant, WD-40, as you can. Remember to think *fluidly* (generating a quantity of ideas) and flexibly (generating unconventional ideas).

3. A major maker of breakfast cereals was about to introduce a new multigrain cereal. Its principal selling point is that it features "three great tastes" in every bowl: corn, rice, and wheat. Because a cereal's name is an integral part of its marketing campaign, the company hired a very costly consulting firm to come up with the right name for the new product. The consulting firm tackled the job using "a combination of structural linguistics and personal creativity." One year and many dollars later, the consulting firm gave its recommendation.

   Take 20 minutes to list names that you think would be appropriate for this cereal. Make brief notes about why you think each name is appropriate.

   Your professor may choose to prepare a list of names from all of the members of your class and may take a vote to determine the winner.

4. Each hemisphere of the brain processes information differently, and one hemisphere tends to dominate the other. Consider the following lists of words and decide which one best describes the way you make decisions and solve problems:

Metaphor	Logic
Dream	Reason
Humor	Precision
Ambiguity	Consistency
Play	Work
Approximate	Exact
Fantasy	Reality
Paradox	Direct
Diffuse	Focused
Hunch	Analysis
Generalization	Specific
Child	Adult

If you chose the list on the left, you tend to engage in "soft" thinking, which suggests a right-brain orientation. If you chose the list on the right, you tend to engage in "hard" thinking, which suggests a left-brain orientation.

Creativity relies on both "soft" and "hard" thinking. Each plays an important role in the creative process but at different phases.

A. Identify which type of thinking—"soft" or "hard"—would be most useful in each of the seven stages of the creative process.

B. List five things you can do to develop your thinking skills in the area ("soft" or "hard") that least describes your decision-making style.

5. Interview at least two entrepreneurs about their experiences as business owners. Where did their business ideas originate? How important are creativity and innovation to their success? How do they encourage an environment of creativity in their businesses?

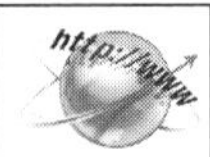

We invite you to visit this book's companion Web site at **www.prenhall.com/Zimmerer.**

Strategic Management and the Entrepreneur

LEARNING OBJECTIVES

Upon completion of this chapter, you will be able to:

1. Explain why and how a small business must build a competitive advantage in the market.
2. Create a strategic plan for a business using the 10 steps in the strategic management process.
3. Know how to write a meaningful mission statement and why it is important.
4. Understand how to identify a company's SWOT—strengths, weaknesses, opportunities, and threats.
5. Establish meaningful goals and objectives.
6. Discuss the three basic strategies—low cost, differentiation, and focus—and know when and how to employ them.
7. Understand the importance of controls such as the balanced scorecard in the planning process.

If you know the enemy and know yourself, you need not fear the results of a hundred battles.

—Sun Tzu

You either have to be first, best, or different.

—Loretta Lynn

Few activities in the life of a business are as vital—or as overlooked—as that of developing a strategy for success. Too often, entrepreneurs brimming with optimism and enthusiasm launch businesses destined for failure because their founders never stop to define a workable strategy that sets them apart from their competition. Because they tend to be people of action, entrepreneurs often find the process of developing a strategy dull and unnecessary. Their tendency is to start a business, try several approaches, and see what works. Without a cohesive plan of action, however, these entrepreneurs have as much chance of building a successful business as a defense contractor attempting to build a jet fighter without blueprints. Companies lacking clear strategies may achieve some success in the short run, but as soon as competitive conditions stiffen or an unanticipated threat arises, they usually "hit the wall" and fold. Without a basis for differentiating itself from a pack of similar competitors, the best a company can hope for is mediocrity in the marketplace.

In today's globally competitive environment, any business, large or small, that is not thinking and acting strategically is extremely vulnerable. From sweeping political changes around the planet and the explosion of the World Wide Web as a business tool to more intense competition and newly emerging global markets, the business environment has become more turbulent and challenging to business owners. Every business is exposed to the forces of a rapidly changing competitive environment, and in the future small business executives can expect even greater competition. Although this market turbulence creates many challenges for small companies, it also creates opportunities for those companies that have strategies in place to capitalize on them. Historically important, entrepreneurs' willingness to create change, to experiment with new business models, and to break traditional business rules has become more crucial than ever.

Gateway Inc.

In the personal computer business, for example, a fierce battle is raging. Plummeting prices of the chips that serve as the "brains" of computers and the rapid proliferation of e-commerce have spawned new companies offering computers for just a few hundred dollars and, in some cases, for free. That means fierce competition for established PC makers such as Gateway, Dell, and Compaq, especially now that most customers see computers as a commodity product. To succeed in this dynamic market, a company must constantly adapt its strategy to changing market and competitive conditions. Ted Waitt, founder of Gateway, says, "Every year for the past 14 years, we've been a new company." Waitt's strategy for the future is to shift Gateway's emphasis from selling the PC itself toward providing services, training, support, software, and financing—in essence, building a relationship with customers.[1]

Perhaps the biggest change entrepreneurs face is unfolding now: the shift in the world's economy from a base of *financial* to *intellectual* capital. "Knowledge is no longer just a factor of production," says futurist Alvin Toffler. "It is the *critical* factor of production."[2] That shift will create as much change in the world's business systems as the Industrial Revolution did in the agriculture-based economies of the 1800s. This knowledge revolution will spell disaster for those companies that are not prepared for it, but it will spawn tremendous opportunities for those entrepreneurs equipped with the strategies to exploit these opportunities.

Horton Interpreting Services

Juana Horton is an entrepreneur who is making the most of the knowledge revolution. Horton, who once worked for a company that helps immigrants become acclimated to the United States, saw an opportunity to put her bilingual skills to work. She formed Horton Interpreting Services, a company specializing in providing Spanish/English translation services. Horton soon saw the opportunity to expand into other languages and began hiring translators on a contract basis. Today Horton Interpreting Services relies on a network of more than 200 translators who can handle more than 70 languages ranging from Spanish and French to Gujarati and Amharic.[3]

In short, the rules of the competitive game of business have been dramatically altered. To be successful, entrepreneurs can no longer do things in the way they've always done them; the new economy requires strategic innovation as much as market success requires product and service innovation. Consequently, the successful small business manager needs a powerful weapon to cope with such a hostile environment: the process of strategic management. **Strategic management** involves developing a game plan to guide a company as it strives to accomplish its vision, mission, goals, and objectives and to keep it from straying off its desired course. Amy Miller, founder of Amy's Ice Creams, a highly successful chain of seven ice cream stores, explains:

strategic management—*the process of developing a game plan to guide a company as it strives to accomplish its vision, mission, goals, and objectives and to keep it from straying off course.*

> Progress and sustainable profitability are reflected not so much by rising numbers of stores and sales as by a company's responsiveness to changes in the marketplace and the community, its ability to maintain commitments to founding principles such as innovative employee management and constantly improving customer service, and its effectiveness in addressing corporate infrastructure needs.[4]

The idea is to give owners a blueprint for matching their companies' strengths and weaknesses to the opportunities and threats in the environment.

One study of 500 small companies concluded that one of the most significant factors in distinguishing growing companies and those in decline was the use of a written business plan.[5] Unfortunately, a survey of more than 500 small companies by Willard & Shullman Group Ltd found that only 12 percent of the companies had a long-range plan in writing. Nearly 60 percent of the small companies surveyed had no written plans at all![6]

1. Explain why and how a small business must build a competitive advantage in the market.

THE SEARCH FOR A COMPETITIVE ADVANTAGE

The goal of developing a strategic plan is to create for the small company a **competitive advantage**—the aggregation of factors that sets a small business apart from its competitors and gives it a unique position in the market. Every small firm must establish a plan for creating a unique image in the minds of its potential customers. No business can be everything to everyone. In fact, one of the biggest pitfalls many entrepreneurs stumble into is failing to differentiate their companies from the crowd of competitors.

competitive advantage—*the aggregation of factors that sets a small business apart from its competitors and gives it a unique image in the market.*

Curtis Universal Joint

For instance, Rick Hartmann is president of Curtis Universal Joint, a company that makes the joints that transfer power through an angle (for example, from your car's driveshaft to its wheels). Hartmann realizes that because the product his company makes is almost identical to those made by competitors, Curtis Universal Joint must find other ways to differentiate itself in a highly competitive industry. Surveying the industry, Hartmann noted that companies filled customers' orders at one of two speeds—slow and slower. If a universal joint broke, customers often watched in frustration as an expensive piece of equipment that could be turning out thousands of dollars of products sat idle, waiting for the $15 part. As part of a strategy to differentiate his company from its competitors, Hartmann began offering The Curtis Guarantee, which promises that any order received by 3:30 (Eastern time) will be shipped the same day or the customer gets a $50 credit. On custom orders, Curtis promises to provide price quotations within four hours, compared to the industry standard of one to two weeks. Adding value by delivering finished goods in the time it takes most of its competitors to submit estimates gives Curtis a distinct competitive advantage. Since implementing its new strategy, not only have Curtis's sales climbed 20 percent but the company also has been able to raise prices. "To boost business," says Hartmann, "you must offer something truly important to the customer and then get the word out so that [they] understand what sets your firm apart."[7]

When it comes to developing a strategic plan, small companies have a variety of natural advantages over their larger competitors. The typical small business has fewer product lines, a better-defined customer base, and a specific geographic market area. Small business owners usually are in close contact with their customers, giving them valuable knowledge on how to best serve their needs and wants. Consequently, small businesses should find that strategic management comes more naturally to them than to larger companies.

Strategic management can increase a small firm's effectiveness, but owners first must have a procedure designed to meet their needs and their business's special characteristics. It is a mistake to attempt to apply a big business's strategic development techniques to a small business because a small business is not a little big business. Because of their size and their particular characteristics—resource poverty, a flexible managerial style, an informal organizational structure, and adaptability to change—small businesses need a different approach to the strategic management process. The strategic management procedure for a small business should include the following features:

- Use a relatively short planning horizon—two years or less for most small companies.
- Be informal and not overly structured; a "shirtsleeve" approach is ideal.
- Encourage the participation of employees and outside parties to improve the reliability and creativity of the resulting plan.
- Focus on the customer. One long-term study of companies around the world found that the most successful firms were those that built their strategies around their customers rather than around their competitors' actions. The resulting strategies made their competitors irrelevant by giving customers exactly what they wanted.[8]
- Do not begin with setting objectives because extensive objective setting early on may interfere with the creative process of strategic management.
- Focus on strategic *thinking,* not just planning, by linking long-range goals to day-to-day operations. Strategic thinking encourages creativity, innovation, and employee involvement in the entire process.

2. Create a strategic plan using the 10 steps in the strategic management process.

THE STRATEGIC MANAGEMENT PROCESS

Strategic planning is not a result or an outcome but an ongoing process. Gary Hamel, a leading strategy consultant and author of *Competing for the Future,* says, "Strategizing is not a once-a-year rain dance, nor is it a once-a-decade consulting project."[9] To be useful, it must become part of the bedrock of a company. The strategic management process consists of 10 steps:

Step 1. Develop a clear vision and translate it into a meaningful mission statement.

Step 2. Define the firm's core competencies and target market segment, and position the business to compete effectively.

Step 3. Assess the company's strengths and weaknesses.

Step 4. Scan the environment for significant opportunities and threats facing the business.

Step 5. Identify the key factors for success in the business.

Step 6. Analyze the competition.

Step 7. Create company goals and objectives.

Step 8. Formulate strategic options and select the appropriate strategies.

Step 9. Translate strategic plans into action plans.

Step 10. Establish accurate controls.

Step 1. Develop a Clear Vision and Translate It into a Meaningful Mission Statement

3. Know how to write a meaningful mission statement and why it is important.

VISION. Throughout history, the greatest political and business leaders have been visionaries. Whether the vision is as grand as Martin Luther King, Jr.'s "I have a dream" speech or as simple as Ray Kroc's devotion to quality, service, cleanliness, and value at McDonald's, the purpose is the same: to focus everyone's attention on the same target and to inspire them to reach it. The vision touches everyone associated with the company—employees, investors, lenders, customers, and the community. It is an expression of what the owner stands for and believes in. Highly successful entrepreneurs are able to communicate their vision and their enthusiasm about that vision to those around them.

A vision is the result of an entrepreneur's dream of something that does not exist yet and the ability to paint a compelling picture of that dream for everyone to see. A clearly defined vision helps a company in three ways:

1. *Vision provides direction.* Entrepreneurs who spell out the vision for their company focus everyone's attention on the future and determine the path the business will take to get there.
2. *Vision determines decisions.* The vision influences the decisions, no matter how big or how small, that owners, managers, and employees make every day in a business. This influence can be positive or negative, depending on how well defined the vision is.
3. *Vision motivates people.* A clear vision excites and ignites people to action. People want to work for a company that sets its sights high.

Vision is based on an entrepreneur's values. Explaining how an entrepreneur's values are the nucleus around which a company grows, author and consultant Ken Blanchard says, "Winning companies first emphasize values—the beliefs that you, as the business owner, have about your employees, customers, quality, ethics, integrity, social responsibility, growth, stability, innovation, and flexibility. Managing by values—not by profits—is a powerful process."[10] Successful entrepreneurs build their businesses around a set of three to six core values, which might range from respect for the individual and innovation to creating satisfied customers and making the world a better place. Indeed, truly visionary entrepreneurs see their companies' primary purpose as more than just "making money." One writer explains, "Almost all workers are making decisions, not just filling out weekly sales reports or tightening screws. They will do what they think best. If you want them to do as the company thinks best too, then you must [see to it that] they have an inner gyro-

Source: Reprinted with special permission of North American Syndicate.

scope aligned with the corporate compass."[11] That gyroscope's alignment depends on the entrepreneur's values and how well he or she transmits them throughout the company.

The best way to put values into action is to create a written mission statement that communicates those values to everyone the company touches.

Mission

mission statement—*an enduring declaration of a company's purpose that addresses the first question of any business venture: What business am I in?*

The **mission statement** addresses the first question of any business venture: What business am I in? Establishing the purpose of the business in writing must come first in order to give the company a sense of direction. "If you don't reduce [your company's purpose] to paper, it just doesn't stick," says the owner of an architecture firm. "Reducing it to paper really forces you to think about what you are doing."[12] As an enduring declaration of a company's purpose, a mission statement is the mechanism for making it clear to everyone the company touches "why we are here" and "where we are going."

MobileFitness

After her company survived two crises that nearly put her out of business, Judy Creiner recognized the importance of creating a written mission statement that would crystallize her vision for MobileFitness, which provides fitness programs and health and fitness instruction for companies. Her mission reads in part: "To be preeminent in the health and wellness arena. To provide our members with unlimited opportunities to make healthy lifestyle changes in a success-oriented and supportive environment."[13]

Without a concise, meaningful mission statement, a small business risks wandering aimlessly in the marketplace, with no idea of where to go or how to get there. The mission statement sets the tone for the entire company.

Elements of a Mission Statement. A sound mission statement need not be lengthy to be effective. Some of the key issues an entrepreneur and his employees should address as they develop a mission statement for the company include:

- What are the basic beliefs and values of the organization? What do we stand for?
- Who are the company's target customers?
- What are our basic products and services? What customer needs and wants do they satisfy?
- Why should customers do business with us rather than the competitor down the street (or across town, on the other coast, on the other side of the globe)?
- What constitutes value to our customers? How can we offer them better value?
- What is our competitive advantage? What is its source?
- In which markets (or market segments) will we choose to compete?
- Who are the key stakeholders in our company and what effect do they have on it?

By answering such basic questions, the company will have a much clearer picture of what it is and what it wants to become.

Norstan Inc.

Norstan Inc., a telecommunications company, discovered the importance of its mission statement as a unifying theme when it experienced rapid growth and made several acquisitions of smaller companies. The owners of the company translated their values and vision into a mission statement for the company this way: "Norstan is a full-range provider of integrated voice, data, and video solutions that satisfy both today's and tomorrow's business needs. Through ethical, responsive, and profitable actions, Norstan will provide a fulfilling work environment for our employees, legendary service for our customers, enhanced value for our shareholders, and a spirit of shared responsibility with our community."[14]

A company's mission statement may be the most essential and basic communications that it puts forward. If the people on the plant, shop, retail, or warehouse floor don't know what a company's mission is, then, for all practical purposes, it does not have one! The mission statement expresses the firm's character, identity, and scope of operations, but writing it is only half the battle at best. The most difficult part is living that mission every day. *That's* how employees decide what really matters. To be effective, a mission statement must become a natural part of the organization, embodied in the minds, habits, attitudes, and decisions of everyone in the company every day.

Ben & Jerry's Homemade Inc.

Ben & Jerry's Homemade relies on a three-part mission statement; consider the message it sends to company stakeholders:[15]

> Product: To make, distribute and sell the finest quality all natural ice cream and related products in a wide variety of innovative flavors made from Vermont dairy products.
>
> Economic: To operate the Company on a sound financial basis of profitable growth, increasing value for our shareholders, and creating career opportunities and financial rewards for our employees.
>
> Social: To operate the Company in a way that actively recognizes the central role that business plays in the structure of society by initiating innovative ways to improve the quality of life of a broad community—local, national, and international.
>
> Underlying the mission of Ben & Jerry's is the determination to seek new and creative ways of addressing all three parts, while holding a deep respect for individuals inside and outside the Company and for the communities of which they are a part.

A company may have a powerful competitive advantage, but it is wasted unless (1) the owner has communicated that advantage to workers, who, in turn, are working hard to communicate it to customers and potential customers and (2) customers are recommending the company to their friends because they understand the benefits they are getting from it that they cannot get elsewhere. *That's* the real power of a mission statement. Table 3.1 offers some useful tips on writing a mission statement.

Step 2: Define the Firm's Core Competencies and Target Market

CORE COMPETENCIES. In the long run, what sets a company apart from its competition is the ability to develop a set of core competencies that enables it to serve its selected target customers better. **Core competencies** are a unique set of lasting capabilities that a company develops in key operational areas, such as quality, service, innovation, team building, flexibility, responsiveness, and others, which allow it to vault past competitors. Typically, a company is likely to build core competencies in no more than five or six (often fewer) areas. These core competencies become the nucleus of a company's competitive advantage and are usually quite enduring over time. To be effective, these competencies should be difficult for competitors to duplicate, and they must provide customers with some kind of perceived benefit. Small companies' core competencies often have to do with the advantages of their size—agility, speed, closeness to their customers, superior service, and ability to innovate. In short, their smallness is an advantage, allowing them to do things that their larger rivals cannot do. The key to success is building these core competencies (or identifying the ones a company already has) and then concentrating them on providing superior service and value for its target customers.

core competencies—*a unique set of lasting capabilities that a company develops in key operational areas that allow it to vault past competitors.*

Developing core competencies does *not* necessarily require a company to spend a great deal of money. It does, however, require an entrepreneur to use creativity, imagination, and vision to identify those things that it does best and that are most important to its target customers. Building a company's strategy around its core competencies allows a business to gain a sustainable competitive edge over its rivals and to ride its strategy to victory.

TABLE 3.1

Tips for Writing a Powerful Mission Statement

Sources: Adapted from Ken Blanchard, "The New Bottom Line," Entrepreneur, *February 1998, pp. 127–131; Alan Farnham, "Brushing Up Your Vision Thing,"* Fortune, *May 1, 1995, p. 129; Sharon Nelton, "Put Your Purpose in Writing,"* Nation's Business, *February 1994, pp. 61–64; Jacquelyn Lynn, "Single-Minded,"* Entrepreneur, *January 1996, p. 97.*

A mission statement is a useful tool for getting everyone fired up and heading in the same direction, but writing one is not as easy as it may first appear. Here are some tips for writing a powerful mission statement:

- *Keep it short.* The best mission statements are just a few sentences long. If they are short, people will tend to remember them better.
- *Keep it simple.* Avoid using fancy jargon just to impress outsiders such as customers or suppliers. The first and most important use of a mission statement is inside a company.
- *Get everyone involved.* If the boss writes the company mission statement, who is going to criticize it? Although the entrepreneur has to be the driving force behind the mission statement, everyone in the company needs the opportunity to have a voice in creating it. Expect to write several drafts before you arrive at a finished product.
- *Keep it current.* Mission statements can get stale over time. As business and competitive conditions change, so should your mission statement. Make a habit of evaluating your mission statement periodically so that it stays fresh.
- *Make sure your mission statement reflects the values and beliefs you hold dear.* They are the foundation on which your company is built.
- *Make sure your mission statement includes values that are worthy of your employees' best efforts.* One entrepreneur says that a mission statement should "send a message to employees, suppliers, and customers as to what the purpose of the company is aside from just making profits."
- *Make sure your mission statement reflects a concern for the future.* Business owners can get so focused on the present that they forget about the future. A mission statement should be the first link to the company's future.
- *Keep the tone of the mission statement positive and upbeat.* No one wants to work for a business with a pessimistic outlook of the world.
- *Consider using your mission statement to lay an ethical foundation for your company.* This is the ideal time to let employees know what you company stands for—and what it won't stand for.
- *Look at other companies' mission statements to generate ideas for your own.* Two books, *Say It and Live It: The 50 Corporate Mission Statements That Hit the Mark* (Currency/Doubleday) and *Mission Statements: A Guide to the Corporate and Nonprofit Sectors* (Garland Publishing), are useful resources.
- *Make sure that your mission statement is appropriate for your company's culture.* Although you should look at other companies' mission statements, do not make the mistake of trying to copy them. Your company's mission statement is unique to you and your company.
- *Use it.* Don't go to all of the trouble of writing a mission statement just to let it collect dust. Post it on bulletin boards, print it on buttons and business cards, stuff it into employees' pay envelopes. Talk about your mission statement often, and use it to develop your company's strategic plan. That's what it's for!

Indian Rock Produce

For example, Albie Buehrer, owner of Indian Rock Produce, has cultivated a profitable niche selling high-quality, organically grown, unusual fruits, herbs, and vegetables to the nation's top restaurant chefs. Drawing on a lifetime of experience in the food industry (from farmer to restaurateur), Buehrer has developed a strategy for his business that emphasizes quality and service over price. In addition to the produce he grows on his own farm (which includes everything from green zebra tomatoes to magenta spinach), Buehrer also offers hard-to-find products from suppliers across the globe. Relying on his company's core competencies, which include his extensive knowledge of and experience in the business and the rich network of contacts and relationships he has cultivated in the industry over the years, Buehrer has become the supplier of preference for exotic produce. Building Indian Rock's strategies on core competencies has allowed Buehrer to push sales from $1.5 million in 1988 to more than $20 million today.[16]

Successful small businesses know the market segment(s) in which they compete and build and retain core competencies that directly contribute to their long-term effectiveness. Answering the following questions will help entrepreneurs focus their resources on creating or reinforcing their companies' core competencies.

- What are our target customers' characteristics (e.g., age, income, buying habits, location)?
- Why do they buy our goods or use our service?
- What unique skills, knowledge, service, or other resources do we possess that would improve our target customers' lives?
- How can we use those resources to offer value to customers that our competitors cannot?
- How loyal are they to their present supplier(s)?
- What factors cause them to increase or decrease purchases?
- To what extent does our market focus build on skills that we already have?
- What skills must we develop to serve our customers in the future?

market segmentation— *a strategy that involves carving up the mass market into smaller, more homogeneous units and then attacking certain segments with a marketing strategy designed to appeal to its members.*

MARKET SEGMENTATION. **Market segmentation** simply means carving up the mass market into smaller, more homogeneous units and then attacking certain segments with a specific marketing strategy designed to appeal to its members. This requires information—knowing who the firm's customers are, their characteristics, and their likes and dislikes. To segment a market successfully, an entrepreneur must first identify the characteristics of two or more groups of customers with similar needs or wants. The key is to develop a basis for segmenting the market—benefits sought, product usage, brand preference, purchase patterns, and so on—and use this basis to identify the various submarkets to enter. Then the owner must verify that the segments are large enough and have enough purchasing power to generate a profit for the firm because segmentation is useless if the firm cannot earn a profit serving its segments. Finally, the owner must reach the market. To be profitable, a segment must be accessible. Typical market segments might be college students, retired people, young singles, ethnic groups, or high-income baby boomers.

Small companies that focus on particular target segments and take the time to learn their customers' habits, wants, and needs can market their goods and services more effectively.

Veterinary Pet Insurance

For instance, in the $23 billion per year pet industry, many small companies have achieved success by concentrating on specific market segments. When he launched Veterinary Pet Insurance in 1982, Jack Stephens targeted the segment of the pet-owning market that treats pets like members of the family. (He sold his first policy to dog star Lassie.) The company struggled in the early years, selling basic accident and illness insurance policies for $33. Since then, the market for pet insurance has exploded, and Stephens's company has issued more than 850,000 policies in 46 states. A law firm in Virginia is also targeting this pampered pet market segment, offering clients estate planning services for their pets. The firm of Gabeler, Battocchi, and Griggs LLC has developed a specialty in estate planning for pets. Senior partner Lane Gabeler creates for her clients wills, letters of instruction, and trusts that provide for the care of pets.[17]

positioning— *a technique that involves influencing customers' perceptions to create the desired image for a business and its goods and services.*

POSITIONING. **Positioning** the company in the market involves influencing customers' perceptions to create the desired image for the business and its goods and services. Proper positioning gives the small business a way of setting itself apart from the competition, the foundation for developing a competitive advantage. Lower prices are a common method of establishing a competitive advantage, but this can be especially dangerous for small businesses that cannot rely on the economies of scale that larger businesses can. A smarter tactic for small business owners is to rely on a natural advantage, such as a small firm's flexibility in reaching the market, a wider variety of customer services, or special knowledge of the good or service.

Healthy Planet Products

Bruce Wilson changed the entire focus of his company, Healthy Planet Products, when he discovered that sales of its traditional greeting cards were growing at 3 percent a year and that sales of its wildlife and environmental cards (printed on high-quality, recycled paper with stunning images of wildlife and nature) were growing at 30 percent a year. "We were trying to be everything to everyone," recalls Wilson, "but there was no way we could compete with Hallmark, American Greetings, and Gibson." Wilson decided to position Healthy Planet Products as "a marketer of cause-related greeting cards." Within three years, 90 percent of the company's cards and stationery were linked to organizations supporting environmental causes such as the Sierra Club, and sales had climbed 80 percent to $5.8 million. Healthy Planet Products' primary target audience is baby boomers who are concerned about environmental issues and who prefer to do business with companies that support environmental causes.[18]

4. Understand how to identify a company's SWOT—strengths, weaknesses, opportunities, and threats.

Step 3: Assess the Company's Strengths and Weaknesses

Having identified the firm's core competencies and desired position in the market, an entrepreneur can turn her attention to assessing company strengths and weaknesses. Building a successful competitive strategy demands that a business magnify its strengths and overcome or compensate for its weaknesses. **Strengths** are positive internal factors that a company can use to accomplish its mission, goals, and objectives. They might include special skills or knowledge, a positive public image, an experienced sales force, and many other factors. **Weaknesses** are negative internal factors that inhibit the accomplishment of a company's mission, goals, and objectives. Lack of capital, a shortage of skilled workers, and an inferior location are examples of weaknesses.

strengths—*positive internal factors that a company can use to accomplish its mission, goals, and objectives.*

weaknesses—*negative internal factors that inhibit the accomplishment of a company's mission, goals, and objectives.*

Identifying strengths and weaknesses helps an owner understand her business as it exists (or will exist). An organization's strengths should originate in the core competencies that are essential to remaining competitive in each of the market segments in which the firm competes. The key to building a successful strategy is using the company's underlying strengths as its foundation and matching those strengths against competitors' weaknesses.

One effective technique for taking this strategic inventory is to prepare a "balance sheet" of the company's strengths and weaknesses (see Table 3.2). The positive side should reflect important skills, knowledge, and resources that contribute to the firm's success. The negative side should record honestly any limitations that detract from the company's ability to compete. This balance sheet should analyze all key performance areas of the busi-

TABLE 3.2
Identifying Company Strengths and Weaknesses

Strengths (Positive Internal Factors)	Weaknesses (Negative Internal Factors)

ness—personnel, finance, production, marketing, product development, organization, and others. This analysis should give owners a more realistic perspective of their businesses, pointing out foundations on which they can build future strengths and obstacles that they must remove for business progress. This exercise can help entrepreneurs move from their current position to future actions.

Step 4: Scan the Environment for Significant Opportunities and Threats

OPPORTUNITIES. Once entrepreneurs have taken an internal inventory of company strengths and weaknesses, they must turn to the external environment to identify any opportunities and threats that might have a significant impact on the business. **Opportunities** are positive external options that a firm could exploit to accomplish its mission, goals, and objectives. The number of potential opportunities is limitless, so entrepreneurs need analyze only those factors that are most significant to the business (probably two or three at most).

opportunities—*positive external options that a firm can exploit to accomplish its mission, goals, and objectives.*

When identifying opportunities, an entrepreneur must pay close attention to new potential markets. Are competitors overlooking a niche in the market? Is there a better way to reach customers? Can we develop new products that offer customers better value? What opportunities are trends in the industry creating?

Citrix Systems Inc.

A few years ago, Citrix Systems Inc., a small Florida-based software company, spotted an important trend in the computer market: a shift away from stand-alone desktop PCs to networks of terminals linked to centralized servers, especially among corporate users. As Citrix managers explored the implications of this trend for their company's future, they saw an opportunity to capitalize on a revolutionary idea. Rather than buy costly software packages for each stand-alone computer, customers could rent only the programs they need over the Internet. Building on expertise in software development that already existed in the company (a strength), Citrix developed a way to separate the computing functions of a program from what a user sees on the screen. Using technology known as independent computing architecture, Citrix's innovation allows users to run the latest versions of popular software packages without constantly upgrading them. Also, because their computers actually do little computing (the server handles this), customers do not have to purchase the latest, most powerful hardware, a source of major savings.[19]

THREATS. **Threats** are negative external forces that inhibit a company's ability to achieve its mission, goals, and objectives. Threats to the business can take a variety of forms, such as new competitors entering the local market, a government mandate regulating a business activity, an economic recession, rising interest rates, technological advances making a company's product obsolete, and many others.

threats—*negative external forces that inhibit a company's ability to achieve its mission, goals, and objectives.*

DiamondBack and Lewis Brothers Stages

For instance, when the team owners in the National Basketball Association (NBA) engaged in a six-month lockout over players' salaries, the impact reached far beyond the players' wallets and the basketball court. Entrepreneurs across the country whose livelihoods depend on professional basketball agonized as they watched their sales and profits dry up. At the DiamondBack, a huge restaurant near the Cleveland Cavaliers' Gund Arena, co-owner David Allen Hill says that traffic from Cavalier basketball games normally accounts for 35 percent of DiamondBack's profits. The company struggled when the games were canceled. In Salt Lake City, revenues at Lewis Brothers Stages, a family-owned motor coach line, fell 10 percent because of the lockout. Lewis Brothers Stages provides bus transportation for visiting teams playing the Utah Jazz.[20]

Although they cannot control the threats themselves, entrepreneurs must prepare a plan for shielding their businesses from these threats.

FIGURE 3.1
The Power of External Forces

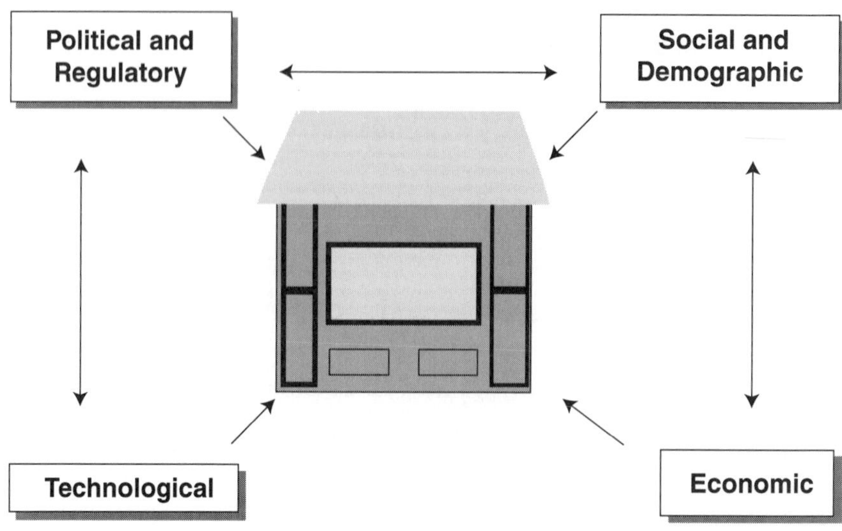

Figure 3.1 illustrates that opportunities and threats are products of the interactions of forces, trends, and events outside the direct control of the business. These external forces will have direct impact on the behavior of the markets in which the business operates, the behavior of competitors, and the behavior of customers. Table 3.3 provides a form that allows business owners to take a strategic inventory of the opportunities and threats facing their companies.

AlumiPlate Inc.

As part of updating the business plan for his small metal-plating business, AlumiPlate Inc., David Dayton prepared an analysis of the company's strengths, weaknesses, opportunities, and threats (a SWOT analysis) and found it to be an extremely useful part of the planning process. Dayton and his 14 employees identified high barriers to new competitors as one of AlumiPlate's major strengths and its proprietary aluminum-coating technology as its greatest opportunity. The team saw the inability to produce a high-volume production demonstration as the company's greatest weakness, and its greatest threat was the

TABLE 3.3
Identifying Opportunities and Threats

Opportunities (Positive External Factors)	Threats (Negative External Factors)

YOU BE THE CONSULTANT . . .

A Different Tune on the Internet

The Internet is threatening to change the face of the music industry, and executives at major music companies such as Atlantic Group and Sony are running scared. Music entrepreneurs, however, find the opportunities the Internet offers them exciting and filled with promise. Traditional music companies make their money the same way they always have: by finding and developing new bands, producing their recordings, and marketing their CDs through stores and the World Wide Web. Music entrepreneurs such as Michael Robertson, CEO of MP3.com, see a different future for the industry, thanks to the Internet and digital formats such as MP3, which allow listeners to download songs from the Web with ease. In their world, music lovers can pick songs off the Web, store them on their computers, play them on their computers and on a variety of other devices, and share them with their friends and others—at no charge! Every year, listeners download billions of songs from the Web and pay for virtually none of them. Although digital downloading of music from the Web provides the ultimate in convenience for listeners and creates many opportunities for entrepreneurs, it threatens to make the traditional product of the recording industry—the venerable record-company-produced CD—irrelevant.

Although many Web sites illegally offer pirated songs for downloading, several sites have sprung up to provide music fans the chance to download songs legally and give struggling young artists the chance to introduce their work. One of the best-known sites is Robertson's MP3.com, which is creating a new business model in the recording industry. When Robertson, who is not a music industry veteran nor a Java programmer, began to learn how the traditional record industry worked, he thought, "The system is broken, and we can fix it." For instance, he discovered that musicians typically get less than 10 percent of a CD's retail price and that most artists are locked into long-term contracts with recording studios that control which songs are produced and recorded. Robertson also discovered that record companies lose money on 85 percent of their artists and depend on a few hit bands to produce their profits. Although major record companies may one day use the Web to deliver music to millions of fans, virtually all of them see the Web strictly as a promotional and advertising tool for now.

Robertson sees things differently and created MP3.com as an alternative to the traditional methods in the recording industry. For instance, when artists sign on with Robertson, they agree to give away one song, which listeners can download for free on the MP3.com Web site **<www.mp3.com>**. If a listener wants to buy a CD, MP3.com presses it and ships it. The artist sets the CD's price, gets 50 percent of the final price, and maintains control of the master recording. Robertson's site has become one of the most popular on the Web, attracting 250,000 visitors a day. Listeners have downloaded free of charge more than 18 million songs from the MP3.com site.

Generating Web traffic and producing profit-generating sales are two different things, however, and the latter is where MP3.com has problems. The tiny start-up has attracted $10 million in venture capital and is planning an initial public offering but like many "dot-com" companies has never earned a profit. Robertson says that MP3.com sells just over 200 CDs a day at an average price of $7, only enough to generate sales volume of about $700,000 a year. The cost of pressing and shipping the CDs, marketing expenses, and payroll for the company's 50 employees doesn't leave much room for generating a profit. Robertson says that most of MP3.com's revenue comes from companies that pay to advertise on his Web site.

Although he refers to the major recording companies as "dinosaurs," Robertson recognizes that the future of his company and others like it may depend on cooperation with the dinosaurs. Val Azzoli, co-CEO of the Atlantic Group, a major player in the industry, agrees, seeing companies such as MP3.com as a way to develop new talent. "Rather than plunk down $1 million to break a new band," he says, "why not test its popularity on the Web first?" Only time will tell what role the Web will play in the music industry. Whatever the future holds, those companies, large or small, that are strategically poised to capitalize on the changes it will create will be most successful.

1. Work with a team of your classmates to develop a list of opportunities and threats that the World Wide Web is creating for companies of all sizes in the music industry.
2. What future do you predict for MP3.com? Explain. What must Michael Robertson do to maintain his company's viability?
3. Visit MP3.com's Web site and then use the resources of the Web to learn more about the company and the industry in which it operates. Conduct a SWOT analysis for MP3.com. What strategic recommendations would you make for the company?

Source: Adapted from Jodi Mardesich, "How the Internet Hits Big Music," *Fortune*, May 10, 1999, pp. 96–102.

heavy demands being placed on key personnel. Dayton and his employees went on to explore the ways AlumiPlate could use its strengths to exploit the best opportunities facing it; they also considered the ways in which its weaknesses make it vulnerable to threats.[21]

These interactions of strengths and weaknesses and opportunities and threats can be the most revealing aspects of using a SWOT analysis as part of a strategic plan. This analysis also requires entrepreneurs to take an objective look at their businesses and the environment in which they operate as they address many issues fundamental to their companies success in the future.

Step 5: Identify the Key Factors for Success in the Business

KEY SUCCESS FACTORS. Every business is characterized by controllable variables that determine the relative success of market participants. Identifying and manipulating these variables is how a small business gains a competitive advantage. By focusing efforts to maximize their companies' performance on these key success factors, entrepreneurs can achieve dramatic market advantages over their competitors. Companies that understand these key success factors tend to be leaders of the pack, whereas those that fail to recognize them become also-rans.

key success factors—*relationships between a controllable variable and a critical factor influencing the firm's ability to compete in the market.*

Key success factors come in a variety of different patterns depending on the industry. Simply stated, they are relationships between a controllable variable (e.g., plant size, size of sales force, advertising expenditures, product packaging) and a critical factor influencing the firm's ability to compete in the market. Many of these sources of competitive advantages are based on cost factors such as manufacturing cost per unit, distribution cost per unit, or development cost per unit. Some are less tangible and less obvious but are just as important, such as product quality, services offered, store location, and customer credit. For example, one restaurant owner identified the following key success factors:

- Tight cost control (labor costs, 15 to 18 percent of sales and food costs, 35 to 40 percent of sales).
- Trained, dependable, honest in-store managers.
- Close monitoring of waste.
- Careful site selection (the right location).
- Maintenance of food quality.
- Consistency.
- Cleanliness.
- Friendly and attentive service from a well-trained waitstaff.

These controllable variables determine the ability of any restaurant in this entrepreneur's market segment to compete. Restaurants lacking these key success factors are not likely to survive, but those that build their strategies with these factors in mind will prosper. However, before any small entrepreneur can build a strategy on the foundation of the industry's key success factors, she must identify them. Table 3.4 presents a form to help owners identify the most important success factors in the industry and their implications for their companies.

Entrepreneurs must use the information gathered to analyze their businesses, their competitors, and their industries in order to isolate these sources of competitive advantage. They must then determine how well their business meets these criteria for successfully competing in the market. Highly successful companies know and understand these relationships, but marginal competitors are mystified by which factors determine success in that particular business. For example, a small manufacturer of cosmetics may discover that

TABLE 3.4
Identifying Key Success Factors

List the specific skills, characteristics, and core competencies that your business must possess if it is to be successful in its market segment.

Key Success Factor	How your company rates . . .
1	Low 1 2 3 4 5 6 7 8 9 10 High
2	Low 1 2 3 4 5 6 7 8 9 10 High
3	Low 1 2 3 4 5 6 7 8 9 10 High
4	Low 1 2 3 4 5 6 7 8 9 10 High
5	Low 1 2 3 4 5 6 7 8 9 10 High
Conclusions:	

shelf space, broad exposure, efficient distribution, and long production runs are crucial to business success. On the other hand, a small retail chain owner may find that broad product lines, customer credit, personalized service, capable store management, and low distribution costs determine success in his business.

Step 6. Analyze the Competition

When a recent survey asked small business owners to identify the greatest challenge they faced in the upcoming year, the overwhelming response was *competition.*[22] In another survey, CEOs across the globe said the World Wide Web and the trend toward e-commerce it is driving will make competition even more fierce in the future. Twenty percent said that e-commerce will *completely* reshape the ways in which they do business.[23] As these studies suggest, keeping tabs on rivals' movements through competitive intelligence programs is a vital strategic activity. "Business is like any battlefield. If you want to win the war, you have to know who you're up against," says one small business consultant.[24] The primary goals of a competitive intelligence program include the following:

- Avoiding surprises from existing competitors' new strategies and tactics.
- Identifying potential new competitors.
- Improving reaction time to competitors' actions.
- Anticipating rivals' next strategic moves.

COMPETITOR ANALYSIS. Sizing up the competition gives a business owner a more realistic view of the market and her company's position in it. A competitive intelligence exercise enables entrepreneurs to update their knowledge of competitors by answering the following questions:

- Who are your major competitors? Where are they located? (The Yellow Pages is a great place to start.)
- What distinctive competencies have they developed?

- How do their cost structures compare to yours? Their financial resources?
- How do they market their products and services?
- What do customers say about them? How do customers describe their products or services, their way of doing business, and the additional services they might supply?
- What are their key strategies?
- What are their strengths? How can your company surpass them?
- What are their primary weaknesses? How can your company capitalize on them?
- Are new competitors entering the business?

A small business owner can collect a great deal of information about competitors through low-cost methods including the following:

- Read industry trade publications for announcements from competitors.
- Ask questions of customers and suppliers on what they hear competitors may be doing. In many cases, this information is easy to gather because some people love to gossip.
- Talk to employees, especially sales representatives and purchasing agents. Experts estimate that 70 to 90 percent of the competitive information a company needs already resides with employees who collect it in their routine dealings with suppliers, customers, and other industry contacts.[25]
- Attend trade shows and collect the competitors' sales literature.
- If appropriate, buy the competitors' products and assess their quality and features. Benchmark their products against yours. The owner of a mail-order gourmet brownie business periodically places orders from her primary rivals and compares their packaging, pricing, service, and quality to her own.[26]
- Obtain credit reports from Dun & Bradstreet on each of your major competitors to evaluate their financial condition.
- Check out the resources of your local library, including articles, computerized databases, and online searches. For local competitors, review back issues of the area newspaper for articles on and advertisements by competitors.
- Use the vast resources of the World Wide Web to learn more about your competitors. The Web enables small companies to uncover valuable competitive information at little or no cost. (Refer to our Web site at **<www.prenhall.com/scarbzim>** for an extensive listing of more than 1,200 useful small business Web sites.)
- Visit competing businesses periodically to observe their operations. Tom Stemberg, CEO of Staples, a chain of office supply superstores, says, "I've never visited a store where I didn't learn something."[27]

Using the information gathered, a business owner can set up teams of managers and employees to evaluate each competitor and make recommendations on specific strategic actions that will improve the firm's competitive position against each.

The owner can use the results of the competitor intelligence analysis to construct a competitive profile matrix for each market segment in which the firm operates. A **competitive profile matrix** allows the owner to evaluate her firm against major competitors on the key success factors for that market segment (refer to Table 3.4). The first step is to list the key success factors identified in Step 5 of the strategic planning process and to attach weights to them reflecting their relative importance. (For simplicity, the weights in this matrix add up to 1.00.) In this example, notice that product quality is weighted twice as heavily (twice as important) as is price competitiveness.

competitive profile matrix—*a tool that allows a business owner to evaluate his or her company against major competitors on the key success factors for that market.*

The next step is to identify the company's major competitors and to rate each one (and your own company) on each of the key success factors:

If factor is a:	Rating is:
Major weakness	1
Minor weakness	2
Minor strength	3
Major strength	4

Once the rating is completed, the owner simply multiplies the weight by the rating for each factor to get a weighted score, and then adds up each competitor's weighted scores to get a total weighted score. Table 3.5 shows a sample competitive profile matrix for a small company. The results should show which company is strongest, which is weakest, and which of the key success factors each one is best and worst at meeting. By carefully studying and interpreting the results, an entrepreneur can begin to envision the ideal strategy for building a competitive edge in her market segment.

KNOWLEDGE MANAGEMENT. Unfortunately, many small companies fail to gather competitive intelligence because their owners mistakenly assume that it is too costly or simply unnecessary. In reality, the cost of collecting information about competitors and the competitive environment typically is minimal, but it does require discipline. "In today's world," says competitive intelligence consultant Leonard Fuld, "all companies, large and small, have virtually the same access to information."[28] Once again, the great equalizer for harnessing information is the Internet. The key is learning how to manage the knowledge a company accumulates. **Knowledge management** is the practice of gathering, organizing, and disseminating the collective wisdom and experience of a company's employees for the purpose of strengthening its competitive position. "Knowledge management allows you to determine the explicit knowledge that is somewhere in your organization and that you can leverage rather than having to reinvent the wheel," says Dorothy Leonard-Barton, author of *Wellsprings of Knowledge.*[29] Because of their size and simplicity, small businesses have an advantage over large companies when it comes to managing knowledge.

knowledge management— *the practice of gathering, organizing, and disseminating the collective wisdom and experience of a company's employees for the purpose of strengthening its competitive position.*

The first step in creating a knowledge management program is to take an inventory of the special knowledge a company possesses that gives it a competitive advantage. This involves assessing the knowledge bank that employees have compiled over time. The second step is to organize the essential knowledge and disseminate it throughout the company to those who need it. High-tech solutions such as e-mail, computerized databases, and software that allow many different employees to work on a project simultaneously are important tools, but low-tech methods such as whiteboards, Post-it notes, and face-to-face meetings can be just as effective in small companies.

TABLE 3.5
Sample Competitive Profile Matrix

Key Success Factors		Your Business		Competitor 1		Competitor 2	
(from Step 5)	Weight	Rating	Weighted Score	Rating	Weighted Score	Rating	Weighted Score
Market Share	0.10	3	0.30	2	0.20	3	0.30
Price Competitiveness	0.20	1	0.20	3	0.60	4	0.80
Financial Strength	0.10	2	0.20	3	0.30	2	0.20
Product Quality	0.40	4	1.60	2	0.80	1	0.40
Customer Loyalty	0.20	3	0.60	3	0.60	2	0.40
Total	1.00		2.90		2.50		2.10

Phase Two Strategies

For Ben Farrell, owner of Phase Two Strategies, a San Francisco public relations firm, keeping up with news stories about clients and their industries is essential. Farrell and his staff used to spend many hours poring over stacks of magazines and newspapers to sift out the information they needed. Recently, however, Phase Two Strategies switched to Lexis-Nexis Tracker, an online news retrieval service that allows staffers to set up search criteria and then creates a Web page with hyperlinks to relevant stories. The new system not only saves time and increases productivity, but it also allows Phase Two Strategies to serve its customers more effectively.[30]

Performance Personnel

Shari Franey, CEO of Performance Personnel, a staffing company with offices in six locations across Pennsylvania, also uses e-mail and voice-mail systems as part of her company's knowledge management program. These tools worked well, but Franey quickly saw their limitations and instituted a series of meetings designed exclusively to allow employees to share useful information with one another. The meetings disseminate vital information throughout the company and build a sense of camaraderie among employees.[31]

5. Establish meaningful goals and objectives.

Step 7. Create Company Goals and Objectives

Before an entrepreneur can build a comprehensive set of strategies, he must first establish business goals and objectives, which give targets to aim for and provide a basis for evaluating a company's performance. Without them, the owner cannot know where the business is going or how well it is performing. The following conversation between Alice and the Cheshire Cat, taken from Lewis Carroll's *Alice in Wonderland,* illustrates the importance of creating meaningful goals and objectives as part of the strategic management process:

> "Would you tell me please, which way I ought to go from here?" asked Alice.
>
> "That depends a good deal on where you want to get to," said the Cat.
>
> "I don't much care where . . . ," said Alice.
>
> "Then it doesn't matter which way you go," said the Cat.

A small business that "doesn't much care where" it wants to go (i.e., has no goals and objectives) will find that "it really doesn't matter which way" it chooses to go (i.e., strategy is irrelevant).

goals—*the broad, long-range attributes a business seeks to accomplish; they tend to be general and sometimes even abstract.*

GOALS. **Goals** are the broad, long-range attributes that a business seeks to accomplish; they tend to be general and sometimes even abstract. Goals are not intended to be specific enough for a manager to act on but simply state the general level of accomplishment sought. Do you want to boost your market share? Does your cash balance need strengthening? Would you like to enter a new market or increase sales in a current one? Do you want to develop new products or services? Addressing these broad issues will help you focus on the next phase—developing specific, realistic objectives.

objectives—*more specific targets of performance, commonly addressing such issues as profitability, productivity, growth, and other key aspects of a business.*

OBJECTIVES. **Objectives** are more specific targets of performance. Common objectives concern profitability, productivity, growth, efficiency, markets, financial resources, physical facilities, organizational structure, employee welfare, and social responsibility. Because some of these objectives might conflict with one another, it is important to establish priorities. Which objectives are most important? Which are least important? Arranging objectives in a hierarchy according to their priority can help an entrepreneur resolve conflicts when they arise. Well-written objectives have the following characteristics:

They are specific. Objectives should be quantifiable and precise. For example, "to achieve a healthy growth in sales" is not a meaningful objective; whereas "to increase retail sales by

YOU BE THE CONSULTANT . . .

Life, the Universe, and Everything

When Duncan Highsmith, CEO of Highsmith Inc., the nation's leading direct-mail supplier of audio-visual tools and educational supplies, sits down to read, his subject matter is not always the current best-seller on the business list. In fact, it's more likely that Highsmith is sifting through an eclectic mix of reading material, ranging from juvenile crime to the wing construction of dragonflies. Why? He's looking for connections among seemingly unrelated topics, emerging trends, and provocative ideas that might eventually reshape his business. For instance, after reading that dragonflies have four wings that move independently of one another, Highsmith says that he began to think differently about the autonomy of several of his company's business units.

Highsmith has dubbed his weekly reading and researching exercise "Life, the Universe, and Everything," a name that aptly describes the breadth of his subject matter. He got the idea in the early 1990s when his company was blindsided by a sharp drop in school budgets, which led to a significant decline in sales at Highsmith Inc. Looking back, Highsmith says that he could have easily foreseen the threat this event posed for his company had he been tracking a surging trend in taxpayers' discontent with ever-rising education budgets. He had fallen victim to a problem that afflicts practically every business owner: the tyranny of the immediate. He was so focused on the internal operations of his company and all of the immediate demands it placed on his time that he never took the time to look outside the business for threats or opportunities that might be looming on the horizon. In 1996, he vowed that he would not let it happen again and created "Life, the Universe, and Everything" to give some structure to the process strategists call environmental scanning.

To help him scan the universe, Highsmith began working with the company's head librarian, Lisa Guedea Carreño. (Highsmith has a library with more than 2,500 books and some 700 magazine subscriptions, and it is located at the center of corporate headquarters.) Guedea Carreño and her library staff spend hours scanning newspapers, online databases, magazines, and Web sites for items of interest, which they forward to Highsmith and others. Every week, Highsmith and Guedea Carreño sit down for two hours and review the information, sharing their ideas and impressions of what they have read. They write short statements about the significance of the most interesting and most promising items, which Guedea Carreño then enters into a database designed specifically for the project. The database is divided into eight broad categories and 77 subcategories—ranging from global environment and adult education to humor and metaphors—that the two have defined over the years.

Highsmith's job is to see the "big picture" for his company, and he has found the exercise to be so helpful that he has expanded "Life, the Universe, and Everything" to include other top managers. "It's starting to create a demand on the part of executives to spend time in the long-term development of the business rather than on routine operations," he says. Ultimately, Highsmith's goal is to have all of his employees thinking strategically about the company—its customers, the overall industry in which it operates, its competitors, potential markets it might capture, and many other vital issues. "I want to make the most of [our employees] by helping them become decision makers, by providing them with information and the context to make good decisions." To provide that information and context, Guedea Carreño and her library staff track 68 different topics, from competitors' activities to trade show practices, for other Highsmith employees. Each person receives a report customized to suit his or her individual preferences.

"Life, the Universe, and Everything" is paying off. A few years ago, using material that Guedea Carreño and her staff had supplied, a manager spotted a potential opportunity in nursing homes for some of Highsmith's 25,000 products. He asked the librarians to gather more detailed information, and, he says, they returned with "the whole nine yards"—market size, major players, public and private ownership, geographic distribution, vendors used, customer demographics—everything needed to make a strategic decision.

Duncan Highsmith may be the king of kings when it comes to knowledge management in small companies, but he continues to look for ways to improve the "Life, the Universe, and Everything" exercise in his company. "The thing about information is that it never stops coming," he says. "We're here to help people integrate information into their jobs as seamlessly as possible. That way, they can *keep* doing their jobs."

1. How does knowledge management benefit a small company?
2. Select a local small business and develop a list of the types of information you would recommend that the owner track. Where would you suggest the owner look for this information?
3. What are the advantages of using the World Wide Web as a source of information? What are the disadvantages? Work with a team of your classmates to develop a list of criteria for evaluating the quality and validity of a Web site.

Source: Adapted from Leigh Buchanan, "The Smartest Little Company in America," *Inc.*, January 1999, pp. 43–54; Highsmith Inc., **<www.highsmith.com>.**

12 percent and wholesale sales by 10 percent in the next fiscal year" is precise and spells out exactly what management wants to accomplish.

They are measurable. Managers should be able to plot the organization's progress toward its objectives; this requires a well-defined reference point from which to start and a scale for measuring progress.

They are assignable. Unless an entrepreneur assigns responsibility for an objective to an individual, it is unlikely that the company will ever achieve it. Creating objectives without giving someone responsibility for accomplishing them is futile.

They are realistic yet challenging. Objectives must be within the reach of the organization or motivation will disappear. In any case, managerial expectations must remain high. In other words, the more challenging an objective is (within realistic limits), the higher the performance will be. Set objectives that will challenge your business and its employees.

They are timely. Objectives must specify not only what is to be accomplished but also when it is to be accomplished. A time frame for achievement is important.

They are written down. This writing process does not have to be complex; in fact, the manager should make the number of objectives relatively small, from five to fifteen.

The strategic planning process works best when managers and employees are actively involved jointly in setting objectives. Developing a plan is top management's responsibility, but executing it falls to managers and employees; therefore, encouraging them to participate broadens the plan's perspective and increases the motivation to make the plan work. In addition, managers and employees know a great deal about the organization and usually are willing to share this knowledge.

6. Discuss the three basic strategies—low cost, differentiation, and focus—and know when and how to employ them.

Step 8. Formulate Strategic Options and Select the Appropriate Strategies

By now, the entrepreneur should have a clear picture of what her business does best and what its competitive advantages are. Similarly, she should know her firm's weaknesses and limitations as well as those of its competitors. The next step is to evaluate strategic options and then prepare a game plan designed to achieve the business's objectives.

strategy—*a road map of the actions an entrepreneur draws up to fulfill a company's mission, goals, and objectives.*

STRATEGY. A **strategy** is a road map of the actions an entrepreneur draws up to fulfill a company's mission, goals, and objectives. In other words, the mission, goals, and objectives spell out the ends, and the strategy defines the means for reaching them. A strategy is the master plan that covers all of the major parts of the organization and ties them together into a unified whole. The plan must be action oriented—that is, it should breathe life into the entire planning process. An entrepreneur must build a sound strategy based on the preceding steps that uses the company's core competencies and strengths as the springboard to success. Joseph Picken and Gregory Dess, authors of *Mission Critical: The 7 Strategic Traps That Derail Even the Smartest Companies,* write, "A flawed strategy—no matter how brilliant the leadership, no matter how effective the implementation—is doomed to fail. A sound strategy, implemented without error, wins every time."[32]

A successful strategy is comprehensive and well integrated, focusing on establishing the key success factors that the manager identified in Step 5. For instance, if maximum shelf space is a key success factor for a small manufacturer's product, the strategy must identify techniques for gaining more in-store shelf space (e.g., offering higher margins to distributors and brokers than competitors do, assisting retailers with in-store displays, or redesigning a wider, more attractive package).

THREE STRATEGIC OPTIONS. Obviously, the number of strategies from which the small business owner can choose is infinite. When all the glitter is stripped away, however, three basic strategies remain. In his classic book, *Competitive Strategy,* Michael Porter

ing campaign that emphasized the benefits of organic milk, which it sells in old-fashioned, reusable, environmentally friendly bottles. Today Straus Family Creamery is a success because it has created a unique position in the market. The company sells more than $4 million worth of its organic dairy products through upscale health food stores and supermarkets and its Web site **<www.strausmilk.com>**. *"I don't think we'd be in business if we hadn't made the change," says Straus.*[35]

If a small company can improve a product's (or service's) performance or reduce the customer's cost and risk of purchasing it, or both, it has the potential to differentiate. To be successful, a business must make its product or service truly different, at least in the eyes of its customers.

Ice Hotel

Entrepreneur Yngve Bergqvist has no trouble setting his hotel in Jukkasjärvi, Sweden, apart from others. Located 125 miles above the Arctic Circle, the aptly named Ice Hotel is the only one if its kind in the world. Everything in the hotel—walls, beds, night tables, chairs, cinema, bars—is made from 22,000 tons of ice harvested from the Torne River! Guests sleep in insulated sleeping bags on ice beds covered with thin mattresses and plenty of reindeer blankets. The 13,000-square-foot Ice Hotel is open from December through April (it melts in the spring), but during its brief existence, it will accommodate some 5,000 guests at rates ranging from $165 to $250 per night! The rock group Van Halen even shot one of its music videos at the Ice Hotel.[36]

Although few businesses are innately as unique as the Ice Hotel, the goal for a company pursuing a differentiation strategy is to create that kind of uniqueness in the minds of its customers. The key to a successful differentiation strategy is to build it on a *distinctive competence*—something the small company is uniquely good at doing in comparison to its competitors. Common bases for differentiation include superior customer service, special product features, complete product lines, instantaneous parts availability, absolute product reliability, supreme product quality, and extensive product knowledge. To be successful, a differentiation strategy must create the perception of value in the customer's eyes. No customer will purchase a good or service that fails to produce its perceived value, no matter how real that value may be. One business consultant advises, "Make sure you tell your customers and prospects what it is about your business that makes you different. Make sure that difference is in the form of a true benefit to the customer."[37]

There are risks in pursuing a differentiation strategy. One danger is trying to differentiate a product or service on the basis of something that does not boost its performance or lower its cost to the buyer. Business owners also must consider how long they can sustain a product's or service's differentiation; changing customer tastes make the basis for differentiation temporary at best. Imitations and knockoffs from competitors also pose a threat to a successful differentiation strategy. Another pitfall is overdifferentiating and charging so much that the company prices its products out of the market. The final risk is focusing only on the physical characteristics of a product or service and ignoring important psychological factors—status, prestige, image, and customer service.

Focus. A **focus strategy** recognizes that not all markets are homogeneous. In fact, in any given market, there are many different customer segments, each having different needs, wants, and characteristics. The principal idea of this strategy is to select one (or more) segment(s), identify customers' special needs, wants, and interests, and approach them with a good or service designed to excel in meeting these needs, wants, and interests. Focus strategies build on *differences* among market segments.

focus strategy—*a strategy in which a company selects one or more market segments, identifies customers' special needs, wants, and interests, and approaches them with a good or service designed to excel in meeting those needs, wants, and interests.*

A successful focus strategy depends on a small company's ability to identify the changing needs of its targeted customer group and to develop the skills required to serve these customers. That means an entrepreneur and everyone in the organization must have a clear understanding of how to add value to the product or service for customers. How does the product or service meet customers' needs at each stage—from raw material to final sale?

Rather than attempting to serve the total market, the focusing firm specializes in serving a specific target segment or niche. A focus strategy is ideally suited to many small businesses, which often lack the resources to reach the overall market. Their goal is to serve their narrow target markets more effectively and efficiently than do competitors that pound away at the broad market. Common bases for building a focus strategy include zeroing in on a small geographic area, targeting a group of customers with similar needs or interests (e.g., left-handed people), or specializing in a specific product or service (e.g., Batteries Plus, a store that sells and services every kind of battery imaginable).

Replacements Limited

For example, Bob Page, founder of Replacements Limited, has built a multimillion dollar business that specializes in stocking and locating more than 95,000 china, crystal, and flatware patterns for customers. Started as a hobby in Page's attic in the 1970s, Replacements Limited now occupies a 12,000-square-foot showroom and a warehouse the size of four football fields! The company's 6 million-piece inventory is made up of 125,000 china patterns, 13,000 crystal patterns, and 11,000 flatware patterns. Replacements Limited employs 600 people, among whom are skilled artisans who reglaze, repair, and repaint chipped and broken china and crystal. Customers have included Mother Teresa, Ted Kennedy, England's royal family, and the Vatican. Page's focus strategy has been extremely successful. Sales in 1981, the company's first full year of operation, were $150,000; today, sales top $60 million.[38]

The most successful focusers build a competitive edge by concentrating on specific market niches and serving them better than any other competitor can. Essentially, this strategy depends on creating value for the customer either by being the lowest-cost producer or by differentiating the product or service in a unique fashion but doing it in a narrow target segment.

Explorean Hotels

Entrepreneur Gaston Azcarraga, head of Grupo Posadas, is counting on a focus strategy for success in the hotly competitive resort hotel market. With his chain of Mexican hotels called Explorean, Azcarraga is targeting young, college-educated Americans with high incomes who are looking for "soft-adventure travel." Rather than trying to compete in the traditional glitzy Mexican tourist resort business, Explorean's goal is to appeal to adventure travelers seeking high-energy activities such as mountain biking and kayaking coupled with luxurious quarters, gourmet meals, and fine wines. Azcarraga bypassed the typical tourist resort market because he says it is "a commodity business" and chose the soft-adventure travel niche because adventure travel is the fastest-growing segment of the travel market. "The challenge is to come up with a product that has a competitive advantage and, at the same time, is more profitable," says Azcarraga. Rates at Explorean start at $440 per night, including adventure activities, an amount that is three times more than traditional Mexican resorts. Trips range from mountain bike tours to ancient Mayan ruins and kayak trips to pools fed by underground rivers. The company faces a challenge as it attempts to balance a varied slate of outdoor activities, which require remote locations, and a full complement of luxury and convenience in out-of-the-way locations. Explorean's strategy "is cutting edge," says one industry analyst. "If they are successful, others will follow."[39]

As Azcarraga's venture suggests, pursuing a focus strategy is not without risks. Companies sometimes must struggle to capture a large enough share of a small market to be profitable. If a small company is successful in a niche, there is also the danger of larger competitors entering the market and eroding it. The small volume of business that some niches support can raise production costs, making a company vulnerable to lower-cost competitors. Sometimes a company with a successful niche strategy gets distracted by its success and tries to branch out into other areas. As it drifts farther away from its core strategy, it loses its competitive edge and runs the risk of confusing or alienating its customers.

Victoria's Secret, the mail-order company once known for its niche in lingerie, has lost much of its appeal to its traditional customers because the business has strayed too far from its roots. In addition to its wide selection of lingerie, Victoria's Secret sells ball gowns, jeans and casual wear, and career clothing. Muddying its image with customers puts a company in danger of losing its identity.

Victoria's Secret

An effective strategic plan identifies a complete set of success factors—financial, operating, and marketing—that, taken together, produce a competitive advantage for the small business. The resulting action plan distinguishes the firm from its competitors by exploiting its competitive advantage. The focal point of this entire strategic plan is the customer. The customer is the nucleus of the business, so a competitive strategy will succeed only if it is aimed at serving customers better than the competitor does. An effective strategy draws out the competitive advantage in a small company by building on its strengths and by making the customer its focus. It also designates methods for overcoming the firm's weaknesses, and it identifies opportunities and threats that demand action.

STRATEGY IN ACTION. The strategies a small business selects depend on its competitive advantages in the market segments in which it competes. In some cases, the business will be implementing multiple strategies across several segments. When a business has a well-defined strategic advantage, it may pursue highly aggressive growth strategies in an attempt to increase its market share. This is especially true when a business achieves a "first-mover" advantage in a market with little direct competition. However, aggressive strategies can backfire if larger competitors decide to fight back. In many cases, the old adage of being the "big fish in a small pond" allows a small business to earn a handsome profit in a market niche without attracting the attention of larger competitors.

Small companies must develop strategies that exploit all of the competitive advantages of their size by:

- Responding quickly to customers' needs.
- Remaining flexible and willing to change.
- Continually searching for new emerging market segments.
- Building and defending market niches.
- Erecting "switching costs" through personal service and loyalty.
- Remaining entrepreneurial and willing to take risks and act with lightning speed.
- Constantly innovating.

Step 9. Translate Strategic Plans into Action Plans

7. Understand the importance of controls such as the balanced scorecard in the planning process.

No strategic plan is complete until it is put into action. The small business manager must convert strategic plans into operating plans that guide the company on a daily basis and become a visible, active part of the business. No small business can benefit from a strategic plan sitting on a shelf collecting dust.

IMPLEMENT THE STRATEGY. To make the plan workable, the business owner should divide the plan into projects, carefully defining each one by the following:

Purpose. What is the project designed to accomplish?

Scope. Which areas of the company will be involved in the project?

Contribution. How does the project relate to other projects and to the overall strategic plan?

Resource requirements. What human and financial resources are needed to complete the project successfully?

Timing. Which schedules and deadlines will ensure project completion?

Once entrepreneurs assign priorities to projects, they can begin to implement the strategic plan.

YOU BE THE CONSULTANT . . .

Today, Buffalo. Tomorrow, the World?

Starting an airline from scratch is no easy task. It requires lots of capital (airplanes aren't cheap!), a skilled and experienced management team, and a solid strategy designed to beat the competition. Bill Schriber, Greg Aretakis, and Dave Hackett are betting that they have the right combination of these factors and have launched Shuttle America from their headquarters (a small Quonset hut with orange shag carpet) at Houston's Hobby Airport.

Because an airline is so capital intensive, the partners' search for capital is never ending—and sometimes downright discouraging. Recently, while cold-calling venture capital firms in an attempt to attract more financing, Schriber explained the Shuttle America concept to a prospective investor. "Excuse me," said the venture capitalist, "but you just used the words 'airline' and 'start-up' in the same sentence. I think I'll hang up now." That attitude is reflected in the opinions of many industry analysts, who consider the airline business to be "mature," not an ideal environment for incubating successful start-ups. So far, however, Shuttle America has beat the odds, not only staying in business but expanding its routes. Schriber, Aretakis, and Hackett have won approval from the Federal Aviation Administration and have managed to attract $8.75 million in financing. The start-up is flying some 26,000 passengers each month to seven East Coast cities and has relocated its headquarters to Bradley International Airport in Hartford, Connecticut.

The three partners learned a great deal about running an airline working for Continental Airlines and its maverick CEO Frank Lorenzo. By 1996, they were formulating plans for launching Shuttle America. They invested $300,000 of their own money (from selling airline stock they owned) as seed capital. Their strategy is to stay away from the industry giants such as American Airlines and Delta Airlines. Instead, their goal is to create a low-fare airline that serves cities with populations large enough to generate the volume they need to be profitable but small enough to be off the radar of the major carriers. Shuttle America is targeting cities with populations of at least 1.5 million people within a 20-mile radius that have either no airline service or only high-fare commuter service. The partners look for markets in which the number of airport passengers has declined dramatically in recent years because of limited flights or high fares. "It's a neat little niche," says Hackett. Although several airlines serve most major cities on the East Coast, smaller cities, such as Buffalo, New York; Hartford, Connecticut; and Norfolk, Virginia, are passed over. "We want to get people to come back and fly," says Hackett.

To keep costs low, Shuttle America flies only one type of airplane: Bombadier's 50-seat Dash-8 turboprop. Schriber, Aretakis, and Hackett chose the turboprop over the 50-seat jets that are so popular with many regional carriers because the turboprops offer lower costs. The Dash-8s cost just $10 million to lease, far less than the $20 million needed to lease a similar-sized jet. The turboprops are much more fuel efficient as well, which allows Shuttle America to break even with only half of its seats full.

As with any start-up business, there are plenty of risks in launching Shuttle America. Perhaps the biggest threat is a price war with a larger, more powerful airline. Recent history is littered with small airlines driven out of business by larger carriers that matched the start-ups' fares and simply outlasted them. Schriber, Aretakis, and Hackett recognize that one way to combat the possibility of a price war is to build name recognition for Shuttle America in the markets in which they compete, and the company has launched an advertising campaign built around several catchy slogans. Other goals include increasing the percentage of flights booked by travel agents (20 percent for Shuttle America versus 80 percent for the industry average) and landing more corporate travel accounts.

Another concern is reassuring the public that Shuttle America is serious about safety and quality. Since the crash of a Valu-Jet airplane several years ago, most small airlines have struggled to avoid being branded as unsafe simply because they are small. Hackett notes that all of Shuttle America's planes are new (even though used ones would have been *much* cheaper). The company also performs all of its own maintenance rather than hiring it out to subcontractors whose work is harder to control. Shuttle America also spends an average of $15,000 to train each of its pilots and pays them the average salary for regional airlines, about $50,000 a year.

Despite the obstacles it faces in an extremely competitive industry, Shuttle America earned a profit in its first year. Schriber, Aretakis, and Hackett see a bright future for their company because there are plenty of other cities that offer opportunities for expansion. Also, cities along the East Coast have been calling Schriber, asking when Shuttle America would start offering flights at their airports. Schriber also has managed to attract an additional $5 million in capital and has begun planning an initial public offering of Shuttle America's stock to raise money for expansion.

1. Which strategy—cost leadership, differentiation, or focus—is Shuttle America following? Explain.
2. Perform a SWOT analysis for Shuttle America.
3. On a scale of 0 to 100, how would you assess Shuttle America's chances of business success? Explain.

Source: Adapted from Julie Rose, "Pie in the Sky?" *Your Company*, October 1999, pp. 71–74.

Involving employees and delegating adequate authority to them is essential because these projects affect them most directly. If the organization's people have been involved in the strategic management process to this point, they will have a better grasp of the steps they must take to achieve the organization's goals as well as their own professional goals. Early involvement of the workforce in the strategic management process is a luxury that larger businesses cannot achieve. Commitment to reaching the company's objectives is a powerful force, but involvement is a prerequisite for achieving total employee commitment. Without a team of committed, dedicated employees, an organization's strategy usually fails.

Step 10. Establish Accurate Controls

So far, the planning process has created company objectives and has developed a strategy for reaching them, but rarely, if ever, will the company's actual performance match stated objectives. Entrepreneurs quickly realize the need to control actual results that deviate from plans.

CONTROLLING THE STRATEGY. Planning without control has little operational value, and so a sound planning program requires a practical control process. The plans created in the strategic planning process become the standards against which actual performance is measured. It is important for everyone in the organization to understand—and to be involved in—the planning and controlling process.

Controlling projects and keeping them on schedule means that an entrepreneur must identify and track key performance indicators. The source of these indicators is the operating data from the company's normal business activity; they are the guideposts for detecting deviations from established standards. Accounting, production, sales, inventory, and other operating records are primary sources of data the manager can use for controlling activities. For example, on a customer service project, performance indicators might include the number of customer complaints, the number of orders returned, the percentage of on-time shipments, and a measure of order accuracy.

To evaluate the effectiveness of their strategies, some companies are developing **balanced scorecards,** a set of measurements unique to a company that includes both financial and operational measures and gives managers a quick yet comprehensive picture of the company's total performance. One writer says that a balanced scorecard:

balanced scorecards—*a set of measurements unique to a company that includes both financial and operational measures and gives managers a quick yet comprehensive picture of the company's total performance.*

> is a sophisticated business model that helps a company understand what's really driving its success. It acts a bit like the control panel on a spaceship—the business equivalent of a flight speedometer, odometer, and temperature gauge all rolled into one. It keeps track of many things, including financial progress and softer measurements—everything from customer satisfaction to return on investment—that need to be managed to reach the final destination: profitable growth.[40]

Rather than sticking solely to the traditional financial measures of a company's performance, the balanced scorecard gives managers a comprehensive view from *both* a financial and an operational perspective. The premise behind such a scorecard is that relying on any single measure of company performance is dangerous. Just as a pilot in command of a jet cannot fly safely by focusing on a single instrument, an entrepreneur cannot manage a company by concentrating on a single measurement. The complexity of managing a business demands that an entrepreneur be able to see performance measures in several areas simultaneously.

When creating a balanced scorecard for his or her company, an entrepreneur should establish goals for each critical indicator of company performance and then create meaningful measures for each one.

Certifiedmail.com

For example, Court Coursey, founder of Certifiedmail.com, a company that delivers certified mail electronically, has developed a scorecard that encompasses measures on everything from financial performance to employee satisfaction. Every quarter, Coursey presents Certifiedmail.com's one-page scorecard to his 10 employees for review. "It's a good way to get a grasp on the company and how it's performing," he says. The scorecard gives Coursey important feedback that allows him to adjust his management style and the company's direction when necessary. The scorecard already has improved Certifiedmail.com's performance. One of Coursey's top priorities is cost control, and the scorecard recently pointed out a wasteful practice that he halted. "[The scorecard] showed me a way to save money," he says. "And it was something I may not have seen without this feedback."[41]

Ideally, a balanced scorecard looks at a business from four important perspectives as shown in Figure 3.3.[42]

Customer Perspective: How do customers see us? Customers judge companies by at least four standards: time (how long it takes the company to deliver a good or service), quality (how well a company's product or service performs in terms of reliability, durability, and accuracy), performance (the extent to which a good or service performs as expected), and service (how well a company meets or exceeds customers' expectations of value). Because customer-related goals are external, managers must translate them into measures of what the company must do to meet customers' expectations.

FIGURE 3.3
The Balanced Scorecard Links Performance Measures

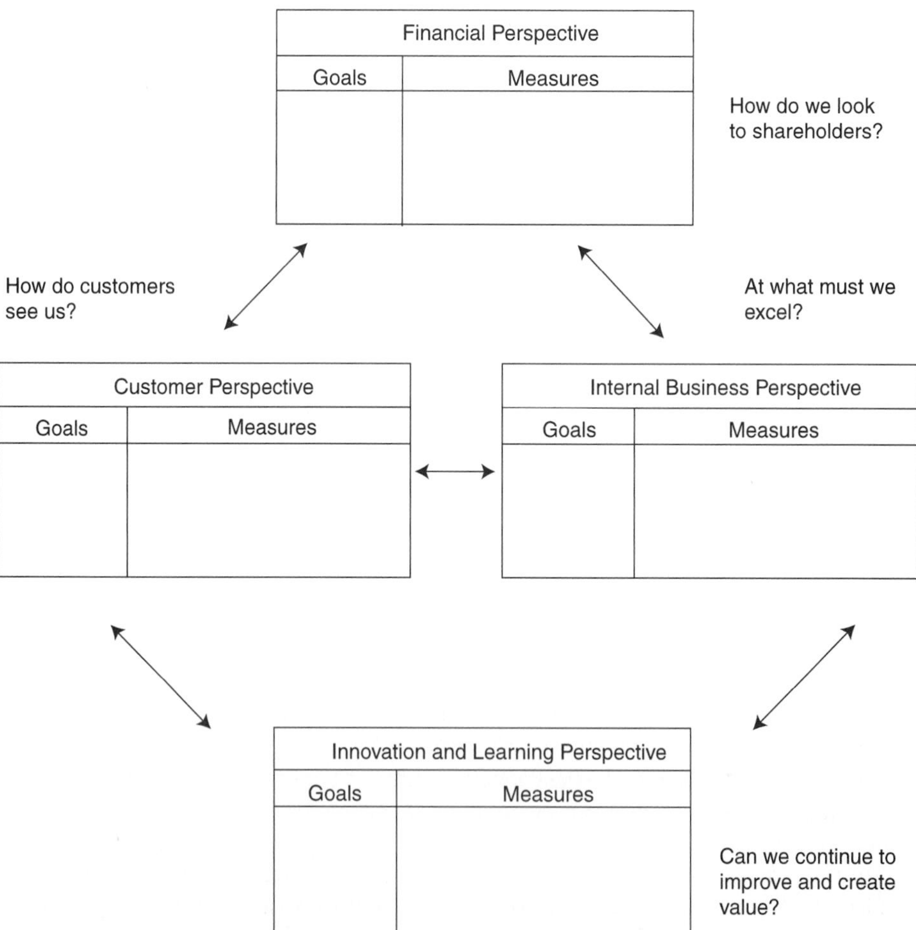

Internal Business Perspective: At what must we excel? The internal factors that managers should focus on are those that have the greatest impact on customer satisfaction and retention and on company effectiveness and efficiency. Developing goals and measures for factors such as quality, cycle time, productivity, costs, and others that employees directly influence is essential.

Innovation and Learning Perspective: Can we continue to improve and create value? This view of a company recognizes that the targets required for success are never static; they are constantly changing. If a company wants to continue its pattern of success, it cannot stand still; it must continuously improve. A company's ability to innovate, learn, and improve determines its future. These goals and measures emphasize the importance of continuous improvement in customer satisfaction and internal business operations.

Financial Perspective: How do we look to shareholders? The most traditional performance measures—financial standards—tell how much the company's overall strategy and its execution are contributing to its bottom line. These measures focus on such factors as profitability, growth, and shareholder value. On balanced scorecards, companies often break their financial goals into three categories: survival, success, and growth.

Although the balanced scorecard is a vital tool that helps managers keep their companies on track, it is also an important tool for changing behavior in an organization and for keeping everyone focused on what really matters. As conditions change, managers must make corrections in performances, policies, strategies, and objectives to get performance back on track. A practical control system is also economical to operate. Most small businesses have no need for a sophisticated, expensive control system. The system should be so practical that it becomes a natural part of the management process.

CONCLUSION

The strategic planning process does *not* end with the 10 steps outlined here; it is an ongoing procedure that the small business owner must repeat. With each round, he or she gains experience, and the steps become much easier. The planning process outlined here is designed to be as simple as possible. No small business should be burdened with an elaborate, detailed, formal planning process that it cannot easily use. Such programs require excessive amounts of time to operate, and they generate a sea of paperwork. The small business manager needs neither.

What does this strategic planning process lead to? It teaches the small business owner a degree of discipline that is important to business survival. It helps him in learning about his business, his competitors, and, most important, his customers. Although strategic planning cannot guarantee success, it does dramatically increase the small firm's chances of survival in a hostile business environment.

CHAPTER SUMMARY

1. Explain why and how a small business must create a competitive advantage in the market.

   The goal of developing a strategic plan is to create for the small company a competitive, unique image in the minds of its potential customers.

2. Develop a strategic plan for a business using the 10 steps in the strategic management process.

   Small businesses need a strategic planning process designed to suit their particular needs.

   Step 1. Developing a clear vision and translating it into a meaningful mission statement sets the tone for the entire company.

   Step 2. Define the firm's core competencies and its target market segment(s), and position the business to compete effectively. Core competencies are a unique set of capabilities that a company develops in key operational areas, such as quality, service, innovation, team building, flexibility, responsiveness, and others, which allows the company to vault past competitors. They are what the company does best and are the focal point of the strategy. This step must identify target market segments and determine how to position the firm in those markets. The owner must identify some way to differentiate the business from its competitors.

Step 3: Assess the company's strengths and weaknesses. Strengths are positive internal factors; weaknesses are negative internal factors.

Step 4: Scan the environment for significant opportunities and threats facing the business. Opportunities are positive external options; threats are negative external forces.

Step 5: Identify the key factors for success in the business. In every business, key factors determine the success of the firms in it, and so they must be an integral part of a company' strategy. Key success factors are relationships between a controllable variable and a critical factor influencing the firm's ability to compete in the market.

Step 6: Analyze the competition. Business owners should know their competitors almost as well as they know their own business. A competitive profile matrix is a helpful tool for analyzing competitors strengths and weaknesses.

Step 7: Create company goals and objectives. Goals are the broad, long-range attributes that the firm seeks to accomplish. Objectives are quantifiable and more precise; they should be specific, measurable, assignable, realistic, timely, and written down. The process works best when managers and employees are actively involved.

Step 8: Formulate strategic options and select the appropriate strategies.

Step 9: Translate strategic plans into action plans. No strategic plan is complete until the owner puts it into action.

Step 10: Establish accurate controls. Actual performance rarely, if ever, matches plans exactly. Operating data from the business assembled into a comprehensive scorecard serve as an important guidepost for determining how effective a company's strategy is. This information is especially helpful when plotting future strategies.

The strategic planning process does not end with these 10 steps; rather, it is an ongoing process that an entrepreneur will repeat.

3. Know how to create a meaningful mission statement and why it is important. Highly successful entrepreneurs are able to communicate their vision to those around them. A firm's mission statement answers the first question of any venture: What business am I in?
4. Understand how to identify a company's SWOT—strengths, weaknesses, opportunities, and threats.

   Developing a sound strategy requires quality information. Strengths are positive internal factors; weaknesses are negative internal factors. Opportunities are positive external options; threats are negative external factors.
5. Establish meaningful goals and objectives.

   Goals are broad, long-range attributes a company seeks to accomplish; objectives are quantifiable and more precise. They should be specific, measurable, assignable, realistic, timely, and in writing.
6. Discuss the characteristics of three basic strategies: low cost, differentiation, and focus.

   Three basic strategic options are cost leadership, differentiation, and focus. A company pursuing a cost leadership strategy strives to be the lowest-cost producer relative to its competitors in the industry. A company following a differentiation strategy seeks to build customer loyalty by positioning its goods or services in a unique or different fashion. In other words, the firm strives to be better than its competitors at something that customers value. A focus strategy recognizes that not all markets are homogeneous. The principal idea of this strategy is to select one (or more) segment(s), identify customers' special needs, wants, and interests, and approach them with a good or service designed to excel in meeting these needs, wants, and interests. Focus strategies build on *differences* among market segments.
7. Understand the importance of controls such as the balanced scorecard in the planning process.

   Just as a pilot in command of a jet cannot fly safely by focusing on a single instrument, an entrepreneur cannot manage a company by concentrating on a single measurement. A balanced scorecard is a set of measurements unique to a company that includes both financial and operational measures and gives managers a quick yet comprehensive picture of the company's total performance.

DISCUSSION QUESTIONS

1. Why is strategic planning important to a small company?
2. What is a competitive advantage? Why is it important for a small business to establish one?
3. What are the steps in the strategic management process?
4. "Our customers don't just like our ice cream," write Ben Cohen and Jerry Greenfield, cofounders of Ben & Jerry's Homemade Inc. "They like what our company stands for. They like how doing business with us makes them feel." What do they mean?
5. What are strengths, weaknesses, opportunities, and threats? Give an example of each.
6. Explain the characteristics of effective objectives. Why is setting objectives important?
7. What are business strategies?
8. Describe the three basic strategies available to small

companies. Under what conditions is each most successful?

9. Explain how a company can gain a competitive advantage using each of the three strategies described in this chapter: cost leadership, differentiation, and focus. Give an example of a company that is using each strategy.

10. How is the controlling process related to the planning process?

11. What is a balanced scorecard? What value does it offer entrepreneurs who are evaluating the success of their current strategies?

Beyond the Classroom . . .

1. Contact the owner of a small business that competes directly with an industry giant (such as Home Depot, Wal-Mart, Barnes and Noble, or others). What does the owner see as his or her competitive advantage? How does the business communicate this advantage to its customers? What competitive strategy is the owner using? How successful is it? What changes would you suggest the owner make?

2. Contact a local entrepreneur and help him or her devise a balanced scorecard for his or her company. What goals did you and the owner establish in each of the four perspectives? What measures did you use to judge progress toward those goals?

3. Use the strategic tools provided in this chapter to help a local small business owner discover his or her firm's strengths, weaknesses, opportunities, and threats. Identify the relevant key success factors and analyze its competitors. Help the owner devise a strategy for success for his or her business.

4. Choose an entrepreneur in your community and interview him or her. Does the company have a strategic plan? A mission statement? Why or why not? What does the owner consider the company's strengths and weaknesses to be? What opportunities and threats does the owner perceive? What image is the owner trying to create for the business? Has the effort been successful? (Do you agree?) Which of the generic competitive strategies is the company following? Who are the company's primary competitors? How does the owner rate his or her chances for success in the future [use a low (1) to high (10) scale]. When you have completed the interview, use the following evaluation questionnaire to rate the company's strategic orientation. Compare your evaluation with other classmates. What, if any, generalizations can you draw from the interview?

Is the Owner Managing the Business Strategically?

Rate your present managerial actions on each of the following questions:

1. In the past two years have you written or reviewed your firm's mission statement?

    Yes (10 pts.)
    No (0 pts.) Q.1. _______

2. Are you confident that your employees are aware of the key underlying values that drive the business?

    Absolutely (10 pts.)
    Generally (7 pts.)
    Not sure (3 pts.)
    I have never shared with them my values (0 pts.) Q.2. _______

3. Does each manager have a clear set of performance objectives for his area of responsibility?

Yes (10 pts.)
Some do (5 pts.)
No (0 pts.) Q. 3. _______

4. Do you regularly meet with your key managers and employees to discuss the behaviors of your competitors?

Regularly and often (10 pts.)
Informally, but not a scheduled event (5 pts.)
Never have done so (0 pts.) Q. 4. _______

5. Would your employees be able to accurately describe the strategies your firm is attempting to employ?

Definitely (10 pts.)
Most of them (5 pts.)
The firm's strategies have never been explained to them (0 pts.)
Q. 5. _______

6. Do all employees understand that through the achievement of success for the organization they enhance the opportunity for achieving their own personal goals?

Definitely (10 pts.)
Most do (7 pts.)
A few do (4 pts.)
It has never been explained to them (0 pts.) Q. 6. _______

7. Do you annually conduct an environmental scanning exercise with your managers in an attempt to identify future opportunities for the firm?

Yes (10 pts.)
Informally (5 pts.)
No (0 pts.) Q. 7. _______

8. Can all of your managers explain the impact of their performance, and that of their staff, on the performance of the total organization?

Absolutely (10 pts.)
Generally (7 pts.)
Not sure (3 pts.)
No (0 pts.) Q. 8. _______

9. Has your business been moving in a clear and positive direction over the past three years?

Definitely (10 pts.)
Generally (7 pts.)
Not sure (3 pts.)
No (0 pts.) Q. 9. _______

10. Do you and your key managers think and behave strategically?

Always (10 pts.)
Generally (7 pts.)
Not sure (3 pts.)
Seldom (0 pts.) Q. 10. _______

Total points _______

Maximum Score 100

Minimum Score 0

Grading Your Firm:

A+	95–100 pts.
A	90–94 pts.
B+	85–89 pts.
B	80–84 pts.
C+	75–79 pts.
C	70–74 pts.
D+	65–69 pts.
D	60–64 pts.
F	below 60 pts.

Your recommendations:

We invite you to visit this book's companion Web site at **www.prenhall.com/Zimmerer.**

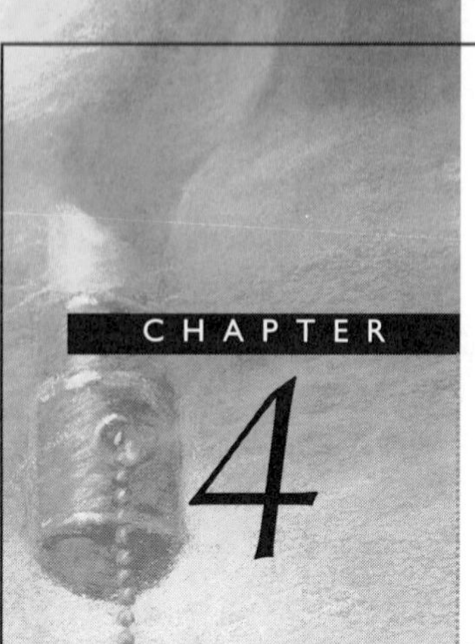

CHAPTER 4

Forms of Business Ownership and Franchising

Before you run in double harness, look well to the other horse.

—Ovid

A prudent question is one-half of wisdom.

—Francis Bacon

LEARNING OBJECTIVES

Upon completion of this chapter, you will be able to:

1. Explain the advantages and the disadvantages of the three major forms of ownership: the sole proprietorship, the partnership, and the corporation.
2. Discuss the advantages and the disadvantages of the S corporation, the limited liability company, the professional corporation, and the joint venture.
3. Describe the three types of franchising: trade name, product distribution, and pure.
4. Explain the benefits and the drawbacks of buying a franchise.
5. Understand the laws covering franchise purchases.
6. Discuss the *right* way to buy a franchise.
7. Outline the major trends shaping franchising.

One of the first decisions an entrepreneur faces when starting a new business is selecting the form of ownership for the new business venture. Too often, entrepreneurs give little thought to choosing a form of ownership and simply select the form that is most popular, even though it may not suit their needs best. Although the decision is not irreversible, changing from one form of ownership to another once a business is up and running can be difficult, expensive, and complicated. That's why it is so important for an entrepreneur to make the right choice at the outset. This seemingly mundane decision can have a significant impact on almost every aspect of a business and its owner(s)—from the taxes the company pays and how it raises money to the owner's liability for the company's debts and her ability to transfer the business to the next generation. Each form of ownership has its own unique set of advantages and disadvantages. The key to choosing the "right" form of ownership is understanding the characteristics of each one and knowing how they affect an entrepreneur's business and personal circumstances. Although there is no best form of ownership, there may be a form of ownership that is best for each entrepreneur's circumstances.

The following are a few considerations that every entrepreneur should review prior to making the final form of ownership choice:

Tax considerations. The graduated tax rates under each form of ownership, the government's constant tinkering with the tax code, and the year-to-year fluctuations in a company's income mean that an entrepreneur must calculate the firm's tax bill under each ownership option every year.

Liability exposure. Certain forms of ownership offer business owners greater protection from personal liability due to financial problems, faulty products, and a host of other difficulties. Entrepreneurs must decide the extent to which they are willing to assume personal responsibility for their companies' obligations.

Start-up capital requirements. Forms of ownership differ in their ability to raise start-up capital. Depending on how much capital an entrepreneur needs and where she plans to get it, some forms are superior to others.

Control. By choosing certain forms of ownership, an entiepreneur automatically gives up some control over the company. Entrepreneurs must decide early on how much control they are willing to sacrifice in exchange for help from other people in building a successful business.

Business goals. How big and how profitable an entrepreneur plans for the business to become will influence the form of ownership chosen. Businesses often switch forms of ownership as they grow, but moving from some formats to others can be extremely complex and expensive.

Management succession plans. When choosing a form of ownership, business owners must look ahead to the day when they will pass their companies on to the next generation or to a buyer. Some forms of ownership make this transition much smoother than others.

Cost of formation. Some forms of ownership are much more costly and involved to create. An entrepreneur must weigh carefully the benefits and the costs of the particular form he or she chooses.

Entrepreneurs have a wide choice of forms of ownership. In recent years, various hybrid forms of business ownership have emerged. This chapter will attempt to outline the key features of the most common forms of ownership, beginning with the sole proprietorship, the partnership, and the corporation.

1-A. Explain the advantages and disadvantages of the sole proprietorship.

THE SOLE PROPRIETORSHIP

The **sole proprietorship** is a business owned and managed by one individual. This form of ownership is by far the most popular. Approximately 73 percent of all businesses in the United States are proprietorships (see Figure 4.1).

sole proprietorship—*a business owned and managed by one individual.*

FIGURE 4.1
Forms of Ownership
Percent of Businesses

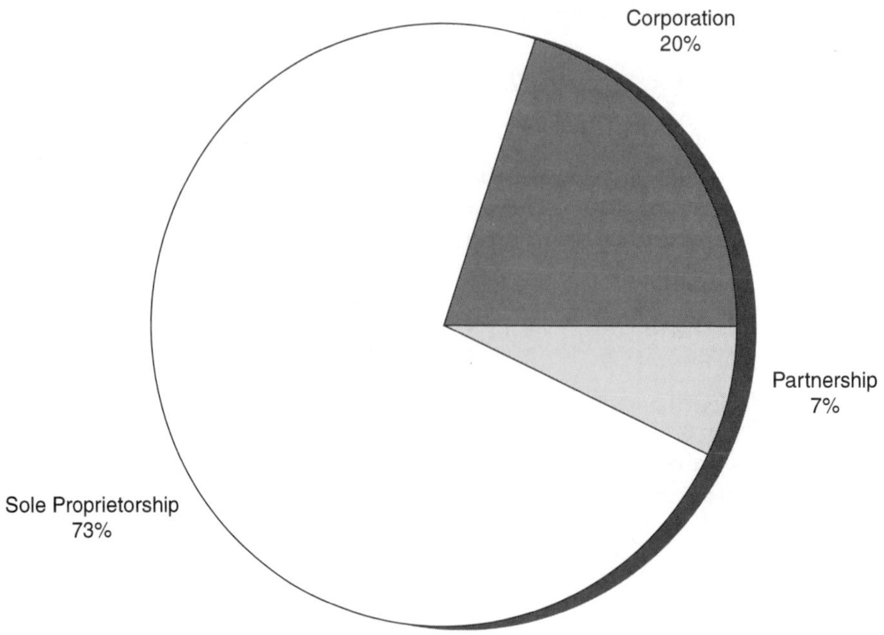

The Advantages of a Proprietorship

SIMPLE TO CREATE. One of the most attractive features of a proprietorship is how fast and simple it is to begin. If an entrepreneur wants to operate a business under his own name (e.g., Strossner's Bakery), he simply obtains the necessary licenses from state, county, and/or local governments and begins operation! For most entrepreneurs, it would not be impossible to start a proprietorship in a single day.

LEAST COSTLY FORM OF OWNERSHIP TO BEGIN. In addition to being easy to begin, the proprietorship is generally the least expensive form of ownership to establish. There is no need to create and file legal documents that are recommended for partnerships and required for corporations. An entrepreneur simply goes to the city or county government, states the nature of the business he will start, and pays the appropriate fees and license costs. Paying these fees and license costs gives the entrepreneur the right to conduct business in that particular jurisdiction.

Someone planning to conduct business under a trade name should acquire a certificate of doing business under an assumed name from the secretary of state. The fee for filing this certificate usually is nominal. Acquiring this certificate involves conducting a legal search to ensure that the name chosen is not already registered as a trademark or a service mark with the secretary of state. Filing this certificate also notifies the state whom the owner of the business is. In a proprietorship, the owner *is* the business.

PROFIT INCENTIVE. One major advantage of the proprietorship is that once the owner pays all of the company's expenses, she can keep the remaining profits (less taxes, of course). The profit incentive is a powerful one, and profits represent an excellent way of "keeping score" in the game of the business.

TOTAL DECISION-MAKING AUTHORITY. Because the sole proprietor is in total control of operations, she can respond quickly to changes, which is an asset in a rapidly shifting market. The freedom to set the company's course of action is a major motivational force. For those who thrive on the enjoyment of seeking new opportunities in business, the freedom of fast, flexible decision making is vital. Sole proprietor Max Gouge of Industrial

Propane & Petroleum says, "I like the feeling of being on my own . . . I make this company work."[1]

NO SPECIAL LEGAL RESTRICTIONS. The proprietorship is the least regulated form of business ownership. In a time when government requests for information seem never-ending, this feature has much merit.

EASY TO DISCONTINUE. If the entrepreneur decides to discontinue operations, he can terminate the business quickly, even though he will still be personally liable for any outstanding debts and obligations that the business cannot pay.

The Disadvantages of a Proprietorship

UNLIMITED PERSONAL LIABILITY. Probably the greatest disadvantage of a sole proprietorship is the **unlimited personal liability** of the owner, which means that the sole proprietor is personally liable for all of the business's debts. Remember: In a proprietorship, the owner *is* the business. He owns all of the business's assets, and if the business fails, creditors can force the sale of these assets to cover its debts. If unpaid business debts remain, creditors can also force the sale of the proprietor's *personal* assets to recover payment. In short, the company's debts are the owner's debts. Laws vary from one state to another, but most states require creditors to leave the failed business owner a minimum amount of equity in a home, a car, and some personal items. The reality: *Failure of a business can ruin a sole proprietor financially.*

unlimited personal liability—*a situation in which the sole proprietor is personally liable for all of the business's debts.*

LIMITED SKILLS AND CAPABILITIES. A sole proprietor may not have the wide range of skills running a successful business requires. Each of us has areas in which our education, training, and work experiences have taught us a great deal; yet there are other areas in which our decision-making ability is weak. Many business failures occur because owners lack the skills, knowledge, and experience in areas that are vital to business success. Owners tend to push aside problems they don't understand or don't feel comfortable with in favor of those they can solve more easily. Unfortunately, the problems they set aside seldom solve themselves. By the time an owner decides to ask for help in addressing these problems, it may be too late to save the company.

FEELINGS OF ISOLATION. Running a business alone allows an entrepreneur maximum flexibility, but it also creates feelings of isolation that there is no one else to turn to for help in solving problems or getting feedback on a new idea. Lee Gardner, the sole proprietor of a company that arranges sponsorships for sporting events, says, "After I set up my company, I realized I was all by myself and responsible for everything. Building a business brick by brick, alone, is not easy."[2]

LIMITED ACCESS TO CAPITAL. If the business is to grow and expand, a sole proprietor generally needs additional financial resources. However, many proprietors have already put all they have into their businesses and have used their personal resources as collateral on existing loans, making it difficult to borrow additional funds. A sole proprietorship is limited to whatever capital the owner can contribute and whatever money he can borrow. In short, proprietors, unless they have great personal wealth, find it difficult to raise additional money while maintaining sole ownership. Most banks and other lending institutions have well-defined formulas for determining borrowers' eligibility. Unfortunately, many sole proprietorships cannot meet those borrowing requirements, especially in the early days of business.

LACK OF CONTINUITY FOR THE BUSINESS. Lack of continuity is inherent in a sole proprietorship. If the proprietor dies, retires, or becomes incapacitated, the business automatically terminates. Unless a family member or employee can take over (which means that person is now a sole proprietor), the business could be in jeopardy. Because people look for secure employment and an opportunity for advancement, proprietorships, being small, often have trouble recruiting and retaining good employees. If no one is trained to run the business, creditors can petition the courts to liquidate the assets of the dissolved business to pay outstanding debts.

Some entrepreneurs find that forming partnerships is one way to overcome the disadvantages of the sole proprietorship. For instance, when one person lacks specific managerial skills or has insufficient access to needed capital, he can compensate for these weaknesses by forming a partnership with someone with complementary management skills or money to invest.

1-B. Explain the advantages and disadvantages of the partnership.

THE PARTNERSHIP

partnership—*an association of two or more people who co-own a business for the purpose of making a profit.*

partnership agreement—*a document that states in writing all of the terms of operating the partnership and protects the interest of each partner.*

A **partnership** is an association of two or more people who co-own a business for the purpose of making a profit. In a partnership, the co-owners (partners) share the business's assets, liabilities, and profits according to the terms of a previously established partnership agreement.

The law does not require a partnership agreement (also known as the articles of partnership), but it is wise to work with an attorney to develop one that spells out the exact status and responsibility of each partner. All too often the parties think they know what they are agreeing to, only to find later that no real meeting of the minds took place. The **partnership agreement** is a document that states in writing all of the terms of operating the partnership and protects each partner involved. Every partnership should be based on a written agreement. "When two entrepreneurial personalities are combined, there is a tremendous amount of strength and energy, but it must be focused in the same direction, or it will tear the relationship apart," explains one business writer. "A good partnership agreement will guide you through the good times, provide you with a method for handling problems, and serve as the infrastructure for a successful operation."[3]

When no partnership agreement exists, the Uniform Partnership Act (UPA) governs a partnership, but its provisions may not be as favorable as a specific agreement hammered out among the partners. Creating a partnership agreement is not costly. In most cases, the partners can discuss each of the provisions in advance. Once they have reached an agreement, an attorney can draft the formal document. Banks will often want to see a copy of the partnership agreement before lending the business money. Probably the most important feature of the partnership agreement is that it resolves potential sources of conflict that, if not addressed in advance, could later result in partnership battles and the dissolution of an otherwise successful business. Spelling out details—especially sticky ones such as profit splits, contributions, workloads, decision-making authority, dispute resolution, dissolution, and others—in a written agreement at the outset will help avoid damaging tension in a partnership that could lead to a business "divorce." Business divorces, like marital ones, are almost always costly and unpleasant for everyone involved.

Unfortunately, the tendency for partners just starting out is to ignore writing a partnership agreement as they ride the emotional high of launching a company together. According to one writer, "In the eager, hectic days of startup, when two people come together with a 'brilliant idea,' they never imagine that some day, they may not want to be partners anymore. Instead, their thoughts race to marketing strategies, product development, sales pitches, and customer service."[4] The result? Every year, thousands of partners find themselves mired in irreconcilable disputes that damage their businesses because they failed to establish a partnership agreement.

Generally, a partnership agreement can include any terms the partners want (unless they are illegal). The standard partnership agreement will likely include the following:

1. *Name of the partnership.*
2. *Purpose of the business.* What is the reason the business was brought into being?
3. *Domicile of the business.* Where will the principal business be located?
4. *Duration of the partnership.* How long will the partnership last?
5. *Names of the partners and their legal addresses.*
6. *Contributions of each partner to the business* at the creation of the partnership and later. This would include each partner's investment in the business. In some situations, a partner may contribute assets that are not likely to appear on a balance sheet. Experience, sales contacts, or a good reputation in the community may be reasons for asking a person to join in partnership.
7. Agreement on *how the profits or losses will be distributed.*
8. An agreement on *salaries or drawing rights* against profits for each partner.
9. Procedure for *expansion through the addition of new partners.*
10. If the partners *voluntarily dissolve the partnership, how will the partnership's assets be distributed?*
11. *Sale of partnership interest.* The articles of partnership should include terms defining how a partner can sell his or her interest in the business.
12. *Salaries, draws, and expense accounts for the partners.* How much money will each partner draw from the business? Under what circumstances? How often?
13. *Absence or disability of one of the partners.* If a partner is absent or disabled for an extended period of time, should the partnership continue? Will the absent or disabled partner receive the same share of profits as she did prior to her absence or disability? Should the absent or disabled partner be held responsible for debts incurred while unable to participate?
14. *Dissolution of the partnership.* Under what circumstances will the partnership dissolve?
15. *Alterations or modifications of the partnership agreement.* No document is written to last forever. Partnership agreements should contain provisions for alterations or modifications.

THE UNIFORM PARTNERSHIP ACT. The Uniform Partnership Act (UPA) codifies the body of law dealing with partnerships in the United States (except in Louisiana, which has not adopted the UPA and where state law governs in the absence of a partnership agreement). Under the UPA, the three key elements of any partnership are common ownership interest in a business, sharing the business's profits and losses, and the right to participate in managing the operation of the partnership. Under the act, each partner has the *right* to:

1. share in the management and operations of the business.
2. share in any profits the business might earn from operations.
3. receive interest on additional advances made to the business.
4. be compensated for expenses incurred in the name of the partnership.
5. have access to the business's books and records.
6. receive a formal accounting of the partnership's business affairs.

The UPA also sets forth the partners' general obligations. Each partner is *obligated* to:

1. share in any losses sustained by the business.
2. work for the partnership without salary.
3. submit differences that may arise in the conduct of the business to majority vote or arbitration.

4. give the other partner complete information about all business affairs.
5. give a formal accounting of the partnership's business affairs.

Beyond what the law prescribes, a partnership is based above all else on mutual trust and respect. Any partnership missing these elements is destined to fail.

The Advantages of the Partnership

EASY TO ESTABLISH. Like the proprietorship, the partnership is easy and inexpensive to establish. The owners must obtain the necessary business licenses and submit a minimal number of forms. In most states, partners must file a certificate for conducting business as partners if the business is run under a trade name.

COMPLEMENTARY SKILLS. In a sole proprietorship, the owner must wear lots of different hats, and not all of them will fit well. In successful partnerships, the parties' skills and abilities usually complement one another, strengthening the company's managerial foundation.

Raging Bull Inc.

Bill Martin and Greg Wright, friends since high school, relied on their complementary skills to build a successful partnership, a Web site for investors called Raging Bull Inc. **<www.ragingbull.com>.** *While still in college, the two decided to combine their passion for investing and the Internet into a business. Wright used his computer skills (and those of his college roommate) to work out the operational and technical aspects of creating the Web site, while Martin used his network of connections through an investment club to locate the material for the site's contents. Traffic on their site started slowly but began to build over time, ultimately attracting so many users that @Ventures, a venture capital firm, invested $2 million in the start-up company. Today Raging Bull Inc. is a multimillion-dollar business thanks to the complementary skills of its founders.*[5]

DIVISION OF PROFITS. There are no restrictions on how partners distribute the company's profits as long as they are consistent with the partnership agreement and do not violate the rights of any partner. The partnership agreement should articulate the nature of each partner's contribution and proportional share of the profits. If the partners fail to create an agreement, the UPA says that the partners share equally in the partnership's profits, even if their original capital contributions are unequal.

LARGER POOL OF CAPITAL. The partnership form of ownership can significantly broaden the pool of capital available to a business. Each partner's asset base improves the business's ability to borrow needed funds; together the partners' personal assets will support a larger borrowing capacity.

general partners—*partners who share in owning, operating, and managing a business and who have unlimited personal liability for the partnership's debts.*

limited partners—*partners who do not take an active role in managing a business and whose liability for the partnership's debts is limited to the amount they have invested.*

ABILITY TO ATTRACT LIMITED PARTNERS. When partners share in owning, operating, and managing a business, they are **general partners.** General partners have unlimited liability for the partnership's debts and usually take an active role in managing the business. Every partnership must have at least one general partner, although there is no limit on the number of general partners a business can have.

Limited partners cannot participate in the day-to-day management of a company, and they have limited liability for the partnership's debts. If the business fails, they lose only what they have invested in it and no more. Limited partners usually are just financial investors in a business. A limited partnership can attract investors by offering them limited liability and the potential to realize a substantial return on their investments if the business is successful. Many individuals find it very profitable to invest in high-potential small businesses, but only if they avoid the disadvantages of unlimited liability while doing so.

potential into syndicates and then selling shares of ownership in each syndicate to limited partners. Dogwood Stable holds 5 percent of every syndicate as the general partner and sells four 23.75 percent shares to limited partners at prices ranging from $11,000 to $77,000 each. Although only about 10 percent of individual racehorse owners earn a profit each year, investors in limited partnerships such as those offered by Dogwood Stable have a 25 percent chance of at least breaking even. The star of Dogwood Stable's limited partnerships so far is Summer Squall, whose winnings and stud fees totaled more than $2.5 million. Limited partners in this syndicate earned many times their original $55,900 investments (although most investors admit that the excitement of the race is the real reason they invest).[7]

Limited Liability Partnerships

Many states now recognize **limited liability partnerships (LLPs)** in which *all* partners in a business are limited partners, having only limited liability for the debts of the partnership. Most states restrict LLPs to certain types of professionals such as attorneys, physicians, dentists, accountants, and others. Just as with any limited partnership, the partners must file a certificate of limited partnership in the state in which the partnership will conduct business, and the partnership must identify itself as an LLP to those with whom it does business. Also, like every partnership, an LLP does not pay taxes; its income is passed through to the limited partners, who pay taxes on their shares of the company's income.

limited liability partnership—*a special type of limited partnership in which* all *partners, who in many states must be professionals, are limited partners.*

Master Limited Partnership

A relatively new form of business structure, **master limited partnership (MLP),** is just like regular limited partnerships, except its shares are traded just like shares of common stock. An MLP provides most of the same advantages to investors as a corporation—including limited liability. One analyst says that a master limited partnership "looks like a corporation, acts like a corporation, and trades on major stock exchanges like a corporation."[8] Congress originally allowed MLPs to be taxed as partnerships. However, in 1987, it ruled that any MLP not involved in natural resources or real estate would be taxed as a corporation, eliminating their ability to avoid the "double taxation" disadvantages. MLP profits typically must be divided among thousands of partners.

master limited partnership—*a partnership whose shares are traded on stock exchanges, just like a corporation's.*

1-C. Explain the advantages and disadvantages of the corporation.

CORPORATIONS

The **corporation** is the most complex of the three major forms of business ownership. It is a separate entity apart from its owners and may engage in business, make contracts, sue and be sued, own property, and pay taxes. The Supreme Court has defined the corporation as "an artificial being, invisible, intangible, and existing only in contemplation of the law."[9] Because the life of the corporation is independent of its owners, the shareholders can sell their interests in the business without affecting its continuation.

Corporations (also known as "C corporations") are creations of the state. When a corporation is founded, it accepts the regulations and restrictions of the state in which it is incorporated and any other state in which it chooses to do business. A corporation doing business in the state in which it is incorporated is a **domestic corporation.** When a corporation conducts business in another state, that state considers it to be a **foreign corporation.** Corporations that are formed in other countries but do business in the United States are **alien corporations.**

Generally, the corporation must report annually its financial operations to its home state's secretary of state. These financial reports become public record. If a corporation's

corporation—*a separate legal entity apart from its owners that receives the right to exist from the state in which it is incorporated.*

domestic corporation—*a corporation doing business in the state in which it is incorporated.*

foreign corporation—*a corporation doing business in a state other than the one in which it is incorporated.*

alien corporation—*a corporation formed in another country but doing business in the United States.*

stock is sold in more than one state, the corporation must comply with federal regulations governing the sale of corporate securities. There are substantially more reporting requirements for a corporation than for the other forms of ownership.

How to Incorporate

Most states allow entrepreneurs to incorporate without the assistance of an attorney. Some states even provide incorporation kits to help in the incorporation process. Although it is cheaper for entrepreneurs to complete the process themselves, it is not always the best idea. In some states, the application process is complex, and the required forms are confusing. The price for filing incorrectly can be high. If an entrepreneur completes the incorporation process improperly, it is generally invalid.

Once the owners decide to form a corporation, they must choose a state in which to incorporate. If the business will operate within a single state, it is probably most logical to incorporate in that state. States differ—sometimes rather dramatically—in the requirements they place on the corporations they charter and how they treat corporations chartered in other states. They also differ in the tax rate they impose on corporations, the restrictions placed on their activities, the capital required to incorporate, and the fees or organization tax charged to incorporate. Delaware, for instance, offers low incorporation fees and minimal legal requirements.

Every state requires a certificate of incorporation or charter to be filed with the secretary of state. The following information is generally required to be in the certificate of incorporation:

The corporation's name. The corporation must choose a name that is not so similar to that of another firm in that state that it causes confusion or lends itself to deception. It must also include a term such as *corporation, incorporated, company,* or *limited* to notify the public that they are dealing with a corporation.

The corporation's statement of purpose. The incorporators must state in general terms the intended nature of the business. The purpose must, of course, be lawful. An illustration might be "to engage in the sale of office furniture and fixtures." The purpose should be broad enough to allow for some expansion in the activities of the business as it develops.

The corporation's time horizon. In most cases, corporations are formed with no specific termination date; they are formed "for perpetuity." However, it is possible to incorporate for a specific duration (e.g., 50 years).

Names and addresses of the incorporators. The incorporators must be identified in the articles of incorporation and are liable under the law to attest that all information in the articles of incorporation is correct. In some states, one or more of the incorporators must reside in the state in which the corporation is being created.

Place of business. The street and mailing addresses of the corporation's principal office must be listed. For a domestic corporation, this address must be in the state in which incorporation takes place.

Capital stock authorization. The articles of incorporation must include the amount and class (or type) of capital stock the corporation wants to be authorized to issue. This is not the number of shares it must issue; a corporation can issue any number of shares up to the amount authorized. This section must also define the different classifications of stock and any special rights, preferences, or limits each class has.

Capital required at the time of incorporation. Some states require a newly formed corporation to deposit in a bank a specific percentage of the stock's par value prior to incorporating.

Provisions for preemptive rights, if any, that are granted to stockholders.

treasury stock—*the shares of its own stock that a corporation owns.*

Restrictions on transferring shares. Many closely held corporations—those owned by a few shareholders, often family members—require shareholders interested in selling their stock to offer it first to the corporation. (Shares the corporation itself owns are called **treasury**

stock.) To maintain control over their ownership, many closely held corporations exercise their right, known as the **right of first refusal.**

Names and addresses of the officers and directors of the corporation.

Rules under which the corporation will operate. **Bylaws** are the rules and regulations the officers and directors establish for the corporation's internal management and operation.

right of first refusal—*a provision requiring shareholders who want to sell their stock to offer it first to the corporation.*

bylaws—*the rules and regulations the officers and directors establish for a corporation's internal management and operation.*

Once the secretary of state of the incorporating state has approved a request for incorporation and the corporation pays its fees, the approved articles of incorporation become its charter. With the charter in hand, the next order of business is to hold an organizational meeting for the stockholders to formally elect directors who in turn will appoint the corporate officers.

The Advantages of the Corporation

LIMITED LIABILITY OF STOCKHOLDERS. Because it is a separate legal entity, a corporation allows investors to limit their liability to the total amount of their investment in the business. This legal protection of personal assets beyond the business is of critical concern to many potential investors.

This shield of limited liability may not be impenetrable, however. Because start-up companies are so risky, lenders and other creditors require the owners to personally guarantee loans made to the corporation. Robert Morris Associates, a national organization of bank loan officers, estimates that 95 percent of small business owners have to sign personal guarantees to get the financing they need. By making these guarantees, owners are putting their personal assets at risk (just as in a proprietorship) despite choosing the corporate form of ownership.

Recent court decisions have extended the personal liability of small corporation owners beyond the financial guarantees that banks and other lenders require, "piercing the corporate veil" much more than ever before. Increasingly, courts are holding entrepreneurs personally liable for environmental, pension, and legal claims against their corporations—much to the surprise of the owners, who chose the corporate form of ownership to shield themselves from such liability.[10] Problems usually arise when entrepreneurs fail to "maintain the integrity" of a corporation by failing to capitalize it sufficiently, neglecting corporate formalities such as holding annual meetings or filing required reports, or commingling their personal assets and those of the corporation. For example, the owner of a Los Angeles boatyard often paid his personal expenses with checks written on his corporation's account. When a customer sued the company and won, the court ruled that the judgment applied not only to the corporation's assets but also to the owner's personal assets because he had failed to keep the two separated.[11]

ABILITY TO ATTRACT CAPITAL. Based on the protection of limited liability, corporations have proved to be the most effective form of ownership for accumulating large amounts of capital. Limited only by the number of shares authorized in its charter (which can be amended), the corporation can raise money to begin business and expand as opportunity dictates by selling shares of its stock to investors. A corporation can sell its stock to a limited number of private investors (a private placement) or to the public (a public offering).

ABILITY TO CONTINUE INDEFINITELY. Unless a corporation fails to pay its taxes or is limited to a specific length of life by its charter, it can continue indefinitely. The corporation's existence does not depend on the fate of any single individual. Unlike a proprietorship or partnership in which the death of a founder ends the business, a corporation lives beyond the lives of those who gave it life. This perpetual life gives rise to the next major advantage—transferable ownership.

TRANSFERABLE OWNERSHIP. If stockholders in a corporation are displeased with the business's progress, they can sell their shares to someone else. Millions of shares of stock representing ownership in companies are traded daily on the world's stock exchanges. Shareholders can also transfer their stock through inheritance to a new generation of owners. During all of these transfers of ownership, the corporation continues to conduct business as usual.

Unlike that of large corporations whose shares are traded on organized stock exchanges, the stock of many small corporations is held by a small number of people ("closely held"), often company founders, family members, or employees. The small number of people holding the stock means that the resale market for shares is limited, which could make the transfer of ownership more difficult.

The Disadvantages of Corporations

COST AND TIME INVOLVED IN THE INCORPORATION PROCESS. Corporations can be costly and time-consuming to establish. The owners are giving birth to an artificial legal entity, and the gestation period can be prolonged for the novice. In some states an attorney must handle the incorporation process, but in most states entrepreneurs can complete all of the required forms alone. However, an owner must exercise great caution when incorporating without the help of an attorney. Also, incorporating a business requires various fees that are not applicable to proprietorships or partnerships. Creating a corporation can cost between $500 and $2,500, typically averaging around $1,000.

DOUBLE TAXATION. Because a corporation is a separate legal entity, it must pay taxes on its net income at the federal level, in most states, and to some local governments as well. Before stockholders receive a penny of its net income as dividends, a corporation must pay these taxes at the *corporate* tax rate. Then stockholders must pay taxes on the dividends they receive from these same profits at the *individual* tax rate. Thus, a corporation's profits are taxed twice. This **double taxation** is a distinct disadvantage of the corporate form of ownership.

double taxation—*a disadvantage of the corporate form of ownership in which a corporation's profits are taxed twice: at the corporate rate and at the individual rate (on the portion of profits distributed as dividends).*

POTENTIAL FOR DIMINISHED MANAGERIAL INCENTIVES. As corporations grow, they often require additional managerial expertise beyond that which the founder can provide. Because she created the company and often has most of her personal wealth tied up in it, the entrepreneur has an intense interest in making it a success and is willing to make sacrifices for it. Professional managers the entrepreneur brings in to help run the business as it grows do not always have the same degree of interest in or loyalty to the company. As a result, the business may suffer without the founder's energy, care, and devotion. One way to minimize this potential problem is to link managers' (and even employees') compensation to the company's financial performance through a profit-sharing or bonus plan. Corporations can also stimulate managers' and employees' incentive on the job by creating an employee stock ownership plan (ESOP) in which managers and employees become part or whole owners in the company.

LEGAL REQUIREMENTS AND REGULATORY RED TAPE. Corporations are subject to more legal, reporting, and financial requirements than other forms of ownership. Corporate officers must meet more stringent requirements for recording and reporting management decisions and actions. They must also hold annual meetings and consult the board of directors about major decisions that are beyond day-to-day operations. Managers may be required to submit some major decisions to the stockholders for approval. Corporations that are publicly held must file quarterly and annual reports with the Securities and Exchange Commission (SEC).

POTENTIAL LOSS OF CONTROL BY THE FOUNDER(S). When entrepreneurs sell shares of ownership in their companies, they relinquish some control. Especially when they need large capital infusions for start-up or growth, entrepreneurs may have to give up *significant* amounts of control, so much, in fact, that the founder becomes a minority shareholder. Losing majority ownership—and, therefore, control—in her company leaves the founder in a precarious position. She no longer has the power to determine the company's direction; "outsiders" do. In some cases, founders' shares have been so diluted that majority shareholders actually vote them out of their jobs!

Microsoft Inc.

Even Bill Gates, one of the wealthiest people in the world, has seen his ownership in Microsoft Inc., the company he founded with Paul Allen as a partnership in 1975, dwindle from 50 percent at start-up to 44.8 percent when the company went public in 1986, to 18.5 percent today. Over the years, Gates's ownership in Microsoft was diluted as he sold stock in the company to raise the capital needed to fuel its rapid growth. Don't feel too sorry for Bill Gates, however. His 18.5 percent stake in the company he cofounded is now worth more than $75 billion dollars![12]

OTHER FORMS OF OWNERSHIP

2. Discuss the advantages and disadvantages of the S corporation, the limited liability company, the professional corporation, and the joint venture.

In addition to the sole proprietorship, the partnership, and the corporation, entrepreneurs can choose from other forms of ownership, including the S corporation, the limited liability company, the professional corporation, and the joint venture.

The S Corporation

In 1954, the Internal Revenue Service Code created the subchapter S corporation. In recent years, the IRS has changed the title to S corporation and has made a few modifications in its qualifications. An **S corporation** is only a distinction that is made for federal income tax purposes and is, in terms of legal characteristics, no different from any other corporation. Although Congress recently simplified some of the rules and requirements for S corporations, a business seeking "S" status still must meet the following criteria:

S corporation—*a corporation that retains the legal characteristics of a regular (C) corporation but has the advantage of being taxed as a partnership if it meets certain criteria.*

1. It must be a domestic (U.S.) corporation.
2. It cannot have a nonresident alien as a shareholder.
3. It can issue only one class of common stock, which means that all shares must carry the same rights (e.g., the right to dividends or liquidation rights). The exception is voting rights, which may differ. In other words, an S corporation can issue voting and nonvoting common stock.
4. It must limit its shareholders to individuals, estates, and certain trusts, although tax-exempt creations such as employee stock ownership plans (ESOPs) and pension plans can now be shareholders.
5. It cannot have more than 75 shareholders (increased from 35), which is an important benefit for family businesses making the transition from one generation of owners to another.

Violating any of these terms *automatically* terminates a company's "S" status. If a corporation satisfies the definition for an S corporation, the owners must actually elect to be treated as one. The election is made by filing IRS Form 2553 at any time during the year, and *all* shareholders must consent to have the corporation treated as an S corporation.

THE ADVANTAGES OF AN S CORPORATION. The S corporation retains all of the advantages of a regular corporation, such as continuity of existence, transferability of ownership, and limited personal liability for its owners. The most notable provision of the S corporation is that it passes all of its profits or losses through to the individual shareholders, and its income is taxed only once at the individual tax rate. Thus, electing S corporation status avoids a primary disadvantage of the regular (or "C") corporation—double taxation. In essence, the tax treatment of an S corporation is exactly like that of a partnership; its owners report their proportional shares of the company's profits on their individual income tax returns and pay taxes on those profits at the individual rate (even if they never take the money out of the business).

Another advantage the S corporation offers is avoiding the tax C corporations pay on assets that have appreciated in value and are sold. Also, owners of S corporations enjoy the ability to make year-end payouts to themselves if earnings are high. In a C corporation, owners have no such luxury because the IRS watches for excessive compensation to owners/managers.

One significant change to the laws governing S corporations that benefits entrepreneurs involves subsidiary companies. Before 1998, if an entrepreneur owned separate but affiliated companies, she had to maintain each one as a distinct S corporation with its own accounting records and tax return. Under current law, that business owner can set up all of these affiliated companies as qualified S corporation subsidiaries ("Q Subs") under the umbrella of a single company, each with its own separate legal identity, and still file a single tax return for the parent company. For entrepreneurs with several lines of businesses, this change means greatly simplified tax filing. Owners also can use losses from one subsidiary company to offset profits from another to minimize their tax bills. "The advent of the Q Sub has made [S corporations] more useful and popular than ever," says one tax expert.[13]

DISADVANTAGES OF AN S CORPORATION. When the Tax Reform Act (TRA) of 1986 restructured individual and corporate tax rates, many business owners switched to S corporations to lower their tax bills. For the first time since Congress enacted the federal income tax in 1913, the maximum individual rate was lower than the maximum corporate rate. However, in 1993, Congress realigned the tax structure by raising the maximum personal tax rate to 39.6 percent from 31 percent. This new rate is 4.6 percent *higher* than the maximum corporate tax rate of 35 percent. Although these changes make S corporation status much less attractive than before, entrepreneurs considering switching to C corporation status must consider the total impact of such a change on their companies, especially if they pay out a significant amount of earnings to owners. In addition to the tax implications of making the switch from an S corporation, owners should consider the size of the company's net income, the tax rates of its shareholders, plans (and their timing) to sell the company, and the impact of the C corporation's double-taxation penalty on income distributed as dividends.

Another disadvantage of the S corporation is that the costs of many fringe benefits—insurance, meals, lodging, and so on—paid to shareholders with 2 percent or more of stock cannot be deducted as business expenses for tax purposes; these benefits are then considered to be taxable income. In addition, S corporations offer shareholders only a limited range of retirement benefits, whereas regular corporations make a wide range of retirement plans available.

WHEN IS AN S CORPORATION A WISE CHOICE? Choosing S corporation status is usually beneficial to start-up companies anticipating net losses and to highly profitable firms with substantial dividends to pay out to shareholders. In these cases the owner can use the loss to offset other income or is in a lower tax bracket than the corporation, thus saving money in the long run. Companies that plan to reinvest most of their earnings to finance growth also find S corporation status favorable. Small business owners who intend to sell their companies in the near future will prefer "S" over "C" status because the taxable gains on the sale of an S corporation are generally lower than those of a C corporation.

On the other hand, small companies with the following characteristics are *not* likely to benefit from S corporation status:

- highly profitable personal service companies with large numbers of shareholders, in which most of the profits are passed on to shareholders as compensation or retirement benefits.
- fast-growing companies that must retain most of their earnings to finance growth and capital spending.
- corporations in which the loss of fringe benefits to shareholders exceeds tax savings.
- corporations in which the income before any compensation to shareholders is less than $100,000 per year.
- corporations with sizable net operating losses that cannot be used against S corporation earnings.

The Limited Liability Company (LLC)

limited liability company (LLC)—*a relatively new form of ownership that, like an S corporation, is a cross between a partnership and a corporation; it is not subject to many of the restrictions imposed on S corporations.*

A relatively new creation, the **limited liability company (LLC)** is, like an S corporation, a cross between a partnership and a corporation. LLCs, however, are not subject to many of the restrictions currently imposed on S corporations and offer more flexibility than S corporations. For example, S corporations cannot have more than 75 shareholders, none of whom can be foreigners or corporations. S corporations are also limited to only one class of stock. LLCs eliminate those restrictions. An LLC must have at least two owners (called "members"), but it offers its owners limited liability without imposing any requirements on their characteristics or any ceiling on their numbers. Unlike a limited partnership, which prohibits limited partners from participating in the day-to-day management of the business, an LLC does not restrict its members' ability to become involved in managing the company.

In addition to offering its members the advantage of limited liability, LLCs also avoid the double taxation imposed on C corporations. Like an S corporation, an LLC does not pay income taxes; its income flows through to the members, who are responsible for paying income taxes on their shares of the LLC's net income. Because they are not subject to the many restrictions imposed on other forms of ownership, LLCs offer entrepreneurs another significant advantage: flexibility. Like a partnership, an LLC permits its members to divide income (and, thus, tax liability) as they see fit.

These advantages make the LLC an ideal form of ownership for small companies in virtually any industry—retail, wholesale, manufacturing, real estate, or service. Because they offer the tax advantage of a partnership, the legal protection of a corporation, and maximum flexibility, LLCs have become an extremely popular form of ownership among entrepreneurs.

Let's Go Party

For example, Marian Fletcher launched a profitable party planning and catering service in 1995 as a sole proprietorship. Her company, Let's Go Party, grew quickly, and Fletcher wanted to bring her daughter into the business as an owner. Reviewing the advantages and disadvantages of each form of ownership led Fletcher to create an LLC. "We decided this was the best way to go for us," she says. "In case anything happens, my daughter and I won't be liable for anything more than what we have invested in the company already." Fletcher, who set up her LLC without the help of an attorney for just $50, also found the LLC's tax treatment to be a major advantage for her and her daughter.[14]

Creating an LLC is much like creating a corporation. Forming an LLC requires an entrepreneur to file two documents with the secretary of state: the articles of organization

articles of organization—*the document that creates an LLC by establishing its name, its method of management, its duration, and other details.*

operating agreement—*the document that establishes for an LLC the provisions governing the way it will conduct business.*

and the operating agreement. The LLC's **articles of organization,** similar to the corporation's articles of incorporation, actually creates the LLC by establishing its name and address, its method of management (board managed or member managed), its duration, and the names and addresses of each organizer. In most states the company's name must contain the words "limited liability company," "limited company," or the letters "L.L.C." or "L.C." Unlike a corporation, an LLC does not have perpetual life; in most states an LLC's charter may not exceed 30 years. However, the same factors that would cause a partnership to dissolve would also cause the dissolution of an LLC before its charter expires.

The **operating agreement,** similar to a corporation's bylaws, outlines the provisions governing the way the LLC will conduct business, such as members' capital contributions to the LLC, the admission or withdrawal of members, distributions from the business, and how the LLC will be managed. To ensure that their LLCs are classified as a partnership for tax purposes, entrepreneurs must draft the operating agreement carefully. The operating agreement must create an LLC that has more characteristics of a partnership than of a corporation to maintain this favorable tax treatment. Specifically, an LLC cannot have any more than *two* of the following four corporate characteristics:

1. *Limited liability.* Limited liability exists if no member of the LLC is personally liable for the debts or claims against the company. Because entrepreneurs choosing this form of ownership usually do so to get limited liability protection, the operating agreement almost always contains this characteristic.
2. *Continuity of life.* Continuity of life exists if the company continues to exist in spite of changes in stock ownership. To avoid continuity of life, any LLC member must have the power to dissolve the company. Most entrepreneurs choose to omit this characteristic from their LLC's operating agreements.
3. *Free transferability of interest.* Free transferability of interest exists if each LLC member has the power to transfer his ownership to another person freely and without the consent of other members. To avoid this characteristic, the operating agreement must state that a recipient of a member's LLC stock cannot become a substitute member without the consent of the remaining members.
4. *Centralized management.* Centralized management exists if a group that does not include all LLC members has the authority to make management decisions and to conduct company business. To avoid this characteristic, the operating agreement must state that the company elects to be "member managed."

Despite their universal appeal to entrepreneurs, LLCs suffer some disadvantages. They can be expensive to create, often costing between $1,500 and $5,000. Although an LLC may be ideally suited for an entrepreneur launching a new company, it may pose problems for business owners considering converting an existing business to an LLC. Switching to an LLC from a general partnership, a limited partnership, or a sole proprietorship by reorganizing to bring in new owners is usually not a problem. However, owners of corporations and S corporations would incur large tax obligations if they converted their companies to LLCs.

To date, the biggest disadvantage of the LLC stems from its newness. As yet, no uniform legislation for LLCs exists (although a Uniform Limited Liability Act is pending at the federal level). Every state now recognizes the LLC as a legal form of ownership.

The Professional Corporation

Professional corporations are designed to offer professionals—lawyers, doctors, dentists, accountants, and others—the advantages of the corporate form of ownership. They are ideally suited for professionals, who must always be concerned about malpractice lawsuits, because they offer limited liability. For example, if three doctors formed a professional corporation, none of them would be liable for the others' malpractice. (Of course, each would

YOU BE THE CONSULTANT . . .

Which Form Is Best?

Watoma Kinsey and her daughter Katrina are about to launch a business that specializes in children's parties. Their target audience is upscale families who want to throw unique, memorable parties to celebrate special occasions for their children between the ages of 5 and 15. The Kinseys have leased a large building and have renovated it to include many features designed to appeal to kids, including special gym equipment, a skating rink, an obstacle course, a mockup of a pirate ship, a ball crawl, and even a moveable haunted house. They can offer simple birthday parties (cake and ice cream included) or special theme parties as elaborate as the customer wants. Their company will provide magicians, clowns, comedians, jugglers, tumblers, and a variety of other entertainers.

Watoma and Katrina have invested $45,000 each to get the business ready to launch. Based on the quality of their business plan and their preparation, the Kinseys have negotiated a $40,000 bank loan. Because they both have families, the Kinseys want to minimize their exposure to potential legal and financial problems. A large portion of their start-up costs went to purchase a liability insurance policy to cover the Kinseys in case a child is injured at a party. If their business plan is accurate, the Kinseys will earn a small profit in their first year (about $1,500) and a more attractive profit of $16,000 in their second year of operation. Within five years, they expect their company to generate as much as $50,000 in profits. The Kinseys have agreed to split the profits—and the workload—equally.

If the business is as successful as they think it will be, the Kinseys eventually want to franchise their company. That, however, is part of their long-range plan. For now, they want to perfect their business system and prove that it can be profitable before they try to duplicate it in the form of franchises.

As they move closer to the launch date for their business, the Kinseys are reviewing the different forms of ownership.

1. Which form(s) of ownership would you recommend to the Kinseys? Explain.
2. Which form(s) of ownership would you recommend the Kinseys *avoid*? Explain.
3. What factors should the Kinseys consider as they try to choose the form of ownership that is best for them?

be liable for her own actions.) Owners create a professional corporation in the same way as a regular corporation. Such corporations are often identified by the abbreviations P.C. (professional corporation), P.A. (professional association), or S.C. (service corporation).

The Joint Venture

A joint venture is very much like a partnership, except that it is formed for a specific, limited purpose. For instance, suppose that you have a 500-acre tract of land 60 miles from Chicago that has been cleared and is normally used in agricultural production. You have a friend who has solid contacts among major musical groups and would like to put on a concert. You expect prices for your agricultural products to be low this summer, so you and your friend form a joint venture for the specific purpose of staging a three-day concert. Your contribution will be the exclusive use of the land for one month, and your friend will provide all the performers as well as technicians, facilities, and equipment. All costs will be paid out of receipts and the net profits will be split, with you receiving 20 percent for the use of your land. When the concert is over, the facilities removed, and the accounting for all costs completed, you and your friend split the profits 20-80, and the joint venture terminates.

In any endeavor in which neither party can effectively achieve the purpose alone, a joint venture becomes a common form of ownership. The "partners" form a new joint venture for each new project they undertake. The income derived from a joint venture is taxed as if it arose from a partnership.

Table 4.1 provides a summary of the key features of the major forms of ownership discussed in this chapter.

TABLE 4.1
Characteristics of the Major Forms of Ownership

Feature	Sole Proprietorship	Partnership	C Corporation	S Corporation	Limited Liability Company
Owner's personal liability	Unlimited	Unlimited for general partners Limited for limited partners	Limited	Limited	Limited
Number of owners	1	2 or more (at least 1 general partner required)	Any number	Maximum of 75 (with restriction on who they are)	2 or more
Tax liability	Single tax: proprietor pays at individual rate	Single tax: partners pay on their proportional shares at individual rate	Double tax: corporation pays tax and shareholders pay tax on dividends distributed	Single tax: owners pay on their proportional shares at individual rate	Single tax: members pay on their proportional shares at individual rate
Maximum tax rate	39.6%	39.6%	35% (39.6% on dividends distributed)	39.6%	39.6%
Transferability of ownership	Fully transferable through sale or transfer of company assets	May require consent of all partners	Fully transferable	Transferable (but transfer may affect S status)	Usually requires consent of all members
Continuity of business	Ends on death or insanity of proprietor or upon termination by proprietor	Dissolves upon death, insanity, or retirement of a general partner (business may continue)	Perpetual life	Perpetual life	Perpetual life
Cost of formation	Low	Moderate	High	High	High
Liquidity of owner's investment in business	Poor to average	Poor to average	High	High	High
Complexity of formation	Extremely low	Moderate	high	High	High
Ability to raise capital	Low	Moderate	Very high	Moderate to high	High
Formation procedure	No special steps required other than buying necessary licenses	No written partnership agreements required (but highly advisable)	Must meet formal requirements specified by state law	Must follow same procedures as C corporation, then elect S status with IRS	Must meet formal requirements specified by state law

FRANCHISING

Franchising has come a long way from its beginnings in the 1850s when the Singer Sewing Machine Company began licensing distributors to sell its sewing machines. Today, approximately 4,500 franchisers operate more than 600,000 franchise outlets throughout the world, and more are opening at an incredible pace. A new franchise opens somewhere in the world every 6.5 minutes![15] Franchises account for 44 percent of all retail sales, totaling more than *$1 trillion,* and they employ some 8 million people in more than 100 major industries.[16] Much of franchising's popularity stems from its ability to offer those who lack business experience the chance to own and operate a business with a high probability of success. This booming industry has moved far beyond the traditional boundaries of fast food into fields as diverse as maid services and bakeries to computer sales and pet-sitting.

In **franchising,** semi-independent business owners (franchisees) pay fees and royalties to a parent company (franchiser) in return for the right to become identified with its trademark, to sell its products or services, and often to use its business format and system. Franchisees do not establish their own autonomous businesses; instead, they buy a "success package" from the franchiser, who shows them how to use it. Franchisees, unlike independent business owners, don't have the freedom to change the way they run their businesses—for example, shifting advertising strategies or adjusting product lines—but they do have a formula for success that the franchiser has worked out. "The secret to success in franchising is following the formula precisely," says one writer. "Successful franchisers claim that neglecting to follow the formula is one of the chief reasons that franchisees fail."[17]

franchising—*a system of distribution in which semi-independent business owners (franchisees) pay fees and royalties to a parent company (franchiser) in return for the right to become identified with its trademark, to sell its products or services, and often to use its business format and system.*

Schlachter's Maaco Auto Painting and Bodyworks

Anita Schlachter, co-owner of a highly successful Maaco (automotive services) franchise with her husband and her son, is convinced that the system the franchiser taught them is the key to their company's progress and growth to date. The Schlachters follow the franchiser's plan, using it as a road map to success. "If you listen to what your franchiser says and follow its policies and procedures, you'll be successful," she says. "Those who think they know more should not go into franchising."[18]

Franchising is based on a continuing relationship between a franchiser and a franchisee. The franchiser provides valuable services such as market research, a proven business system, name recognition, and many other forms of assistance; in return, the franchisee pays an initial franchise fee as well as an ongoing percentage of his sales to the franchiser as royalties and agrees to operate his outlet according to the franchiser's system. Because franchisers develop the business systems their franchisees use and direct their distribution methods, they maintain substantial control over their franchisees. This standardization lies at the core of franchising's success as a method of distribution.

3. Describe the three types of franchising: trade name, product distribution, and pure.

TYPES OF FRANCHISING

There are three basic types of franchising: trade-name franchising, product distribution franchising, and pure franchising. **Trade-name franchising** involves a brand name such as True Value Hardware or Western Auto. Here the franchisee purchases the right to use the franchiser's trade name without distributing particular products exclusively under the franchiser's name. **Product distribution franchising** involves a franchiser's licensing a franchisee to sell specific products under the franchiser's brand name and trademark through a selective, limited distribution network. This system is commonly used to market automobiles (Chevrolet, Oldsmobile, Chrysler), gasoline products (ExxonMobil, Sunoco, Texaco), soft drinks (Pepsi-Cola, Coca-Cola), bicycles (Schwinn), appliances, cosmetics, and other products. These two methods of franchising allow franchisees to acquire some of the parent company's identity.

Pure (or comprehensive or business format) **franchising** involves providing the franchisee with a complete business format, including a license for a trade name, the products or services to be sold, the physical plant, the methods of operation, a marketing strategy plan, a quality control process, a two-way communications system, and the necessary business services. The franchisee purchases the right to use all the elements of a fully integrated business operation. Pure franchising is the most rapidly growing of all types of franchising and is common among fast-food restaurants, hotels, business service firms, car rental agencies, educational institutions, beauty aid retailers, and many others. Although product and trade-name franchises annually ring up more sales than pure franchisees, pure franchising outlets' sales are growing much faster.

trade-name franchising—*a system of franchising in which a franchisee purchases the right to use the franchiser's trade name without distributing particular products under the franchiser's name.*

product distribution franchising—*a system of franchising in which a franchiser licenses a franchisee to sell its products under the franchiser's brand name and trademark through a selective, limited distribution network.*

pure franchising—*a system of franchising in which a franchiser sells a franchisee a complete business format and system.*

4-A. Explain the benefits of buying a franchise.

THE BENEFITS OF BUYING A FRANCHISE

A franchisee gets the opportunity to own a small business relatively quickly, and, because of the identification with an established product and brand name, a franchise often reaches the breakeven point faster than an independent business would. Still, most new franchise outlets don't break even for at least six to eighteen months.

Franchisees also benefit from the franchiser's business experience. In fact, experience is the essence of what a franchisee is buying from a franchiser. Many entrepreneurs go into business by themselves and make many costly mistakes. Given the thin margin for error in the typical start-up, a new business owner cannot afford to make many mistakes. In a franchising arrangement, the franchiser already has worked out the kinks in the system by trial and error, and franchisees benefit from that experience. A franchiser has climbed up the learning curve and can share with franchisees the secrets of success they have discovered in the industry. Gary Mandichak, owner of a successful Petland franchise, says, "[Franchisers] have the experience, they know what works and what doesn't, and they know what's happening in the market."[19]

Franchisees also earn a great deal of satisfaction from their work. According to a recent Gallup survey of franchise owners, 82 percent of franchisees said they were "somewhat satisfied" to "very satisfied" with their work. Plus, 75 percent said they would purchase their franchises again if given the opportunity (compared to just 39 percent of Americans who say they would choose the same job or business again).[20] Another survey reported that 94 percent of franchise owners rated their operations as "very successful" or "successful."[21]

Before jumping at a franchise opportunity, an entrepreneur should consider carefully the question, "What can a franchise do for me that I cannot do for myself?" The answer to this question will depend on the particular situation and is not as important as the systematic evaluation of the franchise opportunity. After careful deliberation, one person may conclude that the franchise offers nothing that she could not do independently, and another may decide that a franchise is the key to success as a business owner. Franchisees often cite the following advantages that are discussed next.

Management Training and Support

Recall from Chapter 1 that one of the leading causes of business failure is incompetent management. Franchisers are well aware of this and, in an attempt to reduce the number of franchise casualties, offer managerial training programs to franchisees prior to opening a new outlet. Many franchisers, especially the well-established ones, also provide follow-up training and counseling services. This service is vital since most franchisers do not require a franchisee to have experience in the business. These programs teach franchisees the details they need to know for day-to-day operations as well as the nuances of running their businesses successfully.

Training programs often involve both classroom and on-site instruction to teach franchisees the basic operations of the business. Before beginning operations, McDonald's franchisees spend 14 days in Illinois at Hamburger University where they learn everything from how to scrape the grill correctly to "how to manage a $1.6 million business."[22] Maaco franchisees spend four weeks at the company's headquarters delving into a five-volume set of operations manuals and learning to run an auto services shop. H & R Block trains its franchisees to unravel the mysteries of tax preparation, whereas Dunkin' Donuts trains a franchisee for as long as five weeks in everything from accounting to dough making. To ensure franchisees' continued success, many franchisers supplement their start-up training programs with ongoing instruction and support. Franchisers offer these training programs because they realize that their ultimate success depends on the franchisee's success.

Despite the positive features of training, inherent dangers exist in the trainer/trainee relationship. Every would-be franchisee should be aware that, in some cases, "assistance" from the franchiser tends to drift into "control" over the franchisee's business. Some franchisers also charge fees for their training services, so the franchisee should know exactly what she is agreeing to and what it costs.

Brand-Name Appeal

A licensed franchisee purchases the right to use a nationally known and advertised brand name for a product or service. Thus, the franchisee has the advantage of identifying his business with a widely recognized trademark, which usually provides a great deal of drawing power. Customers recognize the identifying trademark, the standard symbols, the store design, and the products of an established franchise. Indeed, one of franchising's basic tenets is cloning the franchiser's success. For example, nearly everyone is familiar with the golden arches of McDonald's or the red roof of the Red Roof Inn, and the standard products and quality offered at each. A customer is confident that the quality and content of a meal at McDonald's in Fort Lauderdale will be consistent with a meal at a San Francisco McDonald's. "It's a tremendous advantage to open a business with a recognizable trademark that creates almost instant foot traffic," says franchise attorney and expert Andrew Caffey.[23]

Standardized Quality of Goods and Services

Because a franchisee purchases a license to sell the franchiser's product or service and the privilege of using the associated brand name, the quality of the goods or service sold determines the franchiser's reputation. Building a sound reputation in business is not achieved quickly, although destroying a good reputation takes no time at all. If some franchisees were allowed to operate at substandard levels, the image of the entire chain would suffer irreparable damage; therefore, franchisers normally demand compliance with uniform standards of quality and service throughout the entire chain. In many cases, the franchiser conducts periodic inspections of local facilities to assist in maintaining acceptable levels of performance.

Papa John's Pizza

For instance, John Schnatter, founder of Papa John's, a fast-growing pizza franchise, makes personal visits to some of his franchisees' stores four to five times each week to

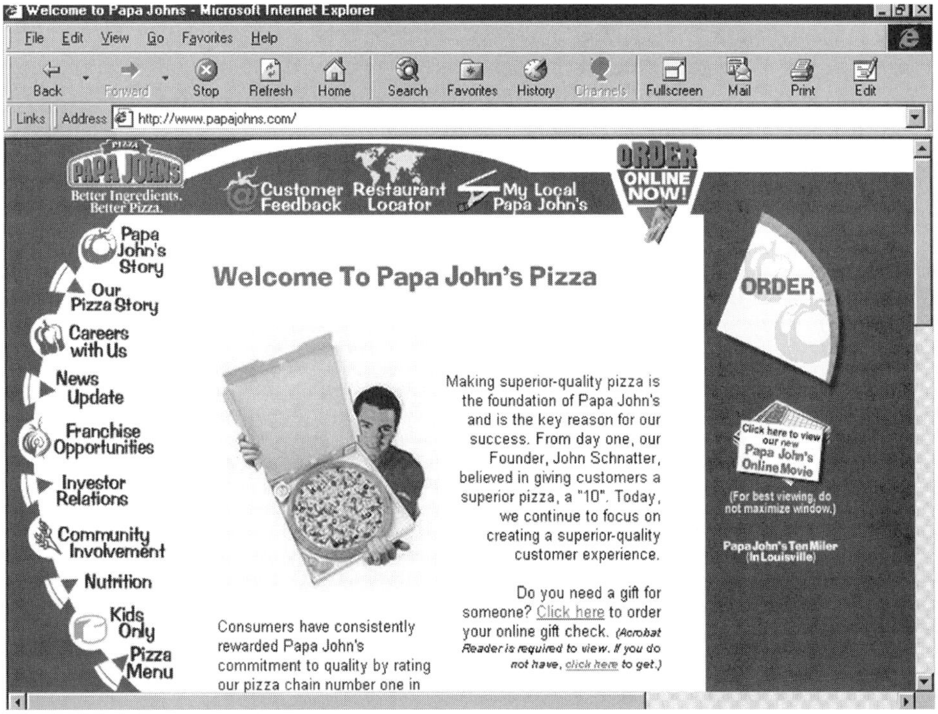

make sure they are performing up to the company's high-quality standards. Franchisees say that Schnatter, known for his attention to detail, often checks pizzas for air bubbles in the crust or tomato sauce for freshness. "Pizza is Schnatter's life, and he takes it very seriously," says one industry analyst.[24]

Maintaining quality is so important that most franchisers retain the right to terminate the franchise contract and to repurchase the outlet if the franchisee fails to comply with established standards.

National Advertising Programs

An effective advertising program is essential to the success of virtually all franchise operations. Marketing a brand-name product or service over a wide geographic area requires a far-reaching advertising campaign. A regional or national advertising program benefits all franchisees. Normally, such an advertising campaign is organized and controlled by the franchiser. It is financed by each franchisee's contribution of a percentage of monthly sales, usually 1 to 5 percent, or a flat monthly fee. For example, Subway franchisees must pay 3.5 percent of gross revenues to the Subway national advertising program. These funds are pooled and used for a cooperative advertising program, which has more impact than if the franchisees spent the same amount of money separately.

Many franchisers also require franchisees to spend a minimum amount on local advertising. To supplement their national advertising efforts, both Wendy's and Burger King require franchisees to spend at least 3 percent of gross sales on local advertising. Some franchisers assist each franchisee in designing and producing its local ads. Many companies help franchisees create promotional plans and provide press releases and advertisements for grand openings.

Financial Assistance

Because they rely on their franchisees' money to grow their businesses, franchisers typically do not provide any extensive financial help for franchisees. Franchisers rarely make loans to enable franchisees to pay the initial franchise fee. However, once a franchiser locates a suitable prospective franchisee, it may offer the qualified candidate direct financial assistance in specific areas, such as purchasing equipment, inventory, or even the franchise fee. Because the start-up costs of some franchises are already at breathtaking levels, some franchisers find that they must offer direct financial assistance.

US Franchise Systems

For example, US Franchise Systems, franchiser of Microtel Inn and Hawthorn Suites hotels, has set up a subsidiary, US Funding Corporation, that makes available to its franchisees $200 million in construction and mortgage financing. Not only has the in-house financing program cut the time required to open a new hotel franchise, but it also has accelerated the franchise's growth rate.[25]

Nearly half of the International Franchise Association's members indicate that they offer some type of financial assistance to their franchises; however, only one-fourth offer direct financial assistance. In most instances, financial assistance from franchisers takes a form other than direct loans, leases, or short-term credit. Franchisers usually are willing to assist qualified franchisees in establishing relationships with banks, private investors, and other sources of funds. Such support and connections from the franchiser enhance a franchisee's credit standing because lenders recognize the lower failure rate among established franchises.

Preferred relationships between lenders and franchisers can be critical because finding financing for a franchise can be challenging, just like attracting capital for any business start-up.

For instance, when Jana Sappenfield began searching for $1.6 million of the $1.9 million needed to purchase a Primrose School franchise, the franchiser helped her connect with Newcourt/AT&T, a Small Business Administration–certified lender that has established preferred relationships with about 25 different franchised companies. "They were familiar with Primrose," says Sappenfield, "so no time was wasted researching or approving the franchiser." Because Primrose School had already accepted Sappenfield's application for a franchise, her loan request sailed easily through Newcourt/AT&T's approval process. "We know the leadership and have an understanding of the selection criteria at the franchises we work with regularly," says a top executive at Newcourt/AT&T. "Consequently, when an approved loan application comes in from a [preferred franchise], we are certain the candidate is qualified." Sappenfield's first Primrose School franchise was so successful that she has since purchased a second one.[26]

Primrose School

Proven Products and Business Formats

What a franchisee essentially purchases is a franchiser's experience, expertise, and products. A franchise owner does not have to build the business from scratch. Instead of being forced to rely solely on personal ability to establish a business and attract a clientele, a franchisee can depend on the methods and techniques of an established business. These standardized procedures and operations greatly enhance the franchisee's chances of success and avoid the most inefficient type of learning—trial and error.

With a franchise, a franchisee does not have to struggle for recognition in the local marketplace as much as an independent owner might.

Kenneth Gabler's independent video rental store had the largest share of the local market when his landlord leased space in the same shopping center to a nationally known video franchise, West Coast Video. When he discovered that the unit was company owned, Gabler offered to buy it. "I figured that if I stayed an independent and tried to compete, West Coast would take away 30 percent of my business anyway. So it was cheaper for me to pay the $15,000 initial fee and a 7 percent royalty every month," he says. West Coast Video's broader tape selection, marketing techniques, and recognized name "have helped tremendously," according to Gabler. Since he converted his business to a franchise, Gabler's sales have tripled![27]

West Coast Video

Centralized Buying Power

A significant advantage a franchisee has over an independent small business owner is participation in the franchiser's centralized and large-volume buying power. If franchisers sell goods and supplies to franchisees (not all do), they may pass on to franchisees any cost savings from quantity discounts they earn by buying in volume. For example, it is unlikely that a small, independent ice cream parlor could match the buying power of Baskin-Robbins with its 3,000-plus retail ice cream stores. In many instances, economies of scale simply preclude the independent owner from competing head-to-head with a franchise operation.

Site Selection and Territorial Protection

A proper location is critical to the success of any small business, and franchises are no exception. In fact, franchise experts consider the three most important factors in franchising to be *location, location,* and *location.* Becoming affiliated with a franchiser may be the best way to get into prime locations. Many franchisers will make an extensive location analysis for each new outlet, including researching traffic patterns, zoning ordinances, accessibility, and population density. McDonald's, for example, is well known for its ability to obtain prime locations in high-traffic areas. Although choosing a location is the franchisee's responsibility, the franchiser usually reserves the right to approve the final site. Choosing a suitable location requires a location analysis, including studies of traffic patterns, zoning ordinances, accessibility, population density, and demographics.

Some franchisers offer franchisees territorial protection, which gives existing franchisees the right to exclusive distribution of brand-name goods or services within a particular geographic area. A clause establishing such a protective zone that bars other outlets from the same franchise gives franchisees significant protection and security. The size of a franchisee's territory varies from industry to industry. For example, one national fast-food restaurant agrees not to license another franchisee within 1.5 miles of existing locations. But one soft-serve ice cream franchiser defines its franchisees' territories on the basis of zip code designations. The purpose of such protection is to prevent an invasion of the existing franchisee's territory and the accompanying dilution of sales. As existing markets have become increasingly saturated with franchise outlets, the placement of new outlets has become a source of friction between franchisers and franchisees. Existing franchisees charge that franchisers are encroaching on their territories by granting new franchises so close to them that their sales are diluted. Although most franchises offer their franchisees some type of territorial protection, the contract of one popular submarine sandwich company offers no such protection and states that the franchiser may compete with its franchisees, even if it "adversely affects" their sales.[28]

Greater Chance for Success

Investing in a franchise is not risk free. Between 200 and 300 new franchise companies enter the market each year, and not all of them survive. But available statistics suggest that franchising is less risky than building a business from the ground up. One expert says that "becoming a franchisee can be the safest way to scratch the entrepreneurial itch."[29] Approximately 24 percent of new businesses fail by the second year of operation; in contrast, only about 7 percent of all franchises will fail by the second year. After six years, 85 percent of franchises are still in business compared to just 50 percent of independent businesses.[30] This impressive success rate for franchises is attributed to the broad range of services, assistance, and guidelines the franchiser provides. These statistics must be interpreted carefully, however, because when a franchise is in danger of failing, the franchiser often repurchases or relocates the outlet and does not report it as a failure. As a result, some franchisers boast of never experiencing a failure. According to the American Bar Association's Franchise Committee, one-third of the franchisees in a typical franchise system are making a decent profit, one-third are breaking even, and one-third are losing money.[31]

The risk of purchasing a franchise is two-pronged: success—or failure—depends on the entrepreneur's managerial skills and motivation and on the franchiser's business experience and system. Many owners are convinced that franchising has been a crucial part of their success. "It's the opportunity to be in business for yourself but not by yourself," says one franchiser.[32]

4-B. Explain the drawbacks of buying a franchise.

THE DRAWBACKS OF BUYING A FRANCHISE

Obviously, the benefits of franchising can mean the difference between success and failure for a small business. However, the franchisee must sacrifice some freedom to the franchiser. The prospective franchisee must explore other limitations of franchising before undertaking this form of ownership.

Franchise Fees and Profit Sharing

Virtually all franchisers impose some type of fees and demand a share of the franchisee's sales revenues in return for the use of the franchiser's name, products or services, and business system. The fees and the initial capital requirements vary among the different franchisers. The Commerce Department reports that total investments for franchises range from $1,000 for business services up to $10 million for hotel and motel franchises. For example, H & R Block requires a capital investment of $2,000 to $3,000, and the Atlanta Bread Company estimates the total cost of opening a franchise to range from $362,000 to $584,000, depending on the size and location of the outlet. A McDonald's franchise requires an investment of $408,600 to $647,000 (but McDonald's owns the land and the building). The average start-up cost for a franchise is between $150,000 and $200,000.[33]

Start-up costs for franchises often include numerous additional fees. Most franchises impose a franchise fee up front for the right to use the company name. Other start-up costs might include site purchase and preparation, construction, signs, fixtures, equipment, management assistance, and training. Some franchise fees include these costs, whereas others do not. For example, Closets by Design, a company that designs and installs closet- and garage-organizers, entertainment centers, and home office systems, charges a franchise fee ranging from $19,500 to $34,900, which includes both a license for an exclusive territory and management training and support. Before signing any contract, a prospective franchisee should determine the total cost of a franchise, something every franchiser is required to disclose in item 10 of its Uniform Franchising Offering Circular (see "Franchising and the Law" on page 128).

Franchisers also impose continuing royalty fees as profit-sharing devices. The royalty usually involves a percentage of gross sales with a required minimum, or a flat fee levied on the franchise. Royalty fees range from 1 percent to 11 percent, although most franchises assess a rate between 3 percent and 7 percent. The Atlanta Bread Company, for example, charges franchisees a royalty of 5 percent of gross sales, which is payable weekly. These ongoing royalties can increase a franchisee's overhead expenses significantly. Because the franchiser's royalties and fees are calculated as a percentage of a franchisee's sales, the franchiser gets paid—even if the franchisee fails to earn a profit. Sometimes unprepared franchisees discover (too late) that a franchiser's royalties and fees are the equivalent of the normal profit margin for a franchise. To avoid such problems, a prospective franchisee should find out which fees are required (some are merely recommended) and then determine what services and benefits the fees cover. One of the best ways to do this is to itemize what you are getting for your money, and then determine whether the cost corresponds to the benefits provided. Be sure to get the details on all expenses—amount, time of payment, and financing arrangements; find out which items, if any, are included in the initial franchise fee and which ones are "extra."

Strict Adherence to Standardized Operations

Although the franchisee owns the business, she does not have the autonomy of an independent owner. To protect its public image, the franchiser requires that the franchisee maintain certain operating standards. If a franchise constantly fails to meet the minimum standards established for the business, the franchiser may terminate its license. Determining compliance with standards is usually accomplished by periodic inspections. At times, strict adherence to franchise standards may become a burden to the franchisee. The owner may believe that the written reports the franchiser demands require an excessive amount of time. In other instances, the owner may be required to enforce specific rules she believes are inappropriate or unfair.

Restrictions on Purchasing

In the interest of maintaining quality standards, franchisees may be required to purchase products, special equipment, or other items from the franchiser or from an "approved" supplier. For example, Kentucky Fried Chicken requires that franchisees use only seasonings blended by a particular company because a poor image could result from franchisees using inferior products to cut costs. Under some conditions, such purchase arrangements may be challenged in court as a violation of antitrust laws, but generally, franchisers have a legal right to see that franchisees maintain acceptable quality standards. Franchisees at several chains have filed antitrust suits alleging that franchisers overcharge their outlets for supplies and equipment and eliminate competition by failing to approve alternative suppliers.[34] A franchiser may legally set the prices paid for the products it sells but may not establish the retail prices to be charged on products sold by the franchisee. A franchiser can suggest retail prices for franchisee's products and services but cannot force the franchisee to abide by them.

Limited Product Line

In most cases, the franchise agreement stipulates that the franchise can sell only those products approved by the franchiser. Unless willing to risk license cancellation, a franchisee must avoid selling any unapproved products through the franchise.

A franchise may be required to carry an unpopular product or be prevented from introducing a desirable one by the franchise agreement. A franchisee's freedom to adapt a product line to local market conditions is restricted. However, some franchisers solicit product suggestions from their franchisees.

McDonald's

In fact, a McDonald's franchisee, Herb Peterson, created the highly successful Egg McMuffin while experimenting with a Teflon-coated egg ring that gave fried eggs rounded corners and a poached appearance. Peterson put his round eggs on English muffins, adorned them with Canadian bacon and melted cheese, and showed his creation to McDonald's chief Ray Kroc. Kroc devoured two of them and was sold on the idea when Peterson's wife suggested the catchy name. In 1975, McDonald's became the first fast-food franchise to open its doors for breakfast, and the Egg McMuffin became a staple on the breakfast menu.[35]

Unsatisfactory Training Programs

Every would-be franchisee must be wary of the unscrupulous franchiser who promises extensive services, advice, and assistance but delivers nothing. For example, one owner relied on the franchiser to provide what had been described as an "extensive, rigorous training program" after paying a handsome technical assistance fee. The program was nothing but a set of pamphlets and do-it-yourself study guides. Other examples include those impatient entrepreneurs who paid initial franchise fees without investigating the business and never heard from the franchiser again. Although disclosure rules have reduced the severity of the problem, dishonest characters still thrive on unprepared prospective franchisees.

Market Saturation

As the owners of many fast-food and yogurt and ice cream franchises have discovered, market saturation is a very real danger. Although some franchisers offer franchisees territorial protection, others do not. Territorial encroachment has become a hotly contested issue in franchising as growth-seeking franchisers have exhausted most of the prime locations and are now setting up new franchises in close proximity to existing ones. In some areas of the country, franchisees are upset, claiming that their markets are oversaturated and their sales are suffering.

Less Freedom

When franchisees sign a contract, they agree to sell the franchiser's product or service by following its prescribed formula. This feature of franchising is the source of the system's success, but it also gives many franchisees the feeling that they are reporting to a "boss." Franchisers want to ensure success, and most monitor their franchisees' performances closely to make sure franchisees follow the system's specifications. Strict uniformity is the rule rather than the exception. "There is no independence. Successful franchisees are happy prisoners," says one writer.[36] Entrepreneurs who want to be their own bosses often are disappointed with a franchise. "I've seen too many people buy a franchise, and the reason they're unsuccessful is that they think they have a better idea how to run that McDonald's than McDonald's has," says one franchising expert.[37] Highly independent, "go-my-own-way" individuals probably should *not* choose the franchise route to business ownership. Table 4.2 describes ten myths of franchising.

TABLE 4.2

Ten Myths of Franchising

Sources: Adapted from Andrew A. Caffey, "There's More to a Franchise Than Meets the Eye," Entrepreneur, **<http://www.entrepreneurmag.com>**; *Andrew A. Caffey, "Myth vs. Reality,* Entrepreneur, **<http://www.entrepreneurmag.com/page.hts?N=7118&Ad=S>**; *Chieh Chieng, "Do You Want to Know a Secret?"* Entrepreneur, *January 1999, pp. 174–178; "Ten Most Common Mistakes Made by Franchise Buyers,"* Franchise Doctor, **<http://www.franchisedoc.com/mistakes.html>**.

Myth #1. Franchising is the safest way to go into business because franchises never fail. Although the failure rate for franchises is lower than that of independent businesses, there are no guarantees of success. Franchises can—and do—fail. Potential franchisees must exercise the same degree of caution in judging the risk of a franchise as they would any other business.

Myth #2. I'll be able to open my franchise for less money than the franchiser estimates. Launching a business, including a franchise, normally takes more money and more time than entrepreneurs estimate. Be prepared. One franchisee of a retail computer store advises, "If a franchiser tells you you'll need $100,000 to get started, you better have $150,000."

Myth #3. The bigger the franchise organization, the more successful I'll be. Bigger is not always better in the franchise industry. Some of the largest franchise operations are struggling to maintain their growth rates because the best locations are already taken. Market saturation is a significant problem for many large franchises, and smaller franchises are accounting for much of the growth in the industry.

Myth #4. I'll use 80 percent of the franchiser's business system, but I'll improve on it by substituting my experience and know-how. When franchisees buy a franchise, they are buying, in essence, the franchiser's experience and know-how. Why pay all of that money to a franchiser if you aren't willing to use their system?

Myth #5. All franchises are the same. Each franchise has its own unique requirements, procedures, and culture. Naturally, some will suit you better than others. Avoid the tendency to select the franchise offering the lowest cost; ask the franchiser and existing franchisees lots of questions to determine whether you'll be comfortable in that system.

Myth #6. I don't have to be a "hands-on" manager. I can be an absentee owner and still be very successful. Most franchisers shy away from absentee owners. They know that franchise success requires lots of hands-on attention, and the owner is the best person to provide that.

Myth #7. Anyone can be a satisfied, successful franchise owner. With more than 4,500 franchises available, the odds of finding a franchise that appeals to your tastes is high. However, not everyone is cut out to be a franchisee. Those "free spirits" who insist on doing things their way will most likely be miserable in a franchise.

Myth #8. Franchising is the cheapest way to get into business for yourself. Although bargains do exist in franchising, the price tag for buying into some systems is breathtaking, sometimes running into several hundreds of thousands of dollars. Franchisers look for candidates who are on solid financial footing.

Myth #9. The franchiser will solve my business problems for me; after all, that's why I pay an ongoing royalty. Although franchisers offer franchisees start-up and ongoing training programs, they will not run their franchisees' businesses for them. Your job is to take the formula that the franchiser has developed and make it work in your location. Expect to solve many of your own problems.

Myth #10. Once I open my franchise, I'll be able to run things the way *I* want to. Franchisees are not free to run their businesses any way they see fit. Every franchisee signs a contract that requires him or her to run the business according to the franchiser's requirements. Franchisees who violate the terms of that agreement run the risk of having their franchise relationship cancelled.

5. Understand the laws covering franchise purchases.

FRANCHISING AND THE LAW

The franchising boom spearheaded by McDonald's and others in the late 1950s brought with it many prime investment opportunities. However, the explosion of legitimate franchises also ushered in with it numerous fly-by-night franchisers who defrauded their franchisees. In response to these specific incidents and to the potential for deception inherent in a franchise relationship, California in 1971 enacted the first Franchise Investment Law. The law (and those of 16 other states that have since passed similar laws) requires franchisers to register a **Uniform Franchise Offering Circular (UFOC)** and deliver a copy to prospective franchisees before any offer or sale of a franchise. The UFOC establishes full disclosure guidelines for any company selling franchises.

Uniform Franchise Offering Circular (UFOC)—*a document that every franchiser is required by law to give prospective franchisees before any offer or sale of a franchise; it outlines 23 important pieces of information.*

In October 1979, the Federal Trade Commission (FTC) enacted the Trade Regulation Rule, requiring all franchisers to disclose detailed information on their operations at the first personal meeting, or at least 10 days before a franchise contract is signed, or before any money is paid. The FTC rule covers *all* franchisers, even those in the 33 states lacking franchise disclosure laws. The purpose of the regulation is to assist the potential franchisee's investigation of the franchise deal and to introduce consistency into the franchiser's disclosure statements. In 1994, the FTC modified the requirements for the UFOC, making more information available to prospective franchisees and making the document shorter and easier to read and understand. The FTC's philosophy is not so much to prosecute abusers as to provide information to prospective franchisees and help them make intelligent decisions. Although the FTC requires each franchiser to provide a potential franchisee with this information, it does not verify its accuracy. Prospective franchisees should use these data only as a starting point for the investigation. The Trade Regulation Rule requires a franchiser to include 23 major topics in its disclosure statement:

1. Information identifying the franchiser and its affiliates and describing their business experience and the franchises being sold.
2. Information identifying and describing the business experience of each of the franchiser's officers, directors, and management personnel responsible for the franchise program.
3. A description of the lawsuits in which the franchiser and its officers, directors, and managers have been involved. Although most franchisers will have been involved in some type of litigation, an excessive number of lawsuits, particularly if they relate to the same problem, is alarming. "The history of the litigation will tell you the future of your relationship [with the franchiser]," says the founder of a maid-service franchise.[38]
4. Information about any bankruptcies in which the franchiser and its officers, directors, and managers have been involved.
5. Information about the initial franchise fee and other payments required to obtain the franchise, including the intended use of the fees. Initial fees typically range from $10,000 to $30,000.
6. A description of any continuing payments franchisees are required to make after start-up, including royalties, service fees, training fees, lease payments, advertising or marketing charges, and others.
7. A detailed description of the payments a franchisee must make to fulfill the initial investment requirement and how and to whom they are made. The categories covered are the initial franchise fee, equipment, opening inventory, initial advertising fee, signs, training, real estate, working capital, legal, accounting, and utilities. These estimates, usually stated in the form of a range of numbers, give prospective franchisees an idea of how much their total start-up costs will be.
8. Information about quality restrictions on goods, services, equipment, supplies, inventory, and other items used in the franchise and where franchisees may purchase them, including restricted purchases from the franchiser.

defines these strategies: (1) cost leadership, (2) differentiation, and (3) focus[33] (see Figure 3.2).

cost leadership strategy— *a strategy in which a company strives to be the low-cost producer relative to its competitors in the industry.*

Cost Leadership. A company pursuing a **cost leadership strategy** strives to be the lowest-cost producer relative to its competitors in the industry. Low-cost leaders have a competitive advantage in reaching buyers whose primary purchase criterion is price, and they have the power to set the industry's price floor. Such a strategy works well when buyers are sensitive to price changes, when competing firms sell the same commodity products, and when companies can benefit from economies of scale. Not only is a low-cost leader in the best position to defend itself in a price war, but it also can use its power to attack competitors with the lowest price in the industry.

There are many ways to build a low-cost strategy, but the most successful cost leaders know where they have cost advantages over their competitors, and they use these as the foundation for their strategies. For example, a small nonunion airline is likely to have a significant advantage in labor costs, but not in fuel costs, over its larger, unionized competitors.

Fastenal Company

At Fastenal Company, a Minnesota-based maker and distributor of nuts and bolts, CEO Bob Kierlin takes a fanatical approach to cost control, constantly looking for new opportunities to reduce expenses. After analyzing insurance costs on Fastenal's fleet of 1,100 pickup trucks, Kierlin dropped collision insurance on the vehicles, saving the company $300,000 per year. "We can lose 20 trucks this year, complete losses, and we'd break even," he says. "We're guessing that's not going to happen." Office furniture at Fastenal is secondhand, often purchased at government auctions. Also, the company produces annual reports in-house at just 40 cents per copy, a fraction of what most companies spend. Rather than buy scratchpads from an office supply store, employees make their own out of scrap paper and a little glue. Workers use pens that suppliers and sales representatives give Kierlin. "There are always ways to save money," says Fastenal's corporate secretary. "We're never satisfied." Yet, when it comes to spending money where it counts, Kierlin is willing to do so. Because on-time deliveries are a crucial part of customer service, Fastenal keeps a relatively new fleet of delivery trucks to avoid breakdowns and expensive repairs. The company also invests wisely in efficient equipment and technology because these investments increase productivity and keep costs low. For instance, Fastenal recently put $8 million into a new computer system designed to improve the company's efficiency.

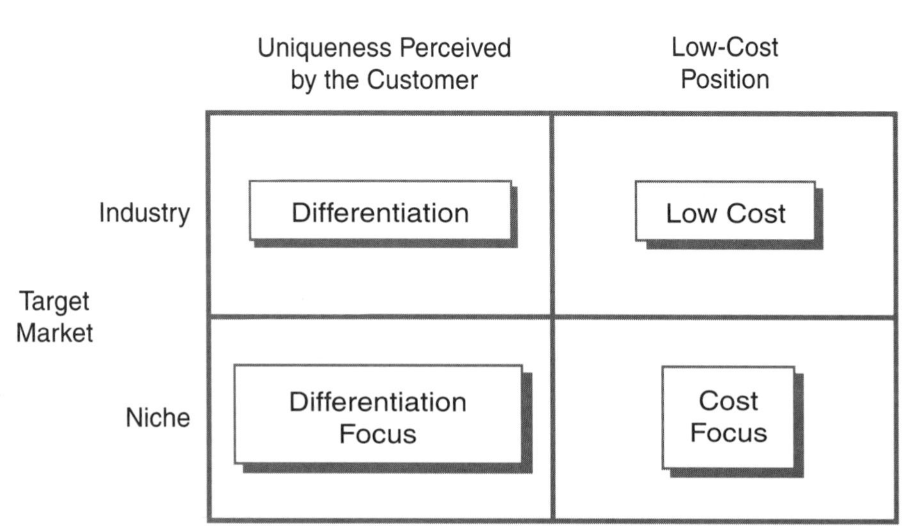

FIGURE 1.2
Entrepreneurial Activity Across the Globe
Source: 1999 Global Entrepreneurship Monitor.

"Either you do a good job of cost control in all aspects of your business, or you start losing it," says Kierlin. Fastenal's cost leadership strategy is ideal given the commodity product it sells and the price sensitivity of its customers. It is also the cornerstone of the company's stellar financial performance: a compound annual earnings growth rate that exceeds 35 percent since the company went public in 1987.[34]

Of course, there are dangers in following a cost leadership strategy. Sometimes a company focuses exclusively on lower manufacturing costs without considering the impact of purchasing, distribution, or overhead costs. Another danger is misunderstanding the firm's true cost drivers. For instance, one food-processing plant drastically underestimated its overhead costs and, as a result, was selling its products at a loss. Finally, a firm may pursue a low-cost leadership strategy so zealously that it essentially locks itself out of other strategic choices.

differentiation strategy— *a strategy in which a company seeks to build customer loyalty by positioning its goods or services in a unique or different fashion.*

Differentiation. A company following a **differentiation strategy** seeks to build customer loyalty by positioning its goods or services in a unique or different fashion. There are many ways to create a differentiation strategy, but the key concept is to be special at something that is important to the customer. In other words, a firm strives to be better than its competitors at something that customers value.

Straus Family Creamery

Albert Straus used a differentiation strategy to save his family's Marin County, California, dairy farm. Like most dairy farms, Straus sold raw milk to a cooperative at a price dictated by the federal government. Facing new environmental regulations that would add to already escalating costs, Straus knew that, unless he made dramatic changes in the farm's strategy, the business would fail. Recognizing a trend toward all-natural foods, Straus and his family decided to launch Straus Family Creamery and to transform the farm into a completely organic dairy with its own product line and brand name, which would give them more control over pricing. "With your own product and your own label, you can set a price that makes a profit," he explains. The Straus Family Creamery faced a steep learning curve because its shift to an organic farm meant no more antibiotics, hormones, parasiticides, or herbicides, but the family was committed to making the strategy work. As the only organic dairy in the area, Straus Family Creamery developed a market-

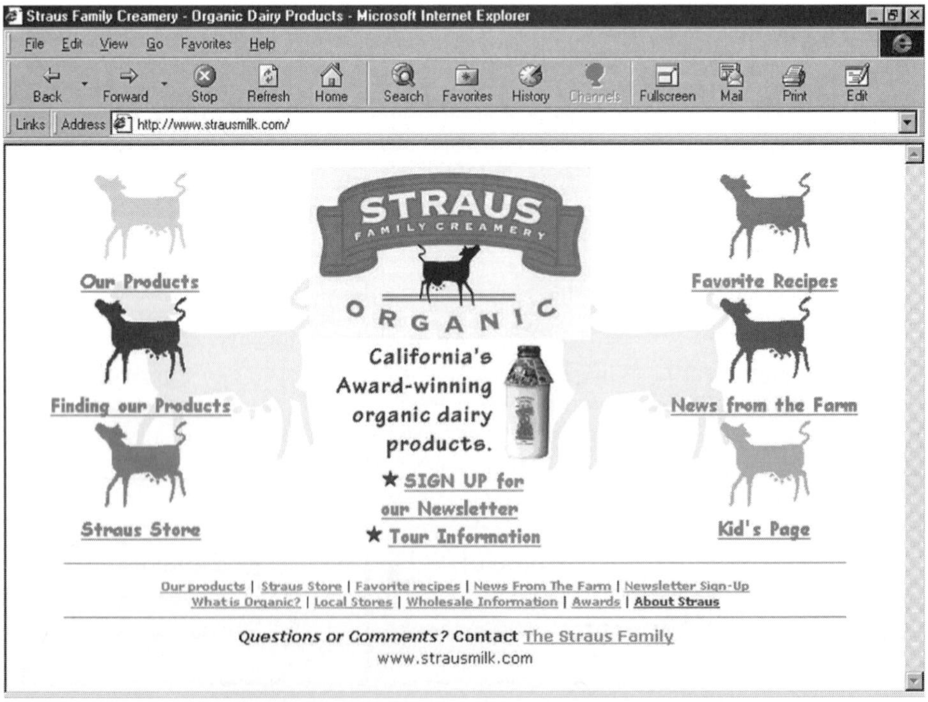

Limited Partnerships

limited partnership—*a partnership composed of at least one general partner and at least one limited partner.*

A **limited partnership,** which is a modification of a general partnership, is composed of at least one general partner and at least one limited partner. In a limited partnership, the general partner is treated, under the law, exactly as in a general partnership. The limited partner is treated more as an investor in the business venture; limited partners have limited liability. They can lose only the amount invested in the business.

Most states have ratified the Revised Uniform Limited Partnership Act. The formation of a limited partnership requires its founder to file a certificate of limited partnership in the state in which the limited partnership plans to conduct business. The certificate of limited partnership should include the following information:

1. the name of the limited partnership.
2. the general character of its business.
3. the address of the office of the firm's agent authorized to receive summonses or other legal notices.
4. the name and business address of each partner, specifying which ones are general partners and which are limited partners.
5. the amount of cash contributions actually made, and agreed to be made in the future, by each partner.
6. a description of the value of noncash contributions made or to be made by each partner.
7. the times at which additional contributions are to be made by any of the partners.
8. whether and under what conditions a limited partner has the right to grant limited partner status to an assignee of his or her interest in the partnership.
9. if agreed upon, the time or the circumstances when a partner may withdraw from the firm (unlike the withdrawal of a general partner, the withdrawal of a limited partner does *not* automatically dissolve a limited partnership).
10. if agreed upon, the amount of, or the method of determining, the funds to be received by a withdrawing partner.
11. any right of a partner to receive distributions of cash or other property from the firm, and the times and circumstances for such distributions.
12. the time or circumstances when the limited partnership is to be dissolved.
13. the rights of the remaining general partners to continue the business after withdrawal of a general partner.
14. any other matters the partners want to include.

The general partner has the same rights and duties as under a general partnership: the right to make decisions for the business, to act as an agent for the partnership, to use the property of the partnership for normal business, and to share in the business's profits. The limited partner does not have the right to manage the business in any way. In fact, if he or she takes part in managing the business, a limited partner may actually forfeit limited liability, taking on the liability status of a general partner. Limited partners can, however, make management suggestions to the general partners, inspect the business, and make copies of business records. A limited partner is, of course, entitled to a share of the business's profits as agreed on and specified in the certificate of limited partnership. The primary disadvantage of limited partnerships is the complexity and the cost of establishing them.

Dogwood Stable

Dogwood Stable of Aiken, South Carolina **<www.dogwoodstable.com>,** *relies on limited partnerships to give sophisticated investors the opportunity to share in the excitement of owning a racehorse. Cot Campbell, owner of Dogwood Stable, reduces the risk of investing in a racehorse by grouping several horses of different ages, price, and breeding*

LITTLE GOVERNMENTAL REGULATION. Like the proprietorship, the partnership form of operation is not burdened with red tape.

FLEXIBILITY. Although not as flexible as sole ownership, the partnership can generally react quickly to changing market conditions because no giant organization stifles quick and creative responses to new opportunities.

TAXATION. The partnership itself is not subject to federal taxation. It serves as a conduit for the profit or losses it earns or incurs; its net income or losses are passed along to the partners as personal income, and the partners pay income tax on their distributive shares. The partnership, like the proprietorship, avoids the "double taxation" disadvantage associated with the corporate form of ownership.

The Disadvantages of the Partnership

UNLIMITED LIABILITY OF AT LEAST ONE PARTNER. At least one member of every partnership must be a general partner. The general partner has unlimited personal liability, even though he is often the partner with the least personal resources.

CAPITAL ACCUMULATION. Although the partnership form of ownership is superior to the proprietorship in its ability to attract capital, it is generally not as effective as the corporate form of ownership, which can raise capital by selling shares of ownership to outside investors.

DIFFICULTY IN DISPOSING OF PARTNERSHIP INTEREST WITHOUT DISSOLVING THE PARTNERSHIP. Most partnership agreements restrict how a partner can dispose of his share of the business. Often, a partner is required to sell his interest to the remaining partner(s). Even if the original agreement contains such a requirement and clearly delineates how the value of each partner's ownership will be determined, there is no guarantee that the other partner(s) will have the financial resources to buy the seller's interest. When the money is not available to purchase a partner's interest, the other partner(s) may be forced either to accept a new partner, or to dissolve the partnership, distribute the remaining assets, and begin again. When a partner withdraws from the partnership, the partnership ceases to exist unless there are specific provisions in the partnership agreement for a smooth transition. When a general partner dies, becomes incompetent, or withdraws from the business, the partnership automatically dissolves, although it may not terminate. Even when there are numerous partners, if one chooses to disassociate her name from the business, the remaining partners will probably form a new partnership.

LACK OF CONTINUITY. If one partner dies, complications arise. Partnership interest is often nontransferable through inheritance because the remaining partner(s) may not want to be in a partnership with the person who inherits the deceased partner's interest. Partners can make provisions in the partnership agreement to avoid dissolution due to death if all parties agree to accept as partners those who inherit the deceased's interest.

POTENTIAL FOR PERSONALITY AND AUTHORITY CONFLICTS. Being in a partnership is much like being in a marriage. Making sure partners' work habits, goals, ethics, and general business philosophy are compatible is an important step in avoiding a nasty business divorce. "People always think you invest in the product or the equipment, but the biggest investment is in the partnership—in each other," says Liz Davidson, who with partner Alex Andrade, runs a successful investment firm in New York City.[6] However, no matter how compatible partners are, friction among them is inevitable. The key is having a mechanism such as a partnership agreement and open lines of communication for controlling it. The demise of many partnerships can often be traced to interpersonal conflicts and the lack of a procedure to resolve those conflicts.

9. A statement (in tabular form) of the franchisee's obligations under the franchise contract, including items such as selecting a site, paying fees, maintaining quality standards, keeping records, transferring or renewing the franchise relationship, and others.
10. A description of any financial assistance available from the franchiser in the purchase of the franchise.
11. A description of all obligations the franchiser must fulfill in helping a franchisee prepare to open and operate a unit. Plus, information covering location selection methods and the training program provided to franchisees. In addition to the training they provide new franchisees, many franchisers offer help with a grand opening for each outlet and on-site management assistance for a short time to get franchisees started.
12. A description of any territorial protection that will be granted to the franchise and a statement as to whether the franchiser may locate a company-owned store or other outlet in that territory.
13. All relevant information about the franchiser's trademarks, service marks, trade names, logos, and commercial symbols, including where they are registered. Look for a strong trademark or service mark that is registered with the U.S. Patent and Trademark Office.
14. Similar information on any patents and copyrights the franchiser owns, and the rights to these transferred to franchisees.
15. A description of the extent to which franchisees must participate personally in the operation of the franchise. Many franchisers look for "hands-on" franchisees and discourage "absentee owners."
16. A description of any restrictions on the goods or services franchises are permitted to sell and with whom franchisees may deal. The agreement usually restricts franchisees to selling only those items approved by the franchiser.
17. A description of the conditions under which the franchise may be repurchased or refused renewal by the franchiser, transferred to a third party by the franchisee, and terminated or modified by either party. This section also addresses the method established for resolving disputes.
18. A description of the involvement of celebrities and public figures in the franchise.
19. A complete statement of the basis for any earnings claims made to the franchisee, including the percentage of existing franchises that have actually achieved the results that are claimed. New rules put two requirements on franchisers making earnings claims: (a) Any earnings claim must be included in the UFOC, and (b) the claim must "have a reasonable basis at the time it is made." However, franchisers are *not* required to make any earnings claims at all; in fact, only about 25 percent of franchisers make earnings claims in their circulars, primarily because of liability concerns about committing such numbers to paper.[39]
20. Statistical information about the present number of franchises; the number of franchises projected for the future; the number of franchises terminated; the number the franchiser has not renewed; the number repurchased in the past; and a list of the names and addresses (organized by state) of other franchisees in the system.
21. The franchiser's financial statements.
22. A copy of all franchise and other contracts (leases, purchase agreements, etc.) the franchisee will be required to sign.
23. A standardized, detachable "receipt" to prove that the prospective franchisee received a copy of the UFOC.

The information contained in the UFOC does not fully protect a potential franchise from deception, nor does it guarantee success. It does, however, provide enough information to begin a thorough investigation of the franchiser and the franchise deal.

6. Discuss the *right* way to buy a franchise.

THE *RIGHT* WAY TO BUY A FRANCHISE

The UFOC is a powerful tool designed to help would-be franchisees select the franchise that is right for them and to avoid being duped by dishonest franchisers. The best defenses a prospective entrepreneur has against unscrupulous franchisers are preparation, common sense, and patience. By investigating thoroughly before investing in a franchise, a potential franchisee minimizes the risk of being hoodwinked into a nonexistent business. Asking the right questions and resisting the urge to rush into an investment decision helps a potential franchisee avoid being taken by unscrupulous operators.

Potential franchisees must beware because franchise fraud still exists in this rapidly growing field. A recent conference of state securities regulators named "illegal franchise offers" as one of the top 10 financial frauds in the United States.[40] The president of one franchise consulting firm estimates that 5 to 10 percent of franchisers are dishonest—"the rogue elephants of franchising." Dishonest franchisers tend to follow certain patterns, and well-prepared franchisees who know what to look for can avoid trouble. The following clues should arouse the suspicion of an entrepreneur about to invest in a franchise:

- Claims that the franchise contract is a standard one and that "you don't need to read it."
- A franchiser who fails to give you a copy of the required disclosure document at your first face-to-face meeting.
- A marginally successful prototype store or no prototype at all.
- A poorly prepared operations manual outlining the franchise system or no manual (or system) at all.
- Oral promises of future earnings without written documentation.
- A high franchisee turnover rate or a high termination rate.
- An unusual amount of litigation brought against the franchiser.
- Attempts to discourage you from allowing an attorney to evaluate the franchise contract before you sign it.
- No written documentation to support claims and promises.
- A high-pressure sale—sign the contract now or lose the opportunity.
- Claiming to be exempt from federal laws requiring complete disclosure of franchise details.
- "Get-rich-quick schemes," promises of huge profits with only minimum effort.
- Reluctance to provide a list of present franchisees for you to interview.
- Evasive, vague answers to your questions about the franchise and its operation.

Not every franchise "horror story" is the result of dishonest franchisers. More often than not, the problems that arise in franchising have more to do with franchisees who buy legitimate franchises without proper research and analysis. They end up in businesses they don't enjoy and that they are not well suited to operate. How can you avoid this mistake? The following steps will help you make the right choice.

Evaluate Yourself

Before looking at any franchise, an entrepreneur should study her own traits, goals, experience, likes, dislikes, risk orientation, income requirements, time and family commitments, and other characteristics. Will you be comfortable working in a structured environment? What kinds of franchises fit your desired lifestyle? In what region of the country or world do you want to live and work? What is your ideal job description? Knowing what you enjoy doing (and what you don't want to do) will help you narrow your search. The goal is to find the franchise that is right—*for you*! One characteristic successful franchisees have in common is that they genuinely enjoy their work. Table 4.3 provides a test for prospective franchisees that helps them evaluate their franchise potential.

TABLE 4.3

A Test for Prospective Franchisees

Sources: Adapted from Erika Kotite, "Is Franchising For You?" Franchise & Business Opportunities 1995, *pp. 14–18; Heather Page, "True Confessions,"* Entrepreneur, *January 1996, pp. 184–186;* Franchise Solutions, **<www.franchisesolutions.com>.**

Of those people who set out to buy a franchise, only 15 percent actually buy one. Some of that 15 percent make the wrong decision. They discover too late that they are not cut out to be franchisees. Do you have what it takes to be a successful franchisee? The following quiz will help you determine your "franchise quotient."

1. You own a company. How much operational detail are you comfortable with?
   a. I want direct control over all operations.
   b. I delegate less than half.
   c. I delegate more than half.
2. You have three job offers with comparable salary and benefits. Choose one.
   a. Small company but high management responsibility and exposure.
   b. Mid-sized company with less personal exposure but more prestigious name.
   c. Large company with least personal exposure but very well-known name.
3. You reach a major stumbling block on a project. You:
   a. Seek help from others immediately.
   b. Think it through and then present possible solutions to your superior.
   c. Keep working until you resolve it on your own.
4. Which investment sounds most appealing?
   a. Five percent fixed return over a period of time.
   b. From -20 percent to +50 percent loss or return over a period of time, depending on changing economic situations.
5. Which business arrangement is most appealing?
   a. You're the sole owner.
   b. You're in a partnership and own a majority of the stock.
   c. You're in an equal partnership.
6. Your company's sales technique increases sales 10 percent per year. You used a technique elsewhere you feel will result in 15 percent to 20 percent annual increases, but it requires extra time and capital. You:
   a. Avoid the risk and stay with the present plan.
   b. Suggest your new method, showing previous results.
   c. Privately use your system, and show the results later.
7. You suggest your system to your boss, and he says, "Don't rock the boat." You:
   a. Drop your different approach.
   b. Approach your boss at a later time.
   c. Go to your boss's boss with your suggestion.
   d. Use your own system anyway.
8. Which would mean the most to you?
   a. Becoming the president of a company.
   b. Becoming the highest-paid employee of a company.
   c. Winning the highest award for achievement in your profession.
9. What three activities do you find most appealing?
   a. Sales and marketing.
   b. Administration.
   c. Payroll.
   d. Training.
   e. Customer service.
   f. Credit and collections.
   g. Management.
10. What work pace do you generally prefer?
    a. Working on one project until it is completed.
    b. Working on several projects at one time.

Scoring: 1. A=5, B=3, C=1. 2. A=3, B=2, C=1. 3. A=1, B=5, C=7. 4. A=2, B=6. 5. A=7, B=5, C=2. 6. A=1, B=6, C=10. 7. A=1, B=5, C=8, D=10. 8. A=8, B=2, C=5. 9. A=10, B=1, C=3, D=3, E=8, F=2, G=5. 10. A=3, B=6.

Total Score:

20–33	You're a corporate player and are happiest in a structured environment. Franchising suits you.
34–71	You're a potentially good franchisee.
72–85	You're an entrepreneur who prefers total independence.

Research Your Market

Before shopping for a franchise, research the market in the area you plan to serve. How fast is the overall area growing? In which areas is that growth occurring fastest? Investing some time at the library developing a profile of the customers in your target area is essential; otherwise, you will be flying blind. Who are your potential customers? What are their characteristics and their income and education levels? What kinds of products and services do they buy? What gaps exist in the market? These gaps represent potential franchise opportunities for you. Market research also should confirm that a franchise is not merely part of a fad that will quickly fade. Steering clear of fads and into long-term trends is one way to sustain the success of a franchise.

Papa John's Pizza

Before Papa John's Pizza allows franchisees to open any store, it requires them to spend six months to a year evaluating the market potential of the local area. "We don't just move into an area and open up 200 stores," says one manager. "We do it one store at a time."[41]

Consider Your Franchise Options

The International Franchise Association publishes the *Franchise Opportunities Guide,* which lists its members and some basic information about them. Many cities host franchise trade shows throughout the year where hundreds of franchisers gather to sell their franchises. Attending one of these franchise showcases is a convenient, efficient way to collect information about a variety of available opportunities. Many business magazines such as *Entrepreneur, Inc., Business Start-Ups, Your Company,* and others devote at least one issue to franchising, in which they often list hundreds of franchises. These guides can help you find a suitable franchise within your price range.

Get a Copy of the Franchiser's UFOC

Once you narrow down your franchise choices, you should contact each franchise and get a copy of its UFOC. Then read it! This document is an important tool in your search for the right franchise, and you should make the most of it. When evaluating a franchise opportunity, what should a potential franchisee look for? Although there's never a guarantee of success, the following characteristics make a franchise stand out.

- *A unique concept or marketing approach.* "Me-too" franchises are no more successful than "me-too" independent businesses. Pizza franchiser Papa John's has achieved an impressive growth rate by emphasizing the quality of its ingredients, whereas Domino's is known for its fast delivery.
- *Profitability.* A franchiser should have a track record of profitability and so should its franchisees. If a franchiser is not profitable, its franchisees are not likely to be either. Franchisees who follow the business format should expect to earn a reasonable rate of return.
- *A registered trademark.* Name recognition is difficult to achieve without a well-known and protected trademark.
- *A business system that works.* A franchiser should have in place a system that is efficient and is well documented in its manuals.
- *A solid training program.* One of the most valuable components of a franchise system is the training it offers franchisees. The system should be relatively easy to teach.
- *Affordability.* A franchisee should not have to take on an excessive amount of debt to purchase a franchise. Being forced to borrow too much money to open a franchise outlet can doom a business from the outset. Respectable franchisers verify prospective franchisees' financial qualifications as part of the screening process.

- *A positive relationship with franchisees.* The most successful franchises are those that see their franchisees as partners and treat them accordingly.

The UFOC covers the 23 items discussed in the previous section and includes a copy of the company's franchise agreement and any contracts accompanying it. Although the law requires a UFOC to be written in plain English rather than "legalese," it is best to have an attorney experienced in franchising to review the UFOC and discuss its provisions with you. Watch for clauses that give the franchiser absolute control and discretion. The franchise contract summarizes the details that will govern the franchiser–franchisee relationship over its life. It outlines *exactly* the rights and the obligations of each party and sets the guidelines that govern the franchise relationship. Still, a recent study by the FTC suggests that 40 percent of new franchisees sign contracts without reading them![42] When one fast-food franchiser took a survey of its franchisees, it discovered that fewer than 10 percent had bothered to read either the UFOC or the franchise contract.[43] Because franchise contracts typically are long term (50 percent run for 15 years or more), it is extremely important for prospective franchisees to understand their terms *before* they sign them.

One of the most revealing items in the UFOC is the **franchisee turnover rate,** the rate at which franchisees leave the system. If the turnover rate is less than 5 percent, the franchise is probably sound. However, a franchise turnover rate approaching 20 percent is a sign of serious, underlying problems in a franchise. Satisfied franchisees are not inclined to leave a successful system.

franchisee turnover rate— *the rate at which franchisees leave a franchise system.*

Talk to Existing Franchisees

One of the best ways to evaluate the reputation of a franchiser is to interview (in person) several franchise owners who have been in business at least one year about the positive and the negative features of the agreement and whether the franchiser delivered what was promised. Did the franchise estimate their start-up costs accurately? Do they get the support the franchiser promised them? Has the franchise met their expectations concerning profitability and return on investment? Knowing what they know now, would they buy the franchise again?

Ranch I

Bob Phillips, a CPA looking to make a career change, wanted to make sure that he purchased the right franchise, so he invested time poring over the UFOCs he had collected from the dozen franchises that interested him. Rather than rely on the documents alone to judge the franchises, Phillips made calls to franchisees that he randomly selected from the lists included in the UFOCs (item 20). His conversations with franchisees convinced him that Ranch 1, a chain of fast-food grilled chicken stores, was the best choice for him. "Almost every one wanted a second location," he says. "That's indicative of a healthy franchise system." Phillips is convinced that his thorough research led him to the right franchise. Today he owns two Ranch 1 franchises that generate more than $2 million in sales, and he plans to open eight more outlets within three years.[44]

Interviewing past franchisees to get their perspectives on the franchiser–franchisee relationship is also helpful. Why did they leave? Franchisees of some companies have formed associations, which might provide prospective franchisees with valuable information. Other sources of information include the American Association of Franchisees and Dealers, the American Franchise Association, and the International Franchise Association.

Ask the Franchiser Some Tough Questions

Take the time to ask the franchiser questions about the company and its relationship with its franchisees. You will be in this relationship a long time, and you need to know as much about it as you possibly can beforehand. What is its philosophy concerning the relation-

YOU BE THE CONSULTANT . . .

The Opportunity of a Lifetime

"Honey, I think I've found it!" said Joe Willingham to his wife Allie. "This is just what I've been looking for, and just in time, too. My severance package from the company runs out next month. The man said that if we invested in this franchise now, we could be bringing in good money by then. It's that easy!"

Allie knew that Joe had been working hard at finding another job since he had been a victim of his company's latest downsizing, but jobs were scarce even for someone with his managerial experience and background in manufacturing. "Nobody wants to hire a 51-year-old man with experience when they can hire 23-year-old college graduates at less than half the salary and teach them what they need to know," Joe told her after months of fruitless job hunting. That's when Joe got the idea of setting up his own business. Rather than start an independent business from scratch, Joe felt more comfortable, given his 26-year corporate career, opening a franchise. "A franchiser can give me the support I need," he told Allie.

"Tell me about this franchise," Allie said.

"It's a phenomenal opportunity for us," Joe said, barely able to contain his excitement. "I saw this booth for American Speedy Print at the Business Expo this morning. There were all kinds of franchises there, but this one really caught my eye," Joe said as he pulled a rather plain-looking photocopy of a brochure from his briefcase.

"Is that their brochure?" asked Allie.

"Well, the company is growing so fast that they have temporarily run out of their normal literature. This is just temporary."

"Oh . . . You would think that a printing franchise could print flashier brochures even on short notice, but I guess. . . ," said Allie.

"The main thing is the profit potential this business has," said Joe. "I met one of their franchisees. I tell you the guy was wearing a $2,000 suit if ever there was one, and he had expensive jewelry dripping from his fingers. He's making a mint with this franchise, and he said we could too!"

Joe continued, "With the severance package I have from the company, we could pay the $10,000 franchise fee and lease most of the equipment we need to get started. It'll take every penny of my package, but, hey, it's an investment in our future. The representative said the company would help us with our grand opening and would help us compile a list of potential customers."

"What would you print?" asked Allie.

"Anything!" said Joe. "The franchisee I talked to does flyers, posters, booklets, newsletters, advertising pieces . . . you name it!"

"Wow! It seems like you'd need lots of specialized equipment to do all of that. How much does the total franchise package cost?" said Allie.

"Well, I'm not exactly sure. He never gave me an exact figure, but we can lease all the equipment we need from the franchiser!"

"Is this all of the material they gave you? I thought franchisers were supposed to have some kind of information packet to give to people," said Allie.

"Yeah, I asked him about that," said Joe. "He said that American Speedy Print is just a small franchise. They'd rather put their money into building a business and helping their franchisees succeed than into useless paperwork that nobody reads anyway. It makes sense to me."

"I guess so. . . ," Allie said reluctantly.

"I think we need to take this opportunity, Hon," Joe said, with a look that spoke of determination and enthusiasm. "Besides, he said that there was another couple in this county that is already looking at this franchise, and that the company will license only one franchisee in this area. They don't want to saturate the market. He thinks they may take it. I think we have to move on this now, or we'll lose the opportunity of a lifetime."

Allie had not seen Joe exhibit this much enthusiasm and excitement for anything since he had lost his job at the plant. Piles of rejection letters from his job search had sapped Joe's zest for living. Allie was glad to see "the old Joe" return, but she still had her doubts about the franchise opportunity Joe was describing.

"It might just be the opportunity of a lifetime, Joe," she said. "But don't you think we need to find out a little more about this franchise before we invest that much money? I mean. . . ."

"Hon, I'd love to do that, but like the man said, we may miss out on the opportunity of a lifetime if we don't sign today. I think we've got to move on this thing now!"

1. What advice would you offer Joe about investing in this franchise?
2. Map out a plan for Joe to use in finding the right franchise for him. What can Joe do to protect himself from making a bad franchise investment?
3. Summarize the advantages and disadvantages Joe can expect if he buys a franchise.

ship? What is the company culture like? How much input do franchisee's have into the system? What are the franchise's future expansion plans? How will they affect your franchise? Are you entitled to an exclusive territory? Under what circumstances can either party terminate the franchise agreement? What happens if you decide to sell your franchise in the future? Under what circumstances would you not be entitled to renew the agreement? What kind of profits can you expect? (If the franchiser made no earnings claims in item 19 of the UFOC, why not?) Does the franchiser have a well-formulated strategic plan?

Make Your Choice

The first lesson in franchising is "Do your homework *before* you get out your checkbook." Once you have done your research, you can make an informed choice about which franchise is right for you. Then it is time to put together a solid business plan that will serve as your road map to success in the franchise you have selected. The plan is also a valuable tool to use as you arrange the financing for your franchise. We will discuss the components of a business plan in Chapter 9.

Appendix A at the end of this chapter offers a checklist of questions a potential franchisee should ask before entering into any franchise agreement.

TRENDS SHAPING FRANCHISING

7. Outline the major trends shaping franchising.

Franchising has experienced three major growth waves since its beginning. The first wave occurred in the early 1970s when fast-food restaurants used the concept to grow rapidly. The fast-food industry was one of the first to discover the power of franchising, but other businesses soon took notice and adapted the franchising concept to their industries. The second wave took place in the mid-1980s as our nation's economy shifted heavily toward the service sector. Franchises followed suit, springing up in every service business imaginable—from maid services and copy centers to mailing services and real estate. The third wave began in the early 1990s and continues today. It is characterized by new, low-cost franchises that focus on specific market niches. In the wake of major corporate downsizing and the burgeoning costs of traditional franchises, these new franchises allow would-be entrepreneurs to get into proven businesses faster and at lower costs. These companies feature start-up costs from $2,000 to $250,000 and span a variety of industries—from leak detection in homes and auto detailing to day care and tile glazing. Other significant trends affecting franchising are discussed next.

Changing Face of Franchisees

Franchisees today are better educated, are more sophisticated, have more business acumen, and are more financially secure than those of just 20 years ago. Franchising is attracting skilled, experienced businesspeople whose goal is to own multiple outlets that cover entire states or regions.

Krispy Kreme Doughnuts

For instance, when Krispy Kreme Doughnuts began to move its popular product north from its southern stronghold, the Lev family—father Howard, sons Russel and Mel, and nephew John Faber—bought the franchise for the entire state of New York. While on a trip to the South, Mel discovered the tasty orbs and brought some back to his family, who quickly devoured them. Once they returned to their home in New York, the Levs decided to become franchisees. All experienced in business (Howard and Mel once owned a shirt-making company), the Levs and Faber have opened 10 stores and have plans for dozens more.[45]

International Opportunities

One of the major trends in franchising is the internationalization of U.S. franchise systems. Increasingly, franchising is becoming a major export industry for the United States. Growing numbers of U.S. franchises are moving into international markets to boost sales and profits as the domestic market becomes saturated. According to a report by Arthur Andersen, 44 percent of U.S. franchisers have international locations, up from 34 percent in 1989. International expansion is a relatively new phenomenon in franchising, however; approximately 75 percent of franchisers established their first foreign outlet within the past 10 years.[46] Canada is the primary market for U.S. franchisers, with Mexico, Japan, and Europe following. These markets are most attractive to franchisers because they are similar to the U.S. market—rising personal incomes, strong demand for consumer goods, growing service economies, and spreading urbanization.

As they venture into foreign markets, franchisers have learned that adaptation is one key to success. Although a franchise's overall business format may not change in foreign markets, some of the details of operating its local outlets must. For instance, fast-food chains in other countries often must make adjustments to their menus to please locals' palates. In Japan, McDonald's (known as "Makudonarudo") outlets sell teriyaki burgers, rice burgers, and katsu burgers (cheese wrapped in a roast pork cutlet topped with katsu sauce and shredded cabbage) in addition to their traditional American fare. In the Philippines, the McDonald's menu includes a spicy Filipino-style burger, spaghetti, and chicken with rice.

Countries that recently have thrown off the chains of communism are turning to franchising to help them move toward a market economy. Some countries of Eastern Europe, including Hungary, Poland, and Yugoslavia, already have attracted franchises. Even Russia is fertile ground for franchising. McDonald's scored a hit with its 700-seat restaurant in Moscow. Despite being one of the largest McDonald's outlets in the world, "the waiting line winds along busy Pushkin Square for well over 500 yards," reports one Soviet magazine.[47] Franchisers in these countries must have patience, however. Lack of capital, archaic infrastructure, and a shortage of hard currencies mean that profits will be slow in coming. Most franchisers recognize the difficulties of developing franchises in foreign markets and start slowly. According to Arthur Anderson, 79 percent of franchisers doing business internationally have fewer than 100 outlets in foreign countries.[48]

Smaller, Nontraditional Locations

intercept marketing—*the principle of putting a franchise's products or services directly in the paths of potential customers, wherever they may be.*

As the high cost of building full-scale locations continues to climb, more franchisers are searching out nontraditional locations in which to build smaller, less expensive outlets. Based on the principle of **intercept marketing,** the idea is to put a franchise's products or services directly in the paths of potential customers, wherever they may be. Locations within locations have become popular. Franchises are putting scaled-down outlets on college campuses, in high school cafeterias, in sports arenas, in hospitals, on airline flights, and in zoos. St. Louis–based Pizzas of Eight already has outlets inside convenience stores, supermarkets, and bowling alleys and plans to open others in video stores.[49] Many franchisees have discovered that smaller outlets in these nontraditional locations generate nearly the same sales volume as full-sized outlets at just a fraction of the cost!

Dunkin' Donuts

Steve Siegel, owner of 35 Dunkin' Donuts shops in the Boston area, recently began branching out into small, nontraditional locations where pedestrian traffic counts are high. One of his most profitable spots measures just 64 square feet, but because it is in a business district filled with office workers, it generates a high volume of sales.[50]

Such locations will be a key to continued franchise growth in the domestic market.

Conversion Franchising

The recent trend toward **conversion franchising,** in which owners of independent businesses become franchisees to gain the advantage of name recognition, will continue. In a franchise conversion, the franchiser gets immediate entry into new markets and experienced operators; franchisees get increased visibility and often a big sales boost. In fact, the average sales gain in the first year for converted franchises is 20 percent.[51] The biggest force in conversion franchising has been Century 21, the real estate sales company.

conversion franchising—*a franchising trend in which owners of independent businesses become franchisees to gain the advantage of name recognition.*

Multiple-Unit Franchising

Multiple-unit franchising (MUF) became extremely popular in the early 1990s. In multiple-unit franchising, a franchisee opens more than one unit in a broad territory within a specific time period. "Multiple ownership of units by franchisees has exploded," says one franchise expert. "Twenty or 30 years ago, it would have been rare for any one franchisee to own 10 or 20 units. Now it's not uncommon . . . for one franchisee to own 60, 70, or even 200 units. Franchisers are finding it's far more efficient in the long run to have one well-trained franchisee operate a number of units than to train many franchises."[52] The popularity of multiple-unit franchising has paralleled the trend toward increasingly experienced, sophisticated franchisees, who set high performance goals that a single outlet cannot meet. The typical multiple-unit franchisee owns between three and six units, but some franchisees own many more.

multiple-unit franchising—*a method of franchising in which a franchisee opens more than one unit in a broad territory within a specific time period.*

Master Franchising

A **master franchise** (or **subfranchise**) gives a franchisee the right to create a semi-independent organization in a particular territory to recruit, sell, and support other franchisees. A master franchisee buys the right to develop subfranchises within a broad geographic area or sometimes an entire country. Subfranchising "turbocharges" a franchiser's growth. Many franchisers use it to open outlets in international markets more quickly and efficiently because the master franchisees understand local laws and the nuances of selling in local markets.

master franchising—*a method of franchising that gives a franchisee the right to create a semi-independent organization in a particular territory to recruit, sell, and support other franchisees.*

TCBY International

For instance, a master franchisee with TCBY International, a yogurt franchise, has opened 21 stores in China and in Hong Kong. Based on his success in these markets, the company has sold him the master franchise in India.[53]

Piggybacking (or Combination Franchising)

Some franchisers also are discovering new ways to reach customers by teaming up with other franchisers selling complementary products or services. A growing number of companies are **piggybacking** outlets—combining two or more distinct franchises under one roof. This "buddy system" approach works best when the two franchise ideas are compatible and appeal to similar customers. For example, franchisers Dunkin' Donuts, Togos' Eatery sandwich shops, and ice cream retailer Baskin-Robbins are working together to build hundreds of combination outlets, a concept that has proved to be highly successful.[54] Properly planned, piggybacked franchises can magnify many times over the sales and profits of individual, self-standing outlets. One Baskin-Robbins franchisee saw his sales climb 25 percent when he added a Blimpie Subs and Salads franchise to his existing ice cream shop. Another enterprising franchisee who combined Shell Oil (gas station), Charley's Steakery (sandwich shop), and TCBY (frozen yogurt) franchises under one roof in Columbus, Ohio, says that sales are running 10 percent more than the three outlets would generate in separate locations.[55]

piggybacking—*a method of franchising in which two or more franchises team up to seel complementary products or services under one roof.*

Serving Aging Baby Boomers

Now that dual-career couples have become the norm, especially among baby boomers, the market for franchises offering convenience and time-saving devices is booming. Customers are willing to pay for products and services that will save them time or trouble, and franchises are ready to provide them. Franchisees of Around Your Neck go into the homes and offices of busy male executives to sell men's apparel and accessories ranging from shirts and ties to custom-made suits. Other areas in which franchising is experiencing rapid growth include home delivery of meals, house-cleaning services, continuing education and training (especially computer and business training), leisure activities (such as hobbies, health spas, and travel-related activities), products and services aimed at home-based businesses, and health care. "People are interested in anything that will make life simpler for them," explains one franchise consultant.[56]

CONCLUSION

Franchising has proved its viability in the U.S. economy and has become a key part of the small business sector because it offers many would-be entrepreneurs the opportunity to own and operate a business with a greater chance for success. Despite its impressive growth rate to date, the franchising industry still has a great deal of room to grow. Describing the future of franchising, one expert says, "Franchising has not yet come close to reaching its full potential in the American marketplace."[57]

CHAPTER SUMMARY

1-A. Explain the advantages and the disadvantages of the sole proprietorship.

A sole proprietorship is a business owned and managed by one individual and is the most popular form of ownership.

Sole proprietorships offer these *advantages*: They are simple to create; they are the least costly form to begin; the owner has total decision-making authority; there are no special legal restrictions; and they are easy to discontinue.

They also suffer from these *disadvantages*: unlimited personal liability of owner; limited managerial skills and capabilities; limited access to capital; and lack of continuity.

1-B. Explain the advantages and the disadvantages of the partnership.

A partnership is an association of two or more people who co-own a business for the purpose of making a profit. Partnerships offer these *advantages*: ease of establishing; complementary skills of partners; division of profits; larger pool of capital available; ability to attract limited partners; little government regulation; flexibility; and tax advantages.

Partnerships suffer from these *disadvantages*: unlimited liability of at least one partner; difficulty in disposing of partnership interest; lack of continuity; potential for personality and authority conflicts; and partners bound by the law of agency.

1-C. Explain the advantages and the disadvantages of the corporation.

A corporation, the most complex of the three basic forms of ownership, is a separate legal entity. To form a corporation, an entrepreneur must file the articles of incorporation with the state in which the company will incorporate.

Corporations offer these *advantages*: limited liability of stockholders; ability to attract capital; ability to continue indefinitely; and transferable ownership.

Corporations suffer from these *disadvantages*: cost and time involved in incorporating; double taxation; potential for diminished managerial incentives; legal requirements and regulatory red tape; and potential loss of control by the founder(s).

2. Discuss the advantages and the disadvantages of the S corporation, the limited liability company, the professional corporation, and the joint venture.

Entrepreneurs can also choose from several other forms of ownership, including S corporations and limited liability companies. An S corporation offers its owners limited liability protection but avoids the double taxation of C corporations.

A limited liability company, like an S corporation, is a cross between a partnership and a corporation, yet it operates without the restrictions imposed on an S corporation. To create an LLC, an entrepreneur must file the articles of organization and the operating agreement with the secretary of state.

A professional corporation offers professionals the benefits of the corporate form of ownership.

A joint venture is like a partnership, except that it is formed for a specific purpose.

3. Describe the three types of franchising: trade name, product distribution, and pure.

   Trade-name franchising involves a franchisee's purchasing the right to become affiliated with a franchiser's trade name without distributing its products exclusively.

   Product distribution franchising involves licensing a franchisee to sell products or services under the franchiser's brand name through a selective, limited distribution network.

   Pure franchising involves selling a franchisee a complete business format.

4. Explain the benefits and the drawbacks of buying a franchise.

   Franchises offer many benefits: management training and support; brand name appeal; standardized quality of goods and services; national advertising programs; financial assistance; proven products and business formats; centralized buying power; territorial protection; and a greater chance of success.

   Franchising also suffers from certain drawbacks: franchise fees and profit sharing; strict adherence to standardized operations; restrictions on purchasing; limited product lines; unsatisfactory training programs; market saturation; and less freedom.

5. Understand the laws covering franchise purchases.

   The Federal Trade Commission (FTC) enacted the Trade Regulation Rule in 1979, which requires all franchisers to disclose detailed information on their operations at the first personal meeting or at least 10 days before a franchise contract is signed, or before any money is paid. The FTC rule covers *all* franchisers. The Trade Regulation Rule requires franchisers to provide information on 23 topics in their disclosure statements.

   Seventeen states have passed their own franchise laws requiring franchisers to provide prospective franchisees a Uniform Franchise Offering Circular (UFOC).

6. Discuss the *right* way to buy a franchise.

   The following steps will help you make the right franchise choice: Evaluate yourself; research your market; consider your franchise options; get a copy of the franchiser's UFOC; talk to existing franchisees; ask the franchiser some tough questions; and make your choice.

7. Outline the major trends shaping franchising.

   Key trends shaping franchising today include the changing face of franchisees; international franchise opportunities; smaller, nontraditional locations; conversion franchising; multiple-unit franchising; master franchising; and piggybacking (or combination franchising).

DISCUSSION QUESTIONS

1. What factors should an entrepreneur consider before choosing a form of ownership?
2. Why are sole proprietorships so popular as a form of ownership?
3. How does personal conflict affect partnerships?
4. What issues should the articles of partnership address? Why are the articles important to a successful partnership?
5. Can one partner commit another to a business deal without the other's consent? Why?
6. What issues should the certificate of incorporation cover?
7. How does an S corporation differ from a regular corporation?
8. What role do limited partners play in a partnership? What happens if a limited partner takes an active role in managing the business?
9. What advantages does a limited liability company offer over an S corporation? A partnership?
10. How is an LLC created? What criteria must an LLC meet to avoid double taxation?
11. Briefly outline the advantages and disadvantages of the major forms of business ownership.
12. What is franchising?
13. Describe the three types of franchising and give an example of each.
14. Discuss the advantages and the limitations of franchising for the franchisee.
15. Why might an independent entrepreneur be dissatisfied with a franchising arrangement?
16. What kinds of clues should tip off a prospective franchisee that he is dealing with a disreputable franchiser?
17. What steps should a potential franchisee take before investing in a franchise?
18. What is the function of the FTC's Trade Regulation Rule? Outline the protection the Trade Regulation Rule gives all prospective franchisees.
19. Describe the current trends in franchising.

20. One franchisee says, "Franchising is helpful because it gives you somebody [the franchiser] to get you going, nurture you, and shove you along a little. But the franchiser won't make you successful. That depends on what you bring to the business, how hard you are prepared to work, and how committed you are to finding the right franchise for you." Do you agree? Explain.

Beyond the Classroom . . .

1. Interview five local small business owners. What form of ownership did each choose? Why? Prepare a brief report summarizing your findings, and explain advantages and disadvantages those owners face because of their choices.

2. Invite entrepreneurs who operate as partners to your classroom. Do they have a written partnership agreement? Are their skills complementary? How do they divide responsibility for running their company? How do they handle decision making? What do they do when disputes and disagreements arise?

3. Visit a local franchise operation. Is it a trade-name, product distribution, or pure franchise? To what extent did the franchisee investigate before investing? What assistance does the franchiser provide? How does the franchisee feel about the franchise contract he signed? What would he do differently now?

4. a. Consult a copy of the International Franchise Association publication *Franchise Opportunities Handbook* (the library should have a copy). Write several franchisers in a particular business category and ask for their franchise packages. Write a report comparing their treatment of the topics covered by the Trade Regulation Rule.

b. Analyze the terms of their franchise contracts. What are the major differences? Are some terms more favorable than others? If you were about to invest in the franchise, which terms would you want to change?

5. Ask a local franchisee to approach his regional franchise representative about leading a class discussion on franchising.

6. Contact the International Franchise Association (1350 New York Avenue, N.W., Suite 900, Washington, D.C., 20005-4709, 202-628-8000) for a copy of *Investigate Before Investing.* Prepare a report outlining what a prospective franchisee should do before buying a franchise.

We invite you to visit this book's companion Web site at **www.prenhall.com/Zimmerer.**

APPENDIX A

A Franchise Evaluation Checklist

The Franchiser and the Franchise

1. Is the potential market for the product or service adequate to support your franchise? Will the prices you charge be in line with the market?
2. Is the market's population growing, remaining static, or shrinking? Is the demand for your product or service growing, remaining static, or shrinking?
3. Is the product or service safe and reputable?
4. Is the product or service a fad, or is it a durable business idea?
5. What will the direct and indirect competition be in your sales territory? Do any other franchisees operate in this general area?
6. Is the franchise international, national, regional, or local in scope? Does it require full- or part-time involvement?
7. How many years has the franchiser been in operation? Does it have a sound reputation for honest dealings with franchisees?
8. How many franchise outlets now exist? How many will there be a year from now? How many outlets are company owned?
9. How many franchises have failed? Why?
10. What service and assistance will the franchiser provide? What training programs are offered? Are they continuous in nature?
11. Will the franchise perform a location analysis to help you find a suitable site?
12. Will the franchiser offer you exclusive distribution rights for the length of the agreement, or may it sell to other franchises in this area?
13. What facilities and equipment are required for the franchise? Who pays for construction? Is there a lease agreement?
14. What is the total cost of the franchise? What are the initial capital requirements? Will the franchiser provide financial assistance? Of what nature? What is the interest rate? Is the franchiser financially sound enough to fulfill all its promises?
15. How much is the franchise fee? Exactly what does it cover? Are there any confining fees? What additional fees are there?
16. Does the franchiser provide an estimate of expenses and income? Are they reasonable for your particular area? Are they sufficiently documented?
17. How risky is the franchise opportunity? Is the return on the investment consistent with the risks?
18. Does the franchiser offer a written contract that covers all the details of the agreement? Have your attorney and your accountant studied its terms and approved it? Do you understand the implications of the contract?
19. What is the length of the franchise agreement? Under what circumstances can it be terminated? If you terminate the contract, what are the costs to you? What are the terms and costs of renewal?
20. Are you allowed to sell the franchise to a third party? If so, will you receive the proceeds?
21. Is there a national advertising program? How is it financed? What media are used? What help is provided for local advertising?
22. Once you open for business, *exactly* what support will the franchiser offer you?
23. How does the franchise handle complaints from and disputes with franchisees? How well has the system worked?

The Franchisees

1. Are you pleased with your investment in this franchise?
2. Has the franchiser lived up to its promises?
3. What was your greatest disappointment after getting into this business?
4. How effective was the training you received in helping you run the franchise?
5. What are your biggest challenges and problems?
6. What is your franchise's cash flow like?
7. How much money are you making on your investment?
8. What do you like most about being a franchisee? Least?
9. Is there a franchisee advisory council that represents franchisees?
10. Knowing what you know now, would you buy this franchise again?

Yourself

1. Are you qualified to operate a franchise successfully? Do you have adequate drive, skills, experience, education, patience, and financial capacity? Are you prepared to work hard?
2. Are you willing to sacrifice some autonomy in operating a business to own a franchise?
3. Can you tolerate the financial risk? Would business failure wipe you out financially?
4. Can you juggle multiple tasks simultaneously and prioritize various projects so that you can accomplish those that are most important?
5. Are you genuinely interested in the product or service you will be selling? Do you enjoy this kind of business? Do you like to sell?
6. Do you enjoy working with and managing people? Are you a "team player"?
7. Will the business generate enough profit to suit you?
8. Has the franchiser investigated your background thoroughly enough to decide if you are qualified to operate the franchise?
9. What can this franchiser do for you that you cannot do for yourself?

CHAPTER 5

Buying an Existing Business

LEARNING OBJECTIVES

Upon completion of this chapter, you will be able to:

1. Understand the advantages and disadvantages of buying an existing business.
2. Define the steps involved in the *right* way to buy a business.
3. Explain the process of evaluating an existing business.
4. Describe the various techniques for determining the value of a business.
5. Understand the seller's side of the buyout decision and how to structure the deal.
6. Understand how the negotiation process works and identify the factors that affect the negotiation process.

Truth will ultimately prevail where there are plans taken to bring it to light.

—George Washington

Experience is something I always think I have until I get more of it.

—Burton Hillis

Starting a business "from scratch" and buying a franchise are not the only options available to an entrepreneur. Every year, more than 500,000 existing businesses are sold—90 percent of which are valued at under $5 million. According to VR Business Brokers, a network of business brokerage firms across the United States, the average selling price of a small company is $160,000.[1] Buying a business is not (and should not be) something to be done quickly or easily, however. Each purchase is unique because each business is unique. In almost every situation, it takes a buyer months to analyze and evaluate the positive and negative aspects of a potential purchase candidate. It may take longer still to complete the final negotiations. The best advice is be patient and do your homework. Be sure that you have answers to the following questions:

- Is the right type of business for sale in a market in which you want to operate?
- What experience do you have in this particular business and the industry in which it operates?
- How critical is experience in the business to your ultimate success? Where should such a business be located?
- What price and payment method are reasonable for you and acceptable to the seller?
- Should you start the business and build it from the ground up or should you shop around to buy an existing company?
- What is this company's potential for success?
- What changes will you have to make—and how extensive will they be—to realize the business's full potential?
- Will the company generate sufficient cash to pay for itself and leave you with a suitable rate of return on your investment?

1-A. Understand the advantages of buying an existing business.

BUYING AN EXISTING BUSINESS

Advantages of Buying an Existing Business

A SUCCESSFUL EXISTING BUSINESS MAY CONTINUE TO BE SUCCESSFUL. Purchasing a thriving business at an acceptable price increases the likelihood of success. The previous management already has established a customer base, built supplier relationships, and set up a business system. The new owner's objective should be to make those modifications that will attract new customers while retaining the firm's existing customers. Maintaining the proper balance of old and new is not an easy task, however. The customer base inherited in a business purchase can carry an entrepreneur while he studies how the business has become successful and how he can build on that success. Time spent learning about the business and its customers before introducing changes will increase the probability that any changes made will be successful.

AN EXISTING BUSINESS MAY ALREADY HAVE THE BEST LOCATION. When the location of the business is critical to its success (as is often the case in retailing), it may be wise to purchase a business that is already in the right place. Opening in a second-choice location and hoping to draw customers may prove fruitless. In fact, an existing business's biggest asset may be its location. If this advantage cannot be matched by other locations, an entrepreneur may have little choice but to buy instead of build. As part of its expansion plans, one fast-food chain recently purchased a smaller chain, not so much for its customer base or other assets as for its prime store locations.

EMPLOYEES AND SUPPLIERS ARE ESTABLISHED. An existing business already has experienced employees, so there are fewer problems associated with the shakedown phase of getting started. Experienced employees can help the company earn money while a new owner learns the business.

BlueJacket Ship Crafters

For example, when Bob Hammer and Sue Crowe, two former executives at major corporations, purchased a small mail-order model-ship-kit manufacturer, BlueJacket Ship Crafters, as a "retirement business," they knew they had a lot to learn about running a small business. Just how much they had to learn, however, was a surprise. Fortunately, the experienced employees they inherited with the company kept it going while Hammer and Crowe got their sea legs. "The learning curve was intense," says Crowe. "We didn't know what we were doing, so we had to keep asking employees how things worked."[2]

In addition, an existing business has an established set of suppliers with a history of business dealings. Those vendors can continue to supply the business while the new owner investigates the products and services of other suppliers. Thus, the new owner is not pressured to choose a supplier quickly without thorough investigation.

EQUIPMENT IS INSTALLED AND PRODUCTIVE CAPACITY IS KNOWN. Acquiring and installing new equipment exerts a tremendous strain on a fledgling company's financial resources. In an existing business, a potential buyer can determine the condition of the plant and equipment and its capacity before buying. The previous owner may have established an efficient production operation through trial and error, although the new owner may need to make modifications to improve it. In many cases, entrepreneurs can purchase physical facilities and equipment at prices significantly below their replacement costs.

INVENTORY IS IN PLACE AND TRADE CREDIT IS ESTABLISHED. The proper amount of inventory is essential to both cost control and sales volume. If a business has too little inventory, it will not have the quantity and variety of products to satisfy customer demand. But if a business has too much inventory, it is tying up excessive capital, thereby increasing costs and reducing profitability. Owners of successful, established businesses have learned to balance these extremes. Previous owners have established trade credit relationships that can benefit the new owner. No supplier wants to lose a good customer.

THE NEW BUSINESS OWNER HITS THE GROUND RUNNING. The entrepreneur who purchases an existing business saves the time, costs, and energy required to plan and launch a new business. The day she takes over the ongoing business is the day her revenues begin. Entrepreneurs who buy an existing business do not have to invest a lifetime building a company to enjoy success.

THE NEW OWNER CAN USE THE EXPERIENCE OF THE PREVIOUS OWNER. Even if the previous owner is not around after the sale, the new owner will have access to all of the business's records, which can guide him until he becomes acclimated to the business and the local market. He can trace the impact on costs and revenues of the major decisions that the previous owner made and can learn from his mistakes and profit from his achievements. In many cases, the previous owner spends time in an orientation period with the new owner, giving the new manager the opportunity to learn about the policies and procedures in place and the reasons for them. Previous owners also can be extremely helpful in unmasking the unwritten rules of business in the area—what types of behavior are acceptable, whom to trust or not, and other important intangibles. After all, most owners who sell out want to see the buyer succeed in carrying on their businesses.

EASIER FINANCING. Attracting financing to purchase an existing business often is easier than finding the money to launch a company from scratch. Many existing businesses already have established relationships with lenders, which may open the door to financing through traditional sources such as banks. As we will see later in this chapter, many business buyers also have access to another important source of financing: the seller.

IT'S A BARGAIN. Some existing businesses may be real bargains. The current owners may need to sell on short notice, which may lead to them selling the business at a low price. Many small companies operate in profitable but tiny niches, making it easy for potential buyers to overlook them. The more specialized the business is, the greater the likelihood is that a bargain might be found. If special skills or training is required to operate the business, the number of potential buyers will be significantly smaller. If the owner wants a substantial down payment or the entire selling price in cash, few buyers may qualify; however, those who do may be able to negotiate a good deal.

1-B. Understand the disadvantages of buying an existing business.

Disadvantages of Buying an Existing Business

"IT'S A LOSER." A business may be for sale because it has never been profitable. Such a situation may be disguised; owners can employ various creative accounting techniques that make the firm's financial picture appear much brighter than it really is. The reason that a business is for sale will seldom be stated honestly as "It's losing money." If there is an area of business in which the maxim "let the buyer beware" still prevails, it is in the sale of a business. Any buyer unprepared to do a complete and thorough analysis of the business may be stuck with a real loser.

Although buying a money-losing business is risky, it is not necessarily taboo. If your analysis of a company shows that it is poorly managed or suffering from neglect, you may be able to turn it around. However, if you do not have a well-defined plan for improving a struggling business, do *not* consider buying it!

Woodplay

For example, entrepreneurs Jim Sally and Tom Marenyi discovered a business that was struggling, but they believed they could turn it around. Before starting their search for a business to buy, Sally and Marenyi established the criteria their acquisition must meet: a quality product, a good name, market potential, and a solid formula upon which they could improve. They soon discovered Woodplay, a small company that manufactured wooden playsets for the residential market. Although the company was known for its outstanding line of well-made redwood products and had good name recognition in an attractive niche, Woodplay had fallen on hard times and was in bankruptcy. Looking beyond the company's immediate financial problems, Sally and Marenyi recognized that Woodplay had great potential. They purchased the company's assets and invested several hundred thousand dollars of their own money in working capital. "The first thing we had to do was stabilize the business," says Marenyi. They quickly eliminated Woodplay's two weakest product lines, added two new ones, and began building a network of national dealers. Within two years, Sally and Marenyi found themselves turning down orders because they could not keep up with the demand for their products! Today Woodplay is thriving, and in addition to expanding their dealer network, Sally and Marenyi are working to build retail locations to sell their state-of-the-art product line.[3]

THE PREVIOUS OWNER MAY HAVE CREATED ILL WILL. Just as ethical, socially responsible business dealings create goodwill for a company, improper business behavior creates ill will. A business may look great on the surface, but customers, suppliers, creditors, or employees may have extremely negative feelings about it. Business relations may have begun to deteriorate, but their long-term effects may not yet appear in the business's financial statements. Ill will can permeate a business for years.

EMPLOYEES INHERITED WITH THE BUSINESS MAY NOT BE SUITABLE. Previous managers may have kept marginal employees because they were close friends or because they started off with the company. The new owner, therefore, may have to make some very unpopular termination decisions. For this reason, employees often do not welcome a new owner because they feel threatened. If the new owner plans to make changes in the business, its current employees may not suit her needs. Others may not be able to adapt to the new owner's management style, and a culture clash results.

For instance, when Bob Hammer and Sue Crowe bought BlueJacket Ship Crafters, they changed the management style in the company from an authoritarian one to one built around empowered work teams. Unfortunately, this new philosophy ran counter to the existing supervisor's management style. Within a year, the supervisor left the company. "She couldn't work with empowered people," recalls Crowe, who describes her as "dictatorial."[4]

BlueJacket Ship Crafters

THE BUSINESS LOCATION MAY HAVE BECOME UNSATISFACTORY. What was once an ideal location may have become obsolete as market and demographic trends changed. Large shopping malls, new competitors, or highway reroutings can spell disaster for small retail shops. Prospective buyers should always evaluate the existing market in the area surrounding an existing business as well as its potential for expansion.

EQUIPMENT AND FACILITIES MAY BE OBSOLETE OR INEFFICIENT. Potential buyers sometimes neglect to have an expert evaluate a firm's facilities and equipment before they purchase it. Only later do they discover that the equipment is obsolete and inefficient, and the business may suffer losses from excessively high costs. The equipment may have been well suited to the business they purchased but not to the business they want to build. Modernizing equipment and facilities is seldom inexpensive.

CHANGE AND INNOVATION ARE DIFFICULT TO IMPLEMENT. It is easier to plan for change than it is to implement it. Methods previously used in a business may have established precedents that are hard to modify. For example, if the previous owner allowed a 10 percent discount to customers purchasing 100 or more units in a single order, it may be almost impossible to eliminate the discount practice without losing some of those customers. The previous owner's policies, even if proven unwise, still affect the changes a new owner can make. Reversing a downward slide in sales can be just as difficult. Implementing changes to bring in new business and convince former clients to return can be an expensive and laborious process.

INVENTORY MAY BE OUTDATED OR OBSOLETE. Inventory is valuable only if it is salable. Smart buyers know better than to trust the inventory valuation on a firm's balance sheet. Some of it may actually appreciate in value in periods of rapid inflation, but more likely it has depreciated. A prospective buyer must judge inventory on the basis of its market value, not its book value.

After Hendrix Neimann had already agreed in principle to purchase Automatic Door Specialists, a security company, from its founder, he and his team of advisers discovered that much of the inventory reported in the company's books was useless scrap and junk. After taking into account the worthless inventory and past-due accounts receivable, Neimann ultimately offered the owner 50 percent of the amount in the original preliminary agreement.[5]

Automatic Door Specialists

Every potential buyer should check the status of a company's inventory to see whether it is outdated and obsolete.

ACCOUNTS RECEIVABLE MAY BE WORTH LESS THAN FACE VALUE. Like inventory, accounts receivable rarely are worth their face value. The prospective buyer should age the accounts receivable (a breakdown of accounts that are 30, 60, 90, and 120 days old and beyond) to determine their collectibility. The older the receivables are, the less likely they are to be collected, and, consequently, the lower their value is. Table 5.1 shows a simple but effective method of evaluating accounts receivable once they have been aged.

When one buyer was considering purchasing an existing business, his research showed that a substantial volume of accounts receivable was well past due. Further investigation revealed that the company and its largest customer were locked in a nasty fight over these outstanding accounts. The buyer decided to withdraw his preliminary offer.[6]

TABLE 5.1
Valuing Accounts Receivable

A prospective buyer asked the current owner of a business about the value of her accounts receivable. The owner's business records showed $101,000 in receivables. But when the prospective buyer aged the accounts and multiplied them by his estimated collection probabilities, he discovered their *real* value.

Age of Accounts	Amount	Collection Probability	Value
0–30 days	$ 40,000	95%	$38,000
31–60 days	25,000	88%	22,000
61–90 days	14,000	70%	9,800
91–120 days	10,000	40%	4,000
121–150 days	7,000	25%	1,750
151-plus days	5,000	10%	500
Total	$101,000		$76,050

Had he blindly accepted the seller's book value of these accounts receivable, this prospective buyer would have overpaid nearly $25,000 for them!

THE BUSINESS MAY BE OVERPRICED. Each year, many people purchase businesses at prices far in excess of their value, which can impair the companies' ability to generate a profit and positive cash flow. If a buyer accurately values a business's accounts receivable, inventories, and other assets, she will be in a better position to negotiate a price that will allow the business to be profitable. Making payments on a business that was overpriced is a millstone around the new owner's neck, making it difficult to carry this excess weight and keep the business afloat.

Although most buyers do not realize it, the price they pay for a company typically is not as crucial to its continued success as the terms on which they make the purchase. Of course, wise business buyers will try to negotiate a reasonable price, but they are much more interested in the deal's terms—how much cash they must pay out and when, how much of the price the seller is willing to finance and for how long, the interest rate at which the deal is financed, and other such terms. Their primary concern is making sure that the deal does not endanger the company's future financial health and that it preserves the company's cash flow.

2. Define the steps involved in the *right* way to buy a business.

THE STEPS IN ACQUIRING A BUSINESS

Buying an existing business can be risky if approached haphazardly. Studies show that more than 50 percent of all business acquisitions fail to meet the buyer's expectations. To avoid costly mistakes, an entrepreneur-to-be should follow a logical, methodical approach:[7]

- Analyze your skills, abilities, and interests to determine what kind(s) of businesses you should consider.
- Prepare a list of potential candidates.
- Investigate those candidates and evaluate the best one(s).
- Explore financing options.
- Ensure a smooth transition.

Analyze Your Skills, Abilities, and Interests

The first step in buying a business is *not* searching out potential acquisition candidates. Every entrepreneur considering buying a business should begin by conducting a self-audit to determine the ideal business for him or her. The primary focus is to identify the type of business *you* will be happiest and most successful owning. Consider, for example, the following questions:

- What business activities do you enjoy most? Least? Why?
- Which industries or markets offer the greatest potential for growth?
- Which industries interest you most? Least? Why?
- What kind of business do you want to buy?
- What kinds of businesses do you want to *avoid?*
- What do you expect to get out of the business?
- How much time, energy, and money can you put into the business?
- What business skills and experience do you have? Which ones do you lack?
- How easily can you transfer your skills and experience to other types of businesses? In what kinds of businesses would that transfer be easiest?
- How much risk are you willing to take?
- Are you willing and able to turn around a struggling business?
- What size company do you want to buy?
- Is there a particular geographic location you desire?

Answering these and other questions beforehand will allow you to develop a list of precise criteria a company must meet before it becomes a purchase candidate. Addressing these issues early in the process will also save a great deal of time, trouble, and confusion as you wade through a multitude of business opportunities.

Prepare a List of Potential Candidates

Once you know what your goals are for acquiring a business, you can begin your search. Do *not* limit yourself to only those businesses that are advertised as being for sale. In fact,

Source: FRANK & ERNEST©NEA

hidden market—*low-profile companies that might be for sale but are not advertised as such.*

the **hidden market** of companies that might be for sale but are not advertised as such is one of the richest sources of top-quality businesses. "About 85 percent of [purchase] opportunities are tucked away within the unadvertised hidden market," says one business broker.[8] Although they maintain a low profile, these hidden businesses represent some of the most attractive purchase targets a prospective buyer may find. How can you tap into this hidden market of potential acquisitions? Typical sources include the following:

- Business brokers
- Bankers
- Accountants
- Investment bankers
- Industry contacts—suppliers, distributors, customers, insurance brokers, and others
- Networking—social and business contact with friends and relatives
- Knocking on the doors of businesses you'd like to buy (even if they're not advertised as being for sale)
- Trade associations
- Newspapers and trade journals listing businesses for sale

In recent years, the World Wide Web also has become an important tool for entrepreneurs looking to buy businesses. In the past, the market for businesses was highly fragmented and unstructured, making it difficult for entrepreneurs to conduct an organized, thorough search for companies that might meet their purchase criteria. Today hundreds of business brokers have established Web sites that list thousands of companies for sale in practically every industry imaginable, enabling entrepreneurs to search the entire country for that perfect business from the comfort of their own homes. Using the Web, potential buyers can eliminate the companies that do not suit them and can conduct preliminary research on those that look most promising. Describing the impact of the Internet on business sales, one broker says, "What we are seeing is *huge.* [The World Wide Web] is going to have major implications for the way we're going to sell companies in the future."[9]

Investigate and Evaluate Candidate Businesses

Finding the right company requires patience. Although some buyers find a company after only a few months of looking, the typical search takes much longer, as much as two or three years. Once you have a list of prospective candidates, it is time to do your homework. The next step is to investigate the candidates in more detail:

- What are the company's strengths? Weaknesses?
- Is the company profitable? What is its overall financial condition?
- What is its cash flow cycle? How much cash will the company generate?
- Who are its major competitors?
- How large is the customer base? Is it growing or shrinking?
- Are the current employees suitable? Will they stay?
- What is the physical condition of the business, its equipment, and its inventory?
- What new skills must you learn to be able to manage this business successfully?

Determining the answers to these (and other questions addressed in this chapter) will allow a prospective buyer to develop a list of the most attractive prospects and to prioritize them in descending order of attractiveness. This process also will make the task of valuing the business much easier.

Explore Financing Options

Placing a value on an existing business (a topic we will discuss later in this chapter) represents a major hurdle for many would-be entrepreneurs. The next challenging task in closing a successful deal is financing the purchase. Although financing the purchase of an existing business usually is easier than financing a new one, some traditional lenders shy away from deals involving the purchase of an existing business. Those that are willing to finance business purchases normally lend only a portion of the value of the assets, so buyers often find themselves searching for alternative sources of funds. Fortunately, most business buyers have access to a ready source of financing: the seller. Once a seller finds a suitable buyer, she typically will agree to finance anywhere from 30 percent to 80 percent of the purchase price. Usually, a deal is structured so that the buyer makes a down payment to the seller, who then finances a note for the balance. The buyer makes regular principal and interest payments over time—perhaps with a larger balloon payment at the end—until the note is paid off. The terms and conditions of such a loan are a vital concern to both buyer and seller. They cannot be so burdensome that they threaten the company's continued existence; that is, the buyer must be able to make the payments to the seller out of the company's cash flow. At the same time, the deal must give the seller the financial security she is seeking from the sale. Defining reasonable terms is the result of the negotiation process between the buyer and the seller.

Ensure a Smooth Transition

Once the parties strike a deal, the challenge of making a smooth transition immediately arises. No matter how well planned the sale is, there are *always* surprises. For instance, the new owner may have ideas for changing the business—sometimes radically—that cause a great deal of stress and anxiety among employees and the previous owner. Charged with such emotion and uncertainty, the transition phase is always difficult and frustrating—and sometimes painful. To avoid a bumpy transition, a business buyer should do the following:

- Concentrate on communicating with employees. Business sales are fraught with uncertainty and anxiety, and employees need reassurance.
- Be honest with employees. Avoid telling them only what they want to hear.
- Listen to employees. They have intimate knowledge of the business and its strengths and weaknesses and usually can offer valuable suggestions.
- Consider asking the seller to act as a consultant until the transition is complete. The previous owner can be a valuable resource, especially to an inexperienced buyer.

Table 5.2 describes 15 steps potential buyers should take to increase the probability that the businesses they buy are the right ones for them.

EVALUATING AN EXISTING BUSINESS

3. Explain the process of evaluating an existing business.

When evaluating an existing business, a lone buyer quickly feels overwhelmed by the tremendous number and complexity of the issues involved. Therefore, a smart buyer will assemble a team of specialists to help in investigating the potential business opportunity. This team is usually composed of a banker, an accountant familiar with the particular industry, an attorney, and perhaps a small business consultant or a business broker. The cost of such a team can range from $3,000 to $20,000, but most buyers agree that using a team significantly lowers the likelihood of making a bad buy. Because making a bad purchase will cost many times the cost of a team of experts, most buyers see it as a wise investment. It is important for a buyer to trust the members of the business evaluation team.

TABLE 5.2

15 Steps to Buying the Company That's Right for You

Source: Jay Finegan, "The Insider's Guide," Inc., October 1999, pp. 26–36. Reprinted with permission of Inc. from "The Insider's Guide," by Jay Finegan, October 1999 © 1999; permission conveyed through Copyright Clearance Center, Inc.

1. *Make sure you shouldn't be starting a company instead.* You should have solid reasons for buying a company rather than starting one—and you should know what they are.
2. *Determine the kind of business you want—and whether you're capable of running it.* This requires an unflinching assessment of your own strengths, weaknesses, personality, and goals.
3. *Consider the lifestyle you want.* What are you expecting from the business? Money? Freedom? Flexibility?
4. *Consider the location you want.* In what part of the country (or world) do you want to live in?
5. *Reconsider lifestyle.* You may own this business for a long, long time; it had better be one you enjoy.
6. *Cozy up to lenders in advance.* Visit potential lenders long before you need to borrow any money. Develop a rapport with them.
7. *Prepare to sell yourself to the sellers.* You're buying their "baby," and they'll want to make sure you're the right person for the job!
8. *Once you've defined the kind of business you're after, find the right company.* Three major sources of potential candidates are: (1) the network of businesspeople and advisers in the area, (2) business brokers specializing in companies of the size or type you want to buy, and (3) businesses that technically are not for sale (but are very attractive).
9. *Choose the right seller.* Is she honest? What's the *real* reason she's selling the business?
10. *Do your research before agreeing to a price.* Ask lots of questions and get the facts to help you estimate the company's value.
11. *Make sure your letter of intent is specific.* It should establish deadlines, escape clauses, payment terms, confidentiality, and many other key issues.
12. *Don't skimp on due diligence.* Don't believe everything you see and hear; a relentless investigation will show whether the seller is telling the truth. Not all of them will.
13. *Be skeptical.* Don't fall in love with the deal; look for reasons *not* to buy the company.
14. *Don't forget to assess the employees.* You're not just buying a company; you're also buying the people who go with it.
15. *Make sure the final price reflects the company's real value.* Don't lower your chances of success by paying too much for the business.

With this team assembled, the potential buyer is ready to explore the business opportunity by examining five critical areas.

1. Why does the owner want to sell?
2. What is the physical condition of the business?
3. What is the potential for the company's products or services?
4. What legal aspects should you consider?
5. Is the business financially sound?

Why Is the Business for Sale?

WHY DOES THE OWNER WANT TO SELL? Every prospective business buyer should investigate the *real* reason the business owner wants to sell. A recent study by the Geneva Corporation found that the most common reasons that owners of small and medium-sized businesses gave for selling were boredom and burnout.[10] Others decided to cash in their business investments and diversify into other types of assets.

and usually their optimism is based in reality. One study by the National Federation of Independent Businesses (NFIB) found that one-third of the entrepreneurs rated their chances of success to be 100 percent![11] This high level of optimism may explain why some of the most successful entrepreneurs have failed in business—often more than once—before finally succeeding.

4. *Desire for immediate feedback.* Entrepreneurs enjoy the challenge of running a business, and they like to know how they are doing and are constantly looking for feedback. "I love being an entrepreneur," says Nick Gleason, cofounder of CitySoft Inc., a Web page design firm based in Cambridge, Massachusetts. "There's something about the sheer creativity and challenge of it that I like."[12]
5. *High level of energy.* Entrepreneurs are more energetic than the average person. That energy may be a critical factor given the incredible effort required to launch a start-up company. Long hours and hard work are the rule rather than the exception.
6. *Future orientation.* Entrepreneurs have a well-defined sense of searching for opportunities. They look ahead and are less concerned with what was done yesterday than with what might be done tomorrow. Entrepreneurs see potential where most people see only problems or nothing at all, a characteristic that often makes them the objects of ridicule (at least until their ideas become huge successes). Whereas traditional managers are concerned with managing available *resources,* entrepreneurs are more interested in spotting and capitalizing on *opportunities.* Sometimes opportunities—and ideas—arise when least expected.

Sandman LLC

For instance, while Stacey Kanzler was watching television coverage of floods that were wreaking havoc in the midwestern United States, she saw crews filling sandbags by hand in a desperate attempt to save homes and businesses. She also saw a business opportunity. "I couldn't believe we didn't have a machine that sewed multiple sandbags simultaneously," she recalls. Drawing on her experience in her husband's earth-moving business, Kanzler developed a prototype sandbagging machine in just two weeks. Her product, the Sandbagger, does the work of 40 people and has saved countless communities from the ravages of floodwaters. Today, Sandman LLC generates annual revenues of more than $2 million.[13]

7. *Skill at organizing.* Building a company "from scratch" is much like piecing together a giant jigsaw puzzle. Entrepreneurs know how to put the right people together to accomplish a task. Effectively combining people and jobs enables entrepreneurs to transform their visions into reality.
8. *Value of achievement over money.* One of the most common misconceptions about entrepreneurs is that they are driven wholly by the desire to make money. To the contrary, *achievement* seems to be entrepreneurs' primary motivating force; money is simply a way of "keeping score" of accomplishments—a symbol of achievement. One business researcher says, "What keeps the entrepreneur moving forward is more complex—and more profound—than mere cash. It's about running your own show. It's about doing what is virtually impossible."[14]

Other characteristics frequently exhibited by entrepreneurs include:

High degree of commitment. Launching a company successfully requires total commitment from an entrepreneur. Business founders often immerse themselves completely in their businesses. Almost every entrepreneur has to overcome seemingly insurmountable barriers to launch a company and to keep it growing. That requires commitment. "I equate commitment with survival," claims one consultant.[15]

Tolerance for ambiguity. Entrepreneurs tend to have a high tolerance for ambiguous, ever-changing situations, the environment in which they most often operate. This ability to handle uncertainty is critical because these business builders constantly make decisions using new, sometimes conflicting information gleaned from a variety of unfamiliar sources.

Flexibility. One hallmark of true entrepreneurs is their ability to adapt to the changing demands of their customers and their businesses. In this rapidly changing global economy, rigidity often leads to failure. As our society, its people, and their tastes change, entrepreneurs also must be willing to adapt their businesses to meet those changes.

Hewlett-Packard

When Bill Hewlett and Dave Packard founded their company in the late 1930s, they had no clear idea of what to make. They knew that they wanted to create a business in the vaguely defined field of electronic engineering. Their company, Hewlett-Packard (now one of the most successful electronics companies in the world), probably survived because of the founders' flexibility. Some of their early product ideas included a clock drive for a telescope, a bowling foul-line indicator, a device to make urinals flush automatically, and a shock machine to make people lose weight![16]

Tenacity. Obstacles, obstructions, and defeat typically do not dissuade entrepreneurs from doggedly pursuing their visions. They simply keep trying. "The ones who make it relish the game and never give up—no matter how tough things get," says one researcher.[17]

What conclusion can we draw from the volumes of research conducted on the entrepreneurial personality? Entrepreneurs are not of one mold; no one set of characteristics can predict who will become entrepreneurs and whether or not they will succeed. Indeed, *diversity* seems to be a central characteristic of entrepreneurs. One researcher of the entrepreneurial personality explains, "Entrepreneurs don't fit any statistical norm. . . Most are aberrant or a bit odd by nature."[18]

As you can see from the examples in this chapter, *anyone*—regardless of age, race, gender, color, national origin, or any other characteristic—can become an entrepreneur (although not everyone should). There are no limitations on this form of economic expression. Entrepreneurship is not a genetic trait; it is a learned skill. The editors of *Inc.* magazine claim, "Entrepreneurship is more mundane than it's sometimes portrayed. . . . You don't need to be a person of mythical proportions to be very, very successful in building a company."[19]

3-A. Describe the benefits of entrepreneurship.

THE BENEFITS OF ENTREPRENEURSHIP

Surveys show that owners of small businesses believe they work harder, earn more money, and are happier than if they worked for a large company. Before launching any business venture, every potential entrepreneur should consider the benefits of small business ownership.

Opportunity to Create Your Own Destiny

Owning a business provides entrepreneurs the independence and the opportunity to achieve what is important to them.

Kate Spade Inc.

After navigating the corporate world for several years and watching many friends in large companies become victims of downsizing, Kate Spade left her post as an editor at Mademoiselle *in 1993 to launch with her husband a trend-setting forerunner in the fashion accessory industry. She explains the move to independence, "We wanted to chase our own destiny." Today Kate Spade Inc. sells its elegant yet functional handbags through upscale retailers such as Barneys, Saks Fifth Avenue, and Neiman Marcus; has retail outlets in New York, Los Angeles, and Tokyo; and rings up annual sales of more than $30 million!*[20]

Like the Spades, entrepreneurs want to "call the shots" in their lives, and they use their businesses to bring this desire to life. They reap the intrinsic rewards of knowing they are the driving forces behind their businesses.

YOU BE THE CONSULTANT . . .

Is This Any Way to Buy a Business?

After reading dozens of entrepreneurial success stories in the press, stockbroker David Clausen decided that he wanted to own a company of his own. He figured that the best way to get into business for himself was to buy an existing company. Clausen did not know where to start, so he called a broker he found listed in the Yellow Pages and began looking at companies. "I had no industry in mind, and I looked at 30 companies," he says.

Looking back, Clausen realizes that he went about buying a business the wrong way. He had no idea what kind of business he wanted to buy, he did not conduct a systematic search for prospects, and he was in a hurry. "I was so eager to get my hands on a business," Clausen admits. "But I was naive. I ran into a lot of obstacles I didn't expect."

Ultimately, it was a friend at church who told Clausen about the company he finally purchased, Barclay Maps, a 40-year-old map-publishing business whose owner had just died. He contacted the former owner's attorney and learned that the asking price was $200,000. Interested, Clausen strolled through the business. He estimated that the equipment he saw was worth about $25,000, added another $15,000 for goodwill, and made an offer of $40,000. To his surprise, the previous owner's family accepted his offer. With just $7,000 of his own money available, he asked the family if he could pay the balance over two years. Again, Clausen was surprised when the family accepted his proposal.

Suddenly a business owner, Clausen was counting heavily on one major asset to keep the company going while he learned the business: a nine-month backlog of orders. "Even if I made no new sales, I had nine months of work to sink or swim," he reasoned. Unfortunately, Clausen soon discovered a host of problems, including a shrinking customer base and woefully outdated equipment, facing Barclay Maps that thorough research before the sale would have uncovered. Clausen figured that the obsolete computers and cartography equipment in the company posed the greatest problem, so he tackled it first. He replaced all of the old machinery with state-of-the-art technology, which not only improved productivity but also enabled Barclay Maps to create digital mapping systems on CDs. Clausen quickly realized that the ability to develop digital maps essentially created a new product line in which his short and shrinking list of customers was keenly interested. He began marketing the digital maps to existing customers before securing new accounts. Despite his shaky start in business, Clausen has managed to increase sales at Barclay Maps from just $190,000 to more than $1 million and has transformed the company into one of the nation's largest suppliers of high-end digital geographic data. Looking back on his purchase of Barclay Maps, Clausen says, "If I were doing this again, I would go about the whole process differently—much smarter."

1. Evaluate the way in which David Clausen went about finding a business to buy, assessing it, and searching for financing. What did he do right? What did he do wrong?
2. What should Clausen have done differently?

Source: Adapted from Gianna Jacobson, "Blind Ambition," *Success*, October 1997, p. 65.

Smart business buyers know that the biggest and most unpleasant surprises can crop up outside the company's financial records and may never appear on the spreadsheets designed to analyze a company's financial position. For instance, a business owner might be looking to sell his business because a powerful new competitor is about to move into the market, a major highway rerouting will cause customer traffic to evaporate, the lease agreement on the ideal location is about to expire, or the primary customer base is declining. Every prospective buyer should investigate thoroughly any reason a seller gives for wanting to sell a business.

Businesses do not last forever, and most owners know when the time has come to sell. Some owners consider their behavior ethical only if they do not make false or misleading statements, but they may not disclose the whole story. In most business sales, the buyer bears the responsibility of determining whether the business is a good value. The best way to do that is to get out into the local community, talk to people, and ask a lot of questions. Visiting local business owners may reveal general patterns about the area and its overall vitality. The local chamber of commerce also may have useful information. Suppliers, customers, and even competitors may be able to shed light on why a business is up for sale. By combining this information with an analysis of the company's financial records, the potential buyer should be able to develop a clearer picture of the business and its real value.

The Condition of the Business

WHAT IS THE PHYSICAL CONDITION OF THE BUSINESS? A prospective buyer should evaluate the business's assets to determine their value. Are they reasonably priced? Are they obsolete? Will they need to be replaced soon? Do they operate efficiently? The potential buyer should check the condition of both the equipment and the building. It may be necessary to hire a professional to evaluate the major components of the building—its structure and its plumbing, electrical, and heating and cooling systems. Unexpected renovations are rarely inexpensive or simple and can punch a gaping hole in a buyer's financial plans.

How fresh is the firm's inventory? Is it consistent with the image the new owner wants to project? How much of it would the buyer have to sell at a loss? A potential buyer may need to get an independent appraisal to determine the value of the firm's inventory and other assets because the current owner may have priced them far above their actual value. These items typically comprise the largest portion of a business's value, and a potential buyer should not accept the seller's asking price blindly. Remember: *Book value is not the same as market value.* Usually, a buyer can purchase equipment and fixtures at substantially lower prices than book value. Value is determined in the market, not on a balance sheet.

Other important factors that the potential buyer should investigate include the following:

Accounts Receivable. If the sale includes accounts receivable, the buyer should check their quality before purchasing them. How creditworthy are the accounts? What portion of them are past due? How likely are you to be able to collect them? By aging the accounts receivable, a buyer can judge their quality and determine their value. (Refer to Table 5.1.)

Lease Arrangements. Is the lease included in the sale? When does it expire? What restrictions does it have on renovation or expansion? The buyer should determine *beforehand* what restrictions the landlord has placed on the lease and negotiate any change prior to purchasing the business.

Business Records. Well-kept business records can be a valuable source of information and can tell a prospective buyer a lot about the company's pattern of success (or lack of it). Unfortunately, many business owners are sloppy recordkeepers. Consequently, the potential buyer and his team may have to reconstruct some critical records. It is important to verify as much information about the business as possible. For instance, does the owner have customer or mailing lists? These lists can be a valuable marketing tool for a new business owner.

Intangible Assets. Does the sale include any intangible assets such as trademarks, patents, copyrights, or goodwill? How long do patents have left to run? Is the trademark threatened by lawsuits for infringement? Does the company have logos or slogans that are unique or widely recognized? Determining the value of such intangibles is much more difficult than computing the value of the tangible assets.

Location and Appearance. The location and the overall appearance of the building are important factors for a prospective buyer to consider. What had been an outstanding location in the past may be totally unacceptable today. Even if the building and equipment are in good condition and are fairly priced, the business may be located in a declining area. What kinds of businesses are in the area? Every buyer should consider the location's suitability several years into the future.

The potential buyer should also check local zoning laws to ensure that any changes he wants to make are legal. In some areas, zoning laws are very difficult to change and, as a result, can restrict the business's growth.

Table 5.3 offers a checklist of items every business buyer should investigate before closing a deal.

TABLE 5.3

A Business Buyer's Checklist

Sources: Adapted from "Look Before You Buy," Business Resale Network, **<www.br-network.com/features/byb1.html>;** *"Making an In-Depth Evaluation," Business Resale Network,* **<www.br-network.com/features/byb1.html>;** *Norm Brodsky, "Caveat Emptor,"* Inc., *August 1998, pp. 31–32; "Basics of Buying a Business," American Express Small Business Exchange,* **<home3.americanexpress.com/smallbusiness/resources/starting/buybiz.shtml>.**

Buildings, furnishings, and fixtures. Every buyer should get a list of all of the fixed assets included in the purchase and then determine their condition, age, usefulness, and value.

Inventory. Inventory may be the biggest part of a business sale, and it can be one of the trickiest parts of the deal. What inventory is on hand? What is its condition? How salable is it? What is its value? (Remember not to confuse *book* value with *market* value.) What is the company's merchandise return policy? How high is its return rate?

Financial statements. Although small business owners are notoriously poor recordkeepers, a business buyer must have access to a company's financial statements for the past five years. This is the only way a buyer can judge the earning power of a company. The most reliable financial statements are those that have been audited by a certified public accountant. Comparing financial ratios against industry standards found in reports from Robert Morris & Associates and Dun & Bradstreet can reveal important patterns.

Tax returns. A good accountant should be able to reconcile the owner's or company's tax returns with its financial statements.

Sales records. A prospective buyer should determine sales patterns by getting a monthly breakdown by product categories, sales representatives, cash versus credit, and any other significant factor for the company for three years. It is also a good idea to identify the company's top 10 customers and review their purchases over the past three years. For what percentage of total sales did these 10 customers account?

Accounts receivable. Age the company's accounts receivable to see how many are current and how many are past due. Identify the top 10 accounts and check their credit ratings.

Accounts payable. Conduct an analysis similar to the one for accounts receivable for the company's accounts payable. Past-due accounts are an indication that a business is experiencing cash flow difficulties.

Legal documents. A prospective buyer should investigate all significant contracts (especially long-term ones) a company has with vendors, suppliers, distributors, lenders, employees, unions, customers, landlords, and others. Can the current owner assign the rights and obligations of these existing contracts to the buyer? If the company is incorporated, it is wise to check the articles of incorporation (or its articles of organization and operating agreement if it is a limited liability company).

Patents, trademarks, and copyrights. Reviewing the documentation for any patents, trademarks, and copyrights the company holds is vital.

Lawsuits. Is the company facing any lawsuits, either current or pending?

Liabilities. It is essential that the seller provide the buyer with a complete list of liabilities that are outstanding against the company, including accounts and notes payable, loans, liens by creditors against business assets, lawsuits, and others.

Advertising and sales literature. A business buyer should study the company's advertising and sales literature to get an idea of the image it is projecting to its customers and the community. Talking to customers, suppliers, bankers, attorneys, and other local business owners will provide clues about the company's reputation.

Organization chart. Current employees can be a vital asset to a business buyer (if they are willing to stay after the sale). Ask the seller to develop an organization chart, showing the company's chain of command, and get copies of employees' job descriptions so you can understand who is responsible for which duties.

Insurance coverage. Evaluate the types and amounts of insurance coverage the company currently has, including workers' compensation. Is it sufficient? If not, will you be able to obtain the necessary coverage at a reasonable price?

Products and Services

WHAT IS THE POTENTIAL FOR THE COMPANY'S PRODUCTS OR SERVICES? No one wants to buy a business with a shrinking customer base. A thorough market analysis can lead to an accurate and realistic sales forecast for an existing business. This research will tell a buyer whether or not he should consider buying a particular business and will help spot trends in the business's sales and customer base.

CUSTOMER CHARACTERISTICS AND COMPOSITION. Before purchasing an existing business, a buyer should analyze both existing and potential customers. Discovering why customers buy from the business and developing a profile of the entire customer base can help the buyer identify a company's strengths and weaknesses. The entrepreneur should determine the answers to the following questions:

- Who are my customers in terms of race, age, gender, and income level? What is their demographic profile?
- Why do they buy?
- What do the customers want the business to do for them? What needs are they satisfying?
- How often do customers buy? Do they buy in seasonal patterns?
- How loyal are my present customers?
- Is it practical or even possible to attract new customers? If so, are the new customers significantly different from existing customers?
- Does the business have a well-defined customer base? Is it growing? Do these customers come from a large geographical area or do they all live near the business?

Analyzing the answers to these questions can help a potential buyer create and implement a more powerful marketing plan. Most likely he will try to keep the business attractive to existing customers, while changing some features of its marketing plan to attract new customers.

COMPETITOR ANALYSIS. A potential buyer must identify the company's direct competition—those businesses in the immediate area that sell similar products or services. The potential profitability and survival of the business may well depend on the behavior of these competitors. An important factor to consider is the trend in the competition. How many competitors have opened in recent years? How many have closed in the past five years? What caused these failures? Has the market already reached the saturation point? Being a latecomer in an already saturated market is not the path to long-term success.

When evaluating the competitive environment, a prospective buyer should address other questions:

- Which competitors have survived, and what characteristics have led to their success?
- How do competitors' sales volumes compare with those of the business under consideration?
- What unique services do competitors offer?
- How well organized and coordinated are the marketing efforts of competitors?
- What are the competitors' reputations?
- What are the strengths and weaknesses of the competition? Which competitor is strongest?
- What competitive edge does each competitor have?
- How can you gain market share in this competitive environment?

Legal Aspects

WHAT LEGAL ASPECTS SHOULD YOU CONSIDER? Business buyers must be careful to avoid several legal pitfalls as they negotiate the final deal. The biggest potential traps include liens, bulk transfers, contract assignments, covenants not to compete, and ongoing legal liabilities.

Liens. The key legal issue in the sale of any asset is typically the proper transfer of good title from seller to buyer. However, because most business sales involve a collection of assorted assets, the transfer of a good title is more complex. Some business assets may have **liens** (creditors' claims) against them and unless they are satisfied before the sale, the buyer must assume them and is financially responsible for them. One way to reduce this potential problem is to include a clause in the sales contract stating that any liability not shown on the balance sheet at the time of sale remains the responsibility of the seller. A prospective buyer should have an attorney thoroughly investigate all of the assets for sale and their lien status before buying any business.

lien—*a creditor's claim against an asset.*

Bulk Transfers. To protect against surprise claims from the seller's creditors after purchasing a business, the buyer should meet the requirements of a **bulk transfer** under Section 6 of the Uniform Commercial Code. Suppose that an owner owing many creditors sells his business to a buyer. The seller, however, does not use the proceeds of the sale to pay his debts to business creditors. Instead, he pockets them to use for his own benefit. Without the protection of a bulk transfer, those creditors could make claim to the assets that the buyer purchased in order to satisfy the previous owner's debts (within six months). To be effective, a bulk transfer must meet the following criteria:

bulk transfer—*protects the buyer of a business's assets from the claims unpaid creditors might have against those assets.*

- The seller must give the buyer a signed, sworn list of existing creditors.
- The buyer and the seller must prepare a list of the property included in the sale.
- The buyer must keep the list of creditors and the list of property for six months.
- The buyer must give written notice of the sale to each creditor at least 10 days before he takes possession of the goods or pays for them (whichever is first).

By meeting these criteria, a buyer acquires free and clear title to the assets purchased, which are not subject to prior claims from the seller's creditors. Because Section 6 can create quite a burden on a business buyer, 16 states have repealed it, and more may follow. About a half-dozen states have revised Section 6 that makes it easier for buyers to notify creditors. Under the revised rule, if a business has more than 200 creditors, the buyer may notify them by public notice rather than by contacting them individually.

Contract Assignments. A buyer must investigate the rights and the obligations he would assume under existing contracts with suppliers, customers, employees, lessors, and others. To continue the smooth operation of the business, the buyer must assume the rights of the seller under many existing contracts. Assuming these rights and obligations means having the seller assign existing contracts to the new owner. For example, the current owner may have four years left on a 10-year lease and will need to assign this contract to the buyer. To protect her interest, the buyer (who is the assignee) should notify the other party involved in the contract of the assignment. In the previous example, the business buyer should notify the landlord promptly of the lease assignment from the previous owner.

Generally, the seller can assign any contractual right to the buyer, unless the contract specifically prohibits the assignment or the contract is personal in nature. For instance, loan contracts sometimes prohibit assignments with **due-on-sale clauses.** These clauses require the buyer to pay the full amount of the remaining loan balance or to finance the balance at prevailing interest rates. Thus, the buyer cannot assume the seller's loan (at a lower

due-on-sale clause—*loan contract provision that prohibits a seller from assigning a loan arrangement to the buyer. Instead, the buyer is required to finance the remaining loan balance at prevailing interest rates.*

interest rate). Also, a seller usually cannot assign his credit arrangements with suppliers to the buyer because they are based on the seller's business reputation and are personal in nature. If such contracts are crucial to the business operation and cannot be assigned, the buyer must renegotiate new contracts. A prospective buyer also should evaluate the terms of any other unique contracts the seller has, including patent, trademark, or copyright registrations, exclusive agent or distributor contracts, real estate leases, financing and loan arrangements, and union contracts.

covenant not to compete (or restrictive covenant)— *an agreement between a buyer and a seller in which the seller agrees not to compete with the buyer within a specific time period and geographic area.*

Covenants Not to Compete. One of the most important and most often overlooked legal considerations for a prospective buyer is negotiating a **covenant not to compete** (or a **restrictive covenant**) with the seller. Under a restrictive covenant, the seller agrees not to open a new competing store within a specific time period and geographic area of the existing one. (The covenant should be negotiated with the *owner,* not with the corporation, because if the corporation signs the agreement, the owner may not be bound.) However, the covenant must be a part of a business sale and must be reasonable in scope in order to be enforceable. Although some states place limitations on the enforceability of restrictive covenants, business buyers should insist on the seller signing one. Without this protection, a buyer may find his new business eroding beneath his feet. For example, Bob purchases a tire business from Alexandra, whose reputation in town for selling tires is unequaled. If Bob fails to negotiate a restrictive covenant, nothing can stop Alexandra from opening a new shop next to her old one and keeping all of her customers, thereby driving Bob out of business. A reasonable covenant in this case might restrict Alexandra from opening a tire store within a three-mile radius for three years. Every business buyer should negotiate a covenant not to compete with the seller.

Ongoing Legal Liabilities. Finally, a potential buyer must look for any potential legal liabilities the purchase might expose. These typically arise from three sources: (1) physical premises, (2) product liability claims, and (3) labor relations. First, the buyer must examine the physical premises for safety. Are employees at risk because of asbestos or some other hazardous material? If a manufacturing environment is involved, does it meet Occupational Safety and Health Administration (OSHA) and other regulatory agency requirements?

Example

One entrepreneur who purchased a retail business located in a building that once housed a gasoline service station was quite surprised when the Environmental Protection Agency informed him that he would have to pay for cleaning up the results of an old, leaking gas tank that still sat beneath the property. Even though he had no part in running the old gas station and did not know the leaking tank was there, he was responsible for the cost of the cleanup! Removing the tank and cleaning up the site cost him several thousand dollars that he had not budgeted.

product liability lawsuits— *lawsuits that claim a company is liable for damages and injuries caused by the products it makes or sells.*

Second, the buyer must consider whether existing products contain defects that could result in **product liability lawsuits,** which claim that a company is liable for damages and injuries caused by the products or services it makes or sells. Existing lawsuits might be an omen of more to follow. In addition, the buyer must explore products that the company has discontinued since he might be liable for them if they prove to be defective. The final bargain between the parties should require the seller to guarantee that the company is not involved in any product liability lawsuits.

Third, what is the relationship between management and employees? Does a union contract exist? The time to discover sour management–labor relations is before the purchase, not after.

If the buyer's investigation reveals such potential liabilities, it does not necessarily eliminate the business from consideration. Insurance coverage can shift such risks from the potential buyer, but the buyer should check to see whether the insurance will cover lawsuits resulting from actions predating the purchase.

Financial Soundness of the Business

IS THE BUSINESS FINANCIALLY SOUND? A prospective buyer must analyze the financial records of a target business to determine its condition. He shouldn't be afraid to ask an accountant for help. Accounting systems and methods can vary tremendously from one type of business to another and can be quite confusing to a novice. Current profits can be inflated by changes in the accounting procedure or in the method for recording sales. For the buyer, the most dependable financial records are audited statements, those prepared by a CPA firm in accordance with generally accepted accounting principles (GAAP). Unfortunately, audited records do not exist in many small companies that are for sale. In some cases, a potential buyer has to hire an accountant to construct reliable financial statements because the owner's accounting and recordkeeping are so sloppy.

When evaluating the financial status of any business prospect, a buyer must remember that any investment in a company should produce a reasonable salary for her, an attractive return on the money she invests, and enough to cover the amount she must borrow to make the purchase. Otherwise, it makes no sense to purchase the business. Because most investors know that they can earn at least 10 percent a year by investing wisely in the stock market, they expect any business they buy to earn at least that amount plus an extra return that reflects the additional risk of buying a business. Many owners expect to earn a return of at least 15 percent to 30 percent on the amount invested in their businesses.

A buyer also must remember that she is purchasing the future profit potential of an existing business. To evaluate the firm's profit potential, she should review past sales, operating expenses, and profits as well as the assets used to generate those profits. She must compare current balance sheets and income statements with previous ones and then develop pro forma statements for the next two or three years. Sales tax records, income tax returns, and financial statements are valuable sources of information.

Are profits consistent over the years, or are they erratic? Is this pattern typical in the industry, or is it a result of unique circumstances or poor management? Can the business survive with such a serious fluctuation in revenues, costs, and profits? If these fluctuations are caused by poor management, can a new manager turn the business around?

Some of the financial records that a potential buyer should examine include the following:

Income statements and balance sheets for the past three to five years. It is important to review data from several years because creative accounting techniques can distort financial data in any single year. Even though buyers are purchasing the future profits of a business, they must remember that many businesses intentionally show low profits in order to minimize the owners' tax bills. Low profits should prompt a buyer to investigate their causes.

Income tax returns for the past three to five years. Comparing basic financial statements with tax returns can reveal discrepancies of which the buyer should be aware. Some small business owners **skim** from their businesses—take money from sales without reporting it as income. Owners who skim will claim their businesses are more profitable than their tax returns show. Although such underreporting is illegal and unethical, it is surprisingly common. Do *not* pay for undocumented, "phantom" profits the seller claims exist. In fact, you should consider whether you want to buy a business from someone who admits to doing business unethically.

skimming—*taking money from sales without reporting it as income.*

Owner's compensation (and that of relatives). The owner's compensation is especially important in small companies; and the smaller the company is, the more important it will be. Although many companies do not pay their owners what they are worth, others compensate their owners lavishly. The buyer must consider the impact of fringe benefits—company cars, insurance contracts, country club memberships, and the like. It is important to adjust the company's income statements for the salary and fringe benefits that the seller has paid himself and others.

Cash Flow. Most buyers understand the importance of evaluating a company's profitability, but fewer recognize the necessity of analyzing its cash flow. They assume that if profits are adequate, there will be sufficient cash to pay all of the bills and to fund an attractive salary for themselves. *That is not necessarily the case!* Before you agree to a deal, you should sit down with an accountant and convert the target company's financial statements into a cash flow forecast. Not only must this forecast take into account existing debts and obligations, but also any modifications the buyer would make in the business. It must also reflect the repayment of any financing the buyer arranges to purchase the company. Will the company generate enough cash to be self-supporting? How much cash will it generate for you?

A potential buyer must look for suspicious deviations from normal (in either direction) for sales, expenses, profits, cash flow, assets, and liabilities. Have sales been increasing or decreasing? Is the equipment really as valuable as it is listed on the balance sheet? Are advertising expenses unusually high or low? How is depreciation reflected in the financial statements?

This financial information gives a buyer the opportunity to verify the seller's claims about the business's performance. Sometimes, however, an owner will take short-term actions that produce a healthy financial statement but weaken the firm's long-term health and profit potential. For example, a seller might lower costs by gradually eliminating equipment maintenance or boost sales by selling to marginal businesses that will never pay their bills. Such techniques can artificially inflate assets and profits, but a well-prepared buyer should be able to see through them.

Finally, a potential buyer should walk away from a deal—no matter how good it may appear on the surface—if the present owner refuses to disclose his company's financial records.

Buying an existing business is a process filled with potential missteps along the way. The expression "Let the buyer beware" should govern your thoughts and actions throughout the entire process. However, by following the foregoing procedure, a buyer can dramatically lower the probability of getting "burned" with a business that does not suit her personality or one that is on the verge of failure. Figure 5.1 illustrates the sequence of events leading up to a successful negotiation with a seller.

4. Describe the various techniques for determining the value of a business.

METHODS FOR DETERMINING THE VALUE OF A BUSINESS

Business valuation is partly an art and partly a science. Part of what makes establishing a reasonable price for a privately held business so difficult is the wide variety of factors that influence its value: the nature of the business itself, its position in the market or industry, the outlook for the market or industry, the company's financial status, its earning capacity, any intangible assets it may own (e.g., patents, trademarks, or copyrights), the value of other similar publicly held companies, and many other factors.

Computing the value of the company's tangible assets normally poses no major problem, but assigning a price to the intangibles, such as goodwill, almost always creates controversy. The seller expects goodwill to reflect the hard work and long hours invested in building the business. The buyer, however, is willing to pay extra only for those intangible assets that produce exceptional income. So how can the buyer and the seller arrive at a fair price? There are few hard-and-fast rules in establishing the value of a business, but the following guidelines are helpful:

YOU BE THE CONSULTANT . . .

Escaping a High-Tech World for a Low-Tech One

Mike and Nancy Lusby knew that it was time for a change in their lives. Mike, the director of operations for a high-tech company in Silicon Valley, had just learned that his $70,000 a year job was being eliminated. Nancy was the manager of the finance department at a high-tech lab in Silicon Valley, and, although she enjoyed her work, she had grown weary of office politics and the three-hour round-trip commutes to work and back. The Lusbys decided that it was time to realize their dream of becoming entrepreneurs.

Rather than start their own company from scratch, however, the Lusbys wanted to buy a business. They knew that they did not want to own a high-tech company and that they did want a business that included living quarters. The couple spent a considerable amount of time scouring advertisements for businesses in magazines and newspapers, ultimately narrowing their choices to three: hardware stores, bed-and-breakfast inns, and general stores. "I've always loved hardware stores," says Mike, "but they don't usually come with a place to live. B&Bs provide you housing, but you're on call 24 hours a day." The couple decided to focus on general stores.

Mike contacted a dozen general stores and visited them but ultimately rejected them all because they were either "boring" or they were too far from good schools for the couple's young daughters. The prospects of finding a suitable general store were fading. "We were down to our last $1,000 in my severance pay, and I spent it on a plane ticket to fly to New Hampshire," Mike says. There he visited the Brick Store, which is listed on the Interior Department's National Register of Historic Places as the oldest continuously operated general store in the United States. Mike immediately recognized the Brick Store's drawing power and marketing potential; he also fell in love with the business, which was started in 1790. The brick building that houses the store today was built in 1804 after a fire destroyed the original location. The two-story, Federal-style building came complete with large white columns and an inviting porch. Its old-world charm was hard for the Lusbys—and for customers—to resist. Plus, there was plenty of room upstairs for the family to live. The Ammonoosuc River flowed by just beyond the Brick Store, and the town of Bath was filled with picturesque, calendar-like scenes of New England. Nearby was the longest covered bridge in New Hampshire.

The Lusbys were ready to buy the Brick Store. The current owner's asking price was $390,000 but he accepted the Lusbys offer of $300,000. The Lusbys took much of their savings and a gift from Nancy's parents to make a down payment of $140,000 and borrowed the balance from a local bank. Although their previous business experience came in handy when they set up a mail-order business to keep revenue coming in during the off-season (January through April), the Lusbys knew they had a lot to learn about retailing. Product lines run into the hundreds—from pocketknives and jellies to weathervanes and worms—all with profit margins as varied as the products themselves. They discovered that the store's tourist traffic arrives in May, swells throughout the summer, and blossoms in September and October. In fact, the Brick House brings in 40 percent of its annual sales in just six weeks during September and October. After that, business slows to a trickle. Fortunately for the Lusbys, three long-time employees agreed to stay on and taught the New England newcomers the daily details of running the store.

After the Lusbys took over the Brick Store, they discovered several problems that caused them so much concern that they actually returned to California for a brief time. They learned that in the future, a new highway will divert approximately 20 percent of the store's traffic. In addition, the Lusbys' early experience in the store did not measure up to the expectations that the previous owner's rather spotty financial records had created. Fortunately, the business broker, whom the Lusbys did not know before buying the store, became a friend and was able to show them that the store could generate enough profits to support itself and them. The Lusbys also discovered how much they enjoyed their new lifestyle and location. "One winter day, [we] sat down and figured out how much we'd have to earn at other jobs to support this kind of life," says Mike. "It came to $75,000 a year." The Lusbys not only are making a comfortable living running the Brick Store, but their commute to work is now much shorter. A short stroll down the steps from the living quarters puts them at work in a beautiful, 200-year-old general store with a tremendous sense of history.

1. Suppose that the Lusbys came to you for advice on buying the Brick Store. What would you have told them?
2. Should the Lusbys have done anything differently in their quest to buy a business? Explain.

Source: Adapted from Lee Smith, "From High Tech . . . to Low Tech," *Fortune*, November 9, 1998, pp. 228[A]–228[D].

FIGURE 5.1
The Acquisition Process

Sources: Adapted from Buying and Selling: A Company Handbook, *PriceWaterhouse, (New York: 1993) pp. 38–42;* *Charles F. Claeys, "The Intent to Buy,"* Small Business Reports, *May 1994, pp. 44–47.*

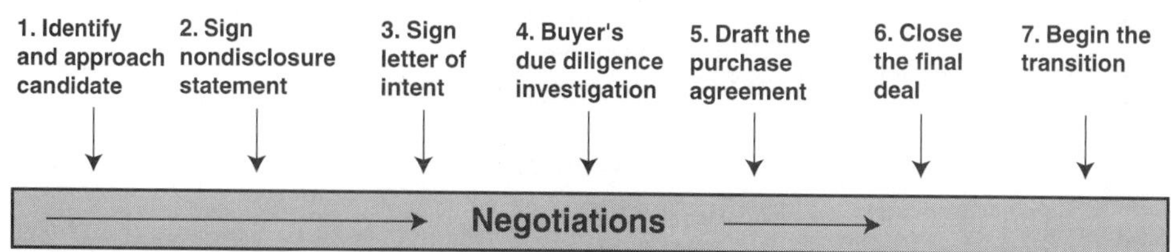

1. *Approach the candidate.* If a business is advertised for sale, the proper approach is through the channel defined in the ad. Sometimes buyers will contact business brokers to help them locate potential target companies. If you have targeted a company in the "hidden market," an introduction from a banker, accountant, or lawyer often is the best approach. During this phase, the seller checks out the buyer's qualifications, and the buyer begins to judge the quality of the company.
2. *Sign a nondisclosure document.* If the buyer and the seller are satisfied with the results of their preliminary research, they are ready to begin serious negotiations. Throughout the negotiation process, the seller expects the buyer to maintain strict confidentiality of all the records, documents, and information he or she receives during the investigation and negotiation process. The nondisclosure document is a legally binding contract that ensures the secrecy of the parties' negotiations.
3. *Sign a letter of intent.* Before a buyer makes a legal offer to buy the company, he or she typically will ask the seller to sign a letter of intent. The letter of intent is a nonbinding document that says that the buyer and the seller have reached a sufficient "meeting of the minds" to justify the time and expense of negotiating a final agreement. The letter should state clearly that it is nonbinding, giving either party the right to walk away from the deal. It should also contain a clause calling for "good faith negotiations" between the parties. A typical letter of intent addresses terms such as price, payment, categories of assets to be sold, and a deadline for closing the final deal.
4. *Buyer's due diligence.* While negotiations are continuing, the buyer is busy studying the business and evaluating its strengths and weaknesses. In short, the buyer must "do his or her homework" to make sure that the business is a good value.
5. *Draft the purchase agreement.* The purchase agreement spells out the parties' final deal. It sets forth all of the details of the agreement and is the final product of the negotiation process.
6. *Close the final deal.* Once the parties have drafted the purchase agreement, all that remains to making the deal official is the closing. Both buyer and seller sign the necessary documents to make the sale final. The buyer delivers the required money, and the seller turns the company over to the buyer.
7. *Begin the transition.* For the buyer, the *real* challenge now begins: making the transition to a successful business owner!

- There is no single best method for determining a business's worth since each business sale is different. The wisest approach is to compute a company's value using several techniques and then to choose the one that makes the most sense.
- The deal must be financially feasible for both parties. The seller must be satisfied with the price received for the business, but the buyer cannot pay an excessively high price.
- Both the buyer and the seller should have access to the business records.
- Valuations should be based on facts, not fiction.
- No surprise is the best surprise. Both parties should deal with one another honestly and in good faith.[11]

The main reason that buyers purchase existing businesses is to get their future earning potential. The second most common reason is to obtain an established asset base; it is much easier to buy assets than to build them. Although evaluation methods should take these characteristics into consideration, too many business sellers and buyers depend on rules of thumb that ignore the unique features of small companies. Often these rules of thumb are based on multiples of a company's net earnings or sales and vary by industry.

For instance, computer service companies are valued at 25 times their earnings; restaurants at 15 times earnings; and travel agencies at .05 to .10 times annual sales.[12] One recent study of small business sales across the United States conducted by Bizcomps found the average sale price was 2.7 times a company's earnings.[13] The problem is that such "one-size-fits-all" approaches seldom work because no two businesses are alike. The best rule of thumb to use when valuing businesses is "Don't use rules of thumb to value businesses." One expert warns, "Businesses are as unique and complex as the people who run them and are not capable of being valued by a simplistic rule of thumb."[14]

The next section describes three basic techniques and several variations on them for determining the value of a hypothetical business, Lewis Electronics.

Basic Balance Sheet Methods: Net Worth = Assets – Liabilities

balance sheet technique—*a method of valuing a business based on the value of the company's net worth (net worth = total assets – total liabilities).*

BALANCE SHEET TECHNIQUE. The **balance sheet technique** is one of the most commonly used methods of evaluating a business, although it is not highly recommended because it oversimplifies the valuation process. This method computes the company's net worth or owner's equity (net worth = total assets – total liabilities) and uses this figure as the value. The problem with this technique is that it fails to recognize reality: Most small businesses have market values that exceed their reported book values.

The first step is to determine which assets are included in the sale. In most cases, the owner has some personal assets that he does not want to sell. Professional business brokers can help the buyer and the seller arrive at a reasonable value for the collection of assets included in the deal. Remember that net worth on a financial statement will likely differ significantly from actual net worth in the market. Figure 5.2 shows the balance sheet for Lewis Electronics. Based on this balance sheet, the company's net worth is \$266,091 – \$114,325 = \$151,766.

adjusted balance sheet technique—*a method of valuing a business based on the market value of the company's net worth (net worth = total assets – total liabilities).*

VARIATION: ADJUSTED BALANCE SHEET TECHNIQUE. A more realistic method for determining a company's value is to adjust the book value of net worth to reflect *actual* market value. The values reported on a company's books may either overstate or understate the true value of assets and liabilities. Typical assets in a business sale include notes and accounts receivable, inventories, supplies, and fixtures. If a buyer purchases notes and accounts receivable, he should estimate the likelihood of their collection and adjust their value accordingly (refer to Table 5.1).

In manufacturing, wholesale, and retail businesses, inventory is usually the largest single asset in the sale. Taking a physical inventory count is the best way to determine accurately the quantity of goods to be transferred. The sale may include three types of inventory, each having its own method of valuation: raw materials, work-in-process, and finished goods. The buyer and the seller must arrive at a method for evaluating the inventory. First-in, first-out (FIFO), last-in, first-out (LIFO), and average costing are three frequently used techniques, but the most common methods use the cost of last purchase and the replacement value of the inventory. Before accepting any inventory value, the buyer should evaluate the condition of the goods.

Example

One young couple purchased a lumber yard without sufficiently examining the inventory. After completing the sale, they discovered that most of the lumber in a warehouse they had neglected to inspect was warped and was of little value as building material. The bargain price they paid for the business turned out not to be the good deal they had expected.

To avoid such problems, some buyers insist on having a knowledgeable representative on an inventory team to count the inventory and check its condition. Nearly every sale involves merchandise that cannot be sold, but by taking this precaution, a buyer minimizes the chance of being stuck with worthless inventory. Fixed assets transferred in a sale might include land, buildings, equipment, and fixtures. Business owners frequently carry real

FIGURE 5.2
Balance Sheet for Lewis Electronics

Lewis Electronics
Balance Sheet
June 30, 200x

Assets			
Current Assets:			
Cash		$11,655	
Accounts Receivable		15,876	
Inventory		56,523	
Supplies		8,574	
Prepaid Insurance		5,587	
Total Current Assets			$ 98,215
Fixed Assets:			
Land		$24,000	
Buildings	$141,000		
less accumulated depreciation	51,500	89,500	
Office Equipment	$ 12,760		
less accumulated depreciation	7,159	5,601	
Factory Equipment	$ 59,085		
less accumulated depreciation	27,850	31,235	
Trucks and Autos	$ 28,730		
less accumulated depreciation	11,190	17,540	
Total Fixed Assets			$167,876
Total Assets			$266,091
Liabilities			
Current Liabilities:			
Accounts Payable		$19,497	
Mortgage Payable (current portion)		5,215	
Salaries Payable		3,671	
Note Payable		10,000	
Total Current Liabilities			$ 38,383
Long-Term Liabilities:			
Mortgage Payable		$54,542	
Note Payable		21,400	
Total Long-Term Liabilities			$ 75,942
Total Liabilities			$114,325
Owners' Equity			
Owners' Equity			$151,766
Total Liabilities and Owners' Equity			$266,091

estate and buildings at prices well below their actual market value. Equipment and fixtures, depending on their condition and usefulness, may increase or decrease the true value of the business. Appraisals of these assets on insurance policies are helpful guidelines for establishing market value. Also, business brokers can be useful in determining the current market value of fixed assets. Some brokers use an estimate of what it would cost to replace a company's physical assets (less a reasonable allowance for depreciation) to determine value. For Lewis Electronics, the adjusted net worth is $274,638 – $114,325 = $160,313 (see the adjusted balance sheet in Figure 5.3), indicating that some of the entries in its books did not accurately reflect true market value.

Business evaluations based on balance sheet methods suffer one major drawback: They do not consider the future earning potential of the business. These techniques

FIGURE 5.3
Balance Sheet for Lewis Electronics Adjusted to Reflect Market Value

Adjusted Balance Sheet
June 30, 200x

Assets			
Current Assets:			
Cash		$ 11,655	
Accounts Receivable		10,051	
Inventory		39,261	
Supplies		7,492	
Prepaid Insurance		5,587	
Total Current Assets			$ 74,046
Fixed Assets:			
Land		$ 39,900	
Buildings	$177,000		
less accumulated depreciation	51,500	125,500	
Office Equipment	$ 11,645		
less accumulated depreciation	7,159	4,486	
Factory Equipment	$ 50,196		
less accumulated depreciation	27,850	22,346	
Trucks and Autos	$ 22,550		
less accumulated depreciation	11,190	11,360	
Total Fixed Assets			$200,592
Total Assets			$274,638
Liabilities			
Current Liabilities:			
Accounts Payable		$ 19,497	
Mortgage Payable (current portion)		5,215	
Salaries Payable		3,671	
Note Payable		10,000	
Total Current Liabilities			$ 38,383
Long-Term Liabilities:			
Mortgage Payable		$ 54,542	
Note Payable		21,400	
Total Long-Term Liabilities			$ 75,942
Total Liabilities			$114,325
Owners' Equity			
Owners' Equity			$160,313
Total Liabilities and Owners' Equity			$274,638

value assets at current prices and do not consider them as tools for creating future profits. The next method for computing the value of a business is based on its expected future earnings.

EARNINGS APPROACH. The buyer of an existing business is essentially purchasing its future income. The **earnings approach** focuses on the future income potential of a business and assumes that a company's value depends on its ability to generate consistent profits over time. There are three variations of the earnings approach.

earnings approach—*a method of valuing a business that recognizes that a buyer is purchasing the future income (earnings) potential of a business.*

Variation 1: Excess Earnings Method. This method combines both the value of a business's existing assets (minus its liabilities) and an estimate of its future earnings potential

goodwill—*an intangible asset that reflects the value of a company's reputation, its established customer and supplier contacts, name recognition, and other factors.*

to determine its selling price. One advantage of this technique is that it offers an estimate of goodwill. **Goodwill** is an intangible asset that often creates problems in a business sale. In fact, the most common method of valuing a business is to compute its tangible net worth and then to add an often arbitrary adjustment for goodwill. In essence, goodwill is the difference between an established, successful business and one that has yet to prove itself. It is based on the company's reputation and its ability to attract customers. A buyer should not accept blindly the seller's arbitrary adjustment for goodwill because it is likely to be inflated. The *real* value of a company's goodwill lies in its financial value to the buyer, not in its emotional value to the seller.

The excess earnings method provides a consistent and realistic approach for determining the value of goodwill. It measures goodwill by the amount of profit the business earns above that of the average firm in the same industry. It also assumes that the owner is entitled to a reasonable return on the firm's adjusted tangible net worth.

Step 1: Compute adjusted tangible net worth. Using the adjusted balance sheet method of valuation, the buyer should compute the firm's adjusted tangible net worth. Total tangible assets (adjusted for market value) minus total liabilities yields adjusted tangible net worth. In the Lewis Electronics example, adjusted tangible net worth is \$274,638 – \$114,325 = \$160,313 (refer to Figure 5.3).

opportunity cost—*the cost of the next best alternative choice; the cost of giving up one alternative to get another.*

Step 2: Calculate the opportunity costs of investing in the business. **Opportunity cost** represents the cost of forgoing a choice. If a buyer chooses to purchase the assets of a business, he cannot invest his money elsewhere. Therefore, the opportunity cost of the purchase would be the amount that the buyer could earn by investing the same amount *in a similar risk investment.*

There are three components in the rate of return used to value a business: (1) the basic, risk-free return, (2) an inflation premium, and (3) the risk allowance for investing in the particular business. The basic, risk-free return and the inflation premium are reflected in investments such as U.S. treasury bonds. To determine the appropriate rate of return for investing in a business, the buyer must add to this base rate a factor reflecting the risk of purchasing the company. The greater the risk is, the higher the rate of return will be. A normal-risk business typically indicates a 25 percent rate of return. In the Lewis Electronics example, the opportunity cost of the investment is \$160,313 × 25% = \$40,078.

The second part of the buyer's opportunity cost is the salary that she could earn working for someone else. For the Lewis Electronics example, if the buyer purchases the business, she must forgo the \$25,000 salary that she could earn working elsewhere. Adding these amounts together yields a total opportunity cost of \$65,078.

Step 3: Project net earnings. The buyer must estimate the company's net earnings for the upcoming year before subtracting the owner's salary. Averages can be misleading, so the buyer must be sure to investigate the trend of net earnings. Have they risen steadily over the past five years, dropped significantly, remained relatively constant, or fluctuated wildly? Past income statements provide useful guidelines for estimating earnings. In the Lewis Electronics example, the buyer and his accountant project net earnings for the upcoming year to be \$74,000.

Step 4: Compute extra earning power. A company's extra earning power is the difference between forecasted earnings (step 3) and total opportunity costs (step 2). Many small businesses that are for sale do not have extra earning power (i.e., excess earnings), and they show marginal or no profits. The extra earning power of Lewis Electronics is \$74,000 – \$65,000 = \$8,922.

Step 5: Estimate the value of intangibles. The owner can use the extra earning power of the business to estimate the value of its intangible assets—that is, its goodwill. Multiplying the extra earning power by a years-of-profit figure yields an estimate of the intangible assets' value. The years-of-profit figure for a normal-risk business ranges from 3 to 4. A very high-risk business may have a years-of-profit figure of 1, whereas a well-established firm might use a figure of 7. For Lewis Electronics, the value of intangibles (assuming normal risk) would be $\$8{,}922 \times 3 = \$26{,}766$.

Step 6: Determine the value of the business. To determine the value of the business, the buyer simply adds together the adjusted tangible net worth (step 1) and the value of the intangibles (step 5). Using this method, the value of Lewis Electronics is $\$160{,}313 + \$26{,}766 = \$187{,}079$.

Both the buyer and seller should consider the tax implications of transferring goodwill. The amount that the seller receives for goodwill is taxed as ordinary income. The buyer cannot count this amount as a deduction because goodwill is a capital asset that cannot be depreciated or amortized for tax purposes. Instead, the buyer would be better off paying the seller for signing a covenant not to compete because its value is fully tax deductible. The success of this approach depends on the accuracy of the buyer's estimates of net earnings and risk, but it does offer a systematic method for assigning a value to goodwill.

Variation 2: Capitalized Earnings Approach. Another earnings approach capitalizes expected net earnings to determine the value of a business. The buyer should prepare his own pro forma income statement and should ask the seller to prepare one also. Many appraisers use a five-year weighted average of past sales (with the greatest weights assigned to the most recent years) to estimate sales for the upcoming year.

Once again, the buyer must evaluate the risk of purchasing the business to determine the appropriate rate of return on the investment. The greater the perceived risk, the higher the return that the buyer requires. Risk determination is always somewhat subjective, but it is necessary for proper evaluation.

capitalized earnings approach—*a method of valuing a business that divides estimated earnings by the rate of return the buyer could earn on a similar risk investment.*

The **capitalized earnings approach** divides estimated net earnings (*after* subtracting the owner's reasonable salary) by the rate of return that reflects the risk level. For Lewis Electronics, the capitalized value (assuming a reasonable salary of $25,000) is:

$$\frac{\text{Net earnings (after deducting owner's salary)}}{\text{Rate of return}} = \frac{\$74{,}000 - \$25{,}000}{25\%} = \$196{,}000$$

Clearly, firms with lower risk factors are more valuable (a 10 percent rate of return would yield a value of $499,000 for Lewis Electronics) than are those with higher risk factors (a 50 percent rate of return would yield a value of $99,800). Most normal-risk businesses use a rate-of-return factor ranging from 25 to 30 percent. The lowest risk factor that most buyers would accept for any business ranges from 15 to 20 percent.

Variation 3: Discounted Future Earnings Approach. This variation of the earnings approach assumes that a dollar earned in the future is worth less than that same dollar today. Therefore, using this approach, the buyer estimates the company's net income for several years into the future and then discounts these future earnings back to their present value. The resulting present value is an estimate of the company's worth.

The reduced value of future dollars represents the cost of the buyer's giving up the opportunity to earn a reasonable rate of return by receiving income in the future instead of today, a concept known as the time value of money. To illustrate the importance of the time value of money, consider two $1 million sweepstakes winners. Rob wins $1 million in a sweepstakes, but he receives it in $50,000 installments over 20 years. If Rob invested every installment at 15 percent interest, he would have accumulated $5,890,505.98 at the end of 20 years. Lisa wins $1 million in another sweepstakes, but she collects her winnings in one lump sum. If Lisa invested her $1 million today at 15 percent, she would have accumulated $16,366,537.39 at the end of 20 years. The difference in their wealth is the result of the time value of money.

discounted future earnings approach—*a method of valuing a business that forecasts a company's earnings several years into the future and then discounts them back to their present value.*

The **discounted future earnings approach** has five steps:

Step 1: Project future earnings for five years into the future. One way is to assume that earnings will grow by a constant amount over the next five years. Perhaps a better method is to develop three forecasts—an optimistic, a pessimistic, and a most likely—for each year and then find a weighted average using the following formula:

$$\text{Forecasted earnings for year } i = \frac{(\text{Optimistic earnings for year } i) + (\text{Most likely forecast for year } i \times 4) + (\text{Pessimistic forecast for year } i)}{6}$$

For Lewis Electronics, the buyer's forecasts are:

Year	Pessimistic	Most Likely	Optimistic	Weighted Average
XXX1	65,000	74,000	92,000	75,500
XXX2	74,000	90,000	101,000	89,167
XXX3	82,000	100,000	112,000	99,000
XXX4	88,000	109,000	120,000	107,333
XXX5	88,000	115,000	122,000	111,667

Buyers must remember that the farther into the future they forecast, the less reliable their estimates will be.

Step 2: Discount these future earnings at the appropriate present value rate. The rate that the buyer selects should reflect the rate he could earn on a similar risk investment. Because Lewis Electronics is a normal-risk business, the buyer chooses a present value rate of 25 percent.

Year	Income Forecast (Weighted Average)	Present Value Factor (at 25%)[a]	Net Present Value
XXX1	75,500	.8000	60,400
XXX2	89,167	.6400	57,067
XXX3	99,000	.5120	50,688
XXX4	107,333	.4096	43,964
XXX5	111,667	.3277	36,593
Total			248,712

$$\text{Present value factor} = \frac{1}{(1+k)^{\pm}}$$

where k = rate of return

t = year ($t = 1, 2, 3 \ldots, n$)

[a] The appropriate present value factor can be found by looking in published present value tables, by using modern calculators or computers, or by solving this formula:

Step 3: Estimate the income stream beyond five years. One technique suggests multiplying the fifth-year income by 1/rate of return. For Lewis Electronics, the estimate is:

$$\text{Income beyond year 5} = \$111{,}667 \times \frac{1}{25\%} = \$446{,}668$$

Step 4: Discount the income estimate beyond five years using the present value factor for the sixth year. For Lewis Electronics:

Present value of income beyond year 5 = $446,668 × 0.2622 = $117,116

Step 5: Compute the total value of the business. Add the present value of the company's estimated earnings for years 1 through 5 (step 2) and the present value of its earnings from years 6 on (step 4):

Total value = $248,712 + $117,116 = $365,828

The primary advantage of this technique is that it evaluates a business solely on the basis of its future earning potential, but its reliability depends on making forecasts of future earnings and on choosing a realistic present value rate. In other words, a company's present value is tied to its future performance, which is not always easy to project. The discounted cash flow technique is especially well suited for valuing service businesses (whose asset bases are often very thin) and for companies experiencing high growth rates.

MARKET APPROACH. The **market** (or price-earnings) **approach** uses the price/earnings ratios of similar businesses to establish the value of a company. The buyer must use businesses whose stocks are publicly traded in order to get a meaningful comparison. A company's price/earnings ratio (or P/E ratio) is the price of one share of its common stock in the market divided by its earnings per share (after deducting preferred stock dividends). To get a representative P/E ratio, the buyer should average the P/E ratios of as many similar businesses as possible.

market approach—*a method of valuing a business that uses the price-earnings (P/E) ratio of similar, publicly held companies to determine value.*

To compute the company's value, the buyer multiplies the average price/earnings ratio by the private company's estimated earnings. For example, suppose that the buyer found four companies comparable to Lewis Electronics but whose stock is publicly traded. Their price/earnings ratios are:

Company 1	3.3
Company 2	3.8
Company 3	4.7
Company 4	4.1
Average P/E ratio	3.975

Using this average P/E ratio produces a value of $294,150:

Value = Average P/E ratio × Estimated net earnings = 3.975 × $74,000 = $294,150

The biggest advantage of the market approach is its simplicity. But this method does have several disadvantages, including the following:

Necessary comparisons between publicly traded and privately owned companies. Because the stock of privately owned companies is illiquid, the P/E ratio used is often subjective and lower than that of publicly held companies.

Unrepresentative earnings estimates. The private company's net earnings may not realistically reflect its true earning potential. To minimize taxes, owners usually attempt to keep profits low and rely on fringe benefits to make up the difference.

Finding similar companies for comparison. Often it is extremely difficult for a buyer to find comparable publicly held companies when estimating the appropriate P/E ratio.

Applying the after-tax earnings of a private company to determine its value. If a prospective buyer is using an after-tax P/E ratio from a public company, he also must use the after-tax earnings from the private company.

Despite its drawbacks, the market approach is useful as a general guideline to establishing a company's value.

Which of these methods is best for determining the value of a small business? Simply stated, there is no single best method. Valuing a business is partly an art and partly a science. Using these techniques, a range of values will emerge. Buyers should look for values that might cluster together and then use their best judgment to determine their offering price. Table 5.4 summarizes the valuation techniques covered in this chapter.

5. Understand the seller's side of the buyout decision and how to structure the deal.

UNDERSTANDING THE SELLER'S SIDE

Few events are more anticipated—and more emotional—for entrepreneurs than selling a business. It often produces vast personal wealth and a completely new lifestyle, and this newly gained wealth offers freedom and the opportunity to catch up on all the things the owners missed out on while building the business. Yet, many entrepreneurs who sell out experience a tremendous void in their lives. One entrepreneur who sold out regretfully explains, "I never realized the role of my business in my life. More than the focal point of my life, it was my very identity."[15]

Selling a business is no simple task. Done properly, it takes time, patience, and preparation to locate a suitable buyer, strike a deal, and make the transition. Too often, business owners put off the selling process until the last minute—at retirement age or when a business crisis looms. One entrepreneur who sold his business says, "Entrepreneurs always think their businesses will be worth more later on. Mistakenly, they hold on [until] it's too late. Know when to walk away, and don't get greedy."[16] Such a "fire sale" approach rarely yields the maximum price for a business. Advance planning and maintaining accurate financial records are keys to a successful sale.

Selling a small, privately owned business is more difficult than it appears. Only about 25 percent to 33 percent of small companies that are up for sale actually get sold, and if the economy is in poor condition, that percentage drops even farther.[17] The reality of the market for businesses is that when many entrepreneurs are ready to sell their companies, they cannot find a qualified buyer! One reason many owners have so much trouble selling their businesses is that they believe their companies are worth much more than they really are. Because they have sacrificed so much and worked so hard to build their businesses, owners naturally think their companies are worth a fortune and set their asking prices accordingly. Sellers must remember that the price they set and the purchase terms they expect must allow the buyer to handle them comfortably and continue to generate a profit.

Before selling her business, an entrepreneur must ask herself some important questions: Do you want to walk away from the business completely, or do you plan to stay on after the sale? If you decide to stay on, how involved do you want to be in running the company? How much can you realistically expect to get for the business? Is this amount of money sufficient to maintain your desired lifestyle? Rather than sell the business to an outsider, should you be transferring ownership to your kids or to your employees? Who are the professionals—business brokers, accountants, attorneys, tax advisers—you will need to help you close the sale successfully? How do you expect the buyer to pay for the company? Are you willing to finance at least some of the purchase price?

Structuring the Deal

Next to picking the right buyer, planning the structure of the deal is one of the most important decisions a seller can make. Entrepreneurs who sell their companies without considering the tax implications of the deal can wind up paying the IRS as much as 70 percent of the proceeds in the form of capital gains and other taxes![18] A skilled tax adviser or finan-

TABLE 5.4

What's It Worth? A Summary of Business Valuation Techniques

Balance Sheet Technique

Book value of net worth = Total assets – Total liabilities
= $266,091 – $114,325 = $151,766

Variation: Adjusted Balance Sheet Technique

Net worth adjusted to reflect market value = $274,638 – $114,325 = $160,313

Earnings Approach

Variation 1: Excess Earnings Method

Step 1: Adjusted tangible net worth = $274,638 – $114,325 = $160,313

Step 2: Opportunity costs = Opportunity cost of investing + Salary forgone
= $160,313 × 25% + $25,000 = $65,078

Step 3: Estimated net earnings = $74,000

Step 4: Extra earning power = Estimated net earnings – Total opportunity costs
= $74,000 – $65,078
= $8,922

Step 5: Value of intangibles (goodwill) = Extra earning power × Years-of-profit figure
= $8,922 × 3
= $26,766

Step 6: Value of business = Tangible net worth + Value of intangibles
= $160,313 + 26,766
= $187,079

Variation 2: Capitalized Earnings Approach

$$\text{Value} = \frac{\text{Net earnings (after deducting owner's salary)}}{\text{Rate of return on a similar risk investment}}$$

$$= \frac{\$74{,}000 - \$25{,}000}{25\%} = \$196{,}000$$

Variation 3: Discounted Future Earnings Approach

Step 1: Project future earnings.

Year	Pessimistic	Most Likely	Optimistic	Weighted Average*
XXX1	$65,000	$ 74,000	$ 94,000	$ 75,500
XXX2	74,000	90,000	101,000	89,167
XXX3	82,000	100,000	112,000	99,000
XXX4	88,000	109,000	120,000	107,333
XXX5	88,000	115,000	122,000	111,667

*Weighted average = $\frac{P + 4 \times ML + O}{6}$

Step 2: Discount future earnings using the appropriate present value factor.

Year	Forecasted Earnings	Present Value Factor	Net Present Value
XXX1	$ 75,500	.8000	$ 60,400
XXX2	89,167	.6400	57,067
XXX3	99,000	.5120	50,688
XXX4	107,333	.4096	43,964
XXX5	111,667	.3277	36,593
Total			$248,712

Step 3: Estimate income stream beyond five years.

$$\text{Income stream} = \text{Fifth-year forecasted income} \times \frac{1}{\text{Rate of return}}$$

$$= \$111{,}667 \times \frac{1}{25\%}$$

$$= \$446{,}668$$

Step 4: Discount income stream beyond five years (using sixth-year present value factor).

Present value of income stream = $446,668 × .2622 = $117,116

Step 5: Compute total value.

Total value = $248,712 + $117,116 = $365,828

Market Approach

Value = Estimated earnings × Average price/earnings ratio of representative companies
= $74,000 × 3.975 = $294,150

Which value is correct? Remember: There is no best method of valuing a business. These techniques provide only estimates of a company's worth. The particular method used depends on the unique qualities of the business and the special circumstances surrounding the sale.

cial planner can help business sellers legally minimize the bite various taxes take out of the proceeds of the sale.

Exit Strategy Options

STRAIGHT BUSINESS SALE. A straight business sale may be best for those entrepreneurs who want to step down and turn over the reins of the company to someone else.

Short Stack Inc.

For instance, Richie Stachowski recently sold his toy company, Short Stack, to Wild Planet Toys of San Francisco because the business had grown so rapidly that Richie wanted more time to focus on other activities. The success of his three-year-old company, which sold worldwide more than 1 million water toys such as the Water Talkie (a device that allows swimmers to communicate underwater) and the Bin-Aqua-Lar (underwater binoculars), had won Richie several national awards and an appearance on The Late Show Starring David Letterman. *But he wanted time to pursue more normal activities—those suited for a 13-year-old boy! (Richie started Short Stack when he was just 10.) The sale of the company to Wild Planet Toys will net Richie an estimated $1 million per year for the next several years.*[19]

One study of small business sales in 60 different categories found that 94 percent were asset sales; the remaining 6 percent involved the sale of stock. About 22 percent were for cash, and 75 percent included a down payment with a note carried by the seller. The remaining 3 percent relied on a note from the seller with no down payment. When the deal included a down payment, it averaged 33 percent of the purchase price. Only 40 percent of the business sales studied included covenants not to compete.[20]

Although selling a business outright is often the safest exit path for an entrepreneur, it usually is the most expensive one. Sellers who cash out and take the money "up front" face an oppressive tax burden. They must pay a 28 percent capital gains tax on the sale price less their investments in the company. Neither is a straight sale an attractive exit strategy for those who want to stay on with the company or for those who want to surrender control of the company gradually rather than all at once.

FORM A FAMILY LIMITED PARTNERSHIP. An entrepreneur could transfer her business to her children but still maintain control over it by forming a family limited partnership. The entrepreneur would take the role of the general partner with the children becoming limited partners in the business. The general partner keeps just 1 percent of the company, but the partnership agreement gives her total control over the business. The children own 99 percent of the company but have little or no say over how to run the business. Until the founder decides to step down and turn over the reins of the company to the next generation, she continues to run the business and sets up significant tax savings for the ultimate transfer of power.

SELL A CONTROLLING INTEREST. Sometimes business owners sell the majority interest in their companies to investors, competitors, suppliers, or large companies with an agreement that they will stay on after the sale as managers or consultants.

Cosmic Pet Products

For instance, Leon and Pam Seidman sold 55 percent of Cosmic Pet Products, a catnip business Leon started while in college, to Four Paws Pet Products, a much larger company. Four Paws gives the Seidmans the autonomy to run the business as they did before the sale, although the Seidmans do work with Four Paws on strategic planning and pricing issues. For both the Seidmans and Four Paws, the sale has produced positive outcomes. The Seidmans still get to run the day-to-day operations of the business they love without having to worry about the financial struggles of keeping a small company going. With the Seidmans' help, Four Paws has improved Cosmic Pet Products' distribution and pricing and built it into the largest catnip company in the country, commanding 60 percent of the market![21]

RESTRUCTURE THE COMPANY. Another way for business owners to cash out gradually is to replace the existing corporation with a new one, formed with other investors. The owner essentially is performing a leveraged buyout of his own company. For example, assume that you own a company worth $15 million. You form a new corporation with $12 million borrowed from a bank and $3 million in equity: $1.5 million of your own equity and $1.5 million in equity from an investor who wants you to stay on with the business. The new company buys your company for $15 million. You net $13.5 in cash ($15 million – your $1.5 million equity investment) and still own 50 percent of the new leveraged business (see Figure 5.4).[22]

SELL TO AN INTERNATIONAL BUYER. In an increasingly global marketplace, small U.S. businesses have become attractive buyout targets for foreign companies. Foreign buyers—mostly European—buy more than 1,000 U.S. businesses each year. Despite the publicity that Japanese buyouts get, England leads the list of nations acquiring U.S. companies. Small business owners are receptive to international offers. According to one survey of entrepreneurs considering selling their businesses, 69 percent said they would sell to a foreign investor.[23]

In most instances, foreign companies buy U.S. businesses to gain access to a lucrative, growing market. They look for a team of capable managers, whom they typically retain for a given time period. They also want companies that are profitable, stable, and growing.

Selling to foreign buyers can have disadvantages, however. They typically purchase 100 percent of a company, thereby making the previous owner merely an employee. Relationships with foreign owners also can be difficult to manage. In a recent survey, executives at foreign-owned small businesses stated that they don't understand what drives their bosses and that their relationships generally worsen over time.[24]

USE A TWO-STEP SALE. For owners wanting the security of a sales contract now but not wanting to step down from the company's helm for several years, a two-step sale may be ideal. The buyer purchases the business in two phases—getting 20 to 70 percent today and agreeing to buy the remainder within a specific time period. Until the final transaction takes place, the entrepreneur retains at least partial control of the company.

ESTABLISH AN EMPLOYEE STOCK OWNERSHIP PLAN (ESOP). Some owners cash out by selling to their employees through an **employee stock ownership plan (ESOP).** An ESOP is a form of employee benefit plan in which a trust created for employees purchases their employer's stock. Here's how an ESOP works: The company transfers shares of its stock to the ESOP trust, and the trust uses the stock as collateral to borrow enough money to purchase the shares from the company. The company guarantees payment of the loan principal and interest and makes tax-deductible contributions to the trust to repay the loan (see Figure 5.5). The company then distributes the stock to employees' accounts based on a predetermined formula. In addition to the tax benefits an ESOP offers,

employee stock ownership plan (ESOP)—*an employee benefit plan in which a trust created for employees purchases stock in their employer's company.*

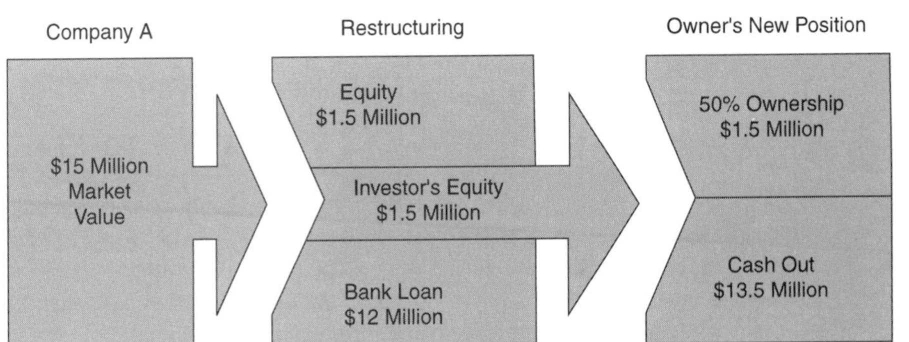

FIGURE 5.4
Restructuring a Business for Sale

Source: Peter Collins, "Cashing Out and Maintaining Control," Small Business Reports, December 1989, p. 28.

YOU BE THE CONSULTANT . . .

A Seller's Tale

Joseph Grassadonia loves the ocean so much that he planned his life around it, including starting businesses that would allow him to have both the time and the money to enjoy the sun and surf of California's beaches. Over the years, Grassadonia launched six magazines, including his most recent, *Dive Travel.* He compares the thrill and challenge of starting and managing a magazine to surfing and catching the ultimate wave. "When you're surfing and you're totally in control of the wave, and the equipment is right and everything is working, it's exhilarating," he says. After five years of running *Dive Travel,* however, Grassadonia says he got to the point where it wasn't fun anymore. "That's when I knew I had to sell," he recalls.

Actually, Grassadonia knew he would eventually sell *Dive Travel* from the day he started it. Managing and growing a magazine is "not my forte," he says. He began shopping for a business broker and settled on a local company to help him sell the company. The first order of business was to put a price tag on *Dive Travel,* something that proved to be a more emotional experience for Grassadonia than he had imagined. Although he knew that a company's value depends on the cash it can generate, he couldn't help but recall all of the energy, time, and talent he had invested in building the magazine from nothing to its current level. "This business is a chunk of my life. How do you put a value on that?" he asks philosophically.

Grassadonia had built *Dive Travel* into a successful publication. "We do business with just about every major advertiser in the marketplace," he says. "It would be very expensive to try and [re]create that." Using *Dive Travel*'s sales of $324,000 and earnings of $50,000, the broker suggested an asking price of $500,000. For the next year, the business attracted very few leads—not an unusual pattern in selling a business. Ads in industry trade journals produced only a few nibbles but no serious buyers. Waiting to sell was wearing on Grassadonia, so he and the broker reduced the price to $450,000. Several more months slipped by with no interest from buyers, and Grassadonia was beginning to wonder if *anyone* wanted to buy *Dive Travel.*

Finally, Susan Wilmink and Thomas Schneck contacted Grassadonia's broker about *Dive Travel.* The couple was living in Germany, where Wilmink worked for a large international magazine publisher and Schneck owned a software company. The only problem was that Wilmink and Schneck couldn't afford to buy *Dive Travel* outright. They proposed that Grassadonia sell them a controlling interest in the company and stay on as a consultant for three years. Grassadonia hesitated at first but then agreed to stay on as long as Wilmink and Schneck took over the day-to-day operations of running the business. A major factor in his decision was Wilmink's presentation on how she and Schneck planned to run the company—from adding a World Wide Web page to repositioning the magazine. "Susan came in with a vision," says Grassadonia.

Negotiating the final deal took another six months, and at times the discussions became heated. At one such emotional moment, Barkley, Grassadonia's 13-year-old Golden Retriever walked over to Wilmink's chair, jumped up, and licked her face. That broke the tension, everyone started laughing, and Wilmink decided to name the new business Barkley Publishing. The final price the parties agreed on was $215,000 for the 51 percent controlling interest Wilmink and Schneck got. Wilmink became the new president and publisher, and Grassadonia agreed to stay on as a paid consultant for three years. At the end of that time, he would sell his stock, with Wilmink and Schneck getting the right of first refusal. In addition, Grassadonia got a percentage of the company's revenues over the three years.

The deal has worked to everyone's satisfaction. Grassadonia has the freedom to surf whenever he pleases, and Wilmink and Schneck have the company they wanted. *Dive Travel*'s circulation has more than doubled, revenues have nearly doubled, and profits are up.

1. Why is the process of valuing a business so difficult for the entrepreneur who founded it?
2. Which method(s) of valuing a business do you think would be most appropriate in placing a realistic value on *Dive Travel*? Explain.
3. Evaluate the final deal the parties struck from both the buyers' and the seller's perspectives. Do you think the deal was fair?

Source: Adapted from Christopher Caggiano, "The Seller," *Inc.,* June 1996, pp. 54–56.

the plan permits the owner to transfer all or part of the company to employees as gradually or as suddenly as preferred.

To use an ESOP successfully, a small business should be profitable (with pretax profits exceeding $100,000) and should have a payroll of more than $500,000 a year. Generally, companies with fewer than 15 to 20 employees do not find ESOPs beneficial. For compa-

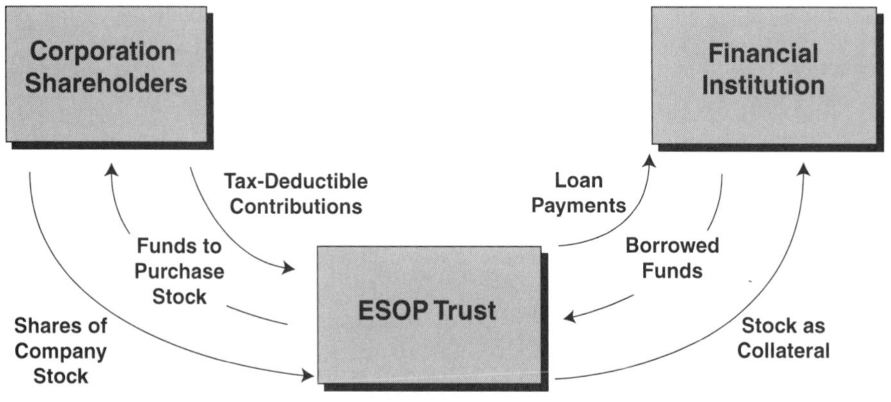

FIGURE 5.5
A Typical Employee Stock Ownership Plan (ESOP)

Source: Corey Rosen, "Sharing Ownership with Employees," Small Business Reports, *December 1990, p. 63.*

nies that prepare properly, however, ESOPs offer significant financial and managerial benefits. "The owner gets to sell off his stock at whatever annual pace appeals to him. There's no cost to the employees, who eventually get to take over the company. And for the company the cost of the buyout is fully deductible," says one consultant.[25]

NEGOTIATING THE DEAL

6. Understand how the negotiation process works and identify the factors that affect the negotiation process.

Although determining the value of a business for sale is an important step in the buying process, it is not the final one. The buyer must sit down with the seller to negotiate the actual selling price for the business and, more importantly, the terms of the deal. The final deal the buyer strikes depends, in large part, on her negotiating skills. The first rule of negotiating a deal is to avoid confusing price with value. Value is what the business is actually worth; price is what the buyer agrees to pay. In a business sale, the party who is the better negotiator usually comes out on top. The seller is looking to:

- get the highest price possible for the business.
- sever all responsibility for the company's liabilities.
- avoid unreasonable contract terms that might limit his future opportunities.
- maximize the cash he gets from the deal.
- minimize the tax burden from the sale.
- make sure the buyer will be able to make all future payments.

The buyer seeks to:

- get the business at the lowest possible price.
- negotiate favorable payment terms, preferably over time.
- get assurances that he is buying the business he thinks he is getting.
- avoid putting the seller in a position to open a competing business.
- minimize the amount of cash paid "up front."

Factors Affecting the Negotiation Process

Before beginning negotiations, a buyer should take stock of some basic issues. How strong is the seller's desire to sell? Is the seller willing to finance part of the purchase price? What terms does the buyer suggest? Which ones are most important to him? Is it urgent that the seller close the deal quickly? What deal structure best suits your needs? What are the tax consequences for both parties? Will the seller sign a restrictive covenant? Is the seller willing to stay on with the company for a time as a consultant? What general economic conditions exist in the industry at the time of the sale? Sellers tend to have the upper hand in good economic times, and buyers will have an advantage during recessionary periods in an industry.

The Negotiation Process

On the surface, the negotiation process appears to be strictly adversarial. Although each party may be trying to accomplish objectives that are at odds with those of the opposing party, the negotiation process does not have to turn into a nasty battle of wits with overtones of "If you win, then I lose." The negotiation process will go much more smoothly and much faster if both parties work to establish a cooperative relationship based on honesty and trust from the outset. A successful deal requires both parties to examine and articulate their respective positions while trying to understand the other party's position. Recognizing that neither of them will benefit without a deal, both parties must work to achieve their objectives while making certain concessions to keep the negotiations alive.

To avoid a stalled deal, a buyer should go into the negotiation with a list of objectives ranked in order of priority. Once she has developed her own list of priorities, it is useful to develop what she perceives to be the seller's list. That requires learning as much as possible about the seller. Knowing which terms are most important (and which are least important) to her and to the seller enables a buyer to make concessions without "giving away the farm" and without getting bogged down in "nit-picking," which often leads to a stalemate. If, for instance, the seller insists on a term to which the buyer cannot agree, she can explain why and then offer to give up something in exchange. The buyer also should identify the one concrete objective that sits at the top of that list, the one thing she absolutely must come away from the negotiations with. The final stage of preparing for the actual negotiation is to study her list and the one she has developed based on her perceptions of the seller to determine where the two mesh and where they conflict. The key to a successful negotiation is to use this analysis to look for areas of mutual benefit and to use them as the foundation for the negotiation.

Figure 5.6 offers five tips on making the negotiation process a successful one.

FIGURE 5.6
The Five Ps of Negotiating
Source: Adapted from Right Associates, Philadelphia, PA.

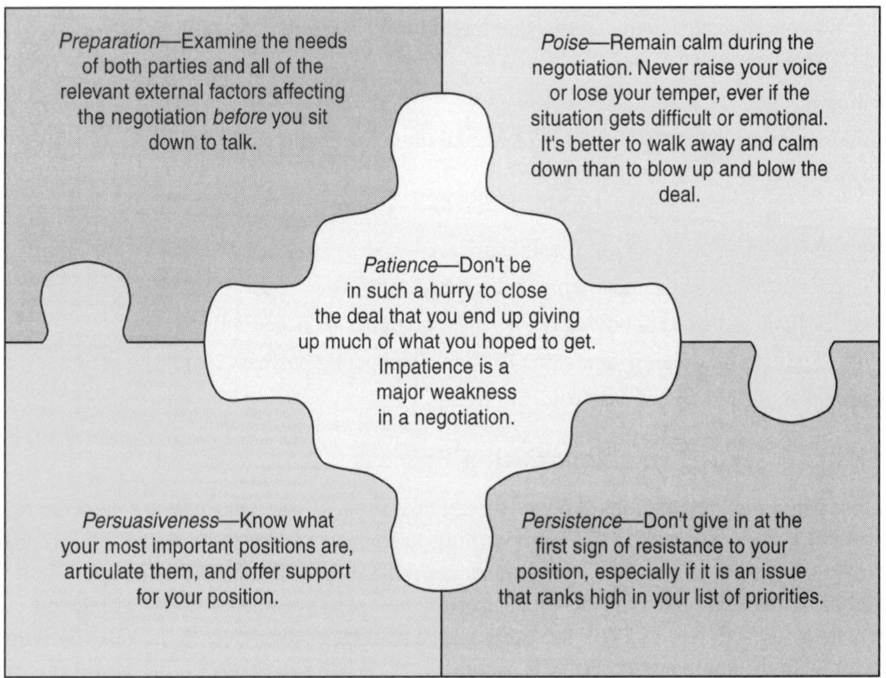

CHAPTER SUMMARY

1. Understand the advantages and disadvantages of buying an existing business.

   The *advantages* of buying an existing business include: A successful business may continue to be successful; the business may already have the best location; employees and suppliers are already established; equipment is installed and its productive capacity known; inventory is in place and trade credit established; the owner hits the ground running; the buyer can use the expertise of the previous owner; and the business may be a bargain.

   The *disadvantages* of buying an existing business include: An existing business may be for sale because it is deteriorating; the previous owner may have created ill will; employees inherited with the business may not be suitable; its location may have become unsuitable; equipment and facilities may be obsolete; change and innovation are hard to implement; inventory may be outdated; accounts receivable may be worth less than face value; and the business may be overpriced.

2. Define the steps involved in the *right* way to buy a business.

   Buying a business can be a treacherous experience unless the buyer is well prepared. The right way to buy a business is to analyze your skills, abilities, and interests to determine the ideal business for you; prepare a list of potential candidates, including those that might be in the hidden market; investigate and evaluate candidate businesses; explore financing options before you actually need the money; and, finally, ensure a smooth transition.

3. Explain the process of evaluating an existing business.

   Rushing into a deal can be the biggest mistake a business buyer can make. Before closing a deal, every business buyer should investigate five critical areas: (1) Why does the owner wish to sell? Look for the *real* reason. (2) Determine the physical condition of the business. Consider both the building and its location. (3) Conduct a thorough analysis of the market for your products or services. Who are the present and potential customers? Conduct an equally thorough analysis of competitors, both direct and indirect. How do they operate and why do customers prefer them? (4) Consider all of the legal aspects that might constrain the expansion and growth of the business. Did you comply with the provisions of a bulk transfer? Negotiate a restrictive covenant? Consider ongoing legal liabilities? (5) Analyze the financial condition of the business, looking at financial statements, income tax returns, and especially cash flow.

4. Describe the various techniques for determining the value of a business.

   Placing a value on a business is partly an art and partly a science. There is no single best method for determining the value of a business. The following techniques (with several variations) are useful: the balance sheet technique (adjusted balance sheet technique); the earnings approach (excess earnings method, capitalized earnings approach, and discounted future savings approach); and the market approach.

5. Understand the seller's side of the buyout decision and how to structure the deal.

   Selling a business takes time, patience, and preparation to locate a suitable buyer, strike a deal, and make the transition. Sellers must always structure the deal with tax consequences in mind. Common exit strategies include a straight business sale, forming a family limited partnership, selling a controlling interest in the business, restructuring the company, selling to an international buyer, using a two-step sale, and establishing an employee stock ownership plan (ESOP).

6. Understand how the negotiation process works and identify the factors that affect the negotiation process.

   The first rule of negotiating is never confuse price with value. In a business sale, the party who is the better negotiator usually comes out on top. Before beginning negotiations, a buyer should identify the factors that are affecting the negotiations and then develop a negotiating strategy. The best deals are the result of a cooperative relationship between the parties based on trust.

DISCUSSION QUESTIONS

1. What advantages can an entrepreneur who buys a business gain over one who starts a business from scratch?
2. How would you go about determining the value of the assets of a business if you were unfamiliar with them?
3. Why do so many entrepreneurs run into trouble when they buy an existing business? Outline the steps involved in the *right* way to buy a business.
4. When evaluating an existing business that is for sale, what areas should an entrepreneur consider? Briefly summarize the key elements of each area.
5. How should a buyer evaluate a business's goodwill?
6. What is a restrictive covenant? Is it fair to ask the seller of a travel agency located in a small town to sign a restrictive covenant for one year covering a 20-square-mile area? Explain.

7. How much negative information can you expect the seller to give you about the business? How can a prospective buyer find out such information?
8. Why is it so difficult for buyers and sellers to agree on a price for a business?
9. Which method of valuing a business is best? Why?
10. Outline the different exit strategy options available to a seller.
11. Explain the 5 Ps of a successful negotiation process. What tips would you offer someone about to enter into negotiations to buy a business?
12. One entrepreneur who recently purchased a business advises buyers to expect some surprises in the deal no matter how well prepared they may be. He says that every potential buyer must build some "wiggle room" into their plans to buy a company. What steps can a buyer take to ensure that he has sufficient "wiggle room"?

Beyond the Classroom ...

1. Ask several new owners who purchased existing businesses the following questions:
   a. How did you determine the value of the business?
   b. How close was the price paid for the business to the value assessed prior to purchase?
   c. What percentage of the accounts receivable was collectible?
   d. How accurate were projections concerning customers (sales volume and number of customers, especially)?
2. Visit a business broker and ask him how he brings a buyer and seller together. What does he do to facilitate the sale? What methods does he use to determine the value of a business?
3. Invite an attorney to speak to your class about the legal aspects of buying a business. How does he recommend a business buyer protect himself legally in a business purchase?

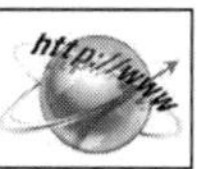

We invite you to visit this book's companion Web site at **www.prenhall.com/Zimmerer.**

SECTION III

Building the Business Plan: Marketing and Financial Considerations

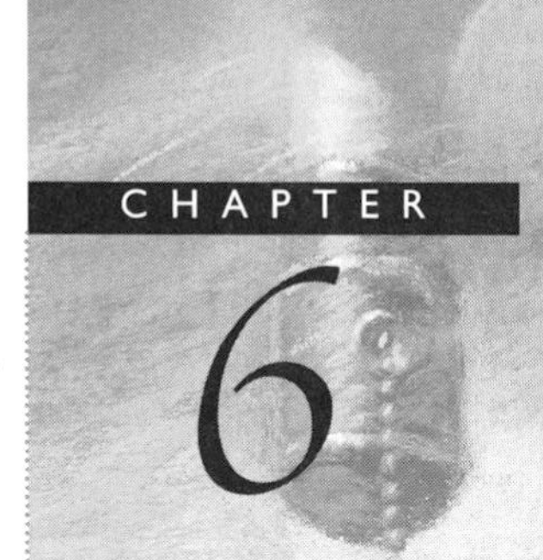

CHAPTER 6

Building a Powerful Marketing Plan

LEARNING OBJECTIVES

Upon completion of this chapter, you will be able to:

1. Describe the principles of building a guerrilla marketing plan and explain the benefits of preparing one.
2. Discuss the role of market research in building a guerrilla marketing plan and outline the market research process.
3. Explain how small businesses can pinpoint their target markets.
4. Describe the factors on which a small business can build a competitive edge in the marketplace: customer focus, quality, convenience, innovation, service, and speed.
5. Discuss the marketing opportunities the World Wide Web (WWW) offers entrepreneurs and how to best take advantage of them.
6. Discuss the "four Ps" of marketing—product, place, price, and promotion—and their role in building a successful marketing strategy.

There is only one boss—the customer. Customers can fire everybody in the company from the chairman on down, simply by spending their money somewhere else.

—Sam Walton

This fishing lure manufacturer I know had all these flashy green and purple lures. I asked, "Do fish take these?" "Charlie," he said, "I don't sell these lures to fish."

—Charles Munger

The culmination of the next five chapters is the creation of a valuable business tool: the *business plan,* a valuable document that defines *what* an entrepreneur plans to accomplish in both quantitative and qualitative terms and of *how* she plans to accomplish it. A business plan consolidates many of the topics we have discussed in preceding chapters with those of the next four chapters to produce a concise statement of how an entrepreneur plans to achieve success in the marketplace.

Too often, business plans describe in great detail what the entrepreneur intends to accomplish (e.g., "the financials") and pay little, if any, attention to the strategies to achieve those targets. Too many entrepreneurs squander enormous effort pulling together capital, people, and other resources to sell their products and services because they fail to determine what it will take to attract and keep a profitable customer base. To be effective, a solid business plan must contain both a financial plan *and* a marketing plan. Like the financial plan, an effective marketing plan projects numbers and analyzes them but from a different perspective. Rather than focus on cash flow, net profits, and owner's equity, the marketing plan concentrates on the *customer.*

This chapter is devoted to creating an effective marketing plan, which is a subset of a total business plan. Before producing reams of computer-generated spreadsheets of financial projections, an entrepreneur must determine what to sell, to whom and how, on what terms and at what price, and how to get the product or service to the customer. In short, a marketing plan identifies a company's target customers and describes how that business will attract and keep them. Its primary focus is capturing and maintaining a competitive edge for a small business.

1. Describe the principles of building a guerrilla marketing plan and explain the benefits of preparing one.

BUILDING A GUERRILLA MARKETING PLAN

marketing—*the process of creating and delivering desired goods and services to customers and involves all of the activities associated with winning and retaining loyal customers.*

Marketing is the process of creating and delivering desired goods and services to customers and involves all of the activities associated with winning and retaining loyal customers. The secret to successful marketing is to understand what your target customers' needs, demands, and wants are before your competitors can; offer them the products and services that will satisfy those needs, demands, and wants; and provide customers service, convenience, and value so that they will keep coming back. Unfortunately, there appears to be a sizable gap between sound marketing principles and actual marketing practices among small businesses. One recent study of small company marketing practices by Dun & Bradstreet revealed many serious weaknesses. For instance, the study found that just one in five small business owners creates a strategic marketing plan and that the most common sales approach is to react to customer orders rather than to proactively seek them out. (Efforts are so passive that walk-in traffic was cited as the most popular sales method.) The study also revealed that word-of-mouth promotion and referrals comprise the typical small company's marketing efforts.[1]

guerrilla marketing strategies—*unconventional, low-cost, creative marketing techniques that allow small companies to compete effectively with larger rivals.*

In a small business, the marketing function cuts across the entire company, affecting every aspect of its operation—from finance and production to hiring and purchasing—as well as the company's ultimate success. As the global business environment becomes more turbulent and competition becomes more intense, small business owners must understand the importance of developing creative marketing strategies; their success and survival depend on it. A marketing plan is *not* just for megacorporations competing in international markets. Although they may be small in size and cannot match their larger rivals' marketing budgets, entrepreneurial companies are not powerless when it comes to developing effective marketing strategies. By using **guerrilla marketing strategies**—unconventional, low-cost, creative techniques—small companies can wring as much or more "bang" from their marketing bucks. For instance, facing the power of discount giants such as Wal-Mart, Kmart, and "category killer" superstores such as Best Buy and Circuit City determined to increase their market shares, small retail shops are turning to guerrilla marketing tactics to lure new customers and to keep existing ones. One small retailer explains, "If the chains are the steamships plowing through the ocean, then we have to be the cigarette [racing] boats zipping around and through them, changing direction on a dime. That must be our advantage when going up against the tremendous cash and resources of the biggies."[2]

Central Market

For example, Central Market, a small chain of supermarkets in southern Texas, relies on a combination of an extensive inventory, wide selection, and a variety of guerrilla marketing strategies to outpace competitors, both big and small. Far from a traditional supermarket, Central Market offers its customers more than just friendly service and a huge selection of grocery products. (The store stocks more than 500 varieties of cheese, 3,000 wines, and 200 types of olive oil.) Unlike the standard grocery store that uses a grid layout of aisles so that shoppers can locate items easily, Central Market customers follow a single path that winds through the 63,000 square-foot building and takes them past virtually every item in the store. Not only does this layout offer 20 percent more shelf space than the typical grocery store layout, but it also allows Central Market to entice customers to buy with lavish, creative displays. Wandering the aisle is a host of "foodies," employees who answer customers' questions, offer free samples of products, and dispense cooking advice (but only after undergoing extensive training). Central Market also draws customers with special events, ranging from taste tests of new products and wine tastings to live entertainment and children's birthday parties. For busy dual-career couples, the store's Café on the Run offers Dinner for Two, a fully prepared meal for two people made from scratch by professional chefs. To broaden its appeal to both experienced and novice cooks, Central Market offers a cooking school that has earned a national reputation by featuring top local, regional, and national chefs. The school, which offers the greatest number of nonprofessional cooking classes in the country, is not designed to be a profit center. Instead, says Vice President John Campbell, "We're trying to make coming to the store an experience that's both educational and entertaining." Central Market has created much more than a grocery store; it has become a collection of exciting, interactive, fun events that happens to sell a lot of groceries! "We want customers to feel uplifted when they walk out of here," says Campbell. Apparently they do. Customers enjoy the unique shopping experience at Central Market so much that they made the stores one of the biggest attractions in southern Texas, generating more than $1 million in sales per week![3]

Guerrilla Marketing Principles

To be successful guerrilla marketers, entrepreneurs must be as innovative in creating their marketing strategies as they are in developing new product and service ideas. The following principles can help business owners create powerful, effective guerrilla marketing strategies.

FIND A NICHE AND FILL IT. As we saw in Chapter 2, "Strategic Management and the Entrepreneur," many successful small companies choose their niches carefully and defend them fiercely rather than compete head-to-head with larger rivals. A niche strategy allows a small company to maximize the advantages of its smallness and to compete effectively even in industries dominated by giants. Focusing on niches that are too small to be attractive to large companies is a common recipe for success among thriving small companies. "Finding such unserved niches is an excellent way to begin 'whupping' the big guys, if not in their own back yard, at least on the same street," says one marketing expert.[4]

Women's Travel Club

As the name of her business implies, Phyllis Stoller, founder of the Women's Travel Club, has targeted that portion of the market that accounts for 41 percent of all travel. Market research told Stoller that women travelers are more interested in safety and sanitary conditions than are men, and she plans every club trip with these factors in mind.

Stoller also discovered that women are more interested in experiencing everyday life than typical tourist activities when traveling in foreign lands. Rather than offer the traditional vacation getaways her competitors sell, Stoller specializes in tours that offer plenty of opportunities for cultural exchanges. Because she knows that women want more information than men do before they make a significant purchase, Stoller publishes a monthly newsletter describing upcoming trips in rich detail, focusing on historical attractions, unusual tourist destinations, and local shopping and dining options. The Women's Travel Club Web site also offers information on every trip, including photos and diaries from past trips.[5]

"Small business is uniquely positioned for niche marketing," says marketing expert Philip Kotler. "If a small business sits down and follows the principles of targeting, segmenting, and differentiating, it doesn't have to collapse to larger companies."[6]

DON'T JUST SELL; ENTERTAIN. Numerous surveys have shown that consumers are bored with shopping and that they are less inclined to spend their scarce leisure time shopping than ever before. Winning customers today requires more than low prices and wide merchandise selection; increasingly, businesses are adopting strategies based on **entertailing,** the notion of drawing customers into a store by creating a kaleidoscope of sights, sounds, smells, and activities, all designed to entertain—and, of course, sell (think Disney). The primary goal of entertailing is to catch customers' attention and engage them in some kind of entertaining experience so that they shop longer and buy more goods or services. Entertailing involves "making [shopping] more fun, more educational, more interactive," says one retail consultant.[7]

entertailing—*a marketing concept designed to draw customers into a store by creating a kaleidoscope of sights, sounds, smells, and activities, all designed to entertain—and, of course, sell.*

Research supports the benefits of entertailing's hands-on, interactive, educational, approach to selling; one study found that, when making a purchase, 34 percent of consumers are driven more by emotional factors such as fun and excitement than by logical factors such as price and convenience.[8] Entertailing's goal, of course, is not only to entertain but also to sell.

Golf Galaxy

One small company that has successfully blended show business with the retail business is Golf Galaxy, a small chain of golf equipment stores stretching from Minnesota to Ohio. In addition to their extensive $1.2 million inventories of every kind of golf gear imaginable, Golf Galaxy locations feature 500-square-foot in-store putting greens complete with an arching bridge modeled after one on the famed Augusta National course that hosts the Masters Tournament. Golfers can try out clubs and equipment in other interactive in-store displays, such as the driving range, the full-sized sand bunker, or the electronic golf simulator that allows customers to "play" a full round of golf on one of the world's 32 most famous courses, no matter what the weather outside is like! Golf Galaxy stores also help customers improve their swing or get the right clubs with the help of an on-staff PGA golf professional and a computer-video swing analysis system. Much of Golf Galaxy's rapid growth stems from the company's unique, sensory experience it offers customers.[9]

STRIVE TO BE UNIQUE. One of the most effective guerrilla marketing tactics is to create an image of uniqueness for your business. Entrepreneurs can achieve a unique place in the market in a variety of ways, including through the products and services they offer, the marketing and promotional campaigns they use, the store layouts they design, and the business strategies they employ. The goal is to stand out from the crowd; few things are as uninspiring to customers as a "me-too" business that offers nothing unique.

Space Adventures

One company that holds a unique place in the travel market is Space Adventures, primarily because of the services it sells. The company's goal is to sell space travel to civilians. Through its Steps to Space programs, the company already has sold about 350 tickets at $95,000 each for suborbital space flights scheduled to begin in 2003.

Until the technology needed to get people into space on a routine basis emerges, the start-up company will generate sales by selling space-related adventure tours such as high-altitude flights at supersonic speed in Russian MiG fighter jets, zero-gravity flights in specially designed jets, video birthday cards from astronauts aboard orbiting space stations, and more mundane earth-bound trips to view solar eclipses and space observatories.[10]

CREATE AN IDENTITY FOR YOUR BUSINESS. Some of the most powerful marketers are those companies that have a clear sense of who they are, what they stand for, and why they exist. Defining their vision for their companies in a meaningful way is one of the most challenging tasks facing entrepreneurs. As we learned in Chapter 2, that vision stems from the beliefs and values of the entrepreneur and is reflected in a company's culture, ethics, and business strategy. Although it is intangible, this vision is a crucial ingredient in a successful guerrilla marketing campaign. Once this vision is firmly planted, guerrilla marketers can use it to market their companies and its products and services. Patagonia, a company that sells a variety of outdoor clothing and gear, has relied on the vision of its founder Yvon Chouinard to build a tremendously loyal base of customers who appreciate quality and the company's dedication to stewardship, social responsibility, and the environment.

CONNECT WITH CUSTOMERS ON AN EMOTIONAL LEVEL. Companies that establish a deeper relationship with their customers than one based merely on making a sale have the capacity to be exceptional guerrilla marketers. These businesses win because customers receive an emotional boost every time they buy these companies' products or services. They connect with their customers emotionally by supporting causes that are important to their customer base, taking exceptional care of their customers, surpassing customers' expectations in quality and service, and making it fun and enjoyable to do business with them.

Ben & Jerry's Homemade

Ben & Jerry's Homemade, the famous maker of premium ice cream products, has become a symbol of small business success because of its ability to connect with its customers on several levels. The company's founders, Ben Cohen and Jerry Greenfield, built their company on principles and values that are important to them and their customers, including superior quality, innovative products (which the company often lets customers name), employee-friendly culture, and strong stance on ethics and social responsibility. Customers feel good about doing business with a company that donates 7.5 percent of its pretax earnings to a variety of philanthropic causes and incorporates a social component in its mission statement.

Much of Ben & Jerry's success is the result of an impressive guerrilla marketing strategy that took root in the company's humble beginnings in a converted gas station in 1978.

Table 6.1 describes several low-cost, highly effective guerrilla marketing tactics small businesses have used to outperform their larger rivals.

A sound guerrilla marketing plan focuses the company's attention on the *customer* and recognizes that satisfying the customer is the foundation of every business. Its purpose is to build a strategy of success for a business—*but from the customer's point of view.* Indeed, the customer is the central player in the cast of every business venture. According to marketing expert Ted Levitt, the primary purpose of a business is not to earn a profit; instead, it is "to create and keep a customer. The rest, given reasonable good sense, will take care of itself."[11] Every area of the business must practice putting the customer first in planning and actions.

A guerrilla marketing plan should accomplish four objectives:

1. It should determine customer needs and wants through market research.
2. It should pinpoint the specific target markets the small company will serve.
3. It should analyze the firm's competitive advantages and build a guerrilla marketing strategy around them.
4. It should help create a marketing mix that meets customer needs and wants.

The rest of this chapter focuses on building a customer orientation into these four objectives of the small company's marketing plan.

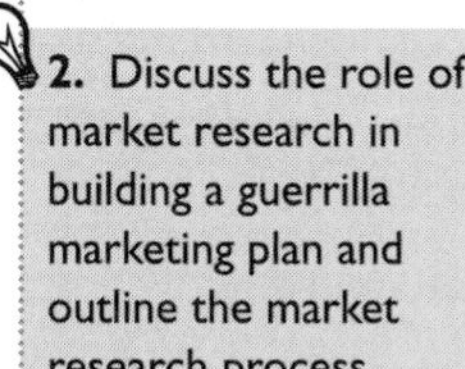
2. Discuss the role of market research in building a guerrilla marketing plan and outline the market research process.

DETERMINING CUSTOMER NEEDS AND WANTS THROUGH MARKET RESEARCH

The changing nature of the U.S. population is a potent force altering the landscape of business. Shifting patterns in age, income, education, race, and other population characteristics, which are the subject of **demographics,** will have a major impact on companies, their customers, and the way they do business with those customers. Businesses that ignore demographic trends and fail to adjust their strategies accordingly run the risk of becoming competitively obsolete.

demographics—*the study of important population characteristics such as age, income, education, race, and others.*

A demographic trend is like a train; a business owner must find out early on where it's going and decide whether or not to get on board. Waiting until the train is roaring down the tracks and gaining speed means it's too late to get on board. However, by checking the schedule early and planning ahead, an entrepreneur may find himself at the train's controls and wearing the engineer's hat! Similarly, small companies that spot demographic trends early and act on them can gain a distinctive edge in the market. An entrepreneur's goal is to make sure her company's marketing plan is on track with the most significant trends that are shaping the industry.

TABLE 6.1
Guerrilla Marketing Tactics

Sources: Adapted from Jay Conrad Levinson, "Attention Getters," Entrepreneur, *March 1998, p. 88; Lynn Beresford, Janean Chun, Cynthia E. Griffin, Heather Page, and Debra Phillips, "Marketing 101,"* Entrepreneur, *May 1996, pp. 104–114; Guen Sublette, "Marketing 101,"* Entrepreneur, *May 1995, pp. 86–98; Denise Osburn, "Bringing Them Back for More,"* Nation's Business, *August 1995, p. 31R; Jay Conrad Levinson, "Survival Tactics,"* Entrepreneur, *March 1996, p. 84; Tom Stein, "Outselling the Giants,"* Success, *May 1996, pp. 38–41.*

- Help organize and sponsor a service- or community-oriented project.
- Sponsor offbeat, memorable events. Build a giant banana split, rent a theater for a morning and invite kids for a free viewing.
- Always be on the lookout for new niches to enter. Try to develop multiple niches.
- Offer to speak about your business, industry, product, or service to local organizations.
- Ask present customers for referrals.
- Sell at every opportunity. One brewery includes a mini-catalog advertising T-shirts and mugs in every six-pack it sells. Orders for catalog items are climbing fast.
- Develop a sales "script" that asks customers a series of questions to hone in on what they are looking for and that will lead them to the conclusion that your product or service is it!
- Offer customers gift certificates. They really boost your cash flow.
- Create samples of your product and give them to customers. You'll increase sales later.
- Offer a 100 percent, money-back, no-hassles guarantee. By removing the customer's risk of buying, you increase your product's attractiveness.
- Create a "frequent buyer" program. Remember how valuable existing customers are. Work hard to keep the customers you have! One coffee shop kept its customers coming back with a punch-card promotion that gave a free pound of coffee after a customer purchased 9 pounds.
- Clip articles that feature your business and send reprints to customers and potential customers. Keep reminding them of who you are and why you're valuable to them.
- Test how well your ads "pull" with coded coupons that customers bring in. Focus your ad expenditures on those media that produce the best results for you.
- Create "tip sheets" to pass out to customers and potential customers (e.g., landscape tips on lawn maintenance).
- Find ways to make your product or service irresistible to your customers. One furniture company mails a Polaroid photo of big-ticket items customers are considering, and sales closing rates have climbed 25 percent.
- Create an award for your community (e.g., a landscape company presented a "best yard" award each season).
- Conduct a contest in the community (e.g., a photographer sponsored a juried photo contest for different age groups).
- Collect testimonials from satisfied customers and use them in ads, brochures, and so on. Testimonials are one of the most effective forms of advertising!
- Get a former journalist to help you write a story "pitch" for local media.
- Show an interest in your customers' needs. If you spot a seminar that would be of interest to them, tell them! Become a valuable resource for them.
- Find unique ways to thank customers (especially first-time buyers) for their business (e.g., a note, a lunch, a gift basket).
- Give loyal customers a "freebie" occasionally. You might be surprised at how long they will remember it.
- Create a newsletter that features your customers or clients and their businesses (e.g., photo of client using your product in his business).
- Cooperate with other businesses selling complementary products and services in marketing efforts and campaigns, a process called fusion marketing. Share mailing lists and advertising time or space, or work together on a special promotion.
- Use major competitors' coupons against them. The owner of an independent sandwich shop routinely pulled business from a nearby national chain by advertising that he would accept its coupons.
- Market your company's uniqueness. Many customers enjoy buying from small companies that are different and unique. The owners of the only tea plantation in the United States used that fact to their advantage in establishing a customer base.

YOU BE THE CONSULTANT . . .

The Man from MARS

Impressed with the true sound from an amplifier he heard at a ZZ Top concert, Mark Begelman went into a local Ace Music store near his home in southern Florida. Begelman, who had played lead guitar in rock bands for more than 30 years, plugged his guitar into the amplifier, cranked up the volume, and started to play. Almost immediately, an impolite clerk approached Begelman and told him to turn the volume down to avoid disturbing other customers. The clerk told Begelman that he could buy the amp, take it home and try it out, and if he was not satisfied, he could return it for store credit. Begelman left the store upset and without the amplifier. "It was one of the great joys of my life to be making music," he says, "and I ended up walking out of a music store feeling bad." Begelman decided to do something about it.

Rather than write a letter to the store owner, Begelman put his substantial financial and managerial resources to work. In 1986, Begelman had founded Office Club, a California-based chain of office supply superstores, which he sold to Office Depot. After serving a four-year stint as CEO of Office Depot, Begelman left and within a few months had purchased the Ace Music chain. Now that he had access to music equipment suppliers, Begelman closed Ace Music and converted it into the kind of store that reflected his love for music and his desire to share that love with others.

Music and Recording Superstore (MARS) is a musician's paradise. Each MARS store, built at a cost of $2.8 million, carries an inventory of $3 million worth of practically every type of musical instrument and equipment, with brand names that include Fender guitars, Pearl drums, Yamaha keyboards, Zildjian cymbals, Marshall speakers, and many others. There is the Guitar Super Wall, the Acoustic Guitar Room, the Keyboard Center, the DJ and Lighting Room, and the Band and Orchestra Department. Every MARS store also contains a recording studio, where musicians are encouraged to try out any piece of equipment they want, a stage where any customer can perform for five minutes, and video screens playing music videos. The service center brings in customers seeking repair work, and MARS entices a variety of customers with concerts, seminars, and theme sessions, such as its weekly Drums for Lunch program, which draws about 100 people for demonstrations and discussions about percussion instruments. Not only are all of the programs MARS has created designed to encourage people to enjoy music but they are also based on sound marketing principles. "By nurturing new musicians and encouraging former players to return to their music, we expand the customer base in the markets we enter," says one manager. At the heart of that philosophy is the MARS Learning Center, which offers lessons and workshops from beginner to advanced on practically every instrument and teaches the joy of performing music.

MARS reaches out to the local community through a variety of programs. The In Tune with Kids program is a cooperative effort with local schools that provides donated instruments to children who cannot afford to buy their own instruments. Through its MARS Music Foundation, the company gives underprivileged children the opportunity to learn about music and how to play musical instruments. The company's outreach efforts are not limited to children; its New Horizons program is aimed at encouraging older adults to learn to play musical instruments.

Through MARS, Mark Begelman is achieving his dream of sharing his love for music with others, and he is doing that by creating a fun, interactive environment for his customers. "I want people to feel great when they walk out of the store," he says. "*I* want to feel great when I walk out of my store!"

1. How would you describe Mark Begelman's marketing strategy for MARS?
2. How would you rate the effectiveness of MARS's marketing strategy? What are its strengths? Its weaknesses?
3. Work with a team of your classmates to brainstorm other ideas that would enhance MARS's marketing efforts.

Sources: Adapted from: "Just Like Mom Said," *Specialty Retail,* **<www.specialtyretail.net/issues/April99.mars.htm>;** Dale D. Buss, "Entertailing," *Nation's Business,* December 1997, pp. 12–18; Lisa Biank Fasig, "Music Megastore Debuts," *Cincinnati Enquirer,* October 1, 1998, **<enquirer.com/editions/1998/10/01/bus_mars01.html>;** Geoffrey Colvin, "MARS and Mark Begelman," *Fortune,* April 9, 1999, p. 248[H].

The increasing cultural diversity in the United States is providing tremendous business opportunities for entrepreneurs who are fast enough and savvy enough to capitalize on them. Demographic patterns indicate that by 2050, Caucasians will make up 53 percent of the nation's population (down from 72 percent in 2000), but the population of Hispanic Americans will be six times its current size and its purchasing power also will climb rapidly.

Latin Girl

Recognizing this demographic trend, Micromedia Affiliates is targeting the Hispanic American female teenage market with its Latin Girl *magazine, which features a heavy emphasis on fashion, makeup, dating, entertainment, and celebrities—all with a Hispanic emphasis. Interestingly,* Latin Girl *is published in English because the company's market research showed that the majority of Hispanic girls prefer reading English.*[12]

The Value of Market Research

By performing some basic market research, small business owners can detect key demographic and market trends. Indeed, *every* business can benefit from a better understanding of its market, customers, and competitors. "Market information is just as much a business asset and just as important as your inventory or the machine you have in the back room," says one marketing consultant.[13] **Market research** is the vehicle for gathering the information that serves as the foundation for the marketing plan. It involves systematically collecting, analyzing, and interpreting data pertaining to a company's market, customers, and competitors. The objective of market research is to learn how to improve the level of satisfaction for existing customers and to find ways to attract new customers. Market research answers questions such as: Who are my customers and potential customers? What are they looking for? What kind of people are they? Where do they live? How often do they buy these products or services? What models, styles, colors, or flavors do they prefer? Why do or don't they buy from my store? How do the strengths of my product or service serve their needs and wants? What hours do they prefer to shop? How do they perceive my business? Which advertising media are likely to reach them? How do customers perceive my business versus competitors? Such information is an integral part of developing a marketing plan that produces sales.

market research—*the vehicle for gathering the information that serves as the foundation for the marketing plan; it involves systematically collecting, analyzing, and interpreting data pertaining to a company's market, customers, and competitors.*

When marketing their goods and services, small companies must avoid mistakes because there is no margin for error when funds are scarce and budgets are tight. Small businesses simply cannot afford to miss their target markets, and market research can help them zero in on the bull's-eye.

Neema Clothing Ltd.

Jim Ammeen, CEO of Neema Clothing Ltd., a small manufacturer of men's tailored clothing, says that the marketing strategy behind his company's impressive growth rate (700 percent since its inception) is the result of deliberate market research. Studying statistics on the U.S. men's clothing industry he had gathered from various sources, Ammeen noticed that "80 percent of the suits retailed for less than $300, yet the majority of manufacturers were pricing their suits in the $500-to-$700 range. I was able to direct Neema's efforts toward capturing business that the competition was overlooking," he says. Neema Clothing continues to thrive by focusing its niche strategy on marketing quality tailored suits and sport coats that fit within this most popular price range.[14]

One of the worst—and most common—mistakes entrepreneurs make is assuming that a market exists for their product or service. The time to find out if customers will buy your product or service is *before* you invest thousands of dollars to launch it! Market research can tell entrepreneurs whether or not a sufficient customer base exists and how likely those customers are to purchase their products or services. In addition to collecting and analyzing demographic data about the people in a particular geographic area and comparing the results to the profile of a typical customer, entrepreneurs can learn a great deal by actually observing, mingling with, and interviewing customers as they shop. Hands-on market research techniques such as these allow entrepreneurs to get past the barriers that consumers often put up and to uncover their true preferences and hidden thoughts.

Galilee Splendor Inc.

Peter Shamir and his partners in Galilee Splendor Inc. used this up-close and personal market research to gauge customers' response to their first product, Bible Bread, a bread modeled after the unleavened bread ("matza") in the Exodus. Long before the partners in Galilee Splendor began selling their bread in the United States, they conducted market research to test Americans' acceptance of the product. Partner Zack Shavin owns a tour company in Jerusalem, and he tested various recipes, packages, and slogans on the thousands of American tourists who visit the Holy Land each year. Billed as "the original fast food," Bible Bread is sold through gourmet, health-food, and kosher stores across the United States and is especially popular throughout the nation's Bible Belt. Why not sell Bible Bread through traditional grocery stores? After Shamir spent hundreds of hours observing and interviewing customers in grocery stores, he concluded that Bible Bread would never be noticed in the vast aisles of large supermarkets. "Research let us know where to put [our product]," he says.[15]

Market research does *not* have to be time consuming, complex, or expensive to be useful. By applying the same type of creativity to market research that they display when creating their businesses, entrepreneurs can perform effective market research "on the cheap."

Urban Outfitters

Urban Outfitters, a fast-growing clothing chain that targets young people in metropolitan areas with its trendy, chic styles, uses cheap market research techniques to stay on the cutting edge of its customers' fashion tastes. Rather than rely on traditional market research techniques such as focus groups and customer surveys, Urban Outfitters gauges its customers' rapidly changing fashion preferences by videotaping and taking snapshots of them in the stores as well as in their own neighborhoods. These "customer profiles" give company merchandisers a clear sense of what its target audience is wearing and allow them to adjust their merchandise mix quickly as tastes change.[16]

Meaningful market research for a small business can be informal; it does not have to be highly sophisticated nor expensive to be valuable.

Faith Popcorn, a marketing consultant, encourages small business owners to be their own "trend-tracking sleuths." Merely by observing their customers' attitudes and actions, small business owners can shift their product lines and services to meet changing tastes in the market. To spot significant trends, Popcorn suggests the following:

- Read as many current publications as possible, especially ones you normally would not read.
- Watch the top 10 TV shows because they are indicators of consumers' attitudes and values and what they're going to be buying.
- See the top 10 movies. They also influence consumer behavior, from language to fashions. In the 1930s, Hollywood star Clark Gable took off his shirt in *It Happened One Night* and revealed a bare chest; undershirt sales soon took a dive. After Will Smith and Tommy Lee Jones donned Ray-Ban sunglasses in *Men in Black,* sales of the sunglasses tripled![17]
- Talk to at least 150 customers a year about what they're buying and why. Make a conscious effort to spend time with some of your target customers, preferably in an informal setting, to find out what they are thinking.
- Talk with the 10 smartest people you know. They can offer valuable insights and fresh perspectives that you may not have considered.
- Listen to your children. ("They can be tremendous guides for you," says Popcorn.)[18]

Next, entrepreneurs should make a list of the major trends spotted and should briefly describe how well their products or services match these trends. "If you see your product falling away from too many trends, you've got to either change your product or dump it, because you know you're going to have a failure," she says.[19]

Owners whose businesses are diverging from major social, demographic, and economic trends, rather than converging with them, run the risk of their markets evaporating before their eyes.

Lady Jane Inc.

A. J. Cohen's business, Lady Jane Inc., a fourth-generation women's apparel store with four locations in downtown Savannah, Georgia, recently closed because it failed to keep pace with fundamental market changes. Over the years, Cohen's customers moved away from the downtown district to shop in the suburbs. Before long, he was competing—unsuccessfully—with suburban shopping malls for his former customers' business. "Our customers' habits changed because of where they were living," says Cohen. "Shopping malls were just more convenient for them than coming back into town to shop at my stores."[20]

Successful business owners constantly watch for shifting market trends and reformulate their marketing strategies to capitalize on them. How can the typical small business owner find the right match between her product or service and the appropriate target market? Market research!

How to Conduct Market Research

The goal of market research is to reduce the risks associated with making business decisions. It can replace misinformation and assumptions with facts. Opinion and hearsay are not viable foundations on which to build a solid marketing strategy. Successful market research consists of four steps: define the problem, collect the data, analyze and interpret the data, and draw conclusions.

STEP 1: DEFINE THE PROBLEM. The first and most crucial step in market research is defining the research problem clearly and concisely. A common error at this stage is to confuse a symptom with the true problem. For example, dwindling sales is not a problem but rather a symptom. To get to the heart of the matter, entrepreneurs must list all the possible factors that could have caused the sales slump. Do we face new competition? Are our sales representatives impolite or unknowledgeable? Have customer tastes changed? Is our product line too narrow? Do customers have trouble finding what they want? Is our Web site giving customers what they want? Is it easy to navigate? One entrepreneur wanting to discover the possible causes of his company's poorly performing Web site videotaped customers as they used it and then interviewed them. After studying the videos and listening to their comments, he redesigned the site to make it easier for users to maneuver through its pages, and he refocused its content.

In some cases, business owners may be interested in researching a specific type of question. What are the characteristics of my customers? What are their income levels? What radio stations do they listen to? Why do they shop here? What factors are most important in their buying decisions?

STEP 2: COLLECT THE DATA. The marketing approach that dominates today is **individualized (or one-to-one) marketing,** gathering data on individual customers and then developing a marketing program designed specifically to appeal to their needs, tastes, and preferences. In a society in which people feel so isolated and interactions are so impersonal, one-to-one marketing gives a business a competitive edge. Companies following this approach know their customers, understand how to give them the value they want, and perhaps most important, know how to make them feel special and important. This marketing approach requires business owners to gather and to assimilate detailed information about their target customers, however. Fortunately, even owners of the smallest businesses can collect and use such information relatively easily with the help of a little creativity and a computerized database.

individualized (one-to-one) marketing—*a system based on gathering data on individual customers and developing a marketing program designed to appeal specifically to their needs, tastes, and preferences.*

Silverman's

For example, at Silverman's, a men's clothing chain in the Dakotas, owner Stephen Silverman and a salesperson recently were reviewing a customer's purchasing history on a computer that doubles as a cash register. The flowchart revealed that he had spent more than $2,000 to date and had shopped four times in the previous six months. Looking at the average time between his visits, they noted that he should be coming in soon. Examining the profile more closely, they saw that this customer prefers double-breasted suits, likes Perry Ellis and Christian Dior suits in gray or blue, and has one shoulder slightly lower than the other. He also was among the customers who received a direct-mail ad featuring the upcoming season's new suits. Then, as if on cue, the customer walked in the door! The salesperson greeted him enthusiastically, personally, and knowledgeably. Within 15 minutes, he completed the sale, and the customer raved about how much he enjoys shopping at Silverman's because they know just what he likes and make it so easy to buy! Silverman's chalks up another sale to a satisfied, loyal customer thanks to its "segment of one" marketing strategy.[21]

Figure 6.1 shows how to develop a one-to-one marketing strategy.

For an effective individualized marketing campaign to be successful, business owners must collect three types of information:

1. *Geographic.* Where are my customers located? Do they tend to be concentrated in one geographic region?
2. *Demographic.* What are the characteristics of my customers (age, education levels, income, gender, marital status, and many other features)?
3. *Psychographic.* What drives my customers' buying behavior? Are they receptive to new products or are they among the last to accept them? What values are most important to them?

How can entrepreneurs collect such valuable market and customer information? Consider the following methods of gathering *primary research,* data you collect yourself,

FIGURE 6.1
How to Become an Effective One-to-One Marketer

Source: Adapted from Susan Greco, "The Road to One-to-One Marketing," Inc., October 1995, pp. 56–66.

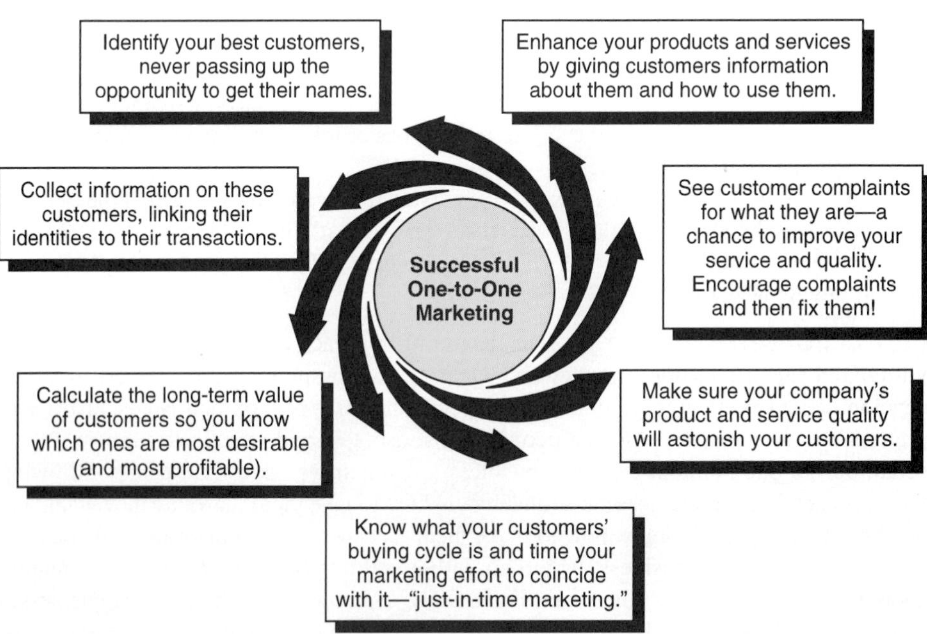

and *secondary research,* data that have already been compiled and are available often at a very reasonable cost (even free). Primary research techniques include:

- *Customer surveys and questionnaires.* Keep them short. Word your questions carefully so that you do not bias the results and use a simple ranking system (e.g., a 1 to 5 scale, with 1 representing "unacceptable" and 5 representing "excellent"). Test your survey for problems on a small number of people before putting it to use.
- *Focus groups.* Enlist a small number of customers to give you feedback on specific issues in your business—quality, convenience, hours of operation, service, and so on. Listen carefully for new marketing opportunities as customers or potential customers tell you what is on their minds. Consider using the Web; one small bicycle company conducts 10 online focus groups each year at no cost and gains valuable marketing information.
- *Daily transactions.* Sift as much data as possible from existing company records and daily transactions—customer warranty cards, personal checks, frequent-buyer clubs, credit applications, and others.
- *Other ideas.* Set up a suggestion system (for customers and employees) and use it. Establish a customer advisory panel to determine how well your company is meeting needs. Talk with suppliers about trends they have spotted in the industry. Contact customers who have not bought anything in a long time and find out why. Contact people who are not customers and find out why. Teach employees to be good listeners and then ask them what they hear.

Secondary research, which is usually less expensive to collect than primary data, includes the following sources:

- *Business directories.* To locate a trade association, use *Business Information Sources* (University of California Press) or the *Encyclopedia of Associations* (Gale Research). To find suppliers, use *The Thomas Register of American Manufacturers* (Thomas Publishing Company) or *Standard and Poor's Register of Corporations, Executives, and Industries* (Standard and Poor Corporation). *The American Wholesalers and Distributors Directory* includes details on more than 18,000 wholesalers and distributors.
- *Direct-mail lists.* You can buy mailing lists for practically any type of business. *The Standard Rates and Data Service (SRDS) Directory of Mailing Lists* (Standard Rates and Data) is a good place to start looking.
- *Demographic data.* To learn more about the demographic characteristics of customers in general, use *The Statistical Abstract of the United States* (Government Printing Office). Profiles of more specific regions are available in *The State and Metropolitan Data Book* (Government Printing Office). *The Sourcebook of Zip Code Demographics* (CACI, Inc.) provides detailed breakdowns of the population in every zip code in the country. *Sales and Marketing Management's Survey of Buying Power* (Bill Communications) has statistics on consumer, retail, and industrial buying.
- *Census data.* The Bureau of the Census publishes a wide variety of reports that summarize the wealth of data found in its census database. Contact the government librarian at your local library for details.
- *Forecasts.* The *U.S. Global Outlook* traces the growth of 200 industries and gives a five-year forecast for each one. Many government agencies including the Department of Commerce offer forecasts on everything from interest rates to the number of housing starts. Again, a government librarian can help you find what you need.
- *Market research.* Someone may already have compiled the market research you need. *The FINDex Worldwide Directory of Market Research Reports, Studies, and Surveys* (Cambridge Information Group) lists more than 10,600 studies available for purchase. Other directories of business research include *Simmons Study of Media and Markets* (Simmons Market Research Bureau Inc.) and the *A. C. Nielsen Retail Index* (A. C. Nielsen Company).

- *Articles.* Magazine and journal articles pertinent to your business are a great source of information. Use the *Reader's Guide to Periodical Literature,* the *Business Periodicals Index* (similar to the *Reader's Guide* but focuses on business periodicals), and *Ulrich's Guide to International Periodicals* to locate the ones you need.
- *Local data.* Your state Department of Commerce and your local chamber of commerce will very likely have useful data on the local market of interest to you. Call to find out what is available.
- *World Wide Web.* Most entrepreneurs are astounded at the marketing information that is available on the World Wide Web (WWW). Using one of the search engines such as Yahoo!, Lycos, Magellan, and others, you can gain access to a world of information—literally!

Much like gold nuggets waiting to be discovered, significant amounts of valuable information about customers and their buying habits is hidden *inside* many small businesses, tucked away in computerized databases. For these business owners, collecting useful information about their target customers and potential new products and markets is simply a matter of sorting and organizing data that are already floating around somewhere in their companies. Thanks to advances in computer hardware and software, data mining, once available only to large companies with vast computer power, is now possible for even very small businesses. **Data mining** is a process in which computer software that uses statistical analysis, database technology, and artificial intelligence finds hidden patterns, trends, and connections in data so that business owners can make better marketing decisions and predictions about customers' behavior. By finding relationships among the many components of a data set, identifying clusters of customers with similar buying habits, and predicting customers' buying patterns, data mining gives entrepreneurs incredible marketing power. Popular data mining software packages include Clementine, DataScope Pro, MineSet, Nuggets, and many others.

data mining—*a process in which computer software that uses statistical analysis, database technology, and artificial intelligence finds hidden patterns, trends, and connections in data so that business owners can make better marketing decisions and predictions about customers' behavior.*

Ammirati, Puris, and Lintas

One small Chicago advertising agency, Ammirati, Puris, and Lintas, uses data mining tools to analyze the results of an extensive survey of customers for its clients. "We mine their responses to segment our clients and to identify profiles for new customers and markets," says Kevin Novak, head of the agency's analytical research department. Not only can the agency provide detailed demographic and statistical breakdowns of their clients' various market segments but it can also profile their buying behavior such as how often they buy a particular product, when and where they buy it, and how many units they buy at a time. Using other features of data mining software to analyze past buying behavior, the agency can rank customer clusters by the likelihood that they will purchase different products and services. "Data mining tools pay off for us because they give us an understanding of our clients' businesses and markets, allowing our agency to compete effectively with much larger agencies," says Novak.[22]

STEP 3: ANALYZE AND INTERPRET THE DATA. The results of market research alone do not provide a solution to the problem; business owners must attach some meaning to them. What do the facts mean? Is there a common thread running through the responses? Do the results suggest any changes needed in the way the business operates? Are there new opportunities the owner can take advantage of? There are no hard-and-fast rules for interpreting market research results; entrepreneurs must use judgment and common sense to determine what the results of their research mean.

STEP 4: DRAW CONCLUSIONS AND ACT. The market research process is not complete until the business owner acts upon the information collected. In many cases, the conclusion is obvious once a small business owner interprets the results of the market research. Based on her understanding of what the facts really mean, the owner must then decide how to use the information in the business. For example, the owner of a retail shop discovered from a survey that her customers preferred evening shopping hours over early morning hours. She made the schedule adjustment, and sales began to climb.

PINPOINTING THE TARGET MARKET

3. Explain how small businesses can pinpoint their target markets.

One of the primary objectives of market research is to identify the small business's **target market**—the specific group of customers at whom the company aims its goods or services. Most marketing experts contend that the greatest marketing mistake small businesses make is failing to define clearly the target market to be served. In other words, most small businesses follow a "shotgun approach" to marketing, firing marketing blasts at every customer that they see, hoping to capture just some of them. Although this approach can work to get a small business established, it can lead to serious problems for a company using it to try to grow. Most entrepreneurs simply cannot use shotgun marketing techniques and compete successfully with larger rivals and their deep pockets. These entrepreneurs develop new products that do not sell because they are not targeted at a specific audience's needs; they broadcast ads that attempt to reach everyone and end up reaching no one; they spend precious time and money trying to reach customers who are not the most profitable; and many of the customers they attract leave because they do not know what the company stands for. "When your resources are limited," says one marketing expert, "you need to develop a more targeted approach."[23]

target market—*the specific group of customers at whom a company aims its goods or services.*

Failing to pinpoint their target markets is especially ironic because small firms are ideally suited to reaching market segments that their larger rivals overlook or consider too small to be profitable. Why, then, is the shotgun approach so popular? Because it is easy and does not require market research or a marketing plan! The problem is that the shotgun approach is a sales-driven rather than a customer-driven strategy. To be customer driven, an effective marketing program must be based on a clear, concise definition of the firm's target customers.

A target-focused marketing strategy can be a powerful strategic weapon for any company that lacks the financial and physical resources of its competitors. Customers respond when companies take the time to learn about their unique needs and offer products and services designed to satisfy them.

Crescendo of New England

For instance, Patrick Mick and Gary Bricker, owners of Crescendo of New England, a small real estate development company, decided to target Generation X professionals with a new apartment complex. Before they began construction, the entrepreneurs first researched the lifestyles and preferences of their 22- to 34-year-old target market. They learned that Generation Xers are highly mobile and engage in a variety of work styles, from telecommuting to running home-based businesses. People in this age group also want product or service information before they make a purchase. After investing enough time to learn about their target customers, Mick and Bricker designed their apartments to include a home office, an extra telephone line, high-speed Internet access, a large exercise facility, a game room, and an on-site business center offering photocopying and teleconferencing. They even set up an informational Web site describing the features and benefits of the new complex. Because of their focused marketing effort, Mick and Bricker had nearly filled the entire apartment complex eight weeks before it was completed![24]

Like Crescendo of New England, the most successful businesses have well-defined portraits of the customers they are seeking to attract. From market research, they know their customers' income levels, lifestyles, buying patterns, likes and dislikes, and even their psychological profiles. The target customer permeates the entire business—from the merchandise sold to the layout and decor of the store. They have an advantage over their larger rivals because the images they have created for their companies appeal to their target customers, and that's why they prosper.

Flying J Travel Plazas

In 1960, Jay Call left college to run his father's gas station that catered to truck drivers. Over the years, Call built the company into a chain of 115 units by concentrating on learning as much as he could about customers and the special needs their on-the-road jobs create, and his efforts have paid off. Flying J Travel Plazas offer truckers 24-hour convenience in clean, *efficient, brightly lit locations. In addition to a full line of diesel fuel pumps and truck repair centers, Flying J units include a lounge with television sets, a buffet restaurant selling reasonably priced, quality meals, and a retail store selling everything from books to long-haul boots. Because truckers often sleep in their trucks to save money, Flying J provides them with spotless private shower rooms where they can freshen up after a long haul and private telephones because truckers rarely use cellular phones. The Flying J Frequent Fueler program keeps truckers coming back to earn fuel discounts and special prizes. The result of Flying J's customer focus? Each travel plaza generates an average of $45,000 per day in revenue!*[25]

Without such a clear picture of its target market and the image it must create to attract those customers, a small company that tries to reach almost everyone usually ends up appealing to almost no one.

The nation's increasingly diverse population offers businesses of all sizes tremendous marketing opportunities if they target specific customers, learn how to reach them, and offer goods and services designed specifically for them. The U.S. Census Bureau projects that Hispanic Americans will be the largest minority in 2050, followed by African Americans and Asian Americans. The U.S. population also will grow older as baby boomers begin to retire in 2011. By 2030, more than 70 million people will be over 65, representing a stunning 13 percent of the population.[26]

Domain

Judy George, founder of the high-fashion furniture chain Domain, is customizing furniture to suit the needs of older customers. For instance, couches and chairs aimed at these customers offer more back support, stand a bit higher, and are not as deep as furniture designed for younger customers. Dressers and cabinets come with slightly oversized knobs that make them easier to open. These modifications make Domain's products ideal for George's elderly clientele.[27]

Sometimes new target markets emerge on their own, much to the surprise of a small business owner.

Example

When Steve Pateman took over the shoe manufacturing company his grandfather had founded, the family business was struggling as a result of intense global competition and rising costs in its core market—high-quality, traditional men's shoes. Pateman was forced to cut the company's workforce from 77 to just 22 employees. Then Pateman received a phone call from a customer with an unusual request: Could he manufacture women's shoes for cross-dressing men? Pateman's company began manufacturing women's shoes in men's sizes and soon developed a complete product line under the Divine label that includes faux leopard thigh boots with seven-and-a-half inch heels! The business has rehired many workers, takes orders from all across the globe, and generates 50 percent of its sales from the transvestite market.[28]

PLOTTING A MARKETING STRATEGY: HOW TO BUILD A COMPETITIVE EDGE

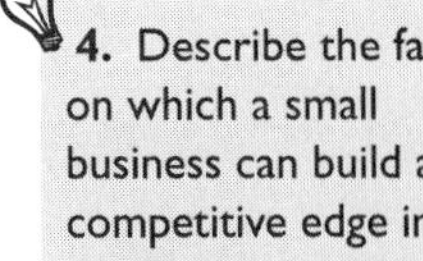
4. Describe the factors on which a small business can build a competitive edge in the marketplace.

A competitive edge is crucial for business success. A small company has a competitive edge when customers perceive that its products or services are superior to those of its competitors. A business owner can create this perception in a variety of ways. Small companies sometimes try to create a competitive edge by offering the lowest prices. This approach may work for many products and services—especially those that customers see as being commodities—but price can be a dangerous criterion upon which to build a competitive edge. Independent hardware stores have discovered that large chains can use their buying power to get volume discounts and undercut the independents' prices. Individual store owners are finding new ways, such as personal service and advice, individual attention, charge accounts, and convenience to differentiate themselves and to retain customer loyalty. "Instead of being forced out of business by the 'category killers,'" says a retail expert, "small retailers are thriving by providing the services and products that larger stores are not able to."[29]

Successful entrepreneurs often use the special advantages that flow from their companies' smallness to build a competitive edge over their larger rivals. Their close contact with the customer, personal attention, focus on service, and organizational and managerial flexibility provide a solid foundation from which to build a towering competitive edge in the market. Small companies are more effective than their larger rivals at **relationship marketing**—developing and maintaining long-term relationships with customers so that they will keep coming back to make repeat purchases. Relationship marketing puts the customer at the center of a company's thinking, planning, and action and shifts the focus from a product or service to customers and their needs and wants. (See Figure 6.2.)

relationship marketing— *the process of developing and maintaining long-term relationships with customers so they will keep coming back to make repeat purchases.*

Business owners are discovering that even though they may be providing their customers with satisfactory service and value, many of their customers do not remain loyal, choosing instead to buy from other companies. Businesses that provide poor customer service are in grave danger. Hepworth, a consulting firm that specializes in customer retention, measures its clients' **revenue at risk,** which calculates the sales revenue a company would lose by measuring the percentage of customers who would leave because of poor service. According to Hepworth's research, for companies that score in the top 25 percent on customer loyalty, revenue at risk averages just 3 percent. However, for companies that rate loyalty scores in the bottom 25 percent, poor customer service puts at risk an average of more than 12 percent of company revenue.[30] Today, earning customers' loyalty requires businesses to take customer focus and service to unprecedented levels, and that requires building long-term relationships with customers. To make relationship marketing work, a

revenue at risk—*a measure that calculates the sales revenue a company would lose by measuring the percentage of customers who would leave because of poor service.*

FIGURE 6.2
The Relationship Marketing Process

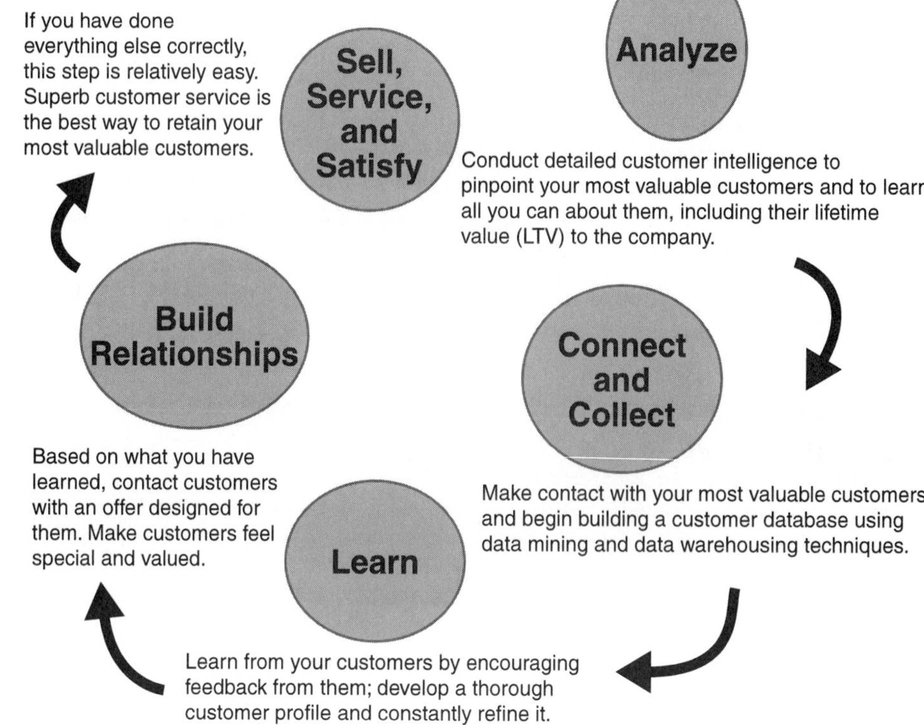

small business must achieve the highest of the following four levels of customer involvement.[31]

Level 1: Customer Awareness. The prevailing attitude in the company is "There's a customer out there." Managers and employees know little about the company's customers and view them only in the most general terms. No one understands the benefits of a close customer–supplier relationship.

Level 2: Customer Sensitivity. A wall stands between the company and its customers. Employees know more about their customers' characteristics, but they have not begun to share much information with them. Similarly, the company doesn't solicit feedback from its customers.

Level 3: Customer Alignment. Managers and employees understand the customer's central role in the business. They spend considerable time talking with, and about, customers. They also seek out customer feedback through surveys, focus groups, and customer interviews and visits.

Level 4: Customer Partnership. The company has refined its customer service attitude from mere techniques to an all-encompassing part of its culture. Customers are part of all major issues. Employees at every level of the organization receive intelligence reports on customers and interact with them whenever possible. Customers play an important role in product development and in other aspects of the business. Managers and employees focus on building lasting relationships with customers.

Table 6.2 describes the differences between relationship marketing and its polar opposite, transaction selling.

Because it is knowledge based, relationship marketing usually requires an investment in technology (e.g., a computer database to track customer behavior, habits, and preferences) and a commitment from the business owner to make it work, but the payoff can be a powerful competitive edge. "You create and add value to a . . . relationship that a big company can't match," explains one business owner who relies on relationship marketing.[32]

To achieve the highest level of customer satisfaction, many small businesses rely on six important sources to develop a competitive edge: a focus on the customer; devotion to quality; attention to convenience; concentration on innovation; dedication to service; and emphasis on speed.

Focus on the Customer

Too many businesses have lost sight of the important component of every business: the customer. Wooing disillusioned customers back will require businesses to focus on them as never before. Businesses must realize that everything in the business—even the business itself—depends on creating a satisfied customer. One entrepreneur says, "If you're not taking care of your customers and nurturing that relationship, you can bet there's someone else out there who will."[33]

Businesses are just beginning to discover the true costs of poor customer relations. For instance:

- Sixty-seven percent of customers who stop patronizing a particular store do so because an indifferent employee treated them poorly.[34]
- Ninety-six percent of dissatisfied customers never complain about rude or discourteous service, but . . .
- Ninety-one percent will not buy from the business again.
- One hundred percent of those unhappy customers will tell their "horror stories" to at least nine other people.

TABLE 6.2
The Differences Between Relationship Marketing and Transaction Selling

Source: Adapted from Timothy M. Baye, "Relationship Marketing: A Six-Step Guide for the Business Start-Up," Small Business Forum, *Spring 1995, pp. 26–41.*

Feature	Relationship Marketing	Transaction Selling
Duration	Ongoing	Distinct beginning and end; one transaction attitude
Key concepts	Collaborate and cooperate	Negotiate
Driven by	Commitment and trust	Making profitable short-term transactions
Style	Mutual dependence	Independence
Business plan implications	Building a network of relationships with dependable suppliers and customers that will lead to long-term profitability	Maximize short-term profits; make the bottom line look good, whatever the long-term costs
Primary advantage	Intimate knowledge of customers' needs, wants, and preferences developed over time	Cash in hand
Primary disadvantage	Dependence on other partners in the web of relationships	Losing the sale if a competitor makes the customer a better offer
Foundation	Knowledge based	Bottom-line oriented
Outlook	Increasing in popularity	On the decline

- Thirteen percent of those unhappy customers will tell their stories to at least twenty other people.[35]

According to the authors of *Keeping Customers for Life,* "The nasty result of this customer indifference costs the average company from 15 to 30 percent of gross sales."[36] Because 70 percent of the average company's sales come from present customers, few can afford to alienate any shoppers. In fact, the typical business loses 20 percent of its customers each year. But a recent study by the consulting firm Bain & Co. shows that companies that retain just 5 percent more customers experience profit increases of at least 25 percent and, in some cases, as much as 95 percent![37] Studies by the Boston Consulting Group also show that customer retention results in above-average profits and superior growth in market share.[38]

Because about 20 percent of a typical company's customers account for about 80 percent of its sales, it makes more sense to focus resources on keeping the best (and most profitable) customers than to spend time trying to chase "fair weather" customers who will defect to any better deal that comes along. Suppose that a company increases its customer base by 20 percent each year, but it retains only 85 percent of its existing customers. Its effective growth rate is just 5 percent per year [20% – (100% – 85%) = 5%]. If this same company can raise its customer retention rate to 95 percent, its net growth rate *triples* to 15 percent [20% – (100% – 95%) = 15%].[39]

Although winning new customers keeps a company growing, keeping existing ones is essential to success. Attracting a new customer actually costs *five times* as much as keeping an existing one. Therefore, small business owners would be better off asking, "How can we improve customer value and service to encourage our existing customers to do more business with us?" rather than "How can we increase our market share by 10 percent?" The *real* key to marketing success lies in a company's existing customer base.

Game-Set-Match

Managers at Game-Set-Match, a company that offers tennis lessons and operates retail stores selling tennis gear and services, recognize the power of marketing to existing customers. With the help of a computerized database, the company identifies its best customers and courts them with special offers, extra service, and additional benefits. As important as technology is to managing Game-Set-Match's customer relationships, the company relies on more than technology to coddle its customers. "Service takes technology, process, and people," says one manager, "and all of them are critical." The payoff for Game-Set-Match is evident; its sales have climbed an average of 45 percent a year for the past four years.[40]

The most successful small businesses have developed a customer focus and have instilled a customer satisfaction attitude *throughout* the company. Companies with world-class customer attitudes set themselves apart by paying attention to "little things" such as remembering a customer's unique preferences or sending a customer a copy of an article of interest to her. For example, at one dentist's office, staff members take photos on a patient's first visit. The photo, placed in the patient's file, allows everyone in the office to call him by name on subsequent visits. When McDonald's opened stores in the financial districts of Los Angeles and New York, it installed stock "ticker boards" and telephones on the tables.[41] A small flower shop offers a special service for customers who forget that special event. The shop will insert a card reading, "Please forgive us! Being short-handed this week, we were unable to deliver this gift on time. We hope the sender's thoughtfulness will not be less appreciated because of our error. Again, we apologize."[42]

How do these companies focus so intently on their customers? They constantly ask customers four basic questions and then act on what they hear:

1. What are we doing right?
2. How can we do that even better?

3. What have we done wrong?
4. What can we do in the future?

For instance, Steve Ettridge, CEO of Temps & Company, an employment services company, regularly surveys existing customers as well as prospects who chose to do business with competitors to determine how well his company is serving them and to identify other needs they have.[43]

Table 6.3 offers some basic strategies for developing and retaining loyal customers.

Devotion to Quality

In this intensely competitive global business environment, quality goods and services are a prerequisite for success—and even survival. According to one marketing axiom, the worst of all marketing catastrophes is to have great advertising and a poor-quality product. Customers have come to expect and demand quality goods and services, and those businesses that provide them consistently have a distinct competitive advantage.

Today, quality is more than just a slogan posted on the company bulletin board; world-class companies treat quality as a strategic objective—an integral part of a company's strat-

TABLE 6.3

Strategies for Developing and Retaining Loyal Customers

Sources: Adapted from Jerry Fisher, "The Secret's Out," Entrepreneur, *May 1998, pp. 112–119; Laura M. Litvan, "Increasing Revenue with Repeat Sales,"* Nation's Business, *January 1996, pp. 36–37. "Encourage Customers to Complain,"* Small Business Reports, *June 1990, p. 7; Dave Zielinski, "Improving Service Doesn't Require a Big Investment,"* Small Business Reports, *February 1991, p. 20; John H. Sheridan, "Out of the Isolation Booth,"* Industry Week, *June 19, 1989, pp. 18–19; Lin Grensing-Pophal, "At Your Service,"* Business Start-Ups, *May 1995, pp. 72–74.*

- Identify your best customers and give them incentives to return. Focus resources on the 20 percent of customers that account for 80 percent of sales.
- When you create a dissatisfied customer, fix the problem fast. One study found that, given the chance to complain, 95 percent of customers will buy again *if* a business handles their complaints promptly and effectively. The worst way to handle a complaint is to ignore it, to pass it off to a subordinate, or to let a lot of time slip by before dealing with it.
- Make sure your business system makes it easy for customers to buy from you. Eliminate unnecessary procedures that challenge customers' patience.
- *Encourage* customer complaints. You can't fix something if you don't know it's broken. Find out what solution the customer wants and try to come as close to that as possible.
- Contact lost customers to find out why they left. You may uncover a problem you never knew existed.
- Ask employees for feedback on improving customer service. A study by Technical Assistance Research Programs (TARP), a customer service research firm, found that front-line service workers can predict nearly 90 percent of the cases that produce customer complaints. Emphasize that *everyone* is part of the customer satisfaction team.
- Get total commitment to superior customer service from top managers—and allocate resources appropriately.
- Allow managers to wait on customers occasionally. It's a great dose of reality. The founder of a small robot manufacturer credits such a strategy with saving his company. "We now require every officer of this company—including myself—to meet with customers at least four times a month," he says.
- Carefully select and train *everyone* who will deal with customers. Never let rude employees work with customers.
- Develop a service theme that communicates your attitude toward customers. Customers want to feel they are getting something special.
- Reward employees "caught" providing exceptional service to the customer.
- Get in the habit of calling customers by name. It's one of the most meaningful ways of connecting with your customers.
- Remember: The customer pays the bills. Special treatment wins customers and keeps them coming back.

total quality management (TQM)—*the philosophy of producing a high-quality product or service and achieving quality in every aspect of the business and its relationship with the customer; the focus is on continuous improvement in the quality delivered to customers.*

egy and culture. This philosophy is called **total quality management (TQM)**—quality not just in the product or service itself but in *every* aspect of the business and its relationship with the customer and *continuous improvement* in the quality delivered to customers.

Companies on the cutting edge of the quality movement are developing new ways to measure quality. Manufacturers were the first to apply TQM techniques, but retail, wholesale, and service organizations have seen the benefits of becoming champions of quality as well. They are tracking customer complaints, contacting "lost" customers, and finding new ways to track the cost of quality (COQ) and their return on quality (ROQ).

The key to developing a successful TQM philosophy is seeing the world from the customer's point of view. In other words, quality must reflect the needs and wants of the customer. How do customers define quality? According to a recent poll, Americans rank quality components in this order: reliability (average time between failures), durability (how long it lasts), ease of use, a known or trusted brand name, and, last, a low price.[44] When buying services, customers look for similar characteristics: tangibles (equipment, facilities, and people), reliability (doing what you say you will do), responsiveness (promptness in helping customers and in solving problems), and assurance and empathy (conveying a caring attitude). For example, the owner of a very successful pest-control company offers his customers a unique, unconditional guarantee: If the company fails to eliminate all roach and rodent breeding and nesting areas on a client's premises, it will refund the customer's last 12 monthly payments and will pay for one year's service by another exterminator. The company has had to honor its guarantee only once in 17 years.

The benefits of a successful TQM philosophy can be substantial, sometimes making the difference between success and failure.

Globe Metallurgical

In the 1980s, Globe Metallurgical, a small maker of ferroalloy and silicon metals, was on the verge of extinction because of poor product quality and mediocre employee relations. To save itself, Globe adopted the TQM philosophy, rewrote workers' job descriptions, flattened its management structure, created worker teams, and focused on customer satisfaction. The changes literally saved the company. Globe turns out 1,100 tons of product per worker-hour compared to an industry average of 500 tons. Productivity is up 50 percent, and sales and profits are hitting record levels. Exports have climbed from 2 percent to 20 percent of sales.[45]

Companies successful in capturing a reputation for top-quality products and services follow certain guidelines to "get it right the first time":

- Build quality into the process; don't rely on inspection to obtain quality.
- Foster teamwork and dismantle the barriers that divide disparate departments.
- Establish long-term ties with select suppliers; don't award contracts on low price alone.
- Provide managers and employees the training needed to participate fully in the quality improvement program.
- Empower workers at all levels of the organization; give them authority and responsibility for making decisions that determine quality.
- Get managers' commitment to the quality philosophy. Otherwise, the program is doomed. Describing his leadership role in his company's TQM philosophy, one CEO says, "People look to see if you just talk about it or actually do it."[46]
- Rethink the processes the company uses now to get its products or services to its customers. Employees at Analog Devices redesigned its production process and significantly lowered the defect rate on its silicon chips and saved $1.2 million a year.[47]
- Reward employees for quality work. Ideally, employees' compensation is linked clearly and directly to key measures of quality and customer satisfaction.
- Develop a company-wide strategy for constant improvement of product and service quality.

Attention to Convenience

Ask customers what they want from the businesses they deal with and one of the most common responses is "convenience." In this busy, fast-paced world of dual-career couples and lengthy commutes to and from work, customers increasingly are looking for convenience. Several studies have found that customers rank easy access to goods and services at the top of their purchase criteria. Unfortunately, too few businesses deliver adequate levels of convenience, and they fail to attract and retain customers. One print and framing shop, for instance, alienated many potential customers with its abbreviated business hours—9 to 5 daily, except for Wednesday afternoons, Saturdays, and Sundays when the shop was closed. Other companies make it a chore to do business with them. In an effort to defend themselves against unscrupulous customers, these businesses have created elaborate procedures for exchanges, refunds, writing checks, and other basic transactions. One researcher claims, "What they're doing is treating the 98 percent of honest customers like crooks to catch the 2 percent who are crooks."[48]

Successful companies go out of their way to make sure that it is easy for customers to do business with them. The HomeBased Warehouse in San Bernadino, California, has borrowed an idea from fast-food restaurants to make buying lumber more convenient for its customers: drive-in windows. More than 200 cars a day pull in and load up with lumber before driving to the cashier's booth to pay. The drive-thru "has increased [sales] volume and enhanced contractor business. They like the time-saving [convenience] of being able to drive in, load up, and cash out at the outside register," says one manager. In Las Vegas, a couple can pull up at the Wedding Window, and an ordained minister in the drive-thru window will marry them![49]

How can a business owner boost the convenience level of her business? By conducting a "convenience audit" from the customer's point of view to get an idea of its ETDBW ("Easy To Do Business With") index:

- Is your business located near your customers? Does it provide easy access?
- Are your business hours suitable to your customers? Should you be open evenings and weekends to serve them better?
- Would customers appreciate pickup and delivery service? The owner of a restaurant located near a major office complex installed a fax machine to receive orders from busy office workers; a crew of employees would deliver lunches to the workers at their desks!
- Does your company make it easy for customers to make purchases on credit or with credit cards?
- Are your employees trained to handle business transactions quickly, efficiently, and politely? Waiting while rude, poorly trained employees fumble through routine transactions destroys customer goodwill.
- Does your company handle telephone calls quickly and efficiently? Long waits "on hold," transfers from one office to another, and too many rings before answering signal customers that they are not important. Jerre Stead, CEO of Ingram Micro Inc., a distributor of computer products, expects every telephone call to the company to be answered within three seconds![50]

Suitable Suits

Urvi Mehta has built a very successful business on the simple premise of offering her customers the ultimate in convenience. Mehta runs Suitable Suits from her New York City office and targets busy professional women in the city who need proper business attire but lack the time or the inclination to shop for it. Mehta and her sales staff measure each customer to ensure a proper fit and interview them about their tastes, preferred styles, and favorite colors. Mehta then checks her inventory of suits and accessories (which she buys directly from vendors), selects several outfits, and takes them to the customer's office or *home for a personal fitting. Because of Suitable Suits' low overhead, Mehta is able to sell professional clothing at prices that are 20 to 40 percent less than specialty stores charge. By offering the convenience her target customers value, Mehta closes a sale on almost every call she makes, selling 100 to 120 suits each month and generating more than $750,000 in sales for her young company.*[51]

Concentration on Innovation

Innovation is the key to future success. Markets change too quickly and competitors move too fast for a small company to stand still and remain competitive. Because they cannot outspend their larger rivals, small companies often turn to superior innovation as the way to gain a competitive edge.

Thanks to their organizational and managerial flexibility, small businesses often can detect and act on new opportunities faster than large companies. Innovation is one of the hallmarks of entrepreneurs, and it shows up in the new products, unique techniques, and unusual marketing approaches they introduce. Despite their limited resources, small businesses frequently are leaders in innovation. For instance, in the hotly competitive pharmaceutical industry, the dominant drugs in most markets were discovered by small companies rather than the industry giants such as Glaxo or Upjohn with their multimillion-dollar R&D budgets.

Obviously, there is more to innovation than spending megadollars on research and development. "It takes money to fund a business," says one small business advisor, "but it's continuous creativity that keeps the venture running smoothly and profitably."[52] How do small businesses manage to maintain their leadership role in innovating new products and services? They use their size to their advantage, maintaining their speed and flexibility much like a martial arts expert does against a larger opponent. Their closeness to their customers enables them to read subtle shifts in the market and to anticipate trends as they unfold. Their ability to concentrate their efforts and attention in one area also gives small businesses an edge in innovation. One venture capitalist explains, "Small companies have an advantage: a dedicated management team totally focused on a new product or market."[53]

G-Vox

Nathaniel Weiss demonstrated the innovative spirit of entrepreneurship and the success it can bring when he invented G-Vox, a unique hardware and software combination that automatically transcribes the notes a guitarist plays into sheet music. Guitarists love G-Vox because it frees them from having to stop in the middle of their creative riffs and write down the notes they are playing. Weiss's product has become so successful that he has been able to forge strategic partnerships with companies such as computer-chip maker Intel, Paramount Studios, and guitar manufacturer Fender. He has also expanded the G-Vox product line to include instructional videos and software that interacts with many other instruments.[54]

Dedication to Service and Customer Satisfaction

In the new economy, companies are discovering that unexpected innovative, customized service can be a powerful strategic weapon. Providing incomparable service—not necessarily a low price—is one of the most effective ways to attract and maintain a growing customer base. In fact, a recent study of consumer behavior reported that 73 percent of customers buy for reasons other than price![55] One business writer explains, "It matters not whether a company creates something you can touch . . . or something you can only experience . . . What counts most is the service built into that something—the way the product is designed and delivered, billed and bundled, explained and installed, repaired and renewed."[56]

USE TECHNOLOGY TO PROVIDE IMPROVED SERVICE. The role of technology is not to create a rigid bureaucracy but to free employees from routine clerical tasks, giving them more time and better tools to serve customers more effectively. Ideally, technology gives workers the information they need to help their customers and the time to serve them.

To use technology effectively, entrepreneurs must ask: "What is the best technology for our strategy?" This question leads to four key service issues: (1) What is our primary service strategy? (i.e., What do we want customers to think of when they hear our name?) (2) What barriers are preventing our company from fully implementing this strategy now? (3) What, if anything, can technology do to overcome these barriers? (4) What is our strategy for encouraging our customers to adopt the new technology?[65]

Best Friends Pet Resorts and Salons

Best Friends Pet Resorts and Salons, a fast-growing chain of pet boarding facilities that more closely resembles a five-star hotel than a kennel, relies on technology to offer both its customers (pet owners) and its clients (pets) incomparable service. Best Friends provides for pets a multitude of personalized services ranging from grooming and supervised play time to special diets and accommodations in comfortable, odor-free suites. CEO Charles Cocotas extends that same level of service to the pet owners who book stays for their pets at Best Friends. To enable employees to keep track of every pet-guests' special needs, habits, and preferences, Cocotas uses a customized version of the same hotel management software that the swankiest hotels use to pamper their human guests. The software gives everyone in the company who interacts with pet owners access to a pet's complete history, down to preferred walking and play times, vaccination schedules, medication needs, and food allergies. When customers call in to check on their pets, employees can call up every detail of the pet's entire day and reassure the owner with a full report. The software also gives Cocotas meaningful management information about which services customers are buying and which promotions caught their attention. Best Friends' investment in technology has enabled the company to accelerate its growth rate and to distinguish itself from its more mundane competition.[66]

REWARD SUPERIOR SERVICE. What gets rewarded gets done. Companies that want employees to provide stellar service must offer rewards for doing so. A recent National Science Foundation study concluded that when pay is linked to performance, employees' motivation and productivity climb by as much as 63 percent.[67]

MasterCare Auto Centers

When MasterCare Auto Centers discovered that its customer service system was failing, it revamped its compensation system, linking it more closely with customer service measures. Employees—including mechanics—who keep loyal customers earn salary bonuses. The new system has raised customer retention 25 percent and lowered employee turnover 40 percent.[68]

GET TOP MANAGERS' SUPPORT. The drive toward superior customer service will fall far short of its target unless top managers support it fully. Success requires more than just a verbal commitment; it calls for managers' involvement and dedication to making service a core company value. Achieving customer satisfaction must become part of the strategic planning process and work its way into every nook and cranny of the organization. Once it does, employees will be able to provide stellar customer service with or without a checklist of "do's and don'ts."

VIEW CUSTOMER SERVICE AS AN INVESTMENT, NOT AN EXPENSE. The companies that lead the way when it comes to retaining their customers view the money they spend on customer service as an investment rather than an expense. One of the most effective ways for entrepreneurs to learn this lesson is to calculate the cost of poor customer service to their companies. Once they calculate it, the cost of lost customers due to poor service is so astonishing to most business owners that they quickly become customer service zealots. For instance, the owner of a small restaurant calculated that if every day he lost to poor service one customer who spent just $5 per week, his business was losing $94,900 in revenue per year! The restaurateur immediately changed his approach to customer service.

Emphasis on Speed

Technology, particularly the Internet, has changed the pace of business so dramatically that speed has become a major competitive weapon. Today's customers expect businesses to serve them at the speed of light! Providing a quality product at a reasonable price once was sufficient to keep customers happy, but that is not enough for modern customers who can find dozens of comparable products with just a few mouse clicks. Speed reigns. World-class companies recognize that reducing the time it takes to develop, design, manufacture, and deliver a product reduces costs, increases quality, improves customer satisfaction, and boosts market share. One study by McKinsey and Company found that high-tech products that come to market on budget but six months late will earn 33 percent less profit over five years. Bringing the product out on time but 50 percent over budget cuts profits just 4 percent![69] Service companies also know that they must build speed into their business system if they are to satisfy their impatient, time-pressured customers.

Victory in this time-obsessed economy goes to the company that can deliver goods and services the fastest, not necessarily those that are the biggest and most powerful. Business is moving so rapidly today that companies "need to accomplish in 90 days what traditionally took a year," explains one entrepreneur.[70] Businesses that can satisfy their customers' insatiable appetites for speed have a distinct advantage.

Santin Engineering

Santin Engineering, a small company that makes prototypes for manufacturers who want a tangible version of their latest designs, relies on speed to satisfy customers, most of whom make components for the fast-paced computer industry. "The pressure is constant to reduce their time frames and to help them get a performing product in the shortest possible period of time," says second-generation owner Drew Santin. "I'm dealing with an industry where the two-year time frame for developing a new product now has become six months or less." Santin defines his company not only in terms of the engineering services it offers but also in terms of the speed at which it performs. Employees are cross-trained for maximum flexibility and are paid extra to work nights and weekends when customers have tight deadlines. The company's investment in computer-controlled equipment enables workers to generate plastic models of proposed products instantly—often during a meeting with the customer![71]

This philosophy of speed is called **time compression management (TCM),** and it involves three aspects: (1) speeding new products to market, (2) shortening customer response time in manufacturing and delivery, and (3) reducing the administrative time required to fill an order. Studies show plenty of room for improvement; most businesses waste 85 to 99 percent of the time it takes to produce products or services without ever realizing it![72]

United Electric Controls

For example, when managers and employees at United Electric Controls, a family-owned maker of temperature and pressure controls and sensors, studied their production process, they were amazed at what they found. In their 50,000-square-foot factory, "We had one product that traveled 12 miles just in our plant," says one manager. Rearranging the plant's layout around products rather than processes solved the problem. "The product that once traveled 12 miles now travels 40 feet," he says. "The outcome was a reduction in lead time from 10 or 12 weeks to just a couple of days."[73]

Although speeding up the manufacturing process is a common goal, companies using TCM have learned that manufacturing takes only 5 percent to 10 percent of the total time between an order and getting the product into the customer's hands. The rest is consumed by clerical and administrative tasks. "The primary opportunity for TCM lies in its application to the administrative process," says one manufacturing plant manager.

Companies relying on TCM to help them turn speed into a competitive edge should:

- Reengineer the entire process rather than attempt to do the same things in the same way—only faster.

tomers.[78] The result is a disproportionately small impact of small companies on the Web. According to Forrester Research, although small businesses make 50 percent of all retail sales in the United States, they account for just 9 percent of all *online* sales! As Web-based sales volume grows, the percentage of sales by small businesses will shrink to just 6 percent by 2003.[79]

Small companies that have established well-designed Web sites understand the Web's power as a marketing tool and are reaping the benefits of e-commerce. The Web magnifies a company's ability to provide superior customer service at minimal cost. An innovative Web site allows customers to gather information about a product or service, have their questions answered, download diagrams and photographs, or track the progress of their orders.

Araujo Estate Wines

When the owner of Araujo Estate Wines, a small California winery, found that employees were spending too much time on the phone answering questions about its different wines and their availability, Araujo modified its Web site to include detailed descriptions of all of its wines (including "tasting notes"), a list of restaurants serving its wines, and a guest comment section. Not only are customer service ratings up, but the winery also has been able to reduce employees' telephone time by 60 percent.[80]

The Web gives small businesses the power to broaden their scope to unbelievable proportions. Web-based businesses are open around the clock seven days a week and can reach customers anywhere in the world.

The Book Corner

"The Web has made me a merchant to the world," says Michael Tennaro, co-owner of the Book Corner, a small bookstore based in Brandon, Florida, with customers in 51 countries around the world. For small businesses such as the Book Corner, selling on the Web can mean the difference between survival and failure. Just a few years ago, the Book Corner, a nondescript retail bookstore located in a strip shopping center struggling to attract customers, was in danger of closing. The decision to move to the Web was an easy one because the Tennaros already had computerized their entire inventory and making their database of books available online was relatively easy. The decision paid big dividends. Today, the Book Corner occupies half of the shopping center, does 50 percent of its business on the Web, and counts giant bookseller Barnes & Noble among its customers.[81]

Small companies that have had the greatest success selling on the Web have marketing strategies that emphasize their existing strengths and core competencies. Their Web marketing strategies reflect their "brick-and-mortar" marketing strategies, often focusing on building relationships with their customers rather than merely scouting for a sale. These companies understand their target customers and know how to reach them using the Web. They create Web sites that provide meaningful information to their customers, that customize themselves based on each customer's interests, and that make it easy for customers to find what they want. In short, their Web sites create the same sense of trust and personal attention customers get when dealing with a local small business.

Using the Web as a marketing tool allows entrepreneurs to provide both existing and potential customers with meaningful information in an interactive rather than a passive setting. Well-designed Web sites include interactive features that allow customers to access information about a company, its products and services, its history, and other features such as question-and-answer sessions with experts or the ability to conduct e-mail conversations with company officials.

Pinnacle Building Systems

For instance, Pinnacle Building Systems, a small company that builds modular homes ranging from 900 square feet to more than 3,000 square feet, has built a Web site that lets customers view floor plans and sketches, detailed specifications on all building materials, photographs of homes the company has built, and information on obtaining financing. Through the Web, Pinnacle can communicate valuable information to potential customers that would be impossible to provide without bringing in an army of sales representatives to *talk with customers one-on-one. When founder Chris Graff launched the site, he had no expectations that it would generate much business for Pinnacle. In its first year, however, the Web site generated $2 million in sales for the company—"beyond anyone's wildest expectations," says Graff. Because of the site's initial success, Graff has upgraded its capabilities, and the company now generates more than $5 million in annual revenues from its Web site.*[82]

The World Wide Web also allows business owners to link their sites to other related Web sites, something advertisements in other media cannot offer. For instance, the homepage of a company selling cookware might include hypertext links to Web pages containing recipes, cookbooks, foods, and other cooking resources. This allows small business owners to engage in cross-marketing with companies on the Web selling complementary products or services. Small businesses also have the ability to get quantifiable results from their Web-based marketing efforts. Many available software packages monitor the number of visitors to a company's Web site and track their movements in the site, telling entrepreneurs which features are most popular with customers.

Small companies have plenty of incentive to set up shop on the World Wide Web. By 2003, more than 500 million people will have access to the Internet, and the number will continue to grow rapidly. Plus, the demographic profile of the typical Web user is very attractive to many entrepreneurs: young, educated, wealthy, and evenly split between males and females. So far, the top-selling items on the Web are computer hardware and accessories, software, travel and financial services, books, music, movies, flowers, and gift items.[83]

Despite all of the hoopla about the marketing potential of the Web, not every business owner should rush out and establish a Web site. In fact, many of those currently trying to sell on the Web are not making any money at it! A recent study by Activemedia found that almost 50 percent of commercial Web sites are profitable.[84] Those companies that have not yet reached profitability through e-commerce are looking to the future, using the Web to connect with their existing customers and, eventually, to attract new ones.

Using the Web as a marketing tool requires more than establishing a Web site and waiting for customers to come calling. Just as in any marketing venture, the key to successful marketing on the World Wide Web is selling the right product or service at the right price to the right target audience. Entrepreneurs on the Web, however, also have two additional challenges: attracting Web users to their Web sites and converting them into paying customers. That requires setting up an electronic storefront that is inviting, easy to navigate, interactive, and offers more than a monotonous laundry list of items. It also requires promoting the Web site in all of a company's marketing material, from print ads and radio spots to business cards and company letterhead. With a solid marketing strategy as a guide, small companies can—and are—selling everything from wine and vacations to jewelry and electronics successfully on the Web. Table 6.4 provides a breakdown of the typical first-year expenses a small company can expect when setting up a Web site.

6. Discuss the "four Ps" of marketing—product, place, price, and promotion—and their role in building a successful marketing strategy.

THE MARKETING MIX

The major elements of a marketing strategy are the four Ps of marketing—**p**roduct, **p**lace, **p**rice, and **p**romotion. These four elements are self-reinforcing, and when coordinated, increase the sales appeal of a product or service. Small business managers must integrate these elements to maximize the impact of their product or service on the consumer. All four Ps must reinforce the image of the product or service the company presents to the potential customer. One longtime retailer claims, "None of the modern marvels of computerized inventory control and point-of-sale telecommunications have replaced the need for the entrepreneur who understands the customer and can translate that into the appropriate merchandise mix."[85]

Setup and maintenance fees	$900
Domain name registration	$70
Design charges for creating logo	$250
Scanner	$150
Photo imaging software	$70
Credit card authorization and processing fees	$600
Total	$2,040
Plus $30 to $70 per month for Web site marketing services	
Plus any start-up fees and per-transaction charges for credit card services	

[a] For a simple Web-based store selling 50 products.

TABLE 6.4
Typical First-Year Operating Expenses for a Small Web-Based Company[a]

Source: PC World, cited in Carla Young Harrington, "Storming the Electronic Marketplace: E-Business," Inc., June 1999, Advertising Supplement.

Product

The product itself is an essential element in marketing. A product is any item or service that satisfies the need of a customer. Products can have form and shape, or they can be services with no physical form. Products travel through various stages of development. The **product life cycle** (see Figure 6.3) describes these stages of growth. Knowing which stage of the life cycle a product is in allows managers to make decisions about whether or not to continue selling the product and when to introduce new follow-up products.

product life cycle—*describes the stages of development, growth, and decline in a product's life.*

introductory stage—*the stage in which a product or service must break into the market and overcome customer inertia.*

growth and acceptance stage—*the stage in which sales and profits materialize.*

In the **introductory stage,** marketers present their product to potential consumers. Initial high levels of acceptance are rare. Generally, new products must break into existing markets and compete with established products. Advertising and promotion help the new product be more quickly recognized. Potential customers must get information about the product, how to use it, and the needs it can satisfy. The cost of marketing a product at this level of the life cycle is usually high because a company must overcome customer resistance and inertia. Thus, profits are generally low, or even negative, in the introductory stage.

After the introductory stage, the product enters the **growth and acceptance stage.** In the growth stage, consumers begin to compare the product in large enough numbers for sales to rise and profits to materialize. Products that reach this stage, however, do not necessarily become successful. If in the introductory or the growth stage the product fails to

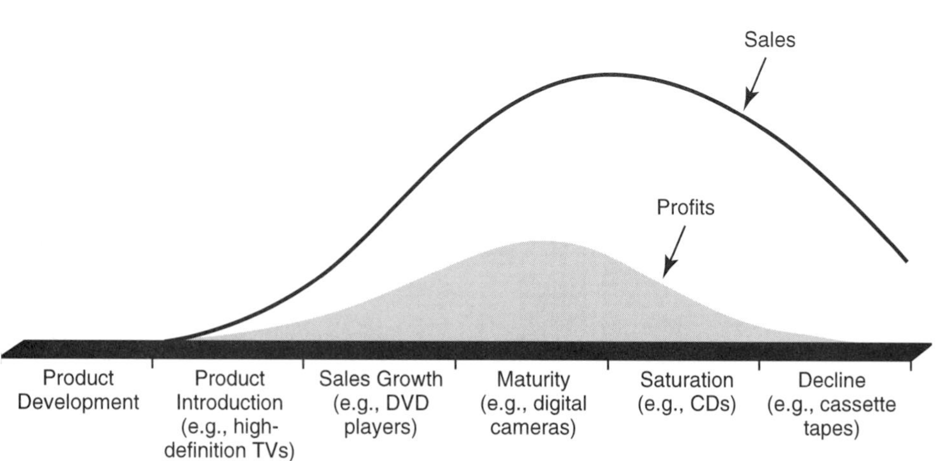

FIGURE 6.3
The Product Life Cycle

meet consumer needs, it does not sell and eventually disappears from the marketplace. According to Greg Stevens, president of a new-product research company, an average of just two new products are launched out of every 3,000 ideas generated; of the two actually launched, only one succeeds.[86] For successful products, sales and profit margins continue to rise through the growth stage.

maturity and competition stage—*the stage in which sales rise, but profits peak and then fall as competitors enter the market.*

market saturation stage—*stage in which sales peak, indicating the time to introduce the next-generation product.*

product decline stage—*the stage in which sales continue to fall and profit margins decline drastically.*

In the **maturity and competition stage,** sales volume continues to rise, but profit margins peak and then begin to fall as competitors enter the market. Normally, this causes a reduction in the product's selling price to meet the competition and to hold its share of the market.

Sales peak in the **market saturation stage** of the product life cycle and give the marketer fair warning that it is time to introduce the next-generation product.

The final stage of the product life cycle is the **product decline stage.** Sales continue to drop, and profit margins fall drastically. However, when a product reaches this stage of the cycle, it does not mean that it is doomed to failure. Products that have remained popular are always being revised. No firm can maintain its sales position without product innovation and change. Even the maker of Silly Putty, first introduced at the 1950 International Toy Fair (with lifetime sales of more than 200 million "eggs"), recently introduced new Day-Glo and glow-in-the-dark colors. These innovations have caused the classic toy's sales to rebound, appealing to new generations of children.

The time span of the stages in the product life cycle depends on the type of products involved. High-fashion and fad clothing have a short product life cycle, lasting for only four to six weeks. Products that are more stable may take years to complete a life cycle. Research conducted by MIT suggests that the typical product's life cycle lasts 10 to 14 years, but the length of that life cycle appears to be shrinking.[87]

Thomas Venable, owner of Spectrum Control, Inc., uses the concept of the product life cycle to plan the introduction of new products to his company's product line. Too often, companies wait too late into the life cycle of one product to introduce another. The result is that they are totally unprepared when a competitor produces "a better mousetrap" and their sales decline. "If you are not developing something new early in the current product's life cycle, you're living on borrowed time," says Venable. "If you wait until your line is mature, you're dead."[88]

In Venable's industry, a 12-year life cycle is common. His company's strategy is to begin turning out prototypes of sequel products two to three years before the maturity phase of the original product (see Figure 6.4). "The whole idea behind the process is to avoid crises," Venable says. "You want to be ready to go with the second product, just as the first one is about to die off."[89]

FIGURE 6.4
Time Between Introduction of Products

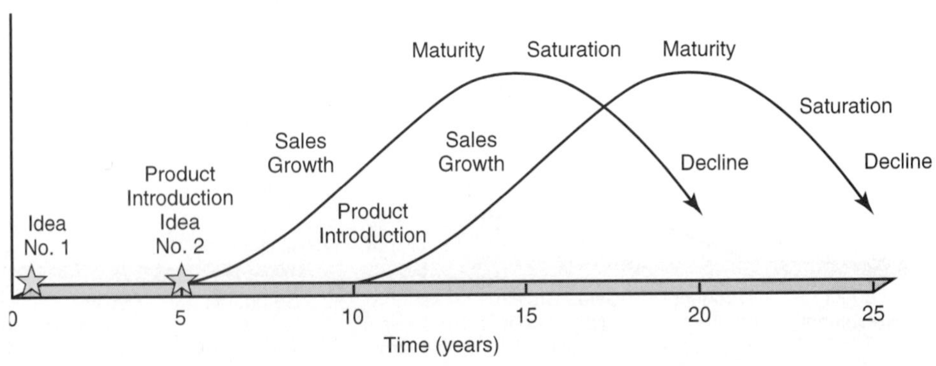

Place

Place (or method of distribution) has grown in importance as customers expect greater service and more convenience from businesses. This trend is one of the forces driving the rapid growth of the World Wide Web as a shopping tool. Entrepreneurs have come up with other clever ways to distribute their products and services and offer their customers more convenience. For instance, many traditionally stationary businesses have added wheels, becoming mobile animal clinics, computer shops, dentist offices, and windshield repair services.

Any activity involving movement of goods to the point of consumer purchase provides place utility. Place utility is directly affected by the marketing channels of distribution, the path that goods or services and their titles take in moving from producer to consumer. Channels typically involve a number of middlemen who perform specialized functions that add valuable utility to the goods or service. These middlemen provide time utility (making the product available when customers want to buy it) and place utility (making the product available where customers want to buy it).

For consumer goods, there are four common channels of distribution (see Figure 6.5).

1. *Manufacturer to Consumer.* In some markets, producers sell their goods or services directly to consumers. Services, by nature, follow this channel of distribution. Dental care and haircuts, for example, go directly from creator to consumer.
2. *Manufacturer to Retailer to Consumer.* Another common channel involves a retailer as a middleman. Many clothing items, books, shoes, and other consumer products are distributed in this manner.
3. *Manufacturer to Wholesaler to Retailer to Consumer.* This is the most common channel of distribution. Prepackaged food products, hardware, toys, and other items are commonly distributed through this channel.
4. *Manufacturer to Wholesaler to Wholesaler to Consumer.* A few consumer goods (e.g., agricultural goods and electrical components) follow this pattern of distribution.

Two channels of distribution are common for industrial goods (see Figure 6.6).

1. *Manufacturer to Industrial User.* The majority of industrial goods are distributed directly from manufacturers to users. In some cases, the goods or services are designed to meet the user's specifications.
2. *Manufacturer to Wholesaler to Industrial User.* Most expense items (paper clips, paper, rubber bands, cleaning fluids) that firms commonly use are distributed through wholesalers. For most small manufacturers, distributing goods through established wholesalers and agents is often the most effective route.

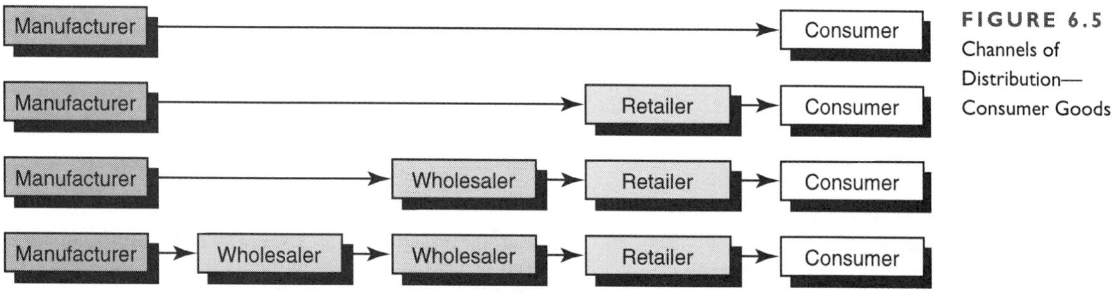

FIGURE 6.5 Channels of Distribution—Consumer Goods

FIGURE 6.6
Channels of Distribution—Industrial Goods

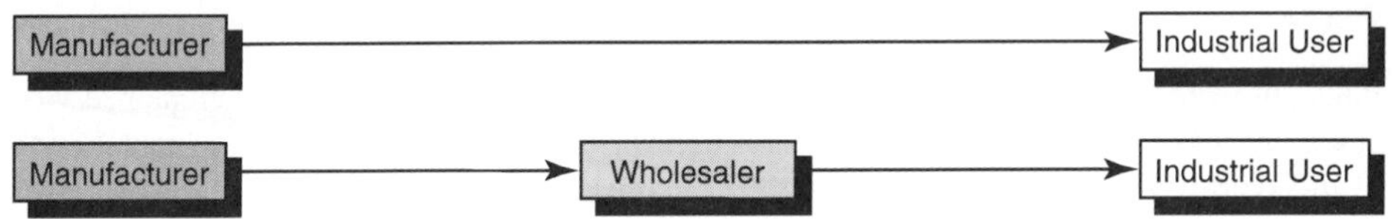

Price

Almost everyone agrees that the price of the product or service is a key factor in the decision to buy. Price affects both sales volume and profits, and without the right price, both sales and profits will suffer. As we will see in the next chapter, the right price for a product or service depends on three factors: (1) a small company's cost structure, (2) an assessment of what the market will bear, and (3) the desired image the company wants to create in its customers' minds.

Price can be a powerful tool for changing a company's image relatively quickly.

D.G. Yuengling & Sons

A decade ago, D.G. Yuengling & Sons, the nation's oldest brewery, was "considered a cheap, coal-region beer," says president Dick Yuengling. But the brewery changed its image to appeal to upscale beer drinkers intrigued by the mystique of nostalgic microbreweries. After a price-cutting campaign failed to slow sliding sales, Yuengling managers reversed their marketing strategy, raising the price of their beer to above-premium levels, focusing promotions on the brewery's rich history, and getting their brew into upscale restaurants and pubs. Today, Yuengling has become the drink of choice in its traditional northeastern territory, and the brewery cannot make enough beer to keep it on the local shelves. The company, which has expanded into the Southeast, now sells more than 500,000 barrels of its premium and light beers annually.[90]

For many small businesses, nonprice competition—focusing on factors other than price—is a more effective strategy than trying to beat larger competitors in a price war. Nonprice competition, such as free trial offers, free delivery, lengthy warranties, and money-back guarantees, intends to play down the product's price and stress its durability, quality, reputation, or special features.

Promotion

Promotion involves both advertising and personal selling. Its goal is to inform and persuade consumers. Advertising communicates to potential customers through some mass medium the benefits of a good or service. Personal selling involves the art of persuasive sales on a one-to-one basis. A small company's promotional program can play a significant role in creating a specific image in its customers' minds—whether it is upscale, discount, or somewhere in between. "Marketing is not a battle of products; it's a battle of perceptions," says one marketing expert.[91] We will discuss promotion in more detail in the next chapter.

CHAPTER SUMMARY

1. Describe the principles of building a guerrilla marketing plan and explain the benefits of preparing one. A major part of the entrepreneur's business plan is the marketing plan, which focuses on a company's target customers and how best to satisfy their needs and wants. A solid marketing plan should:
   - determine customer needs and wants through market research.
   - pinpoint the specific target markets the company will serve.
   - analyze the firm's competitive advantages and build a marketing strategy around them.

- create a marketing mix that meets customer needs and wants.

2. Discuss the role of market research and outline the market research process. Market research is the vehicle for gathering the information that serves as the foundation of the marketing plan. Good research does *not* have to be complex and expensive to be useful. The steps in conducting market research include:
   - defining the problem—"What do you want to know?"
   - collecting the data from either primary or secondary sources.
   - analyzing and interpreting the data.
   - drawing conclusions and acting on them.

3. Explain how small businesses can pinpoint their target markets. Sound market research helps the owner pinpoint his target market. The most successful businesses have well-defined portraits of the customers they are seeking to attract.

4. Describe the factors on which a small business can build a competitive edge in the marketplace: customer focus, quality, convenience, innovation, service, and speed. When plotting a marketing strategy, owners must strive to achieve a competitive advantage—some way to make their companies different from and better than the competition. Successful small businesses rely on six sources to develop a competitive edge:
   - a focus on the customer
   - devotion to quality
   - attention to convenience
   - concentration on innovation
   - dedication to service
   - emphasis on speed

5. Discuss the marketing opportunities the World Wide Web (WWW) offers entrepreneurs and how to best take advantage of them. The Web offers small business owners tremendous marketing potential on a par with their larger rivals. Entrepreneurs are just beginning to uncover the Web's profit potential, which is growing rapidly. Establishing a presence on the Web is important for companies targeting educated, wealthy, young customers. Successful Web sites are attractive, inviting, easy to navigate, interactive, and offer users something of value.

6. Discuss the "four Ps" of marketing—product, place, price, and promotion—and their role in building a successful marketing strategy. The marketing mix consists of the "four Ps":
   - *Product.* Entrepreneurs should understand where in the product life cycle their products are.
   - *Place.* The focus here is on choosing the appropriate channel of distribution and using it most efficiently.
   - *Price.* Setting the right price for a product or service is partly an art and partly a science.
   - *Promotion.* Promotion involves both advertising and personal selling.

DISCUSSION QUESTIONS

1. Define the marketing plan. What lies at its center?
2. What objectives should a marketing plan accomplish?
3. How can market research benefit a small business owner? List some possible sources of market information.
4. Does market research have to be expensive and sophisticated to be valuable? Explain.
5. Describe several market trends that are driving markets into the next decade and their impact on small businesses.
6. Why is it important for small business owners to define their target markets as part of their marketing strategies?
7. What is a competitive advantage? Why is it important for a small business owner to create a plan for establishing one?
8. Describe how a small business owner could use the following sources of a competitive advantage:
   - a focus on the customer
   - devotion to quality
   - attention to convenience
   - concentration on innovation
   - dedication to service
   - emphasis on speed
9. What is the World Wide Web? What marketing potential does it offer small businesses?
10. Explain the concept of the marketing mix. What are the four Ps?
11. List and explain the stages in the product life cycle. How can a small firm extend its product's life?
12. With a 70 percent customer retention rate (average for most U.S. firms, according to the American Management Association) every $1 million of business in 2000 will grow to more than $4 million by the year 2010. If you retain 80 percent of your customers, the $1 million will grow to a little over $6 million. If you can keep 90 percent of your customers, that $1 million will grow to more than $9.5 million. What can the typical small business do to increase its customer retention rate?

Beyond the Classroom . . .

1. Interview the owner of a local restaurant about its marketing strategy. From how large a geographic region does the restaurant draw its clientele? What is the firm's target market? What are its characteristics? Does the restaurant have a competitive edge?

2. Select a local small manufacturing operation and evaluate its primary product. What stage of the product life cycle is it in? What channels of distribution does the product follow after leaving the manufacturer?

3. Obtain a copy of Management Aid #4.012, *Marketing Checklist for Small Retailers,* from the Small Business Administration. Interview a local business owner, using the checklist as a guide. What sources for developing a competitive edge did you find? What weaknesses do you see? How do you recommend overcoming them?

4. Contact three local small business owners and ask them about their marketing strategies. How have they achieved a competitive edge? Develop a series of questions to judge the sources of their competitive edge—a focus on the customer; devotion to quality; attention to convenience; concentration on innovation; dedication to service; and emphasis on speed. How do the businesses compare?

5. Select three local businesses (one large and two small) and play the role of mystery shopper. How easy was it to do business with each company? How would you rate their service, quality, and convenience? Were salespeople helpful and friendly? How would you rate the business's appearance? How would you describe each company's competitive advantage? What future would you predict for each company? Prepare a brief report for your class on your findings and conclusions.

We invite you to visit this book's companion Web site at **www.prenhall.com/Zimmerer.**

CHAPTER 7

Advertising and Pricing for Profit

LEARNING OBJECTIVES

Upon completion of this chapter, you will be able to:

1. Discuss the steps in developing an advertising plan.
2. Explain the differences among promotion, publicity, personal selling, and advertising.
3. Describe the advantages and disadvantages of the various advertising media.
4. Identify four basic methods for preparing an advertising budget.
5. Explain practical methods for stretching a small business owner's advertising budget.
6. Describe effective pricing techniques for introducing new goods or services and for existing ones.
7. Explain the pricing methods and strategies for retailers, manufacturers, and service firms.
8. Describe the impact of credit on pricing.

The business that considers itself immune to the necessity for advertising sooner or later finds itself immune to business.

—Derby Brown

If your price isn't right, you can't sell it regardless of fit, quality, or style.

—Bud Konheim

Some small business owners believe that because of limited budgets they cannot afford the "luxury" of advertising. In their view, advertising is an expense they undertake only when their budgets permit—a leftover expense, something to spend if anything remains after paying the other bills. These owners discover, often after it's too late, that advertising is not just an expense; it is an *investment* in a company's future. Without a steady advertising and promotional campaign, a small business's customer base will soon dry up. Advertising can be an effective means of increasing sales by informing customers of the business and its goods or services; by improving the image of the firm and its products; or by persuading customers to purchase the firm's goods or services. A megabudget is *not* a prerequisite for building an effective advertising campaign. With a little creativity and ingenuity, a small company can make its voice heard above the clamor of its larger competitors—and stay within a limited budget!

The Herbal Remedy

For example, Scott Fiore, owner of The Herbal Remedy, a natural pharmacy in Littleton, Colorado, keeps his company's name in front of customers by using traditional advertising media, writing articles on herbal remedies for local magazines, and generating lots of publicity. Fiore, who spends about $1,400 a month on traditional advertising media, regularly buys radio ads that run during a popular talk show on health because he knows that the show reaches many of his target customers. On several occasions, the show's host has called Fiore to ask questions about a particular herb, giving The Herbal Remedy a promotional boost that normal advertising just cannot buy. Fiore also sponsors a series of free in-store seminars on a variety of health topics, and some have drawn standing-room-only crowds. One of the most effective forms of promotion for Fiore is word-of-mouth advertising from satisfied customers. Their positive experiences with Herbal Remedy lead them to recommend the store to their friends, which has helped Fiore's customer base to grow rapidly. Fiore's promotional efforts are not only fun for both him and his customers, but they also create interest in his store's herbal products and keep his business thriving in the face of larger competitors—and for very little money![1]

Developing an effective advertising program has become more of a challenge for business owners in recent years. Because of media overflow, overwhelming ad clutter, increasingly fragmented audiences, more advertising options, and more skeptical consumers, companies have had to become more innovative and creative in their promotional campaigns. Rather than merely turning up the advertising volume on their campaigns, companies are learning to change their frequencies, trying out new approaches in different advertising media.

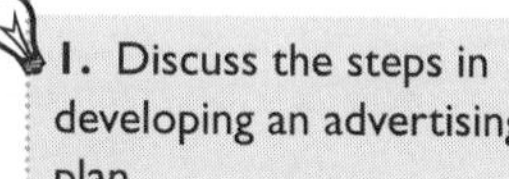

DEVELOPING AN ADVERTISING PLAN

Every small business needs an advertising plan to assure that the money spent on ads is not wasted. A well-developed plan does not guarantee advertising success, but it does increase the likelihood of good results.

The first step is to define the purpose of the company's advertising program by creating specific, measurable objectives. In other words, the owner must decide, "What do I want to accomplish with my advertising?" Some ads are designed to stimulate immediate responses by encouraging customers to purchase a particular product in the immediate future. The object here is to trigger a purchase decision. Other ads seek to build the firm's image among its customers and the general public. These ads try to create goodwill by keeping the firm's name in the public's memory so that customers will recall the small firm's name when they decide to purchase a product or service. Still other ads strive to draw new customers, build mailing lists, increase foot traffic in a store, or introduce a company or a product into a new territory.

The next step in developing an advertising plan is to analyze the firm and its target audience. A business owner who does not know who his advertising target is cannot reach it!

An advertising plan does not have to reach thousands of people to be successful. "It's not how many people see your advertising that counts," says one small business consultant. "It's whether the people who see it are the ones who buy."[2] A small business owner should address the following questions:

- What business am I in?
- What image do I want to project?
- Who are my target customers and what are their characteristics?
- Through which media can they best be reached?
- What do my customers *really* purchase from me?
- What benefits can the customer derive from my goods or services?
- How can I prove those benefits to my target customers?
- What sets my company, products, or services apart from the competition?
- How do I want to position my company in the market?
- What advertising approach do my competitors take?

Answering these questions will help an entrepreneur define her business and profile its customers, which will help her focus the advertising message on a specific target market and get more for her advertising dollar. Defining these issues at the outset enables entrepreneurs to select the media that will reach their target audiences with the least amount of waste.

Example

For instance, Dale Kesel, owner of a small photography studio specializing in portraits, defines his target customers as "parents, ages 25 to 45, with children under 14," but he designs his ads to appeal to the real decision maker in family portraits, "the woman in the household."[3]

Once a business owner has defined her target audience, she can design an advertising message and choose the media for transmitting it. At this stage, the owner decides what to say and how to say it. Creativity counts! One advertising expert claims, "You won't win customers by boring them into buying. You've got to create a desire."[4]

unique selling proposition (USP)—*a key customer benefit of a product or service that sets it apart from its competition; it answers the customer's question: "What's in it for me?"*

Entrepreneurs should build their ads around a **unique selling proposition (USP),** a key customer benefit of a product or service that sets it apart from its competition. To be effective, a USP must be unique—something the competition does not (or cannot) provide—and compelling enough to encourage customers to buy. A successful USP answers the critical question every customer asks: "What's in it for me?" Can your product or service save customers time or money, make their lives easier or more convenient, improve their self-esteem, or make them better? If so, you have the foundation for building a USP. The USP becomes the heart of your advertising message. Unfortunately, many business owners never define their companies' USP, and the result is uninspiring "me-too" advertising that cries out "buy from us" without offering customers any compelling reason to do so. "Most ads are about the product or the company that makes it, [and they] yield disappointing results," says advertising guru Roy H. Williams, author of *The Wizard of Ads.* "The best [ads] are about the customer and how the product will change his life."[5]

The best way to identify a meaningful USP is to describe the primary benefit your product or service offers customers and then to list other secondary benefits it provides. Be sure to look beyond just the physical characteristics of your product or service. Sometimes the most powerful USPs are the *intangible* or *psychological* benefits a product or service offers customers, for example. safety, security, acceptance, status, and others. An advertiser must be careful, however, to avoid stressing minuscule differences that are irrelevant to customers. Before developing advertisements, it is also important to develop a brief list of the facts that support your company's USP, for example, 24-hour service, a fully trained staff, awards won, and others. By focusing ads on these top benefits and the facts supporting them, business owners can communicate their USPs to their target audiences in a meaningful, attention-getting way. Building an ad around a USP spells out for customers the specific benefit they get if they buy that product or service and why they should do business with your company rather than with the competition. "If your audience has to study your ad to figure out what you're trying to say, forget it!" says one expert.[6]

Kesel, for example, offers his customers enduring family memories in the form of high-quality portraits that capture the personalities of the children he photographs. His ads appeal to customers at an emotional level.

Table 7.1 describes a six-sentence advertising strategy designed to create powerful ads that focus on a USP.

The USP around which you build your ad must be truly *unique* to make the ad effective. One technique is to replace your company's name and logo in your ad with those of your top competitor. Does the ad still make sense? If so, the ad is not based on your company's unique selling proposition! Figure 7.1 illustrates the characteristics of a successful ad.

A company's target audience and the nature of its message determine the advertising media it will use. As you learned in the previous section, some messages are much more powerful in some media than in others.

For instance, because Kesel uses samples of portraits in his ads, he relies heavily on ads in the community newspapers nearest his location, although he does supplement his campaign with radio spots.

The process does not end with creating and broadcasting an ad. The final step involves evaluating the ad campaign's effectiveness. Did it accomplish the objectives it was designed to accomplish? Immediate-response ads can be evaluated in a number of ways. For instance, a manager can include coupons that customers redeem to get price reductions on products and services. Dated coupons identify customer responses over certain time periods. Some firms use hidden offers—statements hidden somewhere in an ad that offer customers special deals if they mention an ad or bring in a coupon from an ad. Scott Fiore of The Herbal Remedy puts a "bring this ad in for 10 percent off" message in his print ads so he can track each ad's success rate and adjust his expenditures accordingly.

Business owners can also gauge an ad's effectiveness by measuring the volume of store traffic generated. Effective advertising should increase store traffic, which boosts sales of advertised and nonadvertised items. Of course, if an advertisement promotes a particular

TABLE 7.1
A Six-Sentence Advertising Strategy
Source: Adapted from Jay Conrad Levinson, "The Six-Sentence Strategy," Communication Briefings, *December 1994, p. 4.*

Does your advertising deliver the message you want to the audience you are targeting? If not, try stating your strategy in six sentences:

Primary purpose. What is the primary purpose of this ad? "The purpose of Rainbow Tours' ads is to get people to call or write for a free video brochure."

Primary benefit. What USP can you offer customers? "We will stress the unique and exciting places our customers can visit."

Secondary benefits. What other key benefits support your USP? "We will also stress the convenience and value of our tours and the skill and experience of our tour guides."

Target audience. At whom are we aiming the ad? "We will aim our ads at adventurous male and female singles and couples, 21 to 34, who can afford our tours."

Audience reaction. What response do you want from your target audience? "We expect our audience to call or write to request our video brochure."

Company personality. What image do we want to convey in our ads? "Our ads will reflect our innovation, excitement, conscientiousness, and our warm, caring attitude toward our customers."

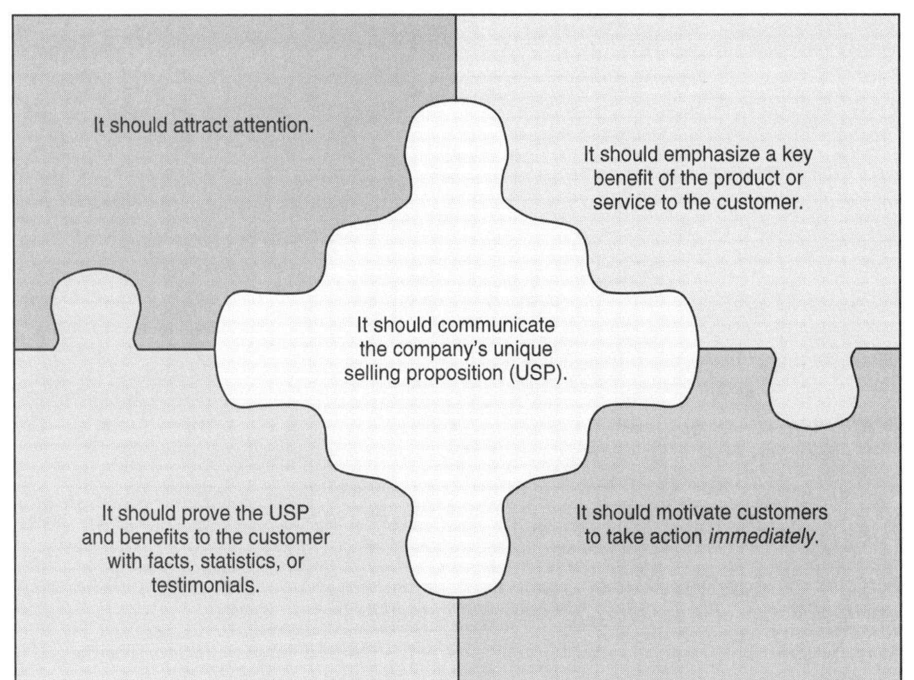

FIGURE 7.1
Five Fundamentals of a Successful Advertisement

Source: Adapted from Jerry Fisher, "Fine Print," Entrepreneur, November 1994, pp. 145–147.

bargain item, the manager can judge its effectiveness by comparing sales of the items to preadvertising sales levels. Remember: The ultimate test of an ad is whether or not it increases sales!

Ad tests can help determine the most effective methods of reaching potential customers. An owner can design two different ads (or use two different media or broadcast times) that are coded for identification and see which one produces more responses. For example, a business owner can use a split run of two different ads in a local newspaper. That is, he can place one ad in part of the paper's press run and another ad in the remainder of the run. Then he can measure the response level to each ad to compare their effectiveness. Table 7.2 describes seven tests every advertisement should pass.

WHAT IS PROMOTION?

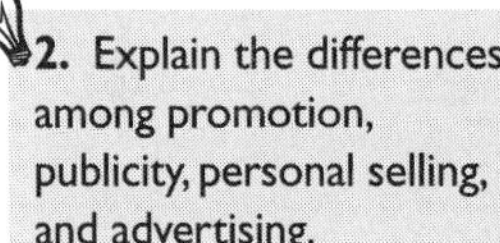

2. Explain the differences among promotion, publicity, personal selling, and advertising.

The terms *advertising* and *promotion* are often confused. **Promotion** is any form of persuasive communication designed to inform consumers about a product or service and to influence them to purchase these goods or services. It includes publicity, personal selling, and advertising.

promotion—*any form of persuasive communication designed to inform consumers about a product or service and to influence them to purchase these goods or services.*

publicity—*any commercial news covered by the media that boosts sales but for which the small business does not pay.*

Publicity

Publicity is any commercial news covered by the media that boosts sales but for which the small business does not pay. "[Publicity] is telling your story to the people you want to reach—namely, the news media, potential customers, and community leaders," says the head of a public relations firm. "It is not . . . haphazard . . . It requires regular and steady attention."[7] Publicity has power; a national survey found that a news feature about a company or a product appearing in a newspaper or magazine would have more impact on people's buying decisions than an advertisement would.[8] Exposure in any medium can raise a company's visibility and boost its sales, and, best of all, publicity is free.

TABLE 7.2

Can Your Advertisement Pass These Seven Tests?

Source: Adapted from Galen Stilson, "Put Your Advertising Through These Quick Tests," Smart Business Supersite, **<www.smartbiz.com/sbs/columns/stil6.htm>.**

Test 1. The scan test. Scan the ad quickly, reading only the headline and any copy that is designed to stand out and looking at the photos or drawings that it includes. Can you tell what the ad is offering, and, more importantly, does the benefit jump out at you?
Test 2. The comprehension test. Give the ad to someone who fits the profile of your target audience but who is unfamiliar with the product or service you are advertising. After reading the ad once, can that person tell you what the product or service is, what benefits it provides, what the offer is, and how to order?
Test 3. The differentiation test. Does the combination of ad copy and graphics differentiate your product or service from those of your competition? If a prospective customer read your ad and one of your chief competitor's ads, would she be able to tell how your product is different and better?
Test 4. The puffery test. Go through your copy and highlight every word or phrase that can be considered "sales puffery," such as "best," "greatest," "finest," and others. Can you eliminate these words and replace them with specific facts? If not, can you support the ad's claims with customer testimonials?
Test 5. The believability test. Give your ad to a potential customer and ask her to read through it. Ask her to highlight any claims in the ad that she finds hard to believe. Can you change them to make them more believable or offer facts to support them?
Test 6. The immediate clarity test. After the potential customer conducts the believability test, ask her to circle any words, phrases, or abbreviations that are not clear to her. Rewrite those parts of your ad.
Test 7. The USP test. Is the ad built around your company's USP? Does the USP come through in the message the ad sends to potential customers?

Pumpkin Masters

After launching Pumpkin Masters, a company that makes pumpkin-carving kits complete with carving tools, elaborate templates, and instructions, John Bardeen was disappointed by the company's lackluster sales. Then, with the help of a loyal customer, the power of publicity changed Pumpkin Masters' fortune. With Bardeen's permission, the cus-

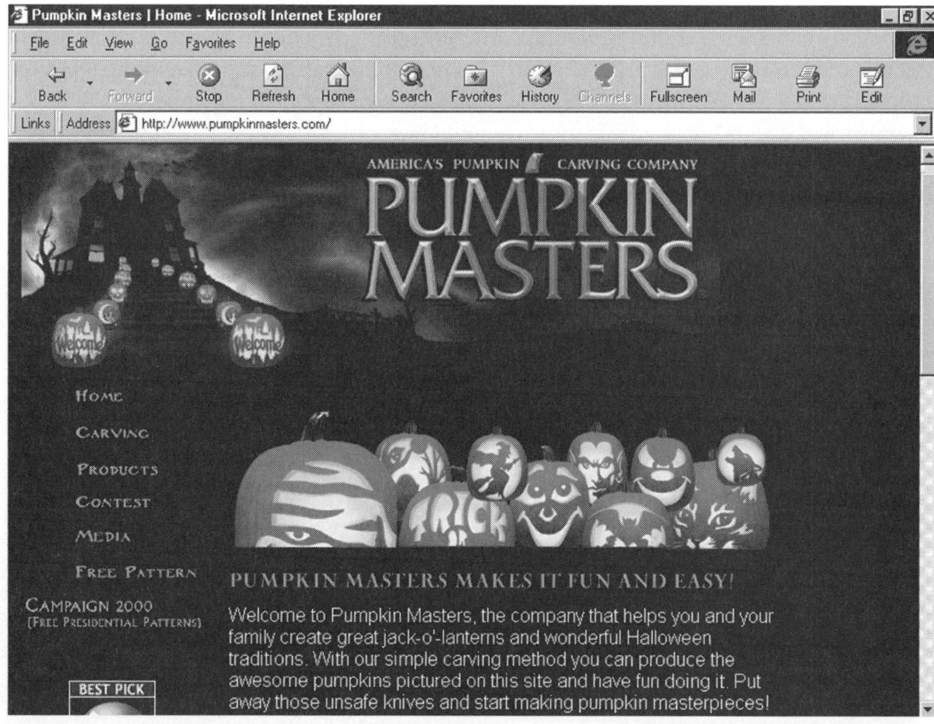

tomer contacted ABC television and convinced the network to display pumpkins carved with the likenesses of the announcers on Monday Night Football. ABC showed the pumpkin carvings throughout the broadcast and opened the show with a scary pumpkin called "Skull" that Bardeen himself had carved. The national exposure jump-started Pumpkin Masters' sales immediately, and the company now sells more than 2 million pumpkin-carving kits each year.[9]

The following tactics can help any small business owner stimulate publicity for her firm.

Write an article that will interest your customers or potential customers. One investment advisor writes a monthly column for the local newspaper on timely topics such as "retirement planning," "minimizing your tax bill," and "investing strategies for the next century." Not only do the articles help build her credibility as an expert, they have attracted new customers to her business.

Sponsor an offbeat event designed to attract attention. Karen Neuburger, owner of Karen Neuburger's Sleepwear, throws pajama parties in stores across the country to promote her line of sleepwear. Local news media almost always cover the party, giving Neuburger's company lots of free exposure.[10]

Involve celebrities "on the cheap." Few small businesses can afford to hire celebrities as spokespersons for their companies. Some companies have discovered other ways to get celebrities to promote their products, however. For instance, when Karen Neuburger learned that Oprah Winfrey is a "pajama connoisseur," she sent the talk show host a pair of her pajamas. The move paid off; Neuburger has appeared on Oprah's popular television show on three separate occasions.[11]

Contact local TV and radio stations and offer to be interviewed. Many local news or talk shows are looking for guests to talk about topics of interest to their audiences (especially in January and February). Even local shows can reach new customers.

Publish a newsletter. With a personal computer and desktop publishing software, any entrepreneur can publish a professional-looking newsletter. Freelancers can offer design and editing advice. Use the newsletter to reach present and potential customers.

Contact local business and civic organizations and offer to speak to them. A powerful, informative presentation can win new business. (Be sure your public speaking skills are up to par first! If not, consider joining Toastmasters.)

Offer or sponsor a seminar. Teaching people about a subject you know a great deal about builds confidence and goodwill among potential customers. The owner of a landscaping service and nursery offers a short course in landscape architecture and always sees sales climb afterward!

Write news releases and fax or e-mail them to the media. The key to having a news release picked up and printed is finding a unique angle on your business or industry that would interest an editor. Keep it short, simple, and interesting. E-mail press releases should be shorter than printed ones—typically four or five paragraphs rather than one or two pages—and they should include a company's Web site address.

LavaMind

Steve Hoffman, cofounder of LavaMind, a CD-ROM game and Web site development company, uses e-mail press releases to generate publicity for his company. Hoffman's e-mail press releases have led to articles in The New York Times, The Wall Street Journal, *and* Business Week, *and others as well as to television coverage on ABC, PBS, and CNBC. Hoffman says that half of LavaMind's sales have come as a result of the publicity generated by his e-mail releases.*[12]

Volunteer to serve on community and industry boards and committees. You can make your town a better place to live and work and raise your company's visibility at the same time.

Sponsor a community project or support a nonprofit organization or charity. Not only will you be giving something back to the community, but you will also gain recognition, goodwill, and, perhaps, customers for your business.

The owner of a dry cleaning business received the equivalent of thousands of dollars worth of advertising from the publicity generated by a program called "Give the gift of warmth." Customers donated winter coats, which the company cleaned for free and then distributed to the needy.

Promote a cause. Joseph Crilley, owner of Crilley's Circle Tavern, was concerned about the dangers of drinking and driving, so he renovated an old school bus and began offering his customers a free shuttle service. Not only has his service made the roads safer, but it also has boosted his business. During off-peak hours, Crilley uses the bus to shuttle school kids on field trips and senior citizens around town to run errands.[13] What started out as a socially responsible act has turned into a successful public relations campaign.

Personal Selling

personal selling—*the personal contact between salespeople and potential customers resulting from sales efforts.*

Advertising often marks the beginning of a sale, but personal selling usually is required to close the sale. **Personal selling** is the personal contact between salespeople and potential customers resulting from sales efforts. Effective personal selling can give the small company a definite advantage over its larger competitors by creating a feeling of personal attention. Personal selling deals with the salesperson's ability to match customer needs to the firm's goods and services. A recent study of top salespeople found that they:

- Are enthusiastic and alert to opportunities. Star sales representatives demonstrate deep concentration, high energy, and drive.
- Are experts in the products or services they sell. They understand how their product lines or services can help their customers.
- Concentrate on select accounts. They focus on customers with the greatest sales potential.
- Plan thoroughly. On every sales call, the best representatives act with a purpose to close the sale.
- Use a direct approach. They get right to the point with customers.
- Work from the customer's perspective. They have empathy for their customers and know their customers' businesses and their needs.
- Use "past success stories." They encourage customers to express their problems and then present solutions using examples of past successes.
- Leave sales material with clients. The material gives the customer the opportunity to study company and product literature in more detail.[14]
- See themselves as problem solvers, not just vendors. They ask, "How can I be a valuable resource for my customers?"
- Measure their success not just by sales volume but by customer satisfaction.[15]

One extensive study of salespeople found that just 20 percent of all salespeople have the ability to sell and are selling the "right" product or service. That 20 percent makes 80 percent of all sales. The study also concluded that 55 percent of sales representatives have "absolutely no ability to sell"; the remaining 25 percent have sales ability but are selling the wrong product or service.[16]

A study by Dartnell Corporation found that it takes an average of 3.9 sales calls to close a deal.[17] Common causes of sales rejections include the representative's failure to determine the customer's needs, talking too much, and neglecting to ask for the order. (Studies show that 60 percent of the time, salespeople never ask the customer to buy!)[18] Unfortunately, the cost of making a sales call exceeds $225, making those "missed opportunities" quite costly.[19]

Small business owners can improve their sales representatives' "batting averages" by following some basic guidelines:

Hire the right people. A successful sales effort starts well before a sales representative calls on a potential customer. The first step is hiring capable salespeople who demonstrate empathy for customers, are motivated, persistent, and focused.

Train sales representatives. Too often, business owners send sales representatives out into the field with little or no training and then wonder why they cannot produce. Training starts with teaching salespeople every aspect of the products or services they will be selling before moving on to teach them how to build relationships with customers. Training must also include the two most important selling skills of all: listening to the customer and closing the sale. Many business owners find that role-playing exercises are an effective sales training technique.

Develop a selling system. One sales consultant recommends a six-step process to increase the likelihood of closing a sale:[20]

1. *Approach.* Establish rapport with the prospect. Customers seldom buy from salespeople they dislike or distrust.
2. *Interview.* Get the prospect to do most of the talking; the goal is to identify his needs, preferences, and problems.
3. *Demonstrate, explain, and show.* Make clear the features and benefits of your product or service and point out how they meet the prospect's needs or solve his problems.
4. *Validate.* Prove the claims about your product or service. If possible, offer the prospect names and numbers of other satisfied customers (with their permission, of course). Testimonials really work.
5. *Negotiate.* Listen for objections from the prospect. Try to determine the *real* objection and confront it. Work to overcome it. Objections can be the salesperson's best friend; they tell her what must be "fixed" before the prospect will commit to an order. Work out the prospect's problems.
6. *Close.* Ask for a decision. Good sales representatives know when the prospect flashes the green light on a sale. They stop talking and ask for the order.

Be empathetic. The best salespeople look at the sale from the customer's viewpoint, not their own! Doing so encourages the sales representative to stress *value* to the customer.

Set multiple objectives. Before making a sales call, salespeople should set three objectives:

1. *The primary objective*—the most reasonable outcome expected from the meeting. It may be to get an order or to learn more about a prospect's needs.
2. *The minimum objective*—the very least the salesperson will leave with. It may be to set another meeting or to identify the prospect's primary objections.
3. *The visionary objective*—the most optimistic outcome of the meeting. This objective forces the salesperson to be open-minded and to shoot for the top.

Monitor sales efforts and results. Selling is just like any other business activity and must be controlled. At a minimum, the small business manager should know:

1. Actual sales versus projected sales.
2. Sales generated per call made.
3. Total sales costs.
4. Sales by product, salesperson, territory, customer, and so on.
5. Profit contribution by product, salesperson, territory, customer, and so on.

Advertising

advertising—*any sales presentation that is nonpersonal in nature and is paid for by an identified sponsor.*

Advertising is any sales presentation that is nonpersonal in nature and is paid for by an identified sponsor. One recent study on the effectiveness of advertising concluded that ads influence purchases of some products for six to nine months. "Advertising can develop long-term brand equity," says the study's author.[21] The remainder of this section will focus on selecting advertising media, developing an advertising plan, and creating an advertising budget.

3. Describe the advantages and disadvantages of the various advertising media.

SELECTING ADVERTISING MEDIA

One of the most important decisions a small business manager must make is which media to use in disseminating the advertising message. The medium used to transmit the message influences the consumer's perception—and reception—of it. By choosing the proper advertising means, a small business owner can reach his target audience effectively at minimum cost. Similarly, the right message communicated in the wrong medium will not increase sales.

Micro Express Inc.

For instance, when they launched Micro Express, a computer services firm, the founders allocated an annual advertising budget of $50,000, most of it for ads in large newspapers. For seven years, major newspapers remained the company's primary advertising medium. Then managers began to examine their customer base more closely and discovered that their customers were large companies rather than the small companies and home users at whom its ads were targeted. Realizing that Micro Express's advertising had been missing its mark, the company switched to direct mailings to Fortune *1000 companies. Not only do the direct-mail ads cost the company less, its sales are climbing again. "We see a much higher return now that we spend $10,000 a year on the right promotional efforts compared to the $50,000 we spent per year targeting the wrong customers," says president Jim Mickel.*[22]

Although no single formula exists for determining the ideal medium to use, there are several important characteristics that make some media better suited than others. Understanding the qualities of the various media available can simplify an owner's decision. Before selecting the vehicle for the message, the owner should consider several questions:

How large is my firm's trading area? How big is the geographical region from which the firm will draw its customers? The size of this area clearly influences the choice of media.

Who are my target customers and what are their characteristics? Determining a customer profile often points to the appropriate medium to use to get the message across most effectively.

Which media are my target customers most likely to watch, listen to, or read? Until he knows who his target audience is, a business owner cannot select the proper advertising media to reach it.

What budget limitations do I face? Every business owner must direct the firm's advertising program within the restrictions of its operating budget. Certain advertising media cost more than others.

What media do my competitors use? It is helpful for the small business manager to know the media his competitors use, although he should *not* automatically assume that they are the best. An approach that differs from the traditional one may produce better results.

How important is repetition and continuity of my advertising message? Generally, an ad becomes effective only after it is repeated several times, and many ads must be continued for some time before they produce results. Some experts suggest that an ad must be run at least six times in most mass media before it becomes effective.

How does each medium compare with others in its audience, its reach, and its frequency? **Audience** measures the number of paid subscribers a particular medium attracts and is called *circulation* in most print media such as newspapers and magazines. **Reach** is the total number of people exposed to an ad at least once in a period of time, usually four weeks. **Frequency** is the average number of times a person is exposed to an ad in that same time period.

What does the advertising medium cost? There are two types of advertising costs the small business manager must consider: the absolute cost and the relative cost. **Absolute cost** is the actual dollar outlay a business owner must make to place an ad in a particular medium for a specific time period. An even more important measure is an ad's **relative cost,** the ad's cost per potential customer reached. Relative cost is most often expressed as **cost per thousand (CPM),** the cost of the ad per 1,000 customers reached. Suppose a manager decides to advertise his product in one of two newspapers in town. The *Sentinel* has a circulation of 21,000 and charges $1,200 for a quarter-page ad. The *Democrat* has a circulation of 18,000 and charges $1,300 for the same space. Reader profiles of the two papers suggest that 25 percent of *Sentinel* readers and 37 percent of the *Democrat* readers are potential customers. Using this information, the manager computes the following relative costs:

audience—*a measure of the number of paid subscribers a particular medium attracts.*

reach—*the total number of people exposed to an ad at least once in a period of time, usually four weeks.*

frequency—*the average number of times a person is exposed to an ad in a period of time.*

absolute cost—*the actual dollar outlay a business owner must make to place an ad in a particular medium for a specific period of time.*

cost per thousand (CPM)—*the cost of an ad per 1,000 customers reached.*

	Sentinel		*Democrat*	
Circulation	21,000		18,000	
Percentage of readers that are potential customers	× 37%		× 25%	
Potential customers reached	5,250		6,660	
Absolute cost of ad	$1,200		$1,300	
Relative cost of ad (CPM)	$1,200 / 5.250	= $228.57 per 1,000 potential customers	$1,300 / 6.660	= $195.20 per 1,000 potential customers

Although the *Sentinel* has a larger circulation and a lower absolute cost for running the ad, the *Democrat* will serve the small business owner better because it offers a lower cost per thousand potential customers (CPM) reached. It is important to note that this technique does not give a reliable comparison across media; it is a meaningful comparison only within a single medium. Differences among the format, presentation, and coverage of ads in different media are so vast that such comparisons are not meaningful.

Media Options

Figure 7.2 gives a breakdown of U.S. business advertising expenditures by medium. Choosing advertising media is no easy task since each has distinctive advantages, disadvantages, and cost. The "right" message in the "wrong" medium will miss its mark.

Word-of-Mouth Advertising

Perhaps the most effective and certainly the least expensive form of advertising is **word-of-mouth advertising** in which satisfied customers recommend a business to friends, family members, and acquaintances. Unsolicited testimonials are powerful because they carry so much weight among potential customers. The best way to generate positive word-of-mouth advertising is to provide the superior quality and service discussed in the previous chapter. Providing that level of service and quality leads to loyal customers who become walking advertisements for the companies they believe in. Word-of-mouth advertising can make or break a business because *dissatisfied* customers also speak out against businesses that treat them poorly. To ensure that the word-of-mouth advertising a company generates is positive, business owners must actually do what they want their customers to say they do!

word-of-mouth advertising—*advertising in which satisfied customers recommend a business to friends, family members, and acquaintances.*

FIGURE 7.2 Advertising Expenditures by Medium

Source: McCann-Erickson, Inc. Statistical Abstract of the United States, 1999.

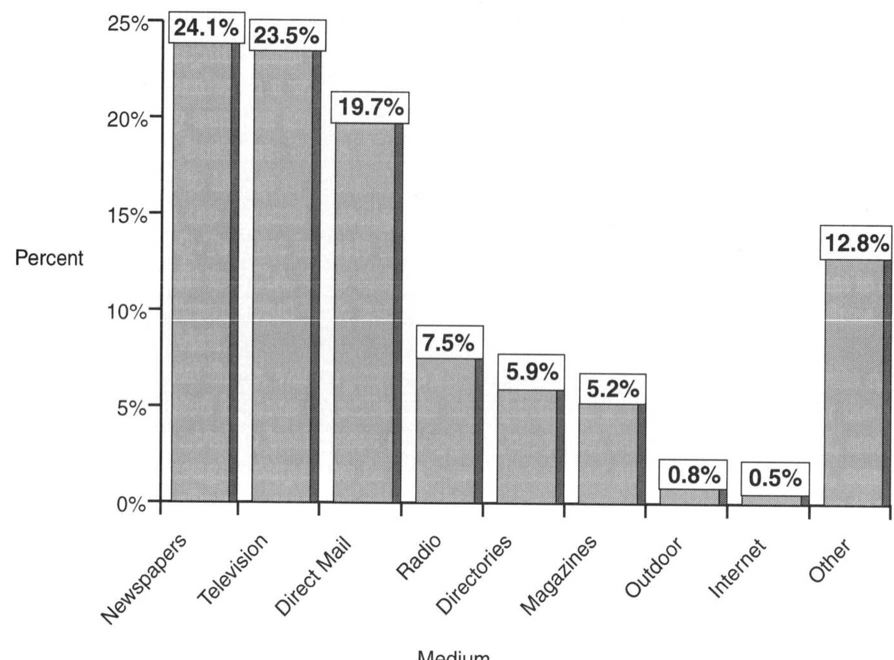

Anderson's Landscape Construction

For instance, Fred Anderson, owner of Anderson's Landscape Construction, a landscape planning and design service that targets upscale homes, relies totally on word-of-mouth advertising for his company's sales. Anderson counts on referrals from professional architects and from satisfied customers to generate new business. If a customer is unhappy about any aspect of a project his company has done, Anderson fixes it to the customer's satisfaction at no extra charge, which surprises some people. "I use a budget others would use for advertising and spend it on making things right," he explains.[23]

The ultimate in word-of-mouth advertising is the holy grail of advertising, something experts call *buzz.* Buzz occurs when a product is hot and everyone is talking about it. From the mood rings of the 1970s to the redesigned Volkswagen Beetle of the 1990s, buzz drives the sales of many products. The Internet has only magnified the power of buzz to influence a product's sales. Buzz on the Web has become a powerful force in influencing the popularity of everything from the Dancing Baby, a computer-animated, diaper-clad, dancing tyke that put a software company called Kinetix on the map to hit movies. (Remember all of the hoopla over the box office hit *The Blair Witch Project* a few years ago? The movie, which cost five enterprising young people just $200,000 to make, grossed $140.5 million, thanks in large part to Internet-based buzz.) What can business owners do to start a buzz about their companies or their products or services? Sometimes buzz starts on its own, leaving a business owner struggling to keep up with the fury it creates. More often than not, however, business owners can give it a nudge by creating interest, mystique, and curiosity in a product or service or by ensuring its scarcity. Ty Inc. has managed to keep collectors interested for years by "retiring" some of its Beanie Baby patterns every year to ensure that demand for them outstrips supply.

NEWSPAPERS. Traditionally, the local newspaper has been the medium that most advertisers rely on to get their messages across to customers. Although the number of newspapers in the United States has declined in recent years, this medium attracts nearly one-fourth of all advertising dollars nationwide, establishing it as the leader among all media.

Newspapers provide several *advantages* to the small business advertiser:

Source: Frank & Ernest © NEA.

Selected geographical coverage. Newspapers are geared to a specific geographic region, and they reach potential customers across all demographic classes.

Flexibility. Newspaper advertisements can be changed readily on very short notice. The owner can select the size of the ad and its location in the paper.

Timeliness. Papers almost always have very short closing times, the publication deadline prior to which the advertising copy must be submitted.

Communication potential. Newspaper ads can convey a great deal of information by employing attractive graphics and copy.

Low costs. Newspapers normally offer advertising space at low absolute cost and, because of their blanket coverage of a geographic area, at low relative cost as well.

Prompt responses. Newspaper ads typically produce relatively quick customer responses. A newspaper ad is likely to generate sales the very next day, and advertisers who use coupons can track the response to an ad.

Of course, newspaper advertisements also have *disadvantages:*

Wasted readership. Because newspapers reach such a variety of people, at least a portion of an ad's coverage will be wasted on those who are not potential customers.

Reproduction limitations. The quality of reproduction in newspapers is limited, especially when it is compared to that of magazines and direct mail.

Lack of prominence. One frequently cited drawback of newspapers is that they carry so many ads that a small company's message might be lost in the crowd. The typical newspaper is 62 percent advertising.

Declining readership. Newspaper circulation as a percentage of U.S. households has dropped from 98 percent in 1970 to 70 percent today. Newspaper ads would be least effective for small businesses targeting young people, who are least likely to read newspapers.

Short ad life. The typical newspaper is soon discarded and, as a result, an ad's life is extremely short. Business owners can increase the effectiveness of their ads by giving them greater continuity. Spot ads can produce results, but maintaining a steady flow of business requires some degree of continuity in advertising.

Buying Newspaper Space. Newspapers typically sell ad space by lines and columns or inches and columns. For instance, a 4-column x 100-line ad occupies four columns and 100 lines of space (14 lines are equal to 1 column inch). For this ad, the small business owner would pay the rate for 400 lines. Most papers offer discounts for bulk, long-term, and frequency contracts and for full-page ads. Advertising rates vary from one paper to another, depending on such factors as circulation and focus. A small business owner would do well to investigate the circulation statements, advertising rates, and reader profiles of the various newspapers available before selecting one.

RADIO. Newspapers offer blanket advertising coverage of a region, but radio permits advertisers to appeal to specific audiences over large geographic areas. By choosing the appropriate station, program, and time for an ad, a small company can reach virtually *any* target market.

Radio advertising offers several *advantages:*

Universal infiltration. Radio's nearly universal presence gives advertisements in this medium a major advantage. Virtually every home and car in the United States is equipped with a radio, which means that these advertising messages receive a tremendous amount of exposure in the target market. Radio reaches 95 percent of all consumers each week![24]

Market segmentation. Radio advertising is flexible and efficient because advertisers can choose stations directed toward a specific market within a broad geographic region. Radio stations design their formats to appeal to specific types of audiences, which makes an advertiser's job much easier.

Flexibility and timeliness. Radio commercials have short closing times and can be changed quickly.

Friendliness. Radio ads are more "active" than ads in printed media because they use the spoken word to influence customers. Vocal subtleties used in radio ads are impossible to convey through printed media. Table 7.3 offers a guide to producing effective radio copy.

Radio advertisements also have a number of *disadvantages:*

Poor listening. Radio's intrusiveness into the public life almost guarantees that customers will hear ads, but they may not listen to them.

Need for repetition. Radio ads must be broadcast repeatedly to be effective.

Limited message. Because radio ads are limited to one minute or less, the message must be brief and not overly complex.

Buying Radio Time. The small business owner can zero in on a specific advertising target by using the appropriate radio station. Stations follow various formats—from rap to rhapsodies—to appeal to specific audiences. Radio advertising time usually sells in 15-second, 30-second, and 60-second increments, with the latter being the most common. Fixed spots are guaranteed to be broadcast at the times specified in the owner's contract with the station. Preemptible spots are cheaper than fixed spots, but the advertiser risks being preempted by an advertiser willing to pay the fixed rate for a time slot. Floating spots are the least expensive, but the advertiser has no control over broadcast times. Many stations offer package plans, using flexible combinations of fixed, preemptible, and floating spots.

Radio rates vary depending on the time of day they are broadcast, and, like television, there are prime-time slots known as drive-time spots. Although exact hours may differ from station to station, the following classifications are common (listed in descending order of cost):

Class AA: Morning drive time—6 A.M. to 10 A.M.

Class A: Evening drive time—4 P.M. to 7 P.M.

Class B: Home worker time—10 A.M. to 4 P.M.

TABLE 7.3
Guidelines for Effective Radio Copy

Source: Radio Basics, Radio Advertising Bureau.

- *Mention the business often.* This is the single most important and inflexible rule in radio advertising. Also make sure listeners know how to find your business. If the address is complicated, use landmarks.
- *Stress the benefit to the listener.* Don't say "Bryson's has new fall fashions." Say "Bryson's fall fashions make you look fabulous."
- *Use attention-getters.* Radio has a whole battery—music, sound effects, unusual voices. Crack the barrier with sound.
- *Zero in on your audience.* Know to whom you're selling. Radio's selectivity attracts the right audience. It's up to you to communicate in the right language.
- *Keep the copy simple and to the point.* Don't try to impress listeners with vocabulary. "To be or not to be" may be the best-known phrase in the language . . . and the longest word has just three letters.
- *Sell early and often.* Don't back into the selling message. At most, you've got 60 seconds. Make the most of them. Don't be subtle.
- *Write for the ear.* Write conversationally.
- *Prepare your copy.* Underline words you want to emphasize.
- *Triple space.* Type clean, legible copy. Make the announcer rehearse.
- *Use positive action words.* Use words such as *now* and *today,* particularly when you're writing copy for a sale. Radio has qualities of urgency and immediacy. Take advantage of them by including a time limit or the date the sale ends.
- *Put the listener in the picture.* Radio's theater of the mind means you don't have to talk about a new car. With sounds and music, you can put the listener behind the wheel.
- *Focus the spot on getting a response.* Make it clear what you want the listener to do. Don't try to get a mail response. Use phone numbers only, and repeat the number three times. End the spot with the phone number.
- *Don't stay with a loser.* Direct-response ads produce results right way—or not at all. Don't stick with a radio spot that is not generating sales. Change it.

Class C: Evening time—7 P.M. to midnight

Class D: Nighttime—midnight to 6 A.M.

Some stations may also have different rates for weekend time slots.

TELEVISION. In advertising dollars spent, television ranks second in popularity of all media. Although the cost of national TV ads precludes their use by most small businesses, local spots can be an extremely effective means of broadcasting a small company's message. A 30-second commercial on network television may cost more than $500,000, but a 30-second spot on local cable television, which now is in 68 percent of all U.S. homes, may go for $200 or less.

Television offers a number of distinct *advantages:*

Broad coverage. Television ads provide extensive coverage of a sizable region, and they reach a significant portion of the population. About 98 percent of the homes in the United States have a television, and the average household spends 7 hours and 12 minutes each day tuned in to television.[25]

Visual advantage. The primary benefit of television is its capacity to present an advertiser's product or service in a graphic, vivid manner with sight, sound, and action. Research shows that 46 percent of television ads result in long-term sales increases and that 70 percent of campaigns boost sales immediately.[26]

Flexibility. Television ads can be modified quickly to meet the rapidly changing conditions in the marketplace. Advertising on TV is the closest substitute for personal selling.

Design and production assistance. Few small business owners have the skills to prepare an effective television commercial. Although professional production firms might easily charge $50,000 for a commercial production, the television station from which a business owner purchases air time may be willing to offer design and production assistance very inexpensively.

Television advertising also has several *disadvantages:*

Brief exposure. Most television ads are on the screen for only a short time and require substantial repetition to achieve the desired effect.

Clutter. The typical person sees 1,500 advertising messages a day, and more ads are on the way. With so many ads beaming across the airwaves, a small business's advertising message could easily become lost in the shuffle.

zappers—*television viewers who flash from one channel to another, especially during commercials.*

Zapping. **Zappers,** television viewers who flash from one channel to another, especially during commercials, pose a real threat to TV advertisers. Zapping means TV advertisers are not reaching the audiences they hope to reach. VCRs, which now are present in 85 percent of U.S. homes, have added to the problem of zapping.[27] The remote control has transformed television viewers into channel surfers during commercial breaks.

Fragmented audience. As the number of channels available proliferates, the question of where to advertise becomes more difficult to answer. Network television has lost audience steadily over the past 20 years to cable television. About 96 percent of cable television households receive more than 30 channels.[28]

Costs. TV commercials can be expensive to create. A 30-second ad can cost several thousand dollars to develop, even before the owner purchases air time. Table 7.4 offers some suggestions for developing creative television commercials.

infomercials—*a full-length television commercial packed with information, testimonials, and a sales pitch.*

Using Television Creatively. Although television ads are not affordable for every small business, many entrepreneurs have found creative ways to use the power of television advertising without spending a fortune. Two popular methods include creating infomercials and using home shopping networks. **Infomercials** (also called direct-response television), full-length television commercials packed with information, testimonials, and a sales pitch, are popular tools for selling everything from mops to computers. Producing

TABLE 7.4

Guidelines for Creative TV Ads

Source: Adapted from How to Make a Creative Television Commercial, *Television Bureau of Advertising, Inc.*

- *Keep it simple.* Avoid confusing the viewer by sticking to a simple concept.
- *Have one basic idea.* The message should focus on a single, important benefit to the customer. Why should people buy from your business?
- *Make your point clear.* The customer benefit should be obvious and easy to understand.
- *Make it unique . . . different.* To be effective, a television ad must reach out and grab the viewer's attention. Take advantage of television's visual experience.
- *Get viewer attention.* Unless viewers watch the ad, its effect is lost.
- *Involve the viewer.* To be most effective, an ad should portray a situation to which the viewer can relate. Common, everyday experiences are easiest for people to identify with.
- *Use emotion.* The most effective ads evoke an emotion from the viewer—a laugh, a tear, or a pleasant memory.
- *Consider production values.* Television offers vivid sights, colors, motions, and sounds. Use them!
- *Prove the benefit.* Television allows an advertiser to prove a product's or service's customer benefit by actually demonstrating it.
- *Identify your company well and often.* Make sure your store's name, location, and product line stand out. The ad should portray your company's image.

and airing a half-hour infomercial can be expensive, often costing $50,000 or more, but entrepreneurs can save money by doing some of the work themselves and hiring freelance professionals for a share of the profits.

Smart Inventions

After he launched Smart Inventions, Jon Nokes set out across the country to promote his latest product, the SmartMop, a unique mop from Finland with a self-wringing feature. In its first year, SmartMop generated $1.8 million in sales, but Nokes knew he could do much better if only he could let customers see the benefits of the SmartMop. Nokes worked with a production company to create a 28-minute infomercial for $60,000 to demonstrate the user-friendly mop. Consumer response to the infomercial amazed even Nokes. Whenever the infomercial aired, orders poured in—so fast, in fact, that Nokes had to invest in a larger manufacturing facility to keep up with demand. After a year of airing the infomercial, sales of the SmartMop had climbed to $44 million![29]

To become an infomercial star, a product should meet the following criteria:[30]

- be unique and of good quality
- solve a common problem
- be easy to use and easy to demonstrate
- appeal to a mass audience
- have an Aha! factor that makes customers think "What a great idea."

Shopping networks such as QVC and the Home Shopping Network offer entrepreneurs another route to television. Time on these networks is free, but getting a product accepted is tough. One buyer for QVC says that the network subjects about 500 products to an extensive review every week, but that only 5 percent are selected to appear on television.[31] Shopping networks look for products that offer quality, have "demonstration appeal," and are typically priced between $15 and $40 (although there are exceptions). Landing a product on one of these networks may be a challenge, but entrepreneurs who do often sell thousands of units in a matter of minutes!

MAGAZINES. Another advertising medium available to the small business owner is magazines. Today, customers have more than 18,600 magazine titles from which to choose.[32] Magazines have a wide reach; today, nearly 9 out of 10 adults read an average of seven different magazines per month. The average magazine attracts 6 hours and 3 minutes of total adult reading time, and studies show that the reader is exposed to 89 percent of the ads in the average copy.[33]

Magazines offer several *advantages* for advertisers:

Long life spans. Magazines have a long reading life because readers tend to keep them longer than other printed media. The result is that each magazine ad has a good chance of being seen several times.

Multiple readership. The average magazine has a readership of 3.9 adult readers, and each reader spends about 1 hour and 33 minutes with each copy. Many magazines have a high "passalong" rate—they are handed down from reader to reader.

Target marketing. By selecting the appropriate special-interest periodical, small business owners can reach customers with a high degree of interest in their goods or services. Specialty magazines have proliferated in recent years, giving businesses the opportunity to advertise in magazines such as *Surfer Girl* or *Ferrets* that target specific audiences.

Ad quality. Magazine ads usually are of high quality, resulting in strong visual appeal. Photographs and drawings can be reproduced very effectively, and color ads are readily available.

Magazines also have several *disadvantages:*

Costs. Magazine advertising rates vary according to their circulation rates; the higher the circulation, the higher the rate. Thus, local magazines, whose rates are often comparable to newspaper rates, may be the best bargain for small businesses.

Long closing times. Another disadvantage of magazines is the relatively long closing times they require. For a weekly periodical, the closing date for an ad may be several weeks before the actual publication date, making it difficult for advertisers to respond quickly to changing market conditions.

Lack of prominence. Another disadvantage of magazine ads arises from their popularity as an advertising vehicle. The effectiveness of a single ad may be reduced because of a lack of prominence; 48.3 percent of the typical magazine content is devoted to advertising.[34] Proper ad positioning, therefore, is critical to an ad's success. Research shows that readers "tune out" right-hand pages and look mainly at left-hand pages.

DIRECT MAIL. Direct mail has long been a popular method of small business advertising and includes such tools as letters, postcards, catalogs, discount coupons, brochures, computer disks, and videotapes mailed to homes or businesses. The earliest known catalogs were printed by fifteenth-century printers. Today, direct-mail marketers sell virtually every kind of product imaginable from Christmas trees and lobsters to furniture and clothing (the most popular mail-order purchase). In fact, the average household in the United States receives 34 pounds of direct mail each year![35] Responding to the convenience of "shopping at home," customers purchase more than $500 billion worth of goods and services through mail order each year!

Direct mail offers a number of distinct *advantages* to the small business owner:

Selectivity. The greatest strength of direct-mail advertising is its ability to target a specific audience to receive the message. Depending on mailing list quality, an owner can select an audience with virtually any set of characteristics. Small business owners can develop, rent, or purchase a mailing list of prospective residential, commercial, or industrial customers.

Grand River Toy Company

When Sandy and Tom Callahan launched their mail-order company, Grand River Toy Company, which markets toys made from environmentally safe materials, they placed newspaper ads and mailed their brief catalog to those who responded. Their list grew—albeit slowly—by word of mouth. In their third year of business, the Callahans purchased mailing lists of upscale, educated buyers concerned about the environment and education from list brokers. Their home-based company has doubled its sales every year since.[36]

Flexibility. Another advantage of direct mail is its capacity to tailor the message to the target. The advertiser's presentation to the customer can be as simple or as elaborate as necessary. In addition, the advertiser controls the timing of the campaign; she can send the ad when it is most appropriate.

Reader attention. With direct mail, the advertiser's message does not have to compete with other ads for the reader's attention. People enjoy getting mail, and one study found that recipients opened and read 48 percent of their direct mail.[37]

Rapid feedback. Direct mail advertisements produce quick results. In most cases the ad will generate sales within three to four days after customers receive it.

Measurable results and testable strategies. Because they control their mailing lists, direct marketers can readily measure the results their ads produce. Also, direct mail allows advertisers to test different ad layouts, designs, and strategies (often within the same "run") to see which one "pulls" the greatest response. Table 7.5 offers guidelines for creating direct-mail ads that really work.

TABLE 7.5

Guidelines for Creating Direct-Mail Ads That Really Work

Sources: Adapted from Kim T. Gordon, "Copy Right," Business Start-Ups, June 1998, pp. 18–19; Paul Hughes, "Profits Due," Entrepreneur, February 1994, pp. 74–78; "Why They Open Direct Mail," Communication Briefings, December 1993, p. 5; Teri Lammers, "The Elements of Perfect Pitch," Inc., March 1992, pp. 53–55; "Special Delivery," Small Business Reports, February 1993, p. 6; Gloria Green and James W. Peltier, "How to Develop a Direct Mail Program," Small Business Forum, Winter 1993/1994, pp. 30–45; Susan Headden, "The Junk Mail Deluge," U.S. News & World Report, December 8, 1997, pp. 40–48.

"Mail order means trend watching, meticulous planning, and devouring news and information on the industry, your niche, technology, politics, and the world—and that's just for starters," says one observer. "You'll have to deal with the laws of a vast federal bureaucracy and 50 states (plus a couple hundred countries if you go international), the intricacies of designing and mailing a catalog, and the fickle nature of a demanding public."

You'll also have to write copy that will get results. Try these proven techniques:

- Promise readers your most important benefit in the headline or first paragraph.
- Use short "action" words and paragraphs.
- Make the copy look easy to read—lots of "white space."
- Use eye-catching words such as *free, you, save, guarantee, new, profit, benefit, improve,* and others.
- Consider using computerized "handwriting" somewhere on the page or envelope; it attracts attention.
- Forget grammatical rules; write as if you were speaking to the reader.
- Repeat the offer three or more times in various ways.
- Back up claims and statements with proof and endorsements whenever possible.
- Ask for the order or a response.
- Ask questions such as "Would you like to lower your home's energy costs?" in the copy.
- Use high-quality paper and envelopes (those with windows are best) because they stand a better chance of being opened and read. Brown envelopes that resemble government correspondence work well.
- Envelopes that resemble bills almost always get opened.
- Address the envelope to an individual, not "Occupant."
- Use stamps if possible. They get more letters opened than metered postage.
- Use a postscript (P.S.) always—they are the most often read part of a printed page. Make sure the P.S. contains a "hook" that will encourage the recipient to read on.
- Make sure the order form is clear and easy to fill out. Include a fax number for ordering, too.

Effectiveness. The right message targeted at the right mailing list can make direct mail one of the most efficient forms of advertising. Studies show that, on average, every dollar a company spends on direct mail produces $10 in sales.[38]

Direct mail ads also suffer from several *disadvantages:*

Inaccurate mailing lists. The key to the success of the entire mailing is the accuracy of the customer list. The Direct Marketing Association estimates that 60 percent of the success of direct marketing is based on the quality of the mailing list.[39]

Clutter. The average person in the United States receives 553 pieces of direct mail each year.[40] With that volume of direct mail, it can be difficult for an advertisement to get customers' attention.

High relative costs. Relative to the size of the audience reached, the cost of designing, producing, and mailing an advertisement via direct mail is high. But if the mailing is well planned and properly executed, it can produce a high percentage of returns, making direct mail one of the least expensive advertising methods in terms of results.

High throwaway rate. Often called junk mail, direct mail ads become "junk" when an advertiser selects the wrong audience or broadcasts the wrong message. In fact, the typical direct mail advertising campaign produces only a 2 percent response rate. To boost returns small business owners can supplement their traditional direct mail pieces with toll-free (800) numbers (an increase of 1 to 2 percent) and carefully timed follow-up phone calls (an increase of 2 to 14 percent).[41]

For instance, Marc Kaner, owner of Fitness Connection, a retailer of vitamin supplements, estimates that his 800 number has increased his sales by 15 percent.[42]

HIGH-TECH DIRECT MAIL. Sending out ads on computer diskettes is an excellent way to reach upscale households and businesses. Not only do computer-based ads give advertisers the power to create flashy, attention-grabbing designs, but they also hold the audience's attention. "Customized diskettes are rarely thrown away," says the founder of one diskette advertising firm. "Human curiosity practically guarantees they will be reviewed." Studies show that recipients of a computer diskette ad spend an average of 26 to 30 minutes interacting with it and that their retention rate is twice that of other ads.[43]

Compact discs (CDs) offer advertisers the same benefits as computer disks with one extra—more space to do it in. Companies are using CDs with interactive ads to sell everything from cars to computers. The ads usually contain videos, computer games, quizzes, animation, music, graphics, and other features to engage more of their audiences' senses. In a world where U.S. households receive *4.5 million tons* of paper each year in the form of direct-mail ads, multimedia ads can offer a distinct advantage: They get noticed. One expert explains the appeal of multimedia ads, "You remember 20 percent of what you see, 30 percent of what you see and hear, and 60 percent of what you interact with."[44]

How to Use Direct Mail. The key to a direct mailing's success is the right mailing list. Even the best direct-mail ad will fail if sent to the "wrong" customers. Owners can develop lists themselves, using customer accounts, telephone books, city and trade directories, and other sources. Other sources for mailing lists include companies selling complementary but not competing products; professional organizations' membership lists; business or professional magazines' subscription lists; and mailing list brokers who sell lists for practically any need. Advertisers can locate list brokers through *The Direct Marketing List Source* from the Standard Rate and Data Service found in most public libraries.

THE WORLD WIDE WEB. The World Wide Web is rapidly reshaping the way companies conduct business and is transforming e-commerce into a major economic force. Just as the Web has become a common tool for conducting business, it also has become a popular medium for advertisers. Increasingly, small businesses are turning to the World Wide Web as a valuable way to reach their customers and to build an awareness of their products and services. According to Jupiter Communications, an Internet research company, online advertising expenses reached $7.7 billion in 2002, up from $1.05 billion in 1998.[45] "The most effective ads are part of a larger campaign that blends various media," says Nat Goldhaber, president of Cybergold, a company that hosts an online shopping mall. "[Just] as the best traditional [advertising] campaigns combine magazines, newspapers, radio, and TV, the best new campaigns also incorporate the Internet."[46] For instance, when lingerie seller Victoria's Secret ran an ad during the Super Bowl to promote its first live lingerie fashion show broadcast over the Web, the response was phenomenal! More than 1.5 million people tuned in to the Victoria's Secret Web site to watch the fashion show, proving the power of combining the Web with traditional advertising media. The Internet has proved to be the fastest-growing advertising medium in history. Using the time required for radio, television, and the Internet to reach 50 million users as a basis for comparing the three media, the Internet is the clear winner. Radio required 38 years to reach that milestone, and television took 13 years; the Internet, however, hit 50 million users in just five years!

The Web's multimedia capabilities make it an ideal medium for companies to demonstrate their products and services with full motion, color, and sound and to get customers involved in the demonstrations. Businesses that normally use direct mail can bring the two-dimensional photos and product descriptions in their print catalogs to life, avoid the expense of mailing them, and attract new customers that traditional mailings might miss.

Charlie Hoeveler, CEO of US Sports Camps, Inc., a company that stages summer camps in a variety of sports on college campuses across the nation, has found the Web to be the ideal vehicle for promoting and managing the administrative details of the hundreds of camps the company runs. For years, US Sports Camps used direct-mail campaigns and ads in sports-oriented magazines to enroll youngsters into its camps. Today, the company touts its Web site **<www.ecamps.com>** *with banner ads on Yahoo! and in all of its other promotional literature. The site, with its online registration form, has attracted hundreds of new customers and has boosted the company's international clientele 200 percent! The sports-specific bulletin boards on the Web site attract potential customers even in the off-season. Hoeveler, who says that he has "a perfect product for the Web," hopes eventually to "see 40 percent or 50 percent of sales come through the site."*[47]

US Sports Camps, Inc.

Advertisements on the Web take five basic forms: banner ads, cookies, full-page ads, "push" technology ads, and e-mail ads. **Banner ads** are small, rectangular ads that reside on Web sites, much like roadside billboards, touting a company's product or service. When visitors to a site click on the banner ad, they go straight to the advertiser's homepage. One measure of a banner ad's effectiveness is the number of impressions it produces. An **impression** occurs every time an ad appears on a Web page, whether or not the user clicks on the ad to explore it. Another common way of judging banner ads is the **click-through rate,** which is calculated by dividing the number of times customers actually click on the banner ad by the number of impressions for that ad. The cost of a banner ad to an advertiser depends on the number of users who actually click on it. For instance, running a banner ad on a high-volume site such as C/Net costs an advertiser from $25 to $75 per thousand clicks. The cost of creating a banner ad ranges from practically nothing for do-it-yourselfers to as much as $3,000 if the ad is designed by a professional and includes animation and high levels of interactivity.

banner ads—*small, rectangular ads that reside on Web sites, much like roadside billboards, touting a company's product or service.*

impression—*occurs every time an ad appears on a Web page, whether or not the user clicks on it.*

click-through rate—*a value calculated by dividing the number of times customers actually click on a banner ad by the number of impressions for that ad.*

Banner ads do not have to be expensive, however. Many small business owners increase the exposure their banner ads receive by joining a banner exchange program, which is similar to an advertising cooperative. In a banner exchange program, member companies can post their banners on each other's sites. These programs work best for companies selling complementary products or services. For instance, a small company selling gourmet food products over the Web might exchange banner ads with a company using the Web to sell fine wines or one selling upscale kitchen tools and appliances. Two of the largest banner exchange Web sites are Microsoft bCentral (formerly LinkExchange) and SmartClicks.

Deborah Edlhuber, owner of Prarie Frontier, a small company selling wildflower and prairie-grass seed, uses a banner exchange program to drive traffic to her company's Web site. Through the exchange, Edlhuber placed banner ads she created herself on several dozen gardening and photographic sites. Prairie Frontier's Web site now draws more than 1,700 hits a day, many of them from her banner exchange partners. "They definitely bring people to my site," says Edlhuber, "and I can track the click-throughs."[48]

Prairie Frontier

The primary disadvantage of banner ads is that Web users can easily ignore them. A recent study by *Advertising Age* magazine found that 49 percent of Web users pay no attention to banner ads.[49] Another study estimates that banner ads produce a click-through rate of just 1 to 1.5 percent.[50] Still, banner ads remain popular; they account for nearly two-thirds of all online advertising expenditures.[51]

Designed properly and placed on the right sites, banner ads can produce results. "Banner ads are a great way for small companies to drive traffic to their sites and then turn that traffic into real revenue," says Bill Lohse, CEO of SmartAge, a full-service Web design firm.[52]

K. B. Lee, owner of the New York Golf Center of Long Island, uses banner ads to draw traffic to his company's Web site. Lee puts his banner ads on a gift-selection site called Perfect Present Picker, and the ads steer a steady stream of customers to the Golf Center

New York Golf Center of Long Island

Web site, boosting sales considerably. "The majority of people who come to my site from presentpicker.com actually end up buying," says Lee.[53]

Studies suggest that the best location for a banner ad is in the lower right-hand corner of the screen and not at the top of the screen, where many are placed.[54]

cookies—*small programs that attach to users' computers when they visit certain Web sites and that track users' Web browsing patterns.*

Cookies are small programs that attach to users' computers when they visit certain Web sites. These programs track the locations users visit while in the site and use this electronic footprint to send pop-up ads that would be of interest to the user. For instance, a Web user who frequently visits garden sites might find ads for garden tools and seed companies popping up on her screen. Many sites that require users to register before they can enter are collecting information to create cookie files. Cookies cannot access a user's computer, read sensitive information such as credit card numbers or passwords and then send that data back to the company that created the cookie. Nor can they alter the files on a computer's hard drive. Cookies can, however, track a user's Web browsing patterns, revealing which pages he views and how often he views them. Because cookies record a person's Web use and habits transparently (and usually without the user's express permission), their use has become somewhat controversial. Some companies use the information they glean from cookies to make inferences about customers' interests and then target ads at them based on those inferences.

full-page ads—*ads that download to users' Web screens before they can access certain Web sites.*

push technology ads—*ads that appear on users' screens when they download information such as news, sports, or entertainment from another site.*

e-mail advertising—*advertising in which companies broadcast their advertising messages via e-mail.*

permission e-mail—*commercial e-mail sent to customers with their consent.*

spam—*unsolicited commercial e-mail.*

Full-page ads are those that download to Web users' screens before they can access certain Web sites. They are common on popular game sites that attract a high volume of Web traffic. **Push technology ads** appear on users' screens when they download information such as news, sports, or entertainment from another site. For instance, a Web user downloading sports information might receive an ad for athletic shoes or T-shirts with the information.

With more than 135 million users, e-mail is the most common application on the Internet, and e-mail advertising capitalizes on that popularity. **E-mail advertising,** in which companies broadcast their advertising messages via e-mail, grew from just 3 percent of total Web advertising expenditures to 15 percent in 2003.[55] E-mail advertising takes two forms: permission e-mail and spam. As its name suggests, **permission e-mail** involves sending e-mail ads to customers with their permission; **spam** is unsolicited commercial e-mail. Approximately 20 percent of all e-mail in the United States is commercial, and it is split evenly between permission e-mail and spam.[56] Because most e-mail users see spam as a nuisance, they often view companies that use it ("spammers") in a negative light. Entrepreneurs would be wise to exclude spam from their Web advertising plans. However, permission e-mail can be an effective—and money-saving—advertising tool. Although a banner ad's response rate is just 1 to 5 percent, permission e-mail messages often produce response rates of 25 percent![57] The cost for traditional direct-mail campaigns ranges from $1 to $2 per piece compared to only $.01 to $.25 per piece for e-mail.[58]

Many companies have success with creative e-mail newsletters sent to customers.

Paul Frederick

For example, Paul Frederick, a maker of fine men's shirts, sends a weekly e-mail newsletter to customers (with their permission) that covers everything from fashion do's and don'ts to the hottest new styles. The electronic newsletter contains links to the company's Web site, where customers can browse through the catalog, use the "Create Your Shirt" feature to design their own shirts, and take advantage of special deals for online customers. The combination of its e-mail advertising campaign and its user-friendly Web site gives Paul Frederick an edge over its rivals.

One advantage of Web advertising is its ability to track the results that an ad produces. Web technology allows advertisers to count the number of visitors to a site and to track the number of people who actually click on the ads placed there.

OUTDOOR ADVERTISING. National advertisers have long used outdoor ads. This medium is proving to be popular among small firms (especially retailers). Spending on outdoor ads is growing at a rate faster than that of most other media, nearly 10 percent a year. Very few small businesses rely solely on outdoor advertising; instead, they supplement other advertising media with billboards. With a creative outdoor campaign, a small company can make a big impact—even on a small budget.

Garcia's Irish Pub

Frank Cipriani, owner of Garcia's Irish Pub, created an incredibly successful outdoor campaign over several months to promote his business. The whimsical "boy-meets-girl at Garcia's" campaign featured a series of messages exchanged among "William," his "Angel in Red," and other characters. The ads had the entire town waiting to see what would happen next! "It really took on a life of its own," says one of the designers. "I wanted something inconspicuous, something that didn't seem like advertising," adds Cipriani.[59]

Outdoor advertising offers certain *advantages* to the small business:

High exposure. Outdoor advertising offers a high-frequency exposure; studies suggest that the typical billboard reaches an adult 29 to 31 times each month. Most people tend to follow the same routes in their daily traveling, and billboards are there waiting for them when they pass by.

Broad reach. The nature of outdoor ads makes them effective devices for reaching a large number of potential customers within a specific area. Not only has the number of cars on the road increased by 147 percent since 1970, but the number of daily vehicle trips people take also has climbed 110 percent.[60] The people outdoor ads reach tend to be younger, wealthier, and better educated than the average person.

Flexibility. Advertisers can buy outdoor advertising units separately or in a number of packages. Through its variety of graphics, design, and unique features, outdoor advertising enables the small advertiser to match his message to the particular audience.

Cost efficiency. Outdoor advertising offers one of the lowest costs per thousand customers reached of all advertising media. Experts estimate the cost per thousand viewers (CPM) for outdoor ads is about $2, compared to $5 for drive-time radio spots, $9 for magazine ads, and $10 to $20 for newspaper ads and prime-time television spots.[61]

Outdoor ads also have several *disadvantages:*

Brief exposure. Because billboards are immobile, the reader is exposed to the advertiser's message for only a short time—typically no more than five seconds. As a result, the message must be short and to the point.

Limited ad recall. Because customers often are zooming past outdoor ads at high speed, they are exposed to an advertising message very briefly, which limits their ability to retain the message.

Legal restrictions. Outdoor billboards are subject to strict regulations and to a high degree of standardization. Many cities place limitations on the number and type of signs and billboards allowed along the roadside.

Lack of prominence. A clutter of billboards and signs along a heavily traveled route tends to reduce the effectiveness of a single ad that loses its prominence among the crowd of billboards.

Using Outdoor Ads. Until the 1990s, billboards were mostly hand-painted. Today, however, technology has changed the face of outdoor advertising dramatically. Computerized painting techniques render truer, crisper, and brighter colors and have improved the quality of outdoor ads significantly. Vinyl surfaces accept print-quality images and are extremely durable. Digital technology, three-dimensional effects, computerized lighting, and other advances allow companies to create animated, continuous motion ads that really capture viewers' attention at reasonable costs. Because the outdoor ad is stationary and the viewer is in motion, the small business owner must pay special attention to its design. An outdoor ad should:

- Identify the product and the company clearly and quickly.
- Use a simple background. The background should not compete with the message.
- Rely on large illustrations that jump out at the viewer.
- Include clear, legible type. All lowercase or a combination of upper- and lowercase letters work best. Very bold or very thin typefaces become illegible at a distance.
- Use black-and-white designs. Research shows that black-and-white outdoor ads are more effective than color ads. If color is important to the message, pick color combinations that contrast both hue and brightness—for example, black on yellow.
- Emphasize simplicity; short copy and short words are best. Don't try to cram too much onto a billboard. One study found that ads with fewer than eight words were most effective, and those containing more than 10 words were least effective.
- Be located on the right-hand side of the highway. Studies show that ads located there draw higher recall scores than those located on the left-hand side.[62]

One of the latest trends in outdoor advertising is "talking billboards," those whose text direct viewers to tune into a specific radio frequency, where they hear a short commercial. Those who tune in hear jokes, skits, and, of course, a commercial for the company and its products. Underwear maker Joe Boxer uses talking billboards with a great deal of success.[63] Entrepreneurs are finding other creative ways to use outdoor advertising to get their messages across to customers. Tom Scott and Tom First, cofounders of Nantucket Nectars, send "mobile marketing squads" out in purple Winnebagos emblazoned with the company's logo to concerts, races, football games, and other events, where they hand out free samples of Nantucket Nectars' products.[64] Beach 'N Billboard, a small company in New Jersey, will imprint company logos and advertisements into the sand at the beach. Some companies now even advertise their products and services using stickers on pieces of fruit sold in grocery stores![65]

TRANSIT ADVERTISING. Transit advertising includes advertising signs inside and outside some 70,000 public transportation vehicles throughout the country's urban areas. The medium is likely to grow as more cities look to public transit systems to relieve transportation problems. Transit ads offer a number of *advantages:*

Wide coverage. Transit advertising offers advertisers mass exposure to a variety of customers. The message literally goes to where the people are. This medium also reaches people with a wide variety of demographic characteristics.

Repeat exposure. Transit ads provide repeated exposure to a message. The typical transit rider averages 24 rides per month and spends 61 minutes per day riding.

Low cost. Even small business owners with limited budgets can afford transit advertising. One study shows that transit advertising costs average only $0.30 per thousand.[66]

Flexibility. Transit ads come in a wide range of sizes, numbers, and durations. With transit ads, an owner can select an individual market or any combination of markets across the country.

Transit ads also have several *disadvantages:*

Generality. Even though a small business can choose the specific transit routes on which to advertise, it cannot target a particular segment of the market through transit advertising. The effectiveness of transit ads depends on the routes that public vehicles travel and on the people they reach, which, unfortunately, the advertiser cannot control.

Limited appeal. Unlike many media, transit ads are not beamed into the potential customer's residence or business. The result is that customers cannot keep them for future reference. Also, these ads do not reach with great frequency the upper-income, highly educated portion of the market.

Brief message. Transit ads do not permit the small advertiser to present a detailed description or a demonstration of the product or service for sale. Although inside ads have a relatively long exposure (the average ride lasts 22.5 minutes), outside ads must be brief and to the point.

DIRECTORIES. Directories are an important advertising medium for reaching those customers who have already made purchase decisions. The directory simply helps these customers locate the specific product or service they have decided to buy. Directories include telephone books, industrial or trade guides, buyer guides, annuals, catalog files, and yearbooks that list various businesses and the products they sell.

Directories offer several *advantages* to advertisers:

Prime prospects. Directory listings reach customers who are prime prospects, since they have already decided to purchase an item. The directory just helps them find what they are looking for.

Long life. Directory listings usually have long lives. A typical directory may be published annually.

However, there are certain *disadvantages* to using directories:

Lack of flexibility. Listings and ads in many directories offer only a limited variety of design features. Business owners may not be as free to create unique ads as in other printed media.

Ad clutter. In many directories, ads from many companies are clustered together so closely that no single ad stands out from the rest.

Obsolescence. Because directories are commonly updated only annually, some of their listings become obsolete. This is a problem for a small firm that changes its name, location, or phone number.

When choosing a directory, the small business owner should evaluate several criteria:

- *Completeness.* Does the directory include enough listings that customers will use it?
- *Convenience.* Are the listings well organized and convenient? Are they cross-referenced?
- *Evidence of use.* To what extent do customers actually use the directory? What evidence of use does the publisher offer?
- *Age.* Is the directory well established and does it have a good reputation?
- *Circulation.* Do users pay for the directory or do they receive complimentary copies? Is there an audited circulation statement?

TRADE SHOWS. Trade shows provide manufacturers and distributors with a unique opportunity to advertise to a preselected audience of potential customers who are inclined to buy. Literally thousands of trade shows are sponsored each year, and carefully evaluating and selecting a few shows can produce profitable results for a business owner. A study by the Center for Exhibition Industry Research found that trade show success does *not* depend on how much an exhibitor spends; instead, success is a function of planning, preparation, and follow-up.[67]

Trade shows offer the following *advantages:*

A natural market. Trade shows bring together buyers and sellers in a setting where products can be explained, demonstrated, and handled. Comparative shopping is easy, and the buying process is more efficient.

Preselected audience. Trade exhibits attract potential customers with a specific interest in the goods or services being displayed. There is a high probability that these prospects will make a purchase.

New customer market. Trade shows offer exhibitors a prime opportunity to reach new customers and to contact people who are not accessible to sales representatives.

Cost advantage. As the cost of making a field sales call continues to escalate, more companies are realizing that trade shows are an economical method for making sales contacts and presentations.

There are, however, certain *disadvantages* associated with trade shows:

Increasing costs. The cost of exhibiting at trade shows is rising quickly. Registration fees, travel and setup costs, sales salaries, and other expenditures may be a barrier to some small firms.

Wasted effort. A poorly planned exhibit ultimately costs the small business more than its benefits are worth. Too many firms enter exhibits in trade shows without proper preparation, and they end up wasting their time, energy, and money on unproductive activities.

To avoid these disadvantages, business owners should:

- Establish objectives for the show. Do you want to generate 100 new sales leads, make new-product presentations to 500 potential customers, or make $5,000 in sales?
- Communicate with key potential customers *before* the show; send them invitations or invite them to stop by your booth for a special gift.
- Make your display memorable. Be sure your exhibit shows your company and its products or services in the best light.
- Have knowledgeable salespeople staffing the booth. Research shows that the most important factor to trade show attendees is knowledgeable, friendly, professional people tending the exhibit.[68]
- Demonstrate your product or service; let customers see it in action.
- Learn to distinguish between serious customers and "tire-kickers."
- Distribute literature that clearly communicates the product or service sold.
- Project a professional image at all times.
- Follow up promptly on sales leads. The most common mistake trade show participants make is failing to follow up on the sales leads the show generated. If you are not going to follow up leads, why bother to attend the show in the first place?

SPECIALTY ADVERTISING. As advertisers have shifted their focus to "narrow casting" their messages to target audiences and away from "broadcasting," specialty advertising has grown in popularity. Advertisers now spend more than $3 billion annually on specialty items. This category includes all customer gift items imprinted with the company's name, address, telephone number, and slogan. Specialty items are best used as reminder ads to supplement other forms of advertising and help to create goodwill among existing and potential customers.

Specialty advertising offers several *advantages:*

Reaching select audiences. Advertisers have the ability to reach specific audiences with well-planned specialty items.

Corhart Refractories Corporation

For instance, Corhart Refractories Corporation wanted to increase the number of steel executives reached at a trade show. The company mailed the executives invitations in a box containing a set of radio earphones. To get the radio (without which the earphones were useless), the executives had to stop by the Corhart's booth. An overflow crowd stopped to get their radios, imprinted with Corhart's logo.[69]

Personalized nature. By carefully choosing a specialty item, a business owner can "personalize" his advertisement. When choosing advertising specialties, a small business owner should use items that are unusual and related to the nature of the business and are meaningful to customers.

Versatility. The rich versatility of specialty advertising is limited only by the business owner's imagination. Advertisers print their logos on everything from pens and scarves to wallets and caps.

There are *disadvantages* to specialty advertising:

Potential for waste. Unless the owner chooses the appropriate specialty item, he will be wasting his time and money. The options are virtually infinite.

Costs. Some specialty items can be quite expensive. Plus, some owners have a tendency to give advertising materials to anyone—even those who are not potential customers.

SPONSORSHIPS AND SPECIAL EVENTS. Although sponsorships of special events are a relatively new advertising medium for small companies, a growing number of small businesses are finding that sponsoring special events attracts a great deal of interest and provides a lasting impression of the company in customers' minds. As customers become increasingly harder to reach through any single advertising medium, companies of all sizes are finding that sponsoring special events—from wine tastings and beach volleyball tournaments to fitness walks and car races—is an excellent way to reach their target audiences. According to the *IEG Sponsorship Report,* companies in North America spend more than $7 billion each year on sponsorships.[70]

Sports events, such as basketball tournaments, soccer matches, and NASCAR races, draw the greatest interest from sponsors. In fact, NASCAR events boast the largest increase in attendance since 1990 of any professional sport, a fact that has not escaped sponsors.[71] Companies also have discovered that NASCAR sponsorships work. Research suggests that NASCAR fans have the highest degree of loyalty to a sponsor's product than any other sport (72 percent versus 52 percent for tennis, 47 percent for golf, and 36 percent for football).[72] Getting your company's name on a race car is not cheap, however. The least expensive part of the car on which to put a company logo is the lower quarter panel, whose cost ranges from $25,000 to $75,000. The most expensive part of the car to sponsor? No surprise: the hood, at a cost of $4 to $6 million![73]

Although most small companies cannot afford the cost of sponsoring a NASCAR race car, there are plenty of more affordable events that generate impressive opportunities for increasing name recognition and customer awareness. For instance, according to the International Festival and Events Association, the number of festivals and events in the United States has doubled to more than 50,000 in the past 15 years.[74] Because of their local character, many of these festivals, fairs, and events are ideally suited for small business sponsors. For instance, the owner of one small art gallery generates thousands of dollars' worth of publicity and recognition for her company with her sponsorship of a local art show. The gala event features a sidewalk art exhibit, a "meet the artists" luncheon, and a competition among local artists. Hundreds of potential customers flock to her gallery on the night the winners are announced. The sponsorship costs the gallery owner a few thousand dollars, but the buzz it generates for her company is worth many times the cost!

Small companies do not have to rely on other organizations' events to generate advertising opportunities; they can create their own special events. Creativity and uniqueness are essential ingredients in any special event promotion, and most entrepreneurs excel at those.

For Paws

For example, the owner of For Paws, a California pet boutique, sponsors free "doggy brunches" each week, complete with "kibble quiche" and "wheat-germ woofies." The shop also caters birthday parties, beach parties (picture a dog with a whistle around his neck, a muscle T-shirt, and a dab of Noxzema on his nose), and other gala events for its four-legged customers and their owners.[75]

The following tips will ensure that a small company gets the most promotional impact from its sponsorship of an event:

- Do not count on sponsorships for your entire advertising campaign. Sponsorships are most effective when they are part of a coordinated advertising effort. Most sponsors spend no more than 10 percent of their advertising budgets on sponsorships.
- Look for an event that is appropriate for your company and its products and services. The owner of a small music store in an upscale mountain resort sponsors a local jazz festival every summer during the busy tourist season and generates lots of business among both residents and tourists. Ideally, an event's audience should match the sponsoring company's target audience. Otherwise, the sponsorship will be a waste of money.
- Research the event and the organization hosting it before agreeing to become a sponsor. How well attended is the event? What is the demographic profile of the event's visitors? Is it well organized?
- Try to become a dominant (or, ideally, the only) sponsor of the event. A small company can be easily lost in a crowd of much larger companies sponsoring the same event. If sole sponsorship is too expensive, make sure that your company is the only one from its industry sponsoring the event.
- Clarify the costs and level of participation required for sponsorship up front.
- Get involved. Do not simply write a check for the sponsorship fee and then walk away. Find an event that is meaningful to you, your company, and its employees and take an active role in it. Your sponsorship dollars will produce a higher return if you do.

POINT-OF-PURCHASE ADS. In the last several years, in-store advertising has become more popular as a way of reaching the customer at a crucial moment—the point of purchase. Research suggests that consumers make 66 percent of all buying decisions at the point of sale.[76] Self-service stores are especially well suited for in-store ads as they remind people of the products as they walk the aisles. These in-store ads are not just blasé signs or glossy photographs of the product in use. Some businesses use in-store music interspersed with household hints and, of course, ads. Another ploy involves tiny devices that sense when a customer passes by and triggers a prerecorded sales message. Other machines emit scents—chocolate chip cookies or pina coladas—to appeal to passing customers' sense of smell.[77] Joe Boxer now sells its boxer shorts in pop-top aluminum cans from vending machines that use motion sensors to detect passing shoppers. When triggered, the machine talks to customers, with comments including, "Hey you! Hey You! Have you changed your underwear lately?"[78]

In sum, small business owners have an endless array of advertising tools, techniques, and media available to them. Even postage stamps, bathroom walls, sides of cows, and parking meters offer advertising space! Table 7.6 summarizes the different advertising media and their suitability for reaching particular customer groups.

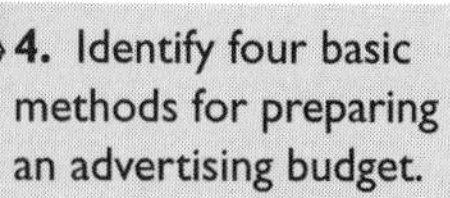

4. Identify four basic methods for preparing an advertising budget.

PREPARING AN ADVERTISING BUDGET

One of the most challenging decisions confronting a small business owner is how much to invest in advertising. The amount the owner wants to spend and the amount the firm can afford to spend on advertising usually differ significantly. There are four methods of determining an advertising budget: what is affordable; matching competitors; percentage of sales; and objective and task.

Under the what-is-affordable method, the owner sees advertising as a luxury. She views advertising completely as an expense, not as an investment that produces sales and profits in the future. Therefore, as the name implies, management spends whatever it can afford on advertising. Too often, the advertising budget is allocated funds after all

YOU BE THE CONSULTANT . . .

Fat Free But Not Famous—Yet

When she was in college, Candace Vanice was a french fry fanatic, but she worried about the fat content of fries cooked the traditional way. "I waited and waited for someone to create fat free French fries, but no one did," recalls Vanice. "So, I got busy in my own kitchen. I explored a great number of approaches that did not work, but one recipe showed great promise." That recipe was based on her mother's recipe for crispy french toast, a dish Vanice had enjoyed while growing up. After much experimenting with seasonings, Vanice created french fries that tasted as good as the ones at fast-food restaurants but with one major advantage: They contained no fat!

In 1994, Vanice applied for and received a patent for her fat-free fries, and she launched a company, Marvel LLC, to market them. She quickly learned that breaking into the food business and getting a new product on grocers' shelves is no easy task. To gain widespread acceptance in supermarkets, a new product needs a food broker to push it. The problem 27-year-old Vanice faced was that both food brokers and supermarkets are reluctant to carry products that are not supported by big-time marketing and advertising campaigns. Vanice's company, like most fledgling start-ups, did not have the financial resources to launch an extensive advertising program.

Vanice had faith in her product, however, and believed that customers would flock to buy her fat-free fries once they tasted them. She contacted several supermarkets in her hometown of Kansas City and started handing out free samples. She also hired a sampling agency to give away free product samples in stores in the surrounding area. As Vanice and the sampling agency handed out fries, they collected customer feedback, asking people to fill out surveys about the fries. According to customers, her fries were an overwhelming hit! The only remaining question was how to raise the visibility of 8th Wonder Fat Free Fries enough to convince food brokers and supermarkets to carry them. That would be a challenge because Marvel LLC had practically no money for advertising.

1. Work with a team of your classmates to develop a creative advertising and promotional plan for Marvel LLC. What unique selling proposition should Vanice use?
2. How should Vanice use publicity to draw attention to her 8th Wonder Fat Free Fries?
3. According to one marketing expert, "A product can be copied or imitated, but a brand cannot." What can entrepreneurs such as Candace Vanice do to build brand name recognition when they do not have the advertising budgets large companies have?

Sources: Adapted from Don Debalak, "French Twist," *Business Start-Ups,* November 1999, pp. 78–81; Marvel LLC, **<www.fatfreefries.com>,** Sheryl Nance-Nash, "Making a Name for Your Brand," *Fortune,* July 20, 1998, pp. 156[L]–156[M].

other budget items have been financed. The result is an inadequate advertising budget. This method also fails to relate the advertising budget to the advertising objective.

Another approach is to match the advertising expenditures of the firm's competitors, either in a flat dollar amount or as a percentage of sales. This method assumes that a firm's advertising needs and strategies are the same as those of its competitors. Although competitors' actions can be helpful in establishing a floor for advertising expenditures, relying on this technique can lead to blind imitation instead of a budget suited to the small firm's circumstances.

The most commonly used method of establishing an advertising budget is the simple percentage-of-sales approach. This method relates advertising expenditures to actual sales results. Tying advertising expenditures to sales is generally preferred to relating them to profits because sales tend to fluctuate less than profits. One expert suggests a useful rule of thumb when establishing an advertising budget: 10 percent of projected sales the first year in business; 7 percent the second year; and at least 5 percent each year after that. Relying totally on such broad rules can be dangerous, however. They may not be representative of a small company's advertising needs.

TABLE 7.6
Advertising Media Comparison Chart

Media	Coverage	Special Characteristics
Newspapers	Selected geographic coverage. Entire city or metropolitan area with major newspapers. Single town with smaller, weekly papers.	Top advertising media; attracts about 23% of advertising expenditures.
Radio	Market area radio station serves. Stations' formats range from country and easy listening to rap and golden oldies.	Ability to reach almost any market by choosing proper station. The average household has 5.6 radios, and 95 percent of the cars in the United States have radios.
Television	Market area TV station serves; could be local (cable) or national (major network).	Powerful medium; especially effective at reaching younger, less educated audiences.
Magazines	Local magazines typically cover a particular city or region.	Magazines usually target specific audiences, from wealthy owners of country estates to low-income apartment dwellers.
Direct mail	Advertiser chooses the audience.	An effective advertising medium for small companies in virtually *any* business.
World Wide Web (WWW)	Anyone in the world who is wired to the WWW.	Reaches upscale, well-educated consumers anywhere in the world; most WWW users are male.
Outdoor advertising	Ranges from a neighborhood to an entire metropolitan area.	An excellent medium to supplement other forms of advertising.
Transit advertising	Urban areas.	Typically does not reach upper-income, well-educated audience.
Directories	Customers who have already made a purchase decision.	Many directories available; the key is picking the right ones.
Trade shows	Preselected audience.	Potential customers are inclined to buy.
Specialty advertising	Advertiser chooses the audience.	Allows advertiser to "narrowcast" message rather than broadcast it.
Special events and promotions	Advertiser chooses the audience.	Allows advertiser maximum flexibility and creativity in ads.
Point-of-purchase ads	Existing customers.	Two-thirds of buying decisions are made at the point of sale.

Advantages	Disadvantages	Tips
Extensive coverage; low absolute and relative costs; timeliness.	Blanket coverage means some ads are wasted on those who are not potential customers; limited reproduction quality; significant ad clutter.	Research newspaper's reader profile; focus on placing ads in proper sections.
Universal infiltration; radio ads are more "active" than print ads, giving advertisers the ability to be more creative with ads.	Need to repeat ads for effectiveness; no visual possibilities; brief ads mean limited message potential.	Make sure station's listener profile matches company's target audience. Keep ad copy simple.
Visual advantage—advertiser can *show* customers product or service benefits; cable stations bring TV ads into price ranges that small businesses can afford.	Brief exposure to ads, often because of zapping; creating TV commercials can be expensive.	Consider infomercials. They may be obnoxious to many, but they work, if properly done. Try to evoke emotion in ads.
Long life spans for ads; most magazines have multiple readers; high ad quality.	Long closing times for ads requires advance planning; ad clutter can reduce ads' effectiveness.	As in newspaper advertising, proper placement is the key. Left-hand pages are best.
Ability to select a specific audience and tailor a message to it; captures reader's attention, at least for a moment.	Will become junk mail if improperly targeted; high relative cost because of low response rates.	Plan direct-mail ads so that you can measure results; use catchy words—*free, save, new.*
Attractive audience profile; rapid growth of the WWW as a marketing tool; ability to use full-color, sound, animation, etc.	Audience may bypass ads without ever seeing them; advertising clutter is a problem and will grow as WWW use grows.	Make site interactive, if possible; games; puzzles, and contests can be effective draws.
Multiple exposures; a bargain because of its low relative cost.	Brief exposure requires limited messages; lack of prominence.	Keep ads short and simple; use clear, legible type.
Wide coverage and repeat exposure to ads; low relative cost.	Difficulty in reaching specific target audiences; brief exposure requires limited message.	Use contrasting colors and designs that give ads a two-dimensional appearance.
Targets prime prospects; long ad life.	Danger of listing or directory becoming obsolete; ad clutter.	Design ad so that it stands out from the crowd.
Ample time for personal selling; ability to demonstrate products.	High cost of traveling to show, setting up, and staffing booth.	Make the most of sales time and follow up leads.
Ability to reach specific audience and to personalize the message.	Potential for waste and high costs.	Specialty items should prompt customer recall.
Reaches some customers when all other attempts fail.	Requires time to plan and coordinate; can be expensive.	Creativity is a must if a specialty promotion is to be successful.
Reaches customer at a crucial moment: the point of purchase.	Require customers to come into the business first.	Capture the customer's attention first; then sell.

The objective-and-task method is the most difficult and least used technique for establishing an advertising budget. It also is the method most often recommended by advertising experts. With this method, an owner links advertising expenditures to specific objectives. Whereas the previous methods break down the total amount of funds allocated to advertising, the task method builds up the advertising funds by analyzing what it will cost to accomplish these objectives. For example, suppose that a manager wants to boost sales of a particular product 10 percent by attracting local college students. He may determine that a nearby rock radio station would be the best medium to use. Then he must decide on the number and frequency of the ads and estimate their costs.

A manager follows this same process for each advertising objective. A common problem with the method is the tendency for the manager to be overly ambitious in setting advertising objectives, which leads to unrealistically high advertising expenditures. The manager may be forced to alter objectives, or the plans to reach them, to bring the advertising budget back to a reasonable level. However, the plan can still be effective.

Most small companies find it useful to plan in advance their advertising expenditures on a weekly basis. This short-term planning ensures a more consistent advertising effort throughout the year. A calendar such as the one pictured in Figure 7.3 can be one of the most valuable tools in planning a small company's advertising program. The calendar enables the owner to prepare for holidays and special events, to monitor actual and budgeted expenditures, and to ensure that ads are scheduled on the appropriate media at the proper times.

FIGURE 7.3
Advertising Planning Calendar

October

Sunday	Monday	Tuesday	Wednesday	Thursday	Friday	Saturday
Advertising Budget for October: 9% of Sales = $2,275 Co-op Ads = $550 Total $2,825		October Advertising Expenditures: $2,845 Under/(Over) Budget: ($20) Remaining Balance: $6,400		1 WPCC Radio 5 Spots $125 Billboard $350	2 The Chronicle 140 lines $100	3
4	5	6	7	8	9 The Chronicle 140 lines $100	10
11	12	13 Meet w/ Leslie Re: November Ad Campaigns 2pm	14	15 Envelope "Stuffer" in Invoices Halloween Sale $175	16 The Chronicle 140 lines $100	17 WPCC Radio 5 Spots $100
18	19	20 WPCC Radio 5 Spots $125	21	22 Direct Mail Halloween Sale Promo "Preferred Customers" $120	23 The Chronicle 140 lines $100	24 WPCC Radio 5 Spots $100
25	26 WPCC Radio 5 Spots $125	27 WPCC Radio 5 Spots $125	28 WPCC Radio 5 Spots $125	29 WPCC Radio 5 Spots $125	30 The Chronicle Half-Page Spread Sale $300	31 Halloween WPCC Radio Live Remote Broadcast $425

HOW TO ADVERTISE BIG ON A SMALL BUDGET

5. Explain practical methods for stretching a small business owner's advertising budget.

The typical small business does not have the luxury of an unlimited advertising budget. Most cannot afford to hire a professional ad agency. This does not mean, however, that the small company should assume a second-class advertising posture. Most advertising experts say that unless a small company spends more than $10,000 a year on advertising, it probably doesn't need an ad agency. For most, hiring freelance copywriters and artists on a per-project basis is a much better bargain. With a little creativity and a dose of ingenuity, small business owners can stretch their advertising dollars and make the most of what they spend. Three useful techniques to do this are cooperative advertising, shared advertising, and publicity.

Cooperative Advertising

In **cooperative advertising,** a manufacturing company shares the cost of advertising with a small retailer if the retailer features its products in those ads. Both the manufacturer and the retailer get more advertising per dollar by sharing expenses.

Example

David Lang, owner of a small lawn equipment store, purchases his inventory from 10 different manufacturers, nine of whom offer cooperative advertising programs. "Without [the manufacturers' help], we could only spend $20,000 a year [on advertising]," says Lang. "But now we can spend $40,000 because we're getting $20,000 back."[79]

Unlike Lang, who uses every dollar of cooperative advertising available to him, most small business owners fail to take advantage of manufacturers' cooperative advertising programs. Manufacturers, whose products cover the entire retail spectrum, make an estimated $15 billion of co-op ad dollars available each year; yet, more than two-thirds of it goes unused![80]

Cahaba Cycles

Barbara Malki, co-owner of Cahaba Cycles, is now a believer in the power of cooperative advertising, although she admits that she had not always been. "Two years ago," she says, "I was leaving co-op money on the table. I'm more aggressive about now. [Now] I . . . use every co-op dollar." Cahaba Cycles recoups about 10 percent of its annual advertising budget through cooperative advertising.[81]

Shared Advertising

In **shared advertising,** a group of similar businesses forms a syndicate to produce generic ads that allow the individual businesses to dub in local information. The technique is especially useful for small businesses that sell relatively standardized products or services such as legal assistance, autos, and furniture. Because the small firms in the syndicate pool their funds, the result usually is higher-quality ads and significantly lower production costs.

cooperative advertising—*an arrangement in which a manufacturing company shares the cost of advertising with a small retailer if the retailer features its products in those ads.*

shared advertising—*an arrangement in which a group of similar businesses forms a syndicate to produce generic ads that allow the individual businesses to dub in local information.*

Other cost-saving suggestions for advertising expenditures include the following:

Repeat ads that have been successful. In addition to reducing the cost of ad preparation, this may create a consistent image in a small firm's advertising program.

Use identical ads in different media. If a billboard has been an effective advertising tool, an owner should consider converting it to a newspaper or magazine ad or a direct-mail flyer.

Hire independent copywriters, graphic designers, photographers, and other media specialists. Many small businesses that cannot afford a full-time advertising staff buy their advertising services à la carte. They work directly with independent specialists and usually receive high-quality work that compares favorably to that of advertising agencies without paying a fee for overhead.

Concentrate advertising during times when customers are most likely to buy. Some small business owners make the mistake of spreading an already small advertising budget evenly—and thinly—over a 12-month period.

Public Relations

The press can be either a valuable friend or a fearsome foe to a small business, depending on how well the owner handles her firm's public relations. Too often, entrepreneurs take the attitude, "My business is too small to be concerned about public relations." However, wise small business managers recognize that investing time and money in public relations benefits both the community and the company. The community gains the support of a good business citizen, and the company earns a positive image in the marketplace.

Many small businesses rely on media attention to get noticed, and getting that attention takes a coordinated effort. Public relations doesn't just happen; an owner must work at getting her company noticed by the media. Although such publicity may not be free, it definitely can lower the company's advertising expenditures and still keep its name before the public. Because small companies' advertising budgets are limited, public relations take on significant importance.

Bob Mayberry Ford

Bob Mayberry, a car dealer in Monroe, North Carolina, recently bought a 1961 Ford squad car like the one used on the 1960s hit TV series, The Andy Griffith Show. *Not only does the car lure potential customers onto his lot, but it also has gotten the dealership into several newspaper articles. "We have sold a lot of cars from it," says Mayberry.*[82]

One successful public relations technique is **cause marketing,** in which a small business sponsors and promotes fund-raising activities of nonprofit groups and charities while raising its own visibility in the community.

Cookies Cook'n

For example, during the Muscular Dystrophy Association's annual telethon, a local shop, Cookies Cook'n, donated over 100 pounds of cookies and brownies to feed telephone volunteers. Several giant cookies were auctioned off during the telethon, and the small cookie shop's name was mentioned frequently. Cookies Cook'n got more television exposure for donating these cookies than it could have gotten spending its entire advertising budget on TV commercials.[83]

cause marketing—*an arrangement in which a small business sponsors and promotes fund-raising activities of nonprofit groups and charities while raising its own visibility in the community.*

PRICING: A CREATIVE BLEND OF ART AND SCIENCE

Deciding how and where to advertise is not the only key to marketing success; small business owners also must determine prices for their goods and services that will draw customers and produce a profit. Unfortunately, too many small business owners set prices according to vague, poorly defined techniques, or even hunches. Price is an important factor in the relationship with customers, and haphazard pricing techniques can confuse and alienate customers and endanger a firm's profitability. Setting prices is not only one of the toughest decisions small business owners face, but it also is one of the most important. Improper pricing has destroyed countless businesses when owners mistakenly thought their prices were sufficient to generate a profit.

Price is the monetary value of a product or service in the marketplace; it is a measure of what the customer must exchange in order to obtain various goods and services. As the media continuously reinforces, this is an era in which shoppers seek value for their money. Price also is a signal of a product's or service's value to an individual, and different customers assign different values to the same goods and services. From an owner's viewpoint, price must be compatible with the customer's perception of value. "Pricing is not just a math problem," says one business writer. "It's a psychology test."[84]

Setting prices with a customer orientation is more important than trying to choose the ideal price for a product. In fact, for most products there is an acceptable price range, not a single ideal price. This price range is the area between the price ceiling defined by customers in the market and the price floor established by the firm's cost structure. A manager's goal should be to position the firm's prices within this acceptable price range. The final price that business owners set depends on the desired image they want to create for the business in the customer's mind—discount, middle-of-the-road, or prestige (see Figure 7.4). "We have to balance our ideal [price] with what the market will pay," says Judy Johnson, co-owner (with husband Doug) of Huckleberry Mountain Company, a manufacturer of specialty candies and preserves. "If we're 40 percent higher than the competition, then we'd better have something really special."[85]

Setting appropriate prices requires more than just choosing a number based solely on intuition. Rather, proper pricing policies require information, facts, and analysis. The factors that small business owners must consider when determining the final price for goods and services include the following:

- Product/service costs
- Market factors—supply and demand
- Sales volume
- Competitors' prices
- The company's competitive advantage
- Economic conditions
- Business location
- Seasonal fluctuations
- Psychological factors
- Credit terms and purchase discounts
- Customers' price sensitivity
- Desired image

Although business owners may not be able to charge the ideal price for a product or service, they should set the price high enough to cover costs and earn a reasonable profit but low enough to attract customers and generate an adequate sales volume. Furthermore, the right price today may be completely inappropriate tomorrow because of changing market and competitive conditions. For many businesses, the pricing decision has become more difficult because the World Wide Web gives customers access to incredible amounts of information about the prices of items ranging from cars to computers. Increasingly, customers are using the Web to find the lowest prices available.

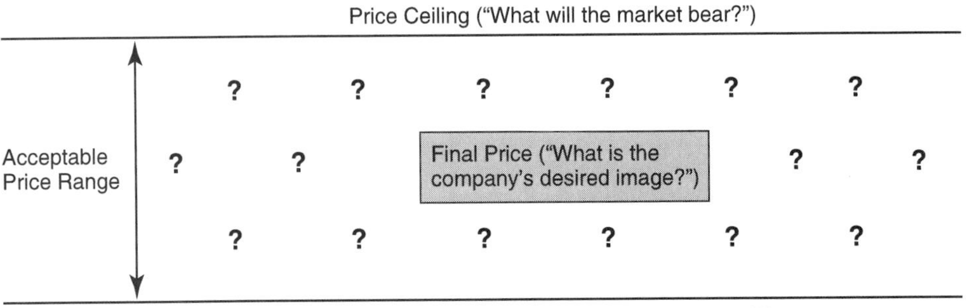

FIGURE 7.4
What Determines Price?

6. Describe effective pricing techniques for introducing new products or services and for existing ones.

PRICING STRATEGIES AND TACTICS

There is no limit to the number of variations in pricing strategies and tactics. This wide variety of options is exactly what allows the small business manager to be so creative. This section will examine some of the more commonly used tactics under a variety of conditions. Pricing always plays a critical role in a firm's overall strategy; pricing policies must be compatible with a company's total marketing plan. "Your price must fit in with the goals and mission of your company," advises one small business owner.[86]

Introducing a New Product

Most small business managers approach setting the price of a new product with a great deal of apprehension because they have no precedent on which to base their decision. If the new product's price is excessively high, it is in danger of failing because of low sales volume. However, if its price is too low, the product's sales revenue might not cover costs. When pricing any new product, the owner should try to satisfy three objectives:

1. *Getting the product accepted.* No matter how unusual a product is, its price must be acceptable to the firm's potential customers.
2. *Maintaining market share as competition grows.* If a new product is successful, competitors will enter the market, and the small company must work to expand or at least maintain its market share. Continuously reappraising the product's price in conjunction with special advertising and promotion techniques helps to retain a satisfactory market share.
3. *Earning a profit.* Obviously, a small firm must establish a price for the new product higher than its cost. Entrepreneurs should not introduce a new product at a price below cost because it is much easier to lower a price than to increase it once the product is on the market.

Calder & Calder Promotions

Linda Calder, owner of Calder & Calder Promotions, a company that produces trade shows, knows how difficult it can be to raise prices. When she launched her company, Calder decided to set her price below the average price of competing trade show production companies because she thought that would give her a competitive edge. "My fee was so low . . . I sold out but did not make a profit," she says. Realizing her mistake, Calder raised prices in her second year, but her customers balked. Her sales fell by 50 percent.[87]

Small business managers have three basic strategies to choose from when establishing a new product's price: a penetration pricing strategy; a skimming pricing strategy; and a sliding-down-the-demand-curve strategy.

PENETRATION. If a small business introduces a product into a highly competitive market in which a large number of similar products are competing for acceptance, the product must penetrate the market to be successful. To gain quick acceptance and extensive distribution in the mass market, the firm should introduce the product with a low price. In other words, it should set the price just above total unit cost to develop a wedge in the market and quickly achieve a high volume of sales. The resulting low profit margins may discourage other competitors from entering the market with similar products.

In most cases, a penetration pricing strategy is used to introduce relatively low-priced goods into a market where no elite segment and little opportunity for differentiation exist. The introduction is usually accompanied by heavy advertising and promotional techniques, special sales, and discounts. Entrepreneurs must recognize that penetration pricing is a long-range strategy; until customers accept the product, profits are likely to be small. If the strategy works and the product achieves mass-market penetration, sales volume will increase, and the company will earn adequate profits. The objectives of the penetration strategy are to break into the market quickly, to generate a high sales volume as soon as possible, and to build market share. Many consumer products, such as soap, shampoo, and light bulbs, are introduced through penetration pricing strategies.

SKIMMING. A skimming pricing strategy often is used when a company introduces a new product into a market with little or no competition. Sometimes the firm employs this tactic when introducing a product into a competitive market that contains an elite group that is able to pay a higher price. Here a firm uses a higher-than-normal price in an effort to quickly recover the initial developmental and promotional costs of the product. Start-up costs usually are substantial due to intensive promotional expenses and high initial production costs. The idea is to set a price well above the total unit cost and to promote the product heavily in order to appeal to the segment of the market that is not sensitive to price. Such a pricing tactic often reinforces the unique, prestigious image of a store and projects a quality picture of the product. Another advantage of this technique is that the manager can correct pricing mistakes quickly and easily. If the firm sets a price that is too low under a penetration strategy, raising the price can be very difficult. If a firm using a skimming strategy sets a price too high to generate sufficient volume, it can always lower the price. Successful skimming strategies require a company to differentiate its products or services from those of the competition, justifying the above-average price.

SLIDING-DOWN-THE-DEMAND-CURVE. One variation of the skimming price strategy is called sliding-down-the-demand-curve. Using this tactic, the small company introduces a product at a high price. Then technological advancements enable the firm to lower its costs quickly and to reduce the product's price before its competition can. By beating other businesses in a price decline, the small company discourages competitors and gradually, over time, becomes a high-volume producer. Computers are a prime example of a product introduced at a high price that quickly cascaded downward as companies forged important technological advances.

Sliding is a short-term pricing strategy that assumes that competition will eventually emerge. But even if no competition arises, the small business almost always lowers the product's price to attract a larger segment of the market. Yet, the initial high price contributes to a rapid return of start-up costs and generates a pool of funds to finance expansion and technological advances.

Pricing Established Goods and Services

Each of the following pricing tactics or techniques can become part of the toolbox of pricing tactics entrepreneurs can use to set prices of established goods and services.

ODD PRICING. Although studies of consumer reactions to prices are mixed and generally inconclusive, many small business managers use the technique known as **odd pricing.** These managers prefer to establish prices that end in odd numbers (5, 7, 9) because they believe that merchandise selling for $12.95 appears to be much cheaper than the item priced at $13.00. Psychological techniques such as odd pricing are designed to appeal to certain customer interests, but their effectiveness remains to be proven.

odd pricing—*a pricing technique that sets prices that end in odd numbers to create the psychological impression of low prices.*

PRICE LINING. **Price lining** is a technique that greatly simplifies the pricing function. Under this system, the manager stocks merchandise in several different price ranges or price lines. Each category of merchandise contains items that are similar in appearance, quality, cost, performance, or other features. For example, most music stores use price lines for their tapes and CDs to make it easier for customers to select items and to simplify stock planning. Most lined products appear in sets of three—good, better, and best—at prices designed to satisfy different market segment needs and incomes.

price lining—*a technique that sets the same price for products that have similar features and appear within the same line.*

leader pricing—*a technique that involves marking down the normal price of a popular item in an attempt to attract more customers who make incidental purchases of other items at regular prices.*

LEADER PRICING. **Leader pricing** is a technique in which the small retailer marks down the customary price (i.e., the price consumers are accustomed to paying) of a popular item in an attempt to attract more customers. The company earns a much smaller profit on each unit because the markup is lower, but purchases of other merchandise by customers seeking the leader item often boost sales and profits. In other words, the incidental purchases that consumers make when shopping for the leader item boost sales revenue enough to offset a lower profit margin on the leader. Grocery stores frequently use leader pricing.

zone pricing—*a technique that involves setting different prices for customers located in different territories because of different transportation costs.*

GEOGRAPHICAL PRICING. Small businesses whose pricing decisions are greatly affected by the costs of shipping merchandise to customers across a wide range of geographical regions frequently employ one of the geographical pricing techniques. For these companies, freight expenses comprise a substantial portion of the cost of doing business and may cut deeply into already narrow profit margins. One type of geographical pricing is **zone pricing,** in which a small company sells its merchandise at different prices to customers located in different territories. For example, a manufacturer might sell at one price to customers east of the Mississippi and at another to those west of the Mississippi. The United States Postal Service's varying parcel post charges offer a good example of zone pricing. The small business must be able to show a legitimate basis (e.g., differences in selling or transporting costs) for the price discrimination or risk violating Section 2 of the Clayton Act.

delivered pricing—*a technique in which a company charges all customers the same price, regardless of their locations and different transportation costs.*

Another variation of geographic pricing is uniform **delivered pricing,** a technique in which a firm charges all of its customers the same price regardless of their location, even though the cost of selling or transporting merchandise varies. The firm calculates the proper freight charges for each region and combines them into a uniform fee. The result is that local customers subsidize the firm's charges for shipping merchandise to distant customers.

FOB-Factory—*a pricing method in which a company sells merchandise to customers on the condition that they pay all shipping costs.*

A final variation of geographical pricing is **FOB-Factory,** in which the small company sells its merchandise to customers on the condition that they pay all shipping costs. In this way, the company can set a uniform price for its product and let each customer cover the freight costs.

opportunistic pricing—*a pricing method that involves charging customers unreasonably high prices when goods or services are in short supply.*

OPPORTUNISTIC PRICING. When products or services are in short supply, customers are willing to pay more for products they need. Some businesses use such circumstances to maximize short-term profits by engaging in price gouging. Many customers have little choice but to pay the higher prices. **Opportunistic pricing** may backfire, however, because customers know that unreasonably high prices mean that a company is exploiting them. For example, after the devastating Los Angeles earthquake, one convenience store jacked up prices on virtually every item, selling small bottles of water for $8 each. Neighborhood residents had no choice but to pay the higher prices. After the incident, many customers remembered the store's unfair prices and began to shop elsewhere. The convenience store's sales slipped and never recovered.

discounts (markdowns)—*reductions from normal list prices.*

DISCOUNTS. Many small business managers use **discounts or markdowns**—reductions from normal list prices—to move stale, outdated, damaged, or slow-moving merchandise. A seasonal discount is a price reduction designed to encourage shoppers to purchase merchandise before an upcoming season. For instance, many retail clothiers offer special sales on winter coats in midsummer. Some firms grant purchase discounts to special groups of customers, such as senior citizens or students, to establish a faithful clientele and to generate repeat business. For example, one small drugstore located near a state university offered a 10 percent student discount on all purchases and was quite successful in developing a large volume of student business.

Multiple pricing is a promotional technique that offers customers discounts if they purchase in quantity. Many products, especially those with relatively low unit value, are sold using multiple pricing. For example, instead of selling an item for 50 cents, a small company might offer 5 for $2.

multiple pricing—*a technique offering customers discounts if they purchase in quantity.*

SUGGESTED RETAIL PRICES. Many manufacturers print suggested retail prices on their products or include them on invoices or in wholesale catalogs. Small business owners frequently follow these suggested retail prices because this eliminates the need to make a pricing decision. Nonetheless, following prices established by a distant manufacturer may create problems for the small firm. For example, a haberdasher may try to create a high-quality, exclusive image through a prestige pricing policy, but manufacturers may suggest discount outlet prices that are incompatible with the small firm's image. Another danger of accepting the manufacturer's suggested price is that it does not take into consideration the small firm's cost structure or competitive situation. A manufacturer cannot force a business to accept a suggested retail price, or require a business to agree not to resell merchandise below a stated price because such practices violate the Sherman Antitrust Act and other legislation.

TWO POTENT FORCES: IMAGE AND COMPETITION

Price Conveys Image

A company's pricing policies communicate important information about its overall image to customers. For example, the prices charged by a posh men's clothing store reflect a completely different image from those charged by a factory outlet. Customers look at prices to determine what type of store they are dealing with. High prices frequently convey the idea of quality, prestige, and uniqueness to the customer. Accordingly, when developing a marketing approach to pricing, a small business manager must establish prices that are compatible with what its customers expect and are willing to pay. Too often, small business owners *underprice* their goods and services, believing that low prices are the only way they can achieve a competitive advantage. One study by the Copernicus consulting firm found that only 15 percent to 35 percent of customers consider price to be the chief criterion when selecting a product or service.[88]

A common mistake small business owners make is failing to recognize the extra value, convenience, service, and quality they give their customers—all things many customers are willing to pay for. These companies fall into the trap of trying to compete solely on the basis of price when they lack the sales volume—and hence, the lower costs—of their larger rivals. It is a recipe for failure. "People want quality," says one merchant selling upscale goods at upscale prices. "They want value. But if you lower prices, they think that you are lowering the value and lowering the quality."[89]

Lacoste

Discounting the prices on its once popular Izod polo shirts nearly cost Lacoste its entire business. Demand for the shirts, which sported a unique crocodile logo, slumped as prices fell. Discounting had eroded the company's distinctive image. Today the company is trying to rebuild its upscale image and the cachet of its crocodile shirts by charging premium prices. Sales have been climbing.[90]

The secret to setting prices properly is based on understanding the firm's target market, the customer groups at which the small company is aiming its goods or services. Target market, business image, and price are closely related.

Crème de la Crème

For instance, Crème de la Crème child care centers charge a staggering $14,000 a year in tuition, compared to a national average tuition of $5,400, and parents are clamoring to *enroll their children. (Some applicants have not even been conceived yet!) Despite its premium prices, Crème de la Crème had a six-month waiting list in only its first year. How did the company manage this spectacular record? The key is differentiating itself from other child care centers and marketing those differences to well-to-do parents who want only the best for their preschool children. A Crème de la Crème center features a 3,600-volume library, a math lab, television and dance studios, and a state-of-the-art computer lab. The company pays 40 percent above the norm for teachers, 90 percent of whom have college degrees, compared to just 31 percent nationwide. Specialized teachers handle important subjects such as music and foreign languages, and keep the student–teacher ratio low. Twenty security monitors ensure students' safety as they play tennis, stage plays in an open-air theater, or frolic in well-equipped playgrounds.*[91]

Competition and Prices

When setting prices, business owners should take into account their competitors' prices, but they should *not* automatically match or beat them. Two factors are vital to studying the effects of competition on the small firm's pricing policies: the location of the competitors and the nature of the competing goods. In most cases, unless a company can differentiate the quality and the quantity of extras it provides, it must match the prices charged by nearby competitors for identical items. For example, if a self-service station charges a nickel more per gallon for gasoline than does another self-service station across the street, customers will simply go across the street to buy. Without the advantage of a unique business image—quality of goods sold, value of services provided, convenient location, favorable credit terms—a small company must match local competitors' prices or lose sales. Although the prices that distant competitors charge are not nearly as critical to the small business as are those of local competitors, it can be helpful to know them and to use them as reference points. Before matching any competitor's prices, however, small business owners should consider the rival's motives. The competition may be establishing its price structure based on a unique set of criteria and a totally different strategy.

The nature of the competitors' goods also influences the small firm's pricing policies. The manager must recognize which products are substitutes for those he sells and then strive to keep his prices in line with them. For example, the local sandwich shop should consider the hamburger restaurant, the taco shop, and the roast beef shop as competitors because they all serve fast foods. Although none of them offers the identical menu of the sandwich shop, they're all competing for the same quick meal dollar. Of course, if a small business can differentiate its products or services by creating a distinctive image in the consumer's mind, it can charge prices higher than those of its competitors. Because competitors' prices can have a dramatic impact on a small company's own prices, entrepreneurs should make it a habit to monitor their rivals' prices, especially on identical items.

Generally, small business managers should avoid head-to-head price competition with other firms that can more easily achieve lower prices through lower cost structures. Most locally owned drugstores cannot compete with the prices of large national drug chains. However, many local drugstores operate successfully by using nonprice competition; these stores offer more personal service, free delivery, credit sales, and other extras that the chains have eliminated. Nonprice competition can be an effective strategy for a small business in the face of larger, more powerful enterprises, especially because there are many dangers in experimenting with price changes. For instance, price shifts cause fluctuations in sales volume that the small firm may not be able to tolerate. Also, frequent price changes may damage the company's image and its customer relations.

One of the most deadly games a small business can get into with competitors is a price war. Price wars can eradicate companies' profit margins and scar an entire industry for years. "Many entrepreneurs cut prices to the point of unprofitablility just to compete," says one business writer. "In doing so, they open the door to catastrophe. Less revenue often translates into lower quality, poorer service, sloppier salesmanship, weaker customer loyalty, and financial disaster."[92] Price wars usually begin when one competitor thinks he can achieve higher volume instantaneously by lowering prices. Rather than sticking to their strategic guns, competitors believe they must follow suit.

Entrepreneurs usually overestimate the power of price cuts, however. Sales volume rarely rises enough to offset the lower profit margins of a lower price. "If you have a 25 percent gross [profit] margin, and . . . you cut your price 10 percent, you have to roughly triple your sales volume just to break even," says one management consultant.[93] In a price war, a company may cut its prices so severely that it is impossible to achieve the volume necessary to offset the lower profit margins. Even when price cuts work, their effects often are temporary. Customers lured by the lowest price usually have almost no loyalty to a business. The lesson: The best way to survive a price war is to stay out of it by emphasizing the unique features, benefits, and value your company offers its customers!

The next three sections will investigate pricing techniques employed in retailing, manufacturing, and service firms.

PRICING CONCEPTS FOR RETAILERS

7-A. Explain the pricing methods and strategies for retailers.

As retail customers have become more price conscious, retailers have changed their pricing strategies to emphasize value. This value/price relationship allows for a wide variety of highly creative pricing and marketing practices. Delivering high levels of recognized value in products and services is one key to retail customer loyalty.

Markup

The basic premise of a successful business operation is selling a good or service for more than it costs to produce it. The difference between the cost of a product or service and its selling price is called **markup** (or **markon**). Markup can be expressed in dollars or as a percentage of either cost or selling price:

markup (markon)—*the difference between the cost of a product or service and its selling price.*

$$\text{Dollar markup} = \text{Retail price} - \text{Cost of the merchandise}$$

$$\text{Percentage (of retail price) markup} = \frac{\text{Dollar markup}}{\text{Retail price}}$$

$$\text{Percentage (of cost) markup} = \frac{\text{Dollar markup}}{\text{Cost of unit}}$$

For example, if a man's shirt costs $15, and the manager plans to sell it for $25, markup would be as follows:

$$\text{Dollar markup} = \$25 - \$15 = \$10$$

$$\text{Percentage (of retail price) markup} = \frac{\$10}{\$25} = 40\%$$

$$\text{Percentage (of cost) markup} = \frac{\$10}{\$15} = 66.67\%$$

Notice that the cost of merchandise used in computing markup includes not only the wholesale price of the merchandise but also any incidental costs (e.g., selling or transportation charges) that the retailer incurs and a profit minus any discounts (quantity, cash) that the wholesaler offers.

Once a business owner has a financial plan, including sales estimates and anticipated expenses, she can compute the firm's initial markup. The initial markup is the *average* markup required on all merchandise to cover the cost of the items, all incidental expenses, and a reasonable profit:

$$\text{Initial dollar markup} = \frac{\text{Operating expenses} + \text{Reductions} + \text{Profits}}{\text{Net sales} + \text{Reductions}}$$

where operating expenses are the cost of doing business, such as rent, utilities, and depreciation; and reductions include employee and customer discounts, markdowns, special sales, and the cost of stockouts.

For example, if a small retailer forecasts sales of $380,000, expenses of $140,000, and $24,000 in reductions, and she expects a profit of $38,000, the initial markup percentage will be:

$$\text{Initial markup percentage} = \frac{140{,}000 + 24{,}000 + 38{,}000}{380{,}000 + 24{,}000} = 50\%$$

This retailer, thus, knows that an average markup of 50 percent is required to cover costs and generate an adequate profit.

Some businesses employ a standard markup on all of their merchandise. This technique, which is usually used in retail stores carrying related products, applies a standard percentage markup to all merchandise. Most stores find it much more practical to use a flexible markup, which assigns various markup percentages to different types of products. Because of the wide range of prices and types of merchandise they sell, department stores frequently rely on a flexible markup. It would be impractical for them to use a standard markup on all items because they have such a divergent cost and volume range. For instance, the markup percentage for socks is not likely to be suitable as a markup for washing machines.

Once an owner determines the desired markup percentage, she can compute the appropriate retail price. Knowing that the markup of a particular item represents 40 percent of the retail price

$$\begin{aligned}\text{Cost} &= \text{Retail price} - \text{Markup}\\ &= 100\% - 40\%\\ &= 60\% \text{ of retail price}\end{aligned}$$

and assuming that the cost of the item is $18.00, the retailer can rearrange the percentage (of retail price) markup formula:

$$\text{Retail price} = \frac{\text{Dollar cost}}{\text{Percentage cost}}$$

Solving for retail price, the retailer computes a price of the following:

$$\text{Retail price} = \frac{\$18.00}{0.60} = \$30.00$$

Thus, the owner establishes a retail price of $30.00 for the item using a 40 percent markup.

Finally, retailers must verify that the retail price they have calculated is consistent with their planned initial markup percentage. Will it cover costs and generate the desired profit? Is it congruent with the firm's overall price image? Is the final price in line with the company's strategy? Is it within an acceptable price range? How does it compare to the prices charged by competitors? And, perhaps most important, are the customers willing and able to pay this price?

Follow-the-Leader Pricing

Some small companies make no effort to be price leaders in their immediate geographic areas and simply follow the prices that their competitors establish. Managers wisely monitor their competitors' pricing policies and individual prices by reviewing their advertisements or by hiring part-time or full-time comparison shoppers. But then these retailers use this information to establish a "me-too" pricing policy, which eradicates any opportunity to create a special price image for their businesses. Although many retailers must match competitors' prices on identical items, maintaining a follow-the-leader pricing policy may not be healthy for a small business because it robs the company of the opportunity to create a distinctive image in its customers' eyes.

Below-Market Pricing

Some small businesses choose to create a discount image in the market by offering goods at below-market prices. By setting prices below those of their competitors, these firms hope to attract a sufficient level of volume to offset the lower profit margins. Many retailers using a below-market pricing strategy eliminate most of the extra services that their above-market-pricing competitors offer. For instance, these businesses trim operating costs by cutting out services such as delivery, installation, credit granting, and sales assistance. Below-market pricing strategies can be risky for small companies because they require them to constantly achieve high sales volume to remain competitive.

PRICING CONCEPTS FOR MANUFACTURERS

7-B. Explain the pricing methods and strategies for manufacturers.

For manufacturers, the pricing decision requires the support of accurate, timely accounting records. The most commonly used pricing technique for manufacturers is cost-plus pricing. Using this method, the manufacturer establishes a price composed of direct materials, direct labor, factory overhead, selling and administrative costs, plus the desired profit margin. Figure 7.5 illustrates the cost-plus pricing components.

The main advantage of the cost-plus pricing method is its simplicity. Given the proper cost accounting data, computing a product's final selling price is relatively easy. Also, because he adds a profit onto the top of the firm's costs, the manufacturer is guaranteed the desired profit margin. This process, however, does not encourage the manufacturer to use his resources efficiently. Even if the company fails to employ its resources in the most effective manner, it will still earn a reasonable profit and, thus, there is no motivation to conserve resources in the manufacturing process. Finally, because manufacturers' cost structures vary so greatly, cost-plus pricing fails to consider the competition sufficiently. But despite its drawbacks, the cost-plus method of establishing prices remains prominent in many industries such as construction and printing.

Direct Costing and Price Formulation

One requisite for a successful pricing policy in manufacturing is a reliable cost accounting system that can generate timely reports to determine the costs of processing raw materials into finished goods. The traditional method of product costing is called **absorption costing** because all manufacturing and overhead costs are absorbed into the finished product's total cost. Absorption costing includes direct materials, direct labor, plus a portion of fixed and variable factory overhead in each unit manufactured. Full-absorption financial statements are used in published annual reports and in tax reports and are very useful in performing financial analysis. But full-absorption statements are of little help to the manufacturer when determining prices or the impact of price changes.

absorption costing—*the traditional method of product costing in which all manufacturing and overhead costs are absorbed into the product's total cost.*

FIGURE 7.5
Cost-Plus Pricing Components

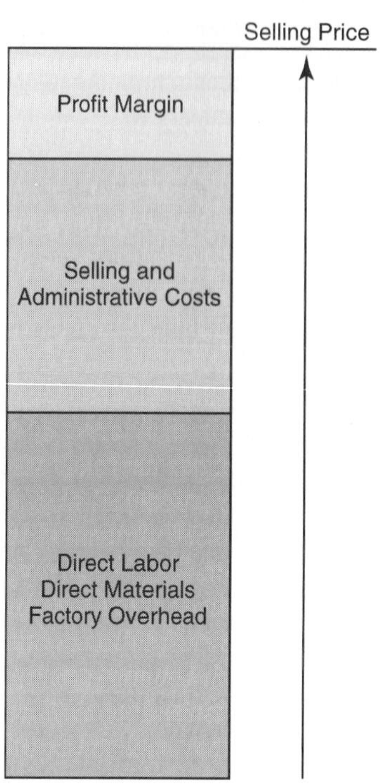

variable (direct) costing—*a method of product costing that includes in the product's cost only those costs that vary directly with the quantity produced.*

A more useful technique for managerial decision making is **variable** (or **direct**) **costing,** in which the cost of the products manufactured includes only those costs that vary directly with the quantity produced. In other words, variable costing encompasses direct materials, direct labor, and factory overhead costs that vary with the level of the firm's output of finished goods. Those factory overhead costs that are fixed (rent, depreciation, insurance) are *not* included in the costs of finished items. Instead, they are considered to be expenses of the period.

The manufacturer's goal when establishing prices is to discover the cost combination of selling price and sales volume that covers the variable costs of producing a product and contributes toward covering fixed costs and earning a profit. The problem with using full-absorption costing for this is that it clouds the true relationships among price, volume, and costs by including fixed expenses in unit cost. Using a direct-costing basis yields a constant unit cost for the product no matter what volume of production. The result is a clearer picture of the price-volume-costs relationship.

The starting point for establishing product prices is the direct cost income statement. As Table 7.7 indicates, the direct-cost statement yields the same net income as does the full-absorption income statement. The only difference between the two statements is the format. The full-absorption statement allocates costs such as advertising, rent, and utilities according to the activity that caused them, but the direct-cost income statement separates expenses into fixed and variable. Fixed expenses remain constant regardless of the production level, but variable expenses fluctuate according to production volume.

When variable costs are subtracted from total revenues, the result is the manufacturer's contribution margin—the amount remaining that contributes to covering fixed expenses and earning a profit. Expressing this contribution margin as a percentage of total revenue yields the firm's contribution percentage. Computing the contribution percentage is a critical step in establishing prices through the direct costing method. This manufacturer's contribution percentage is 36.5 percent.

TABLE 7.7
Full-Absorption Versus Direct-Cost Income Statement

Full-Absorption Income Statement		
Sales Revenue		$790,000
Cost of Goods Sold		
Materials	250,500	
Direct Labor	190,200	
Factory Overhead	120,200	560,900
Gross Profit		$229,100
Operating Expenses		
General and Administrative	66,100	
Selling	112,000	
Other	11,000	
Total Operating Expenses		189,100
Net Income (before taxes)		$ 40,000

Direct-Cost Income Statement		
Sales Revenue (100%)		$790,000
Variable Costs		
Materials	250,500	
Direct Labor	190,200	
Variable Factory Overhead	13,200	
Variable Selling Expenses	48,100	
Total Variable Costs (63.54%)		502,000
Contribution Margin (36.46%)		288,000
Fixed Costs		
Fixed Factory Overhead	107,000	
Fixed Selling Expenses	63,900	
General and Administrative	66,100	
Other Fixed Expenses	11,000	
Total Fixed Expenses (31.39%)		248,000
Net Income (before taxes) (5.06%)		$ 40,000

Computing a Breakeven Selling Price

The manufacturer's contribution percentage tells what portion of total revenues remains after covering variable costs to contribute toward meeting fixed expenses and earning a profit. This manufacturer's contribution percentage is 36.5 percent, which means that variable costs absorb 63.5 percent of total revenues. In other words, variable costs should be 63.5 percent (1.00 – 0.365 = 0.635) of the product's selling price. Suppose that this manufacturer's variable costs include the following:

Material	$2.08/unit
Direct labor	4.12/unit
Variable factory overhead	0.78/unit
Total variable cost	$6.98/unit

The minimum price at which the manufacturer would sell the item for is $6.98. Any price below this would not cover variable costs. To compute the breakeven selling price for this product, find the selling price using the following equation:

$$\text{Profit} = \frac{\left(\begin{matrix}\text{Selling}\\ \text{price}\end{matrix} \times \begin{matrix}\text{Quantity}\\ \text{produced}\end{matrix}\right) + \left(\begin{matrix}\text{Variable cost}\\ \text{per unit}\end{matrix} \times \begin{matrix}\text{Quantity}\\ \text{produced}\end{matrix}\right) + \begin{matrix}\text{Total}\\ \text{fixed cost}\end{matrix}}{\text{Quantity produced}}$$

which becomes:

$$\text{Breakeven selling price} = \text{Profit} + \frac{\left(\begin{matrix}\text{Variable cost}\\ \text{per unit}\end{matrix} \times \begin{matrix}\text{Quantity}\\ \text{produced}\end{matrix}\right) + \begin{matrix}\text{Total}\\ \text{fixed cost}\end{matrix}}{\text{Quantity produced}}$$

To break even, the manufacturer assumes $0 profit. Suppose that his plans are to produce 50,000 units of the product and that fixed costs will be $110,000. The breakeven selling price is as follows

$$\begin{aligned}\text{Breakeven selling price} &= \frac{\$0 + (\$6.98 \times 50{,}000 \text{ units}) + \$110{,}000}{50{,}000 \text{ units}} \\ &= \frac{\$459{,}000}{50{,}000 \text{ units}} \\ &= \$9.18/\text{unit}\end{aligned}$$

Thus, $2.20 ($9.18/unit – $6.98/unit) of the $9.18 breakeven price contributes to meeting fixed production costs. But suppose the manufacturer wants to earn a $50,000 profit. Then the selling price is:

$$\begin{aligned}\text{Selling price} &= \frac{\$50{,}000 + (\$6.98/\text{unit} \times 50{,}000 \text{ units}) + \$110{,}000}{50{,}000 \text{ units}} \\ &= \frac{\$509{,}000}{50{,}000 \text{ units}} \\ &= \$10.18/\text{unit}\end{aligned}$$

Now the manufacturer must decide whether customers will purchase 50,000 units at $10.18. If not, he must decide either to produce a different, more profitable product or to lower the selling price. Any price above $9.18 will generate some profit, although less than that desired. In the short run, the manufacturer could sell the product for less than $9.18 if competitive factors so dictated, but not below $6.98 because this would not cover the variable cost of production.

Because the manufacturer's capacity in the short run is fixed, pricing decisions should be aimed at employing these resources most efficiently. The fixed costs of operating the plant cannot be avoided, and the variable costs can be eliminated only if the firm ceases offering the product. Therefore, the selling price must be at least equal to the variable costs (per unit) of making the product. Any price above this amount contributes to covering fixed costs and providing a reasonable profit.

Of course, over the long run, the manufacturer cannot sell below total costs and continue to survive. So, selling price must cover total product cost—both fixed and variable—and generate a reasonable profit.

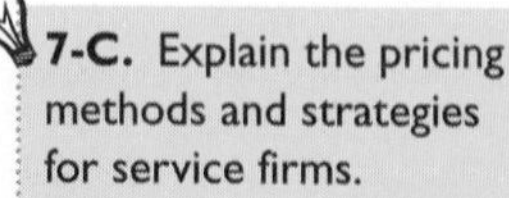

PRICING CONCEPTS FOR SERVICE FIRMS

A service firm must establish a price based on the materials used to provide the service, the labor employed, an allowance for overhead, and a profit. As in the manufacturing operation, a service firm must have a reliable, accurate accounting system to keep a tally of the total costs of providing the service. Most service firms base their prices on an hourly rate, usually the actual number of hours required to perform the service. Some companies, however, base their fees on a standard number of hours, determined by the average number of hours needed to perform the service. For most firms, labor and materials comprise the largest portion of the cost of the service. To establish a reasonable, profitable price for service, the small business owner must know the cost of materials, direct labor, and overhead for each unit of service. Using these basic cost data and a desired profit margin, an owner of the small service firm can determine the appropriate price for the service.

Consider a simple example for pricing a common service—television repair. Ned's T.V. Repair Shop uses the direct-costing method to prepare an income statement for exercising managerial control (see Table 7.8). Ned estimates that he and his employees spent about 12,800 hours in the actual production of television service. So total cost per productive hour for Ned's T.V. Repair Shop comes to the following:

$$\frac{\$172{,}000}{12{,}800 \text{ hours}} = \$13.44/\text{hour}$$

Now Ned must add in an amount for his desired profit. He expects a net operating profit of 18 percent on sales. To compute the final price he uses this equation:

$$\begin{aligned} \frac{\text{Price}}{\text{per hour}} &= \frac{\text{Total cost per}}{\text{productive hour}} \times \frac{1.00}{(1.00 - \text{net profit target as \% of sales})} \\ &= \$13.44 \times 1.219 \\ &= \$16.38/\text{hour} \end{aligned}$$

A price of $16.38 per hour will cover Ned's costs and generate the desired profit. The wise service shop owner computes his cost per production hour at regular intervals throughout the year. Rapidly rising labor costs and material prices dictate that the service firm's price per hour be computed even more frequently. As in the case of the retailer and the manufacturer, Ned must evaluate the pricing policies of competitors, and decide whether his price is consistent with his firm's image.

Of course, the price of $16.38 per hour assumes that each job requires the same amount of materials. If this is not a valid assumption, Ned must recalculate the price per hour *without* including the cost of materials:

$$\begin{aligned} \text{Cost per productive hour} &= \frac{\$172{,}000 - 40{,}500}{12{,}800 \text{ hours}} \\ &= \$10.27/\text{hour} \end{aligned}$$

TABLE 7.8
Direct-Cost Income Statement, Ned's T.V. Repair Shop

Sales Revenue		$199,000
Variable Expenses		
Labor	$52,000	
Materials	40,500	
Variable Factory Overhead	11,500	
Total Variable Expenses		104,000
Fixed Expenses		
Rent	$ 2,500	
Salaries	38,500	
Fixed Overhead	27,000	
Total Fixed Expenses		68,000
Net Income		$27,000

Adding in the desired 18 percent net operating profit on sales:

$$\text{Price per hour} = \$10.27/\text{hour} \times \frac{1.00}{(1.00 - 0.18)}$$
$$= \$10.27/\text{hour} \times 1.219$$
$$= \$12.52/\text{hour}$$

Under these conditions Ned would charge $12.52 per hour plus the actual cost of materials used and any markup on the cost of material. A repair job that takes four hours to complete would have the following price:

Cost of service (4 hours × $12.52/hour)	$50.08
Cost of materials	21.00
Markup on material (10%)	2.10
Total price	$73.18

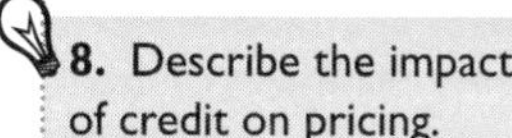
8. Describe the impact of credit on pricing.

THE IMPACT OF CREDIT ON PRICING

Consumers crave convenience when they shop, and one of the most common conveniences they demand is the ability to purchase goods and services on credit. Small businesses that fail to offer customers credit lose sales to competitors who do. Yet, companies that do sell on credit incur additional expenses for offering this convenience. Small companies have three options for selling to customers on credit: credit cards, installment credit, and trade credit.

Credit Cards

Credit cards have become a popular method of payment among customers. Approximately 70 percent of the adult U.S. population uses credit cards to make purchases, and the typical U.S. household has 10 credit cards.[94] The number of credit cards in circulation in the United States exceeds 1 billion, an average of about four cards per person! The average customer uses a credit card 5.5 times per month to charge an average of $547.[95] Customers use credit cards to pay for $28 out of every $100 spent on consumable goods and services.[96] One study found that accepting credit cards increases the probability, speed, and magnitude of customer spending. In addition, surveys show that customers rate businesses offering credit options higher on key performance measures such as reputation, reliability, and service.[97] In short, accepting credit cards broadens a small company's customer base and closes sales it would normally lose if customers had to pay in cash.

The convenience of credit cards is not free to business owners, however. Companies must pay to use the system, typically 1 to 6 percent of the total credit card charges, which they must factor into the prices of their products or services. They also pay a transaction fee of 5 to 25 cents per charge. Given customer expectations, small businesses cannot drop major cards, even when the big card companies raise the fees that merchants must pay. Fees operate on a multistep process. On a $100 Visa or MasterCard purchase, a processing bank buys the credit card slip from the retailer for $97.44. Then that bank sells the slip to the bank that issued the card for about $98.80. The remaining $1.20 discount is called the interchange fee, which is what the processing bank passes along to the issuing bank. Before it can accept credit cards, a business must obtain merchant status from either a bank or an independent sales organization (ISO).

More small businesses also are equipping their stores to handle debit card transactions, which act as electronic checks, automatically deducting the purchase amount from a cus-

YOU BE THE CONSULTANT . . .

Pricing Web Services

Kerry Pinella, a recent business graduate of a small private college, started her career working for a large multinational computer software maker as a sales representative. After two years in sales, Kerry applied for a position on a development team that was working on software applications for the World Wide Web. Kerry thrived on the team atmosphere and learned the technical aspects of the new assignment very quickly. Not only did her team bring their project in on budget, but it also completed it slightly ahead of schedule. Team members give much of the credit for the project's success to Kerry's unofficial role as team leader. Her work ethic and relentless pursuit of quality inspired other team members.

After her team completed their project, however, Kerry had a hard time recapturing the thrill and excitement of developing the World Wide Web software. Subsequent projects simply could not measure up to the "magic" of that first assignment. After talking with several of the members of that software team, Kerry discovered that they felt the same way. Before long, Kerry and two of her former team members left the company to launch their own computer consulting company, Web Consultants. Having worked on the forefront of the Web's commercialization, Kerry and her partners saw the potential it had for revolutionizing business. Their company would specialize in developing, designing, and maintaining Web sites for clients. In their first year of business, Web Consultants accepted jobs from virtually anybody who wanted a Web site. Although they experienced some "growing pains," Web Consultants quickly earned a reputation for producing quality work on time and was more selective in the jobs it bid on.

Halfway into their second year of operation, the partners planned a weekend retreat at a nearby resort so they could get away, review their progress, and plan for the future. As they reviewed their latest financial statements, one of the questions that kept popping up dealt with pricing. Were Web Consultants' pricing policies appropriate? Its sales were growing twice as fast as the industry average, and the company's bid-winning ratio was well above that of practically all of its competitors. For the current year, sales were up, but Web Consultants' net profits were virtually the same as they had been in their first year.

Pulling the records from a computer database for each job they had completed since founding the company, the partners and their employees had spent 22,450 hours developing projects for their clients at a total cost of $951,207. "We were shooting for a net profit of 25 percent on sales," Kerry reminded her partners, "but so far, our net profit margin is just 7.7 percent, only one-third of our target."

"Maybe we could increase our profits if we increased our sales," offered one partner.

The partners began to wonder if their price of $45 per hour was appropriate. Admittedly, they had been so busy completing projects for clients that they had not kept up with what their competitors were charging. Nor had they been as diligent in analyzing their financial statements as they should have been.

As Kerry closed the cover on her laptop computer, she looked at her partners and asked, "What should Web Consultant's hourly price be?"

1. Help Kerry answer the question she has posed.
2. What factors should Kerry and her partners consider when determining Web Consultants' hourly price?
3. Is the company's current price too low? If so, what signals could have alerted Kerry and her partners?

tomer's checking account. The equipment is easy to install and to set up, and the cost to the company is negligible. The payoff can be big, however, in the form of increased sales. "How can you possibly lose when you're offering customers another avenue for purchasing merchandise?" says Mark Knauff, who recently installed a debit card terminal in his guitar shop.[98]

Installment Credit

Small companies that sell big-ticket consumer durables—such as major appliances, cars, and boats—frequently rely on installment credit. Because very few customers can purchase such items in a single lump-sum payment, small businesses finance them over an extended time. The time horizon may range from just a few months up to 30 or more years.

Most companies require customers to make an initial down payment for the merchandise and then finance the balance for the life of the loan. The customer repays the loan principal plus interest on the loan. One advantage of installment loans for a small business is that the owner retains a security interest as collateral on the loan. If a customer defaults on the loan, the owner still holds the title to the merchandise. Because installment credit absorbs a small company's cash, many rely on financial institutions such as banks and credit unions to provide installment credit. When a firm has the financial strength to "carry their own paper," the interest income from the installment loan contract often yields more than the initial profit on the sale of the product. For some businesses, such as furniture stores, this has traditionally been a major source of income.

Trade Credit

Companies that sell small-ticket items frequently offer their customers trade credit—that is, they create customer charge accounts. The typical small business bills its credit customers each month. To speed collections, some offer cash discounts if customers pay their balances early; others impose penalties on late payers. Before deciding to use trade credit as a competitive weapon, the small business owner must make sure that the firm's cash position is strong enough to support the additional pressure.

CHAPTER SUMMARY

1. Explain the differences among promotion, publicity, personal selling, and advertising.
   - Promotion is any form of persuasive communication designed to inform consumers about a product or service and to influence them to purchase these goods or services.
   - Publicity is any commercial news covered by the media that boosts sales but for which the small business does not pay.
   - Personal selling is the personal contact between salespeople and potential customers resulting from sales efforts.
   - Advertising is any sales presentation that is nonpersonal in nature and is paid for by an identified sponsor.
2. Present the steps in developing an advertising plan.
   - The first step is to define the purpose of the company's advertising program by creating specific, measurable objectives.
   - The next step is to analyze the firm and its target audience.
   - The next step involves deciding what to say and how to say it, making sure to build the message around the company's unique selling proposition (USP).
   - The final step involves evaluating the ad campaign's effectiveness.
3. Describe the advantages and disadvantages of the various advertising media.
   - The medium used to transmit an advertising message influences the consumer's perception—and reception—of it.
   - Media options include newspapers, radio, television, magazines, direct mail, the World Wide Web, outdoor advertising, transit advertising, directories, trade shows, special events and promotions, and point-of-purchase ads.
4. Identify four basic methods for preparing an advertisin budget.
   - Establishing an advertising budget presents a real challenge to the small business owner.
   - Here are four basic methods: what is affordable; matching competitors; percentage of sales; objective and task.
5. Explain practical methods for stretching the small business owner's advertising budget.
   - Despite their limited advertising budgets, small businesses do not have to take a second-class approach to advertising. Three techniques that can stretch a small company's advertising dollars are cooperative advertising, shared advertising, and publicity.
6. Describe effective pricing techniques for introducing new goods or services and for existing ones.

- Pricing a new product is often difficult for the small business manager, but it should accomplish three objectives: getting the product accepted; maintaining market share as the competition grows; and earning a profit. Generally, there are three major pricing strategies used to introduce new products into the market: penetration, skimming, and sliding down the demand curve.
- Pricing techniques for existing products and services include odd pricing, price lining, leader pricing, geographical pricing, opportunistic pricing, discounts, and suggested retail pricing.

7. Explain the pricing methods and strategies for retailers, manufacturers, and service firms.
   - Pricing for the retailer means pricing to move merchandise. Markup is the difference between the cost of a product or service and its selling price. Most retailers compute their markup as a percentage of retail price, but some retailers put a standard markup on all their merchandise; more frequently, they use a flexible markup.
   - A manufacturer's pricing decision depends on the support of accurate cost accounting records. The most common technique is cost-plus pricing, in which the manufacturer charges a price that covers the cost of producing a product plus a reasonable profit. Every manufacturer should calculate a product's break-even price, the price which produces neither a profit nor a loss.
   - Service firms often suffer from the effects of vague, unfounded pricing procedures, and frequently charge the going rate without any idea of their costs. A service firm must set a price based on the cost of materials used, labor involved, overhead, and a profit. The proper price reflects the total cost of providing a unit of service.
8. Describe the impact of credit on pricing.
   - Offering consumer credit enhances a small company's reputation and increases the probability, speed, and magnitude of customers' purchases. Small firms offer three types of consumer credit: credit cards, installment credit, and trade credit (charge accounts).

DISCUSSION QUESTIONS

1. What are the four elements of promotion? How do they support one another?
2. Briefly outline the steps in creating an advertising plan. What principles should the small business owner follow when creating an effective advertisement?
3. What factors should a small business manager consider when selecting advertising media?
4. Create a table to summarize the advantages and disadvantages of the following advertising media:

Newspaper	Outdoor advertising
Radio	Transit advertising
Television	Trade shows
Specialty advertising	Sponsorships and promotions
World Wide Web	
Direct mail	

5. What are fixed spots, preemptible spots, and floating spots in radio advertising?
6. Describe the characteristics of an effective outdoor advertisement.
7. Describe the common methods of establishing an advertising budget. Which method is most often used? Which technique is most often recommended? Why?
8. How does pricing affect a small firm's image?
9. What competitive factors must the small firm consider when establishing prices?
10. Describe the strategies a small business could use in setting the price of a new product. What objectives should the strategy seek to achieve?
11. Define the following pricing techniques: odd pricing; price lining; leader pricing; geographical pricing; and discounts.
12. Why do many small businesses use the manufacturer's suggested retail price? What are the disadvantages of this technique?
13. What is a markup? How is it used to determine individual price?
14. What is a standard markup? A flexible markup?
15. What is cost-plus pricing? Why do so many manufacturers use it? What are the disadvantages of using it?
16. Explain the difference between full-absorption costing and direct costing. How does absorption costing help a manufacturer determine a reasonable price?
17. Explain the technique for a small service firm setting an hourly price.
18. What benefits does a small business get by offering customers credit? What costs does it incur?

Beyond the Classroom . . .

1. Contact a small retailer, manufacturer, and a service firm and interview each one about his or her advertising program.
   a. Are there specific advertising objectives?
   b. What media does the owner employ? Why?
   c. How does the manager evaluate an ad's effectiveness?
   d. What assistance does the manager receive in designing ads?
2. Contact several small business owners and determine how they establish their advertising budgets. Why do they use the method they do?
3. Collect two or three advertisements for local small businesses and evaluate them on a scale of 1 (low) to 10 (high) using the following criteria: attention-getting, distinctive, interesting, brevity, personal appeal, credibility, USP-focused, convincing, motivating, and effectiveness. How would you change the ads to make them more effective?
4. Browse through a magazine and find two ads that use sex to sell a good or service—one that you consider effective and one that you consider offensive. Compare your ads and reasoning with those of your classmates. What implications does your discussion have for advertisers?
5. Interview a successful small retailer and ask the following questions: Does the retailer seek a specific image through its prices? What type of outlet would you consider the retailer to be? What role does its competitors play in the business owner's pricing? Does the retailer use specific pricing techniques such as odd pricing, price lining, leader pricing, geographical pricing? How are discounts calculated? What markup percentage does the firm use? How are prices derived? What is the firm's cost structures?
6. Select an industry that has several competing small firms in your area. Contact these firms and compare their approaches to determining prices. Do prices on identical or similar items differ? Why?
7. Use the Web to research the use of cookies in online advertising. What benefits do cookies offer Web users? Web advertisers? What ethical concerns do you have concerning cookies? Explain. Should marketers be able to use cookies?

We invite you to visit this book's companion Web site at **www.prenhall.com/Zimmerer.**

CHAPTER

Managing Cash Flow

8

Whatever you have, spend less.

—Samuel Johnson

A deficit is what you have when you haven't got as much as when you had nothing.

—Gerald F. Lieberman

LEARNING OBJECTIVES

Upon completion of this chapter, you will be able to:

1. Explain the importance of cash management to a small business's success.
2. Differentiate between cash and profits.
3. Understand the five steps in creating a cash budget and use them to create a cash budget.
4. Describe fundamental principles involved in managing the "Big Three" of cash management: accounts receivable, accounts payable, and inventory.
5. Explain the techniques for avoiding a cash crunch in a small company.

Cash—a four-letter word that has become a curse for many small businesses. Lack of this valuable asset has driven countless small companies into bankruptcy. Unfortunately, many more firms will become failure statistics because their owners have neglected the principles of cash management that can spell the difference between success and failure. One small business owner whose company barely survived a cash crisis explains simply, "Cash flow is everything, period."[1] Indeed, developing a cash forecast is essential for new businesses because early profit levels usually do not generate sufficient cash to keep the company afloat. A common cause of business failures is that owners neglect to forecast how much cash their companies will need until they reach the point of generating positive cash flow. Another problem, especially in start-up and fast-growth companies, is overemphasis on increasing sales with little concern for collecting the receivables those sales create. The result is always the same: a cash crisis.

Controlling the financial aspects of a business using the traditional analysis of basic financial statements with ratios (the topic of Chapter 9) is immensely important; however, by themselves, these techniques are insufficient to achieve business success. Entrepreneurs are prone to focus on their companies' income statements—particularly sales and profits. The income statement, of course, shows only part of a company's financial picture. It is entirely possible for a business to earn a profit and still go out of business *by running out of cash.* Managing a company's financial performance effectively requires an entrepreneur to look beyond the "bottom line" and focus on what it takes to keep a company going—cash.

S.T. Lube

"This [monitoring your cash flow statement] is more important than watching your income statement or balance sheet," says Scott Trenner, owner of S.T. Lube, a company that operates six Jiffy Lube franchises. Trenner knows firsthand the importance of positive cash flow. His company ran into serious cash flow problems as he focused on rapid growth. "I was building a multi-million-dollar empire," he recalls, "but my revenues never caught up with my expenses." Cash was so tight that Trenner had trouble meeting the payroll for his company's 65 employees. "I once had to get a two-week, $30,000 loan from my father when we were struggling," he recalls. The turning point came when Trenner created a statement to track and analyze his company's cash flow. "We stopped focusing only on expansion and started paying attention to day-to-day management," he says. "By keeping a close eye on our cash flow statement, we went from a negative cash flow to a positive cash flow of $1,000 a week and turned around a $140,000 deficit in three years."[2]

1. Explain the importance of cash management to a small business's success.

CASH MANAGEMENT

cash management—*the process of forecasting, collecting, disbursing, investing, and planning for the cash a company needs to operate smoothly.*

Cash management involves forecasting, collecting, disbursing, investing, and planning for the cash a company needs to operate smoothly. Cash management is a vital task because cash is the most important yet least productive asset that a small business owns. A business must have enough cash to meet its obligations or it will be declared bankrupt. Creditors, employees, and lenders expect to be paid on time, and cash is the required medium of exchange. But some firms retain an excessive amount of cash to meet any unexpected circumstances that might arise. These dormant dollars have an income-earning potential that the owners are ignoring, and this restricts the firm's growth and lowers its profitability. Proper cash management permits the owner to adequately meet the cash demands of the business, to avoid retaining unnecessarily large cash balances, and to stretch the profit-generating power of each dollar the business owns.

One recent Dun & Bradstreet survey found that 33 percent of small business owners say they have problems managing their cash flow as they build their businesses.[3] Young companies, especially, are "cash sponges," soaking up every available dollar and always hungry for more. "Business owners should be thinking about [cash management] from day one," says the president of a financial consulting company.[4]

Ford Motor Company

Shortly after he launched his new company on June 16, 1903, entrepreneur Henry Ford ran headlong into a cash crisis that nearly wiped out the Ford Motor Company. Start-up expenses (including $10,000 to the Dodge brothers for engines and other parts and $640 to the Hartford Rubber Works for 64 tires) quickly soaked up Ford's $19,500 in start-up capital, and by July 10, the company's cash balance had fallen to a mere $223.65. Another payroll and more parts orders were just around the corner, and the 25-day-old company was already on the brink of a financial collapse. On July 11, an investor saved the day with a $5,000 contribution. Four days later the Ford Motor Company sold its first car to Dr. E. Pfennig of Chicago, pushing the company's cash balance to $6,486.44. From this shaky financial beginning grew one of the largest auto makers in the world![5]

Managing cash flow is also an acute problem for rapidly growing businesses. In fact, fast-track companies are most likely to suffer cash shortages. Many successful, growing, and profitable businesses fail because they become insolvent; they do not have adequate cash to meet the needs of a growing business with a booming sales volume. If a company's sales are up, its owner also must hire more employees, expand plant capacity, increase the sales force, build inventory, and incur other drains on the firm's cash supply. During rapid growth, cash collections often fall behind, compounding the problem. The head of the National Federation of Independent Businesses says that many small business owners "wake up one day to find that the price of success is no cash on hand. They don't understand that if they're successful, inventory and receivables will increase faster than profits can fund them."[6] The resulting cash crisis may force the owner to lose equity control of the business or, ultimately, declare bankruptcy and close. Table 8.1 shows how to calculate the additional cash required to support an increase in sales.

TABLE 8.1

How Much Cash Is Required to Support an Increase in Sales?

Source: Adapted from Norm Brodsky, "Paying for Growth: How Much Cash You Need to Carry New Sales," Inc. *Online Tools & Apps: Worksheet,* **<www.inc.com/tools/details/0,6152,CNT61_HOM1_LOC0_NAVhome_TOL1 1648,00.html>.**

Too often, entrepreneurs believe that increasing sales is the ideal solution to a cash crunch only to discover (often after it is too late) that it takes extra cash to support extra sales. The following worksheet demonstrates how to calculate the amount of additional cash required to support an increase in sales.

To make the calculation, a business owner needs the following information:

- the increase in sales planned ($)
- the time frame for adding new sales (days)
- the company's gross profit margin, gross profit ÷ net sales (%)
- the estimated additional expenses required to generate additional sales ($)
- the company's average collection period (days)

To calculate the amount of additional cash needed, use the following formula:

Extra cash required = ((New sales – Gross profit + Extra overhead) × (Average collection period × 1.20*)) ÷ (Time frame in days for adding new sales)

Consider the following example:

The owner of Ardent Company wants to increase sales by $75,000 over the next year. The company's gross profit margin is 30 percent of sales (so its gross profit on these additional sales would be $75,000 × 30% = $22,500), its average collection period is 47 days, and managers estimate that generating the additional sales will require an increase in expenses of $21,300. The additional cash that Ardent will need to support this higher level of sales is:

Extra cash required = (($75,000 – $22,500 + 21,300) × (47 × 1.2)) ÷ 365 = $11,404

Advent will need $11,404 in extra cash to support the additional sales of $75,000 it plans to bring in over the next year.

* The extra 20 percent is added as a cushion.

cash flow cycle—*the time lag between paying suppliers for merchandise or materials and receiving payment from customers.*

The first step in managing cash more effectively is to understand the company's **cash flow cycle**—the time lag between paying suppliers for merchandise or materials and receiving payment from customers for the product or service (see Figure 8.1). The longer this cash flow cycle, the more likely the business owner is to encounter a cash crisis. Preparing a cash forecast that recognizes this cycle, however, will help avoid a crisis. "To develop a cash management strategy," says one small business owner, "you must understand [the] cash flow patterns [of your business]."[7] Business owners should calculate their cash conversion cycle whenever they prepare their financial statements (or at least quarterly). On a *daily* basis, business owners should generate reports showing the following items: total cash on hand, bank balance, summary of the day's sales, summary of the day's cash receipts and disbursements, and a summary of accounts receivable collections.

The next step in effective cash management is to begin cutting down the length of the cash flow cycle. Reducing the cycle from 240 days to, say, 150 days would free up incredible amounts of cash that this company could use to finance growth and dramatically reduce its borrowing costs. What steps would you suggest the owner of the business whose cash flow cycle is illustrated in Figure 8.1 take to reduce its length?

Table 8.2 describes the five key cash management roles every entrepreneur must fill.

2. Differentiate between cash and profits.

CASH AND PROFITS ARE NOT THE SAME

When analyzing cash flow, entrepreneurs must understand that cash and profits are not the same. "Profit is not cash flow, and cash flow is not profit," says one entrepreneur. "Anyone who tries to glean something about one from looking at the other may be easily misled."[8] Profit (or net income) is the difference between a company's total revenue and its total expenses. It measures how efficiently a business is operating. Cash is the money that is readily available to use in a business. **Cash flow** measures a company's liquidity and its ability to pay its bills and other financial obligations on time by tracking the flow of cash

FIGURE 8.1
The Cash Flow Cycle

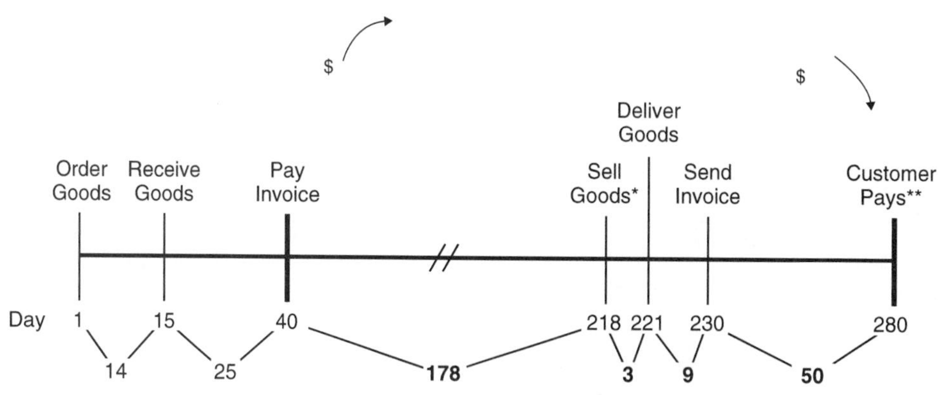

* Based on Average Inventory Turnover:

$$\frac{365 \text{ days}}{2.05 \text{ times/year}} = 178 \text{ days}$$

** Based on Average Collection Period:

$$\frac{365 \text{ days}}{7.31 \text{ times/year}} = 50 \text{ days}$$

TABLE 8.2
Five Cash Management Roles of the Entrepreneur

Source: Adapted from Bruce J. Blechman, "Quick Change Artist," Entrepreneur, *January 1994, pp. 18–21.*

Role 1: Cash Finder. This is the entrepreneur's first and foremost responsibility. You must make sure there is enough capital to pay all present (and future) bills. This is not a one-time task; it is an ongoing job.

Role 2: Cash Planner. As cash planner, an entrepreneur makes sure the company's cash is used properly and efficiently. You must keep track of its cash, make sure it is available to pay bills, and plan for its future use. Planning requires you to forecast the company's cash inflows and outflows for the months ahead with the help of a cash budget (discussed later in this chapter).

Role 3: Cash Distributor. This role requires you to control the cash needed to pay the company's bills and the priority and the timing of those payments. Forecasting cash disbursements accurately and making sure the cash is available when payments come due is essential to keeping the business solvent.

Role 4: Cash Collector. As cash collector, your job is to make sure your customers pay *their* bills on time. Too often, entrepreneurs focus on pumping up sales, while neglecting to collect the cash from those sales. Having someone in your company responsible for collecting accounts receivable is essential. Uncollected accounts drain a small company's pool of cash very quickly.

Role 5: Cash Conserver. This role requires you to make sure your company gets maximum value for the dollars it spends. Whether you are buying inventory to resell or computers to keep track of what you sell, it is important to get the most for your money. Avoiding unnecessary expenditures is an important part of this task. The goal is to spend cash so it will produce a return for the company.

into and out of the business over a period of time. Many small business owners soon discover that profitability does not guarantee liquidity. As important as earning a profit is, no business owner can pay creditors, employees, the government, and lenders in profits; that requires *cash!* Although profits are tied up in many forms, such as inventory, computers, or machinery, cash is the money that flows through a business in a continuous cycle without being tied up in any other asset. "Businesses fail not because they are making or losing money," warns one financial expert, "but because they simply run out of cash."[9]

cash flow—*a method of tracking a company's liquidity and its ability to pay its bills and other financial obligations on time by tracking the flow of cash into and out of the business over a period of time.*

Figure 8.2 shows the flow of cash through a typical small business. Cash flow is the volume of actual cash that comes into and goes out of the business during an accounting period. Decreases in cash occur when the business purchases, on credit or for cash, goods for inventory or materials for use in production. The resulting inventory is sold either for cash or on credit. When cash is taken in or when accounts receivable are collected, the

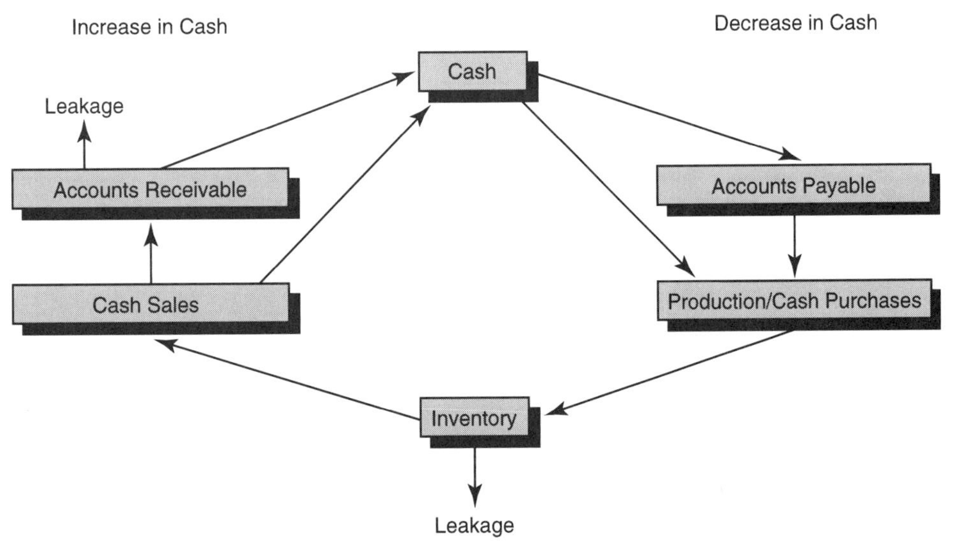

FIGURE 8.2
Cash Flow

firm's cash balance increases. Notice that purchases for inventory and production lead sales; that is, these bills typically must be paid *before* sales are generated. But collection of accounts receivable *lags* behind sales; that is, customers who purchase goods on credit may not pay until next month.

THE CASH BUDGET

The need for a cash budget arises because in every business the cash flowing in is rarely "in sync" with the cash flowing out of the business. This uneven flow of cash creates periodic cash surpluses and shortages, making it necessary for small business owners to track the flow of cash through their businesses so they can project realistically the cash available throughout the year. Many managers operate their businesses without knowing the pattern of their cash flows, believing that the process is too complex or time consuming. In reality, entrepreneurs simply cannot afford to disregard the process of cash management. They must ensure that their businesses have on hand an adequate but not excessive supply of cash to meet their operating needs. "The aim of prudent cash-flow management," says one business writer, "is to make sure there'll be enough cash in the till to meet given demands for that cash at any given time."[10]

How much cash is enough? What is suitable for one business may be totally inadequate for another, depending on each firm's size, nature, and particular situation. The small business manager should prepare a **cash budget,** which is nothing more than a "cash map," showing the amount and the timing of the cash receipts and the cash disbursements day by day, week by week, or month by month. It is used to predict the amount of cash the firm will need to operate smoothly over a specific period of time, and it is a valuable tool in managing a company successfully.

cash budget—*a "cash map," showing the amount and the timing of cash receipts and cash disbursements on a daily, weekly, or monthly basis.*

Example

One consultant recalls how a cash budget helped salvage a once successful service firm that had fallen on hard times. The five-year-old firm with $20 million in annual billings began to lose money and was having trouble paying its bills. After working with the consultant, the company began sending customer invoices much faster and implemented a much stricter collection policy. The new collection system involved employees in collecting overdue payments and took immediate action when an account became overdue. Managers set up a receivables report and reviewed it at weekly staff meetings. They also beefed up the company's financial reports, added a cash budget, and used it to make managerial decisions. Within six months, the company's cash balance had improved dramatically (a turnaround of $1.5 million), managers were able to pay down a line of credit at the bank, and the business was back on track again!

3. Understand the five steps in creating a cash budget and use them to create a cash budget.

PREPARING A CASH BUDGET

Typically, small business owners should prepare a projected monthly cash budget for at least one year into the future and a quarterly estimate several years in advance. It must cover all seasonal sales fluctuations. The more variable a firm's sales pattern, the shorter its planning horizon should be. For example, a firm whose sales fluctuate widely over a relatively short time frame might require a weekly cash budget. The key is to track cash flows over time. The timing of a company's cash flow is as important as the amounts. "An alert cash flow manager keeps an eye not on cash receipts or on cash demands as average quantities but on cash as a function of the *calendar,*" says one business owner.[11]

Regardless of the time frame selected, a cash budget must be in writing for a small business manager to properly visualize the firm's cash position. Creating a written cash plan is not an excessively time-consuming task and can help the owner avoid unexpected cash shortages, a situation that can cause a business to fail. One financial consultant describes "a client who won't be able to make the payroll this month. His bank agreed to meet the payroll for him—but banks don't like to be surprised like that," he adds.[12] Preparing a cash budget will help business owners avoid such adverse surprises and will also let the owner know if he is keeping excessively large amounts of cash on hand. Computer spreadsheets such as Microsoft Excel and Lotus 1-2-3 make the job fast and easy to complete.

The cash budget is based on the cash method of accounting, which means that cash receipts and cash disbursements are recorded in the forecast only when the cash transaction is expected to take place. For example, credit sales to customers are not reported until the company expects to receive the cash from them. Similarly, purchases made on credit are not recorded until the owner expects to pay them. Because depreciation, bad debt expense, and other noncash items involve no cash transfers, they are omitted entirely from the cash budget.

The cash budget is nothing more than a forecast of the firm's cash inflows and outflows for a specific time period, and it will never be completely accurate. But it does give the small business manager a clear picture of the firm's estimated cash balance for the period, pointing out where external cash infusions may be required or where surplus cash balances may be available for investment. Also, by comparing actual cash flows with projections, the owner can revise his forecast so that future cash budgets will be more accurate.

Computer Gallery

Joseph Popper, CEO of Computer Gallery, knows how deadly running out of cash can be for a small company and does everything he can to make sure his business avoids that trap. Popper uses a computer spreadsheet to extract key sales, collection, and disbursement totals and to generate the resulting cash balance each day. Even when he is traveling, Popper keeps up with his company's daily cash balance. He has the spreadsheet results sent to an Internet service, which e-mails them to his alphanumeric pager every day he is out of the office. "We've been paranoid about cash from day one," Popper says. But his system keeps accounts receivable in control, ensures that the company's available cash is working hard, and improves his relationship with the company's banker.[13]

Formats for preparing a cash budget vary depending on the pattern of a company's cash flow. Table 8.3 shows a monthly cash budget for a small department store over a four-month period. Each monthly column should be divided into two sections—estimated and actual (not shown)—so that each succeeding cash forecast can be updated according to actual cash transactions. Comparing forecasted amounts to actual cash flows and learning the causes of any significant discrepancies allows entrepreneurs to improve the accuracy of future cash budgets. There are five basic steps in completing a cash budget:

1. Determining an adequate minimum cash balance.
2. Forecasting sales.
3. Forecasting cash receipts.
4. Forecasting cash disbursements.
5. Determining the end-of-month cash balance.

Step 1: Determining an Adequate Minimum Cash Balance

What is considered an excessive cash balance for one small business may be inadequate for another, even though the two firms are in the same business. Some suggest that a firm's cash balance should equal at least one-fourth of its current debts, but this general rule clearly will not work for all small businesses. The most reliable method of deciding cash balance is based on past experience. Past operating records should indicate the proper cash

TABLE 8.3

Cash Budget for Small Department Store

Assumptions:

Cash balance on December 31 = $12,000

Minimum cash balance desired = $10,000

Sales are 75% credit and 25% cash.

Credit sales are collected in the following manner:

- 60% collected in the first month after the sale
- 30% collected in the second month after the sale
- 5% collected in the third month after the sale
- 5% are never collected

Sales forecasts are as follows:	Pessimistic	Most Likely	Optimistic
October (actual)		$300,000	
November (actual)		350,000	
December (actual)		400,000	
January	$120,000	150,000	$175,000
February	160,000	200,000	250,000
March	160,000	200,000	250,000
April	250,000	300,000	340,000

The store pays 70% of sales price for merchandise purchased and pays for each month's anticipated sales in the preceding month.

Rent is $2,000 per month.

An interest payment of $7,500 is due in March.

A tax prepayment of $50,000 must be made in March.

A capital addition payment of $130,000 is due in February.

Utilities expenses amount to $850 per month.

Miscellaneous expenses are $70 per month.

Interest income of $200 will be received in February.

Wages and salaries are estimated to be

January—$30,000

February—$40,000

March—$45,000

April—$50,000

cushion needed to cover any unexpected expenses after all normal cash outlays are deducted from the month's cash receipts. For example, past records may indicate that it is desirable to maintain a cash balance equal to five days' sales. Seasonal fluctuations may cause the firm's minimum cash balance to change. For example, the desired cash balance for a retailer in December may be greater than in June.

Step 2: Forecasting Sales

The heart of the cash budget is the sales forecast. It is the central factor in creating an accurate picture of the firm's cash position because sales ultimately are transformed into cash receipts and cash disbursements. For most businesses, sales constitute the major source of the cash flowing into the business. Similarly, sales of merchandise require that cash be used to replenish inventory. As a result, the cash budget is only as accurate as the sales forecast from which it is derived.

Cash Budget — Pessimistic Sales Forecast	Oct.	Nov.	Dec.	Jan.	Feb.	Mar.	Apr.
Cash Receipts:							
Sales	$300,000	$350,000	$400,000	$120,000	$160,000	$160,000	$250,000
Credit Sales	225,000	262,500	300,000	90,000	120,000	120,000	187,500
Collections:							
60%—1st month after sale				$180,000	$ 54,000	$ 72,000	$ 72,000
30%—2nd month after sale				78,750	90,000	27,000	36,000
5%—3rd month after sale				11,250	13,125	15,000	4,500
Cash Sales				30,000	40,000	40,000	62,500
Interest				0	200	0	0
Total Cash Receipts				$300,000	$197,325	$154,000	$175,000
Cash Disbursements:							
Purchases				$112,000	$112,000	$175,000	$133,000
Rent				2,000	2,000	2,000	2,000
Utilities				850	850	850	850
Interest				0	0	7,500	0
Tax Prepayment				0	0	50,000	0
Capital Addition				0	130,000	0	0
Miscellaneous				70	70	70	70
Wages/Salaries				30,000	40,000	45,000	50,000
Total Cash Disbursements				$144,920	$284,920	$280,420	$185,920
End-of-Month Balance:							
Cash (beginning of month)				$ 12,000	$167,080	$ 79,485	$ 10,000
+ Cash Receipts				300,000	197,325	154,000	175,000
– Cash Disbursements				144,920	284,920	280,420	185,920
Cash (end of month)				167,080	79,485	(46,935)	(920)
Borrowing/Repayment				0	0	56,935	10,920
Cash (end of month [after borrowing])				$167,080	$ 79,485	$ 10,000	$ 10,000

continues

For an established business, a sales forecast is based on past sales, but owners must be careful not to be excessively optimistic in projecting sales. Economic swings, increased competition, fluctuations in demand, and other factors can drastically alter sales patterns. Several quantitative techniques, which are beyond the scope of this text (linear regression, multiple regression, time series analysis, exponential smoothing), are available to the owner of an existing business with an established sales pattern for forecasting sales. These methods enable the small business owner to extrapolate past and present sales trends to arrive at a fairly accurate sales forecast.

The task of forecasting sales for the new firm is more difficult but not impossible. For example, the new owner might conduct research on similar firms and their sales patterns in the first year of operation to come up with a forecast. The local chamber of commerce and trade associations in the various industries also collect such information. Market research is another source of information that may be used to estimate annual sales for the fledgling firm. Other potential sources that may help predict sales include census reports, newspapers, radio and television customer profiles, polls and surveys, and local government sta-

TABLE 8.3

Cash Budget for Small Department Store *(continued)*

Cash Budget — Most Likely Sales Forecast	**Oct.**	**Nov.**	**Dec.**	**Jan.**	**Feb.**	**Mar.**	**Apr.**
Cash Receipts:							
Sales	$300,000	$350,000	$400,000	$150,000	$200,000	$200,000	$300,000
Credit Sales	225,000	262,500	300,000	112,000	150,000	150,000	225,000
Collections:							
60%—1st month after sale				$180,000	$ 67,500	$ 90,000	$ 90,000
30%—2nd month after sale				78,750	90,000	33,750	45,000
5%—3rd month after sale				11,250	13,125	15,000	5,625
Cash Sales				37,500	50,000	50,000	75,000
Interest				0	200	0	0
Total Cash Receipts				$307,500	$220,825	$188,750	$215,625
Cash Disbursements:							
Purchases				$140,000	$140,000	$210,000	$175,000
Rent				2,000	2,000	2,000	2,000
Utilities				850	850	850	850
Interest				0	0	7,500	0
Tax Prepayment				0	0	50,000	0
Capital Addition				0	130,000	0	0
Miscellaneous				70	70	70	70
Wages/Salaries				30,000	40,000	45,000	50,000
Total Cash Disbursements				$172,920	$312,920	$315,420	$227,920
End-of-Month Balance:							
Cash [beginning of month]				$ 12,000	$146,580	$ 54,485	$ 10,000
+ Cash Receipts				307,500	220,825	188,750	215,625
– Cash Disbursements				172,920	312,920	315,420	227,920
Cash (end of month)				146,580	54,485	(72,185)	(2,295)
Borrowing/Repayment				0	0	82,185	12,295
Cash (end of month [after borrowing])				$146,580	$ 54,485	$ 10,000	$ 10,000

tistics. Table 8.4 provides an example of how one entrepreneur used such marketing information to derive a sales forecast for his first year of operation.

No matter what techniques entrepreneurs employ, they must recognize that even the best sales estimates will be wrong. Many financial analysts suggest that the owner create *three* estimates—an optimistic, a pessimistic, and a most likely sales estimate—and then make a separate cash budget for each forecast (a very simple task with a computer spreadsheet). This dynamic forecast enables the owner to determine the range within which his sales will likely be as the year progresses.

Step 3: Forecasting Cash Receipts

As noted earlier, sales constitute the major source of cash receipts. When a firm sells goods and services on credit, the cash budget must account for the delay between the sale and the actual collection of the proceeds. Remember: You cannot spend cash you

Cash Budget — Optimistic Sales Forecast

	Oct.	Nov.	Dec.	Jan.	Feb.	Mar.	Apr.
Cash Receipts:							
Sales	$300,000	$350,000	$400,000	$175,000	$250,000	$250,000	$340,000
Credit Sales	225,000	262,500	300,000	131,250	187,500	187,500	255,000
Collections:							
60%—1st month after sale				$180,000	$ 78,750	$112,500	$112,500
30%—2nd month after sale				78,750	90,000	39,375	56,250
5%—3rd month after sale				11,250	13,125	15,000	6,563
Cash Sales				43,750	62,500	62,500	85,000
Interest				0	200	0	0
Total Cash Receipts				$313,750	$244,575	$229,375	$260,313
Cash Disbursements:							
Purchases				$175,000	$175,000	$238,000	$217,000
Rent				2,000	2,000	2,000	2,000
Utilities				850	850	850	850
Interest				0	0	7,500	0
Tax Prepayment				0	0	50,000	0
Capital Addition				0	130,000	0	0
Miscellaneous				70	70	70	70
Wages/Salaries				30,000	40,000	45,000	50,000
Total Cash Disbursements				$207,920	$347,920	$343,420	$269,920
End-of-Month Balance:							
Cash [beginning of month]				$ 12,000	$117,830	$ 14,485	$ 10,000
+ Cash Receipts				313,750	244,575	229,375	296,125
– Cash Disbursements				207,920	317,920	343,120	269,920
Cash (end of month)				117,830	14,485	(99,560)	36,205
Borrowing/Repayment				0	0	109,560	0
Cash (end of month [after borrowing])				$117,830	$ 14,485	$ 10,000	$ 36,205

haven't collected yet! For instance, an appliance store might not collect the cash from a refrigerator sold in February until April or May, and the cash budget must reflect this delay. To project accurately the firm's cash receipts, the owner must analyze the accounts receivable to determine the collection pattern. For example, past records may indicate that 20 percent of sales are for cash, 50 percent are paid in the month following the sale, 20 percent are paid two months after the sale, 5 percent after three months, and 5 percent are never collected. In addition to cash and credit sales, the small business may receive cash in a number of forms—interest income, rental income, dividends, and others.

Figure 8.3 demonstrates how vital it is to act promptly once an account becomes past due. Notice how the probability of collecting an outstanding account diminishes the longer the account is delinquent. Table 8.5 illustrates the high cost of failing to collect accounts receivable on time.

TABLE 8.4
Forecasting Sales for a Business Start-Up

Robert Adler wants to open a repair shop for imported cars. The trade association for automotive garages estimates that the owner of an imported car spends an average of $485 per year on repairs and maintenance. The typical garage attracts its clientele from a trading zone (the area from which a business draws its customers) with a 20-mile radius. Census reports show that the families within a 20-mile radius of Robert's proposed location own 84,000 cars, of which 24 percent are imports. Based on a local consultant's market research, Robert believes he can capture 9.9 percent of the market this year. Robert's estimate of his company's first year's sales are as follows:

Number of cars in trading zone	84,000 autos
× Percent of imports	× 24%
= Number of imported cars in trading zone	20,160 imports
Number of imports in trading zone	20,160 imports
× Average expenditure on repairs and maintenance	× $485
= Total import repair sales potential	$9,777,600
Total import repair sales potential	$9,777,600
× Estimated share of the market	× 9.9%
= Sales estimate	$967,982

Now Robert Adler can convert this annual sales estimate of $967,982 into monthly sales estimates for use in his company's cash budget.

Step 4: Forecasting Cash Disbursements

Most owners of established businesses have a clear picture of the firm's pattern of cash disbursements. In fact, many cash payments, such as rent, loan repayments, and interest, are fixed amounts due on specified dates. The key factor in forecasting disbursements for a cash budget is to record them in *the month in which they will be paid, not when the obligation is incurred.* Of course, the number of cash disbursements varies with each particular

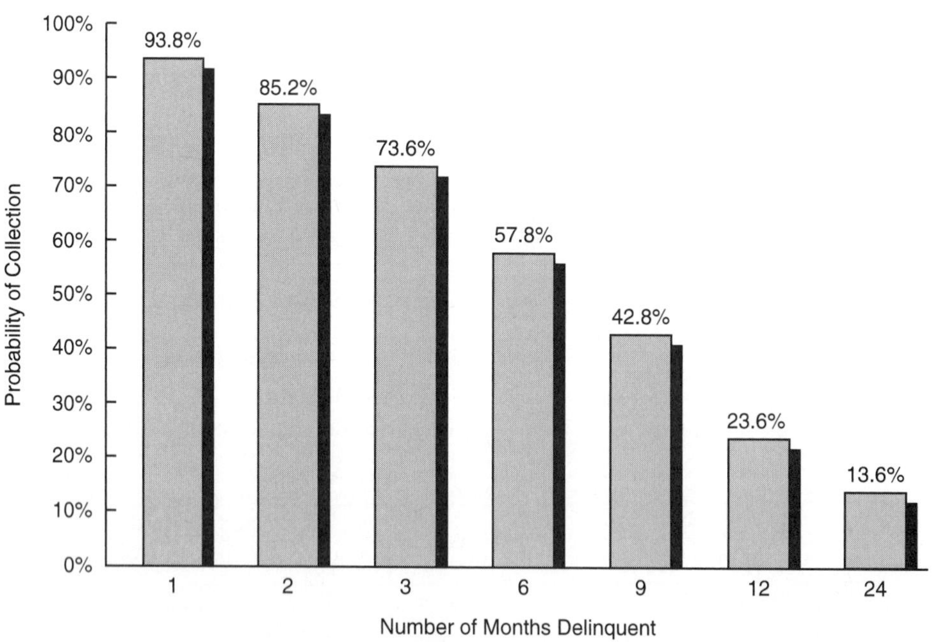

FIGURE 8.3
Collecting Delinquent Accounts

Source: Commercial Collection Agency Section of the Commercial Law League of America.

TABLE 8.5
Managing Accounts Receivable

Source: Adapted from "Financial Control," Inc., reprinted with permission of the publisher.

Are your customers who purchase on credit paying late? If so, these outstanding accounts receivable probably represent a significant leak in your company's cash flow. Slow-paying customers, in effect, are borrowing money from your business interest free. They are using your money without penalty while you forgo opportunities to place it in interest-earning investments, or you must pay interest on money you must borrow to replace the missing funds. Exactly how much is poor credit control costing your company? The answer may surprise you.

The first step is to calculate your company's average collection period ratio (see "Operating Ratios" section in Chapter 9). The second step is to age your accounts receivable to determine how many accounts are current and how many are overdue. The following example shows how to use these numbers to calculate the cost of past-due accounts for a company whose credit terms are "net 30":

Average collection period	65 days
– credit terms	– 30 days
Excess in accounts receivable	35 days
Average daily sales of $21,500[a] × 35 days	$752,500
× Normal rate of return	× 8%
Annual cost of excess	$ 60,200

Slow-paying customers are costing this company more than $60,000 a year! If your business is highly seasonal, quarterly or monthly figures may be more meaningful than annual ones.

[a] Average daily sales = Annual sales ÷ 365 days = $7,847,500 ÷ 365 = $21,500

business, but the following disbursement categories are standard: purchase of inventory or raw materials; wages and salaries; rent, taxes, loans and interest; selling expenses; overhead expenses; and miscellaneous expenses.

Usually, an owner's tendency is to underestimate cash disbursements, which can result in a cash crisis. To prevent this, the wise owner cushions each cash disbursement account, assuming it will be higher than expected. This is particularly true of entrepreneurs opening new businesses. In fact, some financial analysts recommend that a new owner estimate cash disbursements as best he can and then add on another 10 to 25 percent of the total. Whatever forecasting technique is used, the small business manager must avoid underestimating cash disbursements, which may lead to severe cash shortages and possibly bankruptcy.

Sometimes business owners have difficulty developing initial forecasts of cash receipts and cash disbursements. One of the most effective techniques for overcoming the "I don't know where to begin" hurdle is to make a *daily* list of the items that generated cash (receipts) and those that consumed it (disbursements).

Champion Awards

For example, Susan Bowen, CEO of Champion Awards, a $9 million T-shirt screen printer, monitors cash flow by tracking the cash that flows into and out of her company every day. Focusing on keeping the process simple, Bowen sets aside a few minutes each morning to track updates from the previous day on four key numbers:

- *Accounts receivable: 1. What was billed yesterday? 2. How much was actually collected?*
- *Accounts payable: 3. What invoices were received yesterday? 4. How much in total was paid out?*

If Bowen observes the wrong trend—more new bills than new sales or more money going out than coming in—she makes immediate adjustments to protect her cash flow. The benefits produced (not the least of which is the peace of mind knowing no cash crisis is looming) more than outweigh the 10 minutes she invests in the process every day. "I've tried to balance my books every single day since I started my company in 1970," says Bowen.[14]

Step 5: Estimating the End-of-Month Cash Balance

To estimate a firm's cash balance for each month, a small business manager first must determine the cash balance at the beginning of each month. The beginning cash balance includes cash on hand as well as cash in checking and savings accounts. As development of the cash budget progresses, the cash balance at the end of a month becomes the beginning balance for the following month. Next, the owner simply adds total cash receipts and subtracts total cash disbursements to obtain the end-of-month balance before any borrowing takes place. A positive amount indicates that the firm has a cash surplus for the month whereas a negative amount shows a cash shortage will occur unless the manager is able to collect or borrow additional funds.

Normally, a firm's cash balance fluctuates from month to month, reflecting seasonal sales patterns. Such fluctuations are normal, but business owners must watch closely for any increases and decreases in the cash balance over time. A trend of increases indicates that the small firm has ample cash that could be placed in some income-earning investment. On the other hand, a pattern of cash decreases should alert the owner that the business is approaching a cash crisis.

A cash budget not only illustrates the flow of cash into and out of the small business, but it also allows the owner to *anticipate* cash shortages and cash surpluses. "Then," explains a small business consultant, "you can go to the bank and get a 'seasonal' line of credit for six months instead of twelve. Right there you can cut your borrowing costs in half."[15] By planning cash needs ahead of time, a small business is able to achieve the following benefits:

- Increase the amount and the speed of cash flow into the company.
- Reduce the amount and the speed of cash flow out of the company.
- Make the most efficient use of available cash.
- Take advantage of money-saving opportunities, such as quantity and cash discounts.
- Finance seasonal business needs.
- Develop a sound borrowing program.
- Develop a workable program of debt repayment.
- Impress lenders and investors with its ability to plan and repay financing.
- Provide funds for expansion.
- Plan for investing of surplus cash.

"Cash flow spells survival for every business," claims one expert. "Manage cash flow effectively, and your business works. If your cash flow is not well managed, then sooner or later your business goes under. It's that simple."[16] Unfortunately, most small business owners forgo these benefits because they fail to manage their cash properly. One recent study reported that just 26 percent of all small businesses used formal techniques for tracking the level of their cash balances.[17] Because cash flow problems usually sneak up on a business over time, improper cash management often proves to be a costly—and fatal—mistake.

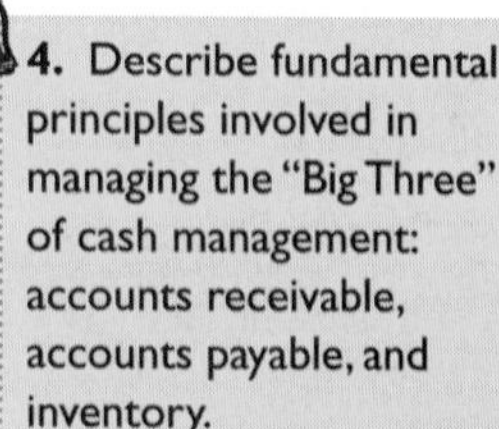
4. Describe fundamental principles involved in managing the "Big Three" of cash management: accounts receivable, accounts payable, and inventory.

THE "BIG THREE" OF CASH MANAGEMENT

It is unrealistic for business owners to expect to trace the flow of every dollar through their businesses. However, by concentrating on the three primary causes of cash flow problems, they can dramatically lower the likelihood of experiencing a devastating cash crisis. The "big three" of cash management are accounts receivable, accounts payable, and inventory. A firm should always try to accelerate its receivables and to stretch out its payables. As one

YOU BE THE CONSULTANT . . .

In Search of a Cash Flow Forecast

"I'll never make that mistake again," Douglas Martinez said to himself as he got into his car. Martinez had just left a meeting with his banker, who had not been optimistic about the chances of Martinez's plumbing supply company getting the loan it needed. "I should have been better prepared for the meeting," he muttered, knowing that he could be angry only at himself. "That consultant at the Small Business Development Center was right. Bankers' primary concern when making loans is cash flow."

"At least I salvaged the meeting by telling him I wasn't ready to officially apply for a loan yet," Martinez thought. "But I've got a lot of work to do. I've got a week to figure out how to put together a cash budget to supplement my loan application. Maybe that consultant can help me."

When he returned to his office, Martinez gathered up the file folders containing all of his fast-growing company's financial reports and printed his projected revenues and expenses using his computer spreadsheet. Then he called the SBDC consultant he had worked with when he was launching his company and explained the situation. When he arrived at the consultant's office that afternoon, they started organizing the information. Here is what they came up with:

Current cash balance	$8,750
Sales pattern	71% on credit and 29% in cash
Collections of credit sales	68% in 1 to 30 days; 19% in 31 to 60 days; 7% in 61 to 90 days; 6% never collected (bad debts).

Sales forecasts:

	Pessimistic	Most Likely	Optimistic
July (actual)	—	$18,750	—
August (actual)	—	$19,200	—
September (actual)	—	$17,840	—
October	$15,000	$17,500	$19,750
November	$14,000	$16,500	$18,500
December	$11,200	$13,000	$14,000
January	$ 9,900	$12,500	$14,900
February	$10,500	$13,800	$15,800
March	$13,500	$17,500	$19,900

Utilities expenses	$800 per month
Rent	$1,200 per month
Truck loan	$317 per month

The company's wages and salaries (including payroll taxes) estimates are:

October	$2,050
November	$1,825
December	$1,725
January	$1,725
February	$1,950
March	$2,425

The company pays 63 percent of the sales price for the inventory it purchases, an amount that it actually pays in the following month. (Martinez has negotiated "net 30" credit terms with his suppliers.)

Other expenses include:

Insurance premiums	$1,200, payable in August and February.
Office supplies	$95 per month
Maintenance	$75 per month
Computer supplies	$75 per month
Advertising	$550 per month
Legal and accounting fees	$250 per month
Miscellaneous expenses	$60 per month

A tax payment of $1,400 is due in December.

Martinez has established a minimum cash balance of $2,000.

"Well, what do you think?" Martinez asked the consultant.

1. Assume the role of the SBDC consultant and help Martinez put together a cash budget for the six months beginning in October.
2. What conclusions can you draw about Martinez's business from this cash budget?
3. What suggestions can you make to help Martinez improve his company's cash flow?

company's chief financial officer stated, the idea is to "get the cash in the door as fast as you can, cut costs, and pay people as late as possible."[18] Business owners also must monitor inventory carefully to avoid tying up valuable cash in an excessive stock of inventory.

Accounts Receivable

Selling merchandise and services on credit is a necessary evil for most small businesses. Many customers expect to buy on credit, so business owners extend it to avoid losing customers to competitors. However, selling to customers on credit is expensive; it requires more paperwork, more staff, and more cash to service accounts receivable. Also, because extending credit is, in essence, lending money, the risk involved is higher. Every business owner who sells on credit will encounter customers who pay late or, worst of all, who never pay at all.

Selling on credit is a common practice in business. Experts estimate that 90 percent of industrial and wholesale sales are on credit and that 40 percent of retail sales are on account.[19] One recent survey of small businesses across a variety of industries reported that 77 percent extend credit to their customers.[20] Because credit sales are so prevalent, an assertive collection program is essential to managing a company's cash flow. A credit policy that is too lenient can destroy a business's cash flow, attracting nothing but slow-paying and "deadbeat" customers. On the other hand, a carefully designed policy can be a powerful selling tool, attracting customers and boosting cash flow. "A sale is not a sale until you collect the money," warns the head of the National Association of Credit Management. "Receivables are the second most important item on the balance sheet. The first is cash. If you don't turn those receivables into cash, you're not going to be in business very long."[21]

HOW TO ESTABLISH A CREDIT AND COLLECTION POLICY. The first step in establishing a workable credit policy is to screen customers carefully *before* granting credit. Unfortunately, few small businesses conduct any kind of credit investigation before selling to a new customer. According to one survey, nearly 95 percent of small firms that sell on credit sell to *anyone* who wants to buy; most have no credit-checking procedure.[22]

HighTech Connect

Rene Siegel, president of HighTech Connect, a public relations firm that focuses on high-technology companies, recognizes the danger of performing services for companies that subsequently fail to pay. The chances of uncollectible accounts are especially high for HighTech Connect because the majority of its customers are risky high-tech start-ups. Before accepting a new client, Siegel invests the time to check out the company's credit rating, its capital base, its financial backers, and its reputation. In addition to a formal credit investigation, Siegel also relies on her extensive network of contacts in Silicon Valley to get the "inside scoop" on the companies wanting to hire HighTech Connect. Her screening diligence has paid off; since she initiated the process, only one customer has failed to pay HighTech Connect for its services, and that was a company that declared bankruptcy.[23]

A detailed credit application is the first line of defense against bad debt losses. Before selling to *any* customer on credit, a business owner should fill out a customized application designed to meet his company's specific needs. After collecting enough information to assemble a credit profile, the business owner should use it by checking the potential customer's credit references! The savings from lower bad debt expenses can more than offset the cost of using a credit reporting service such as TRW or Dun & Bradstreet. The National Association of Credit Management **<www.nacm.org>** is another important source of credit information because it collects information on many small businesses that other reporting services ignore. The cost to check a potential customer's credit at reporting services such as these ranges from $15 to $85, a small price to pay when considering selling thousands of dollars worth of goods or services to a new customer. The Internet has made the job of credit-checking much easier. Sites such as CreditFYI **<www.creditfyi.com>**, Dun & Bradstreet **<www.dnb.com>**, Veritas Credit Corporation **<www.veritas-usa.com>**, and KnowX **<www.knowx.com>** help entrepreneurs gather credit information on potential customers. Unfortunately, few small businesses take the time to conduct a credit check; in one study, just one-third of the businesses protected themselves by checking potential customers' credit.[24]

The next step involves establishing a firm written credit policy and letting every customer know in advance the company's credit terms. Industry practices often dictate credit terms (30 days is common), but a business does not have to abide by industry standards. A credit agreement must state clearly all the terms the business will enforce if the account goes bad—including interest, late charges, attorney's fees, and others. Failure to specify these terms in the contract means they *cannot* be added later after problems arise. When will you invoice? How soon is payment due: immediately, 30 days, 60 days? Will you add a late charge? If so, how much? The credit policies should be as tight as possible and within federal and state credit laws. According to the American Collectors Association, if a business is writing off more than 5 percent of sales as bad debts, the owner should tighten its credit and collection policy.[25]

The third step in an effective credit policy is to send invoices promptly because customers rarely pay *before* they receive their bills. The cornerstone of collecting accounts receivable on time is making sure you invoice your customers or send them their periodic billing statements promptly. "The sooner you mail your invoice, the sooner the check will be in the mail," says one entrepreneur. "In the manufacturing environment, get the invoice en route to the customer as soon as the shipment goes out the door," he advises. "Likewise, service industries with billable hours should keep track of hours daily or weekly and bill as often as the contract or agreement with the client permits."[26] Some businesses use **cycle billing,** in which a company bills a portion of its credit customers each day of the month to smooth out uneven cash receipts.

cycle billing—*a method in which a company bills a portion of its credit customers each day of the month in order to smooth out uneven cash receipts.*

Small business owners can take several steps to encourage prompt payment of invoices:

- Ensure that all invoices are clear, accurate, and timely.
- State clearly a description of the goods or services purchased and an account number.
- Make sure that prices on invoices agree with the price quotations on purchase orders or contracts.
- Highlight the balance due and the terms of sale (e.g., "net 30") on all invoices. One study by Xerox Corporation found that highlighting with color the balance due section of invoices increased the speed of collection by 30 percent.[27]
- Include a telephone number and a contact person in your organization in case the customer has a question or a dispute.

Source: Reprinted with special permission, King Features Syndicate.

When an account becomes overdue, a small business owner must take *immediate* action. The longer an account is past due, the lower is the probability of collecting it. As soon as an account becomes overdue, many business owners send a "second notice" letter requesting immediate payment. If that fails to produce results, the next step is a telephone call. "When you get on the phone, ask for payment in full," advises one expert who claims that a personal phone call "is ten times more productive than a letter."[28] If the customer still refuses to pay the bill after 30 days, collection experts recommend the following:

- Sending a letter from the company's attorney.
- Turning the account over to a collection attorney.
- As a last resort, hiring a collection agency. (The Commercial Law League of America **<www.clla.org>** can provide a list of reputable agencies.)

Although collection agencies and attorneys will take 25 to 50 percent of any accounts they collect, they are often worth the price paid. According to the American Collector's Association, only 5 percent of accounts more than 90 days delinquent will be paid voluntarily. When dealing with delinquent customers, business owners must be sure to abide by the provisions of the federal Fair Debt Collection Practices Act, which prohibits any kind of harassment when collecting debts (e.g., telephoning repeatedly, issuing threats of violence, telling third parties about the debt, or using abusive language). The primary rule when collecting past-due accounts is "Never lose your cool." Establishing a friendly but firm attitude that treats customers with respect is more likely to produce payment than hostile threats.

Table 8.6 outlines 10 collection blunders small business owners typically make and how to avoid them.

OTHER TECHNIQUES FOR ACCELERATING ACCOUNTS RECEIVABLE. Small business owners can rely on a variety of other techniques to speed cash inflow from accounts receivable:

- Speed up orders by having customers e-mail or fax them to you.
- Send invoices when goods are shipped—not a day or a week later; consider faxing or e-mailing invoices to reduce "in transit" time to a minimum. Most small business accounting software has features that allow users to e-mail the invoices they generate.
- Indicate in conspicuous print the invoice due date and any late payment penalties. (Check with an attorney to be sure all finance charges comply with state laws.)
- Restrict a customer's credit until past-due bills are paid.
- Deposit customer checks and credit card receipts *daily.*
- Identify the top 20 percent of your customers (by sales volume), create a separate file system for them, and monitor them closely. Twenty percent of the typical company's customers generate 80 percent of all accounts receivable.
- Ask customers to pay at least a portion of the purchase price up front. To preserve her company's cash flow, Jane Conner, owner of the Whitefish Gymnastics Club for 16 years, required her customers to pay for their 10-week exercise classes after the first session.[29]
- Watch for signs that a customer may be about to declare bankruptcy. If that happens, creditors typically collect only a small fraction, if any, of the debt owed.
- Consider using a bank's lockbox collection service (located near customers) to reduce mail time on collections. In a **lockbox** arrangement, customers send payments to a post office box the company's bank maintains. Several times each day, the bank collects payments and deposits them immediately in the company's account. The procedure sharply reduces processing and clearing times, especially if the lockboxes are located close to the firm's biggest customers' business addresses. The system can be expensive to operate and is most economical for companies with a high volume of large checks.

lockbox—*an arrangement in which customers send payments to a post office box a company's bank maintains; several times a day, the bank collects payments and deposits them in the company's account.*

TABLE 8.6
10 Collection Blunders and How to Avoid Them

Source: Adapted from Janine Latus Musick, "Collecting Payments Due," Nation's Business, *January 1999, pp. 44–46; Bob Weinstein, "Collect Calls,"* Entrepreneur, *August 1995, pp. 66–69; Elaine Pofeldt, "Collect Calls,"* Success, *March 1998, pp. 22–24.*

Blunder 1: Delaying collection phone calls. Many entrepreneurs waste valuable time and resources sending four or five "past-due" letters to delinquent customers, usually with limited effectiveness.

Instead: Once a bill becomes past due, call the customer within a week to verify that he received the bill and that it is accurate. Ask for payment.

Blunder 2: Failing to ask for payment in clear terms. To avoid angering a customer, some entrepreneurs ask meekly, "Do you think you could take care of this bill soon?"

Instead: Firmly, but professionally, ask for payment (the full amount) by a specific date.

Blunder 3: Sounding desperate. Some entrepreneurs show weakness by saying that they must have payment or they "can't meet payroll" or "can't pay bills." That gives the customer more leverage to negotiate additional discounts or time.

Instead: Ask for payment simply because the invoice is past due—without any other explanation. Don't apologize for your request; it's *your* money.

Blunder 4: Talking tough. Getting nasty with delinquent customers does not make them pay any faster and may be a violation of the Fair Debt Collections Practices Act.

Instead: Remain polite and professional when dealing with past-due customers, even if you think they don't deserve it. *Never* lose your temper. Don't ruin your reputation by being rude.

Blunder 5: Trying to find out the customer's problem. Some entrepreneurs think it is necessary to find out why a delinquent customer has not paid a bill.

Instead: Don't waste time playing private investigator. Focus on the business at hand—collecting your money.

Blunder 6: Asking customers how much they can pay. When customers claim that they cannot pay the bill in full, inexperienced entrepreneurs ask, "Well, how much can you pay?" They don't realize that they have just turned control of the situation over to the delinquent customer.

Instead: Take charge of negotiations from the outset. Let the customer know that you expect full payment. If you cannot get full payment immediately, suggest a new deadline. Only as a last resort should you offer an extended payment plan.

Blunder 7: Continuing to talk after you get a promise to pay. Some entrepreneurs "blow the deal" by not knowing when to stop talking. They keep interrogating a customer after they have a promise to pay.

Instead: Wrap up the conversation as soon as you have a commitment. Summarize the agreement, thank the customer, and end the conversation on a positive note.

Blunder 8: Calling without being prepared. Some entrepreneurs call customers without knowing exactly which invoices are past due and what amounts are involved. The effort is usually fruitless.

Instead: Have all account details in front of you when you call and be specific in your requests.

Blunder 9: Trusting your memory. Some entrepreneurs think they can remember previous collection calls, conversations, and agreements.

Instead: Keep accurate records of all calls and conversations. Take notes about each customer contact and resulting agreements.

Blunder 10: Letting your computer control your collection efforts. Inexperienced entrepreneurs tend to think that their computers can manage debt collection for them.

Instead: Recognize that a computer is a valuable tool in collecting accounts but that you are in control. Past-due notices from a computer may collect some accounts, but your efforts will produce more results. Getting to know the people who handle the invoices at your customers' businesses can be a major advantage when collecting accounts.

- Track the results of the company's collection efforts. Managers and key employees should receive a weekly report on the status of the company's outstanding accounts receivable.

Ransom Environmental

Although project managers at Ransom Environmental, an environmental consulting company in Newburyport, Massachusetts, viewed collecting accounts receivable as a necessary evil, CEO Steve Ransom decided his company had to make collections a priority to improve cash flow. Ransom began distributing a receivables status report at the company's weekly operations meetings. Given to every manager, the report features a receivables-aging chart showing whose customers were behind on their payments and by how many days. Ransom Environmental quickly began to see an improvement in its collection patterns and in its cash flow. The company's average collection period has fallen from 75 days to 60 days, and faster collections have boosted cash flow, enabling Ransom to save between $1,000 and $2,000 a month in interest on its line of credit.[30]

Accounts Payable

The second element of the "big three" of cash management is accounts payable. The timing of payables is just as crucial to proper cash management as the timing of receivables, but the objective is exactly the opposite. Entrepreneurs should strive to stretch out payables as long as possible *without damaging their companies' credit rating.* Otherwise, suppliers may begin demanding prepayment or C.O.D. terms, which severely impair a company's cash flow, or they simply stop doing business with it. When one computer manufacturer ran into cash flow problems, it deferred payments to its suppliers for as long as 100 days (compared to an industry average of about 40 days). Because of the company's slow payments, many suppliers simply stopped selling to the computer maker.[31] One cash management consultant claims, "Some companies pay too early and wind up forgoing the interest they could have earned on their cash. Others pay too late and either wind up with late penalties or being forced to buy on a C.O.D. basis, which really kills them."[32] It is perfectly acceptable for small business owners to regulate payments to their companies' advantage. Efficient cash managers set up a payment calendar each month that allows them to pay their bills on time and to take advantage of cash discounts for early payment.

Dunis & Associates

Nancy Dunis, CEO of Dunis & Associates, a Portland, Oregon, marketing firm, recognizes the importance of controlling accounts payable. "Our payables must be functioning just right to keep our cash flow running smoothly," says Dunis. She has set up a simple five-point accounts payable system:[33]

1. Set scheduling goals. *Dunis strives to pay her company's bills 45 days after receiving them and to collect all her receivables within 30 days. Even though "it doesn't always work that way," her goal is to make the most of her cash flow.*
2. Keep paperwork organized. *Dunis dates every invoice she receives and carefully files it according to her payment plan. "This helps us remember when to cut the check," she says, and, "it helps us stagger our payments, over days or weeks"—significantly improving the company's cash flow.*
3. Prioritize. *Dunis cannot stretch out all of her company's creditors for 45 days; some demand payment sooner. Those suppliers are at the top of the accounts payable list.*
4. Be consistent. *"Companies want consistent customers," says Dunis. "With a few exceptions," she explains, "most businesses will be happy to accept 45-day payments, so long as they know you'll always pay your full obligation at that point."*
5. Look for warning signs. *Dunis sees her accounts payable as an early warning system for cash flow problems. "The first indication I get that cash flow is in trouble is when I see I'm*

getting low on cash and could have trouble paying my bills according to my staggered filing system," she says.

Other signs that a business is heading for cash flow problems include difficulty making principal and interest payments on loans and incurring penalties for late payment of routine bills.

Business owners should verify all invoices before paying them. Some unscrupulous vendors will send out invoices for goods they never shipped or services they never rendered, knowing that many business owners will simply pay the bill without checking its authenticity. A common invoice scam aimed at small business owners involves bogus operators sending bills for ads in nonexistent printed or online "yellow pages" directories. In some cases, the directories actually do exist, but their distribution is so limited that ads in them are useless. A recent survey by the real Yellow Pages Publishers Association found that one-third of businesses had received bogus bills for Yellow Pages advertising.[34] To avoid falling victim to such scams, someone in the company—for instance, the accounts payable clerk—should have the responsibility of verifying *every* invoice received.

Generally, it is a good idea for owners to take advantage of cash discounts vendors offer. A cash discount (e.g., "2/10, net 30"—take a 2 percent discount if you pay the invoice within 10 days; otherwise, total payment is due in 30 days) offers a price reduction if the owner pays an invoice early. A clever cash manager also will negotiate the best possible credit terms with his suppliers. Almost all vendors grant their customers trade credit, and small business owners should take advantage of it. However, because trade credit is so easy to get, entrepreneurs must be careful not to overuse and abuse it, putting their businesses in a precarious financial position.

Favorable credit terms can make a tremendous difference in a firm's cash flow. Table 8.7 shows the same most likely cash budget (from Table 8.2) with one exception: instead of purchasing on C.O.D. terms (Table 8.2), the owner has negotiated net 30 payment terms (Table 8.7). Notice the drastic improvement in the company's cash flow resulting from improved credit terms.

If owners do find themselves financially strapped when payment to a vendor is due, they should avoid making empty promises that "the check is in the mail" or sending unsigned checks. Instead, they should openly discuss the situation with the vendor. Most vendors will work out payment terms for extended credit. One small business owner who was experiencing a cash crisis claims:

> One day things got so bad I just called up a supplier and said, "I need your stuff, but I'm going through a tough period and simply can't pay you right now." They said they wanted to keep me as a customer, and they asked if it was okay to bill me in three months. I was dumbfounded: *They didn't even charge me interest.*[35]

Small business owners also can improve their firms' cash flow by scheduling controllable cash disbursements so that they do not come due at the same time. For example, paying employees every two weeks (or every month) rather than every week reduces administrative costs and gives the business more time to use its cash. Owners of fledgling businesses may be able to conserve cash by hiring part-time employees or by using freelance workers rather than full-time, permanent workers. Scheduling insurance premiums monthly or quarterly rather than annually also improves cash flows.

Wise use of business credit cards is another way to stretch the firm's cash balance. However, entrepreneurs should avoid cards that charge transaction fees. Credit cards differ in their interest-charging policies; many begin charging interest from the date of purchase, but some charge interest only from the invoice date.

TABLE 8.7
Cash Budget,[a] Most Likely Sales Forecast

	Jan.	Feb.	Mar.	Apr.
Cash Receipts:				
Sales	$150,000	$200,000	$200,000	$300,000
Credit Sales	112,500	150,000	150,000	225,000
Collections:				
60%—1st month after sale	$180,000	$ 67,500	$ 90,000	$ 90,000
30%—2nd month after sale	78,750	90,000	33,750	45,000
5%—3rd month after sale	11,250	13,125	15,000	5,625
Cash Sales	37,500	50,000	50,000	75,000
Interest	0	200	0	9
Total Cash Receipts	$307,500	$220,825	$188,750	$215,625
Cash Disbursements:				
Purchases[a]	$105,000	$140,000	$140,000	$210,000
Rent	2,000	2,000	2,000	2,000
Utilities	850	850	850	850
Interest	0	0	7,500	0
Tax Prepayment	0	0	50,000	0
Capital Addition	0	130,000	3	0
Miscellaneous	70	70	70	70
Wage/Salaries	30,000	40,000	45,000	50,000
Total Cash Disbursements[a]	$137,920	$312,920	$245,420	$262,920
End-of-Month Balance:				
Cash (beginning of month)[a]	$ 12,000	$181,580	$ 89,485	$ 32,815
+ Cash Receipts	307,500	220,825	188,750	215,625
– Cash Disbursements[a]	137,920	312,920	245,420	262,920
Cash (end of month)[a]	181,580	89,485	32,815	(14,480)
Borrowing	0	0	0	24,480
Cash (end of month [after borrowing])[a]	$181,580	$ 89,485	$ 32,815	$ 10,000

[a] After negotiating "net 30" trade credit terms.

Inventory

Inventory is a significant investment for many small businesses and can create a severe strain on cash flow. Although inventory represents the largest capital investment for most businesses, few owners use any formal methods for managing it. As a result, the typical small business not only has too much inventory but also too much of the *wrong* kind of inventory! Because inventory is illiquid, it can quickly siphon off a company's pool of available cash. "Small companies need cash to grow," says one consultant. "They've got to be able to turn [cash] over quickly. That's difficult to do if a lot of money is tied up in excess inventory."[36]

Surplus inventory yields a zero rate of return and unnecessarily ties up the firm's cash. "The cost of carrying inventory is expensive," says one small business consultant. "A typical manufacturing company pays 25 percent to 30 percent of the value of the inventory for the cost of borrowed money, warehouse space, materials handling, staff, lift-truck expenses, and fixed costs. This shocks a lot of people. Once they realize it, they look at inventory differently."[37] Marking down items that don't sell will keep inventory lean and allow it to turn over frequently. Even though volume discounts lower inventory costs, large purchases may tie up the company's valuable cash. Wise business owners avoid overbuying inventory, recognizing that excess inventory ties up valuable cash unproductively. In fact, only 20 percent of a typical business's inventory turns over quickly, so owners must watch constantly for stale items.[38]

Carrying too little inventory is not desirable because companies with excessive "stock-outs" lose sales (and eventually customers if the problem persists). However, carrying too much inventory usually results in slow-moving inventory and a low inventory turnover ratio. Experienced business owners understand the importance of shedding slow-moving inventory, even if the price they get is below their normal markup.

Channeled Resources Inc.

Recognizing the high cost of holding inventory, Cindy Revenaugh, vice president of sales at Channeled Resources, a company that sells recycled paper products, gives her sales force the power to sell slow-moving items at any price that is not below the company's cost. "We just want to move the stuff and get cash for it," says Revenaugh. "Even if they sell it at cost, it's better than letting it sit here."[39]

Carrying too much inventory increases the chances that a business will run out of cash. "The cash that pays for goods is channeled into inventory," says one business writer, "where its flow is dead-ended until the inventory is sold and the cash is set free again. The cash flow trick is to commit just enough cash to inventory to meet demand."[40] Scheduling inventory deliveries at the latest possible date will prevent premature payment of invoices. Finally, given goods of comparable quality and price, an entrepreneur should purchase goods from the fastest supplier to keep inventory levels low.

Monitoring the "big three" of cash management can help every business owner avoid a cash crisis while making the best use of available cash. According to one expert, maximizing cash flow involves "getting money from customers sooner; paying bills at the last moment possible; consolidating money in a single bank account; managing accounts payable, accounts receivable, and inventory more effectively; and squeezing every penny out of your daily business."[41]

AVOIDING THE CASH CRUNCH

5. Explain the techniques for avoiding a cash crunch in a small company.

Nearly every small business has the potential to improve its cash position with little or no investment. The key is to make an objective evaluation of the company's financial policies, searching for inefficiency in its cash flow. Young firms cannot afford to waste resources, especially one as vital as cash. By utilizing the following techniques, entrepreneurs can get maximum benefit from their companies' pool of available cash.

Barter

bartering—*the exchange of goods and services for other goods and services rather than for cash.*

Bartering, the exchange of goods and services for other goods and services rather than for cash, is an effective way to conserve cash. An ancient concept, bartering regained popularity during recent recessions. Over the last decade, more than 700 barter exchanges have cropped up, catering primarily to small- and medium-sized businesses looking to conserve cash. More than 400,000 companies—most of them small—engage in more than $9.1 billion worth of barter each year.[42] Every day, entrepreneurs across the nation use bartering to buy much needed materials, equipment, and supplies—*without using cash.*

Litho Graphics

For instance, when Jerry Trombo relocated his printing business, Litho Graphics, he traded printing services for moving services, painting, carpeting, furnishings, a computer, and a newly paved driveway. For the year, Litho Graphics conducted more than $50,000 worth of bartering, an amount representing 8 percent of the company's sales—and involving no cash! "I don't buy anything unless I pick up the barter catalogue," says Trombo, who has been bartering through an exchange for more than 11 years. "I'll do anything to avoid spending cash."[43]

In addition to conserving cash, companies that use barter also have the opportunity to transform slow-moving inventory into much-needed products and services. Buying goods

YOU BE THE CONSULTANT . . .

On the Fast Track

Jon Wroten, founder of JWA Security Services, a California-based security guard company, was thrilled when his company landed a two-year contract with the state of California. The $4 million contract accelerated JWA's growth into hyperdrive, and Wroten believed his company was finally on its way to becoming a major player in the industry. Within two years, the JWA had 14 offices, more than 1,000 employees, and $50 million in sales—a far cry from the one-man operation Wroten had launched with $225 in 1981. Wroten began implementing a fast-growth plan that would double JWA's to the $100 million within just four years.

Just as Wroten got his plans underway, however, everything began to unravel. JWA lost its lucrative contract with the state of California, severely affecting its sales and its cash flow. Slow-paying customers further aggravated the company's cash flow woes; some customers took as long as nine months to pay JWA for its security services. The company slipped into a downwardly spiraling cash crisis.

The unfortunate sequence of events proved to be a sobering lesson for Wroten on the difference between generating sales and managing cash flow. Failing to project realistically the amount of cash required to fuel a company's growth and how long it takes to collect accounts receivable can force a company out of business, no matter how fast sales are climbing. In fact, rapid growth usually compounds cash flow problems as a company spends increasing amounts of cash on inventory, supplies, payroll, and other expenses and waits 30 to 45 days or longer to collect its receivables. The result: a serious cash crisis that could destroy a company.

In an attempt to save his company, Wroten began selling JWA's accounts receivable to a factor, and he postponed paying rent and utilities for the company's offices. The future of this once-successful company was in peril.

1. Why does rapid growth often result in cash flow problems for so many small companies?
2. What can entrepreneurs do to avoid the cash flow perils associated with rapid growth?
3. What advice can you offer Jon Wroten about managing his company's accounts receivable? About managing cash flow in general?

Source: Julie Carrick Dalton, "Obit: Flawed Safeguard Sinks Security Company," *Inc.*, September 1, 1999, p. 29. Reprinted with permission of *Inc.* Magazine, from "Obit: Flawed Safeguard Sinks Security Company," by Julie Carrick Dalton, September 1999 © 1999; permission conveyed through Copyright Clearance Center, Inc.

and services with barter also offers the benefit of a built-in discount. Although a company gets credit for the retail value of the goods or services it offers, the real cost to the company is less and depends on its gross profit margin. For instance, the owner of an Italian restaurant bartered $1,000 worth of meals for some new furniture, but his actual cost of the meals was only $680, given his gross profit margin of 32 percent. Business owners who barter also say that joining a barter exchange brings in customers who normally would not buy from them.

In a typical barter exchange, businesses accumulate trade credits when they offer goods or services through the exchange. Then they can use their trade credits to purchase other goods and services from other members of the exchange. The typical exchange charges a $500 membership fee and a 10 percent transaction fee (5 percent from the buyer and 5 percent from the seller) on every deal. The exchange tracks the balance in each member's account and typically sends a monthly statement summarizing account activity.

Trim Overhead Costs

High overhead expenses can strain a small firm's cash supply to the breaking point; simple cost-cutting measures can save big money. Frugal small business owners can trim their overhead in a number of ways.

PERIODICALLY EVALUATE EXPENSES. Business owners not only should attempt to keep their operating costs low, but they also should evaluate them periodically to make sure they have not gotten out of line. Comparing current expenses with past levels is helpful and so is comparing a company's expenses against industry standards. Useful resources for determining typical expenses in an industry include Robert Morris Associates' *Annual Statement Studies,* Dun & Bradstreet's *Industry Norms and Key Business Ratios,* and Prentice Hall's *Almanac of Business and Industrial Financial Ratios.* We will describe these resources in more detail in the next chapter.

Hi-Shear Technology

Linda Nespole, a manager at Hi-Shear Technology, an aerospace subcontractor, used this technique to cut thousands of dollars from her company's operating expenses each year. When Hi-Shear's cash flow was squeezed recently, Nespole began tracking some of the company's largest operating expenses, mostly utility bills, and discovered some unusually large increases. Basic repairs, preventive maintenance, and more efficient fixtures cut costs and generated enough savings to pay for themselves within just a few months. Nespole expanded her list and began charting company expenses and acting on trends she saw. The result: major cost savings in everything from telephone charges to retirement plan costs. Tracking and controlling expenses has become a priority for Hi-Shear's 125 employees, and the company's cash flow has never been better![44]

WHEN PRACTICAL, LEASE INSTEAD OF BUY. By leasing automobiles, computers, office equipment, machinery, and other assets rather than buying them, an entrepreneur can conserve valuable cash. The value of such assets is *not* in owning them but in *using* them. Businesses can lease practically any kind of equipment—from office furniture and computers to construction equipment and manufacturing machinery. Approximately 80 percent of U.S. companies use leasing as a cash management strategy.[45] "These companies are long on ideas, short on capital, and in need of flexibility as they grow and change," says Suzanne Jackson of the Equipment Leasing Association of America. "They lease for efficiency and convenience."[46]

Although total lease payments typically are greater than those for a conventional loan, most leases offer 100 percent financing, which means the owner avoids the large capital outlays required as down payments on most loans. Also, leasing is an "off-the-balance-sheet" method of financing and requires no collateral. A lease is considered an operating expense on the income statement, not a liability on the balance sheet. Thus, leasing conserves a company's borrowing capacity. Lease agreements also are flexible. Leasing companies typically offer a variety of terms and allow businesses to stretch payments over a longer time period than those of a conventional loan. "There are so many ways to tailor a lease agreement to a company's individual equipment and financial needs that you might call it a personalized rental agreement," says the owner of a small construction firm.[47]

Leasing also protects a business against obsolescence, especially when it comes to equipment such as computer hardware and software, whose technological life is limited to perhaps three years.

Sebago Brewing Company

When Kai Adams, Brad Monarch, and Tim Haines opened the Sebago Brewing Company, a restaurant-pub in South Portland, Maine, they borrowed $175,000 through a Small Business Administration loan and invested an equal amount of their own money. Installing beer brewing equipment, oufitting the kitchen, and furnishing the dining room (plus holding some cash in reserve for working capital) took most of their start-up funds. Still, the partners knew that they needed one more crucial ingredient to make their restaurant a success: a sophisticated computer hardware and software system that would track every aspect of its operation minute by minute and give them the control they needed. The only catch was the system cost $30,000 that they did not have! So Adams, Monarch, and Haines decided to lease the computer setup. "It took a lot of money to open this restaurant," says Adams, "and we really had to be selective about what we spent our capital on. Leasing the computer system freed up cash flow for our opening."[48]

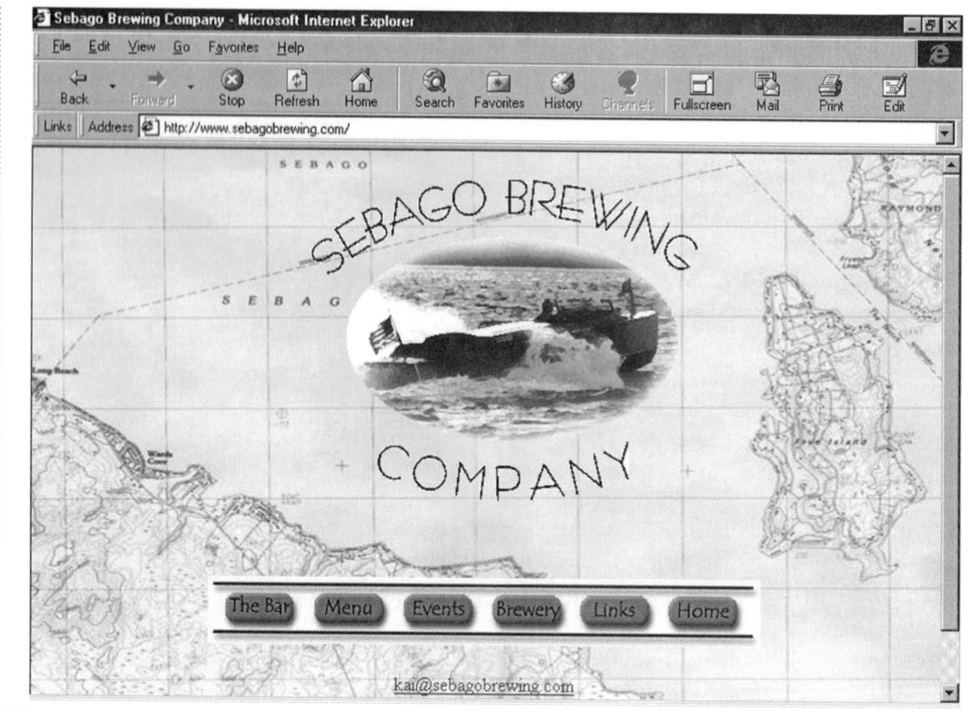

AVOID NONESSENTIAL OUTLAYS. By forgoing costly ego indulgences such as ostentatious office equipment, first-class travel, and flashy company cars, entrepreneurs can make the most efficient use of a company's cash. Before putting scarce cash into an asset, every business owner should put the decision to the acid test: "What will this purchase add to my company's ability to compete and to become more successful?" Making across-the-board spending cuts to conserve cash is dangerous, however, because the owner runs the risk of cutting expenditures that literally drive the business. One common mistake during business slowdowns is cutting marketing and advertising expenditures. "As competitors pull back," says one advisor, "smart marketers will keep their ad budgets on an even keel, which is sufficient to bring increased attention to their products."[49] The secret to success is cutting *nonessential* expenditures. "If the lifeblood of your company is marketing, cut it less," advises one advertising executive. "If it is customer service, that is the last thing you want to cut back on. Cut from areas that are not essential to business growth."[50]

NEGOTIATE FIXED LOAN PAYMENTS TO COINCIDE WITH YOUR COMPANY'S CASH FLOW CYCLE. Many banks allow businesses to structure loans so that they can skip specific payments when their cash flow ebbs to its lowest point. Negotiating such terms gives businesses the opportunity to customize their loan repayments to their cash flow cycles.

Torrington Industries

For example, Ted Zoli, president of Torrington Industries, a construction-materials supplier and contracting business, consistently uses "skipped payment loans" in his highly seasonal business. "Every time we buy a piece of construction machinery," he says, "we set it up so that we're making payments for eight or nine months, and then skipping three or four months during the winter."[51]

BUY USED OR RECONDITIONED EQUIPMENT, ESPECIALLY IF IT IS "BEHIND-THE-SCENES" MACHINERY. One restaurateur saved thousands of dollars in the start-up phase of his business by buying used equipment from a restaurant equipment broker.

HIRE PART-TIME EMPLOYEES AND FREELANCE SPECIALISTS WHENEVER POSSIBLE. Hiring part-time workers and freelancers rather than full-time employees saves on the cost of both salaries and benefits.

CONTROL EMPLOYEE ADVANCES AND LOANS. A manager should grant only those advances and loans that are necessary and should keep accurate records on payments and balances.

ESTABLISH AN INTERNAL SECURITY AND CONTROL SYSTEM. Too many owners encourage employee theft by failing to establish a system of controls. Reconciling the bank statement monthly and requiring special approval for checks over a specific amount, say $1,000, will help minimize losses. Separating recordkeeping and check-writing responsibilities, rather than assigning them to a single employee, offers more protection.

DEVELOP A SYSTEM TO BATTLE CHECK FRAUD. Merchants take more than $13 billion in bad checks each year.[52] About 70 percent of all "bounced" checks occur because nine out of ten customers fail to keep their checkbooks balanced; the remaining 30 percent of bad checks are the result of fraud.[53] The most effective way to battle bad checks is to subscribe to an electronic check approval service. The service works at the cash register, and approval takes about a minute. The fee a small business pays to use the service depends on the volume of checks. For most small companies, charges amount to 1 to 2 percent of the cleared checks' value.

CHANGE YOUR SHIPPING TERMS. Changing the firm's shipping terms from "F.O.B (free on board) buyer," in which the *seller* pays the cost of freight, to "F.O.B seller," in which the *buyer* absorbs all shipping costs, can improve cash flow.

SWITCH TO ZERO-BASED BUDGETING. Zero-based budgeting (ZBB) primarily is a shift in the philosophy of budgeting. Rather than build the current year budget on *increases* from the previous year's budget, ZBB starts from a budget of zero and evaluates the necessity of every item. "Start with zero and review all expenses, asking yourself whether each one is necessary," says one business consultant.[54]

Keep Your Business Plan Current

Before approaching any potential lender or investor, a business owner must prepare a solid business plan. Smart owners keep their plans up-to-date in case an unexpected cash crisis forces them to seek emergency financing. Revising the plan annually also forces the owner to focus on managing the business more effectively.

Invest Surplus Cash

Because of the uneven flow of receipts and disbursements, a company will often temporarily have more cash than it needs—for a week, month, quarter, or even longer. When this happens, most small business owners simply ignore the surplus because they are not sure how soon they will need it. They believe that relatively small amounts of cash sitting around for just a few days or weeks are not worth investing. However, this is not the case. Small business owners who put surplus cash to work *immediately* rather than allowing it to sit idle soon discover that the yield adds up to a significant amount over time. This money can help ease the daily cash crunch during business troughs. "Your goal . . . should be to identify every dollar you don't need to pay today's bills and to keep that money invested to improve your cash flow," explains a consultant.[55]

However, when investing surplus cash, an owner's primary objective should *not* be to earn the maximum yield (which usually carries with it maximum risk); instead, the focus

money market account—*an interest-bearing account that allows depositors to write checks without tying up their money for a specific period of time.*

zero balance account (ZBA)—*a checking account that never has any funds in it. A company keeps its money in an interest-bearing master account tied to the ZBA; when a check is drawn on the ZBA, the bank withdraws enough money from the master account to cover it.*

sweep account—*a checking account that automatically sweeps all funds in a company's checking account above a predetermined minimum into an interest-bearing account.*

should be on the safety and the liquidity of the investments. Making high-risk investments with a company's cash cushion makes no sense and could jeopardize its future. The need to minimize risk and to have ready access to the cash restricts the small business owner's investment options to just a few such as money market accounts, zero balance accounts, and sweep accounts. A **money market account** is an interest-bearing account offered by a variety of financial institutions ranging from banks to mutual funds. Money market accounts pay interest while allowing depositors to write checks (most have minimum check amounts) without tying their money up for a specific period of time. A **zero balance account** (ZBA) is a checking account that technically never has any funds in it but is tied to a master account such as payroll. The company keeps its money in the master account where it earns interest, but it writes checks on the ZBA. At the end of the day, the bank pays all of the checks drawn on the ZBA; then it withdraws enough money from the master account to cover them. ZBAs allow a company to keep more cash working during the float period, the time between a check being issued and its being cashed. A **sweep account** automatically "sweeps" all funds in a company's checking account above a predetermined minimum into an interest-bearing account, enabling it to keep otherwise idle cash invested until it is needed to cover checks.

CONCLUSION

Successful owners run their businesses "lean and mean." Trimming wasteful expenditures, investing surplus funds, and carefully planning and managing the company's cash flow enable them to compete effectively in a hostile market. The simple but effective techniques covered in this chapter can improve every small company's cash position. One business writer says, "In the day-to-day course of running a company, other people's capital flows past an imaginative CEO as opportunity. By looking forward and keeping an analytical eye on your cash account as events unfold (remembering that if there's no real cash there when you need it, you're history), you can generate leverage as surely as if that capital were yours to keep."[56]

CHAPTER SUMMARY

1. Explain the importance of cash management to a small business's success.
   - Cash is the most important but least productive asset the small business has. The manager must maintain enough cash to meet the firm's normal requirements (plus a reserve for emergencies) without retaining excessively large, unproductive cash balances.
   - Without adequate cash, a small business will fail.
2. Differentiate between cash and profits.
   - Cash and profits are *not* the same. More businesses fail for lack of cash than for lack of profits.
   - Profits, the difference between total revenue and total expenses, are an accounting concept. Cash flow represents the flow of actual cash (the only thing businesses can use to pay bills) through a business in a continuous cycle. A business can be earning a profit and be forced out of business because it runs out of cash.
3. Understand the five steps in creating a cash budget and use them to create a cash budget.
   - The cash budgeting procedure outlined in this chapter tracks the flow of cash through the business and enables the owner to project cash surpluses and cash deficits at specific intervals.
   - The five steps in creating a cash budget are as follows: forecasting sales, forecasting cash receipts, forecasting cash disbursements, and determining the end-of-month cash balance.
4. Describe fundamental principles involved in managing the "big three" of cash management: accounts receivable, accounts payable, and inventory.
   - Controlling accounts receivable requires business owners to establish clear, firm credit and collection policies and to screen customers *before* granting them credit. Sending invoices promptly and acting on past-due accounts quickly also improve cash flow. The goal is to collect cash from receivables as quickly as possible.
   - When managing accounts payable, a manager's goal is to stretch out payables as long as possible without damaging the company's credit rating. Other techniques include verifying invoices before paying them, taking advantage of cash discounts, and negotiating the best possible credit terms.

- Inventory frequently causes cash headaches for small business managers. Excess inventory earns a zero rate of return and ties up a company's cash unnecessarily. Owners must watch for stale merchandise.

5. Explain the techniques for avoiding a cash crunch in a small company.

- Trimming overhead costs by bartering, leasing assets, avoiding nonessential outlays, using zero-based budgeting, and implementing an internal control system boost a firm's cash flow position.
- Also, investing surplus cash maximizes the firm's earning power. The primary criteria for investing surplus cash are security and liquidity.

DISCUSSION QUESTIONS

1. Why must entrepreneurs concentrate on effective cash flow management?
2. Explain the difference between cash and profit.
3. Outline the steps involved in developing a cash budget.
4. How can an entrepreneur launching a new business forecast sales?
5. What are the "big three" of cash management? What effect do they have on a company's cash flow?
6. Outline the basic principles of managing a small firm's receivables, payables, and inventory.
7. How can bartering improve a company's cash position?
8. What steps can entrepreneurs take to conserve the cash within their companies?
9. What should be a small business owner's primary concern when investing surplus cash?

Beyond the Classroom . . .

1. Interview several local small business owners about their cash management policies. Do they know how much cash their businesses have during the month? How do they track their cash flows? Do they use some type of cash budget? If not, ask if you can help the owner develop one. Does the owner invest surplus cash?

2. Volunteer to help a small business owner develop a cash budget for his or her company. What patterns do you detect? What recommendations can you make for improving the company's cash management system?

3. Contact the International Reciprocal Trade Association **<www.irta.net>** or the Corporate Barter Council **<www.corporatebarter.com>** and get a list of the barter exchanges in your state. Interview the manager of one of the exchanges and prepare a report on how barter exchanges work and how they benefit small businesses. Ask the manager to refer you to a small business owner who benefits from the barter exchange and interview him or her. How does the owner use the exchange? How much cash has bartering saved? What other benefits has the owner discovered?

4. Use the resources of the World Wide Web to research leasing options for small companies. The Equipment Leasing Association of America **<www.elaonline.com>** is a good place to start. What advantages does leasing offer? Disadvantages? Identify and explain the various types of leases.

5. Contact a local small business owner who sells on credit. Is collecting accounts receivable on time a problem? What steps does the owner take to manage the company's accounts receivable? Do late payers strain the company's cash flow? How does the owner deal with customers who pay late?

We invite you to visit this book's companion Web site at **www.prenhall.com/Zimmerer.**

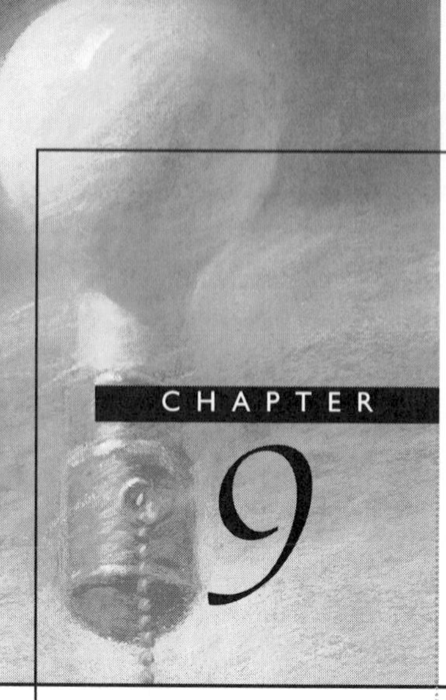

Creating a Successful Financial Plan

The professional's grasp of the numbers is a measure of the control he has over the events that the figures represent.

—Harold S. Geneen

It is better to solve problems than crises.

—John Guinther

LEARNING OBJECTIVES

Upon completion of this chapter, you will be able to:

1. Understand the importance of preparing a financial plan.
2. Describe how to prepare the basic financial statements and use them to manage a small business.
3. Create projected (pro forma) financial statements.
4. Understand the basic financial statements through ratio analysis.
5. Explain how to interpret financial ratios.
6. Conduct a breakeven analysis for a small company.

Fashioning a well-designed, logical financial plan is one of the most important steps to launching a new business venture. The shakeout that has claimed so many dot-com companies in the last few years proves that entrepreneurs who fail to develop a workable strategy for earning a profit within a reasonable time eventually must answer to investors and to creditors. Potential investors demand to see a financial plan before putting their money into a start-up company. More importantly, a financial plan is a vital tool that helps entrepreneurs manage their businesses more effectively, steering their way around the pitfalls that cause failures. Entrepreneurs who ignore the financial aspects of their businesses run the risk of becoming just another failure statistic. One financial expert says of small companies, "Those that don't establish sound controls at the start are setting themselves up to fail."[1]

1. Understand the importance of preparing a financial plan.

Unfortunately, failure to collect and analyze basic financial data is a common mistake among entrepreneurs. According to one survey, one-third of all entrepreneurs run their companies *without any kind of financial plan.*[2] Another study found that only 11 percent of small business owners analyzed their financial statements as part of the managerial planning and decision-making process.[3] To reach profit objectives, entrepreneurs must be aware of their firms' overall financial position and the changes in financial status that occur over time.

This chapter focuses on some very practical tools that will help an entrepreneur develop a workable financial plan, keep her aware of her company's financial plan, and enable her to plan for profit. She can use these tools to help her anticipate changes and plot an appropriate profit strategy to meet them head on. These profit planning techniques are not difficult to master, nor are they overly time consuming. We will discuss the techniques involved in preparing projected (pro forma) financial statements, conducting ratio analysis, and performing breakeven analysis.

BASIC FINANCIAL STATEMENTS

2. Describe how to prepare basic financial statements and use them to manage a small business.

Before we begin building projected financial statements, it would be helpful to review the basic financial reports that measure a company's financial position: the balance sheet, the income statement, and the statement of cash flows. Studies show that the level of financial reporting among small businesses is high; some 81 percent of the companies in one survey regularly produced summary financial information, almost all of it in the form of these traditional financial statements.[4]

The Balance Sheet

The **balance sheet** takes a "snapshot" of a business's financial position, providing owners with an estimate of its worth on a given date. Its two major sections show what assets the business owns and what claims creditors and owners have against those assets. The balance sheet is usually prepared on the last day of the month. Figure 9.1 shows the balance sheet for Sam's Appliance Shop for the year ended December 31, 200X.

balance sheet — *a financial statement that provides a snapshot of a business's financial position, estimating its worth on a given date; it is built on the fundamental accounting equation: Assets = Liabilities + Owner's equity.*

current assets—*assets such as cash and other items to be converted into cash within one year, or within the company's normal operating cycle.*

The balance sheet is built on the fundamental accounting equation: Assets = Liabilities + Owner's equity. Any increase or decrease on one side of the equation must be offset by an increase or decrease on the other side, hence, the name *balance sheet.* It provides a baseline from which to measure future changes in assets, liabilities, and equity. The first section of the balance sheet lists the firm's assets (valued at cost, not actual market value) and shows the total value of everything the business owns. **Current assets** consist of cash and items to be converted into cash within one year or within the normal operating cycle of the

FIGURE 9.1
Balance Sheet, Sam's Appliance Shop

Assets		
Current Assets		
Cash		$ 49,855
Accounts Receivable	$179,225	
Less Allowance for Doubtful Accounts	6,000	$173,225
Inventory		$455,455
Prepaid Expenses		$ 8,450
Total Current Assets		$686,985
Fixed Assets		
Land		$ 59,150
Buildings	$ 74,650	
Less Accumulated Depreciation	7,050	$ 67,600
Equipment	$ 22,375	
Less Accumulated Depreciation	1,250	$ 21,125
Funiture and Fixtures	$ 10,295	
Less Accumulated Depreciation	1,000	$ 9,295
Total Fixed Assets		$157,170
Intangibles (Goodwill)		$ 3,500
Total Assets		$847,655
Liabilities		
Current Liabilities		
Accounts Payable		$152,580
Note Payable		83,920
Accrued Wages/Salaries Payable		38,150
Accrued Interest Payable		42,380
Accrued Taxes Payable		50,820
Total Current Liabilities		$367,850
Long-Term Liabilities		
Mortgage		$127,150
Note Payable		85,000
Total Long-Term Liabilities		$212,150
Owner's Equity		
Sam Lloyd, Capital		$267,655
Total Liabilities and Owner's Equity		$847,655

fixed assets—*assets acquired for long-term use in a business.*

liabilities—*creditors' claims against a company's assets.*

current liabilities—*those debts that must be paid within one year or within the normal operating cycle of a company.*

company, whichever is longer, such as accounts receivable and inventory, and **fixed assets** are those acquired for long-term use in the business. Intangible assets include items that, although valuable, do not have tangible value, such as goodwill, copyrights, and patents.

The second section shows the business's **liabilities**—the creditors' claims against the company's assets. **Current liabilities** are those debts that must be paid within one year or within the normal operating cycle of the company, whichever is longer, and **long-term liabilities** are those that come due after one year. This section of the balance sheet also shows the **owner's equity,** the value of the owner's investment in the business. It is the balancing factor on the balance sheet, representing all of the owner's capital contributions to the business plus all accumulated earnings not distributed to the owner(s).

The Income Statement

The **income statement** (or profit and loss statement or P&L) compares expenses against revenue over a certain period of time to show the firm's net profit (or loss). The income statement is a "moving picture" of the firm's profitability over time. The annual P&L statement reports the bottom line of the business over the fiscal/calendar year. Figure 9.2 shows the income statement for Sam's Appliance Shop for the year ended December 31, 200X.

To calculate net profit or loss, the owner records sales revenues for the year, which include all income that flows into the business from sales of goods and services. Income from other sources (rent, investments, interest) also must be included in the revenue section of the income statement. To determine net sales revenue, owners subtract the value of returned items and refunds from gross revenue. **Cost of goods sold** represents the total cost, including shipping, of the merchandise sold during the accounting period. Manufacturers, wholesalers, and retailers calculate cost of goods sold by adding purchases to beginning inventory and subtracting ending inventory. Service companies typically have no cost of goods sold.

long-term liabilities—*liabilities that come due after one year.*

owner's equity—*the value of the owner's investment in the business.*

income statement—*a financial statement that represents a "moving picture" of a business, comparing its expenses against its revenue over a period of time to show its net profit (or loss).*

Net Sales Revenue	$1,870,841	
Cost of Goods Sold		
Beginning Inventory, 1/1/xx	$ 805,745	
+ Purchases	939,827	
Goods Available for Sale	$1,745,572	
– Ending Inventory, 12/31/xx	455,455	
Cost of Goods Sold		$1,290,117
Gross Profit		$ 580,724
Operating Expenses		
Advertising	$ 139,670	
Insurance	46,125	
Depreciation		
Building	18,700	
Equipment	9,000	
Salaries	224,500	
Travel	4,000	
Entertainment	2,500	
Total Operating Expenses		$ 444,495
General Expenses		
Utilities	$ 5,300	
Telephone	2,500	
Postage	1,200	
Payroll Taxes	25,000	
Total General Expenses		$ 34,000
Other Expenses		
Interest Expense	$ 39,850	
Bad Check Expense	1,750	
Total Other Expenses		$ 41,600
Total Expenses		$ 520,095
Net Income		$ 60,629

FIGURE 9.2
Income Statement, Sam's Appliance Shop

cost of goods sold—*the total cost, including shipping, of the merchandise sold during the accounting period.*

gross profit margin—*gross profit divided by net sales revenue.*

Net sales revenue minus cost of goods sold results in a company's gross profit. Dividing gross profit by net sales revenue produces the **gross profit margin,** a percentage that every small business owner should watch closely. If a company's gross profit margin slips too low, it is likely that it will operate at a loss (negative net income). Many business owners whose companies are losing money mistakenly believe that the problem is inadequate sales volume; therefore, they focus on pumping up sales at any cost. In many cases, however, the losses their companies are incurring are the result of an inadequate gross profit margin, and pumping up sales only deepens their losses! Repairing a poor gross profit margin requires a company to raise prices, cut manufacturing or purchasing costs, refuse orders with low profit margins, or add new products with more attractive profit margins. Monitoring the gross profit margin over time and comparing it to those of other companies in the same industry are important steps to maintaining a company's long-term profitability.

operating expenses—*those costs that contribute directly to the manufacture and distribution of goods.*

Operating expenses include those costs that contribute directly to the manufacture and distribution of goods. General expenses are indirect costs incurred in operating the business. "Other expenses" is a catch-all category covering all other expenses that don't fit into the other two categories. Total revenue minus total expenses gives the net income (or loss) for the accounting period. Figure 9.3 shows how long it takes small companies to become profitable.

The Statement of Cash Flows

statement of cash flow—*a financial statement showing the changes in a company's working capital from the beginning of the year by listing both the sources and the uses of those funds.*

The **statement of cash flows** shows the changes in the firm's working capital from the beginning of the year by listing both the sources of funds and the uses of these funds. Many small businesses never need to prepare such a statement, but in some cases creditors, investors, new owners, or the IRS may require this information.

To prepare the statement, the owner must assemble the balance sheets and the income statements summarizing the present year's operations. She begins with the company's net income for the period (from the income statement). Then she adds the sources of the com-

FIGURE 9.3
How Long to Profitability?
Source: New England Business Service, Inc., 1999.

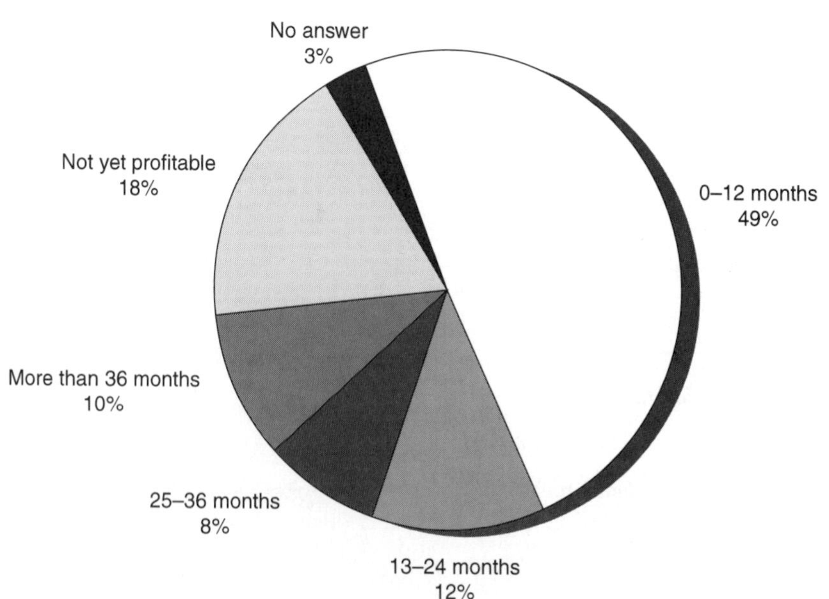

pany's funds—borrowed funds, owner contributions, decreases in accounts receivable, increases in accounts payable, decreases in inventory, depreciation, and any others. Depreciation is listed as a source of funds because it is a noncash expense that has already been deducted as a cost of doing business. But because the owner has already paid for the item being depreciated, its depreciation is a source of funds. Next, the owner subtracts the uses of these funds—plant and equipment purchases, dividends to owners, repayment of debt, increases in accounts receivable, decreases in accounts payable, increases in inventory, and so on. The difference between the total sources and the total uses is the increase or decrease in working capital. By investigating the changes in the firm's working capital and the reasons for them, owners can create a more practical financial action plan for the future of the enterprise.

These financial statements are more than just complex documents used only by accountants and financial officers. When used in conjunction with the analytical tools described in the following sections, they can help entrepreneurs map a firm's financial future and actively plan for profit. Mere preparation of these statements is not enough, however; owners and employees must *understand and use* the information contained in them to make the business more effective and efficient.

CREATING PROJECTED FINANCIAL STATEMENTS

3. Create projected (pro forma) financial statements.

Creating projected financial statements helps the small business owner transform business goals into reality. Budgets answer such questions as: What profit can the business expect to obtain? If the owner's profit objective is *x* dollars, what sales level must she achieve? What fixed and variable expenses can she expect at that level of sales? The answers to these and other questions are critical in formulating a functional financial plan for the small business.

This section will focus on creating projected income statements and balance sheets for the small business. These projected (or pro forma) statements estimate the profitability and the overall financial condition of the business for future months. They are an integral part of convincing potential lenders and investors to provide the financing needed to get the company off the ground. Also, because these statements project a firm's financial position through the end of the forecasted period, they help entrepreneurs plan the route to improved financial strength and healthy business growth.

Because an established business has a history of operating data from which to construct pro forma financial statements, the task is not nearly as difficult as it is for the beginning business. When creating pro forma financial statements for a brand new business, an entrepreneur typically relies on published statistics summarizing the operation of similar-size companies in the same industry. These statistics are available from a number of sources (described later), but this section draws on information found in *Robert Morris Associates Annual Statement Studies,* a compilation of financial data on thousands of companies across hundreds of industries [organized by Standard Industrial Classification (SIC) Code].

Pro Forma Statements for the Small Business

One of the most important tasks confronting the entrepreneur launching a new enterprise is to determine the funds needed to begin operation, as well as those required to keep going through the initial growth period. The amount of money needed to begin a business depends on the type of operation, its location, inventory requirements, sales volume, and other factors. But every new firm must have enough capital to cover all start-up costs, including funds to rent or buy plant, equipment, and tools, as well as pay for advertising, wages, licenses, utilities, and other expenses. In addition, entrepreneurs must maintain a reserve of capital to carry the company until it begins to make a profit. Too often entrepreneurs are overly optimistic in their financial plans and fail to recognize that expenses initially exceed income for most small firms. This period of net losses is normal and may last from just a few months to several years. Owners must be able to meet payrolls, maintain adequate inventory, take advantage of cash discounts, grant customer credit, and meet personal obligations during this time.

THE PRO FORMA INCOME STATEMENT. When creating a projected income statement, an entrepreneur has two options: to develop a sales forecast and work down or set a profit target and work up. Most businesses employ the latter method; the owner targets a profit figure and then determines what sales level he must achieve to reach it. Of course, it is important to compare this sales target against the results of the marketing plan to determine whether it is realistic. Although they are projections, financial forecasts must be based in reality; otherwise, the resulting financial plan is nothing more than a hopeless dream. The next step is to estimate the expenses the business will incur in securing those sales. In any small business, the annual profit must be large enough to produce a return for time the owners spend operating the business, plus a return on their investment in the business.

An entrepreneur who earns less in his own business than he could earn working for someone else must weigh carefully the advantages and disadvantages of choosing the path of entrepreneurship. Why be exposed to all of the risks, sacrifices, and hard work of beginning and operating a small business if the rewards are less than those of remaining in the secure employment of another? Although there are many nonfinancial benefits of owning a business, the net profit after taxes a company generates should be at least as much as an entrepreneur could earn by working for someone else.

An adequate profit must also include a reasonable return on the owner's total investment in the business. The owner's total investment is the amount contributed to the company at its inception plus any retained earnings (profits from previous years funneled back into the operation). If a would-be owner has $70,000 to invest and can invest it in securities and earn 10 percent, she should not consider investing it in a small business that would yield only 3 percent.

An entrepreneur's target income is the sum of a reasonable salary for the time spent running the business and a normal return on the amount invested in the firm. Determining how much this should be is the first step in creating the pro forma income statement.

An entrepreneur then must translate this target profit into a net sales figure for the forecasted period. To calculate net sales from a target profit, the owner needs published statistics for this type of business. Suppose an entrepreneur wants to launch a small retail bookstore and has determined that his target income is $29,000 annually. Statistics gathered from *Robert Morris Associates' Annual Statement Studies* show that the typical bookstore's net profit margin (net profit ÷ net sales) is 9.3 percent. Using this information, he can compute the sales level required to produce a net profit of $29,000:

$$\text{Net profit margin} = \frac{\text{Net profit}}{\text{Net sales (annual)}}$$

$$9.3\% = \frac{\$29{,}000}{\text{Net sales (annual)}}$$

$$\text{Net sales} = \frac{\$29{,}000}{0.093}$$

$$= \$311{,}828$$

Now this entrepreneur knows that to make a net profit of $29,000 (before taxes), he must achieve annual sales of $311,828. To complete the projected income statement, the owner simply applies the appropriate statistics from *Annual Statement Studies* to the annual sales figure. Because the statistics for each income statement item are expressed as percentages of net sales, he merely multiplies the proper percentage by the annual sales figure to obtain the desired value. For example, cost of goods sold usually comprises 61.4 percent of net sales for the typical small bookstore. So the owner of this new bookstore expects his cost of goods sold to be the following:

$$\text{Cost of goods sold} = \$311{,}828 \times 0.614 = \$191{,}462$$

The bookstore's complete projected income statement is shown as follows:

Net sales	(100%)	$311,828
– Cost of goods sold	(61.4%)	191,462
Gross profit margin	(38.6%)	$120,366
– Operating expenses	(29.3%)	91,366
Net profit (before taxes)	(9.3%)	$ 29,000

At this point, the business appears to be a lucrative venture. But remember: This income statement represents a sales goal that the owner may not be able to reach. The next step is to determine whether this required sales volume is reasonable. One useful technique is to break down the required annual sales volume into daily sales figures. Assuming the store will be open six days per week for 52 weeks (312 days), the owner must average $1,039 per day in sales:

$$\text{Average daily sales} = \frac{\$311{,}828}{312 \text{ days}}$$
$$= \$999/\text{day}$$

This calculation gives the owner a better perspective of the sales required to yield an annual profit of $29,000.

To determine whether the profit expected from the business will meet or exceed the entrepreneur's target income, the prospective owner should also create an income statement based on a realistic sales estimate. The previous analysis shows an entrepreneur the sales level needed to reach a desired profit. But what happens if sales are lower? Higher? The entrepreneur requires a reliable sales forecast using the market research techniques described in Chapter 6.

Suppose, for example, that after conducting a marketing survey of local customers and talking with nearby business owners, the prospective bookstore operator projects annual sales for the proposed business to be only $285,000. The entrepreneur must take this expected sales figure and develop a pro forma income statement.

Net sales	(100%)	$285,000
– Cost of goods sold	(61.4%)	174,990
Gross profit margin	(38.6%)	$110,010
– Operating expenses	(29.3%)	83,505
Net profit (before taxes)	(9.3%)	$26,505

Based on sales of $285,000, this entrepreneur should expect a net profit (before taxes) of $26,505. If this amount is acceptable as a return on the investment of time and money in the business, he should proceed with his planning.

At this stage in developing the financial plan, the owner should create a more detailed picture of the firm's expected operating expenses. One common method is to use the operating statistics data found in *Dun & Bradstreet's Cost of Doing Business* reports. These booklets document typical selected operating expenses (expressed as a percentage of net sales) for 190 different lines of businesses.

To ensure that no business expenses have been overlooked in the preparation of the business plan, the entrepreneur should list all of the initial expenses he will incur and have an accountant review the list. Figures 9.4 and 9.5 show two useful forms designed to help entrepreneurs estimate both monthly and start-up expenses. Totals derived from this list of expenses should approximate the total expense figures calculated from published statistics. Naturally, an entrepreneur should be more confident in his own list of expenses because it reflects his particular set of circumstances.

THE PRO FORMA BALANCE SHEET. In addition to projecting the small firm's net profit or loss, an entrepreneur must develop a pro forma balance sheet outlining the fledgling firm's assets and liabilities. The owner primarily is concerned about the profitability, but the importance of the business assets is less obvious. In many cases, small companies begin their lives on weak financial footing because entrepreneurs fail to determine their firms' total asset requirements. To prevent this major oversight, an entrepreneur should prepare a projected balance sheet listing every asset the business will need and all the claims against these assets.

ASSETS. Cash is one of the most useful assets the business owns; it is highly liquid and can quickly be converted into other tangible assets. But how much cash should a small business have at its inception? Obviously, there is no single dollar figure that fits the needs of every small firm. One practical rule of thumb, however, suggests that the company's cash balance should cover its operating expenses (less depreciation, a noncash expense) for one inventory turnover period. Using this guideline, the cash balance for the small bookstore is calculated as follows:

Operating expenses = \$83,505 (from projected income statement)
Less: depreciation (0.9% of annual sales[a]) of \$2,565
Equals: cash expenses (annual) = \$80,940

$$\text{Cash requirement} = \frac{\text{Cash expenses}}{\text{Average inventory turnover}}$$

$$= \frac{\$80{,}940}{3.5^{a}}$$

$$= \$23{,}126$$

[a]*From* RMA Annual Statement Studies.

Notice the inverse relationship between the small firm's average turnover ratio and its cash requirement.

Another decision facing the entrepreneur is how much inventory the business should carry. A rough estimate of the inventory requirement can be calculated from the information found on the projected income statement and from published statistics:

$$\text{Cost of goods sold} = \$174{,}990 \text{ (from projected income statement)}$$

$$\text{Average inventory turnover} = \frac{\text{Cost of goods sold}}{\text{Inventory level}} = 3.5 \text{ times/year}$$

Substituting,

$$3.5 \text{ times/year} = \frac{\$174{,}990}{\text{Inventory level}}$$

Solving algebraically,

$$\text{Inventory level} = \$49{,}997$$

This entrepreneur also includes \$1,800 worth of miscellaneous current assets.

FIGURE 9.4
Anticipated Expenses

Source: U.S. Small Business Administration. Checklist for Going into Business, *Small Marketers Aid no. 71, Washington, DC, 1982, pp. 6–7.*

Worksheet No. 2
Estimated Monthly Expenses

Your estimate of monthly expenses based on sales of $_________ per year

Your estimate of how much cash you need to start your business (see column 3)

What to put in column 2 (These figures are typical for one kind of business. You will have to decide how many months to allow for in your business.)

Item	Column 1	Column 2	Column 3
Salary of owner-manager	$	$	2 times column 1
All other salaries and wages			3 times column 1
Rent			3 times column 1
Advertising			3 times column 1
Delivery expense			3 times column 1
Supplies			3 times column 1
Telephone and telegraph			3 times column 1
Other utilities			3 times column 1
Insurance			Payment required by insurance company
Taxes, including Social Security			4 times column 1
Interest			3 times column 1
Maintenance			3 times column 1
Legal and other professional fees			3 times column 1
Miscellaneous			3 times column 1
Starting Costs You Have to Pay Only Once			Leave column 2 blank
Fixtures and equipment			Fill in worksheet 3 and put the total here
Decorating and remodeling			Talk it over with a contractor
Installation of fixtures and equipment			Talk to suppliers from whom you buy these
Starting inventory			Suppliers will probably help you estimate this
Deposits with public utilities			Find out from utilities companies
Legal and other professional fees			Lawyer, accountant, and so on
Licenses and permits			Find out from city offices what you have to have
Advertising and promotion for opening			Estimate what you'll use
Accounts receivable			What you need to buy more stock until credit customers pay
Cash			For unexpected expenses or losses, special purchases, etc.
Other			Make a separate list and enter total
Total Estimated Cash You Need to Start		$	Add up all the numbers in column 2

FIGURE 9.5
Anticipated Expenditures for Fixtures and Equipment

Source: U.S. Small Business Administration, Checklist for Going into Business, *Small Marketers Aid no. 71, Washington, DC, 1982, p. 12.*

Worksheet No. 3
List of Furniture, Fixtures, and Equipment

Leave out or add items to suit your business. Use separate sheets to list exactly what you need for each of the items below.	If you plan to pay cash in full, enter the full amount below and in the last column.	If you are going to pay by installments, fill out the columns below. Enter in the last column your down payment plus at least one installment.			Estimate of the cash you need for furniture, fixtures, and equipment.
		Price	Down Payment	Amount of each installment	
Counters	$	$	$	$	$
Storage shelves, cabinets					
Display stands, shelves, tables					
Cash register					
Safe					
Window display fixtures					
Special lighting					
Outside sign					
Delivery equipment if needed					
Total Furniture, Fixtures, and Equipment (Enter this figure also in worksheet 2 under "Starting Costs You Have to Pay Only Once.")				$	

Entrepreneurs can use the planning forms shown in Figures 9.3 and 9.4 to estimate fixed assets (land, building, equipment, and fixtures). Suppose the estimate of fixed assets is as follows:

Fixtures	$17,500
Office equipment	2,850
Computers/Cash register	3,125
Signs	3,200
Miscellaneous	1,500
Total	$28,175

LIABILITIES. To complete the projected balance sheet, the owner must record all of the small firm's liabilities, the claims against its assets. The bookstore owner was able to finance 50 percent of the inventory and fixtures through suppliers and has a short-term note payable in the amount of $3,750. The only other major claim against the firm's assets is a long-term note payable to the entrepreneur's father-in-law for $30,000.

The final step is to compile all of these items into a projected balance sheet, as shown in Figure 9.6.

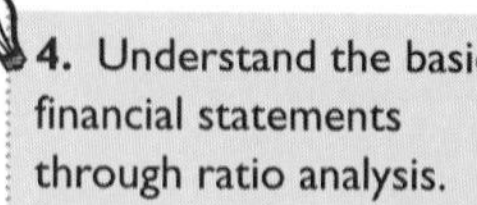
4. Understand the basic financial statements through ratio analysis.

RATIO ANALYSIS

Once an entrepreneur has the business "up and running" with the help of a solid financial plan, the next step is to keep the company moving in the right direction with the help of proper financial controls. Establishing these controls—and using them consistently—is one of the keys to keeping a business vibrant and healthy. "If you don't keep a finger on the pulse of your company's finances, you risk making bad decisions," explains one business writer. "You could be in serious financial trouble and not even realize it."[5]

FIGURE 9.6
Projected Balance Sheet for a Small Bookstore

Assets		Liabilities	
Current Assets		**Current Liabilities**	
Cash	$ 23,126	Accounts Payable	$ 24,998
Inventory	49,997	Note Payable	3,750
Miscellaneous	1,800		
Total Current Assets	$ 74,923	Total Current Liabilities	$ 28,748
Fixed Assets		**Long-Term Liabilities**	
Fixtures	$ 17,500	Note Payable	$ 30,000
Office equipment	2,850		
Computers/Cash register	3,125	Total Liabilities	58,748
Signs	3,200		
Miscellaneous	1,500		
Total Fixed Assets	$ 28,175	**Owner's Equity**	44,350
Total Assets	$103,098	**Total Liabilities and Owner's Equity**	$103,098

A smoothly functioning system of financial controls is essential to achieving business success. Such a system can serve as an early warning device for underlying problems that could destroy a young business. According to one writer:

> A company's financial accounting and reporting systems will provide signals, through comparative analysis, of impending trouble, such as:
>
> - Decreasing sales and falling profit margins.
> - Increasing corporate overhead.
> - Growing inventories and accounts receivable.
>
> These are all signals of declining cash flows from operations, the lifeblood of every business. As cash flows decrease, the squeeze begins:
>
> - Payments to vendors become slower.
> - Maintenance on production equipment lags.
> - Raw material shortages appear.
> - Equipment breakdowns occur.
>
> All of these begin to have a negative impact on productivity. Now the downward spiral has begun in earnest. The key is hearing and focusing on the signals.[6]

What are these signals, and how does an entrepreneur go about hearing and focusing on them? One extremely helpful tool is ratio analysis. **Ratio analysis,** a method of expressing the relationships between any two elements on financial statements, provides a convenient technique for performing financial analysis. When analyzed properly, ratios serve as barometers of a company's financial health. "You owe it to yourself to understand each ratio and what it means to your business," says one accountant. "Ratios point out potential trouble areas so you can correct them before they multiply."[7] Ratio analysis allows a small business manager to determine if her firm is carrying excessive inventory, experiencing heavy operating expenses, overextending credit, taking on too much debt, and managing to pay its bills on time and to answer other questions relating to the efficient operation of the firm. Unfortunately, few business owners actually use ratio analysis; one study discovered

ratio analysis—*a method of expressing the relationship between any two accounting elements that allows business owners to analyze their companies' financial performances.*

that just 2 percent of all entrepreneurs compute financial ratios and use them in managing their businesses![8]

Because they frequently lack an important measure of financial stability—a positive net income—Internet companies have developed their own unique ratios. Because customers ultimately drive the success of every dot-com company, these businesses often express their ratios in terms of the number of customers they attract to their Web sites. Two commonly used ratios in the dot-com world are market capitalization (the total value of a company's outstanding stock) per customer and sales revenue per customer. (To insiders, these ratios are known as "market cap per pair of eyeballs" and "revenue per pair of eyeballs.")

Comparing these ratios for Amazon.com, the Internet company that sells books, CDs, and consumer electronics, and Yahoo!, a pioneering Web portal, shows significant differences:[9]

	Yahoo!	Amazon.com
Market capitalization per customer	$2,038.00	$1,400.00
Sales revenue per customer	$18.99	$160.01
Gross profit per customer	$16.42	$20.79
Minus sales and marketing cost per customer	–$6.11	–$42.47
Minus other operating expenses per customer	–$2.78	–$19.83
Net income (loss) per customer	$7.53	–$41.51

In its bid to become the Wal-Mart of the Web, Amazon.com has become a dominant player in the dot-com world but has yet to show a profit. Yahoo! has been profitable for some time. These ratios give us a clue about the reasons behind these facts.

Clever business owners use financial ratio analysis to identify problems in their businesses while they are still problems, not business-threatening crises. Tracking these ratios over time permits an owner to spot a variety of "red flags" that are indications of these problem areas. This is critical to business success because business owners cannot solve problems they do not know exist!

Atkinson-Baker & Associates

At Atkinson-Baker & Associates, a Los Angeles court-reporting service, every one of the firm's 50 employees is responsible for tracking every day a key financial statistic relating to his or her job. CEO Alan Atkinson-Baker believes that waiting until the month's end to compile financial ratios takes away a company's ability to respond to events as they happen. "Employees have statistics for their jobs, and it helps them see how well they are producing," he says. Because the statistics are linked directly to their jobs, employees quickly learn which numbers to track and how to compile or to calculate them. "Each day everybody reports their statistics," explains Atkinson-Baker. "It all goes into a computer . . . and we keep track of it all." A spreadsheet summarizes the calculations and generates 27 graphs so managers can analyze trends in a meeting the following morning. One rule the company developed from its financial analysis is "Don't spend more today than you brought in yesterday." Atkinson-Baker explains, "You can never run into trouble as long as you stick to that rule." He also notes that effective financial planning would be impossible without timely data. "When we have had problem areas, the statistics have helped us catch them before they became a bigger problem," he says.[10]

Business owners also can use ratio analysis to increase the likelihood of obtaining a bank loan. By analyzing his financial statements with ratios, an owner can anticipate potential problems and identify important strengths in advance. And loan officers *do* use ratios to analyze the financial statements of companies applying for loans. One bank loan officer explains, "We look closely at debt to net worth, debt to net income, and the quick ratio . . . We are primarily interested in trends."[11]

But how many ratios should the small business manager monitor to maintain adequate financial control over the firm? The number of ratios that an owner could calculate is limited only by the number of accounts recorded on a firm's financial statements. However, tracking too many ratios only creates confusion and saps the meaning from an entrepreneur's financial analysis. The secret to successful ratio analysis is *simplicity,* focusing on just enough ratios to provide a clear picture of a company's financial standing.

12 Key Ratios

In keeping with the idea of simplicity, we will describe 12 key ratios that will enable most business owners to monitor their companies' financial positions without becoming bogged down in financial details. This chapter presents explanations of these ratios and examples based on the balance sheet and the income statement for Sam's Appliance Shop shown in Figures 9.1 and 9.2. We will group them into four categories: liquidity ratios, leverage ratios, operating ratios, and profitability ratios.

liquidity ratios—*tell whether a small business will be able to meet its short-term obligations as they come due.*

LIQUIDITY RATIOS. **Liquidity ratios** tell whether the small business will be able to meet its short-term financial obligations as they come due. These ratios can forewarn a business owner of impending cash flow problems. A small company with solid liquidity not only is able to pay its bills on time, but it also has enough cash to take advantage of attractive business opportunities as they arise. The primary measures of liquidity are the current ratio and the quick ratio.

current ratio—*measures a small firm's solvency by indicating its ability to pay current liabilities out of current assets.*

1. Current Ratio. The **current ratio** measures the small firm's solvency by indicating its ability to pay current liabilities (debts) from current assets. It is calculated in the following manner:

$$\text{Current ratio} = \frac{\text{Current assets}}{\text{Current liabilities}}$$

$$= \frac{\$686{,}985}{\$367{,}850}$$

$$= 1.87{:}1$$

Sam's Appliance Shop has $1.87 in current assets for every $1 it has in current liabilities.

Current assets are those that an owner expects to convert into cash in the ordinary business cycle and normally include cash, notes/accounts receivable, inventory, and any other short-term marketable securities. Current liabilities are those short-term obligations that come due within one year and include notes/accounts payable, taxes payable, and accruals.

The current ratio is sometimes called the *working capital ratio* and is the most commonly used measure of short-term solvency. Typically, financial analysts suggest that a small business maintain a current ratio of at least 2:1 (i.e., two dollars of current assets for every one dollar of current liabilities) to maintain a comfortable cushion of working capital. Generally, the higher a company's current ratio, the stronger its financial position; but a high current ratio does not guarantee that a firm's assets are being used in the most profitable manner. For example, a business may be maintaining excessive balances of idle cash or may be overinvesting in inventory.

With its current ratio of 1.87, Sam's Appliance Shop could liquidate its current assets at 53.5 percent (1 ÷ 1.87 = .535) of its book value and still manage to pay its current creditors in full.

quick ratio—*a conservative measure of a firm's liquidity, measuring the extent to which its most liquid assets cover its current liabilities.*

2. Quick Ratio. The current ratio sometimes can be misleading because it does not show the quality of a company's current assets. For instance, a company with a large number of past-due receivables and stale inventory could boast an impressive current ratio and still be on the verge of financial collapse. The **quick ratio** (or the **acid test ratio**) is a more conservative measure of a firm's liquidity because it shows the extent to which its most liquid assets cover its current liabilities. This ratio includes only a company's "quick assets," excluding the most illiquid asset of all—inventory. It is calculated as follows:

$$\text{Quick ratio} = \frac{\text{Quick assets}}{\text{Current liabilities}}$$

$$= \frac{\$686{,}985 - \$455{,}455}{367{,}850}$$

$$= 0.63:1$$

Quick assets include cash, readily marketable securities, and notes/accounts receivables, assets that can be converted into cash immediately if needed. Most small firms determine quick assets by subtracting inventory from current assets because they cannot convert inventory into cash quickly. Also, inventories are the assets on which losses are most likely to occur in case of liquidation.

The quick ratio is a more specific measure of a firm's ability to meet its short-term obligations and is a more rigorous test of its liquidity. It expresses capacity to pay current debts if all sales income ceased immediately. Generally, a quick ratio of 1:1 is considered satisfactory. A ratio of less than 1:1 indicates that the small firm is overly dependent on inventory and on future sales to satisfy short-term debt. A quick ratio of more than 1:1 indicates a greater degree of financial security.

leverage ratios—*measure the financing supplied by a firm's owners against that supplied by its creditors; they are a gauge of the depth of a company's debt.*

LEVERAGE RATIOS. **Leverage ratios** measure the financing supplied by the firm's owners against that supplied by its creditors; they are a gauge of the depth of a company's debt. These ratios show the extent to which an entrepreneur relies on debt capital (rather than equity capital) to finance operating expenses, capital expenditures, and expansion costs. As such, it is a measure of the degree of financial risk in a company. Generally, small businesses with low leverage ratios are less affected by economic downturns, but the returns for these firms are lower during economic booms. Conversely, small firms with high leverage ratios are more vulnerable to economic slides because their debt loads demolish cash flow; however, they have greater potential for large profits.

Over the past decade, U.S. businesses have relied increasingly on debt financing to fuel their growth and expansion. Nonfinancial businesses in the United States have $4.5 trillion in outstanding debt, nearly double the amount in 1995.[12]

LodgeNet Entertainment Corporation

Typical of these debt-laden companies is LodgeNet Entertainment Corporation, which offers pay-per-view movies, video games, cable television, and express checkout to hotel customers. To finance attempts to reach new markets and to take on new partners in strategic alliances, LodgeNet has relied on debt financing so heavily that its debt load has risen twice as fast as its sales over the past six years. (The company's sales are less than $200 million per year, and its total debt is $262 million.) LodgeNet's interest expense eats up $23 million per year, limiting its ability to invest in a new direct Web access service it offers its customers.[13]

debt ratio—*measures the percentage of total assets financed by a company's creditors compared to its owners.*

3. Debt Ratio. A small firm's **debt ratio** measures the percentage of total assets financed by its creditors compared to its owners. The debt ratio is calculated as follows:

$$\text{Debt ratio} = \frac{\text{Total debt (or liabilities)}}{\text{Total assets}}$$

$$= \frac{367{,}850 + 212{,}150}{847{,}655}$$

$$= 0.68:1$$

Total debt includes all current liabilities and any outstanding long-term notes and bonds. Total assets represent the sum of the firm's current assets, fixed assets, and intangible assets. A high debt ratio means that creditors provide a large percentage of the firm's total financing and, therefore, bear most of the company's financial risk. Owners generally prefer higher leverage ratios; otherwise, business funds must come either from the owners' personal assets or from taking on new owners, which means giving up more control over the business. Also, with a greater portion of the firm's assets financed by creditors, the owner is able to generate profits with a smaller personal investment. Creditors, however, typically prefer moderate debt ratios because a lower debt ratio indicates a smaller chance of creditor losses in case of liquidation. To lenders and creditors, high debt ratios mean a higher risk of default.

According to a senior analyst at Dun & Bradstreet's Analytical Services, "If managed properly, debt can be beneficial because it's a great way to have money working for you. You're leveraging your assets, so you're making more money than you're paying out in interest." However, excessive debt can be the downfall of a business. "As we pile up debt on our personal credit cards our lifestyles are squeezed," he says. "The same thing happens to a business. Overpowering debt sinks thousands of businesses each year."[14]

4. Debt to Net Worth Ratio. A small firm's **debt to net worth** (or **debt to equity**) **ratio** also expresses the relationship between the capital contributions from creditors and those from owners and measures how highly leveraged a company is. This ratio shows a company's capital structure by comparing what the business "owes" to what it "owns." It is a measure of the small firm's ability to meet both its creditor and owner obligations in case of liquidation. The debt to net worth ratio is calculated as follows:

debt to net worth ratio— *expresses the relationship between the capital contributions from creditors and those from owners and measures how highly leveraged a company is.*

$$\text{Debt to net worth ratio} = \frac{\text{Total debt (or liabilities)}}{\text{Tangible net worth}}$$

$$= \frac{\$367{,}850 + \$212{,}150}{\$267{,}655 - \$3{,}500}$$

$$= 2.20:1$$

Total debt is the sum of current liabilities and long-term liabilities, and tangible net worth represents the owners' investment in the business (capital + capital stock + earned surplus + retained earnings) less any intangible assets (e.g., goodwill) the firm owns.

The higher this ratio, the more leverage a business is using, and the lower the degree of protection afforded creditors if the business should fail. Also, a higher debt to net worth ratio means that the firm has less capacity to borrow; lenders and creditors see the firm as being "borrowed up." Conversely, a low ratio typically is associated with a higher level of financial security, giving the business greater borrowing potential.

As a firm's debt to net worth ratio approaches 1:1, the creditors' interest in the business approaches that of the owners'. If the ratio is greater than 1:1, creditors' claims exceed those of the owners' and the business may be undercapitalized. In other words, the owner has not supplied an adequate amount of capital, forcing the business to be overextended in terms of debt.

times interest earned ratio—*measures a small firm's ability to make the interest payments on its debt.*

5. Times Interest Earned. The **times interest earned ratio** is a measure of a small firm's ability to make the interest payments on its debt. It tells how many times the company's earnings cover the interest payments on the debt it is carrying. This ratio measures the size of the cushion a company has in covering the interest cost of its debt load. The times interest earned ratio is calculated as follows:

$$\text{Times interest earned} = \frac{\text{Earnings before interest and taxes (or EBIT)}}{\text{Total interest expense}}$$

$$= \frac{\$60{,}629 + \$39{,}850}{\$39{,}850}$$

$$= 2.52{:}1$$

EBIT is the firm's profit *before* deducting interest expense and taxes; the denominator measures the amount the business paid in interest over the accounting period.

A high ratio suggests that the company would have little difficulty meeting the interest payments on its loans; creditors would see this as a sign of safety for future loans. Conversely, a low ratio is an indication that the company is overextended in its debts; earnings will not be able to cover its debt service if this ratio is less than 1. "I look for a [times interest earned] ratio of higher than three-to-one," says one financial analyst, "which indicates that management has considerable breathing room to make its debt payments. When the ratio drops below one-to-one, it clearly indicates management is under tremendous pressure to raise cash. The risk of default or bankruptcy is very high."[15] Many creditors look for a times interest earned ratio of at least 4:1 to 6:1 before pronouncing a company a good credit risk.

Although low to moderate levels of debt can boost a company's financial performance, trouble looms on the horizon for businesses whose debt loads are so heavy that they must starve critical operations, research and development, customer service, and others just to pay interest on the debt. Because their interest payments are so large, highly leveraged companies find that they are restricted when it comes to spending cash, whether on an acquisition, normal operations, or capital spending.

Debt is a powerful financial tool, but companies must handle it carefully—just as a demolitionist handles dynamite. And, like dynamite, too much debt can be deadly. Unfortunately, some companies have pushed their debt loads beyond the safety barrier (see Figure 9.7) and are struggling to survive. Managed carefully, however, debt can boost a company's performance and improve its productivity. Its treatment in the tax code also makes debt a much cheaper means of financing growth than equity. When companies with AA financial ratings borrow at 9.2 percent, the after-tax cost is just 6.6 percent (because interest payments to lenders are tax deductible); equity financing costs more than twice that.

Table 9.1 describes how lenders view liquidity and leverage.

operating ratios—*help an entrepreneur evaluate a small company's overall performance and indicate how effectively the business employs its resources.*

average inventory turnover ratio—*measures the number of times its average inventory is sold out, or turned over, during an accounting period.*

OPERATING RATIOS. **Operating ratios** help an entrepreneur evaluate a small firm's overall performance and indicate how effectively the business employs its resources. The more effectively its resources are used, the less capital a small business will require. These five operating ratios are designed to help an entrepreneur spot those areas she must improve if her business is to remain competitive.

6. Average Inventory Turnover. A small firm's **average inventory turnover ratio** measures the number of times its average inventory is sold out, or turned over, during the accounting period. This ratio tells the owner whether or not the firm's inventory is being

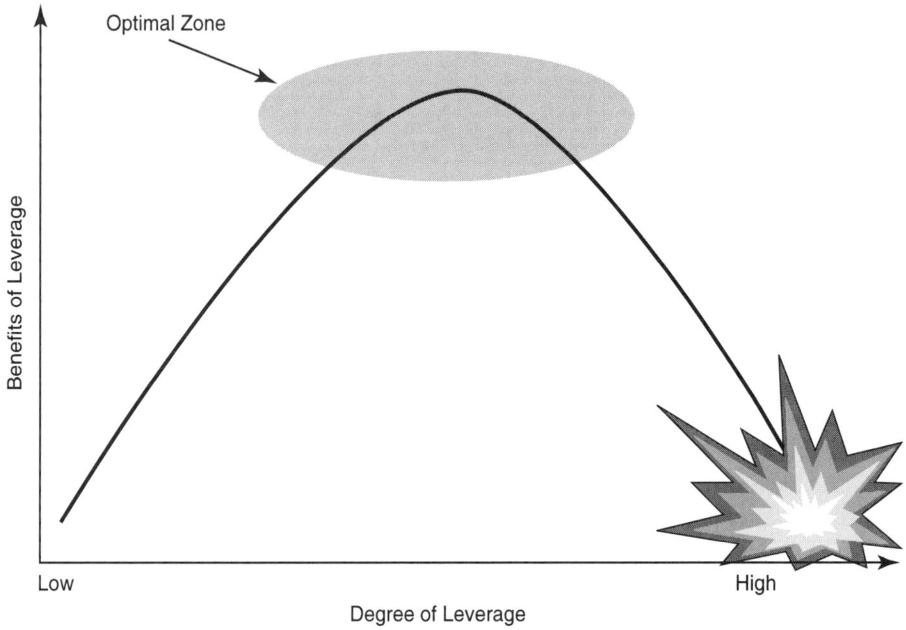

FIGURE 9.7
The Right Amount of Debt Is a Balancing Act

TABLE 9.1
How Lenders View Liquidity and Leverage

Source: Adapted from David H. Bangs, Jr., Financial Troubleshooting *(Dover, NH: Upstart Publishing Company, 1992), p. 124.*

	Liquidity	Leverage
Low	If chronic, this is often evidence of mismanagement. It is a sign that the owner has not planned for the company's working capital needs. In most businesses characterized by low liquidity, there is usually no financial plan. This situation is often associated with last-minute or "Friday night" financing.	This is a very conservative position. With this kind of leverage, lenders are likely to lend money to satisfy a company's capital needs. Owners in this position should have no trouble borrowing money.
Average	This is an indication of good management. The company is using its current assets wisely and productively. Although they may not be impressed, lenders feel comfortable making loans to companies with adequate liquidity.	If a company's leverage is comparable to that of other businesses of similar size in the same industry, lenders are comfortable making loans. The company is not overburdened with debt and is demonstrating its ability to use its resources to grow.
High	Some lenders look for this because it indicates a most conservative company. However, companies that constantly operate this way usually are forgoing growth opportunities because they are not making the most of their assets.	Businesses that carry excessive levels of debt scare most lenders off. Companies in this position normally will have a difficult time borrowing money unless they can show lenders good reasons for making loans. Owners of these companies must be prepared to sell lenders on their ability to repay.

managed properly. It apprises the owner of whether the business inventory is understocked, overstocked, or obsolete. The average inventory turnover ratio is calculated as follows:

$$\text{Average inventory turnover ratio} = \frac{\text{Cost of goods sold}}{\text{Average inventory}}$$

$$= \frac{\$1,290,117}{(\$805,745 + \$455,455) \div 2}$$

$$= 2.05 \text{ times/year}$$

Average inventory is the sum of the value of the firm's inventory at the beginning of the accounting period and its value at the end of the accounting period, divided by 2.

This ratio tells the owner how fast the merchandise is moving through the business and helps her balance the company's inventory on the fine line between oversupply and undersupply. To determine the average number of days units remain in inventory, the owner can divide the average inventory turnover ratio into the number of days in the accounting period (e.g., 365 ÷ average inventory turnover ratio). The result is called *days' inventory* (or *average age of inventory*). Auto dealerships often use the average age of inventory as a measure of performance.

An above-average inventory turnover indicates that the small business has a healthy, salable, and liquid inventory and a supply of quality merchandise supported by sound pricing policies. A below-average inventory turnover suggests an illiquid inventory characterized by obsolescence, overstocking, stale merchandise, and poor purchasing procedures.

Businesses that turn their inventories more rapidly require a smaller inventory investment to produce a particular sales volume. That means that these companies tie up less cash in inventory that idly sits on shelves. For instance, if Sam's could turn its inventory *four* times each year instead of just *two*, the company would require an average inventory of just $322,529 instead of the current level of $630,600 to generate sales of $1,870,841. Increasing the number of inventory turns would free up more than $308,000 in cash currently tied up in excess inventory! Sam's would benefit from improved cash flow and higher profits.

The inventory turnover ratio can be misleading, however. For example, an excessively high ratio could mean the firm has a shortage of inventory and is experiencing stockouts. Similarly, a low ratio could be the result of planned inventory stockpiling to meet seasonal peak demand. Another problem is that the ratio is based on an inventory balance calculated from two days out of the entire accounting period. Thus, inventory fluctuations due to seasonal demand patterns are ignored, which may bias the resulting ratio. There is no universal, ideal inventory turnover ratio. Financial analysts suggest that a favorable turnover ratio depends on the type of business, its size, its profitability, its method of inventory valuation, and other relevant factors.

average collection period ratio—*measures the number of days it takes to collect accounts receivable.*

7. Average Collection Period. The small firm's **average collection period ratio** (or **days sales outstanding, DSO**) tells the average number of days it takes to collect accounts receivable. To compute the average collection period ratio, you must first calculate the firm's receivables turnover. Given that Sam's *credit* sales for the year were $1,309,589, then the company's receivables turnover ratio would be as follows:

$$\text{Receivables turnover ratio} = \frac{\text{Credit sales}}{\text{Accounts receivable}}$$

$$= \frac{\$1,309,589}{\$179,225}$$

$$= 7.31 \text{ times/year}$$

This ratio measures the number of times the firm's accounts receivable turn over during the accounting period. Sam's Appliance Shop turns over its receivables 7.31 times per year. The higher the firm's receivables turnover ratio, the shorter the time lag between the sale and the cash collection.

Use the following to calculate the firm's average collection period ratio:

$$\text{Average collection period ratio} = \frac{\text{Days in accounting period}}{\text{Receivables turnover ratio}}$$

$$= \frac{365 \text{ days}}{7.31 \text{ times/year}}$$

$$= 50.0 \text{ days}$$

Sam's Appliance Shop's accounts receivable are outstanding for an average of 50 days. Typically, the higher a firm's average collection period ratio, the greater its chance of incurring bad debt losses.

One of the most useful applications of the collection period ratio is to compare it to the industry average and to the firm's credit terms. Such a comparison will indicate the degree of the small company's control over its credit sales and collection techniques. One rule of thumb suggests that the firm's collection period ratio should be no more than one-third greater than its credit terms. For example, if a small company's credit terms are net 30, its average collection period ratio should be no more than 45 days. A ratio greater than 45 days would indicate poor collection procedures.

Slow payers represent a great risk to many small businesses. Many entrepreneurs proudly point to rapidly rising sales only to find that they must borrow money to keep their companies going because their credit customers are paying their bills in 45, 60, or even 90 days instead of the desired 30. Slow receivables are a real danger because they usually lead to a cash crisis that threatens a company's survival. Table 9.2 shows how to calculate the savings associated with lowering a company's average collection period ratio.

8. Average Payable Period. The converse of the average collection period, the **average payable period ratio,** tells the average number of days it takes a company to pay its accounts payable. Like the average collection period, it is measured in days. To compute this ratio, first calculate the payables turnover ratio. Sam's payables turnover ratio is as follows:

average payable period ratio—*measures the number of days it takes a company to pay its accounts payable.*

$$\text{Payables turnover} = \frac{\text{Purchases}}{\text{Accounts payable}}$$

$$= \frac{\$939{,}827}{\$152{,}580}$$

$$= 6.16 \text{ times/year}$$

To find the average payable period, use the following computation:

$$\text{Average payable period} = \frac{\text{Days in accounting period}}{\text{Payables turnover ratio}}$$

$$= \frac{365 \text{ days}}{6.16 \text{ times/year}}$$

$$= 59.3 \text{ days}$$

Sam's Appliance Shop takes an average of 59 days to pay its accounts with suppliers.

TABLE 9.2
How Lowering Your Average Collection Period Ratio Can Save You Money

Source: "Days Saved, Thousands Earned," Inc., November 1995, p. 98.

Too often, entrepreneurs fail to recognize the importance of collecting their accounts receivable on time. After all, collecting accounts is not as glamorous or as much fun as generating sales. Lowering a company's average collection period ratio, however, *can* produce tangible—and often significant—savings. The following formula shows how to convert an improvement in a company's average collection period ratio into dollar savings:

$$\text{Annual savings} = \frac{(\text{Credit sales} \times \text{annual interest rate} \times \text{number of days average collection period is lowered})}{365}$$

where

credit sales = company's annual credit sales in $

annual interest rate = the interest rate at which the company borrows money

number of days average collection period is lowered = the difference between the previous year's average collection period ratio and the current one

Example:

Sam's Appliance Shop's average collection period ratio is 50 days. Suppose that the previous year's average collection period ratio was 56 days, a six-day improvement. The company's credit sales for the most recent year were $1,309,589. If Sam borrows money at 10.25%, this six-day improvement has generated savings for Sam's Appliance Shop of

$$\text{Savings} = \frac{\$1{,}309{,}589 \times 10.25\% \times 6 \text{ days}}{365 \text{ days}} = \$2{,}207$$

By collecting his accounts receivable just six days faster on the average, Sam has saved his business more than $2,200! Of course, if a company's average collection period ratio rises, the same calculation will tell the owner how much that costs.

An excessively high average payables period ratio indicates the presence of a significant amount of past-due accounts payable. Although sound cash management calls for a business owner to keep her cash as long as possible, slowing payables too drastically can severely damage the company's credit rating. Ideally, the average payable period would match (or exceed) the time it takes to convert inventory into sales and ultimately into cash. In this case, the company's vendors would be financing its inventory and its credit sales.

One of the most meaningful comparisons for this ratio is against the credit terms suppliers offer (or an average of the credit terms offered). If the average payable ratio slips beyond vendors' credit terms, it is an indication that the company is suffering from a sloppy accounts payable procedure or from cash shortages and its credit rating is in danger. If this ratio is significantly lower than vendors' credit terms, it may be a sign that the firm is not using its cash most effectively.

net sales to total assets ratio—*measures a company's ability to generate sales in relation to its asset base.*

9. Net Sales to Total Assets. A small company's **net sales to total assets ratio** (also called the **total assets turnover ratio**) is a general measure of its ability to generate sales in relation to its assets. It describes how productively the firm employs its assets to produce sales revenue. The total assets turnover ratio is calculated as follows:

$$\text{Total assets turnover ratio} = \frac{\text{Net sales}}{\text{Net total assets}}$$

$$= \frac{\$1{,}870{,}841}{\$847{,}655}$$

$$= 2.21{:}1$$

YOU BE THE CONSULTANT . . .

Yes, But Are Those Profits Real?

It was so easy to do . . . and so easy to justify. Then things began to get out of control.

After years at the helm of the high-flying Comptronix Corporation, an Alabama electronics company, William Hebding admitted that he and two other top officers had improperly inflated the company's profits by engaging in fraudulent accounting practices. The managers disclosed that they had recorded as capital assets some expenses such as salaries and start-up costs and had overstated Comptronix's inventory holdings to decrease its cost of goods sold. The reason was to shore up a weakening balance sheet and to give the illusion that profits were holding at the levels to which investors had grown accustomed. After the scandal broke, Mr. Hebding and his two accomplices were quickly fired.

Comptronix's story has become all too common as fierce competitive conditions exert increasing pressure on companies' profits. "When companies are desperate to stay afloat, inventory fraud is the easiest way to produce profits and dress up the balance sheet," says one accounting expert. The tactic is so simple, yet so effective, primarily because detecting fraudulent adjustments to inventory is so difficult, even for auditors at top accounting firms. In a typical audit, accountants take a small sample of the goods and raw materials in stock and compare an actual count with the company's inventory records. One auditor claims that it is extremely difficult, if not impossible, for an outside auditor to spot inventory fraud "if top management is directing it." One accounting expert reports that inventory fraud has increased fourfold within the past five years.

Companies under pressure to perform, such as those who have gone public recently, are often the perpetrators of such scams, which usually are surprisingly simple. For instance, Kendall Square Research Corporation, a maker of supercomputers, recently acknowledged that it counted as sales numerous computers that it knew customers could not pay for. The company had predicted sales of $60 million, but an investigation showed that sales were only $18.1 million. "There is tremendous pressure on companies such as ours to continue their revenue-growth trend," says the company's new chief financial officer.

Many dot-com companies, feeling the same pressure to perform, are engaging in a common practice known as "earnings management," in which managers modify allowances for warranty costs or returned items or reclassify expenses into other categories. Aware that one quarter of unexpected financial results can ruin a dot-com company's prospects for future growth, some managers are tweaking their companies' financial reports. Their goal? To make their companies' financial statements look as good as possible for investors. "We're painting a picture for investors," says one Silicon Valley accountant. "They want to know that it's business as usual."

One common practice among Internet companies involves recognizing barter revenue. For instance, a Web-based company might barter $10,000 worth of banner ads to another company for $10,000 worth of computer equipment. It would report the $10,000 as revenue and then amortize the cost of the equipment over a span of several years. Recorded this way, the transaction artificially inflates the company's sales revenue and makes its income statement look stronger than it really is.

Another frequent technique used by dot-com businesses is categorizing the costs of storing, packaging, and shipping inventory (known as "fulfillment costs") under "sales and marketing expenses" rather than recording them as part of "cost of goods sold" on the income statement. Shifting these fulfillment costs to a company's cost of goods sold would lower *significantly* its gross profit margin, a number that dot-com investors watch very closely. Even though recording these expenses as part of its cost of goods sold would produce a more accurate picture of a company's financial position, a lower gross profit margin would most likely dampen investors' enthusiasm for its stock. "Companies are under a lot of pressure to keep current [financial statements] looking good," rationalizes one accountant. "The business may be trending in one direction or the other, but we have to always make it look good. Companies work hard to protect [their] margins. It's all about painting the picture."

1. Refer to the balance sheet and income statement for Sam's Appliance Shop (Figures 9.1 and 9.2) and do some "creative accounting" of your own. Inflate the inventory values by a significant amount and see what happens to net worth and profits.
2. Recalculate the 12 key ratios for Sam's Appliance Shop. Compare the results. Which version would look better to a banker? Why?
3. Who loses when the managers of a company commit inventory fraud? What are the ethical implications of such practices?
4. What dangers does the practice of "earnings management" hold for dot-com companies and their investors?

Sources: Adapted from David Raymond, "The Number Runners," *Forbes ASAP,* April 3, 2000, pp. 128–129; Tim Kendall, "Show Me the Money," *Forbes ASAP,* November 29, 1999, p. 36; Lee Berton, "Tech Concerns Fudge Figures to Buoy Stocks," *Wall Street Journal,* May 19, 1994, pp. Bl, B2; Lee Berton, "Convenient Fiction," *Wall Street Journal,* December 14, 1992, pp. Al, A4; Eileen Buckley, "No Accounting for Internet Accounting," *The Industry Standard,* April 10, 2000, p. 58; Elizabeth MacDonald, "Are Those Revenues for Real?" *Forbes,* May 29, 2000, pp. 108–110.

The denominator of this ratio, net total assets, is the sum of all of the firm's assets (cash, inventory, land, buildings, equipment, tools, everything owned) less depreciation. This ratio is meaningful only when compared to that of similar firms in the same industry category. A total assets turnover ratio below the industry average indicates that a small firm is not generating an adequate sales volume for its asset size.

net sales to working capital ratio—*measures how many dollars in sales a business generates for every dollar of working capital.*

10. Net Sales to Working Capital. The **net sales to working capital ratio** measures how many dollars in sales the business generates for every dollar of working capital (working capital = current assets − current liabilities). Also called the **turnover of working capital ratio,** this proportion tells the owner how efficiently working capital is being used to generate sales. It is calculated as follows:

$$\text{Net sales to working capital ratio} = \frac{\text{Net sales}}{\text{Current assets} - \text{Current liabilities}}$$

$$= \frac{\$1{,}870{,}841}{\$686{,}985 - \$367{,}850}$$

$$= 5.86{:}1$$

An excessively low net sales to working capital ratio indicates that a small firm is not employing its working capital efficiently or profitably. On the other hand, an extremely high ratio points to an inadequate level of working capital to maintain a suitable level of sales, which puts creditors in a more vulnerable position. This ratio is very helpful in maintaining sufficient working capital as the small business grows. It is critical for the small firm to keep a satisfactory level of working capital to nourish its expansion, and the net sales to working capital ratio helps define the level of working capital required to support higher sales volumes.

profitability ratios—*indicate how efficiently a small company is being managed.*

PROFITABILITY RATIOS. **Profitability ratios** indicate how efficiently a small company is being managed. They provide the owner with information about the company's bottom line; in other words, they describe how successfully the firm is using its available resources to generate a profit.

net profit on sales ratio—*measures a company's profit per dollar of sales.*

11. Net Profit on Sales. The **net profit on sales ratio** (also called the **profit margin on sales** or **net profit margin**) measures the firm's profit per dollar of sales. The computed percentage shows the number of cents of each sales dollar remaining after deducting all expenses and income taxes. The profit margin on sales is calculated as follows:

$$\text{Net profit on sales ratio} = \frac{\text{Net profit}}{\text{Net sales}}$$

$$= \frac{\$60{,}629}{\$1{,}870{,}841}$$

$$= 3.24\%$$

Most small business owners believe that a high profit margin on sales is necessary for a successful business operation, but this is a myth. To evaluate this ratio properly, the owner must consider the firm's asset value, its inventory and receivables turnover ratios, and its total capitalization. For example, the typical small supermarket earns an average net profit of only one cent on each dollar of sales, but its inventory may turn over as many as 25

"I suggest a candlelight vigil."

Source: From the Wall Street Journal*–Permission, Cartoon Features Syndicate.*

times a year. If a firm's profit margin on sales is below the industry average, it may be a sign that its prices are relatively low, or that its costs are excessively high, or both.

If a company's net profit on sales ratio is excessively low, the owner should check the gross profit margin (net sales minus cost of goods sold expressed as a percentage of net sales). Of course, a reasonable gross profit margin varies from industry to industry. For instance, a service company may have a gross profit margin of 75 percent, while a manufacturer's may be 35 percent. The key is to know what a reasonable gross profit margin is for your particular business. If this margin slips too low, it puts a company's future in immediate jeopardy.

Monitoring this ratio is especially important for fast-growing companies in which sales are climbing rapidly. Unbridled growth can cause expenses to rise faster than sales, eroding a company's net profit margin. Success can be deceptive: Sales are rising, but profits are shrinking.

Example

Roger Scherping says that is exactly what happened in the privately owned electrical contracting company where he was chief financial officer. In just two years, sales skyrocketed from just $3 million to more than $22 million, yet the company's net income plunged to nearly zero during this rapid growth as everyone in the company lost their focus on the bottom line. Company owners quickly regained control and got the business back on track. It is critical for entrepreneurs to establish "profit growth, not sales growth as their companies' primary goal," says Scherping.[16]

12. Net Profit to Equity. The **net profit to equity ratio** (or **return on net worth ratio**) measures the owners' rate of return on investment. Because it reports the percentage of the owners' investment in the business that is being returned through profits annually, it is one of the most important indicators of a firm's profitability or a management's efficiency. The net profit to equity ratio is computed as follows on page 323:

net profit to equity ratio— *measures the owners' rate of return on investment.*

YOU BE THE CONSULTANT . . .

All Is Not Paradise in Eden's Garden: Part I

Joe and Kaitlin Eden, co-owners of Eden's Garden, a small nursery, lawn, and garden supply business, have just received their year-end financial statements from their accountant. At their last meeting with their accountant, Shelley Edison, three months ago, the Edens had mentioned that they seemed to be having trouble paying their bills on time. "Some of our suppliers have threatened to put us on credit hold," said Joe.

"I think you need to sit down with me very soon and let me show you how to analyze your financial statements so you can see what's happening in your business," Edison told them at that meeting. Unfortunately, that was the beginning of Eden's Garden's busy season, and the Edens were so busy running the company that they never got around to setting a time to meet with Shelley.

"Now that business has slowed down a little, perhaps we should call Shelley and see what she can do to help us understand what our financial statements are trying to tell us," said Kaitlin.

"Right. Before it's too late to do anything about it . . ." said Joe, pulling out the following financial statements.

1. Assume the role of Shelley Edison. Using the financial statements for Eden's Garden, calculate the 12 ratios covered in this chapter.
2. Do you see any ratios that look suspicious on the surface? Explain.

Balance Sheet, Eden's Garden

Current Assets		Assets
Cash		$ 6,457
Accounts Receivable	$29,152	
Less Allowance for Doubtful Accounts	3,200	25,952
Inventory		88,157
Supplies		7,514
Prepaid Expenses		1,856
Total Current Assets		$129,936
Fixed Assets		
Land		$ 59,150
Buildings	$51,027	
Less Accumulated Depreciation	2,061	48,966
Autos	24,671	
Less Accumulated Depreciation	12,300	12,371
Equipment	22,375	
Less Accumulated Depreciation	1,250	21,125
Furniture and Fixtures	10,295	
Less Accumulated Depreciation	1,000	9,295
Total Fixed Assets		$150,907
Intangibles (Goodwill)		0
Total Assets		$280,843

Current Liabilities	Liabilities
Accounts Payable	$ 54,258
Notes Payable	20,150
Credit Line Payable	8,118
Accrued Wages/Salaries Payable	1,344
Accrued Interest Payable	1,785
Accrued Taxes Payable	1,967
Total Current Liabilities	$ 87,622
Long-Term Liabilities	
Mortgage	72,846
Note Payable	47,000
Total Long-Term Liabilities	$119,846
	Owner's Equity
Sam Lloyd, Capital	$ 73,375
Total Liabilities and Owner's Equity	$280,843

Income Statement, Eden's Garden

Net Sales Revenue[a]		$689,247
Cost of Goods Sold		
Beginning Inventory, 1/1/XX	$78,271	
+ Purchases	403,569	
Goods Available for Sale	481,840	
– Ending Inventory, 12/31/XX	86,157	
Cost of Goods Sold		$395,683
Gross Profit		$293,564
Operating Expenses		
Advertising	$22,150	
Insurance	9,187	
Depreciation		
Building	26,705	
Autos	7,895	
Equipment	11,200	
Salaries	116,541	
Uniforms	4,018	
Repairs and Maintenance	9,097	
Travel	2,658	
Entertainment	2,798	
Total Operating Expenses		$212,249

General Expenses		
Utilities	$7,987	
Telephone	2,753	
Professional Fees	3,000	
Postage	1,892	
Payroll Taxes	11,589	
Total General Expenses		$27,221
Other Expenses		
Interest Expense	$21,978	
Bad Check Expense	679	
Miscellaneous Expense	1,248	
Total Other Expenses		$23,905
Total Expenses		$263,375
Net Income		$30,189

[a] Credit sales represented $289,484 of this total.

$$\text{Net profit to equity} = \frac{\text{Net profit}}{\text{Owners' equity (or net worth)}} = \frac{\$60{,}629}{\$267{,}655} = 22.65\%$$

This ratio compares profits earned during the accounting period with the amount the owner has invested in the business during that time. If this interest rate on the owners' investment is excessively low, some of this capital might be better employed elsewhere.

INTERPRETING BUSINESS RATIOS

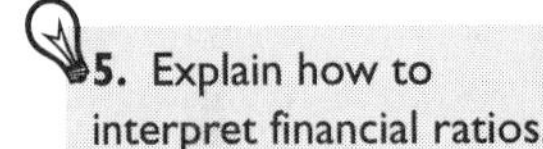

5. Explain how to interpret financial ratios.

Ratios are useful yardsticks in measuring the small firm's performance and can point out potential problems before they develop into serious crises. But calculating these ratios is not enough to ensure proper financial control. In addition to knowing how to calculate these ratios, entrepreneurs must understand how to interpret them and apply them to managing their businesses more effectively and efficiently.

Hi-Shear Technology Inc.

For instance, with the help of financial ratios, Linda Nespole, a top manager at Hi-Shear Technology, an aerospace subcontracting company in Torrance, California, noticed the company's performance beginning to slip. Given the signals her analysis revealed, she immediately devised a strategy to restore Hi-Shear's financial position, focusing first on cost-cutting measures. Simply charting the company's major costs led Nespole to discover leaking water pipes and inefficient lighting that were driving up costs unnecessarily. Some basic repairs lowered utility costs significantly, and a new, more efficient lighting system paid for itself in just six months. Nespole's cost-saving attitude took hold throughout the entire company, and soon all 125 employees were finding ways to keep costs down—from switching long-distance carriers to cutting the cost of its 401(k) retirement plan by 30 percent.[17]

Not every business measures its success with the same ratios. In fact, key performance ratios vary dramatically across industries and even within different segments of the same industry. Every manager must know and understand which ratios are most crucial to his company's success and focus on monitoring and controlling those. Sometimes business owners develop ratios that are unique to their own operations to help them achieve success. One entrepreneur calls them "critical numbers."[18]

AutoLend Group Inc.

For instance, Steve Simon, CEO of AutoLend Group Inc., a used-car financing company, focuses on just a few critical numbers to determine his company's exact financial position every day. He uses several ratios that describe the relationships among his company's cash balance, its total loans outstanding, and its loans in delinquency.

Simon and his top financial staffers developed a spreadsheet to monitor the "key numbers we really needed to keep closest track of," he says. The result is Autolend's "Daily Flash Report," which is available to everyone by 7 A.M. each day! "The relationship between numbers is just as important as the results themselves," says Simon. "We've got very clear goals about how these numbers need to relate for us to achieve profitable growth."[19]

Another valuable way to utilize ratios is to compare them with those of similar businesses in the same industry. By comparing the company's financial statistics to industry averages, the owner is able to locate problem areas and maintain adequate financial controls. "By themselves, these numbers are not that meaningful," says one financial expert of ratios, "but when you compare them to [those of] other businesses in your industry, they suddenly come alive because they put your operation in perspective."[20]

The principle behind calculating these ratios and comparing them to industry norms is the same as that of most medical tests in the health care profession. Just as a healthy person's blood pressure and cholesterol levels should fall within a range of normal values, so should a financially healthy company's ratios. A company cannot deviate too far from these normal values and remain successful for long. When deviations from "normal" do occur (and they will), a business owner should focus on determining the cause of the deviations (see Table 9.3). In some cases, such deviations are the result of sound business decisions, such as taking on inventory in preparation for the busy season, investing heavily in new technology, and others. In other instances, however, ratios that are out of the normal range for a particular type of business are indicators of what could become serious problems for a company. Properly used, ratio analysis can help owners identify potential problem areas in their businesses early on—*before* they become crises that threaten their very survival.

Several organizations regularly compile and publish operating statistics, including key ratios, that summarize the financial performance of many businesses across a wide range of industries. The local library should subscribe to most of these publications:

Robert Morris Associates. Established in 1914, Robert Morris Associates publishes its *Annual Statement Studies,* showing ratios and other financial data for over 350 different industrial, wholesale, retail, and service categories.

Dun & Bradstreet, Inc. Since 1932, Dun & Bradstreet has published *Key Business Ratios,* which covers 22 retail, 32 wholesale, and 71 industrial business categories. Dun & Bradstreet also publishes *Cost of Doing Business,* a series of operating ratios compiled from the Internal Revenue Service's *Statistics of Income.*

Vest Pocket Guide to Financial Ratios. This handy guide, published by Prentice Hall, gives key ratios and financial data for a wide variety of industries.

TABLE 9.3

Putting Your Ratios to the Test

Source: Adapted from George M. Dawson, "Divided We Stand," Business Start-Ups, *May 2000, p. 34.*

When comparing your company's ratios to your industry's standards, ask the following questions:

1. Is there a significant difference in my company's ratio and the industry average?
2. If so, is this a *meaningful* difference?
3. Is the difference good or bad?
4. What are the possible causes of this difference? What is the most likely cause?
5. Does this cause require that I take action?
6. What action should I take to correct the problem?

Industry Spotlight. Published by Schonfeld & Associates, this publication, which can be customized for any one of more than 150 industries, contains financial statement data and key ratios from more than 95,000 tax returns. *Industry Spotlight* also provides detailed financial information for both profitable companies and those with losses.

Trade Associations. Virtually every type of business is represented by a national trade association, which publishes detailed financial data compiled from its membership. For example, owners of small supermarkets could contact the National Association of Retail Grocers or check the *Progressive Grocer,* its trade publication, for financial statistics relevant to their operations.

Government Agencies. Several government agencies (the Federal Trade Commission, Interstate Commerce Commission, Department of Commerce, Department of Agriculture, and Securities and Exchange Commission) offer a great deal of financial operating data on a variety of industries, although the categories are more general. In addition, the Internal Revenue Service (IRS) annually publishes *Statistics of Income,* which includes income statement and balance sheet statistics compiled from income tax returns. The IRS also publishes the *Census of Business,* which gives a limited amount of ratio information.

What Do All of These Numbers Mean?

Learning to interpret financial ratios just takes a little practice! This section will show you how it's done by comparing the ratios from the operating data already computed for Sam's to those taken from *Robert Morris Associates' Annual Statement Studies.* (The industry median is the ratio falling exactly in the middle when sample elements are arranged in ascending or descending order.)

Sam's Appliance Shop	Industry Median

Liquidity Ratios—tell whether or not a small business will be able to meet its maturing obligations as they come due.

1. Current ratio = 1.87:1 — 1.50:1

Sam's Appliance Shop falls short of the rule of thumb of 2:1, but its current ratio is above the industry median by a significant amount. Sam's should have no problem meeting its short-term debts as they come due. By this measure, the company's liquidity is solid.

2. Quick ratio = 0.63:1 — 0.50:1

Again, Sam's is below the rule of thumb of 1:1, but the company passes this test of liquidity when measured against industry standards. Sam's relies on selling inventory to satisfy short-term debt (as do most appliance shops). If sales slump, the result could be liquidity problems for Sam's.

Leverage Ratios—measure the financing supplied by the firm's owners against that supplied by its creditors and serve as a gauge of the depth of a company's debt.

3. Debt ratio = 0.68:1 — 0.64:1

Creditors provide 68 percent of Sam's total assets, very close to the industry median of 64 percent. Although Sam's does not appear to be overburdened with debt, the company might have difficulty borrowing additional money, especially from conservative lenders.

4. Debt to net worth ratio = 2.20:1 — 1.90:1

Sam's Appliance Shop owes creditors $2.20 for every $1.00 the owners have invested in the business (compared to $1.90 in debt to every $1.00 in equity for the typical business). Although this is not an exorbitant amount of debt, many lenders and creditors will see Sam's as "borrowed up." Borrowing capacity is somewhat limited since creditors' claims against the business are more than twice those of the owners.

5. Times interest earned = 2.52:1 — 2.0:1

Sam's earnings are high enough to cover the interest payments on its debt by a factor of 2.52, slightly better than the typical firm in the industry, whose earnings cover its interest payments just two times. Sam's Appliance Shop has a cushion (although a small one) in meeting its interest payments.

Operating Ratios—evaluate the firm's overall performance and show how effectively it is putting its resources to work.

6. Average inventory turnover ratio = 2.05 times/year 4.0 times/year

Inventory is moving through Sam's at a very slow pace, *half* that of the industry median. The company has a problem with slow-moving items in its inventory and, perhaps, too much inventory. Which items are they, and why are they slow moving? Does Sam's need to drop some product lines?

7. Average collection period ratio = 50.0 days 19.3 days

Sam's Appliance Shop collects the average account receivable after 50 days (compared with the industry median of 19 days), more than 2.5 times longer. A more meaningful comparison is against Sam's credit terms; if credit terms are net 30 (or anywhere close to that), Sam's has a dangerous collection problem, one that drains cash and profits and demands *immediate* attention!

8. Average payable period ratio = 59.3 days 43 days

Sam's payables are nearly 40 percent slower than those of the typical firm in the industry. Stretching payables too far could seriously damage the company's credit rating, causing suppliers to cut off future trade credit. This could be a sign of cash flow problems or a sloppy accounts payable procedure. This problem also demands *immediate* attention.

9. Net sales to total assets ratio = 2.21:1 2.7:1

Sam's Appliance Shop is not generating enough sales, given the size of its asset base. This could be the result of a number of factors—improper inventory, inappropriate pricing, poor location, poorly trained sales personnel, and many others. The key is to find the cause . . . *fast*!

10. Net sales to working capital ratio = 5.86:1 10.8:1

Sam's generates just $5.86 in sales for every $1 in working capital, just over half of what the typical firm in the industry does. Given the previous ratio, the message is clear: Sam's simply is not producing an adequate level of sales. Improving the number of inventory turns will boost this ratio; otherwise, Sam's is likely to experience a working capital shortage soon.

Profitability Ratios—measure how efficiently a firm is operating and offer information about its bottom line.

11. Net profit on sales ratio = 3.24% 7.6%

After deducting all expenses, 3.24 cents of each sales dollar remains as profit for Sam's—less than half the industry median. Sam's should check its company's gross profit margin and investigate its operating expenses, checking them against industry standards and looking for those that are out of balance.

12. Net profit to equity ratio = 22.65% 12.6%

Sam's Appliance Shop's owners are earning 22.65 percent on the money they have invested in the business. This yield is nearly twice that of the industry median and, given the previous ratio, is more a result of the owners' relatively low investment in the business than an indication of its superior profitability. Sam is using O.P.M. (other people's money) to generate a profit in his business.

When comparing ratios for their individual businesses to published statistics, small business owners must remember that the comparison is made against averages. The owner must strive to achieve ratios that are at least as good as these average figures. The goal should be to manage the business so that its financial performance is above average. As the owner compares financial performance to those covered in the published statistics, he inevitably will discern differences between them. He should note those items that are substantially out of line from the industry average. However, a ratio that varies from the average does not *necessarily* mean that the small business is in financial jeopardy.

Instead of making drastic changes in financial policy, the owner must explore *why* the figures are out of line.

Petra Group

Greg Smith, CEO of Petra Group, a systems integrator with $1.5 million in annual sales, once gave little thought to comparing his company's financial performance against industry standards. Then Petra Group's sales flattened and Smith's company faced the prospect of losing money for the first time. Smith worked with an accounting firm, using information from Robert Morris Associates and a nonprofit organization that provides similar studies to analyze his company's financial position. Comparing his numbers to industry statistics, Smith quickly saw that his payroll expenses for his 15-person company were too high to allow the company to generate a profit. He also discovered that Petra Group's debt ratio was too high. To restore his company's financial strength, Smith reduced his staff by two and began relying more on temporary employees and independent contractors. He realigned Petra Group's financing, reducing the company's line of credit from $100,000 to just $35,000. The analysis also revealed several strengths for the company. For instance, the company's average collection period was 36.5 days, compared to an industry average of 73 days! Smith continues to use ratio comparisons to make key decisions for his company, and he credits the initial financial analysis with getting his company back on the track to profitability.[21]

In addition to comparing ratios to industry averages, owners should analyze their firms' financial ratios over time. By themselves, these ratios are "snapshots" of the firm's finances at a single instant, but by examining these trends over time, the owner can detect gradual shifts that otherwise might go unnoticed until a financial crisis is looming (see Figure 9.8).

BREAKEVEN ANALYSIS

6. Conduct a breakeven analysis for a small company.

Another key component of every sound financial plan is a breakeven analysis. A small company's **breakeven point** is the level of operation (sales dollars or production quantity) at which it neither earns a profit nor incurs a loss. At this level of activity, sales revenue equals expenses—that is, the firm "breaks even." By analyzing costs and expenses, an entrepreneur can calculate the minimum level of activity required to keep the firm in operation. These techniques can then be refined to project the sales needed to generate the

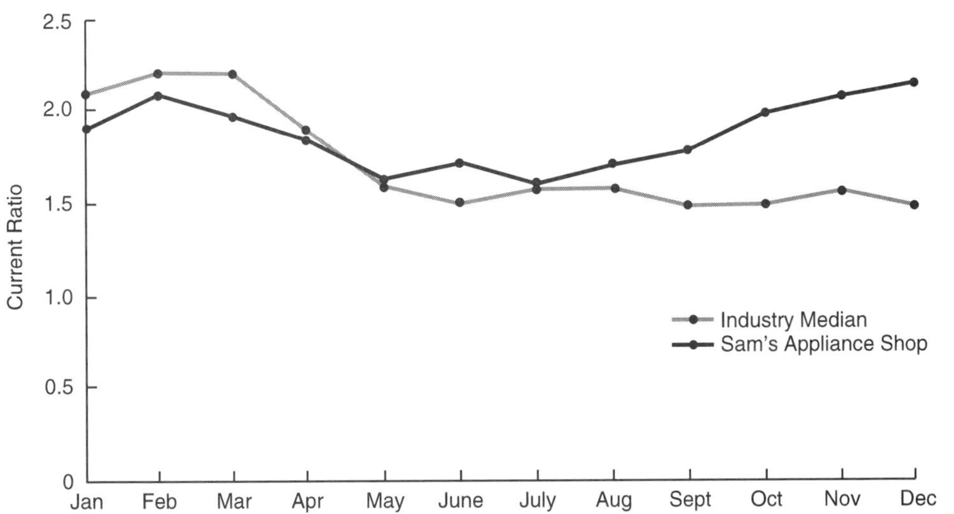

FIGURE 9.8
Trend Analysis of Ratios

breakeven point—*the level of operation (sales dollars or production quantity) at which a company neither earns a profit nor incurs a loss.*

desired profit. Most potential lenders and investors will require the potential owner to prepare a breakeven analysis to assist them in evaluating the earning potential of the new business. In addition to its being a simple, useful screening device for financial institutions, breakeven analysis can also serve as a planning device for the small business owner. It occasionally will show a poorly prepared entrepreneur just how unprofitable a proposed business venture is likely to be.

Calculating the Breakeven Point

fixed expenses—*expenses that do not vary with the volume of sales or production.*

variable expenses—*expenses that vary directly with changes in the volume of sales or production.*

A small business owner can calculate a firm's breakeven point by using a simple mathematical formula. To begin the analysis, the owner must determine fixed costs and variable costs. **Fixed expenses** are those that do not vary with changes in the volume of sales or production (e.g., rent, depreciation expense, interest payments). **Variable expenses,** on the other hand, vary directly with changes in the volume of sales or production (e.g., raw material costs, sales commissions).

Some expenses cannot be neatly categorized as fixed or variable because they contain elements of both. These semivariable expenses change, although not proportionately, with changes in the level of sales or production (electricity would be one example). These costs remain constant up to a particular production or sales volume and then climb as that volume is exceeded. To calculate the breakeven point, the owner must separate these expenses into their fixed and variable components. A number of techniques can be used (which are beyond the scope of this text), but a good cost accounting system can provide the desired results.

Here are the steps an entrepreneur must take to compute the breakeven point using an example of a typical small business, the Magic Shop:

Step 1. Determine the expenses the business can expect to incur. With the help of a budget, an entrepreneur can develop estimates of sales revenue, cost of goods sold, and expenses for the upcoming accounting period. The Magic Shop expects net sales of $950,000 in the upcoming year with a cost of goods sold of $646,000 and total expenses of $236,500.

Step 2. Categorize the expenses estimated in step 1 into fixed expenses and variable expenses. Separate semivariable expenses into their component parts. From the budget, the owner anticipates variable expenses (including the cost of goods sold) of $705,125 and fixed expenses of $177,375.

Step 3. Calculate the ratio of variable expenses to net sales. For the Magic Shop, this percentage is $705,125 ÷ $950,000 = 74 percent. So the Magic Shop uses $0.74 out of every sales dollar to cover variable expenses, leaving $0.26 as a contribution margin to cover fixed costs and make a profit.

Step 4. Compute the breakeven point by inserting this information into the following formula:

$$\text{Breakeven sales (\$)} = \frac{\text{Total fixed cost}}{\text{Contribution margin expressed as a percentage of sales}}$$

YOU BE THE CONSULTANT . . .

All Is Not Paradise in Eden's Garden: Part 2

Remember Joe and Kaitlin Eden, co-owners of Eden's Garden? Assume the role of Shelley Edison, their accountant. You have scheduled a meeting with them tomorrow to review their company's financial statements and to make recommendations about how they can improve their company's financial position. Use the accompanying worksheet to summarize the ratios you calculated earlier in this chapter. Then compare them against the industry averages from *Robert Morris Associates' Annual Statement Studies.*

1. Analyze the comparisons you have made of Eden's Garden's ratios with those from Robert Morris Associates. What red flags do you see?
2. What might be causing the deviations you have observed?
3. What recommendations can you make to the Edens to improve their company's financial performance in the future?

Ratio Comparison			
Ratio	Eden's Garden	Garden Supply Industry Median[a]	
Liquidity Ratios			
Current ratio		1.4	
Quick ratio		0.5	
Leverage Ratios			
Debt ratio		0.6	
Debt to net worth ratio		1.8	
Times interest earned ratio		2.6	
Operating Ratios			
Average inventory turnover ratio		5.6	
Average collection period ratio		9	days
Average payable period ratio		17	days
Net sales to total assets ratio		3.0	
Net sales to working capital ratio		16.6	
Profitability Ratios			
Net profit on sales ratio		7.5%	
Net profit to equity ratio		15.0%	

[a] *Robert Morris Associates Annual Statement Studies.*

For the Magic Shop,

$$\text{Breakeven sales} = \frac{\$177{,}375}{0.26}$$
$$= \$682{,}212$$

The same breakeven point will result from solving the following equation algebraically:

Breakeven sales = Fixed expense + Variable expenses expressed as a percentage of sales

$$S = \$177{,}375 + 0.74$$
$$S = \$682{,}212$$

Thus, the Magic Shop will break even with sales of $682,212. At this point, sales revenue generated will just cover total fixed and variable expense. The Magic Shop will earn no profit and will incur no loss. We can verify this with the following calculations:

Sales at breakeven point	$682,212
– Variable expenses (74% of sales)	–504,837
Contribution margin	177,375
– Fixed expenses	–177,375
Net profit (or net loss)	$ 0

ADDING IN A PROFIT. What if the Magic Shop's owner wants to do *better* than just break even? His analysis can be adjusted to consider such a possibility. Suppose the owner expects a reasonable profit (before taxes) of $80,000. What level of sales must the Magic Shop achieve to generate this? He can calculate this by treating the desired profit as if it were a fixed cost. In other words, he modifies the formula to include the desired net income:

$$\text{Sales (\$)} = \frac{\text{Total fixed expenses} + \text{Desired net income}}{\text{Contribution margin expressed as a percentage of sales}}$$

$$= \frac{\$177{,}375 + \$80{,}000}{\$0.26}$$

$$= \$989{,}904$$

To achieve a net profit of $80,000 (before taxes), the Magic Shop must generate net sales of $989,904.

BREAKEVEN POINT IN UNITS. Some small businesses may prefer to express the breakeven point in units produced or sold instead of in dollars. Manufacturers often find this approach particularly useful. The following formula computes the breakeven point in units:

$$\text{Breakeven volume} = \frac{\text{Total fixed costs}}{\text{Sales price per unit} - \text{Variable cost per unit}}$$

For example, suppose that Trilex Manufacturing Company estimates its fixed costs for producing its line of small appliances at $390,000. The variable costs (including materials, direct labor, and factor overhead) amount to $12.10 per unit, and the selling price per unit is $17.50. So, Trilex computes its contribution margin this way:

$$\text{Contribution margin} = \text{Price per unit} - \text{Variable cost per unit}$$

$$= \$17.50 \text{ per unit} - \$12.10 \text{ per unit}$$

$$= \$5.40 \text{ per unit}$$

So, Trilex's breakeven volume is as follows:

$$\text{Breakeven volume (units)} = \frac{\text{Total fixed costs}}{\text{Per unit contribution margin}}$$

$$= \frac{\$390{,}000}{\$5.40 \text{ per unit}}$$

$$= 72{,}222 \text{ units}$$

To convert this number of units to breakeven sales dollars, Trilex simply multiplies it by the selling price per unit:

$$\text{Breakeven sales} = 72{,}222 \text{ units} \times \$17.50 = \$1{,}263{,}889$$

Trilex could compute the sales required to produce a desired profit by treating the profit as if it were a fixed cost:

$$\text{Sales (units)} = \frac{\text{Total fixed costs} + \text{Desired net income}}{\text{Per unit contribution margin}}$$

For example, if Trilex wanted to earn a $60,000 profit, its required sales would be:

$$\text{Sales (units)} = \frac{390{,}000 + 60{,}000}{5.40}$$

$$= 83{,}333 \text{ units}$$

CONSTRUCTING A BREAKEVEN CHART. The following outlines the procedure for constructing a graph that visually portrays the firm's breakeven point (that point where revenues equal expenses):

Step 1. On the horizontal axis, mark a scale measuring sales volume in dollars (or in units sold or some other measure of volume). The breakeven chart for the Magic Shop shown in Figure 9.9 uses sales volume in dollars because it applies to all types of businesses, departments, and products.

Step 2. On the vertical axis, mark a scale measuring income and expenses in dollars.

Step 3. Draw a fixed expense line intersecting the vertical axis at the proper dollar level parallel to the horizontal axis. The area between this line and the horizontal axis represents the firm's fixed expenses. On the breakeven chart for the Magic Shop shown in Figure 9.9, the fixed expense line is drawn horizontally beginning at $177,375 (point *A*). Because this line is parallel to the horizontal axis, it indicates that fixed expenses remain constant at all levels of activity.

Step 4. Draw a total expense line that slopes upward beginning at the point where the fixed cost line intersects the vertical axis. The precise location of the total expense line is determined by plotting the total cost incurred at a particular sales volume. The total cost for a given sales level is found by the following formula:

$$\text{Total expenses} = \text{Fixed expenses} + \text{Variable expenses expressed as a \% of sales} \times \text{Sales level}$$

Arbitrarily choosing a sales level of $950,000, the Magic Shop's total costs would be as follows:

$$\text{Total expenses} = \$177{,}375 + (0.74 \times \$950{,}000)$$

$$= \$880{,}375$$

FIGURE 9.9
Breakeven Chart,
The Magic Shop

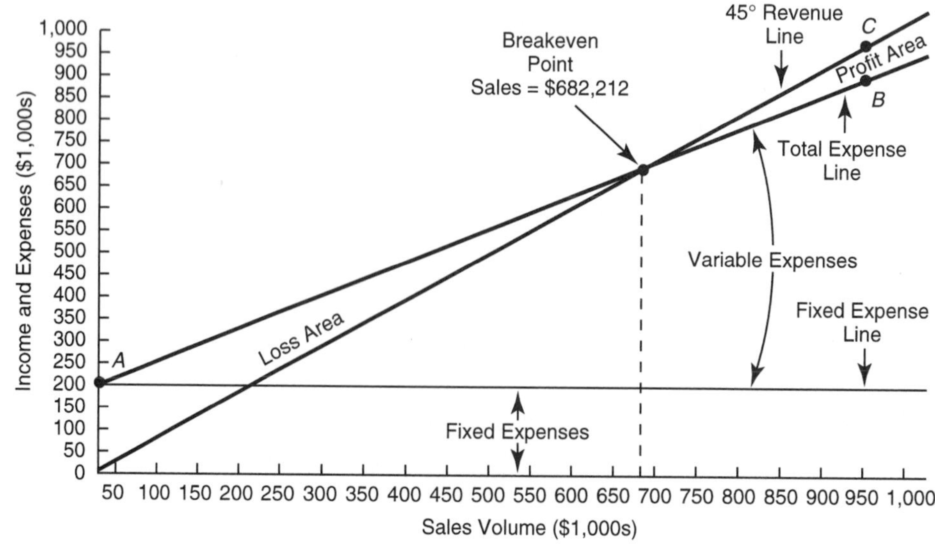

Thus, the Magic Shop's total cost is $880,375 at a net sales level of $950,000 (point *B*). The variable cost line is drawn by connecting points *A* and *B*. The area between the total cost line and the horizontal axis measures the total costs the Magic Shop incurs at various levels of sales. For example, if the Magic Shop's sales are $850,000, its total costs will be $806,375.

Step 5. Beginning at the graph's origin, draw a 45-degree revenue line showing where total sales volume equals total income. For the Magic Shop, point *C* shows that sales = income = $950,000.

Step 6. Locate the breakeven point by finding the intersection of the total expense line and the revenue line. If the Magic Shop operates at a sales volume to the left of the breakeven point, it will incur a loss because the expense line is higher than the revenue line over this range. This is shown by the triangular section labeled *Loss Area.* On the other hand, if the firm operates at a sales volume to the right of the breakeven point, it will earn a profit because the revenue line lies above the expense line over this range. This is shown by the triangular section labeled *Profit Area.*

USING BREAKEVEN ANALYSIS. Breakeven analysis is a useful planning tool for the potential small business owner, especially when approaching potential lenders and investors for funds. It provides an opportunity for integrated analysis of sales volume, expenses, income, and other relevant factors. Breakeven analysis is a simple, preliminary screening device for the entrepreneur faced with the business start-up decision. It is easy to understand and use. With just a few calculations, the small business owner can determine the effects of various financial strategies on the business operation. It is a helpful tool for evaluating the impact of changes in investments and expenditures.

The Mirage

For instance, before Steve Wynn opened the $630 million Mirage, an opulent casino-hotel complex in Las Vegas, a cost revenue analysis showed that the complex needed revenues of $365 million a year—$1 million a day—just to break even! Although many people doubted the casino-hotel's ability to generate that level of revenue, the Mirage has done so consistently. In its first year of operation, the Mirage brought in an average of $1.97 million each day![22]

Although few small companies have breakeven points as high as the Mirage's (much to the relief of entrepreneurs!), the breakeven point can be just as useful. Greg Smith, for instance, knows that Petra Group's breakeven point is $23,000 per week, and he compares sales to that figure every week.[23]

Breakeven analysis does have certain limitations. It is too simple to use as a final screening device because it ignores the importance of cash flows. Also, the accuracy of the analysis depends on the accuracy of the revenue and expense estimates. Finally, the assumptions pertaining to breakeven analysis may not be realistic for some businesses. Breakeven calculations assume the following: Fixed expenses remain constant for all levels of sales volume; variable expenses change in direct proportion to changes in sales volume; and changes in sales volume have no effect on unit sales price. Relaxing these assumptions does not render this tool useless, however. For example, the owner could employ nonlinear breakeven analysis using a graphical approach.

YOU BE THE CONSULTANT . . .

Where Do We Break Even?

Anita Dawson is doing some financial planning for her music store. Based on her budget for the upcoming year, Anita is expecting net sales of $495,000. She estimates that cost of goods sold will be $337,000 and that other variable expenses will total $42,750. Using the past year as a guide, Anita anticipates fixed expenses of $78,100.

Anita recalls an earlier meeting with her accountant, who mentioned that her store had already passed the breakeven point eight-and-one-half months into the year. She was pleased but really didn't know how the accountant had come up with that calculation. Now Anita is considering expanding her store into a vacant building next to her existing location and taking on three new product lines. The company's cost structure would change, adding another $66,000 to fixed costs and $22,400 to variable expenses. Anita believes the expansion could generate additional sales of $102,000.

She wonders what she should do.

1. Calculate Anita's breakeven point without the expansion plans. Draw a breakeven chart.
2. Compute the breakeven point assuming that Anita decides to expand.
3. Would you recommend that Anita expand her business? Explain.

CHAPTER SUMMARY

1. Understand the importance of preparing a financial plan.
   - Launching a successful business requires an entrepreneur to create a solid financial plan. Not only is such a plan an important tool in raising the capital needed to get a company off the ground, but it also is an essential ingredient in managing a growing business.
   - Earning a profit does not occur by accident; it takes planning.
2. Describe how to prepare the basic financial statements and use them to manage the small business.
   - Entrepreneurs rely on three basic financial statements to understand the financial conditions of their companies:
     1. *The balance sheet.* Built on the accounting equation assets = liabilities + owner's equity (capital), it provides an estimate of the company's value on a particular date.
     2. *The income statement.* This statement compares the firm's revenues against its expenses to determine its net profit (or loss). It provides information about the company's bottom line.
     3. *The statement of cash flows.* This statement shows the change in the company's working capital over the accounting period by listing the sources and the uses of funds.
3. Create projected (pro forma) financial statements.

- Projected financial statements are a basic component of a sound financial plan. They help the manager plot the company's financial future by setting operating objectives and by analyzing the reasons for variations from targeted results. Also, the small business in search of start-up funds will need these pro forma statements to present to prospective lenders and investors. They also assist in determining the amount of cash, inventory, fixtures, and other assets the business will need to begin operation.

4. Understand the basic financial statements through ratio analysis.
   - The 12 key ratios described in this chapter are divided into four major categories: *liquidity ratios,* which show the small firm's ability to meet its current obligations; *leverage ratios,* which tell how much of the company's financing is provided by owners and how much by creditors; *operating ratios,* which show how effectively the firm uses its resources; and *profitability ratios,* which disclose the company's profitability.
   - Many agencies and organizations regularly publish such statistics. If there is a discrepancy between the small firm's ratios and those of the typical business, the owner should investigate the reason for the difference. A below-average ratio does not necessarily mean that the business is in trouble.
5. Explain how to interpret financial ratios.
   - To benefit from ratio analysis, the small company should compare its ratios to those of other companies in the same line of business and look for trends over time.
   - When business owners detect deviations in their companies' ratios from industry standards, they should determine the cause of the deviations. In some cases, such deviations are the result of sound business decisions; in other instances, however, ratios that are out of the normal range for a particular type of business are indicators of what could become serious problems for a company.
6. Conduct a breakeven analysis for a small company.
   - Business owners should know their firm's breakeven point, the level of operations at which total revenues equal total costs; it is the point at which companies neither earn a profit nor incur a loss. Although just a simple screening device, breakeven analysis is a useful planning and decision-making tool.

DISCUSSION QUESTIONS

1. Why is developing a financial plan so important to an entrepreneur about to launch a business?
2. How should a small business manager use the 12 ratios discussed in this chapter?
3. Outline the key points of the 12 ratios discussed in this chapter. What signals do each give the manager?
4. Describe the method for building a projected income statement and a projected balance sheet for a beginning business.
5. Why are pro forma financial statements important to the financial planning process?
6. How can breakeven analysis help an entrepreneur planning to launch a business?

Beyond the Classroom . . .

1. Ask the owner of a small business to provide your class with copies of the firm's financial statements (current or past).

- Using these statements, compute the 12 key ratios described in this chapter.
- Compare the firm's ratios with those of the typical firm in this line of business.
- Interpret the ratios and make suggestions for operating improvements.
- Prepare a breakeven analysis for the owner.

2. Find a publicly held company of interest to you that provides its financial statements on the Web. You can conduct a Web search using the company's name or you can find lists of companies at the Securities and Exchange Commission's EDGAR database at <**www.sec.gov/cgi-bin/srch-edgar**>. Analyze the company's financial statements by calculating the 12 ratios covered in this chapter and compare these ratios to industry averages found in *Robert Morris Associates Annual Statement Studies* or Dun & Bradstreet's *The Cost of Doing Business* reports.

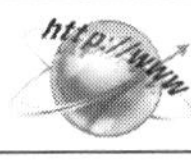

We invite you to visit this book's companion Web site at **www.prenhall.com/Zimmerer.**

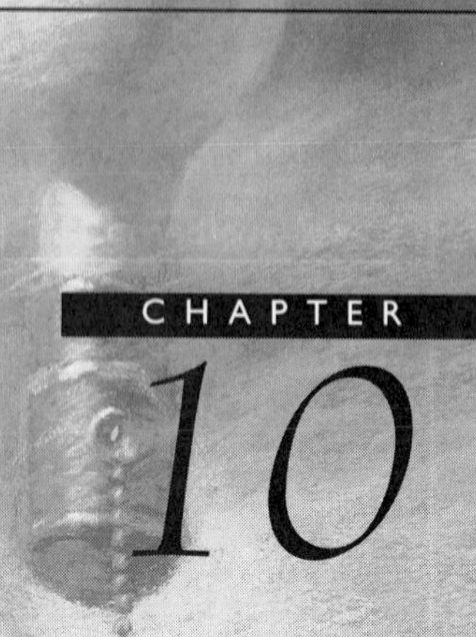

CHAPTER

10 Crafting a Winning Business Plan

The more concrete and complete the plan, the more likely it is to earn the respect of outsiders and their support in necessary financial matters.

—Jesse Werner

The method of the enterprising is to plan with audacity and execute with vigor.

—Christian Bovée

LEARNING OBJECTIVES

Upon completion of this chapter, you will be able to:

1. Explain why every entrepreneur should create a business plan.
2. Describe the elements of a solid business plan.
3. Explain the benefits of preparing a plan.
4. Understand the keys to making an effective business plan presentation.
5. Explain the "five Cs of credit" and why they are important to potential lenders and investors reading business plans.

Too many entrepreneurs dismiss the importance of creating a business plan for their ventures. "I can have the company up and running in the time I'd spend writing a business plan," some say. Or "Our business doesn't need a plan. We're so small, and business plans are only for big companies." Make no mistake, however: *Any* entrepreneur who is in business or is about to launch a business needs a well-conceived business plan to increase the likelihood of success. A large body of research suggest that, whatever their size, companies that engage in business planning outperform those that do not. Unfortunately, studies show that small companies especially are lackadaisical in their approach to developing business plans. A recent survey by the market research company Willard & Shullman Group Ltd. found that only 14 percent of the small companies surveyed had created an annual written business plan. The study also reported that 60 percent of small companies had no written plans of any type![1]

WHY DEVELOP A BUSINESS PLAN?

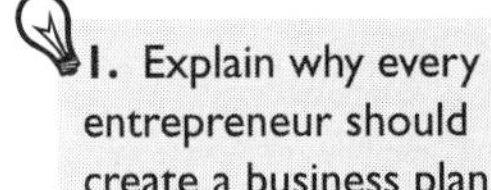
1. Explain why every entrepreneur should create a business plan.

A **business plan** is a written summary of an entrepreneur's proposed business venture, its operational and financial details, its marketing opportunities and strategy, and its managers' skills and abilities. There is no substitute for a well-prepared business plan, and there are no shortcuts to creating one. The plan serves as an entrepreneur's road map on the journey toward building a successful business. It describes the direction the company is taking, what its goals are, where it wants to be, and how it's going to get there. The plan is written proof that the entrepreneur has performed the necessary research and has studied the business opportunity adequately. In short, the business plan is the entrepreneur's best insurance against launching a business destined to fail or mismanaging a potentially successful company.

business plan—*a written summary of an entrepreneur's proposed business venture, its operational and financial details, its marketing opportunities and strategy, and its managers' skills and abilities.*

A business plan serves two essential functions. First and more important, it guides the company's operations by charting its future course and devising a strategy for following it. The plan provides a battery of tools—a mission statement, goals, objectives, budgets, financial forecasts, target markets, strategies—to help entrepreneurs lead a company successfully. It gives managers and employees a sense of direction, but only if everyone is involved in creating, updating, or altering it. As more team members become committed to making the plan work, it takes on special meaning. It gives everyone targets to shoot for, and it provides a yardstick for measuring actual performance against those targets, especially in the crucial and chaotic start-up phase. Creating a plan also forces entrepreneurs to subject their ideas to the test of reality. Can this business idea actually produce a profit?

The second function of the business plan is to attract lenders and investors. Too often small business owners approach potential lenders and investors without having prepared to sell themselves and their business concept. Simply scribbling a few rough figures on a note pad to support a loan application is not enough. Applying for loans or attempting to attract investors without a solid business plan rarely attracts needed capital. Rather, the best way to secure the necessary capital is to prepare a sound business plan. An entrepreneur must pay attention to detail because it is germane to her sales presentation to potential lenders and investors. In most cases, the quality of the firm's business plan weighs heavily in the decision to lend or invest funds. It is also potential lenders' and investors' first impression of the company and its managers. Therefore, the finished product should be highly polished and professional in both form and content.

A business plan must prove to potential lenders and investors that a venture will be able to repay loans and produce an attractive rate of return. Entrepreneur and author Neal Stephenson, who started several high-tech companies before focusing on a writing career, explains his experience writing a business plan:

As I was trying to write my plan, something came into focus for me that should have been obvious from the very beginning. I was proposing to borrow a lot of money from strangers and gamble it on doing something. If it didn't work, these people would lose their money, which is a very sobering prospect. It really shakes you up and makes you think very hard about what it is you are doing. . . . We're using other people's real money, and those people could get hurt.[2]

Stephenson went on to make the process of creating a business plan an important part of his best-selling novel, *Cryptonomicon* (Avon Books, 1999), a multigenerational story that describes the Allied cryptographers who cracked the Axis military codes in World War II and traces the emotional roller-coaster ride of a group of Silicon Valley entrepreneurs creating a start-up.

A business plan is a reflection of its creator. It should demonstrate that the entrepreneur has thought seriously about the venture and what will make it succeed. Preparing a solid plan demonstrates that the entrepreneur has taken the time to commit the idea to paper. Building a plan also forces the entrepreneur to consider both the positive and the negative aspects of the business. A detailed and thoughtfully developed business plan makes a positive first impression on those who read it. In most cases, potential lenders and investors read a business plan before they ever meet with the entrepreneur behind it. Sophisticated investors will not take the time to meet with an entrepreneur whose business plan fails to reflect a serious investment of time and energy. They know that an entrepreneur who lacks the discipline to develop a good business plan likely lacks the discipline to run a business.

An entrepreneur cannot allow others to prepare the business plan for him because outsiders cannot understand the business nor envision the proposed company as well as he can. The entrepreneur is the driving force behind the business idea and is the one who can best convey the vision and the enthusiasm he has for transforming that idea into a successful business. Also, because the entrepreneur will make the presentation to potential lenders and investors, he must understand every detail of the business plan. Otherwise, an entrepreneur cannot present it convincingly and in most cases the financial institution or investor will reject it. Alice Medrich, cofounder of Cocolat, a manufacturer of specialty candies and desserts, recalls her first attempt at presenting her business plan:

First of all, I went to the bank, and I was extremely ill-prepared and so insecure about what I was asking about . . . I was extremely insecure with a banker. I didn't know how to describe what I was doing with any confidence. I did not know how to present a business plan. And, he was condescending to me. Looking back on it, I can understand why: I wasn't prepared . . . We didn't get the loan.[3]

Investors want to feel confident that an entrepreneur has realistically evaluated the risk involved in the new venture and has a strategy for addressing it. They also want to see proof that a business will be profitable and produce a reasonable return on their investment.

Perhaps the best way to understand the need for a business plan is to recognize the validity of the "two-thirds rule," which says that only two-thirds of the entrepreneurs with a sound and viable new business venture will find financial backing. Those who do find financial backing will only get two-thirds of what they initially requested, and it will take them two-thirds longer to get the financing than they anticipated.[4] The most effective strategy for avoiding the two-thirds rule is to build a business plan!

2. Describe the elements of a solid business plan.

THE ELEMENTS OF A BUSINESS PLAN

Smart entrepreneurs recognize that every business plan is unique and must be tailor-made. They avoid the off-the-shelf, "cookie-cutter" approach that produces look-alike plans. The elements of a business plan may be standard, but the way an entrepreneur tells her story should be unique and reflect her personal excitement about the new venture. If this is a first attempt at writing a business plan, it may be very helpful to seek the advice of individuals with experience in this process. Accountants, business professors, attorneys, and consultants with Small Business Development Centers can be excellent sources of advice in creating and refining a plan. (For a list of Small Business Development Center locations, see the Small Business Administration's SBDC Web page at **<www.sba.gov/SBDC>**.) Entrepreneurs also can use business planning software available from several companies to create their plans. Some of the most popular programs include Business Plan Pro* (Palo Alto Software), BizPlan Builder (Jian Tools), PlanMaker (Power Solutions for Business), and Plan Write (Business Resources Software). These planning packages help entrepreneurs organize the material they have researched and gathered, and they provide helpful tips on plan writing and templates for creating financial statements. These planning packages produce professional-looking business plans, but entrepreneurs who use them face one drawback: The plans they produce often look the same, as if they came from the same mold. That can be a turnoff for professional investors, who see hundreds of business plans each year.

Initially, the prospect of writing a business plan may appear to be overwhelming. Many entrepreneurs would rather launch their companies and "see what happens" than invest the necessary time and energy defining and researching their target markets, defining their strategies, and mapping out their finances. After all, building a plan is hard work! However, it is hard work that pays many dividends—not all of them immediately apparent. Entrepreneurs who invest their time and energy building plans are better prepared to face the hostile environment in which their companies will compete than those who do not. Earlier, we said that a business plan is like a road map that guides an entrepreneur on the journey to building a successful business. If you were making a journey to a particular destination through unfamiliar, harsh, and dangerous territory, would you rather ride with someone equipped with a road map and a trip itinerary or with someone who didn't believe in road maps or in planning trips, destinations, and layovers? Although building a business plan does not *guarantee* success, it *does* raise an entrepreneur's chances of succeeding in business.

A business plan typically ranges from 25 to 50 pages in length. Shorter plans usually are too sketchy to be of any value, and those much longer than this run the risk of never getting used or read! This section explains the most common elements of a business plan. However, entrepreneurs must recognize that, like every business venture, every business plan is unique. An entrepreneur should view the following elements as a starting point for building a plan and should modify them as needed to better tell the story of his new venture.

The Executive Summary

To summarize the presentation to each potential financial institution or investors, the entrepreneur should write an executive summary. It should be concise—a maximum of two pages—and should summarize all of the relevant points of the business venture. The executive summary is a synopsis of the entire plan, capturing its essence in a capsulized form. It should explain the basic business model and briefly describe the owners and key employees, target market(s), and financial highlights (e.g., sales projections, dollar amount requested, how the funds will be used, and how and when any loans will be repaid).

The executive summary is a written version of what is known as "the elevator pitch." Imagine yourself on an elevator with a potential lender or investor. Only the two of you are on the elevator, and you have that person's undivided attention for the duration of the ride, but the building is not very tall! To convince the investor that your business is a great

** Business Plan Pro is available at a nominal cost with this textbook.*

investment, you must boil your message down to its essence—key points that you can communicate in just a matter of one or two minutes.

The executive summary *must* capture the reader's attention. If it misses the mark, the chances of the remainder of the plan being read are minimal. A well-developed, coherent summary introducing the financial proposal establishes a favorable first impression of the entrepreneur and the business and can go a long way toward obtaining financing. Although the executive summary is the first part of the business plan, it should be the last section written.

Mission Statement

As you learned in Chapter 3, a mission statement expresses in words an entrepreneur's vision for what her company is and what it is to become. It is the broadest expression of a company's purpose and defines the direction in which it will move. It anchors a company in reality and serves as the thesis statement for the entire business plan.

Company History

The owner of an existing small business should prepare a brief history of the operation, highlighting the significant financial and operational events in the company's life. This section should describe when and why the company was formed, how it has evolved over time, and what the owner envisions for the future. It should highlight the successful accomplishment of past objectives such as developing prototypes, earning patents, achieving market-share targets, or securing long-term customer contracts. This section also should convey the firm's image in the marketplace.

Business and Industry Profile

To acquaint lenders and investors with the industry in which a company competes, an entrepreneur should describe it in the business plan. This section should begin with a statement of the company's general business goals and a narrower definition of its immediate objectives. Together they should spell out what the business plans to accomplish, how, when, and who will do it. **Goals** are broad, long-range statements of what a company plans to achieve in the future that guide its overall direction and express its *raison d'être.* In other words, they address the question: "Why am I in business?" Answering such a basic question appears to be obvious, but, in fact, many entrepreneurs cannot define the basis of their businesses.

goals—*broad, long-range statements of what a company plans to achieve in the future that guide its overall direction and express its* raison d'être.

objectives—*short-term specific performance targets that are attainable, measurable, and controllable.*

Objectives, on the other hand, are short-term, specific performance targets that are attainable, measurable, and controllable. Every objective should reflect some general business goal and include a technique for measuring progress toward its accomplishment. To be meaningful, an objective must have a time frame for achievement. Both goals and objectives should relate to the company's basic mission (see Figure 10.1).

When summarizing a small company's background, an entrepreneur should describe the present state of the art in the industry and what she will need to succeed in the market segment in which her business will compete. She should then identify the current applications of the product or service in the market and include projections for future applications.

This section should provide the reader with an overview of the industry or market segment in which the new venture will operate. Industry data such as market size, growth trends, and the relative economic and competitive strength of the major firms in the industry all set the stage for a better understanding of the viability of the new prod-

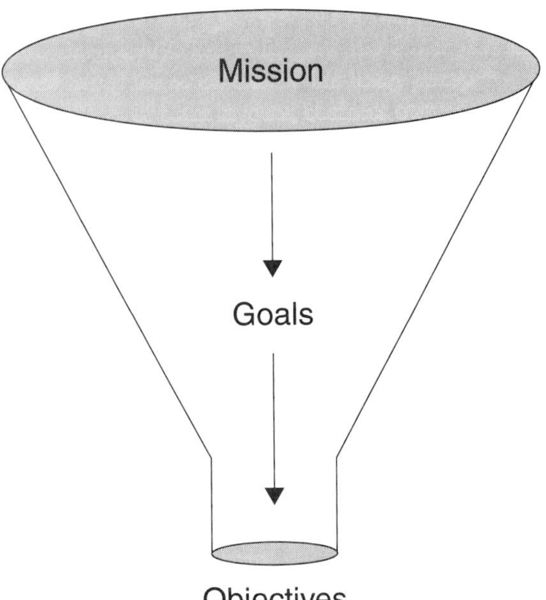

FIGURE 10.1
The Relationship Among Mission, Goals, and Objectives

uct or service. Strategic issues such as ease of market entry and exit, the ability to achieve economies of scale or scope, and the existence of cyclical or seasonal economic trends further help readers evaluate the new venture. This part of the plan also should describe significant industry trends and an overall outlook for its future. Information about the evolution of the industry helps the reader comprehend its competitive dynamics. The *U.S. Industrial Outlook* is an excellent reference that profiles a variety of industries and offers projections for future trends in them. Another useful resource of industry and economic information is the *Summary of Commentary on Current Economic Conditions,* more commonly known as the *Beige Book.* Published eight times a year by the Federal Reserve, it provides detailed statistics and trends in key business sectors and in the overall economy. It offers valuable information on topics ranging from tourism and housing starts to consumer spending and wage rates. Entrepreneurs can find this wealth of information at their fingertips on the Web at **<www.bog.frb.fed.us/fomc/BeigeBook/2000>.**

This section of the plan also should describe the existing and anticipated profitability of the industry. Any significant entry or exit of firms or consolidations and mergers should be discussed in terms of their impact on the competitive behavior of the market. The entrepreneur also should mention any events that have significantly affected the industry in the past 10 years.

Business Strategy

An even more important part of the business plan is the owner's view of the strategy needed to meet—and beat—the competition. In the previous section, the entrepreneur defined *where* he wants to take his business by establishing goals and objectives. This section addresses the question of *how* to get there—business strategy. Here, an entrepreneur must explain how he plans to gain a competitive edge in the market and what sets the business apart from the competition. He should comment on how he plans to achieve business goals and objectives in the face of competition and government regulation and should identify the image that the business will try to project. An important theme in this section is what makes the company unique in the eyes of its customers. One of the quickest routes to business failure is trying to sell "me-too" products or services that offer customers nothing new, better, bigger, faster, or different. The foundation for this part of the business plan comes from the material in Chapter 3, "Strategic Management and the Entrepreneur."

This segment of the business plan should outline the methods the company can use to meet the key success factors cited earlier. If, for example, a strong, well-trained sales force is considered critical to success, the owner must devise a plan of action for assembling one.

Description of Firm's Product/Service

An entrepreneur should describe the company's overall product line, giving an overview of how customers use its goods or services. Drawings, diagrams, and illustrations may be required if the product is highly technical. It is best to write product and service descriptions so that laypeople can understand them. A statement of a product's position in the product life cycle might also be helpful. An entrepreneur should include a summary of any patents, trademarks, or copyrights protecting the product or service from infringement by competitors. Finally, it is helpful to provide an honest comparison of the company's product or service with those of competitors, citing specific advantages or improvements that make the entrepreneur's goods or services unique and indicating plans for creating the next generation of goods and services that will evolve from the present product line.

feature—*a descriptive fact about a product or service.*

benefit—*what a customer gains from the product or service.*

The emphasis of this section should be on defining the *benefits* customers get by purchasing the company's products or services rather than on just a "nuts and bolts" description of the *features* of those products or services. A **feature** is a descriptive fact about a product or service ("an ergonomically designed, more comfortable handle"). A **benefit** is what a customer gains from the product or service feature ("fewer problems with carpal tunnel syndrome and increased productivity"). Advertising legend Leo Burnett once said, "Don't tell the people how good you make the goods; tell them how good your goods make them."[5] This part of the plan must describe how a business will transform tangible product or service *features* into important, but often intangible, customer *benefits*—for example, lower energy bills, faster access to the Internet, less time writing checks to pay monthly bills, greater flexibility in building floating structures, shorter time required to learn a foreign language, or others. Remember: Customers buy benefits, *not* product or service features.

Manufacturers should describe their production process, strategic raw materials required, sources of supply they will use, and their costs. They should also summarize the production method and illustrate the plant layout. If the product is based on a patented or proprietary process, a description (including diagrams, if necessary) of its unique market advantages is helpful. It is also helpful to explain the company's environmental impact and how the entrepreneur plans to mitigate any negative environmental consequences the process may produce.

Marketing Strategy

One crucial concern of entrepreneurs and the potential lenders and investors who finance their companies is whether or not there is a real market for the proposed good or service. Every entrepreneur must, therefore, describe the company's target market and its characteristics. Defining the target market and its potential is one of the most important—and most challenging—parts of building a business plan. Creating a successful business depends on an entrepreneur's ability to attract real customers who are willing and able to spend real money to buy its products or services. Perhaps the worst marketing error an entrepreneur can commit is failing to define his target market and trying to make his business "everything to everybody." Small companies usually are much more successful focusing on a specific market niche where they can excel at meeting customers' special needs or wants.

One popular target market for small businesses is teenagers. By 2010, the number of teens will grow to 35 million, which will make them a larger target market than the much-touted baby boomers. Market research shows that teens are willing to spend and that they have the resources to do so. The typical teenager spends an average of $89 per week, and one teen in nine has a credit card cosigned by a parent.[6]

SKINMARKET

Patsy and Tony Hirsch have tapped into the rich opportunity this market offers with their teen-targeted beauty and multimedia store, SKINMARKET **<www.skinmarket.com>.** *Intrigued by the shopping preferences of their teen daughters and friends, the Hirsches began researching the buying habits of teenage girls. They discovered that teenagers like to try out products before buying them and that they respond to stores that cater to their needs and preferences. In SKINMARKET stores, young women can sample any of the 1,000 or so beauty and makeup products the company has developed to the sounds of the latest music stars. The Hirsches also sell lifestyle books for teens and CDs, all in settings that invite teens to relax, talk, read magazines, linger, and, of course, spend. Comfortable couches, lava lamps, and television screens add to the stores' atmosphere. Not only can teen customers buy breakup kits (complete with ex-boyfriend voodoo dolls and pins), but they also can schedule after-hours birthday parties that offer makeovers. "We understand what it's like to be a teenage girl," says Patsy. "And we built a store around that."*[7]

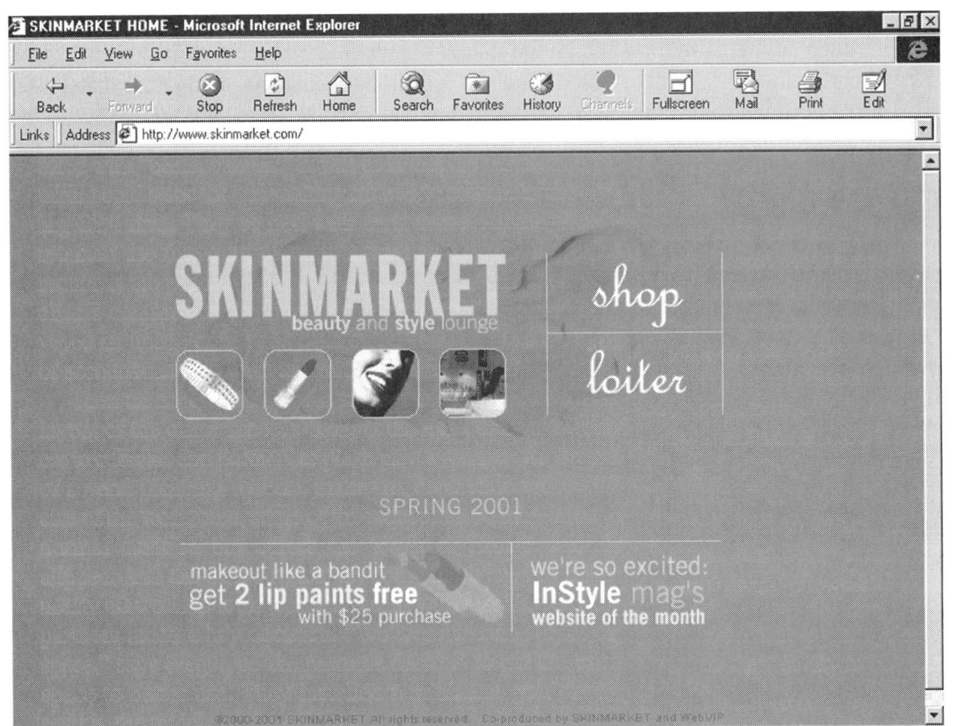

Defining a company's target market involves using the techniques described in Chapter 6, "Building a Powerful Marketing Plan." Questions this part of the business plan should address include:

- Who are my target customers (age, gender, income level, and other demographic characteristics)?
- Where do they live, work, and shop?

- How many potential customers are in my company's trading area?
- Why do they buy? What needs and wants drive their purchase decisions?
- What can my business do to meet those needs and wants better than my competitors?
- Knowing my customers' needs, wants, and habits, what should be the basis for differentiating my business in their minds?

Successful entrepreneurs know that a solid understanding of their target markets is the first step in building an effective marketing strategy. Indeed, every other aspect of marketing depends on their having a clear picture of their customers and their unique needs and wants. Proving that a profitable market exists involves two steps: showing customer interest and documenting market claims.

SHOWING CUSTOMER INTEREST. An entrepreneur must be able to prove that her target customers need or want her good or service and are willing to pay for it. This phase is relatively straightforward for a company with an existing product or service but can be quite difficult for one with only an idea or a prototype. In this case the entrepreneur might offer the prototype to several potential customers in order to get written testimonials and evaluations to show to investors. Or the owner could sell the product to several customers at a discount. This would prove that there are potential customers for the product and would allow demonstrations of the product in operation. Getting a product into customers' hands is also an excellent way to get valuable feedback that can lead to significant design improvements and increased sales down the road.

DOCUMENTING MARKET CLAIMS. Too many business plans rely on vague generalizations such as, "This market is so huge that if we get just 1 percent of it, we will break even in eight months." Such statements are not backed by facts and usually reflect an entrepreneur's unbridled optimism. In most cases, they are also unrealistic! Guy Kawasaki, an experienced entrepreneur/angel investor/venture capitalist criticizes this practice, saying, "You label yourself a bozo because only bozos try this line of reasoning on sophisticated investors."[8]

Entrepreneurs must support claims of market size and growth rates with *facts,* and that requires market research. Results of market surveys, customer questionnaires, and demographic studies lend credibility to an entrepreneur's frequently optimistic sales projections. (Refer to the market research techniques and resources in Chapter 6.) Quantitative market data are important because they form the basis for all of the company's financial projections in the business plan.

Baby Byrd's Q

To get such data before incurring the expense of launching a full-blown barbecue restaurant, entrepreneur Ronald Byrd decided to test the local taste for barbecue by selling his product from a street cart. "This is a marketing research project," he says, pointing to his cart. "I didn't want to invest a lot of money into moving into a restaurant [and have no market]. So, I started with a cart." Sales that outpaced his expectations proved to him (and to bankers) that the demand for his creative barbecue dishes was sufficient to support a restaurant. This aspiring restaurateur also used feedback and suggestions from customers to fine-tune his menu offerings—all before ever opening the doors to his "official" restaurant, Baby Byrd's Q.[9]

One of the essential goals of this section of the plan is to identify the basics for financial forecasts that follow. Sales, profit, and cash forecasts must be founded on more than just wishful thinking. An effective market analysis should identify the following:

Target market: Who are the most promising customers or prospects? What are their characteristics? Where do they live? What do they buy? Why do they buy? When do they buy? What expectations do they have about the product or service? Will the business focus on a niche? How does the company seek to position itself in its market(s)?

Advertising: Once an entrepreneur defines her company's target market, she can design a promotion and advertising campaign to reach those customers most effectively and efficiently. Which media are most effective in reaching the target market? How will they be used? How much will the promotional campaign cost? How can the company benefit from publicity?

Market size and trends: How large is the potential market? Is it growing or shrinking? Why? Are the customer's needs changing? Are sales seasonal? Is demand tied to another product or service?

Location: For many businesses, choosing the right location is a key success factor. For retailers, wholesalers, and service companies, the best location usually is one that is most convenient to their target customers. By combining census data and other market research with digital mapping software, entrepreneurs can locate sites with the greatest concentrations of their customers and the least interference from competitors. Which specific sites put the company in the path of its target customers? Do zoning regulations restrict the use of the site? For manufacturers, the location issue often centers on finding a site near its key raw materials or near its major customers. Using demographic reports and market research to screen potential sites takes the guesswork out of choosing the "right" location for a business.

Pricing: What does the product or service cost to produce or deliver? What is the company's overall pricing strategy? What image is the company trying to create in the market? Will the planned price support the company's strategy and desired image? (See Figure 10.2.) Can it produce a profit? How does the planned price compare to prices of similar products or services? Are customers willing to pay it? What price tiers exist in the market? How sensitive are customers to price changes? Will the business sell to customers on credit? Will it accept credit cards?

Distribution: How will the product or service be distributed? What is the average sale? How many sales calls does it take to close a sale? What are the incentives for salespeople? What can the company do to make it as easy as possible for customers to buy?

This portion of the plan also should describe the channels of distribution that the business will use (mail, in-house sales force, sales agent, retailers). The owner should summarize the firm's overall pricing and promotion strategies, including the advertising budget,

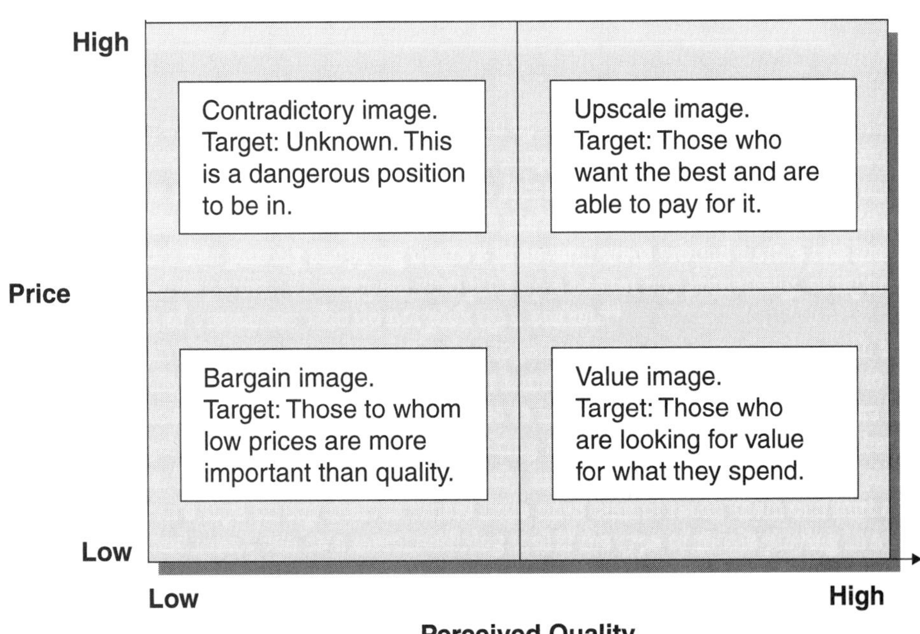

FIGURE 10.2 The Link Between Pricing, Perceived Quality, and Company Image

media used, and publicity efforts. The company's warranties and guarantees for its products and services should be addressed as well.

Competitor Analysis

An entrepreneur should discuss the new venture's competition. Failing to assess competitors realistically makes entrepreneurs appear to be poorly prepared, naive, or dishonest, especially to potential lenders and investors. "A warning bell goes off in the head of sophisticated investors when they hear, 'We have no competition,'" says venture capitalist Guy Kawasaki.[10] Gathering information on competitors' market shares, products, and strategies is usually not difficult. Trade associations, customers, industry journals, marketing representatives, and sales literature are valuable sources of data. This section of the plan should focus on demonstrating that the entrepreneur's company has an advantage over its competitors. Who are the company's key competitors? What are their strengths and weaknesses? What are their strategies? What images do they have in the marketplace? How successful are they? What distinguishes the entrepreneur's product or service from others already on the market, and how will these differences produce a competitive edge? This section of the plan should demonstrate that the firm's strategies are clearly customer focused.

Description of the Management Team

The most important factor in the success of a business venture is the quality of its management, and financial officers and investors weigh heavily the ability and experience of the firm's managers in their financing decisions. Thus, a plan should describe the qualifications of business officers, key directors, and any person with at least 20 percent ownership in the company. *Remember: Lenders and investors prefer experienced managers.* "Deep industry knowledge is what makes today's investors happiest," explains one investment banker.[11]

Résumés in a plan should summarize an individual's education, work history (emphasizing managerial responsibilities and duties), and relevant business experience. When compiling a personal profile, an entrepreneur should review the primary reasons for small business failure (refer to Chapter 1) and show how her team will use its skills and experience to avoid them. Entrepreneurs should not cover up previous business failure, however. Failing in business no longer has a terrible stigma attached to it. In fact, many investors are suspicious of entrepreneurs who have never experienced a business failure.

When considering investing in a business, lenders and investors look for the experience, talent, and integrity of the people who will breathe life into the plan. This portion of the plan should show that the company has the right people organized in the right fashion for success. One experienced private investor advises entrepreneurs to remember the following:

- Ideas and products don't succeed; people do. Show the strength of your management team. A top-notch management team with variety of proven skills is crucial.
- Show the strength of key employees and how you will retain them. Most small companies cannot pay salaries that match those at large businesses, but stock options and other incentives can improve employee retention.
- A board of directors or advisers consisting of industry experts lends credibility and can enhance the value of the management team.[12]

Plan of Operation

To complete the description of the business, the owner should construct an organizational chart identifying the business's key positions and the personnel occupying them. Assembling a management team with the right stuff is difficult, but keeping it together until the company is established may be harder. Thus, the entrepreneur should describe briefly the steps taken to encourage important officers to remain with the company. Employment contracts, shares of ownership, and perks are commonly used to keep and motivate such employees.

Finally, a description of the form of ownership (partnership, joint venture, S corporation, LLC) and of any leases, contracts, and other relevant agreements pertaining to the business is helpful.

Forecasted Financial Statements

One of the most important sections of the business plan is an outline of the proposed company's financial statements—the "dollars and cents" of the proposed venture. For an existing business, lenders and investors use past financial statements to judge the health of the company and its ability to repay loans or generate adequate returns. Therefore, an owner should supply copies of the firm's financial statements from the past three years. Ideally, these statements should be audited by a certified public accountant because most financial institutions prefer that extra reliability, although a financial review of the statements by an accountant sometimes may be acceptable.

Whether assembling a plan for an existing business or for a start-up, an entrepreneur should carefully prepare monthly projected (or pro forma) financial statements for the operation for the next year (and for two or three more years by quarter) using past operating data, published statistics, and judgment to derive three sets of forecasts of the income statement, balance sheet, cash budget (always!), and schedule of planned capital expenditures. (Refer to Chapter 9, "Creating a Successful Financial Plan," for a discussion on creating projected financial statements.) The forecasts should cover pessimistic, most likely, and optimistic conditions to reflect the uncertainty of the future. "In many business plans," says one senior bank officer, "everything is seen through rose-colored glasses. [However], a good plan will provide for contingencies."[13]

It is essential that all three sets of forecasts be realistic. Entrepreneurs must avoid the tendency to "fudge the numbers" just to make their businesses look good. Lenders and investors compare these projections against published industry standards and can detect unrealistic forecasts. In fact, some venture capitalists automatically discount an entrepreneur's financial projections by as much as 50 percent. Upon completing the forecasts, an entrepreneur should perform a breakeven analysis and a ratio analysis on the projected figures.

It is also important to include a statement of the *assumptions* on which these financial projections are based. Potential lenders and investors want to know how an entrepreneur derived forecasts for sales, cost of goods sold, operating expenses, accounts receivable, collections, accounts payable, inventory, taxes, and other items. Spelling out such assumptions gives a plan more credibility and reduces the tendency to include overly optimistic estimates of sales growth and profit margins. In addition to providing valuable information to potential lenders and investors, projected financial statements help an entrepreneur run her business more effectively and more efficiently. They establish important targets for financial performance and make it easier for an entrepreneur to maintain control over routine expenses and capital expenditures.

The Loan or Investment Proposal

The loan or investment proposal section of the business plan should state the purpose of the financing, the amount requested, and the plans for repayment, or, in the case of investors, an attractive exit strategy. When describing the purpose of the loan or investment, an entrepreneur must specify the planned use of the funds. General requests for funds using reasons such as "for modernization," "working capital," or "expansion" are unlikely to win approval. Instead, entrepreneurs should use more detailed descriptions such as "to modernize production facilities by purchasing five new, more efficient looms that will boost productivity by 12 percent" or "to rebuild merchandise inventory for fall sales peak, beginning in early summer." Entrepreneurs should state the precise amount requested and include relevant backup data, such as vendor estimates of costs or past production levels. An entrepreneur should not hesitate to request the amount of money needed but should not inflate the amount anticipating the financial officer to "talk her down." Remember: Lenders and investors are familiar with industry cost structures.

Another important element of the loan or investment proposal is the repayment schedule and exit strategy. A lender's main consideration in granting a loan is the reassurance that the applicant will repay, whereas an investor's major concern is earning a satisfactory rate of return. Financial projections must reflect a firm's ability to repay loans and produce adequate yields. Without this proof, a request for additional funds stands little chance of being accepted. It is necessary for the entrepreneur to produce tangible evidence showing the ability to repay loans or to generate attractive returns. "Plan an exit for the investor," advises the owner of a financial consulting company. "Generally, the equity investor's objective with early stage funding is to earn a 30% to 50% annual return over the life of the investment. To enhance the investor's interest in your enterprise, show how they can 'cash out' perhaps through a public offering or acquisition."[14]

Finally, the owner should have a timetable for implementing the proposed plan. He should present a schedule showing the estimated start-up date for the project and noting any significant milestones along the way. Entrepreneurs tend to be optimistic, so the owner must be sure that his timetable of events is realistic.

It is beneficial to include an evaluation of the risks of a new venture. Evaluating risk in a business plan requires an entrepreneur to walk a fine line, however. Dwelling too much on everything that can go wrong will discourage potential lenders and investors from financing the venture. Ignoring the project's risks makes those who evaluate the plan tend to believe an entrepreneur to be either naive, dishonest, or unprepared. The best strategy is to identify the most significant risks the venture faces and then to describe the plans the entrepreneur has developed to avoid them altogether or to overcome the negative outcome if the event does occur.

There is a difference between a *working* business plan—the one the entrepreneur is using to guide her business—and the *presentation* business plan—the one she is using to attract capital. Although coffee rings and penciled-in changes in a working plan don't matter (in fact, they're a good sign that the entrepreneur is actually using the plan), they have no place on a plan going to someone outside the company. A plan is usually the tool that an entrepreneur uses to make a first impression on potential lenders and investors. To make sure that impression is a favorable one, an entrepreneur should follow these tips:

- First impressions are crucial. Make sure the plan has an attractive (not necessarily expensive) cover.
- Make sure the plan is free of spelling and grammatical errors and "typos." It is a professional document and should read like one.
- Make it visually appealing. Use color charts, figures, and diagrams to illustrate key points. Don't get carried away, however, and end up with a "comic book" plan.

- Include a table of contents to allow readers to navigate the plan easily. Reviewers should be able to look through a plan and quickly locate the sections they want to see.
- Make it interesting. Boring plans seldom get read.
- A plan must prove that the business will make money. In a recent survey of lenders, investors, and financial advisors, 81 percent said that, first and foremost, a plan should prove that a venture will earn a profit.[15] Start-ups do not necessarily have to be profitable immediately, but sooner or later (preferably sooner), they must make money.
- Use computer spreadsheets to generate financial forecasts. They allow entrepreneurs to perform valuable what-if (sensitivity) analysis in just seconds.
- *Always* include cash flow projections. Entrepreneurs sometimes focus excessively on their proposed venture's profit forecasts and ignore cash flow projections. Although profitability is important, lenders and investors are much more interested in cash flow because they know that's where the money to pay them back or to cash them out comes from.
- The ideal plan is "crisp," long enough to say what it should but not so long that it is a chore to read.
- Tell the truth. Absolute honesty is always critical when preparing a business plan.

THE BENEFITS OF PREPARING A PLAN

3. Explain the benefits of preparing a business plan.

Preparing a sound business plan clearly requires time and effort, but the benefits greatly exceed the costs. Building the plan forces a potential entrepreneur to look at her business idea in the harsh light of reality. It also requires the owner to assess the venture's chances of success more objectively. A well-assembled plan helps prove to outsiders that a business idea can be successful. To get external financing, an entrepreneur's plan must pass three tests with potential lenders and investors: (1) the reality test, (2) the competitive test, and (3) the value test.[16] The first two tests have both an external and an internal component.

Reality Test

The external component of the reality test revolves around proving that a market for the product or service really does exist. It focuses on industry attractiveness, market niches, potential customers, market size, degree of competition, and similar factors. Entrepreneurs who pass this part of the reality test prove in the marketing portion of their business plans that there is strong demand for their business idea.

The internal component of the reality test focuses on the product or service itself. Can the company *really* build it for the cost estimates in the business plan? Is it truly different from what competitors are already selling? Does it offer customers something of value?

Competitive Test

The external part of the competitive test evaluates the company's relative position to its key competitors. How do the company's strengths and weaknesses match up with those of the competition? How are existing competitors likely to react when the new business enters the market? Do these reactions threaten the new company's success and survival?

The internal competitive test focuses on management's ability to create a company that will gain an edge over existing rivals. To pass this part of the competitive test, a plan must prove the quality, skills, and experience of the venture's management team. What other resources does the company have that can give it a competitive edge in the market?

CONSULTANT . . .

Planning for a Dot-Com

Should a business plan for a dot-com business be any different from a plan for a regular brick-and-mortar company? Business planning experts say that although every business plan should include certain fundamental elements, dot-com business plans *are* different from traditional plans. Any entrepreneur wanting to launch a successful Internet company should understand these differences before creating a plan and approaching potential investors. Probably the most significant difference between a business plan for a dot-com and a plan for a traditional business is length. Traditional plans typically range from 25 to 50 pages, but an e-business plan should be no more than 30 pages. Some Internet entrepreneurs have attracted millions of dollars in venture capital with plans as short as 10 pages. "Plans have to be light as a feather," says a manager at one Internet investment company.

Several factors are driving the trend toward slimmer, trimmer plans. First, in e-commerce, opportunities emerge at the speed of light, and investors and venture capitalists that once could take months to evaluate a plan now must make decisions in just days or risk missing out on the next big thing. Second, because of the surge in e-commerce, investors are being inundated with dot-com business plans. Reviewing more plans means less time to spend on each one. Finally, sophisticated investors recognize that e-commerce is in its infancy and that entrepreneurs are still trying to work out business models that will produce success in such a fast-paced, dynamic environment. A plan sporting elaborate descriptions of target customers and spreadsheets with detailed financial projections five years into the future simply is not that credible. Investors know that most e-commerce companies will fail, a situation that is not likely to change in the near future.

The financial section of an e-business plan also is much shorter than in a traditional business plan. Rather than producing reams of spreadsheets showing the outcomes of multiple scenarios many years into the future, successful Internet entrepreneurs are sticking with perhaps one or two scenarios projected just two years out. Investors recognize that few e-businesses generate sufficient revenue to generate a profit, especially in the early years when development costs are so high. As e-commerce matures and becomes more stable, investors will expect more traditional types of financial forecasts.

Investors also demand less detail in the section of the plan that describes a company's target market. Normally, an entrepreneur includes in a traditional plan a thorough analysis of the market and the characteristics of the customers that comprise it. A plan for an e-business, however, recognizes that markets and the techniques for reaching customers effectively change rapidly in e-commerce. Investors want entrepreneurs behind Internet companies to summarize the market opportunity and its potential for growth.

Two areas in an e-business plan require more attention than in a traditional plan: the explanation of the business concept and the description of the management team. Before investors put any money into an e-business, they must have a crystal-clear understanding of it and how it is superior to any current business model. "You had better have a very simple way to powerfully differentiate your company," advises venture capitalist Guy Kawasaki. E-commerce plans often include definitions of industry-specific terms, diagrams of technology, hyperlinks to Web sites, and charts showing how a company works.

Just as in a traditional business, investors evaluating an e-commerce plan are looking for a skilled, experienced management team that can prove it has the wherewithal to launch a company and manage it through the tremulous start-up phase. "Launching an e-business is not for the weak-minded nor the weak-hearted," says one expert. Investors are especially interested in how the company will draw customers to its Web site and how it will handle and fulfill orders from them once they arrive. An e-business plan, therefore, should contain a Web site map that shows how all of the pages on the site will look and be linked to one another. It also should describe how the company's back office, the systems that take over once a customer places an order on the site, will work and the volume of traffic it can handle.

Just as with a traditional business plan, the executive summary in an e-business plan is extremely important because it is the first section investors read. If it fails to capture investors' attention and interest, the probability that they will read the rest of the plan is miniscule.

1. In what ways are a plan for a traditional business and one for an e-business similar? Different?
2. Suppose that a good friend comes to you and announces that he is going to launch an Internet business but needs financing to do it. You ask about his business plan. "I don't have the time to write a business plan," he says. What do you tell him?
3. Assume that you convince your friend that he should write a business plan. He asks your advice on how to write the plan. What advice would you offer?

Sources: Adapted from Mark Henricks, "Short and Sweet," *Business Start-Ups,* May 2000, p. 20; Joel Kurtzman, "The New Age of Business Plans," *Fortune,* September 27, 1999, p. 262[N]; Robert Calem, Sheryl Nance-Nash, Michael Scully, and Carlye Adler, "Napkin Plans . . . The Main Street Mayor . . . Silicon Goes Celluloid," *Fortune,* May 24, 1999, p. 296[I]; Guy Kawasaki, "Needbucks.com," *Forbes,* January 10, 2000, p. 188.

Source: Dilbert © UFS.

Value Test

To convince lenders and investors to put their money into the venture, a business plan must prove to them that it offers a high probability of repayment or an attractive rate of return. Entrepreneurs usually see their businesses as good investments because they consider the intangibles of owning a business—gaining control over their own destinies, freedom to do what they enjoy, and others; lenders and investors, however, look at a venture in colder terms: dollar-for-dollar returns. A plan must convince lenders and investors that they will earn an attractive return on their money.

Sometimes the greatest service a business plan provides an entrepreneur is the realization that "it just won't work." The time to find out a potential business idea won't succeed is in the planning stages *before* an entrepreneur commits significant resources to a venture. In other cases it reveals important problems to overcome before launching a company. According to one business consultant, "If you do a really good job of writing your business plan, it's more than just putting words on paper. You do a lot of research, and you expose a lot of flaws. Each one that you expose and treat, you enhance the chances of your success."[17]

The real value in preparing a business plan is not so much in the plan itself as it is in the process an entrepreneur goes through to create the plan. Although the finished product is useful, the process of building a plan requires an entrepreneur to subject his idea to an objective, critical evaluation. What the entrepreneur learns about his company, its target market, its financial requirements, and other factors can be essential to making the venture a success. This process allows the entrepreneur to replace "I think" with "I know" and to make mistakes on paper, which is much cheaper than making them in reality. Simply put, building a business plan reduces the risk and uncertainty in launching a company by teaching the entrepreneur to do it the right way!

Appendix A at the end of this book contains a sample business plan for The Hundred Story House, A Reading Adventure for Children.

MAKING THE BUSINESS PLAN PRESENTATION

4. Understand the keys to making an effective business plan presentation.

Lenders and investors are favorably impressed by entrepreneurs who are informed and prepared when requesting a loan or investment. When attempting to secure funds from professional venture capitalists or private investors, the written business plan almost always precedes the opportunity to meet "face-to-face." Typically, an entrepreneur's time for presenting her business opportunity will be quite limited. (When presenting a plan to a venture capital forum, the allotted time is usually no more than 15 to 20 minutes, and at some forums, the time limit is a mere 5 or 6 minutes.). When the opportunity arises, an entrepreneur must be well prepared. It is important to rehearse, rehearse, and then rehearse more. It is a mistake to begin by leading the audience into a long-winded explanation about the technology on which the product or service is based. Within minutes most of the audience will be lost, and so is any chance the entrepreneur has of obtaining the necessary financing for her new venture.

Some helpful tips for making a business plan presentation to potential lenders and investors include:

- Demonstrate enthusiasm about the venture but don't be overemotional.
- Know your audience thoroughly and work to establish a rapport with them.
- "Hook" investors quickly with an up-front explanation of the new venture, its opportunities, and the anticipated benefits to them.
- Hit the highlights; specific questions will bring out the details later. Don't get caught up in too much detail in early meetings with lenders and investors.
- Keep your presentation simple by limiting it to the two or three (no more) major points you must get across to your audience. "Most people put too much material into their presentations for the amount of time they have," says a consultant who has coached hundreds of entrepreneurs for business plan presentations.[18]
- Avoid the use of technological terms that will likely be above most of the audience. Do at least one rehearsal before someone who has no special technical training. Tell him to stop you anytime he does not understand what you are talking about. When this occurs (and it likely will) rewrite that portion of your presentation.
- Use visual aids. They make it easier for people to follow your presentation, but do not make the visual aids the "star" of the presentation. They should merely support and enhance your message.
- Close by reinforcing the nature of the opportunity. Be sure you have sold the benefits the investors will realize when the business is a success.
- Be prepared for questions. In many cases, there is seldom time for a long "Q&A" session, but interested investors may want to get you aside to discuss the details of the plan.
- Follow up with every investor to whom you make a presentation. Don't sit back and wait; be proactive. They have what you need—investment capital. Demonstrate that you have confidence in your plan and have the initiative necessary to run a business successfully.

A common problem facing entrepreneurs, especially the founders of dot-com companies, is making their business plan presentations stand out from the crowd. As e-commerce has exploded, potential lenders and investors have heard so many variations of "Invest in us. We're the hottest new Internet company" that they are a highly skeptical audience. Some entrepreneurs are giving their presentations unique, creative twists to differentiate themselves. For instance, one entrepreneur, a former drummer for a rock band, opened his six-minute presentation before a venture capital forum with a drum solo. He then went on to explain how his company's decision-support software can transform managers from solo drummers into one-person symphonies.[19] Although unusual twists in a presentation can make it more memorable, they also run the risk of alienating the audience or making the message seem unimportant.

5. Explain the "five Cs of credit" and why they are important to potential lenders and investors reading business plans.

WHAT LENDERS AND INVESTORS LOOK FOR IN A BUSINESS PLAN

Banks will rarely be a new venture's sole source of capital because a bank's return is limited by the interest rate it negotiates, but its risk could be the entire amount of the loan if the new business fails. Once a business is operational and has established a financial track record, however, banks become a regular source of financing. For this reason the small business owner needs to be aware of the criteria lenders and investors use when evaluating the credit-

YOU BE THE CONSULTANT . . .

Battle of the Plans

Unlike most summer campers, the girls attending Camp Startup in Wellesley, Massachusetts, do not take lessons in handling canoes, tying knots, or ornithology. Instead, these entrepreneurs-to-be are learning how to put together a business plan for a fictitious company they plan to launch. Like the participants in Camp Startup, students in colleges and universities across the United States are also creating business plans for companies they hope to start or, in some cases, have already launched. For some, what is at stake involves much more than just a good grade. They are competing for real start-up money and valuable feedback from judges in business plan competitions. In the typical business plan competition, students submit plans and make presentations to panels of judges that include venture capitalists, successful entrepreneurs, private investors, and potential lenders.

More than 50 colleges and universities across the United States sponsor business plan competitions, and it is not uncommon for the winners to attract impressive amounts of venture capital from judges. "I have been amazed at the quality of the plans and the companies coming out of these competitions," says Steve Kaplan of the University of Chicago. One student team at Harvard's business plan competition went on to launch the company for which they created the plan, Chemdex, an e-commerce site that buys and sells life science products. The young entrepreneurs raised $13 million from one of the nation's most well-known venture capital firms and has since made a public stock offering . . . and it was only a *runner-up* in the competition! The winning company was an Internet consulting company named Zefer that attracted $100 million in start-up capital, the largest private funding ever for an Internet start-up.

Although most of the leading schools in the field of entrepreneurship sponsor business plan competitions, perhaps the most famous contest is MIT's $50K Entrepreneurship Competition, which has stimulated the creation of more than 50 companies that have gone on to attract $175 million in venture financing and have created more than 600 jobs! When Mike Cassidy and his two partners won the $50K competition with their plan for Stylus Innovation, a computer software company, Cassidy and his team parlayed the status of their victory into $125,000 in additional venture capital. Cassidy managed the fast-growing company for several years before selling it for $13 million. Unwilling to retire at age 33, he began looking for an Internet company to manage. Cassidy returned to MIT's Web site, where he found descriptions of the businesses the student teams were proposing for the $50K competition. One business in particular, Direct Hit Technologies, an Internet search engine company, caught Cassidy's attention. He approached Gary Culliss, who came up with the idea for Direct Hit, and within days signed on as the company's CEO. Culliss's team did not win a warm-up round of the $50K competition it entered, but with Cassidy's help, the entrepreneurs began reworking the business plan. The retooling worked, and Direct Hit scored a direct hit, winning $30,000 in the competition. Culliss and Cassidy went on to raise $1.4 million in venture capital and to launch Direct Hit successfully, at which time they graciously returned the $30,000 prize money that got them started.

1. If your school does not already have a business plan competition, work with a team of your classmates in a brainstorming session to develop ideas for creating one. What would you offer as a prize? How would you finance the competition? Whom would you invite to judge it? How would you structure the competition?
2. Use the World Wide Web to research business plan competitions at other colleges and universities across the nation. Using the competitions at these schools as benchmarks and the ideas you generated in question 1, develop a format for a business plan competition at your school.
3. Assume that you are a member of team of entrepreneurial students entered in a prestigious business plan competition. Outline your team's strategy for winning the competition.

Sources: Adapted from Jane Hodges, "Eat S'Mores? No. Draft a Business Plan," *Fortune,* September 27, 1999, p. 294; Marc Ballon, "MIT Springboard Sends Internet Company Aloft," *Inc.*, December 1998, pp. 23–25; MIT $50K Entrepreneurship Competition, **<50k.mit.edu>**; Alex Frankel, "Battle of the Business Plans," *Forbes ASAP,* August 23, 1999, pp. 22–24; Michael Warshaw, "The Best Business Plan on the Planet," *Inc.*, August 1999, pp. 80–90.

five Cs of credit—*criteria lenders and investors use to evaluate the creditworthiness of entrepreneurs seeking financing: capital, capacity, collateral, character, and conditions.*

worthiness of entrepreneurs seeking financing. Lenders and investors refer to these criteria as the **five Cs of credit:** capital, capacity, collateral, character, and conditions.

Capital

A small business must have a stable capital base before any lender is willing to grant a loan. Otherwise the lender would be making, in effect, a capital investment in the business. Most banks refuse to make loans that are capital investments because the potential for return on the investment is limited strictly to the interest on the loan, and the potential loss would probably exceed the reward. In fact, the most common reasons that banks give for rejecting small business loan applications are undercapitalization or too much debt. Lenders expect a small company to have an equity base of investment by the owner(s) that will help support the venture during times of financial strain, which are common during the start-up and growth phases of a business. Lenders and investors see capital as a risk-sharing strategy with entrepreneurs.

Capacity

A synonym for capacity is cash flow. Lenders and investors must be convinced of the firm's ability to meet its regular financial obligations and to repay loans, and that takes cash. In Chapter 8, we saw that more small businesses fail from lack of cash than from lack of profit. It is possible for a company to be showing a profit and still have no cash—that is, to be technically bankrupt. Lenders expect small businesses to pass the test of liquidity, especially for short-term loans. Potential lenders and investors examine closely a small company's cash flow position to decide whether it has the capacity necessary to survive until it can sustain itself.

Collateral

Collateral includes any assets an entrepreneur pledges to a lender as security for repayment of a loan. If the company defaults on the loan, the lender has the right to sell the collateral and use the proceeds to satisfy the loan. Typically, banks make very few unsecured loans (those not backed by collateral) to business start-ups. Bankers view the entrepreneurs' willingness to pledge collateral (personal or business assets) as an indication of their dedication to making the venture a success. A sound business plan can improve lenders' and investors' attitudes toward the venture.

Character

Before extending a loan to or making an investment in a small business, lenders and investors must be satisfied with an entrepreneur's character. The evaluation of character frequently is based on intangible factors such as honesty, integrity, competence, polish, determination, intelligence, and ability. Although the qualities judged are abstract, this evaluation plays a critical role in the decision of whether to put money into a business.

Lenders and investors know that most small businesses fail because of incompetent management, and they try to avoid extending loans to high-risk entrepreneurs. A solid business plan and a polished presentation by the entrepreneur can go far in convincing the banker of the owner's capability.

Conditions

The conditions surrounding a funding request also affect an entrepreneur's chances of receiving financing. Lenders and investors consider factors relating to a business's operation such as potential growth in the market, competition, location, strengths, weaknesses, opportunities, and threats. Again, the best way to provide this relevant information is in a business plan. Another important condition influencing the banker's decision is the shape of the overall economy, including interest rate levels, inflation rate, and demand for money. Although these factors are beyond an entrepreneur's control, they still are an important component in a banker's decision.

The higher a small business scores on these five Cs, the greater its chance will be of receiving a loan. The wise entrepreneur keeps this in mind when preparing a business plan and presentation.

CONCLUSION

Although there is no guarantee of success when launching a business, the best way to ensure against failure is to create a business plan. A good plan serves as an entrepreneurial strategic compass that keeps a business on course as it travels into an uncertain future. Also, a solid plan is essential to raising the capital needed to start a business; lenders and investors demand it. "There may be no easier way for an entrepreneur to sabotage his or her request for capital than by failing to produce a comprehensive, well-researched, and, above all, credible business plan," says one small business expert.[20] Of course, building a plan is just one step along the path to launching a business. Building a successful business requires entrepreneurs to put the plan into action. "A successful business is about execution," says Jeff Parker, founder of CCBN.com, a highly successful Internet service that delivers investment-related information to corporations. "You need laser focus and then do everything you can possibly do to stay on your business plan."[21] The remaining chapters in this book focus on putting your business plan to work.

BUSINESS PLAN FORMAT

Although every company's business plan will be unique, reflecting its individual circumstances, certain elements are universal. The following outline summarizes these components.

I. Executive Summary (not to exceed two pages)
   A. Company name, address, and phone number
   B. Names, addresses, phone numbers, and e-mail addresses of all key people
   C. Brief description of the business
   D. Brief overview of the market for your product
   E. Brief overview of the strategy to make your firm a success
   F. Brief description of the managerial and technical experience of your key people
   G. Brief statement of what the financial needs are and planned use of the money

II. Detailed Business Plan
   A. Industry analysis
      1. Industry background and overview
      2. Trends
      3. Growth rate
      4. Outlook for the future
   B. Background of your business

1. Brief history of the business
2. Current situation

C. Entrepreneurial vision
   1. Your company's mission statement
   2. Performance goals and objectives needed to accomplish the mission
   3. What makes your business unique: sources of competitive advantage
   4. How does your company create value for customers?
   5. Describe the key factors that will dictate the success of your business (i.e., price competitiveness, quality, durability, dependability, technical superiority)
   6. Control procedures you will establish to keep the company on track, including measures of performance

D. Strategic analysis
   1. Core competencies
   2. Market positioning and image
   3. SWOT analysis
      a. Strengths
      b. Weaknesses
      c. Opportunities
      d. Threats
   4. Business strategy: How will you compete successfully?
      a. Cost leadership
      b. Differentiation
      c. Focus

E. Market analysis
   1. Your company's target market
      a. Demographic profile
      b. Other significant customer characteristics
   2. What motivates customers to buy?
   3. Which product features (tangible or intangible) influence customers' buying decisions?
   4. How many customers does the market contain? (How large is the market?)
   5. What are their potential annual purchases?
   6. What is the nature of the buying cycle?
      a. Is this product a durable good that lasts for years or a product that is repurchased on a regular basis?
      b. Is the product likely to be purchased at only seasonal periods during the year?
      c. Do customers have a preference concerning where they purchase comparable products? How strong is this preference?
   7. Pricing strategies
      a. Cost structure—fixed and variable
      b. Desired image in market
      c. Your prices versus competitors' prices
   8. Advertising and promotion strategies
      a. Which media are most effective in reaching your target audience? Why?
      b. Media costs

c. Frequency of usage

d. How will you generate publicity for your business?

9. Distribution strategy

a. Channels of distribution

b. How will you get the product or service into the customers' hands?

c. Sales techniques and incentives

10. External market influences: How does each of the following external forces affect the sale or profitability of your product?

a. Economic factors affecting your business

(1) Inflation

(2) Recession

(3) High or low unemployment

(4) Interest rates

b. Social factors affecting your business

(1) Age of customers

(2) Location demographics

(3) Income levels

(4) Size of household

(5) Social attitudes

c. Technological factors affecting your business

(1) The World Wide Web

(2) Hardware and software

F. Competitor analysis

1. Describe each of the following factors and discuss how these factors will influence your success.

a. Existing competitors

(1) Who are they? List major known competitors

(2) Why do the potential customers in your target market buy from them now?

b. Future competitors: firms that might enter the market

(1) Who are they and when and why might they enter the market?

(2) What would be the impact in your target market segment if they enter?

c. What are the strengths and weaknesses of each key competitor?

G. Specifics of your organization and management

1. How is your business organized?

a. Legally (corporation, S corporation, LLC, partnership, sole proprietorship)

b. Functionally

2. Who are the key people in your organization?

a. What are their backgrounds, and what do they bring to the business that will enhance the chance of success?

b. Résumés of key managers and employees

3. Organization chart

H. Financial plans

1. How much money do you need to make this product and your business a long-term success?

a. Tie the response to this question to your production and marketing plan
b. Be realistic and specific
2. Create a budget. Show the lender or investor how much money you need, why you need it, when you need it, and how and when you plan to generate revenues from operations and sales
3. Have a realistic projection of the cost of operating the business
a. Materials
b. Labor
c. Equipment
d. Marketing
e. Overhead
f. Other (i.e., unique start-up costs)
4. Present actual (existing businesses only) and projected balance sheets and income statements
5. Prepare a breakeven analysis
6. Prepare a ratio analysis; compare to industry standards
7. Create cash flow projections

I. Loan proposal
1. Loan purpose
2. Amount requested
3. Repayment or "cash out" schedule (exit strategy)
4. Timetable for implementation

J. Appendices: Marketing research, financial forecasts (balance sheets, income statements, and cash flow forecasts), and other supporting documents.

CHAPTER SUMMARY

1. Explain why every entrepreneur should create a business plan.
   - A business plan serves two essential functions. First and most important, it guides the company's operations by charting its future course and devising a strategy for following it. The second function of the business plan is to attract lenders and investors. Applying for loans or attempting to attract investors without a solid business plan rarely attracts needed capital.
2. Describe the elements of a solid business plan.
   - Although a business plan should be unique and tailor-made to suit the particular needs of a small company, it should cover these basic elements: an executive summary, a mission statement, a company history, a business and industry profile, a description of the company's business strategy, a profile of its products or services, a statement explaining its marketing strategy, a competitor analysis, owners' and officers' résumés, a plan of operation, financial data, and the loan or investment proposal.
3. Explain the benefits of preparing a plan.
   - Preparing a sound business plan clearly requires time and effort, but the benefits greatly exceed the costs. Building the plan forces a potential entrepreneur to look at her business idea in the harsh light of reality. It also requires the owner to assess the venture's chances of success more objectively. A well-assembled plan helps prove to outsiders that a business idea can be successful.
   - The *real* value in preparing a business plan is not so much in the plan itself as it is in the process the entrepreneur goes through to create the plan. Although the finished product is useful, the process of building a plan requires an entrepreneur to subject his idea to an objective, critical evaluation. What the entrepreneur learns about his company, its target market, its financial requirements, and other factors can be essential to making the venture a success.
4. Understand the keys to making an effective business plan presentation.

- Lenders and investors are favorably impressed by entrepreneurs who are informed and prepared when requesting a loan or investment.
- Tips include demonstrate enthusiasm about the venture, but don't be overemotional; "hook" investors quickly with an up-front explanation of the new venture, its opportunities, and the anticipated benefits to them; use visual aids; hit the highlights of your venture; don't get caught up in too much detail in early meetings with lenders and investors; avoid the use of technological terms that will likely be above most of the audience; rehearse your presentation before giving it; close by reinforcing the nature of the opportunity; and be prepared for questions.

5. Explain the five Cs of credit and why they are important to potential lenders and investors reading business plans.
   - Small business owners needs to be aware of the criteria bankers use in evaluating the creditworthiness of loan applicants—the five Cs of credit: capital, capacity, collateral, character, and conditions.
   - Capital—Lenders expect small businesses to have an equity base of investment by the owner(s) that will help support the venture during times of financial strain.
   - Capacity—A synonym for capacity is cash flow. The bank must be convinced of the firm's ability to meet its regular financial obligations and to repay the bank loan, and that takes cash.
   - Collateral—Collateral includes any assets the owner pledges to the bank as security for repayment of the loan.
   - Character—Before approving a loan to a small business, the banker must be satisfied with the owner's character.
   - Conditions—The conditions (interest rates, the health of the nation's economy, industry growth rates, etc.) surrounding a loan request also affect the owner's chance of receiving funds.

DISCUSSION QUESTIONS

1. Why should an entrepreneur develop a business plan?
2. Describe the major components of a business plan.
3. How can an entrepreneur seeking funds to launch a business convince potential lenders and investors that a market for the product or service really does exist?
4. How would you prepare to make a formal presentation of your business plan to a venture capital forum?
5. What are the five Cs of credit? How does a banker use them when evaluating a loan request?

Beyond the Classroom . . .

1. Contact a local entrepreneur who recently launched a business. Did he or she prepare a business plan before starting the company? Why or why not? If the entrepreneur did not create a plan, is he or she considering doing so now? If the entrepreneur did create a plan, what benefits did he or she gain from the process? How long did it take to complete the plan? How did he or she put the plan to use during the start-up phase? Does he or she intend to keep the business plan updated? What advice does he or she have to offer another entrepreneur about to begin writing a business plan?

2. Interview a local banker who has experience in making loans to small businesses. Ask him or her the following questions.

   a. How important is a well-prepared business plan?
   b. How important is a smooth presentation?
   c. How does the banker evaluate the owner's character?
   d. How heavily does the bank weigh the five Cs of credit?
   e. What percentage of small business owners are well prepared to request a bank loan?
   f. What are the major reasons for the bank's rejection of small business loan applications?

3. Interview a small business owner who has requested a bank loan or an equity investment from external sources. Ask him or her these questions:

   a. Did you prepare a written business plan before approaching the financial officer?
   b. If the answer is "yes" to part a, did you have outside or professional help in preparing it?
   c. How many times have your requests for additional funds been rejected? What reasons were given for the rejection?

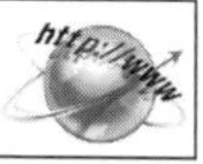

We invite you to visit this book's companion Web site at **www.prenhall.com/Zimmerer.**

Sources of Funds: Debt and Equity

LEARNING OBJECTIVES

Upon completion of this chapter, you will be able to:

1. Explain the differences among the three types of capital small businesses require: fixed, working, and growth.
2. Describe the differences between equity capital and debt capital and the advantages and disadvantages of each.
3. Discuss the various sources of equity capital available to entrepreneurs, including personal savings, friends and relatives, angels, partners, corporations, venture capital, and public stock offerings.
4. Describe the process of "going public," as well as its advantages and disadvantages and the various simplified registrations and exemptions from registration available to small businesses wanting to sell securities to investors.
5. Describe the various sources of debt capital and the advantages and disadvantages of each: banks, asset-based lenders, vendors (trade credit), equipment suppliers, commercial finance companies, savings and loan associations, stockbrokers, insurance companies, credit unions, bonds, private placements, Small Business Investment Companies (SBICs), and Small Business Lending Companies (SBLCs).
6. Identify the various federal loan programs aimed at small businesses.
7. Describe the various loan programs available from the Small Business Administration.
8. Discuss valuable methods of financing growth and expansion internally.

If you don't know who the fool is in a deal, it's you.
—Michael Wolff

There's many a pessimist who got that way by financing an optimist.
—Anonymous

Raising the money to launch a new business venture has always been a challenge for entrepreneurs. Capital markets rise and fall with the stock market, overall economic conditions, and investors' fortunes. These swells and troughs in the availability of capital make the search for financing look like a wild roller-coaster ride. For instance, during the late 1990s, founders of dot-com companies were able to attract mountains of cash from private and professional investors, even if their businesses existed only on paper! Investors flocked to initial public offerings from practically any dot-com company. The market for capital became bipolar: easy-money times for dot-coms and tight-money times for "not-coms." Even established, profitable companies in "old economy" industries such as manufacturing, distribution, real estate, and brick-and-mortar retail could not raise the capital they needed to grow. Then, early in 2000, the dot-com bubble burst, and financing an Internet business also became extremely challenging. During both the boom and the bust of Internet companies, not-com companies, especially those in low-tech industries, found attracting capital very difficult.

A stock market that has smiled on investors for years, a growing economy, and entrepreneurial success that has produced untold numbers of millionaires willing to invest in other entrepreneurial ventures have collaborated to create unprecedented wealth in the United States. Yet, most entrepreneurs, especially those in less glamorous industries or those just starting out, face difficulty finding outside sources of financing. "If you're starting a new venture with only an idea," says one veteran entrepreneur, "you'll probably have to start with only your money."[1] Many banks shy away from making loans to start-ups, venture capitalists are looking for ever-larger deals, private investors have grown cautious, and making a public stock offering remains a viable option for only a handful of promising companies with good track records and fast-growth futures. The result has been a credit crunch for entrepreneurs looking for small to moderate amounts of start-up capital. Entrepreneurs and business owners needing between $100,000 and $3 million are especially hard hit because of the vacuum that exists at that level of financing.

In the face of this capital crunch, business's need for capital has never been greater. Experts estimate the small business financing market to be $170 billion a year; yet, that still is not enough to satisfy the capital appetites of entrepreneurs and their cash-hungry businesses.[2] When searching for the capital to launch their companies, entrepreneurs must remember the following "secrets" to successful financing:

- Choosing the right sources of capital for a business can be just as important as choosing the right form of ownership or the right location. It is a decision that will influence a company for a lifetime, so entrepreneurs must weigh their options carefully before committing to a particular funding source. "It is important that companies in need of capital align themselves with sources that best fit their needs," says one financial consultant. "The success of a company often depends on the success of that relationship."[3]
- The money is out there; the key is knowing where to look. Entrepreneurs must do their homework *before* they set out to raise money for their ventures. Understanding which sources of funding are best suited to the various stages of a company's growth and then taking the time to learn how those sources work are essential to success.
- Creativity counts. Although some traditional sources of funds now play a lesser role in small business finance than in the past, other sources—from large corporations and customers to international venture capitalists and state or local programs—are taking up the slack. To find the financing their businesses demand, entrepreneurs must use as much creativity in attracting financing as they did in generating the ideas for their products and services.
- The World Wide Web puts at entrepreneurs' fingertips vast resources of information that can lead to financing. The Web often offers entrepreneurs, especially those looking for relatively small amounts of money, the opportunity to discover sources of funds that they otherwise might miss. The Web site created for this book **<www.prenhall.com/scarborough>** provides links to many useful sites related to raising both start-up and growth capital. The Web

also provides a low-cost, convenient way for entrepreneurs to get their business plans into potential investors' hands anywhere in the world. When searching for sources of capital, entrepreneurs must not overlook this valuable tool!

- Be thoroughly prepared before approaching potential lenders and investors.

Example

The founder of an online magazine missed a prime opportunity with a potential investor because he was ill-prepared to pitch his business venture effectively. The investor started the meeting (which the entrepreneur had forgotten about) by asking, "What will your total revenue be in five years?" and "Name your five most favored strategic partners in order of priority." The entrepreneur's response was weak. "There'll be lots of revenue; I can assure you of that," he said. "We are particularly keen on partnering with European media companies." The potential investor chatted for a few minutes, politely excused himself, and left, never to be heard from again.[4]

In the hunt for capital, tracking down leads is tough enough; don't blow a potential deal by failing to be ready to present your business idea to potential lenders and investors in a clear, concise, convincing way. That, of course, requires a solid business plan.

- Entrepreneurs cannot overestimate the importance of making sure that the "chemistry" between themselves, their companies, and their funding sources is a good one. Too many entrepreneurs get into financial deals because they needed the money to keep their businesses growing only to discover that their plans do not match those of their financial partners.

Rather than rely primarily on a single source of funds as they have in the past, entrepreneurs must piece together capital from multiple sources, a method known as **layered financing.** They have discovered that raising capital successfully requires them to cast a wide net to capture the financing they need to launch their businesses.

layered financing—*the technique of raising capital from multiple sources.*

Med-Channel Inc.

The founders of Med-Channel, an Internet-based company that focuses on the medical supply industry, demonstrate the "patchwork" of start-up financing that has become so common. In addition to the initial capital the founders provided, the company raised $42 million in its early stages from 11 private investors. Then Med-Channel received a cash infusion from two venture capital firms. As the company grew, it turned to two investment banks and large corporations, including Johnson & Johnson and an Italian pharmaceutical company, to satisfy its capital requirements.[5]

This chapter will guide you through the myriad of financing options available to entrepreneurs, focusing on both sources of equity (ownership) and debt (borrowed) financing.

PLANNING FOR CAPITAL NEEDS

1. Explain the differences among the three types of capital small businesses require: fixed, working, and growth.

Becoming a successful entrepreneur requires one to become a skilled fund-raiser, a job that usually requires more time and energy than most business founders think. In start-up companies, raising capital can easily consume as much as one-half of the entrepreneur's time and can take many months to complete. Most entrepreneurs are seeking less than $1 million (indeed, most need less than $100,000), which may be the toughest money to secure. Where to find this seed money depends, in part, on the nature of the proposed business and on the amount of money required. For example, the originator of a computer software firm would have different capital requirements than the founder of a coal mining operation. Although both entrepreneurs might approach some of the same types of lenders or investors, each would be more successful targeting specific sources of funds best suited to their particular financial needs.

Capital is any form of wealth employed to produce more wealth. It exists in many forms in a typical business, including cash, inventory, plant, and equipment. Entrepreneurs need three different types of capital:

capital—*any form of wealth employed to produce more wealth.*

Fixed Capital

fixed capital—*capital needed to purchase a business's permanent or fixed assets such as land, buildings, computers, and equipment.*

Fixed capital is needed to purchase a business's permanent or fixed assets such as buildings, land, computers, and equipment. Money invested in these fixed assets tends to be frozen since it cannot be used for any other purpose. Typically, large sums of money are involved in purchasing fixed assets, and credit terms usually are lengthy. Lenders of fixed capital expect the assets purchased to improve the efficiency and, thus, the profitability of the business, and to create improved cash flows that ensure repayment.

Working Capital

working capital—*capital needed to support a business's short-term operations; it represents a company's temporary funds.*

Working capital represents a business's temporary funds; it is the capital used to support a company's normal short-term operations. Accountants define working capital as current assets minus current liabilities. The need for working capital arises because of the uneven flow of cash into and out of the business due to normal seasonal fluctuations. Credit sales, seasonal sales swings, or unforeseeable changes in demand will create fluctuations in *any* small company's cash flow. Working capital normally is used to buy inventory, pay bills, finance credit sales, pay wages and salaries, and take care of any unexpected emergencies. Lenders of working capital expect it to produce higher cash flows to ensure repayment at the end of the production/sales cycle.

Growth Capital

growth capital—*capital needed to finance a company's growth or its expansion in a new direction.*

Growth capital, unlike working capital, is not related to the seasonal fluctuations of a small business. Instead, growth capital requirements surface when an existing business is expanding or changing its primary direction. For example, a small manufacturer of silicon microchips for computers saw his business skyrocket in a short time period. With orders for chips rushing in, the growing business needed a sizable cash infusion to increase plant size, expand its sales and production workforce, and buy more equipment. During times of such rapid expansion, a growing company's capital requirements are similar to those of a business start-up. Like lenders of fixed capital, growth capital lenders expect the funds to improve a company's profitability and cash flow position, thus ensuring repayment.

Although these three types of capital are interdependent, each has certain sources, characteristics, and effects on the business and its long-term growth that entrepreneurs must recognize.

2. Describe the differences between equity capital and debt capital and the advantages and disadvantages of each.

EQUITY CAPITAL VERSUS DEBT CAPITAL

Equity capital represents the personal investment of the owner (or owners) in a business and is sometimes called *risk* capital because these investors assume the primary risk of losing their funds if the business fails.

NetFax

For instance, private investor Victor Lombardi lost the $3.5 million he invested in a start-up called NetFax, a company that was developing the technology to send faxes over the Internet. However, when NetFax's patent application stalled, the company foundered. Just three years after its launch, NetFax ceased operations, leaving Lombardi's investment worthless.[6]

equity capital—*represents the personal investment of the owner(s) in a business and is sometimes called risk capital.*

If a venture succeeds, however, founders and investors share in the benefits, which can be quite substantial. The founders of and early investors in Yahoo!, Sun Microsystems, Federal Express, Intel, and Microsoft became multimillionaires when the companies went public and their equity investments finally paid off. To entrepreneurs, the primary advantage of equity capital is that it does not have to be repaid like a loan does. Equity investors are entitled to share in the company's earnings (if there are any) and usually to have a voice in the company's future direction.

The primary disadvantage of equity capital is that the entrepreneur must give up some—perhaps *most*—of the ownership in the business to outsiders. Although 50 percent of something is better than 100 percent of nothing, giving up control of your company can be disconcerting and dangerous.

Bookstop Inc.

For instance, when Gary Hoover launched Bookstop Inc., a book superstore, he relied on equity financing so much that he was left with just 6 percent of his company's stock. Seven years after start-up, the venture capitalists who owned most of the stock fired Hoover from the company he founded![7]

Entrepreneurs are more likely to give up equity in their businesses in the start-up phase than in any other (see Figure 11.1).

debt capital—*the financing that a small business owner has borrowed and must repay with interest.*

Debt capital is the financing that a small business owner has borrowed and must repay with interest. Very few entrepreneurs have adequate personal savings to finance the complete start-up costs of a small business; many of them must rely on some form of debt capital to launch their companies. Lenders of capital are more numerous than investors, although small business loans can be just as difficult (if not more difficult) to obtain. Although borrowed capital allows entrepreneurs to maintain complete ownership of their businesses, it must be carried as a liability on the balance sheet as well as be repaid with interest at some point in the future. In addition, because lenders consider small businesses to be greater risks than bigger corporate customers, they require higher interest rates on loans to small companies because of the risk–return trade-off—the higher the risk, the greater the return demanded. Most small firms pay the prime rate—the interest rate banks charge their most creditworthy customers—*plus* a few percentage points. Still, the cost of debt financing often is lower than that of equity financing. Because of the higher risks associated with providing equity capital to small companies, investors demand greater returns than lenders. Also, unlike equity financing, debt financing does not require an entrepreneur to dilute her ownership interest in the company.

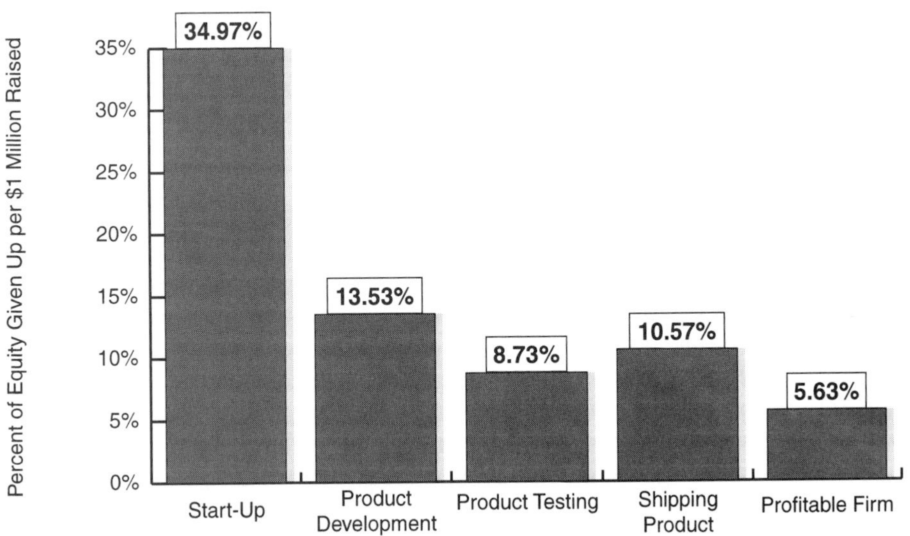

FIGURE 11.1
Average Equity Given Up by Entrepreneurs Seeking Capital (%)
Source: Adapted from VentureOne, San Francisco, California.

At one time, financing a business depended almost solely on an entrepreneur's ability to get a bank loan. Then, in the early 1990s, entrepreneurs began turning more to equity financing to get their businesses up and running. We now turn our attention to nine common sources of equity capital.

3. Discuss the various sources of equity capital and the advantages and disadvantages of each.

SOURCES OF EQUITY FINANCING

Personal Savings

The *first* place entrepreneurs should look for start-up money is in their own pockets. It's the least expensive source of funds available! "The sooner you take outside money, the more ownership in your company you'll have to surrender," warns one small business expert.[8] Entrepreneurs apparently see the benefits of self-sufficiency; the most common source of equity funds used to start a small business is the entrepreneur's pool of personal savings.

Kiss My Face

In 1979, when Robert MacLeod and Stephen Byckiewicz launched Kiss My Face, a company that sold a line of soaps and shampoos, they could not persuade a bank to lend them any money, so they pooled all they had—just $10,000—and invested it in the business. Sales were thin in the early years, but they climbed steadily with the help of creative marketing and the strategic partnerships with larger companies that MacLeod and Byckiewicz forged. The entrepreneurs financed their company's growth with retained earnings and some debt but retained 100 percent ownership. Today, Kiss My Face is debt free and tallies sales of more than $18 million. "We're very happy to have maintained complete control of our business," says MacLeod.[9]

Lenders and investors *expect* entrepreneurs to put their own money into a business start-up. If an entrepreneur is not willing to risk his own money, potential investors are not likely to risk their money in the business either. Furthermore, failing to put up sufficient capital of their own means that entrepreneurs must either borrow an excessive amount of capital or give up a significant portion of ownership to outsiders to fund the business properly. Excessive borrowing in the early days of a business puts intense pressure on its cash flow, and becoming a minority shareholder may dampen a founder's enthusiasm for making a business successful. Neither outcome presents a bright future for the company involved.

Friends and Family Members

Although most entrepreneurs look to their own bank accounts first to finance a business, few have sufficient resources to launch their businesses alone. In fact, three out of four people who start businesses do so with capital from outside sources.[10] After emptying their own pockets, where should entrepreneurs turn for capital? The second place most entrepreneurs look is to friends and family members who might be willing to invest in a business venture. Because of their relationships with the founder, these people are most likely to invest. According to the Census Bureau, nearly 10 percent of small business owners say they rely on relatives and friends for capital.[11] Often, they are more patient than other outside investors and are less meddlesome in a business's affairs than many other types of investors. "Most of our relatives just told us to pay them back when we could," says an entrepreneur who used $30,000 from family members to launch a gourmet coffee business.[12]

Investments from family and friends are an excellent source of seed capital and can get a start-up far enough along to attract money from private investors or venture capital companies. Inherent dangers lurk in family business investments, however. Unrealistic expectations or misunderstood risks have destroyed many friendships and have ruined many family reunions. To avoid such problems, an entrepreneur must honestly present the investment opportunity and the nature of the risks involved to avoid alienating friends and family members if the business fails. On the other hand, some investments return more than friends and family members ever could have imagined. In 1995, Mike and Jackie Bezos invested $300,000 in their son Jeff's start-up business, Amazon.com. Today, Mike and Jackie own 6 percent of Amazon.com's stock, and their shares are worth billions of dollars![13] Table 11.1 offers suggestions for structuring family or friendship financing deals.

Angels

After dipping into their own pockets and convincing friends and relatives to invest in their business ventures, many entrepreneurs still find themselves short of the seed capital they need. Frequently, the next stop on the road to business financing is private investors. These **private investors** or **angels** are wealthy individuals, often entrepreneurs themselves, who invest in business start-ups in exchange for equity stakes in the companies. In many cases, angels invest in businesses for more than purely economic reasons (because they have a

angels—*wealthy individuals, often entrepreneurs themselves, who invest in business start-ups in exchange for equity stakes in the companies.*

TABLE 11.1

Suggestions for Structuring Family and Friendship Financing Deals

Sources: Adapted from Paul Kvinta, "Frogskins, Shekels, Bucks, Moolah, Cash, Simoleans, Dough, Dinero: Everybody Wants It. Your Business Needs It. Here's How to Get It," Smart Business, *August 2000, pp. 74–89. Alex Markels, "A Little Help from Their Friends,"* Wall Street Journal, *May 22, 1995, p. R10; Heather Chaplin, "Friends and Family,"* Your Company, *September 1999, p. 26.*

Tapping family members and friends for start-up capital, whether in the form of equity or debt financing, is a popular method of financing business ideas. Unfortunately, these deals don't always work to the satisfaction of both parties. For instance, when actor Don Johnson needed seed capital to launch DJ Racing, a company that designs and races speedboats, he approached a wealthy Miami friend who made a $300,000 interest-free loan on nothing but a handshake. Within a year, a dispute arose over when Johnson was to pay back the loan. A lawsuit followed, which the two now former friends settled out of court. The following suggestions can help entrepreneurs avoid needlessly destroying family relationships and friendships:

- *Consider the impact of the investment on everyone involved.* Will it work a hardship on anyone? Is the investor putting up the money because he wants to or because he feels obligated to? Can both parties afford the loan if the business folds? Lynn McPhee used $250,000 from family members to launch Xuny, a Web-based clothing store. "Our basic rule of thumb was if [the investment is] going to strap someone, we won't take it," she says.
- *Keep the arrangement strictly business.* The parties should treat all loans and investments in a business-like manner, no matter how close the friendship or family relationship, to avoid problems down the line. If the transaction is a loan exceeding $10,000, it must carry a rate of interest at least as high as the market rate; otherwise the IRS may consider the loan a gift and penalize the lender.
- *Settle the details up front.* Before any money changes hands, both parties must agree on the details of the deal. How much money is involved? Is it a loan or an investment? How will the investor cash out? How will the loan be paid off? What happens if the business fails?
- *Create a written contract.* Don't make the mistake of closing a financial deal with just a handshake. The probability of misunderstandings skyrockets! Putting an agreement in writing demonstrates both parties' commitment to the deal and minimizes the chances of disputes.
- *Treat the money as bridge financing.* Although family and friends can help you launch your business, it is unlikely that they can provide enough capital to sustain it over the long term. Sooner or later, you will need to establish a relationship with other sources of credit if your company is to survive and thrive. Consider money from family and friends as a bridge to take your company to the next level of financing.
- *Develop a payment schedule that suits both the entrepreneur and the lender or investor.* Although lenders and investors may want to get their money back as quickly as possible, a rapid repayment or cash-out schedule can jeopardize a fledgling company's survival. Establish a realistic repayment plan that works for both parties without putting excessive strain on the young company's cash flow.

Doonesbury, reprinted in Your Company *(Now FSB), December 1998/January 1999, p. 51.*

personal interest in the industry), and they are willing to put money into companies in the earliest stages, long before venture capital firms and institutional investors jump in. Angel financing, the fastest-growing segment of the small business capital market, is ideal for companies that have outgrown the capacity of investments from friends and family but are still too small to attract the interest of venture capital companies. For instance, after raising the money to launch Amazon.com from family and friends, Jeff Bezos turned to angels because venture capital firms were not interested in a business start-up. Bezos attracted $1.2 million from a dozen angels before landing $8 million from venture capital firms a year later.[14]

Angels are a primary source of start-up capital for companies in the embryonic stage through the growth stage, and their role in financing small businesses is significant. Experts estimate that 400,000 angels invest $50 billion a year in 30,000 to 60,000 small companies, most of them in the start-up phase.[15] Because the angel market is so fragmented and disorganized, we may never get a completely accurate estimate of its investment in business start-ups. Although they may disagree on the exact amount of angel investments, experts concur on one fact: Angels are the largest single source of external equity capital for small businesses. Their investments in young companies dwarf those of professional venture capitalists, providing at least two to five times more capital to 20 to 30 times as many companies.[16]

Angels fill a significant gap in the seed capital market. They are most likely to finance start-ups with capital requirements in the $10,000 to $2 million range, well below the $3 million to $10 million minimum investments most professional venture capitalists prefer. Because a $500,000 deal requires about as much of a venture capitalist's time to research and evaluate as a $5 million deal does, venture capitalists tend to focus on big deals in which their returns are bigger. Angels also tolerate risk levels that would make venture capitalists shudder; as many as 80 percent of angel-backed companies fail.[17] One angel investor, a former executive at Oracle Corporation, says that of the 10 companies in which he has invested, seven have flopped. Three of the start-ups, however, have produced fifty-fold returns![18] Because of the inherent risks in start-up companies, many venture capitalists have shifted their investment portfolios away from start-ups toward more established firms. That's why angel financing is so important: Angels often finance deals that no venture capitalist will consider.

Drdrew.com

When Curtis Geisen teamed up with boyhood friend Drew Pinsky to launch a Web site based on Pinsky's television and radio persona, the pair could find no willing investors. Even though Pinsky was well known among MTV viewers for his show Loveline, *not one venture capital firm showed any interest in the start-up's business plan. "I must have pitched it a 100 times in a year," recalls Geisen. Then Geisen submitted the plan to Garage.com, an online angel network, where it was listed in "heaven," a password-protected section of the site where investors can locate companies that match their investment criteria. Before long, Geisen and Pinsky closed a deal in which five angels purchased 20 percent of Drdrew.com for $1 million.*[19]

As Geisen and Pinsky's experience suggests, the real challenge lies in *finding* these angels. Most angels have substantial business and financial experience, and many of them are entrepreneurs or former entrepreneurs. The typical angel invests in companies at the start-up or infant growth stage and accepts 30 percent of the investment opportunities presented; makes an average of two investments every three years; and has invested an average of $131,000 of equity in 3.5 firms. Ninety percent say they're satisfied with their investment decisions.[20] When evaluating a proposal, angels look for qualified managers, a business with a clearly defined niche, market potential, and a competitive advantage. They also want to see market research that proves the existence of a sizeable customer base.

Because angels frown on "cold calls" from entrepreneurs they don't know, locating them boils down to making the right contacts. Asking friends, attorneys, bankers, stockbrokers, accountants, other business owners, and consultants for suggestions and introductions is a good way to start. "It's all a networking issue," says one active angel.[21] Angels almost always invest their money locally, so entrepreneurs should look close to home for them—typically within a 50- to 100-mile radius. Angels also look for businesses they know something about and most expect to invest their knowledge, experience, and energy as well as their money in a company. In fact, the advice and the network of contacts that angels bring to a deal can sometimes be as valuable as their money!

VetExchange

John McCallum, founder of VetExchange, an Internet-based service provider for veterinarians, found the contacts and the advice angel investors brought to his company to be invaluable. "Our angels are networked across the country," says McCallum. "They have relationships you can't imagine." One angel, a former entrepreneur, gave McCallum valuable advice on a key strategic issue recently. "He's dealt with the same issue five times before," he says.[22]

Angels tend to invest in clusters as well, many of them through one of the nation's 110 angel capital networks. With the right approach, an entrepreneur can attract an angel who might share the deal with some of his cronies.

Band of Angels

In 1995, Hans Severiens, a professional investor, created the Band of Angels, a group of about 50 angels (mostly Silicon Valley millionaires) who meet monthly in Portola Valley, California, to listen to entrepreneurs pitch their business plans. The Band of Angels reviews about 30 proposals each month before inviting a handful of entrepreneurs to make brief presentations at their monthly meeting. Interested members often team up with one another to invest in the businesses they consider most promising. The Band of Angels' average investment is $600,000, which usually nets them between 15 percent and 20 percent of a company's stock.[23]

The Internet has expanded greatly the ability of entrepreneurs in search of capital and angels in search of businesses to find one another. Dozens of angel networks have opened on the World Wide Web, including AngelMoney.com, Business Angels International, Garage.com, the Capital Network, JumpStart Investments, the Capital Connection, WomenAngels.net, and many others.

Angels are an excellent source of "patient money," often willing to wait seven years or longer to cash out their investments. They earn their returns through the increased value of the business, not through dividends and interest. For example, more than 1,000 early investors in Microsoft Inc. are now millionaires, and the original investors in Genentech Inc. (a genetic engineering company) have seen their investments increase more than 500 times![24] Angels' return-on-investment targets tend to be lower than those of professional venture capitalists. Although venture capitalists shoot for 60 percent to 75 percent returns annually, private investors usually settle for 20 percent to 50 percent (depending on the level of risk involved in the venture). Private investors typically take less than 50 percent ownership, leaving the majority of ownership to the company founder(s). The lesson: If an entrepreneur needs relatively small amounts of money to launch a company, angels are a primary source.

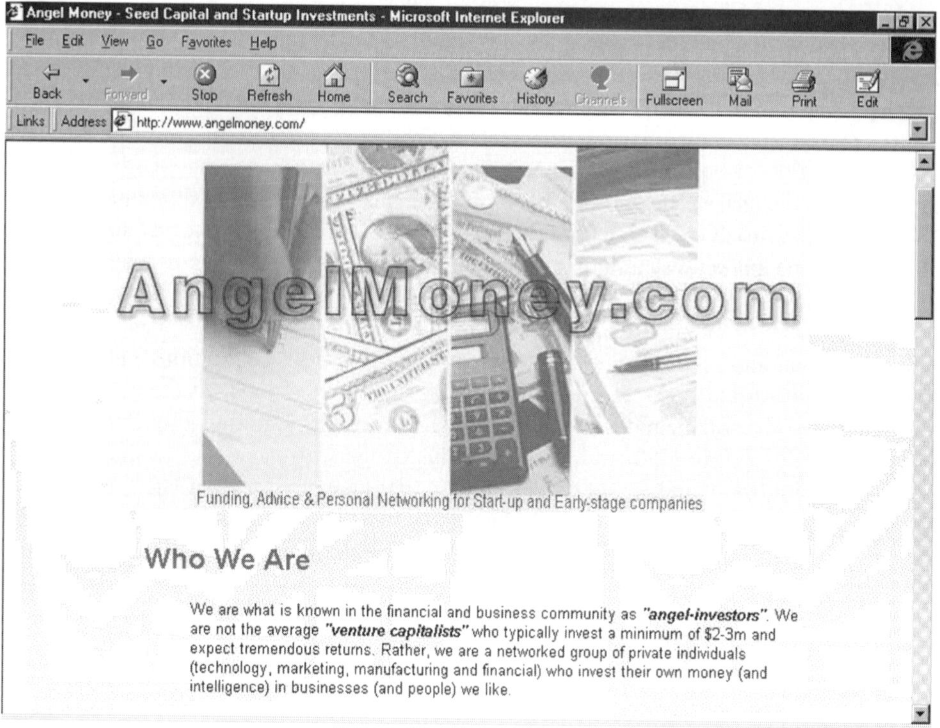

Partners

As we saw in Chapter 4, entrepreneurs can take on partners to expand the capital foundation of a business.

CME Conference Video

When Lou Bucelli and Tim Crouse were searching for the money to launch CME Conference Video, a company that produces and distributes videotapes of educational conferences for physicians, they found an angel willing to put up $250,000 for 40 percent of the business. Unfortunately, their investor backed out when some of his real estate investments went bad, leaving the partners with commitments for several conferences but no cash to produce and distribute the videos. With little time to spare, Bucelli and Crouse decided to form a series of limited partnerships with people they knew, one for each videotape they would produce. Six limited partnerships produced $400,000 in financing, and the tapes generated $9.1 million in sales for the year. As the general partners, Bucelli and Crouse retained 80 percent of each partnership. The limited partners earned returns of up to 80 percent in just six months. Within two years, their company was so successful that venture capitalists started calling. To finance their next round of growth, Bucelli and Crouse sold 35 percent of their company to a venture capital firm for $1.3 million.[25]

Before entering into any partnership arrangement, however, entrepreneurs must consider the impact of giving up some personal control over operations and of sharing profits with others. Whenever entrepreneurs give up equity in their businesses (through whatever mechanism), they run the risk of losing control over it. As the founder's ownership in a company becomes increasingly diluted, the probability of losing control of its future direction and the entire decision-making process increases.

Rollerblades Inc.

At age 19, Scott Olson started a company that manufactured in-line skates—a company for which he had big dreams. Rollerblades Inc. grew quickly but soon ran into the problem that plagues so many fast-growing companies—insufficient cash flow. Through a series of unfortunate incidents, Olson began selling shares of ownership in the company for the money he desperately needed to bring his innovative skate designs to market. Ultimately, investors ended up with 95 percent of the company, leaving Olson with the remaining scant 5 percent. Frustrated at not being able to determine the company's direction, Olson soon left to start another company. "It's tough to keep control," he says. "For every penny you get in the door, you have to give something up."[26]

Corporate Venture Capital

Large corporations have gotten into the business of financing small companies. Today, 900 large corporations across the globe, including Intel, Motorola, Cisco Systems, UPS, and General Electric, invest in start-up companies. According to the National Venture Capital Association, 30 percent of all venture capital investments comes from corporations.[27] Start-up companies not only get a boost from the capital injections large companies give them, but they also stand to gain many other benefits from the relationship. The right corporate partner may share technical expertise, distribution channels, and marketing know-how and provide introductions to important customers and suppliers. Another intangible yet highly important advantage an investment from a large corporate partner gives a start-up is credibility. Doors that otherwise would be closed to a small company magically open when the right corporation becomes a strategic partner.

BuildSoft Inc.

When Keith Brown launched BuildSoft Inc., a company that links residential builders, suppliers, and subcontractors over the Internet, he began looking for corporate investors who would also serve as partners, giving BuildSoft the tools it needed to gain a competitive advantage. Within seven months, Brown had negotiated a $104 million deal with 12 giants in the construction industry, including Lennar and Owens Corning. Not only did the corporations supply valuable capital to the growing company, but they also attracted customers and provided access to products and marketing and distribution expertise.[28]

Foreign corporations are also interested in investing in small U.S. businesses. Often, these corporations are seeking strategic partnerships to gain access to new technology, new products, or access to lucrative U.S. markets. In return, the small companies they invest in benefit from the capital infusion as well as from their partners' international experience and connections. In other cases, small companies are turning to their customers for the resources they need to fuel their rapid growth. Recognizing how interwoven their success is with that of their suppliers, corporate giants such as AT&T, JCPenney, and Ford now offer financial support to many of the small businesses they buy from.

Learning Productions

When Scott Mitchell and Steve Goodman were looking for capital to launch Learning Productions, they made an exploratory sales call on Avnet Computer Marketing Group, a business they hoped would become the first customer for their training software that simulates actual business experiences. Not only did Mitchell and Goodman walk away with an order for their software, but they also secured a commitment from Avnet managers to help launch the start-up. Avnet agreed to provide Learning Productions with free office space and computer access and to pick up the first payroll and the cost of employee benefits. Mitchell and Goodman estimate that Avnet's assistance saved them from having to raise $1.5 million in equity capital and, more importantly, saved them valuable time. "We got at least a three-month jump start," says Mitchell, "and the whole game nowadays is speed to market."[29]

Venture Capital Companies

Venture capital companies are private, for-profit organizations that purchase equity positions in young businesses they believe have high-growth and high-profit potential,

venture capital companies—*private, for-profit organizations that purchase equity positions in young businesses they believe have high-growth and high-profit potential.*

producing annual returns of 300 to 500 percent over five to seven years. More than 3,000 venture capital firms operate across the United States today, investing in promising small companies in a wide variety of industries (see Figure 11.2). Seeking to boost the returns they earn on their endowments, colleges and universities have entered the venture capital business. More than 100 colleges across the nation now have venture funds designed to invest in promising businesses started by their students, alumni, and faculty.[30] Even the Central Intelligence Agency (CIA) has launched a venture capital firm called In-Q-Tel that invests in companies that are developing new technologies that could benefit the CIA. One of In-Q-Tel's investments is in a company that is developing a three-dimensional Web browser that allows users to see "live" versions of the Web sites they visit.[31]

Venture capital firms, which provide about 7 percent of all funding for private companies, have invested billions of dollars in high-potential small companies over the years, including such notable businesses as Apple Computer, Microsoft Inc., Intel, and Data General.[32] Although companies in high-tech industries such as the Internet, computer hardware and software, medical care, biotechnology, and communications are the most popular targets of venture capital, a company with extraordinary growth prospects has the potential to attract venture capital, whatever its industry. Table 11.2 offers a humorous look at how venture capitalists decipher the language of sometimes overly optimistic entrepreneurs.

POLICIES AND INVESTMENT STRATEGIES. Venture capital firms usually establish stringent policies to implement their overall investment strategies.

Investment Size and Screening. Depending on the size of the venture capital corporation and its cost structure, minimum investments range from \$50,000 to \$5 million. Investment ceilings, in effect, do not exist. Most firms seek investments in the \$3 million to \$10 million range to justify the cost of investigating the large number of proposals they receive. "[Venture capital] firms *want* to put more money into a deal," says one expert,

FIGURE 11.2
Venture Capital Financing
Source: PriceWaterhouse-Coopers Moneytree Report, **<www.pwc.moneytree.com>**.

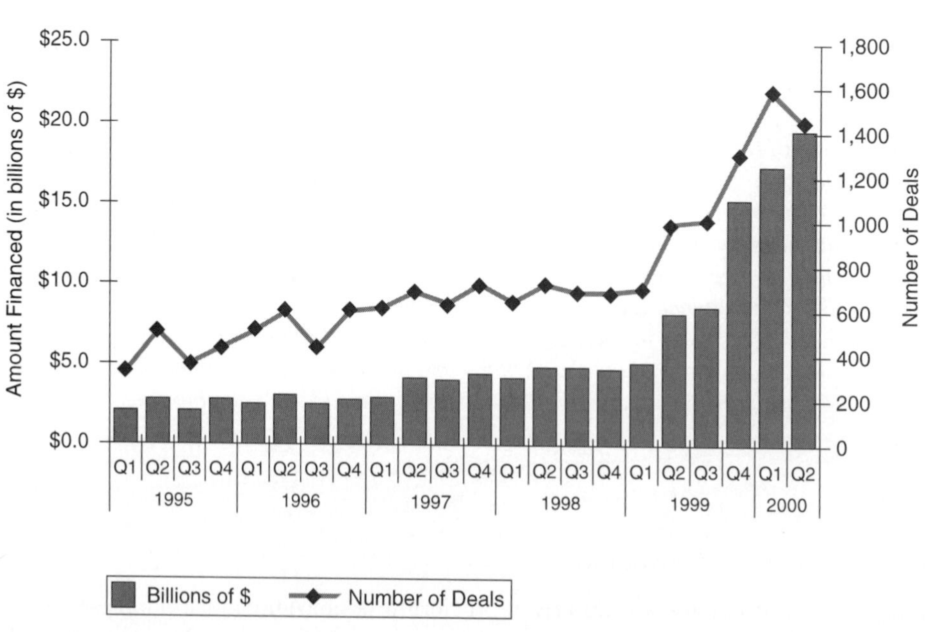

TABLE 11.2
Deciphering the Language of the Venture Capital Industry

Sources: Adapted from Suzanne McGee, "A Devil's Dictionary of Financing," Wall Street Journal, *June 12, 2000, p. C13; John F. Budd Jr., "Cracking the CEO's Code,"* Wall Street Journal, *March 27, 1995, p. A20; "Venture-Speak Defined,"* Teleconnect, *October 1990, p. 42; Cynthia E. Griffin, "Figuratively Speaking,"* Entrepreneur, *August 1999, p. 26.*

By nature, entrepreneurs tend to be optimistic. When screening business plans, venture capitalists must make an allowance for entrepreneurial enthusiasm. Here's a dictionary of phrases commonly found in business plans and their accompanying venture capital translations.

Exploring an acquisition strategy—Our current products have no market.

We're on a clear P2P (pathway to profitability)—We're still years away from earning a profit.

Basically on plan—We're expecting a revenue shortfall of 25 percent.

Internet business model—Potential bigger fools have been identified.

A challenging year—Competitors are eating our lunch.

Considerably ahead of plan—Hit our plan in one of the last three months.

Company's underlying strength and resilience—we still lost money, but look how we cut our losses.

Core business—Our product line is obsolete.

Currently revising budget—The financial plan is in total chaos.

Cyclical industry—We posted a huge loss last year.

Entrepreneurial CEO—He is totally uncontrollable, bordering on maniacal.

Facing unprecedented economic, political, and structural shifts—It's a tough world out there, but we're coping the best we can.

Highly leverageable network—No longer works but has friends who do.

Ingredients are there—Given two years, we might find a workable strategy.

Investing heavily in R&D—We're trying desperately to catch the competition.

Limited downside—Things can't get much worse.

Long sales cycle—Yet to find a customer who likes the product enough to buy it.

Major opportunity—It's our last chance.

Niche strategy—A small-time player.

On a manufacturing learning curve—We can't make the product with positive margins.

Passive investor—She phones once a year to see if we're still in business.

Positive results—Our losses were less than last year.

Repositioning the business—We've recently written off a multimillion-dollar investment.

Selective investment strategy—The board is spending more time on yachts than on planes.

Solid operating performance in a difficult year—Yes, we lost money and market share, but look how hard we tried.

Somewhat below plan—We expect a revenue shortfall of 75 percent.

Expenses were unexpectedly high—We grossly overestimated our profit margins.

Strategic investor—One who will pay a preposterous price for an equity share in the business.

Strongest fourth quarter ever—Don't quibble over the losses in the first three quarters.

Sufficient opportunity to market this product no longer exists—Nobody will buy the thing.

Too early to tell—Results to date have been grim.

A team of skilled, motivated, and dedicated people—We've laid off most of our staff, and those who are left should be glad they still have jobs.

Turnaround opportunity—It's a lost cause.

Unique—We have no more than six strong competitors.

Volume sensitive—Our company has massive fixed costs.

Window of opportunity—Without more money fast, this company is dead.

Work closely with the management—We talk to them on the phone once a month.

A year in which we confronted challenges—At least we know the questions even if we haven't got the answers.

"because they figure their investment is going to take the same attention to watch whether they put in $1 million or $5 million or $25 million."[33]

The venture capital screening process is *extremely* rigorous. The typical venture capital company invests in less than 1 percent of the applications it receives! For example, the average venture capital firm screens about 1,200 proposals a year, but over 90 percent are rejected immediately because they do not match the firm's investment criteria. The remaining 10 percent are investigated more thoroughly at a cost ranging from $2,000 to $3,000 per proposal. At this time, approximately 10 to 15 proposals will have passed the screening process, and these are subjected to comprehensive review. The venture capital firm will invest in three to six of these remaining proposals.

Ownership. Most venture capitalists prefer to purchase ownership in a small business through common stock or convertible preferred stock. The share of ownership a venture capital company purchases may be less than 5 percent for a profitable company to possibly 100 percent for a financially unstable firm. Usually, venture capital firms do not buy a majority of a company's shares; instead, a typical venture capital company seeks to purchase 20 percent to 40 percent of a business. Anything more incurs the risk of draining the entrepreneur's dedication and enthusiasm for managing the firm. Still, the entrepreneur must weigh the positive aspects of receiving needed financing against the negative features of owning a smaller share of the business.

Stage of Investment. Most venture capital firms invest in companies that are either in the early stages of development (called early-stage investing) or in the rapid-growth phase (called expansion-stage investing). Others specialize in acquisitions, providing the financing for managers and employees of a business to buy it out. On average, 91 percent of all venture capital goes to businesses in these stages, although some venture capital firms are showing more interest in companies in the start-up phase because of the tremendous returns that are possible by investing then.[34] Most venture capital firms do not make just a single investment in a company. Instead, they invest in a company over time across several stages, where their investments often total $10 to $15 million.

Control. Although the entrepreneur must sacrifice a portion of the business to the venture capitalist, he usually can retain a majority interest and control of its operations. Most venture capitalists prefer to let the founding team of managers employ its skills to operate a business. However, many venture capitalists join the boards of directors of the companies they invest in or send in new managers or a new management team to protect their investments. Sometimes venture capitalists serve as financial and managerial advisors, while others take an active role in the managing of the company—recruiting employees, providing sales leads, choosing attorneys and advertising agencies, and making daily decisions. One survey found that 90 percent of venture capitalists eventually either become directly involved in managing or select outside managers for the companies in which they invest. Seventy-five percent of these active venture capitalists say they are forced to step in because the existing management team lacked the talent to achieve growth targets.[35] One cautionary note for every entrepreneur seeking venture capital is to find out before the deal is done *exactly* how much control and "hands-on" management investors plan to assume.

Investment Preferences. The venture capital industry has undergone important changes over the past decade. Venture capital funds are larger, more numerous, and more specialized. As the industry grows, more venture capital funds are focusing their investments in niches—everything from low-calorie custards to the Internet. Some will invest in almost any industry but prefer companies in particular stages, including the start-up phase. Traditionally, however, only 9 percent of the companies receiving venture capital financing are in the start-up (seed) stage when entrepreneurs are forming a company or developing a product or service. Most of the start-up businesses that attract venture capital are technology companies.[36]

WHAT VENTURE CAPITALISTS LOOK FOR. Small business owners must realize that it is very difficult for any small business, especially fledgling or struggling firms, to pass the intense screening process of a venture capital company and qualify for an investment. Venture capital firms finance only about 2,600 deals in a typical year.[37] Two factors make a deal attractive to venture capitalists: high returns and a convenient (and profitable) exit strategy. When evaluating potential investments, venture capitalists look for the following features.

Competent Management. The most important ingredient in the success of any business is the ability of the management team, and venture capitalists recognize this. To venture capitalists, the ideal management team has experience, managerial skills, commitment, and the ability to build teams. One financing expert explains, "Venture capitalists are really buying into the management of your company. If the light isn't on at the top, it's dim all the way down."[38]

Competitive Edge. Investors are searching for some factor that will enable a small business to set itself apart from its competitors. This distinctive competence may range from an innovative product or service that satisfies unmet customer needs to a unique marketing or R&D approach. It must be something with the potential to make the business a leader in its field. "You need not apply for VC dough if your product is third, fourth, or later to hit the market," says one financing expert.[39]

Growth Industry. Hot industries attract profits—and venture capital. Most venture capital firms focus their searches for prospects in rapidly expanding fields because they believe the profit potential is greater in these areas. Venture capital firms are most interested in young companies that have enough growth potential to become at least $100 million businesses within three to five years. Venture capitalists know that most of the businesses they invest in will flop, so their winners have to be *big* winners.

Viable Exit Strategy. Venture capitalists not only look for promising companies with the ability to dominate a market, they also want to see a plan for a feasible exit strategy, typically to be executed within three to five years. Venture capital firms realize the return on their investments when the companies they invest in either make an initial public offering or sell out to another business.

Intangible Factors. Some other important factors considered in the screening process are not easily measured; they are the intuitive, intangible factors the venture capitalist detects by gut feeling. This feeling might be the result of the small firm's solid sense of direction, its strategic planning process, the chemistry of its management team, or a number of other factors.

Entrepreneurs in search of financing must understand the implications of accepting venture capital.

GlobalFood Exchange.com

Christopher Swan, cofounder of GlobalFoodExchange.com, an Internet-based food broker, signed a deal for $12.2 million from three venture capital firms in exchange for "a sizeable chunk of equity" in his business. Two of the venture capitalists also sit on the company's board of directors. Swan expresses concern about giving up that much control over the company he helped create but believes the benefits of the capital infusion outweigh the costs.[40]

Despite its many benefits, venture capital is not suited for every entrepreneur. "VC money comes at a price," warns one entrepreneur. "Before boarding a one-way money train, ask yourself if this is the best route for your business and personal desires, because investors are like department stores the day after Christmas—they expect a lot of returns in a short period of time."[41]

4. Describe the process of "going public" as well as its advantages and disadvanages and the various simplified registrations and exemptions from registration available to small businesses.

Public Stock Sale ("Going Public")

In some cases, entrepreneurs can "go public" by selling shares of stock in their corporations to outside investors. In an **initial public offering,** a company raises capital by selling shares of its stock to the general public for the first time. A public offering is an effective method of raising large amounts of capital, but it can be an expensive and time-consuming process filled with regulatory nightmares. "An IPO can be a wonderful thing," says one investment banker. "But it's not all sweetness and light."[42] Once a company makes an initial public offering (IPO), *nothing* will ever be the same again. Managers must consider the impact of their decisions not only on the company and its employees, but also on its shareholders and the value of their stock.

initial public offering— *a method of raising equity capital in which a company sells shares of its stock to the general public for the first time.*

Going public isn't for every business. In fact, most small companies do not meet the criteria for making a successful public stock offering. In a typical year, only about 550 companies manage to make initial public offerings of their stock, and only 20,000 companies in the United States—less than 1 percent of the total—are publicly held. Few companies with less than $10 million in annual sales manage to go public successfully. It is extremely difficult for a start-up company with no track record of success to raise money with a public offering, although some dot-com companies have been able to do so (see Table 11.3). Instead, the investment bankers who underwrite public stock offerings typically look for established companies with the following characteristics:

- consistently high growth rates
- strong record of earnings
- three to five years of audited financial statements
- a solid position in rapidly growing markets
- a sound management team and a strong board of directors

TABLE 11.3
IPOs in the New Economy and in the Old Economy
Source: "What a Difference a Generation Makes," FSB, September 2000, p. 34.

What a difference an economy makes! The following table shows for a sample of both Old Economy and New Economy companies the number of years before the company went public and the price at which the initial public offering was made.

	Company Name	Years to IPO	IPO Price
Old Economy	Starbucks	21.43	$21.50
	Walt Disney	16.46	$25.00
	Merck	13.88	$28.80
	Microsoft	11.20	$21.00
	McDonald's	9.94	$22.50
	FedEx	6.79	$24.00
New Economy	Hotjobs.com	2.52	$ 8.00
	Priceline.com	1.69	$16.00
	MP3.com	1.39	$28.00
	Drugstore.com	1.32	$18.00
	Yahoo!	1.01	$13.00
	NetZero	0.97	$16.00

Meet State Requirements. In addition to satisfying the SEC's requirements, a company also must meet the securities laws in all states in which the issue is sold. These state laws (or "blue-sky" laws) vary drastically from one state to another, and the company must comply with them.

Simplified Registrations and Exemptions

The IPO process described previously (called an S-1 filing) requires maximum disclosure in the initial filing and discourages most small businesses from using it. Fortunately, the SEC allows several exemptions from this full-disclosure process for small businesses. Many small businesses that go public choose one of these simplified options the SEC has designed for small companies. The SEC has established the following simplified registration statements and exemptions from the registration process.

REGULATION S-B. Regulation S-B is a simplified registration process for small companies seeking to make initial or subsequent public offerings. Not only does this regulation simplify the initial filing requirements with the SEC, it also reduces the ongoing disclosure and filings required of companies. Its primary goals are to open the doors to capital markets to smaller companies by cutting the paperwork and the costs of raising capital. Companies using the simplified registration process have two options: Form SB-1, a "transitional" registration statement for companies issuing less than $10 million worth of securities over a 12-month period, and Form SB-2, reserved for small companies seeking more than $10 million in a 12-month period.

To be eligible for the simplified registration process under Regulation S-B, a company must:

- be based in the United States or Canada.
- have revenues of less than $25 million.
- have outstanding publicly held stock worth no more than $25 million.
- not be an investment company.
- provide audited financial statements for two fiscal years.

The goal of Regulation S-B's simplified registration requirements is to enable smaller companies to go public without incurring the expense of a full-blown registration. Total costs for a Regulation S-B are approximately $35,000.

REGULATION D (RULE 504): SMALL COMPANY OFFERING REGISTRATION. Created in the late 1980s, the Small Company Offering Registration (SCOR) (also known as the Uniform Limited Offering Registration, ULOR) now is available in 47 states. A little known tool, SCOR is designed to make it easier and less expensive for small companies to sell their stock to the public by eliminating the requirement for registering the offering with the SEC. The whole process typically costs less than half of what a traditional public offering costs. Entrepreneurs using SCOR will need an attorney and an accountant to help them with the issue, but many can get by without a securities lawyer, which can save tens of thousands of dollars. Some entrepreneurs even choose to market their companies' securities themselves (for example, to customers), saving the expense of hiring a broker. However, selling an issue is both time and energy consuming, and most SCOR experts recommend hiring a professional securities or brokerage firm to sell the company's shares. The SEC's objective in creating SCOR was to give small companies the same access to equity financing that large companies have via the stock market while bypassing many of the same costs and filing requirements.

The capital ceiling on an SCOR issue is $1 million, and the price of each share must be at least $5. That means that a company can sell no more than 200,000 shares (making the stock less attractive to stock manipulators). An SCOR offering requires only minimal notification to the SEC. The company must file a standardized disclosure statement, the U-7, which consists of 50 fill-in-the-blank questions. The form, which asks for information such as how much money the company needs, what the money will be used for, what investors receive, how investors can sell their investments, and other pertinent questions, also serves as a business plan, a state securities offering registration, a disclosure document, and a prospectus. Entrepreneurs using SCOR may advertise their companies' offerings and can sell them directly to any investor with no restrictions and no minimums. An entrepreneur can sell practically any kind of security through an SCOR, including common stock, preferred stock, convertible preferred stock, stock options, stock warrants, and others.

CorpHQ

Steve Crane and Art Aviles, Jr., cofounders of CorpHQ, a Web portal that links small and home-based business owners in an online community, decided to bypass venture capital and relied on an SCOR offering to attract their first round of outside capital. The entrepreneurs believed that taking their company public not only would save them money, but also would create greater opportunities for future financing efforts, both of which have proved to be true. Early on, Crane and Aviles recognized the need to promote their newly public company, whose shares trade on the OTC Bulletin Board, in the investment community. "Our success as a public company depends not only on how well we do financially but also how well we market our company and our story to the financial markets," says Crane.[51]

An SCOR offering provides entrepreneurs needing equity financing the following *advantages:*

- Access to a sizeable pool of equity funds without the expense of full registration with the SEC. Companies often can complete an SCOR offering for less than $25,000.
- Few restrictions on the securities to be sold and on the investors to whom they can be sold.
- The ability to market the offering through advertisements to the public.
- New or start-up companies can qualify.
- No requirement of audited financial statements for offerings less than $500,000.
- Faster approval of the issue from regulatory agencies.
- The ability to make the offering in several states at once.

There are, of course, some *disadvantages* to using SCOR to raise needed funds:

- Not every state yet recognizes SCOR offerings.
- Partnerships cannot make SCOR offerings.
- A company can raise no more than $1 million in a 12-month period.
- An entrepreneur must register the offering in every state in which shares of stock will be sold, although current regulations allow simultaneous registration in multiple states.
- The process can be time consuming, distracting an entrepreneur from the daily routine of running the company. A limited secondary market for the securities may limit investors' interest. Currently, SCOR shares must be traded through brokerage firms that make small markets in specific stocks. However, the Pacific Stock Exchange and the NASDAQ's electronic bulletin board recently began listing SCOR stocks, so the secondary market for them has broadened.

REGULATION D (RULES 505 AND 506): PRIVATE PLACEMENTS. Rules 505 and 506 are exemptions from federal registration requirements that give emerging companies

INVENTORY FINANCING. Here, a small business loan is secured by its inventory of raw materials, work in process, and finished goods. If an owner defaults on the loan, the lender can claim the firm's inventory, sell it, and use the proceeds to satisfy the loan (assuming the bank's claim is superior to the claims of other creditors). Because inventory usually is not a highly liquid asset and its value can be difficult to determine, lenders are willing to lend only a portion of its worth, usually no more than 50 percent of the inventory's value. Most asset-based lenders avoid inventory-only deals; they prefer to make loans backed by inventory *and* more secure accounts receivable.

Asset-based financing is a powerful tool. A small business that could obtain a $1 million line of credit with a bank would be able to borrow as much as $3 million by using accounts receivable as collateral.[66] It is also an efficient method of borrowing because a small business owner has the money he needs when he needs it. In other words, the business pays only for the capital it actually needs and uses.

To ensure the quality of the assets supporting the loans they make, lenders must monitor borrowers' assets, perhaps as often as once a month, making paperwork requirements on these loans intimidating, especially to first-time borrowers. Also, asset-based loans are more expensive than traditional bank loans because of the cost of originating and maintaining them and the higher risk involved. Rates usually run from two to seven percentage points above the prime rate. Because of this rate differential, small business owners should not use asset-based loans over the long term; their goal should be to establish their credit through asset-based financing and then to move up to a line of credit.

Trade Credit

Because of its ready availability, trade credit is an extremely important source of financing to most entrepreneurs. When banks refuse to lend money to a start-up business because they see it as a bad credit risk, an entrepreneur may be able to turn to trade credit for capital. Getting vendors to extend credit in the form of delayed payments (e.g., "net 30" credit terms) usually is much easier for small businesses than obtaining bank financing. Essentially, a company receiving trade credit from a supplier is getting a short-term, interest-free loan for the amount of the goods purchased.

It is no surprise that businesses receive three dollars of credit from suppliers for every two dollars they receive from banks as loans.[67] Vendors and suppliers usually are willing to finance a small business owner's purchase of goods from 30 to 90 days, interest free.

AMCAL

For instance, Gus Walboldt, owner of AMCAL, a fine-art publishing company, uses supplier financing as an integral part of his company's 20-year growth plan. Because calendars represent a large portion of AMCAL's sales, its business is highly seasonal, which creates significant cash flow problems. "We would spend half the year flush with cash [and the other half] cash poor," says Walboldt. Walboldt worked out a financing arrangement with the companies that print the calendars. AMCAL pays the printers' labor and material costs when the calendars are printed during the summer months and then covers their profit margins when its cash flow swells in the fall.[68]

The key to maintaining trade credit as a source of funds is establishing a consistent and reliable payment history with every vendor.

Equipment Suppliers

Most equipment vendors encourage business owners to purchase their equipment by offering to finance the purchase. This method of financing is similar to trade credit but with slightly different terms. Usually, equipment vendors offer reasonable credit terms with only a modest down payment with the balance financed over the life of the equipment (often several years). In some cases, the vendor will repurchase equipment for salvage value at the end of its useful life and offer the business owner another credit agreement on new equipment. Start-up companies often use trade credit from equipment suppliers to purchase equipment and fixtures such as counters, display cases, refrigeration units, machinery, and the like. It pays to scrutinize vendors' credit terms, however; they may be less attractive than those of other lenders.

Commercial Finance Companies

When denied a bank loan, small business owners often look to commercial finance companies for the same type of loan. Commercial finance companies are second only to banks in making loans to small businesses and, unlike their conservative counterparts, are willing to tolerate more risk in their loan portfolios.[69] Of course, their primary consideration is collecting their loans, but finance companies tend to rely more on obtaining a security interest in some type of collateral, given the higher-risk loans that make up their portfolios. Because commercial finance companies depend on collateral to recover most of their losses, they do not require the complete financial projections of future operations that most banks do. However, this does *not* mean that they do not carefully evaluate a company's financial position before making a loan.

Approximately 150 large commercial finance companies such as AT&T Small Business Lending, GE Capital Small Business Finance, and others make a variety of loans to small companies, ranging from asset-based loans and business leases to construction and Small Business Administration loans. Dubbed "the Wal-Marts of finance," commercial finance companies usually offer many of the same credit options that commercial banks do. However, because their loans are subject to more risks, finance companies charge a higher interest rate than commercial banks (usually at least prime plus 4 percent). Their most common methods of providing credit to small businesses are asset based—accounts receivable financing and inventory loans. Specific rates on these loans vary but can be as high as 20 to 30 percent (including fees), depending on the risk a particular business presents and the quality of the assets involved.

In addition to short-term financing for small businesses, commercial finance companies also extend intermediate and long-term loans for real estate and fixed assets.

AMK Manufacturing

When Anna Kinney wanted to build a new building to house her metal fabrication business, AMK Manufacturing, 20 banks rejected her loan application, even though she owned all of the equipment in her company and had a track record of success. Kinney then turned to Allied Capital, a Washington, DC–based commercial finance company, that quickly approved a $300,000, 25-year loan backed by a guarantee from the Small Business Administration.[70]

Savings and Loan Associations

Savings and loan associations (S&Ls) specialize in loans for real property. In addition to their traditional role of providing mortgages for personal residences, S&Ls offer financing on commercial and industrial property. In the typical commercial or industrial loan, the S&L will lend up to 80 percent of the property's value with a repayment schedule of up to 30 years. Minimum loan amounts are typically $50,000, but most S&Ls hesitate to lend money for buildings specially designed for a particular customer's needs. S&Ls expect the mortgage to be repaid from the firm's future profits.

margin loans—*loans from stockbrokers that use the stocks and bonds in the borrower's portfolio as collateral.*

Stock Brokerage Houses

Stockbrokers are getting into the lending business, too, and many of them offer loans to their customers at lower interest rates than banks. These **margin loans** carry lower rates because the collateral supporting them—the stocks and bonds in the customer's portfolio—is of high quality and is highly liquid. "There isn't a bank in the country that can lend more cheaply than you can borrow on margin," claims one stockbroker.[71] Moreover, brokerage firms make it easy to borrow. Usually, brokers set up a line of credit for their customers when they open a brokerage account. To tap that line of credit, the customer simply writes a check or uses a debit card. Typically, there is no fixed repayment schedule for a margin loan; the debt can remain outstanding indefinitely, as long as the market value of the borrower's portfolio of collateral meets minimum requirements. Aspiring entrepreneurs can borrow up to 50 percent of the value of their stock portfolios, up to 70 percent of the value of their bond portfolios, and up to 90 percent of the value of their government securities. For example, one woman borrowed $60,000 to buy equipment for her New York health club, and a St. Louis doctor borrowed $1 million against his brokerage account to help finance a medical clinic.[72]

There is risk involved in using stocks and bonds as collateral on a loan. Brokers typically require a 30 percent cushion on margin loans. If the value of the borrower's portfolio drops, the broker can make a **margin call**—that is, the broker can call the loan in and require the borrower to provide more cash and securities as collateral. Recent swings in the stock market have translated into margin calls for many entrepreneurs, requiring them to repay a significant portion of their loan balances within a matter of days—or hours. If an account lacks adequate collateral, the broker can sell off the customer's portfolio to pay off the loan.

margin call—*occurs when the value of a borrower's portfolio drops and the broker calls the loan in, requiring the borrower to put up more cash and securities as collateral.*

Insurance Companies

For many small businesses, life insurance companies can be an important source of business capital. Insurance companies offer two basic types of loans: policy loans and mortgage loans. **Policy loans** are extended on the basis of the amount of money paid through premiums into the insurance policy. It usually takes about two years for an insurance policy to accumulate enough cash surrender value to justify a loan against it. Once he accumulates cash value in a policy, an entrepreneur may borrow up to 95 percent of that value for any length of time. Interest is levied annually, but repayment may be deferred indefinitely. However, the amount of insurance coverage is reduced by the amount of the loan. Policy loans typically offer very favorable interest rates—often around 8 percent or less. Only insurance policies that build cash value—that is, combine a savings plan with insurance coverage—offer the option of borrowing. These include whole life (permanent insurance), variable life, universal life, and many corporate-owned life insurance policies. Term life insurance, which offers only pure insurance coverage, has no borrowing capacity.

policy loan—*a loan insurance companies make on the basis of the amount of money a customer has paid into a policy in the form of premiums.*

Insurance companies make **mortgage loans** on a long-term basis on real property worth a minimum of $500,000. They are based primarily on the value of the real property being purchased. The insurance company will extend a loan of up to 75 or 80 percent of the real estate's value and will allow a lengthy repayment schedule over 25 or 30 years so that payments do not strain the firm's cash flows excessively.

mortgage loan—*a loan insurance companies make on a long-term basis for real property worth at least $500,000.*

Credit Unions

Credit unions, nonprofit financial cooperatives that promote saving and provide loans to their members, are best known for making consumer and car loans. However, many are also willing to lend money to their members to launch businesses, especially since many banks have restricted loans to higher-risk start-ups. Of the 11,000 state and federally chartered credit unions operating in the United States, about 1,600 are actively making business loans, those of more than $25,000 granted without personal collateral for the purpose

credit union—*a nonprofit financial cooperative that promotes saving and provides loans to its members.*

of starting a business, to their members. Credit unions make almost $3 billion in small business loans each year.[73]

Credit unions don't make loans to just anyone; to qualify for a loan, an entrepreneur must be a member. Lending practices at credit unions are very much like those at banks, but they usually are willing to make smaller loans. Entrepreneurs around the globe are turning to credit unions to finance their businesses, sometimes borrowing tiny amounts of money.

Joseph Ogwal

When Joseph Ogwal, a refugee of war-torn Sudan, arrived in South Africa, he had nothing—literally. Ogwal, who has a degree in electronics engineering, wanted to start his own business to earn enough money to bring his family to South Africa, so he turned to the Cape Metropole South African Credit Co-operative (SACCO) for a small loan. With his $115 loan, Ogwal launched a consumer electronics repair business that already is earning a profit. With another loan from the credit union, he plans to expand his business, launching a training center for repair technicians.[74]

Bonds

Bonds, which are corporate IOUs, have always been a popular source of debt financing for large companies. Few small business owners realize that they can also tap this valuable source of capital. Although the smallest businesses are not viable candidates for issuing bonds, a growing number of small companies are finding the funding they need through bonds when banks and other lenders say no. Because of the costs involved, issuing bonds usually is best suited for companies generating sales between $5 million and $30 million and have capital requirements between $1.5 million and $10 million. Although they can help small companies raise much needed capital, bonds have certain disadvantages. The issuing company must follow the same regulations that govern businesses selling stock to public investors. Even if the bond issue is private, the company must register the offering and file periodic reports with the SEC.

Small manufacturers needing money for fixed assets have access to an attractive, relatively inexpensive source of funds in industrial development bonds (IDBs). A company wanting to issue IDBs must get authorization from the appropriate municipality and the state before proceeding. Typically, the amount of money small companies issuing IDBs seek to raise is at least $1 million, but some small manufacturers have raised as little as $500,000 using IDBs. Even though the paperwork and legal costs associated with making an IDB issue can run up to 2 to 3 percent of the financing amount, that is a relative bargain for borrowing long-term money at a fixed interest rate.

To open IDBs up to even smaller companies, some states pool the industrial bonds of several small companies too small to make an issue. By joining together to issue composite industrial bonds, companies can reduce their issuing fees and attract a greater number of investors. The issuing companies typically pay lower interest rates than they would on conventional bank loans, often below the prime interest rate.

Private Placements

Earlier in this chapter, we saw how companies can raise capital by making private placements of their stock (equity). Private placements are also available for debt instruments. A private placement involves selling debt to one or a small number of investors, usually insurance companies or pension funds. Private placement debt is a hybrid between a conventional loan and a bond. At its heart, it is a bond, but its terms are tailored to the borrower's individual needs, as a loan would be.

Privately placed securities offer several advantages over standard bank loans. First, they usually carry fixed interest rates rather than the variable rates banks often charge. Second, the maturity of private placements is longer than most bank loans: 15 years rather than five. Private placements do not require hiring expensive investment bankers. Finally, because private investors can afford to take greater risks than banks, they are willing to finance deals for fledgling small companies.

Small Business Investment Companies

Small Business Investment Companies (SBICs), created in 1958 when Congress passed the Small Business Investment Act, are privately owned financial institutions that are licensed and regulated by the SBA. Their function is to use a combination of private capital and federally guaranteed debt to provide long-term capital to small businesses. There are two types of SBICs: regular SBICs and specialized SBICs (SSBICs). Approximately 103 SSBICs provide credit and capital to small businesses that are at least 51 percent owned by minorities and socially or economically disadvantaged people. Since their inception in 1969, SSBICs have helped finance more than 19,000 minority-owned companies with investments totaling $1.86 billion. Most SBICs prefer later-round financing (mezzanine financing) and leveraged buyouts (LBOs) over funding raw start-ups. Because of changes in their financial structure made a few years ago, however, SBICs now are better equipped to invest in start-up companies. In fact, about 53 percent of SBIC investments go to companies that are no more than three years old.[75] Funding from SBICs helped launch companies such as Apple Computer, Federal Express, Sun Microsystems, and Outback Steakhouse.

Small Business Investment Companies (SBICs)—*privately owned financial institutions that are licensed and regulated by the SBA; they use a combination of private and public funds to provide long-term capital to small businesses.*

Since 1960, SBICs have provided more than $22 billion in long-term debt and equity financing to some 86,000 small businesses, adding many thousands of jobs to the U.S. economy. Both SBICs and SSBICs must be capitalized privately with a minimum of $5 to $10 million, at which point they qualify for up to four dollars in long-term SBA loans for every dollar of private capital invested in small businesses. As a general rule, both SBICs and SSBICs may provide financial assistance only to small businesses with a net worth of less than $18 million and average after-tax earnings of $6 million during its past two years. However, employment and total annual sales standards vary from industry to industry. SBICs are limited to a maximum investment or loan amount of 20 percent of their private capital to a single client, while SSBICs may lend or invest up to 30 percent of their private capital in a single small business.

SBICs can provide both debt and equity financing to small businesses. But, because of SBA regulations affecting the financing arrangements an SBIC can offer, most SBICs extend their investments as loans with an option to convert the debt instrument into an equity interest later. Most SBIC loans are between $100,000 and $5 million and carry interest rates that can be as high as 17 or 18 percent, but the loan term is longer than most banks allow. When they make equity investments, SBICs are prohibited from obtaining a controlling interest in the companies in which they invest (no more than 49 percent ownership). The average SBIC investment is $583,200. The most common forms of SBIC financing (in order of their frequency) are a loan with an option to buy stock, a convertible debenture, a straight loan, and preferred stock.

Callaway Golf Company

Callaway Golf Company, now the world's largest maker of premium golf clubs, received much of its early financing from SBICs. Ely Callaway, an avid golfer, founded the company at age 63 because he believed that his revolutionary design for a new club would be a huge success. After putting up $400,000 of his own money, Callaway convinced two SBICs, Mventure Corporation and National City Capital Corporation, to invest more than $1 million in the company over the next several years. When Gallaway Golf went public, both SBICs sold their holdings in the company, generating impressive returns on their investments. Today, Callaway Golf employs 2,400 people and generates more than $2 billion a year in sales from 70 countries.[76]

Small Business Lending Companies

Small Business Lending Companies (SBLCs) make only intermediate and long-term SBA-guaranteed loans. They specialize in loans that many banks would not consider and operate on a nationwide basis. For instance, most SBLC loans have terms extending for at least 10 years. The maximum interest rate for loans of seven years or longer is 2.75 percent above the prime rate; for shorter-term loans, the ceiling is 2.25 percent above prime. Another feature of SBLC loans is the expertise the SBLC offers borrowing companies in critical areas.

SBLCs also screen potential investors carefully, and most of them specialize in particular industries. The result is a low loan default rate of roughly 4 percent. Corporations own most of the nation's SBLCs, giving them a solid capital base.

6. Identify the various federal loan programs aimed at small companies.

FEDERALLY SPONSORED PROGRAMS

Federally sponsored lending programs have suffered from budget reductions in the past several years. Current trends suggest that the federal government is reducing its involvement in the lending business, but many programs are still quite active and some are actually growing.

Economic Development Administration

The Economic Development Administration (EDA), a branch of the Commerce Department, offers loan guarantees to create new business and to expand existing businesses in areas with below-average income and high unemployment. Focusing on economically distressed communities, the EDA finances long-term investment projects needed to stimulate economic growth and to create jobs by making loan guarantees. The EDA guarantees up to 80 percent of business loans between $750,000 and $10 million. Entrepreneurs apply for loans through private lenders, for whom an EDA guarantee significantly reduces the risk of lending. Start-up companies must supply 15 percent of the guaranteed amount in the form of equity, and established businesses must make equity investments of at least 15 percent of the guaranteed amount. Small businesses can use the loan proceeds in a variety of ways, including supplementing working capital and purchasing equipment to buying land and renovating buildings.

EDA business loans are designed to help replenish economically distressed areas by creating or expanding small businesses that provide employment opportunities in local communities. To qualify for a loan, the business must be located in the disadvantaged area, and its presence must directly benefit local residents. Some communities experiencing high unemployment or suffering from the effects of devastating natural disasters have received EDA Revolving Loan Fund Grants to create loan pools for local small businesses. Since 1972, the EDA has funded nearly 600 Revolving Loan Fund Grants that have, in turn, made loans to more than 7,200 private businesses.[77]

Department of Housing and Urban Development

The Department of Housing and Urban Development (HUD) sponsors several loan programs to assist qualified entrepreneurs in raising needed capital. The Community Development Block Grants (CDBGs) are extended to cities and towns that, in turn, lend or grant money to entrepreneurs to start small businesses that will strengthen the local economy. Grants are aimed at cities and towns in need of revitalization and economic stimulation. Some grants are used to construct buildings and plants to be leased to entrepreneurs, sometimes with an option to buy. Others are earmarked for revitalizing crime-ridden areas or making start-up loans to entrepreneurs or expansion loans to existing business owners. No ceilings or geographic limitations are placed on CDBG loans and grants, but projects must benefit low- and moderate-income families.

CDBG loan and grant terms are negotiated individually between a town and an entrepreneur. An entrepreneur might negotiate a low-interest, long-term loan, whereas another might arrange for a grant in return for a promise to share a portion of the company's profits for several years with the town.

U.S. Department of Agriculture's Rural Business-Cooperative Service

The U.S. Department of Agriculture provides financial assistance to certain small businesses through its Rural Business-Cooperative Service (RBS). The RBS program is open to all types of businesses (not just farms) and is designed to create nonfarm employment opportunities in rural areas—those with populations below 50,000 and not adjacent to a city where densities exceed 100 people per square mile. Entrepreneurs in many small towns, especially those with populations below 25,000, are eligible to apply for loans through the RBS program, which makes about $850 million in loan guarantees each year.

The RBS does make a limited number of direct loans to small businesses, but the majority of its activity is in loan guarantees. The RBS will guarantee as much as 90 percent of a bank's loan up to $25 million (although actual guarantee amounts are almost always far less) for qualified applicants. Entrepreneurs apply for loans through private lenders, who view applicants with loan guarantees much more favorably than those without such guarantees. The RBS guarantee reduces the lender's risk dramatically because the guarantee means that the government agency would pay off the loan balance (up to the ceiling) if the entrepreneur defaults on the loan.

To make a loan guarantee, the RBS requires much of the same documentation as most banks and most other loan guarantee programs. Because of its emphasis on developing employment in rural areas, the RBS requires an environmental impact statement describing the jobs created and the effect the business has on the area.

Local Development Companies

The federal government encourages local residents to organize and fund **local development companies (LDCs)** on either a profit or nonprofit basis. After raising initial capital by selling stock to at least 25 residents, the company seeks loans from banks and from the SBA. Each LDC can qualify for up to $1 million per year in loans and guarantees from the SBA to assist in starting small businesses in the community. Most LDCs are certified to operate locally or regionally, but each state may have one LDC that can operate *anywhere* within its boundaries. LDCs enable towns to maintain a solid foundation of small businesses even when other attractive benefits such as trade zones and tax breaks are not available.

local development companies (LDCs)—*profit-seeking or nonprofit organizations that combine private funds and public funds to lend money to small businesses.*

Three parties are involved in providing the typical LDC loan—the LDC, the SBA, and a participating bank. An LDC normally requires the small business owner to assist by supplying about 10 percent of a project's cost and then arranges for the remaining capital through SBA guarantees and bank loans. LDCs finance only the fixed assets of a small business—acquiring land or buildings and modernizing, renovating, or restoring existing facilities and sites. They cannot provide funds for working capital to supply inventory, supplies, or equipment, but they can help arrange loans from banks for working capital. LDCs usually purchase real estate, refurbish or construct buildings and plants, equip them, and then lease the entire facility to the small business. The lessee's payments extend for 20 to 25 years to allow repayment of SBA, bank, and LDC loans. When the lease expires, the

LDC normally gives the small business owners an option to purchase the facility, sometimes at prices well below market value.

Small Business Innovation Research Program

Started as a pilot program by the National Science Foundation in the 1970s, the Small Business Innovation Research (SBIR) Program has expanded to 11 federal agencies, ranging from NASA to the Department of Defense, and has an annual budget of $1.2 billion. These agencies award cash grants or long-term contracts to small companies wanting to initiate or to expand their research and development (R&D) efforts. SBIR grants give innovative small companies the opportunity to attract early-stage capital investments *without* having to give up significant equity stakes or take on burdensome levels of debt. The SBIR process includes three phases. Phase I grants, which determine the feasibility and commercial potential of a technology or product, last for up to six months and have a ceiling of $100,000. Phase II grants, designed to develop the concept into a specific technology or product, run for up to 24 months with a ceiling of $750,000. Approximately 40 percent of all Phase II applicants receive funding. Phase III is the commercialization phase, in which the company pursues commercial applications of the research and development conducted in Phases I and II and must use private or non-SBIR federal funding to bring a product to market.

Competition for SBIR funding is intense; only 12 percent of the small companies that apply receive funding. So far, more than 30,000 SBIR awards totaling in excess of $7 billion have gone to small companies, which traditionally have had difficulty competing with big corporations for federal R&D dollars. The government's dollars have been well invested. About one in four small businesses receiving SBIR awards have achieved commercial success for their products.[78]

Active Control Experts Inc.

Active Control Experts Inc. received a $500,000 grant from the Department of Defense to develop a vibration control device that would stabilize the tails of jet fighters. Active Control Experts went on to apply the technology it developed through the SBIR to a new product that makes snowboards more stable.[79]

The Small Business Technology Transfer Program

The Small Business Technology Transfer (STTR) Program complements the SBIR Program. Whereas the SBIR focuses on commercially promising ideas that originate in small businesses, the STTR uses companies to exploit the vast reservoir of commercially promising ideas that originate in universities, federally funded R&D centers, and nonprofit research institutions. Researchers at these institutions can join forces with small businesses and can spin off commercially promising ideas while remaining employed at their research institutions. Five federal agencies award grants of up to $500,000 in three phases to these research partnerships. The STTR's annual budget is approximately $5 million.

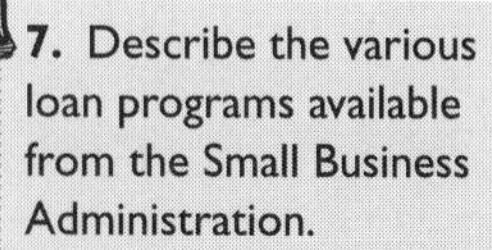
7. Describe the various loan programs available from the Small Business Administration.

SMALL BUSINESS ADMINISTRATION

The Small Business Administration (SBA) has several programs designed to help finance both start-up and existing small companies that cannot qualify for traditional loans because of their thin asset base and their high risk of failure. In its 45-plus years of operation, the SBA has helped more than 14 million companies get the financing they need for start-up or for growth. To be eligible for SBA funds, a business must be within the SBA's criteria for defining a small business. Also, some types of businesses, such as those engaged in gam-

YOU BE THE CONSULTANT . . .

Will $45 Million Get This Car Off the Ground?

For more than 40 years, Paul Moller has been a successful entrepreneur. A gifted mechanical engineer, he has made millions of dollars from several ventures, including the Supertrapp muffler (which became one of the most successful after-market accessories ever made for motorcycles), real estate development projects, and government contracts for flying camera platforms that can perform a variety of duties ranging from inspecting bridges to scouting enemy troops. "[My wife] doesn't understand how I can make so much money and still be broke," jokes Moller.

Understanding Moller's perpetual state of near insolvency is much easier when one understands the dream he has pursued so passionately since his youth. Moller, now in his sixties, is the inventor of the Skycar, a personal vertical takeoff and landing vehicle that he believes is the gateway to the next era of mass transportation. Moller continues to be amazed that people all over the world spend hours stuck in road traffic in machines that were invented in the nineteenth century while the skies above them are wide open. His Skycar is a "roadable aircraft" that, in theory, is capable of lifting off in the length of a standard driveway, flying its occupants to their destination at 350 mph, and landing vertically like a helicopter—all while getting 20 miles to a gallon of fuel!

Moller's vision of the future is filled with Skycars crossing the sky under the automated control of supercomputers and Global Positioning System satellites. Passengers simply punch in their desired destinations, sit back, and let the computers take over. At first glance, his vision may sound like the rantings of a crazed inventor. (After all, people once scoffed at the notion of space travel and landing people on the moon.) But Moller has achieved many breakthroughs with his flying car concept.

Moller's mechanical genius shone through at an early age. When he was just 11, Moller built a working four-person Ferris wheel, and at age 15, after an encounter with a hummingbird, he built a primitive helicopter. His fascination with making machines that can fly never left him.

In 1965, in his workshop, Moller built and flew, briefly, a small two-engine hovering platform, the XM-2. By 1968, he had completed the XM-3, a more stable version of his hovering saucerlike platform. Although the platform was not capable of sustained, controlled flight, it proved that Moller's idea was feasible. To transform these early successes into his dream car, however, would take money—and lots of it. The struggle to attract capital would become a major theme for the rest of Moller's life, a struggle that continues to this day.

One of Moller's greatest successes came on May 10, 1989, when he flew the prototype for his Skycar, the M200X, to a height of 50 feet. The M220X went on to make more than 200 successful flights and led to the development of Moller's current Skycar, also known as the M400. Looking like a cross between a Cessna airplane and the Batmobile, the Skycar sports a bubbled cockpit, is the size of a standard sport utility vehicle, weighs in at 2,400 pounds, and seats four adults. It uses standard automobile fuel and includes emergency parachutes (of course). Twenty-eight different computers running more than 27,000 lines of code control the Skycar's operation, including steering and the flow of fuel to its eight light but powerful engines. Although early production models would be expensive, Moller estimates that once in full production, the Skycar would sell for $40,000 to $60,000, about the price of a quality luxury car.

Moller's company has teetered on the verge of bankruptcy on more than one occasion, and employee turnover has been a problem because the business sometimes has to delay issuing paychecks due to a lack of cash. Still, Moller refuses to give up and is always looking for ways to finance the research and development of the Skycar, a task he regrets because it takes precious time away from his work on the car.

Moller has already plowed $100 million into the Skycar over the years, which, when compared to the $1 billion automakers spend just to redesign one model, is not quite as much as it seems. He estimates that getting the car into production will require another $45 million. To reach the full production volume needed to bring the cost of the Skycar down to earthly levels will take $500 million. The major question is: Where will the money come from?

1. Would you be willing to invest in Moller International? Explain.
2. If you were advising Moller on raising capital for his company, would you recommend that he pursue debt capital or equity capital? Why?
3. Develop a list (in descending order of importance) of possible sources of capital you would suggest to Moller International, and briefly explain your reasoning for including each one.

Sources: Adapted from Moller International Inc., **<www.moller.com>**; Peter Waldman, "Great Idea . . . If It Flies," *Wall Street Journal,* June 24, 1999, pp. B1, B4; David H. Freedman, "This *Is* Rocket Science," *Inc.,* July 2000, **<www.inc.com/articles/details/printable/0,3535, ART9546,00.html>**; John Pearley Huffman, "The Amazing Flying Car of Tomorrow," *Car and Driver,* June 2000, **<www.caranddriver. com/FrameSet/0,1350,_sl_NewArticle_sl_0_cm _1633_cm_3767_ 1_16_cm_00,00.html>**; Jordan Raphael, "The Audacious Mr. Moller," *Los Angeles Times Magazine,* June 2000, **<www.latimes.com/news/ state/updates/lat_flyingcar000625.htm>.**

bling, pyramid sales schemes, or real estate investment, among others, are ineligible for SBA loans.

The loan application process can take from between three days to many months, depending on how well prepared the entrepreneur is and which bank is involved. To speed up processing times, the SBA has established a Certified Lender Program (CLP) and a Preferred Lender Program (PLP). Both are designed to encourage banks to become frequent SBA lenders. When a bank makes enough good loans to qualify as a certified lender, the SBA promises a fast turnaround time for the loan decision—typically three to ten business days. When a bank becomes a preferred lender, it makes the final lending decision itself, subject to SBA review. In essence, the SBA delegates the application process, the lending decision, and other details to the preferred lender. The SBA guarantees up to 75 percent of PLP loans in case the borrower fails and defaults on the loan. The minimum PLP loan guarantee is $100,000, while the maximum is $500,000. Using certified or preferred lenders can reduce the processing time for an SBA loan considerably.

Low Doc Loan Program— *a program initiated by the SBA in an attempt to simplify and streamline the application process for small business loans.*

To further reduce the paperwork requirements involved in its loans, the SBA recently instituted the **Low Doc** (for "low documentation") **Loan Program,** which allows small businesses to use a simple one-page application for all loan applications. Before the Low Doc Program, a typical SBA loan application required an entrepreneur to complete at least 10 forms, and the SBA often took 45 to 90 days to make a decision about an application. Under the Low Doc Program, response time is just three days.

To qualify for a Low Doc loan, a company must have average sales below $5 million during the previous three years and employ fewer than 100 people. Businesses can use Low Doc loans for working capital, machinery, equipment, and real estate. The SBA guarantees 80 percent of loans up to $100,000 and 75 percent of loans over that amount.

"I'm having an out-of-money experience."

Borrowers must be willing to provide a personal guarantee for repayment of the loan principal. Interest rates are prime plus 2.75 percent on loans of seven years or longer and prime plus 2.25 percent on loans of less than seven years. The average Low Doc loan is $79,500.

Example

Richard Smith, owner of a whitewater rafting business, needed money to expand his 20-year-old company and to buy new equipment. Smith, however, was hesitant to approach the SBA because he wanted to avoid "myriads of paperwork." At his banker's urging, Smith decided to try the Low Doc Program, and within days of submitting his application, he received a $100,000 loan.[80]

Another program designed to streamline the application process for SBA loan guarantees is the **SBA*Express* Program,** in which participating lenders use their own loan procedures and applications to make loans of up to $150,000 to small businesses. Because the SBA guarantees up to 50 percent of the loan, banks are often more willing to make smaller loans to entrepreneurs who might otherwise have difficulty meeting lenders' standards. Loan maturities on SBA*Express* loans typically are between five and 10 years.

SBA*Express* Program—*an SBA program that allows participating lenders to use their own loan procedures to make SBA-guaranteed loans.*

SBA Loan Programs

7(A) LOAN GUARANTY PROGRAM. The SBA works with local lenders (both bank and nonbank) to offer a variety of loan programs designed to help entrepreneurs who cannot get capital from traditional sources gain access to the financing they need to launch and grow their businesses. By far, the most popular SBA loan program is the **7(A) Loan Guaranty Program** (see Figure 11.4). Private lenders extend these loans to small businesses, but the SBA guarantees them (80 percent of loans up to $100,000; 75 percent of loans above $100,000 up to the loan guarantee ceiling of $750,000). In other words, the SBA does not actually lend any money; it merely acts as an insurer, guaranteeing the lender a certain repayment in case the borrower defaults on the loan. Because the SBA assumes most of the credit risk, lenders are more willing to consider riskier deals that they normally would refuse.

7(A) Loan Guaranty Program—*an SBA loan program in which loans made by private lenders to small businesses are guaranteed up to a ceiling by the SBA.*

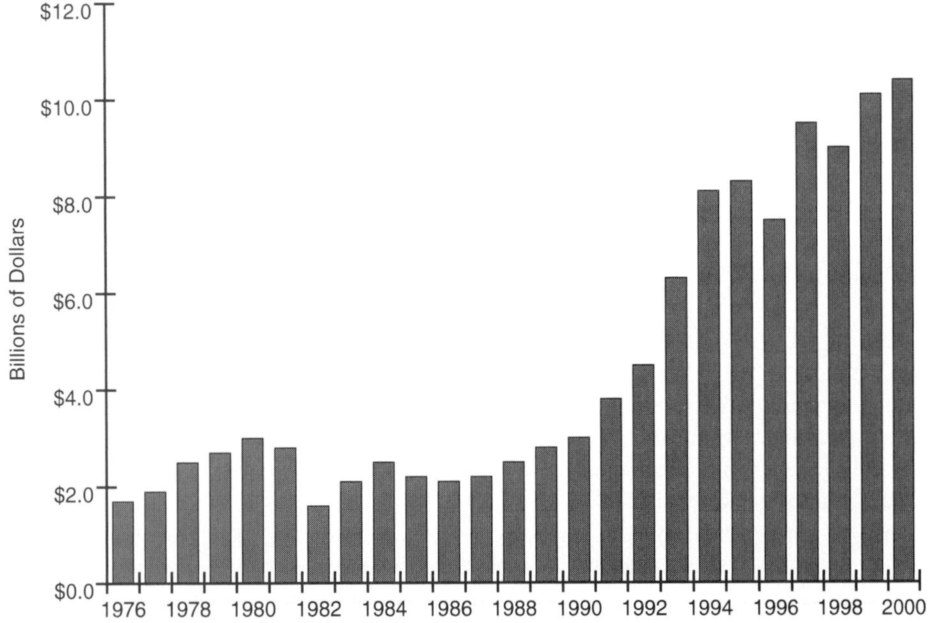

FIGURE 11.4
SBA 7(A) Guaranteed Loans

Source: U.S. Small Business Administration.

Buck's Bags

For instance, when their sports-equipment-bag company, Buck's Bags, began to experience explosive growth that outstripped cash flow, Larry Lee and Dara Lee Howerton applied for an SBA-guaranteed loan at their banker's suggestion. They have received four SBA-guaranteed loans totaling more than $600,000, using the loans to move into a larger plant, buy new equipment, and hire new workers. With the SBA loan guarantees, Buck's Bags's sales have soared. "The SBA was very helpful in getting us through our rapid-growth years," says Larry Lee. "I don't know what we would have done without them."[81]

Qualifying for an SBA-guaranteed loan requires cooperation among the entrepreneur, the participating bank, and the SBA. The participating bank determines the loan's terms and sets the interest rate within SBA limits. Contrary to popular belief, SBA-guaranteed loans do *not* carry special deals on interest rates. Typically, rates are negotiated with the participating bank, with a ceiling of prime plus 2.25 percent on loans of less than seven years and prime plus 2.75 percent on loans of seven to 25 years. Interest rates on loans of less than $25,000 can run up to prime plus 4.75 percent. The average interest rate on SBA-guaranteed loans is prime plus 2 percent (compared to prime plus 1 percent on conventional bank loans). The SBA also assesses a one-time guaranty fee of up to 3.875 percent for all loan guarantees.

The average loan through the 7(A) Loan Guaranty Program is $232,500, and the average duration of an SBA loan is 12 years—longer than the average commercial small business loan. In fact, longer loan terms are a distinct advantage of SBA loans. At least half of all bank business loans are for less than one year. By contrast, SBA real estate loans can extend for up to 25 years (compared to just 10 to 15 years for a conventional loan), and working capital loans have maturities of seven years (compared with two to five years at most banks). These longer terms translate into lower payments, which are better suited for young, fast-growing, cash-strapped companies.

CAPLine Program—*an SBA program that makes short-term capital loans to growing companies needing to finance seasonal buildups in inventory or accounts receivable.*

THE CAPLINE PROGRAM. In addition to its basic 7(A) Loan Guaranty Program (through which the SBA makes about 84 percent of its loans), the SBA provides guarantees on small business loans for start-up, real estate, machinery and equipment, fixtures, working capital, exporting, and restructuring debt through several other methods. About two-thirds of all SBA's loan guarantees are for machinery and equipment or working capital. The **CAPLine Program** offers short-term capital to growing companies needing to finance seasonal buildups in inventory or accounts receivable under five separate programs, each with maturities up to five years: seasonal line of credit (provides advances against inventory and accounts receivable to help businesses weather seasonal sales fluctuations), contract line of credit (finances the cost of direct labor and materials costs associated with performing contracts), builder's line of credit (helps small contractors and builders finance labor and materials costs), standard asset-based line of credit (an asset-based revolving line of credit for financing short-term needs), and small asset-based line of credit (an asset-based revolving line of credit up to $200,000). CAPLine is aimed at helping cash-hungry small businesses by giving them a credit line to draw on when they need it. These loans built around lines of credit are what small companies need most because they are so flexible, efficient, and, unfortunately, so hard for small businesses to get from traditional lenders.

Export Working Capital Program—*an SBA loan program that is designed to provide working capital to small exporters.*

LOANS INVOLVING INTERNATIONAL TRADE. For small businesses going global, the SBA has the **Export Working Capital (EWC) Program,** which is designed to provide working capital to small exporters. The SBA works in conjunction with the Export-Import Bank to administer this loan guarantee program. Applicants file a one-page loan application, and the response time normally is 10 days or less. Loan proceeds must be used to finance small business exports.

Crown Products Inc.

Crown Products Inc., a small company generating more than $16 million in annual sales by exporting grocery products to more than 70 countries, typifies the small companies that benefit most from the EWC Program. In its early years, Crown's retained earnings and contributions from its owners financed the company's growth. But as its growth *accelerated, the company's cash needs began to outstrip its internal funding sources. With the help of the Hibernia National Bank, owners Kee Lee, Sun Kim, and Jeffrey Teague were able to land a $750,000 line of credit that fueled the company's international growth.*[82]

The **International Trade Program** is for small businesses that are engaging in international trade or are adversely affected by competition from imports. The SBA allows global entrepreneurs to combine loans from the EWC Program with those from the International Trade Program for a maximum guarantee of $1.25 million. Loan maturities range from one to 25 years.

International Trade Program—*an SBA loan program for small businesses that are engaging in international trade or are adversely affected by competition from imports.*

SECTION 504 CERTIFIED DEVELOPMENT COMPANY PROGRAM. The SBA's Section 504 program is designed to encourage small businesses to expand their facilities and to create jobs. Section 504 loans provide long-term, fixed-asset financing to small companies to purchase land, buildings, or equipment. Three lenders play a role in every 504 loan: a bank, the SBA, and a **certified development company (CDC).** A CDC is a nonprofit organization licensed by the SBA and designed to promote economic growth in local communities. Some 270 CDCs operate across the United States. An entrepreneur generally is required to make a down payment of just 10 percent of the total project cost. The CDC puts up 40 percent at a long-term fixed rate, supported by an SBA loan guarantee in case the entrepreneur defaults. The bank provides long-term financing for the remaining 50 percent, also supported by an SBA guarantee. The major advantages of Section 504 loans is their fixed rates and terms, their 10- to 20-year maturities, and the low down payment required.

certified development company—*a nonprofit organization licensed by the SBA and designed to promote growth in local communities by working with commercial banks and the SBA to make long-term loans to small businesses.*

Center Fresh Egg Farms

When Jim Dean and seven partners decided to launch an egg-production business in Sioux City, Iowa, they approached a local bank and a CDC for most of the $2.4 million needed to finance the project. The Siouxland Economic Development Corporation (a CDC) loaned $736,000 (which the SBA guaranteed), and American State Bank put $1.2 million into the loan pool. Dean and his partners in Center Fresh Egg Farms contributed the remaining $480,000.[83]

As attractive as they are, 504 loans are not for every business owner. The SBA imposes several restrictions on 504 loans:

- For every $35,000 the CDC loans, the project must create at least one new job or achieve a public policy goal such as rural development, expansion of exports, minority business development, and others.
- Machinery and equipment financed must have a useful life of at least 10 years.
- The borrower must occupy at least two-thirds of a building constructed with the loan, or the borrower must occupy at least half of a building purchased or remodeled with the loan.
- The borrower must qualify as a small business under the SBA's definition and must not have a tangible net worth in excess of $6 million and must not have an average net income in excess of $2 million after taxes for the preceding two years.

Because of strict equity requirements, existing small businesses usually find it easier to qualify for 504 loans than do start-ups.

MICROLOAN PROGRAM. Recall that about three-fourths of all entrepreneurs need less than $100,000 to launch their businesses. Indeed, research suggests that most entrepreneurs require less than $50,000 to start their companies. Unfortunately, loans of that amount can be the most difficult to get. Lending these relatively small amounts to entrepreneurs starting businesses is the purpose of the SBA's **Microloan Program**. Called *microloans* because they range from just $100 to as much as $25,000, these loans have helped thousands of people take their first steps toward entrepreneurship. Banks typically have shunned loans in such small amounts because they considered them to be unprofitable. In 1992, the SBA began funding microloan programs at 96 private nonprofit lenders

Microloan Program—*an SBA program that makes small loans, some as small as $100, to entrepreneurs.*

in 44 states in an attempt to "fill the void" in small loans to start-up companies. The average microloan is $10,000 with a maturity of three years (the maximum term is six years), and lenders' standards are less demanding than those on conventional loans. All microloans are made through nonprofit intermediaries approved by the SBA.

Prequalification Loan Program—*an SBA program designed to help disadvantaged entrepreneurs "prequalify" for SBA loan guarantees before approaching commercial lenders.*

PREQUALIFICATION LOAN PROGRAM. The **Prequalification Loan Program** is designed to help disadvantaged entrepreneurs, such as those in rural areas, minorities, women, the disabled, those with low incomes, veterans, and others, prepare loan applications and "prequalify" for SBA loan guarantees before approaching banks and lending institutions for business loans. Because lenders are much more likely to approve loans that the SBA has prequalified, these entrepreneurs have greater access to the capital they need. The maximum loan under this program is $250,000, and loan maturities range from seven to 25 years. A local Small Business Development Center usually helps entrepreneurs prepare their loan applications at no charge.

Howerton Funeral Home

Lola Howerton, owner of a small funeral home in Virginia, had to turn down several large funerals because she did not have the facilities to accommodate them. When she approached two banks for a $225,000 loan to expand her business, both rejected her application. Then Howerton learned about the SBA's prequalification program. She met with a representative from a local Small Business Development Center who helped her prepare a business plan and then received a letter from the SBA prequalifying her for a loan guarantee. With her business plan and the prequalifying letter, Howerton found banks very receptive to her loan request. Four banks offered to lend her the money she needed, and the terms were better than Howerton expected.[84]

disaster loans—*an SBA loan program that makes loans to small businesses devastated by some kind of financial or physical loss.*

DISASTER LOANS. As their name implies, **disaster loans** are made to small businesses devastated by some kind of financial or physical loss. The maximum disaster loan usually is $500,000, but Congress often raises that ceiling when circumstances warrant. Disaster loans carry below-market interest rates (e.g., 4 percent on the loans to small companies after the Los Angeles earthquakes). Loans for physical damage above $10,000 and financial damage of more than $5,000 require the entrepreneur to pledge some kind of collateral, usually a lien on the business property. The SBA's coffers have been stretched thin by a string of disasters in recent years, ranging from hurricanes on the southeastern coast and earthquakes on the western coast to floods and tornadoes in the Midwest and droughts across the nation.

SBA'S 8(A) PROGRAM. The SBA's 8(A) Program is designed to help minority-owned businesses get a fair share of federal government contracts. Through this program, the SBA directs about $4 million each year to small businesses with "socially and economically disadvantaged" owners. Once a small business convinces the SBA that it meets the program's criteria, it finds a government agency needing work done. The SBA then approaches the federal agency that needs the work done and arranges for a contract to go to the SBA. The agency then subcontracts the work to the small business. Government agencies cooperate with the SBA in its 8(A) Program because the law requires them to set aside a portion of their work for minority-owned firms.

STATE AND LOCAL LOAN DEVELOPMENT PROGRAMS

Just when many federally funded programs are facing cutbacks, state-sponsored loan and development programs are becoming more active in providing funds for business start-ups and expansions. Many states have decided that their funds are better spent encouraging small business growth rather than "chasing smokestacks"—trying to entice large businesses to locate in their boundaries. These programs come in a wide variety of forms, but they all tend to focus on developing small businesses that create the greatest number of jobs and economic benefits. For example, South Carolina's Jobs Economic Development Authority (JEDA) is a direct lending arm of the state, offering low-interest loans to manufacturing, industrial, and service businesses. JEDA also provides financial and technical assistance to small companies seeking to develop export markets.

Although each state's approach to economic development is somewhat special, one common element is some kind of small business financing program: loans, loan guarantees, development grants, venture capital pools, and others. One approach many states have had success with is **Capital Access Programs (CAPs).** First introduced in Michigan in 1986, 22 states now offer CAPs that are designed to encourage lending institutions to make loans to businesses that do not qualify for traditional financing. Under a CAP, the bank and the borrower each pay an up-front fee (a portion of the loan amount) into a loan-loss reserve fund at the participating bank, and the state matches this amount. The reserve fund, which normally ranges from 6 to 14 percent of the loan amount, acts as an insurance policy against the potential loss a bank might experience on a loan and frees the bank to make loans that it otherwise might refuse. One study of CAPs found that 55 percent of the entrepreneurs who received loans under a CAP would not have been granted loans without the backing of the program.[85]

Capital Access Program— *a lending program available in 22 states that encourages lending institutions to make loans to businesses that do not qualify for traditional financing.*

Even cities and small towns have joined in the effort to develop small businesses and help them grow. More than 7,500 communities across the United States operate **revolving loan funds (RLFs)** that combine private and public funds to make loans to small businesses, often at below-market interest rates. As money is repaid into the funds, it is loaned back out to other entrepreneurs. A study by the Corporation for Enterprise Development of RLFs in seven states found that the median RLF loan was $40,000 with a maturity of five years.[86]

revolving loan fund— *a program offered by communities that combine private and public funds to make loans to small businesses, often at below-market interest rates.*

Ag Services

Arlis Hanson, owner of Ag Services, a soybean-processing business in Huffton, South Dakota, received a $150,000 loan from a revolving loan fund, Rural Electric Economic Development Inc. (REED). Hanson used the loan to purchase new equipment and inventory and to increase his company's production of soybean oil.[87]

INTERNAL METHODS OF FINANCING

Small business owners do not have to rely solely on financial institutions and government agencies for capital. Instead, the business itself has the capacity to generate capital. This type of financing, called **bootstrap financing,** is available to virtually every small business and encompasses factoring, leasing rather than purchasing equipment, using credit cards, and managing the business frugally.

bootstrap financing— *internal methods of financing a company's need for capital.*

FACTORING ACCOUNTS RECEIVABLE. Instead of carrying credit sales on its own books (some of which may never be collected), a small business can sell outright its accounts receivable to a factor. A **factor** buys a company's accounts receivable and pays for them in two parts. The first payment, which the factor makes immediately, is for 50 to 80 percent of the accounts' agreed-upon (and usually discounted) value. The factor makes the second payment, which makes up the balance less the factor's service fees, when the original customer pays the invoice. Factoring is a more expensive type of financing than loans from either banks or commercial finance companies, but for businesses that cannot qualify for those loans, factoring may be the only choice!

factor— *a financial institution that buys a business's accounts receivable at a discount.*

Factoring deals are either with recourse or without recourse. Under deals arranged with recourse, a small business owner retains the responsibility for customers who fail to pay their accounts. The business owner must take back these uncollectible invoices. Under deals arranged without recourse, however, the owner is relieved of the responsibility for collecting them. If customers fail to pay their accounts, the factor bears the loss. Because the factoring company assumes the risk of collecting the accounts, it normally screens the firm's credit customers, accepts those judged to be creditworthy, and advances the small business owner a portion of the value of the accounts receivable. Factors will discount anywhere from 5 to 40 percent of the face value of a company's accounts receivable, depending on a small company's:

- customers' financial strength and credit ratings.
- industry and its customers' industries because some industries have a reputation for slow payments.
- history and financial strength, especially in deals arranged with recourse.
- credit policies.[88]

Factoring is ideally suited for fast-growing companies—especially start-ups that cannot qualify for bank loans.

firstPro Inc.

For example, when Phil Nagel, founder of firstPro*, a temporary staffing company in Atlanta, needed cash to finance his business's rapid growth, he began selling his accounts receivable to a factor each week. Short-term financing is crucial to Nagel because of the gap between paying his temporary workers and collecting payment from his customers, but in the early days, his asset-poor fledgling firm could not qualify for a bank loan. Nagel used factoring as his primary source of capital for a decade before his company "graduated" to bank financing. "Factoring allowed me to grow at a faster pace than would have been possible otherwise," he says. "It was perfect for us."*[89]

LEASING. Leasing is another common bootstrap financing technique. Today, small businesses can lease virtually any kind of asset—from office space and telephones to computers and heavy equipment. By leasing expensive assets, the small business owner is able to use them without locking in valuable capital for an extended period of time. In other words, the manager can reduce the long-term capital requirements of the business by leasing equipment and facilities, and she is not investing her capital in depreciating assets. Also, because no down payment is required and because the cost of the asset is spread over a longer time (lowering monthly payments), the firm's cash flow improves.

CREDIT CARDS. Unable to find financing elsewhere, some entrepreneurs have launched their companies using the fastest and most convenient source of debt capital available: credit cards! A survey by Arthur Andersen and National Small Business United found that 50 percent of the owners of small and medium-sized businesses used credit cards as a source of funds.[90] Putting business start-up costs on credit cards charging 21 percent or more in annual interest is expensive and risky, but some entrepreneurs have no other choice.

Vital Resources Inc.

Charlene Connell used 10 credit cards with a total credit limit of $15,000 to make payroll when she launched her computer consulting company, Vital Resources Inc. Although it was a struggle in some months to meet the cards' minimum payments, Connell managed to do so. Today, Vital Resources is a thriving business that owes its early success to a very simple form of financing.[91]

Figure 11.5 summarizes the results of a recent survey of the owners of small and medium-sized businesses concerning their sources of financing.

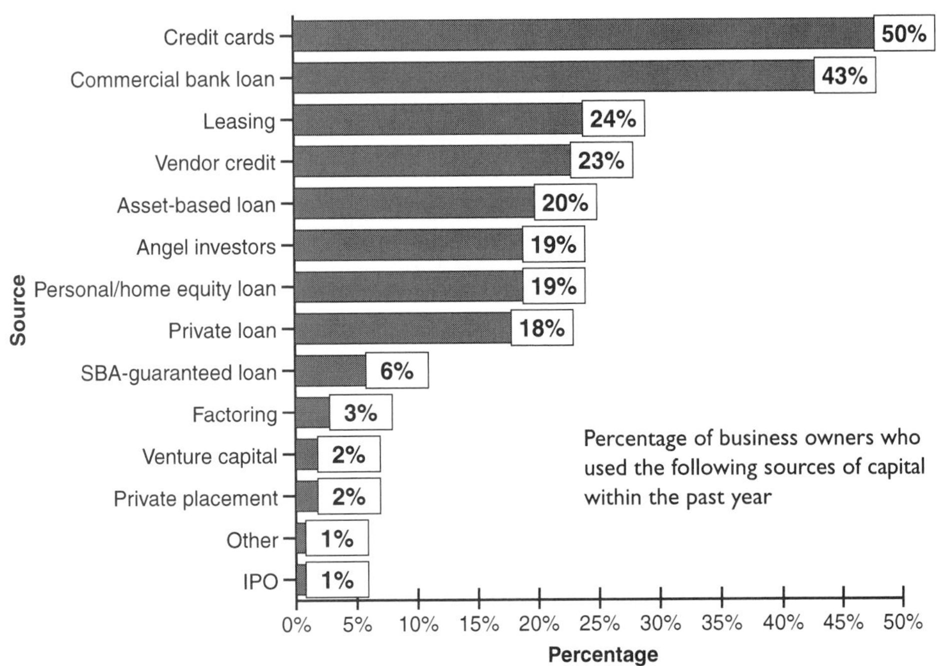

FIGURE 11.5 Where Do Small Businesses Get Their Financing?

Source: Trends for 2000, *a survey by Arthur Andersen and National Small Business United.*

CHAPTER SUMMARY

1. Explain the differences in the three types of capital small businesses require: fixed, working, and growth.
   - Capital is any form of wealth employed to produce more wealth. Three forms of capital are commonly identified as fixed capital, working capital, and growth capital.
   - Fixed capital is used to purchase a company's permanent or fixed assets; working capital represents the business's temporary funds and is used to support the business's normal short-term operations; growth capital requirements surface when an existing business is expanding or changing its primary direction.
2. Describe the differences between equity capital and debt capital and the advantages and disadvantages of each.
   - Equity financing represents the personal investment of the owner (or owners), and it offers the advantage of not having to be repaid with interest.
   - Debt capital is the financing that a small business owner has borrowed and must repay with interest. It does not require entrepreneurs to give up ownership in their companies.
3. Describe the various sources of equity capital available to entrepreneurs, including personal savings, friends and relatives, angels, partners, corporations, venture capital, and public stock offerings.
   - The most common source of financing a business is the owner's personal savings. After emptying their own pockets, the next place entrepreneurs turn for capital is family members and friends. Angels are private investors who not only invest their money in small companies, but they also offer valuable advice and counsel to them. Some business owners have success financing their companies by taking on limited partners as investors or by forming an alliance with a corporation, often a customer or a supplier. Venture capital companies are for-profit, professional investors looking for fast-growing companies in "hot" industries. When screening prospects, venture capital firms look for competent management, a competitive edge, a growth industry, and important intangibles that will make a business successful. Some owners choose to attract capital by taking their companies public, which requires registering the public offering with the SEC.
4. Describe the process of "going public," as well as its advantages and disadvantages, and the various simplified registrations and exemptions from registration available to small businesses wanting to sell securities to investors.
   - Going public involves (1) choosing the underwriter, (2) negotiating a letter of intent, (3) preparing the registration statement, (4) filing with the SEC, and (5) meeting state requirements.

- Going public offers the advantages of raising large amounts of capital, improving access to future financing, improving corporate image, and gaining listing on a stock exchange. The disadvantages include dilution of the founder's ownership, loss of privacy, reporting to the SEC, filing expenses, and accountability to shareholders.
- Rather than go through the complete registration process, some companies use one of the simplified registration options and exemptions available to small companies: Regulation S-B, Regulation D (Rule 504) see pg. 381 Small Company Offering Registration (SCOR), Regulation D (Rule 505 and Rule 506) Private Placements, Section 4(6), Rule 147, Regulation A, direct stock offerings, and foreign stock markets.

5. Describe the various sources of debt capital and the advantages and disadvantages of each: banks, asset-based lenders, vendors (trade credit), equipment suppliers, commercial finance companies, savings and loan associations, stockbrokers, insurance companies, credit unions, bonds, private placements, Small Business Investment Companies (SBICs), and Small Business Lending Companies (SBLCs).
   - Commercial banks offer the greatest variety of loans, although they are conservative lenders. Typical short-term bank loans include commercial loans, lines of credit, discounting accounts receivable, inventory financing, and floor planning.
   - Trade credit is used extensively by small businesses as a source of financing. Vendors and suppliers commonly finance sales to businesses for 30, 60, or even 90 days.
   - Equipment suppliers offer small businesses financing similar to trade credit but with slightly different terms.
   - Commercial finance companies offer many of the same types of loans that banks do, but they are more risk oriented in their lending practices. They emphasize accounts receivable financing and inventory loans.
   - Savings and loan associations specialize in loans to purchase real property—commercial and industrial mortgages—for up to 30 years.
   - Brokerage houses offer loans to prospective entrepreneurs at lower interest rates than banks because they have high quality, liquid collateral—stocks and bonds in the borrower's portfolio.
   - Insurance companies provide financing through policy loans and mortgage loans. Policy loans are extended to the owner against the cash surrender value of insurance policies. Mortgage loans are made for large amounts and are based on the value of the land being purchased.
   - Small Business Investment Companies are privately owned companies licensed and regulated by the SBA that qualify for SBA loans to be invested in or loaned to small businesses.
   - Small Business Lending Companies make only intermediate and long-term loans that are guaranteed by the SBA.
6. Identify the various federal loan programs aimed at small businesses.
   - The Economic Development Administration, a branch of the Commerce Department, makes loan guarantees to create and expand small businesses in economically depressed areas.
   - The Department of Housing and Urban Development extends grants (such as Community Development Block Grants) to cities that, in turn, lend and grant money to small businesses in an attempt to strengthen the local economy.
   - The Department of Agriculture's Rural Business-Cooperative Service loan program is designed to create nonfarm employment opportunities in rural areas through loans and loan guarantees.
   - Local development companies receive loans from banks and guarantees from the SBA and then make loans to small businesses for fixed assets. The goal is to stimulate economic growth and to create jobs in the local communities.
   - The Small Business Innovation Research Program involves 11 federal agencies that award cash grants or long-term contracts to small companies wanting to initiate or to expand their research and development (R&D) efforts.
   - The Small Business Technology Transfer Program allows researchers at universities, federally funded R&D centers, and nonprofit research institutions to join forces with small businesses and develop commercially promising ideas.
7. Describe the various loan programs available from the Small Business Administration.
   - Almost all SBA loan activity is in the form of loan guarantees rather than direct loans. Popular SBA programs include the Low Doc Loan Program, the SBA*Express* Program, the 7(A) Loan Guaranty Program, the CAPLine Program, the Export Working Capital Program, the Section 504 Certified Development Company Program, the Microloan Program, the Prequalification Loan Program, the Disaster Loan Program, and the 8(a) Program. See p. 405
   - Many state and local loan and development programs such as Capital Access Programs and revolving loan funds complement those sponsored by federal agencies.
8. Discuss valuable methods of financing growth and expansion internally.
   - Small business owners may also look inside their firms for capital. By factoring accounts receivable, leasing equipment instead of buying it, and by minimizing costs, owners can stretch their supplies of capital.

DISCUSSION QUESTIONS

1. Why is it so difficult for most small business owners to raise the capital needed to start, operate, or expand their ventures?
2. What is capital? List and describe the three types of capital a small business needs for its operations.
3. Define equity financing. What advantage does it offer over debt financing?
4. What is the most common source of equity funds in a typical small business? If an owner lacks sufficient equity capital to invest in the firm, what options are available for raising it?
5. What guidelines should an entrepreneur follow if friends and relatives choose to invest in her business?
6. What is an angel investor? Assemble a brief profile of the typical private investor. How can entrepreneurs locate potential angels to invest in their businesses?
7. What advice would you offer an entrepreneur about to strike a deal with a private investor to avoid problems?
8. What types of businesses are most likely to attract venture capital? What investment criteria do venture capitalists use when screening potential businesses? How do these compare to the typical angel's criteria?
9. How do venture capital firms operate? Describe their procedure for screening investment proposals.
10. Summarize the major exemptions and simplified registrations available to small companies wanting to make public offerings of their stock.
11. What role do commercial banks play in providing debt financing to small businesses? Outline and briefly describe the major types of short-term, intermediate, and long-term loans commercial banks offer.
12. What is trade credit? How important is it as a source of debt financing to small firms?
13. What function do SBICs serve? How does an SBIC operate? What methods of financing do SBICs rely on most heavily?
14. Briefly describe the loan programs offered by the following:
    a. Economic Development Administration
    b. Department of Housing and Urban Development
    c. Department of Agriculture
    d. local development companies
15. Explain the purpose and the methods of operation of the Small Business Innovation Research Program and the Small Business Technology Transfer Program.
16. How can a firm employ bootstrap financing to stretch its current capital supply?
17. What is a factor? How does the typical factor operate? Explain the advantages and the disadvantages of factoring.

Beyond the Classroom ...

1. Interview several local business owners about how they financed their businesses. From where did their initial capital come? Ask the following questions:
   a. How did you raise your starting capital? What percentage did you supply on your own?
   b. What percentage was debt capital and what percentage was equity capital?
   c. Which of the sources of funds described in this chapter do you use? Are they used to finance fixed, working, or growth capital needs?
   d. How much money did you need to launch your businesses? Where did you get subsequent capital? What advice do you offer others seeking capital?
2. Contact a local private investor and ask him or her to address your class. (You may have to search to locate one!) In what kinds of businesses does this angel prefer to invest? What screening criteria does he or she use? How are the deals typically structured?
3. Contact a local venture capitalist and ask him or her to address your class. In what kinds of businesses does his or her company invest? What screening criteria does the company use? How are deals typically structured?
4. Invite an investment banker or a financing expert from a local accounting firm to address your class about the process of taking a company public. What do they look for in a potential IPO candidate? What is the process, and how long does it usually take?
5. After a personal visit, prepare a short report on a nearby factor's operation. How is the value of the accounts receivable purchased determined? Who bears the loss on uncollected accounts?
6. Interview the administrator of a financial institution program offering a method of financing with which you are unfamiliar and prepare a short report on its method of operation.
7. Contact your state's business development board and prepare a report on the financial assistance programs it offers small businesses.

We invite you to visit this book's companion Web site at **www.prenhall.com/Zimmerer.**

CHAPTER 12

Choosing the Right Location and Layout

LEARNING OBJECTIVES

Upon completion of this chapter, you will be able to:

1. Explain the stages in the location decision: choosing the region, the state, the city, and the specific site.
2. Describe the location criteria for retail and service businesses.
3. Outline the location options for retail and service businesses: central business districts (CBDs), neighborhoods, shopping centers and malls, near competitors, outlying areas, and at home.
4. Explain the site selection process for manufacturers.
5. Describe the criteria used to analyze the layout and design considerations of a building, including the Americans with Disabilities Act.
6. Explain the principles of effective layouts for retailers, service businesses, and manufacturers.
7. Evaluate the advantages and disadvantages of building, buying, and leasing a building.

How little do they see what is, who frame their hasty judgments upon that which seems.

—Robert Southey

Nothing looks as good close up as it does from far away.

—Anonymous

1. Explain the stages in the location decision: choosing the region, the state, the city, and the specific site.

LOCATION: A SOURCE OF COMPETITIVE ADVANTAGE

Much like choosing a form of ownership and selecting particular sources of financing, the location decision has far-reaching and often long-lasting effects on a small company's future. Entrepreneurs who choose their locations wisely—with their customers' preferences and their companies' needs in mind—can establish an important competitive edge over rivals who choose their locations haphazardly. Because the availability of qualified workers, tax rates, the quality of infrastructure, traffic patterns, and many other factors vary from one site to another, the location decision is an important one that can influence the growth rate and the ultimate success of a company.

The location selection process is like an interactive computer game in which each decision opens the way to make another decision on the way to solving the puzzle. The answer to the puzzle, of course, is the best location for a business. At each step in the decision process, entrepreneurs must analyze how well the characteristics of a particular location match the unique requirements of their businesses. Because of their significant impact on a company, location decisions can be difficult; however, like the interactive computer game, there are lots of clues that guide entrepreneurs to the best decision.

The location decision resembles an inverted pyramid. The first level of the decision is the broadest, requiring an entrepreneur to select a particular region of the country. (We will address locating a business in a foreign country in Chapter 13, "Global Aspects of Entrepreneurship.") From there, an entrepreneur must choose the right state, then the right city, and, finally, the right site within the city. The "secret" to selecting the ideal location lies in knowing which factors are most important to a company's success and then finding a location that satisfies as many of them as possible, particularly those that are most critical. For instance, one of the most important location factors for high-tech companies is the availability of a skilled labor force, and their choice of location reflects this. If locating near customers is vital to a company's success, then an entrepreneur's goal is to find a site that makes it most convenient for her target customers to do business with the company.

Coastal Cotton

David Chang, owner of Coastal Cotton, a small retail chain specializing in casual cotton clothing, has seen his company grow from a single store in Hialeah, Florida, to 12 locations in outlet centers across the Southeast and in California. Because Coastal Cotton's primary target is bargain-hunting tourists, Chang chooses locations with high concentrations of potential customers. "You have to know your customer base and be strategic about choosing sites," Chang explains.[1]

The characteristics that make for an ideal location often vary dramatically from one company to another and can change over time. In the old economy, companies once looked for ready supplies of water or access to railroads; today, they are more likely to look for sites that are close to universities and offer high-speed Internet access. In a recent study of 50 metropolitan areas, Cognetics Inc. determined that the factors that made an area most suitable for starting and growing small companies included access to dynamic universities, an ample supply of skilled workers, a nearby airport, and a high quality of life.[2] The key to finding a suitable location is identifying the characteristics that can give a company a competitive edge and then searching out potential sites that meet those criteria.

Choosing the Region

The first step in selecting the best location is to focus at the regional level. Which region of the country has the characteristics necessary for a new business to succeed? Common requirements include rapid growth in the population of a certain age group, rising disposable incomes, the existence of necessary infrastructure, a nonunion environment, and low costs. At the broadest level of the location decision, entrepreneurs usually determine which regions of the country are experiencing substantial growth. Every year many popular business publications prepare reports on the various regions of the nation—which ones are growing, which are stagnant, and which are declining. Studying shifts in population and industrial growth will give an entrepreneur an idea of where the action is—and isn't. For example: How large is the population? How fast is it growing? What is the makeup of the overall population? Which segments are growing fastest? Slowest? What is the population's income? Is it increasing or decreasing? Are other businesses moving into the region? If so, what kind of businesses? Generally, entrepreneurs want to avoid dying regions; they simply cannot support a broad base of potential customers. A firm's customers will be people, businesses, and industry, and if it is to be successful, it must locate in a place that is convenient to them.

One of the first stops entrepreneurs should make when conducting a regional evaluation is the U.S. Census Bureau. Excellent sources of basic demographic and population data include the *U.S. Statistical Abstract* and the *County and City Data Book.* The *U.S. Statistical Abstract* provides entrepreneurs looking for the right location with a great deal of helpful information, ranging from basic population characteristics and projections to poverty rates and energy consumption. Every state also publishes its own statistical abstract, which provides the same type of data for its own population. The *County and City Data Book* contains useful statistics on the populations of all of the nation's 3,141 counties

Source: From the Wall Street Journal*—Permission, Cartoon Features Syndicate.*

and 12,175 cities with populations exceeding 2,500. In addition to the numerous publications it offers, the Census Bureau makes most of the information contained in its valuable data banks available to entrepreneurs researching potential sites through its easy-to-use World Wide Web site **<www.census.gov>**. There entrepreneurs can access for specific locations vital demographic information such as age, income, educational level, employment level, occupation, ancestry, commuting times, housing data (house value, number of rooms, mortgage or rent status, number of vehicles owned, and so on), and many other characteristics. Sorting through each report's 95 fields, entrepreneurs can prepare customized reports on the potential sites they are considering. Oregon State University has compiled much of the data from the Census Bureau, the Bureau of Economic Analysis, the National Center for Education Statistics, and the Mesa Group into the World Wide Web's Government Information Sharing Project **<govinfo.kerr.orst.edu>**. This Web site gives users an easy and powerful system for mining information from the vast and valuable resources the U.S. government has collected and compiled. These Web-based resources give entrepreneurs instant access to important site-location information that only a few years ago would have taken many hours of intense research to compile!

The Herbal Remedy

When Scott Fiore was looking for a location for his natural pharmacy, The Herbal Remedy, he turned first to the demographic data from the U.S. Census Bureau. Not only did his analysis provide him with a picture of the potential customers in each area, but it also pointed him to Douglas County, Colorado, the fastest-growing county in the nation for the second year in a row. The profile that emerged from the demographic data for the county was one of young, affluent, well-educated residents, a perfect fit with Fiore's definition of his target customer. As he drove around the area, Fiore noticed that Douglas County and neighboring Arapaho County were "very sports-oriented, athletic places," which was also consistent with his target audience. More research led Fiore to the town of Littleton, which is conveniently located for customers in both counties but offers relatively low rental rates.[3]

Other sources of demographic data include *Sales and Marketing Management's Survey of Buying Power, Editor and Publisher Market Guide, The American Marketplace: Demographics and Spending Patterns, Rand McNally's Commercial Atlas and Marketing Guide,* and *Zip Code Atlas and Market Planner.* Published every September, the *Survey of Buying Power* provides a detailed breakdown of population, retail sales, spendable income, and other characteristics for census regions, states, metropolitan areas, counties, and cities. The survey includes highlights and summary sections, analyses of changes in metro markets, projections for metro markets, descriptions of newspaper and television markets, and summaries of sales of certain merchandise.

The *Editor and Publisher Market Guide* is similar to the *Survey of Buying Power* but provides additional information on markets. The guide includes detailed economic and demographic information, ranging from population and income statistics to information on climate and transportation networks for more than 1,500 key cities in both the United States and Canada.

The American Marketplace: Demographics and Spending Patterns provides useful demographic information in eight areas: education, health, income, labor force, living arrangements, population, race and ethnicity, and spending and wealth. Most of the tables in the book are derived from government statistics, but *The American Marketplace* also includes a discussion of the data in each table as well as a forecast of future trends.

The *Commercial Atlas and Marketing Guide* reports on more than 128,000 places in the United States, many of which are not available through Census Bureau reports. It includes 11 economic indicators for every major geographic market; tables showing population trends, income, buying power, trade, and manufacturing activity; and large, cross-reference maps. Its format makes it easy to collect large amounts of valuable data on any region in the country (and specific areas within a region).

The *Zip Code Atlas and Market Planner* is an extremely useful location and market-planning tool. It combines a breakdown of zip codes (often the basis of psychographic customer profiles) with maps featuring physical features such as mountains, rivers, and major highways. The planner contains loose-leaf, full color maps, each with a reusable acetate overlay showing five-digit zip code boundaries for all 50 states and more detailed inset maps for 240 major cities and metropolitan areas.

The task of analyzing various potential locations—gathering and synthesizing data on a wide variety of demographic and geographic variables—is one ideally suited for a computer. In fact, a growing number of entrepreneurs are relying on geographic information systems (GIS), powerful software programs that combine map drawing with database management capability, to pinpoint the ideal location for their businesses. GIS packages allow users to search through virtually any database containing a wealth of information and plot the results on a map of the country, an individual state, a specific city, or even a single city block. The visual display highlights what otherwise would be indiscernible business trends. For instance, using a GIS program, an entrepreneur could plot her existing customer base on a map, with various colors representing the different population densities. Then she could zoom in on those areas with the greatest concentration of customers, mapping a detailed view of zip code borders or even city streets. GIS street files originate in the U.S. Census Department's TIGER (Topographically Integrated Geographic Encoding Referencing) file, which contains map information broken down for every square foot of Metropolitan Statistical Areas (MSAs). TIGER files contain the name and location of every street in the country and detailed block statistics for the 345 largest urban areas. In essence, TIGER is a massive database of geographic features such as roads, railways, and political boundaries across the entire United States that, when linked with mapping programs and demographic databases, gives entrepreneurs incredible power to pinpoint existing and potential customers on easy-to-read digital maps.

The Small Business Administration's (SBA's) Small Business Development Center (SBDC) program also offers location analysis assistance to entrepreneurs. These centers, numbering more than 1,000 nationwide, provide training, counseling, research, and other specialized assistance to entrepreneurs and existing business owners on a wide variety of subjects—all at no charge! They are an important resource, especially for those entrepreneurs who may not have access to a computer. (To locate the SBA nearest you, contact the SBA office in your state or go to the SBA's home page at **<www.sba.gov/SBDC>**.

Once an entrepreneur has identified the best region of the country, the next step is to evaluate the individual states in that region.

Choosing the State

Every state has an economic development office to recruit new businesses to that state. Even though the publications produced by these offices will be biased in favor of locating in that state, they still are an excellent source of facts and can help entrepreneurs assess the business climate in each state. Some of the key issues to explore include the laws, regulations, and taxes that govern businesses and any incentives or investment credits the state may offer to businesses locating there. Other factors to consider include proximity to markets, proximity to raw materials, wage rates, quantity and quality of the labor supply, general business climate, tax rates, and Internet access.

PROXIMITY TO MARKETS. Locating close to markets they plan to serve is extremely critical to manufacturers, especially when the cost of transporting finished goods is high relative to their value. Locating near customers is necessary to remain competitive. Service firms often find that proximity to their clients is essential. If a business is involved in repairing equipment used in a specific industry, it should be located where that industry is concentrated. The more specialized a business, or the greater the relative cost of transporting the product to the customer, the more likely it is that proximity to the market will be of critical importance in the location decision. For instance, with its location in the center of the country and its ready access to a variety of transportation systems, St. Louis, Missouri, has become home to many companies' distribution centers. Not only do businesses in St. Louis benefit from a well-educated workforce, they also can ship to customers anywhere in the country quickly and efficiently.

PROXIMITY TO NEEDED RAW MATERIALS. If a business requires raw materials that are difficult or expensive to transport, it may need a location near the source of those raw materials. For instance, one producer of kitty litter chose a location on a major vein of kaolin, the highly absorbent clay from which kitty litter is made. Transporting the heavy, low-value material over long distances would be impractical—and unprofitable. In other situations in which bulk or weight is not a factor, locating in close proximity to suppliers can facilitate quick deliveries and reduce holding costs for inventories. The value of products and materials, their cost of transportation, and their unique function all interact in determining how close a business needs to be to its source of supplies.

WAGE RATES. Existing wage rates will provide another measure for comparison among states. Wages can sometimes vary significantly from one state or region to another, significantly affecting a company's cost of doing business. For instance, according to the Bureau of Labor Statistics, the average hourly compensation for workers (including wages and benefits) ranges from a low of $17.81 in the South to a high of $22.67 in the Northeast.[4] Wage differentials within geographic regions can be even more drastic. When reviewing wage rates, entrepreneurs must be sure to measure the wage rates for jobs that relate to their particular industries or companies. In addition to government surveys, local newspaper ads can give entrepreneurs an idea of the pay scale in an area. Entrepreneurs should study not only prevailing wage rates, but also *trends* in rates. How does the rate of increase in wage rates compare to those in other states? Another factor influencing wage rates is the level of union activity in a state. How much union organizing activity has the state seen within the past two years? Is it increasing or decreasing? Which industries have unions targeted in the recent past?

Gateway

Gateway, the personal computer seller offering high-performance hardware at bargain-basement prices, uses its location to gain a competitive edge in a hotly competitive industry. With constant downward pressure on computer prices, Gateway must keep its costs low. The company's home for its manufacturing operations, North Sioux City, South Dakota—not exactly the heart of Silicon Valley—is one variable in its low-cost formula. South Dakota has no state corporate or personal income taxes, and the low cost of living appeals to employees. Gateway's starting wage for assembly workers—a bargain by national standards—is quite attractive in the local market. Most of the company's workers come from Iowa, known for the quality of its schools. The company's mid-continent location also keeps shipping costs low for a company selling computers nationwide, and managers are pleased with their employees' midwestern work ethic.[5]

LABOR SUPPLY NEEDS. For many businesses, especially "new economy" companies, one of the most important characteristics of a potential location is the composition of the local workforce. Entrepreneurs must consider two factors when analyzing the labor supply in a potential location: the number of workers available in the area and their levels of education, training, adaptability, and experience.

When Gateway founder Ted Waite realized that attracting top managers and staying on top of the dynamic computer industry were difficult to do from the company's South Dakota location, he moved the administrative hub to San Diego, California, a hotbed of skilled workers and high-tech activity. Since moving Gateway's headquarters, Waite has filled nearly all of the top-management posts with local talent. "It really came down to this being a great place to recruit people, with a quality of life [that is] unmatched," says Waite.[6]

Of course, an entrepreneur wants to know how many qualified people are available in the area to do the work required in the business. However, unemployment and labor cost statistics can be misleading if a company needs people with specific qualifications. Some states have attempted to attract industry with the promise of cheap labor. Unfortunately, businesses locating there found exactly what the term implied—unskilled, low-wage labor that is ill-suited for performing the work the companies needed.

Knowing the exact nature of the labor needed and preparing job descriptions and job specifications in advance will help a business owner determine whether there is a good match with the available labor pool. Reviewing the major industries already operating in an area will provide clues about the characteristics of the local workforce as well. Checking with the high schools, colleges, and universities in the state to determine the number of graduates in relevant fields of study will provide an idea of the local supply of qualified workers. Such planning will result in choosing a location with a steady source of quality labor.

BUSINESS CLIMATE. What is the state's overall attitude toward your kind of business? Has it passed laws that impose restrictions on the way a company can operate? Does the state impose a corporate income tax? Is there an inventory tax? Are there "blue laws" that prohibit certain business activity on Sundays? Does the state offer small business support programs or financial assistance to entrepreneurs? These are just some of the issues an owner must compare on a state-by-state basis to determine the most suitable location.

Some states are more "small business friendly" than others. For instance, *Entrepreneur* magazine recently named Fort Worth–Arlington, Texas, as one of the best areas for small businesses, citing a positive attitude toward growing and developing small companies as a major asset. Many factors make Fort Worth (once known as Cowtown because of its stockyards) a desirable location, including its diversified economic base, a strong core of more than two dozen *Fortune* 500 companies, significant population of private investors anxious to invest in promising small companies, and several state and local government support systems offering entrepreneurial assistance and advice. The renaissance of the downtown business district is creating new opportunities for small businesses, and both Dallas–Fort Worth International Airport and Alliance Airport (a specialized commercial air facility) provide important pieces of business infrastructure.[7]

TAX RATES. Another important factor entrepreneurs must consider when screening states for potential locations is the tax burden they impose on businesses and individuals. Income taxes may be the most obvious tax states impose on both business and individual residents, but entrepreneurs also must evaluate the impact of payroll taxes, sales taxes, property taxes, and specialized taxes on the cost of their operations. Currently, seven states impose no income tax on their residents, but state governments always impose taxes of some sort on businesses and individuals. In some cases, states offer special tax rates or are willing to negotiate fees in lieu of taxes for companies that will create jobs and stimulate the local economy.

INTERNET ACCESS. Speedy and reliable Internet access is an increasingly important factor in the location decision. Fast Internet access through cable, DSL, or T1 lines is essential for high-tech companies and those engaging in e-commerce. Even those companies that may not do business over the Web currently are finding the odds very high that they will use the Web as a business tool within the near future. Companies that fall behind in high-tech communication will find themselves at a severe competitive disadvantage.

Darryl Lyons

When Darryl Lyons, a third-generation rancher, began raising Angus cattle to sell from his ranch in Okmulgee, Oklahoma, he made all of his first-year sales of $140,000 to customers located within a 100-mile radius. Then Lyons began using the Web as a marketing tool, and sales climbed to $600,000. Now reaching customers across the globe, Lyons expects sales to reach more than $1.5 million! One problem Lyons faces in his remote location, however, is fast, reliable Internet service. Bad weather interrupts his telephone and Internet service about a dozen times a year, costing him an estimated $3,000 to $4,000 in lost sales each day it is out.[8]

Most entrepreneurs are amazed at the amount of helpful information that exists about each state if they search the right places and ask the right questions. Obtaining and analyzing the information about a region and the states in it provide the entrepreneur with a clear picture of the most favorable location. The next phase of the location selection process concentrates on selecting the best city.

Choosing the City

POPULATION TRENDS. Entrepreneurs should know more about the cities in which their businesses are located than do the people who live there. By analyzing population and other demographic data, an entrepreneur can examine a city in detail, and the location decision becomes more than a shot in the dark. Studying the characteristics of a city's residents, including population size and density, growth trends, family size, age breakdowns, education, income levels, job categories, gender, religion, race, and nationality, gives an entrepreneur the facts she needs to make an informed location decision. In fact, using only basic census data, entrepreneurs can determine the value of the homes in an area, how many rooms they contain, how many bedrooms they contain, what percentage of the population owns their homes, and how much residents' monthly rental or mortgage payments are. Imagine how useful such information would be to someone about to launch a bed and bath shop!

A company's location should match the market for its products or services, and assembling a demographic profile will tell an entrepreneur how well a particular site measures up to her target market's profile. For instance, an entrepreneur planning to open a fine china shop would likely want specific information on family income, size, age, and education. Such a shop would need to be in an area where people appreciate the product and have the discretionary income to purchase it.

Trends or shifts in population components may have more meaning than total population trends. For example, if a city's population is aging rapidly, its disposable income may be decreasing and the city may be gradually dying. On the other hand, a city may be experiencing rapid growth in the population of high-income, young professionals. For example, because it has one of the best telecommunications infrastructures in the world and offers low cost of doing business and ready access to venture capital, Atlanta, Georgia, is attracting droves of young people, many of them entrepreneurs. As a result, the city, where the median age of inhabitants is 30, has seen an explosion of new businesses aimed at young people with rising incomes and hearty appetites for consumption.

The amount of available data on the population of any city or town is staggering. These statistics allow a potential business owner to compare a wide variety of cities or towns and to narrow the choices to those few that warrant further investigation. The mass of data may make it possible to screen out undesirable locations, but it does not make a decision for an entrepreneur. Entrepreneurs need to see potential locations firsthand. Only by personal investigation will an entrepreneur be able to add that intangible factor of intuition into the decision-making process. Spending time at a potential location will tell an entrepreneur not only how many people frequent it, but also what they are like, how long they stay, and what they buy. Walking or driving around the area will give an entrepreneur clues about the people who live and work there. What are their houses like? What kinds of cars do they drive? What stage of life are they in? Do they have children? Is the area on the rise or is it past its prime?

When evaluating cities as possible business locations, entrepreneurs should consider the following factors.

COMPETITION. For some retailers, it makes sense to locate near competitors because similar businesses located near one another may serve to increase traffic flow to all businesses. This location strategy works well for products for which customers are most likely to comparison shop. For instance, in many cities, auto dealers locate next to one another in a "motor mile," trying to create a shopping magnet for customers. The convenience of being able to shop for dozens of brands of cars all within a few hundred yards of one another draws customers from a sizeable trading area. Of course, this strategy has limits. Overcrowding of businesses of the same type in an area can create an undesirable impact on the profitability of all competing firms. Consider the nature of the businesses in the area. Do they offer the same quality merchandise or comparable services? The products or services of a business may be superior to those that competitors currently offer, giving it a competitive edge.

Studying the size of the market for a product or service and the number of existing competitors will help an entrepreneur determine whether she can capture a sufficiently large market share to earn a profit. Again, census reports can be a valuable source of information. The *County Business Patterns* shows the breakdown of businesses in manufacturing, wholesale, retail, and service categories and estimates companies' annual payrolls and number of employees broken down by county. *Zip Code Business Patterns* provides the same data as *County Business Patterns* except it organizes the data by zip code. The *Economic Census,* which is produced for years that end in "2" and "7," gives an overview of the businesses in an area—their sales (or other measure of output), employment, payroll, and form of organization. It covers eight industry categories, including retail, wholesale, service, manufacturing, construction, and others, and gives statistics not only at the national level, but also by state, MSA, county, places with more than 2,500 inhabitants, and zip code. The *Economic Census* is a useful tool for helping entrepreneurs determine whether an area they are considering as a location is already saturated with competitors.

CLUSTERING. Some cities have characteristics that attract certain industries, and, as a result, companies tend to cluster there. With its highly trained, well-educated, and technologically literate workforce, Austin, Texas, has become a mecca for high-tech companies. Home to Dell Computer and Hewlett-Packard, Austin offers computer hardware and software companies exactly what they need to succeed.

Once a concentration of companies takes root in a city, other businesses in those industries tend to spring up there as well. For instance, New York has long been the center of the advertising, fashion, finance, and publishing industries.

The Book Report Network

Carol Fitzgerald, owner of The Book Report Network, an online provider of book reviews and other services, knew that her company had to be located in New York City because that is where all of the major book publishers' headquarters are located. "We're in publishing," says Fitzgerald. "We have to have an office in the city to get books quickly from the publishers."[9]

COMPATIBILITY WITH THE COMMUNITY. One of the intangibles that can be determined only by a visit to an area is the degree of compatibility a business has with the surrounding community. In other words, a company's image must fit in with the character of a town and the needs and wants of its residents. For example, Beverly Hills' ritzy Rodeo Drive (with its 90210 zip code) is home to shops that match the characteristics of the area's wealthy residents. Shops such as Cartier and Tiffany and Company (luxury jewelers), Hammacher Schlemmer (unique, innovative, and expensive gifts), Neiman Marcus (an upscale department store), and McCormick and Schmick (a restaurant touting "the most prestigious business address in Beverly Hills") cater to the area's rich and famous residents.

LOCAL LAWS AND REGULATIONS. Before settling on a city, an entrepreneur must consider the regulatory burden local government might impose. Government regulations affect many aspects of a small business's operation, from acquiring business licenses and building permits to erecting business signs and dumping trash. Some cities are regulatory activists, creating so many rules that they discourage business creation; others take a more lasseiz-faire approach, imposing few restrictions on businesses.

Scanivalve Company

Managers at the Scanivalve Company, a maker of air pressure measurement equipment, decided that the regulatory environment in San Diego was too oppressive for the company to operate efficiently. Managers complained about convoluted fire inspections and redundant hazardous materials handling inspections, but they decided to move their business when the Traffic Demand Management Agency threatened to impose $96,000 in annual fines on Scanivalve for workers who failed to carpool to work. The company moved to Spokane, Washington, lured by its favorable tax structure, well-educated labor force, good transportation infrastructure, and, of course, reasonable regulatory environment.[10]

zoning—*a system that divides a city or county into small cells or districts to control the use of land, buildings, and sites.*

variance—*a special exemption to a zoning ordinance.*

Zoning laws can have a major impact on an entrepreneur's location decision. **Zoning** is a system that divides a city or county into small cells or districts to control the use of land, buildings, and sites. Its purpose is to contain similar activities in suitable locations. For instance, one section of a city may be zoned residential, while the primary retail district is zoned commercial and another is zoned industrial to house manufacturing operations. Before selecting a particular site within a city, an entrepreneur must explore local zoning laws to determine if there are any ordinances that would place restrictions on business activity or that would prohibit establishing a business altogether. Zoning regulations may make a particular location "out of bounds." In some cases, an entrepreneur may appeal to the local zoning commission to rezone a site or to grant a **variance** (a special exemption to a zoning ordinance), but this is risky and could be devastating if the board disallows the variance.

TRANSPORTATION NETWORKS. Business owners must investigate the quality of local transportation systems. Is an airport located nearby? Are flights available to the necessary cities and are the schedules convenient? If a company needs access to a railroad spur, is one available in the city? How convenient is the area's access to major highways? What about travel distances to major customers? How long will it take to deliver shipments to them? Are the transportation rates reasonable? Where is the nearest seaport? In some situations, double or triple handling of merchandise and inventory causes transportation costs to skyrocket. For retailers, the availability of loading and unloading zones is an important feature of a suitable location. Some downtown locations suffer from a lack of sufficient space for carriers to unload deliveries of merchandise.

POLICE AND FIRE PROTECTION. Does the community in which you plan to locate offer adequate police and fire protection? If these services are not adequate and crime rates are high, the cost of the company's business insurance will reflect that.

COST OF UTILITIES AND PUBLIC SERVICES. A location should be served by a governmental unit that provides water and sewer services, trash and garbage collection, and other necessary utilities at a reasonable cost. The streets should be in good repair with adequate drainage. If the location is not within the jurisdiction of a municipality that provides these services, they will become a continuing cost to the business.

QUALITY OF LIFE. A final consideration when selecting a city is the quality of life it offers. For many entrepreneurs, quality of life is one of the key determinants of their choice of locale. Cities that offer comfortable weather, cultural events, museums, outdoor activities, concerts, restaurants, and an interesting nightlife have become magnets for entrepreneurs looking to start companies. Not only can a location in a city offering a high quality of life be attractive to an entrepreneur, but it can also make recruiting employees much easier.

Zefer Corporation

Matthew Burkley, CEO of Zefer Corporation, an Internet consulting firm, chose to locate his company's headquarters in an area in downtown Boston where high-tech companies are concentrated. As Zefer established offices across the country, managers chose locations where they could attract the most qualified workers—San Francisco's South of Market, Chicago's Bucktown, and lower Manhattan. Burkley discovered that the workers the company wants most are young people who want to live and work in neighborhoods filled with people like them and offering the shops, clubs, galleries, and restaurants they enjoy. "In today's labor market, you have to be where your team members want to be," says Burkley.[11]

Choosing the Site

The final step in the location selection process is choosing the actual site for the business. Again, facts will guide an entrepreneur to the best location decision. Each type of business has different evaluation criteria for what makes an ideal location. A manufacturer's prime consideration may be access to raw materials, suppliers, labor, transportation, and customers. Service firms need access to customers but can generally survive in lower-rent properties. A retailer's prime consideration is sufficient customer traffic. The one element common to all three is the need to locate where customers want to do business.

The site location decision draws on the most precise information available on the makeup of the area. Through the use of the published statistics mentioned earlier in this chapter, an entrepreneur can develop valuable insights regarding the characteristics of people and businesses in the immediate community.

Would you like to know how many people or families are living in your trading area, what type of jobs they have, how much money they make, their ages, the value of their homes, and their education level, as well as a variety of other useful information? Sometimes businesses pay large fees to firms and consultants for this market research information. However, this information is available free from public libraries and on the Web. Every decade, the U.S. government undertakes one of the most ambitious market research projects in the world, collecting incredibly detailed statistics on the nation's 276 million residents and compiling it into easy-to-read reports! The Census Bureau has divided the United States into 255 Metropolitan Statistical Areas (MSAs). These MSAs are then subdivided into census tracts, which contain an average of 4,000 to 5,000 people. These census tracts are subdivided into block statistics and are extremely useful for entrepreneurs considering sites in urban areas.

This mother lode of market research is available to entrepreneurs through some 1,300 state data centers across the country. Two reports entrepreneurs find especially useful when choosing locations are *Summary Population,* which provides a broad demographic look at an area, and *Housing Characteristics,* which offers a detailed breakdown of areas as small as city blocks. Nationally, the average block contains about 100 people. The data are available both on CD-ROM and on the World Wide Web at the Census Bureau's Web site. Any entrepreneur with a computer can access this incredible wealth of data with just a few clicks of a mouse.

2. Describe the location criteria for retail and service businesses.

LOCATION CRITERIA FOR RETAIL AND SERVICE BUSINESSES

Few decisions are as important for retailers and service firms than the choice of a location. Because their success depends on a steady flow of customers, these businesses must choose a location with their target customers' convenience and preferences in mind. Following are important considerations.

Trade Area Size

trading area—*the region from which a business can expect to draw customers over a reasonable time span.*

Every retail and service business should determine the extent of its **trading area,** the region from which a business can expect to draw customers over a reasonable time span. The primary variables that influence the scope of the trading area are the type and the size of the business. If a retail store specializes in a particular product line offering a wide selection and knowledgeable salespeople, it may draw customers from a great distance. In contrast, a convenience store with a general line of merchandise may have a small trading area because it is unlikely that customers would drive across town to purchase what is available within blocks of their homes or businesses. As a rule, the larger the store, the greater its selection, and the better its service, the broader is its trading area.

AMC Grand

For example, the typical movie theater draws its customers from an area of five to seven miles; however, the AMC Grand, a collection of 24 screens under one roof in Dallas, Texas, draws customers from as far as 25 miles away. This freestanding "megaplex" has expanded the normal theater trading area and attracts an amazing 3 million moviegoers a year even though it is not located near a shopping mall, as most theaters are. AMC Grand's attendance per screen averages 38 percent more than do AMC Entertainment's traditional theaters; its revenue per customer is 10 percent higher; and its profit margins are 12.5 percent higher.[12]

The following environmental factors also influence trading area size.

Retail Compatibility

retail compatibility—*the benefits a company receives by locating near other businesses selling complementary products and services.*

Shoppers tend to be drawn to clusters of related businesses. That's one reason shopping malls and outlet shopping centers are popular destinations for shoppers and are attractive locations for retailers. The concentration of businesses pulls customers from a larger trading area than a single freestanding business does. **Retail compatibility** describes the benefits a company receives by locating near other businesses selling complementary products and services. Clever business owners choose their locations with an eye on the surrounding mix of businesses.

The Herbal Remedy

Once Scott Fiore decided that Littleton, Colorado, was the ideal city in which to locate his natural pharmacy, The Herbal Remedy, he began a more detailed site analysis that led him to South Bridge Shopping Plaza. This strip shopping center proved to be the ideal location for The Herbal Remedy because of its ready access from a local interstate highway and the complementary nature of the surrounding businesses. A message therapist, a health club, a chiropractor, a rehabilitation center, and a gourmet meat market in the shopping center attract the same customers that Fiore targets. Plus, the Littleton Hospital is directly across the street. "It really is perfect," says Fiore. "We're getting referrals from all those places."[13]

Degree of Competition

The size, location, and activity of competing businesses also influence the size of a company's trading area. If a business will be the first of its kind in a location, its trading area might be quite extensive. However, if the area already has eight or 10 nearby stores that directly compete with a business, its trading area might be very small because the market is saturated with competitors. Market saturation is a problem for businesses in many industries, ranging from fast-food restaurants to convenience stores. A study by *Convenience Store News,* a trade publication of the convenience store industry, found that if the number of customers per convenience store in an area dropped below 3,000, the stores in that area suffered, and many were forced to close.[14]

The Index of Retail Saturation

One of the best ways to measure the level of saturation in an area is the index of retail saturation (IRS), which evaluates both the number of customers and the intensity of competition in a trading area.[15] The **index of retail saturation** is a measure of the potential sales per square foot of store space for a given product within a specific trading area. The index is the ratio of a trading area's sales potential for a particular product or service to its sales capacity:

index of retail saturation— *a measure of the potential sales per square foot of store space for a given product within a specific trading area; it is the ratio of a trading area's sales potential for a product or service to its sales capacity.*

$$IRS = \frac{C \times RE}{RF}$$

where

C = number of customers in the trading area
RE = retail expenditures, or the average expenditure per person ($) for the product in the trading area
RF = retail facilities, or the total square feet of selling space allocated to the product in the trading area

This computation is an important one for every retailer to make. Locating in an area already saturated with competitors results in dismal sales volume and often leads to failure.

To illustrate the index of retail saturation, suppose that an entrepreneur looking at two sites for a shoe store finds that he needs sales of $175 per square foot to be profitable. Site 1 has a trading area with 25,875 potential customers who spend an average of $42 on shoes annually; the only competitor in the trading area has 6,000 square feet of selling space. Site 2 has 27,750 potential customers spending an average of $43.50 on shoes annually; two competitors occupy 8,400 square feet of space.

Site 1

$$IRS = \frac{25{,}875 \times 42}{6{,}000}$$

$$= \$181.12 \text{ sales potential per square foot}$$

Site 2

$$IRS = \frac{27{,}750 \times 43.50}{8{,}400}$$

$$= \$143.71 \text{ sales potential per square foot}$$

Although site 2 appears to be more favorable on the surface, the index shows that site 1 is preferable; site 2 fails to meet the minimum standard of $175 per square foot.

Transportation Network

The transportation networks are the highways, roads, and public service routes that presently exist or are planned. If customers find it inconvenient to get to a location, the store's trading area is reduced. Entrepreneurs should check to see if the transportation system works smoothly and is free of barriers that might prevent customers from reaching their stores. Is it easy for customers traveling in the opposite direction to cross traffic? Do signs and traffic lights allow traffic to flow smoothly?

Physical, Racial, or Emotional Barriers

Trading area shape and size also are influenced by physical, racial, or political barriers that may exist. Physical barriers may be parks, rivers, lakes, or any other natural or other obstruction that hinders customers' access to the area. Locating on one side of a large park may reduce the number of customers that will drive around it to get to the store. If high-crime areas exist in any direction from the site, most of a company's potential customers will not travel through those neighborhoods to reach the business.

In urban areas, new immigrants tend to cluster together, sharing a common culture and language. Some areas are defined by cultural barriers, where inhabitants patronize only the businesses in their neighborhoods. The Little Havana section of Miami or the Chinatown sections of San Francisco, New York, and Los Angeles are examples.

One of the most powerful emotional barriers affecting a location is fear. Businesses in areas where crime is a problem suffer because customers are not willing to travel into them. In South Central Los Angeles, an area once decimated by riots, only a handful of businesses have reopened to serve the local population. Business owners, afraid that the area's burned-out buildings and reputation for crime will dissuade customers from patronizing their businesses, have chosen locations in other parts of the city.

Political Barriers

Political barriers are creations of law. County, city, or state boundaries—and the laws within those boundaries—are examples. State tax laws sometimes create conditions that cause customers to cross over to the next state to save money. For instance, North Carolina imposes a very low cigarette tax, and shops located near the state line do a brisk business in the product selling to customers from bordering states.

Other factors retailers should consider when evaluating potential sites follow.

Customer Traffic

Perhaps the most important screening criterion for a potential retail (and often for a service) location is the number of potential customers passing by the site during business hours. To be successful, a business must be able to generate sufficient sales to surpass its breakeven point, and that requires an ample volume of customer traffic going past its doors. One of the key success factors for a convenience store, for instance, is a high-volume location with easy accessibility. Entrepreneurs should know the traffic counts (pedestrian and/or auto) and traffic patterns at the sites they are considering as potential locations.

The Better Way Boutique

When Lucindia Nobles was looking for a location for The Better Way Boutique, an upscale clothing consignment shop, she thought she had found the perfect site in a strip shopping center. While waiting for a bank to process her loan application, Nobles began to examine the shopping center more closely, and what she saw alerted her to a serious problem: declining customer traffic. Finally, she concluded that the shopping center did not attract enough customers to make her shop a success. Nobles's search for a new location led her to a busy street in downtown College Park, Maryland, not far from the University of Maryland, that is "alive with shoppers," she says. "This is a much better site for us."[16]

Adequate Parking

If customers cannot find convenient and safe parking, they are not likely to stop in the area. Many downtown areas have lost customers because of inadequate parking. Although shopping malls average five parking spaces per 1,000 square feet of shopping space, many central business districts get by with 3.5 spaces per 1,000 square feet. Customers generally will not pay to park if parking is free at shopping centers or in front of competitive stores. Even when free parking is provided, some potential customers may not feel safe on the streets, especially after dark. Many large city downtown business districts become virtual ghost towns at the end of the business day. A location where traffic vanishes after 6 P.M. may not be as valuable as mall and shopping center locations that mark the beginning of the prime sales time at 6 P.M.

Reputation

Like people, a site can have a bad reputation. In some cases, the reputation of the previous business will lower the value of the location. Sites where businesses have failed repeatedly create negative impressions in customers' minds; people view the business as just another that soon will be gone. One restaurateur struggled early on to overcome the negative image his new location had acquired over the years as one restaurant after another had failed there. He eventually established a base of loyal customers and succeeded, but it was a slow and trying process.

Room for Expansion

A location should be flexible enough to provide for expansion if success warrants it. Failure to consider this factor can result in a successful business's being forced to open a second store when it would have been better to expand in its original location.

Visibility

No matter what a small business sells and how well it serves customers' needs, it cannot survive without visibility. Highly visible locations simply make it easy for customers to make purchases. A site lacking visibility puts a company at a major disadvantage before it ever opens its doors for business.

Coffee, Etc.

Consider the story of Coffee, Etc., a small gourmet coffee store/restaurant in San Francisco. Located on the outside of a suburban mall, the store attracted shoppers and mall employees. Then mall owners remodeled the center, building a large department store over the old parking lot. Coffee, Etc. found itself literally hidden in the shadow of the new store, completely invisible to automobile traffic. Sales dropped off, and within a year the store went out of business. Several other restaurants tried the location, but all of them failed. The site remains vacant.[17]

LOCATION OPTIONS FOR RETAIL AND SERVICE BUSINESSES

3. Outline the location options for retail and service businesses.

There are six basic areas where retail and service business owners can locate: the central business district (CBD); neighborhoods; shopping centers and malls; near competitors; outlying areas; and at home. According to the International Council of Shopping Centers, the average cost to lease space in a shopping center is about $15 per square foot. At a regional mall, rental rates run from $20 to $40 per square foot, and in central business locations, the average cost is $43 per square foot (although rental rates can vary significantly from that average, depending on the city).[18] Of course, cost is just one factor a business owner must consider when choosing a location.

Central Business District

The central business district (CBD) is the traditional center of town—the downtown concentration of businesses established early in the development of most towns and cities. Entrepreneurs derive several advantages from a downtown location. Because the firm is centrally located, it attracts customers from the entire trading area of the city. Also, a small business usually benefits from the customer traffic generated by the other stores in the district. However, locating in a CBD does have certain disadvantages. Many CBDs are characterized by intense competition, high rental rates, traffic congestion, and inadequate parking facilities.

Beginning in the 1950s, many cities saw their older downtown business districts begin to decay as residents moved to the suburbs and began shopping at newer, more convenient malls. Today, however, many of these CBDs are experiencing rebirth as cities restore them to their former splendor and shoppers return. Many customers find irresistible the charming atmosphere that traditional downtown districts offer with their rich mix of stores, their unique architecture and streetscapes, and their historic character. One real estate developer experienced in Main Street locations says that his research shows that the best downtown streets for retailers are located in densely populated, affluent areas, are one-way, offer on-street parking, and are shaded by mature trees.[19]

Main Street of Burlington, Inc.

Working through the National Main Street Program, residents in Burlington, Iowa, have revitalized their downtown district. When three historic buildings, including an old stone mill, that had fallen into disrepair were about to be demolished, residents sprang into action and began a cooperative program to refurbish the old buildings and to recruit businesses to them. The effort was successful, and Burlington has since seen 80 new businesses open downtown, representing a total investment of $4.5 million![20]

Neighborhood Locations

Small businesses that locate near residential areas rely heavily on the local trading areas for business. For example, many convenience stores located just outside residential subdivisions count on local clientele for successful operation. One study of food stores found that the majority of the typical grocer's customers live within a five-mile radius. The primary advantages of a neighborhood location include relatively low operating costs and rents and close contact with customers.

Shopping Centers and Malls

The first regional shopping mall, Northgate Shopping Center in Seattle, Washington, was built in 1950 and featured a full-service department store as its anchor and a central pedestrian walkway. Since then, shopping centers and malls have become a mainstay of the American landscape. Since 1970, the number of shopping malls and centers in the United States has climbed from 11,000 to more than 44,400, and they occupy 5.46 billion square feet of retail space.[21] Because many different types of stores exist under one roof, shopping malls give meaning to the term *one-stop shopping*. In a typical month, some 190 million adults visit a mall or shopping center.[22] There are four types of shopping centers:

- *Neighborhood Shopping Centers.* The typical neighborhood shopping center is relatively small, containing from 3 to 12 stores and serving a population of up to 40,000 people who live within a 10-minute drive. The anchor store in these centers is usually a supermarket or a drugstore.
- *Community Shopping Centers.* The community shopping center contains from 12 to 50 stores and serves a population ranging from 40,000 to 150,000 people. The leading tenant is a department or variety store.
- *Regional Shopping Malls.* The regional shopping mall serves a much larger trading area, usually from 10 to 15 miles or more in all directions. It contains from 50 to 100 stores and serves a population in excess of 150,000 people living within a 20- to 40-minute drive. The anchor is typically one or more major department stores.
- *Power Centers.* A power center combines the drawing strength of a large regional mall with the convenience of a neighborhood shopping center. Anchored by large specialty retailers, these centers target older, wealthier baby boomers, who want selection and convenience. Anchor stores usually account for 80 percent of power center space, compared with 50 percent in the typical strip shopping center. Just as in a shopping mall, small businesses can benefit from the traffic generated by anchor stores, but they must choose their locations carefully so that they are not overshadowed by their larger neighbors.

When evaluating a mall or shopping center location, an entrepreneur should consider the following questions:

- Is there a good fit with other products and brands sold in the mall or center?
- Who are the other tenants? Which stores are the anchors that will bring people into the mall or center?
- Demographically, is the center a good fit for your products or services? What are its customer demographics?
- How much foot traffic does the mall or center generate? How much traffic passes the specific site you are considering?
- How much vehicle traffic does the mall or center generate? Check its proximity to major population centers, the volume of tourists it draws, and the volume of drive-by freeway traffic. A mall or center that scores well on all three is probably a winner.
- What is the vacancy rate? The turnover rate?
- How much is the rent and how is it calculated? Most mall tenants pay a base amount of rent plus a percentage of their sales.
- Is the mall or center successful? How many dollars in sales does it generate per square foot? Compare its record against industry averages. (The International Council of Shopping Centers in New York **<www.icsc.org>** is a good source of industry information.)

A mall location does not guarantee success. Malls have been under pressure lately, and many weaker ones have closed. Others have undergone extensive renovations, adding entertainment features to their existing retail space in an attempt to generate more traffic. The basic problem is an oversupply of malls; the United States has 20 feet of mall retail space for every person in the United States!

Near Competitors

One of the most important factors in choosing a retail or service location is the compatibility of nearby stores with the retail or service customer. For example, stores selling high-priced goods find it advantageous to locate near competitors to facilitate comparison shopping. Locating near competitors might be a key factor for success in those businesses selling goods that customers shop for and compare on the basis of price, quality, color, and other factors.

Although some business owners avoid locations near direct competitors, others see locating near rivals as an advantage. For instance, restaurateurs know that successful restaurants attract other restaurants, which, in turn, attract more customers. Many cities have at least one "restaurant row," where restaurants cluster together; each restaurant feeds customers to the others.

Locating near competitors has its limits, however. Clustering too many businesses of a single type into a small area ultimately will erode their sales once the market reaches the saturation point. When an area becomes saturated with competitors, the shops cannibalize sales from one another, making it difficult for any of them to be successful.

Outlying Areas

Generally, it is not advisable for a small business to locate in a remote area because accessibility and traffic flow are vital to retail and service success, but there are exceptions. Some small firms have turned their remote locations into trademarks. One small gun shop was able to use its extremely remote location to its advantage by incorporating this into its advertising to distinguish itself from its competitors.

Home-Based Businesses

For more than 24 million people, home is where the business is, and their numbers are swelling. According to the Department of Commerce, home-based businesses represent the fastest-growing segment of the U.S. economy.[23] One recent study found that 52 percent of all small companies are home based.[24] Although a home-based retail business is usually not feasible, locating a service business at home is quite popular. Many service companies do not have customers come to their places of business, so an expensive office location is unnecessary. For instance, customers typically contact plumbers or exterminators by telephone, and the work is performed in customers' homes.

Entrepreneurs locating their businesses at home reap several benefits. Perhaps the biggest benefit is the low cost of setting up the business. Most often, home-based entrepreneurs set up shop in a spare bedroom or basement, avoiding the cost of renting, leasing, or buying a building. With a few basic pieces of office equipment—a computer, printer, fax machine, copier, telephone answering system, and scanner—a lone entrepreneur can perform just like a major corporation.

Truth and Fun Inc.

For instance, David Gans runs Truth and Fun Inc., a state-of-the-art production studio, from a spare bedroom in his Oakland, California, home. From his high-tech, in-home studio, Gans produces a weekly radio show, the Grateful Dead Hour, *that he beams by satellite to 90 radio stations across the country. "The equipment has gotten so powerful and inexpensive that one human being working from home can produce the exact same quality program as National Public Radio," says Gans.*[25]

Choosing a home location has certain disadvantages, however. Interruptions are more frequent, the refrigerator is all too handy, work is always just a few steps away, and isolation can be a problem. Another difficulty facing some home-based entrepreneurs involves zoning laws. As their businesses grow and become more successful, entrepreneurs' neighbors often begin to complain about the increased traffic, noise, and disruptions from deliveries, employees, and customers who drive through their residential neighborhoods to conduct business.

Propaganda

David Tyreman and Keith Walton started Propaganda, a props-supply business, from their home without neighbors even noticing. But as the business grew, evidence of the home-based entrepreneurs' venture became increasingly obvious. Tyreman recalls the day a truck delivered a 40-foot container that blocked the entire street![26]

Many states now face the challenge of passing updated zoning laws that reflect the reality of today's home-based businesses while protecting the interests of residential homeowners.

THE LOCATION DECISION FOR MANUFACTURERS

4. Explain the site selection process for manufacturers.

The criteria for the location decision for manufacturers are very different from those of retailers and service businesses; however, the decision can have just as much impact on the company's success. In some cases, a manufacturer has special needs that influence the choice of a location. For instance, when one manufacturer of photographic plates and film was searching for a location for a new plant, it had to limit its search only to those sites with a large supply of available fresh water, a necessary part of its process. In other cases, the location decision is controlled by zoning ordinances. If a manufacturer's process creates offensive odors or excessive noise, it may be even further restricted in its choices.

Zoning maps show potential manufacturers the areas of the city or county set aside for industrial development. Some cities have developed industrial parks in cooperation with private industry. These industrial parks typically are equipped with sewage and electrical power sufficient for manufacturing. Many locations are not so equipped, and it can be extremely expensive for a small manufacturer to have such utilities brought to an existing site.

Location of a plant, in some cases, is dictated by the type of transportation facilities required. Some manufacturers may need to locate on a railroad siding, whereas others may only need reliable trucking service. If raw materials are purchased by the carload, for economies of scale, the location must be convenient to a railroad siding. Bulk materials are sometimes shipped by barge and, consequently, require a facility convenient to a navigable river or lake. The added cost of using multiple shipping (i.e., rail-to-truck or barge-to-truck) can significantly increase shipping costs and make a location unfeasible for a manufacturer.

In some cases, the perishability of the product dictates location. Vegetables and fruits must be canned in close proximity to the fields in which they are harvested. Fish must be processed and canned at the water's edge. Location is determined by quick and easy access to the perishable products.

Table 12.1 provides a rating system to determine the suitability of various locations.

Foreign Trade Zones

Foreign trade zones can be an attractive location for small manufacturers that engage in global trade and are looking to minimize the tariffs they pay on the materials and parts they import and the goods they export. A **foreign trade zone** is a specially designated area in or near a U.S. customs port of entry that allows resident companies to import materials and components from foreign countries; assemble, process, manufacture, or package them; and then ship the finished product while either reducing or eliminating tariffs and duties. As far as tariffs and duties are concerned, a company located in a foreign trade zone is treated as if it is located outside the United States. For instance, a maker of speakers might import components from around the world and assemble them at its plant located in a foreign trade zone. The company would pay no duties on the components it imports or on the speakers it exports to other markets. The only duties the manufacturer would pay are on the speakers it sells in the United States.

foreign trade zone—*a specially designated area in or near a U.S. customs port of entry that allows resident companies to import materials and components from foreign countries; assemble, process, manufacture, or package them; and then ship the finished product while either reducing or eliminating tariffs and duties.*

TABLE 12.1
Rating the Suitability of Sites for a Business

Common Factors	Factor Importance (10 high—1 low)
Located to serve the customer (demographic trends)	
Cost of the location (rent or purchase price)	
Quantity and quality of the labor supply	
Zoning restrictions	
General business climate	
Transportation —For customers (highways, public transportation)	
—For raw material or inventories (rail, barge, air freight)	
Proximity to raw material or inventory	
Quality of public services (fire and police protection)	
Taxes (if owning)	
Adequacy for future expansion	
Value of the site in future years	
Labor cost and anticipated productivity	

empowerment zone—*an area designated as economically disadvantaged in which businesses are given tax breaks on the investments they make within zone boundaries.*

business incubator—*an organization that combines low-cost, flexible rental space with a multitude of support services for its small business residents.*

Empowerment Zones

Originally created to encourage companies to locate in economically blighted areas, **empowerment zones** offer businesses tax breaks on the investments they make within zone boundaries. Companies can get federal tax credits, grants, and loans for hiring workers living in empowerment zones and for investments they make in plant and equipment in the zones. Empowerment zones operate in both urban and rural areas, ranging from Los Angeles, California, to Sumter, South Carolina.

Business Incubators

For many start-up companies, a business incubator may make the ideal initial location. A **business incubator** is an organization that combines low-cost, flexible rental space with a multitude of support services for its small business residents. The overwhelming reason for establishing an incubator is to enhance economic development in an area and to diversify

	Actual Scores for Alternative Sites (10 high—1 low)				Total Scores for Alternative Sites (Factor Importance x Actual Score)			
	Site A	Site B	Site C	Site D	Site A	Site B	Site C	Site D
			TOTAL		_____	_____	_____	_____
					_____	_____	_____	_____

Highest-scoring site is:____________________

the local economy. An incubator's goal is to nurture young companies during the volatile start-up period and to help them survive until they are strong enough to go out on their own. Common sponsors of incubators include government agencies (51 percent); colleges or universities (27 percent); partnerships among government, nonprofit agencies, and/or private developers (16 percent); and private investment groups (8 percent). Technology incubators account for 40 percent of all incubators, and 30 percent are mixed-use operations, attracting a wide variety of businesses. The remaining 30 percent focus on service companies and those engaged in light manufacturing or specific niches.[27]

The shared resources incubators typically provide their tenants include secretarial services, a telephone system, computers and software, fax machines, and meeting facilities and, sometimes, management consulting services and financing. Not only do these services save young companies money, they also save them valuable time. Entrepreneurs can focus on getting their products and services to market faster than competitors rather than searching for the resources they need to build their companies. The typical incubator has entry requirements that prospective residents must meet. Incubators also have criteria that establish the conditions a business must maintain to remain in the facility as well as the expectations for "graduation" into the business community.

More than 900 incubators operate across the United States, and four new incubators open, on average, every week. Perhaps the greatest advantage of choosing to locate a start-up company in an incubator is a greater chance for success; according to the National Business Incubation Association, graduates from incubators have a success rate of 87 percent. The average incubator houses 20 ongoing businesses employing 55 people.[28]

Comedicus, Inc.

When the biotech company that he ran from a spare bedroom in his home acquired the exclusive license to a breakthrough system that delivers medicine straight to the heart, James Grabek knew it was time to take his company, Comedicus, Inc., to the next level. Fearful of losing control of his business, Grabek ultimately turned to Genesis Business Centers, a business incubator in Minneapolis, Minnesota. Harlon T. Jacobs, president of Genesis, offered Grabek access to $50,000 in financing, free office space, and management assistance in exchange for just 0.5 percent of the company's stock. Grabek decided to nurture his business in the incubator and quickly accepted the offer. Within 15 months, Genesis had helped Comedicus raise $1 million in a private placement and land $4 million in licensing agreements with major pharmaceutical companies. "It was a turning point that catapulted us into the corporate world," Grabek says of his decision to move into the incubator.[29]

5. Describe the criteria used to analyze the layout and design considerations of a building, including the Americans with Disabilities Act.

LAYOUT AND DESIGN CONSIDERATIONS

Once an entrepreneur chooses the best location for her business, the next question deals with designing the proper layout for the building to maximize sales (retail) or productivity (manufacturing or service). **Layout** is the logical arrangement of the physical facilities in a business that contributes to efficient operations, increased productivity, and higher sales. Planning for the most effective and efficient layout in a business environment can produce dramatic improvements in a company's operating effectiveness and efficiency. An attractive, effective layout can help a company's recruiting efforts. One study conducted by the American Association of Interior Designers found that employees rated the look and feel of their work spaces as the third most important consideration (after salary and benefits) when deciding whether or not to accept or to quit a job.[30] The following factors have a significant impact on a building's layout and design.

layout—*the logical arrangement of the physical facilities in a business that contributes to efficient operations, increased productivity, and higher sales.*

Size

A building must be large enough to accommodate a business's daily operations comfortably. If it is too small at the outset of operations, efficiency will suffer. There must be room enough for customers' movement, inventory, displays, storage, work areas, offices, and restrooms. Haphazard layouts undermine employee productivity and create organizational chaos. Too many small business owners start their operations in locations that are already overcrowded and lack the ability to be expanded. The result is that an owner is forced to make a costly move to a new location within the first few years of operation.

If an entrepreneur plans to expand, will the building accommodate it? Will hiring new employees, purchasing new equipment, expanding production areas, increasing service areas, and other growth require a new location? How fast is the company expected to grow over the next three to five years? Lack of adequate room in the building may become a limitation on a company's growth. Most small businesses wait too long before moving into larger quarters, and they fail to plan their new space arrangements properly. To avoid such

YOU BE THE CONSULTANT . . .

The *Cheers* of Bel Air

Downtown Bel Air, Maryland, faces many of the same challenges that thousands of other small towns and large cities across the United States are facing. Located about 40 minutes northeast of Baltimore, Bel Air is in a fast-growing area, but little of that growth is occurring in the town's central business district. The five-and-dime store, the shoe shop, the hardware store, and Richardson's Pharmacy (which boasted an old-fashioned soda fountain) either closed or moved to suburban malls years ago. Most of the buildings in the downtown area are filled with municipal government offices, law firms, accounting firms, and insurance agencies.

Although few merchants remain in downtown locations, David Wolff and his wife Jane chose a storefront in the middle of Main Street as the location for their coffee shop, Fine Grind. "We definitely wanted a Main Street location," says Wolff, who rejected the higher-priced sites in several malls near town. He points to the high concentration of white-collar workers in the downtown area who would serve as potential customers for the Fine Grind.

Wolff has higher aspirations than mere business success. He wants to be the cornerstone in Bel Air's revitalization effort and to bring "a sense of community" to the town that seems to have lost that. "I'm hoping there's going to be a renaissance on Main Street," he says. "I think I'm the beginning." Wolff was able to supplement the money he invested in the business with a low-interest loan from a state program aimed at revitalizing downtown areas.

Before launching his business, Wolff spent many hours studying the layout, the techniques, and the unique personalities that the proprietors of old-fashioned candy stores, drug stores, and other retail operations used in the early days of the last century. He read books and pored over old photographs and then began applying what he learned to the design of his own shop. He brought in glass canisters of Tootsie Rolls, licorice, jelly beans, and other colorful candies. He bought a large brass espresso machine and put it behind a beautiful long bar hand-crafted from polished wood from an old gymnasium floor. The tables in the Fine Grind are made from the same wood.

Not long after opening, people began coming to Bel Air's downtown district just to visit the Fine Grind, which is exactly what Wolff wanted to happen. To lure customers in, Wolff allows local artists to display their work on the walls of his shop. One Saturday each month, he stays open later than normal to host an art exhibit with entertainment by a local musician. Although only three people (the artist, the musician, and Mr. Wolff) came to the first opening, the events now draw standing-room-only crowds. Wolff also dedicates one evening each month to a local book club (a large bookstore chain in a nearby mall refused to let the book club meet in its store), and another evening the members of a poetry club come in for a poetry reading. During the summer months, Wolff offers live music every Saturday night. Every Saturday morning, Wolff and his family get up early and head to the local farmer's market where they sell coffee and snacks from a booth. Customers also can buy the Fine Grind's products from the company's Web site **<www.finegrind.net>**.

Customers have turned the Fine Grind into a local hangout, and, like a good bartender, Wolff knows all of his regular customers' favorite drinks. "We call this the *Cheers* of Bel Air," says Bonnie Maivelett, a regular who comes in with her husband Bob practically every morning, referring to the popular TV show from the 1980s about a Boston pub "where everybody knows your name." Since the Fine Grind opened, several other entrepreneurs have opened businesses in the downtown area, including several restaurants, an Irish pub, a T-shirt shop, and others. That's exactly what David Wolff hoped would happen when he launched the Fine Grind.

1. What advantages and disadvantages does choosing a downtown location offer an entrepreneur like David Wolff?
2. Assume the role of consultant. Suppose that officials in a town with which you are familiar approached you about revitalizing the central business district. What advice would you offer them?
3. What factors should entrepreneurs evaluate when comparing a downtown location against a location in a shopping center or mall?

Source: Adapted from Hilary Stout, "When Building Up a Business Means Turning Around a Town," *Wall Street Journal,* June 11, 2000 p. B1.

problems, some experts recommend that new businesses plan their space requirements one to two years ahead and update the estimates every six months. When preparing the plan, managers should include the expected growth in the number of employees; manufacturing, selling, or storage space requirements; and the number and location of branches to be opened.

Construction and External Appearance

Is the construction of the building sound? It pays to have an expert look it over before buying or leasing the property. Beyond the soundness of construction, does the building have attractive external and internal appearances? The physical appearance of the building provides customers with their first impression of a business. This is especially true in retail businesses. Many retailers provide the customer with a consistent building appearance as they expand (e.g., fast-food restaurants and motels). Is the building's appearance consistent with the entrepreneur's desired image for the business?

Small retailers must recognize the importance of creating the proper image for their stores and how their shops' layouts and physical facilities influence this image. The store's external appearance contributes significantly to establishing its identity in the customer's mind. In many ways, the building's appearance sets the tone for what the customer can expect in the way of quality and service. The appearance should, therefore, reflect the business's "personality." Should the building project an exclusive image or an economical one? Is the atmosphere informal and relaxed or formal and businesslike? Physical facilities send important messages to customers. Communicating the right signals through layout and physical facilities is an important step in attracting a steady stream of customers. Retail consultant Paco Underhill advises merchants to "seduce" passersby with their storefronts. "The seduction process should start a minimum of 10 paces away," he says.[31]

A store's window display can be a powerful selling tool if used properly. Often, a store's display window is an afterthought, and many business owners neglect to change their displays often enough. The following tips will help entrepreneurs create displays that will sell.

- *Keep displays simple.* Simple, uncluttered, and creative arrangements of merchandise draw the most attention and have the greatest impact on potential customers.
- *Keep displays clean and current.* Dusty, dingy displays or designs that are outdated send a negative message to passersby.
- *Change displays frequently.* Customers do not want to see the same merchandise on display every time they enter a store. Experts recommend changing displays at least quarterly, but stores selling trendy items should change their displays twice a month.
- *Get expert help, if necessary.* Not every business owner has a knack for designing window displays. Their best bet is to hire a professional or to work with the design department at a local college or university.

Entrances

All entrances to a business should invite customers in. Wide entry ways and attractive merchandise displays that are set back from the doorway can draw customers into a business. A store's entrance must catch customers' attention and draw them inside. "That's where you want somebody to slam on the brakes and realize they're going someplace new," says retail consultant Paco Underhill.[32] Retailers with heavy traffic flows such as supermarkets or drugstores often install automatic doors to ensure a smooth traffic flow into and out of their stores. Retailers should remove any barriers that interfere with customers' easy access to the storefront. Broken sidewalks, sagging steps, mud puddles, and sticking or heavy doors not only create obstacles that might discourage potential customers, they also create legal hazards for a business if they cause customers to be injured.

Americans with Disabilities Act—*a law that requires businesses with 15 or more employees to make their facilities available to physically challenged customers and employees.*

The Americans with Disabilities Act

The **Americans with Disabilities Act (ADA),** passed in July 1990, requires practically all businesses to make their facilities available to physically challenged customers and employees. In addition, the law requires businesses with 15 or more employees to accommodate physically challenged candidates in their hiring practices. Most states have similar laws, many of them more stringent than the ADA, that apply to smaller companies as well. The rules of these state laws and the ADA's Title III are designed to ensure that mentally and physically challenged customers have equal access to a firm's goods or services. For instance, the act requires business owners to remove architectural and communication barriers when "readily achievable." The ADA allows flexibility in how a business achieves this equal access, however. For example, a restaurant could either provide menus in Braille or could offer to have a staff member read the menu to blind customers. A small dry cleaner might not be able to add a wheelchair ramp to its storefront without incurring significant expense, but the owner could comply with the ADA by offering curbside pickup and delivery services for disabled customers at no extra charge.

Although the law allows a good deal of flexibility in retrofitting existing structures, buildings that were occupied after January 25, 1993, must be designed to comply with all aspects of the law. For example, buildings with three stories or more must have elevators; anywhere the floor level changes by more than one-half inch, an access ramp must be in place. In retail stores, checkout aisles must be wide enough—at least 36 inches—to accommodate wheelchairs. Restaurants must have 5 percent of their tables accessible to wheelchair-bound patrons.

Complying with the ADA does not necessarily require businesses to spend large amounts of money. The Justice Department estimates that more than 20 percent of the cases customers have filed under Title III involved changes the business owners could have made at no cost, and another 60 percent would have cost less than $1,000![33] In addition, companies with $1 million or less in annual sales or with 30 or fewer full-time employees that invest in making their locations more accessible to all qualify for a tax credit. The credit is 50 percent of their expenses between $250 and $10,500. Businesses that remove physical, structural, and transportation barriers for disabled employees and customers also qualify for a tax deduction of up to $15,000.

The ADA also prohibits any kind of employment discrimination against anyone with a physical or mental disability. A physically challenged person is considered to be "qualified" if he can perform the essential functions of the job. The employer must make "reasonable accommodation" for a physically challenged candidate or employee without causing "undue hardship" to the business.

Casey Martin

When a rare circulatory disease forced professional golfer Casey Martin to use a golf cart to move from one hole to another on a golf course, the Professional Golf Association (PGA) refused to change its rule that prohibits golfers from using carts in tournaments. Martin filed a lawsuit against the PGA under the ADA, claiming that his use of a golf cart constituted a reasonable accommodation for his disability. Both a trial court and a federal appeals court agreed with Martin, who now plays golf (with the help of a cart) alongside some of the greatest golfers of today. The PGA has filed an appeal with the U.S. Supreme Court.[34]

The ADA has affected, in a positive way, how businesses deal with this segment of its customers and employees. The Department of Justice offers a technical assistance program that provides business owners with free information and technical assistance concerning the ADA. The Department of Justice also has an ADA Hotline that owners can call for information and publications on the ADA (800-514-0301).

Signs

One of the lowest-cost and most effective methods of communicating with customers is a business sign. Signs tell potential customers what a business does, where it is, and what it is selling. America is a very mobile society, and a well-designed, well-placed sign can be a powerful tool for reaching potential customers.

A sign should be large enough for passersby to read it from a distance, taking into consideration the location and speed of surrounding traffic arteries. To be most effective, the message should be short, simple, and clear. A sign should be legible in both daylight and at night; proper illumination is a must. Contrasting colors and simple typefaces are best. The most common problems with business signs are that they are illegible, poorly designed, improperly located, and poorly maintained and have color schemes that are unattractive or are hard to read.

Before investing in a sign, an entrepreneur should investigate the local community's sign ordinance. In some cities and towns, local regulations impose restrictions on the size, location, height, and construction materials used in business signs.

Building Interiors

Like exterior considerations, the functional aspects of building interiors are very important and require careful attention to detail. Designing a functional, efficient interior is not easy. Technology has changed drastically the way employees, customers, and the environment interact with one another.

ergonomics—*the science of adapting work and the work environment to complement employees' strengths and to suit customers' needs.*

Piecing together an effective layout is not a haphazard process. **Ergonomics,** the science of adapting work and the work environment to complement employees' strengths and to suit customers' needs, is an integral part of a successful design. For example, chairs, desks, and table heights that allow people to work comfortably can help employees perform their jobs faster and more easily. Design experts claim that improved lighting, better acoustics, and proper climate control benefit the company as well as employees. An ergonomically designed workplace can improve workers' productivity significantly and lower days lost due to injuries and accidents. Unfortunately, many businesses fail to incorporate ergonomic design principles into their layouts, and the result is costly. The most frequent and most expensive workplace injuries are musculoskeletal disorders (MSDs), which cost U.S. businesses $20 billion in workers' compensation claims each year. According to the Occupational Safety and Health Administration (OSHA), MSDs account for 34 percent of all lost-workday injuries and illnesses and one-third of all workers' compensation claims.[35] Workers who spend their days staring at computer monitors (a significant and growing proportion of the workforce) often are victims of MSDs.

The most common MSD is carpal tunnel syndrome (CTS), which occurs when repetitive motion causes swelling in the wrist that pinches the nerves in the arm and hand. Studies by the Bureau of Labor Statistics show that more than 42 percent of CTS cases require more than 30 days away from work.[36] The good news for employers, however, is that preventing injuries, accidents, and lost days does *not* require spending thousands of dollars on ergonomically correct solutions. Most of the solutions to MSDs are actually quite simple and inexpensive.

Sequins International

Sequins International, a maker of sequined fabrics and trimmings in Woodside, New York, uses adjustable chairs and machinery as well as automatic spooling devices to reduce workers' repetitive motions and taxing physical demands. These simple changes eliminated carpal tunnel syndrome and cut workers' compensation costs to just $800, down from $98,000 in 1994.[37]

Other solutions are decidedly low tech.

Designer Checks

For instance, when Designer Checks, a maker of custom checks based in Anniston, Alabama, consulted with an occupational therapist, owner Grady Burrow learned that one of the best ways to fight MSDs among its computer-dependent workforce is simply to take frequent breaks and to move around. Department heads began scheduling regular exercise breaks designed to stretch employees' necks, shoulders, and hands. Before long, many managers began livening up their exercise breaks with music and dancing! Visitors to the Designer Checks' plant are likely to see managers and employees take to the production floor for a rousing rendition of the macarena or the hokey pokey.[38]

When planning store, office, or plant layouts, business owners usually focus on minimizing costs. Although staying within a budget is important, minimizing injuries and enhancing employees' productivity with an effective layout should be the overriding issues. One extensive six-year study concluded that changes in office design have a direct impact on workers' performance, job satisfaction, and ease of communication. The report also concluded that the savings generated by effective layouts are substantial and, conversely, that poorly planned designs involve significant costs.[39] In a reversal of the trend toward open offices separated by nothing more than cubicles, businesses are once again creating private offices in their work spaces. Many businesses embraced open designs, hoping that they would lead to greater interaction among workers. Many companies, however, have discovered that most office workers need privacy and quiet surroundings to be productive. Michael Brill, an office space consultant, studied 11,000 workers to determine the factors that most affect their productivity and found that the ability to do distraction-free work topped the list.[40] Rather than encourage teamwork, open offices leave workers distracted, frustrated, and less productive—just like the characters in the Dilbert cartoon strip.

Flyswat Inc.

Flyswat Inc., a company that develops customized tools and services for Internet browsing, designed the interior of its building to appeal to its twenty-something, high-tech workforce. Cofounders John Rodkin, Leo Chang, and Raymond Crouse created a 150-square-foot indoor beach, complete with 3,000 pounds of sand, in their third-floor San Francisco office! Employees can scrunch the sand between their toes while gazing at banana trees, bird-of-paradise plants, tiki torches, and walls, floors, and ceilings painted to resemble grass and sky. "Why bother?" visitors ask. Because Flyswat employees often spend 60-plus hours a week there, the company founders want to give them a fun, enjoyable place to work. The company buys dinner for its workers four nights a week, maintains a fully stocked kitchen, and offers showers and a laundry room.[41]

When evaluating an existing building's interior, an entrepreneur must be sure to determine the integrity of its structural components. Are the building's floors sufficiently strong to hold the business's equipment, inventories, and personnel? Strength is an especially critical factor for manufacturing firms that use heavy equipment. When multiple floors exist, are the upper floors anchored as solidly as the primary floor? Can inventory be moved safely and easily from one area of the plant to another? Is the floor space adequate for safe and efficient movement of goods and people? Consider the cost of maintaining the floors. Hardwood floors may be extremely attractive but require expensive and time-consuming maintenance. Carpeted floors may be extremely attractive in a retail business but may be totally impractical for a quality manufacturing firm. Entrepreneurs must consider the utility, durability, maintenance requirements, attractiveness, and, if important, the effectiveness in reducing noise of the building's flooring.

Like floors, walls and ceilings must be both functional and attractive. On the functional side, walls and ceilings should be fireproof and soundproof. Are the colors of walls and ceilings compatible, and do they create an attractive atmosphere for customers and employees? For instance, many Web-related companies use bright, bold colors in their designs because they appeal to their young employees. On the other hand, more conservative firms such as accounting firms and law offices decorate with more subtle, subdued tones because they convey an image of trustworthiness and honesty. Upscale restaurants that want their patrons to linger over dinner use deep, luxurious tones and soft lighting to create the proper ambiance. Fast-food restaurants, on the other hand, use strong, vibrant colors and bright lighting to encourage customers to get in and out quickly, ensuring the fast table turnover they require to be successful. In most cases, ceilings should be done in light colors to reflect the store's lighting.

For many businesses, a drive-through window adds another dimension to the concept of customer convenience and is a relatively inexpensive way to increase sales. Although drive-through windows are staples at fast-food restaurants and banks, they can add value for customers in a surprising number of businesses.

Steel Supply Company

For instance, when Marshall Hoffman relocated his business, Steel Supply Company, to a building that had been used as a bank, the idea of using the drive-through window intrigued him. Looking for a way to improve customer service, Hoffman transformed the former bank lobby into his showroom floor and began advertising the convenience of buying steel at the drive-through window. Customers place their steel orders by telephone, pull up to the window and pay, and receive a ticket. The order goes by computer to a warehouse Hoffman built on the site. By the time the customer pulls up to the warehouse, the order is waiting! The window has been a hit with customers. Since moving into its new location, Steel Supply's sales have grown from $3.5 million to more than $6 million.[42]

Lights and Fixtures

Good lighting allows employees to work at maximum efficiency. Proper lighting is measured by what is ideal for the job being done. Proper lighting in a factory may be quite different from that required in an office or retail shop. Retailers often use creative lighting to attract customers to a specific display. Jewelry stores provide excellent examples of how lighting can be used to display merchandise.

Lighting is often an inexpensive investment when considering its impact on the overall appearance of the business. Few people seek out businesses that are dimly lit because they convey an image of untrustworthiness. The use of natural and artificial light in combination can give a business an open and cheerful look. Many restaurant chains have added greenhouse glass additions to accomplish this.

6. Explain the principles of effective layouts for retailers, service businesses, and manufacturers.

LAYOUT: MAXIMIZING REVENUES, INCREASING EFFICIENCY, AND REDUCING COST

The ideal layout for a building depends on the type of business it houses and on the entrepreneur's strategy for gaining a competitive edge. Retailers design their layouts with the goal of maximizing sales revenue; manufacturers see layout as an opportunity to increase efficiency and productivity and to lower costs.

Layout for Retailers

Retail layout is the arrangement of merchandise in a store and its method of display. A retailer's success depends, in part, on a well-designed floor display. A retail layout should pull customers into the store and make it easy for them to locate merchandise; compare prices, quality, and features; and ultimately make a purchase. In addition; the floor plan should take customers past displays of other items that they may buy on impulse. Between 65 and 70 percent of all buying decisions are made once a customer enters a store, which means that the right layout can boost sales significantly. One study found that 68 percent of the items bought on major shopping trips (and 54 percent on smaller trips) were impulse purchases. Shoppers in this study were heavily influenced by in-store displays, especially those at the ends of aisles (called end-cap displays.)[43]

Retailers have always recognized that some locations within a store are superior to others. Customer traffic patterns give the owner a clue to the best location for the highest gross margin items. Merchandise purchased on impulse and convenience goods should be

YOU BE THE CONSULTANT . . .

Not Your Typical CPA Firm

Lipschulz, Levin and Gray (LLG) is not the typical public accounting firm, a fact that is obvious to even the most casual observer who enters the company's offices in Northbrook, Illinois. Rather than the traditional conservative decor found in most CPA offices, LLG's is quite contemporary and very different. First, there are no offices. No employees (officially called "team members") have enclosed offices; nor do they reside in honeycombs of Dilbert-like cubicles. The same holds true of LLG's partners (called "members"). *Everyone* in the company works in an open expanse with no private offices. The flexible work space the owners created *really* is flexible. Even the office furniture, including desks, is on wheels so that team members can move it around as needed to collaborate with colleagues.

The transformation from a staid, traditional accounting firm began in 1988, when the partners did some soul-searching in an attempt to find out why the company was earning so little money, employee turnover was high, morale was low, and attracting quality workers was virtually impossible. "We ended up with everybody else's dregs," says managing partner Steve Siegel. A survey of the company's clients revealed that most of them stereotyped LLG as just another boring accounting firm filled with "bean counters." It was then that the partners began taking bold steps toward shaking off every remnant of the boring CPA firm. They started with their name. Although they retained the founding partners names as the firm's official moniker, the partners adopted a nickname that most of their clients continue to use: the Bean Counters. The name conveyed an image of fun and confronted head-on the stereotype of accountants who were as exciting as airline food.

Then managers made some important decisions about the layout of the office space, which, at the time, assigned workers to cubicles and partners to plush private offices. As a result of several planning retreats, managers decided to reduce the size of the workforce, some of the reductions coming through normal attrition but others the result of firings. Morale slipped, and the office space the company leased to house nearly 60 workers looked rather vacant with just 32. Then the partners made a key decision. "We were wasting [a lot of] space," says Siegel, so the partners decided to put the extra space to better use. They installed a miniature golf course right in the middle of the office!

One goal managers hoped to achieve was to get employees out of their offices and cubicles so they could communicate more effectively and be more creative. A "closed door mentality" continued to prevail at LLG, however. Siegel decided that if people were intimidated by doors, the doors would come down. Before long, walls and cubicles began to disappear as well. One day, at a brainstorming session around the miniature golf course, a partner half-jokingly suggested that one way to increase the level of communication in the office was to put the office furniture on wheels. Almost as soon as he suggested it, the manager looked up and said, "Oh gosh. We're going to do this, aren't we?" They did.

Given the drastic changes in office design the partners were making, it became obvious that the company needed a more suitable space to make them all work. Fortunately, the lease was about to end, so LLG hired an architect to help them find and then create a suitable space. Within two years, the architect presented the partners with a set of plans for an office that was 60 percent smaller, was minimalist in nature, but was extremely functional and comfortable. The partners of LLG were sold on the design, and today that office is home to the Bean Counters. It is an open community without cubicles or offices, yet its creative use of space encourages interaction among team members while allowing them to concentrate on their work when necessary. The space is wired for every type of technology, including a "Welcome Wall" dominated by a big-screen television that constantly flashes quotations about various topics such as business, life, and creativity. Architects also incorporated the company's sense of humor into the design. A four-by-nine-foot abacus made of steel conduit and brightly colored plastic balls graces one wall. The entire work space is designed to encourage the continued development of LLG's most valuable resource: the intellectual capital of its team members.

The new layout is working. In addition to its traditional accounting work, LLG has launched four new business consulting divisions, called Sharp Circles. Client referrals have doubled and income has tripled over the past decade. Communication among team members has never been better, and a distinct sense of innovation pervades the office. In addition, employee turnover has plummeted, and clients are more satisfied with the Bean Counters' work. Siegel and the other partners say that the new office and its layout are an important part of LLG's success. "We could not have gotten those Sharp Circle businesses up and running in the old building," he says. "The old building was such a huge impediment to sitting and meeting and just talking about things. Just being next to each other and hearing what's going on has allowed us to get things going."

1. What impact does the space in which people work have on their ability to do their jobs effectively?
2. Use the resources in your library and on the World Wide Web to learn more about ergonomics and layout. Then select a work space (perhaps on your campus or in a local business) and spend some time watching how people work in it. Finally, develop a list of recommendations for improving the design of the space to enhance workers' ability to do their jobs.

Source: Adapted from Nancy K. Austin, "Tear Down the Walls," *Inc.*, April 1999, pp. 66–76.

located near the front of the store. Items people shop around for before buying and specialty goods will attract their own customers and should not be placed in prime space. Prime selling space should be restricted to products that carry the highest markups.

Layout in a retail store evolves from a clear understanding of customers' buying habits. If customers come into the store for specific products and have a tendency to walk directly to those items, placing complementary products in their path will boost sales. Observing customer behavior can help the owner identify the "hot spots" where merchandise sells briskly and "cold spots where it may sit indefinitely. By experimenting with factors such as traffic flow, lighting, aisle size, noise levels, signs, and colors, an owner can discover the most productive store layout.

grid layout—*a formal arrangement of displays arranged in a rectangular fashion so that aisles are parallel.*

Retailers have three basic patterns from which to choose: the grid, the free-form, and the boutique layouts. The **grid layout** arranges displays in rectangular fashion so that aisles are parallel. It is a formal layout that controls the traffic flow through the store. Supermarkets and discount stores use the grid layout because it is well suited to self-sevice stores. This layout uses the available selling space most efficiently; creates a neat, organized environment; and facilitates shopping by standardizing the location of items. Figure 12.1 shows a typical grid layout.

free-form layout—*an informal arrangement of displays of various shapes and sizes.*

Unlike the grid layout, the **free-form layout** is informal, using displays of various shapes and sizes. Its primary advantage is the relaxed, friendly shopping atmosphere it creates, which encourages customers to shop longer and increases the number of impulse purchases they make. Still, the free-form layout is not as efficient as the grid layout in using selling space, and it can create security problems if not properly planned. Figure 12.2 illustrates a free-form layout.

boutique layout—*an arrangement that divides a store into a series of individual shopping areas, each with its own theme.*

The **boutique layout** divides the store into a series of individual shopping areas, each with its own theme. It is like building a series of specialty shops into a single store. The boutique layout is more informal and can create a unique shopping environment for customers; small department stores sometimes use this layout (see Figure 12.3).

Business owners should display merchandise as attractively as their budgets allow. Customers' eyes focus on displays, which tell them the type of merchandise the business sells. It is easier for customers to relate to one display than to a rack or shelf of merchandise. Open displays of merchandise can surround the focus display, creating an attractive

FIGURE 12.1
The Grid Layout

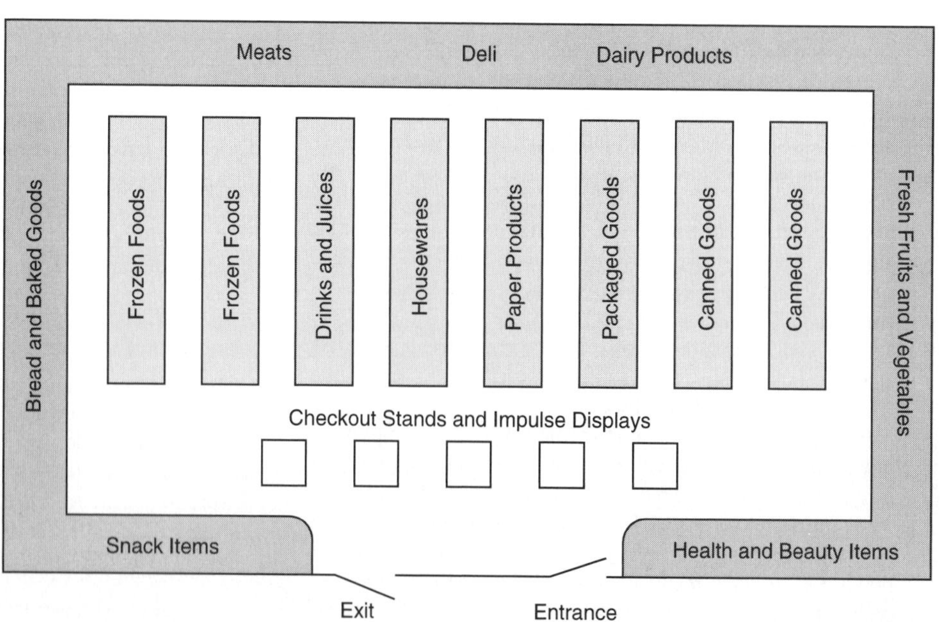

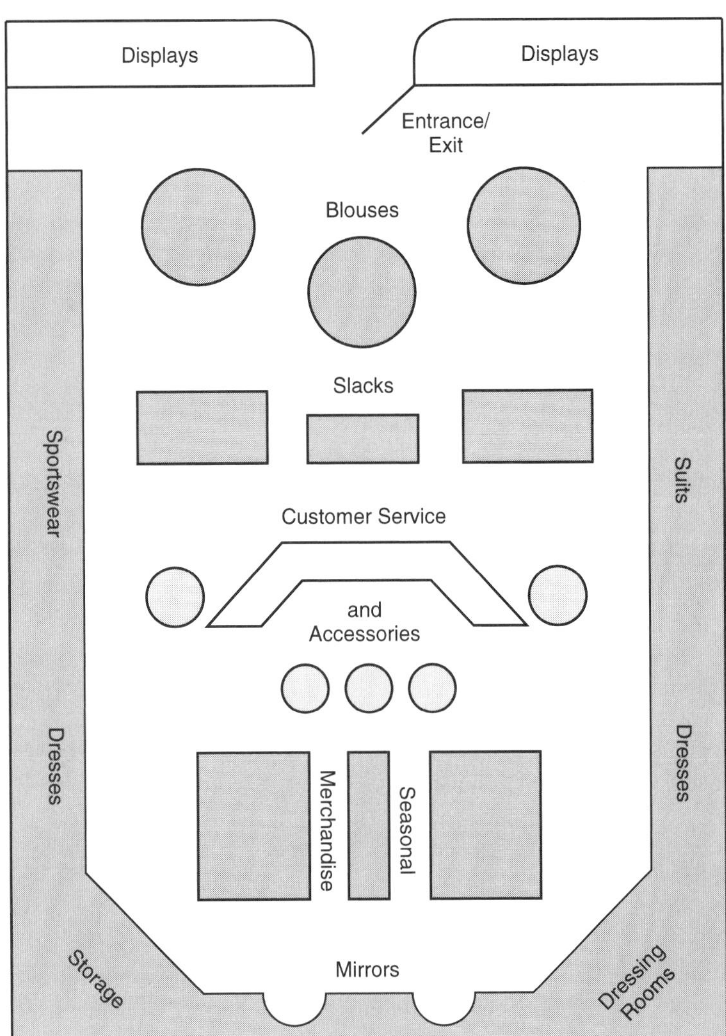

FIGURE 12.2
The Free-Form Layout

selling area. Spacious aisles provide shoppers an open view of merchandise and reduce the likelihood of shoplifting. One study found that shoppers, especially women, are reluctant to enter narrow aisles in a store. Narrow aisles force customers to jostle past one another (experts call this the "butt-brush factor"), which makes them extremely nervous. The same study also found that placing shopping baskets in several areas around a store can increase sales. Seventy-five percent of shoppers who pick up a basket buy something, compared to just 34 percent of customers who do not pick up a basket.[44]

Retailers can also boost sales by displaying together items that complement each other. For example, displaying ties near dress shirts or handbags next to shoes often leads to multiple sales. Placement of items on store shelves is important, too, and store owners must keep their target customers in mind when stocking shelves. For example, putting hearing aid batteries on bottom shelves where the elderly have trouble getting to them or placing popular children's toys on top shelves where little ones cannot reach them can hurt sales. Even background music can be a merchandising tool if the type of music playing in a store matches the demographics of its target customers.

Retailers must remember to separate the selling and nonselling areas of a store. Never waste prime selling space with nonselling functions (storage, office, dressing area, etc.).

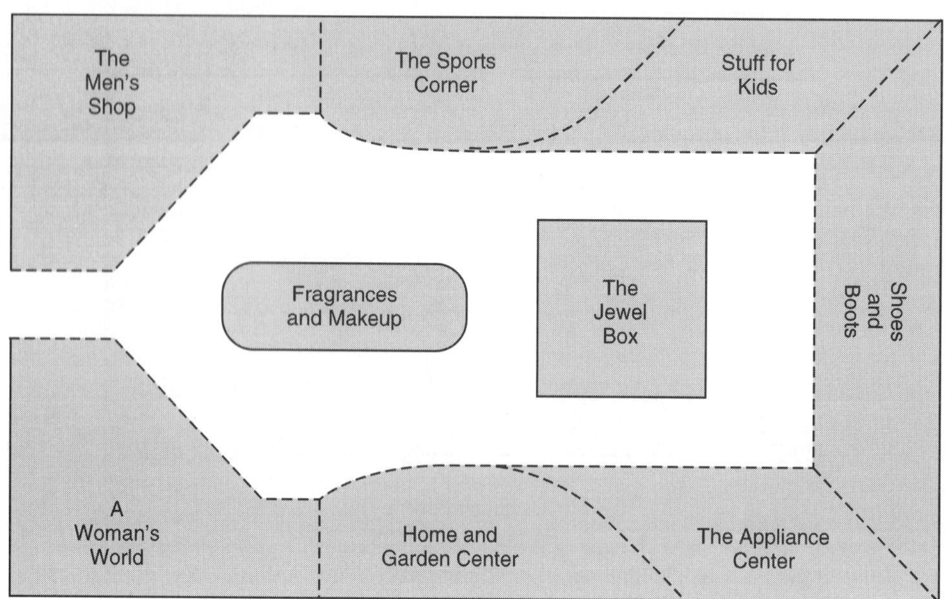

FIGURE 12.3
The Boutique Layout

Although nonselling activities are necessary for a successful retail operation, they should not take precedence and occupy valuable selling space. Many retailers place their nonselling departments in the rear of the building, recognizing the value of each foot of space in a retail store and locating their most profitable items in the best selling areas.

Clearly, not every portion of a small store's interior space is of equal value in generating sales revenue. Certain areas contribute more to revenue than others. The value of store space depends on floor location in a multistory building, location with respect to aisles and walkways, and proximity to entrances. Space values decrease as distance from the main entry-level floor increases. Selling areas on the main level contribute a greater portion to sales than those on other floors in the building because they offer greater exposure to customers than either basement or higher-level locations. Therefore, main-level locations carry a greater share of rent than other levels. Figure 12.4 offers one example of how rent and sales could be allocated by floors.

The layout of aisles in the store has a major impact on the customer exposure merchandise receives. Items located on primary walkways should be assigned a higher share of rental costs and should contribute a greater portion to sales revenue than those displayed along secondary aisles. Figure 12.5 shows that high-value areas are exposed to two secondary aisles.

Space values also depend on their relative position to the store entrance. Typically, the farther away an area is from the entrance, the lower its value. Another consideration is that most shoppers turn to the right entering a store and move around it counterclockwise. (This apparently is culturally determined. Studies of shoppers in Australia and Great Britain find that they turn *left* upon entering a store.) Finally, only about one-fourth of a store's customers will go more than halfway into the store. Using these characteristics, Figure 12.6 illustrates space values for a typical small store layout.

Understanding the value of store space ensures proper placement of merchandise. The items placed in the high-rent areas of the store should generate adequate sales and contribute enough profit to justify their high-value locations.

The decline in value of store space from front to back of the shop is expressed in the 40-30-20-10 rule. This rule assigns 40 percent of a store's rental cost to the front quarter of the

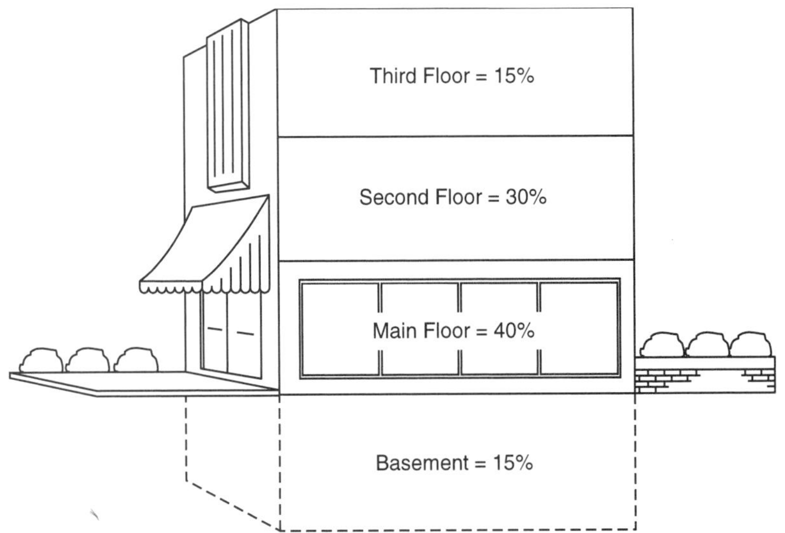

FIGURE 12.4
Rent Allocation by Floors
Source: Retailing, *6th ed. 1997 Prentice Hall. © Dale M. Lewison.*

shop, 30 percent to the second quarter, 20 percent to the third quarter, and 10 percent to the final quarter. Similarly, each quarter of the store should contribute the same percentage of sales revenue.

For example, suppose that a small department store anticipates $720,000 in sales this year. Each quarter of the store should generate the following sales volume:

Front quarter	$720,000 × 0.40 = $288,000
Second quarter	$120,000 × 0.30 = $216,000
Third quarter	$120,000 × 0.20 = $144,000
Fourth quarter	$120,000 × 0.10 = $ 72,000
Total	$720,000

FIGURE 12.5
Rent Allocation Based on Traffic Aisles
Source: Retailing, *6th ed. 1997 Prentice Hall. © Dale M. Lewison.*

FIGURE 12.6
Space Values for a Small Store

Source: Retailing, *6th ed. 1997 Prentice Hall.* © *Dale M. Lewison.*

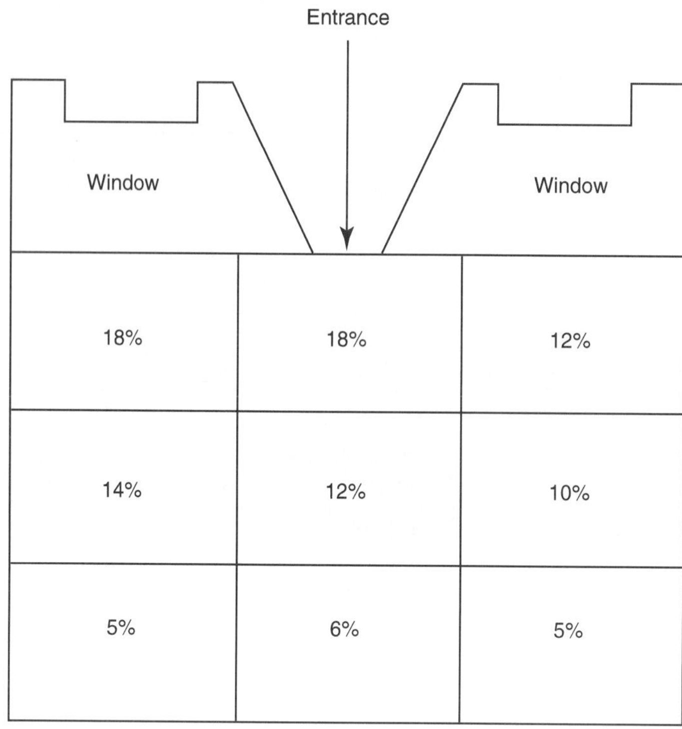

Layout for Manufacturers

Manufacturing layout decisions take into consideration the arrangement of departments, workstations, machines, and stock-holding points within a production facility. The general objective is to arrange these elements to ensure a smooth work flow (in a production facility) or a particular traffic pattern (in a service facility or organization).

Manufacturing facilities have come under increasing scrutiny as firms attempt to improve quality, decrease inventories, and increase productivity through facilities that are integrated, flexible, and controlled. Facility layout has a dramatic effect on product mix, product processing, and material handling, storage, and control, as well as production volume and quality.

FACTORS IN MANUFACTURING LAYOUT. The ideal layout for a manufacturing operation depends on a number of factors, including the following:

- *Type of product.* Product design and quality standards; whether the product is produced for inventory or for order; and the physical properties such as the size of materials and products, special handling requirements, susceptibility to damage, and perishability.
- *Type of production process.* Technology used; types of materials handled; means of providing a service; and processing requirements in terms of number of operations involved and amount of interaction between departments and work centers.
- *Ergonomic considerations.* To ensure worker safety; to avoid unnecessary injuries and accidents; and to increase productivity.
- *Economic considerations.* Volume of production; costs of materials, machines, workstations, and labor; pattern and variability of demand; and length of permissible delays.
- *Space availability within the facility itself.*

TYPES OF MANUFACTURING LAYOUTS. Manufacturing layouts are categorized by either the work flow in a plant or by the production system's function. There are three basic types of layouts that manufacturers can use separately or in combination—product, process, and fixed position—and they are differentiated by their applicability to different conditions of manufacturing volume.

Product Layouts. In a **product (or line) layout,** a manufacturer arranges workers and equipment according to the sequence of operations performed on the product (see Figure 12.7). Conceptually, the flow is an unbroken line from raw material input or customer arrival to finished goods or customer's departure. This type of layout is applicable to rigid-flow, high-volume, continuous, or mass-production operations, or when the service or product is highly standard. Automobile assembly plants, paper mills, and oil refineries are examples of product layouts.

product (line) layout—*an arrangement of workers and equipment according to the sequence of operations performed on a product.*

Product layouts offer the advantages of lower material handling costs; simplified tasks that can be done with low-cost, lower-skilled labor; reduced amounts of work-in-process inventory; and relatively simplified production control activities. All units are routed along the same fixed path, and scheduling consists primarily of setting a production rate.

Disadvantages of product layouts are their inflexibility, monotony of job tasks, high fixed investment in specialized equipment, and heavy interdependence of all operations. A breakdown in one machine or at one workstation can idle the entire line. This layout also requires business owners to duplicate many pieces of equipment in the manufacturing facility, which for a small firm can be cost prohibitive.

Process Layouts. In a **process layout,** a manufacturer groups workers and equipment according to the general function they perform, without regard to any particular product or customer (see Figure 12.8). Process layouts are appropriate when production runs are short, when demand shows considerable variation and the costs of holding finished goods inventory are high, or when the service or product is customized.

process layout—*an arrangement of workers and equipment according to the general function they perform, without regard to any particular product or customer.*

Process layouts have the advantages of being flexible for doing custom work and promoting job satisfaction by offering employees diverse and challenging tasks. Its disadvantages are the higher costs of materials handling, more skilled labor, lower productivity, and more complex production control. Because the work flow is intermittent, each job must be individually routed through the system, scheduled at the various work centers, and have its status monitored.

Fixed Position Layouts. In **fixed position layouts,** materials do not move down a line as in a production layout but rather, due to the weight, size, or bulk of the final product, are assembled in one spot. In other words, workers and equipment go to the material rather

fixed position layout—*an arrangement in which materials do not move down a production line but rather, because of their weight, size, or bulk, are assembled in one spot.*

Assembly	Testing	Touch-up and Packaging
Assembly	Testing	Touch-up and Packaging
Assembly	Testing	Touch-up and Packaging
Assembly	Testing	Touch-up and Packaging

FIGURE 12.7
Product Layout

FIGURE 12.8
Process Layout

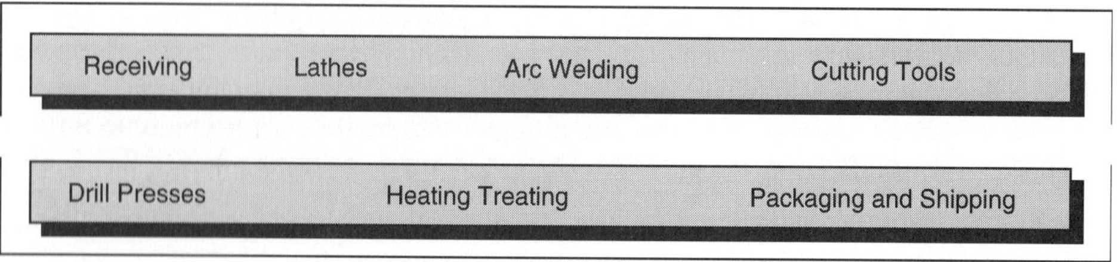

than having the material flow down a line to them. Aircraft assembly shops and shipyards typify this kind of layout.

Functional Layouts. Many layouts are designed with more than one objective or function in mind and, therefore, combinations of the various layouts are common. For example, a supermarket, though primarily arranged on the basis of marketing, is partly a storage layout; a cafeteria represents not only a layout by marketing function but also by work flow (a food assembly line); and a factory may arrange its machinery in a process layout but perform assembly operations in a fixed sequence, as in a product layout.

Designing Layouts

The starting point in layout design is determining how and in what sequence product parts or service tasks flow together. One of the most effective techniques is to create an overall picture of the manufacturing process using assembly charts and process flowcharts. Given the tasks and their sequence, plus knowledge of the volume of products to be produced or of customers to be served, an entrepreneur can analyze space and equipment needs to get an idea of the facility's demands. When using a product or line layout, these demands take precedence, and manufacturers must arrange equipment and workstations to fit the production tasks and their sequence. With a process or functional layout, different products or customers with different needs place demands on the facility. Rather than having a single best flow, there may be one flow for each product or customer, and compromises are necessary. As a result, any one product or customer may not get the ideal layout.

ANALYZING PRODUCTION LAYOUTS. Although there is no general procedure for analyzing the numerous interdependent factors that enter into layout design, specific layout problems lend themselves to detailed analysis. Two important criteria for selecting and designing a layout are worker effectiveness and materials handling costs. A layout should be designed to improve job satisfaction and to use workers at the highest skill level for which they are being paid. This applies just as much to an office layout, where an engineer may spend half of a working day delivering blueprints, as it does to a plant layout, where a machinist must travel a long distance for tools.

Alexander Doll Company

When a team of manufacturing specialists purchased the Alexander Doll Company, a maker of collectible dolls that was founded in 1923, the company's six-story manufacturing operation in New York's Harlem needed a major overhaul. The new owners were experts in designing lean, efficient production systems, and they immediately set about creating one for this classic and well-known maker of dolls. An analysis of the existing layout revealed the use of many archaic principles, which resulted in a work-in-process inventory of more than 90,000 partly finished dolls and a cycle time (the time between receiving a customer's order and delivering a finished doll) of 16 weeks. As they redesigned the factory layout, the new owners involved the 470 employees, who now work in teams of seven or eight. With the new design, work-in-process inventory has fallen by 96 percent, and the company now fills orders within one or two weeks. The new layout played a major role in the company's revitalization.[45]

Manufacturers can lower materials handling costs by using layouts designed so that product flow is automated whenever possible and flow distances and times are minimized. The extent of automation depends on the level of technology and amount of capital available, as well as behavioral considerations of employees. Flow distances and times are usually minimized by locating sequential processing activities or interrelated departments in adjacent areas. The following features are important to a good manufacturing layout:

1. planned materials flow pattern
2. straight-line layout where possible
3. straight, clearly marked aisles
4. backtracking kept to a minimum
5. related operations close together
6. minimum of in-process inventory
7. easy adjustment to changing conditions
8. minimum materials handling distances
9. minimum of manual handling
10. no unnecessary rehandling of material
11. minimum handling between operations
12. materials delivered to production employees
13. material efficiently removed from the work area
14. materials handling being done by indirect labor
15. orderly materials handling and storage
16. good housekeeping

BUILD, BUY, OR LEASE?

7. Evaluate the advantages and disadvantages of building, buying, and leasing a building.

Once an entrepreneur has a good idea of the specific criteria to be met for a building to serve the needs of her business, the issue turns to what she can afford to spend. The ability to obtain the best possible physical facilities in relation to available cash may depend largely on whether an entrepreneur decides to build, buy, or lease a building.

The Decision to Build

If a business had unlimited funds, the owner could design and build a perfect facility. However, few new business owners have this luxury. Constructing a new facility can project a positive image to potential customers. The business looks new and, consequently, creates an image of being modern, efficient, and top quality. A new building can incorporate the most modern features during construction, and these might significantly lower operating costs. When such costs are critical to remaining competitive, it may be reasonable to build.

In some rapidly growing areas, there are few existing buildings to buy or lease that meet an entrepreneur's requirements. In these situations, a business owner must consider the cost of constructing a building as a significant factor in her initial estimates of capital needs and breakeven point. Constructing a building has high initial fixed expenses that an owner must weigh against the facility's ability to attract additional sales revenue and to reduce operating costs.

The Decision to Buy

In many cases, there may be an ideal building in the area where an entrepreneur wants to locate. Buying the facility allows her to remodel it without seeking permission from anyone else. As with building, buying can put a drain on the business's financial resources, but the owner knows exactly what her monthly payments will be. Under a lease, rental rates can (and usually do) increase over time. If an owner believes that the property will actually appreciate in value, purchasing it can be a wise investment. In addition, an owner can depreciate the building each year, and both depreciation and interest are tax-deductible expenses.

When considering purchasing a building, the owner should use the same outline of facilities requirements developed for the building option to ensure that this property will not be excessively expensive to modify for his use. Remodeling can add a significant initial expense. The layout of the building may be suitable in many ways, but it may not be ideal for a particular business. Even if a building housed the same kind of business, its existing layout may be completely unsuitable for the way the new owner plans to operate.

Building or buying a building greatly limits an entrepreneur's mobility, however. Some business owners prefer to stay out of the real estate business to retain maximum flexibility and mobility. Plus, not all real estate appreciates in value. Surrounding property can become run down and, consequently, lower a property's value despite the owner's efforts to keep it in excellent condition.

The Decision to Lease

The major advantage of leasing is that it requires no large initial cash outlay, so the business's funds are available for purchasing inventory or for current operations. Firms that are short on cash will inevitably be forced to lease facilities. All lease expenses are tax deductible.

One major disadvantage of leasing is that the property owner might choose not to renew the lease. A successful business might be forced to move to a new location, and such relocation can be extremely costly and could result in a significant loss of established customers. In many cases it is almost like starting the business again. Also, if a business is successful, the property owner may ask for a significant increase in rent when the lease renewal is negotiated. The owner of the building is well aware of the costs associated with moving and has the upper hand in the negotiations. In some lease arrangements the owner is compensated, in addition to a monthly rental fee, by a percentage of the tenant's gross sales. This is common in malls and shopping centers.

Still another disadvantage to leasing is the limitation on remodeling. If the building owner believes that modifications will reduce the future rental value of the property, he will likely require a long-term lease at increased rent. In addition, all permanent modifications of the structure become the property of the building owner.

CHAPTER SUMMARY

1. Explain the stages in the location decision—choosing the region, the state, the city, and the final site.
   - The location decision is one of the most important decisions an entrepreneur will make, given its long-term effects on the company. An entrepreneur should look at the choice as a series of increasingly narrow decisions: Which region of the country? Which state? Which city? Which site? Choosing the right location requires an entrepreneur to evaluate potential sites with her target customers in mind. Demographic statistics are available from a wide variety of sources, but government agencies such as the Census Bureau have a wealth of detailed data that can guide an entrepreneur in her location decision.
2. Describe the location criteria for retail and service businesses.

- For retailers, the location decision is especially crucial. Retailers must consider the size of the trade area, the volume of customer traffic, number of parking spots, availability of room for expansion, and the visibility of a site.

3. Outline the basic location options for retail and service businesses.
   - Retail and service businesses have six basic location options: central business districts (CBDs), neighborhoods, shopping centers and malls, near competitors, outlying areas, and at home.
4. Explain the site selection process for manufacturers.
   - A manufacturer's location decision is strongly influenced by local zoning ordinances. Some areas offer industrial parks designed specifically to attract manufacturers. Two crucial factors for most manufacturers are the reliability (and the cost of transporting) raw materials and the quality and quantity of available labor.
   - A foreign trade zone is a specially designated area in or near a U.S. customs port of entry that allows resident companies to import materials and components from foreign countries; assemble, process, manufacture, or package them; and then ship the finished product while either reducing or eliminating tariffs and duties.
   - Empowerment zones offer businesses tax breaks on the investments they make within zone boundaries.
   - Business incubators are locations that offer flexible, low-cost rental space to their tenants as well as business and consulting services. Their goal is to nurture small companies until they are ready to "graduate" into the business community. Many government agencies and universities offer incubator locations.
5. Describe the criteria used to analyze the layout and design considerations of a building, including the Americans with Disabilities Act.
   - When evaluating the suitability of a particular building, an entrepreneur should consider several factors: size (is it large enough to accommodate the business with some room for growth?); construction and external appearance (is the building structurally sound and does it create the right impression for the business?); entrances (are they inviting?); legal issues (does the building comply with the Americans with Disabilities Act, and if not, how much will it cost to bring it up to standard?); signs (are they legible, well located, and easy to see?); interior (does the interior design contribute to the ability to make sales and is it ergonomically designed?); lights and fixtures (is the lighting adequate for the tasks workers will be performing and what is the estimated cost of lighting?).
6. Explain the principles of effective layouts for retailers, service businesses, and manufacturers.
   - Layout for retail stores and service businesses depends on the owner's understanding of her customers' buying habits. Retailers have three basic layout options from which to choose: grid, free-form, and boutique. Some areas of a retail store generate more sales per square foot and are, therefore, more valuable.
   - The goal of a manufacturer's layout is to create a smooth, efficient work flow. Three basic options exist: product layout, process layout, and fixed position layout. Two key considerations are worker productivity and materials handling costs.
7. Evaluate the advantages and disadvantages of building, buying, and leasing a building.
   - Building a new building gives an entrepreneur the opportunity to design exactly what he wants in a brand-new facility; however, not every small business owner can afford to tie up significant amounts of cash in fixed assets. Buying an existing building gives a business owner the freedom to renovate as needed, but this can be an expensive alternative. Leasing a location is a common choice because it is economical, but the business owner faces the uncertainty of lease renewals, rising rents, and renovation problems

DISCUSSION QUESTIONS

1. How do most small business owners choose a location? Is this wise?
2. What factors should a manager consider when evaluating a region in which to locate a business? Where are such data available?
3. Outline the important factors in selecting a state in which to locate a business.
4. What factors should a seafood-processing plant, a beauty shop, and an exclusive jewelry store consider in choosing a location? List factors for each type of business.
5. What intangible factors might enter into the entrepreneur's location decision?
6. What are zoning laws? How do they affect the location decision?
7. What is the trade area? What determines a small retailer's trade area?
8. Why is it important to discover more than just the number of passersby in a traffic count?
9. What types of information can the entrepreneur collect from census data?
10. Why may a "cheap location" not be the best location?
11. What is a foreign trade zone? An empowerment zone? A business incubator? What advantages and disadvantages does each one of these offer a small business locating there?
12. Why is it costly for a small firm to choose a location that is too small?

13. What function does a small firm's sign serve? What are the characteristics of an effective business sign?
14. Explain the Americans with Disabilities Act. Which businesses does it affect? What is its purpose?
15. What is ergonomics? Why should entrepreneurs utilize the principles of ergonomics in the design of their facilities?
16. Explain the statement: "Not every portion of a small store's interior space is of equal value in generating sales revenue." What areas are most valuable?
17. What are some of the key features that determine a good manufacturing layout?
18. Summarize the advantages and disadvantages of building, buying, and leasing a building.

Beyond the Classroom . . .

1. Select a specific type of business you would like to go into one day and use census data and Commerce Department reports from the World Wide Web or the local library to choose a specific site for the business in the local region. What location factors are critical to the success of this business? Would it be likely to succeed in your hometown?

2. Interview a sample of local small business owners. How did they decide on their particular locations? What are the positive and negative features of their existing locations?

3. Locate the most recent issue of either *Entrepreneur* or *Fortune* describing the "best cities for (small) business." (For *Entrepreneur,* it is usually the October issue, and for *Fortune,* it is normally an issue in November.) Which cities are in the top 10? What factors did the magazine use to select these cities? Pick a city and explain what makes it an attractive destination for locating a business there.

4. Select a manufacturing operation, a wholesale business, or a retail store, and evaluate its layouts using the guidelines presented in this chapter. What changes would you recommend? Why? Does the changed layout contribute to a more effective operation?

5. Choose one of the businesses you studied in exercise 4 and design an improved layout for the operation. How expensive would these alterations be?

6. Visit the Web site for the Census Bureau at <**www.census.gov**>. Go to the census data for your town and use it to discuss its suitability as a location for the following types of businesses:

- a new motel with 25 units
- a bookstore
- an exclusive women's clothing shop
- a Mexican restaurant
- a residential plumber
- a day-care center
- a high-quality stereo shop
- a family hair care center

7. Use the resources on the World Wide Web or the local library to prepare a demographic profile of your hometown or city or of the town or city in which you attend college. Using the demographic profile as an analytical tool, what kinds of businesses do you think would be successful there? Unsuccessful? Explain. Use these same resources to prepare an analysis of the competition in the area.

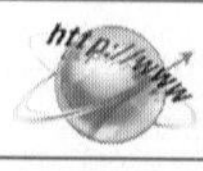

We invite you to visit this book's companion Web site at **www.prenhall.com/Zimmerer.**

CHAPTER

Global Aspects of Entrepreneurship 13

In international business, the foreign country in which you're trading is like the dealer in poker. It decides the house rules and the wild cards. And that means that while every hand remains a gamble, your chances of winning increase with your knowledge of the game.

—Paul and Cheryl Stuart Ruine

A small business owner experienced in conducting international business was talking to another business owner about the benefits of going global. Unconvinced, the novice asked his well-traveled friend what he regarded as the most important language for world trade. Expecting the answer to be English, he was quite surprised when his colleague said, "My customer's language."

—Bits & Pieces

LEARNING OBJECTIVES

Upon completion of this chapter, you will be able to:

1. Explain why "going global" has become an integral part of many small companies' strategies.
2. Describe the eight principal strategies small businesses have for going global: launching a World Wide Web site, relying on trade intermediaries, joint ventures, foreign licensing, international franchising, countertrading and bartering, exporting, and establishing international locations.
3. Explain how to build a thriving export program.
4. Discuss the major barriers to international trade and their impact on the global economy.
5. Describe the trade agreements that will have the greatest influence on foreign trade into the twenty-first century—GATT and NAFTA.

Until recently, the world of international business was much like the world of astronomy before Copernicus, who revolutionized the study of the planets and the stars with his theory of planetary motion. In the sixteenth century, the Copernican system replaced the Ptolemaic system, which held that the earth was the center of the universe with the sun and all the other planets revolving around it. The Copernican system, however, placed the sun at the center of the solar system with all of the planets, including the earth, revolving around it. Astronomy would never be the same.

In the same sense, business owners across the globe have been guilty of having Ptolemaic tunnel vision when it came to viewing international business opportunities. Like their pre-Copernican counterparts, owners saw an economy that revolved around the nations that served as their home bases. Market opportunities stopped at their homeland's borders. Global trade was only for giant corporations that had the money and the management to tap foreign markets and enough resources to survive if the venture flopped.

But no more.

Today, the global marketplace is as much the territory of small, upstart companies as it is that of giant multinational corporations. Powerful, affordable technology, increased access to information on conducting global business, and the growing interdependence of the world's economies have made it easier for companies of all sizes to engage in international trade.

Medical Resources Inc.

When Randy Reichenbach and his wife started Medical Resources Inc. in 1986, their goal was to sell new and refurbished medical equipment to physicians across central Ohio. As far as international sales were concerned, "we never thought of it," says Reichenbach. Today, however, Medical Resources is an experienced exporter with sales of more than $1 million to Saudi Arabia and other Middle Eastern nations. The company's global sales effort began simply enough: It started receiving calls, faxes, and e-mails from international companies interested in its products. Despite the opportunities for global sales that came in every week, the Reichenbachs could not capitalize on them. "We did not know how to handle international inquiries," says Reichenbach, who turned to the Columbus Export Assistance Center for help. The center is one of more than 100 offices in the United States operated under the Department of Commerce's U.S. Commercial Service program and is designed to help small companies break into international trade. International trade specialist Mary Beth Double advised the Reichenbachs on topics ranging from basic export techniques and international payments to shipping requirements and designing the company Web site to attract more international customers. "We were set up to do business overseas and didn't even know it," says Reichenbach. Building on its success in the Middle East, Medical Resources is now expanding into other international markets.[1]

Political, social, cultural, and economic changes are sweeping the world, creating a new world order—and a legion of both problems and opportunities for businesses of all sizes. The challenges can be daunting enough to make businesses of any size hesitant to go global, but profitable opportunities await the small companies that are ready to capitalize on them. Ninety-six percent of the world's population and 67 percent of the world's purchasing power lie outside of the borders of the United States![2] Plus, going global produces huge benefits for small companies. For instance, research suggests that expanding a business beyond its domestic borders may actually enhance a company's overall performance. One study by The Conference Board concluded that American manufacturers with global operations earn more and grow faster than those that remain purely domestic. In addition, multinational firms were 50 percent more likely to survive the decade than those that limited their businesses to American borders.[3] Studies by the U.S. Small Business Administration show that companies engaged in international trade are 20 percent more productive and 9 percent more likely to stay financially solvent than firms that are not.[4] Another study from the Commerce Department found that companies that export create better, higher-paying jobs for their workers than their purely domestic counterparts.[5] The

Figure 11.3 shows the number of IPOs since 1981, along with the amount of capital raised during that time.

Entrepreneurs who are considering taking their companies public should first consider carefully the advantages and the disadvantages of an IPO. The advantages include the following.

Ability to Raise Large Amounts of Capital. The biggest benefit of a public offering is the capital infusion the company receives. After going public, the corporation has the cash to fund R&D projects, expand plant and facilities, repay debt, or boost working capital balances without incurring the interest expense and the obligation to repay associated with debt financing. For instance, when homemaking maven Martha Stewart took her company, Martha Stewart Living Omnimedia, public recently, the sale of 7.2 million shares at $18 per share generated more than $129 million for the company.[43]

Improved Corporate Image. All of the media attention a company receives during the registration process makes it more visible. Plus, becoming a public company in some industries improves its prestige and enhances its competitive position, one of the most widely recognized, intangible benefits of going public.

Improved Access to Future Financing. Going public boosts a company's net worth and broadens its equity base. Its improved stature and financial strength make it easier for the firm to attract more capital—both debt and equity—and to grow.

Attracting and Retaining Key Employees. Public companies often use stock-based compensation plans to attract and retain quality employees. Stock options and bonuses are excellent methods for winning employees' loyalty and for instilling a healthy ownership attitude among them. Employee stock ownership plans (ESOPs) and stock purchase plans

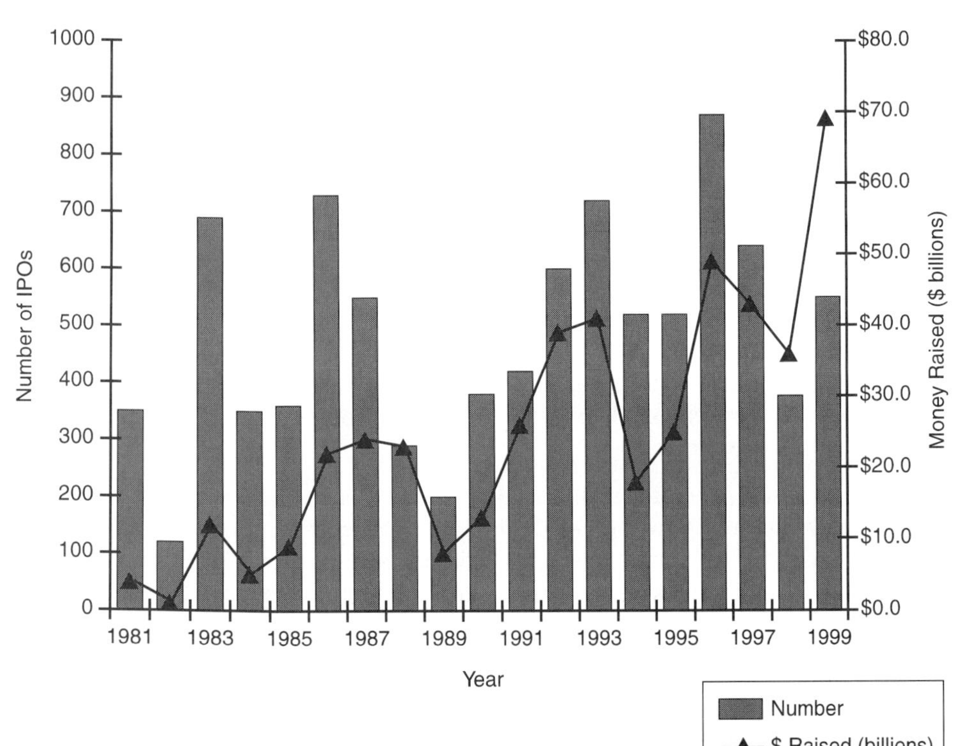

FIGURE 11.3
Initial Public Offerings
Source: Thomson Financial Securities Data, 2000.

are popular recruiting and motivational tools in many small corporations, enabling them to hire top-flight talent they otherwise would not be able to afford.

Using Stock for Acquisitions. A company whose stock is publicly traded can acquire other businesses by offering its own shares rather than cash. Acquiring other companies with shares of stock eliminates the need to incur additional debt.

Listing on a Stock Exchange. Being listed on an organized stock exchange, even a small regional one, improves the marketability of a company's shares and enhances its image. Most publicly held companies' stocks do not qualify for listing on the nation's largest exchanges—the New York Stock Exchange (NYSE) and the American Stock Exchange (AMEX). However, the AMEX recently created a new market for small-company stocks, the Emerging Company Marketplace. Most small companies' stocks are traded on either the National Association of Securities Dealers Automated Quotation (NASDAQ) system's National Market System (NMS) and its emerging small-capitalization exchange or one of the nation's regional stock exchanges. The most popular regional exchanges include the Midwest (MSE), Philadelphia (PHLX), Boston (BSE), and Pacific (PSE).

Despite these advantages, many factors can spoil a company's attempted IPO. In fact, only 5 percent of the companies that attempt to go public ever complete the process.[44] The disadvantages of going public include the following.

Dilution of Founder's Ownership. Whenever an entrepreneur sells stock to the public, he automatically dilutes his ownership in the business. Most owners retain a majority interest in the business, but they may still run the risk of unfriendly takeovers years later after selling more stock.

Loss of Control. If enough shares are sold in a public offering, a founder risks losing control of the company. If a large block of shares falls into the hands of dissident stockholders, they could vote the existing management team (including the founder) out.

Loss of Privacy. Taking their companies public can be a big ego boost for owners, but they must realize that their companies are no longer solely theirs. Information that was once private must be available for public scrutiny. The initial prospectus and the continuous reports filed with the Securities and Exchange Commission (SEC) disclose a variety of information about the company and its operations—from financial data and raw material sources to legal matters and patents to *anyone*—including competitors. One study found that loss of privacy and loss of control were the most commonly cited reasons that CEOs choose not to attempt IPOs.[45]

Reporting to the SEC. Operating as a publicly held company is expensive. Publicly held companies must file periodic reports with the SEC, which often requires a more powerful accounting system, a larger accounting staff, and greater use of attorneys and other professionals. The cost of complying with the SEC's accounting and filing requirements alone can cost $150,000 a year.

Filing Expenses. A public stock offering usually is an expensive way to generate funds for start-up or expansion. For the typical small company, the cost of a public offering is around 12 percent of the capital raised. On small offerings, costs can eat up as much as 40 percent of the capital raised, while on offerings above $20 million, just 5 percent will go to cover expenses.[46] Once an offering exceeds $10 million, its relative issuing costs drop. The largest cost is the underwriter's commission, which is typically 7 percent of the proceeds on offerings less than $10 million and 13 percent on those over that amount.

TABLE 11.4
Simplified Registration and Exemptions: Comparative Table

Source: Deciding to Go Public, *New York: Ernst & Young, 1993, pp. 70–71.*

Private and Limited Offerings Regulation D

	Rule 504	**Rule 505**	**Rule 506**
Dollar Limit	$5 million in any 12-month period	$5 million in any 12-month period	None
Limit on Number of Purchasers	No	35 nonaccredited, unlimited accredited	35 nonaccredited, unlimited accredited
Qualification for Purchasers	No	No	Nonaccredited must be sophisticated
Qualifications of Issuers	Not available for investment companies, blank check companies, or reporting companies	Not available for investment companies or those disqualified by "bad boy" provisions	No
Disclosure Requirements	Not specified	Only if one or more nonaccredited purchasers	Only if one or more nonaccredited purchasers
Financial Statement Requirements	Not specified	Period varies for audited statements	Period varies for audited statements
General Solicitation and Advertising Prohibited	No	Yes	Yes
Resale Restrictions	No	Yes	Yes

Private Placements Section 4(6)	**Intrastate Offerings Rule 147**	**Unregistered Public Offerings Regulation A**	**Small Business Issuers Registration Form SB-1**	**Small Business Issuers Registration Form SB-2**
$5 million	None	$5 million in any 12-month period	$10 million in any 12-month period	None
No	No	No	No	No
All must be accredited	All must be registrants of a single state	No	No	No
No	Must be resident and do business in same state as purchasers	Available for U.S. and Canadian companies only; not available for reporting companies, blank check companies, investment companies, sale of oil and gas or mineral rights, or those disqualified by "bad boy" provisions	Available for U.S. and Canadian companies with revenue and public float of less than $25 million; not available for investment com panies or susidiaries whose parent is not qualified to use the form	Available for U.S. and Canadian companies with revenue and public float of less than $25 million; not available for investment companies or subsidiaries whose parent is not qualified to use the form
Not specified	Not specified	Yes	Yes	Yes
Not specified	Not specified	2 years of unaudited statements	2 years of unaudited statements	2 years of unaudited statements
Yes	No	No	No	No
Yes	Yes	Yes	No	No

YOU BE THE CONSULTANT . . .

A Tale of Two Businesses

The Herbal Remedy

Scott Fiore is determined to launch The Herbal Remedy, a natural pharmacy selling herbs and holistic medicines, in Littleton, Colorado, but he needs $170,000 to do it. Fiore began planning his entrepreneurial venture months before leaving a secure job at Rosemont Pharmaceutical Corporation, and he quickly realized that his search for capital would take longer than he had anticipated. First, he approached his bank and talked with a loan officer there. The bank official reviewed Fiore's business plan and said it looked great and that Fiore could get a business loan—in a year or two. "Our bank doesn't make loans to start-up businesses," explained the loan officer. "The risks are just too high."

Fiore was committed to making his business a reality—and a success. He had gone to Dover, New Hampshire, for several months, where he "interned" in a natural pharmacy owned by a fraternity brother. There, he had learned firsthand the daily details of running a natural pharmacy. After returning to Colorado, Fiore took what he had learned and used it to polish his business plan. He was confident that he could make The Herbal Remedy a successful business. Fiore already had invested $20,000 of his own money, but most of that had gone to finance initial expenses and to cover the cost of incorporating the company. He wanted to form a corporation to protect his family's personal assets in case the business failed.

Fiore is eager to launch the company but needs the capital to do it.

Bizrate.com

Farhad Mohit intended to finish his MBA, get a PhD, and then pursue a career in teaching. Then he discovered the World Wide Web, where "all the knowledge of the world is available." "This is incredible," he thought. While taking a course in entrepreneurship in graduate school, Mohit and friends Dave Schaller and Henri Asseily had prepared a business plan for a Web-based business that would survey e-shoppers about their buying experiences with e-tailers and then make the data available to the marketplace.

After graduation, the trio decided to develop their idea into a real business they called Bizrate.com. Through Bizrate.com, customers not only could find the products they wanted to buy, but they also could find out how other shoppers rated their buying experiences with a particular online store. Working out of Schaller's apartment, the young entrepreneurs designed a Web site, created the infrastructure to support it, and began collecting data from online customers. The frugal entrepreneurial path was not an easy one, however. "Here I was, 27 years old," says Mohit, "moving back into my parents' house, with $80,000 in school debts. I thought my world had come to an end."

When Schaller decided to return to his job at Boston Consulting Group, Mohit and Asseily convinced their former professor at the Wharton School of Business, David Reibstein, to join the company's board of directors and to make an investment in Bizrate.com. Then they raised $220,000 in seed capital from family members and friends, money that would support the fledgling company for several more months. However, Mohit and Asseily knew that they needed big money to take Bizrate.com into the big time. Their business plan indicated that they would need nearly $5 million to take their company to the next level and then as much as $20 to $25 million to establish Bizrate.com as a player in the world of e-commerce.

1. Work with a team of your classmates to develop a plan for The Herbal Remedy and for Bizrate.com for raising the capital they need.
2. Do you recommend sources of debt capital or equity capital or a combination of the two for these entrepreneurs? Explain.
3. Create a list of the factors you considered as you prepared a plan for raising capital for these two companies. How did these factors influence your recommendations for the various sources of capital?

Sources: Adapted from Cynthia Harrington, "Hold 'Em," *Entrepreneur,* July 2000, pp. 78–83; Michelle Prather, "Green Days," *Business Start-Ups,* March 1999, p. 96.

nation's total workforce also benefits from international trade. Every $1 billion in exports of manufactured goods creates an estimated 22,000 new jobs.[6]

WHY GO GLOBAL?

1. Explain why "going global" has become an integral part of many small companies' strategies.

Businesses can no longer consider themselves to be purely domestic companies in this hotly competitive, global environment. "In the global economy, the competitor six time zones away is potentially as serious a threat as the competitor six blocks away," says one expert.[7] For companies across the world, going global is a matter of survival, not preference. No matter where a company's home base is, competitors are forcing it to think globally. For example, the executives of a small Oregon company manufacturing robotic-vision systems to cut french fries discovered that a Belgian company had developed a similar, competing device.[8] "There are an awful lot of people in the rest of the world who think they are pretty good at doing your business," warns Lester Thurow.[9] For instance, in the 1950s just 5 percent of the goods made in America faced foreign competition; today, 80 percent will go up against foreign goods.[10] To succeed in a world market that is becoming increasingly interdependent, companies must go global.

Failure to cultivate global markets can be a lethal mistake for modern businesses, whatever their size. To thrive in the twenty-first century, small businesses must take their place in the world market. Globalization is no longer on the horizon; it is already here. Increasingly, small businesses will be under pressure to expand into international markets. To be successful, companies must consider themselves businesses without borders. "If a company really is a global competitor, it is going to be shipping all over the place from all over the place," says one executive.[11]

Entrepreneurs who take the plunge into global business can reap the following benefits:

- *Offset sales declines in the domestic market.* Markets in foreign countries may be booming when those in the United States are sagging.
- *Increase sales and profits.* Companies that limit themselves to the domestic market are passing up the opportunity to serve nearly 6 billion potential customers around the globe. "Most companies now realize [that] they cannot live by the domestic market alone," says one international expert.[12]
- *Extend their products' life cycles.* Some companies have been able to take products that had reached the maturity stage of the product life cycle in the United States and sell them very successfully in foreign markets.
- *Lower manufacturing costs.* In industries characterized by high levels of fixed costs, businesses that expand into global markets can lower their manufacturing costs by spreading these fixed costs over a larger number of units.
- *Improve competitive position.* Going up against some of the toughest competition in the world forces a company to hone its competitive skills. "Yours will be a bigger and better company if you go international," says one expert.[13]
- *Raise quality levels.* Customers in many global markets are much tougher to satisfy than those in the United States. One reason Japanese products have done so well worldwide is that Japanese companies must build products to satisfy their customers at home, who demand extremely high quality and are sticklers for detail. Businesses that compete in global markets learn very quickly how to boost their quality levels to world-class standards.
- *Become more customer oriented.* Delving into global markets teaches business owners about the unique tastes, customs, preferences, and habits of customers in many different cultures. Responding to these differences imbues these businesses with a degree of sensitivity toward their customers, both domestic and foreign.

Unfortunately, not enough entrepreneurs have learned to see their companies from a global perspective. A recent report from the Competitiveness Policy Council warns that "an absence of global thinking is one of the elements that permeates our society and most directly hurt(s) its competitive position."[14] Indeed, learning to *think globally* may be the first—and most threatening—obstacle an entrepreneur must overcome on the way to creating a truly global business. Global thinking is the ability to appreciate, understand, and respect the different beliefs, values, behavior, and business practices of companies and people in different cultures and countries. A British manager explains:

> If you are operating in South America, you'd better know how to operate in conditions of hyperinflation. If you're operating in Africa, you'd better know a lot about government relations and the use of local partners. If you're operating in Germany, you'd better understand the mechanics of codetermination and some of the special tax systems that one finds in that country. If you're operating in China, it's quite useful in trademark matters to know how the People's Court of Shanghai works. . . . If you're operating in Japan, you'd better understand the different trade structures.[15]

DSP Communications

Davidi Gilo, founder of DSP Communications, a maker of chip sets for wireless communication equipment, operates his highly successful business from a global perspective. Although DSP Communications' headquarters is in Cupertino, California, most of the company's engineers and designers are in Gilo's homeland of Israel, and the bulk of its customer base is in Japan! Early on in the business, Gilo discovered that to break into the Japanese market, he needed a local partner so he forged a joint venture with a Japanese distribution company, Marubun. Recently named as one of the 200 best small businesses by Forbes *magazine, DSP Communications owes much of its success to Gilo's global vision.*[16]

Gaining a foothold in newly opened foreign markets or maintaining a position in an existing one is no easy task, however. "The key to the problem of how to truly become global can be summarized in one word: *attitude*," says one U.S. manager. "Until you have the attitude that you are truly an international company, not just a U.S. company also doing business abroad, you cannot achieve your goals."[17] Success in the global economy also requires constant innovation; staying nimble enough to use speed as a competitive weapon; maintaining a high level of quality and constantly improving it; being sensitive to foreign customers' unique requirements; adopting a more respectful attitude toward foreign habits and customs; hiring motivated, multilingual employees; and retaining a desire to learn constantly about global markets. In short, the path to success requires businesses to become "insiders" rather than just "exporters."

Before venturing into the global marketplace, a small business owner should consider four questions:[18]

1. Are we willing to commit adequate resources of time, people, and capital to our international campaign?
2. Can we make money there? If so, can we get it out? (That is, is the currency convertible?)
3. Will we feel comfortable doing business there? (That is, are we sensitive to the cultural differences of conducting international business?)
4. Can we afford not to go global?

2. Describe the eight principal strategies small businesses have for going global.

GOING GLOBAL: STRATEGIES FOR SMALL BUSINESSES

A growing number of small businesses are recognizing that "going global" is not a strategy reserved solely for industry giants such as General Motors, IBM, and Boeing. In fact, John Naisbitt, trend-spotting author of *The Global Paradox,* says that the increasing globalization of business actually favors smaller companies. "In the huge global economy, there will be smaller and smaller market niches," says Naisbitt. "In this global economy, . . . the competitive edge is swiftness to market and innovation. Small units are much better at speed to market and innovation . . . As a result, they can innovate faster, not just in products but in internal operations, to take advantage of the new technologies."[19] Their agility and adaptability give small firms the edge in today's highly interactive, fast-paced global economy. "The bigger the world economy, the more powerful its smallest players," concludes Naisbitt.[20]

Small companies go global for a variety of reasons. Some move into foreign markets because their domestic sales have sagged.

Artais Weather Check Inc.

For example, after Artais Weather Check Inc. captured 80 percent of the U.S. market in airport weather-observation systems, sales reached a plateau. That's when Artais turned its attention to building sales in foreign markets. The payoff was immediate—and large. Foreign sales jumped to $3.7 million, two-thirds of the company's total sales. So far, Artais has sold its computerized airport information systems in Taiwan, Ecuador, China, Saudi Arabia, and Egypt. Charles Shanklin, president of the family-owned company, expects foreign sales to grow as many developing nations increase expenditures on upgrading their airports' technology.[21]

Other small businesses have discovered soaring demand for their products and services among foreign customers.

Pentaura Ltd.

For instance, Pentaura Ltd., a 15-employee maker of high-quality, handmade furniture, recently began exporting its line of chairs, tables, credenzas, and curio cabinets to Japan after president Jeffrey Weiss discovered how much the Japanese value quality and craftsmanship. With no prior experience in international markets, the Greenville, South Carolina–based company turned to the Japan External Trade Organization (JETRO), a division of the Japanese government that helps companies export their products to Japan. Not only did JETRO help Pentaura navigate the complexities of the Japanese economy, but the organization also advised the small manufacturer to make a few slight modifications in its products. For instance, Pentaura lowers the height of the tables it exports to Japan from 30 inches to 27.5 inches to accommodate customers' smaller stature and more compact living spaces.[22]

Becoming a global business depends on instilling a global culture throughout the organization so that it permeates everything the company does. Entrepreneurs who routinely conduct international business have developed a global mindset for themselves and their companies. As one business writer explains:

> The global [business] . . . looks at the whole world as one market. It manufactures, conducts research, raises capital, and buys supplies wherever it can do the job best. It keeps in touch with technology and market trends around the world. National boundaries and regulations tend to be irrelevant, or a mere hindrance. [Company] headquarters might be anywhere.[23]

As cultures from around the globe become increasingly interwoven, the ability to "go global" will determine the relative degree of success (or lack of it!) for more and more small businesses.

Small companies pursuing a global presence have eight principal strategies available: launching a World Wide Web site, relying on trade intermediaries, joint ventures, foreign licensing, franchising, countertrading and bartering, exporting, and establishing international locations (see Figure 13.1).

Launching a World Wide Web Site

Perhaps the simplest and least expensive way for a small company to launch a global business effort is to create a Web site. The Web gives businesses of any size tremendous mar-

FIGURE 13.1
Eight Strategies for Going Global

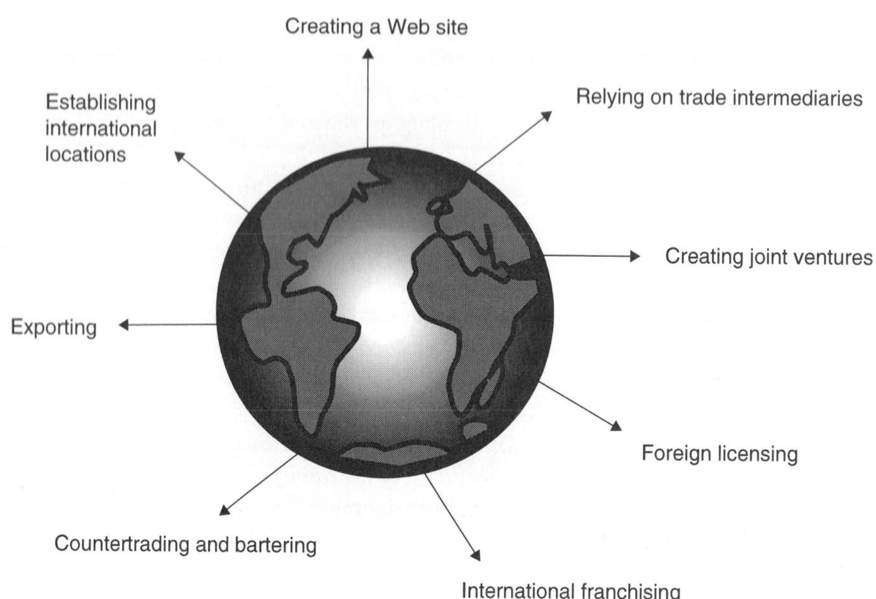

keting potential all over the globe. With a well-designed Web site, a small company can extend its reach to customers anywhere in the world—and without breaking the budget! A company's Web site is available to anyone anywhere in the world and provides exposure 24 hours a day to its products or services seven days a week. For many small companies, the Web has become a tool that is as essential to doing business as the telephone and the fax machine.

Establishing a presence on the Web has become an important part of a company's strategy for reaching customers outside the United States. A study by the International Development Conference estimates the number of World Wide Web users to be 320 million worldwide. Approximately 136 million of them live in the United States, leaving 184 million potential Web customers outside this country's borders.[24] Figure 13.2 provides a breakdown of the Web-using population by region.

Most small companies follow a three-step evolutionary approach to conducting global business on the Web:

Step 1. Connecting to e-mail. Even though it lacks the ability to provide the engaging images, sounds, and animation available on the Web, e-mail gives entrepreneurs the ability to communicate with customers anywhere in the world quickly and easily. E-mail correspondence often is the first step to establishing lasting relationships with international customers. Not only is e-mail communication less expensive than international telephone calls, but it also overcomes many of the problems associated with different time zones.

Eastern Avionics International

James Cantor, CEO of Eastern Avionics International, a small company that markets navigation and communication equipment to private pilots, has used e-mail to boost his company's sales in foreign markets. Because he speaks only English, Cantor relies on a Web-based translation program to help him translate the e-mail orders and inquiries he often gets from customers written in French, German, Spanish, Italian, and Portuguese into English. In just 10 weeks, Eastern Avionics' international sales had climbed 60 percent![25]

Step 2. Using the Web to conduct international market research. Once they discover the power of the Internet through e-mail, entrepreneurs soon begin to explore the Web's capacity as a market research tool. At this point, entrepreneurs become interested in using the Web to generate sales leads by researching customers and market characteristics in other countries. With the help of the Web, they begin to see the world as their market.

Vellus Products, Inc.

After experiencing initial success with her company's Web site among domestic customers, Sharon Doherty, owner of Vellus Products, Inc., a maker of pet-grooming products in Columbus, Ohio, began using the Web to explore potential markets abroad. She spends an average of two hours a day researching foreign markets on the Web, studying competitors, and scouting for potential customers in foreign countries. Her efforts have paid off; international sales now account for more than half of Vellus Products' revenues.[26]

As Doherty's experience shows, the Web offers entrepreneurs the power to collect meaningful information on foreign markets quite easily. For links to many of the most useful international business sites on the Web, go to the Web site for this book at **<www.prenhall.com/scarborough>**.

Step 3. Building a global Web site. Entrepreneurs soon see the need to set up secure Web sites that educate their international customers about the features and the benefits of their products and services and that generate orders from customers anywhere in the world. Combining e-mail with a Web site can be a very effective marketing tool. A small company can answer inquiries from potential customers or introduce its products or services through e-mail and then refer customers to its Web site for more detailed information. Unfortunately, nearly half of all U.S.-based Web sites turn away international orders because they are not set up to process them, a flaw that costs these companies an estimated $10 million in annual sales.[27]

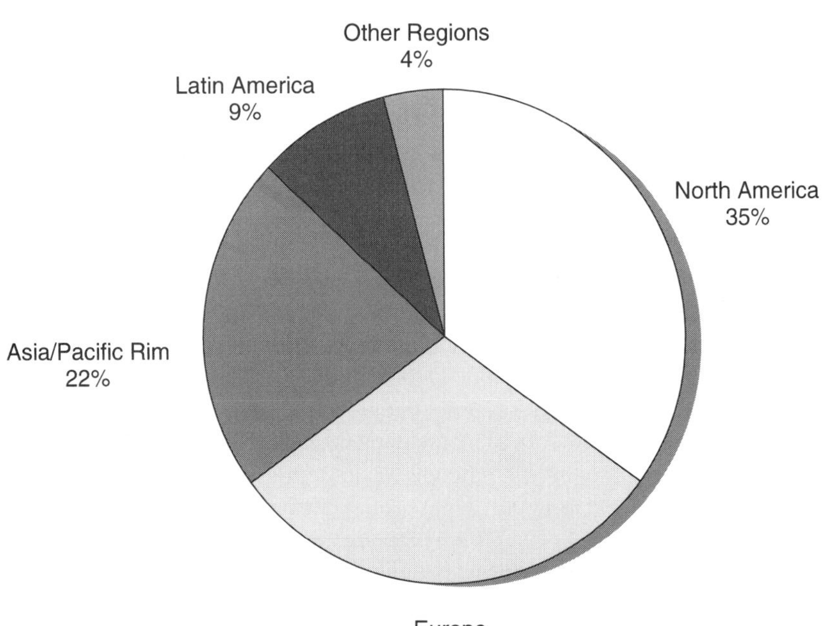

FIGURE 13.2
World Wide Web Users Worldwide by Region
Source: Emarketer.com ***<www.emarketer.com> 2000***

A well-designed Web site can boost sales from international customers; however, a poorly designed site can dissuade or even insult foreign customers. "Don't assume that the site you have now will work in another country," says Greg Koorhan, a consultant specializing in global Web site design. "Entering the global marketplace on the Internet is tricky business."[28] Even something as simple as a site's background color can carry negative connotations for foreign customers. For instance, in Middle Eastern countries, green is considered to be a sacred color and would not be appropriate to use as a background on a commercial Web site. Icons commonly used on Web sites in the United States also can take on different meanings in other lands. An icon of a raised hand with the palm facing forward would be offensive to Web customers in Greece; similarly, a graphic of a hand making an "OK" sign (thumb circling to index finger with remaining fingers raised) is considered vulgar in Brazil. Entrepreneurs must also be careful when translating the content of their Web pages into other languages.

PhotoAccess.com

When managers at PhotoAccess.com, a small company that sells online tools for sending photographs electronically, spotted the opportunity to generate sales in Japan, their first move was to revamp the company's Web site to make it more suitable for Asian customers. They hired a consultant to help them translate the site's content properly and even tailored the text to suit the Japanese market. With the consultant's help, managers changed the site's color schemes and images to make it more suitable for their foreign target customers. One major change involved the payment method to reflect the way that Japanese customers do business. "Rather than taking a credit card number online, we deliver the product to our Japanese customers and then invoice them to pay the balance at a local convenience store," says Paul Souza, design director of the company's Internet products.[29]

In Chapter 15, "E-Commerce and the Entrepreneur," you will learn more about designing a Web site that not only draws customers but also generates sales.

Relying on Trade Intermediaries

trade intermediaries—*domestic agencies that serve as distributors in foreign countries for domestic companies of all sizes.*

Another relatively easy way to break into international markets is by using a trade intermediary. **Trade intermediaries** are domestic agencies that serve as distributors in foreign countries for domestic companies of all sizes. They rely on their networks of contacts, their extensive knowledge of local customs and markets, and their experience in international trade to market products effectively and efficiently all across the globe. Trade intermediaries currently account for about 10 percent of all U.S. exports. Although a broad array of trade intermediaries is available, the following are ideally suited for small businesses.

export management companies (EMCs)—*merchant intermediaries that provide small businesses with a low-cost, efficient, off-site international marketing department.*

EXPORT MANAGEMENT COMPANIES (EMCS). **Export management companies (EMCs)** are an important channel of foreign distribution for small companies just getting started in international trade or for those lacking the resources to assign their own people to foreign markets. Most EMCs are merchant intermediaries, working on a buy-and-sell arrangement with noncompeting domestic small companies. They provide small businesses with a low-cost, efficient, off-site international marketing department, offering services ranging from market research and advice on patent protection to arranging financing and handling shipping. More than 1,000 EMCs operate across the United States, and many of them specialize in particular products or product lines.

The greatest benefits EMCs offer small companies are ready access to global markets and an extensive knowledge base on foreign trade, both of which are vital for entrepreneurs who are inexperienced in conducting global business. In return for their services, EMCs usually earn an extra discount on the goods they buy from their clients or, if they operate on a commission rate, a higher commission than domestic distributors earn on what they sell. Finding an EMC is not difficult. The Federation of International Trade Associations (FITA) provides a searchable list of EMCs on its Web site **<fita.org/**

emc_list_all.html>. Industry trade associations and publications and the U.S. Department of Commerce's Export Assistance Centers* also can help entrepreneurs locate EMCs and other trade intermediaries.

Hamilton Manufacturing Corporation

Hamilton Manufacturing Corporation, a small maker of machines that exchange coins for paper currency, used an export management company to break into foreign markets. James Nesmith, president of the small concern, turned to International Projects Inc., a Toledo-based EMC, for help in selling Hamilton's newly developed machines designed to exchange foreign currency. Going global alone "was a lot more than I could handle," says Nesmith. So Hamilton signed a five-year agreement with International Projects to sell the machines abroad, and its foreign sales are climbing rapidly.[30]

EXPORT TRADING COMPANIES (ETCS). Another tactic for getting into international markets with a minimum of cost and effort is through an export trading company (ETC). ETCs have been an important vehicle in international trade throughout history. The Hudson Bay Company and the East India Company were dominant powers in world trade as early as the 1600s. The East India Company, which was so powerful that it once had its own army and navy, introduced tea to Great Britain and spices to the West Indies. The company continues to help businesses trade in a wide variety of products all across the globe.[31]

export trading companies—*businesses that buy and sell products in a number of countries and offer a wide variety of services to their clients.*

Export trading companies are businesses that buy and sell products in a number of countries, and they typically offer a wide range of services—exporting, importing, shipping, storing, distributing, and others to their clients. Unlike EMCs, which tend to focus on exporting, ETCs usually perform both import and export trades across many countries' borders. ETCs also differ from EMCs in that ETCs often handle products from competing companies. However, like EMCs, ETCs lower the risk of exporting for small businesses. Some of the largest trading companies in the world are based in the United States and Japan. In fact, many businesses that have navigated Japan's complex distribution system successfully have done so with the help of ETCs.

In 1982, Congress passed the Export Trading Company Act to allow producers of similar products to form ETC cooperatives without the fear of violating antitrust laws. The goal was to encourage U.S. companies to export more goods by allowing businesses in the same industry to band together to form export trading companies. The Association for Manufacturing Technology and the Outdoor Power Equipment Institute are two examples of ETC cooperatives.

MANUFACTURER'S EXPORT AGENTS (MEAS). Manufacturer's export agents (MEAs) act as international sales representatives in a limited number of markets for various noncompeting domestic companies. Unlike the close, long-term partnering relationship formed with most EMCs, the relationship between an MEA and a small company is a short-term one, in which the MEA typically operates on a commission basis.

Export Merchants. Export merchants are domestic wholesalers who do business in foreign markets. They buy goods from many domestic manufacturers and then market them in foreign markets. Unlike MEAs, export merchants often carry competing lines, which means they have little loyalty to suppliers. Most export merchants specialize in particular industries—office equipment, computers, industrial supplies, and others.

Resident Buying Offices. Another approach to exporting is to sell to a resident buying office, a government or privately owned operation established in a country for the purpose of buying goods made there. Many foreign governments and businesses have set up buying

* A searchable list of the Export Assistance Centers is available at the USATrade.gov Web site **<www2.usatrade.gov/website/website.nsf>.**

offices in the United States. Selling to them is just like selling to domestic customers because the buying office handles all the details of exporting.

Foreign Distributors. Many small businesses work through foreign distributors to reach international markets. Domestic small companies export their products to these distributors who handle all of the marketing, distribution, and service functions in the foreign country. Distributors often request contracts giving them exclusive distribution rights for a company's product in their market. They offer exporting small businesses the benefits of knowledge of their local markets, the ability to cover a given territory thoroughly, and prompt sales and service support.

Encore Orthopedics

For instance, when managers at Encore Orthopedics in Austin, Texas, decided to sell their company's synthetic knee, hip, and shoulder joints in Germany, they hired local distributors to handle the transactions. CEO Nick Cindrich says his company is pleased with the relationships it has forged with its distributors. About one-third of Encore's sales come from foreign markets, and the company is now expanding into France.[32]

Trade intermediaries such as these are becoming increasingly popular among businesses attempting to branch out into world markets because they make that transition so much faster and easier. Most small businesses simply do not have the knowledge, resources, confidence, or the connections to go global alone. Intermediaries' global networks of buyers and sellers allow their small business customers to build their international sales efforts much faster and with fewer hassles and mistakes. Foreign distributors can help small companies learn the nuances of foreign cultures and land prime selling space for their products and services.

The key to establishing a successful relationship with a trade intermediary is conducting a thorough screening to determine which type of intermediary—and which one in particular—will best serve a small company's needs. A company looking for an intermediary should compile a list of criteria by which to measure candidates' suitability. After compiling a list of potential intermediaries, an entrepreneur should evaluate each one using the criteria list to narrow the field to the most promising ones. Interviewing a principal from each intermediary on the final list should tell an entrepreneur which one is best able to meet the company's needs. For instance, when managers at Tennessee Log Homes, a maker of unassembled log cabins, were trying to locate a distributor in Germany, their research led them to a business that was selling complementary products and had a licensed builder and a realtor on staff.[33]

Finally, before signing any agreement with a trade intermediary, it is wise to conduct thorough background and credit checks. When one entrepreneur signed an agreement with a Mexican distributor interested in selling her company's bird cages there, she discovered that he had lied about owning an established family business with contacts in the industry.[34] Entrepreneurs with experience in global trade also suggest entering short-term agreements of about a year with new trade intermediaries to allow time to test their ability and willingness to live up to their promises.

Joint Ventures

Joint ventures, both domestic and foreign, lower the risk of entering global markets for small businesses. They also give small companies more clout and important connections in foreign lands. In a **domestic joint venture,** two or more U.S. small businesses form an alliance for the purpose of exporting their goods and services abroad. For export ventures, participating companies get antitrust immunity, allowing them to cooperate freely. The businesses share the responsibility and the costs of getting export licenses and permits, and they split the venture's profits. Establishing a joint venture with the right partner has become an essential part of maintaining a competitive position in global markets for a growing number of industries.

domestic joint venture—*an alliance of two or more U.S. small companies for the purpose of exporting their goods and services abroad.*

Yamas Controls Inc., a small California maker of environmental control systems, formed a joint venture with Bechtel Group Inc., the giant construction and engineering company, to provide its systems to the Chinese government. Without the joint venture, Yamas most likely would not have been able to break into the Chinese market. With it, the company's annual sales have grown from $4 million to $40 million in just eight years. Not only did the joint venture lower Yamas's risk of selling in foreign markets, but it also opened the door for similar projects with several American, European, and Chinese firms.[35]

Yamas Controls Inc.

In a **foreign joint venture,** a domestic small business forms an alliance with a company in the target nation. The host partner brings to the joint venture valuable knowledge of the local market and its method of operation as well as of the customs and the tastes of local customers. Sometimes foreign countries place certain limitations on joint ventures. Some nations, for example, require host companies to own at least 51 percent of the venture. "The only way to be German in Germany, Canadian in Canada, and Japanese in Japan is through alliances," says one international manager.[36]

foreign joint venture—*an alliance between a U.S. small business and a company in the target nation.*

Yahoo!, the highly successful Internet portal, established foreign joint ventures early in its existence to break into foreign markets. Yahoo! owns 34 percent of Yahoo Japan, 60 percent of its joint ventures in Great Britain, France, and Germany, and 70 percent of its joint venture in South Korea. Internet giant Amazon.com also used foreign joint ventures to establish its presence in Great Britain and Germany.[37]

Yahoo! and Amazon.com

The most important ingredient in the recipe for a successful joint venture is choosing the right partner. A productive joint venture is much like a marriage, requiring commitment and understanding. In addition to picking the right partner(s), a second key to creating a successful alliance is to establish common objectives. Defining exactly what each party in the joint venture hopes to accomplish at the outset will minimize the opportunity for misunderstandings and disagreements later on. One important objective should always be to use the joint venture as a learning experience.

Unfortunately, most joint ventures fail. According to a recent study, the average success rate is just 43 percent; the average life of a joint venture is only 3.5 years.[38] That makes it essential for the companies in an alliance to establish a contingency plan for getting out in case the joint venture doesn't work. Common problems leading to failure include improper selection of partners, incompatible management styles, failure to establish common goals, inability to be flexible, and failure to trust one another. "The usual problem," says one recent study of joint ventures, "is growing discontent between the partners as they discover how differently they view the world, how hard it is to keep their relationships in balance, and how easy it is . . . to forget what [they have] learned about making alliances work."[39]

Foreign Licensing

Rather than sell their products or services directly to customers overseas, some small companies enter foreign markets by licensing businesses in other nations to use their patents, trademarks, copyrights, technology, processes, or products. In return for licensing these assets, the small company collects royalties from the sales of its foreign licenses. Licensing is a relatively simple way for even the most inexperienced business owner to extend his reach into global markets. Eugene M. Lang, a foreign licensing expert, says, "Many small companies can't afford to invest capital in foreign facilities, and they don't have the personnel to send over there. Often, small company owners don't even have the time to acquaint themselves with foreign markets. The alternative is to license—to find someone who can capture the market for you who is already at home in that market."[40]

Marvel Comics, publisher of comic books featuring superheroes such as Spiderman, the X-Men, and the Incredible Hulk, licenses its comic books in countries across the globe.

Marvel Comics

Panini S.p.A., an entertainment publishing company headquartered in Italy, publishes Marvel comics in Europe, Latin America, Asia, and Africa.[41]

Although many business owners consider licensing only their products to foreign companies, the licensing potential for intangibles such as processes, technology, copyrights, and trademarks often is greater. "You often make more money from licensing your know-how for production or product control than you could from actually selling your finished product in a highly competitive market," explains Lang.[42] Disney often licenses its famous cartoon characters, including Mickey and Minnie Mouse, Goofy, Roger Rabbit, and others, to manufacturers in countries across the world.

Peace Frogs

Catesby Jones, president of Peace Frogs, a small retailer, explains why his company used a foreign licensing arrangement for its copyrighted designs in Spain. "We export our Peace Frogs T-shirts directly to Japan, but in Spain per capita income is lower, competition from domestic producers is stronger, and tariffs are high, so we licensed a Barcelona-based company the rights to manufacture our product," he says.[43]

Foreign licensing enables a small business to enter foreign markets quickly, easily, and with virtually no capital investment. Risks to the company include the potential of losing control over its manufacturing and marketing and creating a competitor if the licensee gains too much knowledge and control. Securing proper patent, trademark, and copyright protection beforehand can minimize these risks, however.

International Franchising

Franchising has become a major export industry for the United States. The International Franchise Association estimates that more than 20 percent of the nation's 4,000 franchisers have outlets in foreign countries.[44] Over the past decade, growing numbers of franchisers have been attracted to international markets to boost sales and profits as the domestic market has become increasingly saturated with outlets and much tougher to wring growth from. International franchisers sell virtually every kind of product or service imaginable—from fast food to child day care—in international markets.

Tumbleweed Southwest Mesquite Bar & Grill

Tumbleweed Southwest Mesquite Bar & Grill, a chain of franchised casual restaurants serving southwestern food, recently opened an outlet in a theme park in Cairo, Egypt, and in a shopping district in downtown London. Tumbleweed also has franchise outlets in Istanbul, Turkey; Amman, Jordan; and Jeddah, Saudi Arabia.[45]

In some cases, the products and services sold in international markets are identical to those sold in the United States. However, most franchisers have learned that they must modify their products and services to suit local tastes and customs.

Domino's Pizza and McDonald's

For instance, Domino's Pizza operates 1,670 restaurants in 64 countries, where local franchises offer pizza toppings that are quite different from the traditional ones used in the United States, including squid (Japan), pickled ginger (India), green peas (Brazil), and reindeer sausage (Iceland), to cater to customers' palates. The dough, the sauce, and the cheese are standard in every location, however.[46] *Although McDonald's builds its foreign menus around the same items and standardized assembly-line approach that have made it such a success in the United States, it makes changes to accommodate local tastes. In Germany, McDonald's restaurants sell beer, and in Great Britain they offer British Cadbury chocolate sticks.*

Although franchise outlets span the globe, Canada is the primary market for U.S. franchisers, with Japan and Europe following. These markets are most attractive to franchisers because they are similar to the U.S. market—rising personal incomes, strong demand for consumer goods, growing service economies, and spreading urbanization. Europe holds special interest for many American franchises as trade barriers there continue to topple, opening up the largest—and one of the most affluent—markets in the world. Although large franchisers are already well established in many European nations, a new wave of smaller franchisers is seeking to establish a foothold there. Growth potential is the primary attraction.

Countertrading and Bartering

As business becomes increasingly global, companies are discovering that attracting customers is just one part of the battle. Another problem global businesses face when selling to some developing countries is that their currencies are virtually worthless outside their borders, so getting paid in a valuable currency is a real challenge! In fact, 70 percent of all countries do not have either convertible currencies or sufficient cash flow to pay for imported goods.[47] Companies wanting to reach these markets must countertrade or barter. A **countertrade** is a transaction in which a company selling goods and services in a foreign country agrees to help promote investment and trade in that country. The goal of the transaction is to help offset the capital drain from the foreign country's purchases. Experts estimate that countertrading accounts for 15 to 20 percent of all global trade, and its use will continue to escalate.[48] Big businesses are accustomed to countertrading to reach certain markets, but small- and medium-sized companies usually lack the skills and the resources needed to conduct countertrades on their own. However, they can tie into deals made by large corporations.

countertrade—*a transaction in which a company selling goods in a foreign country agrees to promote investment and trade in that country.*

Cornnuts, Inc.

For instance, when export giant McDonnell Douglas sold $1.5 billion worth of jets to Spain, it agreed to a countertrade. As part of the deal, Cornnuts, Inc., a small maker of snack foods, agreed to open an office in Spain and to introduce hybrid corn technology there. Cornnuts had been eyeing Spain as an export market but didn't know how to get started. McDonnell Douglas arranged key meetings with Spanish officials and even helped the small company write its presentation and translate it into Spanish. The countertrade has proved to be a winner for Spain, McDonnell Douglas, and Cornnuts.[49]

Countertrading does suffer from numerous drawbacks. Countertrade transactions can be complicated, cumbersome, and time consuming. They also increase the chances that a company will get stuck with useless merchandise that it cannot move. They can lead to unpleasant surprises concerning the quantity and quality of products required in the countertrade. Still, countertrading offers one major advantage: Sometimes it's the only way to make a sale!

Entrepreneurs must weigh the advantages against the disadvantages for their companies before committing to a countertrade deal. Because of its complexity and the risks involved, countertrading is not the best choice for a novice entrepreneur looking to break into the global marketplace.

Bartering, the exchange of goods and services for other goods and services, is another way of trading with countries lacking convertible currency. In a barter exchange, a company that manufactures electronics components might trade its products for the coffee that a business in a foreign country processes, which it then sells to a third company for cash. Barter transactions require finding a business with complementary needs, but they are much simpler than countertrade transactions.

bartering—*the exchange of goods and services for other goods and services.*

Exporting

3. Explain how to build a thriving export program.

For years, small businesses in the United States could afford the luxury of conducting business at home in the world's largest market, never having to venture outside its borders. With increased global competition putting pressure on domestic markets and trade agreements opening up foreign markets as never before, small companies increasingly are looking toward exporting as a global business strategy. Large companies still dominate exporting. Although small businesses account for 97 percent of the companies involved in exporting, they generate only 31 percent of the dollar value of the nation's exports.[50]

YOU BE THE CONSULTANT . . .

Where Do We Start?

Specialty Building Supplies is a small company with $6.4 million in annual sales that manufactures and sells a line of building supply products such as foundation vents, innovative insulation materials, and fireplace blowers to building supply stores in the northeastern United States. The eight-year-old company, founded by Tad Meyers, has won several awards for its unique and innovative products and has earned a solid reputation among its supply store customers and the builders and homeowners who ultimately buy its products. Before launching the company, Meyers had been a home builder. As he watched the price of home heating fuels climb dramatically over time, Meyers began to incorporate into the houses he built simple, inexpensive ways to help homeowners save energy. He began tinkering with existing products, looking for ways to improve them. The first product he designed (and the product that ultimately led him to launch Specialty Building Supplies) was an automatic foundation vent that was thermostatically controlled (no electricity needed). The vent would automatically open and close based on the outside temperature, keeping cold drafts from blowing under a house. Simple and inexpensive in its design, the Autovent was a big hit in newly constructed homes in the Northeast because it not only saved energy but it also avoided a major headache for homeowners in cold climates: water pipes that would freeze and burst. Before long, Meyers stopped building houses and focused on selling the Autovent. Its success prompted him to add other products to the company's line.

Specialty's sales have been lackluster for more than a year now, primarily due to a slump in new home construction in its primary market. Tad Meyers recently met with the company's top marketing managers and salespeople to talk about their options for getting Specialty's sales and profit growth back on track. "What about selling our products in international markets?" asked Dee Rada, the company's marketing manager. "I read an article just last week about small companies doing good business in other countries, and many of them were smaller than we are."

"Interesting idea," Meyers said, pondering the concept. "I've never really thought about selling anything overseas. In fact, other than my years in the military, I've never traveled overseas and don't know anything about doing business there."

"It's a big world out there. Where should we sell our products?" said Hal Milam, Specialty's sales manager. "How do we find out what the building codes are in foreign countries? Would we have to modify our designs to meet foreign standards?"

"I don't know," shrugged Meyers. "Those are some good questions."

"How would we distribute our products?" asked Rada. "We have an established network of distributors here in the United States, but how do we find foreign distributors?"

"I wonder if exporting is our only option," said Meyers. "There must be other ways to get into the global market besides exporting. What do you think? Where do we start?"

1. What advice would you offer Meyers and the other managers at Specialty Building Supplies about their prospects of "going global"?
2. How would you suggest these managers go about finding the answers to the questions they have posed? What other questions would you advise them to answer?
3. Outline the steps these managers should take to assemble an international marketing plan.

However, small companies, realizing the incredible profit potential it offers, are making exporting an ever-expanding part of their marketing plans. In fact, the number of small companies that export has tripled over the last decade, and these companies sell products in practically every industrial classification. In short, there is plenty of opportunity for small businesses looking to grow, and much of that opportunity lies outside the borders of the United States.

Winderosa Manufacturing and Distribution Company

Rachel Carignan, CEO of Winderosa, a maker of small engine gaskets based in Peru, Maine, knows that exporting is not meant only for giants such as Boeing and Ford. Winderosa, with 11 employees who work in a newly remodeled plant that was once a chicken barn, exports 40 percent of its gaskets to 40 countries around the world. The company's Web site features translations in Spanish, German, French, Italian, and Japanese. Because of its global success, Winderosa recently won the State of Maine Small Business Exporter of the Year award.[51]

More than 200,000 U.S. companies currently export; however, only 1 percent of all small and medium-sized businesses are active exporters. Experts estimate that at least twice as many businesses are capable of exporting but are not doing so.[52] The biggest barrier facing companies that have never exported is not knowing where or how to start. Paul Hsu, whose company sells ginseng across the globe, explains, "Exporting . . . starts with a global mind-set, which unfortunately, is not all that common among owners of small- and medium-sized businesses in the United States. . . . Most entrepreneurs in the United States envision markets only within domestic and sometimes even state borders, while Japanese and other foreign entrepreneurs look at export markets first."[53] Breaking the psychological barrier to exporting is the first—and most difficult—step to setting up a successful program. What other steps must an entrepreneur take to get an export program underway?

1. *Recognize that even the tiniest companies and least experienced entrepreneurs have the potential to export.*

   Windchimes by Russco III

   Richie Harral, owner of Windchimes by Russco III, started making wind chimes with his brother at age 10 in 1978 in the cellar of his home. Their company started really small—two kids selling wind chimes to neighbors door-to-door. Their big break came seven years later when Wal-Mart ordered 30,000 chimes. In 1992, Windchimes experienced another stroke of luck when a British distributor, whose parents had bought a chime in a Missouri Wal-Mart, placed a $2,500 order. Today, the United Kingdom accounts for 6 percent of the company's $2 million in sales, and Harral predicts that exports soon will comprise 30 percent of sales.[54]

   Exporting not only can boost a small company's sales, but it also can accelerate its growth rate. A recent study found that small companies that export grow markedly faster than those that do not. The study also concluded that the growth gap is widening as business becomes increasingly global in scope.[55]

2. *Analyze your product or service.* Is it special? New? Unique? High quality? Priced favorably due to lower costs or exchange rates? In which countries would there be sufficient demand for it?

   Creative Bakers of Brooklyn

   Ron Schutte, president of Creative Bakers of Brooklyn, a company that makes presliced cheesecakes for restaurants, saw an opportunity to sell in Japan. The only modification Schutte made to his high-quality cheesecakes was reducing the portion size from 4.5 ounces to 2.25 ounces. "The Japanese aren't as gluttonous as we are," he explains.[56]

3. *Analyze your commitment.* Selling products or services in foreign markets usually takes more time, energy, and money than selling them in the domestic market. Are you willing to devote the time and the energy to develop export markets? Does your company have the necessary resources? Few business owners realize "the amount of management resources it will suck up at the top levels of the company," says one export consultant.[57] Export start-ups can take from six to eight months (or longer), but entering foreign markets isn't as tough as most entrepreneurs think, and the payoffs can be huge. Table 13.1 summarizes key issues managers must address in the export decision.

4. *Research markets and pick your target.* Nearly two-thirds of small businesses export their products to just one country.[58] (See Figure 13.3.) Before investing in a costly sales trip abroad, however, entrepreneurs should make a trip to the local library or the nearest branch of the Department of Commerce. Exporters can choose from a multitude of Web sites, guides, manuals, books, newsletters, videos, and other resources to help them research potential markets. Some of the most helpful tools for researching foreign markets are the Country Commercial Guides prepared annually by U.S. Embassy staff. These valuable guides, available at the International Trade Association's Web site **<www.ita.doc.gov>,** provide detailed information on the economic, political, regulatory, and investment environment for countries ranging from Albania to Zimbabwe. Another extremely useful site is TradeNet's Export Advisor **<www.tradenet.gov>,** a site that answers basic questions about exporting and provides useful information on export resources, financing, and a host of related topics. Armed

TABLE 13.1
Management Issues in the Export Decision

Source: Adapted from A Basic Guide to Exporting *(Washington, DC: U.S. Department of Commerce, 1998),* **<www.unzco.com/basicguide/index.html>.**

Management Objectives

- What are your company's reasons for pursuing export markets? Are they solid objectives (e.g., increasing sales volume or developing a broader, more stable customer base) or are they frivolous (e.g., the owner wants an excuse to travel)?
- How committed is top management to an export effort? Is exporting viewed as a quick fix for a slump in domestic sales? Will the company neglect its export customers if domestic sales pick up?
- What are management's expectations for the export effort? How quickly does management expect export operations to become self-sustaining? What level of return on investment do you expect from the export program?

Experience

- With what countries does your company already conduct business, or from what countries have you received inquiries?
- Which product lines are mentioned most often?
- Are any domestic customers buying the product for sale or shipment overseas? If so, to what countries?
- Is the trend of sales and inquiries increasing or decreasing?
- Who are the primary domestic and foreign competitors?
- What lessons has your company learned from past export attempts or experiences?

Management and Personnel

- What in-house international expertise does your company have (international sales experience, language capabilities, and others)?
- Who will be responsible for the export department's organization and staff? (Do you have an export "champion"?)
- How much senior management time
  a. *should* you allocate to exporting?
  b. *can* you allocate to exporting?
- What organizational structure is required to ensure that export sales are adequately serviced?
- Who will implement the plan?

Production Capacity

- How is your company using its present capacity? Is there any excess capacity? If so, how much?
- Will filling export orders hurt your company's ability to make and service domestic sales?
- What will additional production for export markets cost your company?
- Are there seasonal or cyclical fluctuations in your company's workload? When? Why? Would exporting help smooth these fluctuations?
- Is there a minimum quantity foreign customers must order for a sale to be profitable?
- To what extent would your company need to modify its products, packaging, and design specifically for its export targets? Is your product quality adequate for foreign customers?
- What pricing structure will you use? Will your prices be competitive?
- How will your company collect payment on its export sales?

Financial Capacity

- How much capital will your company need to begin exporting? Where will it come from?
- How will you allocate the initial cost of your company's export effort?
- Does your company have other expansion plans in the works that would compete with an export effort?
- By what date must your export effort pay for itself?
- How important is establishing a global presence to your company's future success?

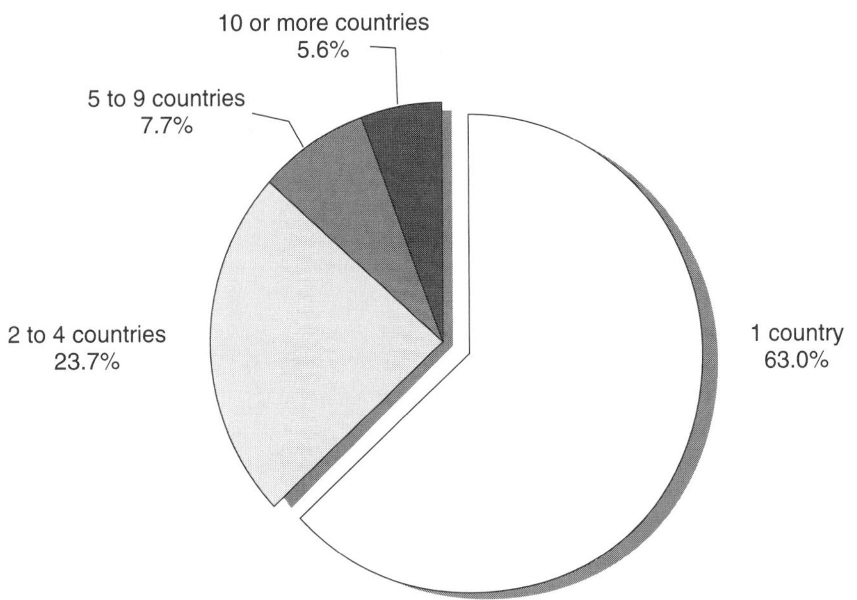

FIGURE 13.3
Number of Countries to Which Small Businesses Export

Source: Exporter Data Base, U.S. Department of Commerce, Office of Trade and Economic Analysis, Trade Development/International Trade Agency, 2000.

with research, entrepreneurs can avoid wasting valuable resources on markets with limited potential for their products or services and can concentrate on those with the greatest promise. Table 13.2 shows the countries that currently top the list of targets for exporting small companies and the foreign markets where small business exports are growing the fastest.

EkkWill Waterlife Resources

Managers at EkkWill Waterlife Resources, a wholesale fish supplier, discovered through research that collecting fish is an even more popular hobby in Japan than in the United States. EkkWill now flies one-third of its production, some 1,440 tons of fish each year, to Japan as well as to Latin America, Asia, Canada, and the West Indies. Its best-selling fish in international markets are Florida gars, red swordtails, and new world cichlids, all common breeds in North America but considered exotic in other lands.[59]

Research shows export entrepreneurs whether they need to modify their existing products and services to suit the tastes and preferences of their foreign target customers.

Robbins Industries

For instance, when Rodney Robbins, CEO of Robbins Industries, a measuring-cup-and-spoon maker, was negotiating with a distributor prior to entering the Swedish and British markets, he learned that he would have to modify his products slightly. The British use measuring utensils labeled in milliliters while the Swedes prefer deciliters.[60]

These modifications can sometimes spell the difference between success and failure in the global market.

TABLE 13.2
Where in the World Do Small Exporters Conduct Business?

Source: "America's Small Businesses and International Trade: A Report," U.S. Small Business Administration Office of International Trade, November 1999, p. 7.

Top 10 Markets for U.S. Small Business Exporters	Top 10 Fastest-Growing Markets for U.S. Small Business Exporters
1. Canada	1. Brazil
2. United Kingdom	2. Malaysia
3. Japan	3. China
4. Mexico	4. Philippines
5. Germany	5. Canada
6. Australia	6. Thailand
7. Hong Kong	7. Israel
8. France	8. Argentina
9. Taiwan	9. United Kingdom
10. Singapore	10. Hong Kong

In other cases, products destined for export need little or no modification. For example, for more than 40 years the W.F. Bassett Company has been exporting its TRIM line of manicure and pedicure products to more than 70 countries in exactly the same form it sells them in the United States.[61] Experts estimate that one-half of exported products require little modification; one-third require moderate modification; only a few require major changes.[62] Entrepreneurs should let market research be their guide when deciding how to modify their products for global markets.

Table 13.3 offers questions to guide entrepreneurs conducting export research.

5. *Develop a distribution strategy.* Should you use an export intermediary or sell directly to foreign customers? Small companies just entering international markets may prefer to rely on export intermediaries to break new ground.

BFW

Lynn Cooper, president of BFW, a 25-year-old medical lighting supplier, uses wholesale distributors to sell her company's products in 25 countries. Exports account for 30 percent of BFW's sales, and Cooper is happy with her method of distribution. "With distributors, the risk to us is minimal, but we still know just where the products are going," she says.[63]

6. *Find your customer.* Small businesses can rely on a host of export specialists to help them track down foreign customers. The U.S. Department of Commerce and the International Trade Administration should be the first stops on an entrepreneur's agenda for going global. These agencies have the market research available for locating the best target markets for a particular company and specific customers in those markets. Industry Sector Analysis (ISAs), International Market Insights (IMIs), and Customized Market Analysis (CMAs) are just some of the reports and services global entrepreneurs find most useful for locating potential customers. In addition, the Department of Commerce offers export-ready companies its Gold Key Service, in which experienced trade professionals arrange meetings with prescreened potential customers and contacts in target countries.

TABLE 13.3
Questions to Guide International Market Research

Source: Adapted from A Basic Guide to Exporting *(Washington, DC: U.S. Department of Commerce, 1998),* **<www.unzco.com/basicguide/index.html>.**

- Is there an overseas market for your company's products or services?
- Are there specific target markets that look most promising?
- Which new markets abroad are most likely to open up or expand?
- How big is the market(s) your company is targeting and how fast is it growing?
- What are the major economic, political, legal, social, technological, and other environmental factors affecting this market?
- What are the demographic and cultural factors affecting this market (e.g., disposable income, occupation, age, sex, opinions, activities, interests, tastes, and values)?
- Who are your company's present—and potential—customers abroad?
- What are their needs and desires? What factors influence their buying decisions (e.g., price, credit terms, delivery terms, quality, brand name, etc.)?
- How would they use your company's product or service? What modifications, if any, would be necessary to sell to your target customers?
- Who are your primary competitors in the foreign market?
- How do competitors distribute, sell, and promote their products? What are their prices?
- What are the best channels of distribution for your product?
- What is the best way for your company to gain exposure in this market?
- Are there any barriers such as tariffs, quotas, duties, or regulations to selling your products in this market? Are their any incentives?
- Are there any potential licensing or joint venture partners already in this market?

Mediafour

The Gold Key program paved the way to global markets for Mediafour, a small software company that makes MacDrive, a program that allows Windows-based PC users to access files created on Apple Macintosh computers. Using the connections made through the Gold Key program, Mediafour's international sales went from virtually nothing to 35 percent of the company's sales in less than two years! Mediafour sells MacDrive in 65 countries and has exclusive distributors for the software in 15 countries, including the United Kingdom, Germany, and Japan. The company's success in exporting has been phenomenal, having captured, for instance, 75 percent of the market in Japan, with sales expected to double with the release of the latest version of its software. To meet the demand from international markets, Mediafour has hired more workers, adding many of them in its new international department.[64]

Other entrepreneurs search out customers on their own.

Electronic Liquid Fillers, Inc.

For instance, Jeff Ake, co-owner of Electronic Liquid Fillers, Inc., a small packaging equipment company, spent seven weeks calling on potential customers in the Pacific Rim. He identified his target customers with the help of foreign-based English language industry trade magazines. During his travels, Ake used the local English-language equivalent of the Yellow Pages to find others.[65]

7. *Find financing.* One of the biggest barriers to small business exports is lack of financing. Access to adequate financing is a crucial ingredient in a successful export program because the cost of generating foreign sales often is higher and collection cycles are longer. The trouble is that bankers and other sources of capital don't always understand the intricacies of international sales and view financing them as excessively risky. Also, among major industrialized nations, the U.S. government spends the least per capita to promote exports.

   Several federal, state, and private programs are operating to fill this export financing void, however. Programs such as the SBA's Export Working Capital Program (guarantees on short-term loans up to $1,250,000) and its International Trade Loan Program (a combination of fixed asset and working capital financing), as well as those offered by the Export-Import Bank (loan guarantees), the Overseas Private Investment Corporation (loans and loan guarantees), and a variety of state agencies give export-minded entrepreneurs much needed access to export financing. To qualify for many of these programs, a company must have at least one year of export experience. The International Trade Administration provides an export finance matchmaking service at its Web site **<www.ita.doc.gov/td/efm>**. A list of all state foreign trade assistance offices is available on the Trade Information Center's National Export Directory Web site at **<infoserv2.ita.doc.gov/NEDHomeP.nsf>**. The Bankers Association for Foreign Trade **<www.baft.org>** is an association of 450 banks that matches exporters needing foreign trade financing with interested banks.

8. *Ship your goods.* Export novices usually rely on freight-forwarders and custom-house agents—experienced specialists in overseas shipping—for help in navigating the bureaucratic morass of packaging requirements and paperwork demanded by customs. These specialists are to exporters what travel agents are to passengers and normally charge relatively small fees for a valuable service.

   Shipping terms, always important for determining which party in a transaction pays the cost of shipping and bears the risk of loss or damage to the goods, take on heightened importance in international transactions. Table 13.4 explains the implications of some of the most common shipping terms used in international transactions.

9. *Collect your money.* Collecting foreign accounts can be more complex than collecting domestic ones, but by picking their customers carefully and checking their credit references closely, entrepreneurs can minimize bad-debt losses. Financing foreign sales often involves special credit arrangements such as letters of credit and bank (or documentary) drafts. A **letter of credit** is an agreement between an exporter's bank and the foreign buyer's bank that guarantees payment to the exporter for a shipment of goods once the exporter delivers specific documents about the shipment. In essence, a letter of credit reduces the financial risk for the exporter by substituting a bank's creditworthiness for that of the purchaser (see Figure 13.4). A **bank draft** is a document the seller draws on the

letter of credit—*an agreement between an exporter's bank and the foreign buyer's bank that guarantees payment to the exporter for a shipment of goods once the exporter delivers specific documents about the shipment.*

bank draft—*a document the seller draws on the buyer, requiring the buyer to pay the face amount (the purchase price of the goods) either on sight (a sight draft) or on a specified date (a time draft).*

TABLE 13.4

Common International Shipping Terms and Their Meanings

Source: Adapted from Guide to the Finance of International Trade, *Edited by Gordon Platt (HBSC Trade Services, Marine Midland Bank, and* The Journal of Commerce), ***<infoserv2.ita.doc.gov/efm/efm.nsf/503d177e3c63f0b48525675900112e24/6218a8703573b32985256759004c41f3/$FILE/Finance_.pdf>,*** *pp. 6–10.*

Shipping Term	Seller's Responsibility	Buyer's Responsibility	Shipping Method(s) Used
FOB ("Free on Board") Seller	Deliver goods to carrier and provide export license and clean on-board receipt. Bear risk of loss until goods are delivered to carrier.	Pay shipping, freight, and insurance charges. Bear risk of loss while goods are in transit.	All
FOB ("Free on Board") Buyer	Deliver goods to the buyer's place of business and provide export license and clean on-board receipt. Pay shipping, freight, and insurance charges.	Accept delivery of goods after documents are tendered.	All
FAS ("Free Along Side"), vessel	Deliver goods alongside ship. Provide an "alongside" receipt.	Provide export license and proof of delivery of the goods to the carrier. Bear risk of loss once goods are delivered to carrier.	Ship
CFR ("Cost and Freight")	Deliver goods to carrier, obtain export licenses, and pay export taxes. Provide buyer with clean bill of lading. Pay shipping and freight charges. Bear risk of loss until goods are delivered to buyer.	Pay insurance charges. Accept delivery of goods after documents are tendered.	Ship
CIF ("Cost, Insurance, and Freight")	Same as for CFR plus pay insurance charges and provide buyer with insurance policy.	Accept delivery of goods after documents are tendered.	Ship
CPT ("Carriage Paid to . . .")	Deliver goods to carrier, obtain export licenses, and pay export taxes. Provide buyer with clean transportation documents. Pay shipping and freight charges.	Pay insurance charges. Accept delivery of goods after documents are tendered.	All
CIP ("Carriage and Insurance Paid to . . .")	Same as for CPT plus pay insurance charges and provide buyer with insurance policy.	Accept delivery of goods after documents are tendered.	All
DDU ("Delivered Duty Unpaid")	Obtain export license, pay insurance charges, and provide buyer documents for taking delivery.	Take delivery of goods and pay import duties.	All
DDP ("Delivered Duty Paid")	Obtain export license and pay import duty, pay insurance charges, and provide buyer documents for taking delivery.	Take delivery of goods.	All

buyer, requiring the buyer to pay the face amount (the purchase price of the goods) either on sight (a sight draft) or on a specified date (a time draft) once the goods are shipped. Rather than use letters of credit or drafts, some exporters simply require cash in advance or cash on delivery (COD). Insisting on cash payments up front, however, may cause some foreign buyers to reject a deal. The parties to an international deal should always come to an agreement in advance on an acceptable method of payment.

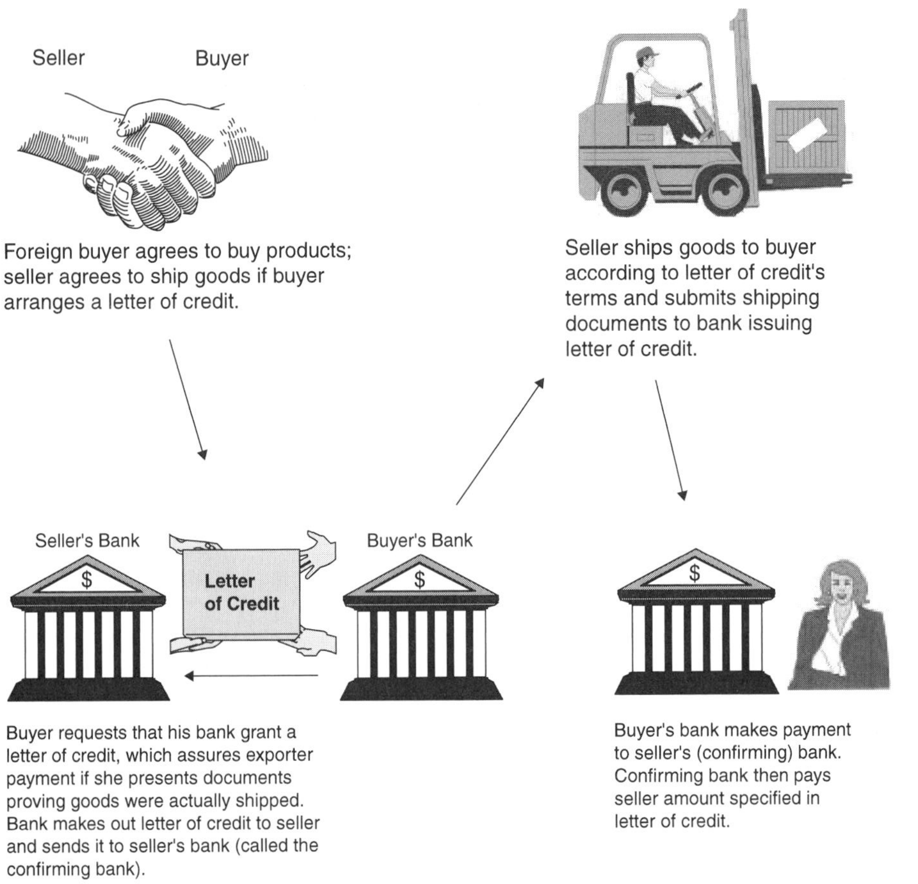

Seller

Buyer

Foreign buyer agrees to buy products; seller agrees to ship goods if buyer arranges a letter of credit.

Seller ships goods to buyer according to letter of credit's terms and submits shipping documents to bank issuing letter of credit.

Seller's Bank

Letter of Credit

Buyer's Bank

Buyer requests that his bank grant a letter of credit, which assures exporter payment if she presents documents proving goods were actually shipped. Bank makes out letter of credit to seller and sends it to seller's bank (called the confirming bank).

Buyer's bank makes payment to seller's (confirming) bank. Confirming bank then pays seller amount specified in letter of credit.

FIGURE 13.4
How a Letter of Credit Works

Many small companies are forming **foreign sales corporations** (FSCs, pronounced "fisks") to take advantage of a tax benefit designed to stimulate exports. Although large companies have used the tax advantages of FSCs for many years, a rapidly growing number of small exporters are beginning to catch on to them. By forming a FSC, a company can reduce its federal income tax liability (and sometimes its state tax liability as well) by 15 percent to 30 percent on earnings from foreign sales. More than 7,100 corporations have created FSCs since they were established in the Tax Reform Act of 1984. Setting up a FSC requires a company to establish a shell corporation in one of four tax-friendly U.S. territories or 32 foreign countries such as the U.S. Virgin Islands, Barbados, Guam, or Jamaica that have tax treaties with the United States. Because of the convenience of doing so, about half of all FSCs are formed in the Virgin Islands. However, experts recommend that companies whose export sales exceed $10 million form FSCs in Barbados. Small companies with $5 million or less in export sales can create small FSCs, which offer the same benefits as regular FSCs but are subject to less stringent procedural requirements. Most companies that establish FSCs use a FSC management company in the designated territory or country to do so. Once it establishes a FSC, a small company can allocate up to 23 percent of its export profits to the FSC, where these profits are taxed at lower rates than normal. Because it costs about $2,000 to set up a small FSC and about $3,000 per year to maintain one, a business should earn at least $50,000 in export profits a year to make the tax savings from a FSC worthwhile.

foreign sales corporations—*a shell company created in an approved U.S. territory or a foreign country that allows a business to reduce its income tax liability by 15 percent to 30 percent on earnings from foreign sales.*

Planned carefully and taken one step at a time, exporting can be a highly profitable route for small businesses. Table 13.5 describes the 12 most common mistakes exporters make.

TABLE 13.5

The 12 Most Common Mistakes Exporters Make

Sources: Adapted from Denis Csizmadia, "Exporters Can Avoid 12 Common Mistakes," Upstate Business, *August 11, 1996, p. 3; Martha Mangelsdorf, "Unfair Trade,"* Inc., *April 1991, pp. 28–36; A Basic Guide to Exporting (Washington, DC: U.S. Department of Commerce, 1998),* **<www.unzco.com/basicguide/index.html>.**

Exporting can be intimidating, especially for an inexperienced small business owner, and overcoming export barriers puts an extra burden on small companies that usually have thin resources. When a small company runs into export trouble, it is usually because it fell victim to one or more of the 12 most common mistakes exporters make:

1. *Not obtaining qualified export counseling and developing a master international marketing plan before starting an export business.* To become a successful exporter, a business must first define its global goals and objectives and identify the problems it is likely to encounter in its global expansion. Then it must develop a workable plan to achieve these objectives and to overcome the problems. Unless a small firm is fortunate enough to have a staff with considerable export expertise, it may not be able to take this crucial first step without qualified outside assistance.

2. *Not obtaining enough commitment from top management to overcome the initial difficulties and financial requirements of exporting.* Although the early delays, costs, and problems may seem difficult to justify when compared to established domestic markets, the long-term benefits of establishing a successful export program will be worth it. Wise exporters take a long-term view and shepherd their international marketing efforts through these early difficulties (which will occur). That takes total support from top managers in the company.

3. *Not taking sufficient care in selecting overseas distributors.* The choice of every foreign distributor is crucial. The sheer distance and resulting complications with communication and transportation require a company's distributors to act with greater independence than their domestic counterparts do. Also, because a new exporter's products, trademarks, and reputation are usually unknown in foreign markets, customers may buy on the strength of distributors' reputations. A company must evaluate carefully every distributor handling its products or services, its reputation, and its facilities.

4. *Chasing orders from around the world instead of establishing a basis for profitable international operations and orderly growth.* If exporters expect distributors to sell their products successfully, they must train them, motivate them, and evaluate their performances. Often this requires putting a marketing executive in a distributor's geographic territory. New exporters should concentrate on one or two markets initially before expanding into multiple markets to avoid stretching their managerial and financial resources too thin.

5. *Neglecting export business when the U.S. market booms.* Many small companies turn to export markets when business falls off in the United States. Then when their domestic business picks up again, some neglect their export customers or relegate them to a secondary place. Such neglect can seriously harm an exporter's reputation in the global market and can jeopardize its long-term global business prospects. Even if its domestic business remains strong, the exporter usually realizes that it has closed off a valuable source of additional sales and profits.

6. *Not treating international distributors on an equal basis with their domestic counterparts.* Often companies have institutional advertising campaigns, special discount offers, sales incentive programs, special credit terms, warranty offers, and the like in the domestic market but fail to offer similar assistance to their international distributors. This is a mistake that can destroy the vitality of overseas marketing efforts.

7. *Assuming that a given marketing technique and product will be successful in all countries.* What works in one market may not work in another, so an exporter must treat each target market separately. Successful exporters are willing to modify their products, packaging, and promotion techniques to suit local tastes, preferences, and habits.

8. *Not being willing to modify products to meet other countries' regulations or cultural preferences.* Exporters cannot ignore the regulations, customs, tastes, preferences, and import restrictions affecting their products in foreign markets. Although most products exporters sell need only minor modifications to be suitable for their target customers, the key to their success lies in the exporter's willingness to make those modifications. Successful exporters are not so arrogant as to think that the domestic way is the best and only way of using or selling a product.

9. *Not printing service, sales, and warranty messages in the local language.* Although a foreign distributor's top managers may speak English, it is unlikely that all sales and service people have this ability. Without a clear understanding of the sales or service message in their own language, these people will be unable to perform their jobs effectively. Smart exporters use locals to translate these messages so that they retain their accuracy.

10. *Not using an export management company or other trade intermediary.* If a company decides that it cannot afford its own export department (or has tried to organize one unsuccessfully), it should consider using an export management company or other appropriate trade intermediary.

11. *Not considering licensing or joint venture arrangements.* Import restrictions in some countries, insufficient personnel or financial resources, or limited product lines cause many companies to dismiss international marketing as unfeasible. Yet, many products that are successful in the United States can be successful in the global marketplace as well. Perhaps the best way to break into the global market may be a licensing arrangement or a joint venture with a foreign partner.

12. *Not providing readily available sales and service support for a product.* A product without proper sales and service support is doomed to failure. When planning its venture into foreign markets, companies must address not only the sales issue but also its service aspects.

Establishing International Locations

Once established in international markets, some small businesses set up permanent locations there. Establishing an office or a factory in a foreign land can require a substantial investment reaching beyond the budgets of many small companies. Plus, setting up an international office can be an incredibly frustrating experience in some countries. Business infrastructures are in disrepair or are nonexistent. Getting a telephone line installed can take months in some places and finding reliable equipment to move goods to customers is nearly impossible. Securing necessary licenses and permits from bureaucrats often takes more than filing the necessary paperwork; in some nations, bureaucrats expect payments to "grease the wheels of justice." Finding the right person to manage an international office is crucial to success; it also is a major challenge, especially for small businesses. Small companies usually have lean management staffs and cannot afford to send key people abroad without running the risk of losing their focus.

Few small businesses begin their global ventures by establishing international locations, preferring, instead, to build a customer base through some of the other strategies covered in this section.

Santec Inc.

For example, in 1984, managers at Santec Inc., a U.S.-based manufacturer of electronic connectors, saw the tremendous potential the European market offered. Rather than plunge into the market by establishing a location on the Continent, however, they decided to begin by exporting. "We have worked our way up to full-scale manufacturing," says Santec's president John Shine. The sales channels the company established in Europe in 1984 have evolved into a full-fledged manufacturing facility at Cumbernauld, Scotland. The move was a natural extension of Santec's globalization strategy. To ensure its long-term success, "it's just a necessity" to have operations for sales, service, and manufacturing in North America, Europe, and Asia, which is Santec's next stop on its global agenda, according to Shine.[66]

Small companies that establish international locations can reap significant benefits. Start-up costs often are lower in many foreign countries, and lower labor costs can produce significant savings as well. Robert Brooker and Adam Haven-Weiss launched their New York Bagel Company in Budapest, Hungary, with just $40,000 in seed money, a fraction of what it would have cost in the United States.[67]

Going global by employing one or more of these eight strategies can put tremendous strain on a small company, but the benefits of cracking international markets can be significant. Not only does going global offer attractive sales and profit possibilities, but it also strengthens the company's competitive skills and enhances its overall reputation. Pleasing tough foreign customers also keeps companies on their competitive toes.

"We have two offices throughout the world."

Source: ©The New York Collection 1990 Robert Weber from cartoonbank.com. All rights reserved.

4. Discuss the major barriers to international trade and their impact on the global economy.

BARRIERS TO INTERNATIONAL TRADE

The world has never had a truly free system of trade because governments have always used a variety of barriers to block free trade among nations in an attempt to protect businesses within their own borders. The benefit of protecting their own companies, however, comes at the expense of foreign businesses, which face limited access to global markets. Numerous trade barriers—both domestic and international—restrict the freedom of businesses in global trading. Although these barriers restrain companies in every country from selling their goods anywhere in the world, international trade grew at a healthy 6 percent per year from 1990 to 2000 and totals more than $7 *trillion* a year!

Domestic Barriers

Sometimes the biggest barriers potential exporters face are right here at home. Three major domestic roadblocks are common: attitude, information, and financing. Perhaps the biggest barrier to small businesses exporting is the attitude: "I'm too small to export. That's just for big corporations." The first lesson of exporting is "Take nothing for granted about who can export and what you can and cannot export." The first step to building an export program is recognizing that the opportunity to export exists.

Another reason entrepreneurs neglect international markets is a lack of information about how to get started. The key to success in international markets is choosing the correct target market and designing the appropriate strategy to reach it. That requires access to information and research. Although a variety of government and private organizations make volumes of exporting and international marketing information available, many small business owners never use it. A successful global marketing strategy also recognizes that not all markets are the same. Companies must be flexible, willing to make necessary adjustments to their products and services, promotional campaigns, packaging, and sales techniques.

Another significant obstacle is the lack of export financing available. One study of exporters found that 53 percent said they had lost export business because they couldn't get financing.[68]

N & N Contact Lens International, Inc.

For example, N & N Contact Lens International, Inc. recently got an order from a Brazilian customer for $247,000 worth of contact lenses. The buyer had good credit with its Brazilian bank, and a credit check produced a favorable report. But N & N's bank refused to finance the deal. "We just don't finance foreign receivables," explained one bank official. N & N's president laments, "[Yet] I can get an order from Atlanta from a guy who went bankrupt and the bank will finance it, without question."[69]

International Barriers

Domestic barriers aren't the only ones export-minded entrepreneurs must overcome. Trading nations also erect obstacles to free trade. Two types of international barriers are common: tariff and nontariff.

TARIFF BARRIERS. A **tariff** is a tax, or duty, that a government imposes on goods and services imported into that country. Imposing tariffs raises the price of the imported goods—making them less attractive to consumers—and protects the makers of comparable domestic products and services. Established in the United States in 1790 by Alexander Hamilton, the tariff system generated the majority of federal revenues for about 100 years. Today, the U.S. tariff code lists duties on 8,753 items—from brooms and olives to flashlights and teacups.[70]

tariff—*a tax, or duty, that a government imposes on goods and services imported into that country.*

NONTARIFF BARRIERS. Many nations have lowered the tariffs they impose on products and services brought into their borders, but they rely on other nontariff structures as protectionist trade barriers.

Quotas. Rather than impose a direct tariff on certain imported products, nations often use quotas to protect their industries. A **quota** is a limit on the amount of a product imported into a country. Every country imposes quotas on some of the products they import. The United States, for instance, imposes more than 3,000 quotas on clothing and textile imports from 40 countries.[71] These quotas, for example, limit the number of cotton knit shirts imported to the United States to 28 million.[72] Whatever their intentions may be, quotas can restrict a company's ability to do business in the global community. David Dyer, CEO of Lands' End, a catalog and online retailer that sells millions of clothing items a year, says "Apparel quotas are very onerous for us."[73]

quota—*a limit on the amount of product imported into a country.*

Japan, often criticized for its protectionist attitude toward imports, traditionally used tariffs and quotas to keep foreign competitors out. However, Japan's average tariff rate is now among the world's lowest—averaging just 1.9 percent (compared to 2.5 percent in the United States)—but quotas still exist on many products.

Dexter Shoe Company

The Dexter Shoe Company faces a formidable trade barrier in its attempt to sell its leather shoes in Japanese markets. Because leather-working is a traditional craft of a Japanese social underclass called the burakumin, *the shoe industry is protected by a strong quota-tariff system. Every year, Dexter must fight for even a modest expansion in its quota allotment, which now stands at a measly 50,000 pairs.*[74]

embargo—*a total ban on imports of certain products.*

Embargoes. An **embargo** is a total ban on imports of certain products. The motivation for embargoes is not always economic. For instance, because of South Africa's history of apartheid policies, many nations have embargoed imports of Krugerrands (gold coins). Traditionally, Taiwan, South Korea, and Israel have banned imports of Japanese autos.

dumping—*the practice of selling large quantities of products in foreign countries below cost in an attempt to gain market share.*

DUMPING. In an effort to grab market share quickly, some companies have been guilty of **dumping** products, selling large quantities of them in foreign countries below cost. The United States has been a dumping target for steel, televisions, shoes, and computer chips in the past. Under the U.S. Antidumping Act, a company must prove that the foreign company's prices are lower here than in the home country and that U.S. companies are directly harmed.

Political Barriers

Entrepreneurs who go global quickly discover a labyrinth of political tangles. Although many American business owners complain of excessive government regulation in the United States, they are often astounded by the complex web of governmental and legal regulations and barriers they encounter in foreign countries.

Companies doing business in politically risky lands face the very real dangers of government takeovers of private property; attempts at coups to overthrow ruling parties; kidnappings, bombings, and other violent acts against businesses and their employees; and other threatening events. Their investments of millions of dollars may evaporate overnight in the wake of a government coup or the passage of a law nationalizing an industry (giving control of an entire industry to the government).

Some nations welcome foreign business investment, but others do everything they can to discourage competition from foreign companies.

International Game Technology

For example, the Japanese recently used a web of complex regulations and bizarre rules to prevent International Game Technology (IGT), an American manufacturer of slot machines, from competing in their home market. IGT battled one ridiculous rule (most of them unwritten) after another for four years to no avail. Finally, with the help of a former Japanese official (whose job had been to keep competitors such as IGT out of the Japanese market), IGT was able to file its legal documents with regulators. After 19 modifications (none affecting its machines' performance and one because the paper was not the right size), IGT finally won the right to sell its slot machines in Japan.[75]

Cultural Barriers

culture—*the beliefs, values, views, and mores that the inhabitants of a country share.*

The **culture** of a nation includes the beliefs, values, views, and mores that its inhabitants share. Differences in cultures among nations create another barrier to international trade. The diversity of languages, business philosophies, practices, and traditions makes international trade more complex than selling to the business down the street. Entrepreneurs who want to succeed in international markets must understand the culture in which they plan to do business and adapt their business styles and their products to suit that culture. Many international deals collapse simply because a businessperson fails to understand the differences in one culture from another. "A lot of times problems come from the assumption that the American way of doing business is universal when, in fact, it is not," says one international business expert.[76] Consider the following examples:

- An American businesswoman in London was invited to a party hosted by an advertising agency. Unsure of her ability to navigate the streets and subways of London alone, she approached a British colleague who was driving to the party and asked him, "Could I get a ride with you?" After he turned bright red from embarrassment, he regained his composure and politely said, "Lucky for you I know what you meant." Unknowingly, the young woman had requested a sexual encounter with her colleague, not a lift to the party![77]

- One American businessman grew tired of trying to speak over the persistent chanting of a nearby group of Islamic men. Exasperated, he looked harshly at the group and said to his Muslim host, "Can't somebody shut those guys up?" Only then did he discover that "those guys" were Islamic priests chanting a call to prayer—and that he had just blown the deal he was trying to land.[78]
- In another incident, an American went to Malaysia to close a sizeable contract. In an elaborate ceremony, he was introduced to a man he thought was named "Roger." Throughout the negotiations, he called the man "Rog," not realizing that his potential client was a "rajah," a title of nobility, not a name.[79]
- On his first trip to the Middle East, an American executive was touring the city with his Arab business contact. As they strolled along the dusty streets, the host reached over, took the executive's hand in his, and the two continued to walk, the host's hand holding the executive's. Totally stunned, the American didn't even have the presence of mind to jerk his hand away—much to his good fortune. He learned later that in his host's country, taking his hand was a sign of great respect and friendship. Jerking his hand away from his host would have been considered a major insult.[80]
- One company selling a razor aimed at women in Holland created a television commercial showing a woman's leg and the product's name. Unfortunately, the ad was completely ineffective because the product's name was slang for "homosexual," and Dutch viewers thought the leg belonged to a transvestite.[81]
- One CEO and a group of managers in a Silicon Valley company went on a business trip to Asia dressed as they normally would in California. Casually attired in T-shirts and baseball caps, the CEO and his aides wanted to show their hosts that they were not restricted to doing business the traditional way. Their conservative Asian hosts, however, saw the young managers as arrogant and buffoonish.[82]

Entrepreneurs who fail to learn the differences in the habits and customs of the cultures in which they hope to do business are at a distinct disadvantage. "In the business arena . . . a lack of understanding of cultures and business practices can be as great an impediment to structuring and implementing a business transaction as an error in the basic assumptions of the deal," says one international expert.[83]

When American businesspeople enter international markets for the first time, they often are amazed at the differences in foreign cultures' habits and customs. Understanding and heeding these often subtle cultural differences is one of the most important keys to international business success. Conducting a business meeting with a foreign executive in the same manner as one with an American businessperson could doom the deal from the outset. "People can be on their best American behavior and go overseas and offend the locals," says one expert in international etiquette.[84] Business customs and behaviors that are acceptable—even expected—in this country may be taboo in others. For instance, American businesspeople usually conduct business in an informal fashion, using slang and calling one another by their first names (or nicknames). Executives in France, England, and Japan, however, would consider such behavior to be rude and highly improper. In many countries such as Spain, China, and Japan, entrepreneurs will need an ample dose of the "three Ps": patience, patience, patience. Unlike the United States, nothing in these cultures, including business, happens fast!

YOU BE THE CONSULTANT . . .

On to Japan . . .

"It's hard to believe how far we've come in just 14 months," said Tad Meyers, president of Specialty Building Supplies.

"That's true," chimed in Dee Rada, the company's sales manager. "When we started this whole international business idea, we had no notion of how complicated and time-consuming it would be. We were total rookies! Which one of us would have thought we'd be trying to sell our products in Japan?"

"True. But now it looks like the big payoff is just around the corner," said Hal Milam, the company's sales manager.

As the three celebrated their success to date in taking their company into the exciting world of international business, each was proud of what they had accomplished and how much they had learned in just a short time. Yet, their excitement was tinged with anxiety because Meyers and Rada were about to travel abroad to meet with several potential distributors for the company's building supplies. In one week, they would be in Japan, negotiating deals with businesspeople they had never met before and whose native language neither spoke.

"I do know how to say 'thank you' in Japanese," said Rada. "It's pronounced 'Du-omo ah-ree-gha-toe.'"

"You should probably find out how to say, 'Where's the bathroom?' and 'We're lost. Will you take us home?' in Japanese too," joked Milam.

"You know, we probably should find out as much as possible about how the Japanese do business," said Meyers. "I understand their way is very different from what we're used to."

"Such as . . . ?" said Milam.

"You know . . . little things," said Rada. "I do know that they make a big deal out of exchanging business cards. They call it *meishi.* In fact, I've had cards printed for Tad and me with English on one side and Japanese on the other. When you take their cards, don't just stick them in your pocket or scribble notes on the backs of them. That's an insult."

"No kidding?" said Meyers. "I didn't know that."

"I thought we'd take some gifts along to give to our guests," said Rada. "I've had them wrapped in pure white paper with these big red ribbons."

"What are you going to give them?" asked Milam.

"I had some nice golf shirts printed up with our logo, and then I had them add the U.S. and Japanese flags crossing one another."

"Cool! They ought to love that."

"We're taking along some brochures detailing our product line, emphasizing its unique nature and superb quality," said Rada. "I had them printed in Japanese just for this trip. Full color, lots of pictures. They cost a few bucks, but I thought it would be a wise investment."

"We will be on a tight schedule while we're there," said Meyers. "We'll have to get right down to business, close the deal, and then get on to the next appointment. There won't be a lot of time for sight-seeing or small talk. I hope we can get these deals done fast and we can get back on the plane for home."

"I just hope they don't try to impress us with authentic Japanese meals while we're there," said Meyers. "I'm pretty much a 'meat-and-potatoes' kind of guy. I don't do sushi. But I hear that McDonald's has restaurants in Japan. I just hope there's one nearby!"

"Where's your sense of adventure?" teased Rada. "Remember: We can't afford to offend our guests. We need to be sensitive to their culture, habits, and tastes. I just hope we don't do something unintentional that upsets somebody."

1. Evaluate the preparations that Meyers and Rada have made for their upcoming trip to Japan.
2. Using the library and the World Wide Web as resources,* read about Japanese culture and Japanese business practices. Based on what you learn, would you advise them to change any of their plans? Explain.

**The Do's and Taboos of International Trade, Gestures: The Do's and Taboos of Body Language Around the World,* and *Do's and Taboos Around the World: A Guide to International Behavior,* all by Roger Axtell, are excellent resources.

INTERNATIONAL TRADE AGREEMENTS

5. Describe the trade agreements that will have the greatest influence on foreign trade in the twenty-first century: GATT and NAFTA.

In an attempt to boost world trade, nations have created a variety of trade agreements over the years. While hundreds of agreements are paving the way for freer trade across the world, two stand out with particular significance: the General Agreement on Tariffs and Trade (GATT) and the North American Free Trade Agreement (NAFTA).

GATT

Created in 1947, the General Agreement on Tariffs and Trade (GATT) became the first global tariff agreement. It was designed to reduce tariffs among member nations and to facilitate trade across the globe. Originally signed by the United States and 22 other nations, GATT has grown to include 124 member countries today. Together, they account for nearly 90 percent of world trade. The latest round of GATT negotiations, called the Uruguay Round, was completed in December 1993 and took effect on July 1, 1995. Prior to this round, the trade agreement had been successful in reducing trade barriers around the world by 90 percent since its inception. Average tariffs in industrial countries had fallen to just 4.7 percent, down from an average of 40 percent in 1947.

The Uruguay Round continues this trend. Negotiators reduced the remaining industrial tariffs by 40 percent, established new rules governing dumping goods at unfairly low prices, strengthened the global protection of patents, and cut the level of government subsidies on agricultural products. In addition, negotiators agreed to form a World Trade Organization (WTO) with more power to settle trade disputes among member nations than GATT had.

NAFTA

The North American Free Trade Agreement (NAFTA) created a free trade area among Canada, Mexico, and the United States. A free trade area is an association of countries that have agreed to knock down trade barriers—both tariff and nontariff—among partner nations. Under the provisions of NAFTA, these barriers were eliminated for trade among the three countries, but each remained free to set its own tariffs on imports from nonmember nations.

NAFTA forged a unified U.S.–Canada–Mexico market of 370 million people with a total annual output of $6.5 trillion dollars of goods and services. This important trade agreement binds together the three nations on the North American continent into a single trading unit stretching from the Yukon to the Yucatan. Because Canada and the United States already had a free trade agreement in effect, the businesses that have benefited most from NAFTA are those already doing business—or those wanting to do business—with Mexico. Before NAFTA took effect on January 1, 1994, the average tariff on U.S. goods entering Mexico was 10 percent. Under NAFTA, these tariffs will be reduced to zero on most goods over the next 10 to 15 years.[85]

NAFTA's provisions have encouraged trade among the three nations, have made that trade more profitable and less cumbersome, and have opened up new opportunities for a wide assortment of companies. In its first five years, NAFTA has spurred an increase in trade among the three nations, but small businesses have been slow to benefit from this trade agreement. A study by FedEx concludes that the treaty has helped only about 20 percent of U.S. small businesses.[86]

Treatment Products Limited

Jeff Victor, manager of Treatment Products Limited, a manufacturer of car cleaners and waxes, says that NAFTA is the primary force behind his company's boom in exports to Mexico. Treatment Products had tried to enter the Mexican market years earlier but met with limited success, primarily because of stiff Mexican tariffs that ran as high as 20 percent. Within months of NAFTA's passage, the tariffs began dropping, and the company's export sales to Mexico began climbing, ultimately totaling 20 percent of company sales. Today, Treatment Products has landed contracts with every major retail chain in Mexico.[87]

Among NAFTA's provisions are:

- *Tariff reductions.* Immediate reductions—then gradual phasing out—of most tariffs on goods traded among the three countries.
- *Nontariff barriers eliminated.* Elimination of most nontariff barriers to free trade by 2008.
- *Simplified border processing.* Mexico, in particular, opens its border and interior to U.S. truckers and simplifies border processing.
- *Tougher health and safety standards.* Industrial standards involving worker health and safety become more stringent and more uniform.
- *Increased protection of patents, copyrights, and trademarks.* Under NAFTA, companies have greater protection of their patents, trademarks, and copyrights across national borders.

CONCLUSION

For a rapidly growing number of small businesses, conducting business on a global basis will be the key to future success. To remain competitive, businesses must assume a global posture. Global effectiveness requires managers to be able to leverage workers' skills, company resources, and customer know-how across borders and throughout cultures across the world. Managers also must concentrate on maintaining competitive costs structures and a focus on the core of every business—the customer! Robert G. Shaw, CEO of International Jensen Inc., a global maker of home and automobile stereo speakers, explains the importance of retaining that customer focus as his company pursues its global strategy: "We want [our customers] to have the attitude of [our] being across the street. If we're going to have a global company, we have to behave in that mode—whether [the customer is] across the street—or seven miles, seven minutes, or 7,000 miles away."[88]

Few businesses can afford the luxury of basing the definition of their target market on the boundaries of their home nation's borders. The manager of one global business, who discourages the use of the word *domestic* among his employees, says, "Where's 'domestic' when the world is your market?"[89] Although there are no sure-fire rules for going global, small businesses wanting to become successful international competitors should observe these guidelines:[90]

- Make yourself at home in all three of the world's key markets—North America, Europe, and Asia. This triad of regions is forging a new world order in trade that will dominate global markets for years to come.
- Develop new products for the world market.
- Familiarize yourself with foreign customs and languages; constantly scan, clip, and build a file on other cultures—their lifestyles, values, customs, and business practices.
- "Glocalize"—make global decisions about products, markets, and management, but allow local employees to make tactical decisions about packaging, advertising, and service.
- Train employees to think globally, send them on international trips, and equip them with state-of-the-art communications technology.
- Hire local managers to staff foreign offices and branches.
- Do whatever seems best wherever it seems best, even if people at home lose jobs or responsibilities.
- Consider using partners and joint ventures to break into foreign markets you cannot penetrate on your own.

By its very nature, going global can be a frightening experience for an entrepreneur considering the jump into international markets. Most of those who have already made the jump, however, have found that the benefits outweigh the risks and that their companies are much stronger because of it.

CHAPTER SUMMARY

1. Explain why "going global" has become an integral part of many small companies' strategies.
   - Businesses large and small can no longer consider themselves to be domestic companies in this hotly competitive, global environment. But gaining a foothold in foreign markets is no easy task for a small company.
   - Companies that move into international business can reap many benefits, including offsetting sales declines in the domestic market; increasing sales and profits; extending their products' life cycles; lowering manufacturing costs; improving competitive position; raising quality levels; and becoming more customer oriented.
2. Describe the eight principal strategies small businesses have for going global (launching a World Wide Web site, relying on trade intermediaries, joint ventures, foreign licensing, international franchising, countertrading and bartering, exporting, and establishing international locations).
   - One of the simplest and least expensive ways for a small company to launch a global business effort is to create a Web site. The Web gives businesses of any size tremendous marketing potential all over the globe. With a well-designed Web site, a small company can extend its reach to customers anywhere in the world at a reasonable cost. Of the 320 million World Wide Web users across the globe, 184 million of them live outside the United States.
   - Businesses looking to "go global" do not have to chart their courses alone. Trade intermediaries such as export management companies, export trading companies, manufacturer's export agents, export merchants, and resident buying offices can serve as a small company's "export department."
   - In a domestic joint venture, two or more U.S. small companies form an alliance for the purpose of exporting their goods and services abroad. In a foreign joint venture, a domestic small business forms an alliance with a company in the target nation.
   - Some small businesses enter foreign markets by licensing businesses in other nations to use their patents, trademarks, copyrights, technology, processes, or products.
   - Franchising has become a major export industry for the United States. The International Franchise Association estimates that more than 20 percent of the nation's 4,000 franchisers have outlets in foreign countries.
   - Some countries lack a hard currency that is convertible into other currencies, so companies doing business there must rely on countertrading or bartering. A countertrade is a transaction in which a business selling its goods in a foreign country agrees to promote investment and trade in that country. Bartering involves trading goods and services for other goods and services.
   - Although small companies account for 97 percent of the companies involved in exporting, they generate only 31 percent of the dollar value of the nation's exports. However, small companies, realizing the incredible profit potential it offers, are making exporting an ever-expanding part of their marketing plans.
   - Once established in international markets, some small businesses set up permanent locations there. Although they can be very expensive to establish and maintain, international locations give businesses the opportunity to stay in close contact with their international customers.
3. Explain how to build a thriving export program.
   - Building a successful export program takes patience and research. Steps include realizing that even the tiniest firms have the potential to export; analyzing your product or service; analyzing your commitment to exporting; researching markets and picking your target; developing a distribution strategy; finding your customer; finding financing; shipping your goods; and collecting your money.
4. Discuss the major barriers to international trade and their impact on the global economy.
   - Three domestic barriers to international trade are common: the attitude that "we're too small to export"; lack of information on how to get started in global trade; and a lack of available financing.
   - International barriers include tariffs, quotas, embargoes, dumping, political barriers, and cultural barriers.
5. Describe the trade agreements that will have the greatest influence on foreign trade into the twenty-first century—GATT and NAFTA.
   - Created in 1947, the General Agreement on Tariffs and Trade (GATT), the first global tariff agreement, was designed to reduce tariffs among member nations and to facilitate trade across the globe.
   - The North American Free Trade Agreement (NAFTA) created a free trade area among Canada, Mexico, and the United States. The agreement created an association that knocked down trade barriers—both tariff and non-tariff—among these partner nations.

DISCUSSION QUESTIONS

1. What is "global thinking"? Why must small businesses think globally?
2. What forces are driving small businesses into international markets?
3. What advantages does going global offer a small business owner? Risks?
4. Outline the eight strategies that small businesses can use to go global.
5. Describe the various types of trade intermediaries small business owners can use. What functions do they perform?
6. What is a domestic joint venture? A foreign joint venture? What advantages does taking on an international partner through a joint venture offer? Disadvantages?
7. What mistakes are first-time exporters most likely to make? Outline the steps a small company should follow to establish a successful export program.
8. What are the benefits of establishing international locations? Disadvantages?
9. Describe the barriers businesses face when trying to conduct business internationally. How can a small business owner overcome these obstacles?
10. What is a tariff? A quota? What impact do they have on international trade?
11. What impact have the GATT and NAFTA trade agreements had on small companies wanting to go global? What provisions are included in these trade agreements?
12. What advice would you offer an entrepreneur interested in launching a global business effort?

Beyond the Classroom...

1. Talk to a student from a foreign country. What products and services are most needed? How does the business system there differ from ours? How much government regulation affects business? What cultural differences exist? What trade barriers has the government erected?

2. a. Review several current business publications and prepare a brief report on which nations seem to be the most promising for U.S. entrepreneurs. What steps should a small business owner take to break into those markets?

   b. Which nations are the least promising? Why?

3. Select a nation that interests you (perhaps one to which you have traveled) and prepare a report on its business customs and practices. How are they different from those in the United States? Similar? What advice would you offer an entrepreneur interested in conducting business there?

4. Interview a small business owner whose company is engaged in international trade. On which of the eight strategies outlined in this chapter does he or she rely? How did the company get started in international trade? To which countries does the company sell its products and services? What cultural differences exist in the way business is conducted there and in the United States? What barriers does the company face in international trade?

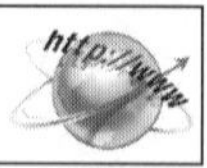

We invite you to visit this book's companion Web site at **www.prenhall.com/Zimmerer.**

Leading the Growing Company and Planning for Management Succession

CHAPTER 14

LEARNING OBJECTIVES

Upon completion of this chapter, you will be able to:

1. Explain the challenges involved in the entrepreneur's role as leader and what it takes to be a successful leader.
2. Describe the importance of hiring the right employees and how to avoid making hiring mistakes.
3. Explain how to build the kind of company culture and structure to support the entrepreneur's mission and goals and to motivate employees to achieve them.
4. Discuss the ways in which entrepreneurs can motivate their workers to higher levels of performance.
5. Describe the steps in developing a management succession plan for a growing business that will allow a smooth transition of leadership to the next generation.

The best leadership does not generate followers; it generates other leaders.

—David Stauffer

Next to doing a good job yourself, the greatest joy is in having someone else do a first-class job under your direction.

—William Feather

1. Explain the challenges involved in the entrepreneur's role as leader and what it takes to be a successful leader.

leadership—*the process of influencing and inspiring others to work to achieve a common goal and then giving them the power and the freedom to achieve it.*

LEADERSHIP IN THE NEW ECONOMY

To be successful, an entrepreneur must assume a wide range of roles, tasks, and responsibilities, but none is more important than the role of leader. Some entrepreneurs are uncomfortable in this role, but they must learn to be effective leaders if their companies are to grow and reach their potential. **Leadership** is the process of influencing and inspiring others to work to achieve a common goal and then giving them the power and the freedom to achieve it. Without leadership ability, entrepreneurs—and their companies—never rise above mediocrity. Yet, leadership is not an easy role to learn; the skills needed to do it well are constantly changing. In the past, many small business managers relied on fear and intimidation as their primary leadership tools. Today, however, the workforce is more knowledgeable, more skilled, and demands a more sophisticated style of leadership.

The rapid pace of change in the new economy also is placing new demands on leaders. Technology is changing the ways in which people work, the ways in which the various parts of an organization operate and interconnect, and the ways in which competitors strive for market dominance. To remain in the game, companies must operate at this new speed of business, and that requires a new style of leadership. Leaders of small companies must gather information and make decisions with lightning speed, and they must give workers the resources and the freedom to solve problems and exploit opportunities as they arise.

eBay, Inc.

Meg Whitman, president and CEO of Internet marketplace eBay, Inc., says that her company's rapid growth rate of 40 to 50 percent per quarter creates new challenges for its workforce, especially its leaders. "That pace absolutely changes the leadership challenge," she says. "Every three months we become a different company." With virtually endless opportunities opening up, eBay, like many companies in the new economy, faces the danger of losing its focus and becoming sidetracked. Whitman claims that "one of my most important jobs is keeping the company focused on our core values and on the business that we want to exploit."[1]

Like Meg Whitman, many entrepreneurs have discovered that the old style of leadership has lost its effectiveness and that they must develop a new, more fluid and flexible style of leadership that better fits the needs of modern workers and competitive conditions.

Until recently, experts compared the leader's job to that of a symphony orchestra conductor. Like the symphony leader, an entrepreneur made sure that everyone in the company was playing the same score; coordinated individual efforts to produce a harmonious sound; and directed the orchestra members as they played. The conductor (entrepreneur) retained virtually all of the power and made all of the decisions about how the orchestra would play the music without any input from the musicians themselves. Today's successful entrepreneur, however, is more like the leader of a jazz band, which is known for its improvisation, innovation, creativity, and free-wheeling style. Max DePree, former head of Herman Miller, Inc., a highly successful office furniture manufacturer, explains the connection this way:

> Jazz band leaders must choose the music, find the right musicians, and perform—in public. But the effect of the performance depends on so many things—the environment, the volunteers playing in the band, the need for everybody to perform as individuals and as a group, the absolute dependence of the leader on the members of the band, the need for the followers to play well. . . . The leader of the jazz band has the beautiful opportunity to draw the best out of the other musicians. We have much to learn from jazz-band leaders, for jazz, like leadership, combines the unpredictability of the future with the gifts of individuals.[2]

Management and leadership are not the same, yet both are essential to a small company's success. Leadership without management is unbridled; management without leadership is uninspired. Leadership gets a small business going; management keeps it going.

Source: Reprinted with permission of Kings Feature Syndicate

In other words, leaders are the architects of small businesses; managers are the builders. Some entrepreneurs are good managers yet are poor leaders; others are powerful leaders but are weak managers. The best bet for the latter is to hire people with solid management skills to help them execute the vision they have for their companies. Stephen Covey, author of *Principle-Centered Leadership,* explains the difference between management and leadership this way:

> Leadership deals with people; management deals with things. You manage things; you lead people. Leadership deals with vision; management deals with logistics toward that vision. Leadership deals with doing the right things; management focuses on doing things right. Leadership deals with examining the paradigms on which you are operating; management operates within those paradigms. Leadership comes first, then management, but both are necessary.[3]

Leadership and management are intertwined; one without the other means that a small business is going nowhere. Leadership is especially important for companies in the growth phase, when entrepreneurs are hiring employees (often for the first time) and must keep the company and everyone in it focused on its mission as growth tests every seam in the organizational structure. At this stage, selling everyone in the company on the mission, goals, and objectives for which the leader is aiming is crucial to a business's survival and success.

Effective leaders should exhibit the following behaviors:

- *Create a set of values and beliefs for employees and passionately pursue them.* Employees look to their leaders for guidance in making decisions. Leaders should be like beacons in the night, constantly shining light on the principles, values, and beliefs on which they founded their companies. Herb Kelleher, CEO of Southwest Airlines, one of the most successful airline companies in the world, says, "It's up to the CEO to set an inspirational example of how workers should behave."[4]

- *Define and then constantly reinforce the vision they have for the company.* Effective leaders have a clear vision of where they want their companies to go, and they concentrate on communicating that vision to those around them. Michael Useem, an expert on leadership and author of *The Leadership Moment,* says, "You can't tell people too often where you're going, what the vision is."[5]
- *Respect and support their employees.* To gain the respect of their employees, leaders must first respect those who work for them. Successful leaders put their employees first. They know that a loyal, dedicated workforce is a company's most valuable resource, and they treat their employees that way.
- *Set the example for their employees.* A leader's words ring hollow if he fails to "practice what he preaches." Few signals are transmitted to workers faster than a leader who sells employees on one set of values and principles and then acts according to a different set. One manager explains, "You've got to walk the talk. If there is ambiguity about your message or values, people will opt out."[6] That is why integrity is perhaps the most important determinant of a leader's effectiveness.
- *Create a climate of trust in the organization.* Leaders who demonstrate integrity soon win the trust of their employees, an essential ingredient in the success of any organization. Honest, open communication and a consistent pattern of leaders doing what they say they will do serve to build trust in a business. An environment of trust becomes especially important when a company encounters a crisis. Workers are willing to band together to tackle the problem facing the company without sensing the need to protect their turf.
- *Focus employees' efforts on challenging goals and keep them driving toward those goals.* When asked by a student intern to define leadership, one entrepreneur said, "Leadership is the ability to convince people to follow a path they have never taken before to a place they have never been—and upon finding it to be successful, to do it over and over again."[7]
- *Provide the resources employees need to achieve their goals.* Effective leaders know that workers cannot do their jobs well unless they have the tools they need. They not only provide workers with the physical resources they need to excel but also the necessary intangible resources such as training, coaching, and mentoring.
- *Communicate with their employees.* Leaders recognize that helping workers see the company's overarching goal is just one part of effective communication; encouraging employee feedback and then listening is just as vital. In other words, they know that communication is a two-way street. Open communication takes on even greater importance when a company faces a difficult or uncertain future.
- *Value the diversity of their workers.* Smart business leaders recognize the value of their workers' varied skills, abilities, backgrounds, and interests. When channeled in the right direction, diversity can be a powerful weapon in achieving innovation and maintaining a competitive edge. Good leaders get to know their workers and to understand the diversity of their strengths. Especially important to young workers in the new economy is a leader's capacity for empathy, the ability to see things from another person's viewpoint (see Figure 14.1).
- *Celebrate their workers' successes.* Effective leaders recognize that workers want to be winners and do everything they can to encourage top performance among their people. The rewards they give are not always financial; in many cases, it may be as simple as a handwritten congratulatory note.
- *Encourage creativity among their workers.* Rather than punish workers who take risks and fail, effective leaders are willing to accept failure as a natural part of innovation and creativity. They know that innovative behavior is the key to future success and do everything they can to encourage it among workers.
- *Maintain a sense of humor.* One of the most important tools a leader can have is a sense of humor. Without it, work can become dull and unexciting for everyone.

Southwest Airlines

Southwest Airlines' Herb Kelleher is famous for creating a work environment where fun is the watchword. Kelleher, who appeared at one employee function on a Harley-Davidson motorcycle and at another dressed as Elvis Presley, encourages employees to have fun at

Accountability to Shareholders. The capital that the entrepreneur manages and risks is no longer just his own. The manager of a publicly held firm is accountable to the company's shareholders. Indeed, the law requires that he recognize and abide by a relationship built on trust. Profit and return on investment become the primary concerns for investors. If the stock price of a newly public company falls, shareholder lawsuits are inevitable. Investors whose shares decline in value often sue the company's managers for fraud and the failure to disclose the potential risks to which their investment exposes them.

Pressure for Short-Term Performance. In privately held companies, entrepreneurs are free to follow their strategies for success, even if those strategies take years to produce results. When a company goes public, however, entrepreneurs quickly learn that shareholders are impatient and expect results immediately. Founders are under constant pressure to produce growth in profits and in market share, which requires them to maintain a delicate balance between short-term results and long-term strategy.

Timing. As impatient as they can be, entrepreneurs often find the time demands of an IPO frustrating and distracting. Managing the IPO takes time away from managing the company. Working on an IPO can consume as much as 75 percent of top managers' time.

Example

When one company that produced sports entertainment software decided to go public, managers spent so much time focusing on the demands of the IPO that the company failed to get a new product to market in time for the Christmas season. Because it missed this crucial deadline, the company never recovered and went out of business.[47]

During this time, the company also runs the risk that the market for IPOs or for a particular issue may go sour. Factors beyond managers' control, such as declines in the stock market and potential investors' jitters, can quickly slam shut a company's "window of opportunity" for an IPO. For instance, when the market for high-tech stocks soured recently, several companies planning IPOs, including InternetConnect (broadband networking services) and Inventa technologies (business-to-business e-commerce solutions), withdrew their proposed stock offerings.[48]

THE REGISTRATION PROCESS. Taking a company public is a complicated, bureaucratic process that usually takes several months to complete. Many experts compare the IPO process to running a corporate marathon, and both the company and its management team must be in shape and up to the grueling task. Two years after his company's IPO, Michael Hislop, CEO of Il Fornaio, a chain of upscale Italian restaurants in California, has some regrets about operating as a publicly held company. "We'd [still] be a private company if I knew then what I know today," he says.[49]

The typical entrepreneur *cannot* take his company public alone. It requires a coordinated effort from a team of professionals, including company executives, an accountant, a securities attorney, a financial printer, and at least one underwriter. The key steps in taking a company public follow.

Choose the Underwriter. The single most important ingredient in making a successful IPO is selecting a capable **underwriter (or investment banker).** The underwriter serves two primary roles: helping to prepare the registration statement for the issue and promoting the company's stock to potential investors. The underwriter works with company managers as an advisor in preparing the registration statement that must be filed with the SEC, promoting the issue, pricing the stock, and providing after-market support. Once the registration statement is finished, the underwriter's primary job is selling the company's stock through an underwriting syndicate of other investment bankers it develops.

underwriter (or investment banker)—*a financial company that serves two important roles: helping to prepare the registration statement for an issue and promoting the company's stock to potential investors.*

letter of intent—*an agreement between the underwriter and the company about to go public that outlines the details of the deal.*

Negotiate a Letter of Intent. To begin an offering, the entrepreneur and the underwriter must negotiate a **letter of intent,** which outlines the details of the deal. The letter of intent covers a variety of important issues, including the type of underwriting, its size and price range, the underwriter's commission, and any warrants and options included. It almost always states that the underwriter is not bound to the offering until it is executed—usually the day before or the day of the offering. However, the letter usually creates a binding obligation for the company to pay any direct expenses the underwriter incurs relating to the offer.

registration statement—*the document a company must file with the SEC that describes both the company and its stock offering and discloses information about the risks of investing.*

Prepare the Registration Statement. After a company signs the letter of intent, the next task is to prepare the **registration statement** to be filed with the Securities and Exchange Commission (SEC). This document describes both the company and the stock offering and discloses information about the risks of investing. It includes information on the use of the proceeds, the company's history, its financial position, its capital structure, any risks it faces, its managers, and many other details. The statement is extremely comprehensive and may take months to develop. To prepare the statement, entrepreneurs must rely on their team of professionals.

File with the SEC. When the statement is finished (with the exception of pricing the shares, proceeds, and commissions, which cannot be determined until just before the issue goes to market), the company officially files the statement with the SEC and awaits the review of the Division of Corporate Finance. The division sends notice of any deficiencies in the registration statement to the company's attorney in a comment letter. The company and its team of professionals must correct all of the deficiencies in the statement noted by the comment letter. Finally, the company files the revised registration statement, along with a pricing amendment (giving the price of the shares, the proceeds, and the commissions).

Wait to Go Effective. While waiting for the SEC's approval, the managers and the underwriters are busy. The underwriters are building a syndicate of other underwriters who will market the company's stock. (No sales can be made prior to the effective date of the offering, however.) The SEC also limits the publicity and information a company may release during this quiet period (which officially starts when the company reaches a preliminary agreement with the managing underwriter and ends 90 days after the effective date).

road show—*a gathering of potential syndicate members sponsored by the managing underwriter for the purpose of promoting a company's initial public offering.*

Securities laws do permit a **road show,** a gathering of potential syndicate members sponsored by the managing underwriter. Its purpose is to promote interest among potential underwriters in the IPO by featuring the company, its management, and the proposed deal. The managing underwriter and key company officials barnstorm major financial centers at a grueling pace.

Ashford.com

During the road show for Ashford.com, an online retailer of luxury goods that raised $75 million in its IPO, top managers courted potential investors on two continents, hitting 24 cities in just 14 days! "In one day, we had a breakfast meeting in Frankfurt, flew to Paris for lunch meetings, then to New York, and finally to Baltimore," says David Gow, Ashford's chief financial officer. "We kept gaining hours. It was the never-ending day."[50]

On the last day before the registration statement becomes effective, the company signs the formal underwriting agreement. The final settlement, or closing, takes place a few days after the effective date for the issue. At this meeting, the underwriters receive their shares to sell and the company receives the proceeds of the offering.

Typically, the entire process of going public takes from 60 to 180 days, but it can take much longer if the issuing company is not properly prepared for the process.

the opportunity to sell stock through private placements without actually going public. In a private placement, the company sells its shares directly to private investors without having to register them with the SEC.

PatchLink.com

For example, PatchLink.com, a company that provides software solutions for businesses over the Internet, raised $5.6 million in a private equity placement made through online broker-dealer OffRoad Capital. PatchLink used the money to expand its engineering, sales, and marketing staff and to launch new products. "We ended up raising more money than we expected to without giving up any more of the company," says CEO Sean Moshir.[52]

A *Rule 505* offering has a higher capital ceiling than an SCOR offering ($5 million) in a 12-month period but imposes more restrictions (no more than 35 nonaccredited investors, no advertising of the offer, and more stringent disclosure requirements).

Rule 506 imposes no ceiling on the amount that can be raised, but, like a Rule 505 offering, it limits the issue to 35 nonaccredited investors and prohibits advertising the offer to the public. There is no limit on the number of accredited investors, however. Rule 506 also requires detailed disclosure of relative information, but the extent depends on the amount of the offering.

These Regulation D rules minimize the expense and the time required to raise equity capital for small businesses. Fees for private placements typically range from 1 to 5 percent rather than the 7 to 13 percent underwriters normally charge for managing a public offering. Offerings made under Regulation D do impose limitations and demand certain disclosures, but they only require a company to file a simple form (Form D) with the SEC within 15 days of the first sale of stock.

SECTION 4(6). Section 4(6) covers private placements and is similar to Regulation D, Rules 505 and 506. It does not require registration on offers up to $5 million if they are made only to accredited investors.

INTRASTATE OFFERINGS (RULE 147). Rule 147 governs intrastate offerings, those sold only to investors in a single state by a company doing business in that state. To qualify, a company must be incorporated in the state, maintain its executive offices there, have 80 percent of its assets there, derive 80 percent of its revenues from the state, and use 80 percent of the offering proceeds for business in the state. There is no ceiling on the amount of the offering.

TravelFest

Gary Hoover put up just $5,000 of his own money and convinced several private investors to purchase $850,000 worth of preferred stock to launch TravelFest, a retail store that caters to travelers. As the company grew, Hoover decided to make an intrastate offering under Rule 147 to raise the money he needed for expansion. He registered the offering in TravelFest's home state of Texas, where resident investors purchased $5.6 million in convertible preferred stock.[53]

REGULATION A. Regulation A, although currently not used often, allows an exemption for offerings up to $5 million over a 12-month period. Regulation A imposes few restrictions, but it is more costly than the other types of exempted offerings, usually running between $80,000 and $120,000. The primary difference between an SCOR offering and a Regulation A offering is that a company must register its SCOR offering only in the states in which it will sell its stock; in a Regulation A offering, the company also must file an offering statement with the SEC. Like an SCOR offering, a Regulation A offering allows a company to sell its shares directly to investors.

Blue Fish Clothing Inc.

For instance, when Blue Fish Clothing Inc., an all-natural women's clothing company, needed money to fuel its rapid growth, founder Jennifer Barclay decided to make a direct public offering under Regulation A, selling 800,000 shares at $5 each. "Banks wouldn't provide the funds, and venture capital firms wanted a huge percentage of the company," says Barclay. Blue Fish publicized its $4 million offering through mailings, advertise-

ments, fish-shaped hanging tags on its garments, and word of mouth among its base of 30,000 loyal customers and supporters. Blue Fish, whose shares are traded on the Chicago Stock Exchange, used the offering's proceeds to build new retail stores, to install a computerized information system, and to expand its management team.[54]

DIRECT STOCK OFFERINGS. Many of the simplified registrations and exemptions discussed previously give entrepreneurs the power to sidestep investment bankers and sell their companies' stock offerings directly to investors and, in the process, save themselves thousands of dollars in underwriting fees. By cutting out the underwriter's commission and many legal and most registration fees, entrepreneurs willing to handle the paperwork requirements and to market their own shares can make direct public offerings (DPOs) for about 6 percent of the total amount of the issue, compared with 13 percent for a traditional stock offering.

Real Goods Trading Company

Real Goods Trading Company, a retailer of environmentally friendly products, was a pioneer of direct public offerings over the Web. In 1991, the company engineered a successful DPO that raised $1 million and followed with a second DPO two years later that generated $3.6 million. Many of the company's customers became investors. In fact, managers discovered that once customers became shareholders, they purchased nearly twice as much merchandise as customers who were not shareholders! Managers at Real Goods found that using the Web to reach potential investors was not only one of the best bargains, but also one of the most effective methods for selling its stock to the public. Real Goods Trading Company's stock is traded on both the NASDAQ and on the Pacific Stock Exchange.[55]

The World Wide Web (WWW) has opened a new avenue for DPOs and is one of the fastest-growing sources of capital for small businesses. Much of the Web's appeal as a fund-raising tool stems from its ability to reach large numbers of prospective investors very quickly and at a low cost. "This is the only form of instantaneous international contact with an enormous population," says one Web expert. "You can put your prospectus out to the world."[56] Companies making direct stock offerings on the Web most often make them under either Regulation A or Regulation D. DPOs work best for companies that have a single product or related product lines and a base of customers who are loyal to the company. In fact, the first company to make a successful DPO over the Internet was Spring Street Brewing, a microbrewery founded by Andy Klein. Klein raised $1.6 million in a Regulation A offering in 1996. Companies that make successful DPOs of their stock over the Web must meet the same standards as companies making stock offerings using more traditional methods. Experts caution Web-based fund seekers to make sure their electronic prospectuses meet SEC and state requirements.

Table 11.4 provides a summary of the major types of exemptions and simplified offerings. Of these, the limited offerings and private placements are most commonly used.

Foreign Stock Markets

Sometimes foreign stock markets offer entrepreneurs access to equity funds more readily than U.S. markets. The United Kingdom's Unlisted Securities Market and the Vancouver Stock Exchange are especially attractive to small companies. Both encourage equity listings of small companies, and the costs of offerings are usually lower than in the United States. Kim Jones raised $2.5 million for his software development company with an initial public offering made through the Vancouver Stock Exchange. Jones, who had explored the possibility of a U.S. IPO, found that he could get a better price for his company's stock on the Vancouver market.[57]

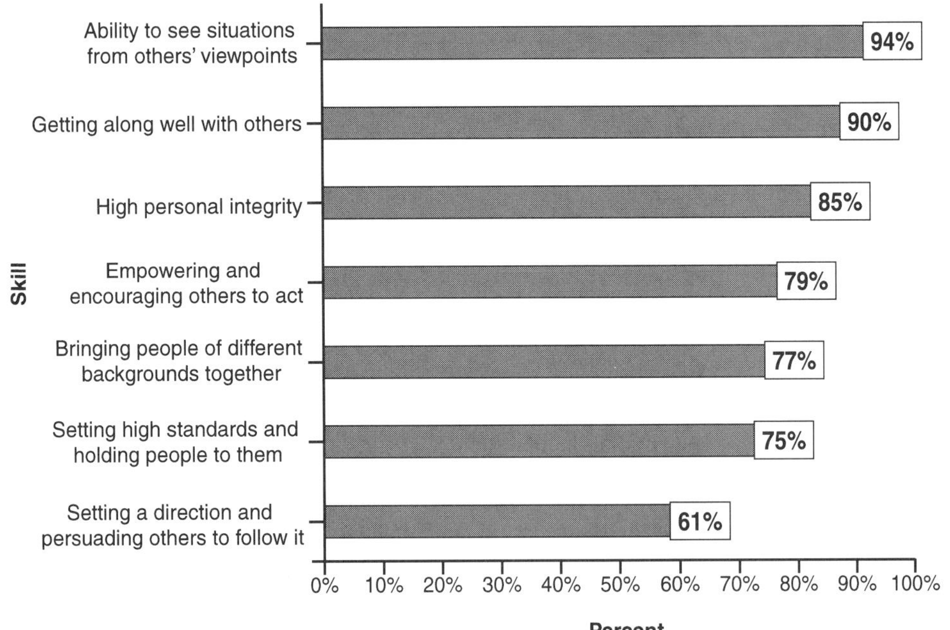

FIGURE 14.1 Generation X on Leadership: Skills That Gen Xers Value Most in Leaders

Source: Peter D. Hart Research Associates, Inc., 1999.

work. Flight attendants sometimes pop out of overhead bins as passengers board, or they tell jokes over the plane's public address system. Crews have been known to liven up the preflight safety demonstrations with song and dance routines. On Halloween, employees dress up in costumes and hand out cake to passengers. The culture of fun at Southwest Airlines has built an esprit de corps that gives Southwest a unique advantage that competitors cannot match, and crown prince Herb Kelleher is its architect.[8]

- *Create an environment in which people have the motivation, the training, and the freedom to achieve the goals they have set.* Richard Teerlink, retired CEO of motorcycle maker Harley-Davidson, warns leaders against focusing excessively on ensuring their own success at the expense of the company and their subordinates. "As a leader, your principal job is to create an operating environment where *others* can do great things," he says.[9] Great leaders know that *their* success is determined by the success of their followers.
- *Become a catalyst for change when change is needed.* With market and competitive climates changing so rapidly, small company leaders must make sure that their companies change along with them. Although leaders must cling to the values and principles that form the bedrock of their companies, they must be willing to change, sometimes radically, the policies, procedures, and processes within their businesses. If a company is headed in the wrong direction, the leader's job is to recognize that and to get the company moving in the right direction. Effective leaders understand that to preserve their businesses, they must change them constantly.
- *Keep their eyes on the horizon.* Effective leaders are never satisfied with what they and their employees accomplished yesterday. They know that yesterday's successes are not enough to sustain their companies indefinitely. They see the importance of building and maintaining sufficient momentum to carry their companies to the next level. A proactive stance is essential. "Your job is to look around corners and see the future," says one expert on leadership.[10]

Leading an organization, whatever its size, is one of the biggest challenges any manager faces. Yet, for an entrepreneur, leadership success is one of the key determinants of the company's success. In addition to the uncertainties of dealing with people, the job of the organizational leader is constantly changing. One business writer explains, "The new leader is . . . the one who sees clearly the goal, shares repeatedly and forcefully the vision, provides the tools, trains and enables co-workers to manage and improve their processes, remains persistent in the face of adversity, and inspires others to take an ownership position in the completion of the mission—by example."[11]

Table 14.1 offers useful tips on how to become a successful leader in the new economy. To be effective, a small business leader must perform four vital tasks:

- Hire the right employees and constantly improve their skills.

TABLE 14.1
Tips for Becoming a Successful Leader in the New Economy

Source: Adapted from "Make Yourself a Leader," Fast Company, June 1999, tear-out booklet.

Leadership in the old economy often meant that leaders had all of the answers and that employees were to follow them to the "promised land." The new economy and its workers, however, require a different style of leadership, one that involves more listening, empowering, delegating, and team building. The following tips can help you become a more effective leader in the new economy.

1. *Leaders are both confident and modest.* Being a leader is not about making yourself more powerful; it's about making the people around you more powerful.

2. *Leaders are authentic.* No one believes in a leader who fails to "walk the talk." Leadership requires integrity and sincerity. These characteristics are the building blocks of trust.

3. *Leaders are good listeners.* Successful leaders know that some of the best ideas come from the people who actually do a job every day, and these leaders are willing to listen to employees. The chief enemy of involving workers in decision making is grandiosity, the belief that the leader has all of the answers.

4. *Leaders are good at giving encouragement, and they are never satisfied.* Leaders constantly test their own stamina and courage and those of the people in their organizations by raising the standards of performance. They are an organization's top cheerleaders when people succeed and are supportive when people fail.

5. *Leaders make unexpected connections.* Leaders arrange for interaction among people who otherwise might not get together. Then they listen for innovative ideas that result from those interactions and act on them.

6. *Leaders provide direction.* However, that does not mean that they have all of the answers, as the Wizard of Oz seemed to have. Modern leaders know how to ask probing, revealing questions of others that provide insight into the best course of action. Steve Miller, a manager at Royal Dutch Shell, says, "No leader can have all the answers . . . The actual solutions about how best to meet the challenges of the moment have to be made by the people closest to the action . . . The leader has to empower these frontline people, to challenge them, to provide them with the resources they need, and then hold them accountable."

7. *Leaders protect their people from danger and expose them to reality.* The surest way leaders can protect their organizations from danger is to keep everyone focused on the vision. Exposing people to reality means forcing the organization to face up to the need for change. Although many people are uncomfortable with and resistant to change, leaders know that their organizations must change or risk being left behind.

8. *Leaders create change and stand for values that don't change.* Although change is essential to an organization's survival, a leader must protect those values and principles that are central to the company's core. Losing these would cause the company to lose its identity. However, leaders must always watch for habits and assumptions that the company must change if it is to continue to prosper.

9. *Leaders lead by example.* Leaders recognize that they are always under the microscope and that workers are always interpreting leaders' actions. That is why leaders must live by the principles they espouse. Leaders use small gestures to send big messages.

10. *Leaders don't blame; they learn.* Leaders know that creativity and innovation carry with them the risk of failure. They also understand that creativity and innovation are essential to the organization's survival and do not punish people just because they tried and failed. Their attitude is: Try, fail, learn, and try again.

11. *Leaders look for and network with other leaders.* Successful leaders are *not* Lone Rangers. They look for allies and the opportunity to network with others so they can learn to become more effective leaders. Leaders build relationships.

12. *The job of the leader is to make more leaders.* In the old economy, the assumption was that an organization needed just one strong leader. In the new economy, the organization with the most leaders usually wins! Your ultimate challenge is not just to become an effective leader but to create more leaders in your company.

- Build an organizational culture and structure that allow both workers and the company to reach their potential.
- Motivate workers to higher levels of performance.
- Plan for "passing the torch" to the next generation of leadership.

HIRING THE RIGHT EMPLOYEES

2. Describe the importance of hiring the right employees and how to avoid making hiring mistakes.

The decision to hire a new employee is an important one for every business, but its impact is magnified many times in a small company. Every new hire a business owner makes determines the heights to which the company can climb—or the depths to which it will plunge. "Bad hires" can poison a small company's culture. They are also incredibly expensive, and no organization, especially small ones, can afford too many of them. One study concluded that an employee hired into a typical entry-level position who quits after six months costs a company about $17,000 in salary, benefits, and training. In addition, the intangible costs—time invested in the new employee, lost opportunities, reduced morale among coworkers, and business setbacks—are seven times the direct costs of a "bad hire." In other words, the total price tag for this "bad hire" is about $136,000![12]

Avoiding Hiring Mistakes

As crucial as finding good employees is to a small company's future, it is no easy task. In the new economy, increased demand for skilled knowledge workers and relatively low levels of unemployment have combined to create a hiring crisis for business owners. The severity of this labor shortage will worsen, too, thanks to demographic trends. Currently, the ratio of workers to retirees is 4:1. By 2011, when baby boomers begin retiring, this ratio will begin dropping, reaching 3:1 in 2020 before bottoming out at 2:1 in 2030.[13] Competition among businesses for quality workers is intense, and the battle for talent has taken on higher stakes. Rapidly advancing technology and increasing globalization give companies of all sizes access to most of the same resources so that the balance of competitive power shifts to those companies with superior human resources. Under these circumstances, the tendency is for companies to lower their hiring standards just to fill jobs, but that can be dangerous. One expert estimates that under normal conditions, one out of every three employees a business hires makes a solid contribution, one is a marginal worker, and one is a hiring mistake.[14] However, if an entrepreneur circumvents the normal selection process, seven out of ten employment decisions fail.[15]

PowerPick International

Richard Froelich, president of PowerPick International, a consulting company that helps manufacturers and distributors reengineer their operations, says that this type of hiring mistake cost his company thousands of dollars. Froelich's poor hiring decision was especially harmful because his 35-employee company relies on recommendations from satisfied customers to bring in new business. "If our most recent project doesn't end up with an enthusiastic referral, we have a problem," he says.[16]

Even though the importance of hiring decisions is magnified in small companies, small businesses are most likely to make hiring mistakes because they lack the human resources experts and the disciplined hiring procedures large companies have. The hiring process is informal and its results are often unpredictable. In the early days of a company, entrepreneurs rarely take the time to create job descriptions and specifications; instead, they usually hire people because they know or trust them rather than for their job skills. Then, as the company grows, business owners hire people to fit in around these existing employees, often creating a very unusual, inefficient organizational structure built around jobs that are poorly planned and designed.

The following guidelines can help small business managers avoid making costly hiring mistakes.

ELEVATE RECRUITING TO A STRATEGIC POSITION IN THE COMPANY. Assembling a quality workforce begins with a sound recruiting effort. By investing time and money at this crucial phase of the staffing process, entrepreneurs can generate spectacular savings down the road by avoiding costly hiring mistakes. The recruiting process also is the starting point for building quality into a company. "The first few people you recruit into key positions determine the DNA for the growing company," says Brad Smart, a recruiting expert.[17] Recruiting is so important that smart top managers no longer leave the task to human resource managers, choosing instead to become actively involved in the process themselves. In many companies, managers never stop recruiting, even though they may not be looking to hire at that moment.

Hoffman Agency

After one top post in his Silicon Valley public relations company remained vacant for 10 months, president Lou Hoffman decided to make his recruiting efforts more systematic and consistent. He now recruits constantly because Hoffman knows that by the time he finds a suitable candidate, a job will be open. Hoffman compares his recruiting strategy to painting the Golden Gate Bridge. By the time the paint crews finish the job, it's time to start over again.[18]

Attracting a pool of qualified job candidates requires not only constant attention but also creativity, especially among small companies that find it difficult to match the more generous offers large companies make. With a sound recruiting strategy and a willingness to look in new places, however, small companies can hire and retain high-caliber employees. The following techniques will help.

Look inside the company first. One of the best sources for top prospects is right inside the company itself. A promotion-from-within policy not only serves as an incentive for existing workers to upgrade their skills but it also avoids nasty surprises: An entrepreneur already knows the employee's work habits, and the employee already understands the company's culture.

Encourage employee referrals. To cope with the shortage of available talent, many companies are offering their employees (and others) bonuses for referring candidates who come to work and stay for a certain time period. Employees serve as reliable screens because they do not want to jeopardize their reputations with their employer. Rewards companies offer to employees for successful referrals range from weekend getaways to cash. At Redback Network, a high-tech networking company, referral bonuses range from $2,500 to $10,000 (for especially hard-to-fill positions)![19]

Perficient

Perficient, an Internet services company, was growing so fast that CEO Jack McDonnell needed to increase the company's workforce from just nine workers to 180 in just 10 months. Using outside recruiters proved to be too time-consuming and costly, so McDonnell offered employees $5,000 referral bonuses. The incentive worked so well that one team leader posted an ad on an Internet job bulletin board and began interviewing candidates who responded on weekends. His efforts led to three new hires for Perficient and $15,000 in bonuses for himself![20]

Make employment advertisements stand out. Getting employment ads noticed in traditional media is becoming more difficult because they get lost in the swarm of ads from other companies.

Signal Corporation

Roger Mody, founder of Signal Corporation, an information technology provider, uses humor to make his employment ads stand out and to communicate the sense of fun in the company's culture. One recent ad ran a photo of Mody after a company pie-eating contest with the tag line "And you should see us on casual day."

Although newspaper ads still top employers' list of ad placement, some businesses are attracting candidates through other media. For instance, Michael Pehl, CEO of I-Cube, an information technology company in Boston, dropped newspaper ads in favor of a series of billboards (including one targeting drivers leaving Logan Airport) that advertise I-Cube as "An Incredible Place to Work."[21]

Use the Internet as a recruiting tool. The Internet is one of the fastest-growing media for employment ads because it offers tremendous reach at a relatively low cost and is effective, especially for companies recruiting high-tech workers. Many companies post jobs on several of the many job bulletin boards on the Web, including Monster Board, Career Mosaic, Career Web, and Headhunter. Darlene Chapin, recruiting manager at Cheetah Technologies, a computer network-management company, says the Internet has proved to be the most effective recruiting tool she uses. Chapin emphasizes that the Internet is just one part of a comprehensive recruiting effort. Cheetah also uses ads in newspapers and technical publications, employee referrals, career fairs, college visits, and other methods to find employees.[22]

The wording of Internet ads is extremely important. In their ads, entrepreneurs should be specific about the qualifications a candidate must have and should describe the benefits their companies offer in an honest but appealing manner. One Internet start-up company was very successful in attracting high-quality applicants with an Internet ad that read: "Salary 10 percent over the going rate. Total autonomy and challenging assignments. All the resources you need. Flexibility on when and where you work."[23]

Recruit on campus. For many employers college and university campuses remain an excellent source of workers, especially for entry-level positions. After screening résumés, a recruiter can interview a dozen or more high-potential students in just one day. On some campuses, competition for the best students is so intense that companies are going to extreme measures. One dot-com business searching for high-demand computer science majors on a prestigious West coast campus offered new BMWs as a signing bonus for its new hires![24]

Forge relationships with schools and other sources of workers. Some employers have found that forging long-term relationships with schools and other institutions to be a valuable source of workers.

Advanced Micro-Electronics

Steve Burkhart, CEO of Advanced Micro-Electronics, a computer maintenance and networking company, works closely with the students and faculty at nearby Vincennes University to create a computer repair program. Internships, part-time jobs, and faculty sabbaticals benefit both the university and Advanced Micro-Electronics. Students get hands-on experience, and Burkhart has a pool of quality workers from which to draw. More than 50 of Burkhart's 150 employees are Vincennes graduates.[25]

Recruit "retired" workers. Many businesses are drawing on a pool of workers that has much to offer: senior citizens. With a lifetime of work experience and time on their hands, "retired" workers can be the ideal solution to many entrepreneurs' labor problems. Currently, only 13 percent of Americans over the age of 65 work, but changes in Social Security laws now allow them to earn more.

Bonne Bell

Bonne Bell, a small cosmetics firm in Lakewood, Ohio, has 87 senior citizens on its payroll. (The oldest is 89, and 30 percent of them are over 70.) The company's owner, Jess Bell, who is 75, says the program has been a huge success for the seniors and her company. "We realized that many seniors are simply not ready to retire when they reach 65," she says.[26]

Consider using offbeat recruiting techniques. To attract the workers they need to support their growing businesses, some entrepreneurs have resorted to rather unconventional recruiting techniques, such as the following:[27]

- Sending young recruiters to party with college students on spring break.
- Having an airplane tow a banner over competitors' offices that reads "Don't make a career mistake."
- Launching a monthly industry networking meeting for local workers at Internet companies.

- Keeping a file of all of the workers mentioned in the "People on the Move" column in the business section of the local newspaper and then contacting them a year later to see if they are happy in their jobs.

Offer what workers want. Of course, adequate compensation is an important consideration for job candidates, but other less tangible factors also weigh in a prospect's decision to accept a job. For young knowledge workers especially, a fun work environment can be as important as salary. "Fun and a sense of humor are becoming minimum job requirements," says one staffing professional.[28] In fact, a survey by O'Conner Kenny Partners found that the factor topping college students' list when evaluating a job offer is "a fun working environment."[29]

Sterling Direct

That's why Bill Ziercher, CEO of Sterling Direct, a direct-marketing company, emphasizes having fun in his business. Employees have a contest for the sloppiest desk of the week, in which the winner has the privilege of displaying "Pat the Pig" (a Beanie Baby) on his or her desk. Ziercher also holds regular events such as the recent on-site beach party, complete with karaoke machine and Super Soaker water guns, and often gives away tickets to sporting events as part of other contests.[30]

CREATE PRACTICAL JOB DESCRIPTIONS AND JOB SPECIFICATIONS. Small business owners must recognize that what they do *before* they ever start interviewing candidates for a position determines to a great extent how successful they will be at hiring winners. The first step is to perform a **job analysis,** the process by which a firm determines the duties and nature of the jobs to be filled and the skills and experience required of the people who are to fill them. Without a proper job analysis, a hiring decision is, at best, a coin toss. The first objective of a job analysis is to develop a **job description,** a written statement of the duties, responsibilities, reporting relationships, working conditions, methods and techniques used, and materials and equipment used in a job. A results-oriented job description explains what a job entails and the duties the person filling it is expected to perform. One business owner uses the following "recipe" for writing job descriptions in his company: job title, job summary, duties to be performed, nature of supervision, job's relationship to others in the company, working conditions, definitions of job-specific terms, and general comments needed to clarify any of the preceding categories.[31]

job analysis—*the process by which a firm determines the duties and nature of the jobs to be filled and the skills and experience required of the people who are to fill them.*

job description—*a written statement of the duties, responsibilities, working conditions, and materials and equipment used in a job.*

Preparing job descriptions is a task most small business owners overlook; however, this may be one of the most important parts of the hiring process because it creates a "blueprint" for the job. One hiring consultant explains, "It's important for a small company to spend a good amount of time defining the tasks that need to be accomplished." If they do, he says, "they've gone a long way toward finding the right person."[32] Without this blueprint, a manager tends to hire the person with experience whom they like the best. Useful sources of information for writing job descriptions include the manager's knowledge of the job, the worker(s) currently holding the job, and the *Dictionary of Occupational Titles (D.O.T),* available at most libraries. The *Dictionary of Occupational Titles,* published by the Department of Labor, lists more than 20,000 job titles and descriptions and serves as a useful tool for getting a small business owner started when writing job descriptions. Table 14.2 provides an example of the description drawn from the *D.O.T.* for an unusual job.

TABLE 14.2
A Sample Job Description from the *Dictionary of Occupational Titles*
 # 413.687—014 in D.O.T.

Worm Picker—gathers worms to be used as fish bait; walks about grassy areas, such as gardens, parks, and golf courses and picks up earthworms (commonly called dew worms and nightcrawlers). Sprinkles chlorinated water on lawn to cause worms to come to the surface and locates worms by use of lantern or flashlight. Counts worms, sorts them, and packs them into containers for shipment.

The second objective of a job analysis is to create a **job specification,** a written statement of the qualifications and characteristics needed for a job stated in terms such as education, skills, and experience. A job specification shows the small business manager what kind of person to recruit and establishes the standards an applicant must meet to be hired. When writing job specifications, some managers define the traits a candidate needs to do a job well. Does the person have to be a good listener, empathetic, well organized, decisive, a "self-starter?" Should she have experience in Java or C++ programming? One of the best ways to develop a list of these traits is to study the top performers currently working for your company, focusing on the characteristics that make them successful. Table 14.3 provides an example that links the tasks for a sales representative's job (drawn from a job description) to the traits or characteristics a small business owner identified as necessary to succeed in that job.

job specification—*a written statement of the qualifications and characteristics needed for a job stated in terms such as education, skills, and experience.*

PLAN AN EFFECTIVE INTERVIEW. Once an entrepreneur knows what she must look for in a job candidate, she can develop a plan for conducting an informative job interview. Too often, small business owners go into an interview unprepared, and as a result, they fail to get the information they need to judge the candidate's qualifications, qualities, and suitability for the job. Conducting an effective interview requires an entrepreneur to know what she wants to get out of the interview in the first place and to develop a series of questions to extract that information. The following guidelines will help an owner develop interview questions that will give her meaningful insight into an applicant's qualifications, personality, and character.

Develop a series of core questions and ask them of every candidate. To give the screening process more consistency, smart business owners rely on a set of relevant questions they ask in every interview. Of course, they also customize each interview using impromptu questions based on an individual's responses.

Ask open-ended questions (including on-the-job scenarios) rather than questions calling for "yes or no" answers. These types of questions are most effective because they encourage candidates to talk about their work experience in a way that will disclose the presence or the absence of the traits and characteristics the business owner is seeking.

Create hypothetical situations candidates would be likely to encounter on the job and ask how they would handle them. Building the interview around such questions gives the owner a preview of the candidate's work habits and attitudes.

Probe for specific examples in the candidate's past work experience that demonstrate the necessary traits and characteristics. A common mistake interviewers make is failing to get candidates to provide the details they need to make an informed decision.

Ask candidates to describe a recent success and a recent failure and how they dealt with them. Smart entrepreneurs look for candidates who describe both success and failure with

TABLE 14.3
Linking Tasks from a Job Description to the Traits Necessary to Perform a Job Successfully

Job Task	Trait or Characteristic
Generate and close new sales	"outgoing"; persuasive; friendly
Make 15 "cold calls" per week	"self-starter"; determined; optimistic; independent; confident
Analyze customers' needs and recommend proper equipment	good listener; patient; empathetic
Counsel customers about options and features needed	organized; polished speaker; "other oriented"
Prepare and explain financing methods	honest; "numbers oriented"; comfortable with computers and spreadsheets
Retain existing customers	customer oriented; relationship builder

equal enthusiasm because they know that peak performers put as much into their failures as they do their successes and usually learn something valuable from their failures.

Table 14.4 shows an example of some interview questions one manager uses to uncover the traits and characteristics he seeks in a top-performing sales representative.

CONDUCT THE INTERVIEW. An effective interview contains three phases: breaking the ice, asking questions, and selling the candidate on the company.

Breaking the ice. In the opening phase of the interview the manager's primary job is to diffuse the tension that exists because of the nervousness of both parties. Many skilled interviewers use the job description to explain the nature of the job and the company's culture to the applicant. Then they use "icebreakers," questions about a hobby or special interest, to get the candidate to relax. For instance, to loosen up one very tense but promising candidate, one entrepreneur asked about his hobby, military history. "He launched into a description of the Battle of Midway that was so enthralling, I told him, 'Since you can come across like that, I'm going to give you a shot,'" recalls the business owner. "He went on to be a star salesman."[33]

Asking questions. During the second phase of the interview, the employer asks the questions from her question bank to determine the applicant's suitability for the job. Her primary job at this point is to listen. Effective interviewers spend about 25 percent of the interview talking and about 75 percent listening. They also take notes during the interview to help them ask follow-up questions based on a candidate's comments and to evaluate a candidate after the interview is over. Experienced interviewers also pay close attention to a candidate's nonverbal clues, or body language, during the interview. They know that candidates may be able to say exactly what they want with their words, but that their body language does not lie! One interviewer refers to an applicant's body language as "music," saying, "An interviewer who listened only to the words without taking the music . . . into account would miss [much] make-or-break data about the candidate."[34]

Small business owners must be careful to make sure they avoid asking candidates illegal questions. At one time, interviewers could ask wide-ranging questions covering just about every area of an applicant's background. Today interviewing is a veritable minefield of legal liabilities, waiting to explode in the unsuspecting interviewer's face. Although the Equal Employment Opportunity Commission (EEOC), the government agency responsible for

TABLE 14.4
Interview Questions for Candidates for a Sales Representative Position

Trait or Characteristic	Question
"outgoing"; persuasive; friendly; "self-starter"; determined; optimistic; independent; confident	How do you persuade reluctant prospects to buy?
good listener; patient; empathetic; organized; polished speaker; "other oriented"	What would you say to a fellow salesperson who was getting more than his share of rejections and was having difficulty getting appointments?
honest; customer oriented, relationship builder	How do you feel when someone questions the truth of what you say? What do you do in such situations?
Other questions:	If you owned a company, why would you hire yourself? If you were head of your department, what would you do differently? How do you recognize the contributions of others in your department? If you weren't in sales, in what other job would you be?

enforcing employment laws, does not outlaw specific questions, it does recognize that some questions can result in employment discrimination. If a candidate files charges of employment discrimination against a company, the burden of proof shifts to the employer to prove that all preemployment questions are job related and are nondiscriminatory. In addition, many states have passed laws that forbid the use of certain questions or screening tools in interviews. To avoid trouble, business owners should keep in mind why they are asking a particular question. The goal is to find someone who is qualified to do the job well. For instance, to test job candidates' ability to reason and to think quickly, Tony Petricciani, CEO of Single Source Systems, a computer systems integration company, asks "Why do they make manhole covers round?" (Answer: Any other geometric shape could fall through the hole if it shifts.) To test candidates' creativity, Robert Baden, owner of a software development company, likes to ask applicants, "If we were standing next to a skyscraper, and I gave you a barometer, how could you figure out how tall the building is?" (Answer: There isn't one really, but one innovative candidate said he would locate the building's janitor and offer to exchange the barometer for the information about the building's height.)[35] By steering clear of questions about subjects that are peripheral to the job itself, employers are less likely to ask questions that will land them in court. Wise business owners ask their attorneys to review their bank of questions before using them in an interview. Table 14.5 offers a quiz entitled "Is It Legal?" to help you understand the kinds of questions that are most likely to create charges of discrimination.

Selling the candidate on the company. In the final phase of the interview, the employer tries to sell her company to desirable candidates. This phase begins by allowing the candidate to ask questions about the company, the job, or other issues. Again, experienced interviewers note the nature of these questions and the insights they give into the candidate's personality. This part of the interview offers the employer a prime opportunity to explain to the candidate why her company is an attractive place to work. Remember: The best candidates will have other offers, and it's up to you to make sure they leave the interview wanting to work for your company. Finally, before closing the interview, the employer should thank the candidate and tell him what happens next (e.g., "We'll be contacting you about our decision within two weeks.")

Table 14.6 describes 10 interviewing mistakes small business owners must avoid.

CHECK REFERENCES. Small business owners should take the time to check every applicant's references. Although many business owners see checking references as a formality and pay little attention to it, others realize the need to protect themselves (and their customers) from hiring unscrupulous workers. Is it really necessary? Yes! According to the Society for Human Resource Management, more than half of candidates either exaggerate or falsify information about their previous employment on their résumés or job application.[36] Checking references thoroughly can help employers uncover false or exaggerated information. Rather than contacting only the references listed, experienced employers call applicants' previous employers and talk to their immediate supervisors to get a clear picture of the applicant's job performance, character, and work habits. After talking with the references a candidate for a top financial position in his company had listed, one entrepreneur took the time to contact the applicant's previous employers. He soon discovered that the candidate had stolen money and misused company credit cards in a previous job. None of the references listed mentioned the incident.

Experienced small business owners understand that the hiring process provides them with one of the most valuable raw materials their companies count on for success—capable, hardworking people. They know that hiring an employee is not a single event but the beginning of a long-term relationship. Table 14.7 on page 498 features some strange but true incidents that employers have encountered during the selection process.

TABLE 14.5

Is It Legal?

Some interview questions can land an employer in legal hot water. Review the following interview questions and then decide whether you think each one is "legal" or "illegal."

Legal	Illegal	
❑	❑	1. Are you currently using illegal drugs?
❑	❑	2. Have you ever been arrested?
❑	❑	3. Do you have any children or are you planning to have children?
❑	❑	4. When and where were you born?
❑	❑	5. Is there any limit on your ability to work overtime or to travel?
❑	❑	6. How tall are you? How much do you weigh?
❑	❑	7. Do you drink alcohol?
❑	❑	8. How much alcohol do you drink per week?
❑	❑	9. Would your religious beliefs interfere with your ability to do this job?
❑	❑	10. What contraceptive practices do you employ?
❑	❑	11. Are you HIV-positive?
❑	❑	12. Have you ever filed a lawsuit or a workers' compensation claim against a former employer?
❑	❑	13. Do you have any physical or mental disabilities that would interfere with your doing this job?
❑	❑	14. Are you a U.S. citizen?
❑	❑	15. What is your race?

Small business owners can use the "OUCH" test as a guide for determining whether an interview question might be considered discriminatory:

- Does the question *Omit* references to race, religion, color, sex, or national origin?
- Does the question *Unfairly* screen out a particular class of people?
- Can you *Consistently* apply the question to every applicant?
- Does the question *Have* job-relatedness and business necessity?

Answers: 1. Legal. 2. Illegal. Employers cannot ask about an applicant's arrest record, but they can ask if a candidate has ever been convicted of a crime. 3. Illegal. Employers cannot ask questions that would lead to discrimination against a particular group (e.g., women). 4. Illegal. The Civil Rights Act of 1964 bans discrimination on the basis of race, color, sex, religion, or national origin. 5. Legal. 6. Illegal. Unless a person's physical characteristics are important for high job performance (e.g., lifting 100-pound sacks of flour), employers cannot ask candidates such questions. 7. Legal. 8. Illegal. Notice the fine line between question 7 and question 8; this is what makes interviewing a challenge! 9. Illegal. This question would violate the Civil Rights Act of 1964. 10. Illegal. What relevance would this have to an employee's job performance? 11. Illegal. Under the Americans with Disabilities Act, which prohibits discrimination against people with disabilities, people with HIV or AIDS are considered "disabled." 12. Illegal. Workers who file such suits are protected from retribution by a variety of federal and state laws. 13. Illegal. This question also would violate the Americans with Disabilities Act. 14. Illegal. This question violates the Civil Rights Act of 1964. 15. Illegal. Employers cannot ask questions about a job applicant's race. The Civil Rights Act of 1964 bans discrimination on the basis of race, color, sex, religion, or national origin.

TABLE 14.6
10 Interviewing Mistakes

1. Succumbing to pressure to hire fast, which often arises as a result of failing to begin the search process far enough in advance. Plan ahead!

2. Falling victim to the halo effect, the tendency to attribute a host of positive attributes (e.g., intelligence, sense of humor, honesty, etc.) to a candidate based on one positive attribute (e.g., well-spoken). This tendency is called the horn effect when it works in a negative fashion.

3. Asking leading or "canned" questions, those in which it is obvious to everyone involved, including the job applicant, what the "right" answer should be.

4. Talking too much. A common mistake inexperienced interviewers make is doing most of the talking while the candidate has to work hard just to become part of the conversation. Remember the 25/75 rule!

5. Failing to take notes during the interview. Jotting down key points, questions, and impressions as they occur will be of tremendous value when it's time to make a final decision about a particular candidate.

6. Accepting generalizations from a candidate. Effective interviewers probe for specific results and examples from candidates so they can verify applicants' qualifications and characteristics more objectively.

7. Asking questions that could lead to charges of discrimination and land the company in a nasty lawsuit. Keep questions job focused and consistent.

8. Failing to check a candidate's references. This routine procedure may uncover inconsistencies and falsehoods in the candidate's background. It can help small business owners avoid making a "bad hire" and lawsuits charging them with "negligent hiring." Ask former employers, "Would you hire him or her again?"

9. Making snap judgments. A common tendency among novice interviewers is to make a decision about a candidate in the first few minutes of an interview and then to spend the rest of the interview justifying that decision.

10. Committing candidate-order error. Experienced interviewers know that the order in which they interview candidates can affect their evaluations of them. Most recent candidates tend to have the advantage. Be aware of this tendency.

BUILDING THE RIGHT CULTURE AND STRUCTURE

3. Explain how to build the kind of company culture and structure that support an entrepreneur's mission and goals and motivate employees to achieve them.

Culture

A company's **culture** is the distinctive, unwritten, informal code of conduct that governs its behavior, attitudes, relationships, and style. It is the essence of "the way we do things around here" and often originates with the founder. In many small companies, culture plays as important a part in gaining a competitive edge as strategy does. It has a powerful impact on the way people work together in a business, how they do their jobs, and how they treat their customers. Company culture manifests itself in many ways—from how workers dress and act to the language they use. For instance, at some companies, the unspoken dress code requires workers to wear suits and ties, but at many companies such as Trilogy Software, employees routinely come to work in jeans and T-shirts. Employees at this unique software maker set their own hours and eat catered lunches and dinners in the company conference room, and every Friday afternoon, Trilogy gives employees a chance to mix and mingle at its Party on the Patio. The culture at Trilogy is more an extension of college life than a transition to corporate life, which suits the company's young, college-educated workforce just fine![37]

culture—*the distinctive, unwritten, informal code of conduct that governs an organization's behavior, attitudes, relationships, and style.*

In many companies, the culture creates its own language. At Disney, for instance, workers are not "employees"; they are "cast members." They don't merely go to work; their jobs are "parts in a performance." Disney's customers are "guests." When a cast member treats someone to lunch, it's "on the mouse." Anything negative—such as a cigarette butt on a walkway—is "a bad Mickey," and anything positive is "a good Mickey."

TABLE 14.7
Strange but True!

Sources: "Hiring Horrors," Your Company, April 1999, p. 14; Mike B. Hall, "From Job Applicants," Joke-of-the-Day, **<wwwjoke oftheday.com>,** *December 8, 2000; Karen Axelton, "L-L-L-Losers!" Business Start-Ups, April 2000, p. 13.*

If you read enough résumés, conduct enough interviews, and check enough references, sooner or later you will encounter something bizarre. Consider the following examples (all true).

- After having lunch with a job candidate, a business owner took the applicant to her office for more discussion. The discussion ended, however, when the applicant dozed off and began snoring.
- On his résumé, one candidate wrote, "It's best for employers if I not work with people." Another included the following note: "Please don't misconstrue my 14 jobs as job hopping. I have never quit a job."
- An interviewer told a man applying for a clerical job to relax before taking a typing test. He flexed his fingers and then took off his shirt!
- An applicant at a warehouse proudly reviewed his prison record for the interviewer, adding that he had gotten much better: Rather than steal from his grandmother, he stole only from her friends and beat her up only if she refused to give him money.
- When asked about his personal interests, one candidate proudly replied, "Donating blood. Fourteen gallons so far!"
- At the end of an interview, the interviewer asked the candidate if he had any questions. His only question: "Is the office close enough so I can run home three times a day to Water Pik my teeth?"
- One candidate asked if he could bring his rabbit to work with him, adding that the rabbit was focused and reliable but that he himself had been fired before.
- When asked about why he had been fired from several jobs, one candidate said that his previous employers had conspired to place an evil curse on him.
- When asked what his ideal job would be, another candidate showed his lack of motivation, saying, "To lie in bed all day, eat chocolate, and get paid."

Recommendations from previous employers can sometimes be quite entertaining, too. The following are statements from managers about workers.

- "Works well when under constant supervision and cornered like a rat in a trap."
- "This young lady has delusions of adequacy."
- "A photographic memory but with the lens cover glued on."
- "If you were to give him a penny for his thoughts, you'd get change."
- "If you stand close enough to him, you can hear the ocean."

Creating a culture that supports a company's strategy is no easy task, but the entrepreneurs that have been most successful at it "have a set of overarching beliefs that serve as powerful guides for everyday action—and that are reinforced in a hundred different ways, both symbolic and substantive," explains one business writer.[38] Culture arises from an entrepreneur's consistent and relentless pursuit of a set of core values that everyone in the company can believe in.

Amy's Ice Creams

For instance, Amy Miller, founder of Amy's Ice Creams, a seven-store chain of gourmet ice cream shops, knows that her company's competitive edge comes not only from selling quality products and friendly service but also from selling entertainment. Miller hires employees who enjoy performing for customers. They juggle their serving spades, toss scoops of ice cream to one another behind the counter, and dance on top of the freezer. They offer free ice cream to customers who will sing, dance, or recite poetry. Walking into an Amy's Ice Cream shop, customers might see employees wearing pajamas (on Sleep-Over Night) or masks (on Star Wars Night); candles decorating the store (on Romance Night) or strobe lights (on Disco Night). Because of the culture Miller has created, employees know that part of their jobs is to create fun and entertainment for their customers; that's what keeps them coming back! Amy Miller has created a culture that values creativity in her company. It allows her employees to have fun, entertains the customers, and keeps the company growing at 30 percent a year![39]

YOU BE THE CONSULTANT . . .

Last Resort Workers

Tim Rock, owner of Rock Communications, a small printing company in Newton, Iowa, was concerned about the growth prospects of his business, not because of a lack of customers but because of a lack of employees. Rock was constantly short of workers. "Every day we'd be one or two or five people short," says Rock. Then one day, while driving down Interstate 80, Rock thought of the prison just outside of town and the number of men there with plenty of time on their hands. Why not hire some of the inmates to work at his company? Rock wrote a letter to the warden, and soon a dozen inmates arrived at Rock Communications for work. It was an extreme solution to Rock's labor problems, but it is one that has worked out well. In the five years that Rock has been hiring workers from the prison, he has seen dozens of men cycle through his business. Most stayed only a few months, but 13 former prisoners are now full-time employees. Rock also has a team of 60 part-time senior adults who assemble advertising inserts the company prints every week.

Like Tim Rock, Jerry Strahan is always in desperate need of employees. Strahan, general manager of Lucky Dogs, Inc., a 52-year-old hot dog vending company in New Orleans, is constantly looking for vendors to take the company's 22 pushcarts out into the streets of the French Quarter. Although the work requires no special skills other than the ability to make change, finding workers in New Orleans willing to push 650-pound carts shaped like a giant hot dog is tougher than it sounds. "We've tried ads and employment agencies," says Strahan, "but most people can't take the streets." Lucky Dogs now recruits at mission centers for the homeless and at the Salvation Army. "We've tried to get better people," Strahan says, "but with no success." Many show up on Lucky Dogs' doorstep after hearing about the opportunity for work from current employees.

The result is a rather motley workforce made up of drifters, alcoholics, petty thieves, and brawlers that is, at best, a challenge to manage and to motivate. "I tell the vendors, 'You need to be neat, you need to be clean, you need to be on time, you need to be polite, and you need to be conscientious,'" says Strahan. "But the vendors say to me, 'Jerry, if I could be all those things, I'd be working in an office on Poydras Street. Can we go for three out of five?'" One off-and-on employee has stayed with the company for 14 years, despite his occasional tendency to show up for work dressed like Doris Day or John Wayne.

Strahan is willing to go for three out of five and, frankly, is happy when he gets it. Erratic behavior and actions that would get workers fired on the spot in most companies is acceptable at Lucky Dogs. "We make a set of rules, and they're good for about 10 minutes," says Strahan, only half joking. "You have to be very forgiving when they're not followed; otherwise, you don't have the carts out. You can't eliminate the madness. Sometimes you can control it." At Lucky Dogs, for instance, it's not unusual for employees to scream at their supervisors, to show up drunk, or to fail to show up for work altogether. "Most companies will say, 'If you show up for work drunk, you're fired,'" says Strahan. "Here, if you show up for work drunk, I've got to give you a C-minus because you showed up."

With the pool of potential workers so small, Lucky Dogs does not turn away many applicants. Those who are clean, able to make change, and have an ID get a chance to work. Strahan does not bother to check references on applicants, either. In an attempt to keep employee theft to a minimum, Lucky Dogs requires vendors to turn in their receipts often during a shift. Strahan does have one rule that, if broken, results in immediate dismissal: Any vendor caught stealing from another vendor will be fired.

To manage (if you can call it that) this rather unruly crew of workers, Strahan admits that he breaks almost every conventional rule in the field of human resources management. Yet, he somehow manages to pull it off. He's been involved in shouting matches with employees and then a few minutes later ends up lending them money. When one worker showed up for his shift so intoxicated that he could barely stand, Strahan asked him to explain. "I thought I was pregnant," said the man. Without missing a beat, Strahan deadpanned, "In your condition, you probably shouldn't be working. Why don't you go home and we'll talk about it tomorrow?" Perhaps Strahan's style is best described as management by looking the other way. Although he has worked in his current job at Lucky Dogs for more than 28 years, he doubts that he could succeed at another company. "I don't think my skills would translate to a normal company," he says.

1. Why must employers such as Tim Rock and Jerry Strahan resort to such extreme measures to find workers?
2. What techniques would you recommend for motivating workers such as those described in this feature?
3. Are there other options for recruiting employees that you might suggest Rock and Strahan explore?

Sources: Adapted from Ann Harrington, "Does Anybody Here Want a Job?" *Fortune,* May 15, 2000, pp. 489–498; Leigh Buchanan, "The Taming of the Crew," *Inc.,* August 1999, pp. 27–40.

Nurturing the right culture in a company can enhance a company's competitive position by improving its ability to attract and retain quality workers and by creating an environment in which workers can grow and develop. In fact, as a younger generation of employees enters the workforce, companies are finding that offering a "cool" culture gives them an edge in attracting the best workers. Like Amy's Ice Creams, these companies embrace nontraditional, relaxed, fun cultures that incorporate concepts such as casual dress, virtual teams, telecommuting, flexible work schedules, on-site massages, cappucinos in company cafeterias, and other cutting-edge concepts. Although creating a "cool" culture involves both art and science, the companies that have been most successful tend to rely on certain principles, which follow.[40]

RESPECT FOR WORK AND LIFE BALANCE. Cool companies recognize that their employees have lives away from work. One recent study of Generation X workers found that those companies that people most wanted to work for erased the traditional barriers between home life and work life by making it easier for employees to deal with the pressures they face away from their jobs. These businesses offer flexible work schedules, part-time jobs, job sharing, telecommuting, sabbaticals, on-site day care, and dry cleaning.

Ipswitch, Inc.

Roger Greene, founder of Ipswitch, Inc., a software company in Lexington, Massachusetts, has built his company on the concept of work–life balance. Company policy discourages employees from working late into the night and on weekends, and Greene recently raised the minimum vacation period for employees to five weeks a year. "Live life as it goes along and do neat things while you're working and enjoy every year of your life," he advises his employees. Ipswitch's rate of employee turnover is half that of the industry average.[41]

A SENSE OF PURPOSE. As you learned in Chapter 3, "Strategic Management and the Entrepreneur," one of the most important jobs an entrepreneur faces is defining the company's vision and then communicating it effectively to everyone the company touches. Cool companies use a strong sense of purpose to make employees feel connected to the company's mission. At motorcycle legend Harley-Davidson, employees are so in tune with the company's mission that some of them have tatooed the company's name on their bodies!

A SENSE OF FUN. At cool companies, the barriers between work and play are blurred. The founders of these businesses see no reason for work and fun to be mutually exclusive. In fact, they believe that workplaces that create a sense of fun make it easier to recruit quality workers and encourage them to be more productive and more customer oriented. At OddzOn Products, a small toy manufacturer, managers recently closed the office in the middle of the day and took all 100 employees to a movie! At Red Sky Interactive, a design and production company in San Francisco, employees are free to bring their dogs to work.[42] Employees at DigitalThink move around among the company's three buildings on company-issued electric scooters called Zappies.[43] In short, cool companies see that work can be fun and do everything they can to make it so.

DIVERSITY. Cool companies not only accept cultural diversity in their workforces, they embrace it, actively seeking out workers with different backgrounds. As one researcher puts it, "Cool companies are *a part* of the world rather than *apart* from the world."[44] They recognize that a workforce that has a rich mix of cultural diversity gives their companies more talent, skills, and abilities from which to draw. The result is a stronger company.

Metasys, Inc.

For example, Patrick Thean, founder of Metasys, Inc., a small company producing transportation software, says that his company's culturally diverse workforce has become one of its greatest strengths. "A diverse team increases my speed," says Thean, himself an immigrant from Singapore. He considers the entire globe his hiring ground. His employees hail from such places as India, Nigeria, Wales, the United States, and many other nations.[45]

INTERGRITY. Employees want to work for companies that stand for honesty and integrity. They do not want to check their own personal values systems at the door when they report to work. Indeed, many workers take pride in the fact that they work for companies that are ethical and socially responsible. They expect their companies to communicate with them openly and honestly about issues that matter to them.

PARTICIPATIVE MANAGEMENT. According to a recent study, one of the primary characteristics of a cool company is a participative management style. Company owners and managers trust and empower employees at all levels of the organization to make decisions and to take the actions they need to do their jobs well. "These companies realize that employees on the front lines often have the best ideas," says the study's author.[46] For instance, at Nantucket Nectars, a small juice company, the management style is so participative that there is no established organizational hierarchy and no secretaries.

LEARNING ENVIRONMENT. Cool companies encourage and support lifelong learning among their employees. "These are companies in which employees leave at the end of the day knowing more than when they started," says the author of the study.[47] That attitude is a strong magnet for the best and the brightest young workers, who know that to stay at the top of their fields, they must always be learning.

Does it really matter how cool a company is? Netscape Communications' Margie Mader, whose official title is Director of Bringing in the Cool People, believes that it is. "With all the competition in hiring, you need to give yourself an edge," she says.[48] Cool companies find it much easier to attract, retain, and motivate workers. In short, the right culture helps a small company compete more effectively.

Managing Growth and a Changing Culture

As companies grow from seedling businesses into leggy saplings and beyond (perhaps into giants in the business forest), they often experience dramatic changes in their cultures. Procedures become more formal, operations grow more widespread, jobs take on more structure, communication becomes more difficult, and the company's personality begins to change. As more workers come on board, employees find it more difficult to know everyone in the company and what their jobs are. Unless an entrepreneur works hard to maintain her company's unique culture, she may wake up one day to find that she has sacrificed that culture—and the competitive edge that goes with it—in the name of growth.

Ironically, growth can sometimes be a small company's biggest enemy, causing a once successful business to spiral out of control into oblivion. The problem stems from the fact that the organizational structure (or lack of it!) and the style of management that make an entrepreneurial start-up so successful often cannot support the business as it grows into adolescence and maturity. As a company grows, not only does its culture tend to change but so does its need for a management infrastructure capable of supporting that growth. Compounding the problem is the entrepreneur's tendency to see all growth as good. After all, who wouldn't want to be the founder of a small company whose rapid growth makes it destined to become the next rising star in the industry? Yet, achieving rapid growth and managing it are two distinct challenges. Entrepreneurs must be aware of the challenges rapid growth brings with it; otherwise they may find their companies crumbling around them as they reach warp speed.

In many cases, small companies achieve impressive growth because they bypass the traditional organizational structures, forgo rigid policies and procedures, and maintain maximum flexibility. One study of business growth found that small companies have the edge over their larger rivals:[49]

- Large companies' inability to react quickly is a major barrier to their growth. Small companies are naturally quick to respond.
- Rigid internal structures keep big companies from growing rapidly. Small companies typically bypass traditional structures.
- Large companies focus on expanding existing product and service lines, while small businesses concentrate more on creating new ones.
- Large companies are concerned with minimizing risks and defending their market share. Small companies are more willing to takes the risks necessary to conquer new markets.
- Large companies are reluctant to eradicate market research and technology that have worked in the past. Entrepreneurial companies have more of a "clean-slate" approach to research and technology.

But growth brings with it change: changes in management style, organizational strategy, and methods of operations. Growth produces organizational complexity. In this period of transition, the entrepreneur's challenge is to walk a fine line between retaining the small-company traits that are the seeds of the business's success and incorporating the elements of the infrastructure essential to supporting and sustaining the company's growth.

Structure

Entrepreneurs rely on six different management styles to guide their companies as they grow. The first three (craftsman, classic, and coordinator) involve running a company without any management assistance and are best suited for small companies in the early stages of growth; the last three (entrepreneur-plus-employee team, small partnership, big-team venture) rely on a team approach to run the company as its growth rate heats up.[50]

THE CRAFTSMAN. One of the earliest management styles to emerge was the craftsman. These entrepreneurs literally run a one-man (or one-woman) show; they do everything themselves because their primary concern is with the quality of the products or services they produce. Woodworkers, cabinetmakers, glassblowers, and other craftsmen rely on this style of management. The benefits of this style include minimal operating expenses (no employees to pay), very simple operations (no workers' compensation, incentive plans, or organization charts), no supervision problems, and the entrepreneur's total control over both the business and its quality.

Of course, one disadvantages of the craftsman management style is that the entrepreneur must do everything in the business, including those tasks that she does not enjoy. The biggest disadvantage of this style, however, is the limitations it puts on a company's ability to grow. A business can grow only so big without the craftsman taking on other workers and delegating authority to them. Before choosing this management style, a craftsman must decide: "How large do I want my business to become?"

THE CLASSIC. As business opportunities arise, a craftsman quickly realizes that she could magnify the company's capacity to grow by hiring other people to work. The classic entrepreneur brings in other people but does not delegate any significant authority to them, choosing instead to "watch over everything" herself. She insists on tight supervision, constantly monitors employees' work, and performs all of the critical tasks herself. Classic entrepreneurs do not feel comfortable delegating the power and the authority for making decisions to anyone else; they prefer to keep a tight rein on the business and on everyone who works there.

Even though this management style gives a business more growth potential than the craftsman style, there is a limit to how much an entrepreneur can accomplish. Therefore, entrepreneurs who choose to operate this way must limit the complexity of their businesses if they are to grow at all. An inherent danger of this style is the entrepreneur's tendency to "micromanage" every aspect of the business rather than spend her time focusing on those tasks that are most important and most productive for the company.

THE COORDINATOR. The coordinator style of management gives an entrepreneur the ability to create a fairly large company with very few employees. In this type of business (often called a virtual corporation because the company is actually quite "hollow"), the entrepreneur farms out a large portion of the work to other companies and then coordinates all of the activities from "headquarters." By hiring out at least some of the work (in some cases, most of the work), the entrepreneur is free to focus on pumping up sales and pushing the business to higher levels. Some coordinators hire someone to manufacture their products, pay brokers to sell them, and arrange for someone to collect their accounts receivable! With the help of just a few workers, a coordinator can build a multimillion-dollar business!

Although the coordinator style sounds like an easy way to build a business, it can be very challenging to implement. The business's success is highly dependent on its suppliers and their ability to produce quality products and services in a timely fashion. Getting suppliers to perform on time is one of the hardest tasks. Plus, if the entrepreneur hires someone else to manufacture the product, she loses control over its quality.

THE ENTREPRENEUR-PLUS-EMPLOYEE TEAM. As their companies grow, many entrepreneurs see the need to shift to a team-based management style. The entrepreneur-plus-employee team gives an entrepreneur the power to grow the business beyond the scope of the manager-only styles. In this style, the entrepreneur delegates authority to key employees, but she retains the final decision-making authority in the company. Of course, the transition from a management style in which the entrepreneur retains almost total authority to one based on delegation requires some adjustments for employees and especially for the entrepreneur! Employees have to learn to make decisions on their own, and the manager must learn to give workers the authority, the responsibility, and the information to make them. Delegating requires a manager to realize that there are several ways to accomplish a task and that sometimes employees will make mistakes. Still, delegation allows a manager to get the maximum benefit from each employee while freeing herself up to focus on the most important tasks in the business.

THE SMALL PARTNERSHIP. As the business world grows more complex and interrelated, many entrepreneurs find that there is strength in numbers. Rather than manage a company alone, they choose to share the managerial responsibilities with one or more partners (or shareholders). As we saw in Chapter 3 concerning forms of ownership, the benefits are many. Perhaps the biggest advantage is the ability to share responsibility for the company with others who have a real stake in the company and are willing to work hard to make it a success. Some of the most effective partnerships are those in which the owners' skills complement one another, creating natural "fault lines" for dividing responsibilities. Of course, the downside to this management style includes the necessity of giving up total control over the business and the potential for personality conflicts and disputes over the company's direction.

THE BIG-TEAM VENTURE. The broadest-based management style is the big-team venture, which typically emerges over time as a company grows. The workload demands on a small number of partners can quickly outstrip the time and energy they can devote to them, even if they are effective delegators. Once a company reaches this point, managers must expand the breadth of the management team's experience to handle the increasing level of responsibility that results from the sheer size of the company. If the company's operations have become global in scope as it has grown, the need for such a management team is even more pronounced. For entrepreneurial ventures that have grown to this size, the big-team venture is almost a necessity.

Any of these management styles can be successful for an entrepreneur if it matches her personality and the company's goals. The key is to plan for the company's growth and to lay out a strategy for managing the changes the company will experience as it grows. "Ask yourself whether your management style is really effective for a business of this particular size, shape, and complexity," advise the authors of *The New Venture Handbook.* "If the answer is no, modify your plan."[51]

Making Teams Work

Large companies have been using self-directed work teams for years to improve quality, increase productivity, raise morale, lower costs, and boost motivation; yet, team-based management only recently began to catch on in small firms. In fact, a team approach may be best suited for small companies. Even though converting a traditional company to teams requires a major change in management style, it is usually easier to implement with a small number of workers. A **self-directed work team** is a group of workers from different functional areas of a company who work together as a unit largely without supervision, making decisions and performing tasks that once belonged only to managers. Some teams may be temporary, attacking and solving a specific problem, but many are permanent components of an organization's structure. As their name implies, these teams manage themselves, performing such functions as setting work schedules, ordering raw materials, evaluating and purchasing equipment, developing budgets, hiring and firing team members, solving problems, and a host of other activities. The goal is to get people working together to serve customers better.

self-directed work team—*a group of workers from different functional areas of a company who work together as a unit largely without supervision, making decisions and performing tasks that once belonged only to managers.*

Managers in companies using teams don't just sit around drinking coffee, however. In fact, they work just as hard as before, but the nature of their work changes dramatically. Before teams, managers were "bosses" who made most of the decisions affecting their subordinates alone and hoarded information and power for themselves. In a team environment, managers take on the role of "coaches" who empower those around them to make decisions affecting their work and share information with workers. As facilitators, their job is to support and to serve the teams functioning in the organization and to make sure they produce results. Not every entrepreneur feels comfortable in the roles of facilitator and coach, but for a team-based approach to succeed, an entrepreneur must learn to adapt.

Companies have strong competitive reasons for using team-based management. Companies that use teams effectively report significant gains in quality, reductions in cycle time, lower costs, increased customer satisfaction, and improved employee motivation and morale. A team-based approach is not for every organization, however. Teams are not easy to start, and switching from a traditional organizational structure to a team-based one is filled with potential pitfalls. Teams work best in environments in which the work is interdependent and people must interact with one another to accomplish their goals. Although a team approach might succeed in a small plant making gas grills, it would most likely fail miserably in a real estate office, where salespeople work independently of one another with little interaction required to make a sale.

In some cases, teams have been a company's salvation from failure and extinction; in others, the team approach has flopped. What's the difference? What causes teams to fail? The following errors are common:[52]

- *Assigning teams inappropriate tasks.* One of the biggest mistakes managers make with teams is assigning them tasks that individuals ought to be performing.

- *Creating "make-nice" teams.* For a team to perform effectively, it must have a clear purpose, and every team member must understand it. Unfortunately, managers sometimes create a team but fail to give it any meaningful work assignments other than to "make nice with one another."
- *Failing to provide adequate training for team members and team leaders.* Some organizations form teams and then expect employees, long accustomed to individual responsibilities, to magically become team players and contributors. Teams are very complex social systems influenced by pressures from within and buffeted by forces from without, and workers need training to become effective team players.
- *Sabotaging teams with underperformers.* Rather than fire poor performers (always an unpleasant task), some managers put them on teams, hoping that the members will either discipline them or get rid of them. It never works. Underperfomers undermine team performance.
- *Switching to team responsibilities but keeping pay individually oriented.* One of the quickest ways to destroy a team system is to pay team members based on their individual performances.

Teams work best in creative environments, and entrepreneurs who use them must establish an organizational structure that supports them. Teams do not fit naturally into a company's layers of hierarchy, and managers must adjust appraisal, compensation, and motivation systems to suit a team-based approach. Employees serving on teams also need support in the form of training in the team process. Successful teams do not just happen; they require planning, adequate resources, and managerial support. In essence, building a successful team-based structure requires some effort on an entrepreneur's part. To ensure teams' success, managers must:

- *Make sure that teams are appropriate for the company and the nature of its work.* A good starting point is to create a "map" of the company's work flow that shows how workers build a product or deliver a service. Is the work interdependent, complex, and interactive? Would teamwork improve the company's performance?
- *Make sure that teams are appropriate for the task to be accomplished.* Nothing ensures the failure of a team faster than assigning it a task that individuals should be performing.
- *Form teams around the natural work flow and give them specific tasks to accomplish.* Teams can be effective only if managers challenge them to accomplish specific, measurable objectives.
- *Provide adequate support and training for team members and leaders.* Team success requires a new set of skills. Workers must learn how to communicate, resolve conflict, support one another, and solve problems as a team. Smart managers see that workers get the training they need.
- *Involve team members in determining how their performances will be measured, what will be measured, and when it will be measured.* Doing so gives team members a sense of ownership and pride about what they are accomplishing.
- *Make at least part of team members' pay dependent on team performance.* Companies that have used teams successfully still pay members individually, but they make successful team work a major part of an individual's performance review. For teams to succeed, at least part of team members' compensation must be based on the team's performance.

Whole Foods

Whole Foods, a natural foods supermarket founded in 1978, relies on employees' participation in self-directed work teams to run its more than 200 stores. Company founders John Mackey, Craig Weller, and Mark Skiles decided to use a highly decentralized management structure built around self-directed teams early in the life of the business, creating the team structure when they opened their second store. Their goal was to allow decisions to be made at the level closest to customers and to help workers feel connected to the com-

pany. Whole Foods' growth has been phenomenal over the years, but the company still uses the team concept; in fact, its workers are known as team members, not employees. Stores have an average of 10 teams, and every employee, including part-time workers, is a member of a team. Teams handle their own hiring, firing, training, purchasing, and scheduling. Management shares extensive financial information with teams, and a part of every team member's compensation is based on the team's performance. Managers at Whole Foods credit the team structure with maintaining an innovative atmosphere, with keeping team members highly motivated, and with sustaining the company's growth and above-average profitability.[53]

Table 14.8 shows the four stages that teams go through on their way to performing effectively and accomplishing results.

4. Discuss the ways in which entrepreneurs can motivate their workers to higher levels of performance.

THE CHALLENGE OF MOTIVATING WORKERS

Motivation is the degree of effort an employee exerts to accomplish a task; it shows up as excitement about work. Motivating workers to higher levels of performance is one of the most difficult and challenging tasks facing a small business manager. Few things are more frustrating to a business owner than an employee with a tremendous amount of talent who lacks the desire to use it. This section discusses four aspects of motivation: empowerment; job design; rewards and compensation; and feedback.

motivation—*the degree of effort an employee exerts to accomplish a task; it shows up as excitement about work.*

Empowerment

One of the principles underlying the team-based management style discussed in the previous section is empowerment. **Empowerment** involves giving workers at every level of the organization the power, the freedom, and the responsibility to control their own work, to make decisions, and to take action to meet the company's objectives. Competitive forces

TABLE 14.8
The Stages of Team Development
Source: Mark Frohman, "Do Teams . . . But Do Them Right," Industry Week, April 3, 1995, p. 22.

Stage	Description	Leader Focus
1. Start-up	High expectations Unclear goals and roles	Task focus Provide goals and structure Supervise start-up and define accountability
2. Reality strikes	Recognition of time and effort required Roadblocks Frustration	Task and process emphasis Clarify expectations and roles Encourage open discussions and address concerns Ensure proper skills and resources
3. Realigning expectations	Goals and roles reset Cooperation and trust begin to produce progress	Process focus Promote participation and team decision making Encourage peer support Provide feedback
4. Performance	Involvement, openness, and teamwork. Commitment to process and task achievement	Monitoring and feedback focus Let team take responsibility for solving problems and making decisions Monitor progress and supply feedback

and a more demanding workforce challenge business owners and managers to share power with everyone in the organization, whether they use a team-based approach or not.

empowerment—*the process of giving workers at every level of the organization the power, the freedom, and the responsibility to control their own work, to make decisions, and to take action to meet the company's objectives.*

Empowering employees requires a different style of management and leadership from that of the traditional manager. Many old-style managers are unwilling to share power with anyone because they fear doing so weakens their authority and reduces their influence. In fact, exactly the opposite is true! Business owners who share information, responsibility, authority, and power soon discover that their success (and their companies' success, too) is magnified many times over. Empowered workers become more successful on the job, which means the entrepreneur also becomes more successful.

Empowerment builds on what real business leaders already know: The people in their organizations bring with them to work an amazing array of talents, skills, knowledge, and abilities. Workers are willing—even anxious—to put these to use; unfortunately, in too many small businesses, suffocating management styles and poorly designed jobs quash workers' enthusiasm and motivation. Enlightened business owners recognize their workers' abilities, develop them, and then give workers the freedom and the power to use those abilities. "Employees work best when you give them the opportunity to use their own creativity and imagination," explains one manager.[54]

When implemented properly, empowerment can produce impressive results, not only for the small business but also for newly empowered employees. For the business, benefits typically include significant productivity gains, quality improvements, more satisfied customers, improved morale, and increased employee motivation. When one manufacturing plant switched to empowered process improvement teams, workers used their newfound freedom to unleash a torrent of new ideas aimed at improving the company's performance. The teams were able to reduce cycle time for several key products by as much as 33 percent to 60 percent, producing huge savings and improving customer satisfaction. Other suggestions by the teams enabled the materials storage department to triple its productivity![55]

For workers, empowerment offers the chance to do a greater variety of work that is more interesting and challenging. Empowerment challenges workers to make the most of their creativity, imagination, knowledge, and skills. This method of management encourages them to take the initiative to identify and solve problems on their own and as part of a team. As empowered workers see how the various parts of a company's manufacturing or service systems fit together, they realize their need to acquire more skills and knowledge to do their jobs well. Entrepreneurs must realize that empowerment and training go hand in hand.

Not every worker wants to be empowered, however. Some will resist, wanting only to "put in their eight hours and go home." One expert estimates that companies moving to empowerment can expect to lose about 5 percent of their workforce. "Out of every 100 employees, five are diehards who will be impossible to change," he says. Another 75 percent will accept empowerment and thrive under it, if it is done properly. The remaining 20 percent will pounce eagerly on empowerment because it is something they "have been waiting to do . . . their whole [work] lives," he says.[56] Empowerment works best when a business owner:

- *Is confident enough to give workers all of the authority and responsibility they can handle.* Early on, this may mean giving workers the power to tackle relatively simple assignments. But, as their confidence and ability grow, most workers are eager to take on more responsibility.
- *Plays the role of coach and facilitator, not the role of meddlesome boss.* One surefire way to make empowerment fail is to give associates the power to attack a problem and then to hover over them, criticizing every move they make. Smart owners empower their workers and then get out of the way so they can do their jobs!
- *Recognizes that empowered employees will make mistakes.* The worst thing an owner can do when empowered employees make mistakes is to hunt them down and punish them. That

teaches everyone in the company to avoid taking risks and to always play it safe—something no innovative small business can afford.

- *Hires people who can blossom in an empowered environment.* Empowerment is not for everyone. Owners quickly learn that as costly as hiring mistakes are, such errors are even more costly in an empowered environment. Ideal candidates are high-energy self-starters who enjoy the opportunity to grow and to enhance their skills.
- *Trains workers continuously to upgrade their skills.* Empowerment demands more of workers than traditional work methods. Managers are asking workers to solve problems and make decisions they have never made before. To handle these problems well, workers need training, especially in effective problem-solving techniques, communication, teamwork, and technical skills. Investing in employee training also improves employee retention.
- *Trusts workers to do their jobs.* Once workers are trained to do their jobs, owners must learn to trust them to assume responsibility for their jobs. After all, they are the *real* experts; they face the problems and challenges every day. One Japanese study found that workers "in the trenches" knew 100 percent of the problems in a company; supervisors knew 74 percent; and top managers knew just 4 percent![57]
- *Listens to workers when they have ideas, solutions, or suggestions.* Because they are the experts on the jobs, employees often come up with incredibly insightful, innovative ideas for improving them—if business owners give them the chance. Failing to acknowledge or to act on employees' ideas sends them a clear message: Your ideas really don't count.
- *Shares information with workers.* For empowerment to succeed, business owners must make sure workers get adequate information, the raw material for good decision making. Some companies have gone beyond sharing information to embrace **open-book management,** in which employees have access to all of a company's records, including its financial statements. The goal of open-book management is to enable employees to understand why they need to raise productivity, improve quality, cut costs, and improve customer service. "Open-book management is really the ultimate form of employee involvement," says one expert.[58] Under open-book management, employees (1) see and learn to understand the company's financial statements and other critical numbers in measuring its performance; (2) learn that a significant part of their jobs is making sure those critical numbers move in the right direction; and (3) have a direct stake in the company's success through profit sharing, ESOPs, or performance-based bonuses. To work, open-book management must not only make sure that workers understand how their company makes a profit but also how they can influence its financial results. One expert writes, "Instead of telling employees how to cut defects, [open-book management] asks them to boosts profits—and lets them figure out how. Instead of giving them a reengineered job, it turns them into businesspeople. They experience the challenge—and the sheer fun and excitement—of matching wits with the marketplace, toting up the score, and sharing in the proceeds. . . . There's no better motivation."[59]

open-book management—*the process of giving employees access to all of a company's records, including its financial statements, so they can understand why they need to raise productivity, improve quality, cut costs, and improve customer service.*

- *Recognizes workers' contributions.* One of the most important tasks a business owner has is to recognize jobs well done. Some businesses reward workers with monetary awards; others rely on recognition and praise; still others use a combination of money and praise. Whatever system an owner chooses, the key to keeping a steady flow of ideas, improvements, suggestions, and solutions is to recognize the people who supply them.

Job Design

Over the years, managers have learned that the job itself and the way it is designed can be a source of motivation (or demotivation!) for workers. In some companies, work is organized on the principle of **job simplification,** breaking the work down into its simplest form and standardizing each task, as in some assembly-line operations. The scope of jobs organized in such a way is extremely narrow, resulting in impersonal, monotonous, and boring work that creates little challenge or motivation for workers. Job simplification invites workers to "check their brains at the door" and offers them little opportunity for excite-

job simplification—*the type of job design that breaks work down into its simplest form and standardizes each task.*

ment, enthusiasm, or pride in their work. The result can be apathetic, unmotivated workers who don't care about quality, customers, or costs.

To break this destructive cycle, some companies have redesigned jobs so that they offer workers intrinsic rewards and motivation. Three strategies are common: job enlargement, job rotation, and job enrichment.

Job enlargement (or **horizontal job loading**) adds more tasks to a job to broaden its scope. For instance, rather than an employee simply mounting four screws in computers coming down an assembly line, a worker might assemble, install and test the entire motherboard (perhaps as part of a team). The idea is to make the job more varied and to allow employees to perform a more complete unit of work.

job enlargement—*the type of job design that adds more tasks to a job to broaden its scope.*

Job rotation involves cross-training employees so they can move from one job in the company to others, giving them a greater number and variety of tasks to perform. As employees learn other jobs within an organization, both their skills and their understanding of the company's purpose and processes rise. Cross-trained workers are more valuable because they give a company the flexibility to shift workers from low-demand jobs to those in which they are most needed. As an incentive for workers to learn to perform other jobs within an operation, some companies offer skill-based pay, a system under which the more skills workers acquire, the more they earn.

job rotation—*the type of job design that involves cross-training employees so they can move from one job in the company to others, giving them a greater number and variety of tasks to perform.*

Job enrichment (or **vertical job loading**) involves building motivators into a job by increasing the planning, decision-making, organizing, and controlling functions—traditional managerial tasks—workers perform. The idea is to make every employee a manager—at least a manager of his own job. Notice that empowerment, the management technique discussed in the previous section, is based on the principle of job enrichment.

job enrichment—*the type of job design that involves building motivators into a job by increasing the planning, decision-making, organizing, and controlling functions workers perform.*

To enrich employees' jobs, a business owner must build the following five core characteristics into them.

- *Skill variety* is the degree to which a job requires a variety of different skills, talents, and activities from the worker. Does the job require the worker to perform a variety of tasks that demand a variety of skills and abilities or does it force him to perform the same task repeatedly?
- *Task identity* is the degree to which a job allows the worker to complete a whole or identifiable piece of work. Does the employee build an entire piece of furniture (perhaps as part of a team) or does he merely attach four screws?
- *Task significance* is the degree to which a job substantially influences the lives or work of others—employees or final customers. Does the employee get to deal with customers, either internal or external? One effective way to establish task significance is to put employees in touch with customers so they can see how customers use the product or service they make.
- *Autonomy* is the degree to which a job gives a worker the freedom, independence, and discretion in planning and performing tasks. Does the employee make decisions affecting his work or must he rely on someone else (e.g., the owner, a manager, or a supervisor) to "call the shots?"
- *Feedback* is the degree to which a job gives the worker direct, timely information about the quality of his performance. Does the job give employees feedback about the quality of their work or does the product (and all information about it) simply disappear after it leaves the worker's station?

Warner Corporation

Tom Warner, a fourth-generation plumber who took over his father's heating, ventilation, and air-conditioning (HVAC) company in 1989, has used innovative job designs to transform his employees' motivation and attitudes toward their jobs and, in the process, to revitalize the company's sales and profits. Until 1992, Warner Corporation was a traditional HVAC business with a crew of workers waiting for "the boss" to tell them where to go, what to do, and when to do it. Warner Corporation was also a company headed for financial trouble. That's when Warner decided to redesign the jobs in his company. The

HVAC technicians, plumbers, and electricians would become area technical directors (ATDs), who would, in essence, manage their own businesses within Warner Corporation. ATDs got their own territories (based on zip codes) in which they developed customer relationships, handled their own equipment, did their own sales work, and collected their own accounts. By transforming his technicians into businesspeople who make decisions and are responsible for generating profits and keeping customers happy, Warner has instilled in them a sense of pride and ownership in their work that was missing before. "This program is a real ego booster," he says. "Running their own businesses, these guys really feel good about themselves." They also take better care of their customers, which shows up in the form of rising sales, profits, and market share. Warner credits the job redesign for turning his company around.[60]

As the nation's workers and the companies employing them continue to change, business is changing the way people work, moving away from a legion of full-time employees in traditional 9-to-5, full-time, on-site jobs. Significant changes in the demographic profile of the nation's workforce are requiring employers to change the way they organize jobs. By 2005, workers will be older, more racially and culturally diverse, and less loyal to any individual employer. In addition, the shortage of workers will worsen. The effect of these changes on business owners will be significant. Companies will be required to offer an ever broader array of work schedules and structures, including flextime, job sharing, flexplace, and telecommuting.

flextime—*an arrangement under which employees work a normal number of hours but have flexibility about when they start and stop work.*

Flextime is an arrangement under which employees work a normal number of hours but have flexibility about when they start and stop work. Most flextime arrangements require employees to build their work schedules around a set of "core hours," such as 11 A.M. to 2 P.M., but give them the freedom to set their schedules outside of those core hours. For instance, one worker might choose to come in at 7 A.M. and leave at 3 P.M. to attend her son's soccer game, while another may work from 11 A.M. to 7 P.M. Flextime not only raises worker morale, but it also makes it easier for companies to attract high-quality young workers who want rewarding careers without sacrificing their lifestyles. In addition, companies using flextime schedules often experience lower levels of tardiness, turnover, and absenteeism. Linda Field, founder of Field & Associates, a marketing and public relations firm in Houston, Texas, says that offering flextime helps her employees keep their work and their lives in balance and brings her company a larger pool of more qualified applicants.[61]

Flextime is becoming a popular job design strategy. A recent survey by the Society for Human Resource Management found that 55 percent of the nation's workers have flexible schedules, up from just 15 percent in 1991.[62] That percentage will grow because flextime is an important job design strategy for some companies that find it difficult to recruit capable, qualified full-time workers. Research shows that when considering job offers candidates weigh heavily the flexibility of the work schedule companies offer. "Offer flextime, and it will definitely help your recruiting efforts," says one human resources consultant.[63]

job sharing—*a work arrangement in which two or more people share a single full-time job.*

Job sharing is a work arrangement in which two or more people share a single full-time job. For instance, two college students might share the same 40-hour-a-week job, one working mornings and the other working afternoons. Salary and benefits are prorated between the workers sharing a job. Because job sharing is a simple solution to the growing challenge of work-life balance, it will become more popular in the future. A recent study by the Society of Human Resource Management found that 22 percent of companies in the United States currently offer job sharing.[64] Companies already using it are finding it easier to recruit and retain qualified workers. "Employers get the combined strengths of two people, but they only have to pay for one," says one hotel sales manager, herself a job sharer.[65]

flexplace—*a work arrangement in which employees work at a place other than the traditional office, such as a satellite branch closer to their homes or at home.*

Flexplace is a work arrangement in which employees work at a place other than the traditional office, such as a satellite branch closer to their homes or, in many cases, at home. Flexplace is an easy job design strategy for companies to use because of **telecommuting.**

Using modern communication technology such as e-mail, voice mail, fax machines, and portable computers, employees have more flexibility in choosing where they work. Today, it is quite simple for workers to hook up electronically to their workplaces (and to all of the people and the information there) from practically anywhere on the planet! Telecommuting employees get the flexibility they seek, and they also benefit from reduced commuting times and expenses, not to mention a less expensive wardrobe (bathrobes and bunny slippers compared to business suits and wingtips). Companies reap many benefits as well, including improved employee morale, less absenteeism, lower turnover, and higher productivity. One study of companies using telecommuting found that employee turnover fell by 20 percent and that productivity climbed between 15 percent and 20 percent.[66]

telecommuting—*an arrangement under which employees working from their homes use modern communications equipment to hook up electronically to their workplaces.*

Despite the many benefits that telecommuting offers both employers and employees, small companies are less likely to use it as a job design strategy than large businesses. Although 90 percent of companies with more than 5,000 employees use telecommuting, only 40 percent of small businesses do.[67]

Callison Architecture

Callison Architecture is one small business that is benefiting from telecommuting. Although just 10 of the architectural firm's employees telecommute from home, CEO William Karst says that "at least 25 percent of our staff is working remotely at any given time" to deliver projects to customers around the world. "Whether working from home, a remote job site, airport, or hotel, our people can be fully integrated with the firm and their project teams," says Karst. Before starting to telecommute, Callison employees must enter into an individually negotiated telecommuting agreement that spells out the parameters of their redesigned jobs.[68]

Before implementing telecommuting, entrepreneurs must address the following important issues.

- Does the nature of the work fit telecommuting? Obviously, some jobs are better suited to telecommuting than others.
- Have you selected the right employees for telecommuting? Telecommuting is not suitable for every job or for every worker. Experienced managers say that employees who handle it best are experienced workers who know their jobs well, are self-disciplined, and are good communicators.
- Can you monitor compliance with federal wage and hour laws for telecommuters? Generally, employers must keep the same employment records for telecommuters that they do for traditional office workers.
- Are you adequately insured? Employers should be sure that the telecommuting equipment employees use in their homes is covered under their insurance policies.
- Can you keep in touch? Telecommuting works well as long as long-distance employees stay in touch with headquarters.
- Have you created an equitable telecommuting policy? One danger of telecommuting is that it can create resentment among employees who remain office-bound.

A variation of telecommuting that is growing in popularity is **hoteling,** in which employees who spend most of their time away from the office use the same office space at different times, just as travelers use the same hotel room on different days. Hoteling requires advance planning and coordination, but businesses that use it have been able to reduce the cost of leasing office space, sometimes by as much as 50 percent. Flexible office designs and furnishings allow workers to configure these "hot offices" (so called because they usually turn over so quickly that the seats are still hot from the previous user) to suit their particular needs.

hoteling—*an arrangement in which employees who spend most of their time away from the office use the same office space at different times.*

Hoffman Agency

When Lou Hoffman, founder of a professional services firm in San Jose, California, realized that employees were using only 45 percent of the company's existing office space regularly, he implemented hoteling. One-third of the company's 65 employees began shar-

ing office space on a rotating basis, and Hoffman added temporary workstations to handle the occasional overflows and schedule conflicts. Hoffman estimates that hoteling saved his company $130,000 in less than one year![69]

Rewards and Compensation

The rewards an employee gets from the job itself are intrinsic rewards, but managers have at their disposal a wide variety of extrinsic rewards (those outside the job itself) to motivate workers. The key to using rewards to motivate involves tailoring them to the needs and characteristics of the workers. "The core of successful motivation is tapping into the things that are really important to people—taking the time to find out what those are, and structuring your recognition around those in the context of the job," says one motivation expert.[70] For instance, to a technician making $25,000 a chance to earn a $3,000 performance bonus would most likely be a powerful motivator. To an executive earning $175,000 a year, it would not be.

pay-for-performance compensation system—*a compensation system in which employees' pay depends on how well they perform their jobs.*

One of the most popular rewards is money. Cash is an effective motivator—up to a point. Over the last 20 years, many companies have moved to **pay-for-performance compensation systems,** in which employees' pay depends on how well they perform their jobs. In other words, extra productivity equals extra pay. By linking employees' compensation directly to the company's financial performance, a business owner increases the likelihood that workers will achieve performance targets that are in their best interest and in the company's best interest. These systems work only when employees see a clear connection between their performances and their pay, however. That's where small businesses have an advantage over large businesses. Because they work for small companies, employees can see more clearly the impact their performances have on the company's profitability and ultimate success than their counterparts at large corporations.

Tape Resources Inc.

Seph Barnard, founder of Tape Resources Inc., a company that sells blank audiotapes and videotapes to television stations and production companies, recently revamped his company's compensation system to one that rewards teamwork and superior performance. Because Tape Resources' competitive advantage is its guaranteed in-stock policy and its fast delivery, its success depends on everyone in the company, from sales representatives to shipping clerks, working together. Workers earn monthly bonuses if the company meets its sales objectives and a significant annual bonus if it meets broader financial targets. Under the new compensation system, the attitude among workers is "we're all in this together," says David Durovy, president of sales. In addition to improved teamwork, sales at the company are climbing.[71]

To make sure that the salaries they pay are competitive, entrepreneurs can consult a variety of sources. The Bureau of Labor Statistics publishes the *Occupational Outlook Handbook,* which provides pay rates and job forecasts for hundreds of occupations. The Bureau of Labor Statistics Web site **<www.bls.gov>** contains wage and salary data by region. Other useful sources are *American Wages and Salary Survey* published by Gale Research, *American Almanac of Jobs and Salaries* from JobStar **<www.jobsmart.org>,** and Wageweb **<www.wageweb.com>.**

stock options—*a plan under which employees can purchase shares of a company's stock at a fixed price.*

Money isn't the only motivator business owners have at their disposal, of course. In fact, money tends to be only a short-term motivator. In addition to the financial compensation they provide, most companies offer their employees a wide array of benefits, ranging from stock options and medical insurance to retirement plans and tuition reimbursement. **Stock options,** a plan under which the employees can purchase shares of a company's stock at a fixed price, have become a popular benefit for employees, especially in the new economy. Stock options take on real value once the fair market price of a company's stock exceeds the exercise price, the price at which employees can purchase stock. (Note that if the fair market price of a stock never exceeds the exercise price, the stock option is useless.) When trying to attract and retain quality employees, many small companies rely on stock options to gain an edge over larger companies offering bigger salaries.

Spencer Reed Group, Inc.

For example, Dick Plodzien, CEO of Spencer Reed Group, Inc., a privately owned executive search and staffing company in Overland Park, Kansas, uses stock options to attract and retain quality employees. Not only has the stock option plan slowed the number of employees defecting to larger companies offering bigger salaries, but it also has enabled Plodzien to entice several executives to leave billion-dollar companies to join Spencer Reed.[72]

Sometimes stock options produce a huge payoff for employees. Workers at highly successful companies such as Microsoft and Dell have retired early as multimillionaires thanks to stock options.

Netscape Communications

When James Clark left Silicon Graphics to launch his own company, Mosaic Communications, he asked his secretary, D'Anne Schjerning, to go with him. He would not be able to pay her any more than she was already earning at Silicon Graphics, but he could offer her stock options. Schjerning decided to take a chance on the new company and accepted the offer to buy 10,000 shares of Mosaic's stock at half-a-penny each. Within a year, Clark had changed the name of his company to Netscape Communications and had made an initial public offering of its stock. On the day of the initial public offering, the stock options that Schjerning had exercised were worth more than $1 million, putting her among the ranks of other millionaire secretaries at high-tech companies![73]

In an economy in which they must compete aggressively for employees, entrepreneurs must recognize that compensation and benefits are no longer "one-size-fits-all" issues. The diversity of today's workforce requires employers to be highly flexible and innovative in the compensation and benefits they provide. To attract and retain quality workers, creative entrepreneurs offer employees a set of benefits designed to appeal to their individual needs and preferences. This diversity has led to the popularity of cafeteria benefit plans, in which employers provide certain base benefits and then allocate a specific dollar amount for employees to select the benefits that suit their needs best. Beyond flexible benefits plans, many small companies are setting themselves apart from others by offering unique benefits such as the following:[74]

- Clothing retailer Eddie Bauer offers employees on-site massages to ease tension and to enhance creativity.
- Starbucks, a chain of coffee shops, provides its employees with a personal concierge service that handles employees' errands. Need to make reservations at a restaurant and to order flowers for your friend's birthday celebration? The concierge will take care of it for you!
- Numerous Silicon Valley companies provide catered meals, on-site kitchens filled with fruit and snacks, and gymnasiums and athletic fields for employees. At Clif Bar, a 65-employee company that makes energy bars, employees on breaks can scale the 22-foot-high climbing wall located in the company gym. Clif Bar also hires trainers to conduct classes in aerobics, weightlifting, and other workouts on company time.
- At its San Jose, California, headquarters, Cisco Systems Inc. operates a child care center for its employees' children, complete with Internet cameras so parents can connect to the Internet and check on their kids.
- One company that writes software for the insurance industry has an ultramodern exercise facility open 24 hours a day for its employees. Not only does the facility help recruit and retain workers, but the company's health insurance costs also have declined since it opened.
- Employees at Adobe Systems get a three-week paid sabbatical leave every five years to pursue some topic of interest to them.
- When workers at Gould Evans Goodman Associates, a Kansas City architectural firm, need a break, they can retreat to one of the company's "spent tents," camping tents set up in a corner complete with pillows, sleeping bags, soothing music, and alarm clocks (of course!).

YOU BE THE CONSULTANT . . .

The New Company Town

The company office complex in the new economy looks very different from the nondescript, open offices so popular in the 1980s and 1990s with their walls painted institutional tan and lined with the cubicles that cartoon character Dilbert toils in every day. With a war raging among companies to attract the most qualified workers, many businesses are using their offices and a host of unique perks as recruiting and retention tools. Some companies provide their employees with in-house or take-home meals to free them from the drudgery of cooking for themselves. Others offer concierge services to help employees take care of the thousands of details that make up everyday life such as buying gifts, picking up laundry, or making reservations. Some offer on-site child care facilities and classes on gardening, sculpting, public speaking, karate, or scuba diving. The goal of these benefits is not only to attract and retain quality workers but also to free them up to focus on doing their jobs. Companies know that many workers will be on site from dawn to dusk and are doing everything they can to make employees' lives easier and more manageable. "Companies are taking the best aspects of home and incorporating them into work," says one expert.

What's behind these companies' efforts? Workers in the United States seem to be busier than ever, leaving little time for fun activities. Taking up that precious time with mundane tasks makes no sense, and that is the appeal of on-site services at work. "Time is a commodity I don't have a lot of," says Sheila Childs, a product manager in BMC software's research and development department and the mother of four children. "The amenities definitely make it comfortable for you to be [at work]." Childs's story is echoed in millions of homes across the United States. A study by the International Labor Organization found that the typical worker in the United States works 1,966 hours per year, even more than the 1,889 hours the legendary workaholic Japanese employee does!

BMC Software in Houston, Texas, has created a unique company campus designed to appeal to every aspect of its high-tech workers' busy lives. BMC has built what comes close to being a self-contained community so complete that one worker says, "You never have to leave the place." When employees are not in their offices, they can lounge on hammocks strung between trees on the company's grounds, lift weights in the gym, play a pickup game on the basketball court, practice their putting on the green, play horseshoes, or get in a friendly game of beach volleyball. Walking past the herb garden, employees might see cooks busily gathering fresh oregano to use in company-provided lunch. On each floor of BMC's two glass towers is a large kitchen well stocked with fruit, popcorn, soft drinks, and coffee. Employees can dine in spacious booths and watch television on the big-screen TV. A sign in a hallway says "Massage Therapy This Way." In the lobby, a Steinway player piano plays a repertoire of both snappy tunes and relaxing minuets as employees and guests move about. A company valet picks up employees' cars scheduled for washes and oil changes. Also within the office complex are a bank, a store, a dry cleaner, a hairdresser, and a nail salon.

1. What are the benefits to companies and to workers of the services and facilities such as the one at BMC Software? What potential disadvantages do you see with companies offering these services and facilities?
2. Would *you* want to work at a company such as BMC Software? Explain.

Source: Jerry Useem, "Welcome to the New Company Store," *Fortune*, January 10, 2000, pp. 62–70.

Besides the wages, salaries, and attractive benefits they use as motivators, creative entrepreneurs have discovered that intangible incentives can be more important sources of employee motivation. After its initial impact, money does not have a lasting motivational effect (which for small businesses, with their limited resources, is a plus). Often for workers, the most meaningful motivational factors are the simplest ones—praise, recognition, feedback, job security, promotions, and others—things that any small business, no matter how limited its budget, can do. "To get the right kind of people, you have to put together a compensation package for them," says one entrepreneur, "but what people really work for is appreciation and the feeling that success brings to them."[75] For instance, one innovative home builder rewards his employees for exceptional work by naming streets after them in his subdivisions.[76] As a source of both fun and motivation, Kathy Keenan, founder of Oak Ridge Public Relations, Inc., gives her employees zany job titles. Oak Ridge is home to the

Mistress of Chaos, Commander Data, the Duchess of Danger, and Empress of the Universe (Keenan herself).[77]

Entrepreneurs find that younger workers, especially "Generation Xers," respond best to intangible rewards and not to monetary rewards. Wanting more balance in their work and personal lives than their baby-boomer parents, Generation X workers are looking for workplaces that offer challenging assignments coupled with a sense of fun. They respond best to constant feedback that is specific and accurate and to managers who take the time to celebrate their successes. The following suggestions will help entrepreneurs motivate and reward their Generation X employees.

- Give them challenging assignments that allow them to learn more skills. Generation X workers value education and want to upgrade their knowledge continuously.
- Give them jobs that require diverse skills and have an observable impact on the company's mission.
- Treat them as individuals and allow them to express their individuality at work.
- Avoid an authoritarian approach. They thrive in a participative work environment.
- Trust them. One of the biggest turnoffs for Generation X employees is a manager who constantly checks up on them, indicating a lack of trust.
- Offer them varied assignments and frequent rewards (not necessarily money). Generation X workers want to be challenged by a variety of tasks, and they expect frequent feedback on their performance.

Trinity Communications

When Trinity Communications, a small marketing communications company, surveyed its 11 Generation X employees to find out what attracts and motivates them, managers were a bit surprised to find that employees ranked a good 401(k) retirement plan, not salary, at the top of their financial concerns. Other motivating factors the employees ranked high were opportunities to learn, access to up-to-date technology, workforce diversity, and flexibility in job design and schedules. Based on the results of its survey, Trinity changed its benefits package to one more consistent with its employees' desires, including a more aggressive 401(k) plan, a more generous and flexible vacation policy, and home computers with Internet access for all workers.[78]

Praise is another simple yet powerful motivational tool. People enjoy getting praise, especially from a manager or business owner; it's just human nature. As Mark Twain once said, "I can live for two months on a good compliment." Praise is an easy and inexpensive reward for employees producing extraordinary work. A short note to an employee for a job well done costs practically nothing; yet it can be a potent source of motivation. One experienced executive says, "The biggest error most managers make is forgetting to say 'Thank you.'"[79]

Mary Kay Cosmetics

At Mary Kay Cosmetics' annual meeting, praise and saying "thank you" are the watchwords. Indeed, they are the main reasons more than 36,000 beauty consultants from around the world gather in Dallas every year. At the meeting, superstar saleswomen receive praise and recognition from their peers and from company founder Mary Kay Ash in sessions that resemble a cross between an awards banquet and a tent revival. Women come away with crowns, sashes, pins, bracelets, and, of course, those coveted pink Cadillacs—and a zealous fervor to go out and sell lots of makeup! "This is a company that understands that positive emotions can be good for the soul," says Gloria Mayfield Hayes, senior sales director.[80]

One of the surest ways to kill high performance is simply to fail to recognize it and the employees responsible for it. Yet, one study found that 18 percent of employees say they have never been rewarded for special incentives by their employers.[81] Failing to praise good work eventually conveys the message that an entrepreneur either doesn't care about exceptional performance or cannot distinguish between good work and poor work. In either case, through inaction, the business owner destroys employees' motivation to excel.

Because they lack the financial resources of bigger companies, small business owners must be more creative when it comes to giving rewards that motivate workers. In many cases, however, using rewards other than money gives small businesses an advantage because they usually have more impact on employee performance over time. One expert on employee motivation says, "To consistently enjoy [high] levels of performance, you've got to give them more than a paycheck. What gets people to excel on a daily basis, to stay late, to work weekends in a pinch is when you regularly communicate to them that you value what they do."[82] In short, rewards do not have to be expensive to be effective.

Mackay Envelope Corporation

At Mackay Envelope Corporation, managers "go around and try to catch people in the act of doing something right," says owner Harvey Mackay. "Managers have a fistful of tickets to Vikings and Timberwolves games, to the opera and to Broadway shows, and we reward them right on the spot. We praise them in front of mother, God, and country!" he says.[83]

In the future, managers will rely more on nonmonetary rewards such as praise, recognition, game tickets, dinners, letters of commendation, and other rewards to create a work environment in which employees take pride in their work, enjoy it, are challenged by it, and get excited about it: in other words, act like owners of the business themselves. The goal is to let employees know that "every person is important" (see Table 14.9).

Table 14.10 offers the 20 top ways to motivate employees, which are based on the results of a survey of some of the nation's leading motivational experts.

Feedback

Business owners not only must motivate employees to excel in their jobs, but they must also focus their efforts on the right targets. Providing feedback on progress toward those targets can be a powerful motivating force in a company. To ensure that the link between her vision for the company and its operations is strong, an entrepreneur must build a series of specific performance measures that serve as periodic monitoring points. For each critical element of the organization's performance (e.g., product or service quality, financial performance, market position, productivity, employee development, etc.), the owner should develop specific measures that connect daily operational responsibilities with the company's overall strategic direction. These measures become the benchmarks for measuring employees' performances and the company's progress. The adage "what gets measured and monitored gets done" is true for most organizations. By connecting the company's long-term strategy to its daily operations and measuring performance, an entrepreneur makes it clear to everyone in the company what is most important. Jack Stack, CEO of Springfield Remanufacturing Corporation, explains the importance of focusing every employee's attention on key performance targets:

TABLE 14.9

Xvxry Pxrson Is Important

Source: "You Arx a Kxy Pxrson," Pasadena Weekly Journal of Business, *155 S. El Molino Avenue, Suite 101, Pasadena, California 91101.*

One business owner let employees know how valuable they are with the following memo:

You Arx a Kxy Pxrson

Xvxn though my typxwritxr is an old modxl, it works vxry wxll—xxcxpt for onx kxy. You would not think that with all thx othxr kxys functioning propxrly, onx kxy not working would hardly bx noticxd; but just onx kxy out of whack sxxms to ruin thx wholx xffort.

You may say to yoursxlf—"Wxll, I'm only onx pxrson. No onx will noticx if I don't do my bxst." But it doxs makx a diffxrxnce bxcausx to bx xffxctivx, an orgnization nxxds activx participation by xvxry onx to thx bxst of his or hxr ability.

So thx nxxt timx you think you arx not important, rxmxbxr my old typxwritxr. You arx a kxy pxrson.

TABLE 14.10
The Top 20 Ways to Motivate Employees

Source: Shari Caudron, "The Top 20 Ways to Motivate Employees," Industry Week, *April 3, 1995, pp. 12–18.*

1. Give employees the information they need to do a good job. Employees need timely information to do their jobs, starting with the company's mission and goals and moving on to information on their specific job responsibilities.
2. Provide regular feedback. Communication should be an ongoing event, giving employees the opportunity to measure and improve their performances.
3. Ask employees for their input and involve them in the decisions that affect their jobs. The people who are performing a job are the real experts, so why not involve them in the decision-making process? At one manufacturing plant, workers, not managers, made all of the decisions relating to the purchase of a $3 million piece of equipment. After all, they were the ones who would be using it.
4. Establish easy-to-use channels of communication. Managers should give employees the opportunity to express their ideas and suggestions on workplace issues. Effective managers learn to become good listeners.
5. Learn from employees themselves what motivates them. Because what motivates each employee is different, managers must customize the rewards they offer. The best way to find out what employees want is to get to know them and then ask them.
6. Learn what on-the-job activities employees choose to do when they have free time and then create opportunities for them to perform those activities on a more regular basis. Employees do well at those tasks they enjoy most.
7. Personally congratulate employees for jobs well done. A survey of 1,500 employees from a variety of work settings found that the most powerful motivator was recognition. Not only is it powerful, but it also doesn't cost anything.
8. Recognize the power of a manager's presence. Employees like frequent contact with their managers, however brief, because it indicates that the manager recognizes the importance of their work.
9. Write personal notes to employees about their performances. Such tangible recognition is a powerful motivator. These notes often make it to the home hall of fame—the refrigerator door.
10. Publicly recognize employees for good work. Given that one-on-one recognition is such an important motivator, consider the power of public recognition to accelerate an employee's performance.
11. Include morale-building meetings that celebrate team success. Although they don't have to be elaborate, team success celebrations help employees build camaraderie and a sense of togetherness.
12. Give employees good jobs to do. Boring, routine, unchallenging work saps employee motivation faster than anything. Proper job design is an important part of effective motivation.
13. Make sure employees have the tools available to do their best work. Like good mechanics, smart managers know that doing a job well requires the right tools. Plus, when managers provide good equipment, employees see it as an investment in their abilities.
14. Recognize employees' personal needs. With so many dual-career families in our society, workers appreciate companies that acknowledge and care for their personal needs by offering flextime, on-site day care, personal time allowances, and other conveniences.
15. Use performance as the basis for promotions. Although it makes sense to promote those employees who are the best and the most productive, too many companies continue to use seniority or politics to determine who gets promoted.
16. Establish a comprehensive promote-from-within policy. One of the best ways to spur employees to higher levels of performance is to show them that doing so leads to promotions within the company.
17. Emphasize the company's commitment to long-term employment. Although no company can offer a blanket "no-layoff" guarantee in this age, managers can communicate a "lifetime employment without guarantees" attitude. Job security for top performers is an important source of motivation.
18. Foster a sense of community. Forming a company around teams is a great way to start, but encouraging employees to recognize fellow workers for top performances can do wonders.
19. Pay people competitively based on what they are worth. If employees believe they are compensated fairly, they won't be preoccupied with their paychecks, and a company can get the most from its nonfinancial awards.
20. Give employees a financial reason to excel by offering them a share of the profits or a share of the company. Employees begin to act like owners when they are owners. Sharing ownership—or at least profits—gives them a major incentive to do everything they can to see that the company prospers.

> To be successful in business, you have to be going somewhere, and everyone involved in getting you there has to know where it is. That's a basic rule, a higher law, but most companies miss . . . the fact that you have a much better chance of winning if everyone knows what it takes to win.[84]

In other words, getting or giving feedback implies that a business owner has established meaningful targets that serve as standards of performance for her, her employees, and the company as a whole. One characteristic successful people have in common is that they set goals and objectives—usually challenging ones—for themselves. Business owners are no different. Successful entrepreneurs usually set targets for performance that make them stretch to achieve, and then they encourage their employees to do the same. The result is that they keep their companies constantly moving forward.

TableTalk

J.J. Stupp, founder of TableTalk, a company that produces decks of cards imprinted with fascinating facts and questions designed to stimulate meaningful conversations, makes goal setting a regular part of her business routine. "Goals are vital to the work plan of any small business," she says. "Writing down short-term and long-term goals for my business helps me stay focused."[85]

For feedback to have impact as a motivating force in a business requires business owners to follow the procedure illustrated in Figure 14.2.

DECIDING WHAT TO MEASURE. The first step in the feedback loop is deciding what to measure. Every business is characterized by a set of numbers that are critical to its success, and these "critical numbers" are what the entrepreneur should focus on. Obvious crit-

FIGURE 14.2
The Feedback Loop

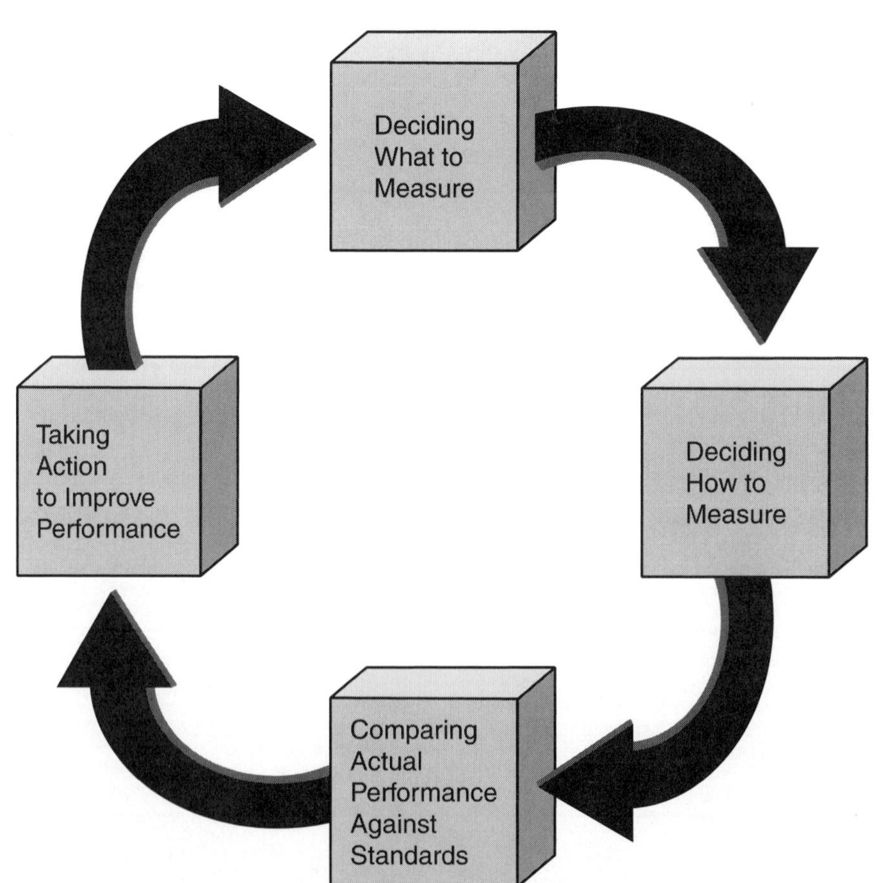

ical numbers include sales, profits, profit margins, cash flow, and other standard financial measures. However, running beneath these standard and somewhat universal measures of performance is an undercurrent of critical numbers that are unique to a company's operations. In most cases, these are the numbers that actually drive profits, cash flow, and other financial measures and are the company's real critical numbers.

Example

For instance, in a conversation with another business owner, a hotel franchisee said that his company's critical number was profit and that the way to earn a profit was to control costs. His managerial efforts focused on making sure that his employees knew exactly what to do, how to do it, and how much they could spend doing it. The only problem was that the hotel was losing money.

"Tell me," said his friend, "how do you make money in this business?"

"We fill rooms," said the hotelier.

"How many rooms do you have to fill to break even?"

"Seventy-one percent," came the reply, "but we're only running at 67 percent."

"How many people know that?" asked his friend.

"Two," he said.

"Maybe that's your problem," observed his friend.

The hotel owner quickly realized that one of his company's most critical numbers was occupancy rate; that's what drove profits! His managerial focus had been misguided, and he had failed to get his employees involved in solving the problem. The hotel owner put together an incentive plan for employees based on occupancy rate. Once the rate surpassed 71 percent, employees qualified for bonuses; the higher the occupancy rate, the bigger the bonuses. He also involved employees in identifying other critical numbers, such as customer retention rates and customer satisfaction levels, and began tracking results and posting them for everyone to see. Before long, every employee in the hotel was involved in and excited about exceeding their targets. The occupancy rate, customer retention rate, customer satisfaction scores and profit all shot up. The hotel owner had learned not only what his company's critical numbers were but how to use them to motivate employees![86]

DECIDING HOW TO MEASURE. Once a business owner identifies his company's critical numbers, the issue of how to best measure them arises. In some cases, identifying the critical numbers defines the measurements the owner must make (e.g., the occupancy rate at the hotel mentioned in the preceding example), and measuring them simply becomes a matter of collecting and analyzing data. In other cases, the method of measurement is not as obvious—or as tangible. For instance, in some businesses, social responsibility is a key factor, but how should a manager measure his company's performance on such an intangible concept? One of the best ways to develop methods for measuring such factors is to use brainstorming sessions involving employees, customers, and even outsiders. For example, one company used this technique to develop a "fun index," which used the results of an employee survey to measure how much fun employees had at work (and, by extension, how satisfied they were with their work, the company, and their managers).

Whatever method a business owner designs to measure a company's critical numbers, it must meet two criteria: validity and reliability. **Validity** is the extent to which a measuring device or technique actually measures what it is intended to measure and how well it measures that factor. **Reliability** is the extent to which a measurement device or technique produces consistent measurements of a factor over time. To be reliable, a measurement technique must be stable. Without measurements that are both valid and reliable, a company could be chasing after solutions to performance gaps that do not really exist! The performance gap appears only because the measurements are faulty or misleading. To avoid this

validity—*the extent to which a measuring device or technique actually measures what it is intended to measure and how well it measures that factor.*

reliability—*the extent to which a measurement device or technique produces consistent measurements of a factor over time.*

problem, managers and employees should carefully define the measurements they will use to track performance and determine the procedure used to collect and to analyze the data.

COMPARING ACTUAL RESULTS WITH STANDARDS. In this stage of the feedback loop, the idea is to look for deviations in either direction from the performance standards the company has set for itself. In other words, opportunities to improve performance arise when there is a gap between "what should be" and "what is." The most serious deviations usually are those for which actual performance falls far below the standard. Managers and employees must focus their efforts on figuring out why actual performance is substandard. The goal is not to hunt down the guilty party (or parties) for punishment but to discover the cause of the subpar performance and fix it! Managers should not ignore deviations in the other direction, however. When actual performance consistently exceeds the company's standards, it is an indication that the standards are set too low. The company should look closely at "raising the bar another notch" to spur motivation.

TAKING ACTION TO IMPROVE PERFORMANCE. When managers or employees detect a performance gap, their next challenge is to decide which course of action will eliminate it most effectively. Typically, several suitable alternatives to solving a performance problem exist; the key is finding an acceptable solution that solves the problem quickly, efficiently, and effectively.

Performance Appraisal

performance appraisal— *the process of evaluating an employee's performance against desired performance standards.*

One of the most common methods of providing feedback on employee performance is through **performance appraisal,** the process of evaluating an employee's actual performance against desired performance standards. Most performance appraisal programs strive to accomplish three goals: (1) to give employees feedback about how they are doing their jobs, which can be an important source of motivation; (2) to provide a business owner and an employee the opportunity to develop a plan for developing the employee's skills and abilities and for improving his performance; and (3) to establish a basis for determining promotions and salary increases. Although the primary purpose of performance appraisals is to encourage and to help employees improve their performances, too often they turn into uncomfortable confrontations that do nothing more than upset the employee, aggravate the business owner, and destroy trust and morale. Why? Because most business owners don't understand how to conduct an effective performance appraisal.

Although American businesses have been conducting performance appraisals for more than 85 years, most companies, their managers, and their employees are dissatisfied with the entire process. Common complaints include unclear standards and objectives; managers who lack information about employees' performances; managers who are unprepared or who lack honesty and sincerity; and managers who use general, ambiguous terms to describe employees' performances. Perhaps the biggest complaint concerning appraisals is that they happen only periodically—most often just once a year. Employees do not have the opportunity to receive any ongoing feedback on a regular basis. All too often, a manager saves up all of the negative feedback to give an employee and then dumps it on him in the annual performance review. Not only does it destroy the employee's motivation, but it does nothing to improve the employee's performance. What good does it do to tell an employee that six months before, he botched an assignment that caused the company to lose a customer. One writer compares the lack of ongoing feedback to asking employees to bowl in the dark. They can hear some pins falling, but they have no idea which ones are left standing for the next frame. "Two pins left," comments the manager. "Which ones?" asks the employee. "Don't bother me. Just keep bowling," says the manager. "I'll be back tomorrow to tell you how you did." At the end of the next day, the manager tells the worker, "You bowled poorly yesterday." "What was my score?" asks the employee. "I don't know,

Source: DILBERT @ UFS

but it was terrible," the manager replies.[87] How motivated would you be to keep bowling? Managers should address problems when they occur rather than wait until the performance appraisal session. Continuous feedback, both positive and negative, is a much more effective way to improve employees' performances and to increase their motivation to produce.

MAKING PERFORMANCE APPRAISALS WORK. If done properly, performance appraisals can be effective ways to provide employee feedback and to improve workers' performances. However, it takes planning and preparation on the business owner's part. The following guidelines can help a business owner create a performance appraisal system that actually works:

- *Link the employee's performance criteria to the job description discussed earlier in this chapter.* To evaluate an employee's performance effectively, a manager must understand the job he is in very well.
- *Establish meaningful, job-related, observable, measurable, and fair performance criteria.* The criteria should describe behaviors and actions, not traits and characteristics. What kind of behavior constitutes a solid performance in this job?
- *Prepare for the appraisal session by outlining the key points you want to cover with the employee.* Important points to include are the employee's strengths and weaknesses and developing a plan for improving his performance.
- *Invite the employee to provide an evaluation of his own job performance based on the performance criteria.* In one small company, workers rate themselves on a one-to-five scale in categories of job-related behavior and skills as part of the performance appraisal system. Then they meet with their supervisors to compare their evaluations with those of their supervisors and discuss them. Workers also evaluate their bosses as part of the review process.[88]
- *Be specific.* One of the most common complaints employees have about the appraisal process is that managers' comments are too general to be of any value. Offer the employee specific examples of his desirable or undesirable behavior.
- *Keep a record of employees' critical incidents—both positive and negative.* The most productive evaluations are those based on a manager's direct observation of their employees' on-the-job performances. Such records also can be vital in case legal problems arise.
- *Discuss an employee's strengths and weaknesses.* An appraisal session is not the time to "unload" about everything an employee has done wrong over the past year. Use it as an opportunity to design a plan for improvement and to recognize employees' strengths, efforts, and achievements.
- *Incorporate employees' goals into the appraisal.* Ideally, the standard against which to measure an employee's performance is against the goals he has played a role in setting. Workers are more likely to be motivated to achieve goals that they have helped establish.
- *Keep the evaluation constructive.* Avoid the tendency to belittle employees. Do not dwell on past failures. Instead, point out specific things they should do better and help them develop meaningful goals for the future and a strategy for getting there.

- *Focus on behaviors, actions, and results.* Problems arise when managers move away from tangible results and actions and begin to critique employees' abilities and attitudes. Such criticism creates a negative tone for the appraisal session and undercuts its primary purpose.
- *No surprises.* If a business owner is doing her job well, performance appraisals should contain no surprises for employees or the business owner. The ideal time to correct improper behavior or slumping performance is when it happens, not months later. Managers should provide employees with continuous feedback on their performances and use the appraisal session to keep employees on the right track.
- *Plan for the future.* Smart business owners use appraisal sessions as gateways to workers' future success. They spend only about 20 percent of the time discussing past performance; they use the remaining 80 percent of the time to develop goals, objectives and a plan for the future.

peer reviews—*an appraisal technique in which an employee's coworkers evaluate his job performance.*

upward feedback—*an appraisal technique in which employees evaluate their manager's job performance.*

Many companies are encouraging employees to evaluate each other in **peer reviews** or to evaluate their bosses in **upward feedback,** both part of a technique called 360-degree feedback in which employees get feedback from above, from below, and from all around. Studies suggest that 13 percent of U.S. companies use 360-degree evaluations as part of their performance appraisal systems.[89] For instance, at W.L. Gore and Associates, the maker of Gore-Tex fabric, employees' pay increases depend on biannual peer reviews.[90] Peer appraisals such as those at W.L. Gore can be especially useful because an employee's coworkers see his on-the-job performance every day. As a result, peer evaluations tend to be more accurate and more valid than those of some managers. Plus, they may capture behavior that managers might miss. Disadvantages of peer appraisals include potential retaliation against coworkers who criticize, the possibility that appraisals will be reduced to "popularity contests," and workers who refuse to offer any criticism because they feel uncomfortable evaluating others. Some bosses using upward feedback report similar problems, including personal attacks and extreme evaluations by vengeful subordinates.

5. Describe the steps in developing a management succession plan for a growing business that will allow a smooth transition of leadership to the next generation.

MANAGEMENT SUCCESSION: PASSING THE TORCH OF LEADERSHIP

More than 90 percent of all companies in the United States are family owned. Not all family-owned businesses are small, however; one-third of the *Fortune* 500 companies are family businesses. Unfortunately, 70 percent of first-generation businesses fail to survive into the second generation; of those that do survive, only 12 percent make it to the third generation, and just 3 percent make it to the fourth generation and beyond.[91] Sibling rivalries, fights over control of the business, and personality conflicts often lead to nasty battles that can tear families apart and destroy once-thriving businesses.

The best way to avoid deadly turf battles and conflicts is to develop a succession plan for the company. Although business founders inevitably want their businesses to survive them and almost 81 percent intend to pass them on to their children, they seldom support their intentions by a plan to accomplish that goal. About 25 percent of all family business owners do *not* have a formal management succession plan![92] These owners dream of their businesses continuing in the family but take no significant steps to make their dreams a reality.

Most of the family businesses in existence today were started after World War II, and their founders are ready to pass the torch of leadership on to the next generation. Experts estimate that between 1993 and 2013, $4.8 trillion in wealth will be transferred from one generation to the next, much of it through family businesses.[93] For a smooth transition from one generation to the next, these companies need a succession plan. Without a succession plan, family businesses face an increased risk of faltering or failing in the next generation. Those businesses with the greatest probability of surviving are the ones whose owners prepare a succession plan well before it is time to "pass the torch of leadership" to the next generation. Succession planning also allows business owners to minimize the impact of taxes on their businesses, their estates, and their successors' wealth as well. With tax rates on gifts and estates as high as 55 percent, a plan that reduces the bite taxes take out of a business transfer is no small matter.

Succession planning reduces the tension and stress created by these conflicts by gradually "changing the guard." A well-developed succession plan is like the smooth, graceful exchange of a baton between runners in a relay race. The new runner still has maximum energy; the concluding runner has already spent her energy by running at maximum speed. The athletes never come to a stop to exchange the baton; instead, the handoff takes place on the move. The race is a skillful blend of the talents of all team members—an exchange of leadership that is so smooth and powerful that the business never falters, but accelerates, fueled by a new source of energy at each leg of the race.

How to Develop a Management Succession Plan

Creating a succession plan involves the following steps.

Step 1: Select the successor. Entrepreneurs should never assume that their children want to take control of the business. Above all, they should not be afraid to ask the question: "Do you really want to take over the family business?" Too often, children in this situation tell Mom and Dad what they want to hear out of loyalty, pressure, or guilt. It is critical to remember at this juncture in the life of a business that children do not necessarily inherit their parents' entrepreneurial skills and desires. By leveling with the children about the business and their options regarding a family succession, the owner will know which heirs, if any, are willing to assume leadership of the business. When naming a successor, merit is a better standard to use than birth order. When considering a successor, an entrepreneur should consider taking the following actions.

- Make it clear to all involved that they are not required to join the business on a full-time basis. Family members' goals, ambitions, and talents should be foremost in their career decisions.
- Do not assume that a successor must always come from within the family. Simply being born into a family does *not* guarantee that a person will make a good business leader. For instance, when Bill France stepped down as president of NASCAR, Inc., the stock car racing business France took over from his father, he named a nonfamily member, Mike Helton, to succeed him. Helton had served as the company's chief operating officer for years under France.[94]
- Give family members the opportunity to work outside the business first to learn first-hand how others conduct business. Working for others will allow them to develop knowledge, confidence, and credibility before stepping back into the family business.

One of the worst mistakes entrepreneurs can make is to postpone naming a successor until just before they are ready to step down. The problem is especially acute when more than one family member works for the company and is interested in assuming leadership of it. Sometimes founders avoid naming successors because they don't want to hurt the family members who are not chosen to succeed them. However, both the business and the family will be better off if, after observing the family members as they work in the business, the founder picks a successor based on that person's skills and abilities.

One-Hour Martinizing

For instance, Fred Jones, owner of 26 family-owned One-Hour Martinizing Dry Cleaning stores, faced what could have been a difficult succession decision because all five of his children were involved in running the business. After carefully evaluating each child's strengths and weaknesses, Jones named his son Tom as his successor. Tom, who is not the oldest of the Jones children, was well qualified, having earned both business experience as a CPA and the trust and respect of the company's employees. None of Tom's brothers and sisters were surprised or upset at their father's decision.[95]

Step 2: Create a survival kit for the successor. Once he identifies a successor, an entrepreneur should prepare a survival kit and then brief the future leader on its contents, which should include all of the company's critical documents (wills, trusts, insurance policies, financial statements, bank accounts, key contracts, corporate bylaws, etc.). The founder should be sure that the successor reads and understands all the relevant documents in the kit. Other important steps the owner should take to prepare the successor to take over leadership of the business include:

- Create a strategic analysis for the future. Working with the successor, entrepreneurs should identify the primary opportunities and the challenges facing the company and the requirements for meeting them.
- On a regular basis, share with the successor the vision of the business's future direction, describing key factors that have led to its success and those that will bring future success.
- Be open and listen to the successor's views and concerns.
- Teach and learn at the same time.
- Relate specifically how the firm's key success factors have produced tangible results.
- Tie the key success factors to performance and profitability.
- Explain the strategies of the business and the operational key success factors.
- Discuss the values and philosophy of the business and how they have inspired and influenced past actions.
- Discuss the people in the business and their strengths and weaknesses.
- Discuss the philosophy underlying the firm's compensation policy and explain why employees are paid what they are.
- Make a list of the firm's most important customers and its key suppliers or vendors and review the history of all dealings with the parties on both lists.
- Discuss how to treat these key players to ensure the company's continued success and its smooth and error-free ownership transition.
- Develop a job analysis by taking an inventory of the activities involved in leading the company. This analysis can show successors those activities on which they should be spending most of their time.
- Document as much process knowledge—"how we do things"—as possible. After many years in their jobs, business owners are not even aware of their vast reservoirs of knowledge. For them, making decisions is a natural part of their business lives. They do it effortlessly because they have so much knowledge and experience. It is easy to forget that a successor will not have the benefit of those years of experience unless the founder communicates it.

Camp Echo Lake

Morry Stein, the head of Camp Echo Lake, a family-run youth camp, took the time to develop a successor's survival kit in case something happened to him. When he was killed tragically in an airplane crash, Stein's sons, Tony and George, and his wife were able to use the written instructions to help make the difficult transition. In the kit he left behind, Stein included the names of his most trusted advisors, advice for handling different employees, where to find important company documents, and a touching pep talk for his family. The transition went smoothly not only because of the survival kit Stein had prepared, but also because he had taken the time to sit down regularly with both of his sons to discuss "the state of the camp" as he called it. "About ten years ago, we started having business meetings around the dining room table at my parents' house," explains Tony. "We talked about new program ideas, the future of camping, how we could raise tuition, when we would enter the business, what our strengths were, and what we liked to do."[96]

Step 3: Groom the successor. The discussions that set the stage for the transition of leadership are time-consuming and require openness by both parties. This is the process by which business founders transfer their knowledge to the next generation. In fact, grooming the successor is the founder's greatest teaching and development responsibility, and it takes time. To implement the succession plan, the founder must be:

- Patient, realizing that the transfer of power is gradual and evolutionary and that the successor should earn responsibility and authority one step at a time until the final transfer of power takes place.
- Willing to accept that the successor will make mistakes.
- Skillful at using the successor's mistakes as a teaching tool.
- An effective communicator and an especially tolerant listener.
- Capable of establishing reasonable expectations for the successor's performance.
- Able to articulate the keys to the successor's performance.

Grooming a successor can begin at an early age simply by involving children in the family business and observing which ones have the greatest ability and interest in the company.

Alexander Machinery

At age 9, Jay Alexander started going to work with his father at the family business, Alexander Machinery, a maker of textile and road construction equipment. At 11, Jay approached his father and asked for a job in the company, beginning a long succession of jobs over the next 12 years. "I've worked practically every job in the company," says Jay. "I've never worked anywhere else." When Jay's father, Bill, decided to step away from the business he founded, Jay was the natural choice as his successor, although Jay's sister also works for the company. "This business has come naturally to him," says Bill.[97]

Step 4: Promote an environment of trust and respect. Another priceless gift a founder can leave a successor is an environment of trust and respect. Trust and respect on the part of the founder and others fuel the successor's desire to learn and excel and build the successor's confidence in making decisions. Developing a competent successor over a five- to ten-year period is realistic. Empowering the successor by gradually delegating responsibilities creates an environment in which all parties can objectively view the growth and development of the successor. Customers, creditors, suppliers, and staff members can gradually develop confidence in the successor. The final transfer of power is not a dramatic, wrenching change but a smooth, coordinated passage.

Step 5: Cope with the financial realities of estate and gift taxes. The final step in developing a workable management succession plan involves structuring the transition so as to minimize the impact of estate, gift, and inheritance taxes on family members and the business. Entrepreneurs who fail to consider the impact of these taxes may force their heirs to sell a successful business just to pay the estate's tax bill. In a recent survey of small busi-

YOU BE THE CONSULTANT . . .

Who's Next?

Dick Strossner wants the family business to continue into the next generation, but so far, none of the younger members in the family have shown much interest in taking over the bakery started by his father in 1947. Strossner, 57, owns 80 percent of the bakery's stock. His sister, who manages the business's financial affairs, owns 10 percent, and Strossner's son, Richard, owns the remaining 10 percent. Both Dick and his sister have worked in Strossner's Bakery since they were teenagers.

When Strossner's parents decided to gradually get out of the business in 1976, Dick was the natural choice to take over management of the bakery because he had been working in the family business for nearly two decades. "Dad taught me almost everything I know about baking," he says. "He did a lot of things I didn't respect and understand until I took over." Although Dick took control of the company, his father continued to work in the family business until he died at the age of 82. The transition from one generation of leadership to the next was not always smooth. Strossner began to experiment with the business, trying new products and different approaches, some of which his father said would never work. He introduced computers to the bakery (an idea Dad was against) and shifted its product mix from bread and Danish pastries to cakes and Danish pastries. Although his father disagreed with some of the experiments, Strossner says, he never interfered, allowing Dick to try whatever he wanted. In most cases, Strossner recalls, his father was right about which ideas would work and which ones would not. "Dad was a major asset for the business," says Strossner, "I really needed him." Under Dick's leadership, the bakery has grown and now includes both a catering business and a florist operation.

With his own retirement not too far away, Strossner is now considering the best way to deal with the issue of management succession. He hopes his son, who currently is not working in the bakery, will take over the leadership reins for the next generation. "I'm thinking he will be back," Strossner says. "He's worked in every single facet of the business." If his son chooses not to return to the bakery, Strossner says his employees are skilled enough and experienced enough to run the business without him. He also wants to start relinquishing control of the family business in time to avoid the bite of heavy estate taxes. Currently, Strossner's estate planning is based on insurance policies. "If I were to go away today, I have enough insurance to cover the taxes," he says.

1. What advice would you offer Dick Strossner concerning a management succession plan?
2. What steps should Strossner take to develop a management succession plan?
3. What tools would you suggest Strossner use for minimizing estate taxes?

Source: Adapted from Jenny Munro, "Bridging the Generation Gap," *Upstate Business,* October 8, 2000, pp. 8–9.

ness owners by researchers at Kennesaw State University, more than half believed that their estates would be hit with a tax bill that would limit their companies' growth potential. One-third said that paying the expected estate tax would require their heirs to sell either part or all of their businesses![98]

Perkins Flowers

Ella Perkins, co-owner of Perkins Flowers, and her son Gordon saw the need to develop an estate plan to minimize the impact of estate and gift taxes on the company, which Gordon was running. Each year, Ella gave Gordon $10,000 worth of stock in the company, the maximum amount the law allows without triggering gift taxes. She also transferred majority ownership in the company to Gordon using other estate planning tools so that estate taxes would be smaller on her minority share of the business. Gordon also purchased enough life insurance for his mother to pay the estimated estate tax bill. When Ella died at age 83, Gordon discovered that despite their attempts at estate planning, the amount of tax due was more than he had expected. "At the very least," he says, "it's going to repress the growth of my business for some significant amount of time." He says that he may have to sell a 43-acre tree farm the company owns to pay the full tax bill.[99]

Although tax laws currently allow individuals to pass up to $1 million of assets to their heirs without incurring any estate taxes, the tax rate on transfers above that amount *starts* at 37 percent! The tax rate climbs to 55 percent for estates valued at more than $3 million. Without proper estate planning, an entrepreneur's family members will incur a painful tax bite when they inherit the business. Yet, according to the Arthur Andersen/MassMutual Survey of American Family Businesses, only 25 percent of all small business owners have completed an estate plan, even though they have 70 to 80 percent of their net worth tied up in their businesses![100] Entrepreneurs should be actively engaged in estate planning no later than age 45; those who start businesses early in their lives or whose businesses grow rapidly may need to begin as early as age 30. A variety of options exists that may prove to be helpful in reducing the estate tax liability. Each operates in a different fashion, but their objective remains the same: to remove a portion of business owners' assets out of their estates so that when they die, those assets will not be subject to estate taxes. Many of these estate planning tools need time to work their magic, so the key is to put them in place early on in the life of the business.

BUY/SELL AGREEMENT. One of the most popular estate planning techniques is the buy/sell agreement. A survey by the Chartered Life Underwriters and the Chartered Life Financial Consultants found that 76 percent of small business owners who have estate plans have created buy/sell agreements.[101] A **buy/sell agreement** is a contract that co-owners often rely on to ensure the continuity of a business. In a typical arrangement, the co-owners create a contract stating that each agrees to buy the others out in case of the death or disability of one. That way, the heirs of the deceased or disabled owner can "cash out" of the business while leaving control of the business in the hands of the remaining owners. The buy/sell agreement specifies a formula for determining the value of the business at the time the agreement is to be executed. One problem with buy/sell agreements is that the remaining co-owners may not have the cash available to buy out the disabled or deceased owner. To resolve this issue, many businesses buy life and disability insurance for each of the owners in amounts large enough to cover the purchase price of their respective shares of the business.

buy/sell agreement—*a contract among co-owners of a business stating that each agrees to buy out the others in case of the death or disability of one.*

LIFETIME GIFTING. The owners of a successful business may transfer money to their children (or other recipients) from their estate throughout the parents' lives. Current federal tax regulations allow individuals to make gifts of $10,000 per year, per parent, per recipient, that are exempt from federal gift taxes. Each child would be required to pay income taxes on the $10,000 gift they receive, but the children are usually in lower tax brackets than those of the giver. For instance, husband-and-wife business owners could give $1.2 million worth of stock to their three children and their spouses over a period of 10 years without incurring any estate or gift taxes at all.

SETTING UP A TRUST. A **trust** is a contract between a grantor (the company founder) and a trustee (generally a bank officer or an attorney) in which the grantor gives to the trustee legal title to assets (e.g., stock in the company), which the trustee agrees to hold for the beneficiaries (children). The beneficiaries can receive income from the trust, or they can receive the property in the trust, or both, at some specified time. Trusts can take a wide variety of forms, but two broad categories of trusts are available: revocable trusts and irrevocable trusts. A **revocable trust** is one that a grantor can change or revoke during his lifetime. Under present tax laws, however, the only trust that provides a tax benefit is an **irrevocable trust,** in which the grantor cannot require the trustee to return the assets held in trust. The value of the grantor's estate is lowered because the assets in an irrevocable trust are excluded from the value of the estate. However, an irrevocable trust places severe restrictions on the grantor's control of the property placed in the trust. Business owners use several types of irrevocable trusts to lower their estate tax liabilities:

trust—*a contract between a grantor (the company founder) and a trustee in which the grantor gives the trustee assets (e.g., company stock), which for trustee holds for the trust's beneficiaries (e.g., the grantor's heirs).*

revocable trust—*a trust that a grantor can change or revoke during his lifetime.*

irrevocable trust—*a trust in which a grantor cannot require the trustee to return the assets held in trust.*

- *Bypass trust.* The most basic type of trust is the bypass trust, which allows a business owner to put $1.3 million into trust naming his spouse as the beneficiary upon his death. The spouse receives the income from the trust throughout her life, but the principal in the trust goes to the couple's heirs free of estate taxes upon the spouse's death.
- *Irrevocable life insurance trust.* This type of trust allows a business owner to keep the proceeds of a life insurance policy out of his estate and away from estate taxes, freeing up that money to pay the taxes on the remainder of the estate. To get the tax benefit, business owners must be sure that the business or the trust (rather than themselves) own the insurance policy. The disadvantage of an irrevocable life insurance trust is that if the owner dies within three years of establishing it, the insurance proceeds do become part of his estate and are subject to estate taxes.
- *Irrevocable asset trust.* An irrevocable asset trust is similar to a life insurance trust except that it is designed to pass the assets in the parents' estate on to their children. The children do not have control of the assets while the parents are still living, but they do receive the income from those assets. Upon the parents' death, the assets in the trust go to the children without being subjected to the estate tax.
- *Grantor retained annuity trust (GRAT).* A grantor retained annuity trust (GRAT) is a special type of irrevocable trust and has become one of the most popular tools for entrepreneurs to transfer ownership of a business while maintaining control over it and minimizing estate taxes. Under a GRAT, an owner can put property in an irrevocable trust for a maximum of 10 years. While the trust is in effect, the grantor retains the voting power and receives the interest income from the property in the trust. At the end of the trust (not to exceed 10 years), the property passes to the beneficiaries (heirs). The beneficiaries are required to pay a gift tax on the value of the assets placed in the GRAT. However, the IRS taxes GRAT gifts only according to their discounted present value because the heirs did not receive use of the property while it was in trust. The primary disadvantage of using a GRAT in estate planning is that if the grantor dies during the life of the GRAT, its assets pass back into the grantor's estate. These assets then become subject to the full estate tax.

Establishing a trust requires meeting many specific legal requirements and is not something business owners should do on their own. It is much better to hire experienced attorneys, accountants, and financial advisors to assist. Although the cost of establishing a trust can be high, the tax savings they generate are well worth the expense.

estate freeze—*a strategy that minimizes estate taxes by creating two classes of stock for a business: preferred voting stock for the parents and nonvoting common stock for the children.*

ESTATE FREEZE. An **estate freeze** minimizes estate taxes by having family members create two classes of stock for the business: (1) preferred voting stock for the parents and (2) nonvoting common stock for the children. The value of the preferred stock is frozen while the common stock reflects the anticipated increased market value of the business. Any appreciation in the value of the business after the transfer is not subject to estate taxes. However, the parent must pay gift taxes on the value of the common stock given to the children. The value of the common stock is the total value of the business less the value of the voting preferred stock retained by the parent. The parents also must accept taxable dividends at the market rate on the preferred stock they own.

family limited partnership—*a strategy that allows business-owning parents to transfer their company to their children (lowering their estate taxes) while still retaining control over it for themselves.*

FAMILY LIMITED PARTNERSHIP. Creating a **family limited partnership (FLP)** allows business-owning parents to transfer their company to their children (thus lowering their estate taxes) while still retaining control over it for themselves. To create a family limited partnership, the parents (or parent) set up a partnership among themselves and their children. The parents retain the general partnership interest, which can be as low as 1 percent, and the children become the limited partners. As general partners, the parents control both the limited partnership and the family business. In other words, nothing in the way the company operates has to change. Over time, the parents can transfer company stock into the limited partnership, ultimately passing ownership of the company to their children. One of the principal tax benefits of an FLP is that it allows discounts on the value of the shares of company stock the parents transfer into the limited partnership. Because a family business is closely held, shares of ownership in it, especially minority shares, are not as marketable as those of a publicly held company. As a result, company shares transferred into the limited partnership are discounted at 20 to 50 percent of their full market value, producing a large tax savings for everyone involved. The average discount is 40 percent, but that amount varies based on the industry and the individual company involved. An FLP is an ideal part of a succession plan when there has been a buildup of substantial value in a business and the older generation has a substantial amount of liquidity. Because of their ability to reduce estate and gift taxes, family limited partnerships have become one of the most popular estate planning tools in recent years.

Developing a succession plan and preparing a successor require a wide variety of skills, some of which the business founder will not have. That's what it is important to bring into the process experts when necessary. Entrepreneurs often call on their attorneys, accountants, insurance agents, and financial planners to help them build a succession plan that works best for their particular situations. Because the issues involved can be highly complex and charged with emotion, bringing in trusted advisors to help improves the quality of the process and provides an objective perspective.

CHAPTER SUMMARY

1. Explain the challenges involved in the entrepreneur's role as leader and what it takes to be a successful leader.
   - Leadership is the process of influencing and inspiring others to work to achieve a common goal and then giving them the power and the freedom to achieve it.
   - Management and leadership are not the same, yet both are essential to a small company's success. Leadership without management is unbridled; management without leadership is uninspired. Leadership gets a small business going; management keeps it going.
2. Describe the importance of hiring the right employees and how to avoid making hiring mistakes.
   - The decision to hire a new employee is an important one for every business, but its impact is magnified many times in a small company. Every "new hire" a business owner makes determines the heights to which the company can climb—or the depths to which it will plunge.
   - To avoid making hiring mistakes, entrepreneurs should develop meaningful job descriptions and job specifications; plan and conduct an effective interview; and check references before hiring any employee.
3. Explain how to build the kind of company culture and structure to support the entrepreneur's mission and goals and to motivate employees to achieve them.
   - Company culture is the distinctive, unwritten code of conduct that governs the behavior, attitudes, relationships, and style of an organization. Culture arises from an entrepreneur's consistent and relentless pursuit of a set of core values that everyone in the company can believe in. Small companies' flexible structures can be a major competitive weapon.
   - Entrepreneurs rely on six different management styles to guide their companies as they grow. The first three (craftsman, classic, and coordinator) involve running a company without any management assistance and are best suited for small companies in the early stages of growth; the last three (entrepreneur-plus-employee team, small partnership, big-team venture) rely on a team approach to run the company as its growth rate heats up.
   - Team-based management is growing in popularity among small firms. Companies that use teams effectively report significant gains in quality, reductions in cycle time, lower costs, increased customer satisfaction, and improved employee motivation and morale.
4. Discuss the ways in which entrepreneurs can motivate their workers to higher levels of performance.
   - Motivation is the degree of effort an employee exerts to accomplish a task; it shows up as excitement about work. Four important tools of motivation include empowerment, job design, rewards and compensation, and feedback.
   - Empowerment involves giving workers at every level of the organization the power, the freedom, and the responsibility to control their own work, to make decisions, and to take action to meet the company's objectives.
   - Job design techniques for enhancing employee motivation include job enlargement, job rotation, job enrichment, flextime, job sharing, and flexplace (which includes telecommuting).
   - Money is an important motivator for many workers, but it is not the only one. The key to using rewards such as recognition and praise and to motivate involves tailoring them to the needs and characteristics of the workers.

- Giving employees timely, relevant feedback about their job performances through a performance appraisal system can also be a powerful motivator.

5. Describe the steps in developing a management succession plan for a growing business that will allow a smooth transition of leadership to the next generation.
   - As their companies grow, entrepreneurs must begin to plan for passing the leadership baton to the next generation well in advance. A succession plan is a crucial element in successfully transferring a company to the next generation. Preparing a succession plan involves five steps: (1) Select the successor; (2) create a survival kit for the successor; (3) groom the successor; (4) promote an environment of trust and respect; and (5) cope with the financial realities of estate taxes.

DISCUSSION QUESTIONS

1. What is leadership? What is the difference between leadership and management?
2. What behaviors do effective leaders exhibit?
3. Why is it so important for small companies to hire the right employees? What can small business owners do to avoid making hiring mistakes?
4. What is a job description? A job specification? What functions do they serve in the hiring process?
5. Outline the procedure for conducting an effective interview.
6. What is company culture? What role does it play in a small company's success? What threats does rapid growth pose for a company's culture?
7. Explain the six different management styles entrepreneurs rely on to guide their companies as they grow (craftsman, classic, coordinator, entrepreneur-plus-employee team, small partnership, and big-team venture).
8. What mistakes do companies make when switching to team-based management? What can they do to avoid these mistakes? Explain the four phases teams typically go through.
9. What is empowerment? What benefits does it offer workers? The company? What must a small business manager do to make empowerment work in a company?
10. Explain the differences among job simplification, job enlargement, job rotation, and job enrichment. What impact do these different job designs have on workers?
11. Is money the "best" motivator? How do pay-for-performance compensation systems work? What other rewards are available to small business managers to use as motivators? How effective are they?
12. Suppose that a mail-order catalog company selling environmentally friendly products identifies its performance as a socially responsible company as a "critical number" in its success. Suggest some ways for the owner to measure this company's "social responsibility index."
13. What is performance appraisal? What are the most common mistakes managers make in performance appraisals? What should small business managers do to avoid making these mistakes?
14. Why is it so important for a small business owner to develop a management succession plan? Why is it so difficult for most business owners to develop such a plan? What are the steps that are involved in creating a succession plan?
15. Briefly describe the options a small business owner wanting to pass the family business on to the next generation can take to minimize the impact of estate taxes.

Beyond the Classroom...

1. Visit a local business that has experienced rapid growth in the past three years and ask the owner about the specific problems he or she had to face due to the organization's growth. How did the owner handle these problems? Looking back, what would he or she do differently?

2. Contact a local small business with at least 20 employees. Does the company have job descriptions and job specifications? What process does the owner use to hire a new employee? What questions does the owner typically ask candidates in an interview?

3. Ask the owner of a small manufacturing operation to give you a tour of his or her operation. During your tour, observe the way jobs are organized. To what extent does the company use the following job design concepts: job simplification? job enlargement? job rotation? job enrichment? flextime? job sharing? Based on your observations, what recommendations would you make to the owner about the company's job design?

4. Contact five small business owners about their plans for passing their businesses on to the next generation. Do they intend to pass the business along to a family member? Do they have a management succession plan? When do they plan to name a successor? Have they developed a plan for minimizing the effects of estate taxes? How many more years do they plan to work before retiring?

5. Entrepreneurs say that they have learned much about leadership from the movies! "Films beg to be interpreted and discussed," says one leadership consultant, "and from those discussions businesspeople come up with principles for their own jobs." A recent survey of small company CEOs by *Inc.* magazine resulted in the following list of the best movies for leadership lessons: *Apollo 13* (1995), *The Bridge on the River Kwai* (1957), *Dead Poets Society* (1989), *Elizabeth* (1998), *Glengarry Glen Ross* (1992), *It's a Wonderful Life* (1946), *Norma Rae* (1979), *One Flew Over the Cuckoo's Nest* (1975), *Twelve Angry Men* (1957), and *Twelve O'Clock High* (1949).[102] Rent one of these films and watch it with a group of your classmates. After viewing the movie, discuss the leadership lessons you learned from it and report the results to the other members of your class.

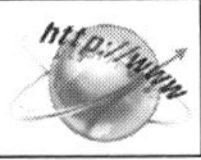

We invite you to visit this book's companion Web site at **www.prenhall.com/Zimmerer.**

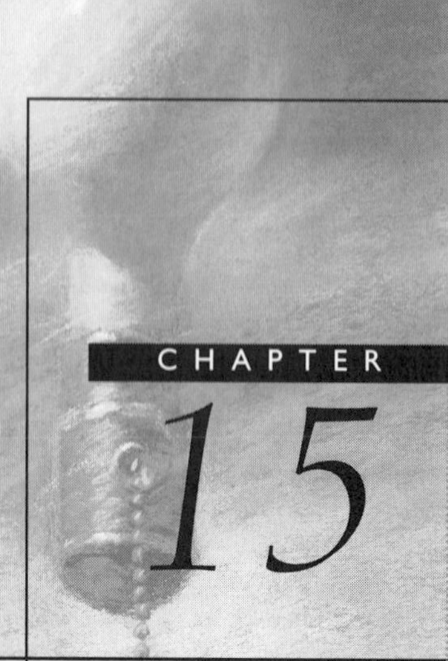

CHAPTER 15

E-Commerce and the Entrepreneur

If you don't believe deeply, wholly, and viscerally that the Net is going to change your business, you're going to lose. And if you don't understand the advantages of starting early and learning fast, you're going to lose.

—Gary Hamel and Jeff Sampler

The sure way to miss success is to miss the opportunity.

—Victor Charles

LEARNING OBJECTIVES

Upon completion of this chapter, you will be able to:

1. Describe the benefits of selling on the World Wide Web.
2. Understand the factors an entrepreneur should consider before launching into e-commerce.
3. Explain the 12 myths of e-commerce and how to avoid falling victim to them.
4. Discuss the five basic approaches available to entrepreneurs wanting to launch an e-commerce effort.
5. Explain the basic strategies entrepreneurs should follow to achieve success in their e-commerce efforts.
6. Learn the techniques of designing a killer Web site.
7. Explain how companies track the results from their Web sites.
8. Describe how e-businesses ensure the privacy and security of the information they collect and store from the Web.
9. Learn how to evaluate the effectiveness of a company's Web site.

As a student of business, you are fortunate to witness the emergence of an event that is reshaping the way companies of all sizes do business: e-commerce. E-commerce is creating a new economy, one that is connecting producers, sellers, and customers via technology in ways that have never before been possible. The result is a whole new set of companies built on business models that are turning traditional methods of commerce and industry on their heads. Companies that ignore the impact of the Internet on their markets run the risk of becoming as outdated to customers today as a rotary-dial telephone. The most successful companies are embracing the Internet, not as merely another advertising medium or marketing tool but as a mechanism for transforming their companies and changing *everything* about the way they do business. As these companies discover new, innovative ways to use the Internet, computers, and communications technology to connect with their suppliers and to serve their customers better, they are creating a new industrial order. In short, e-commerce has launched a revolution. Just as in previous revolutions in the business world, some old established players are being ousted, and new leaders are emerging. The winners are discovering new business opportunities, new ways of designing work, and new ways of organizing and operating their businesses.

Perhaps the most visible changes are occurring in the world of retailing. Although e-commerce will not replace traditional retailing, no retailer, from the smallest corner store to industry giant Wal-Mart, can afford to ignore the impact of the World Wide Web on their business models. Companies can take orders at the speed of light from anywhere in the world and at any time of day. The Internet enables companies to collect more information on customers' shopping and buying habits than any other medium in history. This ability means that companies can focus their marketing efforts like never before—for instance, selling garden supplies to customers who are most likely to buy them and not wasting resources trying to sell to those who have no interest in gardening. The capacity to track customers' Web-based shopping habits allows companies to personalize their approaches to marketing and to realize the benefits of individualized (or one-to-one) marketing (refer to Chapter 6). Ironically, the same Web-based marketing approach that allows companies to get so personal with their customers also can make shopping extremely impersonal. Entrepreneurs who set up shop on the Web will likely never meet their customers face-to-face or even talk to them. Yet, those customers, who can live anywhere in the world, will visit the online store at all hours of the day or night and expect to receive individual attention. Making a Web-based marketing approach succeed requires a business to strike a balance, creating an e-commerce strategy that capitalizes on the strengths of the Web while meeting customers' expectations of convenience and service.

In the world of e-commerce, the new business models recognize the power the Internet gives customers. Pricing, for example, is no longer as simple as it once was for companies. Auction sites such as eBay and Priceline.com mean that entrepreneurs can no longer be content to take into account only local competitors when setting their own prices. With a few mouse clicks, customers can compare the prices of the same or similar products and services from companies across the globe. In the new wired and connected economy, the balance of power is shifting to customers, and new business models recognize this fact. Consider, for example, the challenges auto dealers face when selling to customers armed with dealer cost and pricing information gathered from any one of dozens of Web sites. Because they know the cost of a car to the dealer, these informed customers are taking price out of the buying equation, causing dealers to emphasize other factors such as service or convenience to build long-term relationships. Auto dealerships are not the only companies facing this reality. One study by Ernst and Young found that 64 percent of Internet users research products online before buying them in stores or by telephone.[1]

In this fast-paced world of e-commerce, size no longer matters as much as speed and flexibility do. One of the Web's greatest strengths is its ability to provide companies with instantaneous customer feedback, giving them the opportunity to learn and to make necessary adjustments. Businesses, whatever their size, that are willing to experiment with different approaches to reaching customers and are quick to learn and adapt will grow and prosper; those that cannot will fall by the wayside. The Internet is creating a new industrial order, and companies that fail to adapt to it will soon become extinct.

E-commerce start-ups are redefining even the most traditional industries.

The Knot

When David Liu and Carley Roney began planning their wedding in 1995, they observed firsthand just how antiquated the bridal and wedding industry was. Having to spend countless hours contacting dozens of businesses to arrange for flowers, catering, music, clothing, and other wedding essentials and to register for gifts at various stores in preparation for their wedding, the couple thought, "There's got to be a better way." In 1996, Liu and Roney, along with partners Rob Fassino and Michael Wolfson, launched The Knot, a one-stop Web site **<www.theknot.com>** *for soon-to-wed couples. At The Knot, a couple can create a personalized wedding budget, develop their guest list, register for gifts in an online registry (which includes everything from china to scuba gear), select a honeymoon destination, purchase a wedding gown, and create their own wedding Web page. Brides can view more than 8,000 wedding dresses in a variety of styles (down to the stitching on the seed pearls), get advice on everything from announcements to wine, and join in chat rooms with other brides-to-be. The Knot has revolutionized the way couples plan their weddings and draws more than 250,000 visitors per month, 15 to 20 percent of whom are men. The site also is growing fast, adding more than 1,000 members a day. The Knot has captured the attention of advertisers because its customers spend readily on their weddings. (The average wedding in the United States costs more than $15,000 and has 12 people in the wedding party and 150 guests.) More than 85 percent of The Knot's customers are college educated and between the ages of 18 and 34, and thousands of newlyweds return to the site after their weddings to offer advice and to chat.*[2]

By using an innovative e-commerce business model to create an all-in-one, easy-to-use, online wedding site, The Knot has established a unique position in the market and has changed the way traditional companies in the market must compete.

High-volume, low-margin, commodity products are best suited for selling on the Web. Indeed, the items purchased most often online are books, CDs, computer hardware and software, and airline tickets. However, companies can—and do—sell practically anything over the Web, from antiques and pharmaceuticals to groceries and drug-free urine. A recent survey by Duke University and the Financial Executives Institute predicts that 56 percent of U.S. companies will sell their products online by 2003.[3] The most commonly cited reasons among owners of small and midsized companies for taking their companies to the Web are (1) to reach new customers, (2) to sell goods and services, (3) to disseminate information more quickly, (4) to keep up with competitors, and (5) to reach global markets.[4]

Companies of all sizes are establishing a presence on the Web because that's where their customers are. By 2003, the number of Internet users will grow to more than 500 million, up from 147 million at the end of 1998.[5] In 1998, 16.3 million people actually made purchases over the Internet; by 2003, that number will climb to 85 million! (See Figure 15.1.)[6] Although this torrid pace of growth will not last indefinitely, the Web represents a tremendous opportunity that businesses simply cannot afford to ignore. Forrester Research, an e-commerce research and consulting firm, says that e-commerce will account for 10 percent of the U.S. economy and 5 percent of global sales by 2003.[7]

1. Describe the benefits of selling on the World Wide Web.

BENEFITS OF SELLING ON THE WEB

Although a Web-based sales strategy does not guarantee success, the companies that have pioneered Web-based selling have realized many benefits, including the following (see Figure 15.2):

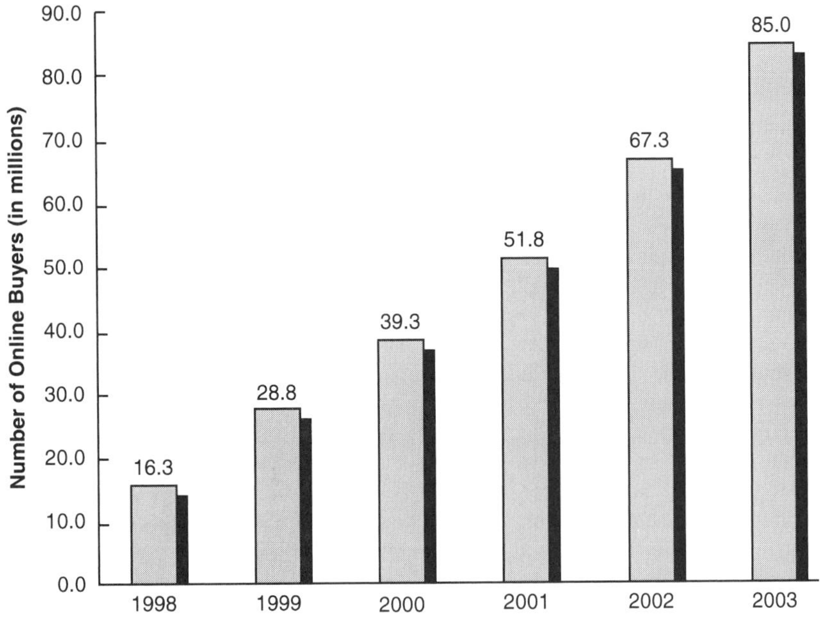

Number of Online Buyers (in millions)

90.0
80.0
70.0
60.0
50.0
40.0
30.0
20.0
10.0
0.0

16.3
28.8
39.3
51.8
67.3
85.0

1998
1999
2000
2001
2002
2003

FIGURE 15.1
Online Buyers
Source: Jupiter Communications, 1999

- *The opportunity to increase revenues.* For many small businesses, launching a Web site is the equivalent of opening a new sales channel. Companies that launch e-commerce efforts soon discover that their sites are generating additional sales from new audiences of customers.
- *The ability to expand their reach into global markets.* The Web is the most efficient way for small businesses to sell their products to the millions of potential customers who live outside the borders of the United States. Tapping into these global markets through more traditional methods would be too complex and too costly for the typical small business. Yet, with the Web, a small company can sell its products efficiently to customers anywhere in the world at any time of day.

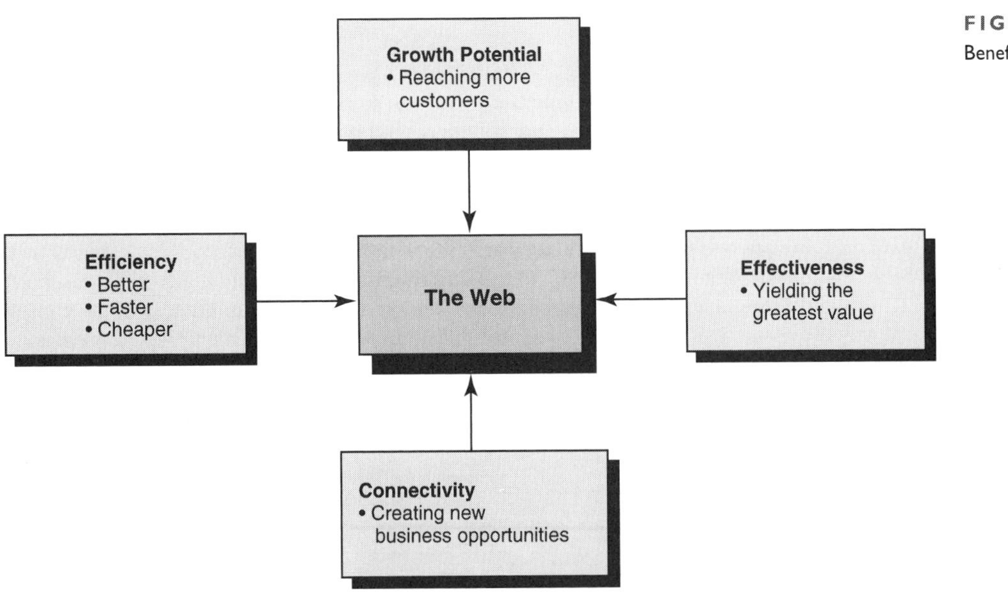

FIGURE 15.2
Benefits of E-Commerce

- *The ability to remain open 24 hours a day, seven days a week.* More than half of all retail sales occur after 6 P.M., when many traditional stores close. Extending the hours a brick-and-mortar store remains open can increase sales, but it also takes a toll on the business owner and the employees. With a Web site up and running, however, a small company can sell around the clock without having to incur additional staffing expenses. Customers never have to worry about whether or not an online store is "open."
- *The capacity to use the Web's interactive nature to enhance customer service.* Although selling on the Web can be highly impersonal because of the lack of human interaction, companies that design their sites properly can create an exciting, interactive experience for their online visitors. Customers can contact a company at any time of the day, can control the flow of information they get, and in some cases can interact with company representatives in real time. In addition, technology now allows companies to "personalize" their sites to suit the tastes and preferences of individual customers. Drawing on a database containing information customers have provided in the past, modern Web sites can be customized, displaying content that appeals to an individual visitor. For instance, a site selling clothing can greet a returning customer by name and ask if she is shopping for herself or for someone on her personal shopping list. Based on her response, the site can recall appropriate sizes and favorite styles and colors and can even make product recommendations.
- *The power to educate and to inform.* Far more than most marketing media, the Web gives entrepreneurs the power to educate and to inform customers. Women and members of Generation Y, especially, crave product information before they make purchases. The Web allows business owners to provide more detailed information to visitors than practically any other medium. For instance, a travel company advertising an Alaskan tour in a newspaper or magazine might include a brief description of the tour, a list of the destinations, a telephone number, the price, and perhaps a photo or two. A Web-based promotion for the same tour could include all of the preceding information as well as a detailed itinerary with dozens of breath-taking photographs; descriptions and photographs of all accommodations; advice on what to pack; airline schedules, seating configurations, and availability; information on optional side trips; comments from customers who have taken this tour; and links to other Web sites about Alaska, the weather, and fun things to do in the region.[8]
- *The ability to lower the cost of doing business.* The Web is one of the most efficient ways of reaching both new and existing customers. Properly promoted, a Web site can reduce a company's cost of generating sales leads, provide customer support, and distribute marketing materials. For instance, sending customers an e-mail newsletter is much less expensive than paying the printing and postage costs of sending the same newsletter by "snail mail." By integrating its Web site with its inventory control system, a company also can reduce its inventory costs by shortening the sales cycle. Finally, linking Web sales activity to suppliers enables a business to cut its purchasing costs.
- *The ability to spot new business opportunities and to capitalize on them.* E-commerce companies are poised to give customers just what they want when they want it. As the number of dual-career couples rises and the amount of available leisure time shrinks, consumers are looking for ways to increase the convenience of shopping, and the Web is fast becoming the solution they seek. Increasingly, customers view shopping as an unpleasant chore that cuts into already scarce leisure time, and they are embracing anything that reduces the amount of time they must spend shopping. "Given the time pressures of balancing work, household duties, child care, and social activities it's not hard to see why the Internet, with its convenience advantage, will increasingly become the smart way to shop," says Geoffrey Ramsey, an expert on e-commerce.[9] Entrepreneurs who tap into customers' need to buy goods more conveniently and with less hassle are winning the battle for market share. New opportunities to serve customers' changing needs and wants are constantly arising, and the Web is the birthplace of many of them.
- *The power to track sales results.* The Web gives businesses the power to track virtually any kind of activity on their Web sites, from the number of visitors to the click-through rates on their banner ads. Because of the Web's ability to monitor traffic continuously, entrepreneurs can judge the value their sites are generating for their companies.

Pom Express

Sherry Rand, founder of Pom Express, a unique business based in Salisbury, Massachusetts, which sells cheerleading equipment exclusively over the Web, is reaping many of these benefits. A cheerleader herself from grade school through college, Rand started with a brick-and-mortar retail store but soon saw the potential the Web offered for selling her products. A few years ago, Rand made the radical decision to shut down her retail store and sell only over the Web. Pom Express **<www.pomexpress.com>** *sells everything a cheerleader could possibly need, from pompoms and hair bows to megaphones and bodysuits. "The smartest thing I've done in business is shutting down my store and going exclusively online," she says. "Online, I don't have to carry the great overhead of a store, and from a quaint little town in northern Massachusetts, I'm selling globally." Many of Pom Express's sales are in Europe where cheerleading is growing in popularity. Rand says her Web-based business "is a great niche, and on the Internet, I can conduct business wherever I want to be."*[10]

FACTORS TO CONSIDER BEFORE LAUNCHING INTO E-COMMERCE

2. Understand the factors an entrepreneur should consider before launching into e-commerce.

Despite the many benefits the Web offers, not every small business owner is ready to embrace e-commerce. A recent survey by GTE Superpages.com found that three out of every four small businesses do not yet have Web sites.[11] Although small companies account for more than half of all retail sales in the United States, they generate only 9 percent of online retail sales, and that number will drop to just 6 percent by 2003.[12] Why are so many small companies hesitant to use the Web as a business tool? For many entrepreneurs, the key barrier is not knowing where or how to start an e-commerce effort, whereas for others cost concerns are a major issue. Other roadblocks include the fear that customers will not use the Web site and the problems associated with ensuring online security.

Whatever their size, traditional companies must realize that selling their products and services on the Web is no longer a luxury. Business owners who are not at least considering creating a Web presence are putting their companies at risk. "Any company that wants to make it in the years ahead must make the technology and the processes of the Internet part of its core competence," says one experienced venture capitalist.[13] However, before launching an e-commerce effort, business owners should consider the following important issues.

- How a company exploits the Web's interconnectivity and the opportunities it creates to transform relationships with its suppliers and vendors, its customers, and other external stakeholders is crucial to its success.
- Web success requires a company to develop a plan for integrating the Web into its overall strategy. The plan should address issues such as site design and maintenance, creating and managing a brand name, marketing and promotional strategies, sales, and customer service.
- Developing deep, lasting relationships with customers takes on even greater importance on the Web. Attracting customers on the Web costs money, and companies must be able to retain their online customers to make their Web sites profitable.
- Creating a meaningful presence on the Web requires an ongoing investment of resources—time, money, energy, and talent. Establishing an attractive Web site brimming with catchy photographs of products is only the beginning.
- Measuring the success of Web-based sales efforts is essential to remaining relevant to customers whose tastes, needs, and preferences are always changing.

Doing business on the Web takes more time and energy than many entrepreneurs think. Answering the following questions will help entrepreneurs make sure they are ready to do business on the Web and avoid unpleasant surprises in their e-commerce efforts:

- What exactly do you expect a Web site to do for your company? Will it provide information only, reach new customers, increase sales to existing customers, improve communication with customers, enhance customer service, or reduce your company's cost of operation? Will customers be able to place orders from the site, or must they call your company to buy?
- How much can you afford to invest in an e-commerce effort?
- What rate of return do you expect to earn on that investment?
- How long can you afford to wait for that return?
- How well suited are your products and services for selling on the Web?
- How will the "back office" of your Web site work? Will your site be tied into your company's inventory control system?
- How will you handle order fulfillment? Can your order fulfillment system handle the increase in volume you are expecting?
- What impact, if any, will your Web site have on your company's traditional channels of distribution?
- What mechanism will your site use to ensure secure customer transactions?
- How will your company handle customer service for the site? What provisions will you make for returned items?
- How do you plan to promote the site to draw traffic to it?
- What information will you collect from the visitors to your site? How will you use it? Will you tell visitors how you intend to use this information?
- Have you developed a privacy policy? Have you posted that policy on your company's Web site for customers?
- Have you tested your site with real, live customers to make sure that it is easy to navigate and easy to order from?
- How will you measure the success of your company's Web site? What objectives have you set for the site?

Table 15.1 provides a set of questions designed to help entrepreneurs assess their companies' potential to become an online success.

3. Explain the 12 myths of e-commerce and how to avoid falling victim to them.

12 MYTHS OF E-COMMERCE

Although many entrepreneurs have made their fortunes through e-commerce, setting up shop on the Web is no guarantee of success. Scores of entrepreneurs have plunged unprepared into the world of e-commerce only to discover that there is more to it than merely setting up a Web site and waiting for the orders to start pouring in. Make sure that you do not fall victim to one of the following e-commerce myths.

Myth 1. Setting Up a Business on the Web Is Easy and Inexpensive

A common misconception is that setting up an effective Web site for an online business is easy and inexpensive. Although practically anyone with the right software can post a static page in just a few minutes, creating an effective, professional, and polished Web site can be an expensive, time-consuming project. Most small businesses set up their Web pages as simple "electronic flyers," pages that post product information, a few photographs, prices, and telephone and fax numbers. Although these simple sites lack the capacity for true electronic commerce, they do provide a company with another way of reaching both new and existing customers.

TABLE 15.1

Assessing Your Company's Online Potential

Sources: Robert McGarvey, "Decision Time," Entrepreneur, March 2000, p. 82; Robert McGarvey, "Connect the Dots," Entrepreneur, March 2000, pp. 78–85; study by Morgan Stanley Dean Witter cited in Joel Kotkin, "Mother of All Malls," Forbes ASAP, April 6, 1998, pp. 60–65.

Considering launching an online company or transforming a brick-and-mortar business into a "dot-com" company? The following questions will help you assess your company's online potential.

1. Does your product have broad appeal to customers everywhere?
2. Do you want to sell your product to customers outside of your immediate geographical area?
3. Can the product you sell be delivered conveniently and economically?
4. Can your company realize significant cost advantages, such as lower rent, labor, inventory, and printing expenses, by going online?
5. Can you draw customers to your company's Web site with a reasonable investment?

The following figure shows several product categories and their e-commerce potential based on the business opportunity they offer and their suitability for selling on the Web. Categories in the upper right quadrant have the greatest Web potential, whereas those in the lower left quadrant offer the least.

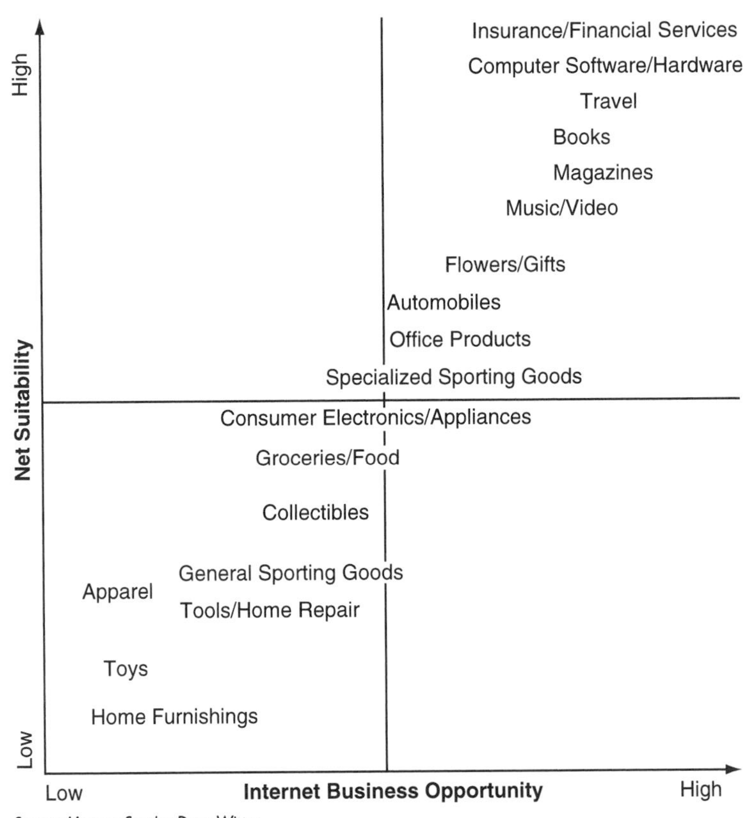

Source: Morgan Stanley Dean Witter

In 1984, Egghead Software established itself as a leader in the computer software business with a chain of retail stores across the country. In the 1990s, however, the business climate changed, and Egghead was in trouble. Facing stiff competition from "big-box" retailers such as Best Buy and CompUSA, which carried thousands of software titles at steeply discounted prices, and from Web-based software sellers, Egghead's sales tumbled. After much research, managers concluded that Egghead was doomed if it maintained its current brick-and-mortar strategy. They decided to reinvent the company into one that sold software exclusively on the Web. Since shuttering its last storefront in early 1998, Egghead's fortunes have reversed, and the company now boasts more than 1 million online customers!

Establishing a true transactional Web site will require several months and an investment ranging from $10,000 up to nearly $1 million, depending upon the features and capacity it incorporates. According to a study by Jupiter Communications, setting up an e-commerce site takes most companies at least six months to complete (see Figure 15.3). The study also revealed that setting up the site was only the first investment required. Companies listed these follow-up investments: (1) redesign the Web site, (2) buy more hardware to support the Web site, (3) automate or expand the warehouse to meet customer demand, (4) integrate the Web site into the inventory control system, and (5) increase customer call center capacity.[14]

Myth 2. If I Launch a Site, Customers Will Flock to It

Some entrepreneurs think that once they set up their Web sites, their expenses end there. Not true! Without promotional support, no Web site will draw enough traffic to support a business. With more than 1 billion Web pages in existence and the number growing daily, getting a site noticed in the crowd has become increasingly difficult. Even listing a site with popular Web search engines cannot guarantee that customers surfing the Web will find your company's site. Just like traditional retail stores seeking to attract customers, virtual companies have discovered that drawing sufficient traffic to a Web site requires promotion—and lots of it! "No one will know you're on the Web unless you tell them and motivate them to visit," explains Mark Layton, owner of a Web-based distributor of computer supplies and author of a book on e-commerce.[15]

Entrepreneurs with both physical and virtual stores must promote their Web sites at every opportunity by printing their URLs on everything related to their physical stores—on signs, in print and broadcast ads, on shopping bags, on merchandise labels, and anywhere else their customers will see. Virtual shop owners should consider buying ads in traditional advertising media as well as using banner ads, banner exchange programs, and cross-marketing arrangements with companies selling complementary products on their own Web sites. Other techniques include creating a Web-based newsletter, writing articles that link to the company's site, or hosting a chat room that allow customers to interact with one another and with company personnel.

FIGURE 15.3
Time Required to Develop an E-Commerce Site
Source: Jupiter Communications

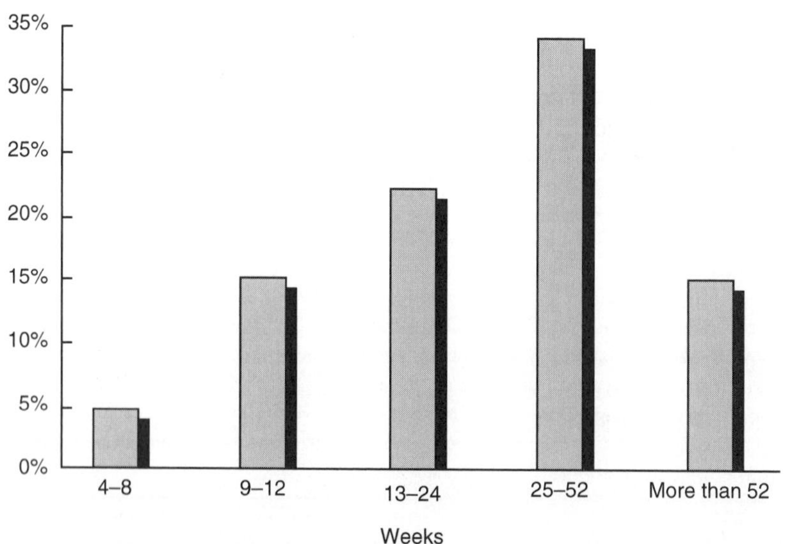

The key to promoting a Web site is networking, building relationships with other companies, customers, trade associations, online directories, and other Web sites your company's customers visit. "You need to create relationships with the businesses and people with whom you share common customers," says Barbara Ling, author of a book on e-commerce. "Then you need to create links between sites to help customers find what they are looking for."[16] For instance, one way Electrasports, a virtual store selling women's exercise and sports clothing, promotes its site **<www.electrasports.com>** is through Banner Women, a network that promotes hundreds of women-oriented Web sites. By linking its site to other sites targeting women, Electrasports reaches its target customers efficiently.

Myth 3. Making Money on the Web Is Easy

Promoters who hawk "get-rich-quick" schemes on the Web lure many entrepreneurs with the promise that making money on the Web is easy. It isn't. One recent study by Activemedia found that just under 50 percent of commercial Web sites are profitable.[17] Making money on the Web is possible, but it takes time and requires an investment up front. As hundreds of new sites spring up every day, getting your company's site noticed requires more effort and marketing muscle than ever before. One study by the Boston Consulting Group, a management consulting firm, and shop.org, an Internet retailing trade association, found that Web retailers invested 65 percent of their revenues in marketing and advertising, compared to their off-line counterparts, who invested just 4 percent.[18]

Myth 4. Privacy Is Not an Important Issue on the Web

The Web allows companies to gain access to almost unbelievable amounts of information about their customers. Many sites offer visitors "freebies" in exchange for information about themselves. Companies then use this information to learn more about their target customers and how to market to them most effectively. Concerns over the privacy of and the use of this information has become the topic of debate by many interested parties, including government agencies, consumer watchdog groups, customers, and industry trade associations.

Companies that collect information from their online customers have a responsibility to safeguard their customers' privacy, to protect that information from unauthorized use, and to use it responsibly. That means that businesses should post a privacy statement on their Web sites, explaining to customers how they intend to use the information they collect. One of the surest ways to alienate online customers is to abuse the information collected from them by selling it to third parties or by spamming customers with unwanted solicitations.

Businesses that publish privacy policies and then adhere to them build trust among their customers, an important facet of doing business on the Web. A study by Jupiter Communications found that 64 percent of Web customers distrust Web sites.[19] According to John Briggs, director of e-commerce for the Yahoo Network, customers "need to trust the brand they are buying and believe that their online purchases will be safe transactions. They need to feel comfortable that [their] personal data will not be sold and that they won't get spammed by giving their e-mail address. They need to know about shipping costs, product availability, and return policies up front."[20] Privacy *does* matter on the Web, and businesses that respect their customers' privacy will win their customers' trust. Trust is the foundation on which the long-term customer relationships that are so crucial to Web success are built.

Myth 5. The Most Important Part of Any E-Commerce Effort Is Technology

Although understanding the technology of e-commerce is an important part of the formula for success, it is *not* the most crucial ingredient. What matters most is the ability to understand the underlying business and to develop a workable business model that offers customers something of value at a reasonable price while producing a reasonable return for the company. The entrepreneurs who are proving to be most successful in e-commerce are those who know how their industries work inside and out and then build an e-business around that knowledge. They know that they can hire Webmasters, database experts, and fulfillment companies to design the technical aspects of their businesses but that nothing can substitute for a solid understanding of their industry, their target market, and the strategy needed to pull the various parts together. The key is seeing the Web for what it really is: another way to reach and serve customers with an effective business model.

Mrs. Beasley's

Ken Harris, CEO of Mrs. Beasley's, a Los Angeles bakery known for its decadent desserts and gift baskets, has been building a loyal customer base over the past 20 years through its retail stores. The company, which has long been a favorite of celebrities such as Charles Bronson, Jody Foster, Cher, and others, also targets corporate buyers who are responsible for purchasing gifts for important customers and clients. When Harris saw the Web's potential for expanding his company's reach and its ability to connect with its target customers efficiently, he forged a partnership with a Web design company to build "a world class Web site." The site **<www.mrsbeasleys.com>** *is actually quite simple but provides customers with a personal address book that provides a complete gift-giving history and allows them to track their orders. When Mrs. Beasley's Web site went online just before the busy holiday season, it generated $2.1 million in sales in just 60 days! The site now accounts for more than 20 percent of Mrs. Beasley's sales, and, according to Harris, is the primary force behind the company's impressive sales growth.*[21]

The key to Ken Harris's success on the Web is his knowledge of and experience in the bakery business to which he applied the technology of the Web. Unfortunately, too many entrepreneurs tackle e-commerce by focusing on technology first and then determine how that technology fits their business idea. "If you start with technology, you're likely to buy a solution in search of a problem," says Kip Martin, program director of META Group's Electronic Business Strategies. Instead, he suggests, "Start with the business and ask yourself what you want to happen and how you'll measure it. *Then* ask how the technology will help you achieve your goals. Remember: Business first, technology second."[22]

Myth 6. "Strategy? I Don't Need a Strategy to Sell on the Web!"

Building a successful e-business is no different than building a successful brick-and-mortar business, and that requires a well-thought-out strategy. Building a strategy means that an entrepreneur must first develop a clear definition of the company's target audience and a thorough understanding of those customers' needs, wants, likes, and dislikes. To be successful, a Web site must be appealing to the customers it seeks to attract just as a traditional store's design and decor must draw foot traffic. Before your Web site can become the foundation for a successful e-business, you must create it with your target audience in mind.

NextPlanetOver.com

Entrepreneurs David Scott and David Reid, cofounders of NextPlanetOver.com, an online business selling comic books, action figures, and related science fiction items, engaged in extensive market research and strategic planning before launching their company. They learned, for example, that the typical adult comic book collector is single, has a median income of $62,000, and is a fan of Star Trek *and* The Simpsons. *To lure these* *prime customers, Scott and Reid designed a Web site that not only has separate stores devoted to each comic book series but also includes reviews of comics and previews of soon-to-be-released books. They also incorporated a section called The Pulse, where visitors can rate new products and chat with one another or with celebrities such as Batman creator, Jeph Loeb. Their research and planning have proved to be a major part of their e-company's success. Their site now draws 10,000 registered users every day, and more than 15 percent of them visit The Pulse before they shop.*[23]

Myth 7. On the Web Customer Service Is Not as Important as It Is in a Traditional Retail Store

Many Web sites treat customer service as an afterthought, and it shows. Sites that are difficult to navigate, slow to load, or confusing will turn customers away quickly, never to return. The fact is that customer service is just as important on the Web as it is in traditional brick-and-mortar stores.

There is plenty of room for improvement in customer service on the Web. Research by BizRate.com found that 75 percent of Web shoppers who fill their online shopping carts become frustrated and leave the site before checking out.[24] The most common reasons for leaving a site without purchasing include the following: The site was too slow (41 percent), the site looked unprofessional (20 percent), the site did not take credit cards (16 percent), the checkout area was too hard to find (14 percent), and the site had no return policy posted (12 percent).[25]

In an attempt to improve the level of service they offer, many sites provide e-mail links to encourage customer interaction. Unfortunately, e-mail takes a very low priority at many e-businesses. A recent study by Jupiter Communications found that 42 percent of business Web sites took longer than five days to respond to e-mail inquiries, never replied at all, or simply were not accessible by e-mail![26] The lesson for e-commerce entrepreneurs is simple: Devote time, energy, and money to developing a functional mechanism for providing superior customer service. Those who do will build a sizeable base of loyal customers who will keep coming back. Forrester Research suggests that the most significant actions online companies can take to bolster their customer service efforts are creating a well-staffed and well-trained customer response team, offering a simple return process, and providing an easy order-tracking process so customers can check the status of their orders at any time.[27]

Table 15.2 summarizes the results of one company's research concerning what both retail and business customers want when shopping on the Web.

Myth 8. Flash Makes a Web Site Better

Businesses that fall into this trap pour most of their e-commerce budgets into designing flashy Web sites with all of the "bells and whistles." The logic is that to stand out on the Web, a site really has to sparkle. That logic leads to a "more is better" mentality when designing a site. On the Web, however, "more" does *not* necessarily equate to "better."

Edler Group

Rick Edler, owner of the Edler Group, a California real estate company, learned this lesson the hard way. Edler's first foray onto the Web was a simple site, one that followed the "electronic flyer" approach and cost just $285. A confessed gadget freak, Edler soon decided to revamp his company's site to incorporate lots of features and lots of flash. "We were going to dazzle everyone with all of the technology," he recalls. The site, which cost $7,000 to design, literally pulsed with color and motion as spinning graphics moved around the screen. It even included movie listings. But the site was a failure, never draw-

TABLE 15.2
What Web Shoppers Want

Source: BizRate.com, 2000. Cited in Bronwyn Fryer and Lee Smith, ".Com or Bust," Forbes Small Business, *December 1999/January 2000, pp. 38–49.*

Retail Customers	Business Customers
1. Competitive product prices	1. On-time delivery
2. Well-designed product presentation	2. Competitive product prices
3. Good product selection	3. Well-designed product presentation
4. Reliable shipping and handling	4. Good product selection
5. On-time delivery	5. Easy ordering
6. Easy ordering	6. Valuable information about products
7. High degree of customer support	7. High degree of customer support
8. Valuable information about products	8. Reliable shipping and handling
9. Posted privacy policy	9. Posted privacy policy
10. User-friendly navigation tools	10. User-friendly navigation tools

ing much traffic at all. The busy design with all of its features meant that the site was very slow to download. "You just stared at it like you were watching a commercial," says Edler. "We were scaring people away." Edler quickly scrapped the site and for $2,000 built a much simpler one that allows buyers to get the details on a listing and take a video tour of a house. The site also includes links to other useful real estate pages. Customer response to the newly designed site **<www.edlergroup.com>** *has been positive, and more importantly, the site is now helping realtors close sales.*[28]

Keep the design of your site simple. Although fancy graphics, bright colors, playful music, and spinning icons can attract attention, they also can be quite distracting and, as Rick Edler learned, very slow to download.

Myth 9. It's What's Up Front That Counts

Designing an attractive Web site is important to building a successful e-business. However, designing the back office, the systems that take over once a customer places an order on a Web site, is just as important as designing the site itself. If the behind-the-scenes support is not in place or cannot handle the traffic from the Web site, a company's entire e-commerce effort will come crashing down. Although e-commerce can lower many costs of doing business, it still requires a basic infrastructure somewhere in the channel of distribution to process orders, maintain inventory, fill orders, and handle customer service. Many entrepreneurs hoping to launch virtual businesses are discovering the need for a "click-and-mortar" approach to provide the necessary infrastructure to serve their customers. "The companies with warehouses, supply-chain management, and solid customer service are going to be the ones that survive," says Daryl Plummer, head of the Gartner Group's Internet and new media division.[29]

To customers, a business is only as good as its last order, and many e-companies are not measuring up. One study suggests that only 30 percent of e-commerce Web sites feature real-time inventory look-up, which gives online shoppers the ability to see if an item they want to purchase is actually in stock.[30] In addition, only 7 percent of Web sites are linked to the back office.[31] These figures will increase as software to integrate Web sites with the back office becomes easier to use and more affordable, but in the meantime customers will have to endure late shipments, incorrect orders, and poor service.

Web-based entrepreneurs often discover that the greatest challenge their businesses face is not necessarily attracting customers on the Web but creating a workable order fulfillment strategy. Order fulfillment involves everything required to get goods from a warehouse into a customer's hands and includes order processing, warehousing, picking and packing, shipping, and billing. Some entrepreneurs choose to handle order fulfillment in-house with their own employees, whereas others find it more economical to hire specialized fulfillment houses to handle these functions.

Pro Se Sports

When Laura Stanford, founder of Pro Se Sports **<www.pro-se-sports.com>**, *an online retailer of women's sports apparel, set up her company's Web site, she had not thought out the issue of order fulfillment. "I had no idea what I was getting into," she says. Contending with long lead times from suppliers and coping with the irregular order patterns have created problems for Stanford's in-house order fulfillment system. Six employees currently process all of Pro Se's orders and ship them out via UPS from the company's small warehouse. Stanford is investigating hiring a fulfillment house to handle Pro Se's orders, but finding a house willing to handle a relatively small volume of orders at a reasonable price has been difficult.*[32]

Myth 10. E-Commerce Will Cause Brick-and-Mortar Retail Stores to Disappear

The rapid growth of e-commerce does pose a serious threat to traditional retailers, especially those who fail to find ways to capitalize on the opportunities the Web offers them. However, it is unlikely that Web-based shopping will replace customers' need and desire to visit real stores selling real merchandise that they can see, touch, and try on. Some products simply lend themselves to selling in real stores more naturally than in online shops. For instance, furniture stores and supermarkets have struggled for success online. On the other hand, other items, particularly standard commodity products for which customers have little loyalty, are ideally suited for online sales. Virtual stores have driven and will continue to drive out of existence some traditional companies that resist creating new business models or are too slow to change. To remain competitive, traditional brick-and-mortar stores must find ways to transform themselves into flexible click-and-mortar operations that can make the convenience, the reach, and the low transaction costs of the Web work for them.

Simon Property

For instance, Simon Property, the nation's largest mall company, uses a device called a Zapstick that is designed to allow customers to blend the convenience of online shopping with the experience of going to the local mall. A graduating senior, for instance, could take a Zapstick to a nearby mall, go into her favorite stores, and scan the bar codes of the products for which she would like to "register." Her choices, including proper sizes and colors as well as prices, are then loaded onto her personal Web page. Her family and friends can visit her site and shop at any time of day from their computers using the selections she has made. The goal of the Zapstick and similar devices is to boost traffic at the mall while giving customers the opportunity to shop online, further blurring the lines between traditional retail and online stores.[33]

Myth 11. The Greatest Opportunities for E-Commerce Lie in the Retail Sector

As impressive as the growth rate and total volume for online retail sales are, they are dwarfed by those in the online business-to-business (B2B) sector, where businesses sell to one another rather than to retail customers. The Gartner Group, an Internet consulting company, projects that online business-to-business transactions will soar from $237 billion in 2000 to more than $2.8 trillion in 2004.[34] That volume of sales is 10 times the amount expected in business-to-consumer e-commerce![35] Entrepreneurs who are looking to sell goods to other businesses on the Web will find plenty of opportunities available in a multitude of industries.

Business-to-business e-commerce is growing so rapidly because of its potential to boost productivity, slash costs, and increase profits. This brand of e-commerce is transforming

Reprinted with special permission of North American Syndicate

the way companies purchase parts, supplies, and materials as well as the way they manage inventory and process transactions. The Web's power to increase the speed and the efficiency of the purchasing function represents a fundamental departure from the past. Experts estimate that transferring purchasing to the Web can cut total procurement costs by 10 percent and transaction costs by as much as 90 percent.[36] For instance, Chris Cogan, CEO of GoCo-op, an Internet purchasing site for hotels, restaurants, and health care companies, explains, "We estimate [that] the average cost of executing a paper purchase order is $115." Businesses using his company's Web-based purchasing system "get that cost down to $10," he says.[37]

Business-to-business e-commerce is growing because of the natural link that exists with business-to-consumer e-commerce. As we have seen, one of the greatest challenges Web-based retailers face is obtaining and delivering the goods their customers order fast enough to satisfy customers' expectations. Increasingly, Web-based retailers are connecting their front office sales systems and their back office purchasing and order fulfillment systems with those of their suppliers. The result is a faster, more efficient method of filling customer orders. So far the most successful online business-to-business companies are those that have discovered ways of tying their front offices, their back offices, their suppliers, and their customers together into a single, smoothly functioning, Web-based network.

Cisco Systems

Cisco Systems, a maker of computer routers, switches, and other hardware, provides a good example of a fully-integrated B2B company. Customers go to the Cisco Web site to check out product specifications and to place orders. Cisco then uses the Internet to transfer those orders directly to its suppliers, who then ship the necessary raw materials to Cisco, or, in many cases, ship products directly to customers. (About 65 percent of Cisco's orders go directly from the supplier to the customer without Cisco ever handling them!) The efficiency of this system minimizes the amount of raw materials inventory that Cisco must carry and allows customers to check on the status of their orders over the Web as well. Cisco keeps its costs low and its customers happy with its innovative Web-based strategy.[38]

Myth 12. It's Too Late to Get on the Web

A common myth, especially among small companies, is that those businesses that have not yet moved onto the Web have missed a golden opportunity. "The reality is that we're in the dawn of the Internet age," says Charles Rutstein, an analyst at Forrester Research. "There's a lot more to come."[39] Companies are still figuring out how to succeed on the Web. In fact, studies show that less than half of all Web sites are profitable.[40] For every e-commerce site that exists, a trio of others has failed. E-commerce is still in its infancy, and an abundance of business opportunities exists for those entrepreneurs insightful enough to spot them and clever enough to capitalize on them.

One fact of e-commerce that has emerged is the importance of speed. Companies doing business on the Web have discovered that those who reach customers first often have a significant advantage over their slower rivals. "The lesson of the Web is not how the big eat the small, but how the fast eat the slow," says a manager at a venture capital firm specializing in Web-based companies.[41]

Succumbing to this myth often leads entrepreneurs to make a fundamental mistake once they finally decide to go online: They believe they have to have a "perfect" site before they can launch it. Few businesses get their sites "right" the first time. In fact, the most successful e-commerce sites are constantly changing, removing what does not work and adding new features to see what does. Successful Web sites are much like a well-designed flower garden, constantly growing and improving, yet changing to reflect the climate of each season. Their creators worry less about creating the perfect site at the outset than about getting a site online and then fixing it, tweaking it, and updating it to meet changing customer demands. "The person trying to create the perfect (online) store will fail," says Gerry Goldsholle, founder of two Web sites aimed at small companies. "Part of the Internet process is 'try it, learn from it, and fix it.' Delay is your biggest enemy. If you delay, someone else will do it."[42]

APPROACHES TO E-COMMERCE

4. Discuss the five basic approaches available to entrepreneurs wanting to launch an e-commerce effort.

A successful e-commerce effort requires much more than merely launching a Web site; entrepreneurs must develop a plan for integrating the Web into their overall business strategy. Many entrepreneurs choose to start their e-commerce efforts small and simply and then expand them as sales grow and their needs become more sophisticated. Others make major investments in creating full-blown, interconnected sites at the onset. The cost of setting up a Web site varies significantly, depending on which options an entrepreneur chooses. Generally, Web experts identify three basic pricing categories for creating a Web site: less than $10,000, between $10,000 and $30,000; and more than $30,000. When it comes to choosing an approach to e-commerce, there are no right or wrong answers; the key is creating a plan that fits into the small company's budget and meets its e-commerce needs as it grows and expands. Entrepreneurs looking to launch an e-commerce effort have five basic choices: (1) online shopping malls, (2) storefront-building services, (3) Internet service providers (ISPs), (4) hiring professionals to design a custom site, and (5) building a site in-house.

Online Shopping Malls

In the under $10,000 category, the simplest way for entrepreneurs to get their businesses online is to rent space for their products at an online shopping mall (also called a shopping portal). Online shopping malls are the equivalent of an electronic strip mall because they list on one site the product offerings from many different small companies. The primary advantages they offer are simplicity and low cost. To join an online mall, an entrepreneur simply provides descriptions and photographs of the products for sale. For a low monthly fee, the mall creates and maintains a virtual storefront for the company and funnels customer orders from it to the company.

The major disadvantages of using an online shopping mall are an individual store's lack of prominence and the lack of control entrepreneurs have over their sites. Most malls host dozens of businesses in a multitude of industries, and standing out in the crowd can be a challenge because all of the sites follow a similar or identical design. In addition, some malls are much more effective than others at promoting their resident businesses.

Storefront-Building Services

Also in the under $10,000 category are storefront-building services that help entrepreneurs create online shops that include features such as Web-hosting services, the ability to handle

YOU BE THE CONSULTANT . . .

Getting Online . . . and into the Green

In 1996, Mammoth Golf was like any other small golf retailer, doing business from a showroom in suburban Baltimore and through a mail-order catalog. Mammoth sold a variety of golf equipment, including custom-built golf clubs, and offered personalized services such as "swing analysis" to make sure each customer's clubs fit his or her individual swing. The 14-employee company was doing well, ringing up annual sales of almost $5 million a year, and cofounders Bill and Stephanie Allbright were pleased with Mammoth's progress. The copreneurs had a bigger vision for their company.

Unlike most entrepreneurs in 1996, the Allbrights understood the potential for growth that the Internet offered small companies that could learn how to harness its power. That year, they devoted a small portion of Mammoth's budget—just $5,000—to hire a company to create and host a Web site. That early site was not an important part of Mammoth's sales, but it was an important part of the company's indoctrination to the Web and what it takes to succeed online. It also proved to be the beginning of the company's transformation from a sleepy little brick-and-mortar store selling golf equipment to a highly successful click-and-mortar retailer with a meaningful e-commerce strategy.

Soon, the Allbrights were watching other retailers achieve explosive growth rates by focusing on e-commerce. What they saw was a new business model: investing heavily early on to create solid technology platforms capable of growing as the company grew and to establish name recognition and brand awareness with customers. "If you want to build a world-class store on the Internet, you have to ask yourself if you're willing to invest both in the site itself and then in the marketing," says Bill. That same year, the Allbrights more than doubled Mammoth's Web site budget to $12,000. However, because the company invested only minimally in advertising the site, sales were puny.

Vice president of marketing Jim Thompson began managing Mammoth's e-commerce effort. His basic strategy was "to make MammothGolf.com its own product" by putting enough money into an advertising campaign for the site. He launched a $250,000 print advertising campaign that placed ads in several golf magazines as well as in *USA Today* and the *Wall Street Journal.* "That's when we started seeing traffic build and started seeing orders," says Thompson.

The campaign worked, but its success pointed out weaknesses in Mammoth's Web site. Thompson redesigned the site with four goals in mind. First, the site had to be fast. Second, navigation within the site had to be simple and easy. Third, the site's content had to offer customers meaningful information, more than just an online catalog interspersed with "Buy Me" buttons. Finally, the site had to be personal, giving customers the sense that they were entering Mammoth's retail store when they logged on to the site. By the end of 1999, Mammoth's online sales had climbed to more than $100,000, with more than half of that coming in December alone! The site was catching on with customers.

At that point, the Allbrights decided to bring the Web site back in-house and manage it there with the help of Jennifer McManus, who had recently been hired as director of Internet operations. As Mammoth was moving its physical store into a new, larger location complete with two golf simulators, an in-store putting green, swing cages, and much more retail space, McManus was moving the Web site to a new technology platform that would support a much larger volume of online business. The system, which can handle 128 transactions a second, is easily expandable and feeds data into a single database.

Today, Mammoth Golf has 14 "techies" working on the e-commerce side of the business. In 1996, when the company first began its Web strategy, it had no "techies" and only two PCs. Sales have more than doubled and now exceed $10 million a year, one-third of which comes from the Web. Thanks to Mammoth's Web site, Bill Allbright estimates that company sales will skyrocket to $50 million within a year and that online sales will account for half of that amount! More than 250,000 visitors stop at **<www.mammothgolf.com>** every year, where they can browse through every item the company has in its physical store. They also can chat in real time with customer service representatives who answer their questions, make recommendations, and steer them to the right pages on the site. Mammoth has even set up a special network for its corporate customers that speeds order processing and delivery times and reduces the cost of placing an order. With its click-and-mortar strategy in place, Mammoth has every intention of expanding its already strong Web presence. None of Mammoth's managers know exactly what the future holds for the Web, but they do know that they will be ready for it!

1. What principles concerning doing business on the Web can you discern from Mammoth Golf's experience that would be useful for other entrepreneurs considering e-commerce?
2. Is it too late for small companies such as Mammoth Golf to get into e-commerce today? What advantages does the "first mover" have in e-commerce? Disadvantages?

Source: Adapted from Jane Hodges, "Putting It All Online," *Small Business Computing,* January 2000, pp. 54–59.

secure credit card transactions, databases for order fulfillment and customer tracking, advertising placement, and search engine registration—all for as little as $100 to $500 per month. Some storefront-building services offer to handle a limited number of transactions for free, although most businesses quickly outgrow the free service and end up paying the monthly fee to the service for site hosting and operation. Most Internet portals such as Yahoo! **<www.store.yahoo.com>** and e-commerce service companies, such as iCat **<www.icat.com>**, Bigstep.com **<www.bigstep.com>**, or BizLand.com **<www.bizland.com>**, offer these e-commerce services.

The major advantages of using these storefront-building services is simplicity and low cost. Setting up a store can take as little as a few hours, and the hosting company shoulders the burden of setting up and running the cyberstore, creating minimal headaches for the entrepreneur behind it. The downside of these services is that most of their sites look as though they came out of the same cookie-cutter approach because they rely on a limited number of templates to create store sites. It is extremely difficult to make a company's Web store stand out when every storefront is stamped from the same mold. Plus, most services limit the number of products they will handle at the base price on these sites to just 50 to 100.

Despite its drawbacks, using a storefront-building service offers a fast and easy way to create a virtual store that is open 24 hours a day, seven days a week.

Internet Wines & Spirits

After trying on his own for several months to set up an online store selling wines and spirits, George Randall turned to Yahoo! Store for help. He selected backgrounds and graphics from Yahoo! Store's templates, answered questions about the items he would sell and how he wanted them shipped, and soon had his virtual store, Internet Wines & Spirits ***<www.internetwines.com>*** *up and running. Each day, as many as 7,000 customers from all over the world visit the company's site, which now sells more than 3,000 items and generates one-third of the company's sales. "Overnight we became an international company," says Randall, noting that Internet Wines & Spirits routinely gets orders from Europe and the Far East.*[43]

Internet Service Providers and Application Service Providers

Another e-commerce option in the under $10,000 category is using an Internet service provider (ISP) or an application service provider (ASP) to create an online store. ISPs and ASPs provide many of the same features as storefront-design services except they offer their small business customers more design flexibility and the ability to customize their Web sites. ISP packages such as MindSpring Complete Commerce or VerioStore are not as easy to use as the templates from storefront-design services and typically require the entrepreneurs using them to know some basics of the hypertext markup language (HTML) used to design most Web sites. Although most ISPs provide basic design templates, experienced HTML users can modify them easily. ISP templates usually include shopping cart and catalog features as well as order and payment processing and report generation capabilities. ASPs' packages provide these same features. However, rather than requiring users to purchase e-commerce software, ASPs "rent" a variety of e-commerce applications, from site building and hosting to purchasing automation and accounting, to their customers on an as-needed basis.

In addition to hosting and running a company's virtual store, ISPs offer the ability to grow with a small company as its online store's sales volume climbs. Most base their fees on the number of visitors a site attracts and the amount of space it takes up on their server, so start-up stores offering a small product line can spend as little as $100 a month (plus initial setup costs). Before choosing an ISP, entrepreneurs should investigate its operating history (specifically the amount of downtime the provider has experienced), the quality of its backup systems (in case of a crash), and its remaining capacity for hosting sites.

DVD Express

When Mike Dubelko launched his online store, DVD Express, in 1996, ISPs were relatively expensive, so Dubelko and his staff created and managed their own small, simple Web site **<www.express.com>**. *Within six months, however, orders for the movies, games, and music the company sold on the site shot up from just 50 per week to more than 2,000 per week, and the system Dubelko and his staff had built could not handle the volume. "We were totally overwhelmed," he recalls. "Our success was killing us." Dubelko located an ISP that could create a site capable of capturing and processing the thousands of orders the site generated. The redesigned site allowed customers to check the availability of any DVD and to track the status of their orders online. Today more than 100,000 online visitors browse through DVD Express's inventory of movies, music, and games each day.*[44]

Hiring Professionals to Design a Custom Site

Businesses able to spend between $10,000 and $30,000 can afford to hire professionals to create their sites. The primary benefit this option offers is the unlimited ability to customize a site, making it anything an entrepreneur wants, including complete front office and back office integration. Just like building a custom-designed house, hiring professionals to design a site from the ground up gives entrepreneurs a high degree of control over the final result. Also, most Web development companies offer complete e-commerce solutions, including consulting and design services, Web hosting, site registration, and listings with search engines and directories.

Because custom-built sites require custom programming, they are much more expensive to create than sites based on preformatted templates. The Gartner Group estimates that building and launching an e-commerce site with complete front office and back office integration now costs more than $500,000![45] Expenses in that range are out of the question for most e-commerce entrepreneurs just starting out. "It's a trial-and-error process," says one e-commerce expert. "So why spend money if you don't have to?"[46]

Building a Web Site In-House

Building a Web site in-house gives an entrepreneur complete control over the site and its design, operation, and maintenance. However, hiring and supporting an in-house staff of Web designers can quickly run up the cost of creating and maintaining a custom Web site into the $250,000 to $500,000 range. Because of the high costs involved in hiring professional Web development companies or in maintaining a staff of Web designers, most entrepreneurs wanting to establish a Web presence do so by using either online shopping malls, storefront-building services, or Internet service providers.

5. Explain the basic strategies entrepreneurs should follow to achieve success in their e-commerce efforts.

STRATEGIES FOR E-SUCCESS

The average Web user spends an average of five hours and 52 minutes online each week. Across a lifetime, the average baby boomer will spend 5 years and 6 months online; the average Generation Xer will spend 9 years and 11 months online; and the average Generation Y user will spend 23 years and 2 months on line, almost one-third of their lives![47] However, converting these Web surfers into online customers requires a business to do more than merely set up a Web site and wait for the hits to start rolling up. Doing business from a Web site is like setting up shop on a dead-end street or a back alley. You may be ready to sell, but no one knows you are there! Building sufficient volume for a site takes energy, time, money, creativity, and, perhaps most importantly, a well-defined strategy. One business writer explains, "[Success in e-commerce] isn't glamorous at all. The difference between Web success and Web failure often hinges on how carefully people sift through details and fine-tune niggling plans. E-businesses that actually get it . . . understand how to use the Web to push the envelope, to create new tools and business models."[48]

Although the Web is a unique medium for creating a company, launching an e-business is not much different from launching a traditional off-line company. The basic drivers of a successful business remain in place on the Web as well as on Main Street. To be successful, both off-line and online companies require solid planning and a well-formulated strategy that emphasizes customer service. The goals of e-commerce are no different from traditional off-line businesses—to increase sales, improve efficiency, and boost profits. Yet, the Web has the power to transform businesses, industries, and commerce itself.

Produce Online

For example, Chuck James, CEO of ProduceOnline **<www.produceonline.com>**, *saw the power to totally remake the produce distribution business that had been in his family for 116 years. James made a bold move, shutting down the family's traditional brick-and-mortar business and moving it entirely to the Web. His site offers buyers and sellers exactly what they need: a marketplace that gives them the power to buy and sell produce* quickly. *"In this business, you either sell it or smell it," quips James.*

In addition to maintaining the fourth-generation family business's record of success, James sees his move to the Web as "an opportunity to reinvent the produce industry." Rather than continuing to count solely on the contacts they have built over the years to locate buyers and sellers, grocers, farmers, and produce dealers can use the search engine on the ProduceOnline Web site to locate one another much more quickly and efficiently. James says his site cuts transaction and processing costs to his customers by 70 percent. ProduceOnline does not charge a subscription fee, choosing instead to collect a 1 percent royalty on completed deals.[49]

How a company integrates the Web into its overall business strategy determines how successful it ultimately will become. Following are some guidelines for building a successful Web strategy for a small e-company.

Consider Focusing on a Niche in the Market

Rather than trying to compete head-to-head with the dominant players on the Web who have the resources and the recognition to squash smaller competitors, entrepreneurs should consider focusing on serving a market niche. Smaller companies' limited resources usually are better spent serving niche markets than trying to be everything to everyone (recall the discussion of the focus strategy in Chapter 3). The idea is to concentrate on serving a small corner of the market that the giants have overlooked. Niches exist in every industry and can be highly profitable, given the right strategy for serving them. A niche can be defined in many ways, including by geography, by customer profile, by product, by product usage, and many others.

Motorcyclebooks.com

Luis Hernandez targets a profitable niche with his online company, Motorcyclebooks.com **<www.motorcyclebooks.com>**, *which sells a complete collection of books—from repair manuals to trip guides—to motorcycle enthusiasts and collectors across the world.*[50]

JustBalls!

Rather than try to sell a complete line of sporting goods, JustBalls! **<www.just balls.com>** *focuses on (as its name suggests) just balls! This e-tailer sells every kind of sports ball imaginable, from autographed collectible balls and cricket balls to tennis balls and balls used to play sepak takraw (a game known as the "sport of kings" in Southeast Asia).*

With its broad reach, the Web is the ideal mechanism for implementing a focus strategy because small companies can reach large numbers of customers with a common interest.

Develop a Community

On the Web, competitors are just a mouse click away. To attract customers and keep them coming back, e-companies have discovered the need to offer more than just quality products and excellent customer service. Many seek to develop a community of customers with similar interests, the nucleus of which is their Web site. The idea is to increase customer loyalty by giving customers the chance to interact with other like-minded visitors or with experts to discuss and learn more on topics about which they are passionate. E-mail lists and chat rooms are powerful tools for building a community of visitors at a site.

Studio B

David Rogelberg, founder of Studio B, a literary agency that specializes in representing authors of computer books, uses mailing list software that circulates ongoing e-mail discussions among subscribers to his site. Rogelberg set up his site **<www.studiob.com>** *with two goals: providing a forum for both published and aspiring authors to ask and answer questions about the publishing business and, of course, attracting clients to his agency. He has succeeded on both counts. Rogelberg's site is now considered to be one of the major resources in the computer book publishing industry and has helped him land 150 new clients for his literary agency.*[51]

Like Studio B, companies that successfully create a community around their Web site turn mere customers into loyal fans who keep coming back and, better yet, invite others to join them.

Attract Visitors by Giving Away "Freebies"

One of the most important words on the Internet is *free.* Many successful e-merchants have discovered the ability to attract visitors to their site by giving away something for free and then selling them something else. One e-commerce consultant calls this cycle of giving something away and then selling something "the rhythm of the Web."[52] The "freebie" must be something customers value, but it does *not* have to be expensive nor does it have to be a product. In fact, one of the most common giveaways on the Web is *information.* (After all, that's what most people on the Web are after!) Creating a free online or e-mail newsletter with links to your company's site, of course, and to others of interest is one of the most effective ways of attracting potential customers to a site. Meaningful content presented in a clear, professional fashion is a must. Experts advise keeping online newsletters short—no more than about 600 words. *Poor Richard's E-Mail Publishing* by Chris Pirillo (Top Floor Publishing) offers much useful advice on creating online newsletters.

Webbers Communication

Gary Foote, owner of Webbers Communication, a small Web site development company, has attracted new customers to his business as a result of his e-mail newsletter, The E-Marketing Digest. Before he created the newsletter, says Foote, "Our customer base came 90 percent from off-line contacts and 10 percent from online contacts. Today it's more like 30 percent off-line and 70 percent online."[53]

Make Creative Use of E-Mail but Avoid Becoming a "Spammer"

Used properly and creatively, e-mail can be an effective way to build traffic on a Web site. Just as with a newsletter, the e-mail's content should offer something of value to recipients. Supported by online newsletters or chat rooms, customers will welcome well-constructed permission e-mail that directs them to a company's site for information or special deals, unlike unsolicited and universally despised e-mails known as "spam."

Companies often collect visitors' e-mail addresses when they register to receive a "freebie." To be successful at collecting a sufficient number of e-mail addresses, a company must make clear to customers that they will receive messages that are meaningful to them and that the company will not sell e-mail addresses to others (which should be part of its posted privacy policy). Once a company has a customer's permission to send information in additional e-mail messages, it has a meaningful marketing opportunity to create a long-term customer relationship. For example, Ticketmaster, which sells 75 million tickets to concerts and performances each year, e-mails its customers the play lists from the most recent concert they attended along with an offer to purchase a concert T-shirt.[54]

Make Sure Your Web Site Says "Credibility"

As we learned earlier in this chapter, nearly two-thirds of customers do not trust Web sites. Unless a company can build trust in its Web site, selling is virtually impossible. Visitors begin to evaluate the credibility of a site as soon as they arrive. Does the site look professional? Are there misspelled words and typographical errors? If the site provides information, does it note the sources of that information? If so, are those sources legitimate? Are they trustworthy? Is the presentation of the information fair and objective, or is it biased? Does the company include a privacy policy posted in an obvious place?

One of the simplest ways to establish credibility with customers is to use brand names they know and trust. Whether a company sells nationally recognized brands or its own well-known private brand, using those names on its site creates a sense of legitimacy. People buy brand names they trust, and online companies can use that to their advantage. Another effective way to build customer confidence is by joining an online seal program such as TRUSTe or BBBOnLine. The online equivalent of the Underwriter Laboratories stamp or the Good Housekeeping Seal of Approval, these seals mean that a company meets certain standards concerning the privacy of customers' information and the resolution of customer complaints. Finally, providing a street address, an e-mail address, and a toll-free telephone number sends a subtle message to shoppers that a legitimate business is behind a Web site. Many small companies include photographs of their brick-and-mortar stores and of their employees to combat the Web's anonymity and to give shoppers the feeling that they are supporting a friendly small business.

Consider Forming Strategic Alliances

Most small companies seeking e-commerce success lack the brand and name recognition that larger, more established companies have. Creating that sort of recognition on the Web requires a significant investment of both time and money, which are two things that most small companies find scarce. If building name recognition is one of the keys to success on the Web, how can small companies with their limited resources hope to compete? One option is to form strategic alliances with bigger companies that can help a small business achieve what it could not accomplish alone. Describing the need for small companies to consider forming strategic alliances, Philip Anderson of Dartmouth's Tuck School of Business says, "You need to build [market] share fast, and that means you have to have more resources than you can get your mitts on by yourself."[55]

Before plunging into a strategic alliance with a larger partner, however, entrepreneurs must understand their dark side. Research shows that 55 percent of strategic alliances unravel within three-and-a-half years.[56] The most common reasons for splitting up? One study found the following causes: incompatible corporate cultures (75 percent), incompatible management personalities (63 percent), and differences in strategic priorities (58 percent).[57]

Petopia.com

Andrea Reisman, cofounder of Petopia.com, an online retailer of pet supplies, saw the need to form an alliance with a larger partner when two key competitors, Pets.com and Pet.net, announced that they had formed partnerships with giants Amazon.com and PetSmart. The threat from these alliances to her company was real and required immediate action. Soon Reisman was talking with Brian Devine, CEO of Petco, the second largest brick-and-mortar pet retailer in the country, about a possible deal of their own. Devine knew that his company had to have a presence on the Web but that building a Petco Web site from scratch would take months and would cost millions of dollars. Reisman knew that Petco's resources and name recognition would help Petopia.com remain a leader in the intensely competitive pet supply market. "Petco is good at bricks-and-mortar; we're good at the dot.com space," explains Reisman. The two CEOs negotiated a deal in which Petco purchased 20 percent of Petopia.com and established Petopia.com as Petco's exclusive online outlet. Then Petco executives got out of Petopia.com managers' way and let them run the e-commerce side of the business **<www.petco.com>**. *The alliance has worked so well that the two companies have now merged, allowing the customer to order more than 5,000 items online, which can be delivered by mail or picked up at any of Petco's 500 stores.*[58]

Table 15.3 offers seven questions every entrepreneur should ask before entering into a strategic alliance with a partner.

Make the Most of the Web's Global Reach

Despite the Web's reputation as an international marketplace, many Web entrepreneurs fail to utilize fully its global reach. More than 20 million potential e-commerce customers and more than 4 million e-business customers reside outside the borders of the United States.[59] "Only 6 percent of the world speaks English," says one expert. "Why limit your Web site to such a small slice of the world?"[60]

E-companies wanting to draw significant sales from foreign markets must design their sites with these foreign customers in mind. A common mechanism is to include several "language buttons" on the opening page of a site that take customers to pages in the language of their choice. Virtual companies trying to establish a foothold in foreign markets by setting up Web sites dedicated to them run the same risk that actual companies do: offending international visitors by using the business conventions and standards they are accustomed to using in the United States. Business practices, even those used on the Web, that are acceptable, even expected, in the United States may be taboo in other countries. A little research into the subtleties of a target country's culture and business practices can save a great deal of embarrassment and money! Creating secure, simple, and reliable payment methods for foreign customers also will boost sales.

When translating the content of their Web pages into other languages, e-companies must use extreme caution. This is *not* the time to pull out their notes from an introductory Spanish course and begin their own translations. Hiring professional translation and localization services to convert a company's Web content into other languages minimizes the likelihood of a company unintentionally offending foreign customers.

Promote Your Web Site Online and Off-Line

E-commerce entrepreneurs have to use every means available—both online and off-line—to promote their Web sites and to drive traffic to them. In addition to using traditional online techniques such as registering with search engines, creating banner ads, and

TABLE 15.3

Questions to Ask *Before* Entering a Strategic Alliance

Source: Robert McGarvey, "Made for Each Other?" Entrepreneur, *February 2000, p. 79.*

Unfortunately, most strategic alliances fail. In his book, *Partnering Intelligence: Creating Value for Your Business by Building Strong Alliances* (Davies-Black Publishing), Stephen M. Dent offers seven questions every entrepreneur should ask *before* forging an alliance.

1. What is your potential partner's business vision?
2. What are its strategies to achieve its vision?
3. Where does it want to go as a company?
4. What are its values and ethics?
5. What kind of corporate culture does it have?
6. What types of relationships and partnerships does it already have and how well are they working out?
7. Has it conducted an internal assessment of its strengths, weaknesses, and culture?

Based on the answers to these seven questions, entrepreneurs can assess how compatible potential partners are with their own business vision and goals.

joining banner exchange programs, Web entrepreneurs must promote their sites off-line as well. Ads in other media such as direct mail or newspapers that mention a site's URL will bring customers to it. It is also a good idea to put the company's Web address on everything a company publishes, from its advertisements and letterhead to shopping bags and business cards. Kozmo, a company that delivers food, videos, books, magazines, and other items in urban areas, even prints its Web address on its delivery workers' uniforms. "Kozmo delivery guys are walking advertisements," quips one advertising expert.[61] A passive approach to generating Web site traffic is a recipe for failure. On the other hand, entrepreneurs who are as innovative at promoting their e-businesses as they are at creating them can attract impressive numbers of visitors to their sites.

DESIGNING A KILLER WEB SITE

6. Learn the techniques of designing a killer Web site.

World Wide Web users are not a patient lot. They sit before their computers, surfing the Internet, their fingers poised on their mouse buttons, daring any Web site to delay them with files that take a long time to load (to many, that's anything more than 5 seconds). Slow-loading sites or sites that don't deliver on their promises will cause a Web user to move on faster than a bolt of lightning can strike. Research shows that most users visit no more than 10 Web sites on a regular basis and that just 4,500 sites attract 70 percent of all Web traffic.[62] With more than 3.6 million Web sites online, how can entrepreneurs design a Web site that will capture and hold potential customers' attention long enough to make a sale? What can they do to keep customers coming back on a regular basis? There is no surefire formula for stopping surfers in their tracks, but the following suggestions will help.

Select the Right Domain Name

Choose a domain name that is consistent with the image you want to create for your company and register it. Entrepreneurs should never underestimate the power of the right domain name or universal resource locator (URL), which is a company's address on the Internet. It not only tells Web surfers where to find a company but it also should suggest something about the company and what it does. Even the casual Web surfer could guess that the "toys.com" name belongs to a company selling children's toys. (It does; it belongs to eToys Inc., which also owns "etoys.com," "e-toys.com," and several other variations of its name.) "Your Web site is part of your brand, and you want your Web address to give a sense of permanence and legitimacy," says one Web marketing expert.[63]

The ideal domain name should be:

- *Short.* Short names are easy for people to remember, so the shorter a company's URL is, the more likely potential customers are to recall it.
- *Memorable.* Not every short domain name is necessarily memorable. Some business owners use their companies' initials as their domain name (for example, **<www.sbfo.com>** for Stanley Brothers Furniture Outlet). The problem with using initials for a domain name is that customers rarely associate the two, which makes a company virtually invisible on the Web.
- *Indicative of a company's business or business name.* Perhaps the best domain name for a company is one that customers can guess easily if they know the company's name. For instance, mail-order catalog company J. Crew's URL is **<www.jcrew.com>,** and New Pig, a maker of absorbent materials for a variety of industrial applications, uses **<www.newpig.com>** as its domain name. (The company carries this concept over to its toll-free number, which is 1-800-HOT-HOGS.)

- *Easy to spell.* Even though a company's domain name may be easy to spell, it is usually wise to buy several variations of the correct spelling simply because some customers are not likely to be good spellers!

Just because entrepreneurs come up with the perfect URL for their company's Web site does not necessarily mean that they can use it. Domain names are given on a first-come, first-served basis. Before business owners can use a domain name, they must ensure that someone else has not already taken it. The simplest way to do that is to go to a domain name registration service such as Network Solutions' Internic at **<www.networksolutions.com>** or Netnames at **<www.netnames.com>** to conduct a name search. Entrepreneurs who find the domain name they have selected already registered to someone else have two choices: They can select another name, or they can try to buy the name from the original registrant.

Eve.com

When Eve.com, an online women's cosmetics and beauty products retailer, attempted to register the domain name **<www.eve.com>**, *company founders Miriam Naficy and Varsha Rao discovered that Evangeline Rogers, a 6-year-old girl in Virginia, already owned it. The cofounders struck a deal with Evangeline for the rights to the URL, but it cost them a family trip to Disneyland, a desktop PC, $500 worth of eToys, an honorary appointment to the company board of directors for 6 months, and an undisclosed sum of money. "It was probably one of the best investments we've made," says Naficy.*[64]

The cofounders of Eve.com bought the rights to their name relatively cheaply, but not every Web start-up is as fortunate. Business incubator eCompanies recently purchased the rights to the domain name "business.com" from an individual for $7.5 million![65]

Finding unregistered domain names is becoming more difficult, but once an entrepreneur finds an unused name that is suitable, he or she must register it (plus any variations of it)—and the sooner, the better! Registering is quite easy: Simply use one of the registration services listed earlier to fill out a form and pay $70, which registers the name for two years. The registration renewal fee is $35 per year. The next step is to register the domain name with the U.S. Patent and Trademark Office (USPTO) at a cost of $245. The USPTO's Web site **<www.uspto.gov/web/menu/tm.html>** not only allows users to register a trademark online, but it also offers useful information on trademarks and the protection they offer.

Make It Easy to Find

With more than a billion pages already on the Web and more coming on every day, making your site easy for people to find is a real challenge. Because the Web is so expansive, many Web users rely on search engines to help them locate sites. In fact, one recent study found that 92 percent of Web surfers use search engines regularly.[66] Smart Web site designers embed codes called meta tags into their homepages that move their sites to the top of the most popular search engines such as Yahoo!, AltaVista, Excite, Google, Infoseek, WebCrawler, and others. Search Engine Watch **<www.searchenginewatch.com>** offers many useful tips on search engine placement and registration as well as on using meta tags to increase the likelihood that a search engine will list a particular site.

Listing a site with the major search engines' indexes can also yield more hits. Entrepreneurs can go to each search engine's Web site to find the instructions for submitting their companies' URLs in the index. Crosslinkz search Engine site **<www.crosslinkz.com/promotion/submit.htm>** provides links to nine of the leading search engine submission sites. Rather than spend time themselves submitting their companies' URLs to search engine sites, entrepreneurs can hire submission services such as SubmitIt **<www.submit-it.com>**, which will submit a site's address to more than 400 search engines for just $59 a year. Registering with multiple search engines is critical because even the largest ones cover less than 20 percent of the Web![67]

Give Customers What They Want

Although Web shoppers are price conscious, they rank fast delivery as the most important criteria in their purchase decisions. Studies also show that surfers look for a large selection of merchandise available to them immediately. Remember that the essence of the selling on the Web is providing convenience to customers. Sites that allow them to shop whenever they want, to find what they are looking for easily, and to pay for it conveniently and securely will keep customers coming back.

Establish Hyperlinks with Other Businesses

Listing the Web addresses of complementary businesses on your company's site and having them list your address on their sites offers customers more value and can bring traffic to your site that you otherwise would have missed. For instance, the owner of a site selling upscale kitchen gadgets should consider a cross-listing arrangement with sites that feature gourmet recipes, wines, and kitchen appliances.

Include E-Mail Options and Telephone Numbers

Customers will appreciate the opportunity to communicate with your company. If you include e-mail access on your site, however, be sure to respond to it promptly. Nothing alienates cyber-customers faster than a company that is slow to respond or fails to respond to their e-mail messages. Also be sure to include a toll-free telephone number for customers who prefer to call with their questions. Unfortunately, many companies either fail to include their telephone numbers on their sites or bury them so deeply within the sites' pages that customers never find them.

Give Shoppers the Ability to Track Orders Online

Many customers who order items online want to track the progress of their orders. One of the most effective ways to keep a customer happy is to send an e-mail confirmation that your company received the order and another e-mail notification when you ship the order. The shipment notice should include the shipper's tracking number and instructions on how to track the order from the shipper's site. Order and shipping confirmations instill confidence in even the most Web-wary shoppers.

Offer Web Specials

Give Web customers a special deal that you don't offer in any other advertising piece. Change your specials often (weekly, if possible) and use clever teasers to draw attention to the offer. Regular special offers available only on the Web give customers an incentive to keep visiting a company's site.

Follow a Simple Design

Catchy graphics and photographs are important to snaring customers, but designers must choose them carefully. Designs that are overly complex take a long time to download, and customers are likely to move on before they appear.

Specific design tips include:

- Avoid clutter. The best designs are simple and elegant with a balance of both text and graphics.
- Avoid huge graphic headers that must download first, prohibiting customers from seeing anything else on your site as they wait (or more likely, *don't* wait). Use graphics judiciously so that the site loads quickly.

- Include a menu bar at the top of the page that makes it easy for customers to find their way around your site.
- Make the site easy to navigate by including navigation buttons at the bottom of pages that enable customers to return to the top of the page or to the menu bar. This avoids what one expert calls "the pogo effect," where visitors bounce from page to page in a Web site looking for what they need.[68] Without navigation buttons or a site map page, a company runs the risk of customers getting lost in its site and leaving.
- Incorporate meaningful content in the site that is useful to visitors, well organized, easy to read, and current. The content should be consistent with the message a company sends in the other advertising media it uses. Although a Web site should be designed to sell, providing useful, current information attracts visitors, keeps them coming back, and establishes a company's reputation as an expert in the field.

poolandspa.com

Dan Harrison, owner of poolandspa.com **<www.poolandspa.com>,** *knows how important informative content is to a successful Web site. From the beginning, Harrison's site has included helpful articles on pools and pool maintenance as well as message boards, chat rooms, and "Ask the Pool Guy" and "Ask the Spa Guy" features, where customers can get answers to their most pressing pool and spa questions from an expert. Harrison's server collects the questions from visitors, and Harrison and his employees post the answers every few days. Poolandspa.com receives an average of 400 questions each day from visitors. Harrison uses the opportunity to interact with visitors through the "Ask the . . ." features to collect valuable information that helps the company target its online and off-line marketing efforts more precisely. Thanks to its interactive Web site, Poolandspa.com now has more than 400,000 names in its database. Harrison, who closed his brick-and-mortar store to focus on the Web, also attributes the company's rapid growth to the success of its e-commerce strategy. "We believe offering information gives us a competitive advantage," he says. "The more information our customers have, the better it is for all of us."*[69]

- Include a "frequently asked questions (FAQ)" section. Adding this section to a page can reduce dramatically the number of telephone calls and e-mail customer service representatives must handle. FAQ sections typically span a wide range of issues—from how to place an order to how to return merchandise—and cover whatever topics customers most often want to know about.
- Be sure to include privacy and return policies as well as product guarantees the company offers.
- Avoid fancy typefaces and small fonts because they are too hard to read.
- Be vigilant for misspelled words, typographical errors, and formatting mistakes; they destroy a site's credibility in no time.
- Don't put small fonts on "busy" backgrounds; no one will read them!
- Use contrasting colors of text and graphics. For instance, blue text on a green background is nearly impossible to read.
- Be careful with frames. Using frames that are so thick that they crowd out text makes for a poor design.

Source: DILBERT © UFS

- Test the site on different Web browsers and on different size monitors. A Web site may look exactly the way it was designed to look on one Web browser and be a garbled mess on another. Sites designed to display correctly on large monitors may not view well on small ones.
- Use your Web site to collect information from visitors, but don't tie up visitors immediately with a tedious registration process. Most will simply leave the site never to return. Offers for a free e-mail newsletter or a contest giveaway can give visitors enough incentive to register with a site.
- Avoid automated music that plays continuously and cannot be cut off.
- Make sure the overall look of the page is appealing. "When a site is poorly designed, lacks information, or cannot support customer needs, that [company's] reputation is seriously jeopardized," says one expert.[70]
- Remember: Simpler usually is better.

Assure Customers That Online Transactions Are Secure

If you are serious about doing business on the Web, make sure that your site includes the proper security software and encryption devices. Computer-savvy customers are not willing to divulge their credit card numbers on sites that are not secure.

Keep Your Site Updated

Customers want to see something new when they visit stores, and they expect the same when they visit virtual stores as well. Delete any hyperlinks that have disappeared and keep the information on your Web site current. One sure way to run off customers on the Web is to continue to advertise your company's "Christmas Special" in August! On the other hand, fresh information and new specials keep customers coming back.

Consider Hiring a Professional to Design Your Site

Pros can do it a lot faster and better than you can. However, don't give designers free rein to do whatever they want to with your site. Make sure it meets your criteria for an effective site that can sell.

Entrepreneurs must remember that on the World Wide Web every company, no matter how big or small it is, has the exact same screen size for its site. What matters most is not the size of your company but how you put that screen size to use.

TRACKING WEB RESULTS

7. Explain how companies track the results from their Web sites.

Software Solutions

As they develop their Web sites, entrepreneurs seek to achieve sites that are both *sticky* and *viral.* In the world of e-commerce, these two concepts are crucial to success, and entrepreneurs are focusing their efforts on trying to design sites that accomplish both goals. A **sticky site** is one that acts like electronic flypaper, capturing visitors' attention and offering them useful, interesting information that makes them stay at the site. The premise of stickiness is that the longer customers stay at a site, the more likely they are to actually purchase something and to come back to it. Customer loyalty is just as important on the Web as it is in traditional brick-and-mortar stores, but it may be harder for online companies to achieve because shopping the competition is much easier on the Web. Another e-store is just a mouse click away! Most Web users visit only a small number of Web sites on a regular basis; the secret to making sure yours is one of them is to design a

sticky site—
one that acts like electronic flypaper, capturing visitors' attention and offering them useful, meaningful information that makes them stay at the site.

viral site— *one that visitors are willing to share with their friends.*

sticky site. A **viral site** is one that visitors are willing to share with their friends. When Web surfers find a site that is useful, informative, or just plain fun, they often share it with their friends. This "word-of-mouse" advertising is one of the most effective ways of generating traffic to a company's site. A friend's recommendation gives the site instant credibility, much like an unsolicited testimonial for a product or service does. Stickiness and viralness are functions of content, features, and design. Following the tips in the previous section on site design will help an entrepreneur design a site that is both sticky and viral.

How can online entrepreneurs know if their sites are viral, sticky, and successful? Answering that question means that entrepreneurs must track visitors to their sites, the paths within the site, and the activity they generate while there. Various methods for tracking Web results are available, but the most commonly used ones include counters and log-analysis software. The simplest technique is a **counter,** which records the number of "hits" a Web site receives. Although counters measure activity on a site, they do so only at the broadest level. If a counter records 10 hits, for instance, there is no way to know if those hits came as a result of 10 different visitors or as a result of just one person making 10 visits. Plus, counters cannot tell Web entrepreneurs where visitors to their sites come from or which pages they look at on the site.

counter— *the simplest mechanism for tracking activity on a Web site by counting the number of "hits" the site receives.*

log-analysis software— *programs to analyze server logs that record visitors' actions on a Web site and then generate meaningful reports for managers.*

A more meaningful way to track activity on a Web site is through **log-analysis software.** Server logs record every page, graphic, audio clip, or photograph that visitors to a site access, and log-analysis software analyzes these logs and generates reports describing how visitors behave when they get to a site. With this software, entrepreneurs can determine how many unique visitors come to their site and how many times repeat visitors come back. Owners of e-stores can discover which FAQ customers click on most often, which part of a site they stayed in the longest, which site they came from, and how the volume of traffic at the site affected the server's speed of operation. The result is the ability to infer what visitors think about a Web site, its products, its content, its design, and other features. Feedback from log-analysis software helps entrepreneurs redesign their sites to eliminate confusing navigation, unnecessary graphics, meaningless content, incomplete information, and other problems that can cause visitors to leave.

All the Right Gifts

Diana and Gregg Shapiro, co-owners of All the Right Gifts **<www.alltherightgifts.com>**, *an online shopping service that helps customers find gifts quickly and conveniently, use log-analysis software to manage their Web site and to keep it fresh and focused on what customers are most interested in. They can access their log reports any time of day and generate statistical analyses, tables, and graphs on practically any aspect of their site. "The data helps us figure out which search engines are generating the best referrals and what key words customers are keying in to find us," says Gregg. "Then we use this information to concentrate our marketing efforts in the best possible way."*[71]

Other tracking methods available to owners of e-businesses include:[72]

- *Clustering.* This software observes visitors to a Web site, analyzes their behavior, and then groups them into narrow categories. Companies then target each category of shoppers with products, specials, and offers designed to appeal to them.
- *Collaborative filtering.* This software uses sophisticated algorithms to analyze visitors' interests by comparing them to other shoppers with similar tastes. Companies then use this information to suggest products in which an individual customer would most likely be interested given his or her profile.
- *Profiling systems.* These programs tag individual customers on a site and note their responses to the various pages in the site. Based on the areas a customer visits most, the software develops a psychographic profile of the shopper. For instance, a visitor who reads an article on massage techniques might receive an offer for a book on alternative medicine or a magazine focusing on environmental issues.
- *Artificial intelligence (AI).* This software, sometimes called neural networking, is the most sophisticated of the group because it actually learns from users' behavior. The more these

time compression management (TCM)—*a philosophy of introducing speed into a company that involves three aspects: (1) speeding new products to market, (2) shortening customer response time in manufacturing and delivery, and (3) reducing the administrative time required to fill an order.*

- Create cross-functional teams of workers and give them the power to attack and solve problems. In world-class companies, product teams include engineers, manufacturing workers, salespeople, quality experts—even customers.
- Set aggressive goals for time reduction and stick to the schedule. Some companies using TCM have been able to reduce cycle time from several weeks to just a few hours!
- Rethink the supply chain. Can you electronically link with your suppliers or your customers to speed up orders and deliveries?
- Instill speed in the culture. At Domino's Pizza, kitchen workers watch videos of the fastest pizza makers in the country.
- Use technology to find shortcuts wherever possible. Properly integrated into a company's strategy for speed, technology can restructure a company's operating timetable. Rather than build costly, time-consuming prototypes, many time-sensitive businesses use computer-aided design and computer-assisted manufacturing (CAD/CAM) to speed product design and testing.
- Put the Internet to work for you. Perhaps nothing symbolizes speed better than the Internet, and companies that harness its lightning-fast power can become leaders in TCM.

PeopleScape

PeopleScape, a Silicon Valley personnel search firm, uses an extensive database of connections in the valley and e-mail to locate potential employees for its customers. "It takes a traditional recruiter two or three weeks to reach someone I can reach within 48 hours," says company cofounder Ben Slick.[74]

5. Discuss the marketing opportunities the World Wide Web (WWW) offers entrepreneurs and how to best take advantage of them.

MARKETING ON THE WORLD WIDE WEB (WWW)

Much like the telephone, the fax machine, and home shopping networks, the World Wide Web (WWW, or the Web) promises to become a revolutionary business tool. Although most entrepreneurs have heard about the **World Wide Web,** the vast network that links computers around the globe via the Internet and opens up endless oceans of information to its users, the majority of them are still struggling to understand what it is, how it can work for them, and how they can establish a meaningful presence on it. Businesses get on the Web by using one of thousands of "electronic gateways" to set up an address (called a Universal Resource Locator, or URL) there. By establishing a creative, attractive **Web site,** the electronic storefront of a company on the Web, even the smallest companies can market their products and services to customers across the globe. The Web is expanding so rapidly that tracking its growth is difficult, but experts estimate that the number of Web pages doubles every six months.[75]

World Wide Web (WWW)—*the vast network that links computers around the globe via the Internet and opens up endless oceans of information to its users.*

Web site—*the electronic storefront of a company on the World Wide Web; its exact location is defined by the site's Universal Resource Locator.*

With its ability to display colorful graphics, sound, animation, and video as well as text, the Web allows small companies to equal—even surpass—their larger rivals' Web presence. Although small companies cannot match the marketing efforts of their larger competitors dollar-for-dollar, a creative Web page can be the "great equalizer" in a small company's marketing program. "It's like advertising your product in the world's largest directory," says the president of the Internet Society. "The [World Wide Web] lets small companies expand far beyond their immediate region. [It is] a phenomenal commercial opportunity that offers businesses a worldwide marketing and distribution system."[76]

Forrester Research estimates that e-commerce will rise from just $50 billion in 1998 to nearly $1.3 trillion in 2003.[77] Unfortunately, most small businesses are not yet taking advantage of the Web's tremendous marketing potential; only one-fourth of small companies have Web sites. The most common reasons small business owners cite for not creating a Web presence are business security concerns and the fear that the site will not draw cus-

YOU BE THE CONSULTANT . . .

The Battle for the Teen Customer

When Stephen Kahn saw an opportunity to sell funky clothing and accessories to girls and young women through a catalog, he knew he had to jump at it. Kahn quit his job as a stockbroker and convinced his ex-college roommate, Christopher Edgar, to help him develop a marketing strategy and write a business plan. Once the pair had finished their plan, they decided to test the conclusion it led them to: that their company would be successful. They took out classified ads in several magazines targeting young women, from *Cosmopolitan* and *Mademoiselle* to *Seventeen* and *YM.* The thousands of requests for catalogs they received in just days surprised even the optimistic entrepreneurs. "Right away we knew we had a consumer group that was waiting to be tapped," says Edgar.

Kahn and Edgar set out to find financing to launch their company, Delia's Inc., but venture capital companies were not interested because they could not imagine the idea of creating a catalog aimed at a target audience that had no credit cards. Kahn and Edgar knew that their target customers spent some $120 billion of their own money on retail purchases, much of it on clothing and accessories, so they put up $100,000 of their own money before turning to family and friends to raise the rest of the $1 million they needed to print and mail their glossy catalog. "I was convinced that this overlooked niche had potential," says Kahn.

Within a year, Delia's had a mailing list of 50,000 names and a base of 10,000 paying customers. Kahn and Edgar hired a staff of young women to handle the flood of calls coming in from across the country. Their move paid off as the young workers found it easy to chat with customers and learn about their preferences, their credit histories, their buying habits, and their e-mail addresses. A team of twenty-something graphic designers and magazine editors kept the magazine fresh, cool, and appealing to Delia's young customer base, whose tastes in clothing and accessories were constantly changing. Kahn and Edgar knew that to succeed, their company had to stay extremely close to their customers and that their inventory had to change as quickly as their customers' tastes.

After three years, the company had cornered 100 percent of the direct-mail teenage girl market, but competitors were catching on to Delia's success. To maintain the company's success as competitors such as MXG Media, Wet Seal, and Claire's Stores moved into the market, Kahn broadened his marketing strategy to include the *brothers* of his existing customers. Delia's soon purchased TSI Soccer, a direct-mail retailer of soccer gear, Screeem, a chain of mall stores targeting young men, and Fulcrum Direct, a collection of catalogs aimed at young men and boys. The moves expanded Delia's database of customers to 16 million, from which the company launched another catalog called Droog aimed at young men.

As part of their ongoing market research, Kahn and Edgar discovered that teenage girls are the fastest growing customer segment on the World Wide Web. "Why not use the Internet to drive business?" he remembers thinking. Not only would the Web be an effective way to reach Delia's customers, but it also would be less costly than creating, printing, and mailing expensive catalogs. Kahn and Edgar purchased **<www.gurl.com>,** a large Web site that features chat rooms, homepage hosting, and e-mail services. Their goal was to build brand awareness for Delia's and to tap into their customers' minds even more effectively. The company has since added Web sites for each of its teen target customers. Recently Kahn negotiated an important deal with Web giant Yahoo! to establish an online store on the Yahoo Shopping service. Web-based sales account for 15 percent of the company's sales and are rising rapidly. Competitors, of course, are following a similar path to reach these same target customers. MXG Media has a Web site that reaches tens of thousands of teen girls and a "magalog," a combination magazine and catalog that it mails to 500,000 girls every quarter.

For now, Delia's marketing strategy, which relies on direct mail, mall stores, and the Web to reach its target customers, has put it in the lead. Will Kahn and Edgar be able to maintain their edge in a market that shifts so rapidly? Missteps in this market can be fatal. "Being uncool is the kiss of death in this business," says an executive at MXG Media.

1. What dangers does Delia's marketing strategy expose the company to?
2. How can the company cope with those dangers?
3. Conduct a Web search to locate several of Delia's Web sites. How effective are they at selling to the company's target customers? What suggestions for improvement can you offer?

Sources: Adapted from Caroline Waxler, "Guys with Moxie," *Forbes,* May 31, 1999, pp. 130–131; David S. Murphy, "Delia's Next Big Step," *Fortune,* February 15, 1999, pp. 192[C]–192[H]; Delia's Inc., **<www.delias.com>.**

TABLE 11.5

The Six Most Common Reasons Bankers Reject Small Business Loan Applications (and How You Can Avoid Them)

Source: Adapted from Anne Field, "Getting the Bank to Say Yes," Success, May *1999, pp. 67–71; J. Tol Broome, Jr., "How to Get a 'Yes' From Your Banker,"* Nation's Business, *April 1996, p. 37.*

Reason 1. "Our bank doesn't make small business loans." Cure: Before applying for a bank loan, research banks to find out which ones actively seek the type of loan you need. Some banks don't emphasize loans under $500,000, while others focus almost exclusively on small company loans. The Small Business Administration's reports, *Micro-Business-Friendly Banks in the United States* and *Small Business Lending in the United States,* are valuable resources for locating the banks in your area that are most likely to make small business loans.

Reason 2. "I don't know enough about you or your business." Cure: Develop a detailed business plan that explains what your company does (or will do) and describes how you will gain a competitive edge over your rivals. Also be prepared to supply business credit references and a personal credit history.

Reason 3. "You haven't told me why you need the money." Cure: A solid business plan will explain how much money you need and how you plan to use it. Make sure your request is specific; avoid requests for loans "for working capital." Don't make the mistake of answering the question, "How much money do you need?" with "How much will you lend me?"

Reason 4. "Your numbers don't support your loan request." Cure: Include a cash flow forecast in your business plan. Bankers analyze a company's balance sheet and income statement to judge the quality of its assets and its profitability, but bankers lend primarily on the basis of cash flow. They know that's how you'll repay the loan. If adequate cash flow isn't available, don't expect a loan. Prove to the banker that you know what your company's cash flow is and how to manage it.

Reason 5. "You don't have enough collateral." Cure: Be prepared to pledge your company's assets—and perhaps your personal assets—as collateral for the loan. Bankers like to have the security of collateral before they make a loan. They also expect more than $1 in collateral for every $1 of money they lend. Banks typically lend 80 to 90 percent of the value of real estate, 70 to 80 percent of the value of accounts receivable, and just 10 to 50 percent of the value of inventory pledged as collateral.

Reason 6. "Your business does not support the loan on its own." Cure: Be prepared to provide a personal guarantee on the loan. By doing so, you're telling the banker that if your business cannot repay the loan, you will. Many bankers see their small business clients and their companies as one and the same. Even if you choose a form of ownership that provides you with limited personal liability, most bankers will ask you to override that protection by personally guaranteeing the loan.

There's no magic to getting a bank to approve your loan request. The secret is proper preparation and building a solid business plan that enhances your credibility as a business owner with your banker. Use your plan to prove that you have what it takes to survive and thrive.

Intermediate and Long-Term Loans

Banks primarily are lenders of short-term capital to small businesses, although they will make certain intermediate and long-term loans. Intermediate and long-term loans are extended for one year or longer and are normally used to increase fixed- and growth-capital balances. Commercial banks grant these loans for starting a business, constructing a plant, purchasing real estate and equipment, and other long-term investments. Loan repayments are normally made monthly or quarterly. One of the most common types of intermediate-term loans is an installment loan, which banks make to small firms for purchasing equipment, facilities, real estate, and other fixed assets. When financing equipment, a bank usually lends the small business from 60 to 80 percent of the equipment's value in return for a security interest in the equipment. The loan's amortization schedule, which is based on a set number of monthly payments, typically coincides with the length of the equipment's usable life. In financing real estate (commercial mortgages), banks typically will lend up to 75 to 80 percent of the property's value and will allow a lengthier repayment schedule of 10 to 30 years.

Another common type of loan banks make to small businesses is a **term loan.** Typically unsecured, banks grant these loans to businesses whose past operating history suggests a high probability of repayment. Some banks make only secured term loans, however. Term

term loan—*a bank loan that imposes restrictions (covenants) on the business decisions an entrepreneur makes concerning the company's operations.*

loans impose restrictions (called covenants) on the business decisions an entrepreneur makes concerning the company's operations. For instance, a term loan may set limits on owners' salaries, prohibit further borrowing without the bank's approval, or submit financial reports and analyses on a specific schedule. An entrepreneur must understand all of the terms attached to a loan before accepting it.

Nonbank Sources of Debt Capital

Although they are usually the first stop for entrepreneurs in search of debt capital, banks are not the only lending game in town. We now turn our attention to other sources of debt capital that entrepreneurs can tap to feed their cash-hungry companies.

ASSET-BASED LENDERS. Asset-based lenders, which are usually smaller commercial banks, commercial finance companies, or specialty lenders, allow small businesses to borrow money by pledging otherwise idle assets such as accounts receivable, inventory, or purchase orders as collateral. This form of financing works especially well for manufacturers, wholesalers, distributors, and other companies with significant stocks of inventory or accounts receivable. Even unprofitable companies whose financial statements could not convince loan officers to make traditional loans can get asset-based loans. These cash-poor but asset-rich companies can use normally unproductive assets—accounts receivable, inventory, fixtures, and purchase orders—to finance rapid growth and the cash crises that often accompany it.

advance rate—*the percentage of an asset's value that a lender will lend.*

Although asset-based lenders consider a company's cash flow, they are more interested in the quality of the assets pledged as collateral. The amount a small business can borrow through asset-based lending depends on the **advance rate,** the percentage of an asset's value that a lender will lend. For example, a company pledging $100,000 of accounts receivable might negotiate a 70 percent advance rate and qualify for a $70,000 asset-based loan. Advance rates can vary dramatically depending on the quality of the assets pledged and the lender. Because inventory is an illiquid asset (i.e., hard to sell), the advance rate on inventory-based loans is quite low, usually 10 percent to 50 percent. A business pledging high-quality accounts receivable as collateral, however, may be able to negotiate up to an 85 percent advance rate. The most common types of asset-based financing are discounting accounts receivable and inventory financing.

DISCOUNTING ACCOUNTS RECEIVABLE. The most common form of secured credit is accounts receivable financing. Under this arrangement, a small business pledges its accounts receivable as collateral; in return, the lender advances a loan against the value of approved accounts receivable. The amount of the loan tendered is not equal to the face value of the accounts receivable, however. Even though the bank screens the firm's accounts and accepts only qualified receivables, it makes an allowance for the risk involved because some will be written off as uncollectible. A small business usually can borrow an amount equal to 55 to 80 percent of its receivables, depending on their quality. Generally, lenders will not accept receivables that are past due.

Many commercial finance companies engage in accounts receivable financing.

Milnucorp

Kyle Jodice, founder of Milnucorp, a small distributor of products ranging from Hula-Hoops to tank parts, uses accounts receivable financing from Action Capital, a commercial finance company in Atlanta, to get the cash he needs to purchase inventory. Action Capital advances money based on Milnucorp's accounts receivable. After Action Capital collects payment from Milnucorp's customers, typically within 40 to 60 days, the commercial finance company remits the payments to Jodice after subtracting the amount of the loan and the interest it charges.[65]

THE NATURE OF DEBT FINANCING

5. Describe the various sources of debt capital and the advantages and disadvantages of each.

Debt financing involves the funds that the small business owner borrows and must repay with interest. Lenders of capital are more numerous than investors, although small business loans can be just as difficult (if not more difficult) to obtain. Although borrowed capital allows entrepreneurs to maintain complete ownership of their businesses, it must be carried as a liability on the balance sheet as well as be repaid with interest at some point in the future. In addition, because small businesses are considered to be greater risks than bigger corporate customers, they must pay higher interest rates because of the risk-return trade-off—the higher the risk, the greater the return demanded. Most small firms pay the **prime rate,** the interest rate banks charge their most creditworthy customers, *plus* two to three percentage points. Still, the cost of debt financing often is lower than that of equity financing. Because of the higher risks associated with providing equity capital to small companies, investors demand greater returns than lenders. Also, unlike equity financing, debt financing does not require an entrepreneur to dilute her ownership interest in the company.

prime rate—*the interest rate banks charge their most creditworthy customers.*

Entrepreneurs seeking debt capital are quickly confronted with an astounding range of credit options varying greatly in complexity, availability, and flexibility. Not all of these sources of debt capital are equally favorable, however. By understanding the various sources of capital—both commercial and government lenders—and their characteristics, entrepreneurs can greatly increase the chances of obtaining a loan.

We now turn to the various sources of debt capital.

Sources of Debt Capital

COMMERCIAL BANKS. Commercial banks are the very heart of the financial market, providing the greatest number and variety of loans to small businesses. Small business loans at commercial banks have been growing at a healthy rate, increasing by 8 percent a year since 1995.[58] One study by the Federal Reserve concluded that commercial banks provide about half the financing available to small businesses and that 80 percent of all loans to existing businesses come from banks![59] For small business owners, banks are lenders of *first* resort.

Banks tend to be conservative in their lending practices and prefer to make loans to established small businesses rather than to high-risk start-ups. One expert estimates that only 5 to 8 percent of business start-ups get bank financing.[60] Bankers want to see evidence of a company's successful track record before committing to a loan. They are concerned with a firm's operating past and will scrutinize its records to project its position in the immediate future. They also want proof of the stability of the firm's sales and of the ability of the product or service to generate adequate cash flows to ensure repayment of the loan. If they do make loans to a start-up venture, banks like to see sufficient cash flows to repay the loan, ample collateral to secure it, or a Small Business Administration (SBA) guarantee to insure it. Studies suggest that small banks (those with less than $300 million in assets) are most likely to lend money to small businesses.[61]

Tasca-Kitchen & Wine Bar

Some banks are willing to extend loans to start-up companies, however. Rasheed Refaey turned to bank financing to cover unexpected cost overruns in the construction and start-up of his restaurant, Tasca-Kitchen & Wine Bar. Refaey already had raised $500,000 from private investors and did not want to give up any more equity in his business, so he turned to a small community bank for a $250,000 loan. His solid business plan coupled with an introduction by consultants at a nearby Small Business Development Center convinced bank officers to make the loan. Business at the restaurant is booming, giving Refaey plenty of cash to repay the loan.[62]

When evaluating a loan application, banks focus on a company's capacity to create positive cash flow because they know that's where the money to repay their loans will come from. The first question in most bankers' minds when reviewing an entrepreneur's business plan is "Can this business generate sufficient cash to repay the loan?" Even though they rely on collateral to secure their loans, the last thing banks want is for a borrower to default, forcing them to sell the collateral (often at "fire sale" prices) and use the proceeds to pay off the loan. *That's* why bankers stress cash flow when analyzing a loan request, especially for a business start-up. "Cash is more important than your mother," jokes one experienced borrower.[63]

Short-Term Loans

Short-term loans, extended for less than one year, are the most common type of commercial loan banks make to small companies. These funds typically are used to replenish the working capital account to finance the purchase of more inventory, boost output, finance credit sales to customers, or take advantage of cash discounts. As a result, an owner repays the loan after converting inventory and receivables into cash. There are several types of short-term loans.

COMMERCIAL LOANS (TRADITIONAL BANK LOANS). The basic short-term loan is the commercial bank's specialty. It is usually repaid as a lump sum within three to six months and is unsecured because secured loans are much more expensive to administer and maintain. In other words, the bank grants a loan to the small business owner without requiring him to pledge any specific collateral to support the loan in case of default. The owner is expected to repay the total amount of the loan at maturity. Sometimes the interest due on the loan is prepaid—deducted from the total amount borrowed. Until a small business is able to prove its financial strength to the bank's satisfaction, it will probably not qualify for this kind of commercial loan.

line of credit—*a short-term bank loan with a preset limit that provides working capital for day-to-day operations.*

LINES OF CREDIT. One of the most common requests entrepreneurs make of banks is to establish a **line of credit,** a short-term loan with a preset limit that provides much needed cash flow for day-to-day operations. With an approved line of credit, a business owner can borrow up to the predetermined ceiling at any time during the year quickly and conveniently by writing himself a loan. Banks usually limit the open line of credit to 40 to 50 percent of the firm's present working capital, although they will lend more for highly seasonal businesses. It is usually extended for one year (or more) and is secured by collateral, although some banks offer unsecured lines of credit to small companies with solid financial track records. A business typically pays a small handling fee (1 to 2 percent of the maximum amount of credit) plus interest on the amount borrowed—usually prime plus three points or more. One study of small businesses with lines of credit found that 76 percent used them; the remaining 24 percent have established their lines as a safety net but had not activated them.[64]

Table 11.5 describes the six most common reasons bankers reject small business loan applications and how to avoid them.

FLOOR PLANNING. Floor planning is a form of financing frequently employed by retailers of "big-ticket items" that are easily distinguishable from one another (usually by serial number), such as automobiles, boats, and major appliances. For example, the commercial bank finances Auto City's purchase of its inventory of automobiles and maintains a security interest in each car in the order by holding its title as collateral. Auto City pays interest on the loan monthly and repays the principal as the cars are sold. The longer a floor-planned item sits in inventory, the more it costs the business owner in interest expense. Banks and other floor planners often discourage retailers from using their money without authorization by performing spot checks to verify prompt repayment of the principal as items are sold.

programs interact with customers, the "smarter" they become. Over time, they can help online marketers know which special offers work best with which customers, when customers are most likely to respond, and how to present the offer.

ENSURING WEB PRIVACY AND SECURITY

8. Describe how e-businesses ensure the privacy and security of the information they collect and store from the Web.

Privacy

The Web's ability to track a customer's every move naturally raises concerns over the privacy of the information companies collect. E-commerce gives businesses access to tremendous volumes of information about their customers, creating a responsibility to protect that information and to use it wisely. A recent survey by Primary Knowledge found that 75 percent of Web users were aware that the sites they visited were collecting personal information about them. Another study by Forrester Research discovered that 90 percent of online customers wanted to control their personal information on the Web.[73] "We are rapidly approaching a corporate version of George Orwell's *1984* when it comes to privacy concerning the Internet and computer databases," says Bruce Methven, an attorney specializing in computer law.[74]

To make sure they are using the information they collect from visitors to their Web sites legally and ethically, companies should take the following steps.

TAKE AN INVENTORY OF THE CUSTOMER DATA COLLECTED. The first step to ensuring proper data handling is to assess exactly the type of data the company is collecting and storing. How are you collecting it? Why are you collecting it? How are you using it? Do visitors know how you are using the data? Do you need to get their permission to use it in this way? Do you use all of the data you are collecting?

DEVELOP A COMPANY PRIVACY POLICY FOR THE INFORMATION YOU COLLECT. A **privacy policy** is a statement explaining the nature of the information a company collects online, what it does with that information, and the recourse customers have if they believe the company is misusing the information. Several Web sites, such as TRUSTe (www.truste.org), an online privacy services firm, offer policy "wizards," automated questionnaires that help e-business owners create comprehensive privacy statements.

privacy policy— *a statement explaining the nature of the information a company collects online, what it does with that information, and the recourse customers have if they believe the company is misusing the information.*

POST YOUR COMPANY'S PRIVACY POLICY PROMINENTLY ON YOUR WEB SITE AND FOLLOW IT. Creating a privacy policy is not sufficient; posting it in a prominent place on the Web site and then abiding by it make a policy meaningful. One of the worst mistakes a company can make is to publish its privacy policy online and then to fail to follow it. Not only is this unethical, but it also can lead to serious damage awards if customers take legal action against the company.

KBKids.com

KBKids.com, an online retailer of children's toys, games, and videos, **<www.kbkids.com>**, *positions its privacy policy in a highly prominent position on its site using a large tab that links to a separate page. The page provides a comprehensive description of its policy, the way it collects information, how customers can view the information the company collects, and its affiliation with two privacy programs, TRUSTe and BBBOnLine. "We established a security and privacy policy to assure our customers that we respect the information they provide to us and that its only use is to help us serve them better," says KBKids.com's marketing vice president.*[75]

Security

A company doing business on the Web faces two conflicting goals: to establish a presence on the Web so that customers from across the globe can have access to its site and to maintain a high level of security so that the business, its site, and the information it collects is safe from hackers and intruders intent on doing harm. Companies have a number of safeguards available to them, but hackers with enough time, talent, and determination usually can beat even the most sophisticated safety measures. If hackers manage to break into a system, they can do irreparable damage, stealing programs and data, modifying or deleting valuable information, changing the look and content of sites, or crashing sites altogether. For instance, authorities recently arrested two hackers in Great Britain who had broken into e-commerce sites in five countries, stealing information on more than 26,000 customers' credit card accounts, and posting it on the Web. FBI experts estimated that the security breach resulted in losses totaling more than $3 million.[76]

YOU BE THE CONSULTANT . . .

Big Brother Online?

It was a simple enough strategy. The company would merge its database of the Web-surfing histories of millions of Americans with the database of names, addresses, and buying habits of those same people, which resided in the database of a recently acquired company. For DoubleClick Inc., the marriage of the two databases would create the perfect marketing tool to sell to its online advertising customers. For advertisers, it would be the ideal way to get the most bang from their advertising dollars, targeting those customers most interested in their products and services. For consumers, merging the two databases would mean seeing online ads for products that fit their consumption patterns, or so thought DoubleClick founder Kevin O'Conner.

Instead O'Conner unleashed a firestorm of protest from consumers and privacy advocates alike when he announced DoubleClick's plan to combine the two databases into one that contained a complete profile of consumers, including their names, addresses, details of every purchase they have made online or from catalogs, and a log of every Web site they have visited in DoubleClick's network. The Web gives marketers the ability to collect incredible volumes of information about customers, including their online surfing and shopping habits. Many companies had been competing in a high-stakes battle to achieve the grail of online advertising, and DoubleClick thought it had gotten there first. It would be able to offer e-commerce businesses the opportunity to conduct one-to-one online marketing campaigns tailored to their target customers' exact needs and interests.

Within days of DoubleClick's announcement, however, privacy groups, congresspeople, and consumer advocacy organizations were up in arms, the state of Michigan had filed a lawsuit, and the Federal Trade Commission announced that it was launching a probe into DoubleClick's actions. In the face of such resistance, O'Conner and DoubleClick quickly backpedaled, announcing that the company was shelving its plans to create a centralized marketing database. "I made a mistake in moving ahead with these plans with no privacy standards in place," O'Conner said.

Within two months of DoubleClick's announcement to delay the development of its centralized marketing database, a small start-up company, Predictive Networks, also raised concerns among privacy advocates by announcing that it had created software that can track every site a Web user visits and then build a "digital silhouette" of that person based on his or her pattern of Web use. Like DoubleClick, Predictive Networks' plan is to sell the profiles to advertisers who could then target their online ads to those customers who are most interested and most likely to buy their products. Unlike DoubleClick, however, customers would sign up for the tracking service. Predictive would offer customers cheap Internet access to Web users in exchange for the privilege of tracking their Web use patterns. Online advertisers are very interested in Predictive's software because market tests show that customers who received ads based on the profile built using the software clicked on 16 percent of the ads they received compared to an industry average of about 1 percent. "We created this company to solve the privacy dilemma," says Predictive Networks founder, Devin Hosea. "People want personalization but also want their privacy."

1. What privacy and ethical issues does the tracking software from DoubleClick and Predictive Networks raise?
2. What benefits do these Web-tracking programs offer advertisers? Web users?
3. Would you be willing to join a tracking program in exchange for cheap Web access? Explain.

Sources: Adapted from Fred Vogelstein, "Minding One's Business," *U.S. News & World Report,* March 13, 2000, p. 45; Andrea Petersen, "DoubleClick Reverses Course After Privacy Outcry," *Wall Street Journal,* March 3, 2000, pp. B1, B6; Julia Agnew, "A Plan to Track Web Use Stirs Privacy Concern," *Wall Street Journal,* May 1, 2000, pp. B1, B18.

To minimize the likelihood of invasion by hackers, e-companies rely on several tools, including virus detection software, intrusion detection software, and firewalls. Perhaps the most basic level of protection, **virus detection software** scans computer drives for viruses, nasty programs written by devious hackers and designed to harm computers and the information they contain. The severity of viruses ranges widely from relatively harmless programs that put humorous messages on a user's screen to those that erase a computer's hard drive or cause the entire system to crash. Because hackers are *always* writing new viruses to attack computer systems, entrepreneurs must keep their virus detection software up-to-date and must run it often. An attack by one virus can bring a company's entire e-commerce platform to a screeching halt in no time!

virus detection software— *programs that scan computer drives for viruses, nasty programs written by devious hackers and designed to harm computers and the information they contain.*

Intrusion detection software is essential for any company doing business on the Web. These packages constantly monitor the activity on a company's network server and sound an alert if they detect someone breaking into the company's computer system or if they detect unusual network activity. Intrusion detection software not only can detect attempts by unauthorized users to break into a computer system while they are happening, but it also can trace the hacker's location. Most packages also have the ability to preserve a record of the attempted break-in that will stand up in court so that companies can take legal action against cyber-intruders.

intrusion detection software— *programs that constantly monitor the activity on a company's network server and sound an alert if they detect someone breaking into the system or if they detect unusual network activity.*

A **firewall** is a combination of hardware and software operating between the Internet and a company's computer network that allows employees to have access to the Internet but keeps unauthorized users from entering a company's network and the programs and data it contains. Establishing a firewall is essential to operating a company on the Web, but entrepreneurs must make sure that their firewalls are set up properly. Otherwise, they are useless! One recent study of more than 2,000 Web sites by ISCA.net, a security consulting firm, found even though every site had a firewall in place, more than 80 percent were vulnerable to attack with commonly available software because they were not properly designed.[77] Even with all of these security measures in place, it is best for a company to run its Web page on a separate server from the network that runs the business. If hackers break into the Web site, they still do not have access to the company's sensitive data and programs.

firewall— *a combination of hardware and software that allows employees to have access to the Internet but keeps unauthorized users from entering a company's network and the programs and data it contains.*

The Computer Security Institute **<www.gocsi.com>** offers articles, information, and seminars to help business owners maintain computer security. The Business Security e-Journal **<www.lubrinco.com>** is a free monthly newsletter on computer security, and *Information Security Magazine* **<www.infosecuritymag.com>,** published by the International Computer Security Association **<www.icsa.net>,** also offers helpful advice on maintaining computer security. For entrepreneurs who want to test their sites' security, the ICSA offers its Security Snapshot system (free of charge) that runs various security tests on a site and then e-mails a "Risk Index" score in six different categories, including the site's risk of hacker intrusion.

In e-commerce just as in traditional retailing, sales do not matter unless a company gets paid! On the Web customers demand transactions they can complete with ease and convenience, and the simplest way to allow customers to pay for e-commerce transactions is with credit cards. From a Web customer's perspective, however, one of the most important issues is the security of their credit card information.

Processing credit card transactions requires a company to obtain an Internet merchant account from a bank or financial intermediary. Setup fees for an Internet merchant account typically range from $500 to $1,000, but companies also pay monthly access and statement fees of between $40 and $80 plus a transaction fee of 10 to 60 cents per transaction.

Once an online company has a merchant account, it can accept credit cards from online customers. To ensure the security of their customers' credit card numbers, online retailers typically use secure sockets layer (SSL) technology to encrypt customers' transaction information as it travels across the Internet. By using secure shopping cart features from storefront-building services or Internet service providers, even the smallest e-commerce stores can offer their customers secure online transactions.

9. Learn how to evaluate the effectiveness of a company's Web site.

EVALUATING THE EFFECTIVENESS OF A SITE

The World Wide Web offers tremendous opportunities to entrepreneurs with the skill and the motivation to create innovative businesses. Just as with every booming opportunity in history, however, not every company seeking success will achieve it. Scores of e-commerce businesses are not reaching their potential, and many will fail. Research by Forrester Research suggests that poorly organized e-commerce sites are underselling by as much as 50 percent and slow-performing sites cause sales to drop off by another 30 percent.[78] Because their founders have failed to create a comprehensive e-commerce strategy, many sites are simply ineffective. One e-commerce expert estimates that "at least 70 percent of Web sites are just up there and don't do much at all."[79]

If their companies are to reach the point of sustaining themselves, online entrepreneurs must learn to evaluate the effectiveness of their e-businesses. The difficulty, however, is that both the investments required for Web success and the payoffs from them are not easy to measure and do not always fit neatly into traditional financial models that calculate return on investment (ROI). For instance, how can a business with both a click-and-brick presence determine exactly how many customers come into its retail store as a result of having visited its Web site? Can it quantify the increase in customer loyalty as a result of its e-commerce efforts? Many companies have discovered that the payoff from their online sales efforts is long term and sometimes intangible.

Owners of e-businesses are developing new models to evaluate the performances of their companies. iGo, an online retailer of mobile computing and communication accessories **<www.igo.com>,** has created an integrated set of performance measures that includes the long-term value (LTV) of its customers and customer retention rates as well as several traditional financial measures.[80] AutoTrader.com, with more than 1.5 million used car listings on its site **<www.autotrader.com>** and 3.5 million visitors each month, established a method that also includes multiple measurements to judge the effectiveness of its site from its initial launch. Jerry Johannesen, manager of MIS at AutoTrader.com, describes it as "a management dashboard" that allows executives to see from a broad perspective how the site is performing and to view summaries of what visitors to the site are doing. This feedback not only tells managers about the Web site's effectiveness, but it also helps them make decisions about improving the site.[81]

CHAPTER SUMMARY

E-commerce is creating a new economy, one that is connecting producers, sellers, and customers via technology in ways that have never been possible before. In this fast-paced world of e-commerce, size no longer matters as much as speed and flexibility do. The Internet is creating a new industrial order, and companies that fail to adapt to it will soon become extinct.

1. Describe the benefits of selling on the World Wide Web. Although a Web-based sales strategy does not guarantee success, the companies that have pioneered Web-based selling have realized many benefits, including the following:
   - The opportunity to increase revenues.
   - The ability to expand their reach into global markets.
   - The ability to remain open 24 hours a day, seven days a week.
   - The capacity to use the Web's interactive nature to enhance customer service.
   - The power to educate and to inform.
   - The ability to lower the cost of doing business.
   - The ability to spot new business opportunities and to capitalize on them.
   - The power to track sales results.
2. Understand the factors an entrepreneur should consider before launching into e-commerce.

   Before launching an e-commerce effort, business owners should consider the following important issues:
   - How a company exploits the Web's interconnectivity and the opportunities it creates to transform relationships with its suppliers and vendors, its customers, and other external stakeholders is crucial to its success.

- Web success requires a company to develop a plan for integrating the Web into its overall strategy. The plan should address issues such as site design and maintenance, creating and managing a brand name, marketing and promotional strategies, sales, and customer service.
- Developing deep, lasting relationships with customers takes on even greater importance on the Web. Attracting customers on the Web costs money, and companies must be able to retain their online customers to make their Web sites profitable.
- Creating a meaningful presence on the Web requires an ongoing investment of resources—time, money, energy, and talent. Establishing an attractive Web site brimming with catchy photographs of products is only the beginning.
- Measuring the success of Web-based sales effort is essential to remaining relevant to customers whose tastes, needs, and preferences are always changing.

3. Explain the 12 myths of e-commerce and how to avoid falling victim to them.

The 12 myths of e-commerce are:

Myth 1. Setting up a business on the Web is easy and inexpensive.

Myth 2. If I launch a site, customers will flock to it.

Myth 3. Making money on the Web is easy.

Myth 4. Privacy is not an important issue on the Web.

Myth 5. The most important part of any e-commerce effort is technology.

Myth 6. "Strategy? I don't need a strategy to sell on the Web! Just give me a Web site, and the rest will take care of itself."

Myth 7. On the Web, customer service is not as important as it is in a traditional retail store.

Myth 8. Flash makes a Web site better.

Myth 9. It's what's up front that counts.

Myth 10. E-commerce will cause brick-and-mortar retail stores to disappear.

Myth 11. The greatest opportunities for e-commerce lie in the retail sector.

Myth 12. It's too late to get on the Web.

4. Discuss the five basic approaches available to entrepreneurs wanting to launch an e-commerce effort.

   Entrepreneurs looking to launch an e-commerce effort have five basic choices: (1) online shopping malls, (2) storefront-building services, (3) Internet service providers (ISPs), (4) hiring professionals to design a custom site, and (5) building a site in-house.

5. Explain the basic strategies entrepreneurs should follow to achieve success in their e-commerce efforts.

   Following are some guidelines for building a successful Web strategy for a small e-company:

   - Consider focusing on a niche in the market.
   - Develop a community of online customers.
   - Attract visitors by giving away "freebies."
   - Make creative use of e-mail but avoid becoming a "spammer."
   - Make sure your Web site says "credibility."
   - Consider forming strategic alliances with larger, more established companies.
   - Make the most of the Web's global reach.
   - Promote your Web site online and off-line.

6. Learn the techniques of designing a killer Web site.

   There is no surefire formula for stopping surfers in their tracks, but the following suggestions will help:

   - Select a domain name that is consistent with the image you want to create for your company and register it.
   - Be easy to find.
   - Give customers what they want.
   - Establish hyperlinks with other businesses, preferably those selling products or services that complement yours.
   - Include an e-mail option and a telephone number in your site.
   - Give shoppers the ability to track their orders online.
   - Offer Web shoppers a special all their own.
   - Follow a simple design for your Web page.
   - Assure customers that their online transactions are secure.
   - Keep your site updated.
   - Consider hiring a professional to design your site.

7. Explain how companies track the results from their Web sites.

   The simplest technique for tracking the results of a Web site is a counter, which records the number of "hits" a Web site receives. Another option for tracking Web activity is through log-analysis software. Server logs record every page, graphic, audio clip, or photograph that visitors to a site access, and log-analysis software analyzes these logs and generates reports describing how visitors behave when they get to a site.

8. Describe how e-businesses ensure the privacy and security of the information they collect and store from the Web.

   To make sure they are using the information they collect from visitors to their Web sites legally and ethically, companies should take the following steps:

   - Take an inventory of the customer data collected.
   - Develop a company privacy policy for the information you collect.
   - Post your company's privacy policy prominently on your Web site and follow it.

   To ensure the security of the information they collect and store from Web transactions, companies should rely on virus and intrusion detection software and firewalls to ward off attacks from hackers.

9. Learn how to evaluate the effectiveness of a company's Web site.

Because the techniques used to evaluate traditional companies do not always fit e-commerce businesses, online entrepreneurs are developing new models to evaluate the performances of their companies that include measures of customer behavior and retention, financial returns, and site performance.

DISCUSSION QUESTIONS

1. How have the Internet and e-commerce changed the ways companies do business?
2. Explain the benefits a company earns by selling on the Web.
3. Discuss the factors entrepreneurs should consider before launching an e-commerce site.
4. What are the 12 myths of e-commerce? What can an entrepreneur do to avoid them?
5. Explain the five basic approaches available to entrepreneurs for launching an e-commerce effort. What are the advantages, the disadvantages, and the costs associated with each one?
6. What strategic advice would you offer an entrepreneur about to start an e-company?
7. What design characteristics make for a successful Web page?
8. Explain the characteristics of an ideal domain name.
9. Describe the techniques that are available to e-companies for tracking results from their Web sites. What advantages does each offer?
10. What steps should e-businesses take to ensure the privacy of the information they collect and store from the Web?
11. What techniques can e-companies use to protect their banks of information and their customers' transaction data from hackers?
12. Why does evaluating the effectiveness of a Web site pose a problem for online entrepreneurs?

Beyond the Classroom . . .

1. Work with a team of your classmates to come up with an Internet business you would be interested in launching. Come up with several suitable domain names for your hypothetical e-company. Once you have chosen a few names, go to a domain name registration service such as Network Solutions' Internic at **<www.networksolutions.com>** or Netnames at **<www.netnames.com>** to conduct a name search. How many of the names your team came up with were already registered to someone? If an entrepreneur's top choice for a domain name is already registered to someone else, what options does he or she have?

2. Select several online companies with which you are familiar and visit their Web sites. What percentage of them have privacy policies posted on their sites? How comprehensive are these policies? What percentage of the sites you visited belonged to a privacy watchdog agency such as TRUSTe or BBBOnLine? How important is a posted privacy policy for e-companies? Explain.

3. Visit five e-commerce sites on the Web and evaluate them on the basis of the Web site design principles described in this chapter. How well do they measure up? What suggestions can you offer for improving the design of each site? If you were a customer trying to make a purchase from each site, how would you respond to the design?

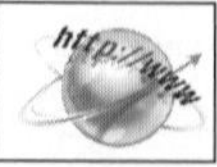

We invite you to visit this book's companion Web site at **www.prenhall.com/Zimmerer.**

END NOTES

Chapter 1

1. Leigh Gallagher, "Moniker's Story," Forbes, April 19, 1999, p. 115.

2. Julia Flynn, "Gap Exists Between Entrepreneurship in Europe, North America, Study Says," Wall Street Journal, July 2, 1999, p. A10.

3. Geoff Williams, "2001: An Entrepreneurial Odyssey," Entrepreneur, April 1999, p. 106; "What's In, What's Out," Success, February 1999, p. 12.

4. Jeffrey A. Tannenbaum, "Like Father, Not Like Son," Wall Street Journal: Small Business, May 24, 1999, p. R27.

5. Howard H. Stevens, "We Create Entrepreneurs," Success, September 1995, p. 51.

6. Flynn, "Gap Exists Between Entrepreneurship in Europe, North America, Study Says," p. A10; "Business Bulletin," Wall Street Journal, June 24, 1999, p. A1.

7. Ibid.

8. Charles Burck, "The Real World of the Entrepreneur," Fortune, April 5, 1993, p. 62.

9. David McClelland, The Achieving Society, (Princeton, NJ: Van Nostrand, 1961), p. 16.

10. Paul Hawken, "A 'New Age' Look at Business," U.S. News & World Report, November 30, 1987, p. 51.

11. Martha E. Manglesdorf, "Insider," Inc., June 1988, p. 14.

12. Gayle Sato Stodder, "Goodbye, Mom & Pop," Entrepreneur, May 1999, p. 112.

13. Debra Phillips, G. David Doran, Elaine W. Teague, and Laura Tiffany, "Young Millionaires," Entrepreneur, November 1998, pp. 118–126.

14. Gayle Sato Stodder, "Never Say Die," Entrepreneur, December 1990, p. 95.

15. Sato Stodder, "Never Say Die," p. 93.

16. James C. Collins, "Sometimes a Great Notion," Inc., July 1993, pp. 90–91; Andrew E. Serwer, "Lessons from America's Fastest-Growing Companies," Fortune, August 8, 1994, pp. 42–62.

17. Bob Weinstein, "Success Secrets," *Business Start-Ups,* August 1995, pp.47–48.

18. Ibid., p. 47.

19. John Case, "The Origins of Entrepreneurship," *Inc.,* June 1989, p. 52.

20. Ron Lieber, "Lessons from America's New Entrepreneurs," *USA Weekend,* August 21–23, 1998, p. 4; Charlotte Mulhern, "Style *And* Substance," *Entrepreneur,* September 1998, p. 18; Michelle Conlin, "It's in the Bag," *Forbes,* December 28, 1998, pp. 86–90.

21. Kathleen Landis, "A New Spin on Outdoor Furniture," *In Business,* March/April 1996, pp. 32–33.

22. Kenneth Labich, "Kissing Off Corporate America," *Fortune,* February 1995, p. 46.

23. Lorayne Fiorillo, "Under the Affluence," *Entrepreneur,* May 1999, pp. 122–125; Mary Beth Grover, "Go Ahead: Buy the Dream," *Forbes,* June 15, 1998.

24. Tony Cook, "Secrets from 'The Millionaire Next Door'," *Reader's Digest,* November 1997, p. 135.

25. Phillips, Doran, Teague, and Tiffany, "Young Millionaires," p. 124.

26. Dave McNary, "Classic Car Obsession Puts Man in Movies," *Greenville News,* September 20, 1997, pp. 1E–2E.

27. Anne Field, "Working Harder," *Fortune,* November 9, 1998, p. 228[H].

28. Robert Johnson, "Owners Pressured to Work Through Vacation Season," *Wall Street Journal,* July 27, 1999, p. B2.

29. Jeremy Main, "A Golden Age for Entrepreneurs," *Fortune,* February 12, 1990, p.126.

30. Rafael J. Garena, "How to Succeed in Business for $49," *Wall Street Journal,* June 12, 1995, p. A12.

31. Pamela Rohland and Elaine W. Teague, "The Price Is Right," *Business Start-Ups,* August 1999, pp. 35–44.

32. Stephanie Barlow, "Making It," *Entrepreneur,* December 1992, pp. 103–106.

33. National Federation of Independent Businesses, "Small Business FAQs," **<http://www.nfib.org/media/faq.asp>.**

34. Robert McGarvey, "Found in Space," *Entrepreneur,* June 1999, pp. 110–117.

35. Cynthia E. Griffin, "Brave New World," *Entrepreneur,* April 1999, p. 49.

36. Christopher D. Lancette, "Sugar Rush," *Entrepreneur,* April 1999, p. 44.

37. Meredith Bagby, "Generation X," *Success,* September 1998, pp. 22–23; Debra Phillips, "Great X-Pectations," *Business Start-Ups,* January 1999, pp. 31–33.

38. Phillips, "Great X-Pectations," pp. 31–33; Geoff Williams, "The Deliberate Entrepreneur," *Business Start-Ups,* May 1999, pp. 37–43.

39. Susan Gregory Thomas, "Mini Computer Moguls," *U.S. News & World Report,* May 19, 1997, pp. 48–49.

40. Luisa Kroll, "Entrepreneur Moms," *Forbes,* May 18, 1998, pp. 84–91.

41. Paulette Thomas, "Closing the Gender Gap," *Wall Street Journal,* May 24, 1999, p. R12; "Work Week," *Wall Street Journal,* June 8, 1999, p. A1.

42. National Foundation for Women Business Owners, "Key Facts," **<http://www.nfwbo.org/key.html>.**

43. Janean Chun, "Hear Them Roar," *Entrepreneur,* June 1995, pp. 10–11; National Foundation for Women Business Owners, "Key Facts," **<http://www.nfwbo.org/key.html>.**

44. Sharon Nelton, "Women's Firms Thrive," *Nation's Business,* August 1998, pp. 38–40; National Foundation for Women Business Owners, "Key Facts," **<http://www.nfwbo.org/key.html>.**

45. Debra Phillips, Cynthia E. Griffin, Heather Page, and Melissa Campanelli, "Quick Guide for Women Entrepreneurs," *Entrepreneur,* January 1999, pp. 23–26.

46. Phillips, Doran, Teague, and Tiffany, "Young Millionaires," p. 125; Geoff Williams, "Keeping Your Cool," *Business Start-Ups,* September 1999, pp. 70–73.

47. Minority Business Entrepreneur, "Statistics," **<www.mbemag.com/html/current.html>.**

48. G. David Doran, Amanda C. Kooser, and Michelle Prather, "The E-List," *Business Start-Ups,* July 1999, pp. 30–38.

49. Debra Phillips, Cynthia E. Griffin, Heather Page, Lynn Beresford, Holly Celeste Fisk, and Charlotte Mulhern, "Entrepreneurial Superstars," *Entrepreneur,* April 1997, pp. 108–139.

50. Eleena De Lisser and Dan Morse, "More Men Work at Home Than Women, Study Shows," *Wall Street Journal,* May 18, 1999, p. B2; Ronaleen Roha, "Home Alone," *Kiplinger's Personal Finance Magazine,* May 1997, pp. 85–89.

51. "Quickstats," *Home Business News Report,* Fall 1994, p. 1.

52. Robert Johnson, "There's No Place Like It," *Wall Street Journal Reports: Small Business,* May 24, 1999, p. R23.

53. Mass Mutual Family Business Network, "Recognizing Why Family Businesses Are Vital to the Future," **<http://www.massmutual.com/fbn/index.htm>;** "Keeping the Firm in the Family," *Upstate Business,* May 18, 1997, p. 8; Annetta Miller, "You Can't Take It with You," *Your Company,* April 1999, pp. 28–34.

54. Erick Calonius, "Blood and Money," *Newsweek: Special Issue,* p. 82.

55. Miller, "You Can't Take It with You," pp. 28–34.

56. Jeff Wuorio, "The Succession Crisis," *Success,* December 1998, pp. 75–81.

57. Udayan Gupta, "And Business Makes Three: Couples Working Together," *Wall Street Journal,* February 26, 1990, p. B2.

58. Bob Weinstein, "For Better or Worse," *Your Company,* Spring 1992, pp. 28–31.

59. Echo M. Garrett, "And Business Makes Three," *Small Business Reports,* September 1993, pp. 27–31.

60. Patricia J. Fry, "Perfect Pairs," *Business Start-Ups,* November 1998, pp. 54–57.

61. "Going Places," *Entrepreneur,* June 1994, p. 14.

62. Charles Stein, "Graduating From Digital," *Your Company,* December 1998/January 1999, pp. 56–60.

63. Donna Kato, "Changing Course, Burning Suits," *Greenville News,* June 6, 1993, p. 1D.

64. Brian O'Reilly, "The New Face of Small Business," *Fortune,* May 2, 1994, p. 82.

65. Kenneth Labich, "The New Low-Risk Entrepreneurs," *Fortune,* July 27, 1992, p. 84.

66. National Federation of Independent Businesses, "Small Business FAQs," **<http://www.nfib.org/media/faq.asp>.**

67. Jeremy Kahn, "Suddenly, Startups Are Chic," *Fortune,* February 15, 1999, p. 110; Small Business Administration, "Small Business Answer Card," **<http://www.sbaonline.sba.gov/ADVO/stats/answer.html>.**

68. Garry Powers, "Wanted: More Small, Fast-Growing Firms," *Business & Economic Review,* April–June 1999, pp. 19–22.

69. Erskine Bowles, "Training Ground," *Entrepreneur,* March 1994, p. 168.

70. Small Business Administration, "Small Business Answer Card," **<http://www.sbaonline.sba.gov/ADVO/stats/answer.html>;** National Federation of Independent Businesses, "Small Business FAQs," **<http://www.nfib.org/media/faq.asp>.**

71. John LaFalce, "The Driving Force," *Entrepreneur,* February 1990, pp. 161–166.

72. Bruce G. Posner, "Why Companies Fail," *Inc.,* June 1993, p. 102.

73. Roy Hoopes, "Mind Your Own Business," *Modern Maturity,* Febrary–March 1991, pp. 26–33.

74. Eugene Carlson, "Spreading Your Wings," *Wall Street Journal,* October 16, 1992, p. R2.

75. Sharon Nelton, "Coming to Grips With Growth," *Nation's Business,* February 1998, pp. 26–32.

76. Charles Stein, "How a Good Idea Went South," *Your Company,* August/September 1998, pp. 60–64.

77. Michael Warshaw, "Great Comebacks," *Success,* July/August 1995, p. 43.

78. Lieber, "Lessons from America's New Entrepreneurs," p. 4.

79. Robert Huber, "Failure: The Seven Mistakes Entrepreneurs Make and How to Avoid Them," *Success,* March 1998, p. 60.

80. Joshua Hyatt, "Should You Start a Business?" *Inc.,* February 1992, p. 50.

81. Stephanie Barlow, "Hang On!" *Entrepreneur,* September 1992, p. 156.

82. G. David Doran, Michelle Prather, Elaine W. Teague, and Laura Tiffany, "Young Guns," *Business Start-Ups,* April 1999, pp. 28–35.

83. Barbara Carton, "Help Wanted," *Wall Street Journal,* May 22, 1995, p. R10.

84. Kirsten Von Kiesler-Bomben, "The Obstacle Course," *Entrepreneur,* July 1990, p. 175.

Chapter 2

1. Carlye Adler, Maria Atanasov, John S. DeMott, Joel Dryfuss, Anne Field, Anne Ashby Gilbert, Sheryl Nance-Nash, and Michael Scully, "More Hot Ideas," *Your Company,* May/June 1999, pp. 34–49.

2. Jennifer Katz, "The Creative Touch," *Nation's Business,* March 1990, p. 43.

3. Warren Bennis, "Cultivating Creative Collaboration," *Industry Week,* August 18, 1997, p. 86.

4. Robert Epstein, "How to Get a Great Idea," *Reader's Digest,* December 1992, p. 103.

5. Roger von Oech, *A Whack on the Side of the Head* (New York: Warner Books, Inc., 1990), p. 108.

6. Peter Carbonara, "30 Great Small Business Ideas," *Your Company,* August/September 1998, pp. 32–58.

7. Robert Fulghum, "Time to Sacrifice the Queen," *Reader's Digest,* August 1993, pp. 136–138.

8. Carla Goodman, "Sparking Your Imagination," *Entrepreneur,* September 1997, p. 32.

9. Ibid.

10. Ibid.

11. Joanne Cleaver, "The 30 Day Launch," *Success,* February 1999, pp. 24–25.

12. Betty Edwards, *Drawing on the Right Side of the Brain* (Los Angeles: J.P. Tarcher, Inc., 1979), p. 32.

13. Von Oech, *A Whack on the Side of the Head,* pp. 21–167; "Obstacles to Creativity," Creativity Web, **<www.oze mail.com.au/~caveman/Creative/Basics/obstacles.htm>.**

14. Erika Kotite, "Gut Reaction," *Entrepreneur,* April 1994, pp. 152–156.

15. Karen Axelton, "Imagine That," *Entrepreneur,* April 1998, p. 96; "Thomas Edison Biography," **<edison-ford-estate.com/ed_bio.htm>.**

16. Sally Fegley, "Painting the Town," *Entrepreneur,* July 1997, p. 14.

17. Joseph Schumpeter, "The Creative Response in Economic History," *Journal of Economic History,* November 1947, pp. 149–159.

18. *Bits & Pieces,* January 1994, p. 6.

19. Epstein, "How to Get a Great Idea," p. 102.

20. Stephanie Barlow, "Turn It On," *Entrepreneur,* May 1993, p, 52.

21. Mark Henricks, "Good Thinking," *Entrepreneur,* May 1996, p. 70.

22. Don Debelak, "Ideas Unlimited," *Business Start-Ups,* May 1999, pp. 57–58.

23. Roy Rowan, "Those Hunches Are More Than Blind Faith," *Fortune,* April 23, 1979, p. 112.

24. Michael Waldholz, "A Hallucination Inspires a Vision for AIDS Drug," *Wall Street Journal,* September 29, 1993, pp. Bl, B5.

25. Goodman, "Sparking Your Imagination," pp. 32–36.

26. Janean Chun, "Theory of Creativity," *Entrepreneur,* October 1997, p. 130.

27. Ibid.

28. Paul Bagne, "When to Follow a Hunch," *Reader's Digest,* May 1994, p. 77.

29. Ibid.

30. "Ceiling Fan Leads to Physics Theory," *Laurens County Advertiser,* December 19, 1993, p. 4.

31. Waldholz, "A Hallucination Inspires a Vision for AIDS Drug," p. 55.

32. *Bits & Pieces,* November 12, 1992, pp. 6–7.

33. Epstein, "How to Get a Great Idea," p. 104.

34. Waldholz, "A Hallucination Inspires a Vision for AIDS Drug," p. 55.

35. Chun, "Theory of Creativity," pp. 130–131.

36. Ed Brown, "A Day at Innovation U." *Fortune,* April 12, 1999, pp. 163–165.

37. Ibid, p. 165.

38. Ibid.

39. *General Information Concerning Patents* (Washington, DC: U.S. Patent and Trademark Office, 1997), p. 15; Tomima Edmark, "Bright Idea," *Entrepreneur,* April 1997, p. 98; Tomima Edmark, "What Price Protection?" *Entrepreneur,* September 1998, pp. 109–110; U.S. Patent and Trademark Office, "Attorneys and Agents," **<www.uspto.gov/web/offices/pac/doc/general/attoney.htm>.**

40. Tomima Edmark, "How Much Is Too Much?" *Entrepreneur,* February 1998, pp. 93–95.

41. Ibid.

42. Tomima Edmark, "On Guard," *Entrepreneur,* August 1997, pp. 92–94; Tomima Edmark, "On Guard," *Entrepreneur,* February 1997, pp.109–111.

43. Michael J. McCarthy, "Fake King Cobras Tee Off Maker of High End Clubs," *Wall Street Journal,* February 11, 1997, pp. A1, A8.

44. Rebecca Quick and Ken Bensinger, "Sleaze E-Commerce," *Wall Street Journal Weekend Journal,* May 14, 1999, pp. W1, W10.

45. Nina Munk, "The Smell of This Magazine Is a Registered Trademark," *Forbes,* May 5, 1997, pp. 39–40.

46. Ron Harris, "Nail Wars Rage Over Modern Shades," *Upstate Business,* April 20, 1997, p. 2; Tara Parker-Pope, "How About a Nail Polish Called 'Bare-Knuckle Trademark Battle'?" *Wall Street Journal,* March 18, 1997, p. B1; Dana Wechsler Linden, "Does Pink Make You Puke?" *Forbes,* August 25, 1997, p. 108.

47. Nancy Ganz, "Protecting Your Good Name," *Nation's Business,* September 1995, p. 6.

48. Philip E. Ross, "Cops versus Robbers in Cyberspace," *Forbes,* September 9, 1996, pp. 134–139.

Chapter 3

1. William J. Holstein and Susan Gregory Thomas, "Gateway Gets Citified," *U.S. News & World Report,* May 3, 1999, pp. 42–44; Elizabeth Corcoran, "Gateway 2005," *Forbes,* March 8, 1999, pp. 52–53.

2. "Shocking Truths About the Future," *Journal of Business Strategy,* July/August 1996, p. 6.

3. Joan Retsinas, "Can You Say, 'Profits'?" *Business Start-Ups,* October 1998, pp. 58–61.

4. Amy Miller, "Here's the Scoop: Small Can Be Good," *Nation's Business,* May 1999, p. 10.

5. Alan W. Jackson, "It's All in the Plan," *Small Business Reports,* June 1994, pp. 38–43.

6. Dan Morse, "Many Small Businesses Don't Devote Time to Planning," *Wall Street Journal,* September 7, 1999, p. B.2.

7. Rick Hartmann, "Separating Your Firm from the Competition," *Nation's Business,* May 1998, p. 8.

8. "The Right Way to Compete," *Communication Briefings,* July 1997, p. 7.

9. Gary Hamel, "Killer Strategies That Make Shareholders Rich," *Fortune,* June 23, 1997, p. 80.

10. Ken Blanchard, "The New Bottom Line," *Entrepreneur,* February 1998, p. 127.

11. Thomas A. Stewart, "Why Values Statements Don't Work," *Fortune,* June 10, 1996, p. 137.

12. Michael Barrier, "Back From the Brink," *Nation's Business,* September 1995, p. 21.

13. Ibid.

14. Blanchard, "The New Bottom Line," p. 129.

15. Ben & Jerry's Homemade, Inc., **<www.benjerry.com/mission.html>.**

16. Bill Sulon, "Selling by Quality and Service," *In Business,* November/December 1998, p. 32; "Pennsylvania Green Grocer Honored for Pioneering Efforts That Influenced Restaurant Industry Evolution," **<www.xpresspress.com/foodnetwork47.html>.**

17. John Marks, "Tail of the Pampered Pooch," *U.S. News & World Report,* May 17, 1999, pp. 46–47; Gabeler, Battocchi, and Griggs, **<cgibin1.erols.com/gabeler/lacy.html>.**

18. Carla Goodman, "Finding Your Niche," *Business Start-Ups,* April 1997, pp. 72–74.

19. Don Clark, "Citrix Helps Lead Drive to Rent Software," *Wall Street Journal,* September 9, 1999, p. B8.

20. Dale D. Buss, "Net Profits Suffer from NBA Lockout," *Nation's Business,* February 1999, pp. 27–29.

21. Mark Henricks, "Analyze This," *Entrepreneur,* June 1999, pp. 72–75.

22. "Survey Shows Competition Is Most Significant Business Worry," *South Carolina Business Journal,* October 1998, p. 8; Stephanie Gruner, "What Worries CEOs," *Inc.,* February 1997, p. 98.

23. "To the Point," *Beyond Computing,* July/August 1998, p. 21.

24. Carolyn Z. Lawrence, "Know Your Competition," *Business Start-Ups,* April 1997, p. 51.

25. Shari Caudron, "I Spy, You Spy," *Industry Week,* October 3, 1994, p. 36.

26. Lawrence, "Know Your Competition," pp. 51–56.

27. Stephanie Gruner, "Spies Like Us," *Inc.,* August 1998, p. 45.

28. John DeVore, "Keeping Up with the Jones Co." *Small Business Computing,* October 1999, p. 26.

29. Laton McCartney, "Getting Smart About Knowledge Management," *Industry Week,* May 4, 1998, p. 30.

30. Tim McCollum, "All the News That's Fit to Net," *Nation's Business,* June 1998, pp. 59–62.

31. Christopher Caggiano, "Low-Tech Smarts," *Inc.,* January 1999, pp. 79–80.

32. Joseph C. Picken and Gregory Dess, "The Seven Traps of Strategic Planning," *Inc.,* November 1996, p. 99.

33. Michael E. Porter, *Competitive Strategy* (New York: Free Press, 1980), Chapter 2.

34. Marc Ballon, "The Cheapest CEO in America," *Inc.,* October 1997, pp. 53–61.

35. Elaine W. Teague, "Cream of the Crop," *Entrepreneur,* November 1998, pp. 113–115.

36. Shelly Branch, "Havin' an Ice Team," *Fortune,* March 1, 1999, pp. 277–278.

37. Debra Phillips, "Leaders of the Pack," *Entrepreneur,* September 1996, p. 127.

38. Laura Fortunato, "Replacing the Irreplaceable," *Region Focus,* Spring 1998, pp. 20–21; Replacements Limited, **<www.replacements.com/default.htm>.**

39. Jonathan Friedland, "A New Hotel Chain Gambles on Adventures in the Jungle," *Wall Street Journal,* September 22, 1999, pp. B1, B16.

40. Joel Kurtzman, "Is Your Company Off Course? Now You Can Find Out Why," *Fortune,* February 17, 1997, p. 128.

41. Mark Henricks, "Who's Counting?" *Entrepreneur,* July 1998, pp. 70–73.

42. Robert S. Kaplan and David P. Norton, "The Balanced Scorecard—Measures That Drive Performance," *Harvard Business Review,* January–February 1992, pp. 71–79.

Chapter 4

1. Barbara Bucholz and Margaret Crane, "One-Man Bands," *Your Company,* Summer 1993, p. 24.

2. Ibid.

3. Jacquelyn Lynn, "Partnership Procedures," *Business Start-Ups,* June 1996, p. 73.

4. Frances Huffman, "Irreconcilable Differences," *Entrepreneur,* February 1992, p. 108.

5. Donna Fenn, "Grand Plans," *Inc.,* August 1999, pp. 43–57.

6. Geoff Williams, "Buddies in Business," *Business Start-Ups,* April 1999, p. 57.

7. Manuel Schiffres, "Partnerships with a Plus," *Changing Times,* October 1989, p. 49.

8. Penny Loeb, "My Paycheck for a Horse," *U.S. News & World Report,* June 7, 1999, pp. 64–65; Dogwood Stable, **<www.dogwoodstable.com>.**

9. Chief Justice John Marshall, cited by Roger L. Miller and Gaylord A. Jentz, *Business Law Today* (St. Paul, MN: West Publishing Co., 1994), p. 632.

10. Anthony J. Mohr, "Take Care to Avoid Liability Traps," *Nation's Business,* November 1997, pp. 32–34; Jane Easter Bahls, "Rethinking Inc." *Entrepreneur,* August 1994, pp. 60–63; Barbara Marsh, "Suits Go After Personal Assets of Firm Owners," *Wall Street Journal,* August 13, 1993, pp. B1–B2.

11. Mohr, "Take Care to Avoid Liability Traps."

12. Andy Serwer, "How Bill Gates Invests His Money," *Fortune,* March 15, 1999, pp. 68–86.

13. Joan Szabo, "Join the Corps," *Entrepreneur,* October 1999, p. 71.

14. Kylo-Patrick Hart, "Step 4: Decide Your Legal Structure," *Business Start-Ups,* August 1996, pp. 62–64.

15. Dale D. Buss, "New Dynamics for a New Era," *Nation's Business,* June 1999, pp. 45–48; "History of Franchising," FranInfo, **<www.franinfo.com/history.html>.**

16. Laura Tiffany, "Breaking the Mold," *Business Start-Ups,* April 1999, pp. 42–47; "Why Buy a Franchise?" The Franchise Doctor, **<www.franchisedoc.com/whybuy.html>;** Buss, "New Dynamics for a New Era," pp. 45–48.

17. Barbara Rudolph, "Franchising Is BIG Business for Small Business," *Your Company,* Spring 1992, p. 44.

18. Chieh Chieng, "Do You Want to Know a Secret?" *Entrepreneur,* January 1999, p. 176.

19. Jacquelyn Lynn, "Franchise Advantage," *Entrepreneur,* February 1995, p. 132.

20. "Why Buy a Franchise?" The Franchise Doctor; Echo M. Garrett, "Reengineering the Franchise," *Inc.,* December 1993, p. 148.

21. "Why Buy a Franchise?" The Franchise Doctor; Kenneth Labich, "The New Low-Risk Entrepreneurs," *Fortune,* July 27, 1992, p. 84.

22. Lynn Beresford, "School Days," *Entrepreneur,* August 1995, p. 200.

23. Tiffany, "Breaking the Mold," p. 45.

24. Anne Field, "Piping-Hot Performance," *Success,* March 1999, pp. 76–80.

25. Andrew A. Caffey, "Franchises That Offer Creative Financing," *Business Start-Ups,* September 1996, pp. 62–68.

26. Paul Deceglie, "Treasure Hunt," *Entrepreneur,* January 1999, pp. 169–173.

27. Nancy Croft Baker, "Independents Try Franchising," *Nation's Business,* June 1989, pp. 31–32.

28. Richard Behar, "Why Subway Is 'The Biggest Problem in Franchising,'" *Fortune,* March 16, 1998, pp. 127–134.

29. Meg Whittemore, "The Franchise Search," *Nation's Business,* April 1993, p. 27.

30. Glen Weisman, "The Choice Is Yours," *Business Start-Ups,* May 1997, pp. 24–30; Dan Morse and Jeffrey Tannenbaum, "Poll on High Success Rate for Franchises Raises Eyebrows," *Wall Street Journal,* March 17, 1998, p. B2.

31. Kirk Shivell and Kent Banning, "What Every Prospective Franchisee Should Know," *Small Business Forum,* Winter 1996/1997, pp. 33–42.

32. Glen Weisman, "The Choice Is Yours," p. 25.

33. Glen Weisman, "The Choice Is Yours," *Business Start-Ups,* May 1997, pp. 24–30; Anne P. Thrower, "Beneath the Golden Arches," *Upstate Business,* June 14, 1998, pp. 1, 10–11.

34. Jeffrey A. Tannenbaum, "Franchisees Balk at High Prices for Supplies from Franchisers," *Wall Street Journal,* July 5, 1995, pp. B1–B2.

35. Gregory Matusky, "The Franchise Hall of Fame," *Inc.,* April 1994, pp. 86–89.

36. Gregory Matusky, "What Every Business Can Learn from Franchising," *Inc.,* January 1994, p. 90.

37. Elaine Pofeldt, "Success Franchisee Satisfaction Survey," *Success,* April 1999, p. 58.

38. Ibid., p. 59.

39. Andrew Caffey, "No Experience Required," *Entrepreneur,* January 1999, pp. 138–145.

40. North American Securities Administrators Association, "State Regulators Identify 'Top Ten Frauds,'" **<www.nasaa.org/whoweare/media/topten.html>.**

41. Field, "Piping Hot Performance," p. 79.

42. Jeannie Ralston, "Before You Bet Your Buns," *Venture,* March 1988, p. 57.

43. Behar, "Why Subway Is 'The Biggest Problem in Franchising,'" pp. 127–134.

44. Steven J. Stark, "Have It Your Way," *Success,* April 1999, pp. 57–59.

45. Chieh Chieng, "No Holes Barred," *Business Start-Ups,* March 1999, p. 64.

46. Asia Pacific Economic Cooperation, "Consultative Survey on Franchising in APEC Member Economies," **<strategis.ic.gc.ca/SSG/ae00275e.html>.**

47. Jeffrey A. Tannenbaum, "Franchisers See a Future in East Bloc," *Wall Street Journal,* June 5, 1990, p. Bl.

48. Asia Pacific Economic Cooperation, "Consultative Survey on Franchising in APEC Member Economies."

49. Buss, "New Dynamics for a New Era," p. 46.

50. Dan Morse, "Franchisees Test the Water Before Taking the Plunge," *Wall Street Journal,* May 11, 1999, p. B2.

51. Carol Steinberg, "Instant Growth," *Success,* July/August 1996, pp. 77–83.

52. Janean Huber, "What's Next?" *Entrepreneur,* September 1994, p. 149.

53. Roberta Maynard, "Why Franchisers Look Abroad," *Nation's Business,* October 1995, pp. 65–72.

54. Gabrielle Solomon, "Co-Branding Alliances: Arranged Marriages Made by Marketers," *Fortune,* October 12, 1998, p. 188[N]; Gordon Williams, "Roadside Attraction," *Financial World,* October 21, 1996, pp. 96–98; Lynn Beresford, "Seeing Double," *Entrepreneur,* October 1995, pp. 164–167; Roberta Maynard, "The Hit Parade for 2000," *Nation's Business,* April 1997, pp. 68–74.

55. Solomon, "Co-Branding Alliances: Arranged Marriages Made by Marketers," p. 188[N].

56. Buss, "New Dynamics for a New Era," p. 46.

57. Huber, "What's Next?" p. 151.

Chapter 5

1. Jill Andresky Fraser, "When It's a Seller's Market," *Inc.,* July 1999, pp. 60–70.

2. Donna Fenn, "The Buyers," *Inc.,* June 1996, p. 48.

3. Elaine W. Teague, "Playing for Keeps," *Entrepreneur,* August 1998, pp. 104–107.

4. Fenn, "The Buyers," p. 48.

5. Hendrix F.C. Neimann, "Buying a Business," *Inc.,* February 1990, pp. 28–38.

6. Fraser, "When It's a Seller's Market."

7. Gianna Jacobson, "Mission: Acquisition," *Success,* October 1997, pp. 62–66; Thomas Owens, "Growth Through Acquisition," *Small Business Reports,* August 1990, p. 63.

8. Steven B. Kaufman, "Before You Buy, Be Careful," *Nation's Business,* March 1996, p. 45.

9. Fraser, "When It's a Seller's Market," p. 67.

10. John Case, "Buy Now—Avoid the Rush," *Inc.,* February 1991, p. 38.

11. Richard M. Rodnick, "Getting the Right Price for Your Firm," *Nation's Business,* March 1984, pp. 70–71.

12. "Business Valuation Methods," American Express Small Business Exchange, **<home3.americanexpress.com/smallbusiness/resources/starting/valbiz.shtml>;** David R. Evanson, "Know Your Worth," *Success,* June 1995, p. 22.

13. Christopher Caggiano, "The 8 Dumbest Ways to Try to Sell Your Company," *Inc.,* November 1994, pp. 73–79.

14. "Business Valuation Methods," American Express Small Business Exchange.

15. Bob Weinstein, "Cashing Out," *Business Start-Ups,* November 1995, p. 93.

16. Ibid.

17. Fraser, "When It's a Seller's Market," p. 60.

18. Peter Nulty, "Smart Ways to Sell Your Business," *Fortune,* March 17, 1996, pp. 97–98.

19. Arthur Lubow, "Mom & Me," *Inc.,* April 1999, pp. 55–63; Michael Liedtke, "Young Inventor Sells Toy Firm," *Upstate Business,* February 7, 1999, p. 3.

20. Shannon P. Pratt, "Business Buyer's Valuation Guide," *In Business,* March–April 1987, p. 59.

21. Laura M. Litvan, "Selling Off, Staying On," *Nation's Business,* August 1995, pp. 29–30.

22. Peter Collins, "Cashing Out and Maintaining Control," *Small Business Reports,* December 1989, p. 28.

23. "More Business Owners May Be Selling Out," *Small Business Reports,* May 1990, p. 26.

24. "Problems with Foreign Owners," *Small Business Reports,* May 1991, p. 11.

25. "The Time Honored ESOP," *Inc.,* June 1991, p. 139.

Chapter 6

1. Mark Henricks, "Soft Sell," *Entrepreneur,* September 1998, pp. 139–144; Neil DiBernado, "D&B Survey Finds the Smaller the Business, the Less Marketing Savvy," **<dnb.com/newsview/0898news1.htm>.**

2. Dale D. Buss, "The Little Guys Strike Back," *Nation's Business,* July 1996, p. 19.

3. Ron Lieber, "Super Market," *Fast Company,* April 1999, pp. 190–201; Central Market, **<www.centralmarket.com>.**

4. Women's Travel Club, **<www.womenstravelclub.com>;** Paul Hughes, "Service Savvy," *Business Start-Ups,* January 1996, pp. 48–51.

5. Lester A. Picker, "Selling to Women," *Your Company,* April/May 1996, pp. 32–38.

6. Roberta Maynard, "Rich Niches," *Nation's Business,* November 1993, pp. 39–42.

7. Dale D. Buss, "Entertailing," *Nation's Business,* December 1997, pp. 18.

8. Ibid., pp. 12–18.

9. Ibid.; Golf Galaxy, **<www.golfgalaxy.com>.**

10. Heidi Ernst, "Space Men," *Your Company,* October 1999, p. 20; Space Adventures, **<www.spaceadventures.com>.**

11. Howard Dana Shaw, "Customer Care Checklist," *In Business,* September/October 1987, p. 28.

12. Hector D. Cantu, "New Magazine for Latina Girls Heeds Ethnic Baby Boom," *Greenville News,* August 29, 1998, p. 16B; **<www.latingirlmag.com>.**

13. Roberta Maynard, "New Directions in Marketing" *Nation's Business,* July 1995, p. 26.

14. Jim Ammeen, "Making a Niche a Perfect Fit," *Nation's Business,* February 1999, p. 8.

15. Joshua Macht, "The New Market Research," *Inc.,* July 1998, pp. 87–94; Galilee Splendor, **<www.galileesplendor.com>.**

16. Justin Martin, "Ignore Your Customer," *Fortune,* May 1, 1995, pp. 121–125; Hoover's Online, **<www.hoovers.com/capsules/16263.html>.**

17. Al Cole, "Cinematic Chic," *Modern Maturity,* March–April 1998, p. 24.

18. Nancy L. Croft, "Smart Selling," *Nation's Business,* March 1988, pp. 51–52.

19. Ibid., p. 51.

20. Meg Whittemore, "Survival Tactics for Retailers," *Nation's Business,* June 1993, p. 23.

21. Stephen M. Silverman, "Retail Retold," *Inc. Technology, Summer 1995, pp. 23–26.*

22. Victoria Hall Smith, "Mine Your Own Business," *Small Business Computing,* November 1999, pp. 60–64.

23. Henricks, "Soft Sell," p. 140.

24. Patricia M. Carey, "Capitalizing on the X Factor," *Success,* May 1999, pp. 61–65.

25. Kelly Barron, "King of the Road," *Forbes,* July 6, 1998, pp. 158–159.

26. Randolph E. Schmid, "Twice as Many Americans by 2100," *Infobeat,* January 13, 2000, **<www.infobeat.com/stories/cgi/story.cgi?id=2563251990-db7>;** Frederick W. Hollmann and Tammany J. Mulder, "Census Bureau Projects Doubling of Nation's Population by 2100," **<www.census.gov/PressRelease/www/2000/cb00-05.html>.**

27. Ann A. Fishman, "Generational Targeted Marketing: How to Grow Bigger by Thinking Smaller," **<chamber.gnofn.org/fishman/menu.html>;** Faye Rice, "Making Generational Marketing Come of Age," *Fortune,* June 26, 1995, pp. 110–114.

28. NPR's "Morning Edition," January 5, 2000.

29. Meg Whittemore, "Retailing Looks to a New Century," *Nation's Business,* December 1994, p. 20.

30. Nick Wreden, "From Customer Satisfaction to Customer Loyalty," *Beyond Computing,* January/February 1999, pp. 12–14.

31. Bradford McKee, "How Much Do You Really Value Your Customers?" *Nation's Business,* August 1993, p. 8.

32. Paul Hughes, "Service Savvy," *Business Start-Ups,* January 1996, p. 48.

33. Aimee L. Stern, "How to Build Customer Loyalty," *Your Company,* Spring 1995, p. 37.

34. "Deadly Game of Losing Customers," *In Business,* May 1988, p. 189.

35. Jerry Fisher, "The Secret's Out," *Entrepreneur,* May 1998, pp. 112–119; Jim Campbell, "Good Customer Service Pays Off," *UP*, November 1988, pp. 12–13.

36. "Keeping Customers for Life," *Communication Briefings,* September 1990, p. 3.

37. Rahul Jacob, "Why Some Customers Are More Equal Than Others," *Fortune,* September 19, 1994, pp. 215–224.

38. Patricia Sellers, "Companies That Serve You Best," *Fortune,* May 31, 1993, p. 75.

39. William A. Sherden, "The Tools of Retention," *Small Business Reports,* November 1994, pp. 43–47.

40. Tim McCollum, "Tools for Targeting Customer Service," *Nation's Business,* November 1998, pp. 49–51.

41. "Be on the Lookout for Changes," *Communication Briefings,* October 1993, p. 4.

42. "Ways & Means," *Reader's Digest,* January 1993, p. 56.

43. Henricks, "Soft Sell," pp. 139–144.

44. Faye Rice, "How to Deal with Tougher Customers," *Fortune,* December 3, 1990, pp. 39–40.

45. Howard Rothman, "Quality's Link to Productivity," *Nation's Business,* February 1994, pp. 33–34.

46. Rahul Jacob, "TQM: More Than a Dying Fad," *Fortune,* October 18, 1993, p. 67.

47. Ibid.

48. Dave Zielinski, "Improving Service Doesn't Require a Big Investment," *Small Business Reports,* February 1991, p. 20.

49. Ibid.

50. Lucy McCauley, "Measure What Matters," *Fast Company,* May 1999, p. 100.

51. Pamela Rohland, "Suits Her," *Business Start-Ups,* October 1999, p. 73.

52. Bob Weinstein, "Bright Ideas," *Business Start-Ups,* August 1995, p. 57.

53. Alan Deutschman, "America's Fastest Risers," *Fortune,* October 7, 1991, p. 58.

54. Don Debelak, "Music for the Masses," *Business Start-Ups,* December 1999, pp. 78–80; G-Vox, **<www.gvox.com>.**

55. "Hold That Price!" *Success,* May 1995, p. 25.

56. Ronald Henkoff, "Service Is Everybody's Business," *Fortune,* June 27, 1994, pp. 48–49.

57. "Keeping Customers for Life," *Communication Briefings,* September 1990, p. 3.

58. Mark Henricks, "Satisfaction Guaranteed," *Entrepreneur,* May 1991, p. 122.

59. Scott McCormack, "Making Waves," *Forbes,* April 5, 1999, pp. 76–78.

60. Jacquelyn Lynn, "Customers," *Business Start-Ups,* December 1995, p. 12.

61. J. Conrad Levinson, "Attention Getters," *Entrepreneur,* March 1998, p. 88.

62. Ron Zemke and Dick Schaaf, "The Service Edge," *Small Business Reports,* July 1990, pp. 57–60.

63. Thomas A. Stewart, "After All You've Done for Your Customers, Why Are They Still NOT HAPPY?" *Fortune,* December 11, 1995, pp. 178–182.

64. Mark Henricks, "5 Best Customer Service Ideas," *Entrepreneur,* March 1999, p. 122.

65. Leonard L. Berry, "Customer Service Solutions," *Success,* July/August 1995, pp. 90–95.

66. Emily Esterson, "Barking Up the High-Tech Tree," *Inc. Technology,* 1998, No. 1, p. 82.

67. Zemke and Schaaf, "The Service Edge," p. 60.

68. David Altany, "Call Me Tom," *Industry Week,* January 22, 1990, p. 14.

69. Brian Dumaine, "How Managers Can Succeed Through Speed," *Fortune,* February 13, 1989, pp. 54–59.

70. Geoff Williams, "Speed Freaks," *Entrepreneur,* September 1999, p. 120.

71. Dale D. Buss, "Embracing Speed," *Nation's Business,* June 1999, pp. 12–17.

72. Mark Henricks, "Time Is Money," *Entrepreneur,* February 1993, p. 44.

73. Ibid.

74. Buss, "Embracing Speed," pp. 12–17.

75. Claire Tristram, "Many Happy Returns," *Small Business Computing,* May 1999, pp. 70–75.

76. Veronica Byrd and Brian L. Clark, "Increasing Your Net Profits," *Your Company,* June/July 1996, p. 24.

77. "E-Business Solutions," *Compass,* Third Quarter 1999, pp. 4–6.

78. "Work Week," *Wall Street Journal,* October 26, 1999, p. A1.

79. David G. Propson, "Small Biz Gets Small Piece of the Pie," *Small Business Computing,* November 1999, p. 24.

80. Carla Young Harrington, "Storming the Electronic Marketplace: E-Business," *Inc.,* June 1999, Advertising Supplement.

81. Courtney Rubin, "Mom 'n Pop Stores Learn How Worldwide the Web Really Is," *USA Weekend,* December 17–19, 1999, p. 4.

82. Leigh Buchanan, "The Best of the Small Business Web: Diamond in the Rough," *Inc. Technology,* 1999, No. 4, pp. 61–107.

83. Gene Koprowski and Heather Page, "E-Reality," *Business Start-Ups,* May 1999, pp. 30–34.

84. David G. Propson, "Intelligence," *Small Business Computing,* November 1999, p. 24.

85. Stanley J. Winkelman, "Why Big-Name Stores Are Losing Out," *Fortune,* May 8, 1989, pp. 14–15.

86. Jeannie Mandelker, "Crush Rivals by Launching Great Products," *Your Company,* October/November 1997, pp. 54–60.

87. Ibid.; "Fast Break," *Success,* September 1998, p. 14.

88. Paul B. Brown, "The Eternal Second Act," *Inc.,* June 1988, pp. 119–120.

89. Ibid., p. 120.

90. Hoover's Online, **<www.hoovers.com/co/capsule/0/0,2163, 53540,00.html>;** Marj Chandler, "Yuengling's Success Defies Convention," *Wall Street Journal,* August 26, 1993, pp. Bl, B8; Yuengling Brewery, **<www.yuengling.com>.**

91. Bob Weinstein, "Set in Stone," *Business Start-Ups,* October 1995, p. 27.

Chapter 7

1. Michelle Prather, "Selling Points," *Business Start-Ups,* July 1999, p. 96.

2. Joel Kurtzman, "Advertising for All the Little Guys," *Fortune,* April 12, 1999, p. 162[L].

3. Sue Clayton, "Handsome Prints," *Business Start-Ups,* October 1995, p. 30.

4. Shelby Meinhardt, "Put It in Print," *Entrepreneur,* January 1989, p. 54.

5. Roy H. Williams, "Advice from the Ad Wizard," *Your Company,* December 1998/January 1999, p. 45.

6. Clayton, "Handsome Prints," p. 32.

7. Meg Whittemore, "PR on a Shoestring," *Nation's Business,* January 1991, p. 31.

8. "Publicity Scores Over Ads," *Communication Briefings,* December 1994, p. 5.

9. Thomas Love, "Creating Demand for a New Product," *Nation's Business,* August 1998, p. 11.

10. Debra Phillips, "Fast Track," *Entrepreneur,* April 1999, p. 42.

11. Ibid.

12. Monique Harris, "Fast Pitch," *Business Start-Ups,* December 1999, pp. 71–75.

13. Lynn Beresford, "Going My Way?" *Entrepreneur,* February 1996, p. 32.

14. Dale D. Buss, "Sell Your Way to Success," *Nation's Business,* February 1999, pp. 14–19; "Traits of Top Salespeople," *Small Business Reports,* December 1990, pp. 7–8; Roberta Maynard, "Finding the Essence of Good Salespeople," *Nation's Business,* February 1998, p. 10; Landy Chase, "2000 and Beyond: The Golden Age of Professional Selling," *The Small Business Journal,* **<www.tsbj.com/editorial/02050601.htm>.**

15. Jaclyn Fierman, "The Death and Rebirth of the Salesman," *Fortune,* July 25, 1994, pp. 80–91.

16. "Most Salespeople Can't Sell," *Small Business Reports,* September 1990, p. 10.

17. "Prepare for Sales Calls," *Success,* May 1996, p. 25.

18. "Those Who Ask, Get," *The Competitive Advantage,* sample issue, p. 7.

19. "The Cost of a Sales Call," *Inc.,* May 1991, p. 86.

20. "Meeting Customer Needs," *In Business,* May/June 1989, p. 14.

21. "Business News," *Wall Street Journal,* July 13, 1995, p. A1.

22. Nancy J. Wagner, "Picking a Medium for Your Message," *Nation's Business,* February 1999, pp. 56–57.

23. Mark Henricks, "Spread the Word," *Entrepreneur,* February 1998, pp. 120–125.

24. "Radio Facts," Radio Advertising Bureau, **<www.rab. com/station/mgfb99/fac2.html>.**

25. "Trends in Television," Television Bureau of Advertising, **<www.tvb.org/tvfacts/trends/tv/executive.html>.**

26. "Ad Suggestion from New Study," *Communication Briefings,* June 1995, p. 2.

27. "Trends in Television," Television Bureau of Advertising, **<www.tvb.org/tvfacts/trends/tv/executive.html>.**

28. "Media Facts," Radio Advertising Bureau, **<www.rab.com/station/mediafact/medfcts98/tv.html>.**

29. G. David Doran, "Station Breaks," *Entrepreneur,* September 1998, pp. 147–151.

30. Ibid.

31. Don Debelak, "Broadcast News," *Business Start-Ups,* September 1998, pp. 90–91; Doran, "Station Breaks," pp. 147–151.

32. "Fact Sheets," Magazine Publishers of America, **<www.magazine.org/resources/fact_sheets/ed1_8_99.html>.**

33. *The Dynamics of Change in Markets and Media,* from a Magazine Publishers Association seminar, New York.

34. "Fact Sheets," Magazine Publishers of America, **<www.magazine.org/resources/fact_sheets/ed3_8_99.html>.**

35. Susan Headden, "The Junk Mail Deluge," *U.S. News & World Report,* December 8, 1997, pp. 40–48.

36. Paul Hughes, "Winning Ways," *Entrepreneur,* February 1994, pp. 80–88.

37. "Why They Open Direct Mail," *Communication Briefings,* December 1993, p. 5.

38. Headden, "The Junk Mail Deluge," pp. 40–48.

39. Ernan Roman, "More for Your Money," *Inc.,* September 1992, p. 116.

40. Headden, "The Junk Mail Deluge," pp. 40–48.

41. Roman, "More for Your Money," p. 116.

42. Nancy Bader, "1-800-4-MO'BIZ," *Your Company,* Summer 1994, p. 4.

43. Ed Nanas, "Computer Diskettes," *Your Company,* Spring 1993, pp. 8–9.

44. Gillian Newson, "Interactive Marketing Is Driven to Succeed," *NewMedia,* June 1993, pp. 73–77; Kristin Davis, "Junk Mail Worthy of the Name," *Kiplinger's Personal Finance Magazine,* March 1993, pp. 56–61.

45. Robert McGarvey, "Site Unseen," *Entrepreneur,* September 1999, p. 34.

46. Jane Weaver, "Marketing Secrets for the New Economy," *PC Computing,* January 2000, p. 98.

47. Leigh Buchanan, "The Best of the Small Business Web: Pitching Camp," *Inc. Technology 1999,* No. 4, pp. 74–75.

48. Bronwyn Fryer, "(Your Message Here)," *Inc. Technology 1999,* No. 1, pp. 76–79; Leigh Buchanan, "The Best of the Small Business Web: Seed Money," *Inc. Technology 1999,* No. 4, pp. 72–74, 108.

49. Fryer, "(Your Message Here)," pp. 76–79.

50. William M. Bulkeley, "New Method for Web Ads Stirs Attention," *Wall Street Journal,* October 22, 1998, pp. B1, B23.

51. Jane Weaver, "Marketing Secrets for the New Economy," *PC Computing,* January 2000, pp. 90–100.

52. Fryer, "(Your Message Here)," p. 78.

53. Melissa Campanelli, "Banner Day," *Entrepreneur,* November 1998, pp. 48–81.

54. Kim Doyle, Anastasia Minor, and Carolyn Weyrich, "Banner Ad Placement Study," Internet.com Corporation, **<webreference.com/dev/banners>.**

55. "E-Mail Marketing Worth $4.6 Billion in 2003," *eMarketer,* February 4, 2000, **<www.emarketer.com/estats/020400_email.html>.**

56. "E-Mail Marketing Report," *eMarketer,* January 2000, **<www.emarketer.com/estats/sell_email.html>.**

57. Weaver, "Marketing Secrets for the New Economy," pp. 90–100.

58. "E-Mail Marketing Worth $4.6 billion in 2003."

59. Cary Kimble, "The Inside Scoop on Outdoor Ads," *IB,* September/October 1990, pp. 14–17.

60. Marc Gunther, "The Great Outdoors," *Fortune,* March 1, 1999, pp. 150–157.

61. Outdoor Advertising Association of America, **<www.oaaa.org>;** Gunther, "The Great Outdoors," pp. 150–157.

62. *The Big Outdoors* (New York: Institute of Outdoor Advertising), p. 15; "Outdoor Ads That Work Best," *Communication Briefings,* October 1993, p. 6.

63. Debra Phillips, "Now Hear This," *Entrepreneur,* July 1999, p. 32.

64. Joel Kurtzman, "Advertising for All the Little Guys."

65. Debra Phillips, "To Infinity and Beyond," *Entrepreneur,* May 1999, p. 46.

66. *TAA Rate Directory of Transit Advertising* (New York: Transit Advertising Association), p. 2.

67. Tad Simons, "Trick of the Trade," *Presentations,* December 1998, pp. 131–135.

68. Leann Anderson, "On with the Show," *Entrepreneur,* August 1998, p. 94.

69. Bernie Ward, "Everything's the Medium," *Sky,* May 1989, pp. 96–110.

70. Harvey Meyer, "And Now, Some Words About Sponsors," *Nation's Business,* March 1999, pp. 38–41.

71. Roy S. Johnson, "Speed Sells," *Fortune,* April 12, 1999, pp. 56–62.

72. Erick Schonfeld, "Coming to a Speedway Near You," *Fortune,* March 31, 1997, p. 38.

73. Cora Daniels, "Not Your Showroom Model," *Fortune,* April 12, 1999, pp. 62–72.

74. Meyer, "And Now, Some Words About Sponsors," pp. 38–41.

75. Carrie Dolan, "Putting on the Dog Just Comes Naturally in Fey Marin County," *Wall Street Journal,* September 20, 1985, p. 1.

76. "Point of Purchase (POP) Advertising," Smart Business Supersite, **<www.smartbiz.com/sbs/arts/hph8.htm>.**

77. Ronald Alsop, "To Share Shoppers, Companies Test Talking, Scented Displays," *Wall Street Journal,* June 12, 1986, p. 31.

78. Rodney Ho, "Vending Machines Make Change," *Wall Street Journal,* July 7, 1999, pp. B1, B4.

79. Denise Osburn and Dawn Kopecki, "A Way to Stretch Ad Dollars," *Nation's Business,* May 1994, p. 68.

80. Ibid.

81. Jane Easter Bahls, "Ad It Up," *Entrepreneur,* December 1994, pp. 47–49.

82. "Advertising Vehicles: Businesses Discover New Use for Old Cars," *The Greenville News,* June 19, 1993, p. 1D.

83. Sara Delano, "Give and You Shall Receive," *Inc.,* February 1983, p. 128.

84. Howard Scott, "The Tricky Art of Raising Prices," *Nation's Business,* February 1999, p. 32.

85. Jan Norman, "How to Set Prices," *Business Start-Ups,* December 1998, p. 45.

86. Carolyn Z. Lawrence, "The Price Is Right," *Business Start-Ups,* February 1996, p. 67.

87. Ibid., p. 66.

88. Robert Shulman and Richard Miniter, "Discounting Is No Bargain," *Wall Street Journal,* December 7, 1998, p. A30.

89. William Echilkson, "The Return of Luxury," *Fortune,* October 17, 1994, p. 18.

90. Shulman and Richard Miniter, "Discounting Is No Bargain."

91. Brenda Biondo, "Think *Your* Day Care Is Expensive?" *USA Weekend,* February 4–6, 2000, p. 10.

92. Gayle Sato Stodder, "Paying the Price," *Entrepreneur,* October 1994, p. 54.

93. Mark Henricks, "War & Price," *Entrepreneur,* June 1995, p. 156.

94. American Consumer Credit Counseling, **<www.consumercredit.com/cardstats.htm>;** Bob Weinstein, "Getting Carded," *Entrepreneur,* September 1995, pp. 76–80.

95. "ICMA Quick Card Facts and Glossary," International Card Manufacturers Association, **<www.icma.com/info/cardfacts.htm>;** Lucy Lazarony, "What Your Address Says About How You Use Credit Cards," Bankrate.com, **<www.bankrate.com/brm/news/cc/19990816.asp>.**

96. "Business Bulletin," *Wall Street Journal,* July 26, 1990, p. A1.

97. Richard J. Maturi, "Charging Ahead," *Entrepreneur,* July 1990, p. 56.

98. Bob Weinstein, "Getting Carded," p. 76.

Chapter 8

1. Mary Baechler, "The Cash-Flow Quagmire," *Inc.,* October 1994, p. 25.

2. "Help! My Firm Is Hemorrhaging Cash," *Your Company,* April/May 1996, pp. 10–11.

3. Ibid.

4. Jill Andresky Fraser, "The Art of Cash Management," *Inc.,* October 1998, p. 124.

5. Jerry Useem, "The Icon That Almost Wasn't," *Inc: That State of Small Business 1998,* p. 142.

6. Daniel Kehrer, "Big Ideas for Your Small Business," *Changing Times,* November 1989, p. 58.

7. William Bak, "I Owe, I Owe," *Entrepreneur,* October 1993, p. 56.

8. Jeannie Mandelker, "Put Numbers on Your Side," *Your Company,* Winter 1994, p. 33.

9. Douglas Bartholomew, "4 Common Financial Management Mistakes . . . And How to Avoid Them," *Your Company,* Fall 1991, p. 9.

10. Robert A. Mamis, "Money In, Money Out," *Inc.,* March 1993, p. 98.

11. Ibid.

12. Bartholomew, "4 Common Financial Management Mistakes . . . And How to Avoid Them," p. 9.

13. Phaedra Hise, "Paging for Cash Flow," *Inc.,* December 1995, p. 131.

14. Jill Andresky Fraser, "Monitoring Daily Cash Trends," *Inc.,* October 1992, p. 49.

15. William G. Shepherd, Jr., "Internal Financial Strategies," *Venture,* September 1985, p. 66.

16. David H. Bangs, *Financial Troubleshooting: An Action Plan for Money Management in the Small Business* (Dover, NH: Upstart Publishing Company, 1992), p. 61.

17. Richard G. P. McMahon and Scott Holmes, "Small Business Financial Management Practices in North America: A Literature Review," *Journal of Small Business Management,* April 1991, p. 21.

18. George Anders, "Truckers Trials: How One Firm Fights to Save Every Penny as Its Profits Plummet," *Wall Street Journal,* April 13, 1982, pp. 1, 22.

19. "Cash Flow/Cash Flow Management," *Small Business Reporter,* No. 9, p. 5.

20. William Bak, "Make 'Em Pay," *Entrepreneur,* November 1992, p. 64.

21. Michael Selz, "Big Customers' Late Bills Choke Small Suppliers," *Wall Street Journal,* June 22, 1994, p. Bl.

22. McMahon and Holmes, "Small Business Financial Management Practices in North America: A Literature Review," p. 21.

23. Ilan Mochari, "Collect from the Worst," *Inc.,* September 1999, p. 101.

24. "The Check Isn't in the Mail," *Small Business Reports,* October 1991, p. 6.

25. Howard Muson, "Collecting Overdue Accounts," *Your Company,* Spring 1993, p. 4.

26. Richard J. Maturi, "Collection Dues and Don'ts," *Entrepreneur,* January 1992, p. 326.

27. Elaine Pofeldt, "Collect Calls," *Success,* March 1998, pp. 22–24.

28. Roger Thompson, "Business Copes with the Recession," *Nation's Business,* January 1991, p. 21.

29. Janine Latis Musick, "Collecting Payments Due," *Nation's Business,* January 1999, pp. 44–46.

30. Ilan Mochari, "Top Billing," *Inc.,* October 1999, p. 89.

31. Jim Carlton, "Tight Squeeze," *Wall Street Journal,* March 26, 1996, pp. A1, A6.

32. Jill Andresky Fraser, "A Confidence Game," *Inc.,* December 1989, p. 178.

33. Jill Andresky Fraser, "How to Get Paid," *Inc.,* March 1992, p. 105.

34. Eleena deLisser, "Yellow-Pages Con Artists Are Pushing Online Editions," *Wall Street Journal,* November 16, 1999, p. B2.

35. Shepherd, "Internal Financial Strategies," p. 68.

36. Stephanie Barlow, "Frozen Assets," *Entrepreneur,* September 1993, p. 53.

37. Roberta Maynard, "Can You Benefit from Barter?" *Nation's Business,* July 1994, p. 6.

38. "33 Ways to Increase Your Cash Flow and Manage Cash Balances," *The Business Owner,* February 1988, p. 8.

39. "301 Great Ideas for Selling Smarter," *Inc.,* January 1, 1998, p. 47.

40. Mamis, "Money In, Money Out," p. 102.

41. Jeffrey Lant, "Cash Is King," *Small Business Reports,* May 1991, p. 49.

42. International Reciprocal Trading Association, **<www.irta.net>.**

43. Ronaleen Roha, "How Bartering Saves Cash," *Kiplinger's Personal Finance Magazine,* February 1996, p. 103.

44. Ilan Mochari, "A Simple Little System," *Inc.,* October 1, 1999, p. 142.

45. Juan Hovey, "Equip Your Future Through a Lease," *Nation's Business,* May 1999, pp. 47–48.

46. Jill Amadio, "To Lease or Not to Lease?" *Entrepreneur,* February 1998, p. 133.

47. Jack Wynn, "To Use but Not to Own," *Nation's Business,* January 1991, p. 38.

48. Michelle Marinan, "Love It, or Lease It," *Small Business Computing,* March 2000, pp. 39–40; Hovey, "Equip Your Future Through a Lease," pp. 47–48.

49. Thompson, "Business Copes with the Recession," p. 20.

50. Ibid.

51. Bruce G. Posner, "Skipped-Payment Loans," *Inc.,* September 1992, p. 40.

52. American Collectors Association, **<www.collector.com/news/fact/check.html>.**

53. "How to Win the Battle of Bad Checks," *Collection,* Fall 1990, p. 3.

54. Thompson, "Business Copes with the Recession," p. 21.

55. Jill Andresky Fraser, "Better Cash Management," *Inc.,* May 1993, p. 42.

56. Mamis, "Money In, Money Out," p. 103.

Chapter 9

1. Eileen Davis, "Dodging the Bullet," *Venture,* December 1988, p. 78.

2. "Odds and Ends," *Wall Street Journal,* July 25, 1990, p. Bl.

3. Richard G. P. McMahon and Scott Holmes, "Small Business Financial Management Practices in North America: A Literature Review," *Journal of Small Business Management,* April 1991, p. 21.

4. Daniel Kehrer, "Big Ideas for Your Small Business," *Changing Times,* November 1989, p. 57.

5. William Bak, "The Numbers Game," *Entrepreneur,* April 1993, p. 54.

6. Diedrich Von Soosten, "The Roots of Financial Destruction," *Industry Week,* April 5, 1993, pp. 33–34.

7. Richard Maturi, "Take Your Pulse," *Business Start-Ups,* January 1996, p. 72.

8. McMahon and Holmes, "*Small Business Financial Management Practices in North America.*"

9. Erik Schonfeld, "How Much Are Your Eyeballs Worth?" *Fortune,* February 21, 2000, pp. 197–204.

10. Jill Andresky Fraser, "When Staffers Track Results," *Inc.,* October 1993, p. 42; Dan Callahan, "Everybody's an Accountant," *Business Ethics,* January/February 1994, p. 37.

11. "Putting Ratios to Work," *In Business,* December 1988, pp. 14–15.

12. Gregory Zuckerman, "Debtor Nation," *Wall Street Journal,* July 5, 2000, pp. C1, C18.

13. Rishawn Biddle, "Gloom Service," *Forbes,* January 24, 2000, p. 140.

14. Bak, "The Numbers Game," p. 57.

15. "Analyzing Creditworthiness," *Inc.,* November 1991, p. 196.

16. James Morrow, "Sales Up, Profits Down," *Success,* November 1997, p. 16.

17. Ilan Mochari, "A Simple Little System," *Inc.,* October 1999, p. 87.

18. Jack Stack, "The Logic of Profit," *Inc.,* March 1996, p. 17.

19. Jill Andresky Fraser, "The No-Surprises Daily Money Watcher," *Inc.*, August 1995, pp. 73–74.

20. William F. Doescher, "Taking Stock," *Entrepreneur,* November 1994, p. 64.

21. Ilan Mochari, "Significant Figures," *Inc.*, July 2000, p. 128.

22. Robert Macy, "Mirage Megaresort Changed Face and Fortunes of Las Vegas," *The Greenville News,* November 25, 1999, p. 22A.

23. Mochari, "Significant Figures."

Chapter 10

1. Dan Morse, "Many Small Businesses Don't Devote Time to Planning," *Wall Street Journal,* September 7, 1999, p. B2.

2. Michael Warshaw, "A Novel Plan," *Inc.*, October 1999, p. 21.

3. Paul Hawken, "Money," *Growing a Business,* KQED, San Francisco, 1988.

4. Steve Marshall Cohen, "Money Rules," *Business Start-Ups,* July 1995, p. 79.

5. "Advice from the Great Ones," *Communication Briefings,* January 1992, p. 5.

6. Cynthia Griffin, Victoria Neal, Heather Page, Michelle Prather, and Laura Tiffany, "Hot Stuff: Teens," *Entrepreneur,* December 1999, p. 78.

7. Cynthia Griffin, Victoria Neal, Heather Page, Michelle Prather, and Laura Tiffany, "Teen Beauty Store," *Entrepreneur,* December 1999, p. 80.

8. Guy Kawasaki, "Needbucks.com," *Forbes,* January 10, 2000, p. 188.

9. "Sales and Marketing," *Venturing,* Vermont Public Television, 1991.

10. Guy Kawasaki, "Time to Money," *Forbes,* March 12, 1999, p. 136.

11. Joel Kurtzman, "The New Age of Business Plans," *Fortune,* September 27, 1999, p. 262[N].

12. Conversation with Charles Burke, CEO, Burke Financial Associates.

13. Alana Odom, "Good Plan Is Vital When Starting Business," *Moneywise,* May 4, 1998, p. 5.

14. Conversation with Charles Burke, CEO, Burke Financial Associates.

15. Karen Axelton, "Good Plan, Stan," *Business Start-Ups,* March 2000, p. 17.

16. Steve Marshall Cohen, "Reality Check," *Business Start-Ups,* October 1995, pp. 74–75.

17. Roger Thompson, "Business Plans: Myth and Reality," *Nation's Business,* August 1988, p. 16.

18. Lisa Falkenberg, "Making Over CEOs," *Fortune,* September 7, 1998, p. 144[L].

19. Andrew Raskin, "There's No Such Thing as a Free Launch," *Inc.*, April 2000, pp. 43–46.

20. Jill Andresky Fraser, "Who Can Help Out with a Business Plan?" *Inc.*, June 1999, p. 115.

21. Thomas Melville, "Success Rules!" *Success,* September 2000, p. 57.

Chapter 11

1. Paul DeCeglie, "What About Me?" Business Start-Ups, June 2000, p. 45.

2. Ibid., pp. 45–51.

3. Udayan Gupta, "The Right Fit," *Wall Street Journal,* May 22, 1995, p. R8.

4. Rufus Griscom, "Blinded by the Spotlight," *Success,* April 1999, p. 96.

5. Luisa Kroll, "P2P or Bust," *Forbes: Best of the Web,* July 17, 2000, pp. 94–96.

6. Silvia Sansoni, "Burned Angels," *Forbes,* April 19, 1999, pp. 182–185.

7. Toni Mack, "They Stole My Baby," *Forbes,* February 12, 1996, pp. 90–91.

8. Elizabeth Fenner, "How to Raise the Cash You Need," *Money Guide,* summer 1991, p. 45.

9. Carrie Coolidge, "The Bootstrap Brigade," *Forbes,* December 28, 1998, pp. 90–91.

10. Ibid.

11. Alex Markels, "A Little Help from Their Friends," *Wall Street Journal,* May 22, 1995, p. R10.

12. Fenner, "How to Raise the Cash You Need," p. 45.

13. Paul Kvinta, "Frogskins, Shekels, Bucks, Moolah, Cash, Simoleans, Dough, Dinero: Everybody Wants It. Your Business Needs It. Here's How to Get It," *Smart Business,* August 2000, pp. 74–89.

14. Pamela Sherrid, "Angels of Capitalism," *U.S. News & World Report,* October 13, 1997, pp. 43–45.

15. Wendy Taylor and Marty Jerome, "Pray," *Smart Business,* July 2000, p. 45; Sherrid, "Angels of Capitalism," pp. 43–45; Kvinta, "Frogskins, Shekels, Bucks, Moolah, Cash, Simoleans, Dough, Dinero: Everybody Wants It. Your Business Needs It. Here's How to Get It," pp. 74–89; Thea Singer, "Where the Money Is," *Inc.*, September 2000, pp. 52–57.

16. Gianna Jacobson, "Capture an Angel," *Success,* November 1995, p. 46.

17. Taylor and Jerome, "Pray," p. 45.

18. Sansoni, "Burned Angels," pp. 182–185.

19. Susan Greco, "Get$$$Now.com," *Inc.*, September 1999, pp. 35–38.

20. Ibid.; "Digging for Dollars," *Wall Street Journal,* February 24, 1989, p. R25.

21. "Digging for Dollars," p. R25.

22. Kvinta, "Frogskins, Shekels, Bucks, Moolah, Cash, Simoleans, Dough, Dinero: Everybody Wants It. Your Business Needs It. Here's How to Get It," p. 78.

23. Anne Ashby Gilbert, "Small Stakes in Small Business," *Fortune,* April 12, 1999, p. 162[H]; Sherrid, "Angels of Capitalism," pp. 43–45.

24. Bruce J. Blechman, "Step Right Up," *Entrepreneur,* June 1993, pp. 20–25.

25. Nancy Scarlato, "Money," *Business Start-Ups,* December 1995, pp. 50–51; Gianna Jacobson, "Raise Money Now," *Success,* November 1995, pp. 39–50.

26. Mark Henricks, "Stand Your Ground," *Entrepreneur,* January 1993, p. 264.

27. Ian Springsteel, "Need More Money? Find a Big White Knight," *FSB,* September 2000, pp. 33–36.

28. Ibid.

29. Mike Hofman, "Capital Customer," *Inc.*, August 2000, p. 129.

30. Arlyn Tobias Gajilan, "Big Money on Campus," *Your Company,* October 1999, p. 34.

31. Warren P. Strobel, "The Spy Who Funded Me (and My Start-Up)," *U.S. News & World Report,* July 17, 2000, pp. 38–39.

32. DeCeglie, "What About Me?" pp. 45–51.

33. Jill Andresky Fraser, "Where Has All the Money Gone?" *Inc.*, April 2000, pp. 101–110.

34. Singer, "Where the Money Is," pp. 52–55; National Venture Capital Association, **<www.nvca.org>.**

35. "Venture Capitalists Take the Reins," *Small Business Reports,* April 1990, p. 23.

36. Singer, "Where the Money Is."

37. Paul DeCeglie, "Hunt It Down," *Business Start-Ups,* May 2000, p. 34.

38. Anne B. Fisher, "Raising Capital for a New Venture," *Fortune,* June 13, 1994, p. 101.

39. Ellyn Spragins, "How VCs Spot Winners (Really)," *Your Company,* February/March 1999, p. 24.

40. Kvinta, "Frogskins, Shekels, Bucks, Moolah, Cash, Simoleans, Dough, Dinero: Everybody Wants It. Your Business Needs It. Here's How to Get It," pp. 74–89.

41. Dave Pell, "What's Old Is New Again," *FSB,* July/August 2000, p. 122.

42. Kvinta, "Frogskins, Shekels, Bucks, Moolah, Cash, Simoleans, Dough, Dinero: Everybody Wants It. Your Business Needs It. Here's How to Get It," p. 87.

43. "Martha, WWF, Satyam Gain," CNN/fn, **<cnnfn.cnn.com/1999/10/19/companies/ipos>.**

44. David R. Evanson, "Tales of Caution in Going Public," *Nation's Business,* June 1996, p. 58.

45. Roberta Maynard, "Are You Ready to Go Public?" *Nation's Business,* January 1995, pp. 30–32.

46. Philip W. Taggart, Roy Alexander, and Robert M. Arnold, "Deciding Whether to Go Public," *Nation's Business,* May 1991, p. 52.

47. David R. Evanson and Art Beroff, "Synchronize Your Watches," *Entrepreneur,* November 1999, pp. 74–77.

48. "Internet Connect Withdraws $100M IPO, Cites Market Conditions," *IPO Monitor,* September 29, 2000, **<www.ipomonitor.com/nt/56966.html>.**

49. Herb Greenberg, "Why Would You Want to Go Public," *Fortune,* May 24, 1999, p. 324.

50. Kvinta, "Frogskins, Shekels, Bucks, Moolah, Cash, Simoleans, Dough, Dinero: Everybody Wants It. Your Business Needs It. Here's How to Get It," p. 88.

51. David R. Evanson and Art Beroff, "It Ain't Over . . ." *Entrepreneur,* December 1999, pp. 66–69; CorpHQ, **<www.corphq.com>.**

52. Andresky Fraser, "Entrepreneurs in Search of a Deal," *Inc.,* April 2000, pp. 116–120; "PatchLink.com Closes $5.6 Million Funding Round Led by OffRoad Capital," **<corporate.patchlink.com/news/Release.asp?ReleaseID=44>.**

53. Mack, "They Stole My Baby," pp. 90–91.

54. Paul DeCeglie, "Public Enemy?" *Business Start-Ups,* November 1999, pp. 38–48; "Small Green Firms Use Direct Public Offerings," *In Business,* May/June 1996, p. 10; "A Fishy Success," *Business Ethics,* July/August 1996, p. 6; Drew Field Direct Public Offerings: Client Summaries, Blue Fish Clothing, **<www.dfdpo.com/clientsum9.htm>.**

55. Paulette Thomas, "Direct Public Offerings Propel Start-Ups to Next Level," *Wall Street Journal,* June 29, 1999, p. B2; Real Goods Trading Company, **<www.real goods.com/stock/index.cfm?sd=1>.**

56. Gianna Jacobson, "Find Your Fortune on the Internet," *Success,* November 1995, p. 50.

57. Debra Phillips, "Northern Exposure," *Entrepreneur,* February 1996, p. 15.

58. "Report to the Congress on Markets for Small Business and Commercial Mortgage Related Securities," Federal Reserve Board of Governors, **<www.federalreserve.gov/boarddocs/RptCongress/markets2000.pdf>.**

59. Michelle L. Kezar, "Big Lending to Small Business," *Cross Sections,* Spring 1995, p. 28; Cynthia E. Griffin, "Breaking the Bank," *Entrepreneur,* March 1998, pp. 110–115.

60. Karen Axelton, "Don't Bank On It," *Business Start-Ups,* May 1998, p. 116.

61. Cynthia E. Griffin, "Money in the Bank," *Entrepreneur,* July 2000, pp. 84–89; Rick Brooks, "Small Banks Lead the Way," *Wall Street Journal,* February 28, 1996, p. S3; "Small Business Lending in the United States, 1999 Edition" Office of Advocacy, U.S. Small Business Administration, **<www.sba.gov/advo/stats/lending/1999/bk_int99.pdf>.**

62. Anne Field, "Getting the Bank to Yes," *Success,* May 1999, pp. 67–71.

63. Daniel M. Clark, "Banks and Bankability," *Venture,* September 1989, p. 29.

64. "Lines of Credit," *Inc.,* July 1990, p. 96.

65. Anne Ashby Gilbert, "Where to Go When the bank Says No," *Fortune,* October 12, 1998, pp. 188[C]–188[F].

66. Teri Agins, "Asset-Based Lending to Firms Has Found Favor with Banks," *Wall Street Journal,* November 5, 1984, p. 35.

67. "What Is Business Credit?" National Association of Credit Management, **<www.nacm.org/aboutnacm/what.html>;** "Financing Small Business," *Small Business Reporter,* c3, p. 9.

68. Jill Andresky Fraser, "When Supplier Credit Helps Fuel Growth," *Inc.,* March 1995, p. 117.

69. "Small Business Lending in the United States, 1999 Edition" Office of Advocacy, U.S. Small Business Administration, **<www.sba.gov/advo/stats/lending/1999/bk_int99.pdf>.**

70. Gilbert, "Where to Go When the Bank Says No," pp. 188 [C]–188[F].

71. Georgette Jasen, "Pros and Cons of Borrowing from Your Broker," *Wall Street Journal,* April 21, 1993, p. Cl.

72. Scott McMurray, "Personal Loans from Brokers Offer Low Rates, " *Wall Street Journal,* January 7, 1986, p. 31.

73. Cynthia E. Griffin, "Give 'Em Credit," *Entrepreneur,* July 1999, p. 26.

74. "Joseph Ogwal: Building a Stable Future for His Family," World Council of Credit Unions, **<www.woccu.org/cudev/microfinance/afr_splt.htm>.**

75. Stephen Barlas, "Something Ventured," *Entrepreneur,* July 2000, pp. 128–129; David R. Evanson and Art Beroff, "No Hot Air," *Entrepreneur,* May 2000, pp. 72–75; U.S. Small Business Administration, **<www.sbaonline.sba.gov/INV/stat/table3.pdf>.**

76. "Success Stories: Callaway Golf Company," National Association of Small Business Investment Companies, **<www.nasbic.org/success/stories/callaway.cfm>.**

77. "Economic Development Administration Fact Sheet," **<www.doc.gov/eda/pdf/1a5_1_99factsheet.pdf>.**

78. "SBA Technolgy: Small Business Innovation Research Program (SBIR)," **<www.sba.gov/SBIR/sbir.html>;** Charles Stein, "A Sugar Daddy for Hungry Start-Ups," *FSB,* May/June 2000, pp. 41–42.

79. Charles Stein, "A Sugar Daddy for Hungry Start-Ups," *FSB,* May/June 2000, pp. 41–42; Department of Defense, SBIR/STTR List, **<www.sbirsttr.com/Awards /SrchResultsDtlsList.asp>.**

80. Laura M. Litvan, "Some Rest for the Paperwork Weary," *Nation's Business,* June 1994, pp. 38–40; Robert W. Casey, "Getting Down to Business," *Your Company,* Summer 1994, pp. 30–33.

81. Anna Barron Billingsley, "Dream Weavers," *Region Focus,* Fall 1999, pp. 20–23.

82. Roberta Reynes, "Borrowing Tailored for Exporters," *Nation's Business,* March 1999, pp. 29–30.

83. Sharon Nelton, "Keeping Money Local with a 504 Loan," *Nation's Business,* September 1998, pp. 40–41.

84. Billingsley, "Dream Weavers," pp. 20–23.

85. Ziona Austrian and Zhongcai Zhang, "An Inventory and Assessment of Pollution Control and Prevention Financing Programs," Great Lakes Environmental Finance Center, Levin College of Urban Affairs, Cleveland State University, **<www.csuohio.edu/glefc/inventor.htm#sba>.**

86. Sharon Nelton, "Loans That Come Full Circle," *Nation's Business,* June 1999, pp. 35–36.

87. Ibid.

88. Roberta Reynes, "A Big Factor in Expansion," *Nation's Business,* January 1999, pp. 31–32; Bruce J. Blechman, "The High Cost of Credit," *Entrepreneur,* January 1993, pp. 22–25.

89. Roberta Reynes, "A Big Factor in Expansion."

90. Phaedra Hise, "Don't Start a Business Without One," *Inc.,* February 1998, pp. 50–53.

91. Hise, "Don't Start a Business Without One," pp. 50–53.

Chapter 12

1. Roberta Maynard, "A Growing Outlet for Small Firms," *Nation's Business,* August 1996, pp. 45–48.

2. Jeffrey A. Tannenbaum, "Phoenix Tops List of Fertile Areas for Small Companies," *Wall Street Journal,* December 7, 1999, p. B.2.

3. Michelle Prather, "Hit the Spot," *Business Start-Ups,* April 1999, p. 104.

4. "Employment Cost Trends," Bureau of Labor Statistics, **<stats.bls.gov/news.release/ecec.t07.htm>.**

5. Tim W. Ferguson, "Sun, Fun, and Ph.D.s, Too," *Forbes,* May 31, 1999, pp. 220–233; Andrew Kupfer, "The Champ of Cheap Clones," *Fortune,* September 23, 1991, pp. 115–120.

6. Ferguson, "Sun, Fun, and Ph.D.s, Too," p. 222.

7. Mark Henricks, "A Tale of 25 Cities," *Entrepreneur,* October 2000, pp. 86–94.

8. Elaine Appleton, "E-Town, USA," *Inc. Technology,* no. 3 (2000), pp. 56–61.

9. Henricks, "A Tale of 25 Cities," pp. 86–94.

10. Leslie Wines, "Escape to Spokane," *Journal of Business Strategy,* May/June 1996, p. 35.

11. Joel Kotkin, "Here Comes the Neighborhood," *Inc.,* July 2000, pp. 113–123.

12. Kevin Helliker, "Monster Movie Theaters Invade the Cinema Landscape," *Wall Street Journal,* May 13, 1997, pp. B1, B13; "It All Started on the Silver Screen," AMC Theaters, **<www.amctheaters.com/about/history.html>.**

13. Prather, "Hit the Spot," p. 104.

14. "C-Store Saturation Analysis," **<www.c-store.com/satration.htm>.**

15. Bernard J. LaLonde, "New Frontiers in Store Location," *Supermarket Merchandising,* February 1963. p. 110.

16. Jan Norman, "How To: Find the Perfect Location," *Business Start-Ups,* February 1998, pp. 54–56.

17. Michael Totty, "'Power' Centers Lure Shoppers by Mixing Elements from Big Malls and Small Plazas," *Wall Street Journal,* December 27, 1988, p. B1.

18. Maynard, "A Growing Outlet for Small Firms."

19. Mitchell Pacelle, "More Stores Spurn Malls for Village Square," *Wall Street Journal,* February 16, 1996, p. B1.

20. "Some Great Things Happening in Main Street Communities," Main Street National Trust for Historic Preservation, **<www.mainst.org/AboutMainStreet/communities.htm>.**

21. *Scope 2000,* International Council of Shopping Centers, **<www.icsc.org/srch/rsrch/scope/current/index.html>.**

22. Ibid.

23. Nichole L. Torres, "No Place Like Home," *Start-Ups,* September 2000, pp. 38–45. "Executive Overview," National Association of Home-Based Business's U.S.A. Home-Based Business Information Superhighway **<www.usahomebusiness.com/homesite2.htm>.**

24. Joanne H. Pratt, "Home-based Business: The Hidden Economy," *Small Business Research Summary,* No. 194, March 2000, U.S. Small Business Administration Office of Advocacy, **<www.sba.gov/ADVO/research/rs194.pdf>.**

25. Susan Gregory Thomas, "Home Offices That Really Do the Job," *U.S. News and World Report,* October 28, 1996, pp. 84–87.

26. Lauren Lipton, "The Home Office That Ate Boston," *Wall Street Journal,* April 23, 1999, p. W.8.

27. "Business Incubation Facts," National Business Incubation Association, **<www.nbia.org/info/fact_sheet.html>.**

28. Ibid.

29. Lori Ioannou, "Start-Ups with a Catch," *Fortune,* July 20, 1998, pp. 156[C]–156[D].

30. Marci McDonald, "The Latte Connections," *U.S. News & World Report,* March 20, 1999, pp. 63–66.

31. Laura Tiffany, "The Rules of . . . Retail," *Business Start-Ups,* December 1999, p. 106.

32. Ibid.

33. "Educational Kit," President's Committee on Employment of People with Disabilities, **<www50.pcepd.gov/pcepd/archives/pubs/ek99/wholedoc.htm#desions>.**

34. "Faces of the ADA," United States Department of Justice, **<www.usdoj.gov/crt/ada/fmartin.htm>.**

35. "Proposal for an Ergonomics Program Standard," The Occupational Health and Safety Administration, **<www.osha-slc.gov/ergonomics-standard/ergofaq.html>.**

36. Melissa J. Perenson, "Straighten Up," *Small Business Computing,* October 1999, pp. 77–80.

37. "Work Week," *Wall Street Journal,* November 16, 1999, p. A1.

38. Shane McLaughlin, "You Put Your Left Foot In," *Inc. Technology,* no. 2 (1998), p. 18.

39. Mitcell Brill and Ceryl Parker, "Office Planning," *Small Business Reports,* December 1988, p. 36.

40. Leigh Gallagher, "Get Out of My Face," *Forbes,* October 18, 1999, pp. 105–106.

41. Laura Tiffany, "Personal Space," *Entrepreneur,* May 2000, p.22; Brenda Moore, "We Don't Want to Know What People Wear to Work," *Wall Street Journal,* California Edition, September 29, 1999, p. CA2.

42. Heather Page, "Pedal to the Metal," *Entrepreneur,* August 1996, p. 15.

43. "Business Bulletin," *Wall Street Journal,* April 15, 1999, p. A1.

44. Kenneth Labich, "This Man Is Watching You," *Fortune,* July 19, 1999, pp. 131–134.

45. Alex Taylor III, "It Worked for Toyota. Can It Work for Toys?" *Fortune,* January 11, 1999, p. 36.

Chapter 13

1. "From Ohio to Yanbu: The Long, Profitable Journey of Medical Resources," U.S. Commercial Service, **<www1.usatrade.gov/Press_Room/Success1.htm>.**

2. "America's Small Businesses and International Trade: A Report," U.S. Small Business Administration Office of International Trade, November 1999, p. 1.

3. "International Incentive," *Small Business Reports,* June 1992, p. 5; "America's Small Businesses and International Trade: A Report."

4. "America's Small Businesses and International Trade: A Report."

5. Rob Norton, "Strategies for the New Export Boom," *Fortune,* August 22, 1994, p. 130; "America's Small Businesses and International Trade: A Report."

6. "America's Small Businesses and International Trade: A Report." "NAFTA's Three-Year Report Card," The Heritage Foundation, **<www.heritage.org/library/categories/trade/bg1117.html>.**

7. Ted Miller, "Can America Compete in the Global Economy?" *Kiplinger's Personal Finance Magazine,* November 1991, p. 8.

8. Bernard Wysocki, Jr., "Going Global in the New World," *Wall Street Journal,* September 21, 1990, p. R3.

9. Preston Townley, "Global Business in the Next Decade," *Across the Board,* January/February 1990, p. 16.

10. Roger E. Axtell, *The Do's and Taboos of International Trade* (New York: John Wiley and Sons, 1994), p. 11.

11. Monci Jo Williams, "Rewriting the Export Rules," *Fortune,* April 23, 1990, p. 90.

12. Charlotte Mulhern, "Going the Distance," *Entrepreneur,* May 1998, p. 129.

13. Mulhern, "Going the Distance."

14. "To Protect or Not to Protect," *FW,* June 1992, p. 56.

15. "Globesmanship," *Across the Board,* January/February 1990, p. 26.

16. Carleen Hawn, "Juggling Act," *Forbes,* November 1, 1999, pp. 242–244.

17. "Globesmanship."

18. "The Best Places to Do Business," *FW,* October 15, 1991, p. 26; *Breaking into the Trade Game: A Small Business Guide To Exporting* (Washington, DC: U.S. Small Business Administration and AT&T, 1994), p. 11.

19. Michael Barrier, "Why Small Looms Large in the Global Economy," *Nation's Business,* February 1994, p. 9; Vivian Pospisil, "Global Paradox: Small Is Powerful," *Industry Week,* July 18, 1994, p. 29.

20. Michael Barrier, "A Global Reach for Small Firms," *Nation's Business,* April 1994, p. 66.

21. Stephanie N. Mehta, "Artais Finds Smallness Isn't Handicap in Global Market," *Wall Street Journal,* June 23, 1994, p. B2.

22. Rudolph Bell, "Japanese Connection," *Upstate Business,* September 5, 1999, pp. 1, 8–9.

23. Jeremy Main, "Hot to Go Global—And Why," *Fortune,* August 28, 1989, p. 70.

24. Larry Pearl and Sandeep Thakrar, "Taking Your Business Worldwide," *FSB,* March 23, 2000, **<www.fsb.com/fotunesb/articles/0,2227,634,00.html>.**

25. Emily Esterson, "United Nations," *Inc. Technology,* no. 2, (1998) p. 88.

26. Roberta Maynard, "Trade Links Via the Internet," *Nation's Business,* December 1997, p. 53.

27. Wendy M. Grossman, "Go Global," *Smart Business,* October 2000, pp. 110–117.

28. Joey Latimer, "Braving the New World," *Small Business Computing,* September 2000, p. 63.

29. Ibid., pp. 63–64.

30. Michael Self, "More Small Firms Are Turning to Trade Intermediaries," *Wall Street Journal,* February 2, 1993, p. B1.

31. The East India Company, **<www.theeastindiacompany.com/company.html>.**

32. Brad W. Ketchum, "Going Global: Now Is No Time to Stay Home," *Inc. Technology,* no. 4, 1999 Ad Supplement.

33. Jeffrey Rothfeder, "Help with Middlemen," *Your Company,* April 1999, pp. 66–67.

34. Mulhern, "Going the Distance," pp. 128–133.

35. "Reducing the Risk of Doing Business in China," *Nation's Business,* November 1994, p. 12.

36. Joseph E . Pattison, "Global Joint Vertures," *Overseas Business,* Winter 1990, p. 25.

37. J. William Gurley, "Like It or Not, Every Start-up Is Now Global," *Fortune,* June 26, 2000, p. 324.

38. Donald L. Burroughs, "Lifting Off with Exports," *U.S. News & World Report,* June 3, 1991, p. 65.

39. "Global Alliances," *Fortune* insert, pp. 67–82.

40. Jeffrey A. Tannenbaum, "Licensing May Be Quickest Route to Foreign Markets," *Wall Street Journal,* September 14, 1990, p. B2.

41. "Marvel Comics Foreign Licensing,"**<www.mavelerope.com/foreign_licensing>.**

42. Tannenbaum, "Licensing May Be Quickest Route to Foreign Makets."

43. *Breaking into the Trade Game: A Small Business Guide To Exporting,* p. 105.

44. Mary E. Tomzack, "Ripe New Markets," *Success,* April 1995, pp. 73–77.

45. Tumbleweed International, LLC, **<www.tumbleweedintl.com/twloc.html>;** "Tumbleweed International Mesquite Bar & Grill Opens in Merrryland Theme Par Helipolis, Egypt," International Franchise Association, **<www.franchise.org/news/pr/03212000i.asp>.**

46. "International Franchises," Domino's Pizza, **<www.dominos.com/Franchise/Internatl.cfm>.**

47. Nathaniel Gilbert, "The Case for Countertrade," *Across the Board,* May 1992, pp. 43–45.

48. Axtell, *The Do's and Taboos of International Trade,* p. 256; Gary Pacific, "Countertrade Basics," Thunderbird Countertrade Club, **<members.tripod.com/T-birdCountertrade/COUNTERTRADEBASIC_files/frame.htm>.**

49. Lourdes Lee Valeriano, "How Small Firms Can Get Free Help from Big Ones," *Wall Street Journal,* July 30, 1991, p. B2.

50. "America's Small Businesses and International Trade: A Report," pp.1–2.

51. "America's Small Businesses and International Trade: A Report," p. 6; Winderosa Manufacturing and Distribution Company, **<www.winderosa.com>.**

52. "America's Small Businesses and International Trade: A Report," p. 6; Axtell, *The Do's and Taboos of International Trade,* p. 10; Grossman, "Going Global," pp. 112–117.

53. Paul C. Hsu, "Profiting from a Global Mindset," *Nation's Business,* June 1994, p. 6.

54. Patricia M. Carey, "Growing Through Exports," *Your Company,* Fall 1994, p. 14.

55. Jeffrey A. Tannenbaum, "Among Fast-Growing Small Concerns, Exporters Expand the Most, Study Says," *Wall Street Journal,* June 19, 1996, p. B2.

56. Jan Alexander, "To Sell Well Overseas, Customize," *Your Company,* Fall 1995, p. 15.

57. Stephanie N. Mehta, "Small Companies Look to Cultivate Foreign Business," *Wall Street Journal,* July 7, 1994, p. B2.

58. "America's Small Businesses and International Trade: A Report," p. 6.

59. EkkWill Waterlife Resources, **<www.petsforum.com/ekkwill>;** Christopher Knowlton, "The New Export Entrepreneurs," *Fortune,* June 6, 1988, p. 98.

60. Alexander, "To Sell Well Overseas, Customize," p. 15.

61. Curt Cultice, "Exporter 'Nails' World Market," *Export America,* **<www.ita.doc.gov/fs_explore.hml>,** p. 8.

62. Becky Mann, "Making Worldly Decisions," *GSA Business,* March 2, 1998, p. 11B; Charlotte Mulhern, "Make No Mistake," *Entrepreneur,* February 1998, p. 38.

63. Jan Alexander, "How to Find an Overseas Distributor," *Your Company,* April/May 1996, pp. 52–54.

64. Samuel Means, "Exporting Peace Talks," *Export America,* **<www.ita.doc.gov/fs_explore.hml>,** pp. 6–7.

65. "The Pacific Rim on a Shoestring," *Inc.,* June 1991, pp. 122–123.

66. John S. McClenahan, "Santec's European Connection," *Industry Week,* October 4, 1993, p. 30.

67. William Echikson, "Young Americans Go Abroad to Strike It Rich," *Fortune,* October 17, 1994, p. 190.

68. Martha E. Mangelsdorf, "Unfair Trade," *Inc.,* April 1991, pp. 28–37.

69. Mark Robichaux, "Exporters Face Big Roadblocks at Home," *Wall Street Journal,* November 7, 1990, p. Bl.

70. National Center for Policy Analysis, **<www.ncpa.org/bg/bg135.html>.**

71. Ibid.

72. Andrew Tanzer, "The Great Quota Hustle," *Forbes,* March 6, 2000, pp. 119–125.

73. Ibid., p. 120.

74. National Center for Policy Analysis, **<www.ncpa.org/bg/bg135.html>;** Christopher J. Chipelo, "Small U.S. Companies Take the Plunge into Japan's Market," *Wall Street Journal,* July 7, 1992, p. B2.

75. Jacob M. Schlesinger, "Tough Gamble," *Wall Street Journal,* May 11, 1993, pp. Al, A8.

76. Charlotte Mulhern, "Culture Shock," *Entrepreneur,* May 1998, p. 46.

77. Lawrence Van Gelder, "It Pays to Watch Words, Gestures While Abroad," *Greenville News,* April 7, 1996, p. 8E.

78. Sandy Asirvatham, "Old World Order," *Success,* October 1998, pp. 73–75.

79. Edward T. Hall, "The Silent Language of Overseas Business," *Harvard Business Review,* May–June 1960, pp. 5–14.

80. Roger E. Axtell, *Gestures: The Do's and Taboos of Body Language Around the World* (New York: John Wiley & Sons, Inc., 1991).

81. Christopher D. Lancette, "Hitting the Spot," *Entrepreneur,* September 1999, p. 40.

82. Asirvatham, "Old World Order."

83. Stephanie Barlow, "Let's Make a Deal," *Entrepreneur,* May 1991, p. 40.

84. Barbara Pachter, "When in Japan Don't Cross Your Legs," *Business Ethics,* March/April 1996, p. 50.

85. William Bak, "Triple Play," *Entrepreneur,* March 1994, p. 60.

86. Lori Ioannou and Sheryl Nance-Nash, "NAFTA: Keeping Score," *Your Company,* February/March 1999, p. 71.

87. Amy Barrett, "It's a Small (Business) World," *Business Week,* April 17, 1995, pp. 96–101.

88. John S. McClenahen, "Sound Thinking," *Industry Week,* May 3, 1993, p. 28.

89. Main, "How to Go Global—And Why."

90. Ibid.

Chapter 14

1. Polly Labarre, "Leaders.com," *Fast Company,* June 1999, p. 96.

2. Max DePree, *Leadership Jazz* (New York: Currency Doubleday, 1992), pp. 8–9.

3. Francis Huffman, "Taking the Lead," *Entrepreneur,* November 1993, p. 101.

4. "The Best of Herb Kelleher," *Your Company,* August/September 1999, p. 70.

5. Michael Barrier, "Leadership Skills Employees Re-spect," *Nation's Business,* January 1999, p. 28.

6. Stratford Sherman, "How Tomorrow's Leaders Are Learning Their Stuff," *Fortune,* November 27, 1995, p. 102.

7. John Mariotti, "The Role of a Leader," *Industry Week,* February 1, 1999, p. 75.

8. Katrina Brooker, "Southwest Airlines: Can Anyone Replace Herb?" *Fortune,* April 17, 2000, **<www.fortune.com/fortune/fortune500/sou.html>;** "The Best of Herb Kelleher," pp. 60–70; Herb Kelleher, "A Culture of Commitment," *Leader to Leader,* no. 4, Spring 1997, **<www.drucker.org/leaderbooks/l2l/spring97/kelleher.html>;** Kathleen Melymuka, "Down-to-Earth Technology Helps Make Herb Kelleher's Southwest Airlines a Soaring Success," *Computerworld,* **<www.idg.net/crd_kelleher_10166.html>.**

9. Michael A. Verespej, "Invest in People," *Industry Week,* February 1, 1999, p. 6.

10. Pierre Mornell, "Nothing Endures But Change," *Inc.,* July 2000, p. 132.

11. Bernard A Nagle, "Wanted: A Leader for the 21st Century," *Industry Week,* November 20, 1995, p.29.

12. Kayte Vanscoy, "The Hiring Crisis," *Smart Business,* July 2000, pp. 85–97; Michael Barrier, "Hire Without Fear," *Nation's Business,* May 1999, pp. 16–23; "Hiring Mistakes," *Practical Supervision,* October 1994, pp. 4–5.

13. Christopher Caggiano, "Recruiting Secrets," *Inc.,* October 1998, pp. 30–42.

14. Richard J. Pinsker, "Hiring Winners," *Small Business Forum,* Fall 1994, pp. 66–84.

15. Barrier, "Hire Without Fear," pp. 16–23.

16. Ibid.

17. "How to Hire Smart," *FSB,* July/August 2000, p. 64.

18. Caggiano, "Recruiting Secrets," pp. 30–42.

19. Karen Southwick, "To Survive: Hire Up," *Forbes ASAP,* April 3, 2000, pp. 117–118.

20. Jill Hecht Maxwell, "An Inside Job," *Inc.,* July 2000, p. 126.

21. Caggiano, "Recruiting Secrets," pp. 30–42.

22. Christopher Caggiano, "The Truth About Internet Recruiting," *Inc.,* December 1999, p. 156.

23. Edward Wakin, "Recruiting the Right People," *Beyond Computing,* May 2000, p. 54.

24. Rebecca Buckman, "What Price a BMW? At Stanford It May Cost Only a Resume," *Wall Street Journal,* May 19, 2000, pp. A1, A12.

25. Christopher Caggiano, "Beyond Campus Recruiting," *Inc.,* April 1998, p. 115.

26. Jane Shealy, "Recruiting & Retaining Top Talent," *Success,* September 2000, p. 86.

27. Caggiano, "Recruiting Secrets," pp. 30–42; Vanscoy, "The Hiring Crisis," pp. 85–97.

28. Wakin, "Recruiting the Right People," p. 55.

29. Lori Francisco, "Extreme Measures," *Business Start-Ups,* June 2000, p. 13.

30. Caggiano, "Recruiting Secrets," pp. 30–42.

31. Jim Johnson, "Take It from Me: Write a Job Description," *Small Business Forum,* Fall 1994, pp. 10–11.

32. Michael Barrier, "Hiring the Right People," *Nation's Business,* June 1996, p. 21.

33. "Making the Most of Job Interviews," *Your Company,* Spring 1993, p. 6.

34. Michael Mercer, "Consider These Guidelines on Conducting Interviews," *Small Business Forum,* Fall 1994, pp.11–14.

35. Christopher Caggiano, "What Were You In For?" *Inc.,* October 1998, p. 117.

36. Jill Hecht Maxwell, "Of Resumes and Rap Sheets," *Inc. Technology 2000,* No. 2, p. 27.

37. Chuck Salter, "Insanity Inc.," *Fast Company,* January 1999, pp. 101–108.

38. John Case, "Corporate Culture," *Inc.,* November 1996, p. 45.

39. Ibid., pp. 42–53.

40. Julie Creswell, "Cool Companies 2000," *Fortune,* June 26, 2000, pp. 98–124; Shari Caudron, "Be Cool!" *Workforce,* April 1998, pp. 50–61; Julie Creswell, "The Coolness Factor," *Fortune,* July 6, 1998, pp. 62–66; Melanie Warner, "Cool Conmpanies 1998," *Fortune,* July 6, 1998, pp. 69–89.

41. Eleena De Lisser, "Start-Up Attracts Staff with a Ban on Midnight Oil," *Wall Street Journal,* August 23, 2000, pp. B1, B6.

42. Debra Phillips, "Working Class Dog," *Entrepreneur,* September 1998, p. 17.

43. Holly J. Morris, "Mom, Dad, and a Scooter," *U.S. News & World Report,* November 6, 2000, p. 86.

44. Caudron, "Be Cool!" p. 56.

45. "Master of Mixology," *Success,* October 1997, p. 27.

46. Caudron, "Be Cool!" p. 58.

47. Ibid.

48. Ibid., p. 61.

49. Anna Brady, "Small Is as Small Does," *Journal of Business Strategy,* January/February 1996, pp. 44–52.

50. Ronald E. Merrill and Henry D. Sedgwick, "To Thine Own Self Be True," *Inc.,* August 1994, pp. 50–56.

51. Ibid., p. 56.

52. Mark Fischetti, "Team Doctors, Report to ER," *Fast Company,* February–March, 1998, pp. 170–177; Robert McGarvey, "Joining Forces," *Entrepreneur,* September 1996, pp. 80–83; "Whoa, Team," *Journal of Business Strategy,* January/February 1996, p. 8.

53. Ed Carberry, "Hypergrowth Strategy: Create an Ownership Culture," *Inc.,* December 12, 1999, **<www.inc.com/casestudies/details/1.345.CAS15825_CNT_GDE65.00.html>.**

54. Brian S. Moskal, "Supervision (Or Lack Of It)," *Industry Week,* December 3, 1990, p. 56.

55. Theodore B. Kinni, "America's Best," *Industry Week,* October 21, 1996, p. 84.

56. Theodore B. Kinni, "The Empowered Workforce," *Industry Week,* September 19, 1994, p. 37.

57. David Maize, "Where It Pays to Have a Great Idea," *Reader's Digest,* June 1995, pp. 100–104.

58. Karen M. Kroll, "By the Books," *Industry Week,* July 21, 1997, p. 47.

59. John Case, "The Open-Book Revolution," *Inc.,* June 1995, pp. 26–43.

60. Jay Finnegan, "Pipe Dreams," *Inc.,* August 1994, pp. 64–70.

61. Linda Field, "A Little Leeway Goes a Long Way," *Nation's Business,* November 1998, p. 6.

62. Robert McGarvey, "Time on Their Side," *Entrepreneur,* July 1999, pp. 79–81.

63. Ibid., p. 79.

64. Carol Kleiman, "Job Sharing Working Its Way into Mainstream," *Greenville News,* August 6, 2000. p. 3G.

65. Ibid.

66. Peg Verone, "House Rules," *Success,* July 1998, pp. 22–24.

67. Eleena De Lisser, "Firms with Virtual Environments Appeal to Workers," *Wall Street Journal,* October 5, 1999, p. B2.

68. Walter A. Kleinschrod, "Telework Overtakes Telecommuting," *Beyond Computing,* November/December 1999, pp. 38–42.

69. Mark Henricks, "Musical Chairs," *Entrepreneur,* April 1999, pp. 77–79.

70. Michael Barrier, "Improving Worker Performance," *Nation's Business,* September 1996, p. 30.

71. Steve Solomon, "Now That We're Not a Start-Up, How Do I Promote Teamwork?" *Inc.,* October 15, 1998, p. 128.

72. Jill Andresky Fraser, "Know Your Options," *Inc.,* February 1998, pp. 112–113.

73. Joshau Harris Prager, "Joining the Ranks of Rich Secretaries in the Internet Age," *Wall Street Journal,* April 22, 1999, pp. A1,A6.

74. Jacquelyn Lynn, "Rub It In," *Entrepreneur,* September 1999, p. 46; Anne Fisher, "The 100 Best Companies to Work For in America," *Fortune,* January 12, 1998, pp. 69–70; Joann S. Lublin, "Climbing the Walls on Company Time," *Wall Street Journal,* December 1, 1998, pp. B1, B16; Pui-Wing Tam, "Silicon Valley Belatedly Boots Up Programs to Ease employees' Lives," *Wall Street Journal,* August 29, 2000, pp. B1, B14; Quentin Hardy, "Aloft in a Career Without Fetters," *Wall Street Journal,* September 29, 1998, pp. B1, B14; Jerry Useem, "Welcome to the New Company Town," *Fortune,* January 10, 2000, pp. 62–70.

75. Michael Barrier, "Improving Worker Performance," *Nation's Business,* September 1996, p. 28.

76. *Bits & Pieces,* July 21, 1994, p. 19.

77. John Brandt, "An Empress Who Doesn't Pull Rank," *Industry Week,* September 16, 1996, p. 6.

78. Donna Fenn, "Managing Generation X," *Inc.,* August 1996, p. 91; Roberta Maynard, "A Less-Stressed Work Force," *Nation's Business,* November 1996, pp. 50–51.

79. Al Marino, "Pay Your Rank and File Fairly," *Industry Week,* February 1, 1999, p. 18.

80. Ronald Lieber, "Why Employees Love These Companies," *Fortune,* January 12, 1998, pp. 72–74; Alan Farnham, "Mary Kay's Lessons in Leadership," *Fortune,* September 20, 1993, pp. 68–77.

81. "Work Week," *Wall Street Journal,* August 3, 1999, p. A1.

82. Robert McGarvey, "Bonus Points," *Entrepreneur,* July 1994, p. 74.

83. Scott Smith, "Mackay's Way," *Success,* September 2000, p. 16.

84. Jack Stack, "That Championship Season," *Inc.,* July 1996, p. 27.

85. Carla Goodman, "Destination: Success," *Business Start-Ups,* December 1996, p. 50.

86. Jack Stack, "The Logic of Profit," *Inc.,* March 1996, p. 17.

87. Ferdinand Fournies, "Why Performance Appraisals Don't Work," *Small Business Forum,* Winter 1993/1994, pp. 69–77.

88. Joan Delaney, "Rave Reviews," *Your Company,* Spring 1994, pp. 12–13.

89. Stephanie Gruner, "Feedback from Everyone," *Inc.,* February 1997, pp. 102–104.

90. Justin Martin, "So, You Want to Work for the Best . . ." *Fortune,* January 12, 1998, pp. 77–78.

91. Janet Moore, "Like Father, Like Daughter," *Upstate Business,* October 8, 2000, p. 9; "Facts on Family Business in the U.S.," Family Firm Institute, **<www.ffi.org>.**

92. "Facts on Family Business in the U.S.," Family Firm Institute, **<www.ffi.org>.**

93. The Arthur Andersen/MassMutual American Family Business Survey, 1997, **<www.massmutual.com/fbn/index.htm>;** Sharon Nelton, "Major Shifts in Leadership Lie Ahead," *Nation's Business,* June 1997, pp. 56–58.

94. "Non-Family Member Elevated to Nascar Presidentcy," *Family Business Magazine,* **<www.familybusinessmagazine.com/inthenews.html#item_5>.**

95. Carol Steinberg, "The Next Generation," *Success,* October 1996, pp. 85–87.

96. Patricia Schiff Estess, "Overnight Succession," *Entrepreneur,* February 1996, pp. 80–83.

97. Woody White, "Planning Eases Transfer of Control of Family Business," *Upstate Business,* October 8, 2000. p. 1.

98. Joan Pryde, "The Estate Tax Toll on Small Firms," *Nation's Business,* August 1997, pp. 20–24.

99. Pryde, "The Estate Tax Toll on Small Firms," pp. 20–24.

100. The Arthur Andersen/MassMutual American Family Business Survey, 1997, **<www.massmutual.com/fbn/index.htm>.**

101. Amanda Walmac, "Get an Estate Plan to Protect Your Family," *Your Company,* Forecast 1997, pp. 48–54.

102. Leigh Buchanan and Mike Hofman, "Everything I Know About Leadership, I Learned from the Movies," *Inc.,* March 2000, pp. 58–70.

Chapter 15

1. Gary Hamel and Jeff Sampler, "The E-Corporation," *Fortune,* December 7, 1998, pp. 81–92.

2. Robert McGarvey, "Found in Space," *Entrepreneur,* June 1999, pp. 110–117; Wendy Bounds, "Here Comes the Bride, Clicking a Mouse," *Wall Street Journal,* January 14, 1999, pp. B1, B3; P. B. Gray, "Really Modern Brides Can Simply Go Online," *Your Company,* December 1998/January 1999, pp. 18–19.

3. Carol Stavraka, "There's No Stopping E-Business. Are You Ready?" *Forbes,* December 13, 1999, Special Advertising Section.

4. Andrew Raskin, "Setting Your Sites," *Inc. Technology,* No. 2, 1999, p. 20.

5. "Stake Your Claims Now with Compaq Nonstop E-Business Solutions," *Compaq Compass,* Third Quarter 1999, p. 4.

6. Julie Koerner, "There's No Stopping E-Business. Are You Ready?" *Forbes,* April 19, 1999, Special Advertising Section: Stavraka, "There's No Stopping E-Business. Are You Ready?" *Forbes.*

7. Fred Vogelstein, "A Cold Bath for Dot-Com Fever," *U.S. News & World Report,* September 13, 1999, pp. 36–38; Steve Bennett, "The ABCs of E-Commerce," *Small Business Computing,* May 1999, pp. 63–68.

8. "Marketing on the World Wide Web," Alaska Internet Marketing, **<www.alaskaoutdoors.com/Misc/info.html>.**

9. Craig Richardson, "Digital Darwinism," *Entrepreneur,* February 1999, p. 135.

10. Robert McGarvey, "Connect the Dots," *Entrepreneur,* March 2000, pp. 78–85.

11. "Work Week," *Wall Street Journal,* October 26, 1999, p. A1.

12. David G. Propson, "Small Biz Gets Small Piece of the Pie," *Small Business Computing,* November 1999, p. 24; "Survival of the Fastest," *Inc. Technology,* No. 4, 1999, pp. 44–57.

13. "e or Be Eaten," *Fortune,* November 8, 1999, p. 87.

14. "Reality Bites" *Wall Street Journal,* May 1, 2000, p. B18.

15. McGarvey, "Connect the Dots," p. 80.

16. Claire Tristram, "Many Happy Returns," *Small Business Computing,* May 1999, p. 73.

17. David G. Propson, "Intelligence," *Small Business Computing,* November 1999, p. 24.

18. Melissa Campanelli, "E-Business Busters," *Entrepr- eneur,* January 2000, pp. 46–50.

19. Jodi Mardesich, "The Web Is No Shopper's Paradise," *Fortune,* November 8, 1999, pp. 188–198.

20. "Survival of the Fastest," *Inc. Technology,* No. 4, 1999, p. 57.

21. Anne Stuart, "Sweet Deals," Inc. Technology 2000, Number 4, pp. 98-109.

22. Steve Bennett and Stacey Miller, "The E-Commerce Plunge," *Small Business Computing,* February 2000, p. 50.

23. Bronwyn Fryer and Lee Smith, ".Com or Bust," *Forbes Small Business,* December 1999/January 2000, pp. 38–49.

24. Robert McGarvey, "Dot Dot Dot," *Entrepreneur,* April 2000, pp. 96–101; Fryer and Smith, ".Com or Bust," pp. 38–49.

25. Melissa Campanelli, "Are You Losing E-Customers?" *Entrepreneur,* November 1999, p. 56.

26. Bronwyn Fryer, "When Something Clicks," *Inc. Technology,* No. 1, 2000, pp. 62–72; Tristram, "Many Happy Returns," pp. 70–75; Mardesich, "The Web Is No Shopper's Paradise," pp. 188–198.

27. "Business Bulletin," *Wall Street Journal,* January 20, 2000, p. A1.

28. Emily Barker, Anne Marie Borrego, and Mike Hoffman, "I Was Seduced by the Web Economy," *Inc.,* February 2000, pp. 48–70.

29. Fred Vogelstein, "A Cold Bath for Dot-Com Fever," *U.S. News & World Report,* September 13, 1999, p. 37.

30. Mardesich, "The Web Is No Shopper's Paradise," pp. 188–198.

31. Bethany McLean, "More Than Just Dot-Coms," *Fortune,* December 6, 1999, pp. 130–138.

32. Julie Vallone, "We've Got a Secret," *Business Start-Ups,* May 2000, pp. 43–46.

33. Chana Schoenberger, "Embracing the Enemy," *Forbes,* December 13, 1999, pp. 334–336.

34. William J. Holstein, "Rewiring the 'Old Economy,'" *U.S. News & World Report,* April 10, 2000, pp. 38–40.

35. Robert McGarvey, "From: Business to: Business," *Entrepreneur,* June 2000, pp. 96–103.

36. McGarvey, "From: Business to: Business," pp. 96–103; Holstein, "Rewiring the 'Old Economy,'" pp. 38–40.

37. McGarvey, "From: Business to: Business," p. 98.

38. Holstein, "Rewiring the 'Old Economy,'" pp. 38–40.

39. Campanelli, "E-Business Busters," p. 50.

40. Robert McGarvey, "In an E-Nutshell," *Entrepreneur's Netpreneur,* June 2000, p. 7.

41. Fryer and Smith, "Dot.com or Bust," p. 41.

42. Dana Dratch, "These E-Gardening Tips Will Help Your Web Site Grow from Sprout to Giant," *Bankrate.com,* February 29, 2000 **<wysiwig://16/http://www.bankrate.com/brm/news/biz/Ecommerce/20000117.asp>.**

43. Brad Grimes, "E-Commerce Made Easy," *Your Company,* April 1999, pp. 71–78; Internet Wines & Spirits **<www.internetwines.com>.**

44. Anne Ashby Gilbert, "Going Small Time," *Fortune,* September 27, 1999, pp. 262[A]- 262[F].

45. Gilbert, "Going Small Time," pp. 262[A]–262[F].

46. Jeffrey A. Tannenbaum, "Web Sites Help Small Companies Open Internet Stores," *Wall Street Journal,* April 25, 2000 p. B2.

47. Michelle Prather, "Life Online," *Business Start-Ups,* May 2000, p. 17.

48. Eryn Brown, "9 Ways to Win on the Web," *Fortune,* May 24, 1999, p. 112.

49. McGarvey, "From: Business to: Business," pp. 96–103; Produce Online, **<www.produceonline.com>.**

50. Melissa Campanelli, "At First Site," *Entrepreneur's Netpreneur,* June 2000, pp. 9–14.

51. J. W. Dysart, "Think Big," *Entrepreneur's Netpreneur,* June 2000, pp. 34–38.

52. Ralph F. Wilson, "The Five Mutable Laws of Web Marketing," *Web Marketing Today* **<http://www.wilsonweb.com/wmta/basic-principles.htm>,** April 1, 1999, pp. 1–7.

53. Shannon Kinnard, "They've Got Mail," *Business Start-Ups,* October 1999, pp. 45–49.

54. Melanie Warner and Daniel Roth, "10 Companies That Get It," *Fortune,* November 8, 1999, pp. 115–117.

55. Robert McGarvey, "Find Your Partner," *Entrepreneur,* February 2000, p. 74.

56. Robert McGarvey, "Irreconcilable Differences," *Entrepreneur,* February 2000, p. 75.

57. Ibid., p. 75.

58. Warner and Roth, "10 Companies That Get It," pp. 115–117; McGarvey, "Irreconcilable Differences," p. 75.

59. Julie Koerner, "There's No Stopping E-Business. Are You Ready?"

60. Dysart, "Think Big," *Entrepreneur's Netpreneur,* June 2000, p. 37.

61. Robert McGarvey, "Lonely?" *Entrepreneur's Netpreneur,* June 2000, pp. 17–24.

62. Susan Gregory Thomas, "Getting to Know You.com," *U.S. News & World Report,* November 15, 1999, pp. 102–112.

63. Tristram, "Many Happy Returns," p. 75.

64. Mike Hofman, "You Are Your URL," *Inc.,* November 1999, pp. 120–124.

65. Robert A. Mamis, "The Name Game," *Inc.'s The State of Small Business 2000,* pp. 141–144.

66. Amy Austin, "Making Your Site Stand Out," *Small Business Computing,* October 1999, advertising insert.

67. Ibid.

68. Doug Gantenbein, "Sites for Sore Eyes," *Small Business Computing,* March 2000, pp. 48–56.

69. Melissa Campanelli, "Content Is King," *Entrepreneur,* October 1999, pp. 46–49.

70. Stavraka, "There's No Stopping E-Business. Are You Ready?"

71. Melissa Campanelli, "Hot on the Trail," *Entrepreneur,* August 1999, pp. 40–43.

72. Susan Gregory Thomas, "Watching While You Click," *U.S. News & World Report,* November 15, 1999, p. 108.

73. Thomas, "Getting to Know You.com," pp. 102–112.

74. J. D. Tuccille, "Don't Be Big Brother," *Small Business Computing,* July 1999, p. 42.

75. Ibid., pp. 42–43.

76. Michael J. Sniffen, "FBI: Losses from Credit Hackers Could Top $3 Million," *Greenville News,* March 25, 2000, p. 6A.

77. Melissa Campanelli, "A Wall of Fire," *Entrepreneur,* February 2000, pp. 48–49.

78. Jenny McCune, "Keeping Tabs on Your Web Site," *Beyond Computing,* March 2000, pp. 45–47.

79. McGarvey, "Dot Dot Dot," p. 96.

80. Nick Wreden, "Computing Your Web Site Payoff," *Beyond Computing,* April 2000, pp. 50–53.

81. McCune, "Keeping Tabs on Your Web Site," pp. 45–47.

INDEX

C

D

E

F

G

H

I

J

K

L

M

N

Q

R

S

T

U

V

Class Notes

Class Notes

Class Notes

Class Notes

Class Notes

Class Notes

Class Notes

Class Notes

Although more companies than ever before are preaching customer service to employees, the reality is that most Americans still rate U.S. companies low on customer service. In a recent survey of 200 companies, 57 percent of the managers said that "customer service" is their top priority. However, 73 percent said that the only way to survive is with "price competition."[57] Such a short-run philosophy short-circuits real progress toward superior customer service. "Sales starts a customer relationship," says one customer service expert. "Service turns it into a profitable or unprofitable relationship."[58]

Successful businesses recognize that superior customer service is only an intermediate step toward the goal of customer *satisfaction*. These companies seek to go beyond customer satisfaction, striving for *customer astonishment!* They concentrate on providing customers with quality, convenience, and service *as their customers define those terms.*

MarineMax

After 26 years in the retail boat business, William McGill, owner of MarineMax, an association of luxury boat retailers, recognized that his industry was characterized by extremely poor service. McGill saw an opportunity to differentiate MarineMax by offering customers unparalleled service and "no-haggle" prices. For inexperienced customers or those who are just plain nervous about taking a new boat out by themselves for the first time, MarineMax will provide a captain at no extra charge. The captain will keep coming back until the customer learns to handle the boat alone. The company also has a staff of repair technicians who are on call 24 hours a day. Every MarineMax boat over 20 feet in length carries a full two-year warranty from bow to stern, twice as long as the typical warranty in the industry. Because McGill has learned that his customers' families influence how often they upgrade to bigger (and more expensive) boats, he sponsors regular seminars and fun events to teach spouses and kids how to get the most out of their boats—and to look at new, larger models. MarineMax also perpetuates customer loyalty through its "getaways," trips that range from one-day outings on a Minnesota lake to two-week trips to the Bahamas. The company services all boats before a trip and sends along a crew of technicians to fix any problems that crop up. All of this superior service costs MarineMax money, and McGill's prices reflect the extra costs. The company figures that 2.5 percent to 6 percent of a boat's price goes to cover the extra service it provides. Customers do not seem to mind slightly higher prices, however; MarineMax's profit margin is more than twice the industry average, and sales are climbing![59]

Certainly the least expensive—and the most effective—way to achieve customer satisfaction is through friendly, personal service. Numerous surveys of customers in a wide diversity of industries—from manufacturing and services to banking and high tech—conclude that the most important element of service is "the personal touch." Calling customers by name, making attentive, friendly contact, and truly caring about their needs and wants are much more essential than any other factor—even convenience, quality, and speed! One entrepreneur explains, "In our society, everything has become so automated that we're starved for personal attention. True customer service means reaching across that automation, recognizing that each person is an individual with needs and doing what it takes to meet those needs."[60]

How can a company achieve stellar customer service and satisfaction?

LISTEN TO CUSTOMERS. The best companies constantly listen to their customers and respond to what they hear! This allows them to keep up with customers' changing needs and expectations. The best way to find out what customers really want and value is to ask them. Businesses rely on a number of techniques including surveys, focus groups, telephone interviews, comment cards, suggestion boxes, toll-free "hot lines," and regular one-on-one conversations (perhaps the best technique). The Internet is another useful tool for getting feedback from customers. One computer software publisher uses an online suggestion box, which has produced several new and profitable ideas for the company.[61]

It is important for entrepreneurs to keep customer feedback in its proper perspective, however. Although listening to customers does produce valuable feedback for business owners in many areas, it is *not* a substitute for an innovative company culture, solid market research, and a well-devised marketing plan. Companies that rely solely on their customers to guide their marketing efforts often find themselves lagging the competition. Customers rarely have the foresight to anticipate market trends and do not always have a clear view of how new products or services could satisfy their needs.

DEFINE SUPERIOR SERVICE. Based on what customers say, managers and employees must decide exactly what "superior service" means in the company. Such a statement should (1) be a strong statement of intent, (2) differentiate the company from others, and (3) have value to customers. Deluxe Corporation, a printer of personal checks, defines superior service quite simply: "Forty-eight hour turnaround; zero defects."[62]

SET STANDARDS AND MEASURE PERFORMANCE. To be able to deliver on its promise of superior service, a business must establish specific standards and measure overall performance against them. Satisfied customers should exhibit at least one of three behaviors: loyalty (increased customer retention rate), increased purchases (climbing sales and sales per customer), and resistance to rivals' attempts to lure them away with lower prices (market share and price tolerance).[63] Companies must track their performance on these and other service standards and reward employees accordingly.

EXAMINE YOUR COMPANY'S SERVICE CYCLE. What steps must a customer go through to get your product or service? Business owners often are surprised at the complexity that has seeped into their customer service systems as they have evolved over time. One of the most effective techniques is to work with employees to flowchart each component in the company's service cycle, including *everything* a customer has to do to get your product or service. The goal is to look for steps and procedures that are unnecessary, redundant, or unreasonable and then to eliminate them.

HIRE THE RIGHT EMPLOYEES. The key ingredient in the superior service equation is *people*. There is no substitute for friendly, courteous sales/service representatives. "You can't create world-class customer care if you hire run-of-the-mill employees," says customer service expert Ron Zemke.[64] Business owners must always be on the lookout for employees who are empathetic, flexible, articulate, creative, and able to think for themselves.

TRAIN EMPLOYEES TO DELIVER SUPERIOR SERVICE. Successful businesses train *every* employee who deals directly with customers; they don't leave customer service to chance. Superior service companies devote 1 to 5 percent of their employees' work hours to training, concentrating on how to meet, greet, and serve customers. Leading mail-order companies such as Lands' End and L.L. Bean spend *many* hours training the employees who handle telephone orders before they deal with their first customer.

EMPOWER EMPLOYEES TO OFFER SUPERIOR SERVICE. One of the single most important variables in determining whether or not employees deliver superior service is the degree to which they perceive they have permission to do so. The goal is to push decision making down the organization to the employees who have contact with customers. This includes giving them the latitude to circumvent "company policy" if it means improving customer satisfaction. If frontline workers don't have this power to solve disgruntled customers' problems, they fear being punished for overstepping their boundaries, become frustrated, and the superior service cycle breaks down. To be empowered, employees need knowledge and information, adequate resources, and managerial support.